THE WORLD AND THE UNITED NATIONS SYSTEM

P9-AQK-581

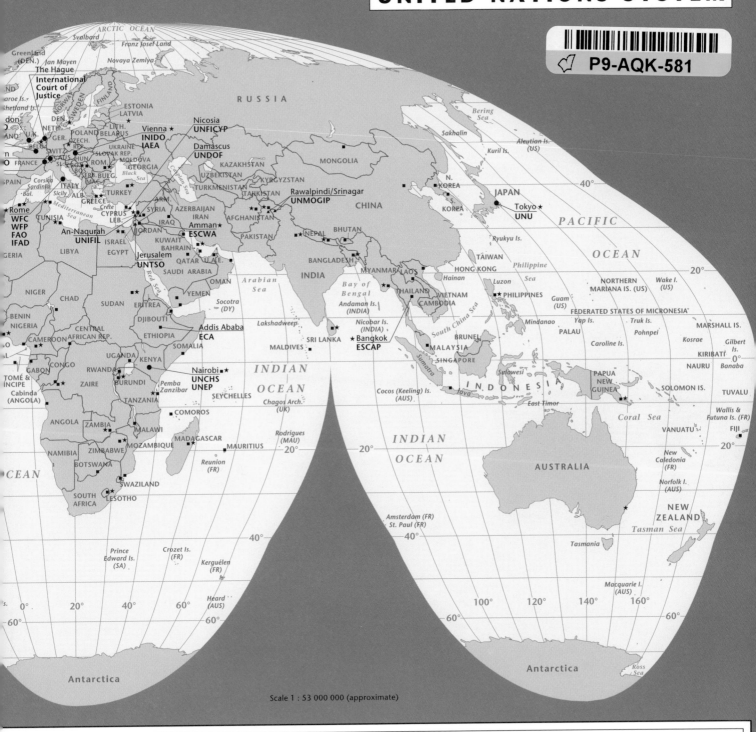

Scale 1 : 53 000 000 (approximate)

SPECIALIZED AGENCIES AND OTHER AUTONOMOUS ORGANIZATIONS WITHIN THE SYSTEM

Berne:
- **UPU** -Universal Postal Union

Geneva:
- **GATT** -General Agreement on Tariffs and Trade
- **ILO** -International Labour Organization
- **ITU** -International Telecommunication Union
- **WHO** -World Health Organization
- **WIPO** -World Intellectual Property Organization
- **WMO** -World Meteorological Organization

London:
- **IMO** -International Maritime Organization

Montreal:
- **ICAO** -International Civil Aviation Organization

Paris:
- **UNESCO** -United Nations Educational, Scientific and Cultural Organization

Rome:
- **FAO** -Food and Agricultural Organization of the United Nations
- **IFAD** -International Fund for Agricultural Development

Vienna:
- **IAEA** -International Atomic Energy Agency
- **UNIDO** -United Nations Industrial Development Organization

Washington:
- **IFC** -International Finance Corporation
- **IMF** -International Monetary Fund
- **The World Bank** { -International Development Association (IDA)
-International Bank for Reconstruction and Development (IBRD)

REGIONAL COMMISSIONS

Addis Ababa:
- **ECA** -Economic Commission for Africa

Bangkok:
- **ESCAP** -Economic and Social Commission for Asia and the Pacific

Geneva:
- **ECE** -Economic Commission for Europe

Santiago:
- **ECLAC** -Economic Commission for Latin America and the Caribbean

WORLDMARK ENCYCLOPEDIA OF THE NATIONS

Volume 1

WORLDMARK
ENCYCLOPEDIA OF THE NATIONS

UNITED NATIONS

Formerly published by Worldmark Press, Ltd.

 Gale Research Inc.

An International Thomson Publishing Company

I(T)P

NEW YORK • LONDON • BONN • BOSTON • DETROIT • MADRID
MELBOURNE • MEXICO CITY • PARIS • SINGAPORE • TOKYO
TORONTO • WASHINGTON • ALBANY NY • BELMONT CA • CINCINNATI OH

Gale Research Inc. Staff

Jane Hoehner, *Developmental Editor*
Allison McNeill, Rebecca Nelson, and Kelle S. Sisung, *Contributing Developmental Editors*
Marie Ellavich, Jolen Gedridge, and Camille Killens, *Associate Developmental Editors*
Lawrence W. Baker, *Senior Developmental Editor*

Mary Beth Trimper, *Production Director*
Evi Seoud, *Assistant Production Manager*
Mary Kelley, *Production Associate*

Cynthia Baldwin, *Product Design Manager*
Barbara J. Yarrow, *Graphic Services Supervisor*
Todd Nessell, *Macintosh Artist*

Library of Congress Cataloging-in-Publication Data

Worldmark encyclopedia of the nations. — 8th ed.
    5 v.
    Includes bibliographical references and index.
    Contents: v. 1. United Nations — v. 2. Africa — v. 3. Americas —
v. 4. Asia & Oceania — v. 5. Europe.
    ISBN 0-8103-9878-8 (set). — ISBN 0-8103-9893-1 (v. 1). — ISBN
0-8103-9880-x (v. 2)
    1. Geography—Encyclopedias. 2. History—Encyclopedias.
3. Economics—Encyclopedias. 4. Political science—Encyclopedias.
5. United Nations—Encyclopedias.
G63.W67 1995
903—dc20
                                          94–38556
                                            CIP

This book is printed on acid-free paper that meets the minimum requirements of American National Standard for Information Sciences—Permanence Paper for Printed Library Materials, ANSI Z39.48-1984. ♾™

ISBN 0-8103-9893-1

Printed in the United States of America by Gale Research Inc.
Published simultaneously in the United Kingdom
by Gale Research International Limited
(An affiliated company of Gale Research Inc.)

10 9 8 7 6 5 4 3 2 1

The trademark **ITP** is used under license.

CONTRIBUTORS

Chairman Ambassador Charles F. Dunbar, President, Cleveland Council on World Affairs

Alberto Benitez, Department of Economics, Florida International University

Evelyn Feretti, Department of Agricultural Economics, Cornell University

Rodger M. Govea, Associate Professor, Department of Political Science, Cleveland State University

Kenneth W. Grundy, Marcus A. Hanna Professor of Political Science, Case Western Reserve University

John W. Guendelsberger, Professor of Law, The Claude W. Pettit College of Law, Ohio Northern University

Nese Guendelsberger, Attorney at Law, Ada, Ohio

Herbert G. Hagerty, Foreign Service Officer (ret.), U.S. Department of State

James J. Heaney, Managing Editor, Webster's New World Dictionary

Gail Junion-Metz, President, Information Age Consultants

Mark N. Katz, Associate Professor of Government and Politics, George Mason University

Catherine Lynch, Assistant Professor, Department of History, Case Western Reserve University

Vincent McHale, Chairman, Department of Political Science, Case Western Reserve University

Glenn McLoughlin, Specialist in Science and Technology Policy, Congressional Research Service, Library of Congress

Raymond E. Metz, Interim Director, University Libraries, Case Western Reserve University

Allan R. Millett, Mason Professor of Military History, The Mershon Center, The Ohio State University

Raul Moncarz, Professor, Department of Economics, Florida International University

Martha Brill Olcott, Professor, Department of Political Science, Colgate University

Henry Precht, Adjunct Associate Professor, Department of Political Science, Case Western Reserve University

John Ranahan, Lake Ridge Academy

Vladimir Rus, Department of Slavic Literature (ret.), Case Western Reserve University

Maria J. Santos, Senior Evaluator, United States General Accounting Office

Joseph W. Stoll, Supervisor, Cartography Laboratory, University of Akron

Jeanne Marie Stumpf-Carome, Department of Sociology, John Carroll University; Department of Anthropology, Kent State University–Geauga Campus

Arthur S. Westneat, School for Public and Environmental Affairs, African Studies Program, Indiana University

Renate Wise, Center for Middle Eastern Studies, The University of Texas at Austin

STAFF

Editor in Chief	Timothy L. Gall
Executive Editor	Susan Bevan Gall
Editor, UN Volume	Lynne Brakeman
Senior Editor	Daniel M. Lucas
Associate Editors	Alana Andrews, Chandra P. Balasubramani, Nelia Dunbar, Robert Halasz, James Henry, Kim Humiston, Roman Jakubowycz, Ann P. Standley, Rosalie Weider, Douglas Wu
Cartographers	Maryland Cartographics, Inc.; Scott B. Edmonds, President Stephanie K. Clark, Deborah G. Freer, Tracy R. Morrill, Justin E. Morrill, Judith G. Nielsen, John P. Radziszewski
Copy Editors	Janet Fenn, Mary Ann Klasen
Typesetting	Brian Rajewski, Deborah Rutti
Data Input	Judith Arth, Dawn Babos, Lee Ann DeWolf, Janis K. Long, Deborah Ridgway
Proofreaders	Deborah Baron, Jan Davis, Janet Fenn, Ruta Marino

ACKNOWLEDGMENTS

A basic part of the editorial preparation of the *Worldmark Encyclopedia of the Nations* consists of keeping continuously abreast of the work of governments. The editors wish to express their gratitude to the many government officials the world over who so kindly gave their cooperation. Grateful acknowledgment is made for the invaluable material, used throughout the encyclopedia, drawn from the mass of documents issued by the United Nations and its specialized agencies. Gratitude is expressed for the assistance given by numerous officials of the UN, the specialized agencies, and the intergovernmental and nongovernmental organizations.

The editors would like to specifically thank the staffs of the United Nations Public Inquiry Unit (headed by Ms. M. Hosali) and the Dag Hammarskjöld Library (headed by Ms. Rima Bordcosh) for the many hours they spent tracking down answers to particularly obscure questions. Special thanks is extended to the following individuals and units for substantive contributions on the work of their organizations: Marie Paul Aristy, Chief Information, Communication and Documentation Unit, INSTRAW; Vera Azar and Lina Arafat, ESCWA, United Nations; Michael Cassandra, Centre for Disarmament Affairs, United Nations; Padraig Czajkowski, Centre for Human Rights, United Nations; Jacqueline Dauchy, Director, Codification Division, Secretariat of the Commission on International Law, United Nations; Lynn Failing, Deputy Chief, Public Information Office, UNRWA; Donald E. Fitzpatrick, Special Assistant to the Under Secretary General for Administration and Management, United Nations; Hirut Gebre-Egziabher, Project Officer, Division of Information, UNICEF; Christine Graves, FAO; Marilla B. Guptil, United Nations Archives; H. J. Frick, Chief, Official Relations Branch, ILO; Nandasiri Jasentuliyana, Director, Office for Outer Space Affairs, United Nations; Mary Lynn Hanley, Chief, Editorial and Audio Visual Branch, Division of Public Affairs, UNDP; Margaret A. Kelly, Secretary, ECOSOC, United Nations; Pamela Maponga, Secretariat of the Special Committee on Apartheid, United Nations; Luciana Marulli-Koenig, Chief Information Support Unit, Dept. of Policy Coordination and Sustainable Development, United Nations; Ian McDonald, Chief Editor, IMF; Mehri Madarshahi, Department of Administration and Management, UN; Allegra Morelli, Director, Information Division, IFAD; Ozdinch Mustafa, Senior Political Affairs Officer, Trusteeship Council, United Nations; Ann Rogers, Senior Economist, Department of Policy Coordination and Sustainable Development, United Nations (for information on the World Food Council); Simeon Sahaydachny, Legal Officer, International Trade Law Branch, Office of Legal Affairs, UNCITRAL; Samir Sanbar, Under Secretary General, Department of Public Information, United Nations; Wesley Scholz, United States Department of State (for information on the Law of the Sea Convention); Maria-Sabina Yeterian-Parisi, Economic Affairs Officer, Policy Coordination and External Relations Service, UNCTAD; David J. Woods, Director, Information Division, GATT; External Relations Division, UNIDO; Communications and External Relations Section, UNIFEM; Division of External Relations, UNHCR; Adrienne Cruz, Publications, Dissemination and Reference Centre, UNRISD; Department of Public Information, UPU; Department of Public Relations and Information, WIPO; and the Secretariat of the World Meteorological Organization.

This encyclopedia greatly benefited from statistics and information requested of the governments of the nations profiled in these volumes. The following persons, personally or through the auspices of their offices, graciously responded to our request for information: Mr. Arben Tashko, Embassy of the Republic of Albania; Mr. Hamid Belhadj, Embassy of the Democratic and Popular Republic of Algeria; Ms. Debbie O.

Profper, Embassy of Antigua and Barbuda; Mr. Garnik Ashotovich Nanagulian, Embassy of the Republic of Armenia; Mr. Christopher Sweeney, Embassy of Australia; Mr. Martin G. Eichtinger, Embassy of Austria; Mr. Djeikhoun Nazim Molla Zade, Embassy of the Republic of Azerbaijan; Mrs. Diane A. Dean, Embassy of the Commonwealth of the Bahamas; Mr. Othman Abdulla Mohammed Rashed, Embassy of the State of Bahrain; Mr. K. M. Ejazul Huq, Embassy of the People's Republic of Bangladesh; Mr. Charles Chesterfield Burnett, Embassy of Barbados; Mrs. Gisele Louise Eggermont, Embassy of Belgium; Mrs. Yvonne Sharman Hyde, Embassy of Belize; Mr. Augustine Moipolai Pone, Embassy of the Republic of Botswana; Mr. Eduardo Botelho Barbosa, Brazilian Embassy; Mr. Ahmad Hajijukin, Embassy of the State of Brunei Darussalam; Ms. Djeneba Yasmine Traore, Embassy of Burkina Faso; Mr. Pierre Ndzengue, Embassy of the Republic of Cameroon; Mr. L. Ian MacDonald, Embassy of Canada; Mrs. Maria I. M. Correa Reynolds, Embassy of Chile; Mr. Antonia F. Copello, Embassy of Colombia; Mr. Kresimir Cosic, Embassy of the Republic of Croatia; Mr. Miltos Miltiadou, Embassy of the Republic of Cyprus; Mr. Joergen Grunnet, Royal Danish Embassy; Mr. Issa Daher Bopuraleh, Embassy of the Republic of Djibouti; Dr. Dario Suro, Embassy of the Dominican Republic; Mr. Kamel Abdel Hamid Mohamed Ahmed, Embassy of the Arab Republic of Egypt; Mr. Eerik Niiles Kross, Embassy of Estonia; Mr. Demissie Segu Segu, Embassy of Ethiopia; His Excellency Pita Kewa Nacuva, Embassy of the Republic of Fiji; Mrs. Pirkko Liisa O'Rourke, Embassy of Finland; Mr. Jean Mendelson, Embassy of France; Mr. Gottfried Haas, Embassy of the Federal Republic of Germany; Miss Mara Marinaki, Embassy of Greece; His Excellency Kenneth Modeste, Embassy of Grenada; His Excellency The Most Reverend Agostino Cacciavillan, Apostolic Nunciature; Mr. Rosny Montoya Flores, Embassy of Honduras; Miss Klara Breuer, Embassy of the Republic of Hungary; Mr. Jon Egill Egilsson, Embassy of Iceland; Mr. Sanjay Bhatnagar, Embassy of India; Mr. Subekti Dhirdjosaputro, Embassy of the Republic of Indonesia; Mr. Nimrod Barkan, Embassy of Israel; Mr. Alessandro Vaciago, Embassy of Italy; Mr. Seiichi Kondo, Embassy of Japan; Mr. Marwan J. Muasher, Embassy of the Hashemite Kingdom of Jordan; Mr. Byong Suh Lee, Embassy of Korea; Dr. Ali Ahmad Al Tarrah, Embassy of the State of Kuwait; Mr. Ints Upmacis, Embassy of Latvia; Mr. Tsepiso Jeffrey Malefane, Embassy of the Kingdom of Lesotho; Dr. Alfonse Eidintas, Embassy of the Republic of Lithuania; Miss Colette Kinnen, Embassy of Luxembourg; Mr. Robert B. Mbaya, Embassy of Malawi; Mr. Alfred M. Falzon, Embassy of Malta; Mr. Banny DeBrum, Embassy of the Republic of the Marshall Islands; Mr. Amadou Diaw, Embassy of the Islamic Republic of Mauritania; Mr. Joaquin Gonzalez Casanova, Embassy of Mexico; Mr. Kodaro M. Gallen, Embassy of the Federated States of Micronesia; Mr. Nadmidyn Bavuu, Embassy of Mongolia; Mr. Antonio Paulo Elias Matonse Jr., Embassy of the Republic of Mozambique; Mr. Japhet Isaack, Embassy of the Republic of Namibia; Mr. Frans L.E. Hulsman, Embassy of the Netherlands; Mr. Robert Carey Moore Jones, Embassy of New Zealand; Mr. Enrique Vanegas, Embassy of Nicaragua; Mr. Adamou Abdou, Embassy of the Republic of Niger; Mr. Tore Tanum, Royal Norwegian Embassy; Mr. Salim Al Mahrooqy, Embassy of the Sultanate of Oman; Mr. Malik Zahoor Ahmad, Embassy of Pakistan; Miss Lerna L. Llerena, Embassy of the Republic of Panama; Mr. Christopher Mero, Embassy of Papua New Guinea; Mr. Jose M. Boza, Embassy of Peru; Mr. Boguslaw M. Majewski, Embassy of the Republic of Poland; Professor Maria Graca S. Almeida Rodrigues, Embassy of Portugal; Mrs. Natal'ya P. Semenikhina, Embassy of the Russian Federation; Mr. John P. Irish, Embassy of St. Kitts and Nevis; Ms. Undine George, Embassy of Saint Lucia; Ms. Cecily A. Norris, Embassy of Saint Vincent and the Grenadines; Dr. Hamad Ibrahim Al Salloom, Embassy of Saudi Arabia; Mr. Marc R. Marengo, Embassy of the the Republic of Seychelles; Miss Siong Fun Lim, Embassy of the Republic of Singapore; Mr. Jaroslav Smiesny, Embassy of the Slovak Republic; Mr. Gregor S. Zore, Embassy of the Republic of Slovenia; Mr. Atukoralalage A. Wijetunga, Embassy of the Democratic Socialist Republic of Sri Lanka; Mr. Abdalla Khidir Bashir, Embassy of the Republic of the Sudan; Mrs. Lindiwe Audrey Nhlabatsi, Embassy of the Kingdom of

Swaziland; Mr. Ingmar J. Bjorksten, Embassy of Sweden; Mr. Francois Barras, Embassy of Switzerland; Ms. Souad Mourazen Al Ayoubi, Embassy of the Syrain Arab Republic; Mr. Ally O. Mjenga, Embassy of the United Republic of Tanzania; Mr. Oussama Romdhani, Embassy of Tunisia; Mr. Ahmet Mahfi Egilmez, Embassy of the Republic of Turkey; Mr. Dmitro Y. Markov, Embassy of Ukraine; Mr. Atiq Mubarak Marzoog Khamis, Embassy of the United Arab Emirates; Mr. Nicholas W. Browne, British Embassy; Mr. Carlos Maria Irigaray, Embassy of Uruguay; Mr. Ramon Hernandez, Embassy of the Republic of Venezuela; Mr. Lazarous Kapambwe, Embassy of the Republic of Zambia; Mr. Mark Grey Marongwe, Embassy of the Republic of Zimbabwe. Special acknowledgment goes to Margaret Hunter, Embassy of Turkmenistan and Veronica Rentmeesters, Embassy of Eritrea for their help in providing current information on their respective countries.

The following individuals and agencies deserve special acknowledgment for their generous assistance: Ernest Carter, USDA, Foreign Agricultural Service; Orlando D. Martino, Chief, Branch of Latin America and Canada, US Department of the Interior, Bureau of Mines, Division of International Minerals; Bernadette Michalski, Energy Analyst, US Department of the Interior, Bureau of Mines, Division of International Minerals; Hendrik G. van Oss, Economic Geologist, US Department of the Interior, Bureau of Mines, Division of International Minerals; Lowell Feld, Energy Information Administration, Energy Markets and Contingency Information Division; Matthew E. Brosius, Deputy Head of Center, Organization for Economic Co-operation and Development; Rosario Benevides, Salomon Brothers; Sarah Baker, BP America, Reference Center.

We would like to thank Elizabeth Gall and Adam Gall for their support and encouragement. Finally, special acknowledgment is given to the Cleveland Council on World Affairs for their generosity in allowing us to tap into their network of experts on the countries of the world. We offer special recognition to Christine E.R. Lucas, who was helpful in the early stages of the revision of this edition.

CONTENTS

FOREWORD

Although the United Nations is often in the news, its basic nature, its possibilities and its limitations are not widely understood. In its first fifty years the organization has enormously expanded, both in membership and in the scope of its work. During that period, both governments and the public have made it responsible for a variety of dangerous and complex problems, usually without providing adequate means to tackle them. This has meant that the United Nations is mostly better known for its shortcomings than for its achievements.

At its foundation the main functions of the UN were the maintenance of international peace and security, disarmament, and various forms of post-war reconstruction. The founders, however, recalling that the part which economic and social disorder had played in creating the conditions for the second world war, provided, in the Charter, a resounding mandate for the promotion of "the economic and social advancement of all peoples" as well as of human rights and fundamental freedoms. The shortcomings of this side of the UN's work, by far the largest part in terms of staff and programs, is perhaps the most serious disappointment of the organization's first fifty years.

The UN itself is only the instrument of its member governments. Apart from the leadership, and the limited powers of initiative, of the Secretary General, the organization depends for its effectiveness and for its development on the support and the political will of the governments. Peacekeeping operations and the intermediary role of the Secretary General have spasmodically enjoyed such support, although there is now a serious controversy as to how much the UN ought to become involved in human disasters which are not threats to international peace. On the economic and social side there has been a far greater reluctance to give the UN a leading role.

The UN is now going through the most important transition of its history. Virtually all of its recent peace and humanitarian operations are concerned with violent situations within the boundaries of a single state, rather than with conflicts between states as in the past. The media and the public seem increasingly to see the organization as the police and rescue organization of a world community that does not yet exist. However reluctant governments may be to authorize and to provide the necessary resources for such a role, there can be little doubt that if the UN fails to carry it out, along with a far more effective lead in economic and social matters, the organization will become increasingly irrelevant to the great global problems which will determine the future of the human race. We already have many problems of "one world." If the UN does not begin to deal with them effectively, it will cease to be useful, and the future will be correspondingly more hazardous.

The so-called UN system covers, in theory at any rate, virtually the entire range of human activity. After fifty years it needs reorganization, reform and renewal. However, its Charter and its fundamental institutions are sound. If the world organization is to be strengthened to meet the enormous challenges of coming years, it is essential that the public understand it, so that it can be both intelligently criticized and strongly supported. This Encyclopedia provides a comprehensive and accessible basis for such understanding.

BRIAN URQUHART
Scholar-in-Residence, The Ford Foundation
August 1994

PREFACE

Carved in stone, opposite the home of the United Nations, is an inscription taken from Isaiah: ". . . and they shall beat their swords into plowshares, and their spears into pruning hooks: nation shall not lift up sword against nation, neither shall they learn war any more." The Prophets' sense of moral justice, which was the foundation of their vision of peace as expressed in this inscription, has not yet been accepted as a basis for political behavior. Indeed, developments in recent years have cast a dark shadow over the United Nations. The passage of resolutions and the toleration of practices inconsistent with the spirit of the Charter have not only instilled doubt about the effectiveness of the organization as a political instrument but have also undermined the spirit of fairness and cooperation that once characterized the work of the specialized agencies. In the 1930s, the world witnessed the loss of moral force and then the political decline of the League of Nations. No friend of peace could wish its successor a similar fate. It is the fervent hope of the editors of this encyclopedia that political influences will not further undermine the substantive achievements of the United Nations.

The problems of peace preoccupy the minds of people everywhere. The ever-intensifying complexities of our times, while serving to increase the responsibility of a larger number of persons, often also augment the individual's feeling of helplessness. Yet, knowledge of other lands and ability to see their people as fellow human beings can enable the individual to overcome this feeling of helplessness and to act for himself and others. In this spirit this work was conceived and is offered, with the hope that it may not only find many specific uses, but may bring into focus a broader world view for the reader, and thus contribute to international understanding.

MOSHE Y. SACHS
Editor and Publisher, First through Seventh Editions

FOREWORD

This encyclopedia is different from all others produced in recent years. It is not simply a collection of miscellaneous facts for ready reference. It resembles more the pioneer work of those encyclopedists who ushered in the era of enlightenment in 18th-century France, in that it mirrors the life of men and nations at a great turning point in history, when the national state system of absolute sovereignties has to find new adjustments under the sovereignty of science. The old safeguards for security—mountains and oceans—no longer hold against the impact of an atomic age. The United Nations is the mirror of this new world in which international life becomes more and more interdependent. The political framework is therefore filled in by a comprehensive survey of the major interests of people everywhere. Such an encyclopedia should prove a valuable guide to the understanding not only of the United Nations but of our time.

JAMES T. SHOTWELL
6 August 1874–17 July 1965
Chairman, Editorial Advisory Board First Edition

INTRODUCTION

The swift course of domestic and world events, part of a hastened process of change, requires an enormous increase of basic understanding by peoples of the multiple factors influencing the tempo and direction of national developments. The pattern of intercultural penetration and cross-fertilizing exchanges of scientific and technological knowledge rests upon a concept of fundamental unity of diverse approaches to the central objective of all human endeavors: the creation of a better world, with general equality of opportunity to all individuals, everywhere.

Within a planet shrunk into community bounds by the progress of communications there are no substantial sectors of mankind still completely isolated from the main currents of 20th-century thought and action. A growing sense of identification among men is fostered by the adoption of certain basic standards of human rights and the slow growth of supranational law rooted in the fundamental principles that are common to all juridical systems.

No period in history has witnessed such accelerated search for adequate answers to the riddles that have so long beset humanity. Metaphysical explanations of the universe and of the individual's place within it vie with each other in the vast and only superficially explored realm of emotions; rationalized conceptions of economic and social philosophies contend in the marketplace of personal loyalties with a violence that frequently threatens to rend asunder the fabric of overall unity; and the march forward of freedoms and improvements in the status of people throughout our earth is largely clouded by the supercharged treatment of political affairs in the media of mass communication.

At a time when people everywhere are truly eager for accurate, comprehensive, and timely information about themselves and their neighbors in the closely related various geographic areas, the vastness and multiplicity of the field to be covered promotes reporting that serves little the needs of the average person: it is either too detailed in breadth and depth, so that only specialists can profit from its availability, or sketchy and fragmentary, to the point where it contributes more to confusion than enlightenment of the users.

A specific reason has made necessary a new approach to analytical and basic data on each country, as a separate political unit, and as a member of the vast family of nations all constitute together: the universality of their interest in the maintenance of international peace and security through the joint exercise of agreed-upon powers to restrain violence; to police disturbed areas where peaceful relations are endangered; to promote the application of legal procedures to the adjudication of their differences; and to strike at the very sources of controversy, which are rooted in the deep chasms among their economic and social standards and their consequent basic inequalities of status.

So-called realists may continue to voice their belief that conflict among nations is an outgrowth of their dynamic development, and that only practical arrangements which create "balances" of power can establish an equilibrium within the diverse segments of the world; and theorists of the biological inevitability of war still proclaim the materialistic concept that only a concentration of authority in the hands of some overwhelmingly strong state can eliminate actual armed conflict and bring to subjected peoples the "benefits" of a freedomless "pax romana." But mankind has made great strides since the days of empires, the conquest of colonial dependencies, the plagues and misery that fixed the general expectation of human life under thirty years, and the spiritual darkness of illiteracy and isolation from the mainstreams of culture of variegated philosophical, religious, and scientific concepts.

Under principles of ethics the peoples and the nations emerged as possessors of rights and bearers of responsibilities, and morality took its place in the councils of power. The advancement toward a universal rule of law has been too slow for the idealists and yet most encouraging to those who believe that peaceful evolutionary progress achieves more durable results than violent revolutionary change. The steady process of codification of generally recognized juridical principles and the formulation of new ones through general consensus constitute one of the most hopeful signs of this restless era of change. International compacts such as the Covenant of the League of Nations and the Charter of the United Nations incorporate moral concepts side by side with legal standards. They recognize that there are both ethical and juridical duties and rights that must be observed by states in their reciprocal relations and in respect of their inhabitants, subjects, and citizens.

So far-reaching are the changes already wrought within the world community, particularly for its less developed segments, that the normal processes of history have lost considerable significance in the face of new realities recently created.

Feeling that none of the encyclopedias and specialized sources of information do sufficient justice to these accomplishments in political freedom, economic development, social progress, and the practice of international cooperation, Worldmark Press, Inc., decided to publish a basically new encyclopedia devoted to the nations.

After identifying the outward symbols of each state: the capital, a map, the flag, the national anthem, the monetary unit, the system of weights and measures, holidays, and time, each article proceeds to cover, as thoroughly as available data permit, 50 individual phases of the country's life, so as to furnish an overall picture of its present as rooted in the past evolution of its institutions, customs, and traditions. A precise definition of location, size, and extent of the individual territory is given, so that the reader can visualize, as a living reality, that which the map depicts graphically. Topography, climate, and flora and fauna supplement the other natural physical features of the respective nation.

More than by any other factor, countries are what they are because of man's exertions to create his own environment, so population, ethnic groups, and language are the next items covered. Together with the section devoted to religion, they give a basic understanding of the demographic phenomena that determine the basic institutions, political, economic, and social, of each sovereign unit.

Transportation and communications follow in the description of the positive factors working for the consolidation of each country's internal unity and of the reconstruction of the wider oneness of mankind.

Next there is a historical survey, in most cases kept brief because of the availability of comprehensive ones in other sources of general information.

As a result of the individual national experience various types of governmental authority have been either adopted from the similar experience of other peoples or created to meet different requirements. In the operation of governments, there are diverse types of machinery which correspond to particular political philosophies and which the citizens control through political parties.

Local governmental structures supplement the system of deliberative and executive authorities in charge of public interests.

Knowledge of the organizational pattern of the judiciary acquires considerable importance for all kinds of individual and corporate activities within a particular nation, so information is furnished thereon.

The internal stability of a country and its international security are made clear by adequate data on the organization and potential of the armed forces.

Because the pattern of migrations has undergone great changes, information on their effect upon demographic developments in each state is of deep significance for any evaluation of manpower prospects and consumer potentials.

No nation is an isolated unit itself. The extent to which each government engages in international cooperation is a useful indicator of its concern with the peaceful handling of potential sources of tensions and conflicts.

One of the phases of internal development with an international impact relates to the wide range of the economy. This encyclopedia deals comprehensively with income, labor, agriculture, animal husbandry, fishing, forestry, mining, energy and power, industry, domestic trade, foreign trade, balance of payments, banking, insurance, securities, public finance, taxation, customs and duties, foreign investment, and economic policy.

It also gives information on health, social welfare, and housing, important in the economically less developed nations as a mainspring of economic activity and financial investment for what is called the infrastructure, vital as a prerequisite of other actions to promote production, employment, higher standards of living and, in general, a broader enjoyment of basic human rights and fundamental freedoms.

The domestic activities mentioned in the two previous paragraphs aim to help in the struggle against illiteracy which, even in more advanced countries, reduces the number of citizens actively engaged in political life and is instrumental in the growth and maintenance of discriminatory practices and arbitrary stereotypes within each nation and between many nations. It is of the utmost importance to know the educational facilities available for supplying trained political leaders, administrators, economists, social workers, medical personnel, and technicians. And to data on teaching establishments is added information on libraries and museums and on the organizations set up by the people of each country to promote their collective interests and welfare.

The press and other media of information and enlightenment constitute an important index of the cultural standing of the people; the degree of their freedom is the best evidence of the intellectual maturity of government and governed, and a significant indicator of the degree to which essential human rights in the field of opinion are truly respected.

Perhaps the most effective way to advance reciprocal understanding is by contacts among peoples of different countries and with each other's natural environment. The conditions which must be met for the purposes of tourism are fully explained.

Dependencies for which each individual state assumes international responsibilities are described in detail. Finally a brief roll of famous persons is a biographical listing of national figures. An up-to-date bibliography closes each nation's description.

But in our day and era nations are not islands unto themselves, busy solely with internal problems of varying magnitude. The field of exclusively domestic concern is shrinking under the tremendous impact of easy communications among nations.

While the United Nations and regional organizations of states, directly or through their subsidiary or associated organs, may and do deal with practically every field of human interest, other organizations restrict their jurisdiction to the more specific areas of economic or social matters. They handle issues at the universal and at the close neighborhood levels and, large or small, they each play a part in the process of international cooperation to improve and give constructive meaning to the relations among peoples. Even military pacts have gradually broadened the scope of their concern as a result of the finding that merely negative aims do not afford by themselves the stability and coherence for which they were brought into being. The Secretary-General of the United Nations, Mr. Dag Hammarskjöld, has repeatedly stated his views that any collective action conducted outside the United Nations, but consonant with the spirit of its charter, can be considered as cooperation toward the fundamental objectives of the world organization.

Because we live under the impact of global issues that affect every individual, for good or for ill, and because also of the advance of democratic processes domestically and internationally, more and more people are now actively concerned with the course of world affairs. The best channels to voice their hopes are the governments democratically elected and responsible to the wishes of the citizenry. When the people disagree with their authorities, whose judgment must necessarily take into account factors not always of public knowledge, the people then can use their nongovernmental bodies to express their prevailing views.

The Worldmark Encyclopedia of the Nations is a pioneer effort. It is our earnest hope that this first edition may prove a truly useful tool to everyone.

BENJAMIN A. COHEN
18 March 1896–12 March 1960
Editor-in-Chief, First Edition

NOTES

GENERAL NOTE: The world has changed dramatically since the publication of the Seventh Edition of the *Worldmark Encyclopedia of the Nations* in 1988. As the world has changed so too has this encyclopedia. The dissolution of the USSR, Czechoslovakia and Yugoslavia; the unification of Germany; the unification of Yemen; and the independence of Eritrea, have led to the creation of 25 new country articles and an additional 570 pages of information in this Eighth Edition. Whereas the First Edition of the *Worldmark Encyclopedia of the Nations,* in one volume, contained 119 country articles, the present edition, in five volumes, now contains 202.

In compiling data for incorporation into the Eighth Edition of the *Worldmark Encyclopedia of the Nations,* substantial efforts were made to enlist the assistance of the government of every nation in the world, as well as of all pertinent UN agencies, who cooperated by supplying data and by revising and updating materials relevant to their sphere of interest. Material received from official sources was reviewed and critically assessed by the editors as part of the process of incorporation. Materials and publications of the UN family and of intergovernmental and nongovernmental organizations throughout the world provided a major fund of geographic, demographic, economic, and social data; in compiling historical and political data, primary materials generated by governments were supplemented by data gathered from numerous other sources.

The reader's attention is directed to the Glossary of Special Terms (pp. 249–50) of this volume) for explanations of key terms and concepts essential to a fuller understanding of the text.

COUNTRY NAMES: Country names are reported (as appropriate) in three forms: the short-form name, as commonly used in the text; the English version of the official name; and the official name in the national language(s). When necessary, textual usages of some short-form names have been rectified, usually through the substitution of an acronym for the official name, in order to strike a better balance between official usages and universal terminology. Thus the following changes in short-form names have been adopted throughout (except in historical context to preserve accuracy): FRG (Federal Republic of Germany); North Korea: DPRK (Democratic People's Republic of Korea); and South Korea: ROK (Republic of Korea). In addition, the following usages have been adopted to reflect official name changes since the Seventh Edition—from Viet-Nam to Viet Nam, from Kampuchea to Cambodia, from Burma to Myanmar.

MAPS: All maps have been redrawn. Spellings on the individual country maps reflect national usages and recognized transliteration practice. To clarify national boundaries and landforms, dark shading has been applied to waters, and lighter shading to lands not within that nation's jurisdiction. Cross-hatching has been used to designate certain disputed areas. Rivers that run dry during certain times of the year are indicated by dashed instead of solid lines. The changes in electronic publishing that have occurred in the last six years have been as dramatic as those that have occurred in national boundaries. To stay current with advanced mapping techniques, the maps have been redrawn in a computerized format in anticipation of an electronic version of this encyclopedia.

FLAGS AND NATIONAL EMBLEMS: All depictions of flags, flag designations, and national emblems have been reviewed and, where necessary, corrected or changed to reflect their official usage as of 1994. In almost all cases the flags and emblems were drawn in an electronic format by One Mile Up, Inc. and are used with their permission. In general, the term "national flag" denotes the civil flag of the nation.

CURRENCY: Currency conversion factors cited in the Eighth Edition are the official exchange rates set by a country's monetary authority, sometimes in a flexible manner. The rates are as reported by the International Monetary Fund in the June 1994 issue of *International Financial Statistics.*

WEIGHTS AND MEASURES: The general world trend toward adoption of the metric system is acknowledged through the use of metric units and their nonmetric (customary or imperial) equivalents throughout the text. The two exceptions to this practice involve territorial sea limits, which are reported in nautical miles, and various production data, for which (unless otherwise stated) units of measure reflect the system in use by the country in question. All tons are metric tons (again, unless otherwise indicated), reflecting the practice of the UN in its statistical reporting. For a complete listing of conversion factors and an explanation of symbols used in the text, see p. 342 of this volume.

HOLIDAYS: Except where noted, all holidays listed are official public holidays, on which government offices are closed that would normally be open. Transliterations of names of Muslim holidays have been standardized. For a fuller discussion on these points, and for a description of religious holidays and their origins and meanings, see the Glossary of Religious Holidays in this volume (pp. 346–348).

INCOME: Data on GNP (gross national product) was compiled from the *World Bank Atlas, 1994.* Data on GDP (gross domestic product) was compiled from *World Tables, 1994,* also a World Bank publication. When a value for GDP was not reported by the World Bank an estimated value reported by the CIA in the 1993 edition of the *World Factbook* was used instead. Percentage contribution to GDP by economic sector was calculated from data reported by the UN in *National Accounts Statistics: Main Aggregates and Detailed Tables, 1991.*

BALANCE OF PAYMENTS: Balance of payments tables were computed from the International Monetary Fund's *Balance of Payments Yearbook.* In some cases, totals are provided even though not all components of those totals have been reported by the government of the country. Accordingly, in some instances numbers in the columns may not add to the total.

PUBLIC FINANCE: Tables reporting government income and expenditures were compiled from *Government Finance Statistics Yearbook, 1993,* published by the International Monetary Fund. As with balance of payments, in some cases, totals are provided income and expenditures even though not all components of those totals have been reported by governments of the country. Accordingly, in some instances, numbers in the columns may not add to the total.

FAMOUS PERSONS: Entries are based on information available through March 1994. Where a person noted in one country is known to have been born in another, the country (or, in some cases, city) of birth follows the personal name, in parentheses.

BIBLIOGRAPHY: Bibliographical listings at the end of country articles are provided as a guide to further reading on the country in question and are not intended as a comprehensive listing of references used in research for the article. Effort was made to provide a broad sampling of works on major subjects and topics as covered by the article; the bibliographies provide, wherever possible, introductory and general works for use by students and general readers, as well as classical studies, recent contributions, and other works regarded as seminal by area specialists. The country article bibliographies were supplemented with information obtained from a search of the OCLC bibliographic database; a process that identified most publications that have been cataloged as of June 1994. An extensive bibliography listing the key references used for this edition appears on page 355 of this volume. However, it is not a complete listing in that many fact sheets, brochures, and other informational materials have been omitted due to space limitations.

CONTRIBUTORS

TO PREVIOUS EDITIONS

Shown below are contributors of country articles to previous editions, in most cases followed by their affiliation or status at the time the contribution was made.

ABOUCHAER, TOUFIC. Second Secretary, Embassy of Syria, Washington, D.C.

ALBA, VICTOR. Author, *Transition in Spain: From Franco to Democracy.*

ALISKY, MARVIN. Director of Center for Latin American Studies and Professor of Political Science, Arizona State University.

ANTHONY, JOHN. Assistant Professor of Middle East Studies, School of Advanced International Studies, Johns Hopkins University.

ARNADE, CHARLES W. Chairman, The American Idea, and Professor of History, University of South Florida.

ASHFORD, DOUGLAS E. Department of Political Science, Cornell University.

AUMANN, MOSHE. Counselor, Embassy of Israel, Washington, D.C.

BARBER, WILLIAM J. Associate Professor of Economics, Wesleyan University.

BARRON, MURIEL T.

BASS, ELIZABETH M. Economist-Editor, Research Project on National Income in East Central Europe, New York.

BENNETT, NORMAN. Professor of History, Boston University.

BERG, ELLIOT J. Professor of Economics, University of Michigan.

BERG, NANCY GUINLOCK.

BERNSTEIN, MARVIN. Professor of History, State University of New York at Buffalo.

BIRNS, LAURENCE R. Director, Council on Hemispheric Affairs.

BOSTON UNIVERSITY, AFRICAN STUDIES CENTER. John Harris, Professor of Economics and Director of African Studies Center; James C. Armstrong, Head, African Studies Library, Editors; Norman Bennett, Professor of History, Boston University; Valerie Plave Bennett, Energy Resources Co.; Heinz A. Bertsch; Edouard Bustin, Professor of Political Science, Boston University; Sid A. Chabawe; Tobias Chizengeni; William D. Coale; Leon Cort; Bernardo P. Ferraz, Fellow, Massachusetts Institute of Technology; Kathleen Langley, Associate Professor of Economics, Boston University; Jay I. Mann; Sandra Mann; Marcos G. Namashulua, Instructor, Political Science, Brandeis University; Jeanne Penvenne; Stella Silverstein; Henry Steady; Dominique Western.

BRADBURY, R. W. Professor of Economics, College of Business Administration, University of Florida.

BUTWELL, RICHARD. Dean for Arts and Science, State University of New York at Fredonia.

CARTER, GWENDOLEN M. Director, Program of African Studies, Northwestern University.

CASTAGNO, ALPHONSO A. Director, African Research and Studies Program, Boston University.

CASTAGNO, MARGARET. Author, *Historical Dictionary of Somalia.*

CHANG, A. S. Hong Kong Correspondent, Institute of Foreign Studies, Tokyo; formerly Professor of Economics, National Chi-nan University, Shanghai.

COLEMAN, JAMES S. Director, African Studies Program, and Professor of Political Science, University of California, Los Angeles.

COLLINS, ROBERT O. Professor of History, University of California, Santa Barbara.

CORBIN, PETER B. Interregional Adviser, UN Department of Technical Cooperation and Development.

CORDERAS, DESCÁRREGA, JOSÉ. Royal Geographical Society, Valverde (Spain).

COWAN, L. GRAY. Dean, School of International Affairs, State University of New York, Albany.

CUMINGS, BRUCE G. Professor of Political Science, Swarthmore College.

CZIRJAK, LASZLO. Associate, Columbia University.

DE GALE, SIR LEO. G.C.M.G., C.B.E., Governor-General, Government of Grenada.

DUNKLE, JOHN R. Associate Professor of Geography and Physical Science, University of Florida.

EVANS, LAURENCE. Professor of History, Harpur College.

EYEK, F. GUNTHER. Professorial Lecturer in History and International Relations, American University.

FALL, BERNARD B. Professor of Government, Howard University.

FINLAND, GOVERNMENT OF. STATISTICAL OFFICE, Helsinki.

FLETCHER, N.E.W. Personal Assistant to the Governor-General, Government of Grenada.

FLETCHER, WILLARD ALLEN. Professor and Chairman, Department of History, College of Arts & Sciences, University of Delaware.

FONER, PHILIP S. Professor of History, Lincoln University.

GANJI, MOHAMMAD H. Chancellor, Amir Showkatul-Mulk University, Birjand, Iran.

GOUTTIERRE, THOMAS E. Dean, International Studies and Programs; Director, Center for Afghanistan, University of Nebraska at Omaha.

GREENHOUSE, RALPH. US Information Agency.

HEINTZEN, HARRY. African Department, Voice of America.

HISPANIC AMERICAN REPORT. Ronald Hilton, Editor; Donald W. Bray, Ronald H. Chilcote, James Cockcroft, Timothy F. Harding, Sir Harold Mitchell, Assistant Editors; Ann Hartfiel, Andrew I. Rematore, Editorial Assistants; Eugene R. Braun, Marjorie Woodford Bray, Lee Ann Campbell, Jorge Caprista, Manuel Carlos, Frances Chilcote, Nancy Clark, Richard L. Cummings, Carlos Darquen, Anthony Dauphinot, Nicholas H. Davis, Joan E. Dowdell, Jerome Durlak, Pan Eimon, Peter L. Eisenberg, Richard Eisman, Claire E. Flaherty, Charles Gauld, Hugh Hamilton, Timothy Harding, Paul Helms, Raymond D. Higgins, Saul Landau, Wendy Lang, Joyce Lobree, Thomas Marks, Marilyn Morrison, Frank Odd, Molly Older, D. Wingate Pike, Gabriel Pinheiro, Luis Ponce de León, Kenneth Posey, James Purks, Lawrence L. Smith, Maud Maria Straub, Linda Striem, David F. Thompson, Pamela Throop, Alice Wexler, Ann Wyckoff, Allen Young, Michael J. Zimmerman, Contributors.

HOFFMAN, GEORGE W. Professor of Geography, University of Texas at Austin.

HUNSBERGER, WARREN S. Professor of Economics, American University (with the assistance of Alan D. Smith, Information Officer, Consulate-General of Japan, New York).

INDOCHINA RESOURCE CENTER. Washington, D.C., D. Gareth Porter, Director.

INGHAM, KENNETH. Director of Studies, Royal Military Academy, Sandhurst.

INGRAMS, HAROLD. Adviser on Overseas Information, Colonial Office, London.

INTERNATIONAL INSTITUTE FOR AERIAL SURVEY AND EARTH SCIENCES. F. J. Ormeling, Head of Cartography Department; C. A. de Bruijn, P. Hofstee, A. B. M. Hijl, Department of Urban Surveys.

ITZKOWITZ, NORMAN. Associate Professor of Oriental Studies, Princeton University.

KANTOR, HARRY. Professor of Political Science, Marquette University.

KAPLAN, FREDRIC M.

KARCH, JOHN J. Professorial Lecturer, Institute for Sino-Soviet Studies, George Washington University.

KINGSBURY, ROBERT C. Assistant Professor of Geography, Indiana University.

KISH, GEORGE. Professor of Geography, University of Michigan.

KOLEHMAINEN, JOHN I. Chairman, Department of Political Science, Heidelberg College.

KOLINSKI, CHARLES J. Professor of History, Florida Atlantic University.

KOSTANICK, HUEY LOUIS. Professor of Geography, University of Southern California.

KRANZ, WALTER. Press and Information Officer, Principality of Liechtenstein.

LEE, ROBERT H.G. Assitant Professor of History, State University of New York at Stony Brook.

LEMARCHAND, RENE. Director, African Studies Center, University of Florida.

LENGYEL, EMIL. Professor of History, Fairleigh Dickinson University (in collaboration with Catherine Logan Camhy).

LEWIS, H. A. G. O.B.E., Fellow, Royal Geographical Society (United Kingdom).

LEWIS, WILLIAM H. Department of Anthropology and Sociology, American University.

LICHTENSTADTER, ILSE. Center for Middle Eastern Studies, Harvard University.

LINDO, WILLIAM. Government Information Services, Government of Belize.

LUX, WILLIAM R. Assistant Professor of History, University of Alabama.

McGUIRE, CARL. Professor of Economics, University of Colorado.

McINTIRE, ROBERT C. Associate Professor and Chairman, Department of Political Science, Millikin University.

McLELLAN, ROBERT S. US Information Agency.

MARKS, HENRY S. Professor of History, Northeast Alabama State Junior College.

MATHEWS, THOMAS G. Secretary-General, Association of Caribbean Universities and Research Institutes, Puerto Rico.

MENDELL, MARCIA EIGEN.

MILLER, NATHAN. Associate Professor of History, University of Wisconsin, Milwaukee.

MILNE, R. S. Professor of Political Science, University of British Columbia.

MORTIMER, MOLLY. Former Commonwealth Correspondent, *The Spectator*, London.

MOSELEY, EDWARD. Assistant Professor of History, University of Alabama.

NEW YORK UNIVERSITY, DEPARTMENT OF POLITICS. I. William Zartman, Editor; John Entelis, Oladipo Coles, Jeffrey Knorr, Marie-Daniele Harmel, Contributors.

NICHOLSON, NORMAN L. Professor of Geography, University of Western Ontario.

O'DELL, ANDREW C. Professor of Geography, University of Aberdeen.

OH, JOHN K. C. Professor of Political Science, Marquette University.

OLIVER, ROBERT T. Head, Department of Speech, Pennsylvania State University.

PANORAMA DDR. Berlin.

PATAI, RAPHAEL. Editor, The Herzl Press.

PAYNE, WALTER A. Professor of History, University of the Pacific.

PETROV, VICTOR P. Professor of Geography, California State College.

POLAND, EMBASSY OF. Washington, D.C.

POLK, WILLIAM R. Director, Adlai E. Stevenson Institute, University of Chicago.

PRAGOPRESS. Prague.

PRICE, GEORGE. Premier, Belize.

RASHIDUZZAMAN, M. Professor of Political Science, Glassboro State College.

REINES, BERNARD.

ROBINSON, KENNETH E. Director, Institute of Commonwealth Studies, and Professor of Commonwealth Affairs, University of London.

ROBINSON, RICHARD D. Lecturer on Middle Eastern Studies, Center for Middle Eastern Studies, Harvard University.

ROSBERG, CARL G., JR. Associate Professor of Political Science, University of California.

ROTBERG, ROBERT I. Professor of Political Science and History, MIT.

RUPEN, ROBERT A. Associate Professor of Political Science, University of North Carolina.

SANDS, WILLIAM. Editor, *The Middle East Journal*.

SHABAD, THEODORE. Correspondent, *The New York Times*.

SHEPHERD, GEORGE. Professor of Political Science, University of Denver.

SMITH, ALAN HEPBURN. Associate Professor of Finance, Marquette University; formerly Permanent Secretary, Ministry of Finance, Ghana.

SORICH, RICHARD. East Asian Institute, Columbia University.

SOVIET ENCYCLOPEDIA PUBLISHING HOUSE.

STEVENS, RICHARD P. Director, African Language and Area Center, Lincoln University.

SYRACUSE UNIVERSITY, FOREIGN AND COMPARATIVE STUDIES PROGRAM. Peter

Dalleo; Thomas C. N. Evans; Robert G. Gregory, Professor of History; Elisabeth Hunt; Roderick J. Macdonald, Professor of History; Thomas F. Taylor.

SYRACUSE UNIVERSITY, PROGRAM OF EAST AFRICAN STUDIES. Fred G. Burke, Director; John R. Nellis, Administrative Assistant; and Gary Gappert, Nikos Georgulas, Richard Kornbluth.

VANDENBOSCH, AMRY. Director Emeritus, Patterson School of Diplomacy and International Commerce, University of Kentucky.

VIVIANI, NANCY. Department of Economics, Australian National University.

WAGNER, EDWARD W. Associate Professor of Korean Studies, Harvard University.

WENNER, MANFRED W. Associate Professor of Political Science, University of Northern Illinois.

WERNSTEDT, FREDERICK L. Associate Professor of Geography, Pennsylvania State University.

WIEDNER, DONALD L. Chairman, Department of History, Temple University.

WILBER, DONALD N. Author, *Iran Past and Present.*

WILMINGTON, MARTIN W. Professor of Economics, Pace College.

WINDER, R. BAYLY. Chairman, Department of Near Eastern Languages and Literatures, New York University.

WOLFE, GREGORY D. Portland State University.

WRIGHT, WINTHROP R. Professor of History, University of Maryland.

YUGOSLAV FEDERAL COMMITTEE FOR INFORMATION.

THE UNITED NATIONS

SYSTEM

THE UNITED NATIONS
FAMILY OF ORGANIZATIONS

INTERNATIONAL COURT OF JUSTICE	GENERAL ASSEMBLY	ECONOMIC AND SOCIAL COUNCIL	SECURITY COUNCIL	SECRETARIAT	TRUSTEESHIP COUNCIL

Main and other
  Sessional committees
Standing committees and ad
  hoc bodies
Other subsidiary organs and related
  bodies

UNRWA
United Nations Relief and
Works Agency for Palestine
Refugees in the Near East

UNARDOL
United Nations Assistance for the
Reconstruction and Development
of Lebanon

IAEA
International Atomic Energy
Agency

Peacekeeping Operations

UNMOSA
UN Military Observer Mission in
South Africa

UNAMIR
UN Assistance Mission in Rwanda

UNMIH II
UN Mission in Haiti II

Agencies, Programs and Funds

INSTRAW
International Research and Training
Institute for the Advancement of
Women

UNCHS (Habitat)
UN Centre for Human Settlements

UNCTAD
UN Conference on Trade and
Development

UNDP
UN Development Programme

UNEP
UN Environment Programme

UNFPA
UN Population Fund

UNHCR
Office of the UN High
Commissioenr for Refugees

UNICEF
UN Children's Fund

UNIFEM
UN Development Fund
for Women

UNITAR
UN Institute for Training and
Research

UNU
United Nations University

WFC
World Food Council

UNDCP
UN International Drug Control
Programme

WFP
World Food Programme
(UN/FAO)

ITC
International Trade Centre
(UNCTAD/GATT)

Functional Commissions
Commission for Social
  Development
Commission on Human Rights
Commission on Narcotic Drugs
Commission on the Status of
  Women
Population Commission
Commission on Sustainable
  Development
Commission on Science and
Technology for Development
Commission on Crime Prevention
  and Criminal Justice

Regional Commissions
Economic Commission for Africa
  (ECA)
Economic Commission for Europe
  (ECE)
Economic Commission for Latin
America and the Caribbean
  (ECLAC)
Economic and Social Commission
  for
Asia and the Pacific (ESCAP)
Economic and Social Commission
for Western Asia (ESCWA)
Sessional and Standing Committees
Expert Committees
Ad Hoc Committees
Related Bodies

Specialized Agencies
ILO
International Labour Organisation
FAO
Food and Agriculture Organisation
of the United Nations
UNESCO
United Nations Educational,
Scientific and Cultural
Organisation
WHO
World Health Organisation

World Bank Group
(Bretton Woods Institutions)
IBRD (World Bank)
International Bank for
  Reconstruction and Development
IDA
International Development
Association
IFC
International Finance Corporation
MIGA
Multilateral Investment Guarantee
Agency

Technical Agencies
IMF
International Monetary Fund
ICAO
International Civil Avaiation
Organisation
UPU
Universal Postal Union
ITU
International Telecommunication
Union
WMO
World Meteorological Organization
IMO
International Maritime
Organisation
WIPO
World Intellectual Property
Organisation
IFAD
International Fund for Agricultural
Development
UNIDO
United Nations Industrial
Development Organisation
GATT/WTO
General Agreement on Tariffs and
Trade/World Trade Organisation

Military Staff Comittee
Standing Committees
Ad Hoc Bodies

International Criminal Tribunal
for the Former Yugoslavia

Peacekeeping operations
(as of July 1994)
UNTSO
UN Truce Supervision Organisation
UNMOGIP
UN Military Oberver Group in
India and Pakistan
UNFICYP
UN Peacekeeping Force in Cyprus
UNDOF
United Nations Disengagement
Observer Force
UNIFIL
United Nations Interim Force
in Lebanon
UNIKOM
United Nations Iraq-Kuwait
Observer Mission
OSGAP
Office of the Secretary General
for Afghanistan and Pakistan
UNAVEM II
United Nations Angola Verification
Mission II
ONUSAL
UN Observer Mission in
El Salvador
MINURSO
UN Mission for the Referendum
in Western Sahara
UNPROFOR I and II
United Nations Protection Force
UNTAC
UN Transnational Authority
in Cambodia
UNOSOM
United Nations Operation
in Somalia
ONUMOZ
UN Operation in Mozambique
MICIVIH
Joint UN/OAS International
Civlian Mission in Haiti
UNMOT
UN Military Observer Mission
to Tajikistan
UNOMUR
UN Observer Mission
in Uganda-Rwanda
UNOMIL
UN Observer Mission in Liberia
UNOMIG I and II
UN Observer Mission to Georgia
UNMIH
UN Mission in Haiti
UNMLT
UN Military Liaison Team
Guatemala
Burundi

STRUCTURE OF THE UNITED NATIONS SYSTEM

The UN system is often referred to as a "family" of organizations. The charter of the UN, signed in San Francisco on 26 June 1945, defined six main organs of the new world body, each with specific tasks and functions. However, because it was impossible to foresee all the demands that might be made on the organization, provision was made for extending its capacities as the need arose. Thus, three of the main organs are specifically empowered to establish "such subsidiary organs" as may be considered necessary for the performance of their functions. In addition, Article 57 of the charter provides that the various specialized agencies established by intergovernmental agreement and having international responsibilities in economic, social, cultural, educational, health, and related fields "shall be brought into relationship" with the UN. Since the signing of the charter, the UN has established numerous subsidiary organs and has entered into relationship with various independent organizations. Reproduced opposite is a chart showing the various organs and bodies within the UN system as of July 1994.

For assistance in interpreting the chart, a brief survey of the UN's main organs, the different categories of subsidiary organs, and the related agencies is given below. A detailed description of the functioning of each of the main organs and an account of the work of selected subsidiary organs are contained in later chapters of the first section of this volume. The structure and work of the UN specialized and technical agencies are described in the second section.

MAIN ORGANS OF THE UN

1. *The General Assembly,* composed of representatives of all member states, is the UN's central deliberative body, empowered to discuss and make recommendations on any subject falling within the scope of the charter itself. It also approves the UN's budget and determines—alone or with the Security Council—part of the composition of the other main organs, including the Security Council.
2. *The Security Council,* a 15-member body, has primary responsibility for maintaining international peace and security. In times of crisis, it is empowered to act on behalf of all member states and to decide on a course of collective action that is mandatory for the entire membership. The charter names five states as permanent members of the Security Council: China, France, the United Kingdom, Russia, and the United States (those that were chiefly responsible for the defeat of the Axis powers in 1945). The remaining Security Council members are elected by the General Assembly for two-year terms.
3. *The Economic and Social Council* is assigned the task of organizing the UN's work on economic and social matters and the promotion of human rights. It consists of 54 members elected for three-year terms by the General Assembly.
4. *The Trusteeship Council* operated the UN trusteeship system established under the charter. It was originally composed of member nations administering trust territories, the permanent members of the Security Council, and a sufficient number of other members, elected by the General Assembly for three-year terms, to ensure an equal division of administering and nonadministering powers. After 1975, it was composed of the five permanent members of the Security Council—the

United States, the sole remaining administering power, and the four permanent nonadministering powers. The last trust territory, the Pacific island of Palau, voted for affiliation with the United States in late 1993. The Trusteeship Council voted in 1994 to convene only at the request of its President, a majority of its member states, the General Assembly, or the Security Council.
5. *The International Court of Justice* is the principal judicial organ of the UN. It consists of 15 judges elected by the General Assembly and the Security Council voting independently.
6. *The Secretariat* is the administrative arm of the organization. It is headed by a Secretary-General appointed by the General Assembly upon the recommendation of the Security Council.

SUBSIDIARY ORGANS OF THE UN

The UN Charter specifically confers the right to create subsidiary organs upon the General Assembly, the Security Council, and the Economic and Social Council. The subsidiary bodies fluctuate in number from year to year, according to the changing requirements of the main organ concerned. Both the General Assembly and the Economic and Social Council, for instance, often create subsidiary bodies to assist them in new fields of concern and dissolve others that have completed their work. Some of the subsidiary organs in turn set up their own subsidiary units—working groups, subcommittees, and the like.

Subsidiary Organs of the General Assembly

The General Assembly's subsidiary organs range in complexity and status from temporary committees to semiautonomous institutions that maintain their own secretariats or administrative departments. The names of the 13 institutions or programs in existence in 1994 (most of which were set up under the joint aegis of the General Assembly and the Economic and Social Council) appear in the lower left-hand column of the chart opposite. The remaining subsidiary organs are too numerous to list; the chart merely indicates their principal types: main and other sessional committees, standing committees and ad hoc bodies, and other subsidiary organs and related bodies.

The main and sessional committees comprise representatives of all member states and are formally reconstituted at each regular General Assembly session to discuss the various items on the agenda for that year. Two sessional committees are not committees of the whole—the 29-member General Committee, which reviews the General Assembly's agenda prior to its adoption at each session, and the nine-member Credentials Committee, which examines the credentials of delegations sent to each General Assembly session.

There are many standing committees, ad hoc bodies, and other subsidiary organs and related bodies. Some of the more important of these are:

- the Advisory Committee on Administrative and Budgetary Questions (ACABQ), a 16-member expert committee which reviews the budgets submitted by the Secretary-General;
- the Committee for Programme and Coordination, a 34-member committee, that reviews the programmatic aspects of the Secretary-General's budget;

- the 18-member Committee on Contributions, which recommends the scale of assessments that nations are required to pay as their share of the United Nations budget;
- the Administrative Committee on Coordination (ACC), established by ECOSOC in 1946. It is composed of the Secretary-General and the executive heads of the specialized agencies and the International Atomic Energy Agency. Its purpose is to supervise implementation of agreements between the UN and the specialized agencies, as well as to ensure the full coordination of activities of these bodies.

The ACC carries out its work through three main committees: the Consultative Committee on Administrative Questions; the Consultative Committee on Programme and Operational Questions; and the Interagency Committee on Sustainable Development. These committees oversee interagency cooperation on topics such as sustainable development, new and renewable sources of energy, international drug abuse control, outer space activities, demographic estimates and projections, women, disabled persons, prevention of crime, youth, water resources, nutrition, statistical activities, long-term development objectives, rural development, and science and technology for development.

An important ACC subcommittee is the Advisory Committee for the Coordination of Information Systems (ACCIS), based in Geneva, which was established in 1983 to facilitate access by member states to United Nations information and to improve the information infrastructure within the UN system. ACCIS advises UN organizations that wish to update or replace their information systems, and promotes the use of common standards to facilitate the electronic exchange of information. ACCIS publishes guides and directories of UN information sources and data bases. It also maintains three important data bases: Database of United Nations Databases and Information Services (DUNDIS), available both online and as a diskette; Database of United Nations Serial Publications (UNSER), available as a diskette; and the Register of Development Activities of the United Nations System (RDA), available as a diskette.

Substantive committees have been set up by General Assembly resolutions to study specific subjects of interest—for example, the peaceful uses of outer space, apartheid in South Africa, and independence for colonial territories. These committees, whose members are elected by the General Assembly or appointed by the its president, usually meet several times a year. At each regular session, they report on their deliberations. They continue as long as is considered necessary. Even when their mandate seems completed, they are not necessarily formally disbanded but may be adjourned indefinitely and reactivated when the need arises. It is through these committees that the General Assembly accomplishes most of its work outside the spheres of responsibility that are specifically entrusted to the Economic and Social Council, the Trusteeship Council, or the various semiautonomous bodies referred to above.

Subsidiary Organs of the Security Council

The Military Staff Committee was established by the charter to advise the Security Council on the military aspects of maintaining international peace. However, the Military Staff Committee secretariat, though it holds regular formal meetings, has never been consulted on any of the UN's peacekeeping operations. The other subsidiary bodies shown on the chart in the top right-hand column were set up, as their names suggest, to conduct the council's peacekeeping operations in the areas specified. (For further information on the work of these bodies, see the chapter on International Peace and Security.)

The Security Council maintains three permanently constituted committees of the whole: one to examine the provisional rules of the council's procedure, the second to consider the admission of new members to the UN, and the third to consider meetings of the council away from the headquarters. The committee on the admission of members did not meet from 1949 to 1971 but since then has met regularly. The committee to examine the council's provisional rules of procedure has not met since 1953. The committee on council meetings away from UN headquarters was constituted in 1972 before the council held meetings in Addis Ababa, and it convened again to prepare for the council session in the following year.

In three cases the Security Council, acting under Chapter VII of the charter, which deals with "action with respect to threats to the peace, breaches of the peace, and acts of aggression," has set up committees to monitor compliance by member states with its resolutions—in 1966, when it imposed mandatory economic sanctions against the illegal regime in Southern Rhodesia; in 1977, when it imposed a mandatory arms embargo against South Africa; and in 1991, after Iraq's unsuccessful invasion of Kuwait, to supervise the elimination of Iraq's weapons of mass destruction.

Subsidiary Organs of the Economic and Social Council

As indicated on the chart, there are four types of subsidiary organs of the Economic and Social Council:

1. the semiautonomous bodies;
2. regional commissions;
3. functional commissions; and
4. sessional, standing, and ad hoc committees.

UN SPECIALIZED AND TECHNICAL AGENCIES

The specialized and technical agencies are separate autonomous organizations with their own policy-making and executive organs, secretariats, and budgets. The precise nature of their relationship with the UN is defined by the terms of special agreements that were established with the Economic and Social Council and subsequently approved by the General Assembly, as provided for in Article 63 of the charter. Since Article 63 also empowers the Economic and Social Council to coordinate the activities of the specialized agencies through consultation and recommendations, they are required to report annually to it.

Mention should be made here of the special status of the General Agreement on Tariffs and Trade (GATT), which will be succeeded by the World Trade Organization. At its inception in 1948, GATT was a treaty establishing a code of conduct in international trade and providing machinery for reducing and stabilizing tariffs. The treaty was concluded pending the creation of a specialized agency to be known as the International Trade Organization, whose draft charter was completed in 1948 but was never ratified by the important trading powers. With the successful conclusion of the Uruguay Round of GATT, a new body, the World Trade Organization, is scheduled to supplant it in 1995. (For further details, see the chapter on the General Agreement on Tariffs and Trade.)

The International Atomic Energy Agency (IAEA) is distinguished from the other agencies in that it was specifically established under the aegis of the UN and is therefore considered in a category by itself. The IAEA reports annually to the General Assembly and only "as appropriate" to the Economic and Social Council. Because of the nature of its work, the IAEA also reports to the Security Council, again only "as appropriate."

THE BRETTON WOODS INSTITUTIONS

These institutions were created before the United Nations itself, at a conference at Bretton Woods, New Hampshire, in the United States in 1944. In the UN Charter, however, they were considered to be an integral part of the system of UN agencies. However, their agreements with the UN bind them only loosely to the rest of the system. The nature of these organizations is very different from the one country, one vote basis of the UN and the other specialized agencies (*see* underWorld Bank and International Monetary Fund (IMF) in the second part of this volume). Membership in the Bretton Woods institutions is subject to financial subscription, and voting is weighted according to members' shares, effectively giving wealthy countries more control than poorer countries. When the World Bank became affiliated with the United Nations, it maintained its complete independence as far as coordination, refused to provide regular information to the UN, limited UN attendance at its meetings, and insisted on a clause eliminating any UN involvement in its budgets. While there is growing cooperation between the World Bank and some UN technical cooperation funds, like the United Nations Development Programme (UNDP), a 1993 study by the Joint Inspection Unit found that there was still not much operational cooperation between the UN system organizations and the World Bank organizations.

THE SIZE AND COST OF THE UN SYSTEM

Since the early 1980s, the United Nations has been criticized for being a "vast, sprawling bureaucracy," and politicians have not hesitated to call it "bloated or "swollen." This perception led to a drive for reform in the mid-1980s during which major contributing countries initiated a 13 percent staff cut. Another round of "rationalization" of the system and its secretariats was initiated in 1991 and continues as this encyclopedia goes to press in the summer of 1994. However, a study by the respected UN authorities Erskine Childers and Sir Brian Urquhart, published by the Dag Hammarskjöld Foundation in 1994, revealed the UN staff around the world, from drivers to directors, numbered 545,000. According to the authors: "The entire UN system world-wide, serving the interests of some 5,500,000,000 [5.5 billion] people in 184 countries, employs no more workers than the civil service in the American state of Wyoming, population 545,000. Its staff is actually smaller than the number of public-service employees of the city of Stockholm in Sweden, with a population of 672,000." While the study concluded that reforms are necessary to render the United Nations system more effective, it points out that the entire budget of the UN and all its agencies was only 0.0005 percent of the world's gross domestic product, representing an expenditure of US$1.90 per human being alive in 1992. By contrast, the world's governments spend approximately US$150 per human being on military expenditures.

COMPARISON WITH THE LEAGUE OF NATIONS

The League of Nations grew out of the catastrophe of World War I (1914–18). Though the idea of the establishment of a body in which the nations of the world could settle their disagreements had been put forth periodically since antiquity, the League, created at the 1919 Paris Peace Conference, was the first organization of sovereign states designed to be universal and devoted to the settlement of disputes and the prevention of war. The League's failure to prevent the outbreak of World War II in 1939 did not destroy the belief in the need for a universal organization. On the contrary, it bred a determination to learn from the mistakes of the past and to build a new world body more adequately equipped to maintain international peace in the future.

The differences between the League of Nations and the UN begin with the circumstances of their creation. First, whereas the Covenant of the League was formulated after hostilities were ended, the main features of the UN were devised while war was still in progress. The more comprehensive powers assigned to the UN for the preservation of peace may owe something to the urgent conditions in which it was conceived. Second, the Covenant was drawn up in an atmosphere of divided attention at the Paris Peace Conference and was incorporated as part of the peace treaty with Germany. Although countries were permitted to ratify the Covenant and the treaty separately, the link between them was not good psychology and contributed, for example, to the unwillingness of the US Senate to ratify the Covenant. In contrast, the UN Charter was drafted as an independent legal instrument at a conference especially convened for the purpose. Third, the Covenant was hammered out behind closed doors, first by the five major powers of the era—France, Italy, Japan, the UK, and the US—and eventually in conjunction with nine other allied nations. The final text of the UN Charter, on the other hand, was the product of combined efforts of 50 states represented at the 1945 San Francisco Conference and therefore took into account the views of the smaller nations, especially their concern to give the new organization far-reaching responsibilities in promoting economic and social cooperation and the independence of colonial peoples.

VOTING

Under the Covenant, decisions of the League could be made only by unanimous vote. This rule applied both to the League's Council, which had special responsibilities for maintaining peace (the equivalent of the UN's Security Council), and to the all-member Assembly (the equivalent of the UN's General Assembly). In effect, each member state of the League had the power of the veto, and, except for procedural matters and a few specified topics, a single "nay" killed any resolution. Learning from this mistake, the founders of the UN decided that all its organs and subsidiary bodies should make decisions by some type of majority vote (though, on occasion, committees dealing with a particularly controversial issue have been known to proceed by consensus). The rule of unanimity applies only to five major powers—France, China, the UK, the US, and the USSR—and then only when they are acting in their capacity as permanent members of the Security Council. The Security Council also proceeds by majority vote, but on substantive (though not on procedural) matters, it must include the concurring votes of all the permanent members. (See the section on Voting in the chapter on the Security Council.)

CONSTITUTIONAL POWERS TO PREVENT WAR AND END AGGRESSION

The Charter was designed to remedy certain constitutional defects and omissions in the Covenant that the founders of the UN believed had been partly responsible for the League's inability to halt the drift toward a second world war in the 1930s. These defects and omissions included the absence of any provision imposing a total ban on war, the provision of an overly rigid procedure for negotiating disputes between states, and the failure to vest the League's Council with sufficient powers to prevent the outbreak of hostilities or to terminate hostilities that had already begun.

The Covenant forbade military aggression but did not reject the limited right of a state to start a war, provided that it had first submitted the dispute to arbitration, judicial decision, or the Council of the League. If one party accepted the findings of the negotiating body and the second did not, the first might then resort to war legally after a "cooling-off" period.

The Charter recognizes no circumstances under which a nation may legally start a war. Article 51 does guarantee the right to individual or collective self-defense, which is a right to respond to an illegal armed attack but not to initiate one. If the Security Council decides that a "threat to the peace" exists, it has the power to order collective enforcement measures. These are mandatory for all member states and may include economic sanctions or military measures, but the power rarely has been invoked. (See the chapter on International Peace and Security.)

MEMBERSHIP

The League never became the universal organization that had been envisaged. Moreover, it failed to secure or retain the membership of certain major powers whose participation and cooperation were essential to make it an effective instrument for preserving the peace. Despite President Wilson's advocacy, the US did not join, and the USSR joined only in 1934, when the League had already shown itself unable to contain the aggressive policies of Germany, Italy, and Japan. The three aggressor states themselves withdrew their membership during the 1930s to pursue their expansionist aims. The UN, on the other hand, is approaching the goal of universality, with only a few smaller countries still unrepresented. By the end of 1987, its membership had reached 159.

PROMOTION OF HUMAN WELFARE

The UN Charter not only lays down specific injunctions for international economic and social cooperation, based on respect for the principle of equal rights and self-determination of peoples, but also has established a special organ—the Economic and Social Council—to conduct the organization's activities in this sphere. Throughout its existence, the UN, together with its specialized agencies, has gradually assumed primary responsibility for assisting the economic and social development of nonindustrialized member nations, most of them former colonial territories that joined the world body long after it was founded. The UN's many projects have become the cornerstone of the development policies adopted by almost all these countries. Since the Covenant of the League contained no provisions for a coordinated program of economic and social cooperation, there can be no comparison between the respective achievements of the two organizations in this respect. Nevertheless, the League performed valuable work in several fields: notably, eliminating the illegal sale of women and children, the "white slave" trade; providing assistance for refugees; reducing traffic in opium and other dangerous narcotics; and getting nations to lessen trade restrictions.

ADMINISTRATION OF COLONIAL TERRITORIES

Instead of sharing the colonial possessions of their defeated enemies as the traditional spoils of victory, the founding members of the League, with admirable foresight and restraint, regarded these territories as international mandates, and certain member states were designated to administer them on behalf of the world organization. This mandate system in a modified form was continued in the trusteeship system evolved by the founders of the UN. However, unlike the Covenant, the Charter expressly stipulates that the administering countries have an obligation to promote the progressive development of the territories placed in their charge toward self-government or independence.

BALANCE SHEET OF THE LEAGUE OF NATIONS

The League failed in its supreme test. It failed to contain the aggressive action of the Axis powers—Japan, Germany, and Italy—and thus failed to halt the drift toward a new world war. Beginning in 1931, Japan, a permanent member of the League's Council, waged a war of aggression against China, in defiance of both the Council and the Assembly. Although the League did impose economic sanctions against Italy, another permanent member of the Council, when it wantonly invaded Ethiopia in 1935, support was halfhearted and the action unsuccessful. The League was unable to do anything against the illegal reoccupation of the Rhineland in 1936 by Germany, still another permanent member of the Council; nor could it offer more than verbal protests against German and Italian intervention in the Spanish Civil War or the forcible incorporation of Austria into Germany in March 1938 and of Czechoslovakia into Germany in the following year. The cumulative effect of these failures strengthened Hitler's belief in the impotence not only of the League itself but also of its principal remaining members. During the summer of 1939, when the world moved ever closer toward war, and even when Hitler's armies marched into Poland on 1 September 1939, not a single member called for a meeting of the League's Council or Assembly.

The League's balance sheet in political matters was not wholly negative, however. It was able, for example, to settle the dispute between Finland and Sweden over the Aland Islands, strategically located in the Gulf of Bothnia; the frontier controversy between Albania, Greece, and Yugoslavia; the potentially explosive border situation between Greece and Bulgaria; and the dangerous conflicts between Poland and Germany over Upper Silesia and between Germany, Poland, and Lithuania over Memel. Through the League's Permanent Court of International Justice, a border controversy between Czechoslovakia and Poland was settled, as were the disputes between Great Britain and Turkey over the Mosul area and between France and Great Britain over the nationality of Maltese residents in the French protectorates of Morocco and Tunisia. The League also stopped the incipient war

between Peru and Colombia over territorial claims in the upper Amazon basin.

In addition to these successful peacekeeping activities, the League financially assisted the reconstruction of certain states, notably Austria, and was responsible for administering the Free City of Danzig and the Saar Territory. (The latter was transferred to Germany following a plebiscite in 1935.) It also carried out important humanitarian work. Some of its nonpolitical activities continued throughout World War II, and its secretariat did valuable preparatory work for the emerging UN. The League of Nations was not officially dissolved until April 1946, five months after the new world body came into being.

THE UN'S GREATER SCOPE

The field of activity and the responsibilities of the UN are considerably more extensive than those of the League. Of the 16 specialized agencies in the UN system, only three—the ILO, the ITU, and the UPU—antedate the UN. The League, furthermore, never sponsored any such enterprises as those undertaken by, for example, the UN Development Program, the UN Environment Program, or the World Food Program. Membership in the League did not oblige a nation to join the Permanent Court of Justice, whereas all members of the UN are automatically parties to the Statute of the International Court of Justice, which is an integral part of the Charter.

Like the League, the UN has recorded several important successes in halting local armed conflicts and the spread of disputes: for example, in the Congo, Kashmir, and, over long periods, Cyprus. However, it has proved unable to take effective action in any situation where the interests of either the US or the former USSR are closely involved or where the two giant powers seem committed to opposite sides of disputes involving smaller nations. Thus, it was unable to check the Soviet invasion of Hungary in 1956 and of Czechoslovakia in 1968; it was unable to take any action to halt the fighting that raged in Indochina during most of its existence; and it has not succeeded in finding a permanent solution to the prolonged crisis that has periodically erupted in Arab-Israeli wars in the Middle East.

The UN's ineffectuality in such situations caused a loss of confidence in its relevance in international political relations. Nor was it a source of consolation that there was no discernible drift toward a world war, for in most cases where the US and the former USSR found themselves almost at the point of actual confrontation, as in the 1962 Cuban crisis, they tended to resolve their differences bilaterally, not under the aegis of the UN.

On the other hand, if the two great powers did not always find it convenient to allow the UN to play too decisive a role in political matters, they found it equally impractical to bypass the world organization altogether.

Unlike the League, the UN is the center of a network of organizations whose activities reach into many aspects of the national life of every member state. As such, it has come to be regarded as an indispensable part of the machinery for conducting multiple-level international relations. In a world transformed by the collapse of the former Soviet bloc, the UN is coming of age and may begin to fulfill the dreams of its founders. While its authority continues to be challenged by countries that remain on the fringe of the world community, the United Nations may be seen as an embryonic world government.

THE MAKING OF THE UNITED NATIONS

The creation of the UN at the San Francisco Conference in June 1945 was the culmination of four years of concentrated preparation. During these years, the idea of a world organization to replace the League of Nations was first debated and then fleshed out. Many of the important principles of the UN adopted at San Francisco were derived from earlier conferences.

DEVELOPMENTS LEADING TO THE SAN FRANCISCO CONFERENCE

1. *The Inter-Allied Declaration (London Declaration) of 12 June 1941.* In a dark hour of World War II, representatives of the UK, Australia, Canada, New Zealand, and the Union of South Africa and of the governments-in-exile of Belgium, Czechoslovakia, France, Greece, Luxembourg, the Netherlands, Norway, Poland, and Yugoslavia assembled at St. James's Palace in London. It was there that they each pledged not to sign a separate peace and declared: "The only true basis of enduring peace is the willing cooperation of free peoples in a world in which, relieved of the menace of aggression, all may enjoy economic and social security. . . . " Ten days later, Hitler launched his attack against the Soviet Union.

2. *The Atlantic Charter of 14 August 1941.* British Prime Minister Winston S. Churchill and US President Franklin D. Roosevelt met aboard the cruiser USS *Atlanta* off the coast of Newfoundland and signed a declaration giving the first indication that the two powers would strive for the creation of a new world organization once peace was restored. In it, they announced "certain common principles . . . of their respective countries . . . for a better future for the world: the need for a secure peace; the abandonment by all nations of the use of force; the disarmament of aggressors; and the establishment of a wider and permanent system of general security."

3. *The Declaration by United Nations of 1 January 1942.* With the Japanese attack on Pearl Harbor on 7 December 1941 and the entry of the US into the war, the conflict assumed even wider dimensions. Japan's initial successes were staggering, and it was clear that the coalition against the Axis powers (Germany, Italy, Japan, and their allies) would need to be strengthened.

   On New Year's Day of 1942 in Washington, DC, representatives of 26 states signed a declaration whose preamble called for subscription "to a common program of purposes and principles embodied in the . . . Atlantic Charter" and explicitly referred to the need for promoting respect for human rights on an international basis. In that declaration, the phrase "united nations" was first used. It had been coined by President Roosevelt to express the unity of the signatory nations in their determination to withstand the onslaught of the Axis powers. The declaration was subsequently signed by the governments of 21 additional states.

4. *The Moscow Declaration of 30 October 1943.* This declaration laid the foundation for the establishment of a new world body to replace the League of Nations. Meeting at a time when victory seemed in sight, the US, British, and Soviet foreign ministers and an ambassador from China drew up the Declaration of Four Nations on General Security, which recognized "the necessity of establishing at the earliest practicable date a general international organization based on the principle of sovereign equality of all peace-loving States, and open to membership by all such States, large and small, for the maintenance of international peace and security."

5. *Dumbarton Oaks Conference, Washington, 21 August–7 October 1944.* The Dumbarton Oaks conference was the first big-power meeting convoked specifically to discuss the establishment of a new world organization. At the beginning of the conference, the delegations offered widely differing proposals. On some of these divergent views they eventually reached agreement. For example, the British and Soviet delegations accepted an American position that favored a strong role for the General Assembly, in which all member states would be represented and which, therefore, would be the most "democratic" of the UN organs. There was agreement that a small Security Council should be "primarily responsible for the maintenance of international peace and security" and that the big powers should have the right of veto in that body. However, a deadlock developed over a Soviet proposal that a big power might exercise this right in disputes in which it was itself involved. This the US and the British refused to accept.

6. *Yalta Conference, February 1945.* The resultant deadlock was resolved at a meeting in Yalta attended by Prime Minister Churchill, President Roosevelt, and Marshal Stalin. The "Yalta formula," actually a compromise proposed by the US and rejected by the USSR at Dumbarton Oaks, provided that if any of the Big Five powers was involved in a dispute, it would not have the right to veto Security Council recommendations for peaceful settlement of the issue but would be able to veto a Security Council decision to invoke sanctions against it. After some initial objections from Churchill, the three leaders at Yalta also managed to agree on the basic principles of a trusteeship system for the administration of certain dependent territories under the aegis of the projected world body.

   On 11 February 1945, the three leaders announced that a conference would be convened in San Francisco on 25 April 1945 for the "earliest possible establishment of a general international organization" along the lines proposed at Dumbarton Oaks.

THE SAN FRANCISCO CONFERENCE, 25 APRIL–26 JUNE 1945

Despite the sudden death of President Roosevelt in early April, the United Nations Conference on International Organization convened as scheduled. President Roosevelt had been working on his speech to the conference before he died. That never-delivered address contains the often-quoted words: "The work, my friends, is peace; more than an end of this war—an end to the beginning of all wars; . . . as we go forward toward the greatest contribution that any generation of human beings can make in this world—the contribution of lasting peace—I ask you to keep up your faith. . . ."

China, the USSR, the UK, and the US acted as the sponsoring powers, and 46 other states participated, comprising all those that had signed the Declaration by United Nations of 1 January

1942 or had declared war on the Axis powers by March 1945. The huge conference was attended by 282 delegates and 1,444 other officially accredited persons from those 50 countries and by representatives of scores of private organizations interested in world affairs (50 from the US alone). The daily output of documents averaged half a million pages.

Major Modifications in the Dumbarton Oaks Draft for the UN Charter

After much debate, the smaller and medium-sized nations succeeded in restricting the Big Five's use of the veto in the Security Council. Herbert V. Evatt, then deputy prime minister of Australia, who was in the forefront of that fight, declared: "In the end our persistence had some good effect. The Great Powers came to realize that the smaller powers would not accept a Charter unless certain minimum demands for restriction of the veto were accepted, viz., that there should be no veto upon the placing of items on the [Security Council] agenda and no veto on discussion [in the Security Council] . . . . If this vital concession had not been won, it is likely that discussion of matters in the open forum of the Security Council would have been rendered impossible: If so, the United Nations might well have broken up."

Another major change resulted from the desire of the smaller nations to give the world organization more responsibilities in social and economic matters and in colonial problems. Accordingly, the Economic and Social Council and the Trusteeship Council were given wider authority than was provided for in the Dumbarton Oaks draft, and they were made principal organs of the UN.

Creation of a New World Court

The San Francisco Conference also unanimously adopted a constitution—called the Statute—for an International Court of Justice to be incorporated as a main organ of the UN and to succeed the Permanent Court of International Justice established by the League of Nations. The Statute, which had originally been drafted by jurists from 44 nations meeting in Washington in April 1945, became part of the Charter of the UN.

Unanimous Acceptance of the Charter

The UN Charter touches on so many delicate and complex matters that its unanimous acceptance has often been ascribed to the particularly auspicious circumstances prevailing in the spring of 1945. In spite of some dissonance, the San Francisco Conference was imbued with a spirit of high mission. The Charter was worked out within two months. It was signed by 50 nations in all its official languages in an impressive ceremony on 26 June 1945. The five official languages at that time were Chinese, English, French, Russian, and Spanish. The sixth official UN language, Arabic, was not adopted until 1973.

ESTABLISHMENT OF THE UN, 24 OCTOBER 1945

The new world body officially came into being on 24 October 1945, when the Charter had been duly ratified by all permanent members of the Security Council and a majority of the other original signatory powers. This date is universally celebrated as United Nations Day.

SUBSEQUENT CHARTER AMENDMENT

Like other political constitutions, the UN Charter contains provisions for its own amendment. Amendments to the Charter come into force when they have been adopted by a vote of two-thirds of the members of the General Assembly and ratified by two-thirds of the UN member states, including all the permanent members of the Security Council.

The amendments that have been adopted are essentially adjustments made to take account of the huge increase in UN membership, which has more than tripled since 1945. As originally constituted, the 11-member Security Council and the 18-member Economic and Social Council were considered adequate to reflect the different interests of the various geographical groupings of states within the organization. However, the admission to the UN during the late 1950s and early 1960s of large numbers of newly independent African, Asian, and Caribbean countries created additional groupings. To accommodate their interests without jeopardizing those of the older groups, the General Assembly, in 1963, adopted amendments to Articles 23, 27, and 61 of the Charter. The first amendment enlarged the membership of the Security Council to 15; the second required that decisions of the Security Council be made by an affirmative vote of nine members (formerly seven); the third enlarged the membership of the Economic and Social Council to 27. All three amendments officially came into force on 31 August 1965.

The Economic and Social Council was enlarged to 54 by an amendment to Article 61 of the Charter, which was adopted by the General Assembly in 1971 and became operative on 24 September 1973.

Charter Review. Under the Charter, a general conference of UN members "for the purpose of reviewing the Charter may be held at a date and place to be fixed by a two-thirds vote of the members of the General Assembly and a vote of any seven members [amended to nine, as of 1965] of the Security Council." In addition, the Charter provided that if such a conference was not held by the tenth regular assembly session (in 1955), the proposal to call such a conference should be placed on the agenda. Accordingly, the 1955 General Assembly considered the matter and decided that a general review conference should be held at an "appropriate" but unspecified date in the future. A committee consisting of the full UN membership was established to consider the time and place at which the conference should be held. The Security Council concurred in the General Assembly's decision by a vote of 9 to 1, with 1 abstention. The committee met every two years until September 1967 without recommending a conference. It then became inactive, recommending that any member state might request it to meet.

At its 1974 session, the General Assembly established a 42-member Ad Hoc Committee on the Charter to consider specific proposals from governments for "enhancing the ability of the United Nations to achieve its purposes." The committee reported to the 1975 Assembly session that there was a fundamental divergence of opinion on the necessity for carrying out a review of the Charter and made no recommendations for action. The General Assembly decided, however, to continue the committee as a Special Committee on the Charter of the UN and on the Strengthening of the Role of the Organization and increased its membership to 47. In pursuit of its mandate, the committee has met every year since 1975 and has reported to each session of the General Assembly.

For example, in 1988 the Special Committee recommended, and the General Assembly adopted, a "Body of Principles for the Protection of All Persons under Any Form of Detention or Imprisonment"; in 1990 it proposed the rationalization of existing UN procedures, which were adopted by the General Assembly; and in 1991, the Special Committee considered the final text of the *Handbook on the Peaceful Settlement of Disputes between States.* That same year the General Assembly requested that the Secretary-General publish and disseminate the handbook.

The Special Committee also considers proposals concerning cooperation between the United Nations and regional organizations in the maintenance of international peace and security, conciliation rules of the United Nations, and assistance to other states affected by the imposition of sanctions by the decision of the Security Council, pursuant to Article 50 of the Charter.

PURPOSES AND PRINCIPLES

The main aims of the UN are set forth in the Preamble to the Charter, in which "the peoples of the United Nations," assembled in San Francisco in June 1945, expressed their determination

"to save succeeding generations from the scourge of war, which twice in our lifetime has brought untold sorrow to mankind, . . .

"to reaffirm faith in fundamental human rights, in the dignity and worth of the human person, in the equal rights of men and women and of nations large and small, . . .

"to establish conditions under which justice and respect for the obligations arising from treaties and other sources of international law can be maintained, and

"to promote social progress and better standards of life in larger freedom. . . ."

To accomplish these goals, they agreed

"to practice tolerance and live together in peace with one another as good neighbors, . . .

"to unite their strength to maintain international peace and security, . . .

"to ensure by the acceptance of principles and the institution of methods, that armed force shall not be used, save in the common interest, and

"to employ international machinery for the promotion of the economic and social advancement of all peoples . . . ."

PURPOSES
The aims of the UN are embodied in a set of purposes and principles contained in Articles 1 and 2 of the Charter, summarized as follows:

1. to maintain international peace and security and, to that end, to take effective collective measures for the prevention and removal of threats to the peace and for the suppression of acts of aggression or other breaches of the peace, and to bring about by peaceful means, and in conformity with the principles of justice and international law, adjustment or set-tlement of international disputes or situations that might lead to a breach of the peace;
2. to develop friendly relations among nations based on respect for the principle of equal rights and self-determination of peoples, and to take other appropriate measures to strengthen universal peace;
3. to achieve international cooperation in solving international economic, social, cultural, or humanitarian problems and in promoting and encouraging respect for human rights and for fundamental freedoms for all without distinction as to race, sex, language, or religion; and
4. to be a center for harmonizing the actions of nations in attaining these common ends.

PRINCIPLES
In pursuit of these purposes, the Charter stipulates that the UN and its members are to act in accordance with the following principles:

1. that the organization is based on the sovereign equality of all its members;
2. that all members are to fulfill in good faith their Charter obligations;
3. that they are to settle their international disputes by peaceful means and without endangering peace, security, and justice;
4. that they are to refrain in their international relations from the threat or use of force against other states;
5. that they are to give the UN every assistance in any action that it takes in accordance with the Charter and shall not assist states against which the UN is taking preventive or enforcement action;
6. that the UN shall also ensure that states that are not members act in accordance with these principles insofar as is necessary to maintain international peace and security; and
7. that nothing in the Charter is to authorize the UN to intervene in matters that are essentially within the domestic jurisdiction of any state, though this principle is not to prejudice the application of enforcement measures made necessary in the event of a threat to or breach of the peace.

MEMBERSHIP

As of 30 April 1994, the UN had 184 member states, including 51 charter members and 133 states that have joined the organization since 1945, the great majority of them former colonial territories that have achieved independence. The table that follows shows the growth of UN membership, the roster lists the members of the UN in alphabetical order and gives the dates of their admission to the UN. The roster does not take account of the several federations or unions of states that were created or dissolved during membership.

Thus, Syria, an original member, ceased independent membership on joining with Egypt to form the United Arab Republic in 1958. On resuming its separate status in 1961, Syria also resumed separate membership, which is still officially dated from the country's original day of entry. Tanganyika and Zanzibar joined the UN as separate states in 1961 and 1963, respectively, but in 1964 merged to form the United Republic of Tanzania, with a single membership officially dated from Tanganyika's day of entry.

Similarly, The Federation of Malaya joined the United Nations on 17 September 1957. On 16 September 1963, its name was changed to Malaysia, following the admission to the new federation of Singapore, Sabah (North Borneo), and Sarawak. Singapore became an independent state on 9 August 1965 and a member of the United Nations on 21 September 1965.

The Federal Republic of Germany and the German Democratic Republic were admitted to membership in the United Nations on 18 September 1973. Through accession of the German Democratic Republic to the Federal Republic of Germany, effective from 3 October 1990, the two German states have united to form one sovereign state.

The unification of the two Germanys began a process of realignment of nations that intensified as communist governments collapsed throughout Eastern Europe. In only two years 15 separate states from the former USSR were admitted to membership. As a result of this sweeping change, the former Union of Soviet Socialist Republics (an original member of the United Nations) became the Russian Federation. In a letter dated 24 December 1991, Boris Yeltsin, the president of the Russian Federation, informed the Secretary-General that the membership of the Soviet Union in the Security Council and all other United Nations organs was being continued by the Russian Federation with the support of the 11 member countries of the Commonwealth of Independent States.

Czechoslovakia also was an original member of the United Nations. On 10 December 1992, its Permanent Representative informed the Secretary-General that the Czech and Slovak Federal Republic would cease to exist on 31 December 1992 and that the Czech Republic and the Slovak Republic, as successor states, would apply for membership in the United Nations. Following the receipt of their applications, the Security Council, on 8 January 1993, recommended to the General Assembly that both the Czech Republic and the Slovak Republic be admitted to United Nations membership. Both were admitted on 19 January 1993.

In 1993, the proposed admission of a part of the former Yugoslavia, which had been known as the Republic of Macedonia, formed the subject of protest from the government of Greece, which considers the name "Macedonia" to pertain to one of its internal states. Now bearing the unwieldy name of "The Former Yugoslav Republic of Macedonia," the new country became a member on 8 April 1993.

ADMISSION OF MEMBERS
In the words of Article 4 of the Charter, membership in the UN is open to all "peace-loving states which accept the obligations contained in the present Charter and, in the judgment of the Organization, are able and willing to carry out these obligations." The original members are the states that participated in the San Francisco Conference, or that had previously signed the Declaration by United Nations, of 1 January 1942, and subsequently signed and ratified the Charter.

The procedure of admission is as follows. A state wishing to join submits an application to the Secretary-General, in which it formally states its acceptance of the Charter obligations. The application is forwarded to the Security Council. If the Security Council, by a vote of at least nine members (formerly seven), including all the permanent members, recommends the application, membership becomes effective on the day that it is approved by a two-thirds majority of the General Assembly. In other words, if any one of the Security Council's permanent members vetoes it, or if it fails to obtain a sufficient majority in the Security Council, the application does not reach the General Assembly at all.

Up to 1955 there were bitter controversies and years of stalemate in the Security Council over the applications of some countries. Usually one or more of the Big Five was on bad terms with the applying state, or it would choose to withhold consent as a bargaining point against the other big powers. Finally, on 14 December 1955, by a compromise, 16 countries were admitted together. Since then, new applications have only exceptionally caused controversy. Most of the applicants have been newly independent states that applied for membership immediately after attaining their independence. In almost all cases they have been admitted without delay and by unanimous vote.

The outstanding exceptions are the applications of the Republic of Korea (ROK), which applied in January 1949; the Democratic People's Republic of Korea (DPRK), which applied in February 1949; South Viet Nam, which applied in December 1951; and North Viet Nam, which applied in December 1951. The two Viet Nams and the ROK sought action on their applications in 1975. The Security Council, by a narrow vote, decided not to take up the ROK's application, and the US subsequently vetoed membership for the Viet Nams, citing as a reason the Security Council's earlier refusal to consider the membership application of the ROK. In response to a General Assembly recommendation, however, the Security Council in 1977 recommended the admission of the newly established Socialist Republic of Viet Nam, and that country became a member in September 1977. The DPRK and the ROK maintained observer status at the General Assembly until September 1991, when both were admitted to membership simultaneously.

WITHDRAWAL FROM MEMBERSHIP
While the Covenant of the League of Nations contained provisions for the legal withdrawal of members, the UN Charter deliberately omits all reference to the subject. The majority feeling at

the San Francisco Conference was that provisions for withdrawal would be contrary to the principle of universality and might provide a loophole for members seeking to evade their obligations under the Charter.

Thus, when the first—and so far the only—case of withdrawal arose, the procedure had to be improvised. On 1 January 1965, Indonesia, which then was pursuing a policy of confrontation against the newly formed Federation of Malaysia, announced that it would withdraw from the UN and its related agencies if Malaysia were to take its elected seat on the Security Council. Three weeks later, Indonesia's foreign minister officially confirmed withdrawal in a letter to the Secretary-General, who, after consultations with the Indonesian mission to the UN, merely noted the decision and expressed hope that Indonesia would in due time "resume full cooperation" with the world body. Following a coup later in 1965, Indonesia sent a telegram to the Secretary-General, just before the opening of the 1966 General Assembly session, announcing its decision to "resume full cooperation with the UN and to resume participation in its activities."

Arrangements were made to ensure that Indonesia's reentry would take place with minimum formality. Hence, it was decided that Indonesia need not make a formal reapplication via the Security Council but that the matter could be handled directly by the General Assembly. Citing the telegram as evidence that Indonesia regarded its absence from the UN as a "cessation of cooperation" rather than an actual withdrawal, the General Assembly's president recommended that the administrative procedure for reinstating Indonesia could be taken. No objections were raised, and Indonesia was immediately invited to resume its seat in the General Assembly. In short, the problems raised by the first case of withdrawal from the UN were solved by treating it as if it had not been a matter of withdrawal at all.

Although South Africa withdrew from three of the UN's related agencies—UNESCO, FAO, and the ILO—because of the antiapartheid sentiments of their members, it did not withdraw from the UN itself, despite numerous General Assembly resolutions condemning apartheid and recommending stringent sanctions.

SUSPENSION AND EXPULSION

The Charter provides that a member against which the Security Council has taken preventive or enforcement action may be suspended from the exercise of the rights and privileges of membership by the General Assembly upon the recommendation of the Security Council. However, only the Security Council, not the General Assembly, has the power to restore these rights. Any member that "has persistently violated the Principles" of the Charter may be expelled from the UN by the same procedure. Up to the end of 1987, no cases of suspension of rights or expulsion had been recommended or considered by the Security Council.

Many states have called for the expulsion of South Africa because of its apartheid policies, but no formal proposal to this effect has been made. In 1974, the General Assembly called upon the Security Council to review the relationship between the UN and South Africa in the light of the constant violation by South Africa of the principles of the Charter and the Universal Declaration of Human Rights. The Security Council considered a draft resolution submitted by Cameroon, Iraq, Kenya, and Mauritania that would have recommended to the General Assembly the immediate expulsion of South Africa under Article 6 of the Charter. Owing to the negative votes of three permanent members (France, UK, US), the draft resolution was not adopted. After the council had reported back to the General Assembly on its failure to adopt a resolution, the president of the General Assembly, Abdelaziz Bouteflika of Algeria, ruled that the delegation of South Africa should be refused participation in the work of the General Assembly. His ruling was upheld by 91 votes to 22, with 19 abstentions. Although remaining a member of the UN, South Africa was not represented at subsequent sessions of the General Assembly. Following South Africa's successful democratic elections of May 1994, after 24 years of refusing to accept the credentials of the South African delegation, the General Assembly unanimously welcomed South Africa back to full participation in the United Nations on 23 June 1994. It also deleted its agenda item on "the elimination of apartheid and the establishment of a united, democratic and non-racial South Africa."

REPRESENTATION OF NATIONS IN THE UN

The members of the UN are nations, not governments. Whereas the UN may concern itself with the character of a government at the time that a nation applies for admission and may occasionally defer admission on these grounds (Spain under the Franco government, for example, applied for membership in 1945–46 but was not admitted until 1955), once a nation becomes a member, any governmental changes thereafter do not affect continuance of membership—provided, of course, that the nation continues to fulfill its Charter obligations. Nor, under the Charter, is the admission of a new nation dependent upon whether other nations individually recognize and have diplomatic relations with the government concerned. Though the relations of individual members with a nation applying for membership will affect the voting in the Security Council and the General Assembly, strictly speaking, the only consideration enjoined by the Charter is the judgment by the members that the applying nation as represented by its government is "willing and able" to carry out its UN obligations. As a result, there are several nations in the UN that do not recognize or have diplomatic relations with each other.

Nations have to be represented at UN proceedings by delegations that are specifically authorized by their governments to speak on their behalf. Thus, when a new ambassador appears, or when a new session of a UN organ convenes, it is necessary to examine the credentials of persons claiming to represent member states. The nine-member Credentials Committee, appointed by the General Assembly at the beginning of each session, must be satisfied that the person was duly appointed by his or her government and that that government is the official government of the respective member nation. The matter can become controversial at the UN if, for example, two rival governments both claim to be the only legitimate government of a member state and each demands that its own representative be seated.

An outstanding case in point was China. The unresolved issue of its representation in the UN had long been one of the most important and controversial items on the General Assembly's agenda. In 1971, however, the General Assembly decided "to restore all its rights to the People's Republic of China and to recognize the representatives of its government as the only legitimate representatives of China to the United Nations, and to expel forthwith the representatives of Chiang Kai-shek from the place which they unlawfully occupy at the United Nations and in all the organizations related to it."

United Nations Member States
(as of 30 April 1994)

MEMBER STATE	DATE OF ADMISSION	SCALE OF ASSESSMENTS (PERCENT)	MEMBER STATE	DATE OF ADMISSION	SCALE OF ASSESSMENTS (PERCENT)
Afghanistan	19 November 1946	0.01	Guyana	20 September 1966	0.01
Albania	14 December 1955	0.01	Haiti	24 October 1945	0.01
Algeria	8 October 1962	0.16	Honduras	17 December 1945	0.01
Andorra	28 July 1993	0.01	Hungary	14 December 1955	0.18
Angola	1 December 1976	0.01	Iceland	19 November 1946	0.03
Antigua and Barbuda	11 November 1981	0.01	India	30 October 1945	0.36
Argentina	24 October 1945	0.57	Indonesia	28 September 1950	0.16
Armenia	2 March 1992	0.13	Iran	24 October 1945	0.77
Australia	1 November 1945	1.51	Iraq	21 December 1945	0.13
Austria	14 December 1955	0.75	Ireland	14 December 1955	0.18
Azerbaijan	2 March 1992	0.22	Israel	11 May 1949	0.23
Bahamas	18 September 1973	0.02	Italy	14 December 1955	4.29
Bahrain	21 September 1971	0.03	Jamaica	18 September 1962	0.01
Bangladesh	17 September 1974	0.01	Japan	18 December 1956	12.45
Barbados	9 December 1966	0.01	Jordan	14 December 1955	0.01
Belarus	24 October 1945	0.48	Kazakhstan	2 March 1992	0.35
Belgium	27 December 1945	1.06	Kenya	16 December 1963	0.01
Belize	25 September 1981	0.01	Korea, Democratic People's Republic of	17 September 1991	0.05
Benin	20 September 1960	0.01	Korea, Republic of	17 September 1991	0.69
Bhutan	21 September 1971	0.01	Kuwait	14 May 1963	0.25
Bolivia	14 November 1945	0.01	Kyrgyz Republic	2 March 1992	0.06
Bosnia and Herzegovina	22 May 1992	0.04	Lao People's Democratic Republic	14 December 1955	0.01
Botswana	17 October 1966	0.01	Latvia	17 September 1991	0.13
Brazil	24 October 1945	1.59	Lebanon	24 October 1945	0.01
Brunei Darussalam	21 September 1984	0.03	Lesotho	17 October 1966	0.01
Bulgaria	14 December 1955	0.13	Liberia	2 November 1945	0.01
Burkina Faso	20 September 1960	0.01	Libyan Arab Jamahiriya	14 December 1955	0.24
Burundi	18 September 1962	0.01	Liechtenstein	18 September 1990	0.01
Cambodia	14 December 1955	0.01	Lithuania	17 September 1991	0.15
Cameroon	20 September 1960	0.01	Luxembourg	24 October 1945	0.06
Canada	9 November 1945	3.11	Madagascar	20 September 1960	0.01
Cape Verde	16 September 1975	0.01	Malawi	1 December 1964	0.01
Central African Republic	20 September 1960	0.01	Malaysia	17 September 1957	0.12
Chad	20 September 1960	0.01	Maldives	21 September 1965	0.01
Chile	24 October 1945	0.08	Mali	28 September 1960	0.01
China	24 October 1945	0.77	Malta	1 December 1964	0.01
Colombia	5 November 1945	0.13	Marshall Islands	17 September 1991	0.01
Comoros	12 November 1975	0.01	Mauritania	27 October 1961	0.01
Congo	20 September 1960	0.01	Mauritius	24 April 1968	0.01
Costa Rica	2 November 1945	0.01	Mexico	7 November 1945	0.88
Côte d'Ivoire	20 September 1960	0.02	Micronesia (Federated States of)	17 September 1991	0.01
Croatia	22 May 1992	0.13	Monaco	28 May 1993	0.01
Cuba	24 October 1945	0.09	Mongolia	27 October 1961	0.01
Cyprus	20 September 1960	0.02	Morocco	12 November 1956	0.03
Czech Republic	19 January 1993	0.42	Mozambique	16 September 1975	0.01
Denmark	24 October 1945	0.65	Myanmar	19 April 1948	0.01
Djibouti	20 September 1977	0.01	Namibia	23 April 1990	0.01
Dominica	18 December 1978	0.01	Nepal	14 December 1955	0.01
Dominican Republic	24 October 1945	0.02	Netherlands	10 December 1945	1.50
Ecuador	21 December 1945	0.03	New Zealand	24 October 1945	0.24
Egypt	24 October 1945	0.07	Nicaragua	24 October 1945	0.01
El Salvador	24 October 1945	0.01	Niger	20 September 1960	0.01
Equatorial Guinea	12 November 1968	0.01	Nigeria	7 October 1960	0.20
Eritrea	28 May 1993	0.01	Norway	27 November 1945	0.55
Estonia	17 September 1991	0.07	Oman	7 October 1971	0.03
Ethiopia	13 November 1945	0.01	Pakistan	30 September 1947	0.06
Fiji	13 October 1970	0.01	Panama	13 November 1945	0.02
Finland	14 December 1955	0.57	Papua New Guinea	10 October 1975	0.01
France	24 October 1945	6.00	Paraguay	24 October 1945	0.02
Gabon	20 September 1960	0.02	Peru	31 October 1945	0.06
Gambia	21 September 1965	0.01	Philippines	24 October 1945	0.07
Georgia	31 July 1992	0.21	Poland	24 October 1945	0.47
Germany	18 September 1973	8.93	Portugal	14 December 1955	0.20
Ghana	8 March 1957	0.01	Qatar	21 September 1971	0.05
Greece	25 October 1945	0.35	Republic of Moldova	2 March 1992	0.15
Grenada	17 September 1974	0.01	Romania	14 December 1955	0.17
Guatemala	21 November 1945	0.02			
Guinea	12 December 1958	0.01			
Guinea-Bissau	17 September 1974	0.01			

United Nations Member States—*cont.*
(as of 30 April 1994)

MEMBER STATE	DATE OF ADMISSION	SCALE OF ASSESSMENTS (PERCENT)	MEMBER STATE	DATE OF ADMISSION	SCALE OF ASSESSMENTS (PERCENT)
Russian Federation	24 October 1945	6.71	Tajikistan	2 March 1992	0.05
Rwanda	18 September 1962	0.01	Thailand	16 December 1946	0.11
St. Kitts and Nevis	23 September 1983	0.01	The Former Yugoslav		
St. Lucia	18 September 1979	0.01	Republic of Macedonia	8 April 1993	0.02
St. Vincent and the			Togo	20 September 1960	0.01
Grenadines	16 September 1980	0.01	Trinidad and Tobago	18 September 1962	0.05
Samoa	15 December 1976	0.01	Tunisia	12 November 1956	0.03
San Marino	2 March 1992	0.01	Turkey	24 October 1945	0.27
São Tomé and Principe	16 September 1975	0.01	Turkmenistan	2 March 1992	0.06
Saudi Arabia	24 October 1945	0.96	Uganda	25 October 1962	0.01
Senegal	28 September 1960	0.01	Ukraine	24 October 1945	1.87
Seychelles	21 September 1976	0.01	United Arab Emirates	9 December 1971	0.21
Sierra Leone	27 September 1961	0.01	United Kingdom	24 October 1945	5.02
Singapore	21 September 1965	0.12	United Republic of Tanzania	14 December 1961	0.01
Slovakia	19 January 1993	0.13	United States of America	24 October 1945	25.00
Slovenia	22 May 1992	0.09	Uruguay	18 December 1945	0.04
Solomon Islands	19 September 1978	0.01	Uzbekistan	2 March 1992	0.26
Somalia	20 September 1960	0.01	Vanuatu	15 September 1981	0.01
South Africa	7 November 1945	0.41	Venezuela	15 November 1945	0.49
Spain	14 December 1955	1.98	Viet Nam	20 September 1977	0.01
Sri Lanka	14 December 1955	0.01	Yemen	30 September 1947	0.01
Sudan	12 November 1956	0.01	Yugoslavia	24 October 1945	0.14
Suriname	4 December 1975	0.01	Zaire	20 September 1960	0.01
Swaziland	24 September 1968	0.01	Zambia	1 December 1964	0.01
Sweden	19 November 1946	1.11	Zimbabwe	25 August 1980	0.01
Syria	24 October 1945	0.04			

Growth of United Nations Membership

YEAR OF ADMISSION	MEMBERS
1945	Argentina, Australia, Belgium, Bolivia, Brazil, Belarus (formerly Byelorussia), Canada, Chile, China, Colombia, Costa Rica, Cuba, Czechoslovakia (readmitted in 1993 as two separate states, the Czech and Slovak Republics), Denmark, Dominican Republic, Ecuador, Egypt, El Salvador, Ethiopia, France, Greece, Guatemala, Haiti, Honduras, India, Iran, Iraq, Lebanon, Liberia, Luxembourg, Mexico, Netherlands, New Zealand, Nicaragua, Norway, Panama, Paraguay, Peru, Philippines, Poland, the Russian Federation (formerly the USSR), Saudi Arabia, South Africa, Syria, Turkey, Ukraine, United Kingdom, United States of America, Uruguay, Venezuela, Yugoslavia
1946	Afghanistan, Iceland, Sweden, Thailand
1947	Pakistan, Yemen (formerly Yemen Arab Republic)
1948	Myanmar (formerly Burma)
1949	Israel
1950	Indonesia
1955	Albania, Austria, Bulgaria, Cambodia (formerly Kampuchea), Finland, Hungary, Ireland, Italy, Jordan, Lao People's Democratic Republic (formerly Laos), Libya, Nepal, Portugal, Romania, Spain, Sri Lanka
1956	Japan, Morocco, Sudan, Tunisia
1957	Ghana, Malaysia
1958	Guinea
1960	Benin, Burkina Faso, Cameroon, Central African Republic, Chad, Congo, Côte d'Ivoire, Cyprus, Gabon, Madagascar, Mali, Niger, Nigeria, Senegal, Somalia, Togo, Zaire
1961	Mauritania, Mongolia, Sierra Leone, Tanzania
1962	Algeria, Burundi, Jamaica, Rwanda, Trinidad and Tobago, Uganda
1963	Kenya, Kuwait
1964	Malawi, Malta, Zambia
1965	Gambia, Maldives, Singapore
1966	Barbados, Botswana, Guyana, Lesotho
1967	People's Democratic Republic of Yemen (since 1990, merged with Yemen)
1968	Equatorial Guinea, Mauritius, Swaziland
1970	Fiji
1971	Bahrain, Bhutan, Oman, Qatar, United Arab Emirates
1973	Bahamas, Germany (formerly the German Democratic Republic and the Federal Republic of Germany)
1974	Bangladesh, Grenada, Guinea-Bissau
1975	Cape Verde, Comoros, Mozambique, Papua New Guinea, Sao Tomé and Principe, Suriname
1976	Angola, Samoa, Seychelles
1977	Djibouti, Viet Nam
1978	Dominica, Solomon Islands
1979	St. Lucia
1980	St. Vincent and the Grenadines, Zimbabwe
1981	Antigua and Barbuda, Belize, Vanuatu
1983	St. Kitts and Nevis
1984	Brunei Darussalam
1990	Liechtenstein, Namibia,
1991	Democratic People's Republic of Korea, Estonia, Federated States of Micronesia, Latvia, Lithuania, Marshall Islands, Republic of Korea
1992	Armenia, Azerbaijan, Bosnia and Herzegovina, Croatia, Georgia, Kazakhstan, Krgyz Republic, Republic of Moldova, San Marino, Slovenia,
1993	Andorra, Czech Republic, Eritrea, Monaco, Slovak Republic, the Former Yugoslav Republic of Macedonia

UNITED NATIONS HEADQUARTERS

THE HEADQUARTERS BUILDINGS

When the UN came into being on 24 October 1945, it had no home. On 11 December 1945, the US Congress unanimously invited the UN to make its headquarters in the US. In February 1946, the General Assembly, meeting for its first session in London, voted for the general vicinity of Fairfield and Westchester counties, near New York City, but sites near Philadelphia, Boston, and San Francisco also were considered during 1946. Then came the dramatic offer by John D. Rockefeller, Jr., to donate $8.5 million toward the purchase of properties along the East River in midtown Manhattan. The City of New York rounded out the zone and granted rights along the river frontage. By November 1947, the General Assembly approved the architectural plans, and nine months later, the UN concluded a $65 million interest-free loan agreement with the US government. The director of planning for UN headquarters was Wallace K. Harrison of the US. The international board of design consultants included G. A. Soilleux, Australia; Gaston Brunfaut, Belgium; Oscar Niemeyer, Brazil; Ernest Cormier, Canada; Ssu-ch'eng Liang, China; Charles le Corbusier, Switzerland; Sven Markelius, Sweden; Nikolai D. Bassow, USSR; Howard Robertson, United Kingdom; and Julio Vilamajo, Uruguay.

The first structure to be completed, in the spring of 1951, was the 39-story marble and glass Secretariat building. In 1952, the conference building (with the three council halls and a number of conference rooms) and the General Assembly building were ready.

Thus, it was five or six years before the UN was permanently housed. In the interim, the Secretariat was established provisionally at Hunter College in the Bronx, New York, and in August 1946, the UN moved to the Sperry Gyroscope plant at Lake Success, Long Island. Several General Assembly sessions took place in the New York City Building at Flushing Meadow, and in 1948 and 1951, the body met at the Palais de Chaillot in Paris.

A library building at the headquarters site, erected and equipped through a $6.6 million donation by the Ford Foundation, was dedicated in 1961 to the memory of former Secretary-General Dag Hammarskjöld.

Various furnishings and works of art for the conference and General Assembly buildings and the library have been donated by member governments. Adjoining the public lobby in the General Assembly building is the Meditation Room, dedicated to those who have given their lives in service to the UN. It includes a stained glass window by Marc Chagall on the theme of "Peace and Man." The public gardens north of the General Assembly building contain sculpture and plantings donated by governments and individuals.

The United Nations headquarters was designed to serve four major groups: delegations, who now represent 184 member states and who send more than 3,000 persons to New York each year for the annual sessions of the General Assembly; the Secretariat, numbering about 6,973 persons in New York out of a total of over 29,891 throughout the world; visitors, who average 1,500 a day; and journalists, of whom more than 450 are permanently accredited while twice that number are present during major meetings.

For a small fee, visitors may join one of the Secretariat's tours of the headquarters buildings, conducted daily in 20 languages by 47 guides from 28 countries.

Capacity

Because of the increase in the number of member states, the seating capacity of the conference rooms and the General Assembly Hall has been enlarged. A major expansion of office and meeting facilities at UN headquarters was undertaken in the 1980s.

About 30,000 men and women from some 150 countries work for the UN and its related organs and agencies—about one-third of them at UN headquarters and the other two-thirds at offices and centers around the globe. (See also the chapter on the Secretariat.)

Conference Services

UN headquarters, together with the organization's offices in Geneva and Vienna, provide the interpreters, translators, writers, editors, and conference personnel required for the many UN meetings throughout the world, as well as for other meetings held under UN auspices.

Telecommunications System

The UN has its own telecommunications system. UN headquarters is linked by radio with the offices in Geneva and Vienna, which, in turn, provide liaison with UN organs and offices in different parts of the world.

Computer System

As part of the fundamental modernization and reorganization of the United Nations, the organization's bank of IBM mainframes, containing information on more than 20,000 UN employees, will be replaced in stages by an Integrated Management Information System (IMIS). The first phase of the replacement, completed in early 1994, implemented a personnel system covering recruiting, hiring, promotions, and moving. Four hundred users at the headquarters were connected to Unix servers with personal computers using Windows software. Eventually all administrative applications will be transferred to four Unix systems organized in client-server architecture. Eventually the system will be extended to the Secretariat's branches in seven other nations and to the peacekeeping missions wordwide, bringing the number of users to more than 2,100. The cost of the system has been estimated at $47 million.

The IMIS system will greatly simplify and centralize the financial management of the organization. For example, the accounting department administers an annual budget of nearly $3 billion, encompassing 90 different currencies. Expenses are estimated in US dollars in the master budget. Converting expenses in foreign countries into US dollars and calculating exchange rates has made it very difficult for the organization to get quality information on the real costs of a proposed operation.

The second phase of the installation, due in June 1994, covers the entitlements system, including special benefits such as housing subsidies, medical insurance, and educational allowances. The formulas for these expenses are frequently updated as living expenses in the various Secretariat locations change. The final components, a financial system and a payroll and budget preparation system, are scheduled to be implemented systemwide in 1995.

UN Postal Administration

UN stamps are issued under separate agreements with the postal authorities of the US, Switzerland, and Austria and are valid for postage only on mail deposited at UN headquarters in New York and at the UN offices in Geneva and Vienna. UN stamps may be obtained by mail, over the counter, or automatically through the Customer Deposit Service in New York, Geneva, or Vienna. Only revenue from the sale of stamps for philatelic purposes is retained by the UN. In addition to producing revenue, UN stamp designs publicize the work of the organization and its related agencies.

RECORDS AND DOCUMENTS

Library

The Dag Hammarskjöld Library contains approximately 400,000 books, 14,500 maps, over 80,000 periodicals and newspapers, and several hundred thousand documents and microfiches. The collection includes not only UN materials but also League of Nations records in its Woodrow Wilson Reading Room, as well as a general reference library on subjects related to the work of the UN. The library is for use by delegations, permanent missions, and the Secretariat and by scholars engaged in advanced research.

Archives

The United Nations Archives, located at 345 Park Avenue South in New York, dates from the establishment of the United Nations. Its 35 linear feet of holdings include both inactive administrative records created by Secretariat offices, as well as archival records that constitute the organization's institutional memory. Each year, approximately 50 researchers cull its archives for information about the UN's predecessors, the Secretary-General's "good offices" role, and the organization's mediating and peacekeeping activities.

The earliest records emanate from predecessor organizations, including the International Penal and Penitentiary Commission (1893–1951); United Nations Relief and Rehabilitation Administration (1943–48), which assisted liberated areas devastated by World War II; United Nations War Crimes Commission (1943–49) whose 17 Allied members together developed procedures for apprehending and punishing war criminals; and the United Nations Conference on International Organization (194), at which the United Nations was chartered.

From its very beginning, a number of regional conflicts required that the new organization assume the role of peacekeeper. Consequently, the UN Archives maintains records associated with a wide variety of peacekeeping missions, ranging from the UN Special Committee on Palestine (1947), to the organization's recently completed electoral mission in Cambodia. Issues arising from colonialism also required early UN involvement. Archival holdings document the establishment of trusteeships for supervising elections and the transition to independence. The organization's technical assistance function in international social and economic development is, likewise, reflected among the archives' records.

Records are generally open for research at the end of 20 years. Strictly confidential records, or those with special restrictions (such as the War Crimes Commission records), require express authorization for access. Those wishing to research UN Archives records should request an appointment by writing to Chief, Archives Unit, United Nations Archives, PK-1200, United Nations, New York, NY 10017.

Documents Services

UN headquarters houses one of the world's largest photocopying and printing plants. Most UN documents are produced in photocopy form for the use of members and the Secretariat. Some documents, as well as many reports and studies, are issued as UN publications for sale to the public. They are available in the bookshop at UN headquarters and from distributors worldwide.

In the United States and Canada, UNIPUB distributes UN publications and publishes scholarly books by the United Nations University Press. It also distributes the publications of the Food and Agricultural Organization (FAO), International Atomic Energy Agency (IAEA), General Agreement on Tariffs and Trade (GATT), and the United Nations Educational, Scientific and Cultural Organization (UNESCO). UNIPUB is located in Lanham, Maryland, and can be reached from the United States at (800) 274-488; from Canada (800) 233-0504. Other UN publications are available from the United Nations Publications Sales Section at UN Headquarters, (212) 963-8302 (for North America, Latin America, Asia, and the Pacific); and from the Geneva Sales Office and Bookshop, (41 22) 734 1473 (for Europe, Africa, and the Middle East).

PUBLIC INFORMATION SERVICES

At its first session, in 1946, the General Assembly decided to create a special Department of Public Information (DPI) in the Secretariat. Recognizing that the UN's aims cannot be achieved unless the world is fully informed of its objectives and activities, the General Assembly directed that DPI should work to promote the fullest possible informed understanding of UN affairs. Accordingly, the UN provides a steady stream of information on its activities, covering virtually all media—press, publications, radio, television, films, photographs, and exhibits.

Press, Publications, and Photographic Services

DPI provides information to news correspondents and facilitates their access to meetings, documents, and other news sources. In any given year, several thousand press releases are issued at UN headquarters, including accounts of meetings, texts of speeches, announcements of special programs, and background or reference papers. DPI holds daily briefings and helps to arrange press conferences for members of delegations and senior members of the Secretariat and the specialized agencies.

Booklets, pamphlets, and leaflets covering the work of the UN are published in many languages. The *UN Chronicle*, issued quarterly in English, French, Spanish, and Arabic, reports on UN activities. DPI also issues a *Yearbook of the United Nations*.

To illustrate UN activities in the field, photo missions are periodically undertaken throughout the world. The photographs obtained, together with extensive coverage of events at UN headquarters and other principal conference centers, are widely used by newspapers, periodicals, book publishers, and government information agencies. Posters and photo display sets are prepared for exhibition at UN headquarters and for worldwide distribution.

DPI press releases, background information releases, and other public information documents are available on the Internet through several electronic networks. In August 1994 these networks included: Agora, Gemnet, Togethernet, and UNDP gopher service. United Nations documents (major reports, and resolutions of the General Assembly, Security Council, and ECOSOC) could be accessed in some 40 countries. Some of these services could be accessed in the United States through commercial electronic carriers with access to the internet like America Online, Delphi, and Prodigy. In the United States, some large libraries in major metropolitan areas provide a free window onto the Internet, allowing access to some of the above documents.

Radio, TV, and Film Services

A major responsibility of DPI is to assist the accredited correspondents of national and commercial broadcasting organizations in their coverage of the UN's work. In radio, correspondents may use studios and recording equipment at UN headquarters, and New York is linked with distant capitals by shortwave or radiotelephone. Film and television correspondents may receive visual coverage of principal meetings of the Security Council and the General Assembly, as well as of press conferences and briefings. Satellite transmissions carry this material around the world.

DPI broadcasts meetings of principal UN organs by shortwave and produces its own radio programs in the six official UN languages (Arabic, Chinese, English, French, Russian, and Spanish), reaching listeners in more than 100 countries. UN films and television programs are produced not only for television but also for groups in schools, universities, and nongovernmental organizations.

Public Inquiries Unit

The Public Inquiries Unit handles individual inquiries from researchers and the general public seeking specific information about the United Nations and its subsidiary organizations. The unit can refer callers to the appropriate UN department or organization, and send by mail UN documents such as reports by the Secretary-General to the General Assembly or Security Council.

UN Information Centers

In 1993, 69 UN Information Centers (23 in Africa; 13 in the Americas; 17 in Asia/Oceania; and 14 in Europe) were disseminating information about UN aims and activities. The centers maintain up-to-date reference libraries of UN publications and documentation and answer public inquiries. DPI material is translated into local languages by the centers, which work closely with local media, information agencies, educational authorities, and nongovernmental organizations in their area. The centers also inform UN headquarters about local UN activities, which, in turn, are publicized by DPI.

PRIVILEGES AND IMMUNITIES

The charter provides that in all territory of its member states, the UN shall hold whatever legal capacity, privileges, and immunities are necessary for the fulfillment of its purposes and that representatives of member states and officials of the UN shall have a status allowing them independent exercise of their functions. On 13 February 1946, the General Assembly adopted the Convention on the Privileges and Immunities of the United Nations. As of 31 December 1993, 184 countries, including the US, had acceded to this convention. UN staff on official business can travel on a *laissez-passer* issued by the UN.

Countries that have acceded to the convention exempt the salaries of UN officials from taxation, except for the US and several other countries, where special reservations apply. These salaries, however, are subject to a "staff assessment," an internal UN taxation. The UN itself is exempt from all direct taxes, customs duties, and export and import restrictions on articles for official use.

Virtually all member states have established permanent missions to the UN in New York. Their personnel enjoy privileges and immunities similar to those of diplomatic missions.

HEADQUARTERS AGREEMENT BETWEEN THE UN AND THE US

A special headquarters agreement, signed by Secretary-General Trygve Lie and US secretary of state George C. Marshall at Lake Success on 26 June 1947, has been in force since 21 November 1947. It defines the 18 acres of land in New York City located between 42nd and 48th Streets and First Avenue and the Franklin D. Roosevelt Drive as the Headquarters District of the United Nations. Subsequently, by supplemental agreements between the UN and the US, additional office space located in buildings in the vicinity has been included in the Headquarters District. The Headquarters District is "under the control and authority of the United Nations as provided in this agreement." It is the seat of the UN, and the agreement stipulates that the district "shall be inviolable." Federal, state, and local personnel on official duty may enter it only with the consent of the Secretary-General. The UN may make regulations for the area. US federal, state, and local law, insofar as it is inconsistent with UN regulations, does not apply here; otherwise, the US courts would have jurisdiction over actions and transactions taking place in the Headquarters District. The UN may expel persons from the district for violations of regulations. In such cases, and generally for the preservation of law and order, US authorities have to provide a sufficient number of police if requested by the Secretary-General. "No form of racial or religious discrimination shall be permitted within the Headquarters District." Other detailed provisions in the agreement between the UN and the US deal with the important matter of the accessibility of the seat of the UN to non-US citizens.

EMBLEM AND FLAG OF THE UN

The General Assembly adopted an official seal and emblem for the organization. The UN emblem depicts in silver against a light blue background a map of the earth, projected from the North Pole, and encircled by two symmetrical olive branches. It is a slight modification of a design selected by the US Office of Strategic Services for buttons used at the San Francisco Conference in 1945. The particular shade of blue is now officially called United Nations blue. The emblem is used only for UN publications and conferences and other officially approved purposes.

The first UN flag was used in Greece in 1947 in a region where there was fighting. The flag has the UN emblem in white against a background of United Nations blue.

The flag may be displayed not only by the UN and the specialized agencies and by governments but also by "organizations and individuals to demonstrate support of the United Nations and to further its principles and purposes." It is considered "especially appropriate" to display the UN flag on national and official holidays; on UN Day, 24 October; and at official events in honor of the UN or related to the UN.

THE UNITED NATIONS BUDGET

Under the Charter, it is the task of the General Assembly to "consider and approve the budget of the Organization" and to apportion the expenses of the UN among the member nations. From an administrative standpoint, the expenditures of the UN may be said to fall into two categories: expenditures that are included in what is termed the "regular budget," to which all members are obliged to contribute; and expenditures for certain high-cost items or programs, for which are established separate, or "extrabudgetary," accounts or funds financed by special arrangements that do not necessarily involve obligatory payments by UN members.

Included in the regular budget are the costs of services and programs carried out at UN headquarters and all overseas UN offices; the expenses of the International Court of Justice; and debt services charges, which are also listed as "special expenses."

Outside the regular budget, member states also are assessed, in accordance with a modified version of the basic scale, for the costs of peacekeeping operations. The number and cost of these operations has been aggravated in recent years, in large part due to political instability in Eastern Europe, Western Asia, and Africa. In the period 1992–93, the Secretary-General estimated the cost for these operations increased sixfold. In a report to the Economic and Social Council, he stated, "It would be mistaken to try to attach an order of importance or priority between peace and security on the one hand, and economic and social development on the other. The two are so closely interlinked as to be indivisible." This underlying philosophy provides the rationale for the growth in the number of peacekeeping operations and the expansion of their mandates beyond the previously traditional observer status, to activities such as disarming and demobilization of forces, humanitarian assistance, human rights monitoring, electoral verification, and civilian police support. Each peacekeeping operation is approved and budgeted separately.

Following is a list of 21 UN observation or peacekeeping operations under way as of April 1994: UN Emergency Force (UNEF); UN Disengagement Observer Force (UNDOF); UN Interim Force in Lebanon (UNIFIL); UN Iran–Iraq Military Observer Group (UNIIMOG); UN Angola Verification Mission (UNAVEM and UNAVEMII); UN Transition Assistance Group (UNTAG); UN Iraq–Kuwait Observation Mission (UNIKOM); UN Mission for the Referendum in Western Sahara (MINURSO); UN Observer Mission in El Salvador (ONUSAL); UN Transitional Authority in Cambodia (UNTAC); UN Protection Force (UNPROFOR); UN Operation in Somalia (UNOSOM and UNOSOM II); UN Operation in Mozambique (ONUMOZ); UN Peace-keeping Force in Cyprus (UNFICYP); UN Observer Mission in Georgia (UNOMIG); UN Mission in Haiti (UNMIH); UN Assistance Mission for Rwanda (UNAMIR); UN Observer Mission Uganda–Rwanda (UNOMUR); UN Military Liaison Team in Cambodia.

As of April 1992, unpaid contributions for the 13 then current or recently completed peacekeeping operations with separate assessed budgets amounted to US$805 million. Shortfalls in the receipt of assessed contributions were met by delaying reimbursements to states that contributed troops, thus placing an unfair burden on them.

United Nations activities that are financed mainly by voluntary contributions outside the regular budget include: the United Nations Development Programme (UNDP), The World Food Program (WFP), The Office of the United Nations High Commissioner for Refugees (UNHCR), the United Nations Children's Fund (UNICEF), the United Nations Relief and Works Agency for Palestine Refugees in the Near East (UNRWA), and the United Nations Population Fund (UNFPA).

The member states of the specialized agencies decide on each agency's budget and scale of assessments separately from the United Nations itself.

COMMITTEES ASSISTING THE GENERAL ASSEMBLY IN FINANCIAL MATTERS

In 1946, the General Assembly established two permanent subsidiary organs concerned with administrative and budgetary affairs. The Advisory Committee on Administrative and Budgetary Questions is responsible for expert examination of the UN budget and the administrative budgets of the specialized agencies. The committee's 16 members, elected by the General Assembly for staggered three-year terms, serve as individuals, not as government representatives. The Committee on Contributions advises the General Assembly on the apportionment of the expenses of the UN among the member nations. Its 18 members are elected for three-year terms and also serve as individuals.

PROCEDURE FOR DETERMINING THE REGULAR BUDGET

Every other year, the Secretary-General presents detailed budget and appropriations estimates for the following biennium. (Until 1974 there were annual budgets.) These estimates are reviewed and sometimes revised by the Advisory Committee. The programmatic aspects are reviewed by the 34-member Committee for Program and Coordination.

Appropriations (Gross) for the Regular Budget of the UN
1946–1995 (in US$)

YEAR	APPROPRIATION	YEAR	APPROPRIATION
1946	$19,390,000	1966	121,080,530
1947	28,616,568	1967	133,084,000
1948	39,285,736	1968	141,787,750
1949	43,204,080	1969	156,967,300
1950	44,520,773	1970	168,956,950
1951	48,925,500	1971	194,627,800
1952	50,547,660	1972	208,650,200
1953	49,869,450	1973	233,820,374
1954	48,528,980	1974–75	606,033,000
1955	50,228,000	1976–77	745,813,800
1956	50,683,350	1978–79	996,372,900
1957	53,174,700	1980–81	1,339,151,200
1958	61,121,900	1982–83	1,472,961,700
1959	61,657,100	1984–85	1,611,551,200
1960	65,734,900	1986–87	1,711,801,200
1961	71,649,300	1988–89	1,748,681,800
1962	85,818,220	1990–91	2,134,072,100
1963	92,876,550	1992–93	2,362,977,700
1964	101,327,600	1994–95	2,580,200,200
1965	108,472,800		

BUDGET FOR THE 1994–95 BIENNIUM

AREA OF EXPENDITURE PURPOSE OF EXPENDITURE	AMOUNT
Overall policymaking, direction and coordination	37,049,800
Political affairs	
Political affairs	67,923,600
Peacekeeping operations and special missions	101,573,200
TOTAL:	169,496,800
International law	
International Court of Justice	18,329,400
Legal activities	32,490,000
TOTAL:	50,819,400
International cooperation for development	
Department for Policy Coordination and Sustainable Development	50,355,600
Department for Economic and Social Information and Policy Analysis	46,815,700
Department for Development Support and Management Services	29,385,800
UN Conference on Trade and Development	108,296,400
International Trade Centre (UNCTAD/GATT)	19,982,200
UN Environment Programme (UNEP)	11,384,500
UN Centre for Human Settlements (HABITAT)	11,854,300
Crime Control	4,638,200
International Drug Control	13,998,700
TOTAL:	296,711,400
Regional cooperation for development	
Economic Commission for Africa (ECA)	78,020,100
Economic and Social Commission for Asia and the Pacific (ESCAP)	59,846,200
Economic Commission for Europe (ECE)	44,684,500
Economic Commission for Latin America and the Caribbean (ECLAC)	79,992,600
Economic and Social Commission for Western Asia (ESCWA)	38,226,600
Regular program of technical cooperation	42,910
TOTAL:	343,680,000
Human rights and humanitarian affairs	
Human rights	36,063,300
Office of the UN High Commissioner for Refugees (UNHCR)	45,329,400
UN Relief and Works Agency for Palestine Refugees in the Near East (UNRWA)	21,007,900
Department of Humanitarian Affairs	18,541,200
TOTAL:	120,941,800
Administrative expenses	
Public information	133,145,300
Administration and management	876,856,000
Jointly financed administrative activities	26,192,800
Special expenses	31,780,400
Staff assessment expenses	404,949,000
Proposed Office for Inspections and Investigations	11,429,100
TOTAL:	1,484,352,600
Capital expenditures	
Technological innovations	18,841,500
Construction and maintenance	58,306,900
TOTAL:	77,148,400
GRAND TOTAL:	US$2,580,200,200

Aside from the regular budget, the General Assembly also allots a certain amount of money for unforeseen and extraordinary expenses and determines the level of the UN's Working Capital Fund, to which member nations advance sums in proportion to their assessed contributions to the regular budget. The fund—US$100 million—is used to finance appropriations pending receipt of contributions and may also be drawn upon by the Secretary-General for other purposes determined by the General Assembly.

Since the expenses of the organization can never be precisely predicted, the Secretary-General reviews actual expenditures for the current year at each regular session of the General Assembly and proposes adjustments in the original appropriations. Usually, a supplemental budget is voted, but occasionally the General Assembly votes reductions.

Income Estimates

It was estimated that expenditures would be offset in the amount of US$477,401,700, to be derived as follows:

1. *income from staff assessment*: US$411,364,200;
2. *general income*: US$59,258,800;
3. *services to public*: US$6,788,700.

Under UN regulations, a percentage of the earnings of the entire UN staff is deducted in lieu of taxes and credited to "income." In order to avoid double taxation of staff members of US nationality, they are reimbursed by the UN for the taxes (federal, state, and city) levied on their UN earnings. The withholdings from the salaries of UN personnel of all other nationalities are credited to the member states' accounts against their assessed contributions. After taking into account staff assessments and other items of income, the net estimated amount remaining to be raised through assessed contributions from member states for the biennium 1994–95 totaled US$1,198,902,550.

ASSESSED CONTRIBUTIONS OF MEMBER STATES TO THE REGULAR BUDGET

The scale of contributions of member states is established by the General Assembly on the recommendation of its Committee on Contributions. The basic original criterion for the apportionment of UN expenses was the ability to pay, with comparative estimates of national income taken as the fairest guide. Other factors, such as the comparative income per capita, the ability of contributors to obtain foreign exchange, and, until 1974, the dislocation of national economies arising out of World War II, also were taken into account. In this way, the US share was at first 39.89 percent, gradually declining to 31.52 percent for 1971–73.

In 1972, the General Assembly established a ceiling on the rate of assessment of the highest contributor, set at 25 percent. At the same time, it lowered the minimum rate of assessment to 0.02 percent (later lowered to 0.01 percent) and requested the Committee on Contributions to give attention to the special economic and financial problems of developing countries.

In an effort to introduce what it termed greater fairness and equity in the scale of assessments, the General Assembly, in 1981, requested the Committee on Contributions to prepare a set of guidelines for the collection of more uniform and comparable data and statistics from member states and to study alternative methods of assessing "the real capacity of member states to pay."

Under the scale of assessments adopted for the period 1994–95, the 10 largest contributors, listed in order, are the United States (25 percent), Japan (12.45 percent), Germany (8.93 percent), Russian Federation (6.71 percent), France (6.0 percent), United Kingdom (5.02 percent), Italy (4.29 percent), Canada (3.11 percent), Spain (1.98 percent), Ukraine (1.87 percent). The complete scale is shown in the table.

Scale of Assessments
(as of 6 May 1994)

MEMBER STATE	PERCENT	MEMBER STATE	PERCENT	MEMBER STATE	PERCENT	MEMBER STATE	PERCENT
Afghanistan	0.01	Dominican Republic	0.02	Liberia	0.01	Samoa	0.01
Albania	0.01	Ecuador	0.03	Libyan Arab Jamahiriya	0.24	San Marino	0.01
Algeria	0.16	Egypt	0.07	Liechtenstein	0.01	São Tomé and	
Andorra	0.01	El Salvador	0.01	Lithuania	0.15	Principe	0.01
Angola	0.01	Equatorial Guinea	0.01	Luxembourg	0.06	Saudi Arabia	0.96
Antigua and Barbuda	0.01	Eritrea	0.01	Madagascar	0.01	Senegal	0.01
Argentina	0.57	Estonia	0.07	Malawi	0.01	Seychelles	0.01
Armenia	0.13	Ethiopia	0.01	Malaysia	0.12	Sierra Leone	0.01
Australia	1.51	Fiji	0.01	Maldives	0.01	Singapore	0.12
Austria	0.75	Finland	0.57	Mali	0.01	Slovakia	0.13
Azerbaijan	0.22	France	6.00	Malta	0.01	Slovenia	0.09
Bahamas	0.02	Gabon	0.02	Marshall Islands	0.01	Solomon Islands	0.01
Bahrain	0.03	Gambia	0.01	Mauritania	0.01	Somalia	0.01
Bangladesh	0.01	Georgia	0.21	Mauritius	0.01	South Africa	0.41
Barbados	0.01	Germany	8.93	Mexico	0.88	Spain	1.98
Belarus	0.48	Ghana	0.01	Micronesia		Sri Lanka	0.01
Belgium	1.06	Greece	0.35	(Federated States of)	0.01	Sudan	0.01
Belize	0.01	Grenada	0.01	Monaco	0.01	Suriname	0.01
Benin	0.01	Guatemala	0.02	Mongolia	0.01	Swaziland	0.01
Bhutan	0.01	Guinea	0.01	Morocco	0.03	Sweden	1.11
Bolivia	0.01	Guinea-Bissau	0.01	Mozambique	0.01	Syria	0.04
Bosnia and Herzegovina	0.04	Guyana	0.01	Myanmar	0.01	Tajikistan	0.05
Botswana	0.01	Haiti	0.01	Namibia	0.01	Thailand	0.11
Brazil	1.59	Honduras	0.01	Nepal	0.01	The Former Yugoslav	
Brunei Darussalam	0.03	Hungary	0.18	Netherlands	1.50	Republic of Macedonia	0.02
Bulgaria	0.13	Iceland	0.03	New Zealand	0.24	Togo	0.01
Burkina Faso	0.01	India	0.36	Nicaragua	0.01	Trinidad and Tobago	0.05
Burundi	0.01	Indonesia	0.16	Niger	0.01	Tunisia	0.03
Cambodia	0.01	Iran	0.77	Nigeria	0.20	Turkey	0.27
Cameroon	0.01	Iraq	0.13	Norway	0.55	Turkmenistan	0.06
Canada	3.11	Ireland	0.18	Oman	0.03	Uganda	0.01
Cape Verde	0.01	Israel	0.23	Pakistan	0.06	Ukraine	1.87
Central African Republic	0.01	Italy	4.29	Panama	0.02	United Arab Emirates	0.21
Chad	0.01	Jamaica	0.01	Papua New Guinea	0.01	United Kingdom	5.02
Chile	0.08	Japan	12.45	Paraguay	0.02	United Republic	
China	0.77	Jordan	0.01	Peru	0.06	of Tanzania	0.01
Colombia	0.13	Kazakhstan	0.35	Philippines	0.07	United States	25.00
Comoros	0.01	Kenya	0.01	Poland	0.47	Uruguay	0.04
Congo	0.01	Korea, Democratic People's		Portugal	0.20	Uzbekistan	0.26
Costa Rica	0.01	Republic of	0.05	Qatar	0.05	Vanuatu	0.01
Côte d'Ivoire	0.02	Korea, Republic of	0.69	Republic of Moldova	0.15	Venezuela	0.49
Croatia	0.13	Kuwait	0.25	Romania	0.17	Viet Nam	0.01
Cuba	0.09	Kyrgyz Republic	0.06	Russian Federation	6.71	Yemen	0.01
Cyprus	0.02	Lao People's Democratic		Rwanda	0.01	Yugoslavia	0.14
Czech Republic	0.42	Republic	0.01	St. Kitts and Nevis	0.01	Zaire	0.01
Denmark	0.65	Latvia	0.13	St. Lucia	0.01	Zambia	0.01
Djibouti	0.01	Lebanon	0.01	St. Vincent and the		Zimbabwe	0.01
Dominica	0.01	Lesotho	0.01	Grenadines	0.01	TOTAL	100.00

Contributions by Nonmember States

States that are not members of the UN but participate in certain of its activities (principally the International Court of Justice, the regional commissions, the UN Conference on Trade and Development, and the control of narcotic drugs) contribute toward expenses of such activities according to a scale of assessments established by the General Assembly. Following are the amounts established for the nonmember states at 30 May 1994:

COUNTRY	US$ ASSESSED
Holy See (Vatican)	10,179
Nauru	1,018
Switzerland	3,542,281
Tonga	5,089

PROPOSALS TO EASE THE UN'S FINANCIAL DIFFICULTIES

By and large, the regular budget has never created major disputes among the member states, and most governments have usually paid their dues relatively punctually. However, beginning in 1963, the USSR refused as a matter of principle to contribute to certain items in the regular budget, such as the UN Commission for the Unification and Rehabilitation of Korea until its dissolution by a consensus vote of the 1973 Assembly, or to those parts of the regular budget devoted to the redemption of UN bonds (a method of raising funds for certain UN peacekeeping operations). France has taken a similar stand in connection with the redemption of the bonds. In addition, a number of countries have refused to contribute to the special accounts for peacekeeping operations in the Congo and the Middle East. It was chiefly these controversial expenditures which precipitated the UN's financial emergency in the mid-1960s.

In July 1962, the International Court of Justice, at the request of the General Assembly, issued an advisory opinion in which it declared that the expenses of the first UN Emergency Force in the Middle East and the UN Force in the Congo constituted expenses of the organization within the meaning of Article 17, paragraph 2, of the Charter and should thus be borne by member states as apportioned by the General Assembly. The Assembly accepted the court's opinion in December 1962, but debate over peacekeeping operations and the financial difficulties continued. A number of other factors, moreover, contributed to the precariousness of the financial position of the organization, notably the lateness of many member states in paying their assessed contributions, the currency fluctuations of the 1970s (marked by two devaluations of the US dollar, on which the UN budget is based), and inflation.

A Group of High-Level Intergovernmental Experts to Review the Efficiency of the Administrative and Financial Functioning of the UN, appointed by the General Assembly in 1985, submitted to the General Assembly in the following year its recommendations for enhancing the efficiency and reducing the expenditures of the organization. Implementation of the group's recommendations was the condition which a number of states, including the US, placed on further payment of their assessments.

The overall financial situation of the United Nations continues to be difficult because many member states still fail to pay their assessed contributions to regular budget or peacekeeping operations in full and on time. Voluntary contributions from some countries and the Working Capital Fund have provided stop-gap solutions; however, as of 30 April 1992, member states' unpaid assessed contributions totalled us$1.89 billion. In April 1992, out of 163 member states, only 39 had paid their assessments for the regular budget in full.

Among the solutions proposed in 1985 were an increase in the Working Capital Fund to us$200 million, the issue of certificates of indebtedness in the amount of the arrears—in effect, borrowing from member states—and borrowing on the open market.

In 1992, Secretary-General Boutros Boutros-Ghali requested the Ford Foundation to assemble an independent advisory group to recommend ways to create a secure, long-term financial base for the organization. The group, co-chaired by Shijuro Ogata, former Deputy Governer of the Japan Development Bank, and Paul Volcker, former Board of Governors' Chairman of the United States Federal Reserve Bank, issued its report in February 1993. Entitled "Financing an Effective United Nations," it suggested the following measures:

- Dividing UN expenditures into three categories: a regular budget financed by assessed contributions; peacekeeping financed by a separate assessment; and humanitarian and development activities financed largely by voluntary contributions.
- Requiring UN member states to pay dues in four quarterly installments, instead of a single lump sum at the beginning of the year; and granting the organization authority to charge interest on late payments.
- Appropriation by some nations of their UN contribution earlier in the year.
- Acceptance by member states of significantly increased peacekeeping costs over the next few years, and financing future cost from national defense budgets.
- Creation by the UN of a $400 million revolving reserve fund for peacekeeping; and consideration of a unified peacekeeping budget, financed by a single annual assessment. The report concluded that proposals for additional, nongovernmental sources of financing the UN were "neither practical nor desirable."

Also in 1993, the Joint Inspection Unit (JIU) of the Secretariat issued a report declaring: "The old financial malaise is emerging with renewed evidence. What was a chronic illness is becoming a critical one." Among JIU proposals:

- Governments should adjust their national legislations to avoid obstacles to paying their UN contributions in full and on time.
- Replenishment of the proposed UN Peace Endowment Fund could take advantage of initiatives, such as the issuance of special stamps by member states, with revenues turned over to the organization.
- Countries could turn over to peacekeeping operations funds earmarked for aid to developing countries in which the existing critical situation is an impediment to using those funds.
- In parallel with financing, cost saving is indispensable to solving the financial crisis. Fighting waste and reducing expenses must take place in all areas of the organization.

The fundamental requirement for the essential financial stability of the UN, however, remained the full and timely payment by all member states of their assessments, in accordance with Article 17, paragraph 2, of the Charter, which states that: "The expenses of the Organization shall be borne by the Members as apportioned by the General Assembly."

THE GENERAL ASSEMBLY

The first of the UN organs established by the charter, the General Assembly is the pivot of the organization. All member states are represented. Each country, large or small, has one vote, and each country chooses its own representatives.

FUNCTIONS AND POWERS

The central position of the General Assembly is firmly established in a series of charter provisions encompassing a wide range of functions and powers. First are the provisions setting forth its powers as the major deliberative body of the UN. With two exceptions (described below), the General Assembly has the right to discuss and make recommendations on any subject that falls within the scope of the charter itself, including the functions and powers of the other organs. Hence, it is in the General Assembly that all of the UN's important projects (except for the Security Council's peacekeeping operations) originate—those dealing with political questions, disarmament, economic and social development, human rights, decolonization of dependent territories, and development of international law.

The second group of charter provisions defining the pivotal position of the General Assembly concerns the financing of the UN. The General Assembly is empowered to "consider and approve" the budget of the organization (which includes that of the International Court of Justice at The Hague), and it also has the right to determine how the expenses shall be apportioned among the member nations.

Lastly, the General Assembly's position is secured by provisions that give it specific powers in relation to the other organs. Thus, both the Economic and Social Council and the Trusteeship Council are constituted under the direct authority of the General Assembly to carry out designated tasks in their respective spheres. The administrative arm of the UN, the Secretariat, is also at the disposition of the General Assembly. The General Assembly's powers, however, are much more limited where the Security Council and the International Court of Justice are concerned. Designed in some respects to be more powerful than the General Assembly, the Security Council is in no way answerable to the body for its activities—although it is required to make an annual report and, when necessary, special reports. Also, whereas the General Assembly is empowered to make recommendations to the council concerning the maintenance of international peace, it cannot give the council instructions. In the case of the International Court of Justice, any attempt to render its activities answerable to the General Assembly would have prejudiced the independent status that is normally accorded to judiciary bodies throughout the world. Nevertheless, inasmuch as the General Assembly not only has budgetary power but also elects the nonpermanent members of the Security Council and, concurrently with the Security Council, all the judges of the International Court, it can be said to exercise an appreciable degree of indirect control over both these bodies.

Thus, the one UN organ on which all member states have the constitutional right to be represented is able to make its will felt throughout the organization, and indeed the entire UN system. Because its powers closely resemble those of a national parliament, the General General Assembly has been described as a "world parliament." Parliamentary powers are not to be con-

fused, though, with governmental powers. Except insofar as the Economic and Social Council, the Trusteeship Council, and the Secretariat are bound to carry out its requests, the General Assembly has no power to legislate and cannot enforce its decisions upon individual member nations. The only sanctions that the General Assembly can wield against an uncooperative member are the suspension of the rights and privileges of membership and expulsion from the organization, but even these sanctions can be invoked only on the recommendation of the Security Council. In effect, then, all General Assembly decisions are purely recommendations that reflect world public opinion; they have moral, though not legal, force. At the end of this chapter, an attempt is made to assess their effectiveness on this score.

Charter Restrictions on the Assembly's Power to Discuss and Recommend

The charter imposes two major restrictions on the General Assembly's powers to discuss and make recommendations. The first is embodied in the principle set out in Article 2, paragraph 7 of the charter, which states: "Nothing contained in the present Charter shall authorize the United Nations to intervene in matters which are essentially within the domestic jurisdiction of any state or shall require the Members to submit such matters to settlement. . . ." This principle is not so restrictive as it might seem, for whether a given issue is or is not of a domestic character is decided by the General Assembly itself. It can and often does override by majority vote the attempt of a member nation to bar a particular topic from debate by invoking Article 2, paragraph 7 of the charter. The most notable case in point was the General Assembly's annual discussion of South Africa's apartheid policy despite South Africa's contention that the matter was within its domestic jurisdiction. (See section on "Apartheid in South Africa" under the chapter "Human Rights.")

The second restriction is to be found in Article 12 of the Charter, which states that while the Security Council is exercising its functions in respect to any international dispute or situation, "the General Assembly shall not make any recommendation with regard to that dispute or situation unless the Security Council so requests." This stipulation, then, clearly establishes the absolute primacy of the Security Council over the General Assembly in times of crisis. Here, the main object of the founders of the UN was to ensure against the possibility of the smaller nations forming a majority bloc to interfere with any decisions that might be taken by the Big Five acting in concert as permanent members of the Security Council, where each possesses the right of veto. (For a discussion of the veto right, see the chapter on the Security Council.)

Extension of the Assembly's Power to Discuss and Recommend through the Uniting for Peace Resolution

Designed to secure maximum unity of action in moments of acute danger, Article 12, in fact, proved to be the chief obstacle to action of any kind during successive crises in the years just after World War II. The effectiveness of the entire system presupposed a spirit of unanimity among the great powers in their determination to end a particular dispute that appeared to threaten international peace and security. However, on each occasion when the great powers might have been expected to display unanimity, the USSR and the four other permanent members of the Security Council took opposite sides in the dispute. As a result, precisely because each of them possessed the veto, all council action was deadlocked. Meanwhile, the General Assembly, prevented from taking action of its own accord because of Article 12, was forced to stand by helplessly.

It was the seriousness of the Korean crisis that finally impelled the General Assembly to take steps to break through its constitutional straitjacket. Following a deadlock in the council in 1950, when the USSR vetoed a United States-sponsored resolution in connection with the entry of the People's Republic of China into the Korean conflict on the side of North Korea, the General Assembly adopted a resolution that enabled it to circumvent the restrictions imposed by Article 12. This act, which came to be known as the "Uniting for Peace Resolution," provides that if the Security Council, because of lack of unanimity among its permanent members, fails to exercise its primary responsibility in the maintenance of peace, in a case where there appears to be a threat to the peace, breach of the peace, or act of aggression, the General Assembly shall consider the matter immediately with a view to making recommendations to members for collective measures, including if necessary the use of armed force. Although the Uniting for Peace Resolution thus considerably extends the General Assembly's powers with respect to maintenance of international peace and security, it in no way represents an attempt to usurp the Security Council's prerogatives. Nor does it attempt to arrogate to the General Assembly the enforcement powers that the charter accorded to the Security Council alone. Even under the Uniting for Peace Resolution, the General Assembly can only recommend that members undertake collective peacekeeping measures; it cannot oblige them to do so. Nor can it impose peacekeeping action against the will of the parties to a dispute. It must obtain their explicit consent to the presence of UN personnel—observer commissions, mediators, troops—in their territories.

The Uniting for Peace Resolution has been invoked in three major crises: the Korean War, the Suez crisis, and the Congo crisis. In all three instances, the Security Council found itself deadlocked, and General Assembly action was deemed essential by the majority of members. Nevertheless, despite its proven usefulness as an instrument of restoring peace in these instances, the resolution seems unlikely to be invoked in future disputes. Certain countries questioned the legality of the resolution and of the General Assembly's action taken under it, and they felt justified on these grounds in refusing to contribute to the costs of the Suez and Congo peacekeeping operations. (See the discussion of peacekeeping operations in the chapter on International Peace and Security.)

ORGANIZATION

Sessions

The General Assembly meets once a year in regular sessions that begin on the third Tuesday in September. Usually these sessions last about three months, ending before Christmas, but there is no fixed time limit, and many times the General Assembly has adjourned, continuing the session after the holidays. Special sessions on a particular topic may be held at the request of the Security Council, or of a majority of UN members, or of one member if the majority of members concur. An emergency special session may be called within 24 hours by the Security Council on the vote of any nine members, or by a majority of UN members, or by one member if the majority concur.

Sessional Committees

Most of the substantive work during regular session is conducted through seven "Main Committees," which are reconstituted at every session. Each is composed of representatives of all member nations.

- The *First Committee* deals with disarmament and related international security matters.
- The *Second Committee* deals with economic and financial matters.
- The *Third Committee* is concerned with social, humanitarian, and cultural matters and human rights.
- The *Fourth Committee* handles questions concerning the granting of independence to colonial territories.
- The *Fifth Committee* deals with the administrative and budgetary matters of the organization.
- The *Sixth Committee* debates legal questions, including the general development and codification of international law.
- The *Special Political Committee,* was created in 1948 as an ad hoc committee of the whole to discuss the Palestine question. Never disbanded, it was subsequently retained as an additional main committee to deal with special political issues.

The General Assembly maintains two other sessional committees, both of which deal with General Assembly procedure. However, neither is a committee of the whole. The 29-member *General Committee,* composed of the General Assembly president, the 21 vice presidents, and the chairmen of the seven main committees, examines the provisional agenda of each session and makes recommendations on the inclusion or exclusion of items and on their assignment to the appropriate main committee. The *Credentials Committee* is a nine-member body appointed by the General Assembly at the beginning of the session to examine the credentials of representatives and to work out any problems that might arise in this connection.

Plenary Meetings

Since all the main committees are committees of the whole, the distinction between the General Assembly meeting in committee and meeting in plenum is largely one of protocol. Always conducted by the president or a vice president, plenary meetings are much more formal affairs. Normally, no one below the rank of head of delegation may actively participate in the proceedings, and no one is allowed to speak from his or her chair but must go to the speaker's rostrum. (None of the conference rooms in which the committees meet is provided with a speaker's rostrum.) The Assembly Hall itself is reserved for plenary meetings and is rarely used by the committees.

It is in plenary meetings that all formal or ceremonial functions occur: opening and closing of the General Assembly session, election of officers and members of other organs, adoption of resolutions and decisions on all agenda items, and addresses by heads of state or government or by other high national officials who visit the UN while the General Assembly is in session. Plenary meetings also constitute the forum for the statements of general policy that the head of each member delegation is entitled to make as part of what is known as the "general debate," which takes place during the first three weeks or so of the regular session. Because of the great number of questions which the General Assembly is called upon to consider (over 150 agenda items at the 1992 session) it allocates most questions to its seven main committees.

Voting Procedure

Each member of the General Assembly and its committees has one vote. Article 18 of the charter decrees that decisions on "important" questions shall be made by a two-thirds majority of the members present and voting. Among the important questions specified are recommendations with regard to maintenance of peace and security; election of the nonpermanent members of the Security Council and of the members of the Economic and Social

Council and the Trusteeship Council; admission of new UN members, suspension of rights and privileges of membership, and expulsion of members; questions relating to the operation of the trusteeship system; and budgetary questions. Decisions on other questions, including the determination of additional categories of important questions requiring a two-thirds majority vote, are made by a simple majority of the members present and voting. The phrase "members present and voting" means members casting either affirmative or negative votes; members who abstain are considered as not voting. Thus, although the number of abstentions is usually listed for information purposes, it does not count in the final tally as to whether a resolution has received the requisite majority—provided that the rules of quorum have been observed. A quorum is constituted when a majority of the members are present; no decision may be taken without one. The president of the General Assembly, however, may declare a meeting open and permit the debate to proceed when at least one-third of the members are present. The chairman of a main committee may open a meeting when one-quarter of the members are present.

Voting may be by a show of hands, by roll call, or, in certain instances such as elections, by secret ballot. The normal method was intended to be by a show of hands, but any member can request a roll call. There has been an increasing tendency to do so, especially on the more contentious issues. Before a roll-call vote is taken, a lot is drawn to determine the country that is to vote first. Starting with that country, voting proceeds according to the alphabetical order of the official names of states in English. Mechanical voting equipment was installed in the Assembly Hall and first used at the 1965 session. Similar equipment is used in some conference rooms.

Seating Arrangements

The charter allows each member state a maximum of five representatives in the General Assembly. Most members, in addition to their five representatives, send five alternative representatives and a number of advisers to each session. Six seats are assigned to every delegation in the Assembly Hall. Both in the hall and in conference rooms, delegations are seated in alphabetical order according to the official names of the countries in English. The seating is rearranged before each session by drawing lots to select the country with which the alphabetical seating will start.

Election of Officers

At each regular session, the General Assembly constitutes itself anew. During the opening meetings, the main officers are elected, who serve until the end of the session. If a special or emergency session is called, it is normally presided over by officers elected in the previous September.

The first officer to be elected is the president. Delegates vote by secret ballot, and a simple majority suffices. In choosing the president, regard has to be paid to the equitable geographical rotation of the office among the following groups of states: African, Asian, Eastern European, Latin American, and Western European and other states. By tacit agreement, no representative of a permanent member of the Security Council ever is elected president of the General Assembly or chairman of a committee.

1.	1946	Paul-Henri Spaak	Belgium
2.	1947	Oswaldo Aranha	Brazil
3.	1948	Herbert V. Evatt	Australia
4.	1949	Carlos P. Romulo	Philippines
5.	1950	Nasrollah Entezam	Iran
6.	1951	Luís Padilla Nervo	Mexico
7.	1952	Lester B. Pearson	Canada
8.	1953	Vijaya Lakshmi Pandit	India
9.	1954	Eelco N. van Kleffens	Netherlands
10.	1955	José Maza	Chile
11.	1956	Prince Wan Waithayakon	Thailand
12.	1957	Sir Leslie Munro	New Zealand
13.	1958	Charles Malik	Lebanon
14.	1959	Víctor Andrés Belaúnde	Peru
15.	1960	Frederick H. Boland	Ireland
16.	1961	Mongi Slim	Tunisia
17.	1962	Sir Muhammad Zafrulla Khan	Pakistan
18.	1963	Carlos Sosa Rodríguez	Venezuela
19.	1964	Alex Quaison-Sackey	Ghana
20	1965	Amintore Fanfani	Italy
21.	1966	Abdul Rahman Pazhwak	Afghanistan
22.	1967	Corneliu Manescu	Romania
23.	1968	Emilio Arenales Catalán	Guatemala
24.	1969	Angie E. Brooks	Liberia
25.	1970	Edvard Hambro	Norway
26.	1971	Adam Malik	Indonesia
27.	1972	Stanislaw Trepczynski	Poland
28.	1973	Leopoldo Benites	Ecuador
29.	1974	Abdelaziz Bouteflika	Algeria
30.	1975	Gaston Thorn	Luxembourg
31.	1976	Hamilton S. Amerasinghe	Sri Lanka
32.	1977	Lazar Mojsov	Yugoslavia
33.	1978	Indalecio Liévano	Colombia
34.	1979	Salim A. Salim	Tanzania
35.	1980	Rüdiger von Wechmar	Federal Republic of Germany
36.	1981	Ismat T. Kittani	Iraq
37.	1982	Imre Hollai	Hungary
38.	1983	Jorge E. Illueca	Panama
39.	1984	Paul J. F. Lusaka	Zambia
40.	1985	Jaime de Piniés	Spain
41.	1986	Humayun Rasheed Choudhury	Bangladesh
42.	1987	Peter Florin	German Democratic Republic
43.	1988	Dante M. Caputa	Argentina
44.	1989	Joseph Nanven Garba	Nigeria
45.	1990	Guido de Marco	Malta
46.	1991	Samir S. Shihabi	Saudi Arabia
47.	1992	Stoyan Ganev	Bulgaria
48.	1993	Samuel R. Insanally	Guyana

Note: General Assembly presidents normally preside over special and emergency special sessions of the world body during their tenure. The exceptions were: José Arce of Argentina, who presided over the second special session in 1948, and Rudecindo Ortega of Chile, who presided over the first and second emergency special sessions held in 1956.

Following the election of the president, the main committees are officially constituted and retire to elect their own officers. Here again the matter of equitable geographical representation arises, and it is precisely regulated by a resolution adopted by the General Assembly in 1963. Of the seven committee chairmen, two must be chosen from African states and one each from Asian, Eastern European, Latin American, and Western European or other states. The seventh chairmanship rotates in alternate years between representatives from Asian and Western European or other states.

The final officers to be elected are the 21 vice presidents. Of these, 16 are elected in accordance with a geographical pattern: six from African states, five from Asian states, three from Latin American states, two from Western European and other states, and one from an Eastern European state. (The election of the president of the General Assembly has the effect, however, of reducing by one the number of vice presidencies allocated to the region from which the president is elected.) The remaining five vice presidents represent the permanent members of the Security Council: China, France, the USSR, the United Kingdom, and the United States.

AGENDA OF THE ASSEMBLY

Under the General Assembly's rules of procedure, the provisional agenda for a regular session must be issued no later than 60 days before the opening. However, up to 30 days before the opening, the Secretary-General, any of the other principal organs of the UN, or any member of the UN may request the inclusion of supplementary items. Additional items may also be included at a later stage, even after the session has started, if a majority of the General Assembly agrees.

Normally, the agenda includes well over 100 items. The great majority of substantive (that is to say, nonprocedural) items arise out of decisions made by previous sessions, and their inclusion in the agenda is automatic. Thus, the General Assembly frequently requests the Secretary-General, a special committee, or another UN organ to submit a special report on a given topic. The report, at the time that it is due, automatically becomes part of the agenda item on the topic. There also are several items that the General Assembly is obliged to consider at each session under the Charter—for example, the annual report of the Secretary-General on the work of the UN and the reports of the three councils. Moreover, certain items placed on the agenda by particular members of the UN come up at session after session because the sponsors are not satisfied with previous action on these matters.

Adoption of the Agenda
The adoption of the agenda is not a mere formality. The General Assembly has to approve the entire agenda and may amend or delete any item by majority vote. A decision to reject a particular member's request to have an item placed on the agenda could have considerable political significance. It is the function of the General Committee (which could be described as the steering committee) to make recommendations to the General Assembly on the inclusion of requested items in the agenda. Most of the pros and cons of including a controversial item in the agenda are thrashed out in this committee rather than in plenary, and the committee's proceedings sometimes afford a preview of the positions that countries will take on certain questions when they come up for substantive debate. Another important function of the General Committee is to recommend the assignment of agenda items to the various main committees for debate. It may also recommend that an important item be debated in plenary without being referred to a committee.

EFFECTIVENESS OF THE ASSEMBLY
Depending on the nature of the question and on the views of the majority, General Assembly debates may lead to one or a combination of the following: recommendations, phrased in varying degrees of urgency, to individual countries or to all countries; initiation of studies and reports; creation of new UN organs, committees of inquiry, and permanent special bodies that are assigned specific tasks; and adoption of international covenants, treaties, and agreements.

Significance of the Enlarged Membership and Changing Voting Patterns
Since 1960, when the impact of the number of newly independent African and Asian nations first began to make itself felt in the UN, the General Assembly's voting patterns have undergone a marked alteration. Until then, the majority of controversial resolutions had tended essentially to reflect a simple East-West division of opinion. In the resulting lineup of votes, the Western view, marshaled under the leadership of the United States, easily attained comfortable majorities on most issues, since it was supported not only by the countries of Western Europe but by the Latin American states as well. The formation of what has come to be known as the "Afro-Asian group," coupled with the general detente in East-West relations, introduced a new element into the voting equation.

Interested in wielding influence within the world body and preoccupied with the problems of development and decolonization rather than with cold war issues as such, African and Asian countries sought to unite themselves into an independent or "nonaligned" voting bloc. On occasion, the unity of the group is split by divided interests. This division occurs most frequently in major political issues of special importance to the big powers, when some small countries may find it expedient to associate themselves with the big power on which they are dependent for financial aid. At other times, notably on items connected with economic development, African and Asian nations may join the developing countries of the Latin American group in order to create a formidable voting bloc that can force through requests to which the highly developed nations, from East and West alike, may be reluctant to accede.

Then again, the emergence of what is in effect a floating third voting force in the General Assembly has resulted in the creation of special alliances as occasion demands. For example, the Soviet bloc and the nonaligned groups often combined to defeat or harry the West on colonial issues. This development also has opened up possibilities for striking voting bargains on individual draft resolutions. Accordingly, one group might support an initiative taken by a second group in exchange for the latter's support on a different item.

The indiscriminate wielding of voting strength by small nations is subject to the law of diminishing returns. Indeed, many small nations have shown indications of growing restraint, realizing that there is little point in pushing through resolutions requiring, for example, increased expenditure on economic development if the big powers, which make the largest financial contributions, are not prepared to implement them. Similarly, these nations have recognized that there is little to be gained from trying to compel the big powers to go beyond their own pace in agreeing upon measures for disarmament or for resolving their differences on peacekeeping issues.

One important outcome of the growing recognition by the small nations of the practical limitations of their voting strength, coupled with the complementary realization by the Western powers that they no longer can be certain of majority support, even on items of particular importance to them, has been a general recourse wherever possible to compromise resolutions that command unanimous or nearly unanimous support. However, notwithstanding this partial solution to the problems created by the emergence of a floating third voting force in the General Assembly, the big powers, especially those from the West, have become increasingly dissatisfied with this situation, and some of their leaders have come to question the principle of "one country, one vote."

While the decisions of the General Assembly have no legally binding force for governments, they carry the weight of world opinion on major international issues, as well as the moral authority of the world community. Even so, the fact that a resolution receives an overwhelming majority vote does not guarantee its effectiveness. Nor does the fact that a resolution was adopted by a slender margin necessarily mean that it will serve no purpose. In general, it may be said that a resolution will be effective insofar as its adoption is not regarded by any country as inimical to its national interests. The most effective resolutions, then, are those that concern matters on which all members are prepared to accept a degree of compromise (though this acceptance may not necessarily be reflected in the actual voting) and that establish goals all members are eager to achieve or to which they have no objection. Like the UN itself, resolutions can be only as effective as the membership wants them to be.

THE SECURITY COUNCIL

Under the charter, the members of the UN vest in the Security Council primary responsibility for maintaining international peace and security. To facilitate its work and to ensure quick and effective action when required, the council has certain powers and attributes not accorded the other organs of the UN. Thus, the council is empowered by the charter to enforce its decisions and prescribe them as a course of action legally binding upon all UN members. However, these prerogatives can be invoked only in times of gravest crisis and under explicit conditions laid down in the charter. Otherwise, the Security Council, like the General Assembly, can only recommend and advise.

Another distinctive feature of the council is the membership and voting privileges accorded to the five countries that were chiefly responsible for the defeat of the Axis nations in World War II and, at the time of the San Francisco Conference, were regarded as militarily the most powerful countries in the world. By the terms of these privileges, China, France, the Russian Federation, the United Kingdom, and the United States were each accorded permanent membership on the Security Council and the right to veto any substantive decision adopted by the majority of the other members. The underlying consideration here was the desire to preserve the unanimity of the Big Five—that is, to ensure that no peacekeeping action would be taken against the will of a country considered sufficiently powerful to oppose the council's decision with military force and so open up the possibility of a third major international war.

Since all five countries were actually specified by name in the relevant charter provisions, an amendment or revision of the charter would be required to name different nations as permanent Security Council members. In turn, a charter amendment requires ratification by all five permanent members of the Security Council before it can come into force. In 1971, a major change was brought about without altering the names of permanent members. The General Assembly voted that the right to represent China belonged to a delegation that the People's Republic of China would name and expelled the delegation from the Republic of China (Taiwan). On 24 December 1991, Boris Yeltsin, president of the new Russian Federation, sent a letter to the Secretary-General informing him that the Russian Federation, as the "continuing state" of the former USSR, would occupy the seat of the former USSR on the Security Council. The letter stated that the Russian Federation had the support of the 11 member countries of the Commonwealth of Independent States, most of whom subsequently became members of the United Nations. The precedent for this switch was cited to be the 1947 accession of the newly independent India to the UN membership held by the former British India.

MEMBERSHIP

To expedite decision and action, the membership of the Security Council was deliberately restricted to a small number. Originally an 11-member body, it was subsequently enlarged to 15 members by a charter amendment that came into effect on 31 August 1965.

With five seats permanently assigned, the remaining 10 are filled by other UN members elected by secret ballot in the General Assembly for two-year terms. Five seats on the Security Council become vacant each year. Nonpermanent members of the council are ineligible for immediate reelection upon retirement. In electing the nonpermanent members of the Security Council, the General Assembly is required to pay due regard to the past and potential contribution of nations to the maintenance of international peace and security, as well as to equitable geographical distribution. In view of the power of the council, nations attach great importance to the choice of the nonpermanent members.

The problem of ensuring equitable geographical distribution of members elected to the Security Council has not been easy to resolve. Prior to the council's enlargement, there had been a long-standing difference of views on a "gentlemen's agreement" reached in the early days of the UN that was intended to guarantee that the six nonpermanent seats would be so distributed that one of the seats would always be held by a Soviet bloc country. However, until 1960, only Poland and the Ukraine were elected, and each served for only one two-year term. In the 1959 election, Poland and Turkey competed for the nonpermanent council seat for the two-year term 1960–61. After 52 ballots, the General Assembly gave the seat to Poland on the basis of the following compromise: though elected for two years, Poland would resign its seat at the end of the first year and Turkey would be the sole candidate to fill the unexpired term. Under a similar arrangement, Romania held a seat for 1962, resigning it for 1963 to the Philippines. To avoid the recurrence of such situations after the enlargement of the council, the General Assembly established a fixed pattern for the geographical distribution of the 10 nonpermanent seats: five from African and Asian nations, one from East European nations, two from Latin American nations, and two from West European and other nations.

The accession of the Russian Federation, a vastly less powerful state than the former USSR, to a permanent seat on the Security Council set off a discussion among the UN membership about the need to make changes to the structure of the Security Council to better reflect the radical changes in the world and the organization's overall membership. The 48th General Assembly established an Open-Ended Working Group on the Question of Equitable Representation on and Increase in the Membership of the Security Council, which held its first meeting in New York on 19 January 1994. The Working Group submitted an informal report to the Secretary-General summarizing the results of its survey of the membership. It found that virtually all member states of the UN favor an increase in the membership of the Security Council. There was little unanimity, however, on the criteria for revising the council's composition. Responses received by the Working Group proposed increasing membership by as few as four (to 19) or more than doubling its size (to 31). Some members suggested the number of permanent members be increased at least by one (to six), or perhaps as much as seven (to 12). Most states responding to the survey agreed that an increase in membership should not diminish the council's efficiency. While most members favored continuing the categories of permanent and nonpermanent memberships, new categories were suggested: permanent seats without power of veto; rotating permanent seats, with or without power of veto; and semipermanent seats or extended membership. Some of the possible criteria put forward for new Security Council permanent membership included size of peacekeeping and financial contributions, the size of population and territory, economic potential, regional importance, geopolitical situation, and military capability.

In January 1994, the Security Council consisted of the five permanent members: China, France, the Russian Federation, the United Kingdom, and the United States. The 10 nonpermanent members, elected for a two-year period, were Brazil, Djibouti, New Zealand, Pakistan, Spain, Argentina, Czech Republic, Nigeria, Oman, and Rwanda.

ORGANIZATION OF THE COUNCIL

The Security Council is organized to function continuously and to meet as often as necessary. Hence, a representative from each member state must always be available so that in an emergency the council can convene at once. Chairmanship rotates among the council's member states according to their English alphabetical order, a new president (as the chairman is called) presiding every month. It is up to the president to decide whether to preside during the discussion of a question that directly concerns his own country.

Council members normally are represented by the heads of their permanent missions to the UN, who have the rank of ambassador. Any state that is not currently a council member but is a party to a dispute under consideration by the council must be invited to send representatives to participate in the proceedings, though without the right to vote. (In these circumstances, the disputing states concerned usually send a high government official, very often the foreign minister.) When the council is discussing a matter other than an actual dispute, the decision to invite the participation of any UN member states whose interests are directly affected is left to its discretion. The council has usually acceded to requests for such invitations. It has also granted representatives of national liberation organizations the opportunity to speak at a number of meetings.

The Security Council has held sessions away from its New York headquarters on two occasions, in Addis Ababa in 1972, to consider questions relating to Africa, and in Panama in 1973, to consider questions relating to Latin America.

VOTING

Each member of the Security Council has one vote. On questions of procedure, a motion is carried if it obtains an affirmative vote of any nine members. On substantive matters, a resolution requires the affirmative votes of nine members, including the concurring votes of the permanent members. However, any member, whether permanent or nonpermanent, must abstain from voting in any decision concerning the peaceful settlement of a dispute to which it is a party.

The Veto

The veto power and its exercise by permanent members remains a central characteristic of the mechanism of the Security Council, although, since the end of the cold war, a new climate of collegiality has made its use rare. Though the word "veto" does not occur in the charter, it is the common-usage term for the power of any of the five permanent members to defeat a resolution by voting "nay."

Negative votes cast in the council by its permanent members constitute an exercise of their veto power only on substantive questions, not on procedural matters. Moreover, by long-standing practice, the charter provision stipulating that all substantive resolutions must obtain the concurring votes of the permanent members has been interpreted to mean that, provided a permanent member does not actually vote "nay," a resolution may still be carried.

The veto power, then, is the constitutional instrument for giving expression to the requirement—discussed at the opening of this chapter—that before the Security Council invokes its authority in peacekeeping action, the big powers should first resolve their differences on how a particular crisis should be handled. However, although the principle of ensuring unanimity among the big powers was the major consideration underlying the institution of the veto, it was not the only one. A complementary consideration was the need of the major powers to ensure that their decisions would not be overridden by a majority vote of the smaller nations. In effect, conferring the right of veto upon a few powerful countries was tacit acknowledgement of the natural conflict that exists between their interests and those of the less powerful nations. It was a recognition of the fact that, despite differing social systems and power rivalry, the large countries often share more interests with each other than they do with smaller nations having social systems and tenets similar to their own. And it was for exactly this reason that the smaller countries represented at the San Francisco Conference made strenuous but unsuccessful efforts to prevent the institution of the veto power in the charter.

FUNCTIONS AND POWERS

The functions and powers assigned to the Security Council under the charter are the following:

- to maintain international peace and security in accordance with the principles and purposes of the UN;
- to investigate any dispute or situation that might lead to international friction and to recommend methods of adjusting such disputes or the terms of settlement;
- to determine the existence of a threat to the peace or an act of aggression and to recommend what action should be taken;
- to call on members to apply economic sanctions and other measures not involving the use of force in order to prevent or stop aggression;
- to take military action against an aggressor; and
- to formulate plans for the establishment of a system to regulate armaments.

The Security council also is empowered to exercise the trusteeship functions of the UN in areas designated as "strategic" (only the Trust Territory of the Pacific Islands was so designated).

Finally, the Council recommends to the General Assembly the admission of new members and the appointment of the Secretary-General and, together with the General Assembly, elects the judges of the International Court of Justice.

MAINTAINING INTERNATIONAL PEACE AND SECURITY

By the very act of joining the UN, all members "confer on the Security Council primary responsibility for the maintenance of international peace and security and agree that in carrying out its duties under this responsibility the Security Council *acts on their behalf*" (italics added). They also consent "to accept and carry out" the decisions of the council on any peacekeeping action that may be required. Under Article 39 of the charter, the Security Council's powers to take such enforceable decisions come into effect only when a definite "threat to the peace," an actual "breach of the peace," or a particular "act of aggression" has occurred. Only if the council decides that one of these circumstances prevails may it invoke its power to take a course of enforcement action that constitutes a legally binding commitment on all UN members. With regard to disputes between states that, in the opinion of the council, have not yet led to a definite threat to the peace or do not constitute an actual breach of the peace or an act of aggression, it may simply recommend measures for a peaceful settlement.

The extreme caution with which the founders of the UN assigned governmental prerogatives to the Security Council is reflected in the fact that its peacekeeping powers are set out in two quite separate chapters of the charter. Chapter VI establishes the council's advisory functions in assisting the peaceful settlement of disputes. Chapter VII defines the kind of action that it may take in the event of threats to the peace, breaches of the peace, and acts of aggression.

Peaceful Settlement of Disputes

Under Chapter VI of the charter, the parties to any dispute "the continuance of which is likely to endanger the maintenance of international peace and security" are enjoined to seek a settlement of their own accord by peaceful means, including "negotiation, enquiry, mediation, conciliation, arbitration, judicial settlement, or resort to regional agencies or arrangements. . . ." When can the Security Council itself intervene? On this point, the charter is as unrestrictive as possible. By no means does every "situation" of conflicting interests lead to an actual dispute. Yet the council need not wait until a situation has given rise to friction before taking action. It may take the initiative of investigating any dispute, or any situation that might lead to international friction or give rise to a dispute, in order to determine whether the continuance of the dispute or situation is likely to endanger the maintenance of international peace and security. Moreover, any nation, whether a member of the UN or not, has the right to bring any dispute or threatening situation before the Security Council (or before the General Assembly). Should the parties to a dispute fail to settle their differences by peaceful means of their own choice, they are bound under the terms of the charter to refer the problem to the council.

Once the council has decided to intervene in a dispute, it can take several courses of action. It may recommend one of the methods of settlement listed in the charter; it may itself determine and recommend other "procedures or methods of adjustment" that it deems appropriate; or, if it considers that the continuance of the dispute is likely to endanger international peace and security, it can decide to recommend substantive terms of settlement.

What is an "appropriate" procedure or method of settlement? And what kind of specific, substantive recommendations can the Security Council make? Purposely, the charter has left these questions to the council's discretion.

An example of a major conflict during which the Security Council recommended both procedures and substantive terms for peaceful settlement was the struggle that eventually led to the independence of the Dutch East Indies. In that instance, the council was unable to prevent bloodshed, but it forestalled the spread of the conflict and it helped in the emergence of the new state of Indonesia.

On 1 August 1947, the Security Council called upon the Netherlands and Indonesia to cease hostilities and to settle their dispute by arbitration or other peaceful means. It then offered, on 25 August 1947, to assist in the settlement through a good offices committee, with whose help a truce was signed. Later, negotiations for a final settlement ran into a snag, and eventually hostilities were resumed. On 28 January 1949, the council called upon the Netherlands to discontinue all military operations and release political prisoners immediately and unconditionally. It also called upon Indonesia to cease guerrilla warfare, and it recommended various measures, including the establishment of an interim federal government of Indonesia and the holding of elections within a certain period of time.

By contrast, in the United Kingdom–Albania case of 1947, a mere recommendation of a method of settlement proved sufficient in a dispute that otherwise might have had serious repercussions. The conflict revolved around the shelling by Albanian coastal batteries of two British warships and the mining of the Corfu Channel by Albania, which caused damage to two British destroyers and loss of life. On 3 April 1947, the Security Council recommended that the case be immediately referred to the International Court of Justice. Both parties complied.

Threats to the Peace, Breaches of the Peace, and Acts of Aggression

If, in its opinion, there is a threat to the peace, the Security Council has the duty to maintain peace and security by preventing the outbreak of actual hostilities. If there has been a breach of the peace or an act of aggression, its duty is to restore international peace and security.

The Security Council is empowered by the charter to call upon the parties to comply with any provisional measures that it deems necessary or desirable. Such immediate instructions to the quarreling states are intended, without prejudice to the rights of the parties, to prevent an aggravation of the conflict. For example, the council may demand the immediate cessation of hostilities and withdrawal of the forces from the invaded territory. If either or both parties do not comply with these demands, the council "shall duly take account" of the failure to comply. In this event, the farthest-reaching prerogative of the Security Council can come into play—namely, its right to institute sanctions against the recalcitrant state or states.

Here again, the discretion of the Security Council is very wide. When the council finds that a threat to the peace, breach of the peace, or act of aggression exists, it is authorized, though not compelled, by the charter to invoke sanctions. Even if its first provisional demands are not heeded, it may continue to press for peaceful settlement or take various other actions, such as the dispatch of a commission of inquiry, short of sanctions. On the other hand, the Security Council is free to invoke whatever enforcement measures it may consider necessary under the circumstances. It need not begin with the mildest but may, as in the Korean conflict, immediately start with the severest type of sanction—namely, the use of military force—if it considers that less drastic measures would be inadequate.

Types of Sanctions. The charter does not provide an exhaustive list of sanctions that the Security Council may invoke, but it mentions two types: sanctions not involving the use of armed forces, and military sanctions.

Sanctions not involving the use of armed forces may be of two kinds. One is the severance of diplomatic relations with one or more of the belligerent states. The other is economic sanctions, including partial or complete interruption of economic relations and communications, such as rail, sea, and air traffic, postal and telegraphic services, and radio. The purpose is to isolate the country or countries against which they are directed, physically, economically, and morally. For example, a would-be aggressor that is denied certain strategic materials may be compelled to cease hostilities. If successful, such measures have great advantages over military sanctions. They impose fewer burdens on the participating countries and fewer hardships on the population of the areas of conflict. They also avoid the danger that once military action on behalf of the UN has been taken, war may spread.

Military sanctions, the charter stipulates, may include demonstrations by air, sea, or land forces; blockade; or "other operations by air, sea, and land forces," the latter including actual military action against the offending country or countries.

Once the Security Council has decided on specific sanctions, all members of the UN are under legal obligation to carry them out. The council may, however, at its discretion, decide that only certain member states shall take an active part, or it may demand that even nonmember states participate in economic sanctions to make them effective. The charter also stipulates that before any member state not represented on the Security Council is called upon to provide armed forces, that country must, upon its request, be invited to participate in the council's deliberations, with a right to vote on the employment of its own contingents.

The Security Council has invoked its powers to impose sanctions judiciously.

In December 1966, the council imposed mandatory economic sanctions against the illegal Smith regime in Southern Rhodesia (now Zimbabwe).

The council instituted a voluntary arms embargo against South Africa in 1963 on the grounds that arms supplied to that country were being used to enforce its policy of apartheid. In November 1977, it imposed a mandatory arms embargo against South Africa. Although the General Assembly requested the Security Council to consider mandatory economic sanctions (in 1977) and a mandatory embargo on oil and oil products (in 1979), the council did not act. (The General Assembly passed a resolution calling for a mandatory oil embargo and economic sanctions against South Africa at its 44th session in 1989.)

On 6 August 1990, in response to Iraq's invasion of Kuwait, the Security Council, in its Resolution 661, imposed the tightest sanctions in its history: a full trade embargo barring all imports from and exports to Iraq, excepting only medical supplies and humanitarian food aid. The Security Council further indicated its resolve by passing Resolution 665 on 25 August 1990, authorizing member states to use force to block shipments of goods to Iraq. Finally, on 25 September, it passed Resolution 670 mandating a complete air transport blockade of Iraq.

In 1991, at the request of the foreign minister of Yugoslavia, the Security Council imposed its first mandatory arms embargo in Europe in an effort to quell the rising tide of insurrection between ethnic groups in that country. By 30 May 1992, Yugoslavia had dissolved into four states: Slovenia, Croatia, Bosnia-Herzegovina, and the Federal Republic of Yugoslavia (Serbia and Montenegro). At that time, Slovenia, Croatia, and Bosnia-Herzegovina were admitted to UN membership and the Security Council, in Resolution 757, imposed mandatory trade sanctions against the Federal Republic of Yugoslavia, excepting only shipments of food and medicine for humanitarian purposes.

On 31 March 1992, the Security Council adopted an arms and air traffic embargo on Libya (Resolution 748) in response to requests by France, the United Kingdom, and the United States. Those countries sought to force Libya to extradite two Libyan nationals indicted in those countries for the 21 December 1988 bombing of Pan Am Flight 103 over Lockerbie, Scotland, in which 270 persons died, and the bombing of UTA Flight 772 on 19 September 1989 in Niger, in which 171 persons died. On 11 November 1993, the Security Council voted to widen those sanctions (Resolution 883) to include freezing Libyan bank accounts, closing the offices of Libyan Arab Airlines, and prohibiting the supply of materials for construction and maintenance of airports. The sanctions also banned the supply of pumps, turbines, and motors used at export terminals and oil refineries.

On 16 June 1993, the Security Council adopted wide-ranging economic and trade sanctions (Resolution 841) against the military regime in Haiti which had unseated Haitian president Jean-Bertrand Aristide in 1991. President Aristide had been elected to office in a UN-supervised election. The council acted in conjunction with similar sanctions imposed by the Organization of American States. In brief, the Security Council directed members not to sell oil, weapons, ammunition, military vehicles, military equipment, and spare parts to Haiti. In addition, it authorized members to blockade the country to prevent those items from being delivered to Haiti. It also authorized member countries to freeze Haitian funds. The sanctions were briefly lifted when negotiations produced the Governors Island agreement of 3 July 1993, in which the military regime agreed to restore President Aristide with the assistance of a UN peacekeeping mission (called the UN Mission in Haiti or UNMIH). On 11 October 1993 the first deployment of UNMIH was prevented from landing at Port au Prince and the sanctions were reinstated three days later.

On 30 May 1993, in its Resolution 918, the Security Council imposed an arms embargo on Rwanda. It imposed the embargo in an effort to protect its UN Assistance Mission for Rwanda (UNAMIR) and other international humanitarian relief workers, as well as the civilian population, from the rampant lawlessness and violence that had broken out in connection with the resumption of that country's civil war between ethnic Hutu and Tutsi factions.

The Security Council's previous reluctance to invoke its ultimate prerogatives is attributable to two main factors. There is a very strong argument that in most cases punitive measures are ineffective and may even harm chances for a peaceful settlement. The provisions on the UN security system make it clear that peace is to be preserved whenever possible without recourse to force. The second major factor is that, before the end of the cold war, one or two of the permanent members would take different positions from the other three or four, so that in most cases the council's sympathies were divided between the opposing parties. Not only did division between the permanent members preclude punitive measures against one side, but it also seriously inhibited definitive action of any kind. For example, the initial action of sending a UN command into Korea was made possible only by the absence of the USSR from the council at the time (in protest against the council's decision on Chinese representation). Had the Soviet Union been there, it would presumably have vetoed the necessary resolutions. An example of the reverse situation is the issue of South Africa's apartheid policies. Beginning in 1960, the African nations appealed regularly to the Security Council to institute mandatory economic sanctions against South Africa in the hope of forcing it to terminate the apartheid system. The former USSR frequently expressed itself in favor of such a move, but the Western permanent members—in particular, South Africa's major trading partners, the United Kingdom and the United States—were reluctant to impose economic sanctions.

In the post-cold war era of collegiality in the Security Council, the Russian Federation and the United States rarely found themselves on opposite poles of an argument, and imposing sanctions as a method to force other member states to comply with Security Council directives was much easier to accomplish.

Armed Forces for the UN

Although the charter contains provisions to equip the Security Council with armed forces in case of need (the Covenant of the League of Nations contained no such provisions), these requirements have not been implemented. Under the charter, all UN members "undertake to make available to the Security Council, on its call and in accordance with a special agreement or agreements, armed forces, assistance, and facilities, including rights of passage, necessary for the purpose of maintaining international peace and security." These agreements were to determine the number and types of military forces to be provided by the nations, their degree of readiness, their location, and so on, and they were to come into effect only after ratification by the countries concerned according to their respective constitutional requirements. (With this provision in mind, the United States Congress in December 1945 passed the "UN Participation Act," authorizing the president of the United States to negotiate a special agreement with the Security Council on the detailed provision of United States forces; the agreement would then require approval by legislative enactment or joint resolution of the United States Congress.) The troops and weapons would remain part of each country's national military establishment. They would not become international forces, but they would be pledged to the UN and, at the request of the Security Council, would be placed at its disposal.

However, the plan to place armed forces at the disposition of the Security Council required wide international agreement on a number of steps before it could be put into operation. The charter provides for the establishment of a Military Staff Committee composed of the chiefs of staff (or their representatives) of the five permanent members to advise and assist the council on all questions relating to its military requirements. The first task that the council assigned the Military Staff Committee was to recommend the military arrangements to be negotiated with member states. The committee was never able to reach agreed positions that could serve as the basis for negotiation and at an early date took on the characteristics of a vestigial organ.

In his 1992 "Agenda for Peace," the Secretary-General called for strengthening UN peacekeeping by reviving these arrangements.

Peacekeeping Practice

Peacekeeping operations are not mentioned in the charter, yet they, as opposed to enforcement measures, are the means that the Security Council has most frequently used to maintain the peace. It has dispatched observer missions and troops in several crises. (The council's major peacekeeping operations and those undertaken by the General Assembly are described in the chapter on International Peace and Security.) Although the arrangements for the provision of armed forces foreseen in the charter have not been realized, the UN has nevertheless been able to establish peacekeeping forces on the basis of voluntary contributions of troops by member states.

Until the end of the cold war, the formula had always been that the disputants themselves must expressly invite the council to take peacekeeping measures (the special situation of Korea being the only exception—see the chapter on International Peace and Security.) The formula permits the Council to act in the maintenance of peace and security even though it may not have resolved its own differences on recommending the terms of a settlement. Generally, the peacekeeping operations undertaken by the council have represented a kind of holding action.

With the eruption of ethnic and nationalistic conflicts in Eastern Europe and Africa after the end of the cold war, the Security Council recognized that the increasing number and complexity of peacekeeping operations warranted review. In May 1993, it requested the Secretary-General to submit a report containing specific new proposals to improve the capacity of the UN in peacekeeping. The Secretary-General submitted his report on "Improving the capacity of the United Nations for peacekeeping" in March 1994. In response to this analysis, on 3 May 1994, the Security Council issued a statement setting forth factors to be considered in establishing UN peacekeeping operations. The factors to be considered in the establishment of new peacekeeping operations included:

- whether a situation exists that presents a threat to international peace and security;
- whether regional or subregional organizations already exist and can assist in resolving the situation;
- whether a cease-fire exists and whether the parties have committed themselves to a peace process intended to reach a political settlement;
- whether a clear political goal exists and whether it can be reflected in the mandate;
- whether a precise mandate for a United Nations operation can be formulated; and
- whether the safety and security of UN personnel can be reasonably insured; in particular, whether the parties to a dispute offer reasonable guarantees of safety to UN personnel.

The council also required an estimate of projected costs for the inital 90 days of a new peacekeeping operation, and for its first six months, and an estimate of the total annual cost, before authorizing any new missions. In the case of mission extensions, it also required estimates of the financial implications.

In both "An Agenda for Peace" (1992) and his March 1994 report, the Secretary-General proposed that a new mechanism had to be developed to enable a quick response to international crises. Under normal circumstances, the process of designing a mission, obtaining committments for troops and equipment, establishing a budget, and obtaining approval for new peacekeeping missions could take as long as three months. The Security Council welcomed the Secretary-General's proposal to devise stand-by arrangements under which member states would maintain an agreed number of troops and equipment ready for quick deployment. A Stand-by Arrangements Management Unit was established to keep track of units and resources available for this purpose.

SUBSIDIARY ORGANS

Besides supervising peacekeeping operations (listed in the chapter on International Peace and Security), the Security Council also has established various standing committees and ad hoc bodies.

United Nations Special Commission (UNSCOM)

After the UN-sanctioned multinational force repulsed Iraq from Kuwait in April 1991, the Security Council passed Resolution 687 setting forth the terms for an official cease-fire. This resolution led the UN into previously uncharted waters. It required Iraq to "unconditionally accept the destruction, removal or rendering harmless of ... all chemical and biological weapons and stocks of agents and all ballistic missiles with a range greater than 150 kilometers...." Iraq also was forced to agree to place all its nuclear weapons materials under the custody of the International Atomic Energy Agency (IAEA). The resolution gave Iraq 15 days to submit a complete inventory of all its weapons of mass destruction.

To verify and implement this condition, the Security Council created the United Nations Special Commission (UNSCOM). Its mandate is to carry out immediate on-site inspections of Iraq's biological, chemical, and missile capabilities; to take possession for destruction, removal, or rendering harmless of all chemical and biological weapons and all materials for research, development, support, and manufacture of such weapons; to supervise the destruction by Iraq of all its ballistic missiles with a range greater than 150km, including major parts, repair, and production facilities; and to monitor and verify Iraq's compliance with its undertaking not to use, develop, construct, or acquire any of the items specified above. UNSCOM also inspectors of the IAEA, who are charged with similar tasks in the area of nuclear armaments.

In October 1991, UNSCOM reported to the Security Council that Iraq at first adopted an attitude of noncooperation, concealment, and outright falsification. The Security Council responded with Resolution 707 (1991) condemning Iraq's violation of Resolution 687 and making nine specific demands. In March 1992, Iraq declared that it was no longer in possession of any of the weapons described in Resolution 687, but the Security Council did not accept this. In June 1992, Iraq again supplied what it said were "full, final and complete reports," on the weapons programs covered by Resolution 687. These reports also were considered to be suspect. Using aggressive surprise inspection techniques, UNSCOM and IAEA were able to compile significant information on Iraq's weapons capabilities.

UNSCOM's investigations revealed that Iraq had acquired a massive stockpile of weapons of mass destruction and ballistic missiles. The international community was horrified to learn that Iraq had established a military research program to develop biological weapons that had long been banned by international disarmament agreements (to which Iraq was ostensibly a party). UNSCOM discovered that the microorganisms involved in this research program included anthrax, botulin toxin, and gas gangere. Although no facilities for the production of these biological weapons were found, UNSCOM did discover huge stockpiles of deadly chemical weapons, including warheads, aerial bombs, and artillery shells meant to deliver a variety of nerve gas agents, tear gas, and mustard gas.

IAEA/UNSCOM inspections also revealed three clandestine uranium enrichment programs and found conclusive evidence of a nuclear weapons development program aimed at an implosion-type weapon. The secret development of these materials, bypassing regular inspections by the IAEA, put Iraq in violation of its undertakings as a member of IAEA. The IAEA also found that Iraq had violated its obligations under the Nuclear Non-Proliferation Treaty. By mid-1992 the IAEA had removed and destroyed most of the materials and facilities and forced Iraq to destroy its nuclear complex at al-Athir, where most of the nuclear weapons research had taken place. The IAEA transported Iraq's nuclear fuel to Russia, where it was diluted from weapons grade to civilian reactor quality.

By the end of January 1993, a total of 772 individuals from 38 countries had served on UNSCOM inspection teams. UNSCOM continues its long-term mission to monitor and verify Iraq's compliance with Resolution 687.

War Crimes

International Tribunal for the Former Yugoslavia. Reports of widespread violations of international humanitarian law in the bloody conflict among the states of the former Yugoslavia led the Security Council to establish a Commission of Experts in October 1992. The commission was established to investigate the reports and submit its findings to the Security Council. In January 1993 the commission sent a first report describing the discovery of a mass grave in Croatia, and thousands of allegations of grave breaches of the Geneva Conventions and international humanitarian law. In February 1993, the Security Council adopted Resolution 808, establishing an international tribunal for the prosecution of persons responsible for the crimes discovered by the Commission, the first such tribunal since the war crimes trials conducted after World War II. By May 1993, the Secretary-General had submitted a detailed report to the Security Council setting forth the tribunal's legal basis, method of proceeding, and its statute. It was established as a subsidiary organ of the Security Council under Chapter VII of the charter. Its headquarters would be at The Hague, Netherlands.

On 25 May 1993, the Security Council passed Resolution 827, approving the report and establishing the tribunal "for the sole purpose of prosecuting persons responsible for the serious violations of international humanitarian law committed in the territory of the former Yugoslavia between 1 January 1991 and a date to be determined by the Security Council upon restoration of peace...." The General Assembly elected 11 judges to the tribunal in September 1993: Georges Michel Abi-Saab (Egypt), Antonio Cassese (Italy), Jules Deschenes (Canada), Adolphus Godwin Karibi-Whyte (Nigeria), Germain le Foyer de Costil (France), Haopei Li (China), Elizabeth Odio Benito (Costa Rica), Rustam S. Sidhwa (Pakistan), Sir Ninian Stephen (Australia), and Mr. Lal Chand Vohrah (Malaysia). However, it was not until 7 July 1994 that South African judge Richard Goldstone was chosen to lead the prosecution team. It was reported that the Russian Federation had opposed nominating a prosecutor from a Western country, because of possible bias against Serbia, its traditional ally.

Commission of Experts on War Crimes in Rwanda. On 1 July 1994, the Security Council requested the Secretary-General establish a three-member Commission of Experts to investigate allegations of mass killings of civilians and genocide in Rwanda, during the re-eruption of civil war in that country in April 1994. It had been reported that as many as 250,000 civilians may have died in ethnic violence. On 8 August 1994, the new government of Rwanda, led by members of the Tutsi ethnic group, notified the Secretary-General that it would cooperate with an international war crimes tribunal. The new government hoped that the promise of an international tribunal under the auspices of the UN would allay the fears of hundreds of thousands of ethnic Hutu citizens who were refusing to return to Rwanda from refugee camps in neighboring countries due to fear of reprisals and prosecution by the new government.

THE ECONOMIC AND SOCIAL COUNCIL

Many of the most outstanding accomplishments of the UN to date are in the economic and social fields. Under Article 55 of the charter, the organization is committed to promote the following goals:

"(a) higher standards of living, full employment, and conditions of economic and social progress and development;

"(b) solutions of international economic, social, health, and related problems; and international cultural and educational cooperation; and

"(c) universal respect for, and observance of, human rights and fundamental freedoms for all without distinction as to race, sex, language, or religion."

The responsibility for UN activities aimed at the achievement of these goals is vested in the General Assembly and, under its authority, the Economic and Social Council.

FIELDS OF ACTIVITY

The activities of the Economic and Social Council, carried out through its subsidiary bodies in cooperation with the specialized agencies, have touched on all aspects of human well-being and affected the lives of people everywhere. A list of the major spheres of activity supervised by the council is given below; the chapters on Economic and Social Development, Technical Cooperation Programs, Social and Humanitarian Assistance, and Human Rights contain further information on matters directly under its purview.

Economic Development. Although this field encompasses both developed and developing nations, emphasis is focused on the problems of the latter group. The activities of the council include evaluating long-term projections for the world economy; fostering international trade, particularly in commodities, between industrialized and nonindustrialized countries; improving the international flow of private and public capital; promoting industrialization and the development of natural resources; resolving related political and legal issues, such as permanent sovereignty over natural resources and land reform; developing programs of technical cooperation for developing nations; and applying the latest innovations of science and technology to improve the industrialization of developing countries.

Social Progress. Among the social problems handled under the aegis of the council are housing, population, international traffic in narcotic drugs, the welfare of children in the developing countries, and the status of the world's refugees, the aging, and the disabled. Particular attention is paid to the role of women in development.

Human Rights. The council and its subsidiary organs have elaborated a series of important principles for the promotion of fundamental freedoms. Measures include the Universal Declaration of Human Rights and a number of declarations and recommendations on specific rights—for example, the rights of women, freedom of information and the press, and racial equality. The most recent declaration was adopted in Vienna in June 1993, namely, the "Vienna Declaration and Programme of Action."

Related Special Problems. An example of a special problem of interest to the council is the improvement of statistical techniques, since efficient statistics are essential to economic and social development. Work in this field includes techniques to improve world statistics in specific economic branches, such as industry and finance; standards of national statistical services; and methods of comparing statistics from different countries.

Problems Dealt with by the UN Related Agencies. The 16 specialized agencies, the General Agreement on Tariffs and Trade (GATT), and the International Atomic Energy Agency (IAEA) undertake a wide range of activities in the economic and social fields. It is a function of the council to coordinate these activities. Accounts of each of the 18 related agencies are given in the separate chapters devoted to them.

FUNCTIONS AND POWERS

Under the charter, the council is authorized to make or initiate studies, reports, and recommendations on economic, social, cultural, educational, health, and related matters; to make recommendations to promote respect for, and observance of, human rights; to prepare draft conventions for submission to the General Assembly on matters within its competence; to call international conferences on matters within its competence and in accordance with rules prescribed by the UN; to enter into agreements, subject to the approval of the General Assembly, with specialized agencies; to coordinate the activities of the specialized agencies and obtain regular reports from them; to perform, with the approval of the General Assembly, services at the request of member nations or the specialized agencies; to consult with nongovernmental agencies whose work is related to matters dealt with by the council; to set up subsidiary organs to assist its work; and to perform any other functions that may be assigned to it by the General Assembly.

COMPOSITION

Originally, the Economic and Social Council consisted of 18 members, but the amendments to the charter that came into force on 31 August 1965 raised the number to 27. Another amendment that came into force on 24 September 1973 increased the membership to 54.

When the council was constituted in January 1946, the General Assembly elected the council's first 18 members for staggered terms: 6 members each for one, two, and three years, respectively. Subsequently, all terms were for three years, so that each year one-third of the membership is elected by the General Assembly.

The General Assembly resolutions adopting the amendments to the charter that increased the membership of the council also laid down an equitable pattern for the geographical distribution of the additional seats. The 54 members are elected so as to include 14 African states, 11 Asian states, 10 Latin American states, 13 Western European and other states, and 6 states from Eastern Europe. Elections are by a two-thirds majority vote on a secret ballot in the General Assembly, and immediate reelection of members is permissible. Although the permanent members of the Security Council have no privileged position on the Economic and Social Council and the charter does not guarantee them membership in the council, it has been the custom to reelect them continuously. In general, the General Assembly has less difficulty in agreeing on its Economic and Social Council selections than in filling Security Council vacancies. Moreover, if, in the opinion of the council, a matter on its agenda is of particular concern to a UN member not represented on the council, it may invite that state to participate in its discussions but without a vote.

In 1994, the council had the following members: Angola, Australia, Bahamas, Bangladesh, Belarus, Belgium, Benin, Bhutan, Brazil, Bulgaria, Canada, Chile, China, Colombia, Costa Rica, Cuba, Denmark, Egypt, Ethiopia, France, Gabon, Germany, Ghana, Greece, India, Indonesia, Ireland, Italy, Japan, Kuwait, Libyan Arab Jamahiriya, Madagascar, Mexico, Nigeria, Norway, Pakistan, Paraguay, Philippines, Poland, Portugal, Republic of Korea, Romania, Russian Federation, Senegal, Sri Lanka, Suriname, Swaziland, Ukraine, United Kingdom, United Republic of Tanzania, United States, Venezuela, Zaire, and Zimbabwe.

PROCEDURE
In 1993, the Economic and Social Council undertook a major restructuring. Whereas it used to hold two sessions each year, one at UN headquarters in the spring and one in Geneva in the summer, it now holds only one meeting per year in summer, rotating each year between Geneva and New York. A president and four vice-presidents are elected by the council for each year. The council also holds an organizational session in January to plan its program of work for the year.

Each of the 54 members of the council has one vote. The big powers possess no veto or other special voting privilege. A proposal or motion before the council may be adopted without a vote unless a member requests one. When a vote is taken, decisions are carried by a simple majority of the members present.

SUBSIDIARY ORGANS
The council accomplishes its substantive work through numerous subsidiary organs in the form of commissions, committees, and ad hoc and special bodies. In Article 68, the charter specifically states that the council "shall set up commissions in economic and social fields and for the promotion of human rights. . . ." Several types of commissions and other organs have been set up within this provision, including the regional commissions, to deal with economic and social problems in the different geographical areas of the world, and the functional commissions, to handle social, human rights, and environmental questions.

Regional Commissions
There are five regional commissions: the Economic Commission for Europe (ECE); the Economic and Social Commission for Asia and the Pacific (ESCAP); the Economic Commission for Latin America and the Caribbean (ECLAC); the Economic Commission for Africa (ECA); and the Economic and Social Commission for Western Asia (ESCWA). Each has its own staff members, who are considered part of the regular staff of the UN. Regional commission expenditures come out of the regular UN budget. The regional commissions are discussed in the chapter on Economic and Social Development.

Functional Commissions
In 1946, the council established six functional commissions and two subcommissions to advise and assist it in its work.

The *Statistical Commission,* with 24 members, assists in developing international statistical services, promoting the development of national statistics and improving their comparability, coordinating the statistical work of the specialized agencies and the central statistical services of the UN Secretariat, and advising the UN organs on general questions relating to the collection, analysis, and dissemination of statistical information.

The *Population Commission,* with 27 members, studies population changes, including migration, and their effect on economic

and social conditions and advises on policies to influence the size and structure of populations and on any other demographic questions on which the UN or its specialized agencies may seek advice.

The *Commission for Social Development,* with 32 members, advises the council on social policies in general and on all matters in the social field not covered by the specialized agencies; it gives priority to the establishment of objectives and programs and to social research in areas affecting social and economic development.

The *Commission on Human Rights,* with 43 members, makes recommendations and prepares reports to the council on human rights questions, including the status of women, the protection of minorities, the prevention of all forms of discrimination, and the implementation of international conventions on human rights. Its Subcommission on Prevention of Discrimination and Protection of Minorities, composed of 25 experts nominated by members, carries out studies and makes recommendations to the commission on the prevention of discrimination of any kind relating to human rights and fundamental freedoms and on the protection of racial, national, religious, and linguistic minorities.

The Commission on Human Rights has also established working groups on specific human rights questions, including apartheid, slavery, indigenous populations, minorities, enforced or involuntary disappearances, and mental health detainees. It also encompasses a Subcommission on Prevention of Discrimination and Protection of Minorities.

The *Commission on the Status of Women,* with 32 members, prepares reports on matters concerning the promotion of women's rights in the political, economic, social, and educational fields and makes recommendations to the council on matters requiring immediate attention in the field of women's rights. The commission has established a working group on communications concerning the status of women.

The *Commission on Narcotic Drugs,* with 40 members, advises the council and prepares draft international agreements on all matters relating to the control of narcotic drugs. Its Subcommission on Illicit Drug Traffic and Related Matters in the Near and Middle East is composed of five persons nominated by their governments in consultation with the Secretary-General and subsequently confirmed by the council.

The *Commission on Science and Technology for Development.* The United Nations has been concerned with the effects of advances in science and technology to world peace and social development since its inception in 1945 at the dawn of the nuclear era. In 1963 the first United Nations Conference on the Application of Science and Technology for the Benefit of the Less Developed Countries met in Geneva and began to form an agenda for international action. This was followed in 1979 by the United Nations Conference on Science and Technology for Development, held in Vienna, which produced the Vienna Programme of Action. In affirmation of the conference's program, the General Assembly established an Intergovernmental Committee on Science and Technology for Development, open to all states, to draw up policy guidelines, monitor activities within the United Nations system, promote implementation of the Vienna Programme, identify priorities, and mobilize resources. In 1989, on the tenth anniversary of the 1979 Conference, the General Assembly expressed its disappointment with the implementation of the Vienna Programme of Action and eventually decided to transform the Intergovernmental Committee and its subsidiary body, the Advisory Committee on Science and Technology for Development, into a functional commission of ECOSOC (General Assembly Resolution 46/235).

The Commission on Science and Technology for Development met for the first time in May 1993. It has 53 members elected by ECOSOC for a term of four years on the principle of equitable geographic distribution. At its first session, the commission recommended to ECOSOC that it be charged with the following tasks:

(a) assisting the council in providing science and technology policy guidelines and recommendations to member states, in particular developing countries;
(b) providing innovative approaches to improving the quality of coordination and cooperation in the area of science and technology within the United Nations system, with a view to ensuring optimum mobilization of resources;
(c) providing expert advice to other parts of the United Nations systems.

The *Commission on Crime Prevention and Criminal Justice* was established in December 1991 by General Assembly Resolution 46/152. An existing ECOSOC Committee on Crime Prevention and Control was dissolved, and its funds were made available to the new commission, which met for the first time in April 1992. The new commission is charged with developing, managing, monitoring, and reviewing implementation of the Crime Prevention and Criminal Justice Programme created at a Ministerial Meeting held in Versailles, France, in 1991. In addition, it will consult member states on the drafting of a convention on crime prevention and criminal justice. Priority areas of the commission include: national and transnational crime; organized crime; economic crime, including money laundering; the role of criminal law in the protection of the environment; crime prevention in urban areas; and juvenile and violent criminality. The main difference between the former committee and the new commission, is that the decisions of the commission will be decisions of the governments, rather than of independent experts. Decisions at this level were considered essential to tackle the problems of drug trafficking, illegal arms sales, terrorism, dumping of industrial waste, and criminal negligence resulting in environmental degradation, corruption, and financial offences.

The *Commission on Sustainable Development.* As a result of the UN Conference on Environment and Development (UNCED) held in Rio de Janeiro in 1992, the council established a new functional commission in February 1993: the Commission on Sustainable Development. The new, 53-member commission began its work of monitoring the implementation of UNCED's Agenda 21 action plan with its first session in New York in June 1993. The commission's mandate includes: monitoring progress towards the UN target of providing 0.7 percent of gross national product of industrialized countries for official development assistance; considering information on the implementation of environmental conventions; and recommending action to the General Assembly. The commission will interact with other UN intergovernmental bodies, regional commissions, and development and financial institutions. A high-level Advisory Board, consisting of eminent persons from all regions of the world, will provide input to the commission and the council through the Secretary-General.

All commissions meet biennially, with the exception of the Commission on Human Rights, which meets annually. The Subcommission on Prevention of Discrimination meets annually, and the Subcommission on Illicit Drug Traffic biennially.

Other Subsidiary Organs
Article 68 of the charter provides that, in addition to the commissions specifically mentioned in the charter, the council should establish "such other commissions as may be required for its functions." With three exceptions, however, the other subsidiary organs created have not been given the name "commission." Instead, they are called "standing committees" or "expert bodies."

In 1994, ECOSOC had standing and expert bodies on the fol-
lowing subjects: Transnational Corporations; Human Settlements; New and Renewable Sources of Energy for Development; Non-Governmental Organizations; Programme and Coordination; Natural Resources; Development Planning; Transport of Dangerous Goods; International Cooperation in Tax Matters; Public Administration and Finance; International Standards of Accounting and Reporting; and Geographical Names.

Semiautonomous bodies, which generally report both to the council and to the General Assembly, include the following: International Research and Training Institute for the Advancement of Women (INSTRAW), UN Conference on Trade and Development (UNCTAD), UN Development Program (UNDP), UN Environment Program (UNEP), UN Population Fund (UNFPA), Office of the UN High Commissioner for Refugees (UNHCR), UN Children's Fund (UNICEF), UN Institute for Training and Research (UNITAR), UN University (UNU), and World Food Council (WFC). The Joint UN/FAO World Food Program (WFP), however, reports to the council only.

RELATIONS WITH NONGOVERNMENTAL ORGANIZATIONS
The charter empowers ECOSOC to make arrangements to consult with international organizations of private citizens, known as nongovernmental organizations (NGOs) and distinguished from intergovernmental organizations. Consultations with NGOs bring informed opinion other than that of governments and their officials before the council and provide it with a source of special experience and technical knowledge. NGOs granted consultative status are divided into two categories. Those in Category I are organizations with a general interest in the work of the council, and their activities are particularly germane to it and to the UN as a whole. Those in Category II are organizations with an interest in some particular aspect of the work of the council. In May 1987, 35 NGOs were listed in Category I and 299 in Category II. Another 490 were listed on the NGO roster for consultation as the occasion arises. By May 1994, 42 NGOs were listed in Category I, 383 in Category II, and 232 were listed on the roster for occasional consultation. All such officially recognized organizations may send observers to the public meetings of the council and its commissions and may submit memoranda for circulation. Representatives of Category I organizations are entitled to participate in council debates and propose items for the agenda. Representatives of Category II organizations may, with the permission of the chair, make oral statements at council meetings.

Consultative status in Category II has been granted to nearly all important international business associations, cooperative societies, farmers' organizations, trade unions, and veterans' organizations; to leading professional groups, such as associations of architects, engineers, lawyers, newspaper publishers and editors, social welfare workers, tax experts, and many others; and to various women's and youth associations. Many associations formed along denominational lines—Greek Orthodox, Jewish, Muslim, Protestant, and Roman Catholic—also have consultative status. Most organizations that enjoy such official UN standing are international, in that they have members in more than one country. An organization whose membership is restricted to one particular country may obtain consultative status in the council only with the consent of the country's government.

The participation of NGOs in the work of the council took a historic turn during preparations for the Conference on Environment and Development (UNCED) held in 1992 in Rio de Janeiro. More than 1,400 NGOs participated in UNCED, and their contributions to the historic conference were acknowledged to be invaluable. In view of this remarkable participation, the Secretary-General recommended that relevant and competent NGOs be accorded unusual participation in and access to ECOSOC's new functional commission, the Commission on Sustainable

Development, which will monitor the progress of implementation of UNCED's Agenda 21 action plan.

Since many delegations expressed the need to transform the United Nations into a forum that was more accessible to NGOs, ECOSOC established a Working Group on the Review of Arrangements for Consultations with Non-Governmental Organizations in 1993. The Working Group held its first session in June 1994 with a mandate to review the arrangemetns for consultation with nongovernmental organizations, arrangements which had not been revised since they were first adopted by the council in 1968.

In his 1994 *Agenda for Development* Secretary-General Boutros Boutros-Ghali noted that NGOs undertake development projects valued at more than US$7 billion annually. He stated: "The time has arrived to bring NGO and United Nations activities into an increasingly productive relationship of consultation and cooperation."

ORGANIZATION OF INTERNATIONAL CONFERENCES

In accordance with a charter provision, the council from time to time calls for international conferences on special world problems falling within its sphere of competence. Thus, in recent years, the UN has held conferences on such subjects as the environment, population, food, housing, and the status of women. These conferences have led to the establishment of the UN Environment Program, the World Food Council, the Center for Human Settlements (Habitat), and other programs and to the adoption of world plans of action for the environment, clean water, population, the aging, the disabled, and other subjects of international concern.

PROPOSED RESTRUCTURING

In his 1992 *Agenda for Peace,* Secretary-General Boutros Boutros-Ghali issued a wide-ranging strategy for the future of the United Nations system, including proposals for changes in ECOSOC. It was suggested that those would reflect changes in the very definition of economic and social progress that had naturally resulted from the dissolution of the former USSR. In addition, a wealth of information now existed on successful and unsuccessful efforts at development, information that in itself called for a fundamental change in the structure of the United Nations so that it could respond more effectively to its members' needs in the area of economic and social development.

In his *Agenda,* the Secretary-General proposed that ECOSOC report to the Security Council on economic and social developments that might pose threats to international peace and security. He also urged the creation of a high-level, intersessional mechanism to enable ECOSOC to react in a timely way to new developments. He also called for lines of communication between the General Assembly and ECOSOC to be clarified and streamlined. In addition, the Secretary-General urged that the relationship between ECOSOC and its subsidiary bodies be redefined. For example, he reported to the General Assembly in 1992 (A/47/434) that members of ECOSOC were frustrated by discussing the same issues four times in the same calendar year: in the council's subsidiary body, in the committee session, in the council plenary, and in the General Assembly).

Intense negotiations occurred during a resumed session of the 47th session of the General Assembly in June 1993. A draft package of reforms was proposed that had as its main aim eliminating duplication of work in the General Assembly and ECOSOC and providing guidelines for a division of labor. For example, it was suggested that the governing bodies of the UN Development Programme (UNDP), UN Population Fund (UNFPA), and the UN Children's Fund (UNICEF) be transformed into smaller executive boards under the overall authority of ECOSOC. Other proposals would have affected the procedures of ECOSOC and would have subsumed the council's two subcommittees (on economic and social issues) into the plenary body.

Although there was clearly a consensus on the need for reform and rationalization, the developing countries (in particular those countries that make up the Group of 77) blocked passage of the package because of concerns over the numerical and regional composition of governing bodies of the different funds and programs of the United Nations. The smallest countries felt that the drastic reduction in representation would exclude them from participation in the decision-making processes of these bodies. The General Assembly adjourned in September 1993 without coming to agreement on these proposals.

THE TRUSTEESHIP COUNCIL

Unlike the other main organs of the UN, the Trusteeship Council was established for the purpose of executing a closely defined system of operations. This is the trusteeship system, which was devised to adapt the League of Nations mandate system to meet the requirements of a new era.

The 1990s witnessed the graduation of the last of the Trusteeship Territories to independence or free association status. This historic achievement represents the official end of colonization as an official political system. In only 50 years the Trusteeship Council presided over the orderly, democratic transfer of power from developed nations to their former colonies.

The Trusteeship Council voted in 1994 to convene only at the request of its President, a majority of its member states, the General Assembly or the Security Council.

THE MANDATE SYSTEM OF THE LEAGUE OF NATIONS

In its political aspect, the history of the world could be read as the history of the creation and disintegration of successive empires, a chain of vicious cause and effect that has brought much bloodshed and wretchedness. After World War I, however, a concerted effort was made for the first time, in a limited way, to break the chain. Recognizing that colonies are a source of friction and jealousy among wealthy nations, the victorious Allies decided not to appropriate for themselves the colonies of their defeated enemies. Instead, those territories belonging to imperial Germany and the Ottoman Empire that were considered unable to function as independent states were placed under international administration supervised by the League of Nations.

The founders of the League created three types of mandates for the administration of these territories by nations acting as "Mandatories of the League of Nations." Class A mandates covered territories that were considered to be ready to receive independence within a relatively short period of time. These territories were all in the Middle East: Iraq, Palestine, and Transjordan, administered by the UK; and Lebanon and Syria, administered by France. Class B mandates covered territories for which the granting of independence was a distant prospect. These territories were all in Africa: the Cameroons and Togoland, each of which was divided between British and French administration; Tanganyika, under British administration; and Ruanda-Urundi, under Belgian administration. To the territories classified under Class C mandates virtually no prospect of self-government, let alone independence, was held out. These territories included South West Africa, administered by the Union of South Africa; New Guinea, administered by Australia; Western Samoa, administered by New Zealand; Nauru, administered by Australia under mandate of the British Empire; and certain Pacific islands, administered by Japan.

The terms of the mandate system implied an acknowledgment of the right of the peoples of the colonial territories belonging to states defeated in war to be granted independence if they were thought to have reached a sufficiently advanced stage of development. However, no provision was made in the League Covenant specifying that the countries designated to administer the mandated territories should take steps to prepare these peoples for eventual self-determination.

THE UN TRUSTEESHIP SYSTEM

Although the Covenant of the League forbade wars of aggression—that is, wars of conquest—the League's founding members did not see the need to underwrite this provision in a positive assertion of the principle of equal rights and self-determination of peoples. The UN Charter embodies an implicit recognition of the belief that denial of equal rights and the right of peoples to self-determination is a potential cause of war.

Thus, Article 1 of the Charter sets forth as a basic purpose of the UN "to develop friendly relations among nations based on respect for the principle of equal rights and self-determination of peoples, and to *take other appropriate measures to strengthen universal peace*" (italics added). Article 76, which sets out the main objectives of the international trusteeship system that was to replace the mandate system of the League, leaves no doubt of the value attached to its role as a means of helping the UN, in the words of the Preamble to the Charter, "to save succeeding generations from the scourge of war." The article reads as follows:

"The basic objectives of the trusteeship system, in accordance with the Purposes of the United Nations laid down in Article 1 of the present Charter, shall be:

"(a) to further international peace and security;

"(b) to promote the political, economic, social, and educational advancement of the inhabitants of the trust territories, and their progressive development towards self-government or independence as may be appropriate to the particular circumstances of each territory and its peoples and the freely expressed wishes of the peoples concerned, and as may be provided by the terms of each trusteeship agreement;

"(c) to encourage respect for human rights and for fundamental freedoms for all without distinction as to race, sex, language, or religion, and to encourage recognition of the interdependence of the peoples of the world; and

"(d) to ensure equal treatment in social, economic, and commercial matters for all Members of the United Nations and their nationals, and also equal treatment for the latter in the administration of justice. . . . "

Thus, in addition to emphasizing the importance of the trusteeship system as an instrument for peace, Article 76 defines the framework for the elaboration of obligations that the countries designated to administer the territories placed under UN trusteeship must undertake toward the peoples concerned. In essence, these obligations amount to a pledge on the part of the administering authorities to work toward the liquidation of the trusteeship system itself by preparing the peoples in trust territories for independence, or at least self-government.

The Trust Territories and Their Administering Authorities

The Charter does not specify the actual territories to be placed under UN trusteeship. Article 77 merely states that the system shall apply to three categories: (1) territories still under mandate, (2) territories "detached from enemy states as a result of the Second World War," and (3) territories voluntarily placed under the system by states responsible for their administration.

On the question of designating the administrators of trust territories, the Charter is equally nonspecific. It states simply that the individual trusteeship agreements shall designate the authority in each case, which may be "one or more states or the Organization itself." The provision that the UN itself may serve as an administering authority is a compromise solution that was adopted when it was decided at the San Francisco Conference to abandon an ambitious plan, originally proposed by China and initially supported by the US, to make the UN directly responsible for the administration of all trust territories.

It was decided that the powers that had administered mandates on behalf of the League of Nations were to conclude agreements with the new world organization and administer the same territories that were still dependent. There was one exception. The Pacific islands, which after World War I had been given to Japan as Class C mandates, were, by a special arrangement embodied in the Charter, classified as a strategic area to be administered by the US under a modified trusteeship.

As a result of agreements worked out by the General Assembly, 11 trust territories were placed under UN trusteeship, and seven countries were designated as administering authorities. These figures exclude the former German colony of South West Africa, which after World War I had been mandated to the Union of South Africa, because South Africa refused to place the territory under UN trusteeship. The distribution of the territories and their respective administering authorities was as follows:

in East Africa: Ruanda-Urundi administered by Belgium, Somaliland by Italy, and Tanganyika by the UK;

in West Africa: Cameroons administered by the UK, Cameroons by France, Togoland by the UK, and Togoland by France;

in the Pacific: Nauru, administered by Australia and on behalf of New Zealand and the UK, New Guinea by Australia, Western Samoa by New Zealand, and the Pacific islands of the Marianas, Marshalls, and Carolines by the US.

In September 1975, when New Guinea acceded to independence, the Trust Territory of the Pacific Islands became the only Territory on the agenda of the Trusteeship Council.

By virtue of a Trusteeship Agreement approved by the Security Council in 1947, the Territory was placed under United States administration as a strategic area under the terms of Article 83 of the Charter. In compliance with the provisions of that Article, the Trusteeship Council reported to the Security Council on all matters concerning the Territory, which was comprised of four entities (Northern Mariana Islands, the Federated States of Micronesia, the Marshall Islands and Palau).

Negotiations on the future political status of the Trust Territory of the Pacific Islands began in 1969. In 1975, the Northern Mariana Islands, in a referendum observed by the Trusteeship Council, chose to become a Commonwealth of the United States. In a series of referendums held in 1983 and duly observed by the Trusteeship Council's Visiting Missions, the Federated States of Micronesia and the Marshall Islands opted for a status of Free Association with the United States, while in Palau, the 75% majority required under its Constitution for the approval of the compact of Free Association with the United States could not be obtained in that and six later referendums.

In 1986, the Trusteeship Council, noting that the "peoples of the Federated States of Micronesia, the Marshall Islands, the Northern Mariana Islands and Palau have established constitutions and democratic political institutions providing the instruments of self governments," recommended an early termination of the Trusteeship Agreement.

In December 1990, the Security Council considered the status of the Trust Territory of the Pacific Islands and adopted, by 14 votes to 1, resolution 683 (1990). By that resolution, the Council determined the objectives of the Trusteeship Agreement had been fully attained with respect to those three entities and that therefore the applicability of the Trusteeship Agreement to them had been terminated. Palau, therefore, remained the only entity under

the 1947 Trusteeship Agreement. The Trusteeship Council at its annual regular sessions continued to review the situation in Palau.

In November, 1993, the Pacific island of Palau, the last of the islands remaining under the Trusteeship Agreement, succeeded in passing a referendum for the approval of the compact of Free Association with the United States. In January 1994, the Council requested the United States and Palau to agree on a date on or about 1 October 1994 for the full entry into force of the Compact of Free Association, and expressed the hope that, in the near future, the Trusteeship Agreement would be terminated by the Security Council (see chapter on Independence of Colonial Peoples).

THE TRUSTEESHIP COUNCIL

The fact that the Trusteeship Council was made a main organ of the UN is evidence of the importance attached to the role of the trusteeship system. The Council's functions, however, are decidedly more limited than those of the other main organs, for it acts, as the case may be, under the direct responsibility of the General Assembly in respect to trusteeships not involving areas designated as strategic or of the Security Council in respect to trusteeships relating to areas designated as strategic. The Charter provisions make it clear that the Trusteeship Council only "assists" the General Assembly and the Security Council in implementing the trusteeship system. It had a purely executive capacity in supervising the day-to-day operations of the system.

Composition

The Charter provides that the Council is to be composed of three groups of members: the countries administering trust territories, permanent members of the Security Council that do not administer trust territories, and a number of other UN members elected for three-year terms by the General Assembly to ensure an equal division between administering and nonadministering countries in the Council.

Until 1960, the Council consisted of 14 members: 7 administering members; 2 permanent nonadministering members; and 5 other nonadministering countries elected for three-year terms by the Assembly. As the various trust territories gained independence, the size and composition of the Council changed. The Assembly decided that after 1968, the Council would be composed only of administering powers and the nonadministering permanent members of the Security Council. On 16 September 1975, when Papua New Guinea, which includes the former trust territory of New Guinea, achieved independence, Australia ceased to be a member of the Council. This change left a membership of five: one administering power, the US, and four nonadministering permanent members of the Security Council—China, France, the USSR, and the UK.

Procedure

Each member of the Trusteeship Council has one vote. Decisions are made by a simple majority vote. The permanent members of the Security Council have no veto or other special voting privileges. Before 1968, the Council held two regular sessions a year, and afterwards, one. Special sessions may be called on the decision of the majority of the members or at the request of the Security Council or the General Assembly. The president and vice-president are elected at the beginning of each regular session and serve for one year.

Powers

In carrying out its supervisory and administrative functions, the Council was specifically authorized under the Charter to consider reports submitted by the administering authority; to accept petitions and examine thin consultation with the administering authority; to provide for periodic visits to the trust territories at times agreeable to the respective administering authorities; and to formulate a questionnaire on the political, economic, social, and educational progress in each trust territory, which the administering authorities were required to answer.

OPERATION OF THE TRUSTEESHIP SYSTEM

Trusteeship and Strategic Area Agreements

Since trusteeship territories were merely entrusted to the administering authorities, the precise terms of the agreement had to be carefully prescribed for each territory and approved by a two-thirds vote of the General Assembly, or by the Security Council in the case of a strategic area.

Article 82 of the Charter provided that there may be designated in any trusteeship agreement a strategic area or areas, which may include part or all of the trust territory concerned. In such cases, all trusteeship functions of the UN were to be exercised by the Security Council.

In fact, there exists only one strategic area agreement—that concluded between the UN and the US government on the Pacific islands mandated to Japan after World War I. Most of the general provisions of the other trusteeship agreements are included in it, but the right of accessibility to the area is curtailed, and supervision by the UN is made dependent on US security requirements. The US is also authorized to close certain areas for security reasons.

The Role of the Administering Authorities

Administering countries were given full legislative, administrative, and judicial powers over the territories entrusted to them. If they so desired, they could administer the trust territory in conjunction with one of their own colonies. Thus, the trust territory of Ruanda-Urundi was united administratively with the Belgian Congo, and Australia established an administrative union between the trust territory of New Guinea and its own dependency, Papua. However, UN trusteeship territories were never considered to be under the sovereignty of the administering authorities, which governed them only on behalf of the UN.

The Work of the Trusteeship Council

In essence, the work of the Council consists in the exercise of the powers specifically granted to it by the Charter for the purpose of supervising the operation of the trusteeship system and ensuring that the administering authority is carrying out its obligations as laid down by the trusteeship agreement.

The work of the Trusteeship Council has diminished progressively as, one by one, the 11 trust territories either achieved independence or, on being granted self-determination, chose to unite with another independent state.

In November 1993, Palau, the last remaining Trusteeship Territory succeeded in passing a referendum approving a Compact of Free Association with the United States. In January, 1994, at its sixty-first session, the Council requested the United States, in consultation with the Government of Palau, the last remaining Trusteeship Territory, to agree on a date on or about October 1, 1994 for the full entry into force of the Compact of Free Association.

The council considered that the United States had satisfactorily discharged its obligations under the terms of the Trusteeship Agreement and that it was appropriate for that Agreement to be terminated with effect from the date referred to above, as agreed upon by the two Governments.

At that session the Trusteeship Council also amended its rules of procedure 1 and 2, which were replaced by the following:

"The Trusteeship Council shall meet as and where occasion may require, by decision of the Trusteeship Council, or by decision of its President, or at the request of a majority of its members, or at the request of the General Assembly, or at the request of the Security Council acting in pursuance of the relevant provisions of the Charter."

THE INTERNATIONAL COURT OF JUSTICE

The International Court of Justice was established at the San Francisco Conference in 1945. It is a successor to and resembles the Permanent Court of International Justice created at the time of the League of Nations, but its competence is wider, because membership in the League did not automatically require a nation to join the Permanent Court. The International Court, however, is a principal organ of the UN, so that all UN members automatically become parties to its statute, which, modeled on that of the Permanent Court, was adopted as an integral part of the Charter. By joining the UN, each country binds itself, in the words of the Charter, "to comply with the decision of the International Court of Justice in any case to which it is a party." If any party to a case violates this obligation, the other party "may have recourse to the Security Council, which may, if it deems necessary, make recommendations or decide upon measures to be taken to give effect to the judgment."

The Charter further provides that nonmembers of the UN may become parties to the statute of the court "on conditions to be determined in each case by the General Assembly upon the recommendation of the Security Council." Two such countries—Nauru and Switzerland—have become parties to the statute in this way.

The rules under which the court is constituted and by which it functions are laid down in the statute and detailed in rules adopted by the court itself. The seat of the court is the Peace Palace at The Hague in the Netherlands, but it can meet elsewhere if it so desires. The judges are bound "to hold themselves permanently at the disposal of the Court."

The court is funded from the regular budget of the UN, to whose members its services are otherwise free of charge.

JUDGES OF THE COURT

The court consists of 15 independent judges, known as "members" of the court. They are elected "from among persons of high moral character" without consideration of nationality, except that no two judges of the same nationality may serve concurrently. They must be persons possessing the qualifications required in their respective countries for appointment to the highest judicial offices or be jurists of recognized competence in international law. No judge of the International Court of Justice may exercise any political or administrative function or engage in any professional occupation. When engaged in the business of the court, judges enjoy diplomatic privileges and immunities. A newly elected judge must "make a solemn declaration in open court that he will exercise his powers impartially and conscientiously." A judge cannot be dismissed except by a unanimous decision of the other judges that "he has ceased to fulfill the required conditions." No such dismissal has ever occurred.

As in any court, a judge may disqualify himself from sitting on a particular case. The statute enumerates certain conditions under which this disqualification is obligatory—for example, if a judge was previously involved in the case as a member of a commission of inquiry.

SIGNIFICANCE OF NATIONALITY OF JUDGES

The statute declares specifically that a judge has the right to sit on a case in which his own country is a party. Furthermore, any country that is a party to a case before the court may add a person to sit as judge on that case if there is not already a judge of its nationality on the court. If there are "several parties in the same interest," they may add only one judge to the bench. Such ad hoc judges are chosen by the respective states themselves and may, or may not, be nationals of the states choosing them.

NOMINATION AND ELECTION OF JUDGES

Two international conferences at The Hague, in 1899 and 1907, contemplated the establishment of a permanent international court, but the conferees were unable to agree on a system for electing judges. They did agree, however, on a convention establishing a Permanent Court of Arbitration. That convention provides that each country that is a party to it shall name four jurists as arbitrators who will be available to consider a concrete matter for international arbitration. When the Permanent Court of International Justice was established after World War I, a solution was found for the difficult problem of electing judges. The legal experts named as potential arbitrators under the Hague convention were given the right to nominate candidates, and the League of Nations elected the judges from among these nominees. This system has in essence been preserved by the UN. To ensure that candidates are not mere government nominees, they are proposed by the groups of jurists already established in the Permanent Court of Arbitration or by similar groups specially constituted in countries not members of that court; no national group may nominate more than four persons, and only two of those may bear the nationality of the group.

The list of candidates so nominated then goes to the UN. To be elected to a judgeship on the court, a candidate must obtain an absolute majority in the Security Council and the General Assembly, both bodies voting independently and simultaneously. If more than one candidate of the same nationality obtains the required votes, the eldest is elected. On these occasions, Nauru and Switzerland, the two nonmembers of the UN that are parties to the statute of the court, vote in the General Assembly. In electing judges to the court, delegates are requested to bear in mind that "the main forms of civilization" and "the principal legal systems of the world" should be represented at all times on the international tribunal.

TERMS OF JUDGESHIPS

Judges are elected for nine years. To stagger the expiration of terms, the terms of five of the judges named in the first election (1946) expired at the end of three years, and the terms of five others at the end of six years, as determined by lot. Hence, five judges are now elected every three years. Reelection is permissible and frequently occurs. Every three years, the court elects its president and vice-president from among the judges. Unless reelected, judges chosen to fill a casual vacancy serve only for the remainder of their predecessor's term.

The composition of the court as of 1 June 1994 was as follows (terms expire on 5 February of the year given in parentheses):

Mohammed Bedjaoui, Algeria (1997), President
Stephen M. Schwebel, United States (1997), Vice-President
Shigeru Oda, Japan (2003)
Sir Robert Yewdall Jennings, United Kingdom (2000)

Nikolai K. Tarassov, Russian Federation (1997)
Gilbert Guillaume, France (2000)
Mohamed Shahabuddeen, Guyana (1997)
Andrés Aguilar Mawdsley, Venezuela (2000)
Christopher G. Weeramantry, Sri Lanka (2000)
Raymond Ranjeva, Madagascar (2000)
Géza Herczegh, Hungary (2003)
Shi Jiuyong, China (2003)
Carl-August Fleischhauer, Germany (2003)
Abdul G. Koroma, Sierra Leone (2003)

Normally, all judges sit to hear a case, but nine judges (not counting an ad hoc judge) constitute a quorum. The statute of the court makes provision for the formation of chambers for summary procedure, for particular categories of cases, or for an individual case. A Chamber for Environmental Matters were established by the court in July 1993. Since 1945, four cases were referred to a chamber. A judgment delivered by a chamber is considered as rendered by the court.

PROCEDURE OF THE COURT

All questions are decided by a majority vote of the judges present. If the votes are equal, the president has the casting, or deciding, vote. The judgments have to be read in open court and are required to state the reasons on which they are based and the names of the judges constituting the majority. Any judge is entitled to append to the judgment a personal opinion explaining his or her concurrence or dissent. All hearings are public unless the court decides, whether at the request of the parties or otherwise, that the public should not be admitted.

Judgments are final and without appeal. An application for revision will be considered by the court only if it is based on the discovery of some decisive fact that at the time of the judgment was unknown to both the court and the party seeking revision. Should a dispute arise concerning the meaning or scope of a judgment, the court shall interpret it at the request of any party.

In order to simplify and expedite recourse to it, the court amended its Rules of Court in 1972. A completely overhauled set of rules, incorporating those amendments, was adopted in 1978.

COMPETENCE AND JURISDICTION OF THE COURT

Only states can be parties in cases before the court. Hence, proceedings may not be instituted by or against an individual, corporation, or other entity that is not a state under international law. However, if certain rules are satisfied, a state may take up a case involving one of its nationals. Thus, the Nottebohm Case (Liechtenstein v. Guatemala), in which a judgment was rendered on 6 April 1955, involved a claim by Liechtenstein in regard to injuries sustained by a German-born, naturalized citizen of Liechtenstein as a result of certain measures that Guatemala had taken during World War II.

All countries that are parties to the statute have automatic access to the court and can refer any case they wish to the court. In addition, the Security Council may recommend that a legal dispute be referred to the court.

Under the Charter, nations are not automatically obliged to submit their legal disputes for judgment. At the San Francisco Conference, it was argued by some that the court should be given compulsory jurisdiction and that UN members should bind themselves to accept the court's right to consider legal disputes between them. This proposal would have meant that if one member filed a case against another member, the court would automatically, and without reference to the second member concerned, have the right to try the case. The proposal was rejected because some delegates feared that such a provision might make the statute unacceptable to their countries. Moreover,

it was generally felt that since the disputants in an international court are sovereign states, they should not be summoned against their will to submit to the court's jurisdiction. Thus, the court cannot proceed to adjudicate a case unless all parties to the dispute have consented that it should do so. Such consent comes about mainly in one of the following three ways.

1. There can be a specific agreement between the parties to submit a dispute to the court. This is the simplest method and the one employed in several recent cases. Since the creation of the court, 10 cases have been brought before it in this way.
2. There can be specific clauses contained in treaties and conventions. Many treaties and conventions expressly stipulate that disputes that may arise under them, such as a claim by one country that a treaty has been violated by another country, will be submitted to the court for decision. More than 430 treaties and conventions, including peace treaties concluded after World War II, contain clauses to this effect, a fact which attests to the readiness of countries to agree in advance to accept judicial settlement.
3. There can be voluntary recognition in advance of the compulsory jurisdiction of the court in specified types of disputes. Article 36 of the statute states that all parties to the statute "may at any time declare that they recognize as compulsory ipso facto and without special agreement, in relation to any other state accepting the same obligation, the jurisdiction of the Court in all legal disputes concerning: (a) the interpretation of a treaty; (b) any question of international law; (c) the existence of any fact which, if established, would constitute a breach of an international obligation; (d) the nature or extent of the reparation to be made for the breach of an international obligation."

Such declarations may be made for only a limited period if desired and with or without any conditions, or they may state that they will become operative only when a particular country or number of countries accept the same obligation. The most far-reaching reservation that has been attached to a declaration is the condition that the court must not adjudicate any dispute that the country itself determines to be an essentially domestic matter. In effect, this reservation leaves the country free to deny the court's jurisdiction in most cases in which it might become involved. In general, the practical significance of many of the declarations is severely limited by the right to make conditions. As of 1 June 1994, declarations recognizing the compulsory jurisdiction of the court had been made by 59 states.

The jurisdiction of the court therefore comprises all legal disputes which the parties to the statute refer to it and all matters specifically provided for in the UN Charter or in treaties and conventions in force. In the event of a dispute as to whether the court has jurisdiction, the statute provides that the matter shall be decided by the court. Article 38 of the statute requires that in deciding the disputes submitted to it, the court shall apply the following: (1) international conventions establishing rules recognized by the contesting states; (2) international custom as evidence of a general practice accepted as law; (3) the general principles of law recognized by civilized nations; and (4) judicial decisions and teachings of the most highly qualified publicists of the various nations as a subsidiary means for determining the rules of law. In certain cases, however, if the parties concerned agree, the court may decide a case *ex aequo et bono*—that is, by a judgment in equity taken simply on the basis of what the court considers is right and good.

ADVISORY OPINIONS

The Charter provides that the General Assembly and the Security Council may request the court to give an advisory opinion on any legal question and that other UN organs and specialized agencies, when authorized by the General Assembly, may also request advisory opinions on legal questions arising within the scope of their activities. In such cases, the court does not render a judgment but provides guidance for the international body concerned. Thus, advisory opinions by their nature are not enforceable, and, although the bodies may receive them with respect, they may not necessarily find it politic to act on them. In some cases, however, the requesting body will be committed to abide by the court's decision.

EXTRAJUDICIAL FUNCTIONS OF THE COURT
Many international conventions, treaties, and other instruments confer upon the International Court of Justice or its president the function of appointing umpires or arbitrators in certain eventualities. Furthermore, even when no treaty provision to this effect exists, the court or individual judges may be requested to carry out functions of this nature.

Review of the Role of the Court
In 1970, citing the relative lack of activity of the court, nine member states sponsored a General Assembly agenda item on a review of the role of the court. In an explanatory memorandum, they noted that the situation at that time was "not commensurate with either the distinction of the judges or the needs of the international community." Proposals for remedying the situation included a revision of the court's statute and rules of procedure, the appointment of younger judges and/or shorter terms of office, and wider acceptance of the court's compulsory jurisdiction.

The subject was debated at four subsequent sessions of the General Assembly, culminating in the adoption in 1974 of a resolution designed to strengthen the role of the court. The recommendations included the possible insertion of clauses in treaties that would provide for submission to the court of disputes arising from differences in their interpretation or application; acceptance of the compulsory jurisdiction of the court with as few reservations as possible; and greater recourse to the court by UN organs and specialized agencies for advisory opinions.

SURVEY OF COURT PRACTICE
Since the court's inauguration in 1946, states have submitted 72 legal disputes to it, and international organizations have requested 21 advisory opinions.

LEGAL DISPUTES
Of the 72 cases submitted to the court by states, 18 were withdrawn by the parties or removed from the list for some other reason. In 11 others, the court found that, under its statute, it lacked jurisdiction. The remaining cases on which the court has rendered judgment encompassed a wide range of topics, including sovereignty over disputed territory or territorial possessions, the international law of the sea, and commercial interests or property rights either of states or of private corporations and persons. (Examples of these types of disputes are given in the case histories below.)

Many of the cases, including some that fall into the three categories just described, involve differences in interpretations of specific bilateral or multilateral treaties and other legal instruments. Thus, in the case of the rights of US citizens in Morocco (France v. US), the court found, on 27 August 1952, that the prohibition of certain imports into Morocco had violated US treaty rights. However, it rejected the US claim that its citizens were not subject in principle to the application of Moroccan laws unless they had received the US's prior assent.

ADVISORY OPINIONS
The 21 advisory opinions requested by the General Assembly,

Security Council, or authorized specialized agencies likewise have dealt with a variety of matters. The court, on 16 October 1975, rendered an opinion in response to a request made by the General Assembly at its 1974 session. The question concerned Western Sahara, which was passing from Spanish administration. Morocco, Mauritania, and Algeria, all bordering states, took conflicting positions on ties of sovereignty that might have existed before the territory came under Spanish administration. The court concluded that no ties of territorial sovereignty between Western Sahara and the Kingdom of Morocco or the Mauritanian entity had existed. In the decolonization of the territory, therefore, the principle of self-determination through the free expression of the will of its people should apply in accordance with the relevant General Assembly resolution.

Another opinion concerned the question of whether the costs of the peacekeeping operations in the Middle East and the Congo could, within the scope of Article 17 of the Charter, be regarded as expenses of the organization to be financed by contributions of member states, as assessed by the General Assembly. In its opinion, issued on 20 July 1962, the court concluded that the expenses of both operations could be regarded as expenses of the UN within the meaning of Article 17 of the Charter.

In other examples, the court rendered an advisory opinion in 1949 on a question put after the assassination of the United Nations mediator in Palestine: the court found that the United Nations had the capacity to maintain a claim against a state for injuries to an agent of the organization. In 1988, the court expressed the opinion that, by virtue of the United Nations Headquarters Agreement, the United States was under obligation to submit to arbitration a dispute with the United Nations concerning an order to close the office maintained by the Palestine Liberation Organization observer mission in New York.

CASES PENDING
As of 1 June 1994, 10 contentious cases were pending:

1. Aerial Incident of 3 July 1988 (Islamic Republic of Iran v. United States of America).
2. East Timor (Portugal v. Australia).
3. Maritime Delimitation between Guinea-Bissau and Senegal (Guinea-Bissau v. Senegal).
4. Maritime Delimitation and Territorial Questions between Qatar and Bahrain (Qatar v. Bahrain).
5. Questions of Interpretation and Application of the 1971 Montreal Convention arising from the Aerial Incident at Lockerbie (Libyan Arab Jamahiriya v. United Kingdom).
6. Questions of Interpretation and Application of the 1971 Montreal Convention arising from the Aerial Incident at Lockerbie (Libyan Arab Jamahiriya v. United States of America).
7. Oil Platforms (Islamic Republic of Iran v. United States of America).
8. Application of the Convention on the Prevention and Punishment of the Crime of Genocide (Bosnia and Herzegovina v. Yugoslavia (Serbia and Montenegro)).
9. Gabčíkovo-Nagymaros Project (Hungary v. Slovakia).
10. Cameroon v. Nigeria.

Also pending is one request from the World Health Organization for an advisory opinion on the Legality of the Use by a State of Nuclear Weapons in Armed Conflict.

SOME CASE HISTORIES OF DISPUTES SUBMITTED TO THE COURT
For convenience, the following sample case histories have been drawn from the three categories of legal disputes indicated above.

Disputes over Territorial Claims and Territorial Possessions

In the Case Concerning Sovereignty over Certain Frontier Land (Belgium v. Netherlands), the court traced developments that had begun before the 1839 separation of the Netherlands from Belgium, and in its judgment, on 20 June 1959, it decided that sovereignty over the disputed plots belonged to Belgium.

In a dispute regarding sovereignty over certain islets and rocks lying between the British Channel island of Jersey and the French coast, the Minquier and Ecrehos Islands Case, the UK and France invoked historical facts going back to the 11th century. The UK started its argument by claiming title from the conquest of England in 1066 by William, Duke of Normandy. France started its argument by pointing out that the dukes of Normandy were vassals of the king of France and that the kings of England after 1066, in their capacity as dukes of Normandy, held the duchy in fee from the French kings. The court decided, on 17 November 1953, that "the sovereignty over the islets and rocks of the Ecrehos and Minquier groups, insofar as these islets and rocks are capable of appropriation, belongs to the United Kingdom."

The first case involving two Asian countries, Cambodia and Thailand, was filed with the court in October 1959, as the Case Concerning the Temple of Preah Vihear. It concerned, as stated by Cambodia, "a sacred place of pilgrimage and worship for the Cambodian population." On 15 June 1962, the court found, 9 to 3, that the temple was in Cambodian territory and that, therefore, Thailand must withdraw any military or police forces or other guards that it had stationed there; it further held, by 7 to 5, that Thailand must restore to Cambodia any works of art that might have been removed since Thailand's occupation of the temple area in 1954.

In 1980, in a case brought by the United States concerning the seizure of its embassy in Teheran and the detention of its diplomatic and consular staff, the court held that Iran must release the hostages, hand back the embassy and make reparations. However, before the court fixed the amount of reparation, the case was withdrawn following agreement reached between the two states.

In the first frontier dispute between two African states, by a special agreement Burkina Faso and Mali submitted to a chamber of the court in October 1983 the question of the delimitation of part of the land frontier between them. In January 1986, the court ordered interim measures of protection in order to restore peace between the two states following armed hostilities at the end of 1985. The court gave its final judgment in December 1986, establishing the coordinates for the delimitation of the frontier.

In 1984, Nicaragua alleged that the United States was using military force against it and intervening in its internal affairs. The United States denied that the court had jurisdiction. After written and oral proceedings, the court found, however, that it had jurisdiction and that Nicaragua's application was admissible. The United States refused to recognize either this ruling or the subsequent 1986 judgment in which the court determined that the United States had acted in breach of its obligations toward Nicaragua, must desist from the actions in question, and should make reparation. The request by Nicaragua that the court determine the form and amount of reparation was withdrawn in 1991.

In a case between Libya and Chad, the two countries submitted to the court a territorial dispute relating to the Aozou Strip in the Sahara. Libya's claim as made in the case extended far to the south of that strip of land. The court, in a judgment of 3 February 1994, found wholly in favor of Chad. After an agreement on the implementation of the judgment had been concluded between the two parties, Libyan forces, monitored by an observer force deployed by the Security Council, withdrew from the Aozou strip by 31 May 1994.

Disputes Relating to the Law of the Sea

The Corfu Channel Case (UK v. Albania), the first case decided by the court, was brought before it at the suggestion of the Security Council. On 22 October 1946, two UK destroyers passing through the Corfu channel off the Albanian coast struck mines whose explosion caused the death of 46 seamen and damage to the ships. The British thereupon mineswept the channel. Albania claimed that it had not laid the mines. The court found Albania "responsible under international law for the explosions . . . and for the damage and loss of human life that resulted therefrom" and determined the compensation due to the UK at £843,947, equivalent to approximately US$2.4 million at that time. The court also found that the British mine-sweeping activities in Albanian territorial waters had violated international law. The unanimous rejection by the court of the British claim that the action was justified under the principle of "self-protection" constituted the first judicial finding that the use of force for self-help is in certain circumstances contrary to international law.

In 1981, Canada and the US submitted to a chamber of the court a question as to the course of the maritime boundary dividing the continental shelf and fisheries zones of the two countries in the Gulf of Maine area. In its judgment of 12 October 1984, the chamber of the court established the coordinates of that boundary.

On 3 June 1985, the court delivered a judgment in a dispute relating to the delimitation of the continental shelf between Libya and Malta that had been referred to the court in 1982 by means of a special agreement specifically concluded for that purpose.

On 14 June 1993, the court delivered a judgment in a dispute relating to the maritime delimitation between Denmark and Norway.

Disputes Involving Commercial Interests and Property Rights

The Anglo-Iranian Oil Co. Case grew out of a law passed by Iran on 1 May 1951, terminating the concessions of the Anglo-Iranian Oil Co. and expropriating the company's refinery at Abadan, the largest in the world. On 26 May, the UK instituted proceedings against Iran before the International Court. On 5 July, the court ordered important "interim measures" enjoining the two governments to refrain from any action that might aggravate the dispute or hinder the operation of the company. The company was to continue under the same management as before nationalization, subject to such modification as agreed to by a special supervisory board, which the court requested the two governments to set up. A year later, however, on 22 July 1952, the court, in its final judgment, ruled that it lacked jurisdiction and lifted the "interim measures." The court found that the 1933 agreement, which gave the Iranian concession to the Anglo-Iranian Oil Co. and which the UK claimed had been violated by the act of nationalization, was merely a concessionary contract between Iran and a foreign corporation. The court ruled that the interpretation of such a contract was not one of the matters in regard to which Iran had accepted the compulsory jurisdiction of the court. The controversy was settled by negotiations in 1953, after the Mossadegh regime in Iran had been replaced by another government.

The Barcelona Traction Case (Belgium v. Spain) arose out of a 1948 adjudication by a provincial Spanish law court of the bankruptcy of a company incorporated in Canada with subsidiaries operating in Barcelona. Belgium was seeking reparation for damages alleged to have been sustained by Belgian shareholders in the company as a result of the Spanish court's adjudication, which Belgium claimed was contrary to international law. The court, on 5 February 1970, found that the Belgian government lacked the standing to exercise diplomatic protection of Belgian shareholders in a Canadian company with respect to measures taken against that company in Spain.

THE SECRETARIAT

CHARTER REQUIREMENTS

The charter lays down very few requirements governing the establishment of the sixth main organ of the UN—the Secretariat. Such requirements as are specified, in Chapter XV, may be conveniently listed under the following headings.

Composition. The charter states simply: "The Secretariat shall comprise a Secretary-General and such staff as the Organization may require."

Appointment of Staff. With regard to the Secretary-General, the charter stipulates that the person to hold the position "shall be appointed by the General Assembly upon the recommendation of the Security Council." In other words, the Security Council first must agree on a candidate, who then must be endorsed by a majority vote in the General Assembly. The other members of the Secretariat are to be appointed by the Secretary-General "under regulations established by the General Assembly." The charter stipulates that the "paramount consideration" in the employment of staff "shall be the necessity of securing the highest standards of efficiency, competence, and integrity." However, to this consideration is added an important rider—namely, that "due regard shall be paid to the importance of recruiting the staff on as wide a geographical basis as possible."

Functions of the Secretariat. The duties of the general staff are not specified beyond an instruction that an appropriate number shall be permanently assigned to the Economic and Social Council and the Trusteeship Council and, "as required, to other organs of the United Nations." With respect to the functions of the Secretary-General, the charter states only that he shall be "the chief administrative officer of the Organization," shall "act in that capacity" at all meetings of the General Assembly and the three councils, and shall also perform "such other functions as are entrusted to him by these organs." Apart from these general requirements, the charter accords the Secretary-General one specific duty and one specific power: to make an annual report to the General Assembly on the work of the organization, and he has the right to bring to the attention of the Security Council any matter that "in his opinion may threaten the maintenance of international peace and security."

The single restriction on the Secretariat is that "in the performance of their duties the Secretary-General and the staff shall not seek or receive instructions from any government or from any other authority external to the Organization," and that "they shall refrain from any action which might reflect on their position as international officials responsible only to the Organization." As a corollary to this injunction, the charter puts member nations under the obligation to "respect the exclusively international character of the responsibilities of the Secretary-General and the staff and not to seek to influence them in the discharge of their responsibilities."

APPOINTMENT OF THE SECRETARY-GENERAL

Since the charter does not specify the qualifications for Secretary-General and the term of office, these decisions had to be made by the first General Assembly, in January 1946. It was agreed that, in making its recommendations to the General Assembly, the Security Council should conduct its discussions in private and vote in secret, for the dignity of the office required avoidance of open debate on the qualifications of the candidate. The General Assembly also decided that the term of office would be five years (the Secretary-General of the League of Nations was elected for 10 years) and that the Secretary-General would be eligible for reappointment.

The permanent members of the Security Council have tacitly agreed that the Secretary-General should not be a national of one of their own countries.

STRUCTURE AND COMPOSITION OF THE SECRETARIAT

The Secretariat services the other organs of the UN and administers the programs and policies laid down by them. As the scope and range of UN activities have widened, the staff of the Secretariat has increased in number and its organizational pattern has increased in complexity. The major elements of the Secretariat, variously designated as offices, departments, programs, conferences, and the like, are headed by officials of the rank, but not necessarily the title, of undersecretary-general or assistant secretary-general. In 1987 there were 48 officials at those two levels in the Secretariat.

As the United Nations grew from its original 51 members in 1945 to 184 members in 1994, the Secretariat necessarily changed and evolved. Between 1945 and 1994 major reform of the Secretariat's structure was undertaken five times: 1953–56; 1964–66; 1974–77; 1985–86; and 1992–94. The latest round of restructuring was requested by the General Assembly in numerous resolutions beginning in 1988 (41/213 ; 44/200; 45/254; 46/232, and 47/212A). Secretary-General Boutros Boutros-Ghali began the restructuring process upon his entry into office in January 1992. Whereas in 1991 there were 48 high-level posts (1 director general, 26 undersecretary-generals, 20 assistant secretary-generals) reporting directly to the Secretary-General, in the 1992–1993 biennium that number had been reduced to 21 undersecretary-generals and 16 assistant secretary-generals for a total of 37. A hiring freeze was also instituted in 1992. In July 1994, the activities of the Secretariat were organized in the following departments:

The Department of Political Affairs (DPA). The functions of five previous offices and units were integrated into the DPA. The department oversees the organization's efforts in preventive diplomacy and peacemaking, collects and analyzes information to alert the General Assembly and Security Council of impending crises, and carries out mandates handed down by the General Assembly and Security Council. DPA provides secretariat services to both bodies. It also provides electoral assistance to countries requesting help in strengthening the democratic process.

The Department of Peacekeeping Operations (DPKO). This department supervises the operations of the United Nations peacekeeping missions around the world. The work of the United Nations in this area has grown exponentially in size and complexity since the end of the cold war. In December 1991, peacekeeping missions involved approximately 11,000 troops and 4,000 civilian personnel with a combined budget of us$500 million. By September 1993, the Department of Peacekeeping Operations was supervising approximately 80,000 military personnel and 12,000 civilian personnel, whose annualized budgets approached US$3 billion. In the reorganization, the Field Operations Division, which had been part of the Department for Administration and Management, was transferred to its main client, the Department of Peacekeeping Operations.

The Department of Humanitarian Affairs (DHA). Humanitarian assistance and assistance for countries affected by natural and man-made disasters accounted for approximately US$5.5 billion throughout all the organizations of the UN system in 1992–93. To handle the increasing number of emergencies the organization's membership requested it to manage, the Secretary-General created the Department of Humanitarian Affairs, incorporating the functions of the UN Disaster Relief Office (UNDRO) and 11 other units of the Secretariat. Two new units were created: the Complex Emergencies Branch and the Inter-Agency Support Unit. The DHA works to improve the delivery of humanitarian assistance to victims of disasters and other emergencies. It also acts as an advocate for humanitarian activities being considered by intergovernmental bodies. It was designed to provide quick needs assessments, field situation analyzes, and early negotiations on access to emergency situations. A major feature of this department is interagency coordination that allows all the organizations of the UN system to make consolidated appeals for humanitarian assistance and to better track contributions from donor governments, UN agencies, and nongovernmental organizations.

The Department for Policy Coordination and Sustainable Development (DPCSD). This department provides support for the Economic and Social Council and the General Assembly's Second Committee (economic and financial matters) and Third Committee (social, humanitarian, and cultural matters). It is responsible for the follow-up to the long-term mandates on promoting sustainable development (known as Agenda 21) handed down by the UN Conference on Environment and Development. It also incorporates the activities of the previously Vienna-based Centre for Social Development and Humanitarian Affairs and the Rome-based World Food Council secretariat. One of DPCSD's main jobs is to promote cooperation with the many nongovernmental organizations that wish to contribute to the work of the organization in economic, social and environmental fields.

The Department of Economic and Social Information and Policy Analysis (DESIPA). This department provides support to the Statistical and Population Commissions of ECOSOC. It is the focal point for economic and social analysis of information about population and statistics. It handles technical cooperation activities in the areas of statistics and population. In addition, it makes projections and identifies emerging issues requiring attention by the international community. DESIPA serves as the lead unit in economic and social information and cooperates closely with the World Bank and the International Monetary Fund (IMF).

The Department of Development Support and Management Services (DDSMS). This department has a two-part mandate. It acts as an executing agency for development projects in the fields of natural resources and energy planing, governance and public management, financial management and accounting, focussing attention on the needs of the least developed countries and the countries of the former Soviet Union (often referred to as "economies in transition"). Its second mandate is to be the focal point for implementing technical cooperation management services.

The Department of Public Information (DPI). Under the reorganization, the Dag Hammarskjöld Library and the publishing services of the organization were transferred from the Office of Conference Services to DPI. The department, which creates press releases, publications, and radio and video programs publicizing the work of the organization, also took on the activities that had been handled by the former Office of the Spokesman for the Secretary-General. Many of DPI's field offices were integrated into the field offices of the UN Development Programme (UNDP) for

substantial savings. DPI's work was facilitated by the installation of an electronic mail system to 210 locations, including peacekeeping missions, information centers and UNDP offices, increasing headquarters' contact with its far-flung staff.

The Department of Administration and Management (DAM). This department has four offices: the Office of Programme Planning, Budget and Accounts; the Office of Human Resources Management; the Office for Conference and Support Services; and the Financial Management Office.

The Office of Internal Oversight Services (OIOS). In August 1993, the Secretary-General announced the creation of a new Office of Inspections and Investigations, headed by an assistant secretary-general, which would incorporate various former units of the DAM dealing with audit, management advisory services, evaluation, and monitoring. In July 1994, the General Assembly strengthened the office, and changed its name to the Office of Internal Oversight Services (resolution A/218B (29 July 1994)). The General Assembly stipulated that the head of the new office, at the level of undersecretary-general, should be an expert in the fields of accounting, auditing, financial analysis and investigations, management, law, or public administration. It further stipulated that the individual should serve only one five-year term, and that the post would not be subject to geographical distribution limits. The new watchdog office was given wider independence to investigate possible fraud and abuse within the organization. It will be assisted in its task by the Integrated Management Information System (IMIS), a major hardware and software upgrade that will allow greater monitoring and audit capabilities through electronic audit trails. The creation of this office had long been sought by industrialized countries concerned that their contributions to the United Nations were being wasted by fraud and abuse.

Each of the above departments is headed by an undersecretary-general, with the exception of the Department for Political Affairs (DPA) which is headed by two undersecretary-generals whose responsibilities are divided geographically.

The Office of Legal Affairs (OLA). This office advises the organization and the Secretary-General on legal matters. Under the 1992 reorganization, it also assumed responsibility for the Office for Ocean Affairs and Law of the Sea.

Besides the above departments, the Centre for Human Rights, formerly a division, had its activities greatly expanded by a series of new mandates by the General Assembly, ECOSOC, the Commission on Human Rights, and expert groups in the human rights field. It is the principal entity of the UN Secretariat dealing with human rights issues, and is responsible for supervising the ratification and implementation of the international human rights agreements. The Secretary-General, in his 1993 report (A/48/428), stated that the activities of the Centre for Human Rights were evolving from standard-setting to furthering the implementation of a universal culture of human rights. The center is responsible for following up the recommendations of the Second World Conference on Human Rights held in Vienna in June 1993. Recognizing this, the 47th session of the General Assembly authorized additional financial resources for the center. The center is headed by an assistant secretary-general who reports directly to the Secretary-General.

Directly below the ranks of undersecretary-general and assistant secretary-general are directors of main subdepartments and chiefs of specific bureaus within the major organizational units. Below them is the professional staff: personnel with qualifications as administrators, specialists, technical experts, statisticians, translators, editors, interpreters, and so on. Staff in the category of general services include administrative assistants, clerical workers, secretaries, typists, and the like. Manual workers, such as building maintenance staff, are separately classified.

Personnel at the professional level and above are recruited in

ORGANIZATIONAL STRUCTURE OF THE UNITED NATIONS SECRETARIAT

(AS OF JULY 1994)

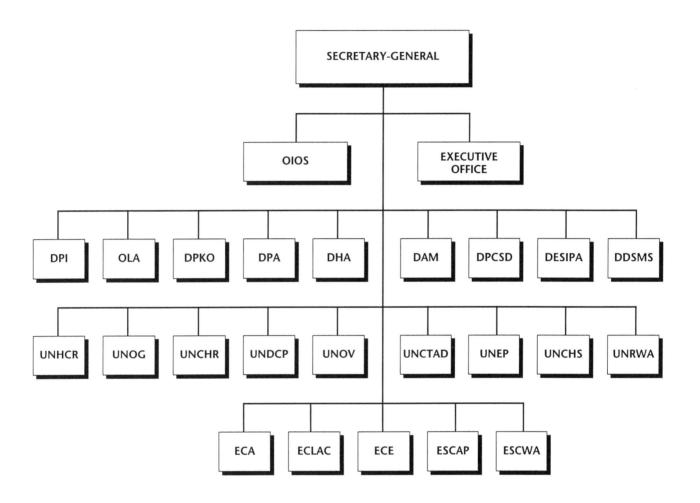

LISTING OF KEY ORGANIZATIONAL UNITS

OIOS	Office of Internal Oversight Services	UNDCP	United Nations International Drug Control Programme
DPI	Department of Public Information		
OLA	Office of Legal Affairs	UNOV	United Nations Office at Vienna
DPKO	Department of Peace-keeping Operations	UNCTAD	United Nations Conference on Trade and Development
DPA	Department of Political Affairs		
DHA	Department of Humanitarian Affairs	UNEP	United Nations Environment Programme
DAM	Department of Administration and Management	UNCHS	United Nations Centre for Human Settlements
DPCSD	Department for Policy Coordination and Sustainable Development	UNRWA	United Nations Relief and Works Agency for Palestinian Refugees in the Near East
DESIPA	Department for Economic and Social Information and Policy Analysis	ECA	Economic Commission for Africa
		ECLAC	Economic Commission for Latin America and the Caribbean
DDSMS	Department for Development Support and Management Services	ECE	Economic Commission for Europe
UNHCR	Office of the United Nations High Commissioner for Refugees	ESCAP	Economic and Social Commission for Asia and the Pacific
UNOG	United Nations Office at Geneva	ESCWA	Economic and Social Commission for Western Asia
UNCHR	United Nations Centre for Human Rights		

the various member countries of the UN and, when serving outside their own country, are entitled to home-leave travel, repatriation grants, and related benefits. General service personnel include a number of nationalities, but they are recruited locally and are not selected according to any principle of geographical representation. The majority of general service staff employed at UN headquarters are US citizens.

Organizational Distribution of Staff

For the 1994–95 biennium, the UN Secretariat consisted of approximately 15,321 staff members holding permanent appointments or temporary appointments of one year or more. Of this total, 10,171 represented posts financed from the regular budget, while 5,149 were in the Secretariat posts financed from extrabudgetary sources (voluntary funds).

Problems of Staff Appointment According to Equitable Geographical Distribution

All UN senior staff members are appointed by the Secretary-General under regulations established by the General Assembly. Some of the appointments, such as the UN High Commissioner for Refugees, are subject to confirmation by the General Assembly. Staff recruitment, in general, is handled by the Office of Personnel, salary scales and other conditions of employment being determined by the General Assembly.

UN member governments attach great importance to having a fair proportion of their nationals employed in the Secretariat. The 1962 General Assembly recommended that in applying the principle of equitable geographical distribution, the Secretary-General should take into account members' financial contributions to the UN, the respective populations of the member countries, the relative importance of posts at different levels, and the need for a more balanced regional composition of the staff at the director level. It further recommended that in confirming permanent contracts (UN staff are initially hired on the basis of one-year contracts), particular account should be taken of the need to reduce underrepresentation of some member states.

The 1975 General Assembly reaffirmed previously defined aims for UN recruitment policy and mentioned the following specifically: development of an international civil service based on the highest standards of efficiency, competence, and integrity; equitable geographic distribution, with no post, department, or unit to be regarded as the exclusive preserve of any member state or region; the recruitment of a greater number of qualified women for professional and senior-level posts; and the correction of imbalances in the age structure of the Secretariat.

One of the United Nations' most disturbing lapses relates to the status of women within the organization's own secretariat. The equality of men and women is a principle enshrined in the UN charter. However, while more than half of the Secretariat's general service (nonprofessional) posts are filled by women, until very recently, few women have been appointed to the highest levels of management. No woman has even been seriously considered for the position of Secretary-General. The General Assembly called in 1978 for an increase in the number of women in posts at the professional level to 25% of total staff. The Secretary-General reported in 1987 that the number of women in the professional and higher categories had increased to 25.7% of the total, compared to 17.9% in 1977. In 1985, at the end of the United Nations Decade for Women, the number of women in professional posts (designated as P-1, P-2, P-3, P-4, P-5, D-1 and D-2)

had risen to 29%. However, women held only 8% of the highest administrative posts (director level, including assistant secretary-general and undersecretary-general; designated D-1 and D-2). In response, the General Assembly raised its goal for women to 35% of all professional level posts, with 25% in the senior, D-level posts by 1995. Some of the United Nations' semiautonomous subsidiary bodies already have achieved encouraging progress in equitable gender representation in their own secretariats. The United Nations Population Fund (UNFPA) reported in 1992 that 43% of its professional posts were occupied by women and set a goal of 50% of professional posts to be filled by women by the year 2000. UNICEF, which had women in 24.6% of its professional posts in 1986, increased that level to 35% in 1992. UNICEF set a goal to have women in 40% of professional posts by 1994. In 1992, in an effort to further strengthen the position of all women in the Secretariat, the first guidelines on sexual harassment were issued.

The International Civil Service Commission, established by the General Assembly in 1972, is responsible for making recommendations to that body for the regulation and coordination of service within the UN, the specialized agencies, and other international organizations that are part of the UN system. The commission is composed of 15 independent experts, appointed in their individual capacities for four-year staggered terms.

THE EVOLVING ROLE OF THE SECRETARIAT

The UN's administrative arm has developed largely in accordance with the demands made upon it. In the process, it has evolved a distinctive character of its own, in keeping with its status as a constitutionally defined organ of the world body.

The Secretary-General has played the most significant part in shaping the character of the Secretariat. As chief administrative officer, the Secretary-General has wide discretionary powers and latitude to administer as he thinks fit. As Eleanor Roosevelt, a former chairman of the UN Commission on Human Rights, noted in 1953, the Secretary-General, "partly because of the relative permanence of his position (unlike the president of the General Assembly who changes every year) and partly because of his widely ramified authority over the whole UN organization, tends to become its chief personality, its embodiment and its spokesman to the world."

Each Secretary-General strives to develop and maintain the positive functions of the Secretariat. Although each has had his own views on the role of the office, all have shared the belief that the Secretariat is the backbone of the UN system. The most eloquent statement of that belief was probably made by Dag Hammarskjöld in an address at the University of California in 1955: ". . . the United Nations is what member nations made it, but within the limits set by government action and government cooperation, much depends on what the Secretariat makes it." In addition to the Secretariat's function of providing services and facilities for governments in their capacity as members of the UN, he said, the Secretariat also "has creative capacity. It can introduce new ideas. It can, in proper forms, take initiatives. It can put before member governments findings which will influence their actions." Stressing the fact that members of the Secretariat serve as international officials rather than as government representatives, Hammarskjöld concluded that "the Secretariat in its independence represents an organ, not only necessary for the life and proper functioning of the body, but of importance also for its growth.

THE SECRETARY-GENERAL

From the outset, the secretary-general of the UN has played an important role in helping to settle crises that have troubled nations since the end of World War II. In practice, the role has gone far beyond what might be anticipated from a reading of the terse Charter provisions for the office. Yet the role has been developed precisely through a skillful exploitation of the potentialities inherent in those provisions.

The deliberative organs of the UN are political bodies intended to function as forums where the interests of governments can be represented and reconciled. The secretary-general and the Secretariat embody the other aspect of the UN: the organization is also intended to be a place where people may speak not for the interests of governments or blocs but as impartial third parties. The secretary-general is consistently working in a political medium but doing so as a catalytic agent who, in person or through special missions, observers, and mediators, uses his influence to promote compromise and conciliation.

Under the Charter, the secretary-general has the right to bring to the attention of the Security Council any matter that, in his opinion, might threaten international peace and security. This right goes beyond any power granted the head of an international organization before the founding of the UN. The Charter requires that he submit to the General Assembly an annual report on the work of the organization. In this report, he can state his views and convey his voice to the world's governments. The secretary-general's role has also been considerably enhanced by exploiting the Charter provision that he shall perform "such other functions" as are entrusted to him by the main organizational units of the United Nations.

THE ROLE OF THE UN SECRETARY-GENERAL

In 1986, then Secretary-General Pérez de Cuéllar was invited to give the Cyril Foster Lecture at Oxford University. His thoughts on the institution of the secretary-general in an era of international evolution deserve attention.

First, he suggested that a secretary-general must avoid two extremes: "On one side is the Scylla of trying to inflate the role through too liberal a reading of the text [of the Charter]: of succumbing, that is, to vanity and wishful thinking. On the other is the Charybdis of trying to limit the role to only those responsibilities which are explicitly conferred by the Charter and are impossible to escape: that is, succumbing to modesty, to the instinct of self-effacement, and to the desire to avoid controversy. Both are equally damaging to the vitality of the institution. I submit that no secretary-general should give way to either of them."

Pérez de Cuéllar stated that he used the annual report to the General Assembly as a way to initiate action and galvanize efforts in other parts of the UN system. He pointed out that the secretary-general sometimes remains the only channel of communication between parties in conflict, and therefore must be able to improvise in the context of "good offices" missions. A disciple of "quiet diplomacy," Pérez de Cuéllar said that the secretary-general must not only be impartial, but must be perceived to be so. He observed that a secretary-general needs enormous patience; he does not have the option of being frustrated or discouraged. He suggested that the secretary-general must "try to understand the roots of insecurity, the fears and resentments and the legitimate

aspirations which inspire a people or a state to take the position they do."

He delineated four priority areas for attention by the world body: (1) disarmament, and particularly, nuclear disarmament; (2) human rights; (3) "the shaming disparity of living standards between those who live in the developed world—the North—and their less fortunate brethren in the developing world—the South"; and (4) the world response to natural and man-made disasters.

In closing, Pérez de Cuéllar set forth his own essential requirements for a secretary-general:
"The Secretary-General is constantly subjected to many and diverse pressures. But in the last analysis, his office is a lonely one. He cannot stand idle. Yet helplessness is often his lot. The idealism and hope of which the Charter is a luminous expression have to confront the narrow dictates of national policies. The Secretary-General's efforts must be based on reason but, behind many a government's allegedly logical position, there are myths and silent fears. The voice of the Charter is often drowned by clashes and conflicts between states. If the Secretary-General is to rise above these contradictions in international life, two qualities are essential.

One is faith that humanity can move—and indeed is moving—towards a less irrational, less violent, more compassionate, and more generous international order. . . .

The other essential quality is to feel that he is a citizen of the world. This sounds [like] a cliché, but the Secretary-General would not deserve his mandate if he did not develop a sense of belonging to every nation or culture, reaching out as best he can to the impulse for peace and good that exists in all of them. He is a world citizen because all world problems are *his* problems; the Charter is his home and his ideology, and its principles are his moral creed."

The role of the secretary-general has varied with the individual and with the time and circumstances. This chapter contains an outline account of the initiatives taken by the five secretaries-general in various international crises and areas of conflict. Additional discussion of some of the main areas of conflict may be found in the chapter on International Peace and Security.

THE SECRETARIES GENERAL

The first secretary-general, Trygve Lie of Norway, was appointed for a five-year term on 1 February 1946. On 1 November 1950, he was reappointed for three years. He resigned on 10 November 1952 and was succeeded by Dag Hammarskjöld of Sweden on 10 April 1953. On 26 September 1957, Hammarskjöld was appointed for a further five-year term beginning on 10 April 1958. After Hammarskjöld's death in a plane crash in Africa on 17 September 1961, U Thant of Burma was appointed secretary-general on 3 November 1961, to complete the unexpired term. In November 1962, U Thant was appointed secretary-general for a five-year term beginning with his assumption of office on 3 November 1961. On 2 December 1966, his mandate was unanimously renewed for another five years. At the end of his second term, U Thant declined to be considered for a third. In December 1971, the General Assembly appointed Kurt Waldheim of Austria for a five-year term beginning on 1 January 1972. In December

1976, Waldheim was reappointed for a second five-year term, which ended on 31 December 1981. He was succeeded by Javier Pérez de Cuéllar of Peru, who was appointed by the Assembly in December 1981 for a five-year term beginning on 1 January 1982. He was reappointed for a second five-year term beginning on 1 January 1987. In late 1991, Pérez de Cuéllar expressed his wish not to be considered for a third term. On 3 December 1991, the General Assembly appointed Boutros Boutros-Ghali of Egypt to a five-year term beginning on 1 January 1992.

Trygve Lie

Born in Oslo, Norway, 1896; died in Geilo, Norway, 30 December 1968. Law degree from Oslo University. Active in his country's trade union movement from the age of 15, when he joined the Norwegian Trade Union Youth Organization. At 23, became assistant to the secretary of the Norwegian Labor Party. Legal adviser to the Norwegian Trade Union Federation (1922–35). Elected to the Norwegian Parliament (1935). Minister of justice (1935–39). Minister of trade, industry, shipping, and fishing (1939–40). After the German occupation of Norway in 1940 and until the liberation of Norway in 1945, he was, successively, acting foreign minister and foreign minister of the Norwegian government in exile in London. A prominent anti-Nazi, he rendered many services in the Allied cause during World War II. For example, he was instrumental in preventing the Norwegian merchant marine, one of the world's largest, from falling into German hands. Reelected to Parliament in 1945. Headed the Norwegian delegation to the San Francisco Conference.

Dag Hjalmar Agne Carl Hammarskjöld

Born in Jönkönpirg, Sweden, 1905; died near Ndola, Northern Rhodesia (now Zambia), 17 September 1961. Studied at Uppsala and Stockholm universities; Ph.D., Stockholm, 1934. Secretary of Commission on Unemployment (1930–34). Assistant professor of political economy, Stockholm University (1933). Secretary of the Sveriges Riksbank (Bank of Sweden, 1935–36); chairman of the board (1941–45). Undersecretary of state in the Swedish ministry of finance (1936–45). Envoy extraordinary and financial adviser to the ministry of foreign affairs (1946–49). Undersecretary of state (1949). Deputy foreign minister (1951–53). Delegate to the Organization for European Economic Cooperation (OEEC; 1948–53). Vice-chairman of the Executive Committee of the OEEC (1948–49). Swedish delegate to the Commission of Ministers of the Council of Europe (1951–52). Hammarskjöld was a member of the Swedish Academy, which grants the Nobel prizes, and vice-president of the Swedish Tourist and Mountaineers' Association.

U Thant

Born in Pantanaw, near Rangoon, Burma (now Myanmar), 1909; died in New York, 25 November 1974. Educated at University College, Rangoon. Started career as teacher of English and modern history at Pantanaw High School; later headmaster. Active in development and modernization of Burma's educational system. Author and freelance journalist. Books include a work on the League of Nations (1932), *Democracy in Schools* (1952), and *History of Post-War Burma* (1961). After Burma's independence, became Burma's press director (1947), director of broadcasting (1948), and secretary in the ministry of information (1949–53). Chief adviser to his government at many international conferences. Member of Burma's delegation to the 1952 General Assembly. In 1957, moved to New York as head of Burma's permanent delegation to the UN.

Kurt Waldheim

Born in Sankt Andrä-Wördern, Austria, 21 December 1918. Studied at the Consular Academy of Vienna and took an LL.D. at the University of Vienna. Member of the delegation of Austria in negotiations for Austrian State Treaty, London, Paris, and Moscow (1945–47). First secretary of Austria's legation to France (1948–51). Counselor and head of personnel division, ministry of foreign affairs, Vienna (1951–55). Permanent observer of Austria to the UN (1955–56). Minister, embassy to Canada, Ottawa (1956–58), and ambassador (1958–60). Director-general, political affairs, ministry of foreign affairs, Vienna (1960–64). Ambassador and permanent representative of Austria to the UN (1964–68 and 1970–71). Austrian minister of foreign affairs (1968–70). Unsuccessful candidate for the presidency of Austria in 1971. Guest Professor of Diplomacy, Georgetown University, Washington, DC, 1982–84. Author of *The Austrian Example*, on Austria's foreign policy in 1973; *Building the Future Order*, in 1980; *In the Eye of the Storm*, 1985.

In 1986, during his second campaign for the Austrian presidency, information about Waldheim's record as a German Army lieutenant in World War II was reported for the first time in the international press. Despite his previous assertions that he had been wounded at the Russian front in 1941 and then returned to Vienna to study law, it was discovered he had served as a lieutenant in the high command of Army Group E, whose commander, General Alexander Loehr, was later hanged for atrocities. The reports indicated that Waldheim had served in Yugoslavia and Greece, a fact that he had hitherto concealed, at a time when reprisals, deportations, and other war crimes were being carried out by the German Army. In 1987, the US Justice Department, on the basis of an examination of US files and of the records of the War Crimes Commission in the UN archives, placed Waldheim on a watch list, which is used to bar entry to the US for people linked to war crimes.

An international commission of historians appointed by Waldheim, after his election to the presidency of Austria in 1986, reported in February 1988 that it had found evidence that Waldheim was aware of war crimes during his service in the Balkans and had concealed his record but had found no evidence that he himself had committed any crime. The commission's report created a national crisis in the government of Austria and deeply divided the Austrian people. A national poll showed that, while the majority of people did not wish him to resign (as many prominent intellectuals and politicians were loudly insisting), most indicated that they would not vote for him again. Waldheim himself insists that the commission cleared him of the charge of committing war crimes, though overstepping its mandate.

However, the debate over which countries did (or did not) know the facts about Waldheim's war service before or during his tenure as secretary-general continued to surface in the press periodically. There was general agreement that public knowledge of the real nature of Waldheim's war service would have disqualified him for consideration for the post of secretary-general. In August 1994, Representative Carolyn B. Maloney, Democrat of Manhattan, introduced the War Crimes Disclosure Act, H.R. 4995, with the intention of forcing the Central Intelligence Agency to disclose parts of the Waldheim dossier which it has withheld, citing national security interests.

Waldheim served as president of Austria for one term, from 1986 to 1992. In July 1994, Pope John Paul II, a long-time friend of Waldheim's, awarded him the Knighthood of the Order of Pius "for outstanding service as secretary-general of the United Nations." The honor is awarded to Catholics or non-Catholics for outstanding services to the church or society, and is largely symbolic.

Javier Pérez de Cuéllar

Born in Lima, Peru, 19 January 1920. Graduated from the law school of Catholic University, Lima (1943). Joined Peruvian ministry of foreign affairs (1940) and the diplomatic service (1944).

Served as secretary at Peruvian embassies in France, the United Kingdom, Bolivia, and Brazil. Returned to Lima (1961) as director of legal and personnel departments, ministry of foreign affairs. Served as ambassador to Venezuela, USSR, Poland, and Switzerland. Member of Peruvian delegation to the 1st General Assembly (1946) and of delegations to the 25th through 30th sessions (1970–75). Permanent representative of Peru to the UN (1971–75). Served as UN secretary-general's special representative in Cyprus (1975–77); UN undersecretary-general for special political affairs (1979–81); and secretary-general's personal representative in Afghanistan (1981). After resigning from the UN, he returned to the ministry of foreign affairs and voluntarily separated from the service of his government on 7 October 1981. In 1992 UNESCO named him chairman of its World Commission on Culture and Development. He has been a director of Republic National Bank of New York since 1992. He is a former professor of diplomatic law at the Academia de Guerra Aérea del Peru. Author of *Manual de derecho diplomático (Manual of International Law),* 1964.

Boutros Boutros-Ghali

Born in Cairo, Egypt, 14 November 1922. Graduated from Cairo University in 1946 with a Bachelor of Law. Received his Ph.D. in international law in 1949 from Paris University. From 1949–77 he was Professor of International Law and International Relations and head of the Department of Political Science at Cairo University. Boutros-Ghali was a Fulbright Research Scholar at Columbia University in 1954–55. He served as director of the Centre of Research of The Hague Academy of International Law from 1963–1964, and was a visiting professor at the Faculty of Law of Paris University from 1967–68. In 1977 he became Egypt's Minister of State for Foreign Affairs, and was present at the Camp David Summit Conference during the negotiations that led to the Camp David accords between Egypt and Israel in 1978. He continued as Minister of State for Foreign Affairs until 1991, when he became Deputy Prime Minister of Foreign Affairs. He became a member of the Egyptian parliament in 1987 and was part of the secretariat of the National Democratic Party since 1980. From 1980–92 he was a member of the Central Committee and Political Bureau of the Arab Socialist Union. From 1970–91 he was a member of the UN's International Law Commission. His professional affiliations include membership in the Institute of International Law, the International Institute of Human Rights, the African Society of Political Studies and the Académie des Sciences Morales et Politiques (Académie Française, Paris). He founded the publication *Al Ahram Iktisadi* and was its editor from 1960 to 1975. Boutros-Ghali has authored more than 30 books and over 100 articles on international affairs, international law, foreign policy, diplomacy, human rights, and economic and social development.

DEVELOPMENTS UNDER TRYGVE LIE, 1946-1952

Trygve Lie had not yet been in office three months when he took the initiative of advising the Security Council on the Secretariat's interpretation of the Charter. The Council was considering its first case, the Iranian complaint against the USSR. The secretary-general delivered a legal opinion that differed sharply from that of the Security Council. The Council did not accept his interpretation, but it upheld his right to present his views. After setting this precedent, Lie submitted legal opinions on other matters.

During Lie's first term as secretary-general, East-West tension charged the UN atmosphere. As the world situation became increasingly threatening, the political role of the secretary-general expanded. Lie took definite stands on three issues, each of which earned him the dislike of some permanent members of the Secu-

rity Council. The issues were Chinese representation, a plan for the general settlement of the cold war, and UN military action in the Korean War.

Chinese Representation. By the end of 1949, a number of states, including the USSR and the United Kingdom—permanent members of the Security Council—had recognized the mainland government, the People's Republic of China. In January 1950, the USSR representatives, having failed to obtain the seating of the representatives of the People's Republic, began boycotting UN meetings at which China was represented by delegates of the Republic of China, based on Taiwan. In private meetings with delegations, Lie tried to solve the impasse. He adduced various reasons, including a ruling of the International Court of Justice, for the thesis that nonrecognition of a government by other governments should not determine its representation in the UN.

Trygve Lie's Twenty-Year Peace Plan. Lie developed an extraordinary initiative during the first half of 1950. In a letter to the Security Council dated 6 June 1950, approximately two weeks before the outbreak of the Korean War, he said: "I felt it my duty to suggest a fresh start to be made towards eventual peaceful solution of outstanding problems." In his *Twenty-Year Program for Achieving Peace Through the United Nations,* Lie proposed new international machinery to control atomic energy and check the competitive production of armaments and also proposed the establishment of a UN force to prevent or stop localized outbreaks of violence.

Armed with these proposals and other memoranda, including the one on Chinese representation, Lie journeyed first to Washington, then to London, to Paris, and finally to Moscow. He held conversations not only with foreign ministers and high-ranking diplomats but also with US President Harry S Truman, British Prime Minister Clement Attlee, French President Vincent Auriol, and Soviet Premier Joseph Stalin. Lie's reception was cordial in Moscow, warm in Paris, and friendly in London, but cool in Washington.

The international picture changed abruptly, however, with the outbreak of the Korean War. The attitude of a number of governments toward Lie changed dramatically as well.

The Korean War. An outstanding example of a secretary-general taking a stand on an issue was Lie's intervention in the emergency meeting of the Security Council on 24 June 1950. He unequivocally labeled the North Korean forces aggressors because they had crossed the 38th parallel, declared that the conflict constituted a threat to international peace, and urged that the Security Council had a "clear duty" to act. After the Council (in the absence of the Soviet delegate) had set in motion military sanctions against North Korea, Lie endorsed this course of action and rallied support from member governments for UN military action in Korea. These moves brought him into sharp conflict with the USSR, which accused him of "slavish obedience to Western imperialism" and to the "aggression" that, in the Soviet view, the US had committed in Korea.

As the Korean conflict grew more ominous with the intervention of the People's Republic of China, Lie played an active role in getting cease-fire negotiations underway in the field. At the same time, he fully identified himself with military intervention in Korea on behalf of the UN.

Extension of Lie's Term as Secretary-General. Lie's first term as secretary-general was to expire on 31 January 1951. In the Security Council, the USSR vetoed a resolution recommending him for a second term and subsequently announced that it would accept anyone other than Lie who was acceptable to the other members of the Council. The US announced that it would veto anyone but Lie. The Council was unable to recommend a candidate for the office of secretary-general to the General Assembly, a situation unforeseen in the Charter. A resolution in the Assembly to extend Lie's term by three years, beginning on 1 February

1951, was carried by 46 votes to 5, with 8 abstentions. The negative votes were cast by the Soviet bloc.

The USSR maintained normal relations with Lie until the expiration of his original term on 31 January 1951. Thereafter, it stood by its previous announcement that the extension of the term was illegal and that it would "not consider him as secretary-general." By the fall of 1951, however, its nonrecognition policy toward Lie subsided. However, other complications were facing Lie, and on 10 November 1952, he tendered his resignation to the General Assembly.

DEVELOPMENTS UNDER DAG HAMMARSKJÖLD, 1953–1961

Hammarskjöld's activities in the political field were more numerous and far-reaching than Lie's had been. Both the General Assembly and the Security Council repeatedly relied on his initiative and advice and entrusted important tasks to him.

The 1954 General Assembly set a precedent when it asked the secretary-general to seek the release of 11 US fliers held prisoners by mainland China. The Assembly resolution left the course of action entirely to his judgment. After various preparations, Hammarskjöld flew to Peking (now Beijing) for personal negotiations with that government, and the 11 fliers were released. This success greatly increased the readiness of the Assembly to rely on the secretary-general as a troubleshooter.

The Suez Crisis. Grave responsibilities were entrusted to the secretary-general by the General Assembly in connection with the establishment and operation of the UN Emergency Force (UNEF). On 4 November 1956, at the height of the crisis resulting from British, French, and Israeli intervention in Egypt, the secretary-general was requested to submit a plan within 48 hours for the establishment of a force "to secure and supervise the cessation of hostilities." The Assembly approved his plan and, at his suggestion, appointed Major-General E. L. M. Burns, Chief of Staff of the UN Truce Supervision Organization, as the chief of UNEF. The Assembly authorized the secretary-general to take appropriate measures to carry out his plan, and an advisory committee of seven UN members was appointed to assist him. Hammarskjöld flew to Egypt to arrange for the Egyptian government's consent for UNEF to be stationed and to operate in Egyptian territory. He was given the task of arranging with Egypt, France, Israel, and the United Kingdom the implementation of the cease-fire and an end to the dispatch of troops and arms into the area and was authorized to issue regulations and instructions for the effective functioning of UNEF.

Hammarskjöld's Views on Developing the Role of Secretary-General. Even before the Middle East crisis of 1956, Hammarskjöld had pointed to the need for the secretary-general to assume a new role in world affairs. On his reelection to a second term, Hammarskjöld told the General Assembly that he considered it to be the duty of the secretary-general, guided by the Charter and by the decisions of the main UN organs, to use his office and the machinery of the organization to the full extent permitted by practical circumstances. But he then declared: "I believe it is in keeping with the philosophy of the Charter that the secretary-general be expected to act also *without such guidance*, should this appear to him necessary in order to help in *filling a vacuum* that may appear in the systems which the Charter and traditional diplomacy provide for the safeguarding of peace and security." (Italics added.) In other words, inaction or a stalemate either at the UN or outside of it may be justification for the secretary-general to act on his own.

Thus, in 1958, Hammarskjöld took an active hand in the Jordan-Lebanon crisis. After a resolution for stronger UN action failed to carry in the Security Council, he announced that he would nevertheless strengthen UN action in Lebanon and "accept the consequences" if members of the Security Council were to dis-

approve; none did. In the fall of 1959, the USSR made it known that it did not favor a visit by the secretary-general to Laos and, in particular, the assignment of a special temporary "UN ambassador" there. Yet Hammarskjöld did go to Laos to orient himself on the situation in that corner of Southeast Asia, and he assigned a high UN official as the head of a special mission to Laos. In March 1959, Hammarskjöld sent a special representative to help Thailand and Cambodia settle a border dispute. He acted at their invitation without specific authorization by the Security Council or the General Assembly. The dispute was settled.

In his report to the 1959 Assembly, he said: "The main significance of the evolution of the Office of the Secretary-General . . . lies in the fact that it has provided means for smooth and fast action . . . of special value in situations in which prior public debate on a proposed course of action might increase the difficulties . . . or in which . . . members may prove hesitant. . . ."

The Congo Crisis. By far the greatest responsibilities Hammarskjöld had to shoulder were in connection with the UN Operation in the Congo (now Zaire).

On 12 and 13 July 1960, respectively, President Joseph Kasavubu and Premier Patrice Lumumba of the newly independent Congo each cabled the secretary-general, asking for UN military assistance because of the arrival of Belgian troops and the impending secession of Katanga. At Hammarskjöld's request, the Security Council met on the night of 13 July. He gave his full support to the Congo's appeal and recommended that the Council authorize him to "take the necessary steps" to set up a UN military assistance force for the Congo, in consultation with the Congolese government and on the basis of the experience gained in connection with the UNEF in the Middle East. The Security Council so decided.

Since the Congo operation thus initiated was of much greater dimensions than the UNEF operation, the responsibilities imposed upon the secretary-general were correspondingly heavier, for, although the Security Council and the General Assembly guided Hammarskjöld, he himself had to make extraordinarily difficult decisions almost daily, often on highly explosive matters that arose as a result of serious rifts within the Congolese government and many other factors.

Various member governments, including the USSR and certain African and Western countries, criticized Hammarskjöld for some actions that the UN took or failed to take in the Congo. At times, he had to face the possibility that some country that had contributed military contingents to the UN force would withdraw them.

When it became known in February 1961 that Lumumba, who had been deposed by Kasavubu early in September 1960 and later detained by the Léopoldville authorities, had been handed over by them to the Katanga authorities and subsequently murdered, Hammarskjöld declared that the UN was not to blame for the "revolting crime." However, several delegates claimed that he should have taken stronger measures to protect Lumumba.

The "Troika" Proposal. The USSR had asked for Hammarskjöld's dismissal long before the assassination of Lumumba. Premier Khrushchev, as head of the Soviet delegation to the 1960 General Assembly, accused Hammarskjöld of lacking impartiality and of violating instructions of the Security Council in his conduct of the UN operation in the Congo. He also proposed a basic change in the very institution of the secretary-general, arguing that since the secretary-general had become "the interpreter and executor of decisions of the General Assembly and the Security Council," this one-man office should be replaced by a "collective executive organ consisting of three persons, each of whom would represent a certain group of states"—namely, the West, the socialist states, and the neutralist countries; the institution of a "troika," he declared, would guarantee that the UN executive organ would not act to the detriment of any of these groups of states.

Hammarskjöld rejected the accusations against his impartiality, declared that he would not resign unless the member states for which the organization was of decisive importance or the uncommitted nations wished him to do so, and received an ovation from the overwhelming majority of the delegations. He also stated that to replace the one-man secretary-general by a three-man body would greatly alter the character and limit the scope of the UN.

Outside the Soviet bloc there had been little support for the "troika" proposal, but some "subtroika" proposals were advanced. Hammarskjöld in turn suggested that his five top aides, including a US and a Soviet citizen, advise the secretary-general on political problems. Discussions of the question were interrupted by his death.

Death of Dag Hammarskjöld. Because of dangerous developments in the Congo, Hammarskjöld flew there in September 1961. On the night of 17 September, the plane carrying him from Léopoldville to a meeting with the Katanga secessionist leader at Ndola, Northern Rhodesia, crashed in a wooded area about 16 km (10 mi) west of Ndola airport. Hammarskjöld and all 15 UN civilian and military personnel traveling with him, including the crew, were killed. The exact cause of the tragedy has not been determined. An investigation commission appointed by the General Assembly reported several possibilities: inadequate technical and security preparations for the flight, an attack on the plane from the air or the ground, sabotage, or human failure by the pilot.

DEVELOPMENTS UNDER U THANT, 1961–1971

U Thant's approach to his office was different from that of Hammarskjöld, whose dynamic conception of the secretary-general's political role had aroused such opposition in the Soviet bloc. Thant did not take the same initiatives as his predecessor, but he consistently sought to use the prestige of his office to help settle disputes. Moreover, both the General Assembly and the Security Council assigned him to mediate extremely delicate situations. In his annual reports, he put forth proposals on basic issues, such as disarmament and economic and social cooperation and many of his suggestions were adopted.

An early example of a successful initiative taken by U Thant was in connection with the long-standing dispute between Indonesia and the Netherlands over the status of West Irian. The territory, formerly known as West New Guinea, had belonged to the Dutch East Indies, and Indonesia now claimed it as its own. In December 1961, fighting broke out between Dutch and Indonesian troops. Appealing to both governments to seek a peaceful solution, the secretary-general helped them arrive at a settlement. That settlement, moreover, brought new responsibilities to the office of the secretary-general: for the first time in UN history, a non-self-governing territory was, for a limited period, administered directly by the world organization.

The Cyprus Operation. Intercommunal clashes broke out in Cyprus on Christmas Eve 1963 and were followed by the withdrawal of the Turkish Cypriots into their enclaves, leaving the central government wholly under Greek Cypriot control. A "peace-making force" established under British command was unable to put an end to the fighting, and a conference on Cyprus held in London in January 1964 ended in disagreement. In the face of the danger of broader hostilities in the area, the Security Council on 4 March 1964 decided unanimously to authorize U Thant to establish a UN Peacekeeping Force in Cyprus (UNFICYP), with a limited three-month mandate to prevent the recurrence of fighting, to help maintain law and order, and to aid in the return to normal conditions. The force was to be financed on the basis of voluntary contributions. The Council also asked the secretary-general to appoint a mediator to seek a peaceful settlement of the Cyprus problem. The report of U Thant's mediator, Galo Plaza Lasso, was transmitted to the Security Council in

March 1965 but was rejected by Turkey. Plaza resigned in December 1965, and the function of mediator lapsed.

Another crisis occurred in November 1967, but threatened military intervention by Turkey was averted, largely as a result of US opposition. Negotiations conducted by Cyrus Vance for the US and José Rolz-Bennett on behalf of the secretary-general led to a settlement. Intercommunal talks were begun in June 1968, through the good offices of the secretary-general, as part of the settlement. The talks bogged down, but U Thant proposed a formula for their reactivation under the auspices of his special representative, B. F. Osorio-Tafall, and they were resumed in 1972, after Thant had left office.

The India-Pakistan War of 1965 and Conflict of 1971. Hostilities between India and Pakistan broke out in Kashmir in early August 1965 and soon spread along the entire length of the international border from the Lahore area to the sea. At the behest of the Security Council, whose calls on 4 and 6 September for a cease-fire had gone unheeded, U Thant visited the subcontinent from 9 to 15 September. In his report to the Council, the secretary-general proposed certain procedures, including a possible meeting between President Ayub of Pakistan and Prime Minister Shastri of India, to resolve the problem and restore the peace.

The Council, on 20 September, demanded a cease-fire and authorized the secretary-general to provide the necessary assistance to ensure supervision of the cease-fire and withdrawal of all armed personnel. For this purpose, U Thant strengthened the existing UN Military Observer Group in India and Pakistan (UNMOGIP), stationed in Kashmir, and established the UN India-Pakistan Observation Mission (UNIPOM) to supervise the cease-fire and withdrawal of troops along the border outside Kashmir.

At a meeting organized by Soviet Premier Kosygin in January 1966 in Tashkent, USSR, the leaders of India and Pakistan agreed on the withdrawal of all troops; this withdrawal was successfully implemented under the supervision of the two UN military observer missions in the area. UNIPOM was disbanded in March 1966, having completed its work.

Following the outbreak of civil strife in East Pakistan in March 1971 and the deterioration of the situation in the subcontinent that summer, U Thant offered his good offices to India and Pakistan and kept the Security Council informed under the broad terms of Article 99 of the Charter. When overt warfare broke out in December, the Security Council appealed to all parties to spare the lives of innocent civilians. Pursuant to a decision by the Council, U Thant appointed a special representative to lend his good offices for the solution of humanitarian problems after the cease-fire of 18 December 1971, which was followed by the independence of Bangladesh.

U Thant's Stand on the Viet Nam War. Throughout his tenure, U Thant was deeply concerned with the question of Viet Nam. By tacit consent, the question was never formally debated in the General Assembly and only cursorily touched upon in the Security Council. Until the opening of the Paris peace talks in 1968, the secretary-general was unremitting in his efforts to persuade the parties in the conflict to initiate negotiations on their own. In 1966, he put forward a three-stage proposal to create the conditions necessary for discussion, but it was ignored by the US.

After the Paris talks began, U Thant deliberately refrained from making any public statements on Viet Nam "in order to avoid creating unnecessary difficulties" for the parties. He broke this silence only once, on 5 May 1970, when he expressed his deep concern "regarding the recent involvement of Cambodia in the war."

U Thant's Second Term. U Thant's second term of office was dominated by the protracted Middle East crisis that arose in the aftermath of the Six-Day War in 1967. His quick action in removing UNEF troops from the Suez area at the request of the United

Arab Republic just before that war began occasioned much criticism and some misunderstanding.

Of the two other major political conflicts during the period 1967–70, the civil war in Nigeria and the Soviet invasion of Czechoslovakia on 20 August 1968, only the latter was debated at the UN. The political aspects of the Nigerian situation were never raised in either the General Assembly or the Security Council out of deference to the African countries themselves, whose main objective was to keep external intervention to a minimum. However, as the troops of the Federal Republic of Nigeria began to penetrate more deeply into the eastern region (which had announced its secession from Nigeria and proclaimed itself an independent state under the name of Biafra), the various humanitarian organs of the UN became increasingly concerned about the plight of the people there. Accordingly, in August 1968, the secretary-general took the initiative of sending a personal representative to Nigeria to help facilitate the distribution of food and medicine.

At the request of its six Western members, the Security Council decided to debate the situation in Czechoslovakia, despite the protests of the USSR. On 23 August 1968, 10 members voted for a resolution condemning the Soviet action, which the USSR vetoed. Another resolution, requesting the secretary-general to send a representative to Prague to seek the release of imprisoned Czechoslovak leaders, was not put to a vote. In view—as one UN text puts it—of the "agreement reached on the substance of the problem during the Soviet-Czechoslovak talks held in Moscow from August 23 to 26," no further action was taken by the Council. However, it is worth noting that U Thant was among the first world figures to denounce the invasion publicly. At a press briefing on 21 August at UN headquarters, he expressed unequivocal dismay, characterizing the invasion as "yet another serious blow to the concepts of international order and morality which form the basis of the Charter of the United Nations . . . and a grave setback to the East-West détente which seemed to be re-emerging in recent months."

DEVELOPMENTS UNDER KURT WALDHEIM, 1972–1981

Two overriding concerns shaped Waldheim's secretary-generalship: concern for the preservation of the peace and concern for the evolution of world economic arrangements that would effect a more equitable distribution of the world's wealth. Two other issues were also of special concern to Waldheim: the financial position of the UN and terrorism. The financial position of the UN had been rendered precarious by the practice of some member states, including the USSR, France, and the US, of withholding or threatening to withhold their share of UN funds for activities that they questioned. When Waldheim took office, the crisis had become an emergency, and he dealt with it vigorously throughout his tenure. In September 1972, he placed the question of terrorism on the agenda of the General Assembly against the wishes of many member states. It was the first time a secretary-general had ever placed a substantive item on the Assembly's agenda.

Peacemaking. In 1972, on his own authority, Waldheim undertook a number of missions on behalf of peace. Visiting Cyprus, he temporarily calmed the Turkish community's concern over reported arms shipments to the Greek-dominated government. He visited the island again in 1973 in pursuit of reconciliation. After the hostilities in 1974, he was able to bring Greek and Turkish leaders together for negotiations, and he presided over the Geneva talks regarding Cyprus.

Waldheim's efforts to conciliate in the Viet Nam War were rebuffed by both sides in 1972. He then tried, without success, to end the war through action by the Security Council. He visited the two Yemens to try to mediate a border dispute in 1972, and in

the same year, he tried to mediate between India and Pakistan.

In the long-standing Arab-Israeli dispute, Waldheim made many efforts toward a satisfactory settlement and organized the UN Emergency Force as a buffer between the armies of Egypt and Israel at the request of the Security Council in October 1973.

Striving for a New International Economic Order. The sixth special session of the Assembly, in the spring of 1974, and the seventh special session, in September 1975, resulted in a number of decisions and proposals for bridging the gap between the rich and the poor nations and building a "new international economic order." The seventh special session was, in Waldheim's words, "a major event, even a turning point, in the history of the United Nations and showed a new and highly promising capacity of the organization to achieve practical results through consensus and through negotiation."

Financial Status of the UN. Waldheim acted both to reduce the costs of running the UN and to bring in contributions from member nations.

The US contribution to the UN, historically the highest single assessment, by the early 1970s stood at 31.5 percent of the budget. In October 1973, the US Congress reduced the US share to 25 percent of the UN budget; 116 other nations also had their contributions reduced by the UN. The difference was made up by increasing the assessments of Japan, China, and 10 other members and by admitting to membership the two Germanys. Waldheim helped to bring these changes about, fostering the notion that any country paying more than 25 percent of the UN's expenses could wield excessive influence.

Terrorism. Incidents of terrorism increased in the early 1970s. In September 1972, during the XXth Olympiad in Munich, 11 Israeli athletes were killed by Palestinians of the Black September group. Waldheim expressed himself strongly about the event and put the question of terrorism on the agenda of the 1972 General Assembly. A number of Arab and African countries took exception to his initiative, arguing that attention should be focused on the causes of terrorism. Although the Assembly had earlier condemned aerial hijacking, the resolution that it adopted on terrorism did not condemn the practice but called for a study of its causes. After OPEC officials were attacked by terrorists in 1975, the sentiment for more ample UN action against terrorism grew among third-world countries.

Waldheim's Second Term. Waldheim entered his second term of office in January 1977 with few illusions about the United Nations. To some extent, he wrote, it was still in search of its identity and its true role: "It tends to react rather than foresee, to deal with the effects of a crisis rather than anticipate and forestall that crisis." The history of the UN since its founding, he wrote, "has essentially been the story of the search for a working balance between national sovereignty and national interests on the one hand and international order and the long-term interests of the world community on the other." He said he was not discouraged, however, and he urged governments—particularly the major powers—to turn away from the age-old struggle for spheres of influence and to honor and respect their obligations and responsibilities under the Charter.

In 1978, Waldheim called for an effort to improve and streamline the workings of the UN, beginning with the General Assembly, the agenda of which should be reviewed, he said, and items of lesser interest removed. He noted that the Assembly had grown in three decades from a body of 50 members with an agenda of 20 items to a gathering of some 150 members and an agenda of more than 130 items.

Waldheim traveled extensively in East Asia in early 1979 and again in 1980 to get a firsthand view of developments in that area, particularly Indo-China, where, in the aftermath of the Viet Nam war, there was an exodus of refugees, by land and sea, from that country. With the tide of these and other refugees from Laos and Kampuchea rising daily, Waldheim convened a meeting in Geneva in June 1979 to help alleviate the problem.

In May 1979, pursuing a "good offices" mission in Cyprus, Waldheim convened a high-level meeting calling for a resumption of intercommunal talks. The talks were subsequently resumed but broke down shortly thereafter. Waldheim again exerted his best efforts beginning in late 1979, as did the UN itself, in search of solutions to unexpected crises touched off by the Soviet invasion of Afghanistan and the taking of US diplomatic personnel as hostages in Iran. From the outset, his efforts were directed at freeing the hostages and settling relations between Iran and the US, and, for this purpose, he went to Tehran himself, as did a UN commission of inquiry. Waldheim noted that the war between Iran and Iraq, which began in September 1980, had resisted all efforts, both within and outside the UN, at finding a peaceful solution. He offered his own good offices for this purpose and appointed Olof Palme, former Swedish prime minister, as his special representative. In regard to the Afghanistan crisis, he appointed Javier Pérez de Cuéllar of Peru as his personal representative.

DEVELOPMENTS UNDER JAVIER PÉREZ DE CUÉLLAR, 1982–1991

Secretary-General Pérez de Cuéllar presided over the United Nations during one of the most remarkable decades in the political history of the world. During his tenure, the stalemate imposed on the United Nations by the rivalries of the Cold War came to an end. The political map of Europe, which had remained stable for more than 40 years since the end of WWII, was completely redrawn when the Soviet Union collapsed in 1989. East and West Germany were united and the Berlin Wall was reduced to rubble. Historic achievements in bilateral arms control and disarmament negotiations lowered the level of confrontation between the West and the East for the first time since the dawn of the nuclear era. A new atmosphere of consensus enabled the Security Council to begin providing the kind of leadership envisioned for it by the founders of the organization, as enshrined in the UN Charter. Long-standing political problems in Namibia, Cambodia, and Latin America were resolved with success by United Nations peacekeeping missions, and the evolution of the organization's activities in helping organize and monitor free and fair elections in new democracies began. The winds of change were also blowing strongly in South Africa, where the *apartheid* system was beginning to crumble after more than 30 years of condemnation by the United Nations.

The story of Pérez de Cuéllar's 10-year term as secretary-general straddles this historic evolution of the world scene at the *fin de siécle*. Upon leaving office in December 1991, in his report on the work of the United Nations, he set forth his own feelings about his experience as secretary-general:

"Peace has won victories on several fronts. . . . New vistas are opening for States to work together in a manner they did not do before. The earlier posture of aloofness and reserve towards the Organization has been replaced by more ardent participation in its endeavors. An era of law and justice may not be around the corner but the United Nations has defined the direction. . . . Today there are far more solid grounds for hope than there are reasons for frustration and fear. The hope arises both from the enduring relevance of the philosophy of the Charter and from the vastly strengthened credentials of the Organization. My credo is anchored in that philosophy and it will remain so. With its return from the doldrums, and with its role no longer peripheral, the United Nations has come nearer to the vision of its Charter. Everyone who contributed to the process is entitled to a measure of exultation and I, for my part, to a feeling of fulfillment. I profoundly appreciate the confidence placed in me through this testing phase of international affairs. I close on that note of faith and gratitude."

The situation had been very different when Pérez de Cuéllar first took office, in 1982. In his first report to the General Assembly, in September 1982, on the work of the organization, Pérez de Cuéllar commented on the inability of the UN to play an effective and decisive role in its capacity to keep the peace and serve as a forum for negotiations. The Falkland Islands crisis and the invasion of Lebanon by Israel, both major events of 1982, were clear examples of the failure of the international community, and its organization, to use the mechanisms of diplomacy to prevent international conflict. Countries seemed unwilling or reluctant to use the United Nations' peacekeeping mechanisms to help them resolve their difficulties without resort to violence. Time after time, he said, "we have seen the Organization set aside or rebuffed, for this reason or for that, in situations in which it should and could have played an important and constructive role." He saw this trend as dangerous for the world community and for the future and criticized the tendency of governments to resort to confrontation, violence, and even war in pursuit of what were perceived as vital interests.

Another clear indication of the organization's lack of stature was the crippling budgetary problems caused by some member states' continuing practice of withholding part or all of their assessed contributions, placing the work of the entire organization in a constant state of uncertainty. Clearly, at the beginning of his term, the United Nations stood in need of a rebirth.

The Middle East

The Iran-Iraq War. In regard to the prolonged war between Iran and Iraq, which had started in 1980 and taken an enormous toll in human lives, Pérez de Cuéllar considered it to be his overriding responsibility under the Charter not only to seek an end to the conflict but also, until that goal was achieved, to try, under international humanitarian rules, to mitigate its effects in such areas as attacks on civilian population centers, use of chemical weapons, treatment of prisoners of war, and safety of navigation and civil aviation. On four occasions between 1984 and 1986, he dispatched specialists to investigate charges of the use of chemical weapons, initially against Iranian forces but later injuring Iranian civilians and Iraqi forces as well. In 1984 and 1985, two UN teams investigated allegations of violations of promises by the two countries to cease deliberate attacks on purely civilian population centers, and in January 1985, the secretary-general dispatched a fact-finding mission to Iran and Iraq to investigate the treatment of prisoners of war and civilian detainees. He himself visited Tehran and Baghdad in April 1985 to discuss proposals he had drawn up to initiate movement toward a comprehensive settlement of the war, and he continued to search for new approaches to this goal.

In July 1987, the Security Council unanimously adopted a resolution (598/1987) asking the secretary-general to send UN observers to verify and supervise a cease-fire between Iran and Iraq and withdrawal to internationally recognized boundaries. Pérez de Cuéllar was also asked by the Council to explore the question of entrusting to an impartial body the task of inquiring into responsibility for the conflict. Subsequent discussions with the two governments in their capitals reaffirmed his conviction that his good offices could be used to facilitate the restoration of peace and stability in the region. On 20 August 1988, the fighting stopped and UN military observers took up the challenge of monitoring compliance with the cease-fire. The secretary-general and his representative continued a "good offices" mission to build confidence and lay the basis for a lasting peace in the region.

The Gulf War. In August 1990, Iraq invaded Kuwait with 100,000 troops and took complete control of the small, underdefended country within 48-hours. In the four months following the invasion the Security Council responded with historic speed and unanimity. It passed 12 resolutions condemning the invasion, invoking Chapter VII of the Charter to impose economic sanctions on Iraq, and addressing aid to refugees and Iraq's taking of hostages. Pérez de Cuéllar remarked in his 1990 annual report that the council "has established that such actions, which are in direct contravention of the principles of the Charter and international law, cannot be committed with impunity." On 29 November 1990, after three weeks of debate, the Security Council passed Resolution 678 "authorizing Member States cooperating with the Government of Kuwait, unless Iraq on or before January 15, 1991, fully implements . . . the foregoing resolutions, to use all necessary means to implement Security Council Resolution 660 and all subsequent relevant resolutions to restore international peace and security in the area."

With the phrase "all necessary means," a new chapter in the history of the UN began. A 680,000-strong multi-national military force, led by 410,000 United States troops, was authorized by this resolution to impose the Security Council's will upon Iraq and restore the national sovereignty of Kuwait. On 16 January 1991, the allies began a six-week aerial bombardment of Iraq and Kuwait in preparation for a land attack on Kuwait. On 25 February, the ground attack began. Twelve days latter the allied forces had decisively defeated Iraq's army of occupation, decimating it and pushing surviving units back into Iraq. Iraqi casualties were estimated in the hundreds of thousands. The United States lost 309 lives, some in pre-combat incidents. On 6 April, Iraq's parliament officially accepted the terms of Resolution 687, which it characterized as "unjust."

Resolution 687 had established a 200-kilometer-long demilitarized zone along the Iraq-Kuwait border, extending 10 kilometers into Iraq and five kilometers into Kuwait, to be patrolled by the UN Iraq-Kuwait Observer Mission (UNIKOM). The secretary-general reported that UNIKOM's 1,400 troops from 36 countries had been fully deployed on 9 May 1991.

In his 1991 report on the work of the organization, Pérez de Cuéllar pointed out that the experience of the Gulf action, moving as it did into areas undefined by the charter, suggested the need for "collective reflection on questions relating to the future use of the powers vested in the Security Council under Chapter VII. In order to preclude controversy, these questions should include the mechanisms required for the Council to satisfy itself that the rule of proportionality in the employment of armed force is observed and the rules of humanitarian law applicable in armed conflicts are complied with." He also warned that the use of Chapter VII measure should not be "overextended," since the imposition of mandatory economic sanctions necessarily created hardships for third-party nations (nations not party to the conflict, but who have important economic partnerships with the sanctioned state).

The Arab-Israeli Conflict. In mid-1982, Israeli forces moved into Lebanese territory, bypassing the UN Interim Force in Lebanon (UNIFIL). In August of that year, at the request of Lebanon and with the authorization of the Security Council, Pérez de Cuéllar deployed military observers to monitor the violence in and around Beirut. He also put forward proposals for expanding the role of UNIFIL—deploying the force, with elements of the Lebanese army and internal security forces, in areas vacated by Israeli forces as they withdrew from Lebanon, and working out arrangements to ensure that southern Lebanon became a zone of peace under the sovereignty and authority of the Lebanese government. These proposals were not accepted by Israel.

Pérez de Cuéllar also attempted to pursue the long-standing goal of convening a peace conference on the Middle East, holding numerous consultations with the partiesinvolved. In December 1987, the diplomatic stalemate was shaken by a massive Palestinian uprising, the *intifadah,* in the Israeli-occupied territories that forced the Palestine National Council (the PLO's parliament in exile) to formally recognize Israel. However, the Israeli govern-

ment declined to reciprocate. Yasser Arafat, the head of the PLO, was asked to address an emergency session of the Security Council, which had to be held in Geneva, since it was feared the United States would deny him an entry-visa. At that session, the United States vetoed the dispatch of a UN mission to the occupied territories to monitor the treatment of Palestinians by Israeli security forces.

In 1990 and 1991, the United States took the lead in trying to reconvene a peace conference. In October 1991, US Secretary of State James Baker made history by convening in Madrid the first-ever direct negotiations between all parties to the conflict. A key group interested in the talks were the former Palestinians, who since 1967 had been residing in territories under the control of Israelis and were represented by the PLO. Since the Israelis had insisted on their exclusion from the Madried talks, little progress was made. In December 1991, the General Assembly repealed its Resolution 3379 (1975) which had equated Zionism with racism. This was only the second time in the history of the UN that the General Assembly had voted to rescind a resolution.

Afghanistan

The secretary-general and his personal representative, Diego Cordovez, acting as mediator, were continuously involved, until early 1988, in discussions and consultations aimed at negotiating a settlement of the situation in Afghanistan that had been brought about by Soviet military intervention in that country in late 1979 and had affected neighboring countries, particularly Pakistan, to which many Afghan refugees had fled. The negotiations revolved around four points: agreement on noninterference and nonintervention; the voluntary return of refugees; international guarantees on the settlement, to be given by the US and the USSR; and the withdrawal of foreign troops.

The General Assembly supported these efforts and appealed to all states and national and international organizations to extend humanitarian relief assistance to alleviate the hardships of the Afghan refugees, in coordination with the UN high commissioner for refugees.

The negotiation efforts met with success in early April 1988, when agreement was reached on a treaty under which the USSR would withdraw its 115,000 troops from Afghanistan, Pakistan and Afghanistan would cease all interference in each other's internal affairs, Afghan refugees would be given a safe return to their country, and Afghanistan would become a neutral and non-aligned state guaranteed by the USSR and the US. A small UN military observer team (UNGOMAP) was to be sent to Afghanistan to monitor compliance with the treaty, which was signed in Geneva on 14 April by Afghanistan, Pakistan, the USSR, and the US. The USSR withdrew its troop in February 1989, however fighting continued, and rebel forces continued to receive aid from the United States and Pakistan. The USSR, for its part, continued to prop up the Marxist government in Kabul. UNGOMAP's mandate ran out in March 1990 and the secretary-general replaced it with a smaller high-level Office of the Secretary-General in Afghanistan and Pakistan, funded out of the UN's regular budget. This office's purpose was to advise the secretary-general on the military and political situation in order to assist him in finding a settlement.

Central America

In Central America, Pérez de Cuéllar and the secretary-general of the Organization of American States extended, in November 1985, a joint offer of services to the five Central American countries concerned—Costa Rica, El Salvador, Guatemala, Honduras, and Nicaragua—as well as to those of the Contadora Group, bringing to their attention the resources that the two organizations could provide, separately and together, to facilitate resolution of the region's problems and complement the Contadora process. The two leaders visited the area in January 1986 in an effort to reactivate the negotiating process. Pérez de Cuéllar welcomed the proposal of President Oscar Arias Sánchez of Costa Rica for a peace plan, put forward in February 1987 and agreed to that August in Guatemala City by the five Central American countries. He agreed to serve as a member of the International Committee for Verification and Follow-up created by the Guatemala agreement and offered to extend any additional assistance that would be appropriate under the UN Charter.

As a result of this initiative, the countries concerned joined in a framework agreement, Esquipulas II, which gave the UN a mandate to verify the commitments made by the parties to each other. In 1989, the secretary-general established the UN Observer Mission (ONUVEN) to supervise the electoral process in Nicaragua. It was the first time the UN had been directly involved in electoral supervision. The UN Observer Group in Central America (ONUCA) was charged with overseeing the demobilization of the Contra guerrillas in Nicaragua. In December 1989, the secretary-general brought together the five Central American presidents in order to resume a dialogue between the government of El Salvador and the FMLN guerrillas. By July 1990, the San José Human Rights Accord was concluded, in which the government of El Salvador agreed to have its compliance monitored by a UN mission (UN Observer Mission in El Salvador—ONUSAL). After 20 months of negotiations, on his very last day in office, Pérez de Cuéllar witnessed the signing of a cease-fire agreement in the 12-year civil war in El Salvador, on 31 December 1991.

The success of the United Nations in monitoring the elections in Nicaragua encouraged Haiti to request the organization to monitor its elections in December 1990. The General Assembly granted the request, and created the UN Observer Group for Verification of Elections in Haiti, known by its French acronym, ONUVEH. Jean-Bertrand Aristide was elected president in elections declared by the United Nations to be free and fair. However, in September 1991, President Aristide was overthrown by a military coup, creating an intransigent problem for Pérez de Cuéllar's successor.

Cambodia
Hostilities between Cambodia (at that time Kampuchea) and Viet Nam had broken out in 1978. The United Nations became deeply involved in a humanitarian mission to assist refugees in the conflict along the border of Thailand and Cambodia. In January 1989, the revitalized Security Council began to take a more active role in the 11-year-old civil war. The secretary-general's special representative, Under Secretary Rafeeuddin Ahmed, played an essential role in the negotiating the framework for a settlement leading to a specific blueprint for the restoration of peace. In August 1989 the Paris Conference on Cambodia was convened, but was suspended within a month. Meetings in New York and Paris in 1990 finally secured the agreement of all the parties to the framework agreement developed by the Security Council. The agreement was signed on 23 October 1991, and two more UN missions were created: the UN Transitional Authority in Cambodia (UNTAC), and the UN Advance Mission in Cambodia (UNAMIC). The scale and cost of the mandate for these missions was unprecedented. It included repatriation of refugees from the Thai border camps, cantonment of all military forces and demobilization of 70 percent of these troops, registration of voters, supervision of elections for a Constituent Assembly, and supervision of the process of drafting and ratifying a new constitution.

Namibia
The change in the players on the world stage led to the resolution of this long-standing issue, nearly twenty-five years after the General Assembly first denounced South Africa's attempted annexation of South West Africa (now Namibia), and a dozen years

after the Security Council laid out the settlement plan for its independence. The Security Council's resolution 435 of 1978 had called for a cease-fire in Namibia, the abolition of apartheid laws, the withdrawal of South Africa from Namibia, the election of a constituent assembly, and the establishment of the United Nations Transitional Assistance Group (UNTAG) to oversee free and fair elections. However, the presence of Cuban troops in Namibia in support of the liberation movement, the South West Africa Peoples' Organization (SWAPO), created another stalemate between East and West. In 1988, the change in the political climate between the two superpowers produced an agreement that led to the withdrawal of the Cuban troops and the implementation of UNTAG. The transition began in April 1989 and 97 percent of the registered voters participated in elections in November. On 21 March 1990, Namibia became an independent state, with SWAPO leader Sam Nujoma as its president. UNTAG withdrew from Namibia in March 1990. As Pérez de Cuéllar reported in 1990, "UNTAG turned out to be something far more than its somewhat pedestrian name implied. It established the workability of democratic procedures even in a terrain which at first looked most unpromising. It also proved the executive ability of the United Nations in successfully managing a complex operation which brought together 8,000 men and women from more than 100 nations . . . ."

Apartheid
The dramatic events that led to the dismantling of the apartheid system and the birth of a new South African nation are chronicled in the chapter on International Peace and Security. However, it was during Pérez de Cuéllar's tenure as secretary-general that the General Assembly held its 16th Special Session (12–14 December 1989) devoted to the question of apartheid. On 11 February 1990, South African President F.W. de Klerk released Nelson Mandela after 27 years of imprisonment. In response to the assembly's Resolution S-16/1, the secretary-general sent a high-level mission to South Africa in June 1990 to investigate the progress that had been made toward dismantling *apartheid*. By the end of his tenure, the process of change that would bear fruit in 1994, was firmly established.

Other Major Developments
Besides the problems of international peace and security listed above, the secretary-general's reports to the General Assembly made it clear he observed a growing appreciation in the international community of the need for cooperative action on a number of problems that transcend country borders and defy the ability of states to solve them independently. The recognition of the HIV/AIDS pandemic, its link to the plague of drug abuse and drug trafficking, and the concomitant links to international terrorism and organized crime all urgently required the attention of the world organization.

It was in the final years of Pérez de Cuéllar's tenure that the stage was set for what he called a new evolution in global society, in which humankind would make international covenants, not only between individuals and nations, but also between humankind and the environment: the 1987 Montreal Protocol on Substances that Deplete the Ozone Layer came into force in 1989; the Basel Convention on the Control of Transboundary Movements of Hazardous Wastes and Their Disposal was adopted in March 1989; the Second World Climate Conference was held in late 1990; and in February 1991, the first negotiations by the International Negotiating Committee on a framework convention on climate change began. Those negotiations would lead to the historic UN Conference on Environment and Development (UNCED), held in Rio de Janeiro in 1992 and dubbed the "Earth Summit." It was during the final years of the 1980s that an entirely new concept for the UN's work was developed: sustainable development.

DEVELOPMENTS UNDER BOUTROS BOUTROS-GHALI 1992–

Secretary-General Boutros Boutros-Ghali took office in an air of general euphoria over the accomplishments of the United Nations in the post-Cold War era. However, his first two years in office witnessed the proliferation of intractable and appalling regional conflicts in Haiti, Somalia, the former Yugoslavia and Rwanda, among others. The multiplicity and savagery of these conflicts cast a pall on the much hoped-for "new world order" which the end of the Cold War had inspired.

Soon after Boutros-Ghali's inauguration, in January 1992, the Security Council met in its first-ever summit session, at which the heads of states of all the members of the council convened in New York, in person. On 31 January 1992, they requested that the secretary-general submit to the Security Council "an analysis and recommendations on ways of strengthening and making more efficient within the framework and provisions of the Charter the capacity of the United Nations for preventive diplomacy, for peacemaking and for peacekeeping." Boutros-Ghali's *An Agenda for Peace* set forth an analysis of the world organization's new situation at a time of global transition with respect to international peace and security. This document is more fully explained in the chapter on International Peace and Security.

In May 1994, Boutros-Ghali responded to a 1992 request of the General Assembly to submit a similar report on development under the agenda item "Development and International Economic Cooperation." He declared that development was not only a fundamental human right, but also the most secure basis for peace. Although the UN had accomplished remarkable achievements in many areas, it was undeniable that after decades of efforts to assist the developing world, the poorest nations were falling even further behind, strangled by debt and social upheaval. Boutros-Ghali said that, although concerns had been expressed that the United Nations put greater emphasis on peacekeeping than development, the numbers of staff and the regular budgetary allocations did not support this fear. He posited that development could not proceed without a fundamental basis in peace, and went on to describe the ideal evolution of a peacekeeping/humanitarian aid operation into a situation of sustainable development.

Boutros-Ghali further maintained that protection of the environment was another fundamental concept for development. "In the developing world, ecological pressure threatens to undermine long-term development. Among many countries in transition, decades of disregard for the environment have left large areas poisoned and unable to sustain economic activity in the long term. Among the wealthiest nations, consumption patterns are depleting world resources in ways that jeopardize the future of world development," observed Boutros-Ghali. The concept of "sustainable development," as elaborated by UNCED in 1992, had to be strengthened as a guiding principle of development. Social justice and democracy were posited as the other pillars of a successfully developing country.

Boutros-Ghali suggested that the international mechanisms to create cooperative momentum in the development process existed in the United Nations system of organization but that it was "caught in a confining cycle. There is a resistance to multilateralism from those who fear a loss of national control. There is a reluctance to provide financial means to achieve agreed ends from those who lack conviction that assessments will benefit their own interests. And there is an unwillingness to engage in difficult operations by those who seek guarantees of perfect clarity and limited duration."

Haiti

Elected in UN-supervised elections in December 1990 and deposed by a military coup in September 1991, Haiti's President Jean-Bertrand Aristide turned to the United Nations and the Orga-nization of American States for assistance. In its Resolution 46/7 (September 1991), the General Assembly strongly condemned the "attempted illegal replacement of the Constitutional President of Haiti" and demanded that President Aristide be restored to power. It requested that the secretary-general cooperate with the Organization of American States (OAS) to restore the legally elected government in Haiti. A trade embargo and a halt to bilateral assistance were imposed on the illegal government, but there was little progress in negotiations. In December 1992, the secretary-general appointed Dante Caputo as Special Envoy for Haiti. The OAS also endorsed Caputo in January 1993. In its Resolution 47/20B (20 April 1993), the General Assembly mandated a joint UN/OAS International Civilian Mission to Haiti (known by its French acronym, MICIVIH) to be deployed throughout Haiti to report on the human rights situation there. On 16 June 1993, the Security Council imposed sanctions on Haiti. In July, talks were held on Governors Island, New York, and an agreement reached on specific measures relating to the return of President Aristide. In August 1993, the Security Council passed a resolution (862/1993) approving the dispatch of an advance team to prepare the way for the UN Mission in Haiti (UNMIH) which would supervise the transition. On 25 August 1993, the Haitian parliament ratified President Aristide's appointment of Robert Malval as prime minister-delegate during the transition period, as provided by the Governors Island Agreement. The Security Council then suspended the sanctions against Haiti.

On 27 September, the Security Council approved the deployment of UNMIH. However, on 11 October, armed civilians (known as "attachés") prevented the mission from debarking upon its arrival in Haiti. The attachés were known to be terrorizing the population through assassinations, attacks on the offices of the prime minister, and a general strike against UNMIH. It was also reported that police had facilitated, and in some cases participated in, these actions.

It became apparent that the military government was reneging on its promises under the Governors Island Agreement. On 13 October 1993, the Security Council reimposed its oil and arms embargo. That same month, most of the personnel of MICIVIH were evacuated, leaving a small administrative team to report on the alarming violence and violations of human rights being perpetuated, particularly against supporters of President Aristide.

In May 1994, the Security Council imposed expanded sanctions on Haiti, including a ban on commercial air travel. On 31 August 1994, the Security Council, in its resolution 940 (1994), authorized the use of a multinational force similar to the one used to repel Iraq from Kuwait. Specifically, the Security Council authorized UN members to: "form a multinational force under unified command and control and, in this framework, to use all necessary means to facilitate the departure from Haiti of the military leadership, consistent with the Governors Island Agreement, the prompt return of the legitimately elected President and the restoration of the legitimate authorities of the Government of Haiti, and to establish and maintain a secure and stable environment that will permit implementation of the Governors Island Agreement, on the understanding that the cost of implementing this temporary operation will be borne by the participating Member States." By the same resolution, the Security Council approved the eventual deployment of the 6,000-strong UNMIH force to assist with the restoration of democracy in Haiti.

At the time of writing, the multinational force had succeeded in landing in Haiti without significant bloodshed, pursuant to a last-minute negotiation headed by former United States President Jimmy Carter at the request of current President Bill Clinton.

Somalia

The downfall of Somalia's President Siad Barre in January 1991 resulted in a power struggle and clan warfare in many parts of

Somalia. In November 1991, the fighting intensified causing widespread death and destruction, and forcing hundreds of thousands of civilians to flee their homes. Almost 4.5 million people in Somalia—over half the estimated population—were threatened by severe malnutrition. It was estimated that as many as 300,000 people had died since November and at least 1.5 million were at immediate risk. The United Nations had instituted humanitarian operations in Somalia, but due to the deteriorating situation, it had been obliged to withdraw its personnel from the country.

In early 1992, Under Secretary-General for Political Affairs, James O.C. Jonah led a team to Somalia for talks aimed at bringing about a cessation of hostilities and securing access by the international relief community to civilians caught in the conflict. During that visit, unanimous support was expressed by all faction leaders for a United Nations role in bringing about national reconciliation. On 23 January 1992, the Security Council (Resolution 733/1992) urged all parties to cease hostilities, called for an embargo on military equipment, and requested the secretary-general to contact all parties involved in the conflict. In February, the secretary-general obtained the agreement of the two main factions in Mogadishu to an immediate cease-fire and on 3 March 1992, Interim President Ali Mahdi and General Mohamed Farah Aidid signed an "Agreement on the Implementation of a Cease-fire." The agreement also included acceptance of a United Nations security component for convoys of humanitarian assistance and deployment of 20 military observers on each side of Mogadishu to monitor the cease-fire.

On 24 April 1992, the Security Council adopted resolution 751 (1992) and established a UN Operation in Somalia (UNOSOM). The total strength of UNOSOM was eventually established at 4,219 troops to protect the representatives of the six main UN organizations at work in Somalia coordinating humanitarian efforts (FAO, UNDP, UNICEF, UNHCR, WFP and WHO). In addition, more than 30 non-governmental organizations were working in Somalia as "implementing partners" of the UN. However, in October the security situation deteriorated, as some factions refused to agree to the deployment of UN troops to assure delivery of humanitarian aid to people in great need. According to some estimates, as many as 3,000 persons a day were dying of starvation, while warehouses remained stocked with food supplied by the humanitarian agencies. On 3 December 1992, the Security Council unanimously adopted Resolution 794 (1992) authorizing the use of "all necessary means to establish as soon as possible a secure environment for humanitarian relief operations in Somalia." A Unified Task Force (UNITAF), led by United States troops, was deployed in Mogadishu on 9 December 1992.

On 3 March 1993, the secretary-general recommended the Security Council establish a new force, UNOSOM II, to take over from UNITAF, which had deployed approximately 37,000 troops in southern and central Somalia. The secretary-general appointed Admiral Jonathan T. Howe (Ret.) of the United States as his new Special Representative for Somalia to oversee the transition from UNITAF to UNOSOM II. A Conference on National Reconciliation in Somalia was convened on 15 March 1993 in Addis Ababa, Ethiopia. It was attended by the leaders of 15 Somali political movements and representatives of regional organizations. After two weeks of intensive negotiations, the 15 Somali leaders signed an Agreement for disarmament and security, rehabilitation and reconstruction, restoration of property and settlement of disputes, and transitional mechanisms.

UNOSOM II took over from UNITAF on 4 May 1993, and proceeded to fulfill its mandate to disarm the Somali factions who were terrorizing the people and obstructing humanitarian activities. This provoked the hostility of a few clan leaders. On 5 June, 25 Pakistani soldiers were killed, 10 were missing and 54 were wounded in a series of ambushes and armed attacks against UNOSOM II troops throughout Mogadishu. The Security Coun-

cil reaffirmed that the secretary-general was authorized to take all necessary measures against those responsible for armed attacks, and on 12 June 1993, UNOSOM II initiated decisive military action in south Mogadishu.

On 3 October 1993, United States Rangers, deployed in support of UNOSOM II, but not under UN command, launched an operation in south Mogadishu aimed at capturing a number of key aides of General Aidid who were suspected of complicity in the 5 June attack, as well as subsequent attacks on UN personnel and facilities. Two US helicopters were shot down by Somali militiamen using automatic weapons and rocket-propelled grenades. While evacuating the detainees, the Rangers came under concentrated fire, and 18 US soldiers were killed and 75 wounded. The bodies of the US soldiers were subjected to humiliating treatment. Following these events, the US both reinforced its Quick Reaction Force in Somalia and announced its intention to withdraw its forces from Somalia by 31 March 1994.

On 9 October 1993, General Aidid's faction declared a unilateral cessation of hostilities against UNOSOM II, but the situation remained tense. It was reported that the major factions were rearming in anticipation of renewed fighting. UNOSOM II's mandate to force the factions to disarm was unenforceable.

In February 1994, the leaders of the two main Somali factions met in Nairobi and signed a Declaration of National Reconciliation on 24 March, committing themselves to repudiate any form of violence. A National Reconciliation Conference was scheduled for 15 May 1994; however, this conference was postponed. As of March 1994, UNOSOM II's strength stood at nearly 18,500 troops.

The Former Yugoslavia

In June 1991, the Republics of Croatia and Slovenia declared themselves independent from Yugoslavia. Fighting broke out when Serbs living in Croatia, supported by the Yugoslavian Army, opposed this move. European Community efforts to end hostilities were unsuccessful. On 25 September 1992, the United Nations Security Council unanimously adopted resolution 713 (1991) calling on all states to implement an arms embargo to Yugoslavia. Then Secretary-General Pérez de Cuéllar appointed former US Secretary of State Cyrus Vance as his personal envoy for Yugoslavia. Vance undertook several missions to Yugoslavia and discussed with the parties the feasibility of deploying a UN peacekeeping operation. An unconditional cease-fire was signed on 2 January 1992, and the Security Council approved the dispatch of a group of 50 military liaison officers to Yugoslavia to use their good offices to promote maintenance of the cease-fire. However, some political groups in Yugoslavia objected to the UN plan for a peacekeeping mission. Nevertheless, on 21 February 1992, the Security Council established the United Nations Protection Force (UNPROFOR) as an interim arrangement to create conditions of peace and security required for the negotiation of an overall settlement of the Yugoslav crisis.

On 30 April 1992, the secretary-general deployed 40 military observers to the Mostar region of Bosnia and Herzegovina in response to the deteriorating security situation there. However, fighting between Bosnian Muslims and Croats on one side, and Bosnian Serbs on the other, intensified. UNPROFOR, which had established its headquarters in Sarajevo, the capital, was obliged to relocate to Zagreb, the capital of Croatia.

A situation tragically similar to that in Somalia quickly developed. UN humanitarian convoys could not reach civilians trapped in the conflict. The Security Council, in its resolution 770 (1992) once again invoked Chapter VII of the Charter and called on states to "take nationally or through regional agencies or arrangements all measures necessary" to facilitate the delivery of humanitarian assistance to Sarajevo and other parts of Bosnia and Herzegovina. The situation continued to deteriorate and the

Security Council declared a "no-fly zone" to prevent the bombing of Sarajevo and other villages. On 13 March 1993 three unidentified aircraft dropped bombs on two villages, the first time that the "no-fly zone" had been violated since its declaration. On 31 March the Security Council extended its ban on flights, and authorized NATO to enforce the no-fly zone. Between the establishment of the no-fly zone and April 1994, 1,620 violations of the ban on flights over Bosnian airspace were registered. On 28 February 1994, NATO fighters in the airspace of Bosnia and Herzegovina shot down four of six jets which had defied the international ban on military flights and ignored two warnings.

On 27 April 1994, the Security Council increased the strength of UNPROFOR to 33,891. Negotiations for a resolution of the crisis in the former Yugoslavia continued in July 1994.

Cambodia

The UN Transitional Authority in Cambodia (UNTAC) successfully undertook its mission to conduct elections and repatriate more than 360,000 refugees. Its 21,000 military, police, and civilian personnel were fully deployed by mid-1992. Elections were held in May 1993, and 96 percent of the eligible population, nearly 4.7 million people, registered to vote. Despite concerns about disruption by the National Army of Democratic Kampuchea, which had withdrawn from the process, a six-week election campaign in which 20 political parties took part was successfully held. On 10 June, the secretary-general's special representative declared that his view that the elections had been free and fair. The newly elected Constituent Assembly held its inaugural meeting on 4 June 1993 to begin its task of drafting and adopting a new constitution. The four Cambodian political parties that won seats in the election agreed to join in an interim administration for the remainder of the transitional period. UNTAC's mandate terminated in November 1993. A small Military Liaison Team remained in the country for six months as observers. The liaison team's mandate expired on 15 May 1994, and they were replaced by three military officers assisting the secretary-general's special representative in Cambodia.

INTERNATIONAL PEACE AND SECURITY

The first purpose of the UN, as stated in Article 1 of its charter, is the maintenance of international peace and security. To this end, the organization is required "to take effective collective measures for the prevention and removal of threats to the peace, and for the suppression of acts of aggression or other breaches of the peace, and to bring about by peaceful means . . . adjustment or settlement of international disputes or situations which might lead to a breach of the peace." The UN has undertaken this heavy responsibility with varying levels of success over the years. However, in the nuclear era, international security in the absence of an organization like the United Nations is unimaginable. More than 800 UN peacekeepers from 43 countries died in the service of international peace and security between 1945 and 1992. In recognition of their invaluable contribution to world peace, the United Nations peacekeeping forces were awarded the Nobel Peace Prize in 1988.

BASIC CHARTER PROVISIONS
The basic provisions of the charter defining the functions of the Security Council and the General Assembly are summarized here, but fuller accounts will be found in the chapters on those bodies, which complement the present chapter.

1. *Relative Powers of the Security Council and the General Assembly.* Under Article 24 of the charter, the Security Council has "primary responsibility" in questions of peace and security. It is invested with special powers enabling it to decide, on behalf of the entire UN membership, to take collective action when peace is threatened (Articles 39–42) and is empowered to negotiate agreements with individual members of the UN for the provision of armed forces necessary to maintain international security and to determine how many members shall participate in any collective action undertaken (Articles 43–48).

The General Assembly, on the other hand, is empowered only to consider and make recommendations, either to the Security Council or to particular states, on matters pertaining to peace and security. Moreover, under Articles 11 and 12, it may discuss but may not make actual recommendations on any special dispute between nations that is currently under consideration by the Security Council. However, though the Assembly is not expressly empowered to take action, neither is it expressly prohibited from doing so. In the only charter provision touching on the subject, paragraph 2 of Article 11—which is the focus of conflicting interpretation in the long-standing constitutional controversy on the financing of certain General Assembly-sponsored peacekeeping operations—the actual wording is as follows: "Any such question [of international peace and security] on which action is necessary shall be referred to the Security Council by the General Assembly either before or after discussion."

2. *Bringing a Dispute or Serious Situation Before the UN.* Although the charter firmly establishes the primacy of the Security Council over the General Assembly in matters of peace and security, it does not stipulate that disputes or serious situations must be discussed in the Security Council before they are discussed by the General Assembly. A dispute may be brought before the UN in a variety of ways specified in the charter without order of preference. One or more of the disputing parties may bring the matter before the Security Council voluntarily, or the council

itself may choose to exercise its constitutional right to investigate a dispute at its own discretion; or any UN member, whether or not it is involved in the dispute, may propose the matter for discussion by the General Assembly; or a non-UN member that is a party to the dispute may—under certain conditions—bring it to the attention of the General Assembly; or the Security Council may ask the General Assembly to discuss the matter.

Despite these liberal provisions, the charter does not stipulate that all political disputes between states should be brought before the UN. Article 33, for example, enjoins UN members "first of all" to seek a solution to their differences on their own initiative (though if they fail to take this initiative, the Security Council is empowered to call upon them to do so). Only after their efforts to achieve a peaceful settlement have proved fruitless are the disputing parties obliged by the charter to refer the matter to the Security Council. Again, the UN was never intended by its founders to be regarded as the sole international agency for dealing with political disputes. Thus, Article 52 states that nothing in the charter "precludes the existence of regional arrangements or agencies for dealing with such matters relating to the maintenance of international peace and security as are appropriate for regional action" and that members participating in such regional arrangements or agencies "shall make every effort to achieve pacific settlement of local disputes through such regional arrangements or by such regional agencies before referring them to the Security Council."

POLITICAL BACKGROUND TO THE UN'S PEACEKEEPING ACTION
The UN's efforts to preserve international peace and security are the most contentious aspect of its entire work, because of the inherently political nature of its role and the fact that both the Security Council and the General Assembly are essentially political bodies, not courts of law that apportion blame and impartially hand down judgments drawn from a set of established legal codes. Their task in disputes brought before them is to find a compromise solution that is at once satisfactory to all parties, based on the political realities of the world situation and consistent with the principles of the charter. In this way, each local dispute brought before the UN automatically becomes a dispute involving the entire membership, as nations express differing views on the appropriate action to be taken by consensus of the membership.

The involvement of the general membership in all disputes is precisely what the founders of the UN intended—as a means of ensuring collective international responsibility for political solutions that are both just and realistic. However, in order to provide a counterweight to the unavoidable taking of sides, they established the principle of unanimity among the great powers by bestowing the right of veto on the permanent members of the Security Council. The workability of this principle in practice presupposed a basic measure of cooperation among the great powers. As events turned out, however, unanimity among the great powers proved to be a chimera. Within a year of the signing of the charter, the world was in the throes of the cold war, and the United States and USSR were engaged in a power struggle. The effects of this unexpected political development on the UN's work in maintaining international peace and security were immediate and devastating. Each dispute between the smaller nations that came before the UN was subsumed under the developing power struggle between the giants. As a result, between 1945 and 1990, the Security Council was deadlocked again and again by 279 vetoes. Furthermore, the charter requirements for agreement on the provision of armed forces for the UN could not be met.

Whereas the USSR looked to the Security Council and the veto as its power instrument in the UN, the United States looked to the support of the majority vote in the General Assembly. In order to circumvent the Soviet veto in the Security Council, and being at that time confident of majority support for most of its substantive policy objectives, the United States spearheaded a drive to turn the General Assembly into a body for action in periods of international crisis. This drive culminated in the adoption in 1950 of the Uniting for Peace Resolution, which empowered the General Assembly to undertake collective measures for maintaining or restoring peace when the Security Council found itself unable to act in times of emergency (for the terms of the resolution, see the chapter on the General Assembly). It was the United States, represented by Secretary of State Dean Acheson, that originated the proposal for the resolution. Although some of the small nations expressed reservations about certain clauses, most of them were eager to participate more fully in the UN's peace and security responsibilities. Only India and Argentina abstained in the vote, and only the Soviet bloc voted against the resolution, branding it as illegal and contrary to the charter.

The Uniting for Peace Resolution has been invoked in three major crises: the Korean War, the Suez crisis, and the Congo crisis (discussed under Case Histories below). In all three instances, the Security Council found itself deadlocked, and General Assembly action was deemed essential by the majority of members. Nevertheless, despite its proven usefulness as an instrument of restoring peace in these instances, the resolution seems unlikely to be invoked in future disputes. Certain countries questioned the legality of the resolution and of the General Assembly's action taken under it, and they felt justified on these grounds in refusing to contribute to the costs of the Suez and Congo peacekeeping operations.

At the end of the 1980s, the demise of the Soviet Union and the cold war dramatically changed this state of affairs. Within a few short years the entire Soviet bloc was dissolved and a new era of cooperation between the United States and the Russian Federation raised hopes that the Security Council would begin to fulfill the function foreseen for it by the organization's founders. However, the political vacuum created by the collapse of the East-West stalemate was followed by an eruption of intransigent, deadly regional conflicts and civil wars, particularly in Africa and Eastern Europe. In the 43 years between 1945 and 1988, the Security Council authorized 13 peacekeeping operations. In only four short years, between 1988 and 1992, it authorized another 13 peacekeeping operations. By the end of 1994, 17 peacekeeping operations were severely taxing the ability and political will of member states to respond with personnel and financial contributions.

TYPES OF ACTION TAKEN BY THE UN

The UN has two main responsibilities with respect to the political disputes that are brought before it by states: helping the parties concerned to arrive at a peaceful settlement of the issue that caused the dispute, and maintaining the peace if animosities threaten to erupt into violence or restoring the peace if hostilities have already broken out.

An Agenda for Peace

In response to the profoundly altered global political situation, on 31 January 1992, the Security Council met in a historic summit session attended by 13 heads of state and two foreign ministers. At that session, the Security Council requested Secretary-General Boutros Boutros-Ghali to prepare an analysis and recommendations on ways to strengthen UN peacekeeping efforts. In June 1992 the Secretary-General submitted *An Agenda for Peace*. This important document challenged member states to adapt their world organization to the new international situation with more effective and rational peacekeeping procedures. The document began by defining four types of peace-related activities:

Preventive Diplomacy. Defined as action to prevent disputes from arising and to prevent existing disputes from escalating into conflicts. The Secretary-General listed a number of different actions that constituted preventive diplomacy: confidence building (exchange of military missions, opening channels for the exchange of information, and providing monitoring for regional arms reduction agreements), fact-finding missions, early warning from regional organizations with observer status at the United Nations, preventive deployment of a UN force before hostilities occur, and the establishment of demilitarized zones.

Peacemaking. Action to bring hostile parties to agreement through peaceful means like those outlined in Chapter VI of the UN Charter, namely: negotiation, enquiry, mediation, conciliation, arbitration, judicial settlement or appealing to regional organizations.

The Secretary-General suggested that the International Court of Justice remained an underused resource for peaceful settlement of international disputes. He recommended that member states that had not accepted the general jurisdiction of the International Court of Justice, do so before the end of the UN Decade of International Law in the year 2000. Another tool for peacemaking was the imposition of economic sanctions under Article 41 of the charter. The main difficulty with this tool was compensating member states that would find their own economies crippled by the imposition of sanctions on an offending state.

Peacekeeping. Defined as the deployment of a UN force to the field, usually with the consent of the parties to the conflict. Peacekeeping could involve military, police, and civilian personnel. The UN pioneered this new form of military deployment during the early conflicts in the Middle East and the Congo. Peacekeeping troops serve at the request of all the parties to a conflict, for example, to monitor implementation of a cease-fire, or to prevent shipments of weapons across borders. They may also serve to monitor a demilitarized zone and provide a buffer between combatants. Peacekeeping forces, however, are only lightly armed and authorized to use force only in self-defense. By its very nature, peacekeeping implies an even-handed treatment of all the parties in a conflict.

Peace Enforcement. Although not officially defined as a separate concept in *An Agenda for Peace*, the Secretary-General did propose the creation, under Article 43 of the charter, of forces which could respond quickly and forcefully to imminent or outright aggression. In fact, the UN had sometimes been called upon to send forces to restore a cease-fire. In the Secretary-General's proposal, these troops would be maintained and specially trained by the armed forces of member states. When called upon, they would be more heavily armed than peacekeeping forces and authorized to use deadly force to stop combatants. The Secretary-General proposed that these special units would be on call for quick response to the early stages of an international crisis. In the post–cold war era, peace enforcement had already found expression in the Security Council's authorization of a multinational force (sanctioned by the UN but not, however, under UN administration) led by the United States to suppress Iraq's 1991 invasion of Kuwait.

However, the concept of peace enforcement remains controversial, as some experts and member countries maintain that there is no basis in the UN charter for an organization dedicated to international peace to settle disputes with military force. Under the charter, member states are meant to settle their disputes by peaceful means.

On the other hand, Article 43 of the charter provides for member states to make military forces available to the Security Council. In fact, it was originally envisioned that the United States alone would provide twenty divisions (over 300,000 troops), a very large naval force, 1,250 bombers, and 2,250 fighters. These provisions were never implemented due to lack of consensus.

In 1993, former Undersecretary-General Brian Urquhart, who participated in the management of 15 peacekeeping operations during his 40-year tenure at the United Nations, proposed the creation of an elite UN-trained military force made up of international volunteers, not soldiers seconded from national forces. Urquhart suggested that such a volunteer force would give the Security Council the ability to back up preventive diplomacy with immediate peace enforcement. "Clearly, a timely intervention by a relatively small but highly trained force, willing and authorized to take combat risks and representing the will of the international community, could make a decisive difference in the early stages of a crisis," said Urquhart in the journal "Foreign Policy." Urquhart suggested that such a force might have been used effectively, for example, during the attempted deployment of the UN Mission in Haiti (UNMIH). When the United States naval ship carrying the first deployment of troops arrived at Port au Prince in October 1993, the ship was prevented from landing by a disorganized and violent demonstration of armed civilians at the port. By August 1994, the escalating crisis in Haiti had led the Security Council to authorize a multinational force, similar to that used in the Iraq-Kuwait crisis, to restore the democratically elected government of Haiti. The escalation might have been prevented if UNMIH had been enabled to carry out its mandate.

Peace Building. Defined as "action to identify and support structures which will tend to strengthen and solidify peace in order to avoid a relapse into conflict."

The UN had already begun to develop the concept of "peace building" as early as 1990, when the UN Observer Group in Central America supervised Nicaraguan elections which were certified to be "free and fair" by the UN Observer Mission to Verify the Electoral Process in Nicaragua (ONUVEN).

Since then the demand for UN electoral assistance has grown enormously. Before 1992, the UN supervised elections in Haiti, Namibia, and Nicaragua. However, between January 1992 and June 1994, the United Nations received 56 requests for electoral assistance. The organization's Electoral Assistance Unit was established in 1992 and operates within the Department of Peacekeeping Operations. It provided assistance to 53 of those states. Following is a list of member states requesting and receiving assistance during this period: Albania, Argentina, Azerbaijan, Brazil, Burundi, Cameroon, Central African Republic, Chad, Colombia, Congo, Djibouti, El Salvador, Equatorial Guinea, Eritrea, Estonia, Ethiopia, Gabon, Ghana, Guinea, Guinea-Bissau, Guyana, Kenya, Latvia, Lesotho, Liberia, Madagascar, Malawi, Mozambique, Namibia, Netherlands Antilles, Nicaragua, Niger, Panama, Paraguay, Peru, Philippines, Romania, Russia, Rwanda, Senegal, Seychelles, Sierra Leone, South Africa, Swaziland, Togo, Uganda, and Western Sahara. The Electoral Assistance Unit is supported by the UN Trust Fund for Electoral Observation, a voluntary fund which, in 1994, was supported by contributions from Austria, Denmark, Iceland, Ireland, Norway, Sweden, Switzerland, and the United Kingdom.

Besides building peace by strengthening a country's democratic infrastructure, the Secretary-General also included the following activities under the concept of peace building: clearing land-mines so that agriculture and transportation may be resumed safely; disarming the warring parties; taking custody of and destroying weapons; repatriating refugees; training security personnel; edu-cational and cultural exchanges; and joint projects to develop agriculture, improve transportation, or utilize shared natural resources.

The Cost of Waging Peace

In *Renewing the United Nations System* (Dag Hammarskjöld Foundation, 1994), co-authors Brian Urquhart and Erskine Childers (former senior adviser to the UN Director General for Development and International Cooperation) cite the following figures: "By early 1993 the UN was deploying four times the number of troops, 70 times more police and over 100 times the number of civilian personnel as in 1987, at nearly 10 times the annual cost. As of 30 April 1994 the UN had contributions from 66 countries of 65,838 troops, 2,400 military observers, and 1,307 civilian and police personnel, with possible further deployments (and costs) evolving almost weekly relative to situations like those in Haiti, Rwanda and the former Yugoslavia. The projected costs of peace-keeping rose from some US$600 million in 1991 to an estimated US$2.3 billion for 1993."

In fact, in May 1994, the Secretary-General was unable to obtain 5,500 troops from African nations to protect refugees and international aid workers caught in the bloody Rwandan civil war. He attributed this to donor fatigue among the countries that frequently assign troops to UN operations.

However, when compared to the costs incurred during international conflicts, the price of peacekeeping shrinks to insignificance. The United States Army spent more to maintain a single division *not* engaged in battle, than the UN's entire 1989 expenditure for peacekeeping (approximately US$638 million). The 1992 budget for peacekeeping roughly equaled the cost of one nuclear-powered attack submarine. In 1991 the United States spent approximately US$63 billion during operation Desert Storm, 100 times more than the amount spent for UN peacekeeping worldwide that year. Global defense expenditures at the end of the 1980s had approached US$1 trillion per year (or US$2 million per minute), monopolizing precious resources that, especially in developing countries, are desperately needed for social programs. Of course, these monetary figures do not adequately take into account the tragic price paid in human death and suffering during war.

Most UN peacekeeping operations are not financed from the organization's regular budget, but from special accounts established by the organization to fund each particular operation. Each member is then assessed for a share of the mission's estimated cost. Special assessments for peacekeeping are divided into three categories. The five permanent members of the Security Council pay about 22 percent more than the regular scale of assessments because of their greater influence over Security Council decisions (by virtue of holding the power of veto). Other developed industrial states pay the same share for peacekeeping as they pay for the regular budget. Wealthier developing countries pay one-fifth of their regular budget share for peacekeeping. The poorest nations (least developed countries, or LDCs) pay one-tenth of their regular share. There are certain inequities to this arrangement. For example, 15 "developing" states with per capita GNPs of $5,000 or more still are assessed only one-fifth of their regular budget assessment for peacekeeping (United Arab Emirates, Kuwait, Qatar, Brunei, Singapore, Bahamas, Israel, Cyprus, Barbados, Bahrain, Saudi Arabia, Malta, Greece, Libya, and Oman).

A recurrent and critical problem for UN peacekeeping has been the consistent shortfall in the payment of members' assessed contributions. In 1992 the unpaid arrears of members to the UN for peacekeeping operations was more than US$800 million. The organization essentially passes the shortfall on to the nations contributing troops, by delaying payments it owes to them. These nations are effectively paying for peacekeeping twice: once with their special assessment, and again when they must pay themselves for the costs of the troops and equipment they contribute.

For the above reasons, the Secretary-General suggested in his *Agenda for Peace* that contributions to UN peacekeeping operations be financed from defence budgets, rather than from foreign affairs budgets. Other innovative proposals in the agenda included obtaining standing commitments from member states as to the numbers and kinds of skilled personnel they can offer the United Nations as new operations arise; new arrangements for training peacekeeping personnel, including indispensable civilian and police staff; stockpiling basic peacekeeping equipment (vehicles, communications equipment, generators, etc.); and air and sea lift capacity to be provided by member states either free of cost or at lower than commercial rates.

Genesis of a Peacekeeping Mission

Many missions are planned in response to a crisis, so the steps in mounting them happen more or less simultaneously. When more time is available, the following sequence of events is usually adhered to:

- Mediation. The Secretary-General may be instructed to dispatch field survey missions, or may choose to send his own special representative to help achieve a political settlement.
- Initial Design. The mission concept is presented to the Security Council for its preliminary approval.
- Security Council Directive. The Security Council directs the Secretary-General to report back within a specified amount of time with a plan for the mission that includes its size, structure, duties, and timeline.
- Mission Design. Units of the Department of Peacekeeping Operations put together a plan for the mission.
- Security Council approval obtained.
- Creation and verification of the mission budget.
- Submission of the budget to the Fifth Committee (Financial).
- Fifth Committee submits the budget to the General Assembly for approval.
- Assessment letters are sent to the member states.

Until approved by the General Assembly, the Secretary-General cannot make contractual commitments for equipment, transport, or other services in excess of a US$10 million annual spending authority for special circumstances. The length of the approval process creates a devastating time lag when an international crisis develops that requires a timely response.

Chronology of Peacekeeping Operations

Since 1945, there have been 33 UN peacekeeping or observer missions. The following is a list of most of the UN peacekeeping operations, arranged in chronological order. Unless otherwise noted, figures are accurate as at 31 October 1993. For more background on the conflicts and the countries receiving UN peacekeeping missions, the reader is referred to the country entries in Volumes I through IV of this encyclopedia.

UNTSO-United Nations Truce Supervision Organization

Duration: June 1948 to present.
Headquarters: Government House, Jerusalem.
Strength: 220 military observers.
Fatalities: 28.
Mandate: Initially to supervise the original truce of 1948; in 1949, following the conclusion of armistice agreements between Israel and its Arab neighbors (Egypt, Jordan, Lebanon and Syria), its responsibility became to assist the parties in supervising the application and observance of those agreements. However, over the years, its activities and responsibilities have expanded to cover a number of UN-supervised emergency situations in Israel, Syria, and Lebanon.
Composition: UNTSO's military observers come from 19 con-

tributing countries: Argentina, Australia, Austria, Belgium, Canada, Chile, China, Denmark, Finland, France, Ireland, Italy, Netherlands, New Zealand, Norway, Russian Federation, Sweden, Switzerland, and United States.
Annual cost: approximately US$31 million.

UNMOGIP-United Nations Military Observer Group in India and Pakistan

Duration: January 1949 to present.
Location: The cease-fire line between India and Pakistan in the state of Jammu and Kashmir.
Strength: 39 military observers.
Fatalities: 6.
Mandate: To observe developments pertaining to the strict observance of the cease-fire of 17 December 1971 and report to the Secretary-General.
Composition: UNMOGIP's military observers come from eight countries: Belgium, Chile, Denmark, Finland, Italy, Norway, Sweden, and Uruguay.
Annual cost: approximately US$7 million.

UNEF I-First United Nations Emergency Force

Duration: November 1956 to June 1967.
Location: Initially the Suez Canal sector and the Sinai peninsula; later, along the Armistice Demarcation Line in the Gaza area and the Egyptian side of the international frontier in the Sinai peninsula..
Strength: At peak: 6,000; at end: 3,400.
Fatalities: 90.
Mandate: To secure and to supervise the cessation of hostilities, including the withdrawal of the armed forces of France, Israel, and the United Kingdom from Egyptian territory, and to serve as a buffer between the Egyptian and Israeli forces.
Composition: Brazil, Canada, Colombia, Denmark, Finland, India, Indonesia, Norway, Sweden, and Yugoslavia.
Total cost: approximately US$199 million.

UNOGIL-United Nations Observation Group in Lebanon

Duration: June 1958 to December 1958.
Location: Beirut, Lebanon.
Strength: 591 military observers (maximum).
Fatalities: None.
Mandate: To ensure that there was no illegal infiltration of personnel or supply of arms across the Lebanese border.
Composition: Forces from 21 countries.
Total cost: approximately US$3.7 million.

ONUC-United Nations Operation in the Congo

Duration: July 1960 to June 1964.
Location: Leopoldville (now Kinshasa), Republic of Congo (now Zaire).
Strength: Peak: 19,825.
Fatalities: 234.
Mandate: Initially, to ensure withdrawal of Belgian forces and assist the government in maintaining law and order; later, to maintain territorial integrity and independence of the Congo and to prevent the occurrence of civil war.
Composition: Argentina, Brazil, Canada, Denmark, Ethiopia, Ghana, Guinea, India, Indonesia, Ireland, Italy, Liberia, Malaysia, Mali, Morocco, Netherlands, Nigeria, Norway, Pakistan, Sudan, Sweden, Tunisia, Yugoslavia.
Total cost: approximately US$408 million.

UNSF-United Nations Security Force in West New Guinea (West Irian)

Duration: October 1962 to April 1963.
Location: Hollandia, West Irian (now Jayaphra, Indonesia).

Strength: 1,600.
Fatalities: None.
Mandate: To maintain peace and security in the territory under the UN Temporary Executive Authority established by agreement between Indonesia and the Netherlands while the administration of the territory was transfered to Indonesia.
Composition: Canada, Pakistan, United States.
Total cost: approximately US$26.4 million (cost borne by Netherlands and Indonesia).

UNYOM-United Nations Yemen Observations Mission
Duration: July 1963 to September 1964.
Location: Sana'a, Yemen.
Strength: 25 military observers; 114 members of a reconnaissance unit; 50 members of an air unit.
Fatalities: None.
Mandate: To observe and certify the implementation of the disengagement agreement between Saudi Arabia and the United Arab Republic (now Egypt and Syria).
Composition: Canada, Yugoslavia.
Total cost: approximately US$1.8 million (cost borne by Saudi Arabia and Egypt).

UNFICYP-United Nations Peacekeeping Force in Cyprus
Duration: March 1964 to present.
Location: Cyprus.
Strength: 1,208 troops and support personnel, 12 military observers and 35 civilian police.
Fatalities: 165.
Mandate: To prevent a recurrence of fighting between Turkish-backed Cypriots and Greek-backed Cypriots; to contribute to the maintenance and restoration of law and order.
Composition: The operational elements of UNFICYP are provided by Argentina, Australia, Austria, Canada, Denmark, Finland, Hungary, Ireland, Sweden, and the United Kingdom. There are also 34 international civilian personnel and 381 locally recruited staff.
Annual cost: approximately US$45 million.

DOMREP-Mission of the Representative of the Secretary-General in the Dominican Republic
Duration: May 1965 to October 1966.
Location: Santo Domingo, Dominican Republic.
Strength: Two military observers.
Fatalities: None.
Mandate: To observe the situation and to report on breaches of the cease-fire between the two *de facto* authorities.
Composition: None.
Annual cost: US$275,831 (through UN regular budget).

UNIPOM-United Nations India-Pakistan Observation Mission
Duration: September 1965 to March 1966.
Location: Lahore, Pakistan, and Amritsar, India (deployed along the India/Pakistan border between Kashmir and the Arabian Sea).
Strength: 96 military observers (maximum).
Fatalities: None.
Mandate: To supervise the cease-fire along the India/Pakistan border (except the State of Jammu and Kashmir where UNMOGIP operates) and the withdrawal of all armed personnel to the positions held before 5 August 1965.
Composition: Australia, Belgium, Brazil, Burma, Canada, Chile, Denmark, Ethiopia, Finland, Ireland, Italy, Nepal, Netherlands, New Zealand, Nigeria, Norway, Sweden, Sri Lanka, Venezuela.
Total cost: US$1,713,280.

UNEF II-Second United Nations Emergency Force.
Duration: October 1973 to July 1979.
Location: Suez Canal sector and later the Sinai peninsula.
Strength: Peak: 7,000; end: 4,000.
Fatalities: 52.
Mandate: To supervise the cease-fire between Egyptian and Israeli forces; later, to supervise the redeployment of those forces and act as a buffer between them.
Composition: Australia, Austria, Canada, Finland, Ghana, Indonesia, Ireland, Nepal, Panama, Peru, Poland, Senegal, Sweden.
Total cost: approximately US$446.5 million.

UNDOF-United Nations Disengagement Observer Force
Duration: June 1974 to present.
Location: Syrian Golan Heights.
Strength: 1,107 troops.
Fatalities: 31.
Mandate: To maintain the cease-fire between Israel and Syria; supervise the disengagement of Israeli and Syrian forces; supervise the areas of separation and limitation.
Composition: Originally composed of Austrian and Peruvian infantry units and Canadian and Polish logistic elements. Currently composed of contingents from Austria, Canada, Finland, and Poland.
Annual cost: approximately US$36 million.

UNIFIL-United Nations Interim Force in Lebanon
Duration: March 1978 to present.
Location: Southern Lebanon.
Strength: 5,266 troops and approximately 520 international and local civilian staff.
Fatalities: 193.
Mandate: To confirm the withdrawal of Israeli forces from southern Lebanon; restore international peace and security; assist the government of Lebanon in ensuring the return of its effective authority in the area.
Composition: Troops provided by Fiji, Finland, France, Ghana, Ireland, Italy, Nepal, Norway, Poland, and Sweden.
Annual cost: approximately US$232 million.

UNGOMAP-United Nations Good Offices Mission in Afghanistan and Pakistan
Duration: April 1988 to March 1990.
Location: Kabul, Afghanistan, and Islamabad, Pakistan.
Strength: 50 military observers.
Fatalities: None.
Mandate: To assist in monitoring the implementation of the 1988 peace settlement between Afghanistan and Pakistan.
Composition: Austria, Canada, Denmark, Finland, Fiji, Ghana, Ireland, Nepal, Poland, and Sweden.
Cost: approximately US$14 million.

UNIIMOG-United Nations Iran-Iraq Military Observer Group
Duration: August 1988 to February 1991.
Location: The 740-mile border between Iran and Iraq (headquarters in both Baghdad, Iraq, and Teheran, Iran).
Strength: 105 observers; 53 military personnel; 93 local staff.
Fatalities: 1.
Mandate: To verify, confirm, and supervise the cease-fire and withdrawal of troops.
Composition: Argentina, Australia, Austria, Bangladesh, Canada, Denmark, Finland, Ghana, Hungary, India, Indonesia, Ireland, Italy, Kenya, Malaysia, New Zealand, Nigeria, Norway, Peru, Poland, Senegal, Sweden, Turkey, Uruguay, Yugoslavia, Zambia.
Total cost: approximately US$235 million.

UNAVEM I-United Nations Angola Verification Mission I
Duration: January 1989 to June 1991.
Location: Luanda, Angola.
Strength: Peak: 70 military observers; 22 international staff; 15 local staff.
Fatalities: None.
Mandate: To monitor the withdrawal of Cuban troops from Angola.
Composition: Algeria, Argentina, Brazil, Congo, Czechoslovakia, India, Jordan, Norway, Spain, Yugoslavia.
Total cost: approximately US$18.8 million.

UNTAG-United Nations Transition Assistance Group.
Duration: April 1989 to March 1990.
Location: Windhoek, Namibia.
Maximum strength: Approximately 4,500 military personnel; 1,500 police; 2,000 civilian personnel; 1,000 election observers.
Fatalities: 19.
Mandate: To monitor and supervise the Namibia independence plan, including supervision of elections to a Constituent Assembly.
Composition: Argentina, Australia, Austria, Bangladesh, Canada, Denmark, Finland, Ghana, Hungary, India, Indonesia, Ireland, Italy, Kenya, Malaysia, New Zealand, Nigeria, Norway, Peru, Poland, Senegal, Sweden, Turkey, Uruguay, Yugoslavia, Zambia.
Total cost: approximately US$368.3 million.

ONUCA-United Nations Observer Group in Central America
Duration: November 1989 to January 1992.
Location: Costa Rica, El Salvador, Guatemala, Honduras, and Nicaragua (headquarters in Tegucigalpa).
Strength: Peak: 1,195; end: 338.
Fatalities: None.
Mandate: Initially, to verify the compliance of the five Central American countries with their security undertakings (the Esquipulas II Agreement, 1987) to cease aid to insurrectionist movements in the region and not to allow their territory to be used for attacks on other states; later, to monitor the demobilization of the Nicaraguan resistance (the "Contras").
Composition: Argentina, Brazil, Canada, Colombia, Ecuador, India, Ireland, Spain, Sweden, Venezuela.
Total cost: approximately US$87 million.

UNIKOM-United Nations Iraq-Kuwait Observation Mission.
Duration: April 1991 to present.
Location: The demilitarized zone along the boundary between Iraq and Kuwait.
Strength: 252 military observers in October 1993, 109 other military personnel, and some 80 international and 106 local civilian staff. Due to repeated Iraqi incursions, in 1993 UNIKOM's mandate was expanded to include taking action against such incursions, and an increase in troop strength to 3,645 was approved by the Security Council.
Fatalities: 2.
Mandate: To monitor the Khawr 'Abd Allah waterway between Iraq and Kuwait and the demilitarized zone; deter violations of the boundary; observe any hostile action; and, as expanded by Security Council resolution 806 (1993), to resist attempts to prevent it by force from discharging its duties.
Annual cost: approximately US$75 million.

UNAVEM II-United Nations Angola Verification Mission II
Duration: June 1991 to present.
Location: Angola.
Strength: 50 military observers, 18 police observers, 11 military paramedics, 43 international civilian staff and 75 local staff.

Fatalities: 3.
Mandate: Initially, monitor the cease-fire between the Angolan Government and UNITA, until general elections were held in 1992; observe the elections scheduled for September 1992. When fighting broke out again after the elections, UNAVEM II's mandate was expanded to include monitoring the new cease-fire between the government and UNITA. However, the political situation continued to deteriorate, until in 1993 UNAVEM II had to evacuate 45 of its 67 monitoring locations. Its mandate was extended three months at a time, as it had become an essential factor in a continuous UN effort to facilitate the resumption of negotiations and support humanitarian activities in the country..
Composition: Military and police personnel are contributed by Argentina, Brazil, Congo, Guinea-Bissau, Hungary, India, Ireland, Jordan, Malaysia, Morocco, Netherlands, Nigeria, Norway, Slovak Republic, Spain, Sweden, and Zimbabwe.
Annual cost: approximately US$107 million between 1 June 1991 and 31 October 1992.

ONUSAL-United Nations Observer Mission in El Salvador
Duration: July 1991 to present.
Location: El Salvador.
Strength: Approximately 350 military and police personnel, 170 international civilian staff, and 187 local staff.
Fatalities: 2.
Mandate: Initially, to verify compliance with the San José Agreement on Human Rights by the government of El Salvador and the Frente Farabundo Marti para la Liberación Nacional (FMLN); monitor the human rights situation in El Salvador; investigate specific cases of alleged human rights violations; promote human rights in the country; make recommendations for the elimination of violations; and report on these matters to the Secretary-General. Subsequent to final peace agreements which were signed in 1992, ONUSAL's mandate was expanded to include verification of the cease-fire and separation of forces; and monitoring the maintenance of public order while a new National Civil Police force was set up. Finally, ONUSAL's mandate was expanded to observe national elections for the presidency, the legislative assembly, mayors, and municipal councils in March 1994.
Composition: ONUSAL military observers are provided by Brazil, Canada, Colombia, Ecuador, India, Ireland, Spain, Sweden, and Venezuela. Police observers come from Austria, Brazil, Chile, Colombia, France, Guyana, Italy, Mexico, Spain, and Sweden.
Annual cost: approximately US$35 million.

MINURSO-United Nations Mission for the Referendum in Western Sahara.
Duration: September 1991 to present.
Location: Western Sahara.
Strength: 226 military observers, 98 military support personal, 26 civilian police officers, and 104 civilian staff members, 69 of whom are internationally recruited.
Fatalities: 4.
Mandate: To verify a cease-fire between the government of Morocco and the Frente Popular para la Liberación de Saguia el-Hamra y de Rio de Oro (Frente Polisario); monitor the confinement of Moroccan and Frente Polisario troops to designated locations; ensure release of all political prisoners or detainees; oversee exchange of prisoners of war; implement a repatriation program; identify and register qualified voters; organize and ensure a free referendum to enable the people of Western Sahara to exercise their right to self-determination, to choose between independence and integration with Morocco.
Composition: Military observers and support personnel are provided by Argentina, Australia, Austria, Bangladesh, Belgium, Canada, China, Egypt, France, Ghana, Greece, Guinea, Hondu-

ras, Ireland, Italy, Kenya, Malaysia, Nigeria, Pakistan, Poland, Russian Federation, Switzerland, Tunisia, United States, and Venezuela. Police officers are contributed by Austria, Belgium, Germany, Malaysia, and Togo.

Annual cost: approximately US$37 million.

UNAMIC-United Nations Advance Mission in Cambodia

Duration: October 1991 to March 1992.

Location: Cambodia.

Strength: 1,504 military and civilian personnel.

Fatalities: None.

Mandate: To immediately deploy a small advance mission to assist the Cambodian parties to maintain a cease-fire while preparations were made for the larger UNTAC force. UNAMIC consisted of civilian and military liaison staff, a military mine-awareness unit, and logistics and support personnel. Its mandate was expanded in January 1992 to include training Cambodians in mine-clearing.

Composition: Algeria, Argentina, Australia, Austria, Bangladesh, Belgium, Canada, China, France, Germany, Ghana, India, Indonesia, Ireland, Malaysia, Netherlands, New Zealand, Pakistan, Poland, Russian Federation, Senegal, Thailand, Tunisia, United Kingdom, United States, And Uruguay.

Annual cost: See UNTAC.

UNPROFOR-United Nations Protection Force

Duration: March 1992 to present.

Location: Bosnia and Herzegovina, Croatia, the Federal Republic of Yugoslavia (Serbia and Montegnegro), and the former Yugoslav Republic of Macedonia.

Strength: 25,000 military personnel, 660 civilian police, 695 international civilian staff, and 974 local staff.

Fatalities: 59.

Mandate: In the wake of the end of the cold war, fighting broke out among ethnic and religious factions in the former Yugoslavia. In January 1992, Secretary-General Boutros Boutros-Ghali sent a 50 military liaison officers to Yugoslavia to promote maintenance of cease-fire by facilitating communication. In February, although some political groups in Yugoslavia were still expressing objections to a UN plan for a peace-keeping operation, the Security Council established UNPROFOR for an initial period of 12 months to create the conditions of peace and security required for the negotiation of an overall settlement of the Yugoslav crisis. UNPROFOR's operational mandate extends to five republics of the former Yugoslavia, as indicated above. In the rapidly deteriorating situation, its mandate has been enlarged in all five republics to include such things as security at Sarajevo airport; protection of humanitarian convoys; monitoring of a "no-fly zone" banning all military flights in the airspace of Bosnia and Herzegovina; border control; the creation of "safe areas" to protect civilians from armed attack.

Composition: Military and/or civilian police personnel are provided by Argentina, Australia, Bangladesh, Belgium, Brazil, Canada, Colombia, Czech Republic, Denmark, Egypt, Finland, France, Ghana, Ireland, Jordan, Kenya, Luxembourg, Nepal, Netherlands, New Zealand, Nigeria, Norway, Poland, Portugal, Russian Federation, Slovak Republic, Spain, Sweden, Switzerland, Tunisia, Ukraine, United Kingdom, United States, and Venezuela.

Annual cost: Approximately US$1.2 billion.

UNTAC-United Nations Transitional Authority in Cambodia

Duration: March 1992 to September 1993.

Location: Cambodia.

Strength: (Peak): 22,000 military and civilian personnel.

Fatalities: 55.

Mandate: To monitor and help implement the Paris Agree-

ments signed in 1991 between the various political entities in Cambodia. The mandate included aspects relating to human rights, the organization and conduct of free and fair general elections, military arrangements, civil administration, the maintenance of law and order, the repatriation and resettlement of the Cambodian refugees, and rehabilitation of essential Cambodian infrastructure. During its mission the Security Council requested UNTAC to play many roles, including human rights oversight and investigation of allegations of human rights abuses during the transitional period; implementing a legal framework for the electoral process; stabilizing the security situation; and ensuring a neutral political environment conducive to free and fair elections. After elections were held in May 1993 and a newly elected Constituent Assembly began work on 14 June 1993, a withdrawal schedule for UNPROFOR was established, leaving a smaller contingent of military police officers and medical units to continue the work of mine clearance and training.

Composition: UNTAC military and/or civilian police personnel were provided by Algeria, Argentina, Australia, Austria, Bangladesh, Belgium, Brunei Darussalam, Bulgaria, Cameroon, Canada, Chile, China, Colombia, Egypt, Fiji, France, Germany, Ghana, Hungary, India, Indonesia, Ireland, Italy, Japan, Jordan, Kenya, Malaysia, Morocco, Namibia, Nepal, Netherlands, New Zealand, Nigeria, Norway, Pakistan, Philippines, Poland, Russian Federation, Senegal, Singapore, Sweden, Thailand, Tunisia, United Kingdom, United States, and Uruguay.

Annual cost: The total cost of both UNAMIC and UNTAC for the period from 1 November 1991 to 24 September 1993 was approximately US$1,500 million.

ONUMOZ-United Nations Operation in Mozambique

Duration: December 1992 to present.

Location: Mozambique.

Strength: Between 7,000 and 8,000.

Fatalities: 6.

Mandate: To help implement the General Peace Agreement signed in 1992 in Rome, after 14 years of devastating civil war between the Republic of Mozambique and the Resisténcia Nacional Moçambicana (RENAMO). ONUMOZ's mandate included four important elements: political, military, electoral, and humanitarian. ONUMOZ military wing would monitor and verify the cease-fire, the separation of forces of the two parties, their demobilization and the collection, storage, and destruction of weapons. It would authorize security arrangements for vital infrastructures and provide security for United Nations and other international activities. ONUMOZ's Electoral Division would monitor and verify all aspects and stages of the electoral process. ONUMOZ's humanitarian component would function as an integrated component of ONUMOZ to make available food and other relief for distribution to soldiers in the assembly area.

Composition: The military component includes 302 military observers and some 6,250 infantry and support personnel from Argentina, Bangladesh, Botswana, Brazil, Canada, Cape Verde, China, Czech Republic, Egypt, Guinea-Bissau, Hungary, India, Italy, Japan, Malaysia, Netherlands, Portugal, Russian Federation, Spain, Sweden, Uruguay, and Zambia. The Electoral Division will include 148 international electoral officers.

Annual cost: Approximately US$290 million.

UNOSOM I-United Nations Operation in Somalia I

Duration: April 1992 to April 1993.

Location: Somalia.

Strength: Originally 50 military observers; expanded to include 500 security personnel, and further expanded to include 719 personnel in logistical units: totalling approximately 4,219.

Fatalities: None.

Mandate: To monitor a cease-fire in the capital, Mogadishu;

provide protection for UN personnel, equipment, and supplies at the seaports and airports; escort deliveries of humanitarian supplies from there to distribution centers in the city and its immediate environs.

Composition: Observers were sent from Australia, Austria, Bangladesh, Belgium, Canada, Czechoslovakia, Egypt, Fiji, Finland, Indonesia, Jordan, Morocco, New Zealand, Norway, Pakistan, and Zimbabwe.

Total cost: Approximately US$109.7 million.

UNOSOM II-United Nations Operation in Somalia II
Duration: June 1993 to present.
Location: Somalia.
Strength: 28,000 military personnel and 2,800 civilian staff.
Fatalities: 81.
Mandate: To establish a secure environment throughout the whole of Somalia; provide assistance to the Somali people in rebuilding their economy and social and political life; help reestablish the country's institutional structure; monitor that all factions continued to respect the various agreements; prevent resumption of violence and, if necessary, take appropriate action against any faction that violated the cessation of hostilities; maintain control of heavy weapons; seize small arms of all unauthorized elements; secure and maintain security at all ports, airports, and lines of communications; protect personnel, installations, and equipment belonging to the UN and other international organizations; take forceful action to neutralize armed elements that attacked or threatened to attack such facilities; assist in repatriation of refugees; continue the program of mine clearance begun under UNISOM I.

Composition: Military personnel are provided by Australia, Bangladesh, Belgium, Botswana, Canada, Egypt, France, Germany, Greece, India, Ireland, Italy, Kuwait, Malaysia, Morocco, Nepal, New Zealand, Nigeria, Norway, Pakistan, Republic of Korea, Romania, Saudi Arabia, Sweden, Tunisia, Turkey, United Arab Emirates, United States, and Zimbabwe.

Note: The United States forces deployed in Mogadishu to support UNOSOM I and UNOSOM II were not under United Nations command or authority. The Unified Task Force (UNITAF) spearheaded by the United States was deployed in Mogadishu on 9 December 1992 and included military units from Australia, Belgium, Botswana, Canada, Egypt, France, Germany, Greece, India, Italy, Kuwait, Morocco, New Zealand, Nigeria, Norway, Pakistan, Saudi Arabia, Sweden, Tunisia, Turkey, United Arab Emirates, United Kingdom, and Zimbabwe.

Annual cost: Approximately US$977 million.

UNOMUR-United Nations Observer Mission in Uganda-Rwanda
Duration: June 1993 to present
Location: Uganda side of the Uganda-Rwanda border.
Strength: 81 military observers, 17 international staff, and 7 locally recruited personnel.
Mandate: To verify that no lethal weapons and ammunitions are transported across the border from Uganda into northern Rwanda.
Composition: Military observers were provided by Bangladesh, Botswana, Brazil, Canada, Hungary, Netherlands, Senegal, and Zimbabwe.
Annual cost: Approximately US$8 million.

UNOMIG-United Nations Observer Mission in Georgia
Duration: August 1993 to present.
Location: Georgia.
Strength: Authorized: 88 military observers and 56 international and 46 local civilian staff. Actual: (on 31 October 1993) 12 military observers and 4 civilians.

Mandate: To verify compliance with a cease-fire agreed to on 27 July 1993 between the government of Georgia and separatists in its northwestern region, Abkhazia. It would also investigate reports of cease-fire violations and attempt to resolve such incidents; and report to the Secretary-General about such violations. Before UNOMIG could be fully deployed, the cease-fire broke down, and, in accordance with the instructions of the Security Council resolution 858 (1993), deployment was halted.

Composition: The following states have expressed their readiness to make troops available to UNOMIG when deployment resumes: Austria, Bangladesh, Czech Republic, Denmark, Germany, Greece, Poland, Sierra Leone, Sweden, and Switzerland.

Annual cost: Estimated to have been approximately US$23 million upon full deployment.

UNOMIL-United Nations Observer Mission in Liberia
Duration: September 1993 to present.
Location: Liberia.
Strength: 303 military observers, 20 military medical personnel, 45 military engineers, 58 United Nations volunteers, 89 international civilian staff, and 136 local civilian staff.
Mandate: To verify the Cotonou Peace Agreement signed in Cotonou, Benin, between the parties to the Liberian conflict that broke out in 1990 when the Liberian president, Samuel Doe, was overthrown, causing a complete breakdown of law and order. The UNOMIL was created at the invitation of the Economic Community of West African States (ECOWAS), which has taken various initiatives to peacefully settle the conflict, including the establishment of its own military observer group, ECOMOG. UNOMIL was to work with ECOMOG in implementing the Cotoneau Peace Agreement. ECOMOG has primary responsibility for the implementation of the agreement's provisions, and UNOMIL's role is to monitor the implementation procedures to verify their impartial application.

Composition: The military component is composed of personnel from Austria, Bangladesh, China, Czech Republic, Ecuador, Egypt, Guinea-Bissau, Hungary, Jordan, Kenya, Malaysia, Pakistan, Slovakia, and Uruguay.

Annual cost: Approximately US$40 million.

UNMIH-United Nations Mission in Haiti
Duration: Originally: September 1993 to February 1996
Location: Haiti.
Strength: Proposed: 6,000 military personnel (as of July 1994).
Mandate: Pending the creation of a new police force, assist the government in monitoring the activities of those members of the armed forces involved in carrying out police functions; provide guidance and advice; monitor the conduct of police operations; ensure that legal requirements are fully met. However, the advance unit of UNMIH was prevented from landing at Port au Prince on 11 October 1993.

Composition: When deployed, military personnel are to be provided by Argentina, Canada, and the United States. Police personnel will be contributed by Algeria, Austria, Canada, France, Indonesia, Madagascar, Russian Federation, Senegal, Spain, Switzerland, Tunisia, and Venezuela.

Annual cost: Estimated at approximately US$100 million.

UNAMIR-United Nations Assistance Mission for Rwanda
Duration: October 1993 to present.
Location: Rwanda.
Strength: 2,548 military personnel, 60 police officers, 110 international civilian staff, and 61 locally recruited civilian staff.
Fatalities: 14.
Mandate: In the context of the Arusha peace agreement concluded in August 1993 between the government of Rwanda and the Rwandese Patriotic Front (RPF), UNAMIR would contribute

to the establishment and maintenance of a climate conducive to the secure installation and subsequent operation of the transitional government; assure the security of the capital city, Kigali; monitor a cease-fire agreement, including establishing an expanded demilitarized zone and demobilization procedures; monitor the security situation leading up to elections; assist with mine clearance. UNAMIR would also investigate alleged noncompliance with provisions of the peace agreement and provide security for the repatriation of Rwandese refugees. It would also escort and protect humanitarian activities.

Composition: At its peak strength UNAMIR was to be composed of 2,217 formed troops and 331 military observers provided by Argentina, Austria, Bangladesh, Belgium, Canada, Congo, Ecuador, Egypt, Fiji, Ghana, Malawi, Mali, Nigeria, Pakistan, Russian Federation, Senegal, Tanzania, Togo, Tunisia, Uruguay, and Zimbabwe.

Annual cost: Estimated at approximately US$98 million.

SOME CASE HISTORIES OF UN ACTION
The cases are arranged in order of the dates when the disputes were first brought before the UN.

The Middle East
Establishment of Israel. In April 1947, the General Assembly, at a special session, established a Special Committee on Palestine to make recommendations for the future status of the British mandate. The resulting partition plan, which divided Palestine into an Arab and a Jewish state, with an international regime for the city of Jerusalem, was adopted by the General Assembly in November of the same year. A UN Palestine Commission was established to carry out the recommendations, and the Security Council was requested to implement the plan. The date for termination of the British mandate and withdrawal of British troops was 1 August 1948. However, violent fighting broke out between the Arab nations and the Jewish community in Palestine. The Security Council thereupon established a Truce Commission consisting of Belgium, France, and the United States, while the General Assembly authorized a UN Mediator for Palestine to replace the Palestine Commission.

On 14 May 1948, the Jewish state of Israel was proclaimed. Almost immediately, the Arab nations instituted full-scale armed action. Following a four-week truce at the request of the Security Council, hostilities were renewed on 8 July. This time, the Security Council, invoking Chapter VII of the charter, ordered the governments concerned to desist from further military action and proclaimed a cease-fire.

Through the UN mediator, Count Folke Bernadotte, the Security Council then established a UN Truce Supervision Organization (UNTSO) of military observers from different countries, with headquarters in Jerusalem, and assigned it the task of patrolling the frontiers. Fighting continued, however, and Count Bernadotte was assassinated in September 1948. During its regular session in the fall of 1948, the General Assembly established a three-member Conciliation Commission (France, Turkey, and the US) to negotiate a settlement and also established the UN Relief for Palestine Refugees (later replaced by UNRWA). Following negotiations with the acting UN mediator, Ralph Bunche, in the first half of 1949, Israel, Egypt, Jordan, Lebanon, and Syria signed armistice agreements. The agreements provided for mixed armistice commissions to check on their implementation. UNTSO continued in operation to observe the cease-fire and is still in existence, investigating complaints of armistice violations and reporting to the Security Council. The Conciliation Commission also continues to function, still trying to fulfill its mandate from the General Assembly to assist the parties concerned to negotiate a final settlement of all issues.

The Suez Crisis. In July 1956, Egypt nationalized the Suez Canal. In September, after Egypt's rejection of the London Conference plan for international control of the canal, France and the United Kingdom informed the Security Council that Egypt's attitude was endangering the peace. Israel invaded Egypt's Gaza Strip the following month, and a Security Council resolution calling for a cease-fire and the withdrawal of Israeli troops was vetoed by France and the United Kingdom. France and the United Kingdom began armed intervention in the area, and thereafter the situation was handled exclusively by the General Assembly under the Uniting for Peace Resolution. In November 1956, the General Assembly established the UN Emergency Force (UNEF) to secure and supervise cessation of hostilities. Since Israel would not permit UNEF contingents on territory under its control, the force was stationed on the Egyptian side of the demarcation line. Withdrawal of British and French forces was completed by December 1956 and of Israeli forces by March 1957. The canal was cleared by April of the same year, and Egypt declared it open to international traffic (Israeli ships were barred, however).

The Six-Day War, 1967. By the mid-1960s, the tension between Israel and the Arab countries had begun to manifest itself in frequent and sometimes major hostilities across the various armistice borders. On 18 May 1967, the United Arab Republic (UAR), which two days earlier had begun deploying troops to the armistice demarcation line in the Sinai peninsula, officially requested Secretary-General U Thant to withdraw all UNEF units from the area. After consultations with the UNEF Advisory Committee, U Thant ordered the withdrawal of the force that evening.

U Thant's prompt compliance with the UAR's request aroused severe criticism in Israel and other quarters. His view was that both legal and practical considerations required him to act without delay. In subsequent reports, he pointed out that UNEF was not an enforcement operation ordered by the Security Council but a peacekeeping operation dependent on the consent of the host country. His unilateral decision to disband the force was, however, probably the most controversial of his career as Secretary-General. Some of his critics challenged the legal validity of his stand, while many others believed that he could have used his office to try to persuade the UAR at least to agree to a postponement of its request for UNEF's withdrawal, which they felt only helped pave the way for the crisis that followed.

The UAR occupied the fortress Sharm el-Sheikh, which commands the Strait of Tiran at the mouth of the Gulf of Aqaba. On 22 May 1967, it declared the gulf closed to Israeli ships and to other ships bound for Israel with strategic goods. Israel found its sole direct access to the Red Sea blockaded and considered the blockade, together with the military agreement that the UAR had recently signed with Jordan, a justified *casus belli*. Regarding the assurances of help that it had received from Western countries in the course of concentrated diplomatic activity intended to avert the impending war as insufficient, it simultaneously attacked the UAR, Jordan, and Syria on 5 June. Within three days, it had deeply penetrated the territory of each country.

The Security Council, in emergency session, demanded a cease-fire on 6 June 1967. Israel announced that it would accept a cease-fire provided that the other parties accepted it. Jordan announced acceptance on 7 June, the UAR on 8 June, and Syria on 9 June, and a cease-fire accordingly took effect on 10 June. Violations of the cease-fire, especially along the Israel-Syria border, continued until 13 June, when Secretary-General U Thant was able to report the "virtual cessation" of all military activity. By then, Israel had voluntarily withdrawn its forces from much of the territory that it had occupied but had retained control of several areas regarded as essential to its security—namely, the whole of the UAR's Sinai peninsula up to the Suez Canal, including Sharm el-Sheikh and the Gaza Strip; the Jordanian part of the city of Jerusalem and the West Bank area of the Jordan River; and the Golan Heights, in Syrian territory overlooking the Sea of Galilee.

On 14 June, the Security Council adopted a resolution calling upon Israel to ensure the "safety, welfare and security" of the inhabitants of the occupied areas and upon the "governments concerned" scrupulously to respect the humanitarian principles governing the treatment of prisoners of war contained in the 1949 Geneva Convention.

An emergency special session of the General Assembly, held from 19 June to 21 July 1967, failed to produce a resolution that might serve as the frame of reference for a settlement. The division of opinion between the supporters of the Arabs, including the Soviet bloc and several African and Asian countries, and the supporters of the Israeli position, including the United States and several Western countries, was too deep to be bridged. However, the General Assembly did adopt, by a vote of 99 in favor with 20 abstentions, a resolution declaring invalid Israel's proclamation on 28 June that Jerusalem would thenceforward be a unified city under Israeli administration.

Resolution 242. For many months, the Security Council was equally unsuccessful in the attempt to devise an acceptable formula for establishing permanent peace in the area. Finally, on 22 November 1967, after weeks of quiet diplomacy and closed discussions, it adopted Resolution 242, which has remained the basis of UN efforts to achieve a definitive settlement. The resolution, based on a British draft, establishes certain principles for a peaceful settlement without going into contentious specifics or prescribing priorities. The principles include withdrawal of Israeli forces from occupied areas (the text deliberately avoided requesting withdrawal from "all" occupied areas, in view of Israel's declaration that it would not give up certain strategic places, including Jordanian Jerusalem); an end to states of belligerency; respect for the rights of all states in the area to peaceful existence; and an affirmation of the need to guarantee free navigation through international waterways, settle the long-standing Palestine refugee problem, and guarantee the territorial integrity and political independence of the countries involved. All parties—except, initially, Syria—accepted the formula.

The October War, 1973. Full-scale hostilities broke out again in the Suez Canal and Israel-Syria sectors on 6 October 1973. The Security Council met four times without considering any draft resolutions and on 12 October decided to reconvene at a later date after consultations. It did so on 21 October at the request of the United States and the USSR and the next day adopted Resolution 338, which called for the immediate cessation of all military activities. It also decided that negotiations between the concerned parties for a just and durable peace should begin at once. China did not participate in this or other votes on the question. Israel, Syria, and Egypt agreed to comply, each stating conditions.

A second UN Emergency Force (UNEF II) was established by the Security Council on 25 October 1973. Its personnel were to be drawn from member states, with the exception of the permanent members of the council, and its eventual strength was to be 7,000. As the force was assembled, it took up stations in zones of disengagement between Israel and Egypt.

A peace conference on the Middle East was convened in December 1973 in Geneva under the auspices of the UN and the co-chairmanship of the United States and the USSR. The work of the conference came to fruition at kilometer 101 on the Cairo-Suez road on 18 January 1974, when the chief of staff of the Egyptian Armed Forces and the chief of staff of the Israel Defense Forces signed an Agreement on Disengagement of Forces, with the UNEF commander as witness. The agreement came into effect on 25 January 1974.

It was not until 31 May 1974, in Geneva, that Syria and Israel signed an Agreement on Disengagement, which called for the creation of a UN Disengagement Observer Force (UNDOF) and specified that it did not represent a peace agreement but a step toward peace. On the same day, after the signing, the Security Council adopted a resolution jointly sponsored by the United States and the USSR that set up UNDOF. China and Iraq did not participate in the vote. The strength of UNDOF was to be 1,250, its components to be drawn from members of the UN that were not permanent members of the Security Council. In 1993, UNDOF comprised some 1,100 troops, provided by Austria, Canada, Finland, and Poland, deployed between the Israeli and Syrian forces on the Golan Heights in accordance with the 1974 disengagement agreement.

Developments in Lebanon. On 15 March 1978, following a Palestinian commando raid in Israel, Israeli forces invaded southern Lebanon. On 19 March, the Security Council called on Israel to cease its military action against Lebanese territory and decided to establish a UN Interim Force in Lebanon (UNIFIL) to confirm the withdrawal of Israeli forces and assist the Lebanese government in ensuring the return of its effective authority in the area.

The mandate of the 6,000-man UNIFIL has been extended by the Security Council every six months since then. Perhaps its greatest crisis occurred on the morning of 6 June 1982, when Israeli forces, comprising two mechanized divisions with air and naval support, moved into Lebanese territory, bypassing positions occupied by UNIFIL. The Israeli invasion was followed by a few days of intensive exchanges of fire with PLO and Syrian forces and by Israeli air attacks on targets in the Beirut area. In subsequent days and weeks, the Security Council met numerous times to demand a cease-fire, withdrawal of Israeli forces, and respect for the rights of the civilian population.

UNIFIL's mandate was enlarged to extend protection and humanitarian assistance to the population of the area; an international survey mission was established to assess the situation on the spot; a UN observer group was deployed in and around Beirut to ensure that a cease-fire was fully observed by all concerned; and, at Lebanon's request, a 4,000-man multinational force, composed of contingents from France, Italy, and the United States (and later the United Kingdom), was deployed in the Beirut area. The force was withdrawn in 1984.

At the end of 1987, UNIFIL comprised some 5,660 troops, provided by Fiji, Finland, France, Ghana, Ireland, Italy, Nepal, Norway, and Sweden. It has continued to assist the Lebanese government in ensuring the return of its effective authority in southern Lebanon.

The Question of Palestinian Rights. Concurrently with its consideration of the situation in the Middle East and of the role of peacekeeping forces in the region, the UN has been concerned with the question of Palestinian rights. In 1968, the General Assembly established the Special Committee to Investigate Israeli Practices Affecting the Human Rights of the Population of the Occupied Territories, which reports annually to it, and in 1974, it reaffirmed "the inalienable rights of the Palestinian people" to unhindered self-determination, national independence, and sovereignty. The General Assembly recognized the Palestinian people as a principal party in the establishment of a just and durable peace in the Middle East, and it invited the PLO to participate as an observer in its work and in UN conferences.

In 1975, the General Assembly established the Committee on the Exercise of the Inalienable Rights of the Palestinian People and asked it to recommend a program for the implementation of those rights. The committee recommended that a timetable be established by the Security Council for the complete withdrawal of Israeli forces from the areas occupied in 1967. The evacuated areas, with all properties and services intact, would be taken over by the UN, which, with the cooperation of the League of Arab States, would subsequently hand them over to the PLO as the representative of the Palestinian people. The General Assembly has endorsed the committee's recommendations at successive sessions since 1976, but the Security Council has not acted on them.

An International Conference on the Question of Palestine, held in Geneva in the summer of 1983, adopted a declaration on Palestine and a program of action for the achievement of Palestinian rights, which was later endorsed by the General Assembly. The conference also called for the convening of an international conference on the Middle East, a proposal which the General Assembly has also endorsed.

At its 1987 session, the General Assembly reaffirmed its conviction that "the question of Palestine is the core of the conflict in the Middle East and that no comprehensive, just and lasting peace in the region will be achieved without the full exercise by the Palestinian people of its inalienable national rights and the immediate, unconditional and total withdrawal of Israel from all the Palestinian and other Arab occupied territories." The General Assembly again called for the convening of an international peace conference on the Middle East under the auspices of the UN and at the invitation of the Secretary-General, with the participation of the five permanent members of the Security Council and all the parties to the Arab-Israeli conflict, including the PLO.

Korea

At the end of World War II, the Allied powers agreed that Soviet troops would accept the Japanese surrender north of the 38th parallel in Korea and that United States forces would accept it south of that line. The two occupying powers established a joint commission to set up a provisional government for the country, but the commission could not come to an agreement, and the United States brought the matter to the General Assembly in September 1947. In November, the General Assembly created a Temporary Commission on Korea to facilitate nationwide elections. However, since the commission was denied access to northern Korea, it was only able to supervise elections in the southern half of the country. These elections took place in May 1948, and in August, the United States transferred governmental and military functions to the duly elected government of the Republic of Korea (ROK). Meanwhile, a separate government was established in the north. In December 1948, the General Assembly, over the objection of the USSR, established a seven-member UN Commission on Korea (UNCOK) to replace the Temporary Commission and to seek reunification.

On 25 June 1950, both UNCOK and the United States informed the Security Council that the Democratic People's Republic of Korea (DPRK) had attacked the ROK that morning. The council met on the same day and (the USSR being absent at the time in protest against a council decision on Chinese representation) declared the attack to be a breach of the peace. It called for a cease-fire, withdrawal of DPRK forces to the 38th parallel, and the assistance of member states to the ROK. As the fighting continued, the Security Council, on 27 June, recommended that UN members furnish assistance to the ROK to repel the attack and restore peace and security. On the same day, the United States announced that it had ordered its own air and sea forces to give cover and support to the South Korean troops. On July 7, the Security Council voted to recommend that states make forces available to a UN Unified Command under the United States. (It should be noted that although the council had used the language of Chapter VII of the charter—"breach of the peace," etc.—it did not specifically invoke the chapter itself or use its constitutional power thereunder to order all states to comply with its decision.) In all, 16 nations supplied troops: Australia, Belgium, Canada, Colombia, Ethiopia, France, Greece, Luxembourg, Netherlands, New Zealand, Philippines, Thailand, Turkey, South Africa, the United Kingdom, and the US; the ROK also placed its troops under the UN Command.

On 1 August 1950, the USSR returned to the Security Council (having by then been absent for six months) and declared that all the actions and decisions that had previously been taken by the council were illegal. On 6 November, the USSR vetoed a resolution proposed by the United States. As a result of the ensuing deadlock, the General Assembly virtually took over the handling of the entire situation (the Security Council even agreeing unanimously, on 31 January 1951, to remove the item from its agenda). The legalistic device by which the General Assembly voted itself competent to continue with collective measures that under the charter are the exclusive preserve of the Security Council was the Uniting for Peace Resolution.

Even before the Security Council became deadlocked, the General Assembly had considered an agenda item entitled "The Problem of the Independence of Korea." Under this item, it established the Commission for the Unification and Rehabilitation of Korea (UNCURK) to replace UNCOK. Then, on 6 November 1950, events were given a new twist when the People's Republic of China entered the war on the side of the DPRK. The General Assembly promptly added the agenda item entitled "Intervention of the Central People's Government of the People's Republic of China in Korea." Under this item, the General Assembly established the UN Korean Reconstruction Agency (UNKRA) and a three-member Cease-fire Group that included the president of the General Assembly to determine a basis for ending hostilities. Following China's refusal to cooperate, the General Assembly, in February 1951, adopted a resolution that that government had engaged in aggression. It also established a Good Offices Committee and an Additional Measures Committee to supplement the Cease-fire Group. Truce negotiations began in July 1951, but fighting continued until 1953, when an armistice agreement was signed on 27 July. A year later, the General Assembly called for the political conference that had been provided for in the armistice agreement. The conference was held between April and June 1954, but it failed to resolve problems and negotiate reunification of the country. UNKRA ceased operations in 1960, and UNCURK was dissolved by a consensus vote of the 1973 General Assembly.

On 18 November 1975, the General Assembly adopted two resolutions—one with Western support, the other with that of the Communist states—which were to some extent conflicting but which both favored dissolution of the UN Command at an early date. The first resolution called for negotiations among the DPRK, the ROK, China, and the United States. The second called for negotiations between the DPRK and the United States. The DPRK declared that it would not participate in negotiations with the ROK.

As of mid-1987, the following countries were still represented on the UN Command: Australia, Canada, Philippines, ROK, Thailand, United Kingdom, and United States.

In his 1987 report to the General Assembly on the work of the UN, Secretary-General Pérez de Cuéllar stated that there had been, during the previous year, a series of proposals emanating from both North and South Korea for the resumption of talks on overcoming the contentious issues between the two sides and that he had had continuing contacts with both sides in an effort to assist in reducing the causes of tension between them and enhancing the prospect of a negotiated settlement.

Kashmir

Kashmir (officially, Jammu and Kashmir) was originally one of the princely states of British India. Under the partition plan and the Indian Independence Act of 1947, it became free to accede to either India or Pakistan, on both of which it borders. On 1 January 1948, India reported to the Security Council that tribesmen were invading Kashmir with the active assistance of Pakistan. After the invasion had begun, the maharajah of Kashmir had requested accession to India and India had accepted on the understanding that, once normal conditions were restored, the question of accession would be settled by a plebiscite. Pakistan declared that Kashmir's accession to India was illegal.

The Security Council, after asking the parties to mediate, called for withdrawal of Pakistani nationals, reduction of Indian forces, and arrangement of a plebiscite on Kashmir's accession to India. A UN Commission for India and Pakistan (UNCIP) was sent to mediate in July 1948. By 1949, UNCIP had effected a cease-fire and was able to state that principles on a plebiscite had been accepted by both governments. In July 1949, agreement was reached on a cease-fire line, and UNCIP appointed a group of military observers to watch for violations. However, it was unable to reach agreement on terms for the demilitarization of Kashmir prior to a plebiscite.

In March 1951, after several attempts at further negotiation had failed, the Security Council decided to continue the observer group—now called the UN Military Observer Group in India and Pakistan (UNMOGIP)—to supervise the cease-fire within Kashmir itself. Despite continued mediation, the differences between the parties remained. The Security Council repeatedly considered the matter without achieving appreciable progress.

In August 1965 there was a sudden outbreak of serious hostilities. UNMOGIP reported clashes between the regular armed forces of both India and Pakistan, and fighting continued into September, although the Security Council had twice called for a cease-fire. Following a report that fighting had spread to the international border between India and West Pakistan, the council, on September 20, requested that both sides issue orders for a cease-fire within two days and withdraw their forces to their previously held positions. The cease-fire was accepted by both states, but continuous complaints of violations were made by each side. Accordingly, the Council requested Secretary-General U Thant to increase the size of UNMOGIP and to establish the UN India-Pakistan Observation Mission (UNIPOM) on the India-West Pakistan border.

On 5 November 1965, the Security Council urged that a meeting between the parties be held as soon as possible and that a plan for withdrawal containing a time limit for execution be developed. U Thant appointed a representative to meet with authorities of both countries on the question. On 17 February 1966, he informed the council that a plan and rules for withdrawals had been worked out. He also stated that, on 10 January, the prime minister of India and the president of Pakistan had agreed at Tashkent, where they had met at the initiative of the USSR, that their respective forces would be withdrawn to their original positions by 25 February. Thus, though the crisis remains quiescent, the conflict itself is unresolved, and UNMOGIP is still in operation, with some 40 military observers stationed in the area.

In 1971, another conflict between the two countries broke out, this time in connection with the civil strife in East Pakistan, which later became the independent state of Bangladesh. As nearly 10 million refugees streamed into neighboring India, tension increased in the subcontinent. U Thant conveyed his serious concern to the president of Pakistan and the prime minister of India and, with the consent of the host governments, set up two large-scale humanitarian programs. One of these, with the UN high commissioner for refugees as the focal point, was for the relief of the refugees in India. The other was for assistance to the distressed population in East Pakistan. U Thant's actions were subsequently unanimously approved by the General Assembly.

On 20 July 1971, the Secretary-General drew the attention of the president of the Security Council to the steady deterioration of the situation in the region, which he described as a potential threat to peace and security. He noted that humanitarian, economic, and political problems were involved, and he indicated that the UN should play a more forthright role to avert further deterioration. In October of that year, he offered his good offices to the governments of India and Pakistan, but India declined. Clashes broke out between the two countries, and on 3 December, U Thant notified the Security Council under Article 99 of the

charter that the situation in the region constituted a threat to international peace and security.

After a cease-fire had put an end to the fighting on 17 December 1971, the Security Council adopted a resolution demanding the strict observance of the cease-fire until withdrawal of all armed forces to their previous positions should take place. The council also called for international assistance to relieve the suffering and for the appointment of a special UN representative to lend his good offices for the solution of humanitarian problems. During 1972, the refugees, with UN assistance, returned to their homeland. The UN relief operation helped pave the way for the rehabilitation of the shattered economy of Bangladesh, which became a member of the UN in 1974.

In 1993 UNMOGIP consisted of 39 military observers from eight countries: Belgium, Chile, Denmark, Finland, Italy, Norway, Sweden, and Uruguay.

The Congo (Zaire)

One week after the Democratic Republic of the Congo (now Zaire), a former Belgian colony, had become independent on 30 June 1960, troops of the Force Publique mutinied against the Belgian officers, demanding higher pay and promotions. As violence and general disorder spread rapidly throughout the country, Belgium rushed troops to the area to protect its extensive mining interests. On 11 July, Katanga, the richest province of the country by virtue of its Belgian-controlled copper mines, proclaimed its secession from the new state. On the following day, President Kasavubu and Prime Minister Patrice Lumumba appealed for UN military assistance "to protect the national territory against acts of aggression committed by Belgian metropolitan troops."

In a series of meetings, the Security Council called for the withdrawal of Belgian troops and authorized Secretary-General Hammarskjöld to provide the Congolese government with such military and technical assistance as might be necessary until the national security forces, through the efforts of the government with UN assistance, might be able, in the government's opinion, to meet their tasks fully.

Within two days, contingents of a UN force provided by a number of countries, including Asian and African states, began to arrive in the Congo, followed by UN civilian experts to help ensure the continued operation of essential services. Over the next four years, the task of the UN Operation in the Congo was to help the Congolese government restore and maintain the political independence and territorial integrity of the country and maintain law and order and also to put into effect a wide and long-term program of training and technical assistance.

At its peak strength, the UN force totaled nearly 20,000 officers and men. The instructions of the Security Council to the force were strengthened early in 1961 after the assassination of Lumumba in Katanga. The force was to protect the Congo from outside interference, particularly by evacuating foreign mercenaries and advisers from Katanga and preventing clashes and civil strife, by force if necessary as a last resort.

Following the reconvening of the Congolese parliament in August 1961 under UN auspices, the main problem was the attempted secession, led and financed by foreign elements, of the province of Katanga, where secessionist gendarmes under the command of foreign mercenaries clashed with UN forces. Secretary-General Hammarskjöld lost his life on 17 September 1961, when his plane crashed on the way to Ndola (in what is now Zambia), where talks were to be held for the cessation of hostilities.

In February 1963, after Katanga had been reintegrated into the national territory of the Congo, a phasing out of the force was begun, aimed at its termination by the end of that year. At the request of the Congolese government, however, the General Assembly authorized the stay of a reduced number of troops for a further six months. The force was completely withdrawn by 30 June 1964. Civilian aid continued in the largest single program of assistance undertaken by the UN up to that time, with some 2,000 experts at work in the nation.

Cyprus

Cyprus was granted independence from British rule in 1960 through agreements signed by the United Kingdom, Greece, and Turkey. Under these agreements, Cyprus was given a constitution containing certain unamendable provisions guaranteeing specified political rights to the Turkish minority community. The three signatory powers were constituted guarantors of Cyprus's independence, each with the right to station troops permanently on the island.

The granting of independence had been preceded by a prolonged conflict between the Greek and Turkish communities on the future status of Cyprus. The Greek Cypriots, comprising 80 percent of the total population, originally had wanted some form of union with Greece, thereby provoking a hostile reaction among the Turkish Cypriots, who countered by demanding partition. Each side was supported in its aims by the country of its ethnic origin. Independence did nothing to alleviate dissension on the island. Both sides were dissatisfied with the constitution that had been granted them, but their aims were diametrically opposed. The Turks wanted partition or a type of federal government, whereas the Greeks wanted a constitution free of outside controls and of provisions perpetuating the division between the two communities.

After three years of continuous tension, the Cyprus government, under Greek Cypriot president Makarios, complained to the Security Council on 27 December 1963 that Turkey was interfering in its internal affairs and committing acts of aggression. Against a background of mounting violence on the island, the council considered the matter but did not immediately take any peacekeeping action.

With the consent of Cyprus, British troops had been trying to restore order during the crisis. However, in mid-February 1964, the United Kingdom informed the Security Council that its efforts to keep the peace would have to be augmented. Accordingly, on 4 March 1964, the council unanimously authorized the establishment of the UN Peacekeeping Force in Cyprus (UNFICYP) for a three-month period and at the same time requested Secretary-General U Thant to designate a UN mediator to promote a substantive settlement. UNFICYP became operational on 27 March 1964, with a mandate to prevent the recurrence of fighting, help maintain law and order, and promote a return to normal conditions.

A coup d'état on 15 July 1974 by Greek Cypriot and Greek elements opposed to President Makarios forced him to flee the country. This was quickly followed by military intervention by Turkey, whose troops subsequently established Turkish Cypriot control over the northern part of Cyprus. Four days after a cease-fire went into effect on 16 August 1974, the UN high commissioner for refugees was asked to coordinate humanitarian assistance in Cyprus, where more than 200,000 persons had been dislocated as a result of the hostilities.

Concurrently with the functioning of UNFICYP, the UN has been active in promoting a peaceful solution and an agreed settlement of the Cyprus problem. This task, first entrusted to a mediator, has been carried out since 1968 through the good offices of the Secretary-General. Within that framework, a series of intercommunal talks between representatives of the Greek and Turkish Cypriot communities, as well as high-level meetings, were held, beginning in 1974, in a effort to reach a just and lasting solution. The intercommunal talks were discontinued after the Turkish Cypriot authorities, on 15 November 1983, proclaimed a "Turkish Republic of Northern Cyprus," a step which the Security Council called legally invalid. Secretary-General Pérez de Cuéllar met separately with representatives of the two sides in an effort to resume the negotiating process. Among the proposals put forward is the establishment of a Federal Republic of Cyprus that would be nonaligned and would enjoy sovereignty, independence, and territorial integrity.

In the meantime, UNFICYP has continued its task of supervising the cease-fire and maintaining surveillance over the buffer zone between the cease-fire lines. In 1993, the force numbered 1,208 troops and support personnel, 12 military observers and 35 civilian police. Its troops were provided by Australia, Austria, Canada, Denmark, Finland, Hungary, Ireland, Sweden, and the United Kingdom.

Apartheid in South Africa

The racial policy of apartheid practiced by the South African government not only violated the political and human rights of its African citizens, it also destabilized the entire southern African region. The government of South Africa's policies towards the independence of surrounding African nations, the flight of South African freedom fighters to those countries, and the possibility that the technologically advanced government of South Africa might acquire nuclear capabilities, led the United Nations to consider apartheid in South Africa as a real threat to international peace and security. More than four decades of effort by the United Nations bore fruit in April 1994, when Nelson Mandela was elected president of South Africa in democratic elections open to South African citizens of all races.

The racial policies of the government of South Africa were a major concern of the UN since its earliest years. Over more than four decades, the General Assembly and the Security Council called for measures by the international community aimed at bringing about the end of apartheid, an Afrikaans word meaning "separateness," and at enabling the Africans of South Africa, who outnumber the whites by more than 4 to 1, to exercise political, economic, and all other rights in their country. In the words of a 1982 General Assembly resolution, the goal of the UN with regard to South Africa was "the total eradication of apartheid and the establishment of a democratic society in which all the people of South Africa as a whole, irrespective of race, color, sex or creed, will enjoy equal and full human rights and fundamental freedoms and participate freely in the determination of their destiny."

The question of South Africa's racial policies was first raised in the General Assembly in 1946, when India complained that the South African government had enacted legislation discriminating against South Africans of Indian origin. The General Assembly expressed the view that the treatment of Indians in South Africa should conform with South Africa's obligations under agreements concluded between that country and India and its obligations under the UN Charter.

The wider question of racial conflict in South Africa arising from that government's apartheid policies was placed on the General Assembly's agenda in 1952. On that question and on India's original complaint, the South African government maintained that the matter was essentially within its domestic jurisdiction and that, under the charter, the UN was barred from considering it.

The Security Council took up the question for the first time in 1960, following an incident at Sharpeville on 21 March in which South African police fired on peaceful demonstrators protesting the requirement that all Africans carry "passes"; 69 people were killed and 180 wounded. The council stated that the situation in South Africa had led to international friction and, if continued, might endanger international peace and security. The council called on the South African government to abandon its policy of apartheid, which it termed "a crime against the conscience and dignity of mankind."

In order to keep the racial policies of South Africa under review, the General Assembly decided, in 1962, to establish the Special Committee Against Apartheid. The committee, composed of 18 members, was subsequently given a wider mandate to review all aspects of South Africa's policies of apartheid and the international repercussions of those policies.

The committee's work included the following activities: holding of meetings and hearings; the sending of missions to member states to gain support for the struggle against apartheid; the organization of international conferences, special sessions, and seminars; and the implementation of the resolutions of the General Assembly and the Security Council, particularly by promoting sports, cultural, consumer, and other boycotts and, with the UN Center Against Apartheid, cooperating with governments, intergovernmental organizations, trade unions, women's organizations, religious leaders, student and youth movements, and antiapartheid groups in mobilizing international public opinion in support of action against apartheid.

The General Assembly also established, in 1965, the UN Trust Fund for South Africa, which, through voluntary contributions, made grants to organizations for legal aid to persons persecuted under South Africa's apartheid laws, relief to such persons and their families, and relief for refugees from South Africa. In 1967, the General Assembly established the UN Educational and Training Program for Southern Africa, which granted scholarships to students from South Africa and Namibia for study and training abroad.

Arms Embargo and Other Sanctions. A voluntary arms embargo against South Africa was instituted by the Security Council in 1963. Noting that some of the arms supplied to South Africa were being used to further its racial policies and repress the African people, the council called on all states to stop the sale and shipment of arms, ammunition of all types, and military vehicles to South Africa. Subsequently, in 1970, the Security Council condemned violations of the arms embargo and called on all states to strengthen and implement it unconditionally; withhold the supply of all vehicles, equipment, and spare parts for use by South African military and paramilitary forces; revoke all licenses and patents granted for South African manufacture of arms, aircraft, or military vehicles; prohibit investment or technical assistance for arms manufacture; and cease military cooperation with South Africa.

Both the Security Council and the General Assembly condemned the shooting, on 26 June 1976, of Africans, including schoolchildren, demonstrating in the township of Soweto.

The following year, the Security Council made the arms embargo against South Africa mandatory, the first time that such action had been taken against a member state under Chapter VII of the charter, which provides for enforcement action in the face of threats to international peace and security. Concerned that South Africa was at the threshold of producing nuclear weapons, the Security Council also decided that states should refrain from any cooperation with South Africa in the manufacture and development of such weapons. It established a committee to keep under constant review the implementation by states of the mandatory arms embargo.

Meanwhile, the General Assembly, in 1970, urged states to terminate diplomatic and other official relations with South Africa, as well as economic and all other types of cooperation, as an expression of international rejection of South Africa's policy of apartheid, which the General Assembly called "a crime against humanity." In 1973, the General Assembly adopted the International Convention on the Suppression and Punishment of the Crime of Apartheid (see the section on Racial Discrimination in the chapter on Human Rights).

In 1974, the General Assembly rejected South Africa's credentials and recommended that South Africa be totally excluded from participation in all international organizations and conferences held under UN auspices until it abandoned its policies of apartheid.

The International Conference on Sanctions Against South Africa, held in Paris in May 1981, called for further international action to isolate South Africa, including the imposition, under Chapter VII of the charter, of sanctions "as the most appropriate and effective means to ensure South Africa's compliance with the decisions of the United Nations." The need for sanctions, including disengagement of transnational corporations operating in South Africa and disinvestment in companies doing business with South Africa, remained the focal point of UN efforts to end that country's policies of apartheid.

Other measures included a sports boycott, embodied in the International Declaration Against Apartheid in Sports, which was adopted by the General Assembly in 1977, and the International Convention Against Apartheid in Sports, which was adopted in 1985 and came into force on 4 April 1988.

Other Action. Other action taken by the UN in support of the African majority of South Africa and against that country's policies of apartheid included:

- condemnation of South Africa's policy of destabilization in southern Africa through its armed incursions into neighboring independent African states that support and assist the efforts of the African majority of South Africa;
- rejection of South Africa's policy of establishing "homelands" as "independent" entities within South Africa where Africans are forced to resettle;
- recognition of the African liberation movements of South Africa—the African National Congress of South Africa (ANC) and the Pan Africanist Congress of Azania (PAC), both banned by South Africa—as "the authentic representatives of the overwhelming majority of the South African people"; and support for persons imprisoned or detained in South Africa for their opposition to apartheid.

The Final Stages. In April 1989, the Special Committee against Apartheid and the Intergovernmental Group to Monitor the Supply of Shipping of Oil and Petroleum Products to South Africa met in New York and recommended that the Security Council impose a mandatory oil embargo. It also recommended that pending action by the Security Council, all oil-producing, shipping, and handling states should enact legislation to stop the flow of oil to South Africa.

From 12–14 December 1989, the General Assembly held a Special Session on Apartheid and its Destructive Consequences in South Africa. It adopted by consensus a historic declaration which listed the steps that the South African regime should take to restore political and human rights in that country. It suggested guidelines for negotiations and for drawing up a new constitution based on the principles of the United Nations Charter and the Declaration of Human Rights. The declaration called upon all South Africans, as a matter of urgency, to join together to negotiate an end to the apartheid system and agree on all the measures necessary to transform their country into a nonracial democracy.

In February 1990, in a dramatic development, most political prisoners in South Africa, including Nelson Mandela, deputy president of the ANC, were released, and the ANC, PAC, and the South African Communist Party were recognized by the government. On 22 June 1990, Nelson Mandela addressed the General Assembly, thanking the United Nations for its efforts to secure his release and that of other South African political prisoners. He urged the UN and individual governments to continue the sanctions which they had imposed on South Africa. In May 1990, the government of South Africa and the ANC adopted the Groote Schuur Minute, which granted indemnity to political exiles and refugees, and paved the way for their return to South Afirca. In August 1990, both parties agreed to the Pretoria Minute under which the government undertook to review emergency and security matters, while the ANC suspended armed actions.

On 1 February 1991, South African president F.W. de Klerk announced that the basic laws of apartheid would be repealed during that session of Parliament. He also issued a Manifesto for the New South Africa, stating that the new nation should be based on justice. The basic laws of apartheid were repealed on 5 June 1991, and later that month a peace summit was held by religious and business leaders, and some of the major parties to political violence. As a result, a preparatory committee, including the government and the ANC, was established and became known as the National Peace Initiative. In August 1991, the National Peace Initiative released a draft national peace accord. Also in August, the government and the office of the UN High Commissioner for Refugees (UNHCR) agreed on a plan for the voluntary repatriation of an estimated 40,000 South african refugees and political exiles.

In spite of the commencement of formal negotiations on constitutional reforms in December 1991, not all political parties participated and violence in the townships continued to escalate. In June 1992, 50 people died in the Boipatong massacre and the ANC suspended its participation in the talks until the government took more decisive action to put an end to the violence.

In July 1992, several political players in South Africa were invited to come and apprise the Security Council of the situation in their country. Subsequently, the Security Council authorized the Secretary-General to appoint a special representative to go to South Africa to find out first hand what what was going on in the country, so that it could be determined how the international community could assist in bringing an end to the violence and create conditions for a peaceful transition in South Africa. As a result of this mission, the Security Council adopted Resolution 772 (1992) authorizing the Secretary-General to deploy the UN Observer Mission in South Africa (UNOMSA), charged with the task of assisting with strengthening the structures set up under the 1991 peace accords. The resolution also invited other international organizations such as the Organization of African Unity (OAU), the Commonwealth and the European Union to consider deploying their own observers in coordination with the United Nations. The first group of 50 UNOMSA observers was deployed in September 1992. It was widely agreed by all parties in South Africa that the presence of international observers greatly helped to reduce political tension, limit violence, and improve the climate for the negotiation process.

In April 1993, a new negotiating framework, the Multiparty Negotiating Council (MPNC) brought together 26 parties and

was the most representative gathering in the history of South Africa. After several months of protracted negotiations, in November 1993, the MPNC adopted a number of constitutional principles and institutions to guide the country during a transitional period lasting until 27 April 1999. This interim constitution set forth plans for elections of a Constitutional Assembly that would draft a new national constitution. In response to all the positive developments, on 8 October 1993, in its Resolution 48/1 (1993), the 184-member General Assembly unanimously ended its 31-year ban on economic and other ties with South Africa in the areas of trade, investment, finance, travel, and transportation. Member states were asked to lift the sanctions they had imposed over the years under numerous UN resolutions and decisions. On 15 October 1993, the Nobel Peace Prize was awarded to South African president F.W. de Klerk and ANC president Nelson Mandela.

Although incidents of violence continued, and some parties to the negotiations threatened to withdraw from the election process, the elections were held successfully from 26–28 April 1994. At the request of the South African Transitional Executive Committee, the Security Council increased the UNOMSA contingent to approximately 1,800 during the election period. Another approximately 900 international observers from foreign governments and international organizations also were deployed across the country to observe the balloting. The UNOMSA observers determined whether voters enjoyed free access to voting stations, whether the secrecy of the vote had been guaranteed, and that ballot boxes had been properly sealed, protected, and transported. It also witnessed the counting of the ballots and the communication of the results to South Africa's Independent Electoral Commission, the body responsible for organizing, administering, and monitoring all aspects of the elections to verify that they were free and fair.

A New Era Dawns. On 27 April 1994 the new six-color flag of a South Africa liberated from apartheid was unfurled at United Nations headquarters in New York. On 10 May 1994, Nelson Rolihlala Mandela was inaugurated as the new president of the Republic of South Africa. On 25 May 1994, the Security Council lifted the mandatory arms embargo it had imposed on South Africa in 1977. On 21 June 1994, the General Assembly, in its Resolution 48/258 (1994), declared that the mandate of the Special Committee against Apartheid had been successfully concluded, and terminated its existence. By the same resolution, it removed the agenda item on the elimination of apartheid from the agenda of its next (49th) session. On 23 June 1994, South Africa was welcomed back to full participation in the work of the General Assembly, after 20 years of banishment.

ARMS REGULATION AND DISARMAMENT

Only days after the signing of the Charter, the world entered the nuclear age. On 6 and 9 August, 1945, respectively, atomic bombs destroyed the Japanese cities of Hiroshima and Nagasaki. The newly formed UN was thus confronted with unprecedented military and political problems. The Charter had envisaged arms limitation and disarmament elements in the progressive establishment of an international security system. It empowered the General Assembly to consider "principles governing disarmament and the regulation of armaments" and assigned to the Security Council the task of formulating plans to establish an appropriate system of controls for the "regulation of armaments," to be submitted to the members of the UN. However, the revolutionary changes brought about by the discovery of atomic power gave the need for disarmament greater immediacy and an enhanced place in the sphere of international politics and security. The UN has reacted progressively to this unfolding of events while the peoples of the world have begun to live under the threat of nuclear annihilation.

Fifty years after the founding of the organization, the tensions that dominated the international political situation during the Cold War period eased, significant progress was achieved in the field of disarmament, and new opportunities opened for the international community to achieve security at lower levels of arms. At the same time, new challenges confronted the members of the UN as the focus of tensions among nations turned from the international to the regional and local level.

In the course of the past five decades, the UN has used a variety of methods, techniques, and approaches in the search for disarmament.

INITIAL EFFORTS

Under Article II of the UN Charter, the General Assembly is empowered to consider "principles governing disarmament and the regulation of armaments" and to recommend action to be taken by member states or the Security Council or both. The General Assembly has undertaken this kind of consideration at every one of its regular sessions since it first met in 1946. The General Assembly's very first resolution, adopted on 24 January 1946, addressed the question of disarmament. It sought the elimination of atomic weapons and other weapons of mass destruction and the assurance that, from then on, atomic energy would be used only for peaceful purposes, and it established the Atomic Energy Commission. In a resolution adopted in December 1946, the General Assembly recognized the connection between the questions of disarmament and of international peace and security.

In 1947, the Security Council set up the Commission for Conventional Armaments in order to regulate armaments and armed forces under an international system of control and inspection, and it called upon the two commissions to take immediate action.

Despite the urgency of the matter, the two commissions did not make much progress. In 1952, the General Assembly, in an attempt to break the impasse, consolidated them into a single 11-member Disarmament Commission, which was entrusted with the task of preparing proposals for the regulation, limitation, and balanced reduction of all armed forces and armaments, by stages, in a coordinated, comprehensive program.

The early debates in the Disarmament Commission ended inconclusively in October 1952. In November, the first hydrogen bomb, with a force that dwarfed that of the Hiroshima-type atomic bomb, was tested by the United States at Eniwetok (now Enewetak), in the Pacific. The following August, a hydrogen bomb was exploded by the USSR.

A subcommittee of the Disarmament Commission, set up by the General Assembly in 1953 and consisting of representatives of Canada, France, the USSR, the United Kingdom, and the US, held a number of meetings, but by the autumn of 1955, efforts aimed at drawing up a comprehensive disarmament plan ended in deadlock. The subcommittee's efforts to consider partial disarmament measures also came to a stalemate over the next two years. In 1957, the General Assembly enlarged the Disarmament Commission from 11 to 25 nations. It was again enlarged, in 1959, to comprise all members of the UN, but it convened only one further time, in 1965.

In 1959, the General Assembly unanimously adopted the first resolution ever to be sponsored by all member states. In it, the General Assembly declared that it was "striving to put an end completely and forever to the armaments race," and it stated that "the question of general and complete disarmament is the most important facing the world today." The resolution aimed at having all proposals and suggestions made during the General Assembly debate transmitted to the Disarmament Commission "for thorough consideration."

Substantive differences in the approach taken to disarmament by the Western powers and the USSR emerged during the subsequent period. A Ten-Nation Committee on Disarmament, based on equal East-West representation, was set up in 1960 outside the framework of the UN to discuss general and complete disarmament but became deadlocked on issues of partial or general measures. As a result, the UN began to pursue disarmament efforts in two ways. While the ultimate goal remained, as it has ever since, "general and complete disarmament under effective international control," measures that would bring about partial disarmament were viewed as integral to that goal and not as hindrances to its achievement. It was felt that devoting parallel, and at times even primary, attention to "collateral" measures designed to reduce tension and build confidence would facilitate the complex task of achieving general and complete disarmament. The immediate hopes and expectations of the majority of nations centered on two such measures: the discontinuance of nuclear-weapon tests and the prevention of the spread of nuclear weapons. By the mid-1960s, the elaboration of partial disarmament measures within the UN began to overshadow all-embracing, long-range efforts.

In 1961, John I. McCloy of the United States and Valerian A. Zorin of the USSR, representing their respective nations in formal disarmament talks, submitted to the General Assembly a Joint Statement of Agreed Principles of Disarmament Negotiations. These eight principles, which were unanimously endorsed by the General Assembly, dealt with: (1) the stated goal of negotiations—a program ensuring that disarmament was to be "general and complete" and was to be accompanied by reliable procedures for the maintenance of peace; (2) the reduction of non-nuclear weapons and facilities to such levels as might be agreed to be necessary for the maintenance of internal order and the provision of personnel for a UN peacekeeping force; (3) an agreed elaboration of the main elements of the disarmament program; (4) implementation of the program in agreed stages, which were to have specified time limits; (5) balance so that at no stage could any state or group maintain an advantage; (6) the need for international control under an international disarmament organization to be created within the framework of the UN; (7) the need during and after disarmament to strengthen institutions for maintaining world peace; and (8) the need to achieve and implement the widest possible agreement in the shortest possible time.

At the same time, the General Assembly also endorsed an agreement to set up, in place of the Ten-Nation Committee, an Eighteen-Nation Committee on Disarmament. When the committee first met in Geneva in early 1962, one member, France, decided not to participate, explaining that it hoped that it might be possible later for the disarmament problem to be discussed among the powers that could contribute effectively to its solution. At the outset, the committee decided to organize so as to permit simultaneous work on general and complete disarmament, confidence-building (collateral) measures, and the discontinuance of nuclear-weapon tests.

In 1969, the committee's membership was enlarged to 26, and its name changed to the Conference of the Committee on Disarmament (CCD). The General Assembly requested the CCD, as the multilateral negotiating body, to work out, while continuing its negotiations on collateral measures, a comprehensive program to deal with the cessation of the arms race and general and complete disarmament under effective international control. In 1975, the CCD was further enlarged, to 31 members, with France still declining to take its seat.

The scant results and continuing difficulties in disarmament negotiations, among other things, led, also in 1969, to the General Assembly's adoption of a resolution declaring the 1970s as a Disarmament Decade.

SPECIAL SESSIONS OF THE GENERAL ASSEMBLY ON DISARMAMENT

First Special Session, 1978

By 1976 it was clear that no real progress had been made to halt the arms race. World military expenditure was estimated at many times more than the amount spent globally on health, education, and economic development. While the nuclear-weapon powers were the major competitors in the arms race, military spending by countries outside the two main military alliances was also rising. Since the end of the Second World War, many millions of people have been killed by conventional weapons in more than 100 wars, most of them fought in the developing areas of the world.

In 1976, the General Assembly, deploring the "meagre achievements" up to that time of the first Disarmament Decade in terms of truly effective agreements, decided, primarily at the initiative of developing countries, to hold a special session in 1978 devoted entirely to disarmament. The aim of the session was to set a new course in international affairs, turn states away from the nuclear and conventional arms race, and obtain agreement on a global strategy for disarmament.

The first special session on disarmament, held at UN headquarters from 23 May to 1 July 1978, was the largest, most representative meeting of nations ever convened to consider the question of disarmament. For the first time in the history of disarmament endeavors, the international community of states as a whole achieved a consensus on a comprehensive disarmament strategy, which was embodied in the Final Document adopted at the session.

The Final Document stressed the central role and primary responsibility of the UN in the field of disarmament and placed disarmament issues in a more comprehensive perspective than

had ever been done before. It reaffirmed the fundamental importance of disarmament to international peace and security and stated that "disarmament and arms limitation agreements should provide for adequate measures of verification satisfactory to all parties." It contained specific measures intended to strengthen the machinery dealing with disarmament within the UN system. Composed of four parts—an introduction, a declaration, a program of action, and a section on machinery—the Final Document set out goals, principles, and priorities in the field of disarmament.

The *Introduction* stated that while the final objective should continue to be general and complete disarmament under effective international control, the immediate goal was the elimination of the danger of a nuclear war and the implementation of measures to halt and reverse the arms race.

The *Declaration* stated that "the increase in weapons, especially nuclear weapons, far from helping to strengthen international security, on the contrary weakens it, . . . heightens the sense of insecurity among all states, including the non-nuclear-weapon states, and increases the threat of nuclear war." It further stated that "genuine and lasting peace can only be created through the effective implementation of the security system provided for in the Charter of the United Nations and the speedy and substantial reduction of arms and armed forces." It emphasized that, in the adoption of disarmament measures, the right of each state to security should be kept in mind and that, at each stage of the disarmament process, "the objective should be undiminished security at the lowest possible level of armaments and military forces."

The *Program of Action* listed priorities and measures that states should undertake as a matter of urgency in the field of disarmament. Priorities included nuclear weapons; other weapons of mass destruction, including chemical weapons; and conventional weapons, including any that might be deemed to be excessively injurious or to have indiscriminate effects. The program called for agreements or other measures to be "resolutely pursued on a bilateral, regional and multilateral basis with the aim of strengthening peace and security," and it recommended that measures be taken and policies pursued to strengthen international peace and security and to build confidence among states. The urgency of preventing the proliferation of nuclear weapons and of halting nuclear tests was stressed. The program called for full implementation of the 1967 Treaty of Tlatelolco, prohibiting nuclear weapons in Latin America, and recommended steps to put into effect the proposals for the establishment of other nuclear-weapon-free zones. Other measures included prohibition of the development, production, and stockpiling of chemical weapons; limits on the international transfer of conventional weapons; agreed reduction of military budgets; and further study of the question of verification. The program also listed measures to be undertaken to mobilize world public opinion on behalf of disarmament.

The final section, on *Machinery*, noted the urgency of revitalizing the disarmament machinery and outlined the consensus reached on the strengthening or establishment of appropriate forums, of suitably representative character, for disarmament deliberations and negotiations, as well as for other activities to be undertaken, including research.

Acting on the recommendations of the special session, the General Assembly established, as a specialized, subsidiary deliberative body, a revitalized Disarmament Commission composed of all UN members. It was assigned the mandate of making recommendations on disarmament problems as requested by the General Assembly, and to follow up the relevant decisions and recommendations of the special session on disarmament.

The special session recognized the continued need for a single multilateral negotiating forum on disarmament and recognized that the Committee on Disarmament in Geneva should continue to fulfil this role and to carry on the work of its predecessors—the Ten-Nation Committee on Disarmament (1959–60), the Eighteen-Nation Committee on Disarmament (1962–69) and the Conference of the Committee on Disarmament (1969–78). Known as the Conference on Disarmament since 1984, it has a membership of 38 countries, including the five nuclear-weapon states and most of the militarily powerful states of the world's regions. In 1994, in recognition of the changed international situation after the Cold War, the conference reviewed the idea of expanding its membership.

Other results of the General Assembly's first special session included the establishment of a program of fellowships on disarmament; an increased flow of information on disarmament to governments, nongovernmental organizations, the media, and the general public; and the designation of the week beginning 24 October (UN Day) to be observed each year as Disarmament Week (see also under Studies, Research, Information, and Training below).

In order to enable the UN to fulfil its role in the field of disarmament and to carry out the tasks assigned to it, the special session took steps to strengthen the role of the section of the UN Secretariat handling disarmament affairs, the Centre for Disarmament Affairs. The centre's main tasks include maintaining a database on conventional armaments transfers, supporting ongoing deliberations and negotiations in New York, Geneva, and elsewhere, fostering regional confidence and security building initiatives, and disseminating information to sources outside the UN.

In 1979, the General Assembly declared the 1980s as the Second Disarmament Decade, stating that its goals should remain consistent with the ultimate objective of general and complete disarmament. The basic goals of the Second Disarmament Decade were set out as follows: halting and reversing the arms race; conclusion of agreements on disarmament according to the objectives and priorities of the 1978 Final Document; strengthening international peace and security in keeping with the UN Charter; and reallocating resources from military to development purposes, particularly in favor of developing countries.

In the four years following the first special session, the international situation in fact deteriorated: numerous events beyond effective UN influence evolved in such a way as to hinder international arms-limitation efforts, particularly in the early 1980s, when military expenditures increased and a lack of confidence permeated disarmament discussions and affected negotiations. After some initial progress, negotiations stalled on virtually every important disarmament issue, and the 1978 Program of Action remained substantially unimplemented.

Second Special Session, 1982

The second special session of the General Assembly devoted to disarmament was held at UN headquarters from 7 June to 10 July 1982. Given the international tension and armed conflicts prevailing at that time, the atmosphere did not bode well for the reaching of further accords on sensitive, substantive issues then relating to the perceived national security interests of states.

At the time of the first special session in 1978, the General Assembly had reaffirmed the goal of general and complete disarmament, a concept that had received considerable attention even before that in the framework of the UN. The emphasis placed on general and complete disarmament slowly gave way to another approach, known as the comprehensive program of disarmament. The intent of the approach was to elaborate a program which would place partial measures of disarmament into a carefully considered plan, setting out objectives, priorities, and timeframes, with a view to the achievement of disarmament on a progressive basis.

A main agenda item of the session—to elaborate the strategy

of the 1978 Program of Action into a Comprehensive Program of Disarmament—was not achieved. Thus, the General Assembly did not agree, as it had in 1978, on a formula for specific action. In the Concluding Document of the session, however, the General Assembly unanimously reaffirmed the validity of the Final Document of the first special session on disarmament. It expressed its profound preoccupation over the danger of war, particularly nuclear war, and urged member states to consider as soon as possible proposals for ensuring prevention of such a war. The General Assembly also stressed again the need for strengthening the central role of the UN in the field of disarmament, for implementing the security system provided for in the Charter of the UN, and for enhancing the effectiveness of the multilateral negotiating body, the Committee on Disarmament.

The committee and then the Conference on Disarmament continued to negotiate the draft comprehensive program of disarmament until 1989. At the end of the conference's session that year, it was agreed to suspend work on the program until the circumstances were more propitious for progress.

Among the other decisions of the second special session was the launching of a World Disarmament Campaign to increase public awareness of disarmament issues (see also under Studies, Research, Information, and Training below). The General Assembly also decided to convene a third special session on disarmament (subsequently scheduled to be held in 1988 at UN headquarters).

Third Special Session, 1988

The third special session took place in 1988 against the background of a considerably improved international climate. The progress that had been recorded in some important fields of disarmament, in particular nuclear disarmament, was welcomed throughout the debates during the session.

The 1987 *Treaty between the former Soviet Union and the United States on the Elimination of Their Intermediate-Range and Shorter-Range Missiles* (INF Treaty); the achievements of the 1986 Stockholm Conference on Confidence- and Security-Building Measures and Disarmament in Europe; and the 1986 *South Pacific Nuclear Free Zone Treaty* (Treaty of Rarotonga) were indicative of the favorable trends in arms control and disarmament.

The progress reported on the negotiations that had begun before the commencement of the special session, between the former Soviet Union and the United States, on a treaty on the reduction and limitation of strategic offensive arms (START) (see below), as well as progress made in the Conference on Disarmament on the complete elimination of chemical weapons, also were highly welcomed. All this notwithstanding, member states were unable to adopt by consensus a final document setting the pace and direction for future negotiations.

DISARMAMENT MACHINERY

General Assembly

The General Assembly, as the main deliberative body of the UN, takes up questions concerning disarmament and related international security matters at each of its annual sessions, through its First Committee, and makes recommendations. In recent years, some 25-30 percent of the resolutions adopted by the General Assembly have been concerned with disarmament and related international security matters; many of these resolutions give mandates to the Disarmament Commission or make requests to the Conference on Disarmament (formerly the Committee on Disarmament) to take into consideration various ideas or questions under negotiation. Both the Disarmament Commission and the Conference on Disarmament report to the General Assembly each year.

Disarmament Commission

The revitalized Disarmament Commission established after the first special session of the General Assembly on disarmament is composed of all members of the UN. It provides a deliberative forum for consideration of specific disarmament issues when the General Assembly is not in session. A subsidiary organ of the General Assembly, it meets annually at UN headquarters for approximately four weeks, usually in May–June, to make recommendations to the General Assembly on specific disarmament problems and to follow up mandates given to it.

Conference on Disarmament

As a result of its first special session on disarmament, the General Assembly mandated the Committee on Disarmament to fulfil the role of a single multilateral negotiating forum and to carry on the work of earlier committees. It enlarged the membership of the committee to 40 countries, including all five nuclear-weapon states (China, France, the USSR, the United Kingdom, and the US). Redesignated the Conference on Disarmament at the end of 1983, it meets in Geneva for approximately six months each year, usually when the General Assembly is not in session. Its Secretary-General is appointed, upon consultation, by the Secretary-General of the UN and also serves as that individual's personal representative.

The Conference on Disarmament has a unique relationship with the UN. It defines its own rules of procedure and develops its own agenda, taking into account the recommendations made by the General Assembly. It agreed on a permanent agenda of 10 items in 1979, and from those items it chooses an annual agenda and fixes its program of work for the year. Its work in plenary meetings and also in subsidiary bodies dealing with specific items is conducted by consensus, since international agreements, if they are to be effective, must be generally acceptable.

MAIN ACHIEVEMENTS

Multilateral Agreements

After World War I, intense efforts were made to translate the 1874 Brussels Declaration and the subsequent Hague Conventions into a ban on chemical weapons and "the use of projectiles, the sole object of which is the diffusion of asphyxiating or deleterious gases." Although a total ban is still to be attained, one of the first achievements, in 1925, was the Protocol for the Prohibition of the Use in War of Asphyxiating, Poisonous or Other Gases, and of Bacteriological Methods of Warfare, generally referred to as the Geneva Protocol. It bans "the use in war of asphyxiating, poisonous or other gases and of all analogous liquids, materials or devices," as well as "the use of bacteriological methods of warfare." The Geneva Protocol, with 110 states parties in 1987, is the point of departure in current efforts toward a ban on the production, possession, and stockpiling of chemical weapons and helped establish the convention banning bacteriological weapons in 1972 (see below).

Concerted efforts by the UN and by governments since 1945 at both the multilateral and bilateral levels, as well as on a regional basis, have led to a body of important agreements, treaties, and conventions committing their parties to various arms limitation and disarmament measures. The multilateral instruments concluded so far are given below (the number of states parties as of 31 December 1987 is shown in parentheses after each title).

- The 1959 *Antarctic Treaty* (37) provides for the demilitarization of Antarctica and is the first treaty to put into practice the concept of the nuclear-weapon-free zone, later applied to Latin America and the South Pacific, as well as to the seabed and outer space. It prohibits any military maneuvers, weapon tests, building of installations, or disposal of radioactive wastes in the Antarctic region.

- The 1963 *Treaty Banning Nuclear Weapon Tests in the Atmosphere, in Outer Space and Under Water* (Partial Test-Ban Treaty) (115) bans all nuclear weapon tests in the three environments designated but does not ban underground tests. Since 1963, the General Assembly has repeatedly urged conclusion of a comprehensive treaty banning all nuclear tests, including those conducted underground.

- The 1967 *Treaty on Principles Governing the Activities of States in the Exploration and Use of Outer Space, Including the Moon and Other Celestial Bodies* (Outer-Space Treaty) (87) bans nuclear and other weapons of mass destruction from the earth's orbit and prohibits the military use of celestial bodies and the placing of such weapons on those bodies.

- The 1967 *Treaty for the Prohibition of Nuclear Weapons in Latin America* (Treaty of Tlatelolco) (31) creates the first nuclear-weapon-free zone in a densely populated area and is the first arms-limitation agreement to provide for control and verification by an international organization, the Agency for the Prohibition of Nuclear Weapons in Latin America, as well as through the safeguards system of the International Atomic Energy Agency (IAEA).

- The 1968 *Treaty on the Non-Proliferation of Nuclear Weapons* (Non-Proliferation Treaty) (138) aims at preventing the spread of nuclear weapons to non-nuclear-weapon states, at guaranteeing all countries access to nuclear technology for peaceful purposes, and at promoting the process of nuclear disarmament. The treaty defines a nuclear-weapon state as one that had manufactured and exploded a nuclear weapon or other nuclear explosive device prior to 1 January 1967. With the broadest adherence of all treaties, it has helped so far to maintain the number of nuclear-weapon states at five.

- The 1971 *Treaty on the Prohibition of the Emplacement of Nuclear Weapons and Other Weapons of Mass Destruction on the Sea-Bed and the Ocean Floor and in the Subsoil Thereof* (Sea-Bed Treaty) (79) bans the placement of nuclear and other weapons of mass destruction and facilities for such weapons on or under the seabed outside a 12-mile coastal zone.

- The 1972 *Convention on the Prohibition of the Development, Production and Stockpiling of Bacteriological (Biological) and Toxin Weapons and on Their Destruction* (109) is the first international agreement providing for actual disarmament, that is, the destruction of existing weapons.

- The 1977 *Convention on the Prohibition of Military or Any Other Hostile Use of Environmental Modification Techniques* (52) prohibits the use of techniques that would have widespread, long-lasting, or severe effects in causing such phenomena as earthquakes, tidal waves, and changes in weather and climate patterns.

- The 1979 *Agreement Governing Activities of States on the Moon and Other Celestial Bodies* (7) goes further than the 1967 Outer-Space Treaty in prohibiting the use of the moon and other celestial bodies for military purposes.

- The 1981 *Convention on Prohibitions or Restrictions on the Use of Certain Conventional Weapons Which May Be Deemed to Be Excessively Injurious or to Have Indiscriminate Effects* (28) restricts or prohibits the use of mines and booby traps, incendiary weapons, and fragments not readily detectable in the human body. These rules range from a complete ban on the use of such weapons to restrictions on their use in conditions that would cause incidental loss of life or injury to civilians or damage to civilian objects.

- The 1985 *South Pacific Nuclear-Free-Zone Treaty* (Treaty of Raratonga) (9), exemplifies a positive regional limitation measure. Its geographical limits are contiguous with those of the two other major zonal treaties, the Treaty of Tlatelolco and the

Antarctic Treaty, the three instruments covering a significant portion of the earth's surface.

- The 1990 *Treaty on Conventional Armed Forces in Europe* (CFE Treaty) (22), was a considerable post-Cold War break-through achieved at a summit meeting of the Conference on Security and Cooperation in Europe (CSCE). It was adopted in Paris in November 1990. The treaty entered into force on 9 November 1992, after it was signed by the original 22 participating states, joined by seven of the new republics formed from the former Soviet Union. It established limits for five categories of weapons within its area of application, which stretches from the Atlantic to the Urals. Chosen for limitation were those categories of weapons systems that would eliminate disparities in force levels and the capability of launching surprise attack or large-scale offensives. The treaty was the first in Europe to provide for the actual reduction of conventional weapons. As called for in the treaty, negotiations among the states party to the CFE Treaty soon began, aimed at limiting the personnel strength of armed forces. Known as the *CFE-1A Agreement*, it was signed in July 1992 at the summit meeting of the CSCE at Helsinki.

Bilateral Agreements

Over the same period, bilateral negotiations between the USSR and the United States have produced a number of agreements between the two powers, including those described below.

- The 1972 *Treaty on the Limitation of Anti-Ballistic Missile Systems* (ABM Treaty and part of the SALT I agreements) restricts in general the development of sea-based, air-based, space-based, or mobile land-based antiballistic missile (ABM) systems and specifically limits development of ABM systems to two sites with no more than 100 launchers each. By a protocol of 1974, the deployment of ABM systems is further limited to a single area, with no more than 100 launchers.
- The 1972 *Interim Agreement on Certain Measures with Respect to the Limitation of Strategic Offensive Arms* (commonly regarded as SALT I) establishes limitations for a five-year period—with a provision for extension—on the number of launchers of strategic weapons.
- Under the 1973 *Agreement on the Prevention of Nuclear War*, the two parties agree to make the removal of the danger of nuclear war and of the use of nuclear weapons an objective of their policies and to make all efforts toward guaranteeing stability and peace.
- The 1974 *Treaty on the Limitation of Underground Nuclear-Weapon Tests* (Threshold Test-Ban Treaty) establishes a nuclear threshold by prohibiting underground nuclear-weapon tests having a yield exceeding 150 kilotons.
- The 1976 *Treaty on Underground Nuclear Explosions for Peaceful Purposes* prohibits the carrying out of any individual nuclear explosion for peaceful purposes having a yield exceeding 150 kilotons or any group explosion with an aggregate yield exceeding 1,500 kilotons, and it includes on-site verification procedures.
- The 1979 *Treaty on the Limitation of Strategic Offensive Arms* (SALT II) establishes limits on the number and types of strategic nuclear-delivery vehicles.
- The 1974, 1976, and 1979 treaties have not come into force, but each party has agreed to adhere to their substantive provisions as long as the other party does likewise.
- The 1987 *Treaty between the Two States on the Elimination of Their Intermediate Range and Shorter-Range Missiles* (INF Treaty) provides for the elimination of an entire class of nuclear weapons with a range between 55 and 5,500 kilometers (3,410 miles). The treaty entered into force on 1 June 1988 and its provisions were implemented before the 1 June 1991 date set by the treaty.

- The 1991 *Treaty on the Reduction and Limitation of Strategic Offensive Arms* (START Treaty) places limits on the two sides' strategic nuclear forces, i.e., inter-continental ballistic missiles (ICBMs). This treaty established an unprecedented reduction of 35 percent to 40 percent of the states' overall nuclear forces at the time and created an elaborate system for verification of compliance.
- The 1993 *Treaty on Further Reduction and Limitation of Strategic Offensive Arms* (START II), once implemented, will bring about deep reductions in the overall levels of ICBMs, submarine-launched ballistic missiles (SLBMs), nuclear armed heavy bombers and nuclear air-launched cruise missiles (ACLMs). The agreement is not yet ratified, as its terms provide that it cannot enter into force before the START Treaty.

MAJOR ISSUES AND DISARMAMENT NEGOTIATION EFFORTS

The Threat of Nuclear Weapons

When the first atomic bombs were exploded on 6 and 9 August 1945, their immense destructive power confronted the world with military and political problems of unprecedented magnitude.

The catastrophic consequences of the use of nuclear weapons would not be confined to the nuclear adversaries but would threaten civilization on a global scale. According to a 1984 World Health Organization (WHO) report on the effects of nuclear war on health and health services, as many as 10,000 megatons of nuclear bombs could be exploded globally in an all-out nuclear war—90 percent of them in Europe, Asia, and North America and 10 percent in Africa, Latin America, and Oceania. As a result, half of the world's population could instantly become war victims. About 1.5 billion people could die and 1.1 billion could be injured. In addition, millions of immediate survivors of an attack would die of radiation effects, disease, cold temperatures, and starvation over the following few years. Thus, the greatest threat to humanity comes from nuclear arsenals, whose total destructive power has reached a level equivalent to more than 1 million Hiroshima bombs. Yet, each of the nuclear powers, albeit with expressed reluctance, considers it essential, either as a strategy or a necessary policy of credible deterrence of war, to possess operational nuclear weapons as long as the others have them.

A 1988 UN study on the climatic and potential physical effects of nuclear war concluded that a major nuclear war would entail the high risk of a global environmental disruption. A 1990 UN report captured the sense of the turning point in history brought about by the development of nuclear weapons. According to that report, nuclear weapons represented a historically new form of weaponry, which, by their multiple and far-reaching effects, provided a means of warfare whose mass destructive potential was unparalleled in human experience. Nuclear technology had made it possible to release more energy in one microsecond from a single nuclear weapon than all the energy released by conventional weapons used in all wars throughout history. The same expert group estimated that, by 1990, the arms race had led to the gradual deployment on land and on the high seas of some 50,000 nuclear warheads. They also estimated that the world stockpile of nuclear weapons was equivalent to some 13,000 million tons of TNT, and that its explosive capacity was 1 million times the explosive energy of the Hiroshima atomic bomb.

In 1945, only the United States had developed the technology to produce nuclear weapons, but by 1949, the USSR had also developed a nuclear-weapon capability, followed by the United Kingdom in 1952, France in 1960, and China in 1964. Throughout the Cold War era, the United States and the former Soviet Union, among the five nuclear-weapon states, held the vast majority of nuclear weapons and the most advanced delivery systems. Indeed, the UN, in a consensus document adopted at the first special session of disarmament in 1978, recognized the special responsibility that these two states bore with respect to nuclear disarmament.

Over the years, concerns have been expressed in UN forums that some non-nuclear-weapon states might develop nuclear-weapon programs (the issue of so-called "threshold" states). After the end of the war in the Persian Gulf in April 1991, it came to light that some of the concerns expressed, at least in the case of Iraq, were warranted. In 1993–94 the defiance of the Democratic Peoples' Republic of Korea (DPRK) touched off an international crisis. The DPRK refused to allow access to IAEA inspectors charged with monitoring peaceful nuclear facilities (see chapter on IAEA). These developments challenged the UN, especially its Security Council, and the IAEA to unprecedented action.

With the dissolution of the Soviet Union at the end of 1991, its nuclear weapons were left on the territories of four of the newly independent states: Belarus, Kazakhstan, Russian Federation, and Ukraine. This state of affairs created a new set of challenges to the international community in the control of nuclear weapons.

Over the years, many measures have been proposed in the UN and other multilateral forums to limit, reduce, and eliminate nuclear weapons and their delivery systems; to assure non-nuclear-weapons states that nuclear weapons will not be used or even threatened to be used against them; to prevent the spread of nuclear weapons to non-nuclear-weapons states; to bring about a halt to all nuclear testing; to ensure the non-use of nuclear weapons; to bring about the cessation of the production of nuclear weapons as well as the production of fissionable material for weapons purposes; to restrict the deployment of nuclear weapons by nuclear-weapon states, and to foster cooperation in the peaceful uses of nuclear energy.

With the close of the Cold War era, a turning point in international political history had been reached and the dramatic international events that occurred had direct repercussions in the area of nuclear disarmament. Bilateral negotiations between the Russian Federation and the United States led to several agreements which, when fully implemented, will result in unprecedented reductions in the nuclear forces of both sides.

These developments served to codify the end of the Cold War and helped to pave the way for further control over the nuclear arsenals of the two major nuclear-weapon states, as well as to encourage the other three declared nuclear-weapon states towards further efforts in the field of nuclear weapons.

In a further sign that the international situation had significantly progressed, the conference decided to begin multilateral negotiations in January 1994 on a comprehensive nuclear test ban treaty. During the regular session of the General Assembly in 1993, the two major powers expressed interest in reaching agreement on a cessation of the production of fissionable material for weapons purposes.

Bilateral Nuclear Arms Reduction Agreements

Although the United Nations did not take part in the historic bilateral negotiations between the former USSR and the United States from 1969 to 1993, member states of the UN have responded with encouragement to the initiatives of the two major powers and have appealed to them to conduct their negotiations with the utmost determination to prevent nuclear war, reduce nuclear arsenals, prevent an arms race in outer space—a long-standing UN objective—and halt the arms race. Other nuclear-weapon states have declared that they would join the process of reducing nuclear weapons once the major powers have reduced theirs. In this context, it is appropriate to review here the sequence of events that brought these negotiations to such a salutary conclusion and their far-reaching implications for global security.

The SALT Treaties

The Strategic Arms Limitation Talks (SALT), which the former Soviet Union and the United States initiated in 1969, led in their first phase to the signing on 26 May 1972 in Moscow of two agreements: the *Treaty on the Limitation of Anti-Ballistic Missile Systems* (ABM Treaty), subsequently amended by a protocol of 3 July 1974, and the *Interim Agreement on Certain Measures With Respect to the Limitation of Strategic Offensive Arms*, with a protocol attached. Both the ABM Treaty and the Interim Agreement entered into force on 3 October 1972.

By signing the ABM Treaty, the United States and the former Soviet Union undertook not to develop, test, or deploy mobile land-based, sea-based, air-based, or space-based ABM systems. They also agreed to limit ABM systems to two sites with no more than 100 launchers at each site. In that way, they would not build nationwide ABM systems, which each side viewed as destabilizing. In 1974, the treaty was amended by a protocol which limited each side to one ABM deployment area only. The former Soviet Union chose to maintain its ABM system in the area centered on its capital, Moscow, and the United States chose to maintain its system in an intercontinental ballistic missile (ICBM) deployment area in North Dakota. Subsequently, the United States decided not to deploy its ABM system.

The second phase of the talks (SALT II) began in November 1972 and ended in June 1979 with the signing in Vienna of the *Treaty on the Limitation of Strategic Offensive Arms*, a protocol which was an integral part of the treaty, and a *Joint Statement of Principles and Basic Guidelines for Subsequent Negotiations on the Limitation of Strategic Arms*. The treaty, designed to remain in force to the end of 1985, defined and identified specific weapons and included numerous detailed limitations on the testing, deployment, modernization and replacement, and conversion of particular weapons systems. A Standing Consultative Commission was set up by the two countries in 1972 to deal with any questions or doubts about compliance with SALT II. Although SALT II was not ratified by either party, each side declared its intention to abide by the provisions of the treaty as long as the other did.

The INF Treaty

Early in the 1980s, the United States and the former Soviet Union opened two new sets of negotiations, one on intermediate-range nuclear forces (INF) and one on the reduction of strategic arms (START). After their discontinuation in December 1983, owing to the strained political situation between the two sides on the question of intermediate forces in Europe, the two powers agreed in January 1985 to hold negotiations on the complex questions concerning space and nuclear arms—both strategic and intermediate range—in order to work out an agreement for preventing an arms race in space and terminating it on earth, at limiting and reducing nuclear arms, and at strengthening strategic stability. This process led first to the signing in December 1987 in Washington of the *Treaty between the Two States on the Elimination of Their Intermediate-Range and Shorter-Range Missiles* (INF Treaty). It provided for the elimination of an entire class of nuclear weapons, namely, those nuclear forces with a range of between 500 and 5,500 kilometres. (Nuclear weapons with a range of more than 5,500 kilometres were considered to be strategic, while those with a range of less than 500 kilometres belonged to the category of tactical nuclear weapons.) The treaty entered into force on 1 June 1988. The INF Treaty is considered the first nuclear disarmament treaty, as it brought about the first actual reductions in the nuclear weapons of the two major powers. It also was considered an important turning point with respect to the strict verification schedule that it established, which included mutual arrangements for on-site inspections. Its provisions were fully implemented before June 1991, the date set by the treaty.

The START Treaties

In parallel to the negotiations being conducted on intermediate nuclear force, a complex series of talks were also held on reducing significantly the two sides' strategic nuclear weapons, in particular inter-continental ballistic missiles (ICBMs). These negotiations were finalized by the signing, at a summit meeting between President Bush and President Gorbachev in Moscow on 31 July 1991, of the *Treaty on the Reduction and Limitation of Strategic Offensive Arms* (START Treaty). The main objective of the treaty was to increase stability in the nuclear relationship between the former USSR and the United States. The interrelated limits and sublimits on the two sides' strategic nuclear forces established by the treaty amounted to an unprecedented reduction of 35 percent to 40 percent of their overall nuclear forces at the time. Furthermore, an elaborate system, including a full range of notifications, inspections, and permanent monitoring, was adopted for the verification of compliance with the terms of the treaty.

At the same time as efforts were being carried forward to ratify the START Treaty and to deal with the problems raised by the dissolution of the former Soviet Union, the Russian Federation and the United States intensified their negotiations on their strategic nuclear weapons. As a result, on 3 January 1993, President Bush and President Yeltsin signed the *Treaty on Further Reduction and Limitation of Strategic Offensive Arms* (START II). The treaty, once implemented, will bring about deep reductions in the overall number of nuclear warheads of the two sides including in their levels of inter-continental ballistic missiles (ICBMs), submarine-launched ballistic missiles (SLBMs), nuclear armed heavy bombers and nuclear air-launched cruise missiles (ACLMs).

Entry into force of the START I Treaty was complicated by the breakup of the USSR in 1989. The Russian Federation ratified the treaty on condition that the new republics of Belarus, Kazakhstan, and Ukraine also ratify the treaty and join the Nuclear Non-Proliferation Treaty (NPT). The START I Treaty was ratified by the United States Senate (1 October 1992), the Russian parliament (4 November 1992), the Belarus parliament (4 February 1993), the Kazakhstan parliament (2 July 1992), and the Ukrainian parliament (3 February 1994). Belarus joined the NPT on 22 July 1993. Kazakhstan joined the NPT on 14 February 1994. As of 1 August 1994, the government of Ukraine had stated that it would join the NPT, but had not yet done so. The treaty will come into force when that final condition is met and a formal exchange of treaty documents takes place.

The START II agreement is not yet ratified as its terms provide that it cannot enter into force before the START Treaty. The treaty provides that, in a two-phased process, the Russian Federation will reduce the number of its strategic nuclear weapons to 3,000 and the United States to 3,500, by the year 2003. If the United States is able to supply financial assistance to the Russian Federation to enable it to carry out the dismantlement of its nuclear weapons, the target treaty date for elimination of the weapons will be the year 2000.

Unilateral Initiatives

In addition to the joint efforts of the two major powers to reduce the level of nuclear confrontation between them, a broad set of unilateral nuclear initiatives was announced by President Bush on 27 September and by President Gorbachev on 5 October 1991, which affected the entire spectrum of nuclear weapons of the United States and the former Soviet Union. The broad unilateral initiatives announced the destruction by both sides of their tactical nuclear weapons throughout the world, as well as other significant moves with respect to their nuclear forces. At the same time, President Gorbachev declared a one-year moratorium on nuclear weapons testing.

Upon the dissolution of the former Soviet Union at the end of 1991, its nuclear arsenal, which was subject to the reductions and limitations agreed under the START Treaty, passed into the jurisdiction of four newly formed states: Belarus, Kazakhstan, the Russian Federation, and Ukraine. To address the questions raised by the new situation, the four states, together with the United States, signed on 23 May 1992 in Lisbon, a protocol to the 1991 START Treaty. In the document, the four states, as successor states of the former USSR, agreed to assume the obligations of the former Soviet Union under the treaty, including working out arrangements among themselves to comply with the limits and restrictions contained in the treaty. While the Russian Federation assumed the status of nuclear-weapon state inherited from the former USSR, Belarus, Kazakhastan, and Ukraine committed themselves to adhere to the non-proliferation treaty as non-nuclear-weapon states in the shortest possible time.

Cessation of Nuclear Testing

It is widely considered that a comprehensive test ban would inhibit the proliferation of nuclear weapons. It would make it difficult, if not impossible, for the nuclear-weapon states to develop new weapon designs and would place constraints on the refinement of existing ones. On the other hand, nuclear-weapon states, including the US, tend to regard at least some form of testing as necessary so long as their security is at all dependent on a strategy of nuclear deterrence.

The question of the discontinuance of nuclear testing has been discussed in the General Assembly since 1945. An estimated 1,622 nuclear-test explosions were detonated between 16 July 1945 and 31 December 1986—815 by the US, 597 by the USSR, 140 by France, 40 by the United Kingdom, 29 by China, and 1 by India, which stated that its nuclear test was an experiment strictly for peaceful purposes.

Partial Test Ban Treaty

Late in 1958, the nuclear powers (then the USSR, the United Kingdom, and the US) began negotiations in Geneva on the discontinuance of nuclear-weapon tests. Although they accomplished nothing definitive, related and subsequent efforts in the General Assembly and the Eighteen-Nation Committee on Disarmament and, finally, further negotiations led to the signing in Moscow on 5 August 1963 of the the *Treaty Banning Nuclear Weapons Tests in the Atmosphere in Outerspace and under Water* (Partial Test-Ban Treaty). The treaty prohibits any nuclear explosions for weapons testing or for any other purpose in the atmosphere or beyond its limits, including outer space; or under water, including territorial waters or high seas. Its prohibitions also extend to nuclear explosions in any other environment if such an explosion produces radioactive debris outside the territorial limits of the state under whose jurisdiction or control the explosion is conducted. Further to the main provisions of the treaty, which did not prohibit the testing of nuclear devices underground, the parties to the treaty also confirmed their intention to seek an end to all testing of nuclear weapons and to continue negotiations towards that end, and declared their desire to end radioactive contamination of the environment.

The treaty was the first international agreement to regulate nuclear arms worldwide, and it has been recognized as an important instrument in reducing international tensions and decreasing radioactive pollution. It also helped to create a climate in which negotiations on other nuclear-arms limitation agreements, notably the *Treaty on the Non-Proliferation of Nuclear Weapons*, were able to take place.

France and China have not become parties to the treaty, but France announced in 1974 that it would not conduct any further atmospheric tests.

Bilateral Agreements on Nuclear Testing

In 1963, the nonaligned states in particular made strenuous efforts to persuade the USSR and the United States to extend the Partial Test Ban Treaty to include a ban on underground tests.

Disagreement about verification prevented such an extension. Even after the Partial Test Ban Treaty came into effect, extensive underground testing continued, particularly by the USSR and the United States.

Two bilateral treaties, between the former Soviet Union and the United States, placed limits on their underground nuclear tests. These were the 1974 *Treaty on the Limitation of Underground Nuclear Weapon Tests* (known as the threshold test-ban treaty) and the 1976 *Treaty on Underground Nuclear Explosions for Peaceful Purposes*. Each party agreed not to test explosives yielding more than the 150-kiloton limit. Because of difficulties with the verification provisions and technology associated with the two treaties, they remained unratified for many years, although the two powers complied with their provisions. Following three years of bilateral negotiations from November 1987 to 1 December 1990 on nuclear testing verification and yield measurement methodology, the two powers exchanged instruments of ratification of the two treaties. The verification arrangements set out in conjunction with those two treaties were unprecedented in their openness and transparency, and helped to set the stage for even greater cooperation between the two major powers in agreements on the reduction of their nuclear-weapon arsenals.

Comprehensive Test Ban Treaty

The question of the complete cessation of all nuclear-weapon tests or of all nuclear explosive tests has been considered as a separate issue in UN bodies since 1963 and is the subject of many General Assembly resolutions. Between 1977 and 1980, the USSR, the United Kingdom, and the United States also undertook trilateral negotiations on a comprehensive test-ban treaty but again did not succeed in completing one. Questions of how to verify compliance with a ban on nuclear-weapon tests, how to treat nuclear explosions for peaceful purposes under the conditions of a ban, and whether to seek to ban all nuclear explosions have presented difficulties both in the Conference on Disarmament, which has been the main focus of efforts since 1980, and in the bilateral discussions that commenced in July 1986 between the USSR and the US. The two powers have discussed the questions of more precise verification, methodologies for measuring the yield of permitted explosions, conditions for ratifying the 1974 and 1976 treaties, and the possibility of lower thresholds for underground explosions leading to a comprehensive ban.

In an effort to add impetus to the ongoing efforts, the USSR halted all nuclear explosions for an 18-month period, from August 1985 to February 1987. The United States did not reciprocate because it believed that such an unverifiable measure was not a substitute for a negotiated, binding treaty.

Unilateral Actions Towards an End to Nuclear Testing

With the end of the Cold War and the improvement in international political climate, important political strides towards the achievement of a comprehensive nuclear test ban were registered. In the early 1990s the number of underground nuclear tests being conducted by the nuclear-weapon states began to decrease considerably. In October 1991, the former Soviet Union declared a unilateral moratorium on nuclear tests, which was extended by the Russian Federation indefinitely. In April 1992 France suspended its nuclear testing. In October 1992 the United States enacted a law which not only declared a unilateral moratorium on its nuclear tests, but also directed that after September 1996, the United States government could no longer conduct nuclear tests. The United Kingdom, which has conducted for several decades its nuclear-weapon tests at the nuclear testing site in the United States, has respected the declared moratorium of the United States and has not conducted any nuclear tests since November 1991. However, China conducted its latest nuclear tests in October 1993 and in June 1994.

Despite the Chinese tests, the developments just mentioned were welcomed by the vast majority of the members of the General Assembly and renewed optimism that a comprehensive nuclear test ban is an achievable goal.

Prevention of Nuclear Proliferation

In the early years of the atomic era, it was widely assumed that only a few highly industrialized nations would be able to afford to manufacture nuclear weapons. However, by the mid-1960s, advancing technology and simplification of nuclear production processes, particularly for electric-power generation, had led to the categorization of some 20 nations, including relatively small ones, as countries possessing a nuclear capability; there are now some 30 so-called "threshold" states. The fear of horizontal nuclear proliferation has thus spawned much discussion in the General Assembly. During 1965 and 1966, the greater part of the General Assembly's debates on disarmament was devoted to this issue, especially with the emergence of China as a nuclear-weapon power.

In 1967, the United States and the USSR, after prolonged negotiations, put forward identical draft non-proliferation treaties in the Eighteen-Nation Committee on Disarmament, and in 1968, after further negotiation, a final joint draft was commended overwhelmingly by the General Assembly as the *Treaty on the Non-Proliferation of Nuclear Weapons*. The treaty came into force in March 1970. By 31 July 1993, it had been ratified by 160 countries, including the five declared nuclear-weapon states: China, France, the Russian Federation, the United Kingdom, and the United States. Though the treaty had received a great deal of support as reflected in the large amount of ratifications to it, challenges to its objectives remained.

The Non-Proliferation Treaty prohibits the spread of nuclear weapons, employing the safeguards system of the IAEA to provide assurance against any diversion or misuse of nuclear materials by non-nuclear-weapon states. It also contains provisions for promoting the peaceful uses of nuclear energy; for making nuclear equipment, materials, and information available on a nondiscriminatory basis to non-nuclear-weapon states for peaceful purposes; and for the pursuit of negotiations relating to the cessation of the nuclear-arms race and to nuclear and general disarmament. All the non-nuclear-weapon parties to the treaty must accept safeguards, through separate agreements, with the IAEA. The safeguards system provides for international inspection of all their nuclear installations. Several states that are not parties to the treaty have also signed safeguards agreements with the IAEA covering all or most of their installations.

Following the disintegration of the former Soviet Union at the end of 1991, the nuclear weapons left on its former territory had fallen under the jurisdiction of Belarus, Kazakhstan, the Russian Federation, and Ukraine. While the Russian Federation assumed the treaty obligations of the former Soviet Union, in a special agreement, the Lisbon Protocol, Belarus, Kazakhstan, and Ukraine had agreed to become non-nuclear-weapon states party to the NPT. As of 1 November 1993, only Belarus had complied with that commitment. In addition, several other states not party to the treaty, among them Argentina, Brazil, India, Israel, and Pakistan, have extensive nuclear programs and facilities, the great majority subject to non-treaty nuclear safeguards agreements with the IAEA. Their lack of participation reflects one of the main criticisms of the treaty, that is, they believe that its organization and structure is discriminatory, dividing the international community into nuclear haves and have-nots.

In the wake of the war in the Persian Gulf, the UN Special Commission (UNSCOM), appointed to eliminate Iraq's capability to use weapons of mass destruction, uncovered the existence of a clandestine nuclear weapons program in that country. This revelation further challenged the NPT regime and in particular the inspection procedures employed by the IAEA.

Four conferences have been held to review the operation of the treaty—in 1975, 1980, 1985, and 1990. In accordance with the terms of the treaty, a conference is to be held 25 years after its entry into force to decide whether it shall continue in force indefinitely or shall be extended for an additional fixed period or periods. Since the treaty's entry into force, the parties and the General Assembly have called in various contexts for universal adherence to the treaty as the best means of further strengthening the non-proliferation regime.

Some of the aspects that are of crucial importance to the extension of the NPT and the strengthening of the non-proliferation regime revolve around the issue of efforts being made towards the cessation of the nuclear arms race and nuclear disarmament. In that connection, the question of the achievement of a comprehensive nuclear test ban treaty has taken on paramount importance for many non-nuclear-weapon states. In addition, the issue of the granting of guarantees to non-nuclear-weapon states that nuclear weapons will not be used against them would make an important contribution to the reinforcement of the NPT structure. Many states have for years supported the call for the nuclear-weapon states to cease production of fissionable material for weapons purposes, which they consider would contribute significantly in a qualitative manner to the ending of the nuclear arms race.

Notwithstanding the above caveats, the Non-Proliferation Treaty remains effective as the cornerstone of an international non-proliferation structure that has grown to embrace the overwhelming majority of countries of the world.

Nuclear-Weapon-Free Zones

The establishment of nuclear-weapon-free zones in various parts of the world has long been considered a possible means for curbing horizontal nuclear proliferation and enhancing peace and security for non-nuclear-weapon states on a regional basis.

Outer Space

The 1967 *Treaty on Principles Governing the Activities of States in the Exploration and Use of Outer Space, including the Moon and Other Celestial Bodies*, while not strictly belonging to that body of law which bans nuclear weapons from a particular area, is relevant nonetheless to the concept of nuclear-free zones. Among other things, it provides that states parties will not place any objects carrying nuclear weapons or any weapon of mass destruction in orbit around the earth, install these weapons on celestial bodies, or station them in outer space.

The Seabed

The 1972 *Treaty on the Prohibition of the Emplacement of Nuclear Weapons and Other Weapons of Mass Destruction on the Sea-Bed and the Ocean Floor and in the Subsoil Thereof* provides that states parties undertake not to place on or under the seabed, beyond the outer limit of a 12-mile coastal zone, any nuclear or other weapons of mass destruction or any facilities for such weapons.

Antarctica

The 1959 *Antarctic Treaty* was the first international agreement to provide for the absence of nuclear weapons in a specified area by having established a demilitarized zone in the Antarctic. Under the terms of the treaty, Antarctica is to be used exclusively for peaceful purposes. All military activity, nuclear explosions, or disposal of radioactive waste in the area are prohibited. The provisions of this treaty appear to have been scrupulously observed.

Latin America and the Caribbean

The *Treaty for the Prohibition of Nuclear Weapons in Latin America and the Caribbean* (Treaty of Tlatelolco), signed on 14 February 1967 at Tlatelolco, Mexico, was the first treaty establishing a nuclear-weapon-free zone in a densely populated area. It is also the first regional agreement to establish its own system of international verification and a permanent supervisory organ, the Agency for the Prohibition of Nuclear Weapons in Latin

America (known by its Spanish acronym OPANAL), which was set up in June 1969. States parties to the treaty agree to use any nuclear material or facilities under their jurisdiction exclusively for peaceful purposes and to prohibit the presence of nuclear weapons in their territories, under any circumstances. They also agree not to engage in, encourage, authorize, directly or indirectly, or in any way participate in, the testing, use, manufacture, production, possession, or control of any nuclear weapon. The treaty's verification system includes the requirement that safeguards agreements be concluded with IAEA in respect of all the nuclear activities undertaken by the parties. Annexed to the treaty are two Additional Protocols. Under Additional Protocol I, France, the Netherlands, the United Kingdom, and the United States agree to guarantee nuclear-weapon-free status to those territories for which they are, *de jure* or *de facto*, internationally responsible. In August 1992, the protocol was signed by France, thus giving it full force as all four countries had now signed. Under Additional Protocol II, nuclear-weapon states pledge to respect fully the denuclearization of Latin America and not to use or threaten to use nuclear weapons against parties to the treaty. By 1979, all five nuclear-weapon states had become parties to it.

The South Pacific

The states party to the 1986 *South Pacific Nuclear Free Zone Treaty* (Treaty of Rarotonga) have undertaken not to manufacture or acquire any nuclear explosive device; to control the export of fissionable material; to ensure that their nuclear activities are exclusively for peaceful and nonexplosive purposes and are conducted under strict safeguards; to ban the testing of nuclear explosive devices in the South Pacific; to prohibit the stationing of nuclear explosive devices in their territories; and to prevent the dumping at sea, in the region, of nuclear waste.

The treaty has three protocols, which are integral to its purposes. Protocol 1 obliges France, the United Kingdom, and the United States to apply the terms of the treaty in respect of the territories for which they are responsible in the region, especially with regard to prohibitions on the manufacture, stationing, and testing of any nuclear explosive device. The three states have not signed this protocol. Protocol 2 commits the five nuclear-weapon states not to use or threaten to use any nuclear explosive device against parties to the treaty. This protocol has been agreed to by China and the Russian Federation. Protocol 3 commits the five nuclear-weapon states not to test any nuclear explosive device anywhere within the zone covered by the treaty. China and the Russian Federation have ratified this protocol.

Proposals for Nuclear-weapon-free Zones

In addition to those areas and zones mentioned above, where there has been success in elaborating treaties prohibiting the use of nuclear weapons, the General Assembly has also discussed, with varying degrees of success, proposals for creating nuclear-weapon-free zones in many other regions of the world. Although these discussions have covered a number of geographic zones, including the Balkans, the Mediterranean, and Northern Europe, most proposals have dealt in particular with Central Europe, the African continent, the Middle East, and South Asia.

Security Assurances to Non-nuclear-weapon States

Since the conclusion of the NPT in 1968, the non-nuclear-weapon states have repeatedly insisted that their promise not to acquire nuclear weapons should be met with an assurance that nuclear weapons would not, under any circumstances, be used against them. On 19 June 1968, the Security Council recognized that aggression using nuclear weapons, or the threat of doing so, against a non-nuclear-weapon state would warrant immediate action by the Security Council, above all its nuclear-weapon state permanent members. The Security Council also reaffirmed the provision of the UN Charter that declares that a state, if the victim of an armed attack, has a right to act in individual or collective self-defense until such time as the Security Council could take action to maintain peace and security.

At the 1978 special session on disarmament, four of the five nuclear-weapon states individually declared their intention not to use, or threaten to use, nuclear weapons against non-nuclear-weapon states, which met the conditions outlined in their respective declarations. At that session also, China reiterated the declaration it made when it conducted its first nuclear test—that it would never use nuclear weapons against a non-nuclear-weapon state. The nuclear-weapon states have refined and reasserted their respective security guarantees several times since then.

Each year since 1979, the Conference on Disarmament has considered proposals for effective international arrangements that would assure non-nuclear-weapon states against the use, or threat of use, of nuclear weapons. Non-nuclear-weapon states have expressed the view that further assurances, in legally binding form, are necessary in order to effectively guarantee their security against nuclear attack. The Western nuclear-weapon states and their allies have been of the view that, in order to receive such negative security assurances, states must have demonstrated a commitment not to acquire nuclear weapons, by forming part of a nuclear-weapon-free zone or by adhering to the Nuclear Non-Proliferation Treaty. Those non-nuclear-weapon states that are party to the NPT consider the issue of pivotal importance to the outcome of the 1995 NPT Conference.

Prohibition of the Production of Fissionable Material
An approach to nuclear disarmament which has received much international attention over the years has been to stop the production of fissionable material for weapons purposes.

The United States submitted proposals on this subject to the Eighteen-Nation Committee on Disarmament and the General Assembly during the 1960s, which included plans for inspection of certain types of nuclear reactors and separation plants; the dismantling of a number of nuclear weapons by both the United States and the former Soviet Union, to be carried out in the presence of observers; and the transfer or conversion of fissionable material to industries or forms in which it could be used for peaceful purposes.

In 1992 the United States announced a unilateral cessation of its national production of plutonium and highly enriched uranium for nuclear weapons. Among the nuclear-weapon states, both the Russian Federation and the United States have recently expressed support for reaching an international agreement to halt the production of weapons-grade fissionable material in the interests of non-proliferation. In 1993, the General Assembly adopted without a vote a resolution recommending negotiation in the most appropriate international forum of a non-discriminatory, multilateral, and internationally and effectively verifiable treaty banning the production of material for nuclear weapons or other nuclear explosive devices.

The dissolution of the Soviet Union and the fact that nuclear weapons are now on the territories of four of the successor states, as well as the vast amount of nuclear material that will need to be removed and monitored owing to the disarmament process of the two major powers, represent challenges which the non-proliferation movement must overcome.

OTHER WEAPONS OF MASS DESTRUCTION
In 1946, the General Assembly envisaged not only the elimination of atomic weapons, but also of all other major weapons of mass destruction. The dangers of such weapons to humanity cannot be underestimated. Even in World War I, "first-generation" chemical agents caused some 1.3 million casualties, of which over 100,000 were fatal. In 1948, the Commission for Conventional Armaments, in setting out the limits of its jurisdiction, also defined weapons of mass destruction as including, besides atomic explo-

sive weapons, radioactive material weapons, lethal chemical and biological weapons, and any weapons developed in the future with comparable destructive effects.

Chemical and Biological Weapons
As mentioned earlier, the powerful sense of outrage generated by the use of chemical weapons during the First World War resulted in the signing of the Geneva Protocol of 1925 banning the use, but not the production, possession, or stockpiling, of chemical or bacteriological weapons. As a consequence, possession and acquisition, particularly of chemical weapons, has continued and, indeed, in recent years has proliferated. Many parties to the Geneva Protocol have included reservations or statements with their signatures that open the door to the possible retaliatory use of such weapons.

The protocol also did not provide for mechanisms to verify compliance or for procedures to deal with violations. Recognizing the shortcomings of the protocol, the international community continued its quest for a complete ban on chemical and biological weapons. Although treated as a single issue previously, it was agreed in 1971 to separate consideration of chemical and biological weapons in the hope that an early ban on biological weapons could be achieved.

Biological Weapons
The *Convention on the Prohibition of the Development, Production and Stockpiling of Bacteriological (Biological) and Toxin Weapons and on Their Destruction* entered into force on 26 March 1975 and was hailed as a first step towards a comprehensive ban on chemical weapons.

The convention prohibits the development, production, stockpiling, acquisition, or retention of microbial or other biological agents, or toxins whatever their origin or methods of production, of types and in quantities that have no justification for prophylactic, protective, or other peaceful purposes. It also prohibits weapons, equipment, or means of delivery designed to use such agents or toxins for hostile purposes or in armed conflict. The agents, toxins, weapons, equipment, and means of delivery held by states that became party to the convention should be destroyed or diverted to peaceful purposes not later than nine months after the entry into force of the convention for that state. Furthermore, any state party that finds that any other state party is not complying with the provisions of the convention may lodge a complaint with the Security Council.

In 1986, states parties decided to initiate a set of confidence-building measures in the form of a voluntary exchange of information and data. The information to be exchanged included data on high-risk research centers and laboratories; outbreaks of infectious diseases; publication of results of biological research; and the promotion of contacts among scientists in biological research.

In 1991, the states parties established an Ad Hoc Group of Governmental Experts to identify and examine potential verification measures from a scientific and technical standpoint. A majority of states parties have requested a special conference to review the results of the expert group in 1994.

Chemical Weapons
In 1966, with the adoption of its first resolution on the question of chemical and bacteriological (biological) warfare, the General Assembly commenced a long process of international discussions and negotiations on issues relevant to the question. The adoption of the resolution reflected growing international awareness of the dangers involved with the possible use of such weapons of mass destruction.

The question of chemical and biological weapons was treated as a single issue requiring a unified approach before 1971. After agreement had been reached on the Biological Weapons Convention in 1972, attention turned more to the chemical weapons aspect and numerous proposals were put forward in the multilateral negotiating body in Geneva, including the complete texts of drafts conventions. In 1980, the Conference on Disarmament began working toward a convention on chemical weapons, but progress was evident only late in the decade. The former Soviet Union and the United States, the only states that had admitted to possessing stockpiles of chemical weapons, began a series of bilateral contacts that led to agreement between them on sensitive issues of verification of implementation of a convention, including the question of challenge and on-site inspection.

The actual use of chemical weapons during the war between Iraq and the Islamic Republic of Iran in the 1980s, confirmed by an investigative team appointed by the Secretary-General, focussed greater international attention on the need to reach early agreement on the prohibition of these weapons. In 1991, the war in the Persian Gulf and the possibility that chemical weapons might again be used added even greater urgency to the efforts to rid the world of chemical weapons as soon as possible.

The *Convention on the Prohibition of the Development, Production, Stockpiling and Use of Chemical Weapons and on Their Destruction* was opened for signature on 13 January 1993 in Paris, France. The convention is of unlimited duration and will enter into force 180 days after the deposit of instruments of ratification by 65 states parties, but not earlier than two years after its opening for signature, that is, not before 13 January 1995.

The convention is considered a genuine disarmament measure in that it provides for the elimination of an entire category of weapons of mass destruction. Its importance lies in the fact that these weapons exist in large quantities, have been used in combat in the past, and are believed to be possessed by a large number of countries. Further, the verification system provided for under the convention is the most comprehensive to have been formulated for a multilateral agreement in the field of disarmament.

By the terms of the convention, states parties undertake never, under any circumstances, to use chemical weapons, nor to develop, produce, otherwise acquire, stockpile, or retain chemical weapons, or transfer them, directly or indirectly, to anyone. They also commit themselves never to engage in any military preparations to use chemical weapons nor to assist, encourage, or induce, in any way, anyone to engage in any activity prohibited under the convention. Within a period of 10 years, each state party undertakes to destroy chemical weapons and production facilities that it may own or possess, or that are located in any place under its jurisdiction or control, as well as all chemical weapons it has abandoned on the territory of another state party. The convention also bans the use of riot control agents as a method of warfare.

The states parties are required to submit detailed declarations on any chemical weapons they might possess, on old and abandoned chemical weapons they might have on their territory, and on any related chemical weapons production facilities, as well as on the plans and implementation of the destruction of such. They have agreed to a comprehensive and graduated system of routine inspections for international monitoring of the implementation of their obligations under the convention. Also provided for is a system of short-notice, challenge inspections, by which each state party may request an international inspection team to monitor any facility or location in the territory of another state party, which is obliged to allow the inspection, for the purpose of clarifying and resolving any questions concerning possible non-compliance. An inspected state party may protect activities and installations that it considers unrelated to the inspection request.

The convention provides for the establishment of the Organization for the Prohibition of Chemical Weapons (OPCW), which will be composed of the Conference of States Parties, as the principal decision-making body; the Executive Council, with a membership of 41 states parties representing five regional groups; and the Technical Secretariat, headed by a director general to conduct

the practical work of the organization. The principal component of the secretariat will be its inspectorate, responsible for carrying out the verification provisions of the convention. In order to enable the organization to fulfill its functions immediately after entry into force of the convention, a Preparatory Commission for the Organization was convened by the Secretary-General in February 1993 in the Hague, Netherlands, the eventual site of the OPCW. The Preparatory Commission will continue working until the formation of the OPCW.

New Weapons of Mass Destruction

The question of new weapons of mass destruction has been under consideration since the mid-1970s in the General Assembly and the Conference on Disarmament, which have stated that effective measures should be taken to prevent the emergence of such weapons. The former USSR and other states favored a general agreement precluding laboratory development of weapons of mass destruction, as well as specific agreements as relevant possibilities are identified; other states feel that meaningful, verifiable agreements are practical only for specific, emergent weapons or systems.

A list of specific types of potential weapons of mass destruction presented by the former USSR in 1979 included the following: radiological weapons, using radiological materials, a possibility already foreseen in 1948; particle-beam weapons, using charged or neutral particles to affect biological targets; and infrasonic "acoustic radiation" weapons and electromagnetic weapons operating at certain radio frequencies, either of which could have injurious effects on human organs.

Radiological Weapons

At the 1976 session of the General Assembly, the United States proposed an instrument prohibiting radioactive weapons. This proposal led to bilateral negotiations with the USSR and the submission in 1979 of an agreed joint initiative for consideration by the then Committee on Disarmament.

Each year from 1980 to 1992, the multilateral negotiating body has considered proposals for reaching agreement on a convention to prohibit the development, production, stockpiling, or use of radiological weapons. Some nonaligned and neutral states of the Conference on Disarmament, while recognizing the potential danger of the development of radiological weapons, considered that a military attack on a civilian nuclear power installation represented a more dangerous risk of mass destruction caused by the release of radiological substances. The former Soviet Union and the United States felt this idea altered the basic concept and content of the joint initiative.

Finding an acceptable way to cover both a ban on radiological weapons in the traditional sense and a prohibition of attacks against peaceful nuclear facilities has since been the main problem in efforts to negotiate a radiological weapons convention. This question has remained on the agenda of the Conference on Disarmament and the General Assembly, but differences of view concerning the question of the prohibition of attacks against nuclear facilities have persisted, and no progress has been made.

PROTECTING THE ENVIRONMENT FROM MILITARY ACTIVITY

In recent history, the world has viewed with mounting concern the specter of deliberate destruction of the environment as a method of warfare. The damage inflicted on the environment during the war in the Persian Gulf in 1991 and 1992 led to the inclusion of a new item on the agenda of the General Assembly, entitled "Exploitation of the environment as a weapon in times of armed conflict and the taking of practical measures to prevent such exploitation." In December 1991, the General Assembly requested the Secretary-General to prepare a report on protecting the environment in times of armed conflict.

Prohibition of Environmental Modification

In July 1974, following a summit meeting between the United States and the USSR, the two powers advocated measures to preclude the use of environmental modification techniques for hostile military purposes. This proposal led to consideration of the question in the General Assembly and the Conference of the Committee on Disarmament and the opening for signature on 18 May 1977 of the Convention on the Prohibition of Military or Any Other Hostile Use of Environmental Modification Techniques. The convention entered into force in 1978. In essence, the convention bolsters existing provisions in international law protecting the environment by outlawing environmental modification techniques that would cause widespread, long-lasting, or severe effects to another state. During the process that led to the convention, many states decided it defined too narrowly the scope of the techniques to be banned. By 1994, the convention had acquired only 55 signatures.

The convening of the UN conference in Rio de Janeiro in 1992 and the specter of oil wells set ablaze and a massive oil spill in the Persian Gulf during the Gulf War of 1991–92 intensified the debate over the environmental consequences of war. Some of the states parties to the convention have made it known that they will ask, sometime before 1995, the Secretary-General of the UN, as depositary (the holder of the legal, certified copies of the treaty), to convene a consultative committee of experts to provide views on the scope and application of the provisions of the convention. The states parties also have confirmed that the use of herbicides as an environmental modification technique was a method of warfare that fell within the scope of the prohibition of the convention if such use upset the ecological balance of a region, thus causing widespread, long-lasting, and severe effects.

CONVENTIONAL WEAPONS

It is a painful reality that, throughout the nuclear era and the cold war, and now in the post-cold war world, all armed conflicts—almost every one of them in developing countries—have been fought with conventional weapons. More than 20 million people have died in those wars. Every year, armed conflicts are waged in some 30 locations on the planet, all fought with conventional weapons. Advances in science and technology have changed the face of conventional warfare and spurred on arms races, most often in already volatile regions. Conventional weapons and armed forces account for some four-fifths of global military expenditures and for approximately 80 percent of the world arms trade.

Thus, while consideration of nuclear questions has dominated disarmament debates in the UN and other forums, the problems posed by the conventional arms race and arms transfers have come increasingly to the fore, particularly in the 1980s. In the disarmament forums at the UN, discussions of the issue of conventional disarmament have focussed on four main elements: (a) limitations on conventional weapons themselves; (b) transparency in international arms transfers and the establishment of a UN Register on Conventional Arms; (c) the regional approach and the building of military confidence and security among states; and (d) the strengthening of international humanitarian and disarmament law with respect to inhumane weapons, including the question of land mines.

In 1986, "conventional disarmament" was considered as a separate item on the agenda of the General Assembly for the first time, and, as a result, in 1987 it appeared on the agenda of the Disarmament Commission, indicating an increasing acceptance of the view that nuclear and conventional disarmament should proceed simultaneously.

When the question of prohibiting the use of certain conventional weapons, such as napalm and other incendiaries, was first raised in the General Assembly in the late 1960s, there were numerous proposals for banning various weapons, such as mines and booby traps, that also were deemed to cause unnecessary suffering or have indiscriminate effects. Considerable work, including some under the auspices of the International Committee of the Red Cross and of diplomatic conferences on protocols to the Geneva Convention of 1949 relating to humanitarian law in armed conflicts, was done in the late 1960s and the 1970s. As noted above, in 1980, a UN conference at Geneva adopted the *Convention on Prohibitions or Restrictions on the Use of Certain Conventional Weapons Which May Be Deemed to Be Excessively Injurious or to Have Indiscriminate Effects*; the convention was opened for signature in 1981 and came into force in December 1983.

UN Register of Conventional Arms

On 1 January 1992 the *UN Register of Conventional Arms* was officially established and the first reports on arms transfers during 1992 were due to be received by the UN Centre for Disarmament Affairs by 30 April 1993. In October of 1993, the Secretary-General presented a consolidated report on the first year of operation of the register to the General Assembly, which brought the information presented by states into the public domain. Information was received from 87 states, including most of the major supplier countries, on arms imports and exports in seven categories of heavy conventional weapons—battle tanks, armored combat vehicles, large calibre artillery systems, combat aircraft, attack helicopters, warships, and missiles and missile launchers. Submissions to the register, which are on a voluntary basis, are to be made by 30 April of each year. Upon the request of the General Assembly, the Secretary-General convened a group of experts in 1994 to examine the continuing operation of the register and its further development. In that connection, many states asserted that the information shared should include information on military holdings, on procurement through national production, and on weapons of mass destruction. They believed that these additions to the register would help to attract wider universality in reporting.

The establishment of the Register of Conventional Arms by the UN was a ground-breaking endeavor. The exchange of information enacted by means of the register has the potential to foster confidence among states and create an atmosphere more conducive to self-restraint and real measures of disarmament. The successful further development and operation of the register could provide the member states of the UN with an effective instrument of preventive diplomacy.

Also in relation to openness and transparency in military matters, the Disarmament Commission completed its work on guidelines and recommendations for objective information on military matters, which were endorsed by the General Assembly. Also in 1992, the Conference on Disarmament took up for the first time an item dealing with conventional weapons under a new agenda item entitled "Transparency in armaments." It continued consideration of the item in 1993 and 1994 in the framework of a subsidiary body of the conference, and presented a report to the General Assembly on its work in 1993.

Inhumane Weapons

Early international humanitarian laws dealt with the effects of inhumane conventional weapons. The St. Petersburg Declaration of 1868 recognized that the object of warfare would not be served by the use of weapons that uselessly aggravate the suffering of disabled soldiers. The "dum-dum" bullet, developed a few years later, was banned by the 1899 Hague Conference as contrary to the St. Petersburg Declaration. Principles enunciated in the St. Petersburg Declaration of 1868 and the Hague Conferences of 1899 and 1907 were repeated in the Geneva Conventions of 1949, prohibiting the employment of weapons, projectiles, and material and methods of warfare of a nature to cause superfluous injury or unnecessary suffering. Between 1974 and 1977, two protocols were negotiated to the Geneva Conventions, but were not considered effective at adopting any prohibitions or restrictions on conventional weapons.

In 1977, the General Assembly decided to convene a UN conference with the aim of reaching an agreement on prohibitions or restrictions of use of certain conventional weapons. The UN Conference, held at Geneva in 1979 and 1980, adopted the convention, which entered into force on 2 December 1983. Annexed Protocol I prohibits the use of any weapons that injure with fragments that are not detectable by X-rays. Protocol II prohibits or sets out restrictions on the use of mines (excluding anti-ship mines), booby-traps, and other delayed action devices. Protocol III prohibits or outlines restrictions on the use of incendiary weapons, that is, weapons designed with the primary purpose of setting fire to objects or causing injury by means of fire.

In accordance with the terms of the convention, upon the request of the states parties submitted in 1993, the Secretary-General, as depositary of the convention, will convene a conference of the states party to the convention and its annexed protocols with the aim of reviewing its scope and operation. Preparations for that conference began in 1994.

Among other items of discussion with respect to the review of the convention, the vast toll in civilian life and bodily injury, together with the devastation of societies and economies in post-conflict situations caused by the massive and indiscriminate use of land mines, has been receiving greater international attention. In 1993, the General Assembly called upon all states to adopt a moratorium on the export of antipersonnel land mines. In a related resolution, the General Assembly requested the Secretary-General to prepare a report on the problems caused by the increasing presence of mines and other unexploded devices resulting from armed conflicts and on the manner in which the United Nations' contribution to the solution of problems relating to mine clearance could be strengthened.

CONFIDENCE-BUILDING MEASURES

Regional Confidence-Building

The objective of confidence-building measures is to contribute toward reducing or eliminating the causes for mistrust, fear, tensions, and hostilities, which are significant factors behind the international arms buildup. A UN study on confidence-building measures, issued in 1981, represented an attempt to clarify and develop the concept of confidence-building and to provide guidelines to governments for introducing and implementing confidence-building measures and promoting public awareness of the concept so as to advance negotiations and enhance peace and security. In that same year, the General Assembly invited all states to consider the possible introduction of confidence-building measures in their particular regions and, where possible, to negotiate among themselves in keeping with conditions and requirements prevailing in the respective regions. In fact, multilateral negotiations on these issues had been under way since the early 1970s.

The Vienna Talks on the Mutual Reduction of Forces and Armaments and Associated Measures in Central Europe, which commenced in 1973 among the member countries of NATO and the Warsaw Pact, were aimed at enhancing stability in the central region of the two alliances and in Europe as a whole while reducing armed forces and equipment but maintaining undiminished security. After decades of unsuccessful efforts in that framework, the two sides agreed to close down the talks in 1989 to pursue efforts in the context of a new set of talks on conventional force reductions within the security pillar of the Conference on Security and Cooperation in Europe (CSCE), ongoing since the adoption of the 1975 Helsinki Act.

The CSCE, held in Geneva and Helsinki from 1972 to 1975 and involving 33 European countries, as well as Canada and the US, further developed the concept of confidence-building measures on a non-UN regional basis; its Final Act, issued at Helsinki in August 1975, included provisions on security, human rights, and scientific cooperation. The final Stockholm Document, adopted in September 1986, constituted the first security agreement for Europe among the 35 states participating in the conference that adopts militarily significant, politically binding, and verifiable confidence-building measures. Under its terms, the CSCE states agreed to a new set of standards on the notification and observation of certain military activities, and, most important, they agreed upon verification of compliance by means of mandatory on-site inspection arrangements.

Reviewed during 1977–78 in Belgrade and again from 1980 to 1983 in Madrid, the conference led to the Stockholm Conference on Confidence- and Security-Building Measures and Disarmament in Europe, held from 1984 to 1986, with the same states participating.

In Vienna in 1989, at the same time that negotiations between the two military alliances were initiated on conventional armed forces in Europe, a new set of negotiations began on confidence- and security-building measures (CSBMs) among all the CSCE participating states. The talks led to the adoption of the Vienna Document of 1990, which incorporated and expanded the provisions of the Stockholm Document. Among its provisions are an exchange of military information among its parties on the command structure of their military forces, plans for the deployment of major weapon and equipment systems, and the military budget plans for the forthcoming year. The CSCE held a summit meeting in Paris immediately following the adoption of the Vienna CSBM document and adopted the Charter of Paris. Among other results, the participating CSCE states decided to establish a Crisis Prevention Centre in Vienna, which became essentially the operational component of the CSBM document'

In order to consolidate further the achievements of the 1990 Charter of Paris, the CSCE held a summit meeting in 1992. It issued an important document relating to confidence-building entitled the *Helsinki Document–1992–The Challenges of Change*, adopted unanimously by its full membership. In Helsinki, the states parties decided *inter alia* to start a new negotiation on arms control, disarmament, and confidence- and security-building; established a new CSCE Forum for Security Cooperation; and strengthened the Conflict Prevention Centre set up in Vienna.

In the interest of improving openness and transparency, and facilitating monitoring and compliance with existing or future arms control agreements and to strengthen the capacity for conflict resolution and crisis management in the CSCE, a *Treaty on Open Skies* was signed in March 1992 by 24 of the CSCE participating states. Covering an area from Vancouver to Vladivostok, the treaty allows observation flights by a state party over the territory of other state parties.

The UN has contributed to the process of confidence-building in a number of ways. The Secretary-General has assisted states parties to arms limitation agreements, at their request, in exchanges of information. This is the case for the newly formed Register of Conventional Arms, for the maintenance of an international system for standardized reporting of military expenditures, for the biological weapons convention as well as for the seabed treaty.

The Secretary-General also has contributed to confidence-building within regions by stimulating informal discussions of regional and global disarmament issues at seminars and conferences organized under the auspices of the Centre for Disarmament Affairs. Further, in order to promote cooperation among regional states towards arms limitation and disarmament, the UN has established three regional centers as follows: UN Regional

Centre for Peace and Disarmament in Africa (Lomé, Togo); UN Regional Centre for Peace and Disarmament in Asia and the Pacific (Kathmandu, Nepal), and the UN Regional Centre for Peace, Disarmament and the Development in Latin America and the Caribbean (Lima, Peru). The centers focus their activities on dissemination of information, training, and regional meetings.

Zones of Peace

The 1971 Declaration of the Indian Ocean as a Zone of Peace is considered annually by an ad hoc Committee on the Indian Ocean, which has proposed the convening of a conference of the regional states. There also have been proposals for zones of peace and cooperation in various other regions, including the Mediterranean and the South Atlantic.

ECONOMIC AND SOCIAL CONSEQUENCES OF THE ARMS RACE

Since the 1950s, the General Assembly has appealed for the reduction of military spending and has suggested that the money thus saved be redeployed for economic and social development activities. A 1981 UN expert study on the relationship between disarmament and development saw a triangular relationship between disarmament, security, and development and concluded that the world could either continue to pursue the arms race or move toward a more sustainable international and political order; it could not do both. A 1982 expert study on the economic and social consequences of the arms race and of military expenditures concluded that UN mechanisms for peaceful settlement of disputes should be strengthened, that the use of the world's finite resources for military ends should be discouraged, and that there should be extensive diversion of these resources from military applications to socioeconomic development.

Conference on Disarmament and Development

In 1984, the General Assembly decided to convene an International Conference on the Relationship Between Disarmament and Development. The conference, which took place at UN headquarters in August–September 1987, considered ways and means of enhancing security and of releasing additional resources for development purposes through disarmament measures.

In particular, the conference called upon the UN to make greater efforts to promote collective knowledge of the nonmilitary threats to international security; to establish an improved and comprehensive database on global and national military expenditures; to continue to analyze the impact of global military expenditures on the world economy and the international economic system; to monitor trends in military spending, and to facilitate an international exchange of views and experience in the field of conversion from military to civilian production. To carry out the above work, a high-level task force was set up within the UN Secretariat. The Secretary-General reports each year to the General Assembly on the efforts carried out in this regard.

The improvement in the East-West relations in the late 1980s and the beginning of significant reductions in armed forces and armaments in the 1990s drew considerable attention to the issue of conversion of weapons, weapons testing and production facilities, and redeployment of armed forces. At its forty-fourth session in 1989, the General Assembly, for the first time, adopted a resolution dealing with the subject of conversion of military resources.

Beginning with the 1990 international conference in Moscow on Conversion: Economic Adjustments in an Era of Arms Reduction, a number of similar conferences on different aspects of conversion of military resources to civilian production have been organized by the Centre for Disarmament Affairs and other interested UN bodies in cooperation with various host countries. The conference in Moscow was followed by an international confer-

ence on International Cooperation in Peaceful Uses of Military Industrial Technology in Beijing, China, in 1991. This was followed by yet another international conference on aerospace complex conversion held in Moscow in 1992.

The UN Institute for Disarmament Research (UNIDIR) submitted to the General Assembly at its forty-seventh session in 1992, through the Secretary-General, a study entitled *Economic aspects of disarmament: disarmament as an investment*. It found that on the cost side disarmament required a fundamental reallocation of resources from military to civilian production, which could result in major problems of unemployment or underemployment of labor, capital, and other resources. Economic dividends of disarmament were likely to be small in the short term, it concluded. In the long term, however, disarmament would lead to significant benefits in the civilian sector through the production of goods and services made possible through the reallocation of resources from the military sector. Thus, in its economic aspects, the report said, disarmament was like an investment process involving short-run costs and long-run benefits.

Reduction of Military Budgets

Proposals for the reduction of military budgets, based on the conviction that such measures would facilitate the disarmament process and help release resources for economic and social development, were made in the General Assembly during the 1950s and 1960s. Throughout the 1970s and 1980s, the General Assembly pursued this question on two tracks. There were those states that pressed for the identification and elaboration of principles for freezing and reducing military budgets, while other states favored an effort by the General Assembly to broaden participation in the standardized reporting system.

During the same period, the General Assembly initiated a series of expert studies and established an Ad Hoc Panel on Military Budgeting, aimed at arriving at a generally acceptable conceptual definition of military budgets and the development of a standardized system of measuring and reporting the military expenditures of states.

An international system for the standardized reporting of military expenditures was introduced in pursuance of resolution 35/142 B of 17 December 1980. A 1982 study reaffirmed that the reporting instrument was a practical method for monitoring and reporting on military expenditures and strongly recommended its continuous use. On the basis of national reports on military expenditures received, the Secretary-General has submitted annually to the General Assembly a document on the operation of the reporting system. The General Assembly also has continued to recommend that member states use the reporting instrument to forward annually to the Secretary-General military expenditures for the latest fiscal year for which data are available.

The Disarmament Commission also considered the reduction of the military budgets from 1979 until 1989. Despite the progress and refinement made on the reporting system, basic differences in approach to the problem of reducing military budgets remained. In the 1986 session of the Disarmament Commission, provisional agreement was achieved on a text embodying a set of principles to govern the action of states in freezing and reducing military budgets. However, there was disagreement on the use of the standardized reporting instrument. The item has not been on the agenda of the Disarmament Commission since 1990.

In 1992, the General Assembly endorsed a set of guidelines and recommendations for objective information on military matters as adopted by the Disarmament Commission at its 1992 session. The "Guidelines" are intended *inter alia* to encourage openness and transparency on military matters, to facilitate the process of arms limitation, reduction, and elimination, as well as to assist verification of compliance with obligations undertaken by states in these fields.

STUDIES, RESEARCH, INFORMATION, AND TRAINING

Studies and Research

Since the early 1960s, the UN has prepared studies on disarmament issues mandated by the General Assembly, usually with the assistance of experts and consultants. The purpose of these studies is to assist the negotiating process through analysis of specific questions, as well as to provide information in order to facilitate better understanding of the issues.

The *UN Institute for Disarmament Research* (UNIDIR), which was established in October 1980 as an autonomous institution within the UN framework, conducts independent research on disarmament problems, aimed at encouraging disarmament by expanding accessible information on proposals and concepts. Located in Geneva, UNIDIR is funded principally by voluntary contributions from governments and public and private organizations.

The *Advisory Board on Disarmament Studies* functions as the board of trustees of UNIDIR. Its other major functions include advising on programs for disarmament studies and research and on implementation of the UN Disarmament Information Programme. It may also advise the Secretary-General of the UN on specific disarmament and related questions.

Information

The Centre for Disarmament Affairs within the UN Secretariat publishes reference and other information materials on disarmament issues, including the *Disarmament Yearbook,* a periodical entitled *Disarmament,* and fact sheets. The department also coordinates the activities of the UN Disarmament Information Programme (launched by the General Assembly 1982 as the World Disarmament Campaign).

The UN Disarmament Information Programme has as its mandate informing, educating, and generating public understanding and support for multilateral action in the field of arms limitation and disarmament. The program focusses on five major constituencies: elected representatives, research institutes, educational communities, nongovernmental organizations, and the media. Its responsibilities include organizing regional conferences, meetings, and seminars to facilitate an exchange of ideas and information between governmental and nongovernmental sectors, and between governmental and other experts. It also disseminates a variety of publications, such as the *Disarmament Yearbook,* periodicals, topical papers, and newsletters. It sponsors training and education programs for young diplomats and student internships. Finally, it coordinates special events such as Disarmament Week (the week of 24 October).

Training

A disarmament fellowships program for young diplomats and public officials from various countries, particularly developing countries, was established by the General Assembly at its first special session on disarmament. The program is aimed at preparing students for work with their governments in the field of disarmament and at enhancing and broadening diplomatic expertise. Disarmament fellows are trained each year under the auspices of the Department for Disarmament Affairs.

PEACEFUL USES OF OUTER SPACE

In October 1957, the USSR launched the first *Sputnik* into orbit around the earth. In the following year, the General Assembly for the first time debated the question of outer space. Two items were proposed for inclusion on the agenda: "The Banning of the Use of Cosmic Space for Military Purposes, the Elimination of Foreign Bases on the Territories of Other Countries, and International Cooperation on the Study of Cosmic Space," proposed by the USSR; and a "Program for International Cooperation in the Field of Outer Space," proposed by the US. The very titles of these items indicate the differences that initially existed between the two powers in regard to an international accord on the uses of outer space. The USSR proposed that the first order of business should be a ban on armaments in space but wished to link this goal with the dismantling of US overseas military bases. The US preferred to avoid the disarmament issue altogether in this connection and wished merely to emphasize that it was the common aim of mankind to ensure the use of outer space for peaceful purposes. This disagreement provoked a series of disputes over the composition and terms of reference of the special UN body that should be established to deal with outer space problems. The USSR wanted a body with East-West parity, while the US preferred a body more broadly geographical in representation.

Owing to these differences, the 1958 General Assembly merely set up an 18-member ad hoc committee to deal with questions of outer space. It included only three member states from the Soviet bloc, which, because of the composition of the committee, declared that they would not take part in its work. The committee eventually was reduced to 13 participants.

After intensive negotiations, the 1959 General Assembly set up the permanent 24-nation Committee on the Peaceful Uses of Outer Space. Its membership was increased to 28 in 1962, 37 in 1973, 47 in 1977, and 53 in 1980. In 1962, the committee organized itself into two subcommittees of the whole, one to deal with scientific and technical cooperation and the other with the task of evolving outer space law. The committee has also set up working groups of the whole to deal with navigation satellites, direct broadcasting satellites, remote sensing satellites, and the use of nuclear power sources in outer space.

DEVELOPMENTS IN SCIENTIFIC AND TECHNICAL COOPERATION

Scientific and technical cooperation within the framework of the UN grew out of General Assembly action on the basis of recommendations of the committee and has increased over the years. It covers various fields of activity, including the following.

Exchange of Information. The UN Secretariat produces annual reports on national and cooperative international projects. Since 1961, a growing number of countries and international organizations have provided the committee with information on space activities and programs.

Public Registry of Launchings of Space Vehicles. An essential requirement for international cooperation in outer space development is that launchings of space vehicles, together with scientific data on the results of such launchings, be made public. In 1961, the General Assembly decided unanimously that the UN "should provide a focal point" for such information and requested the Secretary-General to open a public registry for this purpose. The

information is transmitted to the Committee on the Peaceful Uses of Outer Space for review and is then placed in the registry.

The Russian Federation and the US regularly supply appropriate data, as do Australia, Canada, China, France, Germany, India, Italy, Japan, the UK, and the European Space Agency (ESA).

Cooperation with Specialized Agencies and Other International Organizations. By the terms of its 1961 resolution on outer space, the General Assembly requested the WMO to submit reports to the Committee on the Peaceful Uses of Outer Space on the international cooperation required in weather research. In the following year, it endorsed steps taken under WMO auspices that resulted in the establishment of the World Weather Watch, incorporating meteorological satellites into its operational system. The same resolution also requested the ITU to submit reports on cooperation required to develop effective space communications. In the ensuing years, this cooperative effort embraced other agencies and international organizations having special interests in matters related to outer space, including UNEP, FAO, UNESCO, ESA, the International Telecommunications Satellite Organization (INTELSAT), and the International Maritime Satellite Organization (INMARSAT).

Education and Training. The General Assembly has emphasized the need to train personnel from countries not yet advanced in space activities. The secretariat distributes a periodically revised directory of information taken from UN documents and carries out an educational program on space applications. The program creates an awareness of the potential of space applications for development, especially in developing countries, through technical advisory services, seminars, and workshops and the administration of fellowships offered by member states and international organizations for education and training.

Under the United Nations Programme on Space Applications, the latest efforts are being directed towards the development and enhancement of knowledge and skills in the discipline through the establishment and operation of centers for space science and technology education at the regional level.

INTERNATIONAL SPACE YEAR AND THE UNITED NATIONS CONFERENCE ON ENVIRONMENT

In 1989, the General Assembly recommended that more attention be paid to all aspects related to the protection and preservation of the outer space environment, especially those potentially affecting the earth's environment. In the same year, the General Assembly also endorsed the designation of the year 1992 as International Space Year and its use as a vehicle for promotion of international cooperation, which should be carried out for the benefit and in the interests of all states, with particular emphasis on the needs of developing countries.

Numerous programs were carried out in support of International Space Year and culminated in 1992. "Mission to Planet Earth," which was a central focus of the International Space Year, saw scientists worldwide using space technologies to assess such threats to the earth's environment as global warming, deforestation, and ozone depletion. Subsequently, the General Assembly recommended that the United Nations should actively encourage the continuation of activities initiated for International Space Year and promote broader involvement in those activities by more nations.

Reflecting the growing concern of the international community on environmental security, the United Nations Conference on Environment and Development took place also in 1992 at Rio de Janeiro. Such concern for the protection of environment also was a focus of the activities for International Space Year. The following year, the Secretary-General suggested in his report that it might also be time to examine ways to formalize international cooperation in the utilization of space systems and space technology for environmental purposes, particularly the implementation of the programs recommended in Agenda 21. The product of the Rio conference, Agenda 21 lays out a detailed program of action to be taken by the United Nations, other international organizations, national governments, and intergovernmental organizations. In response to the request by the Committee on the Peaceful Uses of Outer Space, which was subsequently endorsed by the General Assembly, the Secretary-General prepared an analytical report on the role that the committee could play in view of the decisions and recommendations of the United Nations Conference on Environment and Development. The report was well accepted by the committee, and the committee continues its consideration on this subject.

UN CONFERENCES ON OUTER SPACE

Originally recommended by the General Assembly in 1959, the first UN Conference on the Exploration and Peaceful Uses of Outer Space was held in August 1968 in Vienna, with 78 states and a large number of international organizations attending. The conference examined the practical benefits to be derived from space research and the opportunities for international cooperation available to nations without space capability, with special reference to the needs of the developing countries. The participants submitted some 200 papers dealing primarily with space applications. They reviewed 10 years of space research in practical applications—in communications, meteorology, navigation, and education—and practical benefits, as well as economic and legal questions pertaining to international cooperation.

In August 1982, the Second UN Conference on the Exploration and Peaceful Uses of Outer Space (called UNISPACE 82) was held in Vienna, with 94 state participants and 45 observers representing intergovernmental and nongovernmental organizations. The conference dealt with the entire gamut of space sciences, technologies, and applications from scientific, technical, political, economic, social, and organizational points of view. It also considered the legal implications of issues on the agenda and discussed growing international concern relating to military activities in outer space.

The report of the conference, adopted by consensus, dealt with questions relating to the prevention of an arms race in space, the needs and possibilities for technology transfer, coordination in the use of the geostationary orbit, remote sensing of earth resources from space, the use of direct-broadcasting satellites, space transportation and space platform technologies, protection of the near-earth environment, the role of the UN, and other matters. The recommendations of the conference were seen as an agenda for nations and organizations to follow in carrying out space activities.

Recently the Committee on the Peaceful Uses of Outer Space has been discussing the holding of a possible third United Nations conference on the Exploration and Peaceful Uses of Outer Space.

DEVELOPMENT OF INTERNATIONAL LAW ON OUTER SPACE

The early work of the legal subcommittee of the Committee on the Peaceful Uses of Outer Space was marked by disputes that delayed progress on the development of outer space law. The majority of members stressed the dangers of spectacular scientific advances without corresponding legal obligations and safeguards.

In originally proposing the formulation of an international legal code on outer space, the General Assembly had recommended that such a code be based, insofar as possible, on the existing body of international law (including the UN Charter) and the principle of freedom of space exploration for all states. But the USSR and the US differed on certain fundamental issues from the time that the question was first debated in the General Assembly in 1959. The most important difference was on the relation between the prevention of armaments in space and disarmament on earth.

The breakthrough in this quasi-procedural deadlock first came as part of the general East-West détente that followed the partial nuclear test-ban treaty signed in August 1963. During its 1963 session, the General Assembly was able to adopt by acclamation two important measures relating to restricting the use of outer space to peaceful purposes. The first was a resolution calling upon all states to refrain from placing in orbit objects carrying nuclear weapons or other weapons of mass destruction. The second was a resolution embodying a Declaration of Legal Principles Governing the Activities of States in the Exploration and Use of Outer Space. Though not an agreement with binding force, as the USSR had wished, it was regarded as the forerunner to a full legal treaty.

The *Treaty on Principles Governing the Activities of States in the Exploration and Use of Outer Space, Including the Moon and Other Celestial Bodies*, which the General Assembly unanimously acclaimed in 1966 and which came into force on 10 October 1967, was based on drafts submitted individually by both the US and the USSR. The 17 articles of the treaty state that the exploration and use of outer space shall be carried out for the benefit of all countries and shall be the province of all mankind, that outer space and celestial bodies are not subject to national appropriation by claim of sovereignty or any other means, and that exploration shall be carried on in accordance with international law. Parties to the treaty undertake not to place in orbit any objects carrying nuclear weapons, install such weapons on celestial bodies, or otherwise station them in outer space. The moon and other celestial bodies shall be used by all parties exclusively for peaceful purposes, and military bases or maneuvers on celestial bodies shall be forbidden. States shall regard astronauts as envoys of mankind in outer space and shall render them all possible assistance in case of accident, distress, or emergency landing. Parties launching objects into outer space are internationally liable for damage caused by such objects or their component parts. The principle of cooperation and mutual assistance shall be followed in space exploration. Harmful contamination of the moon and other celestial bodies shall be avoided. All stations, installations, equipment, and space vehicles on the moon and other celestial bodies shall be open for inspection to representatives of other states on a reciprocal basis.

Under the 1967 *Agreement on the Rescue of Astronauts, the Return of Astronauts, and the Return of Objects Launched into Outer Space,* which came into force on 3 December 1968, contracting parties agree to procedures for assistance to spacecraft personnel in the event of an accident or emergency landing and for the return of space objects.

The 1971 *Convention on International Liability for Damage Caused by Space Objects*, which came into force on 1 September 1972, provides a procedure for the presentation and settlement of claims.

Under the 1974 *Convention on Registration of Objects Launched into Outer Space*, which came into force on 15 September 1976, a central register of objects launched into space was established and is maintained by the UN Secretary-General, with mandatory registration, as well as notification to the Secretary-General of voluntary markings of such objects. Assistance is provided to states requesting help in the identification of hazardous objects or those causing damage.

The *Agreement Governing Activities of States on the Moon and Other Celestial Bodies*, adopted by the General Assembly on 5 December 1979, describes the moon and its natural resources as the common heritage of mankind, and it reserves the moon for exclusively peaceful purposes. It bars the emplacement of nuclear or other weapons of mass destruction on the moon and also prohibits the placing in orbit, or in any other trajectory to or around the moon, of objects carrying such weapons and the establishment of military bases, the testing of any type of weapons, and the conduct of military activities on the moon.

The General Assembly has adopted three more sets of principles based on the work of the Committee on the Peaceful Uses of Outer Space. The *Principles Governing the Use by States of Artificial Earth Satellites for International Direct Television Broadcasting*, adopted in 1982, condition the establishment of direct-broadcasting satellite services on the prior consent of receiving states. The *Principles Relating to Remote Sensing of the Earth from Outer Space*, adopted in 1986, provide for international cooperation and participation in remote sensing; they specify that such activities will be permitted without the consent of the states being sensed but that the latter will have the right to receive data and information concerning their resources.

Finally, after many years of difficult debate and negotiation within the Committee, the General Assembly adopted in 1992 the *Principles Relevant to the Use of Nuclear Power Sources in Outer Space*. They provide guidelines and criteria for safe use of nuclear power sources in outer space, including the requirement that a safety review be made prior to launching of any nuclear power source and that results of such review be made public through the Secretary-General of the United Nations, who should also be notified of any re-entry of radioactive materials to the earth.

Reflecting the changes in the international political and security environment, which provide new possibilities for the utilization of space technology to promote international peace, there have been more constructive discussions within the committee in recent years on the enhancement of international cooperation in various aspects. Currently, the committee and its Legal Subcommittee are continuing their considerations on the matters relating to the definition and delimitation of outer space and to the character and utilization of the geostationary orbit and on legal framework for sharing the benefits of space exploration by all states.

LAW OF THE SEA

The earth is essentially a liquid planet, with more than 70 percent of its surface covered by water. Although geographically divided and labeled as continents, islands, seas, and oceans, the earth, when viewed from outer space, appears as one large body of water interspersed with lesser land masses. The world's oceans thus provide a common link for the more than 110 nations whose shorelines are washed by their waters. Despite these universal characteristics, however, this last earthly frontier has become an arena for disputes over such matters as fishing rights and varying claims of national jurisdiction, the right of exploitation of the sea's mineral resources, responsibility for the protection of the environment, the right of innocent passage of ships, and free access to the sea for landlocked countries.

For centuries the doctrine that governed ocean space and resources was "freedom of the seas"; coastal state claims were restricted within narrow limits. The first change in this regime came with the emergence of the doctrine of the continental shelf, spurred by the development of offshore oil and gas fields. The US, in 1945, was the first to proclaim jurisdiction over the natural resources of its continental shelf "beneath the high seas" (that is, beyond US territorial limits). Other nations were quick to follow suit, many of them seeking to extend their jurisdiction over fisheries. In order to clarify accepted norms and codify state practice, the UN, in 1958, convened the First Conference on the Law of the Sea. Working on the basis of drafts prepared by the International Law Commission (see the chapter on International Law), the conference adopted the Convention on the Continental Shelf, thus establishing the new doctrine in international law. The conference adopted three other conventions—on the territorial sea and contiguous zone, the high seas, and fishing and conservation of living resources. A further attempt made in 1960, at the Second Conference on the Law of the Sea, failed to define the limits of the territorial sea.

A sense of urgency was again given to problems connected with the deep seas in 1967, when Malta warned the General Assembly that there was a danger that technically equipped countries might wish to appropriate the ocean floor for their national use, not only to develop its immense resources but also for defense and other purposes. Malta's delegate, Arvid Pardo, remarked that the "dark oceans" were "the womb" of life: life had emerged from the protecting oceans. Man was now returning to the ocean depths, and his penetration "could mark the beginning of the end for man, and indeed for life as we know it . . . it could also be a unique opportunity to lay solid foundations for a peaceful and increasingly prosperous future for all peoples."

Reacting to the Maltese call for international solutions, the General Assembly set up the Committee on the Peaceful Uses of the Seabed and the Ocean Floor Beyond the Limits of National Jurisdiction, called the Seabed Committee, to study various aspects of the problem and to indicate practical means to promote international cooperation. The principal results of the committee's work were embodied in a Declaration of Principles, adopted by the General Assembly in 1970, proclaiming that the seabed and ocean floor and its resources beyond national jurisdiction "are the common heritage of mankind" and that no nation should exercise sovereignty or rights over any part of the area.

The declaration also called for the establishment of an international regime to govern the exploration and exploitation of the sea's resources for the benefit of mankind.

Recognizing that the problems of ocean space are interrelated and need to be considered as a whole, the General Assembly also decided, in 1970, to convene a new UN Conference on the Law of the Sea to prepare a single comprehensive treaty. The Seabed Committee, in preparation for the conference, thus had to deal not only with the international seabed area but also with such issues as the regime of the high seas, the continental shelf and territorial sea (including the question of limits), fishing rights, preservation of the marine environment, scientific research, and access to the sea by landlocked states.

THIRD LAW OF THE SEA CONFERENCE

The Third UN Conference on the Law of the Sea opened at UN headquarters in New York in December 1973 with a brief organizational session. Its real work commenced the following year in Caracas, Venezuela, with the important decision to proceed on the basis of a negotiated "package deal"—no one provision or section would be formally approved until all others were in place. This informal approach was dictated not only by the interdependence of the issues involved but also by the need to produce ultimately an overall balance that could command the widest support. The first informal text, as the agreed basis for negotiations, was prepared in 1975. It was followed by a series of revisions progressively developed through special negotiating and working groups, committees, and plenary meetings. The emphasis throughout the negotiations was on informal and flexible working methods and on consensus-building.

UN CONVENTION ON THE LAW OF THE SEA

The final text of the UN Convention on the Law of the Sea (UNCLOS) was approved by the conference at UN headquarters on 30 April 1982, by a vote of 130 in favor, with 4 against (Israel, Turkey, US, and Venezuela) and 17 abstentions. Following the signing of the Final Act of the conference in Jamaica on 10 December 1982, the convention was opened for signature for a period of two years, at the end of which time it had been signed by 159 states and by the UN Council for Namibia, the EEC, the Cook Islands, and Niue. The convention came into force on 16 November 1994, one year after receiving its 60th ratification.

THE CONTENTIOUS ISSUE OF DEEP SEA MINING

Although the United States had been a leader in the international community's effort to develop an overall legal framework for the oceans in the Third United Nations Conference on the Law of the Sea, deep divisions arose between developing and developed nations over the establishment of an international organization to regulate the exploration of deep sea mining in international waters (Part XI of the Treaty). These divisions were so deep that the United States declined to formally sign the treaty, although endorsing the consensus that had been reached by the conference on other areas covered by the treaty.

Negotiations on the issue of deep sea mining were based on

the generally accepted principle, enunciated as early as 1970 by General Assembly Resolution 2749 (XXV): " . . . the seabed and ocean floor and subsoil thereof, beyond the limits of national jurisdiction (hereinafter referred to as the "Area"), as well as the resources of the Area, are the common heritage of mankind." The administrations of Lyndon Johnson and Richard Nixon supported the principle that the resources of the seabed beyond national jurisdiction are the common heritage of mankind, and that an international regime should be established to administer these resources. This principle was affirmed in deep seabed mining legislation enacted by the United States in 1980.

However, in the view of industrialized countries, the details of the establishment of a new organization to carry out this vision, as established by the conference in the treaty, were heavily weighted in favor of developing nations. The objections of the industrialized nations fell into two categories: institutional issues and economic and commercial issues. On the institutional front, industrialized nations objected to what they perceived as inadequate influence within the seabed organization. On the economic and commercial front, the industrialized nations sought a more market-oriented regime. They objected to provisions for mandatory technology transfer, production limitations from the seabed, what they perceived as onerous financial obligations on miners, and the establishment of a subsidized international public enterprise that, it was postulated, would compete unfairly with other commercial enterprises.

In the late 1980s, other nations increasingly began to recognize difficulties in the seabed mining regime, as set forth in the treaty. This shift in attitude reflected general changes in the international political environment: the waning of the Cold War and the explosion of interest in free market reforms in developing countries and within Eastern Europe and the states of the former Soviet Union. The developing countries also came to be concerned about the effectiveness of the treaty without participation by the industrialized countries of the world.

In July 1990, then Secretary-General Javier Pérez de Cuéllar initiated informal consultations aimed at achieving universal participation in UNCLOS. Fifteen meetings were convened in the period 1990 to 1994, resulting in major amendments to UNCLOS. During this time, UNCLOS received its 60th ratification, and entry into force was definitely set for 16 November 1994, in accordance with the terms of the treaty. With the approach of this date, the industrialized nations perceived a window of opportunity to reform the treaty before it entered into force. In early 1993, the Clinton administration in the US decided to take a more active role in the reform effort, deciding that the merit of actively participating would not be to find an answer to every future question regarding the uses of the oceans, but to create a framework and channel discussions of new issues along lines more acceptable to the industrialized nations.

Negotiations on The Agreement Relating to the Implementation of Part XI of the United Nations Convention on the Law of the Sea (hereafter referred to as the "agreement") concluded on 3 June 1994. The agreement avoids establishing a detailed regime anticipating all phases of activity associated with mining of the deep seabed. However, it sets forth economic and commercial principles consistent with a free market philosophy to form the basis for developing rules and regulations at such time as commercial mining develops in international waters.

The agreement retains the institutional outlines of Part XI of the treaty, but scales back the structure and links the activation and operation of institutions to the actual development of concrete interest in seabed mining. It provides the United States, and other states with major economic interests, a voice in decision-making commensurate with those interests. In particular, the United States, acting alone, can block decision on issues of major financial or budgetary significance in a finance committee. It also

can block decisions to distribute revenues from mining to countries or other entities (for example, revolutionary movements) in the executive council.

The mandatory technology transfer provisions are replaced by provisions for the promotion of technology transfer through cooperative arrangements (called "joint ventures") and through procurement on the open market. The agreement now also subjects the exploration and mining arm of the authority (called the "Enterprise") to the same obligations as other miners and removes the obligations of developed nations to finance it.

The agreement limits assistance to land-based producers of minerals to adjustment assistance financed out of a portion of royalties from future seabed mining. It also replaces the production control regime of Part XI by the application of GATT principles on subsidization. The agreement further replaces the detailed financial obligations imposed on miners by a future system for recovering economic rents based on systems applicable to land-based mining, and provides that it be designed to avoid competitive incentives or disincentives for seabed mining.

At the conclusion of the informal consultations, only the Russian Federation made a statement reserving its position, since some of its proposals had not been incorporated into the agreement. It was then decided to convene a resumed 48th session of the General Assembly from 27–29 July 1994 for the purpose of adopting and opening for signature the agreement, at which time most of the abstaining industrialized nations were expected to sign the treaty and the agreement.

Provisions of UNCLOS

The convention covers almost all human uses of the seas—navigation and overflight, resource exploration and exploitation, conservation and pollution, fishing, and shipping. Its 321 articles and nine annexes constitute a guide for behavior by nations in the world's oceans, defining maritime zones, laying down rules for drawing boundaries, assigning legal duties and responsibilities, and providing machinery for settlement of disputes. Some of the main provisions of the convention are the following.

Territorial Sea. Coastal states would exercise sovereignty over their territorial sea of up to 19.3 km (12 mi) in breadth, but foreign vessels would be allowed "innocent passage" through those waters for purposes of peaceful navigation.

Straits Used for International Navigation. Ships and aircraft of all countries would be allowed "transit passage" through straits used for international navigation, as long as they proceeded without delay and without threatening the bordering states; states alongside the straits would be able to regulate navigation and other aspects of passage.

Archipelagic States. Archipelagic states, consisting of a group or groups of closely related islands and interconnecting waters, would have sovereignty over a sea area enclosed by straight lines drawn between the outermost points of the islands; all other states would enjoy the right of passage through sea lanes designated by the archipelagic states.

Exclusive Economic Zone. Coastal states would have sovereign rights in a 322-km (200-mi) exclusive economic zone with respect to natural resources and certain economic activities and would also have certain types of jurisdiction over marine science research and environmental protection; all other states would have freedom of navigation and overflight in the zone, as well as freedom to lay submarine cables and pipelines. Landlocked and other geographically disadvantaged states would have the opportunity to participate in exploiting part of the zone's fisheries when the coastal state could not harvest them all. Highly migratory species of fish and marine mammals would be accorded special protection.

Continental Shelf. Coastal states would have sovereign rights over the continental shelf (the national area of the seabed) for the purpose of exploring and exploiting it; the shelf would extend at least 322 km (200 mi) from shore and 563 km (350 mi) or more under specified circumstances. Coastal states would share with the international community part of the revenue that they would derive from exploiting oil and other resources from any part of their shelf beyond 322 km (200 mi). A Commission on the Limits of the Continental Shelf would make recommendations to states on the shelf's outer boundaries.

High Seas. All states would enjoy the traditional freedoms of navigation, overflight, scientific research, and fishing on the high seas; they would be obliged to adopt, or cooperate with other states in adopting, measures to conserve living resources.

Islands. The territorial sea, exclusive economic zone, and continental shelf of islands would be determined in accordance with rules applicable to land territory, but rocks that could not sustain human habitation or economic life would have no economic zone or continental shelf.

Enclosed or Semienclosed Seas. States bordering enclosed or semi-enclosed seas would be expected to cooperate on management of living resources and on environmental and research policies and activities.

Landlocked States. Landlocked states would have the right of access to and from the sea and would enjoy freedom of transit through the territory of transit states.

International Seabed Area. A "parallel system" would be established for exploring and exploiting the international seabed area. All activities in this area would be under the control of an International Seabed Authority, to be established under the convention. The authority would conduct its own mining operations through its operating arm, called the "Enterprise," and would also contract with private and state ventures to give them mining rights in the area, so that they could operate in parallel with the authority. The first generation of seabed prospectors, called "pioneer investors," would have guarantees of production once mining was authorized.

Marine Pollution. States would be bound to prevent and control marine pollution from any source and would be liable for damage caused by violation of their international obligations to combat marine pollution.

Marine Scientific Research. All marine scientific research in the exclusive economic zone and on the continental shelf would be subject to the consent of the coastal state, but coastal states would in most cases be obliged to grant consent to foreign states when the research was to be conducted for peaceful purposes.

Development and Transfer of Marine Technology. States would be bound to promote the development and transfer of marine technology "on fair and reasonable terms and conditions," with proper regard for all legitimate interests, including the rights and duties of holders, suppliers, and recipients of technology.

States would be obliged to settle their disputes over the interpretation or application of the convention by peaceful means. They would have to submit most types of disputes to a compulsory procedure entailing decisions that would be binding on all parties. Disputes could be submitted to an International Tribunal for the Law of the Sea, to be established under the convention; to the International Court of Justice; or to arbitration. Conciliation also would be available, and, in certain circumstances, submission to conciliation might be compulsory.

PREPARATORY COMMISSION

With the signing of the convention, a preparatory commission was established to pave the way for the two major institutions to be set up under the convention—the International Seabed Authority, with its headquarters in Montego Bay, Jamaica, and the International Tribunal for the Law of the Sea, to be located in Hamburg, Germany. Establishment of the preparatory commission and of the pioneer investment scheme was provided for in two resolutions adopted by the conference on 30 April 1982.

The Preparatory Commission for the International Seabed Authority and for the International Tribunal for the Law of the Sea began its work in 1983, drafting the rules that will govern the two institutions, as well as a mining code to regulate future seabed operations. In addition to such other duties as planning and preparing for the "Enterprise," the commission was charged with the implementation of a special interim regime that allows "pioneer investors" in seabed mining development to pursue their work, short of actual exploitation, and to obtain preferential mining rights from the authority once it is established.

International Acceptance

The new legal regime for the seas is now firmly established throughout the world: by July 1994, 129 states had established 12-mile territorial limits and 91 states had declared exclusive economic zones. Eighteen states had declared fishing zones of 200 miles. Most such national legislation is derived directly from the provisions of the convention. The General Assembly is concerned with ensuring maximum conformity in state practice and each year examines the status of the convention and reviews developments relating to its application.

ECONOMIC AND SOCIAL DEVELOPMENT

Article 55 of the charter, on international economic and social cooperation, calls on the UN to promote higher standards of living, full employment, and conditions of economic and social progress and development. The fostering of economic and social development, however, was only one of several objectives specified in the charter, and no special emphasis was accorded to it. The League of Nations and the early ILO were concerned primarily with defensive or protective action, such as the protection of countries against diseases that might cross international frontiers, prevention of international traffic in women and children and in illicit drugs, and protection of workers against unfair and inhumane conditions of labor. Such early action in the economic and social fields was taken in a climate of thought that hardly recognized the concept of economic and social development.

Toward the middle of this century, however, the concept took root as a major objective of international cooperation, and the primary goal of the UN and the specialized agencies in the economic and social fields came to be promoting the development of the less developed countries.

THE RICH AND THE POOR NATIONS

The UN's preoccupation with development is tied to the division of its membership between rich and poor nations, a division that the Secretary-General has frequently characterized as a leading long-term threat to world peace and security.

In 1945, when the UN was established, this sharp dichotomy could not be drawn. The wealth of Europe had been wasted by the ravages of war. Only the US could claim to be rich, and even the US, with the depression of the 1930s still a fresh memory, could not be confident of lasting prosperity. What made the challenge of development central to the thinking of every aspiring country was the rapidity with which the countries of Western Europe recovered their prosperity and went on to attain higher levels of economic and social well-being than they had ever experienced. Meanwhile, economic expansion continued apace in the more prosperous countries that had not been directly hurt by the war—the US, Canada, Australia, and New Zealand. And within a few years, in Asia, the miracle of Japan's recovery and growth was matching Europe's postwar record.

Nothing comparable occurred among the colonial peoples and former colonial peoples. Tropical Asia, Africa, and Latin America had been cultivated in preceding generations largely as appendages to industrial Europe and North America—on the one hand, supplying essential primary commodities not commonly found in the temperate regions and, on the other hand, serving as profitable markets for consumer goods produced in the temperate regions. The peoples of these economically underdeveloped areas made rapid political progress in the postwar era. Significant economic progress also was recorded in a number of these countries, so that by the late 1950s, it was considered not only tactful but also proper to refer to them as "developing" rather than "underdeveloped" nations. As a group, however, the developing countries were far outdistanced in economic growth by the temperate zone industrialized countries, which were finding the postwar era the most propitious in history for their development. Before the UN had completed its first 15 years, it was abundantly evident that a very disturbing gap had opened up between the industrial-

ized and the developing nations and that, despite very substantial foreign aid efforts, the gap was growing broader year by year.

SCOPE OF THE UN'S WORK

The international community was not slow to recognize the political and economic dangers inherent in such an imbalance of national wealth. As early as 1946, when "recovery" rather than "development" dominated UN thinking on economic matters, the General Assembly requested the Economic and Social Council to study ways and means of furnishing advice to nations desiring help in developing their resources. As a result, the UN, in cooperation with the specialized agencies of the UN system, began its first programs of technical assistance.

This chapter describes the principles and goals of the UN development effort. It also discusses some of the factors influencing development, such as science and technology, the role of transnational corporations, and the use of natural resources, and it summarizes the work of the regional commissions. Programs of technical cooperation undertaken by the UN and its related organizations are described in the chapter on Technical Cooperation Programs, and social and humanitarian programs in the chapter on Social and Humanitarian Assistance. The work of the specialized agencies in supporting economic and social development is described in the separate chapters on those agencies.

FIRST UN DEVELOPMENT DECADE

The first UN Development Decade was launched by the General Assembly in December 1961. It called on all member states to intensify their efforts to mobilize support for measures required to accelerate progress toward self-sustaining economic growth and social advancement in the developing countries. With each developing country setting its own target, the objective would be a minimum annual growth rate of 5 percent in aggregate national income by the end of the decade.

The economically advanced states were asked to pursue policies designed to enable the developing countries to sell more of their products at stable and remunerative prices in expanding markets in order to finance more of their economic development, and to follow policies designed to ensure developing countries an equitable share of earnings from extraction and marketing of their natural resources by foreign capital. Industrialized states were also called on to pursue policies that would lead to an increase in the flow of developmental resources and stimulate the lflow of private capital to developing countries on mutually acceptable terms. The General Assembly recommended that the flow of international capital and assistance to developing countries should be about 1 percent of the combined national incomes of the economically advanced countries.

Throughout the decade of the 1960s, however, the growth rate in the economically advanced market economies accelerated, and the gap between the per capita incomes of the developing countries and those of the developed countries widened. Two-thirds of the world's population living in the less developed regions of the world still had less than one-sixth of the world's income. In 1962, annual per capita income in those regions averaged $136, while that of the economically advanced market economies in North America and Western Europe averaged $2,845 and $1,033, respectively.

In a report issued in 1969, Secretary-General U Thant noted that the slower progress in development had been accompanied by the emergence or aggravation of major imbalances that imperiled future growth. Without greater progress in food production and the more effective control of communicable diseases, the necessary conditions for steady economic and social development could hardly be said to have been created. At the same time, the Secretary-General pointed out, the experience of a few countries had demonstrated that "given a favorable constellation of circumstances and policies, an adequate and sustained pace of development can be achieved," and acceptance of development as a fundamental objective had gradually wrought a desirable change in attitudes and modes of action on the part of developing countries. Public decisions were no longer made solely in response to expediency, and policies and programs previously decided upon in relative isolation were gradually being integrated and harnessed to a common purpose. At the international level, the Secretary-General noted, the institutional machinery for the review and advancement of international policies had been considerably strengthened by the creation of such bodies as the UN Conference on Trade and Development and the Committee for Development Planning.

The first UN Development Decade ended in December 1970 with one of its major goals, the attainment of a 5 percent growth rate, unattained in the developing countries. During the period 1960–67, those countries achieved an annual rate of increase in their total domestic product of about 4.6 percent, but, because of the population increase, the increase in their per capita gross product was only about 2 percent. The General Assembly concluded that one of the reasons for the slow progress was the absence of a framework of international development strategy.

SECOND UN DEVELOPMENT DECADE

At its 25th session, in 1970, the General Assembly adopted a resolution outlining an international development strategy for the second UN Development Decade—the 1970s. The main objectives of the plan were to promote sustained economic growth, particularly in the developing countries; ensure a higher standard of living, and facilitate the process of narrowing the gap between the developed and developing countries. The General Assembly declared that the developing countries bore primary responsibility for their development but that their efforts would be insufficient without increased financial assistance and more favorable economic and commercial policies on the part of the developed countries.

Under the goals and objectives of the second decade, the General Assembly stated that the average annual rate of growth in the gross product of the developing countries as a whole should be at least 6 percent, with the possibility of attaining a higher rate in the second half of the decade. Such a rate of growth would imply an average annual expansion of 4 percent in agricultural output and 8 percent in manufacturing output.

The General Assembly also stated that it was essential to bring about a more equitable distribution of income and wealth in order to promote social justice and efficiency of production; to raise the level of employment substantially; to achieve a greater degree of income security; to expand and improve facilities for education, health, nutrition, housing, and social welfare; and to safeguard the environment. Thus, qualitative and structural changes in society should go hand in hand with rapid economic growth, and existing disparities—regional, sectoral, and social—should be substantially reduced. The General Assembly believed that developing countries must bear the main responsibility for financing their development. To this end, they were asked to pursue sound fiscal and monetary policies and to remove institutional obstacles through the adoption of appropriate legislative and administrative reforms. At the same time, each economically advanced country was called upon to endeavor to provide annually to developing countries financial resource transfers of a minimum net amount of 1 percent of its gross national product (GNP). A major part of financial resource transfers to the developing countries should be provided in the form of official development assistance.

Progress achieved during the first half of the decade was reviewed by the General Assembly in 1975. It noted that the gap between the developed and the developing countries had increased alarmingly during the first half of the decade, but it found the generally gloomy picture lightened by one element—the developing countries had emerged "as a more powerful factor, as a necessary consequence of the new and growing perception of the reality of interdependence." The General Assembly also found that some of the aggregate targets set in the strategy for the decade had been met or exceeded, "owing mainly to the developing countries' own efforts and, to a certain extent, to external factors such as the commodity boom" (a short-lived rise in commodity prices between 1972 and 1974). Those aggregates, however, did not reflect the variation in achievement among developing countries, for many countries did much worse than the average. A major area of shortfall was in agriculture, where less than half the target rate of 4 percent annual growth was realized by the developing countries as a whole.

The General Assembly further noted that the net flow of financial resources from developed countries in the form of official development assistance had decreased in real terms and as a percentage of GNP. At the same time, the burden of debt-service payments of developing countries had continued to increase in relation to their export earnings.

NEW INTERNATIONAL ECONOMIC ORDER

In September 1973, in Algiers, the Arab petroleum-exporting countries discussed the possible uses of oil as a political weapon. When a new Arab-Israeli conflict broke out on 6 October, the Arab countries reduced the flow of oil to Europe and Japan and suspended exports to the US, the Netherlands, and Portugal. The embargo against the US was lifted in March 1974, that against the Netherlands in July 1974, and that against Portugal after a new regime instituted a policy leading to independence for African territories under Portuguese administration in 1974 and 1975. However, the measures taken by the petroleum-exporting countries marked a turning point for the world economy. Members of the Organization of Petroleum-Exporting Countries (OPEC) undertook a long-term study of the collective fixing of oil prices and increased them periodically thereafter.

On 31 January 1974, President Boumedienne of Algeria requested a special session of the General Assembly to consider the question of all raw materials and relations between developed industrial and developing states. Within two weeks, 70 nations endorsed his proposal.

Sixth Special Session of the General Assembly. The special session, held in April–May 1974, adopted a declaration and program of action on the establishment of a new international economic order. The declaration and program of action called for a fundamental change in the international economic order, in the absence of which the gap between developing and developed countries would only continue to widen. Such a change would require the industrial countries to make adjustments in their policies and economies for the benefit of the poorer countries, which in turn were determined to control their own resources.

The program of action called for efforts to link the prices of exports of developing countries to the prices of their imports from developed countries. It suggested the formation of producers' associations, orderly commodity trading, increased export income for producing developing countries, and improvement in their terms of trade. It also looked to the evolution of an equitable relationship between the prices of raw materials, primary commodities, and semimanufactured goods exported by developing countries and the raw materials, primary commodities, food, manufactured and semimanufactured goods, and capital equipment imported by them.

In the declaration, UN member states proclaimed their determination to work urgently for "the establishment of a new international economic order based on equity, sovereign equality, interdependence, common interest, and cooperation among all states, irrespective of their economic and social systems, which shall correct inequalities and redress existing injustices, make it possible to eliminate the widening gap between the developed and the developing countries and ensure steadily accelerating economic and social development in peace and justice for present and future generations."

Though the program and declaration were adopted without a vote and enthusiastically supported by almost all developing and socialist countries, most Western European and other industrialized states with market economies entered reservations, often very far-reaching. They warned against constraints to the flow of trade that might result from the establishment of producers' associations and argued that nationalization should be carried out in accordance with the existing rules of international law.

Charter of Economic Rights and Duties of States. At its regular session in 1974, the General Assembly adopted a charter of Economic Rights and Duties of States. The charter affirmed that every state has the right to exercise freely full permanent sovereignty over its wealth and natural resources, to regulate foreign investment within its national jurisdiction, and to nationalize, expropriate, or transfer the ownership of foreign property. The charter provided that appropriate compensation should be paid in cases of nationalization and that any controversies should be settled under the domestic laws of the nationalizing states unless all states concerned agree to other peaceful means. It also set forth the right of states to associate in organizations of primary producers in order to develop their national economies.

Seventh Special Session of the General Assembly. The General Assembly held a seventh special session devoted to development and international cooperation in September 1975. The polemical atmosphere in which the program and declaration on the new international economic order and the charter on the economic rights and duties of states had been adopted was replaced by a pragmatic approach. Negotiations were carried on chiefly in private meetings between "contact groups" representing the developing countries and the Western European and other states with market economies. Since the market economy states were the buyers of approximately three-quarters of the exports of the developing countries, agreement between the two groups was essential to significant progress. At the close of the session, Secretary-General Kurt Waldheim declared that it had been "about *change* rather than the smoother management of the status quo."

The results of the special session were embodied in a resolution that proposed a large number of initiatives and was unanimously adopted by the General Assembly. It reaffirmed the target, originally defined in the strategy for the second Development Decade, of 1 percent of the GNP of developed countries to be devoted to official assistance to the developing countries, and it called for the accumulation of buffer stocks of commodities in order to offset market fluctuations, combat inflationary tendencies, and ensure grain and food security.

In 1979, the General Assembly called for the launching, at the third special session on development in 1980, of a round of global and sustained negotiations on international economic cooperation for development. The negotiations, however, failed to achieve the hoped-for progress at the special session held in September 1980, but at the regular session that year, an international development strategy for the third UN Development Decade was adopted.

THIRD UN DEVELOPMENT DECADE

In the new international development strategy adopted by the General Assembly for the third UN Development Decade, beginning on 1 January 1981, governments pledged themselves, individually and collectively, to fulfill their commitment to establish a new international economic order based on justice and equity. They agreed to subscribe to the goals and objectives of the strategy and to translate them into reality by adopting a coherent set of interrelated, concrete, and effective policy measures in all sectors of development.

The strategy set forth goals and objectives for an accelerated development of the developing countries in the period 1981–90, including the following: (1) a 7 percent average annual rate of growth of gross domestic product (GDP); (2) a 7.5 percent annual rate of expansion of exports and an 8 percent annual rate of expansion of imports of goods and services; (3) an increase in gross domestic savings to reach about 24 percent of GDP by 1990; (4) a rapid and substantial increase in official development assistance by all developed countries, to reach or surpass the target of 0.7 percent of GNP of developed countries; (5) a 4 percent average annual rate of expansion of agricultural production; and (6) a 9 percent annual rate of expansion of manufacturing output. Other goals and objectives of the strategy included the attainment, by the year 2000, of full employment, of universal primary school enrollment, and of life expectancy of 60 years as a minimum, with infant mortality rates no higher than 50 per 1,000 live births.

The strategy also set out a series of policy measures—in international trade, industrialization, food and agriculture, financial resources for development, international monetary and financial issues, science and technology for development, energy, transportation, environment, human settlements, disaster relief, and social development, as well as in technical cooperation, including cooperation among developing countries themselves, and special measures for the least-developed countries and for geographically disadvantaged countries, such as island and landlocked developing countries.

In fact, the 1980s was a terrible decade for the economies of developing countries. By 1990 only five donor countries had met the UN's target of donating 0.7 percent of their GNP to development: Norway, the Netherlands, Denmark, Sweden, and France. Canada and Germany had achieved a level of 0.4 percent of their GNP. The United States, which had never agreed to the UN target, had given 0.2 percent of its GNP. Intransigent recession in the industrialized world, declining commodity prices, rising interest rates, trade barriers, and crippling international debt meant human suffering for the vast majority of the world's population. By 1990 4.2 billion of the world's 5.3 billion people lived in developing countries. Overall growth in these nations shrank to about 3 percent annually, and per capita growth to 1 percent, compared to averages of 5.5 percent in the 1960s and 3 percent in the 1970s. Lending by the IMF and World Bank group of institutions often came with requirements for "restructuring" that carried a heavy price in terms of human sacrifice. Debt-laden developing countries found themselves spending vastly more on debt service than on social services.

This dismal result was illustrated by the fact that the number of countries designated by the General Assembly as "least developed" had grown from 24 in 1972 to 47 in 1991.

FOURTH UN DEVELOPMENT DECADE

In 1990, the General Assembly concluded that its goals for the Third UN Development Decade had not been attained. It set new priorities and goals for the growth of the developing member nations with its International Development Strategy (IDS) for the Fourth United Nations Development Decade (1991–2000). Within one year of its passage, however, the former USSR had dissolved, forever changing the landscape of international economic relations. Many of the assumptions on which the IDS had been based were upset by the historic forces that were thus set in motion.

In September 1990, the Second United Nations Conference on the Least Developed Countries set targets for official development assistance (ODA) to those nations. The General Assembly, through the new IDS, urged industrialized countries to reach or surpass those targets. It also recommended that developing countries try to raise their rate of industrialization by 8–10 percent and increase their annual food production by 4 percent.

The General Assembly set forth six goals for the new IDS that amounted to an early manifestation of a new philosophy of "sustainable" development that would be vigorously developed at the historic UN Conference on Environment and Development (UNCED), two years later. The goals of the IDS were:

1. To speed up the pace of economic growth in the developing countries;
2. To devise a development process that meets social needs, reduces extreme poverty significantly, develops and uses people's capacity and skills, and is environmentally sound and sustainable;
3. To improve the international systems of money, finance, and trade;
4. To strengthen and stabilize the world economy and establish sound macroeconomic management practices, nationally and internationally;
5. To strengthen international cooperation for development;
6. To make a special effort to deal with the particular problems of the least developed countries.

The philosophy for the new IDS was based on the principle that, because the developed countries have the greatest influence on the international economic environment, they have a special responsibility for the success of development efforts. It also recognized that speeding up development would require strenuous efforts by developing countries to increase domestic savings, raise investment and investment returns, hold down inflation, exercise monetary and fiscal discipline, maintain realistic exchange rates, and allocate resources more efficiently.

Improving the state of international trade was paramount for any development plan. The Uruguay Round of the GATT talks were stalled and protectionism was on the rise in the developed nations. The strategy proposed that the following actions be taken to accelerate international trade in the 1990s:

1. Stand by the commitment made in 1986 to halt and reverse protectionism;
2. Liberalize trade and improve developing countries' access to all markets by reducing or removing tariff barriers;
3. Free up trade in tropical products and products based on natural resources;
4. Bring trade in textiles under the normal rules of GATT;
5. Substantially reduce agricultural subsidies and other protective policies;
6. Implement and improve the generalized system of preferences under which some developing countries' exports are admitted to industrialized countries at reduced rates or duty-free;
7. Ensure that regional economic arrangements and trade blocs conform with GATT rules;
8. Make sure that GATT contracting parties adhere strictly to the agreement's rules and principles.

Other provisions of the IDS included establishing more stable commodity markets, obtaining concessional terms for the transfer of technology to developing countries, and finding agreement on a way that the intellectual property system (which protects own-ership of copyrights, trademarks, industrial designs, and patents) can promote development while protecting intellectual property. It also recommended that work on international rules and standards to govern the exchange of technological information (the code of conduct on the transfer of technology), which had come to a halt at the end of the 1980s, should be completed.

The underlying causes of economic stagnation also were decried. The IDS called for the eradication of poverty, hunger, adult illiteracy, lack of basic education for women, and runaway population growth in developing countries, and noted the catastrophic deterioration of the environment by shortsighted development projects.

In 1992, the Secretary-General gave the General Assembly a guardedly optimistic report on the progress of the IDS to that point. The developed market economies themselves had grown by only about 1 percent in 1991. Although a recovery had begun in 1992, it was considered to be weak. There was concern that the urgent needs of the newly independent countries of the former USSR, often referred to as "economies in transition," would divert assistance from developing countries. Per capita incomes remained stagnant or declined in all the developing regions, except South and East Asia and China. The debt crisis of the developing countries had not worsened, but little progress had been made in terms of debt relief and forgiveness. However, some of the Latin American countries had again become creditworthy.

The 1993 Report on the World Social Situation, commissioned by the General Assembly to review the implementation of the Declaration on Social Progress and Development made 20 years earlier, also was cautiously optimistic. It noted the positive direction of reform in the United Nations system towards coordination between various UN agencies with operations in the same countries. "Although the major development goals, proclaimed more than 20 years ago in the Declaration on Social Progress and Development, have not changed significantly, the priorities, approaches and emphases have been reviewed and renewed, as the understanding of the forces behind development have deepened. Thus, emphasis is now on assisting the recipient countries to strengthen their institutional capacity to sustain the development process" the report said. In other words: helping them learn how to help themselves.

However, by May 1994, as part of a General Assembly–mandated triennial review of progress, it was reported that 1993 had seen a significant reduction in voluntary contributions to operational activities. UNDP saw its contributions reduced 15 percent from 1992 levels, forcing it to restrict its operations by 70 percent; UNICEF experienced a 22 percent drop; and UNFPA saw a reduction of 8 percent. The World Food Programme was 65 percent behind the previous biennium in obtaining contributions. The argument that the system of "voluntary" contributions for specific programs should give way to a more coordinated source of funding from a central pool of resources that would be included in the member states' annual assessment.

THE EARTH SUMMIT—AGENDA 21

The United Nations Conference on Environment and Development (UNCED), popularly dubbed the "Earth Summit," brought together 117 heads of state and government in Rio de Janeiro, Brazil from 3–14 June 1992. The product of this historic meeting, an 800-page document called "Agenda 21," set forth global measures to protect the planet's environment while guaranteeing sustainable economic growth. An important statement of the basic principles of sustainable development, The Rio Declaration on Environment and Development, was adopted by acclamation. The conference also spawned a new functional commission of ECOSOC, the Commission on Sustainable Development, which has a mandate to monitor international treaties on the environment, provide policy direction, and coordinate action within the

United Nations system to achieve the goals of Agenda 21.

In addition to Agenda 21, two important conventions on the environment were opened for signature and received widespread endorsement: the Global Warming Convention, which set guidelines for regulating emissions of gases believed to cause global warming, was signed by 153 nations; and the Biodiversity Convention, which committed signatory nations to protection of endangered species and cooperation on genetic and biological technology, was signed by representatives of 150 countries. The Biodiversity Convention became legally binding in December 1993, after 30 countries had ratified it. Two important documents setting forth the principles behind the concept of sustainable development also were widely adopted at the Earth Summit: the Statement on Forest Principles, recommending preservation of world forests and monitoring of development impact on timberlands; and the Declaration on Environment and Development, a statement of principles that emphasized the coordination of economic and environmental concerns.

More than two years were spent preparing for the Earth Summit and drafting the documents that would achieve widespread international acceptance. However, many controversial propositions had to be deleted or scaled down in the final documents to achieve the final consensus. For example, negotiators removed or excluded specific targets on pollution controls, resource protection, and financial aid to developing countries that restrain their economic development in order to protect their natural resources. Developing countries had sought to establish a "green fund" to support their efforts to implement environmentally sustainable development. However, the G-7 group of industrialized countries succeeded in specifying that such development funds would be channeled through the World Bank's Global Environment Facility (GEF), effectively retaining control of funding in the hands of the industrialized world. The European Community had recommended a tax on fossil fuels in industrialized nations, but, opposition from oil-producing countries killed this provision. Also deemphasized in the final documents were references to population control. Passages referring to contraception were completely deleted at the insistence of an odd coalition that included the Holy See (Vatican), Roman Catholic countries, and Moslem countries.

The sense of urgency that brought 35,000 accredited participants and 117 heads of state to Rio de Janeiro for the Earth Summit is perhaps well summed up by the UNCED secretary-general, Canadian Maurice Strong: "The Earth Summit must establish a whole new basis for relations between rich and poor, North and South, including a concerted attack on poverty as a central priority for the 21st Century. We owe at least this much to future generations, from whom we have borrowed a fragile planet called Earth."

Three other major UN conferences that would deal with the subject of sustainable development were scheduled for 1994 and 1995: the International Conference on Population and Development (Cairo, Egypt, September 1994); the World Summit on Social Development (Copenhagen, Denmark, March 1995); and the Fourth World Conference on Women (Beijing, China, September 1995).

THE 1994 AGENDA FOR DEVELOPMENT

The 47th General Assembly requested the Secretary-General to consult with member states and prepare an "agenda for development." After obtaining submissions from member states, agencies of the UN system and public and private sources worldwide, he presented his report to the 49th General Assembly in 1994. Entitled *Development and International Economic Cooperation: An Agenda for Development*, this wide-ranging document summarized the basic tenets of the experience gained during the UN's 50 years of development work. The agenda was intended to offer guidelines for thought and action by member states.

One reason put forward for creating such a document was that with the end of the cold war, funding development projects as a mechanism for establishing spheres of influence also had ended. The fundamental social, political, and economic changes that had altered the map of Europe and provided a new atmosphere of consensus at the United Nations, also threatened to bewilder and exhaust the potential donors to UN programs for development. Some quarters had even suggested that the UN was expending more for its many new peacekeeping operations than for development. The Secretary-General produced statistics in an annex to the agenda that demonstrated that this was not the case, even exempting the funds expended by the specialized agencies.

Several major themes of the agenda set forth a new underlying philosophy regarding international development programs.

1. National governments bear the major responsibility for development. However, the United Nations' vast experience and global reach made it a unique resource for the developing nations. The United Nations could act as facilitator and communicator, but it could not substitute for the commitment of individual states and their domestic and international partners.

2. However, national governments could no longer be assumed to be paramount economic agents. The internationalization of trade and the ascendance of the market system worldwide meant that governments must, however, provide a regulatory framework for effective operation of a competitive market system. They must also invest in human capital by ensuring that social safety nets are in place.

3. Economic growth should promote full employment and poverty reduction, not just economic growth as an end in itself. If, despite national economic improvement, great poverty continued in a nation, no development effort could be sustainable.

4. No mechanism exists by which the major economies could be induced to make globally beneficial structural change in their own economies, or to adopt more globally responsible economic, fiscal, and monetary policies. This single point represents a sea change in philosophy from the "new international economic order" of the 1970s.

5. UNCED's historic Agenda 21 demonstrated that the environment had finally been recognized by the international community as a resource for development that must be nurtured and protected. Governments had the responsibility to provide the leadership and regulatory structure to protect their natural environment. Successful development required policies that incorporate environmental considerations. The Secretary-General pointed out that pioneering efforts were being made to make local inhabitants incentive partners rather than simply collateral beneficiaries of sustainable development programs. As the keyword and rallying cry of the Earth Summit, "sustainability" must be the guiding principle of development, to be achieved by a true partnership of governments, international organizations, and nongovernmental organizations; a true partnership between humanity and nature.

6. No development could be considered sustainable in the presence of poverty, disease, illiteracy, great unemployment, discrimination against women, armed conflict, or lack of social integration; the manifestations of social integration being discrimination, fanaticism, intolerance, and persecution.

7. Democracy and development are processes (not events) that are fundamentally linked because people's participation in the decision-making processes that affect their lives gives legitimacy to governments and their development programs.

In his conclusions, the Secretary-General admitted that, over the years, absence of clear policy guidance from the General Assembly and the lack of effective policy coordination by ECOSOC had resulted in an overall lack of focus in the UN development system. The fundamental changes under way included the restructuring of development efforts to be channeled through UNDP resident coordinators, by means of the development of one comprehensive "country strategy note." This alone would bring about better (if not perfect) coordination and more rational use of available funds.

However, the Secretary-General also noted the growth of other obstructions to the urgent need for social and economic development in the developing countries: "At present the UN mechanism is caught in a confining cycle. There is a resistance to multilateralism from those who fear a loss of national control. There is a reluctance to provide financial means to achieve agreed ends from those who lack conviction that assessments will benefit their own interests. And there is an unwillingness to engage in difficult operations by those who seek guarantees of perfect clarity and limited duration. Without a new and compelling collective vision, the international community will be unable to break out of this cycle."

DEVELOPMENT PLANNING

Almost all the organizations in the UN family contribute in one way or another to development planning—by helping to evolve and introduce new planning methods, by assisting governments in establishing realistic growth targets, and by trying to ensure that overall plans take account of the needs of the different sectors of society.

Within the UN, problems relating to development planning are the concern of the Economic and Social Council's Committee for Development Planning. The 24-member committee, established in 1966, is a consultative body that meets annually to consider problems encountered in implementing development plans.

The UN Secretariat provides an account of the state of the world economy through its annual publication of the *World Economic and Social Survey*, which has appeared every year since 1948. Since 1990 UNDP has stimulated debate about the concept of human-centered development through the publication of the annual *Human Development Report*, written by an independent team of development specialists and published by Oxford University Press. Statistical data, considered indispensable for economic and social development planning, also appears in a number of UN publications, including the *Statistical Yearbook, Demographic Yearbook, Yearbook of National Accounts Statistics, Yearbook of International Trade Statistics, World Energy Supplies, Commodity Trade Statistics, Population and Vital Statistics Report,* and *Monthly Bulletin of Statistics.*

WORLD FOOD COUNCIL (WFC)

The world food situation in the early 1970s was marked by extreme food shortages in many developing countries in Africa and parts of Southeast Asia, by a general lack of progress in the world fight against hunger and malnutrition, and by very slow progress in the creation of a system of internationally coordinated cereal reserves to meet crop shortfalls and other abnormal situations.

It was against this background that the General Assembly decided, in 1973, to convene a conference to deal with global food problems. The UN World Food Conference, held in Rome in November 1974, called for the creation of a 36-member ministerial-level World Food Council to review annually major problems and policy issues affecting the world food situation and to bring its political influence to bear on governments and UN bodies and agencies alike.

Each year up through 1992 the WFC met in plenary session at the invitation of one of its member states. The council, as a subsidiary body of the UN General Assembly, reports annually to it through the Economic and Social Council.

At first, the WFC's approach to solving world food problems was to encourage the adoption of national food strategies by developing countries. Under this plan, each country would assess its present food situation, including needs, supply, potential for increasing food production, storage, processing, transport, distribution, marketing, and the ability to meet food emergencies. In the early 1980s, this concept was taken over by the World Bank.

In 1989, at its fifteenth session held in Cairo, Egypt, the WFC delineated a Programme of Co-operative Action with four main goals for UN member countries within the next decade: the elimination of starvation and death caused by famine; a substantial reduction of malnutrition and mortality among young children; a tangible reduction in chronic hunger; and the elimination of major nutritional-deficiency diseases. The Programme of Co-Operative Action contained proposals for immediate action to be taken on food-for-work programs in rural areas where employment opportunities are not available and measures to make specific food items affordable to the poor. Over the longer term, the WFC recommended projects to create production and employment opportunities in rural and urban areas; community initiative projects designed to enable the communities themselves to identify and implement projects; vocational training schemes; retraining schemes; food stamp schemes. In the area of nutrition, the WFC recommended the implementation on an emergency basis of supplementary feeding programs for children; primary health care programs, including programs to improve sanitation and drinking water; family planning programs; nutritional education programs; and support to food and nutrition programs undertaken by WHO, UNICEF, and other international agencies.

At its sixteenth session in 1990, held in Bangkok, Thailand, the council observed that most countries had not yet set specific goals and targets to implement its call to action. However, by 1991 those goals had been adopted by all UN member states as part of the International Development Strategy for the Fourth United Nations Development Decade.

The WFC also considered the coordination of the activities of some 35 international agencies that have programs significantly related to hunger problems. The WFC observed that its own role was that of providing a central, undivided focus on hunger and recommended the creation of an inter-secretariat consultative mechanism among the four Rome-based food organizations (FAO, IFAD, WFC, and WFP). In 1991, meeting in Helsingor, Denmark, it reiterated this support. It noted with concern the great financial difficulties facing these international organizations.

The eighteenth session of the WFC met in 1992 in Nairobi, Kenya. Its report to the General Assembly noted that although most developing regions made some headway during the 1980s in reducing hunger and malnutrition, this was not the case for the peoples of Africa where disastrous droughts and civil disturbances had caused widespread starvation in recent years. The council praised the IFAD Special Programme for Sub-Saharan African Countries Affected by Drought and Desertification. In response to the disastrous problems of Africa, the WFC called for a "New Green Revolution," and the intensified transfer of technology to accomplish such a revolution. It recommended that substantial increases in investments in research, extension, and training were needed, particularly in Africa.

In 1992 the WFC also noted the problems of millions of people in Eastern Europe and the Commonwealth of Independent States (formerly the USSR) in gaining access to adequate food as a result of the dislocation of their economies.

In the context of the efforts of the General Assembly to streamline the activities of the United Nations, the WFC considered its future role within the framework of the restructuring process. With disarming frankness, the council stated: "We agree that the council has fallen short of achieving the political leadership and coordination role expected from its founders at the 1974 World Food Conference." It concluded that, in a rapidly changing world, the continuation of the status quo for the World Food Council and the United Nations as a whole was not possible. It established an ad hoc committee to review the mandate and future role of the WFC, which met in New York on 14–15 September 1992 and submitted its report to the 47th Session of the General Assembly (1992). However, the committee could not reach agreement on what the council's future role should be. Views ranged from abolishing it to strengthening it and integrating its mandate with another intergovernmental body. With this the committee referred the matter to the General Assembly, which requested the council members to continue attempts to agree on appropriate measures to be taken. After informal meetings from January to May 1993, the council reported to the General Assembly that "Council members are agreed on a set of principles to guide the United Nations response to global food and hunger problems, but disagreements continue to exist concerning the most effective institutional response to these principles."

In 1993 no formal WFC session was held, nor were any substantive documents prepared by the WFC secretariat. In fact, in December 1993, the secretariat in Rome was abolished as a result of the restructuring of the United Nations. Responsibility for servicing any future meetings of the WFC was given to the newly formed Department for Policy Coordination and Sustainable Development (DPCSD) in New York.

In November 1993 the president of the World Food Council held informal consultations with other WFC ministers of agriculture during the biennial FAO Conference in Rome about the possibility of scheduling the next (19th) session of the council. The consultations were inconclusive and the future of the WFC was not taken up at the General Assembly's 48th regular session in light of these ongoing discussions.

Despite uncertainties about its future role and functioning, the General Assembly elected the following states as members of the World Food Council in November 1993: Bangladesh, Brazil, China, Liberia, Malawi, Mexico, Pakistan, Sudan, Turkey, and the United States.

SCIENCE AND TECHNOLOGY FOR DEVELOPMENT

A major event of the first UN Development Decade was the UN Conference on the Application of Science and Technology for the Benefit of the Less Developed Countries, held in Geneva in 1963. The conference focussed world attention on the practical possibilities of accelerating development through the application of advances in science and technology and on the need for reorienting research toward the requirements of the developing countries.

A second conference, the UN Conference on Science and Technology for Development, held in Vienna in 1979, adopted a program of action (the Vienna Programme) designed to put science and technology to work for the economic development of all countries, particularly the developing countries. It recommended the creation by the General Assembly of a high-level intergovernmental committee on science and technology for development, open to all member states, and the establishment of a voluntary fund to be administered by UNDP.

The Geneva Conference was a predominantly technical or pragmatic conference at which developed countries provided developing countries with state-of-the-art reports on developed-country technologies. By contrast, the Vienna Conference reflected the 1970s discussions between developed and develop-

ing countries over a more equal access of the latter to the world's science and technology. Thus science and technology were placed within the context of international diplomacy. The result, the Vienna Programme of Action was a compromise that did not fully meet the expectations of the developing countries.

The Vienna Programme of Action was divided into three target areas: strengthening the science and technology capacities of developing countries; restructuring the existing pattern of international scientific and technological relations; and strengthening the role of the UN system in the field of science and technology and the provision of increased financial resources.

Endorsing the recommendations of the Vienna conference, the General Assembly decided to establish an Intergovernmental Committee on Science and Technology for Development (ISTD), to be open to all states, and to create within the UN Secretariat a Center for Science and Technology for Development (CSTD) to provide substantive support to the committee and to coordinate activities within the UN system. In 1982, the General Assembly established the UN Financing System for Science and Technology for Development to finance a broad range of activities intended to strengthen the endogenous scientific and technological capacities of developing countries. In 1986, it transferred the responsibilities and resources of the financing system to a newly created UN Fund for Science and Technology for Development, administered by UNDP. In 1992, this new voluntary fund amounted to US$1.56 million and had funded six policy meetings in Cape Verde, Jamaica, Pakistan, Togo, Uganda, and Viet Nam.

In 1989, on the tenth anniversary of the Vienna Conference, the General Assembly expressed its disappointment with the implementation of the Vienna Programme. As part of the effort to rationalize and reform the entire United Nations system, in April 1992, the General Assembly decided to transform the ISTD into a functional commission of ECOSOC, the Commission on Science and Technology for Development. The activities of the Centre for Science and Technology for Development were incorporated into the new Department of Economic and Social Development, within its Division of Science, Technology, Energy, Environment and Natural Resources.

Major objectives of the new commission, which held its first session in April 1993, include:

(a) Assisting ECOSOC in providing science and technology policy guidelines and recommendations to member states, in particular developing countries;
(b) Providing innovative approaches to improving the quality of coordination and cooperation in the area of science and technology within the United Nations system, with a view to ensuring optimum mobilization of resources;
(c) Providing expert advice to other parts of the UN system.

The commission also requested that the Secretary-General prepare proposals to improve the coordination of the different bodies in the UN system, including the World Bank, which are involved in science and technology activities.

New developments, such as the United Nations Conference on Environment and Development in 1992—which had substantial science and technology components—and changing attitudes within intergovernmental bodies regarding the role of government and the private sector in view of the end of the cold war, led to the need for a major restructuring of the United Nations in the economic and social sector (including science and technology). While the General Assembly confirmed the continued validity of the Vienna Programme of Action in its resolution on science and technology for development in December 1993, its objectives were merged with the Technology Programme of the UN Conference on Trade and Development (UNCTAD). UNCTAD thus became responsible for science and technology within the United

Nations system. Major program elements of the revised work program include:

(a) Endogenous capacity-building and resource mobilization in the area of science and technology for development;
(b) Technology assessment and information services;
(c) Issues related to investment and technology transfer.

The new Commission on Science and Technology also decided to adopt themes for study by working groups during the two-year periods between its sessions. For 1993–95, these included technology for small-scale economic activities to address the basic needs of low-income populations, the gender implications of science and technology for developing countries, and the science and technology aspects of work being considered by the Commission on Sustainable Development. The commission also considered studying a variety of other issues, including the role of technology in military conversion, the effect of new and emerging technologies on industrialization, and the role of information technologies in developing countries.

Transnational Corporations

Since the end of World War II, the role of multinational or transnational corporations in international commerce has been growing, but information on their activities has been fragmentary and often closely held. Many of these corporations are household names. They conduct a large portion of their business outside their host country, often recruiting management from their overseas subsidiaries and recruiting shareholders around the world. Some of these corporations command resources greater than those of most governments represented at the UN. In 1989, estimated sales by foreign affiliates of transnationals worldwide were US$4.5 trillion. In comparison, world exports were only US$3 trillion. The relationship of transnational corporations with developing countries frequently has been troubled, but they can provide capital, managerial expertise, and technology that are all urgently required for development and often would be hard to come by in any other way.

In 1972, the Economic and Social Council requested the Secretary-General to appoint a group of eminent persons to study the impact of transnational corporations on development and international relations. The group of 20 economists, government officials, and corporation executives from all parts of the world met in 1973 and heard testimony from 50 witnesses in public hearings—a procedure new to the UN. Its report, issued in 1974, recommended the creation of a permanent commission on transnational corporations under the Economic and Social Council and an information and research center in the UN Secretariat.

In December 1974, the council established an intergovernmental Commission on Transnational Corporations as a standing committee (not a functional commission) to furnish a forum within the UN system regarding such corporations; promote an exchange of views about them among governments, intergovernmental organizations, business, labor, and consumers; assist the council in developing the basis for a code of conduct on the activities of transnational corporations; and develop a comprehensive information system on their activities.

The 48-member commission meets annually. At its second session, held in Lima in March 1976, it gave priority to the elaboration of a code of conduct and recommended that the Economic and Social Council establish an Intergovernmental Working Group on a Code of Conduct. The code was to be the first multilaterally agreed framework governing all aspects of the relations between states and transnational corporations, with standards to protect the interests of both the host countries and investors in those countries. The working group held a number of negotiating sessions between 1977 and 1982. Negotiations continued in

meetings of a special session of the commission, open to all states.

In April 1991, the commission approved a text authorizing the preparation of recommendations on encouraging TNCs to cooperate in efforts to protect and enhance the environment in all countries for submission to the UN Conference on Environment and Development (UNCED) in 1992. The commission agreed that the following issues should be addressed: internationally agreed standards; improving management and regulation of industrial processes; transferring environmentally sound technologies to developing countries on favorable terms; using environment and development accounting and reporting methods; international environmental management; preventive measures to minimize risks to human life, property, and the environment; and the question of reparations for damage. It directed its secretariat, the Center on Transnational Corporations, to prepare its submission to UNCED. However, in early 1992, the center's functions were absorbed into a new department of the Secretariat and eventually transferred altogether to UNCTAD (see below).

At its 1994 Substantive Session, the commission recommended to ECOSOC that it be integrated into the institutional machinery of the UN Conference on Trade and Development (UNCTAD). ECOSOC decided to transmit this recommendation to the General Assembly for action.

An Intergovernmental Group of Experts on International Standards of Accounting and Reporting, established by the Economic and Social Council in 1982, reviews issues that give rise to divergent accounting and reporting practices of transnational corporations and identifies areas where efforts at harmonization appear necessary.

The four other priorities for the commission's program of work are: establishment of an information system to advance understanding of the nature of transnational corporations and their effects on home and host countries; research into the effects of their operations; technical assistance; and work leading to a more precise definition of the term *transnational corporations*.

The UN Center on Transnational Corporations was established by the Economic and Social Council in 1974 as part of the UN Secretariat. The functions of the center were to develop a comprehensive information system on the activities of transnational corporations, using data from governmental, corporate, and other sources; to analyze and disseminate the information to all governments; to provide technical assistance and strengthen the capacity of host countries (especially developing countries) in their dealings with transnational corporations; and to carry out political, legal, economic, and social research, particularly research to help in devising a code of conduct. By 1985, the center had established that the 350 largest transnational corporations (half of which were based in the United States) had combined sales of US$2.7 trillion, a sum which was larger than the combined GNP of all the developing countries, including China.

In 1990 ECOSOC requested the Center on Transnational Corporations to undertake a survey of corporate environmental management to document the most advanced practices as models for companies that had not yet created environmental programs and to submit the results to UNCED. The "Benchmark Corporate Environmental Survey," was submitted to the UNCED preparatory meeting in August 1991. Twenty percent of the 163 firms surveyed responded. The center recommended UNCED consider the following recommendations in preparing its Agenda 21: increased international cooperation to better inform TNCs of the impact of their operations on the greenhouse phenomenon; include TNCs in the consultative process surrounding climate change studies; treat dioxins and PCBs as international, not just local, pollution problems; transnational affiliates in developing countries should handle toxic wastes according to the same rules as in developed countries; TNCs should create safety zones around their facilities to lessen the potential impact of accidents; the oceans should be protected from land-based pollution; TNCs should sponsor programs to save wetlands and rainforests and protect biodiversity; TNCs should help develop a code of conduct on biotechnology. The center also pointed out that environmental rules and regulations differed from country to country. The companies that responded to the survey were interested in the UN setting international guidelines, although many of them were unaware of the existence of current international guidelines.

In 1992, as part of the comprehensive restructuring of the UN secretariat, the functions of the center were incorporated into a new unit: the Transnational Corporations and Management Division of the Department of Economic and Social Development. In May 1993, the General Assembly transferred responsibility for the transnational program again to the secretariat of UNCTAD.

NATURAL RESOURCES AND ENERGY

The importance of natural resources for economic development was emphasized in 1970 when the Economic and Social Council established the Committee on Natural Resources. The committee develops guidelines for advisory services to governments, reviews arrangements to coordinate UN activities in natural resources development, and evaluates trends and issues concerning natural resources exploration and development, as well as prospects for selected energy, water, and mineral resources.

During the 1970s, the Committee on Natural Resources played an important role in focusing world attention on the status of the global stock of water resources to meet human, commercial, and agricultural needs. As a result of an initiative of the committee, the UN Water Conference was convened in 1977 in Mar del Plata, Argentina. The conference adopted an action plan to guide international efforts to effectively manage, develop, and use water resources. To give impetus to the Mar del Plata Action Plan, the General Assembly, in 1980, launched the International Drinking Water Supply and Sanitation Decade (1981–90).

In 1973, the General Assembly established the UN Revolving Fund for Natural Resources Exploration, which began operation in 1975. The fund, financed from voluntary contributions, is intended to provide additional risk capital for mineral exploration in developing countries. In 1981, the fund was authorized to extend its exploration activities to geothermal energy.

During the 1970s, with the rise in and volatility of costs for petroleum, affecting the economies of all countries, particularly those of the poorer countries, and the growing awareness that known supplies of petroleum would, in the long run, be unable to meet global requirements, more attention was focussed on new and renewable sources of energy. This led to the General Assembly's decision to convene, in Nairobi in August 1981, the UN Conference on New and Renewable Sources of Energy. The conference examined alternative forms of energy, including solar, biomass, geothermal, and ocean energy; wind power; hydropower; fuelwood and charcoal; peat; and the use of draft animals for energy purposes. It adopted the Nairobi Program of Action for the Development and Utilization of New and Renewable Sources of Energy as a blueprint for national and international action. The Nairobi Program identified five broad areas for concentrated action: energy assessment and planning; research, development, and demonstration; transfer, adaptation, and application of mature technologies; information flows; and education and training.

Endorsing the Nairobi Program later that year, the General Assembly set up an interim committee to launch immediate implementation and, in 1992, established the Committee on the Development and Utilization of New and Renewable Sources of Energy, open to the participation of all states as full members. Later in 1992, in response to the requirements of implementing UNCED's Agenda 21, this committee was combined with the

energy portion of the Committee on Natural Resources and Energy, and became a new standing committee of ECOSOC: the Committee on New and Renewable Sources of Energy and on Energy for Development. The Committee on Natural Resources now concentrates mainly on water and mineral resources. Each committee has a membership of 24 government-nominated experts who are elected by ECOSOC.

The first session of the new Committee on New and Renewable Resources and Energy met in New York from 7–18 February 1994. The Secretary-General reported to the committee that in 1990 new and renewable energy sources accounted for 17.7 percent of the total energy consumption. The drop in oil prices during the 1980s had led to a decline in investment in renewable energy resources, but growing concern for the fragile state of the world's environment lent urgency to efforts to find alternatives to burning fossil fuels and wood, which were contributing to the threat of global warning.

At its first session, the committee noted that the Nairobi Program had led to progress in the application of large-scale technologies, such as hydropower and geothermal energy, and had helped bring to maturity solar energy and wind technologies. However, the overall impact of these new technologies remained insignificant. The committee identified four domains for action by member states: more efficient use of energy and energy-intensive material; increased use of renewable sources of energy; more efficient production and use of fossil fuels; and fuel substitution from high carbon to low carbon-based fuels. It also called for integrated national action programs for developing energy systems; for removing subsidies on conventional sources of energy; establishing support for new, environmentally sound technologies; and finding ways to use wasted energy, such as waste heat from industrial processes. Its report to ECOSOC also recommended the establishment of regional "centers of excellence" to provide training, technology support, and resource data.

Another positive development in this field in the 1990s was the increasing recognition by the World Bank and the International Monetary Fund (IMF) that energy conservation makes good economic and environmental sense. Public outcry over displacement of local populations by big dams and destruction of rain forests for grazing projects funded by the World Bank had led it to institute an environmental assessment on every project it undertook. In 1992 the IMF also began to study the impact of its policies on its member nations' environment. The bank also branched out into supporting new sources of energy, for example by lending Mauritius US$15 million to support a program to generate 10–20 percent of that nation's future energy needs by burning sugarcane waste product readily available in that country.

Addressing another important area in the energy field—the use of nuclear energy for the economic and social development of developing countries—the General Assembly, in 1977, set in motion arrangements for an international conference on the subject. The first global effort in this field, the UN Conference for the Promotion of International Cooperation in the Peaceful Uses of Nuclear Energy, was held in Geneva in 1987. Although unable to reach agreement on principles acceptable to all, the participants at the conference exchanged views and experience on topics ranging from the production of electricity to the various applications of nuclear techniques in food and agriculture, medicine, hydrology, research, and industry.

The first session of the newly reconstituted Committee on Natural Resources was held in early 1993. Its second session met in New York in early 1994. In the 1990s the focus of the Committee on Natural Resources became the implementation of the recommendations of Agenda 21, particularly measures to promote the more rational and sustainable use of natural resources. In the chairman's summary of the meeting, he noted that mineral and water resources had to be seen as finite and valuable resources, and that their production and consumption affected other constituents of the environment. Therefore, a holistic approach was required to the planning and management of natural resources within the geographical boundaries of each country and also in the consideration of the global impact of national policies or measures. A continued call was made for integrated approaches to water and land management. The committee emphasized the need to consider natural resources as a whole, rather than by individual sectors, such as agriculture and industry.

The committee also noted that the fundamental importance of mineral resources to economic development and quality of life had not been adequately reflected in Agenda 21. It recommended that the need to ensure the sustainable supply of minerals should be a key issue for deliberations on Agenda 21.

The committee's discussion on mineral resources was influenced by the impact of privatization of state mineral enterprises on people in the developing countries and economies in transition. While there seemed to be a new trend toward closer understanding between these countries and transnational corporations, the committee stated that governments should promote measures to reduce destruction of the environment from private mining operations. It also recommended that governments promote measures to encourage better use of existing resources through recycling and substitution.

REGIONAL COMMISSIONS

The five regional commissions—serving Europe, Asia and the Pacific, Latin America and the Caribbean, Africa, and Western Asia—have been established by the Economic and Social Council in recognition of the fact that many economic and social problems are best approached at the regional level. The commissions work to raise the level of economic and social development activity in their respective regions, as well as to maintain and strengthen relations among countries within and outside regions. All actions taken by the commissions are intended to fit within the framework of overall UN economic and social policies. The commissions also are empowered, with the agreement of the governments concerned, to make recommendations directly to member governments and to the specialized agencies.

The commissions are subsidiary organs of the Economic and Social Council, to which they report annually. The secretariats of the commissions—each headed by an executive secretary with the rank of undersecretary-general—are integral parts of the UN staff, and their budgets form part of the regular UN budget.

An important part of the work of all the regional commissions is the preparation of regional studies and surveys, particularly annual economic and social surveys that are published at the headquarters of each commission. Supplementing these are bulletins and periodicals covering a wide range of subjects—such as agriculture, population, transportation and communications, energy, industry, and housing and construction—that are widely used as sources of information by governments, business and industry, educational institutions, other UN organs, and the press.

In the early 1990s, under pressure from both developing and industrialized countries to reform and rationalize the scattered development activities of the United Nations system, Secretary-General Boutros Boutros-Ghali proposed that the activities of all United Nations organs be coordinated. In December 1992, the General Assembly adopted his proposal with its historic Resolution A/47/199 that stressed the need for development activities to "be streamlined and rationalized, especially in the interrelated areas of programming, execution, decentralization, monitoring and evaluation, thus making the UN system more relevant and responsive to the national plans, priorities and objectives of developing countries, and more efficient in its delivery systems." Under this plan, many of the functions carried out by various committees and boards of the specialized agencies and UN funds would be transferred away from headquarters (in New York, or, in the case of the specialized agencies, Geneva or Vienna), to the regional commissions (headquartered in major cities of each region) and the office of the UNDP resident coordinator in the specific countries that were to be served by development programs. As this strategy develops, the role of the regional commissions will become more and more central to the work of the United Nations system.

Economic Commission for Europe (ECE)

The Economic Commission for Europe (ECE), with headquarters in Geneva, was established in 1947 to help mobilize concerted action for the economic reconstruction of postwar Europe and to increase European economic activity among countries both within and outside the region. To these goals was added that of providing governments with economic, technological, and statistical information. Begun as an experiment at a time when severe postwar shortages of some commodities and surpluses of others made economic cooperation in Europe a necessity, ECE soon became the only multilateral forum to deal with cooperation between Eastern and Western Europe. The ECE provides a systematic means of intergovernmental cooperation among the countries of Europe, the United States, Canada, Israel, and the republics of the former Soviet Union.

ECE priority objectives include the development of trade, scientific and technical cooperation, improvement of the environment, and long-term planning and projections as a basis for formulation of economic policy. Through meetings of policymakers and experts, publication of economic analyses and statistics, and study tours and exchanges of technical information, the commission provides a link between governments having different economic and social systems and belonging to different subregional organizations.

Plenary meetings of the commission are held annually; its subsidiary organs meet throughout the year. These include the Committee on Environmental Policy; the Inland Transport Committee; the Conference of European Statisticians; the Committee on the Development of Trade; the Senior Economic Advisers to ECE Governments; the Committee on Energy; the Working Party on Coal; the Working Party on Electric Power; the Working Party on Gas; the Senior Advisers to ECE Governments on Science and Technology; the Working Party on the Chemical Industry; the Working Party on Engineering Industries and Automation; the Working Party on Standardization Policies; the Working Party on Steel; the Committee on Agriculture; the Timber Committee; and the Committee on Human Settlements.

ECE works closely with a number of specialized agencies, particularly the ILO and FAO; with other intergovernmental organizations; and with nongovernmental organizations, which ECE has consulted frequently for their expertise in particular subjects.

The analytical work of the ECE provides both a macro- and micro-economic picture of the state of the region. Its major annual publications are the *Economic Survey of Europe* and the *Economic Bulletin for Europe*. It also publishes statistical bulletins and special reports on the state of markets in industry, timber, and human settlements. It has also published guides for the management of joint ventures, privatization and conditions for foreign direct investment.

The network of committees and working parties mentioned above carries on the ECE's technical cooperation work. The ECE has formulated regionwide strategies and legal instruments in the fields of environment and transportation. One of its most significant accomplishments is the establishment of a standard for electronic data interchange (the UN/EDIFACT or United Nations Electronic Data Interchange for Administration, Commerce and Transport). This international standard for communication between networks of computers paves the way for the development of paperless international trade in the twenty-first century.

The events of 1989–91, during which the entire face of Europe changed beyond recognition, provided enormous challenges for the ECE. War in the former Yugoslavia and the resulting economic sanctions and displacement of 3 million people made a somber picture. The ECE provided technical cooperation to the countries of Eastern Europe in transition to a market economy. By 1994, these countries made up fully one-half of its expanded membership. Hundreds of workshops on transition issues were conducted by the ECE in these countries in 1994 and 1995. The program of workshops was supplemented by the introduction of regional advisory services in each of the ECE's major fields of activity.

Membership and Budget. As of June 1994, the following countries were members of the ECE: Albania, Andorra, Armenia, Austria, Azerbaijan, Belarus, Belgium, Bosnia-Herzegovina, Bulgaria, Canada, Croatia, Cyprus, Czech Republic, Denmark, Estonia, Finland, France, Germany, Georgia, Greece, Hungary, Iceland, Ireland, Israel, Italy, Kazakhstan, Kyrgyzstan, Latvia, Liechtenstein, Lithuania, Luxembourg, Malta, Monaco, Netherlands, Norway, Poland, Portugal, Republic of Moldova, Romania, Russian Federation, San Marino, Slovakia, Slovenia, Spain, Sweden, Switzerland, The Former Yugoslav Republic of Macedonia, Turkey, Turkmenistan, Ukraine, United Kingdom, United States of America, Uzbekistan, and Yugoslavia. In 1993, the ECE decided that, since the former USSR had been a European member of the United Nations, new members of the United Nations that had been constituent republics of the USSR, even if they were located in the Asian part of the former USSR, were entitled to be members of the ECE.

Appropriations for the ECE from the regular UN budget for the 1994–95 biennium totaled US$44,684,500.

Economic and Social Commission for Asia and the Pacific (ESCAP)

The Economic and Social Commission for Asia and the Pacific (ESCAP), with headquarters in Bangkok, and a Pacific Operations Center based in Port Vila, Vanuatu, serves a region that contains more than half the world's population. It was established in 1947 as the Economic Commission for Asia and the Far East to promote reconstruction and economic development of the region. Its name was changed in 1974 to reflect equal concern with economic growth and social progress and to clarify its geographic scope. The commission meets annually.

ESCAP's activities help identify common problems and facilitate cooperation for economic and social development at the regional level. It provides technical assistance and advisory services to governments on request, carries out research on regional issues, and acts as a clearinghouse of information.

The commission, which originally had a structure based around nine separate committees, was restructured in 1992 as follows:

- Three thematic committees dealing respectively with regional economic cooperation, environment and sustainable development, and poverty alleviation through economic growth and social development. These committees meet annually.
- Two technical committees dealing with transport and communications and statistics. These committees meet biennially.
- Two special bodies, the first dealing with least developed and land-locked developing countries, and the second dealing with Pacific island developing countries. These bodies also meet biennially.

Three regional institutions are directly under the commission's jurisdiction: the Statistical Institute for Asia and the Pacific (SIAP) located in Tokyo, Japan; the Asian and Pacific Centre for Transfer of Technology (APCTT) located in New Delhi, India; and the Regional Coordination Centre for Research and Development of Coarse Grains, Pulses, Roots and Tuber Crops in the Humid Tropics of Asia and the Pacific (CGPRT) located in Bogor, Indonesia. The commission also is executing agency for major regional projects in agriculture, energy development, mineral resources development, and remote sensing.

The restructuring which formally began in April 1992, when the commission adopted Resolution 48/2 to reorganize its program and conference structures, had several goals. The core strategy was to de-emphasize a sectoral approach to issues that tended to address agricultural, industrial, and social issues in isolation. The commission instead adopted a holistic thematic approach that it felt would produce pragmatic solutions. For that reason, ESCAP reduced its subprogram structure from 15 topics to only six topics. The main focus is now regional economic cooperation, protecting the environment through sustainable development, and alleviating poverty through economic growth and social development. The programs for transport and communications and statistics are seen to be "cross-cutting" programs that support the others. Finally, a special focus has been mandated for least developed, land-locked, and island developing countries.

The reorganization was completed on 1 January 1994, and the commission's secretariat was reorganized to reflect the new structure. The secretariat now consists of nine "line" divisions and two servicing divisions. The substantive divisions are: International Trade and Economic Cooperation; Industry and Technology; Environment and Natural Resources Management; Social Development; Population; Rural and Urban Development; Transport, Communications and Tourism; Statistics; Development Research and Policy Analysis. The two servicing divisions are: Division of Administration and Programme Management Division. Other units of the secretariat are the ESCAP/UNCTAD Joint Unit on Transnational Corporations and the United Nations Information Service.

One of ESCAP's most significant recent meetings was the Fourth Asian and Pacific Population Conference (Bali, August 1992). The conference was cosponsored by ESCAP and UNFPA, in recognition of the fact that population issues were inextricably linked to the cycles of poverty and the struggle for development. The conference adopted the Declaration on Population and Development (known as the "Bali Declaration"). By this declaration, ESCAP's member countries set goals for themselves to adopt strategies to attain replacement-level fertility (around 2.2 children per woman) by the year 2010 or sooner. They also agreed to reduce the level of infant mortality to 40 per thousand live births or lower by the same time.

Membership and Budget. On 1 April 1994, ESCAP had 49 regional members: Afghanistan, Armenia, Australia, Azerbaijan, Bangladesh, Bhutan, Brunei Darussalam, Cambodia, China, Democratic People's Republic of Korea, Fiji, France, India, Indonesia, Islamic Republic of Iran, Japan, Kazakhstan, Kiribati, Kyrgyzstan, Lao People's Democratic Republic, Malaysia, Maldives, Marshall Islands, Micronesia, Mongolia, Myanmar, Nauru, Nepal, Netherlands, New Zealand, Pakistan, Papua New Guinea, Philippines, Republic of Korea, Russian Federation, Samoa, Singapore, Solomon Islands, Sri Lanka, Tajikistan, Thailand, Tonga, Turkmenistan, Tuvalu, United Kingdom, United States of America, Uzbekistan, Vanuatu, and Viet Nam. It also had 10 associate members: Commonwealth of the Northern Mariana Island, Cook Islands, French Polynesia, Guam, Hong Kong, Macau, New Caledonia, Niue, Republic of Palau, and Territory of American Samoa.

It is worthy of note that ESCAP's membership includes 13 least-developed countries (more than one-quarter of its membership); 11 land-locked countries; and 20 Pacific island developing countries (more than one-third of its membership). The total population of ESCAP's members is roughly 3.2 billion.

ESCAP's share of the budget appropriations for the 1994–95 biennium, as approved by the General Assembly, amounts to US$59.84 million. In addition, ESCAP receives extrabudgetary resources, from both bilateral and multilateral sources, for implementing the work of the commission and its subsidiary regional institutions. Total extrabudgetary cash contributions received by ESCAP for its program of work amounted to US$ 16.02 million in 1993.

Economic Commission for Latin America and the Caribbean (ECLAC)

The Economic Commission for Latin America and the Caribbean (ECLAC), with headquarters in Santiago, was established in 1948 as the Economic Commission for Latin America. In 1983, it formally incorporated the Caribbean region into its name. ECLAC's aim is to help the governments of the region promote the economic development of their countries and improve living standards. To this end, it collaborates with the governments of the region in the investigation and analysis of regional and national economic problems, and provides assistance in the formulation of development plans. It organizes and convenes regional intergovernmental meetings on topics in the field of economic and social development. ECLAC conducts research, executes studies, disseminates information, provides technical assistance, participates in seminars and conferences, and gives training courses.

ECLAC's initial stress on economic growth and trade was later complemented with emphasis on employment, income distribution, and other social aspects of development. In recent years, the commission has expanded its activities to include research in such areas as the environment, the development and transfer of technology, and the role of transnational corporations.

In 1994 ECLAC had divisions and units dealing with the following subject areas: development issues and policies; economic development; environment and human settlements; food and agriculture; international trade, development financing and transport, natural resources and energy; population; production, productivity, and management (transnational corporations); science and technology; social development and humanitarian affairs; and statistics and economic projections. There was a division for documents and publications and one for program planning and operations. The secretariat of ECLAC also maintains the Latin American Economic and Social Documentation Center. ECLAC also has two sub-regional headquarters (in Mexico and Port of Spain), and offices in Bogota, Brasilia, Buenos Aires, Montevideo, and Washington, D.C.

ECLAC meets biennially; a committee of the whole carries on intersessional work. Other permanent bodies include: the Committee of High-Level Government Experts; Caribbean Development and Co-operation Committee; the Regional Conference on the Integration of Women into the Economic and Social Development of Latin America and the Caribbean; and the Regional Council for Planning.

Two other organizations are part of the ECLAC system: the Latin American and Caribbean Institute for Economic and Social Planning (ILPES) in Santiago, Chile; and the Latin American Demographic Center (CELADE), also in Santiago. ILPES was established in 1962 and undertakes research and provides training and advisory services, as well as furthering cooperation among the planning services of the region. CELADE was established in 1957, but became an integral part of the commission in 1975. It collaborates with governments in formulating population policies and provides demographic estimates and projections, documentation, data processing, and training facilities.

The commission carries out its work in close cooperation with UNDP, the International Trade Center (UNCTAD/GATT),

UNESCO, the International Maritime Organization (IMO), UNICEF, and the International Telecommunications Union (ITU).

Following is a list of significant ECLAC publications: *CEPAL Review* (three issues a year in Spanish and English); *Economic Survey of Latin America and the Caribbean* (annual, Spanish and English); *Boletín Demográfico* (twice yearly); *Statistical Yearbook for Latin America and the Caribbean* (annual; bilingual, Spanish and English); *Industrialización y desarrollo tecnológico* (journal).

Membership and Budget. On 1 May 1994, ECLAC had 33 regional members: Antigua and Barbuda, Argentina, Bahamas, Barbados, Belize, Bolivia, Brazil, Chile, Colombia, Costa Rica, Cuba, Dominica, Dominican Republic, Ecuador, El Salvador, Grenada, Guatemala, Guyana, Haiti, Honduras, Jamaica, Mexico, Nicaragua, Panama, Paraguay, Peru, Saint Kitts and Nevis, Saint Lucia, Saint Vincent and the Grenadines, Suriname, Trinidad and Tobago, Uruguay, and Venezuela. There were also eight nonregional members: Canada, France, Italy, Netherlands, Portugal, Spain, United Kingdom, and United States. Finally, there were six associate members: Aruba, British Virgin Islands, Montserrat, Netherlands Antilles, Puerto Rico, and United States Virgin Islands.

Appropriations for ECLAC from the regular UN budget for the 1994–95 biennium totaled US$79,992,600.

Economic Commission for Africa (ECA)

The Economic Commission for Africa, with headquarters in Addis Ababa, Ethiopia, was established in 1958. It was the first intergovernmental organization in Africa whose geographical scope covered the whole of a continent in which economic and social conditions differed widely and where many countries and dependent territories were among the poorest in the world. ECA's chief objective is the modernization of Africa, with emphasis on both rural development and industrialization. Its work has been marked by a sense of urgency and a determination to match the rapid pace of African political progress with economic and social progress. In carrying out its functions, ECA works closely with the Organization of African Unity and various organizations of the UN system.

The commission's sessions are held annually at the ministerial level and are known as the Conference of Ministers.

The approach of ECA is primarily at the level of its four subregions: North Africa, Eastern and Southern Africa, Central Africa, and West Africa. ECA members have made it clear that the subregional approach is to be regarded as a necessary first step and that pan-African economic integration remains the goal. For that reason, five multinational programming and operational centers were established: in Tangier, Morocco, for North Africa; in Niamey, Niger, for West Africa; in Lusaka, Zambia, for Eastern and Southern Africa; in Yaounde, Cameroon, for Central Africa; and a fifth center for the countries of Rwanda, Burundi, and Zaire in Gisenyi, Rwanda.

Work priorities for the 1990s and beyond include the broadened concept of food security and poverty alleviation through sustainable development with emphasis on capacity building; the promotion of economic cooperation among African countries and between African and other developing countries; the physical integration of the continent in line with the goals of the UN Transport and Communications Decade for Africa (1991–2000); and greater control and sovereignty over natural resources and environment. In the field of industrial development, ECA implemented the UN Second Industrial Development Decade in Africa (IDDA) by strengthening the technological and entrepreneurial capabilities of African countries. Special attention was paid to subregional and regional cooperation in small-scale cottage and rural industries and to highly advanced technology.

In 1992 ECA issued a technical publication evaluating the impact of the 1992 European economic integration measures on

African agriculture. The publication discussed the various factors underlying the European single market. The publication underscored the need for galvanizing the cooperation of African nations in the face of moves to strengthen economic integration in other regions, notably Europe and North America. ECA also consulted with the OAU and the African Development Bank on the establishment and functioning of an African Economic Community (AEC).

ECA supervised the African Training and Research Centre for Women, which assisted ECA member states in improving the socioeconomic conditions of African women and enhancing their participation in development. ECA pursued its efforts to establish a regional Federation of African Women Entrepreneurs and a Bank for African Women to support women's entrepreneurial activities.

ECA has developed a Pan-African Development Information System that provides training, advisory services, data base development, and network-building, and produces studies and publications for ECA member states, institutions, and nongovernmental organizations.

Membership and Budget. At 1 July 1994, ECA had 53 members: Algeria, Angola, Benin, Botswana, Burkina Faso, Burundi, Cameroon, Cape Verde, Central African Republic, Chad, Comoros, Congo, Côte d'Ivoire, Djibouti, Egypt, Equatorial Guinea, Eritrea, Ethiopia, Gabon, Gambia, Ghana, Guinea, Guinea-Bissau, Kenya, Lesotho, Liberia, Libya, Madagascar, Malawi, Mali, Mauritania, Mauritius, Morocco, Mozambique, Namibia, Niger, Nigeria, Rwanda, São Tomé and Principe, Senegal, Seychelles, Sierra Leone, Somalia, South Africa, Sudan, Swaziland, Tanzania, Togo, Tunisia, Uganda, Zaire, Zambia, and Zimbabwe. South Africa was suspended from participation in ECA by ECOSOC from 1963 until 1994, when multiracial democracy was restored to that country.

Appropriations for ECA from the regular UN budget for the biennium 1994–95 totaled US$82 million.

Economic and Social Commission for Western Asia (ESCWA)

A regional economic commission for the Middle East was first proposed in 1947–48. A commission that would include the Arab nations and Israel proved to be out of the question, however, and in 1963, the UN Economic and Social Office in Beirut (UNESOB) was set up. For 11 years, UNESOB assisted governments in economic and social development and provided them with consultants in such fields as community development, demography, industrial development planning, and statistics.

In 1972, Lebanon revived the issue of a regional commission for the area, and in August 1973, the Economic and Social Council established the Economic Commission for Western Asia to supersede UNESOB. In 1984, it was renamed the Economic and Social Commission for Western Asia (ESCWA) to reflect the importance of the social aspect of its activities.

The commission began operations on 1 January 1974, with provisional headquarters in Beirut. As defined by the resolution establishing the commission, its task is to initiate and participate in measures for facilitating concerted action for the economic reconstruction and development of Western Asia, for raising the region's level of economic activity, and for maintaining and strengthening the economic relations of countries of the region both among themselves and with other countries of the world.

ESCWA undertakes or sponsors studies of economic and social issues in the region, collects and disseminates information, and provides advisory services at the request of countries of the region on ESCWA's fields of activities. Much of ESCWA's work is carried out in cooperation with other UN bodies. The commissions conducts industrial studies for individual countries in conjunction with UNIDO. It cooperates with FAO in regional planning, food security, and management of agricultural resources. UNDP supports ESCWA's work on household surveys in Western Asia and the Arab Planning Institute in Kuwait. Work is also undertaken with UNFPA and UNIFEM in population and women's programs, with ILO in statistical surveys on labor, with AGFUND in rural development, with UNCTAD in development planning and maritime transport training, with UNEP in integrating environmental aspects (particularly control of desertification) into development programs, and with OIC in natural resources, industry, and trade issues.

The sessions of the commission (held every two years) are attended by representatives of member states and bodies, UN bodies and specialized agencies, regional and intergovernmental organizations, and other states attending as observers.

In 1992, the commission called for the establishment of an Arab and international interagency coordinating committee on environment and development to promote the goals of the UN Conference on Environment and Development's (UNCED) Agenda 21.

Some of ESCWA's significant publications are: the *External Trade Bulletin* (annual); *National Accounts Studies* (annual); *Population Bulletin* (biannual); *Statistical Abstract of ESCWA Region* (annual); *Survey of Economic and Social Development in the ESCWA Region* (annual); *Population Bulletin* (every two years); *Review of Monetary and Banking Policy in ESCWA Region* (annual); and *Survey and Assessment of Energy-Related Activities and Developments in the ESCWA Region* (annual).

ESCWA maintains close liaison with other UN organs and specialized agencies and with intergovernmental organizations in the region, such as the League of Arab States and the Arab Fund for Economic and Social Development.

In 1976, ESCWA decided to move its operations to Amman, Jordan, for one year because of the conflict in Lebanon. Later the same year, it decided to accept the offer of the government of Iraq for Baghdad to be the site of its permanent headquarters. It moved to Baghdad in 1982, only to relocate to Amman during the Gulf War between Iraq and Kuwait in 1991. In 1994 it was still headquartered in Amman.

Membership and Budget. On 1 July 1994, there were 13 members of ESCWA: Bahrain, Egypt, Iraq, Jordan, Kuwait, Lebanon, Oman, Palestine (Palestine Liberation Organization), Qatar, Saudi Arabia, Syria, United Arab Emirates, and Yemen.

Appropriations for ESCWA from the regular UN budget for the 1994–95 biennium totaled US$51 million.

TECHNICAL COOPERATION PROGRAMS

The International Development Strategy for the third UN Development Decade called for a renewed emphasis on technical cooperation and a significant increase in the resources provided for this purpose. It recognized that technical cooperation contributes to the efforts of developing countries to achieve self-reliance by facilitating and supporting investment, research, and training, among other things.

UN programs of technical cooperation may be grouped in three categories: (1) the UN regular program, financed under the portion of the UN regular budget set aside for technical cooperation activities; (2) activities funded by the UN Development Programme (UNDP); and (3) extrabudgetary activities financed by contributions provided directly to the executing agencies by multilateral funding organizations within or outside the UN system, other than UNDP, and by contributions from governments and nongovernmental organizations.

To consolidate the responsibilities and resources within the UN Secretariat in support of technical cooperation activities, the UN General Assembly in March 1978 set up the Department of Technical Cooperation for Development (DTCD). In 1993, under further restructuring of the United Nations, this became the Department for Development Support and Management Services (DDSMS).

DDSMS provides technical and managerial support and advisory services to member states of the UN, relevant research, and parliamentary services to expert groups and intergovernmental bodies. It has a twofold mandate: (i) it acts as an executing agency for programs and projects relating to institution-building and human resource development in areas such as development policies and planning, natural resources and energy planning, governance and public management, and financial management and accounting; (ii) it acts as a focal point for the provision of management services and implementation functions for technical cooperation.

UNITED NATIONS DEVELOPMENT PROGRAMME (UNDP)

Since its earliest days, the UN system has been engaged in a growing effort that has two main thrusts. The first, and most important, is supporting the vigorous drive of the world's developing countries to provide their own people with the essentials of a decent life—including adequate nutrition, housing, employment, income, education, health care, consumer goods, and public services. The second aim, which is closely related, is to help these countries increase their output of commodities, raw materials, and manufactured items, which the world increasingly needs, as well as to ensure them a fair return.

The United Nations Development Programme (UNDP) is the UN's major arm—and the world's largest channel—for international technical cooperation for development provided on a grant basis. Working with the government of nearly every country—and with more than 30 international agencies—UNDP supports the development efforts of 175 countries and territories in Africa, Asia and the Pacific, Latin America and the Caribbean, the Arab states, and Europe and the Commonwealth of Independent States. Under the overall framework of "sustainable human development," the programs it supports focus primarily on building national capacities to eliminate poverty, protect and regenerate the environment, create employment, and empower women. The ultimate goal is to improve the quality of human life.

Evolution of UNDP

Although UNDP came into formal existence only in January 1966, it really began 20 years earlier, for it grew out of two long-established UN institutions.

In 1948, the UN General Assembly (GA) had decided to appropriate funds under its regular budget to enable the UN Secretary-General to supply teams of experts, offer fellowships, and organize seminars to assist national development projects at the request of governments. About the same time, many of the specialized agencies had begun to undertake similar projects. However, no sooner had the Regular Programs of Technical Assistance, as they were called, begun to operate than it became apparent that the money that could be spared from the regular budget would not meet demand. In 1949, the General Assembly set up a separate account for voluntary contributions toward technical assistance and decided to make it a central account to finance the activities not only of the UN itself but also of the specialized agencies. Machinery was established for distributing financial resources and coordinating projects, and the whole enterprise was called the Expanded Programme of Technical Assistance (EPTA), to distinguish it from the UN's technical assistance financed under the regular budget. The venture proved remarkably successful. Ten years after it had begun operations, EPTA was financing technical assistance in some 140 countries and territories. Between 1950 and 1960, the number of governments contributing funds had grown from 54 to 85, and the total annual contributions had risen from $10 million to $33.8 million.

In 1958, the General Assembly felt that it would be desirable to broaden the scope of UN technical assistance to include large-scale preinvestment surveys and feasibility studies on major national development projects that would lay the groundwork for subsequent investment of capital. These surveys and studies involved a much greater financial outlay than the kind of technical assistance then being undertaken, and the General Assembly decided to set up a new institution that would be run along lines similar to those of EPTA. Thus, the Special Fund was established to act as a multilateral channel for voluntary contributions to preinvestment projects, and as a coordinating center for the work of the various UN agencies. The Special Fund began operations in 1959; within three years, 86 governments had pledged over $110 million.

In January 1964, the Secretary-General formally proposed to the Economic and Social Council that EPTA and the Special Fund be merged into a single enterprise. The advantages to be derived from the merger were a pooling of resources, a simplification of procedures, improvement in overall planning, elimination of duplication, reduction in administrative costs, and a general strengthening of UN development aid. By August 1964, the Council had adopted recommendations for the merger, but because of the stalemate at the 1964 General Assembly, no action could be taken until the following year. On 22 November 1965, the General Assembly unanimously voted to consolidate the two operations, effective 1 January 1966, as the United Nations Development Programme.

Structure and Organization

Administrator and Executive Board. UNDP is headed by an administrator, appointed by the UN Secretary-General and confirmed by the General Assembly, who is responsible to a 36-nation Executive Board for all aspects of program operations. The board—representing every geographical region and both contributor and program countries—reports to the General Assembly through the Economic and Social Council. In addition to setting overall policy guidelines, the Executive Board examines and approves the volume of assistance allocated to each country over successive five-year cycles and must similarly approve all country programs. (The Executive Board began its work in 1994, replacing the 48-nation UNDP/UNFPA Governing Council, which had a similar composition and function. The Governing Council's decision-making almost always took place by "consensus" rather than by recorded voting.)

Regional Bureaus. Regional bureaus, located at UN headquarters, cover Africa, Asia and the Pacific, Latin America and the Caribbean, and the Arab states. There is also a Division for Europe and the Commonwealth of Independent States. These offices serve as the administrator's principal links with the program countries. Together with bureaus or divisions for strategic planning, program policy and evaluation, program development and support, and finance and administration, they furnish UNDP's country-based Resident Representatives with day-to-day operational support.

Resident Representatives. Resident Representatives heading 128 program country offices function as field-level leaders of the UN development system. They are responsible for seeing that UNDP-assisted country programs are carried out effectively and efficiently. They act as chief liaison officers between government planning authorities and the executing agencies, help blueprint all activities from formulation to follow-up, and are responsible for ensuring that personnel, equipment, and facilities are utilized to best advantage.

Resident Representatives and other staff in UNDP's country offices also perform a variety of non-project-related development activities that make a significant contribution to UNDP's goals, and to the needs of its national partners. These include engaging in policy dialogue with national officials and providing them with development planning advice; furnishing technical advisory and general problem-solving services, often at the request of concerned sectoral ministries; assisting in mobilizing investment from both internal and external sources, as well as with follow-up investment advice and services; acting as a focal point for government needs in emergencies caused by natural or man-made disasters; assisting in the formulation, management, and evaluation of UNDP country programs; and, upon request, participating in the coordination of external assistance from other sources and in the preparation of well-balanced, effective national development programs.

Training and other support is offered on issues of special concern: UNDP's Division for Gender in Development helps to ensure that programs consider women's needs and interests; the Division for Nongovernmental Organizations promotes increased participation of NGOs and community groups in development activities; the Environment and Natural Resources Group ensures that the environmental impact of all programs is weighed; the Short-Term Advisory Services program sends skilled advisers to provide top-level technical and managerial advice in such sectors as agriculture, transportation, and industry.

Functions and Guiding Principles

The nature of UNDP and its activities has changed over the years. In part, this has been in response to the evolving requirements and interests of the program countries. The changes also have reflected global concerns for particular development problems and issues.

In the early 1970s, UNDP had to demonstrate its ability to replace a basic structure, which had served it well in its formative stages, with a "second generation" mechanism designed to determine the nature of UNDP's market with greater discrimination, and to deliver the required product with more efficiency. The cumulative impact of a number of intensive inquiries into development and development assistance—by the Pearson Commission, the UN Committee for Development Planning, Sir Robert Jackson's study of the capacity of the UN development system, and by some of the major donor countries individually—helped to fashion a new look for UNDP. The various studies agreed on needs for more deliberate matching of country requests for assistance with available resources; the introduction of forward and coordinated planning and programming; more careful and appropriate project design; and greater quality, timeliness, and efficiency of implementation.

The consideration of these matters by the UNDP Governing Council in 1970 produced a consensus on the future of UNDP that was endorsed by the General Assembly in the same year, translated into organizational and procedural changes in 1971, and brought substantially into effect during the next few years. The pivotal change was the introduction of "country programming." This involved the forward programming of UNDP assistance at the country level for periods of up to five years, identification of the role UNDP inputs would play in specified areas related to a country's development objectives, and the phasing of these inputs. Country programming, together with a similar approach to regional, interregional, and global activities, is designed to achieve the most rational and efficient utilization of resources.

A necessary counterpart to the introduction of UNDP country programming was administrative reform. The most important change involved decentralization—a substantial shift of power and responsibility for effective UNDP technical cooperation at all stages away from headquarters and into the program countries, where the UNDP Resident Representatives often play a lead role in UN development system activities within a country. Guidelines for the selection of these officials imply that, first and foremost, they should be effective managers, for it is they who cooperate directly with the governments to ensure the smooth functioning of development programs. In addition, they must intervene to help ensure more efficient implementation and more effective use of the results of project assistance. Upon request, they must be ready to play a vital part in the coordination of assistance from other sources with that provided by UNDP. In fact, under the restructuring of the UN development system mandated by the General Assembly, most UNDP Resident Representatives also are designated by the UN Secretary-General as Resident Coordinators of all UN operational assistance for development.

In 1975, UNDP further revised its programming principles to include "new dimensions" in technical cooperation, designed primarily to foster greater self-sufficiency among developing countries by relying more heavily on their own skills and expertise for development activities. Accordingly, UNDP redefined its role in technical cooperation to stress results achieved, rather than inputs required from the industrialized nations.

Seen from this perspective, the purpose of technical cooperation is to promote increasing autonomy with regard to the managerial, technical, administrative, and research capabilities required to formulate and implement development plans in the light of options available.

In the 1990s, UNDP has made other changes that are having a substantial impact on its programming, as well as on development thinking in general. In 1990 the Governing Council directed UNDP to focus its activities on six themes: poverty eradication and grass roots participation; environment and natural resources management; technical cooperation among developing countries

(TCDC); management development; transfer and adaptation of technology; and women in development. UNDP has also adopted a "program approach," whereby funding is provided for comprehensive programs with integrated components rather than distinct, separate projects. This enables UNDP to deliver assistance that is more focused and has greater impact and sustainability.

Another change has been UNDP's promotion of "human development," which puts people at the center of development, enlarging their choices and creating opportunities through which they can realize their potential and express their creativity. Human development does not measure a country's progress solely by its Gross National Product, but takes into account such factors as its people's access to health services, level of education, and purchasing power. Since 1990 UNDP has stimulated debate about this concept through the publication of an annual Human Development Report, written by an independent team of development specialists and published by Oxford University Press. Since then, a growing number of countries have received UNDP assistance in incorporating human development concerns into planning and the allocation of budgets.

Linking human development with its traditional emphasis on building self-reliance, UNDP has now embraced the concept of "sustainable human development" as the guiding principle underlying all its work. As defined by UNDP's administrator, James Gustave Speth, who took office in July 1993:

"Sustainable human development is development that not only generates economic growth but distributes its benefits equitably; that regenerates the environment rather than destroying it; that empowers people rather than marginalizing them. It gives priority to the poor, enlarging their choices and opportunities and providing for their participation in decisions affecting them. It is development that is pro-poor, pro-nature, pro-jobs and pro-women. In sum, sustainable human development stresses growth, but growth with employment, environment, empowerment and equity."

Within this framework, UNDP has identified three priority goals: (1) strengthening international cooperation for sustainable human development and serving as a substantive resource on how to achieve it; (2) building developing countries' capacities for sustainable human development; and (3) helping the United Nations become a powerful, unified force for sustainable human development.

From its inception, UNDP has been called upon to make its assistance available to all countries where it can be effective in helping to meet priority needs, provided that those countries are members of the UN or one of its affiliated agencies. This broad frame of reference is essential for protecting two of UNDP's most valuable assets—its universality and its large measure of freedom from political problems and pressures.

Planning and Programming

In the planning and programming of UNDP assistance, the largest role is played by the developing countries themselves. The process involves three basic steps.

First, an estimate is made of the core financial resources expected to be available to UNDP over a five-year period. This estimate is then divided up into Indicative Planning Figures (IPFs) for each country assisted, and for regional, interregional, and global programs. The IPFs are approved, and adjusted from time to time, by UNDP's Executive Board.

Second, with its IPF as a guide, each government draws up a "country program," outlining its priorities for UNDP assistance and allocating its share of UNDP resources among those priorities. Country program formulation—in which the UNDP's Resident Representative and locally based officials of other UN agencies usually participate—takes a number of factors into account. Among these are a country's overall development plans, the domestic resources that it can call upon for carrying out those

plans, and the assistance expected from external sources other than UNDP. Each country program is then submitted to the Executive Board for approval.

The third step involves preparation of individual project requests—again usually in consultation with advisers from the UN system. These requests delineate each project's main objectives, its duration, its cost, and the respective responsibilities of the government and the UN system.

Allocation of Funds

UNDP IPFs for 1972–76, the first programming cycle, were largely determined by applying the same percentage of total UNDP resources actually committed to each country from 1967 through 1971 to the total of projected UNDP resources for the years 1972 through 1976.

Completely new criteria were established by the Governing Council for the 1977–81 "second cycle." Of the country programming resources expected to be available during those years, 92.5 percent was allocated largely on the basis of a formula involving each country's population and its per capita gross national product (GNP)—with this second factor being given somewhat greater weight in calculating each country's allocation.

Under the new criteria, about 13 percent of total resources was devoted to regional programs aimed at fostering development cooperation among neighboring countries or at achieving economies by making expertise available to several governments from a single regional base. There was also a separate IPF for global and interregional programs, such as "breakthrough" research on high-yielding strains of staple food grains.

On an overall basis, during the third cycle (1982–86), countries with per capita GNPs of $500 a year or less received 80 percent of total UNDP funding, as compared with 52 percent in the 1977–81 period and 40 percent in the 1971–76 period.

In 1985, the Governing Council decided that for the fourth programming cycle (1987–91), countries with 1983 per capita GNPs of $750 or less a year were to receive 80 percent of IPF resources, reflecting UNDP's emphasis on assisting the poorer countries.

In the fifth programming cycle (1992–96) countries with yearly per capita GNPS of $750 or less received 87 percent of national IPF resources.

Implementation in the Field

UNDP is primarily a funding, programming, monitoring, and coordinating organization. Over the5 years, the bulk of the field work it has supported has been carried out by UN agencies and regional commissions, and by regional development banks and funds. Increasingly, UNDP is also calling upon national institutions and nongovernmental organizations for project execution.

The executing agencies, as they are called, perform three major functions. They serve as "data banks" of development knowledge and techniques in their respective specialties. They help governments plan the individual sectors in their country programs for UNDP assistance. As a rule, they recruit the international experts, purchase the equipment, and procure the specialized contract services needed for project execution.

The choice of a particular agency to implement any given project is made by UNDP in consultation with the government of the developing country. Though a single agency is always in charge of a particular project, often two or more collaborate in providing the services required.

Through its Office for Project Services, UNDP directly implements those activities that are not carried out by other executing agencies, providing a full range of management services, including procurement and finance.

The progress of field work is monitored through periodic reviews, involving UNDP country office staffs, government officials, and experts of the executing agencies. A modern computer-based management information system provides a continuous flow of operational data from the field. When required, special missions are sent to program countries to evaluate project work.

Systematic efforts are made to stimulate follow-up investments on surveys, feasibility studies, and other appropriate projects. These activities—which often begin at very early stages of project implementation—involve cooperation with all likely and acceptable sources of development finance—internal and external, public and private.

In a larger sense, however, most projects have a "built-in" follow-up component because they are deliberately planned to create permanent institutions or facilities that will be taken over by national personnel. Thus, many projects—particularly in training, applied research, and development planning—not only continue but also significantly expand their work after UNDP support ends.

Typically, some 5,000 projects, ranging from two to five years in duration, have been under way in any given year. Since 1993, however, UNDP has been making a deliberate attempt to sharpen its focus. It become more selective in what it would finance, concentrating in particular on capacity-building initiatives that gave priority to the poor, to creating employment, to advancing women, and to regenerating the environment. The largest share of UNDP core resources went to Africa and Asia and the Pacific, followed by Latin America and the Caribbean, the Arab states, and Europe and the Commonwealth of Independent States. In 1993, of total spending, nearly half was for project personnel, 19 percent for subcontracts, 15 percent for equipment, 9 percent for training, and the remainder for miscellaneous costs such as operation and maintenance of equipment.

Total expenditures for technical cooperation activities by UNDP in 1993 were around US$1 billion, covering not only direct country programs but also the costs of UNDP program planning, management, and coordination by 132 offices worldwide and at UNDP headquarters in New York, and project implementation services by 31 executing agencies.

Financing and Expenditures

UNDP is financed in several ways. First, the developing countries themselves pay a large share of the costs of their UNDP-assisted projects. Their funds are used for the salaries of local personnel, construction and maintenance of project buildings and facilities, and the purchase of locally available supplies and services. Second, almost every member of the UN and its associated agencies makes a yearly voluntary contribution to UNDP's core resources. Third, cost-sharing contributions make up a growing portion of UNDP's income. These are resources provided in convertible currency by program country governments, or by another country or organization to share in the costs of particular programs. In 1993 voluntary contributions by member countries to UNDP's core resources amounted to approximately US$910 million. Contributions to non-core resources—UNDP-administered funds, trust funds, and cost-sharing arrangements—raised the total UNDP income to over US$1.4 billion.

Major contributors to UNDP's core resources in 1993
(US$ millions)

COUNTRY	VOLUNTARY CONTRIBUTION
United States	$125.0
Japan	96.1
Denmark	86.5
Netherlands	86.3
Germany	80.6
Norway	71.0
Sweden	70.7
France	50.0
United Kingdom	44.9
Canada	41.4
Switzerland	38.9
Italy	24.9
Belgium	18.6
Austria	13.4
Australia	11.4
Finland	9.1
Spain	8.5

UNDP expenditures in 1993 by region and by economic or social sector were as follows:

UNDP Estimate of Field Program Expenditures by Region, 1993
(US$ millions)

REGION	CORE	COST-SHARING
Africa	$240.0	$26.3
Asia and the Pacific	238.7	31.0
Latin America and the Caribbean	74.3	248.9
Arab states	51.7	20.3
Europe and the Commonwealth of Independent States	9.1	2.3
Global and Interregional	62.1	12.4
TOTAL	$675.9	$341.2

UNDP Estimate of Field Program Expenditures by Sector, 1993*
(US$ millions)

SECTOR	AMOUNT
General Development Issues	$277.9
Agriculture, Forestry and Fisheries	154.5
Environment, Natural Resources and Energy	91.7
Industry	81.1
Health	64.0
Transport	51.6
Education	50.9
Employment	38.3
Population and Human Settlements	37.7
Humanitarian Assistance and Disaster Management	34.8
Science and Technology	34.6
Communications and Information	32.7
Social Development	24.4
Other sectors	42.9
TOTAL	$1,017.1

* Includes cost-sharing and government cash counterpart contributions.

Associated Programs

The UNDP administrator also is responsible for several associated funds and programs:

United Nations Capital Development Fund provides limited amounts of "seed financing" for such social infrastructure as low cost housing, water supply systems, rural schools, and hospitals; and for such "grass roots" productive facilities as agricultural workshops, cottage industry centers, cooperatives, and credit programs.

United Nations Sudano Sahelian Office works with 22 countries across the Sudano Sahelian belt of Africa, from Senegal to Somalia, designing projects in such areas as deforestation control, sand dune stabilization, and rangeland management; mobilizing resources to carry them out; and implementing them in cooperation with other UN agencies.

United Nations Development Fund for Women provides direct assistance to innovative and potentially replicable projects involving women, including those to reduce workload and increase income; helps to raise women's status in society; and works to ensure their involvement in mainstream development activities. (see UNIFEM).

UN Revolving Fund for Natural Resources Exploration helps underwrite searches for economically useful mineral deposits that developing countries could not otherwise carry out because of the high risk factor involved.

United Nations Volunteers program, established by the General Assembly in 1971, is administered by UNDP from its Geneva, Switzerland, office. Volunteers from 115 professions serve in both UNDP and UN-assisted projects, as well as in development programs carried out directly by host governments. Recruited globally, they are sent to a country only at the request, and with the approval, of the host government. Volunteers serve for two years and receive a monthly allowance to cover necessities. The average age of UNV specialists is 39, with an average of 10 years' experience in their field of specialization. The actual age ranges from the mid-20s to the 60s and 70s, as retirees are welcomed for their experience.

The skills most in demand for UNV specialists are: agriculture, agronomy, animal husbandry, appropriate technology, audiovisual arts, business management, cartography, community development, computer programming, construction trades, data processing, demography, development administration, disaster preparedness, economics, education, electronics, employment for the disabled, engineering, environment, export promotion, fisheries, forestry, handicrafts, HIV/AIDS prevention, home economics, horticulture, logistics, marketing/trade promotion, medicine, nursing/midwifery, printing/bookbinding, public administration, public health, social work, statistics, teacher training, teaching English language, teaching math/science, technical trades/skills, urban/regional planning, vehicle/fleet maintenance, veterinary science, vocational training, women in development, and youth work.

In 1994 more than 2,000 men and women of more than 100 nationalities were serving in developing countries as vounteer specialists and field workers. Half were working in Africa, one-third in Asia and the Pacific, and the remainder in the Arab States, the Caribbean, Central and South America, and new programs in Central and Eastern Europe. In the first 20 years of the UNV's existence, its specialists completed 6,000 assignments.

UN CONFERENCE ON TRADE AND DEVELOPMENT (UNCTAD)

The first UN Conference on Trade and Development, which met in Geneva in the spring of 1964, recommended the establishment of a permanent UN body to deal with trade in relation to development. The General Assembly, noting that international trade was an important instrument for economic development and that there was a widespread desire among developing countries for a comprehensive trade organization, decided to establish UNCTAD as one of its permanent organs in December 1964.

The main purpose of UNCTAD is to promote international trade, particularly that of developing countries, with a view to accelerating economic development. UNCTAD is one of the principal instruments of the General Assembly for deliberation and negotiation in respect to international trade and international economic cooperation. It formulates principles and policies on international trade, initiates action for the adoption of multilateral trade agreements, and acts as a center for harmonizing trade and development policies of governments and regional economic groups. The 1992 conference reaffirmed UNCTAD's functions to be policy analysis, intergovernmental deliberation, consensus building, negotiation of international agreements, monitoring, implementation, follow-up, and technical cooperation.

UNCTAD has 187 member states and has granted observer status to a number of organizations. There have been eight sessions of UNCTAD at roughly four-year intervals: Geneva (1964); New Delhi (1968); Santiago (1972); Nairobi (1976); Manila (1979); Belgrade (1983); Geneva (1987); and Cartagena de Indias, Colombia (1992).

Structure

The continuing work of the organization is carried out between sessions by the Trade and Development Board (TDB), UNCTAD's executive body, established by the General Assembly. The TDB implements conference decisions and initiates studies and reports on trade and related development problems. The TDB reports annually to the General Assembly through the Economic and Social Council. It also serves as the preparatory body for sessions of the conference.

The Trade and Development Board has several standing committees that review trends and make recommendations in specific areas, including commodities, poverty alleviation, economic cooperation among developing countries, and developing services sectors. A Special Committee on Preferences and the International Group of Experts on Restrictive Business Practices also report to the TDB.

At the eighth session of UNCTAD, in February 1992, five ad hoc working groups were established to deal with:

• investment and financial flows;
• trade efficiency;
• privatization;
• trading opportunities for developing countries; and
• the relationship between investment and technology transfer.

Secretariat

The UNCTAD secretariat is located at Geneva. It provides service to the conference, the TDB, and its subsidiary bodies. The Secretary-General of UNCTAD is appointed by the Secretary-General of the UN and confirmed by the General Assembly.

In May 1993 the UN General Assembly assigned the UNCTAD secretariat responsibility for servicing two subsidiary bodies of the Economic and Social Council: the Commission on Transnational Corporations and the Commission on Science and Technology for Development (see the section on "Economic and Social Development").

The UNCTAD secretariat also provides technical assistance to developing countries in connection with the Uruguay Round of multilateral trade negotiations which took place under the auspices of the General Agreement on Tariffs and Trade (GATT).

Export Promotion and Marketing

Export promotion and marketing are the responsibility of the International Trade Center in Geneva, which is operated jointly by UNCTAD and GATT. The center focuses attention on export market opportunities and helps developing countries to train personnel in marketing and export-promotion techniques and to set up the institutions and programs necessary to build up modern export-promotion services.

Commodities

In 1980, the Agreement Establishing the Common Fund for Commodities was adopted by the UN Negotiating Conference on a Common Fund. International agreements also have been concluded for nine commodities—cocoa, coffee, tin, olive oil, sugar, natural rubber, wheat, jute and jute products, and tropical timbers. The fund came into operation in September 1989.

At its 1976 session in Nairobi, UNCTAD adopted an an Integrated Program for Commodities aimed at setting prices for the primary commodities of developing countries that would take into account world inflation, monetary changes, and the cost of manufactured imports. As part of the program, the Nairobi session agreed that steps would be taken to negotiate a common fund for the financing of buffer stocks that would be held or sold as conditions required, thus helping to end the wide fluctuation in commodity prices that has plagued developing countries dependent on these products as exports.

The eighth session of UNCTAD in 1992 recognized the need to formulate an effective international commodity policy for the 1990s. Commodity markets remained extremely depressed and most of the commodity agreements achieved by UNCTAD in the 1980s had lapsed. In 1993 UNCTAD began to develop a micro-computer-based commodity analysis and information system (MICAS), which provides comprehensive, up-to-date information on all aspects of commodity use, production, trade, and consumption. The system will assist developing countries in managing their economies and competing more effectively in world markets.

Preferential Tariffs for Developing Countries

UNCTAD adopted the General System of Preferences (GSP) in 1968, giving preferential tariff treatment in developed countries to manufactured goods exported by developing countries. By 1992, 16 programs were in operation, giving preferential treatment to more than us$70 billion worth of exports a year from more than 100 developing countries. However, the conference recognized that the more advanced developing countries benefitted most from the system, and in 1992 efforts were undertaken to include more agricultural products and some "sensitive" industrial products. The conference plans a general policy review of GSP in 1995.

Shipping

UNCTAD initiated the development of the 1978 UN Convention on the Carriage of Goods by Sea (called the Hamburg Rules). By July 1993, the Hamburg Rules had received 21 ratifications and entered into force on 1 November 1993.

The Convention on a Code of Conduct for Liner Conferences (1974) provides for the national shipping lines of developing countries to participate on an equal basis with the shipping lines of developed countries. This convention became effective in 1983. In 1991 the conference reviewed this convention and adopted guidelines towards its more effective implementation. Technical and structural changes in liner shipping since 1974 were taken into account. By July 1993 there were 77 contracting parties to the convention.

The UN Convention on International Multimodal Transport of Goods (1980) establishes a single liability organizational structure for the international carriage of given consignments of goods entailing use of more than one mode of transport. By July 1993 it had received seven ratifications (entry into force requires 30 contracting parties).

The UN Convention on Conditions for Registration of Ships (1986) introduces new standards of responsibility and accountability for the world shipping industry and defines the elements of the genuine link that should exist between a ship and the state whose flag it flies. By July 1993 nine ratifications had been received (entry into force requires 40 contracting parties accounting for 25 percent of the world's tonnage).

UNCTAD also provides technical cooperation and specialized training projects financed in part by UNDP. Training courses cover multimodal transport, improving port performance, and the use of the Advance Cargo Information System (ACIS) to enable shipping lines and railway companies to track the movement of cargo.

Other Multilateral Agreements and Conventions

The Set of Multilaterally Agreed Equitable Principles and Rules for the Control of Restrictive Business Practices (1980) establishes international means for the control of restrictive business practices, including those of transnational corporations, adversely affecting international trade, in particular the trade and economic development of developing countries.

Negotiations were begun in 1978 on an International Code of Conduct on the Transfer of Technology. The provisions of the proposed code fall into two broad groups: those concerning the regulation of the transfer of technology transactions and of the conduct of parties to them, and those relating to steps to be taken by governments to meet their commitments to the code. In 1991 consultations were held on setting up an intergovernmental group of experts to prepare ground for the resumption of negotiations on the code of conduct.

As a result of these consultations, the Trade and Development Board acknowledged that it was impossible at that time to obtain consensus on the outstanding issues for a draft code of conduct. In 1993 the Trade and Development Board established an Ad Hoc Working Group on Interrelationship between Investment and Technology Transfer to examine and encourage new initiatives on investment and technology policies that would facilitate technology transfer. This group adopted a work program aimed at examining issues of investment flows, transfer of technology and competitiveness, technological capacity-building in developing countries, and transfer and development of environmentally sound technologies. In light of the ongoing work of this group, the Secretary-General of UNCTAD recommended to the General Assembly in 1993 that further consultations on the code of conduct take place after the completion of the activities of the Ad Hoc Working Group.

UNCTAD also elaborated the Modes Clauses on Marine Hull and Cargo Insurance, which assists the insurance markets in developing countries to produce their own insurance policy clauses and conditions. UNCTAD also has prepared minimum standards for shipping agents that serve as guidelines for national authorities and professional associations establishing standards.

Debt Relief

In the area of money and finance, UNCTAD devotes particular attention to the debt problems of developing countries and has negotiated measures of debt relief for the poorer among those countries, as well as a set of agreed guidelines for dealing with future debt problems. At its 1987 session in Geneva, UNCTAD recommended a number of policy approaches and measures to deal with debt problems, resources for development, and related monetary issues; commodities; international trade; and the problems of the least developed countries—all aimed at revitalizing development, growth, and international trade in a more predictable and supportive environment through multilateral cooperation.

UNCTAD and the World Bank developed a joint program to extend technical cooperation to developing countries in the field of debt management. UNCTAD is responsible for the software component of the project. The assistance is based on the development and distribution of the Debt Management and Financial Analysis System (DMFAS), software designed to enable debtor countries to analyze data, make projections, and plan strategies for debt repayment. UNCTAD trains operators to use the software. It also provides training for senior officials in raising their awareness of institutional reforms that might be necessary for effective debt management.

Least Developed Countries (LDCs)

In 1993 47 countries were classified as least developed countries (LDCs). UNCTAD has taken a lead role in mobilizing support for LDCs by organizing two UN conferences on LDCs. The first, held in Paris in 1980, adopted the Substantial New Program of Action (SNPA), which defined measures to be taken by LDCs to promote their own development. The second, also held in Paris, in 1990, reviewed the implementation of the SNPA and strengthened the program.

UNCTAD has given political impetus to the setting of official development assistance at 0.7 percent of the GNP of donor countries. It also has recommended improvement of International Monetary Fund's compensatory financing facility for export earnings shortfalls of developing countries and the creation of special drawing rights for LDCs.

The eighth session of UNCTAD in 1992 requested that detailed analyses be made of the socioeconomic situations and domestic policies of the LDCs, their resource needs, and external factors affecting their economies.

Trade in the 21st Century

The 1992 conference identified four priority areas to be analyzed for the four-year period to 1996, when the ninth session of UNCTAD will be held.

1. *New International Partnership for Development.* To assist developing countries and countries in transition to market economies increase their participation in the world economy.
2. *Global Interdependence.* Emphasis to be placed on the international implications of macroeconomic policies, the evolution of international trading, monetary and financial systems, effective management at the international level, and the consequences of enlarged economic spaces and regional integration processes.
3. *Paths to Development.* The conference called for studies of national development experiences with a view to deriving useful lessons to inform future action. The studies would include consideration of general economic management and the relationships between economic progress and market orientation.
4. *Sustainable Development.* The interaction between trade and environmental policies was to be considered. The promotion and implementation of environmentally sound technologies as elaborated at the UN Conference on Environment and Development in 1992 were to be stressed.

The 1992 conference also discussed trade efficiency and the use of electronic data interchange to reduce the cost of transactions. In July 1995, UNCTAD will organize a World Symposium on Trade Efficiency in Columbus, Ohio. The symposium is subtitled "New Technologies for Efficient Global Trade; UNCTAD's Tradepoint Network." The symposium will unite trade ministers, chief executives, and senior officials in focussing on new technologies in the fields of banking, insurance, transport, telecommunications, and information for trade. The promotion of international standards for electronic commerce will be a key component of the symposium. The symposium also will launch a worldwide process of alleviating technical and procedural barriers that prevent poorer countries from fully participating in world trade. UNCTAD is developing a Tradepoint Network of 100 operational trading points to facilitate this process. The Tradepoint Network is scheduled to operate worldwide by October 1994.

WORLD FOOD PROGRAM (WFP)

The World Food Program, which the UN sponsors jointly with the Food and Agriculture Organization (FAO), began operations in 1963. It has since grown from a small experimental program to become the largest multilateral food distributor in the world. In 1993, more than 42 million people received direct assistance through WFP emergency operations and development projects.

Between 1946 and 1960, several attempts were made to establish an international body to regulate international trade and to deal with surpluses produced by food exporting countries. None of these attempts were successful, mainly because some countries objected to interference in their trade relations. In 1955, a study called, "Uses of Agricultural Surpluses to Finance Economic Development in Under-developed Countries," provided the

breakthrough. The report posited that agricultural surpluses could finance additional investment in developing countries without competing with the sales of domestic products or with imports from other countries.

At the 1961 FAO Conference, George McGovern, the head of the US delegation, formally proposed establishing a multilateral program with a fund of US$100 million in commodities and cash, to which the US was willing to contribute US$40 million. This initiative led the FAO and the UN to establish the World Food Program on a three-year experimental basis (January 1963 to December 1965).

WFP uses food commodities, cash, and services contributed by UN member states to back programs of social and economic development, as well as for emergency relief. At the request of governments, WFP provides food aid for development projects to increase agricultural production, rehabilitate roads and other vital infrastructure, protect the environment and improve health and education. WFP food assistance also provides basic sustenance for refugees and other victims of disasters. The aim of the WFP is to apply food aid in ways that will eventually make the recipients self-sufficient in obtaining or producing food. The success of the program's work should ultimately be judged by the number of people who, over time, are able to feed themselves.

In the three decades of its existence, the program has invested approximately US$13 billion (40 million tons of food aid) to combat hunger and to promote economic and social development in the developing world. More than 1,600 development projects and 1,200 emergency operations have been assisted by the WFP. However, in recent years, emergency work has come to dominate WFP's work. In 1992, WFP handled 5.2 million tons of emergency food aid for nearly 28 million people.

WFP supplies for development purposes are used in a variety of ways. Early projects included a land-settlement project in Bolivia, the development of nomadic sheep husbandry in Syria, resettling nomads in Egypt, land reclamation and development in Morocco, and land settlement in Tanzania. Other projects contributed directly to the development of human resources by providing food for school children, expectant and nursing mothers, hospital patients, and adults attending education centers.

The program gave special attention to creating employment and income through food-for-work programs. In Bangladesh, a vulnerable-group development project, begun in 1975, continues to provide training in health, literacy, and income-generation for women. Similar projects were started in Bolivia and Mexico, while major land-development programs commenced in Egypt, Sudan, Korea, and China. The largest single dairy project ever undertaken, "Operation Flood," in India, increased milk production by 50 percent and benefitted 30 million people.

Early in its operations, recipient governments had a major problem in covering the non-food costs of a project, including transport storage and other expenses. The early success of the program (28 formal requests for aid in May 1963 rose to 193 requests by November 1964) led donor countries to increase their contributions to cover these costs. Indeed, the WFP's ability to quickly transport large quantities of food, at short notice, to remote areas of the world, is one of its most important areas of expertise.

In 1973 a worldwide food shortage created a serious lack of resources, and the WFP governing body was unable to approve any new projects that year. The number of existing recipients and the size of their rations also were cut. Despite these measures there was a shortfall of 160,000 tons of commodities. A concerted effort was made to find new funds, and in 1974 King Faisal of Saudi Arabia offered US$50 million, the largest cash donation ever made. This marked a turning point because the donation came from a nonindustrial developing country that was, and still is, a net importer of food commodities. It also marked an important change in the nature of donations, away from the idea of surplus disposal and toward a wider sharing of responsibility for those in need.

In 1975 the UN General Assembly established the International Emergency Food Reserve (IEFR), to be placed at the disposal of WFP. This reserve, which receives contributions from all governments, has a minimum annual target of 500,000 tons, enabling WFP to quickly respond to emergency situations.

In 1988 donor commitments for development activities reached a high point of US$778 million, which represented two-thirds of WFP resources. By 1993 this trend had reversed and emergency situations were consuming more than 60 percent of WFP's resources. Part of this increase is directly attributable to the program's new relationship with the UN body that supervises refugee relief. In January 1992, the UN High Commissioner for Refugees (UNHCR) worked out an agreement giving the WFP the responsibility to procure and deliver food commodities to UNHCR-managed refugee feeding operations.

In the last 30 years, WFP has witnessed the graduation of former food-aid recipients to the status of potential donors. The Republic of Korea, Singapore, Venezuela, Greece, Hungary, and Mexico are all former recipients who now boast growing economies. The program has also developed ways to use its cash contributions creatively. For example, by buying more food in developing countries for relief and development activities it has encouraged and expanded trade between developing countries. In 1993 the WFP was the largest UN purchaser of goods in developing countries.

WFP has its headquarters in Rome and staff posted in 85 countries serving 90 developing nations. It is administered by an executive director. Its governing body is the 42-member Committee for Food Aid Policies and Programmes (CFA). Half of the members of CFA are elected by ECOSOC, the other half by the FAO Council. In 1992 the members of the CFA were: Algeria, Angola, Argentina, Australia, Bangladesh, Belgium, Brazil, Burkina Faso, Burundi, Cameroon, Canada, China, Colombia, Cuba, Democratic People's Republic of Korea, Dominican Republic, Egypt, El Salvador, Ethiopia, Finland, France, Germany, Ghana, Guinea, Hungary, India, Indonesia, Italy, Japan, Mexico, Netherlands, Norway, Pakistan, Romania, Saudi Arabia, Sri Lanka, Sudan, Sweden, Syria, Tanzania, United Kingdom, and United States of America.

For the 1991–92 biennium, WFP had total pledges and contributions worth nearly US$3 billion. In 1993 WFP reported that its administrative expenses were less than 6 percent of annual expenditure.

UNITED NATIONS POPULATION FUND (UNFPA)

The UN has been concerned with population questions since its earliest years, establishing the Population Commission in 1947 as one of the functional commissions of the Economic and Social Council. The early work of the UN on population questions concentrated on the improvement of demographic statistics, which were lacking for many areas of the world, and then began to focus on the application of statistical data in analytical studies and in the preparation of worldwide population estimates and projections. The first *Demographic Yearbook* was published by the UN Statistical Office in 1948.

In the 1960s, however, the extraordinarily rapid rate at which the world's population was growing became an urgent concern (between 1950 and 1960, the world population increased from 2.5 billion to over 3 billion, and it was projected to more than double by the year 2000). In a resolution adopted in 1966, the General Assembly authorized the UN to provide technical assistance in population matters, and the following year, the General Assembly established a Trust Fund for Population Activities,

renamed in 1969 the United Nations Fund for Population Activities (UNFPA), to provide additional resources to the UN system for technical cooperation activities in the population field. In 1972, the fund was placed under the authority of the General Assembly, which designated the Governing Council of UNDP as its administering body. By its resolution number 1763(LIV) of 18 May 1973, the Economic and Social Council of the United Nations defined the mandate of UNFPA, and, in 1979, the General Assembly affirmed that the UNFPA was a subsidiary organ. In 1987, the fund's name was changed to the United Nations Population Fund, but the acronym UNFPA was retained. In 1993, the General Assembly transformed the Governing Council of UNDP into the UNDP/UNFPA Executive Board, which will provide intergovernmental support to and supervision of the UNFPA in accordance with overall policy guidance of the General Assembly and ECOSOC of the United Nations.

The first World Population Conference, held in Bucharest in 1974, adopted a World Population Plan of Action (WPPA) that stressed the relationship between population factors and overall economic and social development. The General Assembly affirmed that the plan was "an instrument of the international community for the promotion of economic development" and urged that assistance in the population field should be expanded, particularly to UNFPA, for the proper implementation of the plan.

The International Conference on Population, held in Mexico City in August 1984, reaffirmed the validity of the WPPA and adopted recommendations for its further implementation. Target mortality rates were adjusted, and emerging issues, such as migration, urbanization, computerized data processing, and aging of populations, were addressed. Also considered was the need for an intersectoral approach to population and development, for policies that respect individual and family rights, and for improvement in the status of women, including their increased participation in all aspects of development.

The third decennial conference, the International Conference on Population and Development, was held in Cairo, 5–13 September 1994. The Programme of Action adopted at the Cairo conference recommended that population concerns be fully integrated into development planning, in order to meet the needs and improve the quality of life of present and future generations. The program builds upon the considerable international awareness and knowledge that has developed since the Bucharest and Mexico City conferences regarding the linkages among population issues, sustained economic growth, and sustainable development. The program also addresses the reproductive health and educational needs of individuals, especially of girls and women, and calls for increased investment in the social sectors, from donor agencies and recipient governments alike.

UNFPA supports a broad range of population activities. Nearly half of the fund's assistance is used for maternal and child health care and family planning programs. Another 20 percent is used for population and family planning communication and education. UNFPA also supports developing countries in their efforts to collect and analyze population data, conduct population censuses, formulate population policies, and undertake research on fertility, mortality, and migration and their relationship to development, as well as on linkages between population and sustainable development. The fund supports special programs concerning women, youth, the aged, AIDS, and population and development. UNFPA is the leading source of population assistance within the United Nations system. The fund's resources come from voluntary contributions from governments.

Some UNFPA projects

The *State of the World Population 1991* report focussed on family planning as the difference between choice and chance. Accordingly, the UNFPA programs in 1992 vigorously promoted the concept of family planning as a basic human right, and helps countries procure, produce, and distribute contraceptive supplies. The fund's "Global Initiative on Contraceptive Requirements and Logistics Management Needs in Developing Countries in the 1990s" grew rapidly. With the financial assistance of the Swedish International Development Authority, the Rockefeller Foundation, and the World Bank, UNFPA organized in-depth studies of contraceptive requirements and logistics management needs in India, Nepal, Pakistan, and Zimbabwe.

In 1992 the UNFPA worked closely with the Arab Gulf Programme for the United Nations Development Organizations (AGFUND), UNDP, and the International Planned Parenthood Federation (IPPF) on preparations to establish the Arab Women's Centre for Training and Research, which opened in Tunis in January 1994.

UNFPA provided support to conduct comparative trials of the safety and effectiveness of two copper intrauterine devices (IUDs) and to introduce once-a-month injectable contraceptives in selected developing countries.

In Africa, the fund supported 40 integrated women, population, and development projects in 28 countries. The projects generally addressed women's reproductive and productive needs. UNFPA also supported 29 national women's organizations active in population activities.

In 1992 UNFPA procured US$31,633,000 worth of oral contraceptive pills, US$9,986,000 worth of contraceptive injectables, US$3,817,000 worth of contraceptive IUDs, and US$2,106,000 worth of condoms for distribution in developing countries.

Budget and Organization

In 1993, UNFPA's resources totalled US$219.6 million, received from 101 countries. Fifteen countries currently contribute more than 95 percent of UNFPA's resources. Approximately 76 percent of UNFPA's funds are allocated to countries most in need of population assistance. At present, 58 countries are designated as "priority countries"—32 in Sub-Saharan Africa, 17 in Asia and the Pacific, 4 in the Arab States, and 5 in Latin America and the Caribbean.

In 1992, UNFPA issued the following publications and reports: *1992/93 Directory of Training Courses in Family Planning and Maternal and Child Health, Women and Micro-enterprise Development*; *Women, Population and the Environment*; *South Asian Women*; a training guide, *Incorporating Women into Population and Development: Knowing Why and Knowing How*; a monthly magazine *POPULI*; the annual *Inventory of Population Projects in Developing Countries Around the World 1991/92*; and its definitive publication, the annual *The State of World Population*, a comprehensive demographic study of patterns in population growth and distribution. The organization also loans films on videotape, including: *Towards a World in Balance*, produced by UNFPA for World Population Day, 11 July 1992; *Planned Families, Better Lives*; *Population: The Challenge Ahead*; and the 70-minute film *The Day of Five Billion*, a music magazine documentary in which celebrities and world leaders celebrate the birth of the world's 5 billionth inhabitant in 1987.

UN ENVIRONMENT PROGRAM (UNEP)

In the course of the twentieth century, and especially after World War II, the increase in the earth's population and the advance of technology, with concomitant changes in patterns of production and consumption, led to pressure on the environment and threats to its stability that were new in human history. For a long time, the implications of these phenomena were largely ignored. In the decade of the 1960s, however, problems such as soil erosion; air, water, and marine pollution; the need for conservation of limited resources; and desiccation of once-fertile zones became acute

enough to awaken the consciousness of governments and people in all parts of the world, but especially in the industrialized countries, to the urgency of the situation. The UN responded with the decision of the 1968 General Assembly to convene a world conference on the human environment.

The first UN Conference on the Human Environment was held in Stockholm in June 1972. The conference was a focus for, rather than the start of, action on environmental problems. At its conclusion, the participants, representing over 90 percent of the world's population, adopted a declaration and a 109-point plan of action for the human environment that became the blueprint for a wide range of national and international programs. The broad intent of the action plan was to define and mobilize "common effort for the preservation and improvement of the human environment." The preamble to the declaration conveys the urgency, magnitude, and complexity of that task.

Later in 1972, on the basis of the conference's recommendations, the General Assembly created the UN Environment Program (UNEP), to monitor significant changes in the environment and to encourage and coordinate sound environmental practices. With headquarters in Nairobi, Kenya, UNEP is the first global UN agency to be headquartered in a developing country. Its mission is to provide leadership and encourage partnership in caring for the environment by inspiring, informing, and enabling nations and peoples to improve their quality of life without compromising that of future generations.

Twenty years after its inception, UNEP's mandate was reaffirmed and strengthened in 1992 at the UN Conference on Environment and Development (UNCED), held in Rio de Janeiro, Brazil. Out of that conference came an ambitious plan of action—Agenda 21—with an emphasis on integrating development and environment into all United Nations program areas.

The UNEP secretariat is headed by an executive director who is elected by the UN General Assembly for a four-year term, upon the recommendation of the Secretary-General. UNEP's professional staff in 1993 numbered around 200. Besides its Nairobi headquarters, UNEP maintains the following offices around the world: UNEP Regional Office for West Asia, Bahrain; UNEP Regional Coordination Unit, Jamaica; UNEP Regional Office for Africa, Nairobi, Kenya; UNEP Regional Office for Latin America, Mexico City; UNEP Regional Office for Europe, Geneva, Switzerland; UNEP Regional Office for Asia and the Pacific, Bangkok, Thailand; UNEP Arab League Liaison Office, Tunis, Tunisia; UNEP Regional Office for North America, New York; UNEP Liaison Office, Washington DC.

UNEP's Governing Council is composed of 58 states elected by the General Assembly for four-year terms on the basis of equitable geographic representation (16 African seats, 13 Asian seats, 10 Latin American and Caribbean seats, 13 seats for Western European and other states). The Governing Council generally meets every two years.

For the 1993–95 biennium, the following states were elected to the Governing Council: Argentina, Australia, Austria, Bangladesh, Barbados, Bhutan, Botswana, Burundi, Cameroon, Chile, China, Congo, Côte d'Ivoire, Czechoslovakia, Denmark, France, Gabon, Gambia, Germany, Guyana, Italy, India, Indonesia, Iran, Japan, Kenya, Kuwait, Lesotho, Malaysia, Mauritius, Mexico, New Zealand, Netherlands, Nigeria, Norway, Pakistan, Philippines, Poland, Portugal, Romania, Russian Federation, Rwanda, Senegal, Spain, Sri Lanka, Thailand, Tunisia, Ukraine, United Kingdom, United States, Uruguay, Venezuela, Yugoslavia, Zaire, and Zimbabwe. Since UNEP is an integral part of the UN Secretariat, all UN member states and accredited observers can take part in its proceedings.

The Council's functions and responsibilities include promoting international cooperation in the field of environment and recommending policies to that end, providing general policy guidance for environmental programs within the UN system, keeping the world environmental situation under review so as to ensure that emerging problems requiring international assistance receive adequate consideration by governments, promoting the contribution by international scientific and other professional communities to knowledge about the environment and the technical aspects of UN environmental programs, keeping under review the impact of national and international development policies, and reviewing and approving the utilization of the resources of the Environment Fund.

The Environment Fund was set up under the authority of the Governing Council to finance wholly or partly the costs of new environmental initiatives within the UN system. It is made up of voluntary contributions and comprises about two-thirds of UNEP's budget. Over the last 10 years, 95 percent of the contributions have come from 15 countries; 60 countries have paid 5 percent; and well over half the UN member states do not contribute at all. The fund is supplemented by trust funds (20 percent), counterpart contributions (8 percent), and the UN regular budget (6 percent), which is meant to bear the costs for servicing the Governing Council. The budget for the biennium 1994–95 was US$120–130 million.

For its first 20 years, UNEP's policy, as set by the Governing Council, has been focused on the three broad areas of environmental assessment, environmental management, and international environmental law. Many parts to the program evolved under these three themes. There was the environmental monitoring capacity built up in the Global Environment Monitoring System (GEMS), and the establishment of a computer-based store of data in the International Register of Potentially Toxic Chemicals (IRPTC). More computer-based capability was developed to show how both natural and human resources are distributed in the Global Resource Information Database (GRID). Another key information system is INFOTERRA, UNEP's international network for the retrieval of global environmental information. It is a worldwide network with national focal points in 160 countries, providing governments, industry, and researchers with access to a vast reservoir of environmental data and information gathered from about 6,000 institutions and experts in more than 1,000 priority subject areas.

Environmental management and legal instruments were developed. The most successful example of international environmental law can be seen in the instruments used to protect the ozone layer: the 1985 Vienna Convention and the 1987 Montreal Protocol. Expert groups convened by UNEP, with the World Meteorological Organization (WMO), the scientific community, and industry, led to the development of the Vienna Convention for the Protection of the Ozone Layer, which was adopted in March 1985. In September 1987 the Montreal Protocol on Substances that Deplete the Ozone Layer was signed, setting limits for the production and consumption of chloro-fluorocarbons (CFCs) and halons. The Montreal Protocol came into force on 1 January 1989 and was amended in London in June 1990, after research showed that ozone depletion was even more severe than previously feared. CFCs, halons, and carbon tetrachloride (another ozone-depleting chemical, used as a solvent) are now to be phased out by 2000 and a timetable has been set for phasing out other harmful substances. A multilateral fund, involving UNEP, UNDP, and the World Bank, was established to help developing countries meet the costs of complying with the revised protocol and to provide for the necessary transfer of technology.

The Mediterranean Action Plan has been the model as UNEP's Regional Seas Programme has spread. Today, nearly 140 countries take part in Regional Seas Programmes catalyzed and coordinated by UNEP. Action Plans cover the Mediterranean, the Kuwait region, the Red Sea, the Caribbean, the Atlantic coast of West and Central Africa, the Eastern African seaboard, the Pacific coast of South America, the islands of the South Pacific, the East-Asian region, and South Asia. Action Plans for the Black Sea and the North-West Pacific are being developed. Coordination is provided through UNEP's Ocean and Coastal Areas Programme Activity Center (OCA/PAC).

UNEP provides the secretariat for the Convention on International Trade in Endangered Species of Wild Fauna and Flora (CITES), which entered into force in 1975 and prohibits or regulates trade in some 20,000 endangered species. The protection of endangered species under the CITES Convention has seen successful international cooperation to stamp out trade in rare plants and animals.

UNEP also provides the secretariat for the Convention on the Conservation of Migratory Species of Wild Animals (CMS), which came into force in 1983. UNEP supports the World Conservation Monitoring Center (WCMC), which assesses the distribution and abundance of the world's species. Action plans for African elephants and rhinos, Asian elephants and rhinos, primates, cats, and polar bears have been published by UNEP and IUCN.

UNEP also has contributed to the drawing up of global conventions on hazardous waste, climate change, biodiversity, and desertification.

In March 1989, the Basel Convention on the Control of Transboundary Movements of Hazardous Wastes and their Disposal, drafted by UNEP, was adopted by 116 governments and the European Community. The convention entered into force on 5 May 1992. Its immediate target is to impose strict controls on the international movement of hazardous wastes and eventually to reduce their production. As of July 1993, 43 countries acceded or had signaled their intention to accede to the convention.

In June 1992, the Convention on Biological Diversity was signed during the UN Conference on Environmental and Development in Rio de Janeiro. The convention was prepared by an Intergovernmental Negotiating Committee, set up by UNEP's Governing Council and assisted by UNEP, FAO, UNESCO, and IUCN. Its main aims are to conserve biological diversity and to ensure that its benefits to mankind are shared equitably. UNEP also supports the International Board for Plant Genetic Resources (IBPGR), which has established a network of gene banks in 30 countries to house the world's 40 base collections. More than 100 countries collaborate and more than 500,000 plant species have been collected, evaluated, and deposited.

A joint venture between UNEP, UNDP, and the UN Sudano-Sahelian Office is assisting 22 Sudano-Sahelian countries to fight desertification. In spite of these efforts, implementation of the Plan of Action to Combat Desertification has been slow. Institutional, administrative, technical, and financial factors all are involved in this delay.

UNEP, along with the World Meteorological Organization (WMO), established the Intergovernmental Panel on Climate Change to provide scientific assessments on the magnitude, timing, and potential environmental and socioeconomic consequences of climate change and realistic response strategies. Negotiations begun in early 1991 led to the formulation of the United Nations Framework Convention on Climate Change, which was signed by 154 governments in Rio de Janeiro during the 1992 United Nations Conference on Environment and Development.

The organization also is responsible for UN activities involving freshwater. Among regional initiatives are the Action Plan for Latin America and the Caribbean and the program for environmentally sound management of inland waters in the Zambezi Basin.

UNEP, along with UNDP and the World Bank, administers the US$2 billion Global Environment Facility (GEF), and is responsible for GEF's Scientific and Technical Advisory Panel (STAP).

GEF was established as a three-year pilot in 1991 to oversee funding for global environment protection in the areas of climate change, biodiversity, international waters, and ozone depletion. In 1992, a restructuring process began that resulted in agreement on fundamentally altered institutional arrangements for the facility, now known as GEFF II. UNEP will play the primary role in catalyzing the development of scientific and technical analysis and in advancing environmental management in GEF-financed activities. It also will be responsible for establishing and supporting the Scientific and Technical Advisory Panel as an advisory body to the GEF. The UNDP is responsible for technical assistance activities and capacity building. The World Bank, the GEF Trust Fund's repository, plays the primary role in ensuring the development and management of investment projects while also mobilizing private sector resources that are consistent with GEF objectives and national sustainable development strategies. The GEF provides the interim funding mechanism for the conventions on climate change and biological diversity, until parties to those conventions agree on a permanent arrangement.

UNCED and Agenda 21 marked a new beginning for the world community as a whole. Agenda 21 reaffirmed UNEP's role as the principal environment body in the UN system and expanded UNEP's role to encompass a vast range of world environmental needs and problems, with an emphasis on regional delivery. Specifically, Agenda 21 set out priority areas that were confirmed by UNEP's Governing Council in 1993:

- Capacity building
- Environmental management of terrestrial ecosystems and their resources
- Data collection and dissemination, assessment of environmental conditions, and early warning of environmental problems
- Promotion of environmental management of marine and coastal areas
- Support and cooperation for environmental action, including global and regional cooperation
- Environmental management of freshwater resources
- Environmental health, settlements, and human welfare
- Industry, energy, and the environment
- Environmental economics, accounting, and management tools
- International law on sustainable development, institutions, and policies
- Toxic chemicals and waste management
- Protection of the atmosphere.

In 1993, UNEP's executive director outlined three priorities for a revitalized UNEP program, with each activity area supported by the interdependence of the application of sound science, the mobilization of social consensus, and the development of effective public policy:
1. Future UNEP activities must build up the capacity of developing nations to manage their environment and its resources in a sustainable way. This will include developing environmental institutions and legislation and better environmental education.
2. UNEP must identify emerging environmental problems and, by bringing governments together, stimulate the development of programs and policies that will set about solving these problems. UNEP will continue to play this role in such areas as biodiversity, climate change, and desertification. UNEP also will seek to realize its potential as an agent to resolve environmental conflict.
3. UNEP will in the future concentrate on the compilation, analysis, and timely dissemination of data that can be used by those who need it, whether as a response to an environmental emergency or for the long-term assessment of the use of natural resources and their degradation.

Bibliography
UNEP Annual Report 1992
"United Nations Environment Programme: Two Decades Of Achievement And Challenge" Source: *Our Planet*, Volume 4, Number 5, 1992
OzonAction (quarterly newsletter)
Climate Change Bulletin (quarterly newsletter)
UNEP/GEMS Environment Library (series)
    The following is an alphabetical listing of some of UNEP's electronic databases available for use by scientists and researchers:
Activities on Wind Effect (ACWIND)
Computerized Industrial Environmental Legislation (CIEL)
Desertification Library (Database) (DELI)
Desertification Mailing List (MAIL)
Desertification Thesaurus (KEYS)
Directory of Organizations dealing with Desertification Control and Dryland Development (DIOR)
Environment Periodicals (EPPER)
Environment Programme Library (Database) (EPLIB)
Global Resource Information Data Base (GRID)
Industry and Environment Data Base (EPBIBL)
INFOTERRA Data Base
International Register of Potentially Toxic Chemicals Data Base (IRPTC)
Marine and Coastal Expertise Database
Network of Researchers and Institutions dealing with Wind Erosion (REWIND)
News and Data (Database)
Query/Response Database (Q/R)
UN Compendium on Dryland Development and Desertification Control Projects (PROCOM)
UNEP Desertification Control Projects (DEPRO)
Worldwide Documentation on Wind Erosion Control (BIWIND)

UN CENTER FOR HUMAN SETTLEMENTS (HABITAT)

UN concern with the problems of human settlements, particularly with the deteriorating quality of living conditions in developing countries and the need to link urban and regional development programs with national development plans, led to the convening of the first international conference on the question in Vancouver, Canada, in May–June 1976. The declaration and plan of action adopted by Habitat: UN Conference on Human Settlements (Habitat I) represented an important commitment on the part of governments and the international community to improve the quality of life for all people through human settlements development. The plan of action contained 64 recommendations for national action concerning settlement policies and planning; provision of shelter, infrastructure, and services; land use and land tenure; the role of popular participation; and effective institutions and management.

Habitat I also recommended the strengthening and consolidation of UN activities in a single organization concerned exclusively with human settlements. Acting on this recommendation, the General Assembly established in 1978 the UN Center for Human Settlements (Habitat), with headquarters in Nairobi, Kenya, to serve as a focal point for human settlements action and to coordinate human settlements activities within the UN system.

The center provides technical assistance to governments; organizes expert meetings, workshops, and training seminars; issues print, audio visual, and electronic publications; and disseminates information worldwide. In 1993 the center had under execution 257 technical cooperation programs and projects in over 90 countries, with an overall budget in excess of US$42 million for the year.

In 1982, the General Assembly proclaimed 1987 as the International Year of Shelter for the Homeless. The objectives were to improve the shelter situation of the poor and disadvantaged at both individual and community levels, particularly in developing countries, and to demonstrate means of continuing those efforts as ongoing national programs beyond 1987.

Beginning in 1986, the tenth anniversary of Habitat I, World Habitat Day has been observed each year on the first Monday in October. As lead agency in the UN system for coordinating activities related to the Global Strategy for Shelter to the Year 2000, the center continues to work toward its goal of facilitating adequate shelter for all by that date.

The Habitat II Conference is scheduled for Istanbul, Turkey, in 1996, 20 years after Habitat I. Subtitled "A Summit for Cities," the UN Conference on the Future of Cities has as its goal making the world's cities, towns, and villages healthy, safe, just, and sustainable. The two central themes to be explored are "sustainable human settlements in an urbanizing world" and "adequate shelter for all."

UN RESEARCH INSTITUTE FOR SOCIAL DEVELOPMENT (UNRISD)

The UN Research Institute for Social Development (UNRISD) was created in 1963 as an autonomous agency within the UN system. It engages in multidisciplinary research on the social dimensions of contemporary problems affecting development. Its work is guided by the conviction that, for effective development policies to be formulated, an understanding of the social and political context is crucial. The institute attempts to provide governments, development agencies, grass roots organizations, and scholars with a better understanding of how development policies and processes of economic, social, and environmental change affect different social groups.

Working through an extensive network of national research centers, UNRISD aims to promote original research and strengthen research capacity in developing countries.

Research themes in 1994 included "Crisis, Adjustment and Social Change"; "Socio-Economic and Political Consequences of the International Trade in Illicit Drugs"; "Environment, Sustainable Development and Social Change"; "Integrating Gender into Development Policy"; "Participation and Changes in Property Relations in Communist and Post-Communist Societies"; and "Political Violence and Social Movements." UNRISD research projects focussed on the 1995 World Summit for Social Development include "Rethinking Social Development in the 1990s"; "Economic Restructuring and New Social Policies"; "Ethnic Diversity and Public Policies"; and "The Challenge of Rebuilding War-Torn Societies."

Although it offers no courses or fellowships, the institute maintains a Reference Centre and publishes books, monographs, a Discussion Paper Series, a Briefing Paper Series on the World Summit for Social Development, and a free newsletter in English, French, and Spanish entitled "UNRISD Social Development News." Publications may be ordered from the Reference Centre.

The institute has approximately 15 staff members at its headquarters in Geneva, and is financed entirely by voluntary contributions.

UN INSTITUTE FOR TRAINING AND RESEARCH (UNITAR)

In 1963, the General Assembly requested the Secretary-General to establish a UN Institute for Training and Research as an autonomous body within the framework of the UN. UNITAR commenced functioning in March 1965. It is headed by an executive director and has a board of trustees appointed by the UN Secretary-General in consultation with the president of the General Assembly and the president of the Economic and Social Council. UNITAR originally had its headquarters in New York and a

European office in Geneva. In 1993 UNITAR's headquarters was transferred to Geneva. It maintains a liaison office in New York to coordinate training activities.

The mandate of UNITAR is to enhance the effectiveness of the UN in attaining its major objectives—particularly the maintenance of peace and the promotion of economic and social development—through training and research. Its functions include ensuring liaison with UN organizations and strengthening cooperation with academic institutions; conducting training programs in multilateral diplomacy and international cooperation for diplomats accredited to the United Nations and national officials; and carrying out a wide range of training programs in social and economic development. In addition, UNITAR responds to ad hoc requests for training. During 1993 UNITAR received requests for programs from UNDP, UNEP, and other UN bodies.

Courses offered by UNITAR in 1993 included: Geographic Information Systems for Natural Resource Management, Implementation of the London Guidelines for the Exchange of Information in International Trade, Promoting the Implementation of the United Nations Framework Convention on Climate Change, Environmental Negotiations and Dispute Resolution, Debt Management, and Training in Disaster Control.

By the end of 1992, UNITAR had trained more than 17,000 diplomats, national civil servants, and international civil servants from 180 nations. In 1993 more than 2,000 persons participated in UNITAR's 66 training programs. In the early 1990s training programs in diplomacy, negotiation, foreign affairs management, and debt and financial management were developed for newly independent countries in Europe and Central Asia; countries in transition in Africa, Asia, and Europe; and for the Palestinian negotiating team.

The institute's research program originally concentrated on three main areas: UN institutional issues, peace and security issues, and economic and social issues. After restructuring in 1992, basic research on training was conducted only if extrabudgetary funds were provided.

UNITAR is supported by voluntary contributions from governments, intergovernmental organizations, foundations, and other nongovernmental organizations.

UN UNIVERSITY (UNU)

In 1969, Secretary-General U Thant proposed that a UN university be established. The Founding Committee was set up two years later, and in December 1973, the General Assembly approved a charter for the university. The following spring, the UNU Council, composed of academic leaders and prominent persons from 24 countries, was appointed. Members of the university council serve in their individual capacities rather than as representatives of governments. UNU commenced operations in September 1975. For 17 years the university maintained its headquarters in a high-rise office building in Tokyo. In 1992 it moved to a new building in the Shibuya district of Tokyo constructed and made available by the government of Japan. The university maintains a liaison office in New York.

UNU is an autonomous organ of the General Assembly. It is jointly sponsored by the UN and UNESCO, whose Secretary-General and Director General, respectively, together appoint the rector and members of the university council. Its charter guarantees academic freedom and emphasizes the primacy of scholarly excellence over any other considerations—for example, choices of programs and personnel—in determining its activities.

Like traditional universities, UNU is concerned with the advancement of knowledge. Unlike traditional universities, however, it has no students of its own, no faculty, and no campus. It is a completely new institution: an international community of scholars engaged in research, postgraduate training, and the dissemination of knowledge to help solve, in the words of its charter, "pressing global problems of human survival, development and welfare." It operates through worldwide networks of academic and research institutions and individual scholars who work together on projects concerned with such problems as peace, development, the environment, science, and technology. The UNU's five areas of concentration for 1990–95 include: universal human values and global responsibilities; the world economy and development; global life-support systems; advances in science and technology; and population dynamics and human welfare.

The academic activities of the university are carried out primarily through a network of its research and training centers: UNU World Institute for Development Economics Research (UNU/WIDER), Helsinki, Finland (established 1985); UNU Institute for New Technologies (UNU/Intech), Maastricht, the Netherlands (established 1990); UNU International Institute for Software Technology (UNU/IIST), Macau (established 1992); UNU Institute for Natural Resources in Africa (UNU/INRA), in Accra, Ghana, and Lusaka, Zambia (established 1990). The university also sponsors the Programme for Biotechnology in Latin America and the Caribbean, located in Caracas, Venezuela (established 1989).

In March 1992, a memorandum of understanding was signed with Canada to study a possible UNU center in Ontario to initiate research on global environment and human health. In the same field, negotiations were under way to establish a research and training center at the University of Ulm, Germany. Negotiations also were held to establish a research and training program at Ulster University, Northern Ireland, in the area of ethnicity and conflict resolution. In 1994, UNU was planning a Centre for Global Governance in Barcelona, Spain.

Between 1976 and 1992, a total of 1,170 UNU fellows received postgraduate training through the university's network. Fellows are selected after recommendation from their home institutions, which must be working in an area of concern to the university, and must be committed to returning to work at those institutions.

The UNU Press publishes scholarly works on the United Nations system in the areas of peace studies, regional studies, technology and development, human and social development, international law, food and nutrition, energy technology, and natural resources and environment. The UNU Press publishes one periodical, *The Food and Nutrition Bulletin*, issued quarterly. UNU publications are distributed in North America by UNIPUB based in Lanham, Maryland.

UNU is supported by voluntary contributions from governments, foundations, and individuals. Its principal source of support is investment income from an endowment fund that ensures academic freedom and financial independence. By 1994, pledges to the endowment fund and operating contributions had been made by 51 governments and seven other benefactors, totalling US$271,660,779. In 1992–93, UNU reported income of US$60.3 million and expenditures of US$55.1 million.

UNIVERSITY FOR PEACE

The University for Peace was established in 1979 in San Jose, Costa Rica, to promote postgraduate studies and research on peace. A General Assembly resolution called on member states, NGOs, and intergovernmental bodies, as well as interested individuals and organizations, to contribute to the university's Trust Fund.

INTERNATIONAL RESEARCH AND TRAINING INSTITUTE FOR THE ADVANCEMENT OF WOMEN (INSTRAW)

On the recommendation of the 1975 World Conference of the International Women's Year, the General Assembly established the International Research and Training Institute for the Advancement of Women (INSTRAW) as an autonomous body within the UN system to carry out research, training, and information activities aimed at the promotion of women as key agents of development. The institute began operations in 1979, with headquarters in Santo Domingo, the Dominican Republic. It works closely with UN and governmental organizations and has developed a worldwide network of focal points and correspondents.

INSTRAW's research and training programs cover a number of areas. One research focus is methodologies and statistics for measuring the contribution of women working outside the formal sector. A major achievement in this area was INSTRAW's publication of *Women in the World Economy,* a study based on research on the role of women in trade, money and finance, technology, industry, and agriculture. To study the contribution of women in developing countries who do unpaid work, INSTRAW produced a technical/methodological study, Methods for Valuating the Contribution of Women to Development. The institute also maintains a documentation center with a collection of UN documents on women and development issues and a computerized bibliographic database.

INSTRAW offers a number of training packages to developing countries. It recently completed a multi-media training package on Women and New and Renewable Sources of Energy, which was used in seminars in the Dominican Republic, Egypt, Ethiopia, Libya, Tanzania, and the former Yugoslavia. INSTRAW is also assessing training needs in some of the newly independent countries of eastern Europe. INSTRAW has completed a *Gender Training Portfolio* that contains material for a Women in Development curriculum for academic institutions. In collaboration with other UN agencies, INSTRAW developed computer modules to assist policymakers in understanding the relationship between certain sectoral policies and the advancement of women. These computer modules include: *Urban Women in Development Model* and *Rural Women in Development Mode*.

By 1992, more than 2,000 people had taken part in INSTRAW training workshops and seminars. The institute publishes *INSTRAW News* twice a year and produces reports, documents, and public information.

The institute is funded by voluntary contributions from member states, intergovernmental and nongovernmental organizations, foundations, and private sources. It is headed by a board of trustees of 11 members, who are nominated by governments and elected by the Economic and Social Council but who serve in their personal capacities, and by a director, appointed by the UN Secretary-General on the recommendation of the board of trustees.

UNITED NATIONS DEVELOPMENT FUND FOR WOMEN (UNIFEM)

In 1976, the UN General Assembly established the Voluntary Fund for the United Nations Decade for Women. The fund was created to provide direct support for women's projects and to promote the inclusion of women in the decision-making processes of mainstream development programs. In 1985 the New York-based organization formally joined the UN family of agencies as UNIFEM.

UNIFEM reports directly to the administrator of UNDP. It is overseen by a five-member Consultative Committee representing UN member states from the world's five principal regional groups. The committee approves large projects and advises on the use of the fund's resources. UNIFEM is administered by a director.

In order to support efforts of the women of the developing world to achieve their objective for economic and social development and for equality, and by so doing to improve the quality of life for women and men alike, the fund supports microprograms run by women in developing countries. For example, UNIFEM estimates that although women grow, process, and market between 50 percent and 80 percent of the food consumed in developing countries, governments rarely record these inputs or support them with financial credit. UNIFEM's programs include: training women in improved agricultural techniques; transfer of appropriate food technologies such as grinding mills, graters, oil presses, solar driers, and fish smokers; obtaining for women increased access to credit for seeds, fertilizers, and equipments; and support for microenterprises. UNIFEM works with the UN High Commisioner for Refugees (UNHCR) in assisting African refugees. At any one time it manages a portfolio of approximately 150 projects and has supported over 750 projects in 100 developing countries.

In 1991 UNIFEM collaborated on the publication of *The World's Women 1970–90: The Trends and Statistics*. Co-authored by the UN Statistical Office, UNICEF, and UNFPA, this publication gathered statistics and interpreted trends on women, families, and households; women in public life and leadership; the status of education and training for women; health and child-bearing; housing, human settlements, and the environment; and women's work and the economy.

Financing is provided by the governments of both industrialized and developing countries, by nongovernmental organizations, foundations, corporations, private individuals, and from UNIFEM's growing number of national committees. In 1990, 30 percent of the funds projects were implemented with contributions by NGOs, many of which are women's organizations. UNIFEM's major government contributors in 1992 were Canada, Finland, Germany, Japan, Netherlands, Norway, Sweden, and the United States.

In 1992, UNIFEM had national committees in Australia, Belgium, Canada, Denmark, Finland, France, Germany, Iceland, Japan, New Zealand, Norway, Philippines, Sweden, Switzerland, and the United States. National committees were forming in Ireland, Italy, Luxembourg, Spain, and the United Kingdom.

UNIFEM reported income in 1992 of US$11.5 million and program expenditures of US$11.5 million. It expended US$2.7 million in Latin America and the Caribbean, US$2.2 million in Asia and the Pacific, US$3.8 million in Africa, and US$2.8 million in other areas of the world.

SOCIAL AND HUMANITARIAN ASSISTANCE

International disaster relief, the special problems of children, refugees, the elderly, youth, the disabled, and families are all subjects for which member states have directed the UN to provide international leadership and expert guidance. The global nature of trade in illicit narcotic drugs and the internationalization of criminal activities were social ills that became so destabilizing at the end of the twentieth century that member states requested their international organization to implement innovative global programs to maintain security and social justice.

INTERNATIONAL DISASTER RELIEF

Background
The international community is faced with the growing challenge of preventing, mitigating the effects of, and providing humanitarian assistance to affected populations in crises that require rapid and effective response. The 1990s saw a dramatic increase in "complex emergencies" that often involved ethnic and civil strife. In mid-1994 more than 30 million people in 29 countries were in dire need of emergency assistance. Severe drought threatening over 20 million people in sub-Saharan Africa added an additional element of suffering to that already faced by millions in Burundi, Liberia, Rwanda, Somalia, southern Sudan, and Zaire. A study released at the World Conference on Natural Disaster Reduction, convened by the General Assembly in May 1994, showed that the previous three decades had seen a steady and rapid increase in the number of significant natural disasters—and in the numbers of people affected.

Office of the United Nations Disaster Relief Coordinator (UNDRO)
Beginning in 1965, proposals were put forward in the General Assembly to increase the UN's ability to help people stricken by disasters, but it was the disasters of 1970 that brought international concern for emergency relief to a head. In 1971, the General Assembly established the Office of the United Nations Disaster Relief Coordinator (UNDRO), with headquarters in Geneva.

UNDRO was not designed to assume all the responsibilities of meeting disasters from its own resources. Its principal function is that of catalyst and coordinator of donors of aid and services. Its data bank and independent telecommunications system, supplemented by the worldwide UN system, give it the capacity to define the specific needs arising from a disaster and to respond rapidly by identifying potential sources of relief. It directs and mobilizes aid emanating from the UN system and coordinates aid from other sources.

UNDRO's mandate also includes assisting governments in preventing disasters or mitigating their effects by contingency planning, in association with similarly concerned voluntary organizations. It promotes the study, prevention, control, and prediction of natural disasters and gathers and disseminates information relevant to disaster relief.

Between its inception in 1972 and 1987, UNDRO helped coordinate relief and raise money for emergency aid in more than 380 major disasters.

The Department of Humanitarian Affairs (DHA)
In December 1991, the General Assembly, by its Resolution 46/182, recognized the need to strengthen coordination for rapid response to humanitarian emergencies. Over the years ad hoc arrangements had sprung up in many of the UN departments and specialized agencies to deal with emergency relief. Sometimes these arrangements were found to be working at cross-purposes or competing for financial support from the same potential donors. The General Assembly requested the Secretary-General to designate an emergency relief coordinator, supported by a secretariat, to ensure that the entire UN system was better prepared for, and more capable of rapid and coherent response to national disasters and other humanitarian emergencies. The resolution also stipulated guiding principles of humanity, neutrality and impartiality for the provision of humanitarian assistance. It also stressed respect for the sovereignty, territorial integrity and national unity of states.

In April 1992, the Secretary-General established the Department of Humanitarian Affairs, incorporating UNDRO, various UN units that had been dealing with specific emergency programs, and the secretariat for the International Decade for Natural Disaster Reduction. The Secretary-General appointed an Emergency Relief Coordinator to head the new department. The DHA has its headquarters in New York and an office in Geneva.

Resolution 46/182 gave the DHA three tools to speed up the response of the international community to emergencies: the Inter-Agency Standing Committee (IASC) to formulate and coordinate policy; the Central Emergency Revolving Fund (CERF) as a quick source of emergency funding; and the Consolidated Appeals Process (CAP), which assesses the needs of a critical situations and prepares a comprehensive interagency response strategy.

The IASC is chaired by the Emergency Relief Coordinator and is composed of the executive heads of the following UN organizations: the United Nations Development Programme (UNDP); the Office of the UN High Commissioner for Refugees (UNHCR); the UN Children's Fund (UNICEF); the World Food Program (WFP); the World Health Organization (WHO), and the Food and Agriculture Organization of the UN (FAO). Other humanitarian organizations such as the International Committee of the Red Cross (ICRC), the International Federation of Red Cross and Red Crescent Societies (IFRC), and the International Organization for Migration (IOM) also take part in the IASC. Representatives of relevant nongovernmental organizations (NGOs) are invited to participate.

In addition to coordinating overall policy on humanitarian assistance, the IASC addresses issues such as: access to victims, security of personnel and relief supplies, ensuring humanitarian imperatives in conflict situations, examining special needs arising from application of UN sanctions, demobilization of combatants, de-mining, resource mobilization, assistance to internally displaced persons, field coordination of international humanitarian responses, and ensuring transition from relief to development.

The Central Emergency Revolving Fund (CERF) of US$50 million was created under the terms of Resolution 46/182 as a cash-flow mechanism for use by operational organizations, especially during the critical initial stages of emergencies. The CERF is financed by voluntary contributions and managed by the Department of Humanitarian Affairs. Agencies draw on the CERF and repay the advances they receive as donors respond to their own fundraising efforts. From its establishment in 1992 until June 1994, the CERF was utilized on 31 occasions, providing operational humanitarian organizations with a total of US$95.5 million, of which US$56.1 million has been reimbursed.

The Consolidated Appeals Process (CAP), coordinated and monitored by DHA, is an interagency exercise by which UN system organizations and other humanitarian organizations assess the full range of requirements for responding to emergencies. The CAP helps the international community to identify the most critical needs of affected people and to determine the most appropriate ways to provide assistance. This process enables donors and agencies to concentrate their efforts where they are needed most and eliminates wasteful competition among agencies for donor funds. In the 1992–94 period, appeals were launched for Afghanistan, Angola, Armenia, Azerbaijan, Burundi, Djibouti, Eritria, Ethiopia, Georgia, Haiti, Iraq, Kenya, Lebanon, Liberia, Mozambique, Rwanda, Somalia, Sudan, Tajikistan, the former Yugoslavia, and Zaire.

The DHA's work takes place where the fields of international security, political affairs, and humanitarian concerns converge. An important responsibility entrusted to DHA involves humanitarian diplomacy in efforts to prevent emergencies and in negotiation with parties to conflicts aimed at ensuring access to those in need. DHA's staff is involved in policy planning and early warning functions, emergency operational support and relief coordination, and disaster mitigation. The DHA maintains close contact with the UN Departments of Political Affairs and Peacekeeping Operations in order to coordinate the security, political, and humanitarian aspects of complex emergencies.

New Initiatives

DHA is developing a centralized information management system on humanitarian emergencies. The International Emergency Readiness and Response Information System (IERRIS) and the Humanitarian Early Warning System (HEWS) are being developed in collaboration with governments and other UN agencies. The United States and Japan donated funds and equipment to establish IERRIS, a modern information network system based in New York, which is linked by satellite to the DHA's office in Geneva and its field operations. The IERRIS will allow international humanitarian partners to exchange information on supplies and readiness, and develop common procedures and compatible technologies.

During the first two years of its operation, several special programs within DHA addressed specific needs. It established a Special Emergency Programme for the Horn of Africa (SEPHA) and a Drought Emergency in South Africa Programme (DESA). In response to the special needs of the newly independent countries of Eastern Europe, it created the Special Emergency Programme for the Newly Independent States (SEP-NIS). DHA also had special programs to coordinate humanitarian assistance for Iraq and Afghanistan.

Other projects within the DHA were established to help governments and international agencies prepare for quick response to the sudden onset of disasters. These activities included the Disaster Management Training Programme (DMTP), managed jointly by DHA and UNDP on behalf of the International Search and Rescue Advisory Group (INSARAG). INSARAG is an interagency task force. The UN Disaster Assessment and Coordination Standby Teams was another project under development by DHA.

Landmines

The removal of land-mines is another important aspect of DHA's work, undertaken in conjunction with the Department of Peace-keeping Operations. In his 1994 report to the General Assembly on humanitarian assistance (GA/49/177), the Secretary-General reported that there were between 85 million and 110 million land-mines scattered in 60 countries around the world. Although de-mining had usually been considered a military operation, the international community has recognized that these land-mines hold up the transition from emergency to development by deterring the repatriation of refugees, making farming impossible, and rendering roads, railroads, and electrical power grids unusable. Beyond this, it was estimated that 400 people were killed each month by uncleared land-mines. Although some types of land-mines could be purchased for as little as US$3, the cost to remove each one was between US$300 and US$1,000. The Secretary-General stated that more than 2 million new land-mines would be laid in 1994 alone. All these factors had combined to shift the removal of land-mines from an exclusively military concern to the area of humanitarian and development assistance.

The Department of Humanitarian Affairs and the Department of Peace-keeping Operations implemented de-mining plans in a number of countries, using three stages: first, bringing in United Nations de-mining resources to conduct de-mining operations in support of humanitarian and peacekeeping objectives; second, informing local populations and returning refugees how to recognize, avoid, mark, and report land-mines; and, third, helping the national government create its own de-mining capability. By training local de-miners, supervisors, instructors, and program management personnel, the United Nations strives to give countries long-term means to deal with their land-mine problems. Besides the DHA, the UNHCR, UNICEF, and UNDP were involved in de-mining activities.

International Decade for Natural Disaster Reduction

Between 1960 and 1990 deaths from natural disasters rose by a factor of 10, with 90 percent of casualties occurring in developing countries ill prepared to respond to natural disasters. Although the World Meteorological Organization has shown that each dollar spent on disaster preparedness is equivalent to 100 dollars spent after a disaster, no mechanisms existed to transfer the huge body of knowledge on disaster preparedness and prevention from the industrialized countries to developing countries. For example, an earthquake of 6.6 magnitude on the Richter scale in California in January 1994 caused fewer than 100 deaths. An earthquake of 6.4 magnitude in India's Maharashtra State in September 1993 caused 10,000 deaths. Most of the deaths in the Indian tragedy were caused by the collapse of homes while people slept. By contrast, California has long been a proving ground for earthquake-resistant architectural innovations.

In 1989, the General Assembly declared the 1990s the International Decade for Natural Disaster Reduction to reduce loss of life and property damage resulting from natural disasters. It established a high-level council of 10 internationally renowned personalities, a scientific and technical committee of 24 scientists from around the world, and approximately 120 national committees to promote the decade and the formulation of disaster preparedness programs. 13 October was declared "International Day for Natural Disaster Reduction," and observed by public gatherings and publicity to raise awareness of the need to implement disaster preparedness.

In May 1994, the World Conference on Natural Disaster Reduction was convened in Yokohama, Japan. Representatives from 147 countries and 37 nongovernmental organizations and observers from UN specialized agencies participated in the conference, which both reviewed implementation of the General Assembly's recommendations during the first half of the decade and adopted the "Guidelines for Natural Disaster Prevention, Preparedness and Mitigation," also called the "Yokohama Strategy." It noted that the first half of the decade had seen some improvement in the field of disaster response, but that the goals for disaster prevention and preparedness had not received wide publicity.

The conference document stated that, while natural phenomena that cause disasters are outside human control, vulnerability of populations was a result of human activity (or nonactivity). In its "Strategy for the Year 2000 and Beyond," the conference called for a global culture of prevention and a policy of self-reliance in each vulnerable country and community. Other elements of the strategy included education and training in disaster prevention, strengthening research and development for disaster reduction and mitigation, and improving awareness in vulnerable communities through more active use of media. Finally the conference called on all countries to express the political commitment to reduce their vulnerability by means of legislation and policy decisions at the highest levels to mobilize domestic resources, develop risk assessment programs, and emergency plans and to design projects for subregional, regional, and international cooperation. It also recommended an improvement in communications capabilities on natural disasters among countries for preparedness and early warning systems.

Man-made Humanitarian Disasters

Perhaps the thorniest problem for the new DHA was the increase in and complexity of humanitarian disasters caused by internal civil strife in places like Angola, the former Yugoslavia, and Rwanda. In the largest exodus ever known, 2 million people in Rwanda abandoned their homes in one week during the resumption of a civil war and the organized slaughter of thousands of civilians in that country in the summer of 1994. The exodus overwhelmed the capacity of international aid organizations to deal with the crisis, and thousands of people died of cholera, dysentery, and other diseases in makeshift camps hurriedly set up along Rwanda's border with other countries. In August 1994, the UN agencies appealed to member states for US$470 million to respond to the disaster. The initial response to the appeal yielded US$137 million. In his report to the 49th General Assembly on "Strengthening of the coordination of emergency humanitarian assistance" (A/49/177), the Secretary-General stated:

> "Complex emergencies are presenting serious new challenges to humanitarian organizations and others involved in providing relief assistance. Disregard for fundamental humanitarian principles, serious violations of humanitarian law and threats to the safety and protection of relief personnel have underscored the need for enhancing awareness of all involved in complex emergencies—including the Security Council—of humanitarian concerns and objectives and for appropriate measures to protect humanitarian mandates in conflict situations. *While the new generation of multifaceted United Nations operations require close interaction between the political, military and humanitarian dimensions, it is important, at the same time, to ensure that the humanitarian component can preserve its unique identity by maintaining neutrality and impartiality.*" (emphasis added).

In this connection, the IASC established a set of guidelines for humanitarian missions in conflict situations:

(a) The need for humanitarian relief assistance to be undertaken in accordance with the principles of impartiality, neutrality, and humanity;

(b) Reaffirmation of free, safe, and unimpeded access for humanitarian assistance and the role of humanitarian diplomacy in that regard;

(c) The need for greater collaboration with nongovernmental organizations engaged in humanitarian relief;

(d) The need to ensure security and protection of all relief personnel;

(e) The need to apprise the Security Council fully on relevant humanitarian issues that should be appropriately reflected in its decisions on complex emergencies;

(f) The importance of shielding humanitarian assistance against the effects of sanctions, particularly in relation to vulnerable groups.

United Nations Sahelian Office (UNSO)

Another UN undertaking in disaster relief developed in response to the desiccation of the Sudano-Sahelian zone of West Africa. Many years of drought in Burkina Faso, Chad, Mali, Mauritania, Niger, and Senegal had, by 1973, resulted in a crisis and the threat of mass starvation in the region. In May, the Secretary-General, acting under resolutions of the General Assembly and the Economic and Social Council, designated FAO as the "focal point" of an emergency operation of the UN system to provide and transport rations, seeds for sowing, animal feed, and vaccines to victims in the six countries. The following month, the UN Sahelian Office (UNSO) was created to promote medium- and long-term recovery in cooperation with the Permanent Interstate Committee on Drought Control in the Sahel, known by its French acronym CILSS and composed of eight affected states—Burkina Faso, Cape Verde, Chad, Gambia, Mali, Mauritania, Niger, and Senegal.

In 1977, UNSO's mandate was expanded to assist the UN Environment Programme (UNEP) in implementing the Plan of Action to Combat Desertification in the Sudano-Sahelian Region. Within its desertification program, UNSO serves 22 countries. In addition to the member states of CILSS, these are Benin, Cameroon, Djibouti, Ethiopia, Ghana, Guinea, Guinea-Bissau, Kenya, Nigeria, Somalia, Sudan, Tanzania, Togo, and Uganda. UNSO mobilizes general and earmarked contributions to promote sustainable management of the natural resources in arid and semi-arid lands. It helps governments plan and coordinate natural resource management and implement field projects on soil and water conservation and integrated land management.

UN CHILDREN'S FUND (UNICEF)

The UN International Children's Emergency Fund (UNICEF) was established by the General Assembly on 11 December 1946 to provide emergency relief assistance in the form of food, medicine, and clothing to the children of postwar Europe and China. In December 1950, the General Assembly extended the life of the fund for three years, changing its mandate to emphasize health and nutrition programs of long-range benefit to children of developing countries. In October 1953, the General Assembly decided that UNICEF should continue its work as a permanent arm of the UN system, and charged the organization to emphasize programs giving long-term benefit to children everywhere, particularly those in developing countries who are in the greatest need. The organization's name was changed to the UN Children's Fund, but the acronym "UNICEF" was retained.

In 1959 the General Assembly unanimously adopted the Declaration of the Rights of the Child, affirming the right of children to special protection and opportunities and facilities for healthy, normal development.

Following a global study of the needs of children in 1961, UNICEF increased the scope and flexibility of its approach to children to include projects that promote the role of children as an invaluable "human resource" in national development, thus making it possible to provide aid for education.

UNICEF was awarded the Nobel Peace Prize in 1965.

In November 1989, the General Assembly voted to transform the rights and obligations under the 1959 Declaration into the Convention on the Rights of the Child, the most comprehensive treaty ever to address the individual rights of children and set universally accepted standards for their children. The convention entered into force as international law in September 1990. By April 1994, 159 member states had ratified the convention.

As the only United Nations agency devoted exclusively to the needs of children, UNICEF promotes the universal ratification and full implementation of the Convention on the Rights of the Child by 1995. UNICEF also participated in the World Conference on Human Rights in Vienna in June 1993, speaking out forcefully on behalf of children and against violation of their rights.

Purposes and Scope of Work

Combining humanitarian and development objectives, UNICEF's primary goal is to help children of the poorest and least developed countries. It helps them directly, by supporting government programs to improve child health, nutrition, education, and social services, and indirectly, by serving as child advocate, appealing to governments and to the consciences of individuals worldwide to find and commit the resources required to protect and prepare children adequately.

UNICEF's mandate from the General Assembly's 1946 resolution for "strengthening . . . the permanent child health and welfare programs of the countries receiving assistance" has been developed and continuously adapted to current conditions. It places strong emphasis on community participation in the development and operation of services for children and has increasingly focused on community-based action. As a funding agency—as distinct from a specialized agency—UNICEF is able to work with various ministries and nongovernmental organizations, maintaining an intersectoral approach to community action in meeting the needs of children.

In 1976, UNICEF adopted an approach to the provision of basic health and welfare services, the key element of which was community participation. This new approach resulted from experiences in economically and politically diverse developing countries showing that services are likely to be not only cheaper but also more effective when community members are involved, because they mobilize hitherto unused abilities within the community and the services can be run at recurrent costs that the country and community can afford. Integration of women into the establishment of community-based services is especially important, since their participation can have a significant impact on the quality of life for their children.

UNICEF gives priority to the establishment of long-term programs and places special emphasis on the use of national expertise wherever feasible.

UNICEF cooperates with developing countries in several ways: it assists in the planning and extension of services benefiting children and in the exchange of experience between countries; it provides funds to strengthen the training and orientation of national personnel, complementing, wherever possible, the work of specialized agencies; and it delivers technical supplies, equipment, and other aid for extending services.

In September 1990, the Convention on the Rights of the Child entered into force, less than one year after its adoption by the General Assembly. That month, UNICEF organized the World Summit for Children, attended by representatives from more than 150 countries, including 71 heads of state or government. It produced a Declaration and a Plan of Action, which recognized the rights of the young to "first call" on nations' resources and set goals for the year 2000, including:

1. A reduction of the 1990 infant and under-five child mortality rates by one third or to 50 to 70 per 1,000 live births respectively, whichever is lower;
2. A reduction by half of the 1990 maternal mortality rate;
3. A reduction by half of the 1990 rate for severe malnutrition among children under the age of five;

4. Universal access to safe drinking water and to sanitary means of excreta disposal, and
5. Universal access to basic education and completion of primary education by at least 80 percent of school-age children.

Some of these goals have been chosen for accelerated achievement by 1995.

Recognizing that survival and development of children is intricately linked to the status of women in developing countries, the Executive Board, at its annual meeting in May 1994, requested the executive director to give high priority to UNICEF efforts to develop gender-sensitive indicators in each sectoral area of development and to set gender-specific goals in national programmes of action. The executive director would support gender equality within the family, organized participation of women at all levels, and capacity-building and mobilization of youth for a more gender-equitable society.

Organization

UNICEF is an integral part of the UN, with semiautonomous status. The Executive Board, which is the governing body of UNICEF, meets once a year to establish policy, review programs, and approve expenditures. Membership comprises 36 governments from all regions, elected in rotation for a three-year term by the United Nations Economic and Social Council (ECOSOC). The 36 members of the Executive Board at the May 1994 annual meeting were: Angola, Azerbaijan, Central African Republic, Colombia, Congo, Denmark, Ethiopia, India, Japan, Netherlands, Pakistan, Republic of Korea, Sweden, United Republic of Tanzania (terms expiring 31 December 1994); Australia, Belarus, Canada, China, Costa Rica, Germany, Mozambique, Philippines, Russian Federation, Suriname, Switzerland (terms expiring 31 December 1995); Brazil, Burkina Faso, France, Ghana, Indonesia, Italy, Jamaica, Lebanon, Romania, United Kingdom, United States (terms expiring 31 December 1996).

The executive director of UNICEF is appointed by the UN Secretary-General in consultation with the Executive Board. The administration of UNICEF and the appointment and direction of staff are the responsibility of the executive director, under policy directives laid down by the Executive Board, and under a broad authority delegated to the executive director by the Secretary-General. In 1994, the executive director was James P. Grant.

UNICEF has a network of country and regional offices serving more than 138 countries and territories. The organization's headquarters is in New York, and it maintains an important office in Geneva. Regional offices are located in Nairobi, Kenya; Abidjan, Côte d'Ivoire; Santa Fe de Bogotá, Colombia; Bangkok, Thailand; Amman, Jordan; and Kathmandu, Nepal. Offices are also located in Sydney, Australia, and Tokyo.

In 1993, UNICEF employed a total staff of almost 7,000 people serving in 207 locations in 115 countries; 40 percent of staff were in sub-Saharan Africa, 23 percent in Asia, 11 percent in the Americas and Caribbean, and 9 percent in the Middle East and North Africa. The remaining 17 percent served in headquarters locations or in offices recently created in the EEC and the countries of the former Soviet Union. Approximately 2,000 UNICEF staff are in the professional category.

UNICEF has decided to improve the representation of women on its international professional staff to 40 percent by 1994 and to 50 percent by the year 2000. In 1985, only 27 percent of international professional posts were filled by women. By 1993, that figure had been raised to 37 percent.

UNICEF is supported by 34 National Committees, mostly in the industrialized countries, whose more than 100,000 volunteer members raise money through various activities, including the sale of greeting cards. The committees also undertake advocacy, education for development, and information activities. Approximately 25 percent of the organization's 1993 budget was contributed through the National Committees.

In 1994 the National Committees maintained offices in Australia, Austria, Belgium, Bulgaria, Canada, Denmark, Finland, France, Germany, Greece, Hong Kong, Hungary, Ireland, Israel, Italy, Japan, Latvia, Lithuania, Luxembourg, Netherlands, New Zealand, Norway, Poland, Portugal, Republic of Korea, Romania, San Marino, Slovakia, Spain, Sweden, Switzerland, Turkey, United Kingdom, and United States.

Cooperation with Other Agencies

UNICEF collaborates closely with the specialized agencies, including the International Labour Organization (ILO), Food and Agriculture Organization (FAO), the United Nations Education, Scientific and Cultural Organization (UNESCO), and World Health Organization (WHO), as well as with the units of the UN Secretariat concerned with services benefiting children. It also works with the funding agencies and programs of the UN system—such as United Nations Development Programme (UNDP), United Nations Population Fund (UNFPA), World Food Programme (WFP), the World Bank, International Fund for Agricultural Development (IFAD), and United Nations Environment Programme (UNEP)—to exchange information, discuss policies of cooperation affecting the situation of children, and explore potential program collaboration.

At its 1994 annual session, the UNICEF Executive Board reaffirmed its support for the International Child Development Centre in Florence, an action-oriented global think-tank on children's and broader development issues.

Close working relations are maintained with the UN Department of Humanitarian Affairs (DHA) and with the United Nations High Commissioner for Refugees (UNHCR) in emergency relief and aid to refugees, respectively. UNICEF also works with regional development banks and the regional economic and social commissions and with bilateral aid agencies.

Of particular importance is UNICEF's cooperation and collaboration in programs with nongovernmental organizations (NGOs), both national and international. The NGO Committee on UNICEF comprises over 100 international professional and voluntary groups involved with children and either directly or indirectly, through concern with aspects of social development. A roster of international and national correspondent organizations is continuing to grow, particularly from developing countries. Some 400 organizations participate in activities and share information through UNICEF/NGO liaison offices in New York and Geneva. Many of these organizations have become important supporters of UNICEF by providing a channel for advocacy on behalf of children and by participating in fund-raising and in UNICEF programs.

Financing

UNICEF's work is accomplished with voluntary contributions from both governments and nongovernmental sources. Total income in 1993 amounted to US$866 million. Income from governments accounted for 68 percent of this. It was projected that total income in 1994 would amount to US$888 million.

UNICEF's income is divided among contributions for general resources, for supplementary funds, and for emergencies. General resources are the funds available to fulfill commitments for cooperation in country programs approved by the Executive Board, and to meet administrative and program support expenditures. They include contributions from 106 governments, the net income from greeting card sales, funds contributed by the public (mainly through National Committees for UNICEF), and other income. These funds amounted to US$509 million in 1993 and were projected to total US$545 million in 1994.

Contributions for supplementary funds are those sought by UNICEF from governments and intergovernmental organizations to support projects for which general resources are insufficient, or for relief and rehabilitation programs in emergency situations. Supplementary funding in 1993 amounted to US$187 million, and was forecast to reach US$201 million in 1994. Funding for emergencies in 1993 amounted to US$170, and was expected to total US$155 million in 1994.

Countries with Government or NGO Contributions to UNICEF Amounting to US$1 Million or More in 1993
(in thousands of US dollars)

COUNTRY	GOVERNMENTAL CONTRIBUTIONS	NONGOVERNMENTAL CONTRIBUTIONS
Australia	9,260.1	4,056.9
Austria	1,771.3	2,664.6
Belgium	3,894.8	9,521.1
Brazil	n/a	5,076.3
Canada	37,216.6	15,575.7
Chile	1,098.2	61.8
Denmark	33,259.8	2,218.6
Finland	7,513.0	2,954.9
France	10,289.7	34,295.5
Germany	13,152.1	51,963.0
Greece	200.0	3,559.5
Hong Kong	29.2	1,353.2
Iraq	3,140.3	690.7
Ireland	1,314.5	330.1
Italy	33,112.1	25,339.5
Japan	28,993.2	28,005.3
Netherlands	31,427.0	38,101.5
Norway	44,498.4	1,792.5
Portugal	147.3	1,616.9
Republic of Korea	900.0	1,688.2
Spain	2,132.1	16,808.2
Sweden	97,942.8	2,725.5
Switzerland	15,263.5	16,351.4
Turkey	100.0	1,268.5
United Kingdom	16,400.3	11,956.4
United States	122,103.8	31,680.9

Expenditure

UNICEF's total expenditure in 1993 amounted to US$804 million. Expenditure by program sector was as follows:

UNICEF Program Expenditure by Sector, 1993
(in millions of US dollars)

SECTOR	EXPENDITURE
Child health	210
Water supply and sanitation	84
Nutrition	31
Community and family-based services for children and women	57
Formal and nonformal education	72
Planning and project support	127
Emergency relief	223
TOTAL	804

PROGRAMS

Primary Health Care

Through its extensive field network in developing countries UNICEF undertakes, in coordination with governments, local communities, and other partners, programs in health, nutrition, education, water and sanitation, the environment, women in development, and other activities that improve the well-being of children. Emphasis is placed on community-based programs in which people participate actively and are trained in such skills as health care, midwifery, and teaching.

UNICEF facilitates the exchange of programming experience among developing countries, and encourages governments to undertake a regular review of the situation of their children and to incorporate a national policy for children in their comprehensive development plans. It also places emphasis on national capacity building and the use of national expertise wherever possible.

UNICEF provides assistance on the basis of mutually agreed priorities for children in collaboration with the governments concerned. Priority is given to the world's most vulnerable—almost all its resources are therefore invested in the poorest developing countries, with the greatest share going to children under five years old. Currently, UNICEF cooperates in programs in 138 countries: 46 in sub-Saharan Africa; 35 in Latin America; 34 in Asia; 14 in the Middle East and North Africa; and 9 in Central and Eastern Europe and Central Asia.

Health
Immunization
In cooperation with the World Health Organization (WHO), UNICEF supports the expanded Program on Immunization that each year prevents an estimated 3.2 million child deaths from six diseases—diphtheria, measles, poliomyelitis, tetanus, tuberculosis, and whooping cough. In October 1991, both agencies announced that their goal of protecting 80 percent of the world's children before their first birthday had been achieved (compared to less than 5 percent in 1975, when the program was launched). UNICEF and WHO are making an effort to raise immunization coverage for the six diseases to this level in all countries, eliminate neonatal tetanus, and substantially reduce measles deaths and cases by the end of 1995.

Oral rehydration therapy
UNICEF works closely with WHO to control diarrheal dehydration, which is the single largest cause of death among children under five years of age in the developing world. UNICEF-assisted programs for the control of diarrheal diseases promote the manufacture and distribution of prepackaged salts—oral rehydration salt (ORS)—or homemade solutions. The use of oral rehydration therapy (ORT) has more than doubled, from 17 percent in 1985 to 38 percent at present, and is believed to prevent more than a million deaths each year. UNICEF and WHO have set a goal of 80 percent ORT use for children by the end of 1995.

Acute respiratory infections (ARI)
ARI, in particular pneumonia, are the single biggest cause of child mortality in the world and account for over 3 million deaths among children under five years of age in developing countries. UNICEF has adopted a comprehensive approach to control ARI, including helping countries to develop national plans and infrastructures; decentralizing activities to substantial level; training health workers; supporting access to essential drugs and appropriate technological devices; and helping with monitoring and communication.

Safe motherhood
Some 500,000 women die every year from causes related to pregnancy and childbirth. In cooperation with WHO, UNICEF works to reduce maternal mortality by 50 percent by the year 2000, to improve prenatal care, and to ensure safe delivery for all pregnant women and access by all couples to family planning services. It also focuses on information, education, and communication on birthspacing, responsible parenthood, and discouraging early marriage and early pregnancy.

HIV/AIDS
By mid-1992, nearly 1 million children had been born infected with the human immunodeficiency virus (HIV), the majority of whom lived in sub-Saharan Africa. A study by WHO has found that in countries where an HIV/AIDS epidemic began early, 60 percent of those newly infected are between 15 and 24 years of age. It is estimated that in 1993 15 million people were HIV-infected worldwide. By the end of the decade, more than 9 million children will have been orphaned in Africa alone.

UNICEF works closely with governments and supports prevention programs such as youth health and development promotion; school-based interventions; sexual and reproductive health promotion; family and community care; and mass communication and mobilization. It also helps AIDS-infected families and AIDS orphans.

In 1994 the Executive Board supported UNICEF's participation in a proposed joint programme on HIV/AIDS, to be cosponsored by several United Nations agencies.

Nutrition
In 1993, 193 million children were malnourished as a result of frequent bouts of diarrhea and other illnesses, bottle-feeding of infants and poor weaning practices, low birth-weight, infrequent feeding and micronutrient deficiencies. UNICEF fights malnutrition by empowering communities; protecting and promoting breastfeeding and appropriate child feeding practices; controlling the three main forms of micronutrient deficiencies—iron, iodine, and vitamin A; improving nutrition information system; and helping countries to reach consensus as to the causes of malnutrition. It aims to achieve universal salt iodization to prevent iodine deficiency disorders, and to eliminate vitamin A deficiency by 1995.

UNICEF participated in the International Conference on Nutrition held in Rome in December 1992 and contributed to the formulation of the World Declaration on Nutrition and the Plan of Action for Nutrition adopted by the conference. The declaration identified children under five years of age as the group most affected by malnutrition.

Breastfeeding
In coordination with WHO, UNICEF launched in June 1991, a "baby-friendly hospital initiative" to promote breastfeeding. The initiative aims at empowering women to breastfeed by ending the distribution of free and low-cost supplies of infant formula in hospitals and maternity facilities by 1995. As of December 1993, 1,274 hospitals and maternity facilities have become "baby-friendly" by implementing the "Ten Steps to Successful Breastfeeding" recommended by UNICEF and WHO. Baby-friendly hospitals encourage mothers to initiate breastfeeding immediately after birth and to continue exclusive breastfeeding, and they do not accept free and low-cost formula from companies.

Water supply and sanitation
Some 1.3 billion people in the developing world today have no access to safe drinking water and 1.9 billion have no sanitary facilities. As a result, water-borne diseases contribute to the death of about 4 million children every year.

To meet the goals of universal access to safe drinking water and to sanitary means of excreta disposal, and elimination of guinea worm disease by the end of the decade, UNICEF allocates the third largest portion of its income to this sector (for the amount see section on expenditure). In addition to provision of effective low-cost water supply and sanitary services, UNICEF promotes hygiene education and environmental protection. UNICEF is working to eliminate the water-borne guinea worm disease (dracunculiasis) by 1995.

Basic education
In 1994, UNICEF reported that education was in a state of crisis in much of the developing world. Almost 130 million children were denied primary education in 1993, and two-thirds were girls. More than 660 million women were illiterate, a statistic that has real bearing on the chances for the survival and development of children. UNICEF works to improve access to primary educa-

tion and to reduce drop-out rates. It gives priority to the education of girls, with the aim of reducing gender disparities.

UNICEF cosponsored (with UNESCO, UNDP, and the World Bank) the World Conference on Education for All in Jomtien, Thailand, in March 1990 and is making efforts to achieve the goals set by the conference for the 1990s. In March 1993, UNICEF participated in National Conference on Education for All in China, which involved the nine most populous countries: Bangladesh, Brazil, China, Egypt, India, Indonesia, Mexico, Nigeria, and Pakistan. UNICEF, UNESCO, and UNFPA sponsored the Education for All Summit of these countries held in New Delhi in December 1993. These countries account for 75 percent of the world's nearly 1 billion illiterates and children who have no opportunity for primary education.

Urban basic services

Almost half of the developing world's urban dwellers are children whose vulnerability over the past decade has increased with the rapid growth of towns and cities amid economic and environmental crisis and recurring conflict. UNICEF revised its policy in 1993 by focusing on poverty reduction, primary environmental care, rehabilitation, and preventive approaches for urban children in especially difficult circumstances. It also provides advocacy and technical support and emphasizes the need for concerted effort at all levels—national, subnational, and community.

Debt swaps

Since 1989, UNICEF, UNCTAD, and UNDP have assisted in the conversion of foreign debt in developing countries to funds that supplement UNICEF's ongoing contributions to child survival and development in basic education, primary health care, and water and sanitation. The essential feature of the program is that the government concerned agrees to spend local currency on programs for children rather than using its scarce foreign exchange to service the debt.

By the end of 1993, UNICEF had assisted in conversion of debt in six countries: Bolivia, Jamaica, Madagascar, the Philippines, Senegal, and the Sudan. In 1994 UNICEF reported that these conversions generated local funds equivalent to US$29.4 million, retiring US$110.3 million worth of debt. In 1994 requests had been received from a number of West African countries for similar assistance.

At its annual meeting in May 1994, the Executive Board invited the Economic and Social Council to discuss thoroughly the "20/20" concept, proposed by the executive director. This proposal, under wide consideration throughout the UN family of organizations, would assure sufficient resource levels for developing countries by allocating 20 percent of developing countries' expenditures and 20 percent of official development assistance (ODA) to priority human concerns, rather than debt-financing. In 1993, only 10 percent of ODA and annual budgets in developing countries were devoted to priority human concerns.

Emergency relief and rehabilitation

Although most UNICEF activities focus on the "silent" emergencies that claim 35,000 children's lives every day, natural disasters and armed conflicts constitute the main "loud" emergencies that challenge the organization's resources. In any emergency situation, UNICEF works closely with other UN agencies and many nongovernmental organizations (NGOs). Despite the end of the cold war, expenditures for emergency programs continued to grow. Emergency programs accounted for 8 percent of UNICEF's budget in 1988; 19 percent in 1991; and 22 percent in 1992. In 1994 emergency programs absorbed 28 percent of all UNICEF program expenditures for the year.

In 1993 UNICEF provided US$223 million worth of emergency assistance to over 64 countries affected by disasters, including Afghanistan, Angola, Ethiopia, Iraq, Kenya, Liberia, Mozambique, Somalia, the Sudan, and the former Yugoslavia.

It is sad to note that in 1993, three UNICEF staff members lost their lives in the line of duty responding to the needs of children in emergency situations. In 1994 seven UNICEF staff members were killed in violent conflicts in Rwanda alone.

Removal of Land-mines

The scale of the land-mine problem almost defies imagination. Due to the persistence of armed conflicts throughout the world, it is estimated that there is one mine for every 20 children in the world today. The region with the highest concentration of land-mines is Africa, in countries such as Angola, Mozambique, and Somalia, but land-mines are also destroying the lives of children in Asia, Central America, the Middle East, and Central and Eastern Europe.

In September 1993, UNICEF Executive Director James P. Grant called for a total ban on the production, marketing, and use of land-mines. That call gave momentum to a vigorous global campaign by more than 80 NGOs. The General Assembly subsequently passed four resolutions calling for greater assistance for UN mine clearing efforts, a moratorium on the export of antipersonnel mines, a study of measures that could be taken to protect children from the indiscriminate use of all weapons of war, and a review of the 1980 Inhumane Weapons Convention.

Major UNICEF Publications

The State of the World's Children (annual)
The Progress of Nations (annual, first appeared 1993). Ranks the nations of the world according to their achievements for children in health, nutrition, and education, as well as progress in the field of family planning and in women's development.
UNICEF Annual Report
First Call For Children (quarterly newsletter)

OFFICE OF UN HIGH COMMISSIONER FOR REFUGEES (UNHCR)

The UN Relief and Rehabilitation Administration (UNRRA) was established on 9 November 1943, to bring material aid to war-stricken areas of the world. Through its services, some 6 million displaced persons were repatriated. The constitution of a successor agency, broader in scope, the International Refugee Organization (IRO), was approved by the General Assembly on 15 December 1946. In addition to the relief and repatriation assistance provided by UNRRA, the IRO was charged with the protection of refugees and displaced persons and with resettlement responsibilities. The IRO Preparatory Commission became operative on 30 June 1947; by 31 December 1951, when IRO's operational activities ceased, more than 1 million persons had been resettled.

As part of a series of initiatives designed to address refugee problems following the dissolution of the IRO, the General Assembly, in December 1949, agreed on the necessity of setting up a body primarily responsible for the international protection of refugees and the search for durable solutions to their plight. As a consequence, the Office of the UN High Commissioner for Refugees (UNHCR) was established as of 1 January 1951 for a limited period of three years. It was soon evident, however, that international assistance was needed, and as new situations that created refugees have continued to arise, UNHCR's mandate has been renewed by the General Assembly for successive periods of five years.

UNHCR was awarded the Nobel Peace Prize in 1954 and again in 1981.

Organization

The UN High Commissioner for Refugees is elected by the General Assembly on the nomination of the Secretary-General and follows policy directives given to him by the General Assembly. The 47-nation Executive Committee of UNHCR meets annually to review activities in the fields of protection and material assistance, approve assistance projects to be included in the next year's annual program, and provide overall guidance. The high commissioner reports to the committee on the implementation of special tasks that he may have been called upon to carry out—often at the request of the Secretary-General—and on the administration of special trust funds. In July 1994, ECOSOC recommended that the General Assembly increase the membership of the Executive Committee to 50 states.

UNHCR headquarters are in Geneva. At the beginning of 1994, it had offices in over 100 countries and a worldwide staff of some 4,450, of whom more than 3,530 were in the field.

Financing

The financial arrangements made at the creation of UNHCR reflected the fundamental difference between it and the IRO. The IRO's budget was separate from that of the UN, while some of the basic administrative costs of UNHCR are covered by the regular UN budget, since UNHCR is an integral part of the Secretariat, rather than a specialized agency. Its substantive activities in the field of protection and material assistance, however, depend entirely on voluntary contributions.

At the outset, UNHCR was not allowed to appeal to governments for funds without the express authorization of the General Assembly. The first funds of any magnitude put at the high commissioner's disposal came from the Ford Foundation in 1952 in the form of a grant of US$2.9 million (later increased to US$3.1 million) for a pilot program of projects intended to promote the local settlement of some 100,000 refugees in Europe through such measures as low-rent housing, small loans, vocational training, and rehabilitation of the handicapped. Subsequently, in 1954, the General Assembly authorized the high commissioner to appeal to governments for a four-year US$16 million program oriented toward permanent solutions and modeled on the Ford experimental undertaking. The target was eventually reached through US$14.5 million in contributions by governments and over US$2 million by private organizations.

Clearing refugee camps in Europe was the main objective of UNHCR at this time, and the funds needed to finish this task were raised to a large extent through World Refugee Year (1959/60), a campaign that extended to 100 countries and areas.

In 1957, UNHCR's capacity to react effectively to unexpected situations was enhanced when the General Assembly authorized the high commissioner to establish an emergency fund not to exceed US$500,000. This innovation grew out of the experience of 1956, when some 200,000 refugees from Hungary crossed into Austria and Yugoslavia within a matter of weeks, prompting the high commissioner to appeal for funds for the emergency. By 1993, the emergency fund's ceiling had been raised to US$25 million, with up to US$8 million available for a single emergency in a given year.

With the exception of a very limited subsidy from the United Nations regular budget (which is used exclusively for administrative costs), UNHCR's assistance programs are funded by voluntary contributions from governments, intergovernmental and nongovernmental organizations, and individuals. These so-called "voluntary funds" finance all UNHCR assistance programs worldwide. UNHCR's annual voluntary funds expenditure has risen rapidly over the last 25 years, reaching US$1.3 billion in 1993.

The High Commissioner's Responsibilities

The high commissioner's primary responsibility is international protection. In addition, he promotes durable solutions to the problems of refugees through voluntary repatriation, local inte-

gration, or resettlement in a third country. Whatever the field of activity, he and his staff are always guided by humanitarian and strictly nonpolitical considerations. UNHCR's ability to adhere to this policy over the years since its inception in 1951 has led the General Assembly to extend the scope of its material assistance activities, in many cases to persons who do not necessarily meet the definition of refugees contained in the high commissioner's statute. This definition describes refugees as persons who, owing to well-founded fear of being persecuted for reasons of race, religion, nationality, or political opinion, are outside their country of nationality and are unable or unwilling, because of such fear, to avail themselves of the protection of that country. In recent years, UNHCR has increasingly been called on to help not only refugees but also persons uprooted by man-made disasters and displaced either outside or within their country of origin. However, UNHCR's competence does not extend to refugees already receiving help from another UN organization, notably the Arab refugees from Palestine who are cared for by UNRWA (see separate section below).

From its outset, UNHCR's work was intended to be undertaken jointly with other members of the international community. UNHCR draws on the expertise of other United Nations organizations in matters such as food production (FAO), health measures (WHO), education (UNESCO), child welfare (UNICEF), and vocational training (ILO). It also cooperates closely with the World Food Programme in providing basic food supplies to refugees, and with the World Bank and the International Fund for Agricultural Development (IFAD) in implementing projects that aim to promote self-reliance. Over the decades, the most sustained and devoted service to the cause of refugees has been provided by nongovernmental organizations (NGOs). Over 200 NGOs cooperate in UNHCR's relief and legal assistance programs. In 1993, the Nansen Medal, awarded for outstanding service to the cause of refugees, recognized the valuable collaboration of one such NGO, Médcins sans Frontières (Doctors without Borders).

Since refugees no longer enjoy the protection of the countries they have fled, they must rely on the international community to provide it. The main vehicle for international protection is the 1951 Convention Relating to the Status of Refugees and its 1967 protocol, which lays down minimum standards for the treatment of refugees by countries that have acceded to it. By April 1994, 118 states were party to both the convention and its protocol; an additional eight had signed one or the other.

One of the most important provisions of the 1951 convention is that refugees must not be sent back to a country where they may face persecution on grounds of race, political opinion, religion, nationality, or membership in a particular social group (the principle of *non-refoulement*). The convention also defines the rights of refugees in the country of asylum with respect to such matters as the right to work, education, access to courts, and social security. Moreover, it provides for the issuance of travel documents by the country of residence to compensate for the fact that refugees are not in a position to use their national passports.

By its statute and under the 1951 convention, UNHCR is given specific responsibility for supervising the application of the provisions of the convention. It is also available to supply technical advice to governments on appropriate legal and administrative measures to give effect to the stipulations of the convention.

Another important legal instrument concerning refugees is the Convention Governing the Specific Aspects of Refugee Problems in Africa, adopted by the Organization of African Unity in 1969. This convention, which came into force on 20 June 1974, emphasizes that the granting of asylum is a peaceful and humanitarian act that should not be regarded as unfriendly by any member state. A similar provision can be found in the Declaration on Territorial Asylum adopted by the General Assembly in December

1967 (see the section on Other Declarations in the chapter on Human Rights).

Asylum is the key aspect of the protection work of the high commissioner's office. A conference of plenipotentiaries convened by the General Assembly in 1977 "to consider and adopt a convention on territorial asylum" failed to achieve its objectives, and the absence of such a convention remains a gap in the legal basis for the protection of asylum-seekers.

In 1975, UNHCR undertook new duties in the field of protection on a provisional basis, following the entry into force on 13 December of the 1961 Convention on the Reduction of Statelessness. Under the terms of the convention, stateless persons may apply to national authorities to have nationality accorded to themselves or to their children or may ask UNHCR's assistance in presenting a claim.

In the same year, UNHCR's Executive Committee established a Subcommittee on International Protection to study in greater detail some of the more technical aspects of the legal protection of refugees. The subcommittee has addressed such questions as the problem of large-scale influxes of refugees and displaced persons and the responses of the international community to such mass movements, the rescue and safety of asylum-seekers at sea, the reunion of refugee families, various legal aspects of the granting of asylum and refugee status, the situation of refugee children, refugee women and the issuance of travel documents for refugees, security from military and other armed attacks on refugee camps and settlements, and UNHCR's involvement with internally displaced persons..

MATERIAL ASSISTANCE ACTIVITIES

UNHCR's material assistance activities include emergency relief, assistance in voluntary repatriation or local integration, and resettlement through migration to other countries, as well as social services.

Africa

UNHCR's involvement in Africa dates from 1957, when thousands of people fled from the fighting in Algeria to Morocco and Tunisia. Working in conjunction with the League of Red Cross Societies, UNHCR provided both immediate and long-term assistance and helped to organize the repatriation of some 200,000 refugees in 1962, after the cessation of hostilities.

By 1967 there were an estimated 750,000 refugees in Africa, many of them victims of the struggles for independence in Guinea-Bissau, Angola, and Mozambique. In 1974–75, UNHCR assisted in repatriating many of these refugees to their newly independent countries. A large-scale repatriation and rehabilitation program involving some 200,000 refugees and displaced persons in Zimbabwe was coordinated by UNHCR in 1980, and a major repatriation to Chad was completed in 1982.

By the early 1990s, Africa harbored over 6 million refugees, or around one-third of the global refugee population. During the previous decade, refugee situations persisted or erupted in the Horn of Africa, West Africa and southern Africa. In some cases, such as for Mozambican refugees in Malawi and in the Horn, these situations were exacerbated by drought.

A number of refugees were able to return home, notably Namibians, Ethiopians, and Ugandans in the Sudan, and Somalis in Ethiopia. The repatriation of some 1.7 million Mozambicans got under way in mid-1993. In the Horn, a cross-border approach was put into action aimed at creating conditions conducive to the voluntary repatriation of refugees and safe return of internally displaced persons. This approach has been characterized by the use of "quick impact projects" (QIPs). QIPs entail the execution of small-scale projects, such as the repair and reconstruction of essential facilities; the provision of livestock, seed, and processing machinery; and the establishment of small-scale

businesses. The projects are designed to bridge the gap between relief and development by helping returnees and their communities regain self-sufficiency. In certain areas such as North-West Somalia and Mozambique, however, repatriation has been bedeviled by the presence of land-mines in the areas of return.

In 1993, violent upheavals in the central African state of Burundi drove some 580,000 persons to seek refuge in neighboring countries. The following year, bloodshed engulfed neighboring Rwanda, creating, by May 1994, over 800,000 refugees. UNHCR launched emergency assistance programs to cope with refugees from both situations.

Principal countries of asylum at 31 December 1993 included the Sudan, which hosted some 745,200 mainly Ethiopian and Eritrean refugees; Malawi, whose population of 713,600 mainly Mozambican refugees was, as a proportion of the national population, the largest in the world; Guinea, with 656,700 mainly Liberian refugees; and Tanzania, with its mix of Burundi, Mozambican, Rwandese, and Zairian refugees.

UNHCR assistance in Africa in 1993 totaled US$325.1 million.

Southwest Asia, North Africa, and the Middle East

In August 1974, following events in Cyprus, the high commissioner was designated to coordinate humanitarian relief for 241,300 people who had been uprooted and displaced. In the absence of a political settlement, aid is still being channeled to the island.

Events in Afghanistan in the late 1970s and the 1980s provoked a tremendous exodus from the country. Despite the unprecedented repatriation of 1.5 million Afghans in 1992, at the beginning of 1993 over 4 million Afghans remained in exile (2.5 million in Iran and 1.5 million in Pakistan). Hopes for their continued repatriation were stymied by a resurgence of fighting in Afghanistan in April 1992. In that year, Afghanistan itself became a country of asylum when some 60,000 Tajiks escaping from their country's civil war found sanctuary in northern Afghanistan.

In 1991, the Gulf War led to a situation of mass displacement, creating, by May 1991, some 1.4 million refugees in Iran and 400,000 on the border with Turkey. UNHCR mounted a massive emergency assistance program for these groups, as well as for internally displaced Kurds in northern Iraq. By the end of 1991, most of the Iraqis in Iran and on the Turkish border had returned home.

UNHCR assistance in South West Asia, North Africa, and the Middle East in 1993 totaled US$115.4 million.

Asia and Oceania

In May 1971, the high commissioner was appointed "focal point" for UN assistance to millions of Bengali refugees from East Pakistan (later Bangladesh) in India. More than US$180 million in cash, goods, or services was channeled through this focal point, mainly for emergency relief in India but also for the repatriation operation that began early in 1972, following the creation of Bangladesh. The operation involved the transfer of non-Bengalis from Bangladesh to Pakistan and of Bengalis from Pakistan to Bangladesh. By the time it was concluded in July 1974, 241,300 people had been moved, nearly all by air, across the subcontinent in either direction.

Another major crisis erupted in mid-1978, when nearly 200,000 refugees from the Arakan state of Burma flooded into Bangladesh. UNHCR was again designated as coordinator of UN assistance. Following an agreement concluded with the Burmese government in July 1978, repatriation began in November of that year. The UNHCR program included assistance to the returnees once they were back in their country of origin.

Early in 1975, the conflict that for almost three decades had involved Vietnam, Cambodia, and Laos came to an end with changes of regime in the three countries of Indochina. Since that time, over 2.8 million Vietnamese, Cambodians, and Lao have left their homes and sought asylum in neighboring countries. These mass movements reached their peak in 1979, when some 393,560 people arrived by boat or overland in various asylum countries throughout the region, and in early 1980, when additional large numbers of Kampucheans moved into the border area with Thailand to escape hostilities in their own country.

UNHCR has undertaken to provide temporary assistance for Indochinese in various countries of Southeast Asia, to ask governments to extend permanent resettlement opportunities, and to facilitate voluntary repatriation where feasible. In addition, large numbers of displaced persons in the Thai-Kampuchean border area have been assisted by other UN agencies and the ICRC. By the beginning of 1994, some 2.7 million Indo-Chinese Refugees and displaced persons had been resettled, repatriated, or integrated locally, while around 88,000 remained in camps throughout the region.

Under the terms of a memorandum of understanding concluded with the Vietnamese government in May 1979, UNHCR has been coordinating a program of orderly departure from Vietnam. A further coordinating role has been played by UNHCR in the funding of a major program to combat piracy against refugee boats and other vessels in the South China Sea.

The Comprehensive Plan of Action for Indo-Chinese Refugees (CPA) was adopted in June 1989 with the objective of discouraging clandestine departures; assuring access to status determination procedures for all asylum-seekers; providing resettlement opportunities for bona fide refugees; and ensuring a safe and dignified repatriation for those not determined to be refugees. The CPA had the effect of dramatically reducing the numbers of Lao and Vietnamese asylum-seekers; the number of Vietnamese asylum-seekers, for example, dropped from 71,364 in 1989 to a mere 55 in 1992.

The repatriation of Cambodians from Thailand, which began in March 1992, resulted in the return home of some 387,000 refugees, or nearly the whole caseload in Thailand. Returnees and the communities receiving them are being assisted, in some cases, by means of QIPs (see the section on Africa, above), to consolidate their reintegration.

In 1991–92, around 250,000 mainly Muslim refugees fled Myanmar to Bangladesh. At the request of the government of Bangladesh, UNHCR began assisting this group in February 1992. At the beginning of 1994, following negotiation between the governments of Myanmar and Bangladesh, and UNHCR, preparations were under way for their repatriation.

Some 140,000 Sri Lankan Tamils sought safety from their country's communal violence in the Indian State of Tamil Nadu. Since 1992, some 40,000 of them have been repatriated. In Sri Lanka, UNHCR assists both the returnees and internally displaced persons.

UNHCR assistance in Asia and Oceania in 1993 amounted to us$144.4 million.

Latin America and the Caribbean

Originally, Latin America was a primary resettlement area for European refugees. However, the events in Chile in September 1973 involved UNHCR in major assistance measures for Latin American refugees. UNHCR had to contend first with the problem of several thousand refugees of various nationalities in Chile, providing relief, care, and maintenance and helping establish "safe havens" where they could live until their resettlement could be arranged.

In addition to ongoing assistance to Chilean refugees, UNHCR was called on to assist an increasing number of Nicaraguans in Costa Rica, Honduras, and Panama in late 1978. By 1979, the number of Nicaraguan refugees receiving such assistance had risen to 100,000. However, following the change of government in Nicaragua in July 1979, voluntary repatriation began, and UNHCR launched a special program to facilitate both the return itself and the rehabilitation of returnees through assistance in areas such as agriculture, health, and housing.

In the early 1980s, Central America became an area of increasingly grave concern to UNHCR. By the end of 1980, 80,000 refugees from El Salvador had sought refuge in neighboring countries. The International Conference on Central American Refugees (CIREFCA), which was convened in May 1989, proved to be of considerable help in facilitating a convergence towards durable solutions for uprooted populations. The move towards democratization in the region, the success of regional peace initiatives, and the CIREFCA process resulted in a reduction in refugee numbers as a result of attainment of durable solutions. In Haiti, however, the overthrow of the country's democratically elected president in September 1991 led to an exodus of Haitians seeking asylum in the region. Despite UNHCR's plea to governments in the region to uphold the principle of *non-refoulement*, Haitian asylum-seekers continued to be interdicted on the high seas.

UNHCR assistance in the Americas and the Caribbean in 1993 amounted to us$38.1 million.

Europe

When UNHCR came into existence in 1951, it inherited responsibility for some 120,000 persons still living in refugee and displaced persons' camps, mainly in the Federal Republic of Germany, Austria, Italy, and Greece. The great majority of these persons had been uprooted during World War II, primarily through the Nazi policies of removing people from occupied territories for forced labor and forcibly shifting populations for racial reasons. Particularly deplorable was the situation of the children born in the camps. Clearance of those camps was long delayed, mainly for lack of funds. Eventually, some 100,000 people, refugees since World War II, were settled as a result of UNHCR's programs.

New movements of refugees have, however, continued to occur. One of the largest of these was the result of the Hungarian crisis in 1956. The high commissioner was called on, in October 1956, to coordinate the activities of governments and voluntary organizations on behalf of the 200,000 Hungarians who sought refuge in Austria and Yugoslavia. From October 1956 until the end of 1959, about 180,000 Hungarian refugees arrived in Austria, and 19,000 in Yugoslavia. The total movement involved 203,100 persons. Of these, 18,000 eventually chose to return to Hungary, 9,600 elected to remain in Austria, 65,400 went to other European countries, and 107,400 emigrated overseas; the whereabouts of 2,700 are unknown.

In November 1991, UNHCR received a mandate from the United Nations Secretary-General to act as the lead United Nations agency to provide protection and assistance to those affected by conflict in the former Yugoslavia, then estimated at half a million people. By the beginning of 1994, this number had jumped to almost 3.8 million. UNHCR continued to assume prime responsibility in favor of this group for logistics/transport, protection/legal assistance, food monitoring, shelter, and other sectors.

The war between Armenia and Azerbaijan in the early 1990s created some 900,000 displaced Azeris and 300,000 displaced ethnic Armenians. The military conflict in Georgia created around 300,000 refugees and displaced persons. UNHCR, in coordination with the United Nations Department of Humanitarian Affairs and other UN agencies, operated emergency response programs in all three countries.

During 1993, UNHCR total expenditure in Europe amounted to us$585.5 million.

UN RELIEF AND WORKS AGENCY FOR PALESTINE REFUGEES IN THE NEAR EAST (UNRWA)

The plight of Palestine refugees has been a serious concern of the UN ever since the Arab-Israeli War of 1948. When a cease-fire came into effect early in 1949, hundreds of thousands of Arabs who lived in the territory that is now Israel were stranded on the other side of the armistice line from their homes. The Arab states claim that the refugees were driven out by the Israelis or fled in fear of reprisals. Israel, on the other hand, asserts that the Arab states told the Arab population to evacuate the area temporarily so that their armies could more easily drive the Israelis into the sea. (For the political background, see the section on the Middle East in the chapter on International Peace and Security.)

Emergency relief was given the refugees at first by the ICRC, the League of Red Cross Societies, and the American Friends Service Committee, using money and supplies provided by the temporary UN Relief for Palestine Refugees, established in December 1948. In December 1949, the General Assembly created a special agency, the United Nations Relief and Works Agency for Palestine Refugees in the Near East (UNRWA), to provide relief and works projects in collaboration with the local governments. In the following year, the General Assembly extended UNRWA's mandate to June 1952 and instructed it to carry out development projects that would enable the refugees to be absorbed into the economy of the region. As originally conceived, UNRWA was a large-scale but definitely temporary operation, to be terminated by the end of 1952. The General Assembly accordingly asked Israel and its neighbors to secure "the permanent reestablishment of the refugees and their removal from relief." In carrying out programs of resettlement, however, all parties concerned, including UNRWA, were to act without prejudice to the rights of those refugees who "wished to return to their homes and live in peace with their neighbors." These were to "be permitted to do so at the earliest practicable date"; those who chose not to do so were to be compensated for their losses.

These goals were not achieved by 1952 and have not been met since then. Large-scale development projects to induce the refugees to leave the camps and enable them to become self-supporting in their host countries were approved by the General Assembly but never realized. Since 1952, UNRWA's mandate has been repeatedly extended, most recently until 30 June 1996.

UNRWA extends its activities over an area of more than 100,000 square miles. It deals with six governmental authorities: Jordan, Lebanon, Syria, and Egypt; the government of Israel as occupying power in the West Bank and the Gaza Strip; and the Palestinian Authority as it assumes powers and responsibilities in the Gaza Strip and the Jericho Area and the remainder of the West Bank. In March 1994 UNRWA was providing essential services to 2,940,181 Palestine refugees.

Organization

UNRWA is a subsidiary organ of the General Assembly, and its policy and functions are determined by that body. It is headed by a commissioner-general, who is assisted by a 10-nation Advisory Commission composed of Belgium, Egypt, France, Japan, Jordan, Lebanon, Syria, Turkey, the United Kingdom, and the United States. The commissioner-general is appointed by the UN Secretary-General in consultation with the governments of the Advisory Commission.

Headquarters are in Vienna and in Amman, Jordan; field offices are located in Jerusalem, Gaza, Amman, Beirut, and Damascus. UNRWA has liaison offices at UN headquarters in New York and in Cairo. Each field office is headed by a representative of the commissioner-general, who is responsible for UNRWA activities in each area. The organization employs over 20,000 local staff, mainly Palestinian refugees, and about 180 international staff.

Financing

UNRWA depends almost entirely on voluntary contributions from governments and the European Union. As of January 1992, UNRWA adopted a biennial budgetary cycle. The regular budget for 1994–95 amounts to US$632.3 million, of which US$552.8 million is in cash and US$79.5 million is in kind. Over 81 percent of the agency's budget is devoted to its three operational programs, in great part to pay educational and medical staff. Administrative costs account for 10.2 percent of the budget. At the beginning of 1994, the agency faced a cash shortfall of over US$21 million.

In recent years, UNRWA has faced cash crises that have been resolved by budget reductions, early payment of pledges by donor countries, and special contributions. The ongoing strife in Lebanon since 1975 and the Israeli invasions of 1978 and 1982 have seriously affected the agency's operations. In June 1982, UNRWA mounted an emergency relief operation, and in 1987, after further violence in Lebanon, it appealed for US$20.6 million in emergency aid.

Number and Geographic Distribution of Refugees

In March 1994, 3,006,787 refugees were registered with UNRWA. Of this total, 1,193,539 were registered in Jordan, 643,600 in the Gaza Strip, 504,070 in the West Bank, 338,290 in Lebanon and 327,288 in the Syrian Arab Republic. Of the nearly 1.2 million refugees in Jordan, about 40 percent fled there from the West Bank and Gaza during and immediately following the June 1967 war or are descendants of those who fled.

For relief purposes, UNRWA defines a "Palestine refugee" as a person whose normal residence was Palestine for a minimum of two years immediately before the outbreak of the Arab-Israeli conflict in 1948 and who, as a result of this conflict, lost both home and means of livelihood. To be eligible for UNRWA assistance, such a person must be registered and in need and must have taken refuge in Jordan, Lebanon, Syria, or the Gaza Strip, the areas contiguous to Israel in which the agency operates. Children and grandchildren of registered refugees also are generally eligible for assistance.

Services Provided

UNRWA's three principal areas of activity are education, health services, and relief and social services.

Education. UNRWA-UNESCO schools for refugee children have been in operation in Jordan, Lebanon, Syria, and the Gaza Strip since 1951. In 1986–87, 349,000 pupils were enrolled in UNRWA-UNESCO elementary and preparatory schools, and another 115,000 refugee children attended state and private schools. By 1994 education accounted for 47 percent of the agency's budget. During 1993/94 there were 398,648 students in 641 UNRWA schools staffed by 12,158 staff. Seventy-seven schools were located in Lebanon, 109 were located in Syria, 201 in Jordan, 100 in the West Bank, and 154 in the Gaza Strip. Eight vocational training centers run by UNRWA offered 5,646 places. In 1993/94, UNRWA awarded 795 scholarships for study at Arab universities.

Health Services. Under an agreement with UNRWA, WHO has been responsible since 1949 for the technical direction of the agency's health services. WHO also provides certain senior medical staff, including the agency's chief medical officer. Preventive and curative health services, as well as health education and environmental sanitation programs, are very extensive. At the end of 1993, there were 120 health units, 105 diabetes clinics, 68 dental clinics, and 108 family planning clinics. UNRWA medical units registered nearly 6 million patient visits during 1993. Health services accounted for about 21 percent of the agency's budget during this period.

Relief and Social Services. The agency delivered food rations, emergency shelter, and welfare programs for about 167,000 of the poorest refugees. UNRWA's social services program operated 71 women's centers, serving more than 5,000 women. It also ran 18 community-based rehabilitation centers for disabled people. These services consumed 13.7 percent of UNRWA's budget in 1994/95.

Although it was once a major part of UNRWA's program, the general distribution of food rations has ceased. Since 1982, UNRWA has distributed food only to special hardship cases, which include widows, orphans, the aged, the physically and mentally handicapped, and the chronically ill.

Emergency shelter was a large part of the agency's early work. At that time, some 30,000 tents provided the principal shelter for the 30 percent of the refugees living in the camps. As funds and the availability of suitable sites permitted, the agency gradually replaced the tents with huts. At first, many refugees objected to using a shelter that they regarded as permanent, but this objection was gradually overcome. By the end of 1959, all the tents in UNRWA camps had been replaced by huts. In 1967, 10 emergency tent camps were established in eastern Jordan and Syria for some 110,000 of the refugees and other persons displaced as a result of the Six-Day War. The tents have since been replaced by shelters. By 1994 roughly one-third of Palestinian refugees were living in 59 refugee camps.

The Promise of Peace in the Gaza Strip and the West Bank
In 1987, a Palestinian uprising in the Israeli-occupied territories of the West Bank and Gaza Strip (the *Intifadah*) created problems in administering UNRWA programs there. Schools in the West Bank have been closed for extended periods since 1988, and UNRWA services in both territories frequently were interrupted when curfews were imposed on camps.

Following the signing of the Declaration of Principles by the Palestine Liberation Organization (PLO) and the government of Israel in September 1993, creating a structure for the gradual implementation of self-rule in the Gaza Strip and Jericho, UNRWA launched a major effort to improve services and infrastructure for Palestine refugees. The agency has identified nearly US$165 million in projects so far for its Peace Implementation Program (PIP). Nearly US$100 million of this amount will be spent in the Gaza Strip and West Bank alone. As funding becomes available, UNRWA plans to spend another US$65 million on projects to improve facilities and services for refugees in Jordan, Lebanon, and the Syrian Arab Republic.

YOUTH
Concern for youth has been expressed within the UN system ever since its inception and particularly since the adoption by the General Assembly in 1965 of the Declaration on the Promotion Among Youth of the Ideals of Peace, Mutual Respect and Understanding Between Peoples. In that declaration, the General Assembly stressed the importance of the role of youth in today's world, especially its potential contribution to development, and proposed that governments give youth an opportunity to take part in preparing and carrying out national development plans and international cooperation programs.

Other recommendations made to member states by the General Assembly relate to the preparation of youth, through education, for full participation in all aspects of life and development; health policies and programs to ensure that young people are able to take advantage of opportunities open to them; the adoption of all possible means to increase employment for youth; the opening up of channels of communication between the UN and youth organizations; and measures aimed at promoting human rights and their enjoyment by youth.

The World Youth Assembly, held at UN headquarters in July 1970, was the first international youth convocation organized by the UN. It brought together some 650 young people to express their views on issues relating to world peace, development, education, and the environment and to discuss ways in which they could support the UN.

In 1979, the General Assembly decided to designate 1985—the twentieth anniversary of the 1965 Declaration—as International Youth Year, with the three themes of participation, development, and peace. The objectives of the year were to bring about widespread awareness of the situation of young people and of their problems and aspirations, and to engage them in the development process. International Youth Year resulted in the endorsement by the General Assembly of guidelines for strategies and activities in favor of youth at the national, regional, and international levels in coming years.

In observance of the tenth anniversary of International Youth Year, in 1995, the General Assembly will devote a plenary meeting to the subject of youth, and will set forth goals for a world youth program of actions towards the year 2000 and beyond. Its principal objective will be to provide a global framework for national and regional action. The plan of action will be drafted by the UN secretariat following the submission of proposals by member states, organizations of the UN system, and nongovernmental organizations.

A trust fund established for International Youth Year and renamed the UN Youth Fund is used to support projects involving young people in the development of their countries.

AGING AND THE ELDERLY
In the 75 years between 1950 and the year 2025, the world elderly population will have increased from 8 percent to 14 percent of the total global population, or 1.2 billion persons. While the total world population will have grown by a factor of a little more than three, the elderly will have grown by a factor of six and the very old by a factor of 10. The developing countries are projected to age more quickly in the coming decades, and are concerned by two factors: a weak institutional infrastructure for accommodating the elderly, and the uncertainty that families will be able to continue providing traditional care for the elderly.

In 1948, Argentina first presented a draft declaration on old age rights to the General Assembly, which referred it to ECOSOC. ECOSOC requested the Secretary-General to draft a report on the matter, and in 1950 he submitted a report entitled "Welfare of the Aged: Old Age Rights." However, the rapid change in the world's population structure was not evident in 1950, and an interval of 20 years elapsed before Malta tabled another initiative on the agenda of the General Assembly in 1969. This initiative was followed throughout the 1970s and led to the convening of the World Assembly on Aging in 1982.

In 1973, the General Assembly considered a comprehensive report that noted the demographic increase in the absolute and relative size of the older populations of the world (a trend that was expected to continue because of medical advances and decreases in birth and death rates) and estimated that the number of persons 60 years of age or over throughout the world would double between 1970 and the year 2000. The General Assembly recommended guidelines to governments in formulating policies for the elderly, including development of programs for the welfare, health, and protection of older people and for their retraining in accordance with their needs, in order to maximize their economic independence and their social integration with other segments of the population.

In 1978, the General Assembly decided to convene a world assembly for the purpose of launching "an international action program aimed at guaranteeing economic and social security to older persons," as well as opportunities for them to contribute to national development. The General Assembly later decided that the conference should also consider the interrelated issue of the aging of whole populations.

The World Assembly on Aging, held in Vienna in July–August 1982, was attended by representatives of more than 120 countries. It adopted an international plan of action, both to help the aging as individuals and to deal with the long-term social and economic effects of aging populations. Recommendations contained in the plan of action covered (1) the need to help the elderly lead independent lives in their own family and community for as long as possible, instead of being excluded and cut off from all activities of society; (2) the importance of giving the elderly a choice in regard to the kind of health care they receive and the importance of preventive care, including nutrition and exercise; (3) the need to provide support services to assist families, particularly low-income families, to continue to care for elderly relatives; and (4) the need to provide social-security schemes, to assist the elderly in finding (or returning to) employment, and to provide appropriate housing. The plan of action also included recommendations for meeting the needs of particularly vulnerable persons, such as elderly refugees and migrant workers.

The Commission for Social Development, which is entrusted with reviewing implementation of the plan of action every four years, noted in 1985 that by the year 2025, more than 70 percent of persons over 60 years of age would live in developing countries. In 2025, experts estimate that the elderly population of the world will number 1.2 billion, six times more than the 200 million elderly worldwide in 1950. The commission listed priorities for action, including the creation of national committees on aging, coordinated planning, strengthening of information exchange, training, research, and education programs.

In 1988, the UN established the International Institute on Aging in Valetta, Malta, to conduct training, research, collection and publication of data, and technical cooperation in the field of aging. In 1990, the General Assembly designated 1 October as the International Day for the Elderly. In 1991, the General Assembly adopted a set of 18 United Nations "Principles for Older Persons" clustered under five themes: independence, participation, care, self-fulfillment, and dignity. The principles mandate that older persons should have the opportunity to work and to determine when to leave the work force; remain integrated in society and participate actively in the formation of policies that affect them; have access to health care to help them maintain the optimum level of physical, mental, and emotional well-being; be able to pursue opportunities for their full development; and be able to live in dignity and security.

In 1992, the General Assembly gave its patronage to the privately-created Banyan Fund Association's World Fund for Aging, in Torcy, France, which assists developing countries, at their request, in activities aimed at formulating and implementing policies and programs on aging. Also in 1992, the General Assembly devoted four special plenary meetings in October to a conference on aging. It issued a Proclamation on Aging (resolution A/47/5), which reaffirmed its previous resolutions and established the year 1999 as the International Year of the Elderly "in recognition of humanity's demographic coming of age and the promise it holds for maturing attitudes and capabilities in social, economic, cultural and spiritual undertakings, not least for global peace and development in the next century." In its Resolution 47/86, the General Assembly adopted a set of global targets on aging for the year 2001 as a practical strategy for countries to provide for the needs of the elderly.

The United Nations Trust Fund for Aging became operational in 1983, and supports training, income-generation, policy-formulation, and needs assessments projects. Governments, nongovernmental organizations, private organizations, and individuals can contribute to the fund, which is managed by the director general of the United Nations Office at Vienna. By January 1991, the United Nations Trust Fund for Aging had disbursed over US$1 million in seed money grants to 42 projects.

DISABLED PERSONS

Under the charter principles of the dignity and worth of the human being and the promotion of social justice, the General Assembly has acted to protect the rights of disabled persons. In 1971, it adopted the Declaration on the Rights of Mentally Retarded Persons, and in 1975, the Declaration on the Rights of Disabled Persons (see the section on Other Declarations in the chapter on Human Rights). In 1976, the General Assembly decided to proclaim 1981 as International Year of Disabled Persons, and it called for a plan of action for the year at the national, regional, and international levels.

The year's purpose, and its theme, was the promotion of "full participation and equality," defined as the right of disabled persons to take part fully in the life and development of their societies, to enjoy living conditions equal to those of other citizens, and to have an equal share in improved conditions resulting from socioeconomic development. Other objectives of the year included increasing public understanding of disability and encouraging disabled persons to organize themselves to express their views effectively.

During the year, national committees were set up in more than 140 countries to map out plans of action to implement the objectives of the year. Regional seminars—for Asia and the Pacific, Africa, Latin America, Western Asia, and Europe—held during the year discussed regional cooperation on behalf of disabled persons. At the international level, organizations of the UN system and other intergovernmental organizations, as well as nongovernmental organizations (NGOs), discussed ways in which the world community could aid the disabled through technical cooperation and other means.

The year's activities were followed by the General Assembly's adoption, in 1982, of a World Program of Action Concerning Disabled Persons, aimed at continuing long-term programs at the national, regional, and international levels. To provide the necessary time frame for implementation of the program, the General Assembly proclaimed the period 1983–92 as the UN Decade of Disabled Persons.

The World Program of Action has proved to be a valuable guide for improving the social, economic, and physical conditions of disabled persons by defining disability issues in the context of human rights and recommending measures aimed at equalizing opportunities for the full participation of disabled persons in society. The program has offered a new approach on disability, representing a step forward in social thinking on such aspects as prevention of disabilities, rehabilitation, equalization of opportunities, and participation of disabled persons in all aspects of life.

During the first five years of the Decade of Disabled Persons, 1983–87, there was a significant growth in the number of organizations of disabled persons throughout the world, which were able to articulate and identify their needs. Governments, NGOs, and regional bodies reported an increased awareness by disabled persons of their rights. There was also an increase in research and exchange of information on the prevention of disabilities and the rehabilitation of the disabled, on the mobility of the disabled, and on their participation in leisure and sports activities.

At the same time, obstacles impeding the implementation of the World Program of Action were identified, including the demographic increase in the number of disabled persons worldwide because of poverty, malnutrition, wars, civil unrest, and deteriorating social and economic conditions in many countries. Because of these obstacles, the General Assembly drew up a set of priority activities to ensure the effective implementation of the program of action during the remaining half of the decade.

Although several specialized agencies in the UN system had prepared guidelines and manuals on key disability issues, those guidelines were not incorporated into national programs in the majority of countries. In order to make the World Program of

Action more operational, the General Assembly called for a long-term strategy setting out standard rules on the equalization of opportunities for disabled persons. In 1990, ECOSOC, in its Resolution 1990/26, authorized the Commission for Social Development to establish a working group to create a set of standard rules for submission to the General Assembly in 1993. This new instrument offered governments clear policy options on how to implement measures for full equalization of opportunities for disabled persons.

In 1992, the last year of the decade, Secretary-General Boutros Boutros-Ghali reported that the 1981 Year for Disabled Persons was so successful in getting the issue of disability and the concerns of disabled people on national agendas that had come to be regarded as a milestone in the long struggle of disabled people for equal rights. Four plenary sessions of the General Assembly in October 1992 were devoted to a celebration and evaluation of the progress made during the decade. Preceding that event, an International Conference of Ministers Responsible for Disability met in Montreal to seek consensus on a framework for action to continue the momentum generated by the decade.

It was clear that the major achievement of the decade was increased public awareness of disability issues among policy-makers, planners, politicians, service providers, parents, and disabled persons themselves. For example, information on disability issues is now included in censuses and 55 countries now maintain statistical information on disability. In 1960, such information was available in only 15 countries. Several European countries set up computerized information networks to share disability-related information. It was also observed that nongovernmental organizations dedicated to the welfare of disabled people were able to increase their influence and gain the respect of their communities. The Voluntary Fund for the United Nations Decade of Disabled Persons had supported 161 projects by the end of 1991, for a total of approximately US$2.9 million.

However, despite its relative success, by the end of the decade, it was estimated that 300 million people with disabilities live in developing countries and that only 1 percent of these have access to basic health, education, and adequate sanitation services.

THE FAMILY—SOCIETY'S BUILDING BLOCK
Although many of the UN's resolutions and instruments deal tangentially with the needs of families, the General Assembly's first formal recognition of the family unit's special status as the basic building block of civilized society came in 1989 when it passed resolution A/44/82 (1989) proclaiming 1994 as the first International Year of the Family. The theme of the year was "Family: resources and responsibilities in a changing world," and its motto was "Building the smallest democracy at the heart of society." In 1993, the General Assembly declared 15 May 1994 the first International Day of Families, to be celebrated annually thereafter.

The General Assembly sought to raise the awareness of governments at the national, local, and regional levels about the threat posed to families and the possible consequences to society of the fragmentation and disintegration of the family unit. The erosion of social safety nets around the world had placed tremendous burdens on families. Abject poverty, which affected 20 percent of the world population, contributed to the destruction of families, for example, when members left the family unit to search for employment. Studies showed that within the space of a few decades the traditional extended family had shrunk to the nuclear family and finally to the single-parent family. In the United Kingdom alone, half of all births in 1990 were to single women. UN agencies called for recognition of the family's contribution towards achieving human development, alleviating poverty, and providing health care, nutrition, education, shelter, and employment for family members. The UN called for governments to formulate "family-sensitive" national policies and to assess how decisions would affect families.

Rather than try to narrowly define the family, the General Assembly took the broadest possible approach, encouraging celebration of the vast diversity observed in families throughout the world. A study showed that average family size varied from 2.2 members in Sweden to 7.1 members in Iraq. In all industrial countries except the former Soviet Union, the average household size shrank between 1970 and 1990. In the United States the average household shrank from 3.1 persons in 1970 to 2.6 persons in 1990. On the other hand, households grew in size in Africa, south Asia, and the Middle East. In Algeria, for example, average household size grew from 5.9 persons in 1966 to 7 persons in 1987. Despite the many cultural and economic differences in families around the world, according to the Secretary-General, some elements of an international consensus regarding families emerged:

- The family is the natural and fundamental group unit of society and is entitled to protection by society and the state;
- Various concepts of the family exist in different social, cultural, and political systems, but it is recognized that families are basic to the social structure and development of all societies. It is also recognized that families around the world exhibit many common problems.
- Gender equality, women's equal participation in employment, and shared parental responsibilities are essential elements of modern family policy;
- Families are the fullest reflection, at the grass-roots level, of the strengths and weaknesses of the social and developmental environment; and
- Families, as basic units of social life, are major agents of sustainable development at all levels of society, and their contribution is crucial for its success.

Besides four regional preparatory meetings and two nongovernmental events held in 1993 to prepare for the International Year of the Family, the General Assembly held an International Conference on Families in October 1994. The secretariat for the International Year, based in Vienna, coordinated technical cooperation projects in Africa and the countries of the former Soviet Union. A world forum of nongovernmental organizations (NGOs) held in Malta in late 1993 called for the UN and its member nations to enter into an ongoing process of building a family-friendly society. It also called for the elaboration of a declaration on the rights and responsibilities of families in the follow-up to the International Year of the Family.

Some of the most important existing international instruments that refer to the family are:

- the 1948 Universal Declaration of Human Rights;
- the 1966 International Covenant on Economic, Social and Cultural Rights;
- the 1979 Convention on the Elimination of All Forms of Discrimination Against Women;
- the 1981 Declaration on the Elimination of All Forms of Intolerance and of Discrimination Based on Religion or Belief; and
- the 1989 Convention on the Rights of the Child.

CRIME PREVENTION AND CRIMINAL JUSTICE
The work of the UN in the field of crime prevention and criminal justice has two main purposes: to lessen the human and material costs of crime and its impact on socioeconomic development and to formulate international standards and norms in crime prevention and criminal justice and promote their observance.

By 1990, United Nations statistics showed that worldwide incidence of assaults had risen from around 150 per 100,000 population in 1970 to nearly 400 per 100,000 population in 1990. The incidence of thefts had more than tripled in the same period. In addition, the number of adults held in legal detention worldwide increased from around 1 million in 1975 to 1,100,000 in 1980, a 10 percent jump. Another UN study showed that developed countries were spending an average of 2 to 3 percent of their budgets on crime control, while developing countries were devoting an average of 9 to 14 percent of their precious national resources to crime control. Traffic in illicit drugs was estimated to total US$500 billion a year. The intertwined expansion of transnational organized crime and the traffic in illicit drugs, and their link to international terrorism, provided the most powerful arguments for international cooperation.

Historical Background

Evidence of systems of criminal justice date back to the dawn of human civilization. Clay tablets from 2400 BC listing a code of conduct have been unearthed in Syria. The ancient civilization of Sumeria left an elaborate set of laws dating back to the twenty-first century BC. Standards for imposing penalties on criminals were handled more informally, rarely being codified into law before the advent of the modern era. The earliest form of international cooperation between sovereign nations may have been efforts to control piracy on the high seas. However, it was the nineteenth century that saw the development of widespread concern about the growth of urban crime, and the proliferation of reformatories and penal institutions.

The First International Congress on the Prevention and Repression of Crime was held in London in 1872 to consider the proper administration of prisons, possible alternatives to imprisonment, modes of rehabilitating criminals, treatment of juvenile offenders, extradition treaties, and the "means of repressing criminal capitalists." These subjects continue to challenge the international community at the end of the twentieth century. The London congress established the International Prison Commission with a mandate to collect penitentiary statistics, encourage penal reform, and convene international conferences every five years. The IPC established an affiliation with the League of Nations and, in 1935, was renamed the International Penal and Penitentiary Commission (IPPC). For 75 years, the IPPC did invaluable work in the collection of research materials, however; at the 1935 congress, it became dominated by adherents of the Nazi government in power in Germany. During the war years a substantial part of its funding came from the Axis powers, and it became a publicist for Fascist theories on the biological roots of crime and draconian measures for its control. When the United Nations was established at the close of World War II, it declined to accept affiliation with the IPPC. The UN did, however, decide that the control and prevention of crime would be one of its areas of concern.

United Nations Activities

On 1 December 1950, by its resolution 415(V), the United Nations dissolved the IPPC and officially assumed its functions. These functions include the convening of international congresses every five years, the formulation of policies, and the development of international programs of action. To discharge these responsibilities, the General Assembly, in 1950, authorized the UN Congress on the Prevention of Crime and the Treatment of Offenders to be convened every five years.

In its resolution 415(V), the General Assembly also created an Ad Hoc Advisory Committee composed of seven experts to formulate programs for study and action in the field of crime prevention and treatment of offenders. This ad hoc committee eventually became the Committee on Crime Prevention and Control (CCPC), established in 1971 in response to the 1970 crime congress (held in Kyoto, Japan), which broadened considerably the scope of issues relating to criminal justice policy. The CCPC had 27 members who were nominated by their governments and elected by ECOSOC. It was charged with coordinating the efforts of UN bodies and prepared for the international crime congresses. It frequently drafted proposed texts for international standards and guidelines concerning criminal justice policy.

In November 1991, a Ministerial Summit, attended by 114 state ministers, was held in Versailles, France, and called for creation of a new UN crime prevention and criminal justice program. The General Assembly responded by transforming the CCPC into a functional commission of ECOSOC: the Commission on Crime Prevention and Criminal Justice. The new 40-member commission held its first session in April 1992 at Vienna. It is charged with developing, monitoring, and reviewing the UN's program on crime prevention and mobilizing support from member states. It coordinates the activities of the UN's regional and interregional institutes on crime prevention and criminal justice. It also is responsible for preparing for UN crime congresses.

The Crime Prevention and Criminal Justice Branch

This branch of the UN Secretariat, headquartered in Vienna, is the UN's central repository of technical expertise in matters of crime prevention, criminal justice, criminal law reform, and major criminological concern. It prepares studies and reports for the quinquennnial congresses and for the Commission on Crime Prevention and Criminal Justice. The branch collects and analyzes statistics and provides technical assistance to member states and regional institutes. It prepares periodic country-by-country surveys of crime trends and criminal justice policies. The branch issues two regular publications: *The International Review of Criminal Policy,* a journal of applied criminology published annually since 1952, and the *Criminal Justice Newsletter,* which disseminates information on United Nations activities in the field, published twice a year.

The Criminal Justice Branch also works closely with various regional centers, a research institute and an international computer information network. The international standards proposed by the UN are meant as springboards to for appropriate national action. Differences in history, culture, economic structures, and governmental institutions dictate against a wholesale adoption of UN guidelines and standards. Regional centers can take into account the differing cultures and traditions of geographically linked countries and can better guide and harmonize national policies.

The *United Nations Interregional Crime and Justice Research Institute (UNICRI)* is based in Rome. It was founded in 1968, in response to concerns voiced by the 1965 Stockholm crime conference, under the name United Nations Social Defence Research Institute. UNICRI is housed in the heart of the old section of Rome, in an edifice built at the order of Pope Innocent X as a model prison for the replacement of dungeons used in the Middle Ages. The Italian government modernized the building's interior and made it available to UNICRI.

UNICRI carries out field research in conjunction with local institutions and experts. The institute is often charged with specific research projects in preparation for international crime congresses. It also holds international seminars and workshops. Its experts execute technical cooperation missions to assist member countries in implementing specific projects. It has a small but highly specialized library on criminology, penology, and related fields of law, sociology, and psychology. It also maintains a collection of United Nations and Council of Europe documents concerning criminal justice affairs. It publishes major research papers and an annual catalog of relevant research from around the world. UNICRI has computerized its *World Directory of Criminological Institutes,* and it has created the software and user manual for a computerized international expert roster. It has taken the lead in developing a UN global information network (see UNCJIN, below). UNICRI is financed by the UN Social Defense Trust Fund, a voluntary fund maintained by donations from governments and other sources. By mid-1989, UNICRI had received contributions and pledges amounting to approximately us$2,484,000.

The *African Regional Institute for the Prevention of Crime and the Treatment of Offenders (UNAFRI)* was established in January 1987, in temporary quarters at Addis Ababa, Ethiopia. It is now based in Kampala, Uganda. It organizes training courses and research and brings together criminal justice officials and development planners from all over Africa. It has conducted a feasibility study on the establishment of a regional, computerized information network to link up with the United Nations Criminal Justice Information Network (UNCJIN) (see below). UNAFRI operates under the auspices of the Economic Commission for Africa with financial assistance from the United Nations Development Program.

The *Asian and Far East Institute for the Prevention of Crime and the Treatment of Offenders (UNAFEI)* was established in 1961 and is based in Tokyo, Japan. It provides facilities for training courses and sends its staff to countries within the region to conduct classes in cooperation with host governments. UNAFEI publishes a regular newsletter and studies such as *Forms and Dimensions of Criminality in Asian Countries, Alternatives to Imprisonment in Asia,* and *Criminal Justice in Asia—the Quest for an Integrated Approach.* Although UNAFEI was initially a joint venture between the United Nations and the government of Japan, financial assistance from the UN was discontinued in 1970. The director of UNAFEI is assigned by the government of Japan in consultation with the UN.

The *European Institute for Crime Prevention and Control (HEUNI)* was established in 1981 in an agreement between the United Nations and the government of Finland. It is based in Helsinki. Its funds are provided by the government of Finland with assistance from other governments. HEUNI conducts training seminars and holds expert meetings to study regional issues in depth. Its expert meetings are often convened in order to offer a European perspective on draft documents of UN criminal justice policy. HEUNI has been actively involved with plans for a global UN information system on crime and criminal justice. Its publications include: *Criminal Justice Systems in Europe, The Role of the Victim of Crime in European Criminal Justice Systems,* and *Non-Custodial Alternatives in Europe.*

The *Latin American Institute for the Prevention of Crime and the Treatment of Delinquency (ILANUD)* was established in 1975 and is based in San José, Costa Rica. ILANUD devises practical strategies taking into account UN recommendations in criminal justice. It organizes regular training courses, workshops, seminars, and conferences for personnel in the criminal justice systems of Latin American governments. In 1987 it established an Agrarian Justice Program that aimed at improving procedures governing agricultural production. ILANUD also implemented a computerized data base in its documentation center. ILANUD was established with financial assistance from the United Nations, but now is supported mainly by the government of Costa Rica.

In 1989, the Criminal Justice Branch the *United Nations Criminal Justice Information Network (UNCJIN)* began operating under the auspices of the Criminal Justice Branch. UNCJIN is a computer network accessible by modem and gopher technology on the Internet. The UNCJIN gopher is resident on the computer system of the State University of New York at Albany. UNCJIN is funded in part by the United States Bureau of Justice Statistics, the State University of New York at Albany, and the Research Foundation of the State University of New York. UNCJIN's goal is to establish a worldwide network to disseminate and exchange information concerning criminal justice and crime prevention

issues. Information available through the UNCJIN gopher is constantly evolving and expanding. In 1994 it included: criminal justice profiles of more than 120 countries; basic constitutional documents of countries; summaries of the latest United States Supreme Court decisions; international criminal justice statistics from the UN World Crime Surveys; United States Bureau of Justice Statistics reports; the entire CIA Factbook; and an annotated list of publication outlets in criminal justice and criminology. One can also search the on-line library catalogs of major criminal justice and law libraries around the world, examine all the major United Nations rules and guidelines on criminal justice, and access other UN on-line resources.

UN Congresses on Prevention of Crime and Treatment of Offenders

Participants in UN crime congresses include criminologists, penologists, and senior police officers as well as experts in criminal law, human rights, and rehabilitation. Representatives of UN member states and of intergovernmental and nongovernmental organizations also attend. Eight crime congresses were held between 1955 and 1990. The ninth congress is scheduled to be held in Tunis, the capital of Tunisia, in 1995.

The *first congress,* held in Geneva in 1955, was attended by delegates from 51 governments and representatives from the ILO, UNESCO, WHO, the Council of Europe, and the League of Arab States. The topics of the first congress reflected the pressing concerns of Europeans recovering from the turmoil of World War II. Many delegates had experienced brutality and deprivation while incarcerated in their own countries by the occupying Fascist powers. It adopted 95 standard minimum rules for the Treatment of Prisoners, which set out what is accepted to be good general principle and practice in the treatment of prisoners and are also intended to guard against mistreatment. An additional rule, adopted in 1977, provides that persons arrested or imprisoned without charge are to be accorded the same protection as persons under arrest or awaiting trial and prisoners under sentence. The success of the Standard Minimum Rules paved the way for many other international models, standards, norms, and guidelines touching on every aspect of criminal justice. The prevention of juvenile delinquency was also considered at the congress, since so many children were growing up abandoned or orphaned.

The *second congress,* held in London in 1960, was attended by representatives of 70 governments and delegates from 60 nongovernmental organizations. In all, there were 1,131 participants. The second congress dealt with a wider range of issues than the first congress. It considered the growing problem of juvenile delinquency, as well as questions of prison labor, parole, and after-care. The addition of new member states to the United Nations required the expansion of the largely European perspective that dominated the first congress. The congress analyzed crime and criminal justice in relation to overall national development. Experts warned that economic improvement alone was not a one-way street leading away from crime. Tumultuous economic growth could lead to a greater prevalence of crime.

The *third congress,* held in Stockholm in 1965, addressed the ambitious theme of "Prevention of Criminality." Topics on the agenda included a continuation of the discussion on social change and criminality; social forces and the prevention of crime; community-based preventive action; measures to curtail recidivism; probation policies; and special preventive and treatment programs for young adults. A total of 1,083 participants, representatives of 74 governments and 39 nongovernmental organizations, attended the third congress. The influence of the increasing numbers of developing member nations made itself felt in 1965. The congress asserted that developing nations should not restrict themselves to mechanically copying criminal justice institutions developed in Western countries.

The *fourth congress*, held in Tokyo in 1970, was the first to take place outside of Europe. Although the number of participants declined slightly, to 1,014, the number of governments represented rose to 85. The fourth congress was convened under the slogan "Crime and Development," reflecting the dramatic increase in the number of developing countries who had become members of the UN during the 1960s. It stressed the need for crime control and prevention measures (referred to as "social defense policies") to be built into development planning. The third congress expanded the theme of community-based prevention, noting the successful utilization of civic involvement in the host nation, Japan. The congress also investigated the nation-by-nation implementation of the Standard Minimum Rules for the Treatment of Prisoners, relying on results of a questionnaire submitted to member states before the opening of the congress.

The *fifth congress*, held in Geneva in 1975, the number of nations represented increased to 101 and the participation of the specialized agencies was augmented by the presence of Interpol and the Organisation for Economic Cooperation and Development (OECD). The congress's theme was "Crime Prevention and Control: the Challenge of the Last Quarter of the Century." Among the many topics considered were:

- changes in the form and dimension of criminality at national and transnational levels;
- crime as a business and organized crime;
- the role of criminal legislation, judicial procedures, and other forms of social control in the prevention of crime;
- the addition of crime-prevention activities to the traditional law enforcement roles of police;
- the implementation of the Standard Minimum Rules for the Treatment of Offenders;
- the economic and social consequences of crime;
- alcohol and drug abuse;
- victim compensation as a substitute for retributive criminal justice.

The fifth congress was responsible for two documents that rank in importance with the standard minimum rules: the "Declaration on the Protection of All Persons from Being Subjected to Torture and Other Cruel, Inhuman or Degrading Treatment or Punishment," which was adopted by the General Assembly by its resolution 3452(XXX); and the "Code of Conduct for Law Enforcement Officials," which has been called a Hippocratic oath for police professionals. The code was adopted by the General Assembly in 1979. The declaration on torture was given binding legal form in 1984, when the General Assembly adopted a convention on the same subject (see the section on Other International Human Rights Conventions in the chapter on Human Rights).

The *sixth congress*, held in Caracas in 1980, was the first UN crime congress to be hosted by a developing nation and the first held in the western hemisphere. Delegations from 102 nations, the ILO, WHO, the Council of Europe, Interpol, the League of Arab States, the Organization for African Unity, and the Pan-Arab Organization for Social Defence attended. The congress's theme was "Crime Prevention and the Quality of Life." It considered the following matters:

- new trends in crime and appropriate prevention strategies;
- the application of juvenile justice measures ;
- offenses by the powerful, who quite often stand beyond the effective reach of the law;
- deinstitutionalization of correction measures;
- the role of UN guidelines and standards in criminal justice;
- capital punishment;
- the importance of international cooperation.

A working group of experts from Latin America and the Caribbean contributed an innovative approach on the classification of crimes. It suggested that the scope of criminal law statutes should be broadened to include willful actions harmful to the national wealth and well-being—destruction of the ecology, or participation in drug trafficking, or trafficking in persons. By way of corollary, the working group recommended a decrease in the number of statutes covering petty crimes or crimes that had little socially destructive effect.

The *seventh congress*, held in Milan in 1985, adopted the Milan Plan of Action as a means of strengthening international cooperation in crime prevention and criminal justice. The plan was approved later the same year by the General Assembly, which also approved international instruments and principles adopted by the Milan Congress. These were the UN Standard Minimum Rules for the Administration of Juvenile Justice (the Beijing Rules), the Declaration of Basic Principles of Justice for Victims of Crime and Abuse of Power, Basic Principles on the Independence of the Judiciary, and a Model Agreement on the Transfer of Foreign Prisoners.

The Beijing Rules aim at promoting juvenile welfare to the greatest possible extent, thereby minimizing the necessity of intervention by the juvenile justice system. The rules set minimum standards for the handling of juvenile offenders, enumerate the rights of juveniles, and include principles for adjudication and disposition of juvenile offenses and for institutional and noninstitutional treatment of juvenile offenders.

The Declaration of Basic Principles of Justice for Victims of Crime and Abuse of Power defines "victims" as persons who, individually or collectively, have suffered harm, including physical or mental injury, emotional suffering, economic loss, or substantial impairment of their fundamental rights, through acts or omissions that are in violation of criminal laws or constitute violations of internationally recognized norms relating to human rights. It sets forth the rights of such victims and their families to restitution, compensation, and social assistance.

The Basic Principles on the Independence of the Judiciary stipulate that the judiciary shall have jurisdiction over all issues of a judicial nature and that judges shall decide matters before them impartially, without any restrictions, improper influences, or interference. The right of everyone to be tried by ordinary courts or tribunals is reaffirmed.

The Model Agreement on the Transfer of Foreign Prisoners is aimed at promoting the social resettlement of offenders by facilitating the return of persons convicted of crimes abroad to their country of nationality or residence to serve their sentence at the earliest possible stage.

The Milan Congress also considered questions relating to human rights in the administration of justice and to the prevention of juvenile delinquency and domestic violence.

The *eighth congress* was held in Havana, Cuba, from 27 August to 7 September 1990. The congress was attended by 1,400 participants from 127 countries, five intergovernmental organizations, and 40 nongovernmental organizations. Its overall theme was "International cooperation in crime prevention and criminal justice for the twenty-first century." The congress considered five topics: (1) crime prevention and criminal justice in the context of development; (2) criminal justice policies in relation to problems of imprisonment, other penal sanctions, and alternative measures; (3) effective national and international action against organized crime, terrorist criminal activities; (4) prevention of juvenile delinquency and protection of the young; and (5) United Nations norms and guidelines in crime prevention and criminal justice.

The eighth congress adopted a number of new instruments and resolutions that the General Assembly promptly approved. These included model treaties on extradition, mutual assistance in criminal matters, the transfer of proceedings in criminal matters, and the supervision of offenders conditionally sentenced or conditionally released. Other instruments passed were:

- A model treaty for the prevention of crimes against a peoples' cultural heritage;
- Basic Principles on the Use of Force and Firearms by Law Enforcement Officials;
- Basic Principles on the Role of Lawyers;
- Guidelines on the Role of Prosecutors;
- United Nations Standard Minimum Rules for Non-custodial Measures (the Tokyo Rules);
- Basic Principles for the Treatment of Prisoners;
- Guidelines for the Prevention of Juvenile Delinquency (the Riyadh Guidelines); and
- Rules for the Protection of Juveniles Deprived of Their Liberty.

The conference also adopted resolutions on computerization, prevention of urban crime, protection of the environment, corruption in government, racketeering and illicit trafficking in narcotic drugs and psychotropic substances, computer-related crimes, measures against drug addiction, organized crime and terrorism, domestic violence, and the instrumental use of children in criminal activities. The congress also requested that guidelines be prepared on the management of prisoners infected with human immunodeficiency virus (HIV) and those with acquired immunodeficiency syndrome (AIDS).

The eighth congress called for the elaboration of an effective international crime and justice program to assist countries in combating problems of national and transnational crime. An important outcome was the creation of the Commission on Crime Prevention as a functional commission of ECOSOC.

INTERNATIONAL COOPERATION FOR NARCOTIC DRUGS CONTROL

"...Let us resolve that at this special session of the General Assembly, words lead to action and that this action leads to success. Drug abuse is a time bomb ticking away in the heart of our civilization. We must now find measures to deal with it before it explodes and destroys us."

Secretary-General Javier Pérez De Cuéllar
Remarks to the 17th Special Session of the General Assembly
20 February 1990

Until the end of the nineteenth century, trade in narcotics was considered a legitimate business. Misuse of addiction-producing substances—opium, coca leaf, and Indian hemp—was thought to be the result of ingrained habits in particular areas of the world. The problem was considered a domestic one. However, modern technology and the expansion of transport and world trade introduced a new dimension. An increasing number of alkaloids and derivatives were being produced from opium and coca leaves and easily distributed. In addition, a large number of psychotropic substances (depressors of the central nervous system such as barbiturates, stimulants of the central nervous system such as amphetamines, and hallucinogens such as lysergic acid diethylamide, or LSD) were developed and their consumption increased enormously; hence, problems once considered local became global.

The UN exercises functions and powers relating to the worldwide control of narcotic drugs in accordance with a number of international treaties concluded since 1912, when the first International Opium Convention was signed at The Hague. By 1994, the majority of countries were parties to one or more of the treaties. The international control system is based on the cooperation of the states that are bound by these treaties in controlling the manufacture and sale of drugs within their jurisdiction. The treaties stipulate that these states are bound to adopt appropriate legislation, introduce necessary administrative and enforcement measures, and cooperate with international control organs as well as with each other.

Narcotics Control Under the League of Nations

The League of Nations Covenant provided that League members should "entrust the League with the general supervision over agreements with regard . . . to the traffic in opium and other dangerous drugs." The first League Assembly created an Advisory Committee on Traffic in Opium and Other Dangerous Drugs to assist and advise the League's Council in its supervisory tasks in the field. The League established a Permanent Central Board, later renamed the Permanent Central Narcotics Board, to supervise the control system introduced by the second International Opium Convention, which came into force in 1928. The board was composed of independent experts, to whom League members were required to submit annual statistics on the production of opium and coca leaves and on the manufacture, consumption, and stocks of narcotic drugs and quarterly reports on the import and export of narcotic drugs. Specific governmental authorizations were required for every import and export of narcotic drugs.

The Convention for Limiting the Manufacture and Regulating the Distribution of Narcotic Drugs, signed at Geneva in 1931, created a new technical organ, also composed of independent experts, the Drug Supervisory Body. The aim of the 1931 convention was to limit world manufacture of drugs to the amount actually needed for medical and scientific purposes.

The Convention for the Suppression of the Illicit Traffic in Dangerous Drugs, signed at Geneva in 1936, called for severe punishment of illicit traffickers in narcotics and extradition for drug offenses.

A protocol signed on 11 December 1946 (and which entered into force on 10 October 1947) transferred to the United Nations the functions previously exercised by the League of Nations under the pre–World War II narcotics treaties.

The United Nations and International Drug Control
Historical Background
The functions of the League's Advisory Committee were transferred to the United Nations Commission on Narcotic Drugs (CND), established in 1946 as a functional commission of the Economic and Social Council. Over the years a number of bodies were created to carry out the work of the United Nations in the field of narcotics control, including the International Narcotics Board (INCB), the Division of Narcotic Drugs (part of the United Nations Secretariat), and the United Nations Fund for Drug Abuse Control (UNFDAC). In addition, several specialized agencies, notably the World Health Organization (WHO) and the United Nations Educational, Scientific and Cultural Organization (UNESCO), also were called on to contribute to the war on illegal drugs.

By the mid-1980s the General Assembly recognized that, while several important treaties had been elaborated (see under The Treaty System below), the system had not produced the desired result. Illicit traffic in drugs had achieved crisis proportions all over the world, threatening the stability of governments and regional peace and security in Africa, Southeast Asia, Latin America, and the Caribbean. In 1984, the General Assembly requested the CND to elaborate a new treaty to explicitly treat the problem of illegal drug trafficking. In 1985 the General Assembly decided to convene an International conference on Drug Abuse and Illicit Trafficking in Vienna in June 1987. That Conference adopted a Declaration and a Comprehensive Multidisciplinary Outline of Future Activities in Drug Abuse Control.

However, the 1987 annual report of INCB revealed that drug-trafficking syndicates now held enough financial power to challenge the elected authorities of some South American countries. In addition, the spread of Acquired Immune Deficiency Syndrome (AIDS) and the HIV virus had assumed pandemic proportions, due in large part to the sharing of infected needles by drug abusers. The INCB noted that international drug traffic was financed and organized by criminal organizations with international links and with accomplices in financial circles who helped "launder" money obtained through the drug trade. Member states proclaimed 26 June 1988 as the first International Day Against Drug Abuse, to begin to focus public attention on the worldwide scope of the problem.

In February 1988, a plenipotentiary conference of the United Nations member states was convened in Vienna. It adopted the 1988 United Nations Convention Against Illicit Trafficking in Narcotic Drugs and Psychotropic Substances (see under The Treaty System below), which was immediately ratified by 43 nations. However, for lack of sufficient ratifications and accessions, the convention would not come into effect until December 1990.

The Global Programme of Action Against Drug Abuse

In November 1989, the General Assembly expressed its alarm at the slow pace of accessions holding up the entry into force of the 1988 convention. To consolidate international efforts, the General Assembly held a four-day special session (its seventeenth special session) in February 1990 to adopt a Political Declaration (A/RES/S-17/2) affirming the determination of the international community to band together to fight drug trafficking. In its declaration the General Assembly recognized the links between drug trafficking and the economic and social conditions of the countries producing drugs. It also voiced its concern about the link between drug trafficking and international terrorism, and the threat posed by transnational crime organizations that corrupted elected governments. The member states resolved to "protect mankind from the scourge of drug abuse and illicit trafficking in narcotic drugs and psychotropic substances...." They reaffirmed their commitment to support the international effort to eradicate drug trafficking both financially and by bringing national laws into line with the various United Nations treaties on narcotics control. The document also noted that international cooperation in restraining drug trafficking should be conducted in accordance with the principles of national sovereignty embodied in the United Nations charter. The General Assembly concluded the document by adopting a Global Programme of Action and declaring the period 1991–2000 the United Nations Decade Against Drug Abuse.

The 100-paragraph Global Programme of Action contained proposals for worldwide cooperation to stem the rising tide of drug abuse. Some of its provisions were based on the Multidisciplinary Outline mentioned above, and included:

- Raising national priorities for drug abuse prevention and reduction programs;
- Commissioning an analysis of the social causes generating drug demand;
- Providing UN financial support to prevent drug abuse by children, and the use of children in the drug trade in developing countries;
- Having the UN act as a global information clearinghouse on treatment and rehabilitation of drug addicts;
- Using high resolution satellite imagery and aerial photography (with the agreement of producing countries) to identify illegal narcotic cultivation;
- Convening an international conference to elaborate ways to prevent the diversion of the chemicals and substances used to process the raw materials of illicit drugs;

- Developing international mechanisms should be developed to prevent drug money laundering and to confiscate funds and property acquired with drug money;
- Promoting through the UN the exchange of information among states on the flows of drug money; coordinating anti-drug operation training.

On 15 February 1990, just before the General Assembly's special session, the United States, Bolivia, Colombia, and Peru met in Cartagena, Colombia, and signed the Cartagena Declaration, agreeing to cooperate to stem the flow of drugs to the United States. The four countries, representing the world's largest consumer (the United States) and the largest suppliers of illicit cocaine, agreed to wage a war on drugs on three fronts: demand reduction, consumption reduction, and supply reduction. The United States agreed to financially support alternative development to replace the coca-growing economy in Peru and Bolivia and to fund emergency social programs. The multilateral cooperation begun at the Cartagena summit was extended in 1992 at a summit held in San Antonio, Texas, to include Mexico in the international struggle against drug trafficking organizations.

1990 World Ministerial Summit

The government of the United Kingdom, in association with the United Nations, organized a three-day World Ministerial Summit to Reduce the Demand for Drugs and to Combat the Cocaine Threat. The summit was held in London from 9–11 April 1990, and was attended by 650 delegates, most at the ministerial level, from 124 countries. The summit adopted the London Declaration committing the nations to giving higher priority to prevention and reduction of illicit drug demand at national and international levels. The London summit produced a consensus that, whereas producing countries had previously felt that drug abuse did not threaten their own populations, developing countries now realized that drug abuse had become a worldwide phenomenon cutting across national boundaries, class, race and income levels.

Some of the London Declaration's provisions include:

- Drug abuse prevention and treatment should be part of national health, social, education, legal and criminal justice strategies;
- Drug education should be developed at all school stages;
- Prevention programs in the workplace should be developed and implemented;
- Mass media campaigns against drugs should be used;
- The United Nations Fund for Drug Abuse Control (later the United Nations International Drug Control Program, see below) should be provided the funds to devise a strategy for the Andean sub-region, where most of the world's coca is grown and illicitly processed into cocaine.
- Nations that had not yet done so should ratify or accede to the 1988 United Nations Convention Against Illicit Traffic in Narcotic Drugs and Psychotropic Substances, and, in the meanwhile, they should try to apply its terms provisionally.

In October 1993, China, Laos, and Myanmar (referred to as the "Golden Triangle") signed a Memorandum of Understanding, expanding existing cooperation on drug control, in cooperation with the UNDCP. The countries aimed to eliminate opium poppy cultivation through economic and social development programs; curb traffic in narcotic drugs and essential chemicals used in manufacturing drugs; and implement programs to reduce the demand for illicit drugs.

Despite the growing alarm of nations, the phenomenon of illicit drug trafficking and drug abuse continued to rise. The 1994 report of the INCB stated that the worldwide drug menace had broken past geographic limits and outgrown its traditional classification as a criminal or social issue and penetrated the spheres of international politics and world economics. Drug organizations had become illegal transnational corporations. In 1994 the CND concluded that UNDCP should, once again, review existing international drug control instruments and activities in order to identify ways to strengthen the system and make appropriate changes. In June 1994, the International Conference on Preventing and Controlling Money Laundering and the Use of the Proceeds of Crime was held in Italy (see Crime Prevention and Criminal Justice, above).

UN Bodies Concerned With Narcotics Control
The United Nations International Drug Control Programme
In December 1990, the General Assembly requested that the Secretary-General merge the various units of the organization that were concerned with drug control into a single, integrated program. In 1991, the United Nations International Drug Control Programme (UNDCP) integrated the functions of the Division of Narcotic Drugs, UNFDAC, and the secretariat for the INCB. Headquartered in Vienna, UNDCP is charged with the responsibility of coordinating and leading United Nations drug control activities. UNDCP is headed by an executive director. The program publishes a quarterly *Bulletin on Narcotics* as well as information letters, scientific notes, and publications on drug abuse control activities. UNDCP's budget comes from both the UN regular budget (US$14.8 million for 1994–95) and from the voluntary Fund of UNDCP (US$187.8 million for 1994–95).

UNDCP's *Treaty Implementation and Legal Affairs Division* monitors and ensures the implementation of the various conventions, decisions, and resolutions entrusted to the United Nations (see The Treaty System below). This division provides secretariat services to the expert meetings, the CND, INCB, ECOSOC, and the General Assembly as required.

The *Division for Operational Activities* manages UNDCP technical cooperation programs worldwide. It assists governments and other institutions in the development and implementation of national, subregional, and regional programs to reduce illicit cultivation, production, manufacture, traffic and abuse of drugs. The division has four regional offices based in Vienna for: Asia and the Pacific; Europe, North America, and the Middle East; Africa; and Latin America and the Caribbean. In 1994, it also had 20 field offices.

The *Technical and Advisory Services Branch* provides technical expertise to CND, expert groups, and INCB. It assists in identifying and formulating technical cooperation projects that will be managed by the Division for Operational Activities. The Technical and Advisory Services Branch keeps a roster of international specialists on drug-related subjects and stays in contact with research institutions and universities for the latest findings in the field of drug abuse.

The Commission on Narcotic Drugs (CND)
The 53-member Commission on Narcotic Drugs is the main policy-making body within the United Nations system for all issues pertaining to international drug abuse control. It analyzes the world drug abuse situation and develops proposals to strengthen international efforts. It is one of the functional commissions of the Economic and Social Council. In addition, it prepares such draft international conventions as may be necessary; assists the council in exercising such powers of supervision over the application of international conventions and agreements dealing with narcotic drugs as may be assumed by or conferred on the council; and considers what changes may be required in the existing machinery for the international control of narcotic drugs and submits proposals thereon to the council. In addition, the commission has special functions under the 1961 Single Convention on Narcotic Drugs (see under The Treaty System, below), such as placing drugs under international control and making recommendations for the implementation of the aims and provisions of the

convention, including programs of scientific research and the exchange of scientific or technical information. The commission also reviews implementation of the Global Programme of Action, provides policy guidance to UNDCP, and monitors its activities. The commission meets annually in regular or in special sessions.

The International Narcotics Control Board (INCB)
The International Narcotics Control Board is responsible for promoting compliance with the provisions of drug control treaties. It was created by the 1961 Single Convention on Narcotic Drugs as a successor to the Permanent Central Board and the Drug Supervisory Body. The 13 members of the board are not government representatives but experts acting in their private, individual capacities. The board has important functions to perform under the treaties. It watches over statistics of drug production, manufacture, trade, and consumption and also over the estimates needed for the coming year that states are required to furnish to it; if a state does not send estimates, the board makes them itself. The board may request any state to explain a condition that in its view indicates an improper accumulation of narcotic drugs. It may even recommend, in case of difficulties created by a country for the international control, that other states stop the shipment of drugs to that country. A most effective means of ensuring compliance is publicity: the reports of the board (and of other international bodies) ensure that the public is made aware of any situation that may contribute to the spread of drug abuse.

Other United Nations Bodies Cooperating with UNDCP
The *United Nations Interregional Crime and Justice Research Institute (UNICRI)* was formerly known as the United Nations Social Defence Research Institute. UNICRI carried out a four-year research study funded by UNDCP on the interaction between criminal behavior and drug abuse and on control measures adopted in individual countries. It conducts research, surveys, and workshops on the criminal aspects of drug abuse for UNDCP. UNICRI is more fully described above, under Crime Prevention and Criminal Justice.

The *International Labour Organisation (ILO)* carries out activities on drug-related problems in the workplace and on the vocational rehabilitation of recovering drug addicts. WHO and UNDCP prepared a multi-media resource kit to assist enterprises in developing solutions to those problems.

The *World Health Organization (WHO)* carries out activities related to drug dependence and other drug control activities assigned to it by international drug control treaties. WHO plays an integral role in determining which substances should be placed under international control, in accordance with the provisions of the 1961 Single Convention on Narcotic Drugs and the 1971 Convention on Psychotropic Substances. WHO's Global Programme on Drug Dependence cooperates with member states in the prevention, treatment, and management of drug addiction. WHO also develops guidelines and manuals for teachers and health professionals.

The *United Nations Educational, Scientific and Cultural Organization (UNESCO)* focuses on the prevention of drug abuse through public education and awareness. UNESCO works with media organizations in producing radio and television programs. With the support of UNDCP, UNESCO is carrying out research projects on drug use and prevention in Africa, Asia and the Pacific, and Latin America and the Caribbean.

The *International Maritime Organization (IMO)* is concerned with the transportation of illicit drugs by ships. IMO has compiled guidelines on the prevention of drug smuggling on ships engaged in international traffic. The guidelines set out security precautions, methods of concealments, actions to be taken when drugs are discovered, identification of addicts, and cooperation with customs.

The *International Civil Aviation Organization (ICAO)* seeks to counteract the shipment of illicit drugs by air. It develops technical specifications and guidance material for civil flights, and suggests measures to ensure that commercial carriers are not used to transport illicit drugs.

The *Universal Postal Union (UPU)* has carried out studies to establish international measures covering the shipment of illicit drugs through the mails.

The *Food and Agriculture Organization of the United Nations (FAO)* manages several multidisciplinary programs financed by UNDCP. FAO covers the agricultural aspects of the drug crisis. Its programs are aimed at raising the income level of farmers, and thereby reducing the incentive to cultivate narcotic crops. It has participated in UNDCP-financed projects in Bolivia, Myanmar, and Pakistan. FAO and UNDCP are studying the potential of remote sensing techniques and satellite imagery (already in use by FAO to predict droughts and other international crop statistics) in the detection of illicit crops.

The *United Nations Development Programme (UNDP)* incorporates drug abuse control programs into its development projects in Asia and the Pacific, and Latin America and the Caribbean. UNDP's resident coordinators and resident representatives work closely with the UNDCP in countries where serious drug problems exist.

The *United Nations Children Fund (UNICEF)* focuses on the world's 100 million street children, who are often drug abusers and/or drug sellers. UNICEF has programs in Latin America and the Caribbean to strengthen families and provide services to children in need.

The Treaty System

One of the tasks of the UN in drug control is to adapt international treaty machinery to changing conditions. Six agreements have been drawn up under United Nations auspices.

The Paris Protocol of 1948. The prewar international conventions on narcotics applied to all addictive products of three plants—the opium poppy, the coca bush, and the cannabis plant—and to products belonging to certain chemical groups known to have addictive properties. By the end of World War II, however, a number of synthetic narcotics not belonging to the defined chemical groups had been developed. A protocol signed in Paris on 19 November 1948 authorized WHO to place under international control any new drug not covered by the previous conventions that was or could be addictive. The Paris protocol came into force on 1 December 1949.

The Opium Protocol of 1953. Despite earlier international treaties on opium, its production continued and found its way into illicit channels. The Commission on Narcotic Drugs first proposed an international opium monopoly, with production quotas and a system of international inspection. It was impossible, however, to obtain agreement on such important questions as the price of opium and inspection rights.

A compromise was worked out by the United Nations Opium Conference, held in New York in May–June 1953, and was embodied in a Protocol for Limiting and Regulating the Cultivation of the Poppy Plant, the Production of, International Trade in, and Use of Opium. Under this protocol, only seven states—Bulgaria, Greece, India, Iran, Turkey, the USSR, and Yugoslavia—were authorized to produce opium for export. Producing states were required to set up a government agency to license opium poppy cultivators and designate the areas to be cultivated. Cultivators were to deliver all opium immediately after harvesting to this agency, the only body with the legal right to trade in opium. The Permanent Central Narcotics Board, under the protocol, was empowered to employ certain supervisory and enforcement measures and, with the consent of the government concerned, to carry out local inquiries. The protocol came into force in December 1964.

The Single Convention on Narcotic Drugs, 1961. On 30 March 1961, a conference at United Nations headquarters adopted and opened for signature the Single Convention on Narcotic Drugs, 1961. This convention, which came into force on 13 December 1964, was a milestone in international narcotics control.

The first objective of the convention—codification of existing multilateral treaty law in this field—was almost achieved. The second goal—simplification of the international control machinery—was achieved: the Permanent Central Board and the Drug Supervisory Body were combined as the International Narcotics Control Board, as described earlier. The third goal was extension of control to cover cultivation of plants grown for narcotics. The treaty continued controls on opium, including national opium monopolies and the obligation of governments to limit production to medical and scientific purposes. Provisions dealing with medical treatment and rehabilitation of addicts were quite new as treaty obligations. Opium smoking, opium eating, coca-leaf chewing, hashish (cannabis) smoking, and the use of cannabis for nonmedical purposes were prohibited. The convention required states that are parties to it to take special control measures for particularly dangerous drugs, such as heroin and ketobemidone. Earlier treaty provisions, requiring (1) that exports and imports of narcotic drugs be made only on government authorization from both sides, (2) that governments report on the working of the treaty, and (3) that they exchange, through the Secretary-General, laws and regulations passed to implement the treaty, were retained. Provisions for controlling the manufacture of narcotic drugs and the trade and distribution of narcotic substances also were continued, together with measures for controlling new synthetic drugs.

The Convention on Psychotropic Substances, 1971. During the 1960s there was increasing concern over the harmful effects of such drugs as barbiturates, amphetamines, LSD, and tranquilizers. WHO and the Commission on Narcotic Drugs recommended that governments take legislative and administrative control measures.

On the basis of a draft drawn up by the Commission on Narcotic Drugs, in close collaboration with WHO, a plenipotentiary conference for the adoption of a protocol on psychotropic substances met in Vienna in 1971, with 71 states represented. On 21 February 1971, it adopted and opened for signature the Convention on Psychotropic Substances, 1971. The convention has been in force since 1976.

The 1971 convention was a major step in the extension of international drug control. It contains a number of prohibitive measures for hallucinogens that present a high risk of abuse and have no therapeutic application. Special provisions regarding substances such as LSD prescribe, among other things, prohibition of their use except for research authorized and supervised by governments.

The requirement of licenses for manufacture, trade, and distribution, the supervision of these activities, and the repression of acts contrary to laws and regulations are applied to all of the drugs enumerated in the 1971 convention. Governments may limit or prohibit the import (and export) of any psychotropic drug. With this regulatory system, governments can protect themselves against unwanted drugs. Psychotropic drugs used in therapy but with great abuse potential, such as sleeping pills, are controlled by requiring medical prescriptions and by supervision of export-import activity. International trade in the most dangerous stimulants—the amphetamines—is subject to a more stringent authorization system. Strict record-keeping of drug movements and statistical reports to the International Narcotics Control Board are also required.

A humane provision in the treaty requires that "all practicable measures for the prevention of abuse, the early identification, treatment, education, after-care, rehabilitation, and social reintegration of persons involved" be taken and that "either as an alternative to conviction or punishment or in addition to conviction or punishment, such abusers shall undergo measures of treatment, education, after-care, rehabilitation, and social reintegration."

The Protocol Amending the 1961 Single Convention on Narcotic Drugs, 1972. A plenipotentiary conference adopted, on 25 March 1972, amendments to strengthen the international narcotics control system and to include new concepts and means.

The International Narcotics Control Board was increased from 11 to 13 members, to serve for five years instead of three. Technical measures included in the protocol concern limitation of the production of opium, seizure and destruction of illicitly cultivated opium poppies, and the option of the board to recommend technical or financial assistance to governments. The protocol, like the 1971 Convention, provides for after-care and rehabilitation of drug abusers. Also, drug offenders are made extraditable in any extradition treaty. The protocol came into force on 8 August 1975.

Convention Against Illicit Trafficking in Narcotic Drugs and Psychotropic Substances, 1988. In recognition of the increasing difficulty faced by law enforcement and other government agencies in coping with the expansion of illicit drug trafficking, the General Assembly, in 1985, requested the Commission on Narcotic Drugs to prepare a new convention covering areas not adequately regulated by existing treaties.

In 1988, the United Nations convened a conference in Vienna that was attended by representatives of 106 nations. The conference adopted the new convention, which was immediately ratified by 43 nations. The convention entered into force on 11 November 1990.

The 34-article convention addresses the issues of tracing, freezing, and confiscating proceeds and property derived from drug trafficking. Courts may seize bank, financial, or commercial records, without the imposition of bank secrecy laws. The convention also provides for extradition of major drug traffickers, mutual legal assistance between states on drug-related investigations, and transfer of proceedings for criminal prosecution. The convention also commits states to eliminate or reduce illicit demand for narcotic drugs and psychotropic substances. One of the most important provisions of the treaty, Article 12, sets forth two tables of substances used to manufacture illicit drugs and agrees to implement controls on the manufacture and shipment of such substances. In essence, Article 12 imposed the same controls on the chemicals used to manufacture illicit drugs as are imposed on the raw materials like opium and cocaine. The substances controlled by the convention included ephedrine, ergometrine, ergotamine, lysergic acid, 1-phenyl-2-proanone, pseudoephedrine, acetic anhydride, acetone, anthranilic acid, ethyl ether, phenylacetic acide, and piperidine.

By April 1993, 72 states had ratified the 1988 convention: Afghanistan, Australia, Bahamas, Bahrain, Bangladesh, Barbados, Belarus, Bhutan, Bolivia, Brazil, Bulgaria, Burkina Faso, Cameroon, Canada, Chile, China, Costa Rica, Côte d'Ivoire, Cyprus, Czechoslovakia, Denmark, Ecuador, Egypt, France, Ghana, Greece, Grenada, Guatemala, Guinea, Honduras, India, Iran, Italy, Japan, Jordan, Kenya, Luxembourg, Madagascar, Mexico, Monaco, Morocco, Myanmar (Burma), Nepal, Nicaragua, Niger, Nigeria, Oman, Pakistan, Paraguay, Peru, Portugal, Qatar, Romania, Russian Federation, Saudi Arabia, Senegal, Seychelles, Slovenia, Spain, Sri Lanka, Suriname, Sweden, Syria, Togo, Tunisia, Uganda, Ukraine, United Arab Emirates, United Kingdom, United States, Venezuela, and Yugoslavia. As of April 1993, the European Community had confirmed only Article 12.

Narcotic Drugs Under International Control

Opium and Its Derivatives. Opium, the coagulated juice of the poppy plant *Papaver somniferum L.*, was known to the Sumerians living in lower Mesopotamia in 3000 BC. It was used by the Greeks and Arabs for medicinal purposes and was probably introduced into China by the Arabs in the ninth or tenth century. The opium poppy can be grown in most of the habitable parts of the world and is often cultivated for its beautiful flowers or its seeds, which are a valuable food. As an addictive drug, opium was originally eaten or drunk as an infusion. The practice of smoking opium is only a few hundred years old.

The best-known derivatives of opium are morphine, codeine, and diacetylmorphine, more commonly called heroin. While morphine and codeine have valuable medicinal properties, heroin has no medical uses for which less dangerous analgesics cannot be substituted, and upon the recommendation of the Commission on Narcotic Drugs, its manufacture has been banned in most countries. A number of drugs are derived from morphine or are compounded with it, including ethylmorphine and benzylmorphine. Some morphine derivatives, such as apomorphine, are not addictive in themselves.

The most important drugs in national and international illicit traffic are still opium and its derivatives, in particular morphine and heroin. As a result of effective international controls, there has been little diversion of opium or opiates from legitimate channels into the illicit trade. There is, however, illicit production of opium in some countries. From these supplies, clandestine factories manufacture morphine that is converted into heroin. Opium contains as an average 10 percent of morphine, which is made into diacetylmorphine or heroin in equal weight by relatively simple methods. Clandestine factories have been moving closer to the opium-producing areas. Morphine can be extracted from poppy capsules whether or not the opium has been extracted; at least 30 percent of licit morphine comes from this process. When Turkey, in 1974, resumed cultivation of the opium poppy, which had been stopped two years earlier, it decided not to produce opium but to use the "poppy-straw method" for extraction of morphine. About 90 percent of the licit morphine is used to make codeine, whereas 90 percent of illicit morphine is used to make heroin. An effective way of eradicating heroin is to stop illicit poppy cultivation. This is the intent of the international treaties and also of crop substitution undertaken in several countries with the support of the UNDCP.

Coca Leaf and Cocaine. Coca leaves grow on an evergreen shrub, *Erythroxylon coca*, native to the mountainous western region of South America. The leaves are the raw material for the manufacture of cocaine. The leaves themselves have been chewed by some of the Andean peoples for centuries to help combat hunger and overcome the fatigue and exhaustion caused by the high altitude.

The Commission on Narcotic Drugs concluded that coca-leaf chewing is a dangerous habit and constitutes a form of addiction. In 1954, the Economic and Social Council recommended that the countries concerned should gradually limit the cultivation and export of coca leaf to medical, scientific, and other legitimate purposes and should progressively abolish the habit of coca-leaf chewing. At the same time, it was recognized that there was little chance of eliminating coca-leaf addiction unless the living conditions of those among whom the habit was widespread could be improved and that the problem must be attacked on this front as well.

Coca leaves are used to make licit cocaine, the production of which has declined to about one ton a year, but they are also used for the illicit market that supplies increasing quantities of this dangerous drug to North America, Western Europe, and other regions.

A new, more addictive, and more deadly form of cocaine called "crack" is an inexpensive, potent form of the base drug in crystalline form. It is usually smoked, giving a quick, intense high, which lasts only a few minutes. "Crack" is harmful to the brain, heart, lungs, and nervous system and produces serious psychological effects.

Cannabis (Marijuana). The plant *Cannabis sativa,* or the crude drug derived from it, is known under almost 200 different names—marijuana, hashish, Indian hemp, charas, ganji, kif, bhang, and maconha, to name a few. Widely used as an intoxicant by millions of people for at least 4,000 years, it can be grown in most parts of the inhabited world. Depending on the soil and cultivation, the plant grows to a height of one to 20 feet. The narcotic resin is found in the flowering tops.

Cannabis is used as a narcotic in many parts of Africa, the Middle East, and the Americas. Because the plant grows wild and is easy to cultivate illicitly, traffickers have little difficulty in obtaining cannabis. Statistics on users are not available, but their number must run well in the millions.

Synthetic Narcotic Drugs. A number of synthetic substitutes, especially for morphine, are widely used. They were placed under control by the 1948 protocol. They may and do give rise to abuse but in a relatively limited way, and there is little, if any, illicit traffic in them. The most widely known are pethidine and methadone.

Psychotropic Substances. Psychotropic substances placed under international control by the 1971 convention are listed, like narcotic drugs, in treaty schedules that may be modified from time to time by the Commission on Narcotic Drugs. They have widely different characteristics, and, according to complex criteria having to do with the dangers they present to the individual and society, they have been placed in four schedules with decreasing severity of control. In Schedule I are found mainly hallucinogens, such as LSD, mescaline, and psilocine. All are made by synthesis, but the last two are also found in plants, the peyotl cactus and the hallucinatory mushroom, respectively. Schedule II contains mainly drugs of the amphetamine type that stimulate the central nervous system. They have limited therapeutic value but are widely abused, especially by young people who inject them intravenously, possibly causing psychoses. In Schedule III are found mainly the most powerful depressants of the central nervous system—barbiturates used as hypnotics (sleeping pills) by a very large number of consumers everywhere. These drugs, if used without therapeutic necessity, produce a form of addiction that can be extremely dangerous. Barbiturates are often used in association with heroin, with alcohol (with an especially dangerous interaction), and even with stimulants. Schedule IV has some barbiturate depressants and a number of tranquilizers. These constitute a very large body of medicaments supposed to eliminate anxiety and nervousness. Large quantities of such drugs as meprobamate and diazepan are consumed without therapeutic need and may alter mood and behavior.

HUMAN RIGHTS

In the Preamble to the Charter, "the peoples of the United Nations" express their determination "to reaffirm faith in fundamental human rights, in the dignity and worth of the human person, in the equal rights of men and women and of nations large and small." Article 1 of the Charter states that one of the purposes of the UN is to promote and encourage "respect for human rights and for fundamental freedoms for all without distinction as to race, sex, language, or religion." In Article 56, "all Members pledge themselves to take joint and separate action in cooperation with the Organization for the achievement" of this purpose. The Charter vests responsibility for assisting in the realization of human rights and fundamental freedoms in three of the principal organs: the General Assembly, the Economic and Social Council, and the Trusteeship Council. The Charter also provides for the establishment of commissions for the promotion of human rights as subsidiary bodies of the Economic and Social Council. As early as 1946, two such commissions were created: the Commission on Human Rights and the Commission on the Status of Women.

THE INTERNATIONAL BILL OF RIGHTS

At the San Francisco Conference, a proposal to embody an international bill of rights in the Charter itself was put forward but was not pursued because it required more detailed consideration. The idea of establishing an international bill of rights, however, was regarded as inherent in the Charter. Even before the Charter was ratified and had entered into force and before the UN as an organization was established, steps were taken toward this goal. The Preparatory Commission of the UN and its Executive Committee, meeting in the fall of 1945, both recommended that the work of the Commission on Human Rights should be directed, in the first place, toward the formulation of an international bill of rights. The General Assembly agreed with these recommendations in January 1946. Accordingly, when the terms of reference of the Commission on Human Rights were laid down in February 1946, "an international bill of rights" was the first item on its work program.

When the Commission on Human Rights and its drafting committee started work on this ambitious project, it turned out that there was disagreement among the members about the form that the draft bill of rights should take. Some members thought the bill should be a "declaration" or "manifesto" that would be proclaimed by a resolution of the General Assembly. Others urged that it take the form of an international treaty, which, in addition to being approved by the General Assembly, would have to be opened for signature and for ratification or accession by governments and would be binding only on those governments that had ratified it or acceded to it. The relevant report of the drafting committee records that it was agreed by those who favored the declaration form that the declaration should be accompanied or followed by one or more conventions. It was also agreed by those who favored the convention form that the General Assembly, in recommending a convention to member nations, might make a declaration wider in content or more general in expression. As a consequence, drafts of a "declaration" and of a "convention" were prepared, and studies were undertaken for the creation of international supervisory and enforcement machinery, called "measures of implementation."

Eventually, the decision emerged that the international bill of rights should not be produced by one single, comprehensive, and final act but should consist of two or more international instruments, namely, a declaration and a convention (or covenant), and measures of implementation. Later, it was decided that there should be not one but two covenants—one on civil and political rights and the other on economic, social, and cultural rights—and that the provisions on the measures of implementation should be embodied in the texts of the covenants. The latter decision was modified somewhat in 1966, when the provisions regulating one specific aspect of the implementation arrangements, the right of petition (communication), were included in a separate optional protocol.

The Universal Declaration of Human Rights

The Universal Declaration of Human Rights was prepared by the Commission on Human Rights in 1947 and 1948 and adopted and proclaimed by the General Assembly on 10 December 1948 by a vote of 48 in favor, none against, with 6 abstentions. Two representatives were absent. One of them stated later that, if he had been present, he would have voted in favor.

The Universal Declaration consists of a preamble and 30 articles. It proclaims—and in this regard it differs from the traditional catalog of the rights of man that are contained in various constitutions and fundamental laws of the 18th and 19th centuries and the first decades of the 20th century—not only civil and political rights but also rights that were eventually regulated in the International Covenant on Economic, Social and Cultural Rights.

The declaration proclaims, in Article 1, that all human beings are born free and equal in dignity and rights and, in Article 2, that everyone is entitled to all the rights and freedoms set forth in the declaration "without distinction of any kind, such as race, color, sex, language, religion, political or other opinion, national or social origin, property, birth or other status" and that "no distinction shall be made on the basis of the political, jurisdictional or international status of the country or territory to which a person belongs, whether it be independent, trust, non-self-governing or under any other limitation of sovereignty."

In Articles 3 to 21, the declaration deals with the traditional civil and political rights, including the right to life, liberty, and security of person; freedom from slavery and servitude; freedom from torture or cruel, inhuman, or degrading treatment or punishment; equality before the law and equal protection of the law; freedom from arbitrary arrest, detention, or exile; the right to be presumed innocent until proved guilty; the right to protection against arbitrary interference with one's privacy, family, home, or correspondence and to protection against attacks upon one's honor and reputation; freedom of movement and residence; the right to leave any country, including one's own; the right to seek and enjoy in other countries asylum from persecution; the right to a nationality and the right to change one's nationality; the right of men and women of full age to marry, without any limitation due to race, nationality, or religion; freedom of thought, conscience, and religion; the right to own property and not to be arbitrarily deprived of it; freedom of opinion and expression; the right to peaceful assembly and association; the right to take part in the government of one's country; and the right to equal access to public service.

Economic, social, and cultural rights (Articles 23 to 27) are introduced by Article 22, which states generally that "everyone, as a member of society, has the right to social security" and is entitled to the realization of "economic, social and cultural rights indispensable for his dignity and the free development of his personality." The article implies, however, that those economic, social, and cultural rights are not everywhere and immediately achievable. It states that the "realization" of these rights is to be brought about "through national effort and international cooperation and in accordance with the organization and resources of each state."

The declaration affirms everyone's right to work, to free choice of employment, to just and favorable conditions of work, and to protection against unemployment. It affirms the right of everyone to equal pay for equal work; to "just and favorable remuneration"; to form and join trade unions; to "a standard of living adequate for the health and well-being of himself and of his family"; and to "rest and leisure, including reasonable limitation of working hours and periodic holidays with pay." It also proclaims "the right to security in the event of unemployment, sickness, disability, widowhood, old age or other lack of livelihood in circumstances beyond [one's] control." Everyone has the right to education, which "shall be free, at least in the elementary and fundamental stages" and compulsory on the elementary level. The declaration affirms everyone's right "freely to participate in the cultural life of the community, to enjoy the arts and to share in scientific advancement and its benefits."

Article 28 asserts that "everyone is entitled to a social and international order in which the rights and freedoms set forth in this Declaration can be fully realized." In the exercise of individual rights and freedoms, everyone shall be subject only to such limitations as are determined by law. Such limitations, according to Article 29, shall be "solely for the purpose of securing due recognition and respect for the rights and freedoms of others and of meeting the just requirements of morality, public order, and the general welfare in a democratic society." Article 30 states that nothing in the declaration may be interpreted as implying for any state, group, or person "any right to engage in any activity or to perform any act aimed at the destruction of any of the rights and freedoms" set forth in the declaration.

The Universal Declaration of Human Rights was adopted, not in the form of an international convention that, when ratified, is legally binding on the states that are parties to it, but in the form of a resolution of the General Assembly, as "a common understanding" of the rights and freedoms that member states have pledged themselves to respect and observe and as "a common standard of achievement for all peoples and all nations." In the view of most of those who were instrumental in its preparation and adoption, the declaration was not meant to be a "binding" instrument. However, as soon as the declaration was adopted, it began to be used as a code of conduct and as a yardstick to measure the compliance by governments with the international standards of human rights.

In countless allegations of human rights violations that it has been called upon to examine, the UN has had recourse to the declaration, whether it was dealing with allegations of forced labor, with discrimination in non-self-governing and trust territories, with customs and practices inconsistent with the dignity of women, or with other violations of human rights. The declaration also has played an important role in the activities of specialized agencies, such as the ILO, UNESCO, and ITU, and in regional organizations, such as the OAS, the Council of Europe, and the OAU.

The declaration has thus acquired a validity beyond that originally contemplated in 1948. The international community, both the states that had been instrumental in its creation and those that later achieved independence, used the declaration for the purpose of fulfilling an assignment greater and more far-reaching than that originally carved out for it. Today, the declaration has acquired the status of customary international law and is valid for all states.

The International Covenants on Human Rights

The Commission on Human Rights, the Economic and Social Council, and the General Assembly devoted 19 years (1947–66) to the preparation of the International Covenants on Human Rights. One problem that created a considerable amount of controversy, particularly in the early years, was whether the treaty that would give legal effect to the rights and freedoms set forth in the Universal Declaration of Human Rights should regulate only those rights that traditionally have been guaranteed in national constitutions or catalogs of rights and are known as "civil and political rights" or whether the treaty should also set forth "economic, social and cultural rights."

As already indicated, it was eventually decided that there should be two covenants dealing with the two sets of provisions, respectively. The principal reason for having two separate instruments regulating the two groups of rights was the fundamentally different character of the rights concerned, which led some even to question whether "economic, social and cultural rights" are, technically, rights at all—in the sense of enforceable and justiciable rights. The different character of these rights made it necessary to provide for a difference in the type of international obligations to be undertaken by states that are parties to one or the other, or both, of the two covenants. Another reason for establishing two different covenants was thought to be the necessity to adjust the arrangements for international supervision—the "measures of implementation"—to the different character of the rights.

In the International Covenant on Civil and Political Rights, each state party undertakes to *respect* and to *ensure* to all individuals within its territory and subject to its jurisdiction the rights recognized in that covenant. In the International Covenant on Economic, Social and Cultural Rights, each state party undertakes only to *take steps*, individually and through international assistance and cooperation, to the maximum of its available resources, *with a view to achieving progressively* the full realization of the rights recognized in that covenant. Subject to certain exceptions and modifications, the International Covenant on Civil and Political Rights imposes upon states parties the obligation to maintain defined standards. The states parties to the International Covenant on Economic, Social and Cultural Rights assume the obligation to promote an objective—the achievement of human rights.

By and large, the two covenants between them cover the rights proclaimed in the Universal Declaration of Human Rights, as they have been described above, but there are considerable differences between the Universal Declaration and the covenants.

The provisions of the Universal Declaration proclaiming that everyone has a right to own property and that everyone has the right to seek and to enjoy in other countries asylum from persecution have no counterpart in the covenants. On the other hand, the covenants deal with a number of questions in regard to which the declaration contains no provision. An example is the provision of both covenants that all peoples have the right to self-determination "by virtue of which they freely determine their political status and freely pursue their economic, social, and cultural development."

The International Covenant on Civil and Political Rights, but not the declaration, protects aliens against expulsion, entitles everyone not to be compelled to testify against himself or herself or to confess guilt, provides for a right to compensation for miscarriage of justice, and also provides that no one shall be liable to be tried or punished again for an offense for which he or she has already been finally convicted or acquitted. The covenant prohibits any propaganda for war and any advocacy of national, racial, or religious hatred. It provides for the protection of ethnic, religious, and linguistic minorities. The declaration does not contain corresponding provisions.

The International Covenant on Economic, Social and Cultural Rights contains provisions on the right to work and to enjoy just and favorable conditions of work; the right to form and join trade unions and, subject to the law of the land, the right to strike; the right to social security, including social insurance and the protection of the family; the right to an adequate standard of living and freedom from hunger; the right to the enjoyment of the highest attainable standards of physical and mental health; the right to education; and the right to take part in cultural life.

The International Covenants on Human Rights were adopted by the General Assembly on 19 December 1966. The International Covenant on Economic, Social and Cultural Rights came into force on 3 January 1976. At 31 December 1993, it had been acceded to or ratified by 127 states. The International Covenant on Civil and Political Rights entered into force on 23 March 1976. At 31 December 1993, it had been acceded to or ratified by 125 states. Its two Optional Protocols had been signed by a total of 94 states.

Measures of Implementation
The states parties to the Covenant on Economic, Social and Cultural Rights undertake to submit to the Economic and Social Council reports on the measures that they have adopted and the progress made in achieving the observance of the rights recognized in that covenant. Until 1986, the Economic and Social Council entrusted the task of examining such reports to a working group. Since then, this task has been carried out by the Committee on Economic, Social and Cultural Rights, an eight-member group of experts elected by the council to serve in their personal capacity. The committee submits to the council a summary of its consideration of the reports of states parties and makes suggestions and recommendations of a general nature.

Under the International Covenant on Civil and Political Rights, an 18-member Human Rights Committee was established to consider reports submitted by states parties on measures taken to implement the covenant's provisions and also to consider communications alleging violations under the Optional Protocol, which provides for consideration of communications from individuals who claim to be victims of violations of any rights set forth in the covenant. However, only claims against states parties to the protocol can be considered.

Apart from the right of individual complaint under the specific procedure of the Optional Protocol, thousands of letters and reports alleging human rights violations are received each year by the UN. Communications containing complaints of violations of human rights are summarized and sent confidentially to the members of the Commission on Human Rights and its Subcommission on Prevention of Discrimination and Protection of Minorities; copies of the complaint also are sent to the member states named. The identity of the writers is not disclosed unless they have consented to disclosure. Any replies from the government are forwarded to the commission and subcommission.

The subcommission, if it finds that the communications appear to reveal "a consistent pattern of gross and reliably attested violations" of human rights, may refer the situation to the commission, which, in turn, can decide to carry out a thorough study of the situation or to name an ad hoc committee to investigate it. All these procedures are confidential and are dealt with in private meetings until a report, if any, is made by the Commission on Human Rights to the Economic and Social Council.

The Commission on Human Rights and its subcommission also consider in public session each year the question of violations of human rights and fundamental freedoms, including racial discrimination and apartheid, in various countries and territories. For example, since 1967, an ad hoc working group of experts of the commission has reported regularly on allegations of ill-treatment of opponents of apartheid and other racist policies, and on the treatment of political prisoners and detainees, in South Africa and Namibia.

Since 1968, the commission has been considering the question of the violation of human rights in the territories occupied by Israel as a result of the 1967 hostilities in the Middle East, including violations of the 1949 Geneva Convention concerning the protection of civilian persons in time of war.

In 1975, the commission established a five-member working group to study the human rights situation in Chile. The group visited Chile in 1978 and submitted a report to the General Assembly and the commission. After the completion of the group's mandate, the commission appointed a special rapporteur in 1979 to continue to study the situation. The commission has also requested that studies or reports be prepared by special rapporteurs or by the Secretary-General on the human rights situation in Afghanistan, Bolivia, El Salvador, Equatorial Guinea, Guatemala, Iran, and Poland.

In addition, the commission and its subcommission have studied specific phenomena of particularly serious violations of human rights. Thus, working groups have been established—on southern Africa, on enforced or involuntary disappearances, on slavery, and on indigenous populations—and special rapporteurs have been appointed to examine the question of summary or arbitrary executions and questions concerning torture, religious intolerance, and the use of mercenaries.

OTHER INTERNATIONAL HUMAN RIGHTS CONVENTIONS
The UN and two of the specialized agencies, the ILO and UNESCO, have prepared and put into force a number of conventions in the human rights field that, while not as comprehensive as the International Bill of Rights, deal with important specific rights. (Conventions on racial discrimination and on the status of women are discussed in separate sections below.)

Prevention and Punishment of Genocide
In 1948, the General Assembly adopted the Convention on the Prevention and Punishment of the Crime of Genocide. The convention entered into force in 1951. At 31 December 1993, it had been acceded to or ratified by 112 states. Under the convention, genocide means any of the following acts committed with intent to destroy in whole or in part a national, ethnic, racial, or religious group as such: (a) killing members of the group; (b) causing serious bodily or mental harm to members of the group; (c) deliberately inflicting on the group conditions of life calculated to bring about its physical destruction in whole or in part; (d) imposing measures intended to prevent births within the group; and (e) forcibly transferring children of the group to another group. One result of the convention is that the states parties place it beyond doubt that genocide (and conspiracy, incitement, and attempt to commit it and complicity in it), even if perpetrated by a government in its own territory against its own citizens, is not a matter essentially within the domestic jurisdiction of states but one of international concern. States parties confirm that genocide, whether committed in time of peace or in time of war, is a crime under international law that they undertake to prevent and to punish. Any contracting party can call upon UN organs to intervene.

Freedom of Association
The Freedom of Association Convention of 1948 (in force since 1950) was the first major achievement of the joint efforts of the UN and the ILO in the field of international legislation on human

rights problems. By this convention, states parties undertake to give effect to the right of workers and employers, without distinction whatsoever, to establish and join organizations of their own choosing without previous authorization. In exercising the rights provided for in the convention, workers and employers and their respective organizations, like other persons or organized groups, shall respect the law of the land. However, the law of the land shall not be such as to impair, nor shall it be so applied as to impair, the guarantees provided in the convention.

Under the Right to Organize and Collective Bargaining Convention of 1949 (in force since 1951), workers shall enjoy adequate protection against acts of antiunion discrimination in their employment, particularly in respect to acts calculated to make the employment of a worker subject to the condition that the worker shall not join a union or shall relinquish trade union membership.

Freedom of Information

Out of the very ambitious legislative program of the UN and the specialized agencies to guarantee through international instruments the right set forth in Article 19 of the Universal Declaration of Human Rights to seek, receive, and impart information and ideas through any medium and regardless of frontiers, only the Convention on the International Right of Correction has been adopted. At a UN Conference on Freedom of Information held in 1948, two additional conventions in this field were drafted—a general Convention on Freedom of Information and a Convention on the International Transmission of News—but these have not yet been opened for signature and ratification, although the General Assembly has approved the latter convention.

The idea underlying the Convention on the International Right of Correction, which was opened for signature in 1953 and has been in force since 1962, is the attempt to transfer to the international level an institution that has been part of national law in a great number of countries. In the convention, the contracting states agree that in cases where a contracting state contends that a news dispatch capable of injuring its relations with other states or its national prestige or dignity, transmitted from one country to another by correspondents or information agencies and published or disseminated abroad, is false or distorted, it may submit its version of the facts (called a communiqué) to the contracting states within whose territories such dispatch has been published or disseminated. The receiving state has the obligation to release the communiqué to the correspondents and information agencies operating in its territory through the channels customarily used for the release of news concerning international affairs for publication.

Protection of Refugees and Stateless Persons

In the Convention Relating to the Status of Refugees of 1951 (in force since 1954, with a protocol of 1967) and the Convention Relating to the Status of Stateless Persons of 1954 (in force since 1969), far-reaching provisions for the protection of refugees and stateless persons were enacted. Two principles are the basis of both conventions: (1) there shall be as little discrimination as possible between nationals on the one hand and refugees or stateless persons on the other, and (2) there shall be no discrimination based on race, religion, or country of origin at all among refugees and stateless persons.

In 1961, a conference of plenipotentiaries adopted the Convention on the Reduction of Statelessness, which entered into force in 1975.

Abolition of Slavery, the Slave Trade, and Forced Labor

The fight against slavery has been an international concern since the beginning of the 19th century. In more recent times, under the auspices of the League of Nations, the Slavery Convention of 1926 was enacted, by which the contracting parties undertook to prevent and suppress the slave trade and to bring about "progressively and as soon as possible" the complete abolition of slavery in all its forms. Under UN auspices, the Supplementary Convention on the Abolition of Slavery, the Slave Trade, and Institutions and Practices Similar to Slavery was adopted in 1956 and has been in force since 1957. Under the convention, states parties undertake to bring about, also "progressively and as soon as possible," the complete abolition or abandonment not only of slavery but also of other objectionable practices, such as debt bondage and serfdom.

By the Convention Concerning the Abolition of Forced Labor, adopted by the International Labor Conference in 1957 and in force since 1959, states parties undertake to suppress and not to make use of any form of forced or compulsory labor as a means of political coercion or education or as a punishment for holding or expressing political views or views ideologically opposed to the established political, social, or economic system; as a punishment for having participated in strikes; or as a means of racial, social, national, or religious discrimination.

Equality in Employment and Occupation

By the Convention on Discrimination in Employment and Occupation, adopted by the International Labor Conference in 1958 (in force since 1960), each state party undertakes to declare and pursue a national policy designed to promote, by methods appropriate to national conditions and practices, equality of opportunity and treatment with respect to employment and occupation, with a view to eliminating discrimination. The fulfillment of the obligations undertaken by this convention is subject to the supervisory arrangements that apply under the constitution of the ILO.

Equality in Education

In 1960, the General Conference of UNESCO adopted the Convention Against Discrimination in Education (in force since 1962). Like the Discrimination (Employment and Occupation) Convention, the Convention Against Discrimination in Education prohibits any distinction, exclusion, limitation, or preference based on race, color, sex, language, religion, political or other opinion, national or social origin, economic condition, or birth that has the purpose or effect of impairing equality of treatment in education. The establishment or maintenance of separate educational systems or institutions for pupils of the two sexes is not prohibited, provided that these systems or institutions offer equivalent access to education and provide teaching staffs meeting the same standards of qualification. A special protocol adopted in 1962 institutes a Conciliation and Good Offices Commission to be responsible for seeking a settlement of any disputes that may arise between the states parties to the convention.

Non-Applicability of Statutory Limitations to War Crimes and Crimes Against Humanity

In 1968, the General Assembly adopted the Convention on the Non-Applicability of Statutory Limitations to War Crimes and Crimes Against Humanity. The convention, in force since 1970, provides that no statutory limitation shall apply to war crimes and crimes against humanity, irrespective of the date of their commission. It also revises and extends the concepts of war crimes and crimes against humanity as they were defined in 1945 in the Charter of the International Military Tribunal and were applied and interpreted by the tribunal. The states parties to the 1968 convention undertake to adopt all necessary domestic measures with a view to making possible the extradition of persons who have committed such crimes.

War Crimes Records. Records of the International Military Tribunal (Nuremberg) and the International Military Tribunal for the Far East (Tokyo) are in the UN Archives in New York. Also deposited there are the records of various national military tribunals that were submitted to the UN War Crimes Commission established in London by a meeting of Allied and Dominion representatives in October 1943, two years before the UN was created. The following 17 countries were members of the commission: Australia, Belgium, Canada, China, Czechoslovakia, Denmark, France, Greece, India, Luxembourg, Netherlands, New Zealand, Norway, Poland, UK, US, and Yugoslavia. The commission's primary task was to collect, investigate, and record evidence of war crimes and to report to the governments concerned those instances where the material available appeared to disclose a prima facie case. The commission took no part in the detention of persons listed or in the prosecution of the cases. It ended its work in March 1948 and deposited its records in the UN Archives with the stipulation that access to the records be limited to requests by governments for information on specific individuals. Following consultations among representatives of the former members of the commission in September/October 1987, its chairman recommended to the UN Secretary-General that the files be opened to governments for research into and investigation and prosecution of war crimes and to individuals, with the permission of the government of which they are nationals or permanent residents, for research into the history and work of the commission and into war crimes.

Prevention and Punishment of Crimes Against Internationally Protected Persons

In 1973, the General Assembly adopted the Convention on the Prevention and Punishment of Crimes Against Internationally Protected Persons, Including Diplomatic Agents. The convention, in force since 1977, aims at preventing the commission of acts of terrorism against heads of state, heads of government, ministers of foreign affairs, representatives of states, and officials of international organizations, as well as members of their families who accompany them or form part of their households. Each state party to the convention agrees to make murder, kidnapping, or other attacks upon the person or liberty of an internationally protected person or a violent attack upon his official premises, private accommodations, or means of transport a punishable crime. States agree to cooperate in the prevention of these crimes and in the prosecution and punishment of offenders.

Prevention of Torture and Other Cruel, Inhuman, or Degrading Treatment or Punishment

In 1975, the General Assembly proclaimed the Declaration on the Protection of All Persons from Being Subjected to Torture and Other Cruel, Inhuman or Degrading Treatment or Punishment. The declaration spells out in greater detail the provisions of the Universal Declaration of Human Rights and the International Covenant on Civil and Political Rights that no one may be subjected to torture or to cruel, inhuman, or degrading treatment or punishment.

The declaration was given binding legal form in 1984, when the General Assembly adopted the Convention Against Torture and Other Cruel, Inhuman or Degrading Treatment or Punishment. In the convention, which came into force on 26 June 1987, torture is defined as any act by which severe physical or mental pain is intentionally inflicted by, at the instigation of, or with the acquiescence of someone acting in an official capacity, whether to obtain information or a confession; to punish, intimidate, or coerce; or for reasons based on discrimination. It does not include pain or suffering arising only from, inherent in, or incidental to lawful sanctions. States parties undertake to prevent torture in their jurisdictions and ensure that it is legally punishable. No exceptional circumstances, such as war, the threat of war, internal political instability, or any other emergency, may be invoked to justify torture, nor can a torturer be excused by virtue of having acted under orders. The convention provides for extradition of persons believed to have committed acts of torture and for protection and compensation for torture victims.

Convention on the Rights of the Child

In November 1989, the General Assembly adopted the Convention on the Rights of the Child, based on the draft proposed by the Commission on Human Rights in March of that year. The convention, which came into force in September 1990, has been signed by 171 states and, at 30 April 1994, 159 states were party to it. The convention recognizes and protects a wide range of civil rights and liberties. It acknowledges the importance of a secure and healthy family or alternative environment; provides for education, leisure, and cultural activities; and states that children in emergencies are entitled to special protection and that children who are in conflict with the law must be guaranteed basic rights. The convention also stipulates that children should be protected from any form of exploitation.

In accordance with article 43 of the Convention, a Committee on the Rights of the Child consisting of 10 members was established in February 1991. The committee meets twice a year to consider periodic reports submitted by states which give details of their effective implementation of the provisions of the convention. The committee submits to the General Assembly, through the Economic and Social Council, a report on its activities every two years.

International Convention on the Protection of the Rights of All Migrant Workers and Members of their Families

In December 1990, the General Assembly adopted a convention that takes into account the importance and extent of the migration phenomenon, which involves millions of people and affects a large number of states in the international community. In particular, the convention stipulates that all migrant workers and members of their families have the same right to equality with nationals of the state where they are engaged in remunerated activity. At 31 December 1993, there were only two states parties to the convention and thus it has not yet entered into force.

REGIONAL HUMAN RIGHTS INSTRUMENTS

The work of the UN in the human rights field, for which the provisions of the Charter have been the point of departure, has also inspired important developments in the protection of human rights on the regional level by the Council of Europe, the Organization of American States, and the Organization of African Unity.

The European Convention on Human Rights

Under the auspices of the Council of Europe, the European Convention on Human Rights was signed in 1950 and entered into force in 1953. The convention is based on an early draft of what is now the International Covenant on Civil and Political Rights. It was concluded by the governments of European countries "to take the first steps for the collective enforcement of certain of the rights stated in the Universal Declaration of Human Rights." It was subsequently supplemented by five additional protocols. As far as the substantive provisions are concerned, the European Convention and the International Covenant on Civil and Political Rights cover, more or less, the same ground, although there are a number of important differences between the two instruments.

The European Convention established two internal organs "to ensure the observance of the engagements undertaken by the High Contracting Parties in the present Convention"—that is, the European Commission on Human Rights and the European Court of Human Rights. Any party to the convention has the right to refer to the commission any alleged breach of the convention by another party. The commission may also receive petitions from any person, nongovernmental organization, or group of individuals claiming to be the victim of a violation, by one of the parties, of the rights set forth in the convention and in the relevant protocols. The exercise of this power by the commission is subject to the condition that the state against which the complaint is directed has recognized this competence of the commission.

If the commission does not succeed in securing a friendly settlement on the basis of respect for human rights as defined in the convention, it draws up a report on the facts and states its opinion as to whether the facts found disclose a breach by the state concerned of its obligations under the convention. The final decision is taken either by the Committee of Ministers of the Council of Europe, a political organ, or, if it has jurisdiction and the matter is referred to it, by the European Court of Human Rights.

The European Social Charter
The European Social Charter is the European counterpart to the International Covenant on Economic, Social and Cultural Rights. The provisions of the European Social Charter, however, are more specific and detailed. It has established a reporting procedure. The reports are examined by a committee of independent experts, which submits its conclusions to a governmental social subcommittee. The Consultative Assembly of the Council of Europe is consulted. In the final stage, the Committee of Ministers may make any recommendation that it considers necessary to any contracting party in the areas of economic, social, and cultural rights.

The American Convention on Human Rights
In 1948, several months before the adoption by the General Assembly of the Universal Declaration of Human Rights, the Ninth International Conference of American States, meeting in Bogotá, adopted the American Declaration of the Rights and Duties of Man. This declaration was followed in 1969 by the signing in San José, Costa Rica, of the American Convention on Human Rights. The convention, in force since 1978, is a very comprehensive instrument, similar to both the European Convention on Human Rights and the International Covenant on Civil and Political Rights. The organs of implementation of the Pact of San José are the Inter-American Commission on Human Rights (corresponding to the European Commission and to the Human Rights Committee under the International Covenant on Civil and Political Rights) and the Inter-American Court of Human Rights. While the right of petition of individuals is optional under the European Convention and the International Covenant on Civil and Political Rights, in the inter-American system, every state party accepts the right of petition automatically.

The African Charter on Human and Peoples' Rights
In 1981, the Assembly of Heads of State and Government of the Organization of African Unity, meeting in Nairobi, Kenya, adopted the African Charter on Human and Peoples' Rights. The charter, which came into force on 21 October 1986, provides for an African Commission on Human and Peoples' Rights, composed of 11 members elected by the assembly, to promote and protect the rights set forth in the charter. The provisions of the charter are similar to those of the Universal Declaration of Human Rights but with special reference to African traditions of rights and freedoms, including the right to self-determination and the right of peoples to dispose of their wealth and natural resources.

THE FIGHT AGAINST RACIAL DISCRIMINATION
The idea of the equality of races emerged as the one that, more than any other, has dominated the thoughts and actions of the post–World War II period. The aim of racial equality has permeated the lawmaking and the standard-setting activities of the UN family of organizations and also the day-to-day work of many of its organs. The Charter, the Universal Declaration of Human

Rights, and the two International Covenants on Human Rights prohibit discrimination on the grounds of race or color, as do the conventions against discrimination in employment and occupation and in education that have already been described.

The Declaration on the Elimination of All Forms of Racial Discrimination
In 1963, the General Assembly proclaimed the Declaration on the Elimination of All Forms of Racial Discrimination, which affirms that discrimination between human beings on the grounds of race, color, or ethnic origin is an offense to human dignity, a denial of Charter principles, a violation of the rights proclaimed in the Universal Declaration of Human Rights, and an obstacle to friendly and peaceful relations among peoples.

The International Convention on the Elimination of All Forms of Racial Discrimination
In 1965, the General Assembly adopted the International Convention on the Elimination of All Forms of Racial Discrimination which entered into force in January 1969. At 31 December 1993, it had been acceded to or ratified by 137 states. Under the convention, states parties undertake not only to condemn racial discrimination and pursue a policy of eliminating it in all its forms but also to prohibit and bring to an end, by all appropriate means, including legislation as required by circumstances, racial discrimination by any individual, group, or organization. States parties undertake to declare it an offense punishable by law to disseminate ideas based on racial superiority or hatred or that are an incitement to racial discrimination. They also commit themselves to declare illegal and prohibit organizations that promote and incite racial discrimination and to recognize participation in such organizations as an offense punishable by law. The convention provides for the establishment of international supervisory machinery similar to that laid down in the International Covenant on Civil and Political Rights but contains tighter provisions.

Under the convention, an 18-member Committee on the Elimination of Racial Discrimination was established, which, like the Human Rights Committee provided for in the International Covenant on Civil and Political Rights, has the function of considering reports by states and allegations by a state party that another state party is not giving effect to the provisions of the convention. States parties to the convention also may recognize the competence of the Committee on the Elimination of Racial Discrimination to receive and consider petitions (communications) from individuals or groups of individuals. In the last instance, the International Court of Justice can be apprised of disputes with respect to the interpretation and application of the convention.

The International Convention on the Suppression and Punishment of the Crime of Apartheid
In 1973, the General Assembly adopted the International Convention on the Suppression and Punishment of the Crime of Apartheid which entered into force in July 1976. At 31 December 1993, it had been acceded to or ratified by 99 states. The convention provides that international responsibility for the crime of apartheid shall apply to individuals, members of organizations and institutions, and representatives of a state, whether residing in the state in which the acts are perpetrated or elsewhere. Persons charged can be tried by any state party to the convention. A three-member group of the Commission on Human Rights meets each year to review progress in implementing the convention.

The International Declaration and the International Convention Against Apartheid in Sports
The International Declaration Against Apartheid in Sports, adopted by the General Assembly in 1977, calls on states to take all appropriate action to cease sporting contacts with any country

practicing apartheid and to exclude or expel any such country from international and regional sports bodies.

The International Convention Against Apartheid in Sports, adopted by the General Assembly in 1985, gave the provisions of the declaration a binding legal form. It entered into force in April 1988. At 31 December 1993, it had been acceded to or ratified by 57 states.

Other Action to Combat Racism and Racial Discrimination

In 1972, the General Assembly decided to launch a Decade for Action to Combat Racism and Racial Discrimination, to begin on 10 December 1973, the 25th anniversary of the Universal Declaration of Human Rights, and in 1973, the General Assembly approved a comprehensive and ambitious program for the decade. Among its goals were the following: to promote human rights for all without distinction of any kind on grounds of race, color, descent, or national or ethnic origin, especially by eradicating racial prejudice, racism, and racial discrimination; to arrest any expansion of racist policies; to identify, isolate, and dispel the fallacious and mythical beliefs, policies, and practices that contribute to racism and racial discrimination; and to put an end to racist regimes.

While there was not necessarily complete unanimity in the General Assembly on every phrase and formulation of the relevant decisions on the decade adopted in 1972, 1973, and 1974, there was a general consensus in support of its goals. However, at the 1975 session of the General Assembly, a resolution was adopted by which the General Assembly determined that "Zionism is a form of racism and racial discrimination." The resolution was adopted by 72 votes to 35, with 32 abstentions. Among those strongly opposed were the nine members of the European Economic Community, as well as the US, Canada, Australia, and New Zealand, and other states of Western Europe, Latin America, and Africa. Many of these states declared that the resolution radically changed the concept of the decade and would therefore change their attitude toward it.

The midpoint of the decade was marked by a world conference held in Geneva in August 1978. The conference adopted recommendations for comprehensive mandatory sanctions against the racist regimes of southern Africa, elimination of all discriminatory laws and practices, adoption of laws to punish dissemination of ideas based on racial superiority or hatred, and promotion of the rights of indigenous peoples and migrant workers. In 1979, the General Assembly adopted a program for the remaining four years of the decade, and in 1982, it decided that a second conference would be held in 1983.

The Second World Conference to Combat Racism and Racial Discrimination, held in Geneva in August 1983, was attended by representatives of 128 states, as well as of UN organs and specialized agencies and of intergovernmental and nongovernmental organizations. The conference adopted a declaration and a program of action in which it noted that "in spite of the efforts of the international community during the Decade, at the national, regional and international levels, racism, racial discrimination and apartheid continue unabated and have shown no sign of diminishing." The program of action contained practical suggestions on matters such as action to combat apartheid; education, teaching, and training; dissemination of information and the role of the mass media in combating racism and racial discrimination; measures for the promotion and protection of the human rights of minority groups, indigenous peoples, and migrant workers who are subject to racial discrimination; recourse procedures for victims of racial discrimination; implementation of the International Convention on the Elimination of All Forms of Racial Discrimination and other related international instruments; national legislation and institutions; seminars and studies; action by nongovernmental organizations; and international cooperation.

On the recommendation of the conference, the General Assembly proclaimed the Second Decade to Combat Racism and Racial Discrimination, on 22 November 1983, and called for renewed and intensified efforts and for implementation of the program of action approved by the conference.

THE WORK OF THE UN RELATING TO THE STATUS OF WOMEN

The work of the UN relating to the status of women, aimed at achieving equal rights for men and women, is an important part of the UN's efforts to promote and to encourage respect for human rights and fundamental freedoms. The organ given the main responsibility in this field is the Commission on the Status of Women, a functional commission of the Economic and Social Council, established in 1946. Almost all the achievements of the UN in this matter are due to the initiative and work of the commission.

The Convention on the Political Rights of Women

The Convention on the Political Rights of Women, adopted in 1952 and in force since 1954, represented the culmination of the endeavors of generations of fighters for women's rights. It provides that women shall be entitled to vote in all elections, that they shall be eligible for election to all publicly elected bodies, and that they shall be entitled to hold public office and to exercise all public functions on equal terms with men and without any discrimination.

The Convention on the Nationality of Married Women

The Convention on the Nationality of Married Women, adopted in 1957 and in force since 1958, provides that neither the celebration nor the dissolution of marriage between a national and an alien, nor the change of nationality by the husband during marriage, shall automatically affect the nationality of the wife.

The Convention on Consent to Marriage, Minimum Age for Marriage, and Registration of Marriages

The Convention on Consent to Marriage, Minimum Age for Marriage, and Registration of Marriages, adopted in 1962 and in force since 1964, provides that no marriage shall be legally entered into without the full and free consent of both parties, such consent to be expressed by them in person after due publicity and in the presence of the authority competent to solemnize the marriage. States parties to the convention are committed to take legislative action to specify a minimum age for marriage. All marriages shall be registered in an official register by a competent authority.

In a recommendation on the same subjects as those of this convention, adopted in 1965, the General Assembly stated that the minimum age shall be not less than 15 years.

The Declaration on the Elimination of Discrimination Against Women

In 1967, the General Assembly solemnly proclaimed the Declaration on the Elimination of Discrimination Against Women. The declaration states that discrimination against women, denying or limiting as it does their equality of rights with men, is fundamentally unjust and constitutes an offense against human dignity. Work was started on a convention to put the principles of the declaration into binding legal form.

The Convention on the Elimination of All Forms of Discrimination Against Women

On 18 December 1979, the General Assembly adopted the Convention on the Elimination of All Forms of Discrimination Against Women. The convention came into force in September 1981; as of 7 February 1994 the following 132 States had ratified the convention: Afghanistan, Angola, Antigua and Barbuda, Argentina, Armenia, Australia, Austria, Bahamas, Bangladesh, Barbados, Belarus, Belgium, Belize, Benin, Bhutan, Bolivia, Bosnia and Herzegovina, Brazil, Bulgaria, Burkina Faso, Burundi, Cambodia, Canada, Cape Verde, Central African Republic, Chile, China, Colombia, Congo, Costa Rica, Croatia, Cuba, Cyprus, Czech Republic, Denmark, Dominica, Dominican Republic, Ecuador, Egypt, El Salvador, Equatorial Guinea, Estonia, Ethiopia, Finland, France, Gabon, Gambia, Germany, Ghana, Greece, Grenada, Guatemala, Guinea, Guinea-Bissau, Guyana, Haiti, Honduras, Hungary, Iceland, India, and Indonesia. Also, Iraq, Ireland, Israel, Italy, Jamaica, Japan, Jordan, Kenya, Lao People's Democratic Republic, Latvia, Liberia, Libya, Lithuania, Luxembourg, Madagascar, Malawi, Maldives, Mali, Malta, Mauritius, Mexico, Mongolia, Morocco, Namibia, Nepal, Netherlands, New Zealand, Nicaragua, Nigeria, Norway, Panama, Paraguay, Peru, Philippines, Poland, Portugal, Republic of Korea, Romania, Russian Federation, Rwanda, Saint Kitts and Nevis, Saint Lucia, Saint Vincent and the Grenadines, Samoa, Senegal, Seychelles, Sierra Leone, Slovak Republic, Slovenia, Spain, Sri Lanka, Suriname, Sweden, Tajikistan, Thailand, Togo, Trinidad and Tobago, Tunisia, Turkey, Uganda, Ukraine, United Kingdom, United Republic of Tanzania, Uruguay, Venezuela, Viet Nam, Yemen, Yugoslavia, Zaire, Zambia, and Zimbabwe.

Under the convention, states parties undertake to adopt all appropriate measures to abolish existing laws, regulations, customs, and practices that are discriminatory against women and to establish legal protection of the rights of women on an equal basis with men. The convention contains detailed provisions concerning equal rights for women in voting and holding public office and in education, employment, and health care. It provides for equality before the law and for the elimination of discrimination against women in all matters relating to marriage and family relations.

The convention established a Committee on the Elimination of Discrimination Against Women to periodically examine reports by states parties on measures that they have taken to implement the convention. The 23-member committee meets annually to consider the reports, which are due within one year of ratification or accession to the convention and every four years thereafter. The committee makes recommendations and observations to states parties on the basis of its consideration of the reports.

International Women's Year
In 1972, the General Assembly proclaimed the year 1975 as the International Women's Year. In 1974, the Economic and Social Council decided to convene an international conference to examine to what extent the organizations of the UN system had implemented the recommendations for the elimination of discrimination against women made by the Commission on the Status of Women since its establishment and to launch an international action program aimed at achieving the integration of women as full and equal partners with men in the total development effort, eliminating discrimination on grounds of sex, and achieving the widest possible involvement of women in strengthening international peace and eliminating racism and racial discrimination.

The World Conference of the International Women's Year took place in June/July 1975 in Mexico City. It was the most representative meeting on women's issues ever held, bringing together more than a thousand representatives, about 70 percent of them women, from more than 130 countries. The conference adopted the "Declaration of Mexico on the Equality of Women and Their Contribution to Development and Peace, 1975"; a world plan of action for implementation of the objectives of the International Women's Year; regional plans of action; and a great number of decisions on concrete problems. In the Declaration of Mexico, the conference affirmed its faith in the objectives of the International Women's Year—equality, development, and peace.

UN Decade for Women
Later in 1975, the General Assembly endorsed the proposals of the Mexico conference and proclaimed the period 1976–85 as the UN Decade for Women: Equality, Development, and Peace. The General Assembly called for the decade to be devoted to effective and sustained action to implement the world plan of action, and it decided to convene in 1980, at the midpoint of the decade, another world conference to review and evaluate the progress made.

The second world conference, held in Copenhagen in July 1980, adopted a program of action for the second half of the decade, 1980–85, to promote the three objectives of equality, development, and peace, with special emphasis on the subtheme—employment, health, and education. It called for specific action to ensure that the objectives of the world plan were met by the end of the decade.

The program of action was endorsed later in 1980 by the General Assembly, which decided to convene in 1985 a world conference to review and appraise the achievements of the decade.

1995 Fourth World Conference on Women
The Fourth World Conference on Women will be held in Beijing, from 4–15 September 1995. It is subtitled "Action for Equality, Development and Peace." At preparatory meetings in 1994, the Secretary-General said a turning point had been reached in the cause of women worldwide. He added that the conference would represent a vital continuation of the work on development issues begun during the United Nations Conference on the Environment and Development (UNCED) in June 1992 and the World Conference on Human Rights held in Vienna in June 1993, and to be continued with the International Conference on Population and Development, to be held in Cairo (5–13 September 1994) and the World Summit for Social Development, to be held in Copenhagen (11–12 March 1995).

Besides receiving reports from virtually all UN organizations on their programs relating to the status of women, the conference will address gender issues in the context of a new vision of the 21st century as one in which gender equality would be achieved. It will also focus on the problems of rural women and the need to facilitate access to resources so that they can improve their lives and, in turn, the lives of their families and communities.

The Nairobi Forward-Looking Strategies
The World Conference to Review and Appraise the Achievements of the UN Decade for Women was held in Nairobi, Kenya, in July 1985, attended by representatives of 157 states, as well as observers from specialized agencies and other organizations. The major achievement of the conference was the adoption, by consensus, of the Nairobi Forward-Looking Strategies for the Advancement of Women to the Year 2000. Measures recommended included technical cooperation, training and advisory services, institutional coordination, research and policy analysis, participation of women in activities at the international and regional levels, and dissemination of information on goals and objectives for the advancement of women.

The Declaration on the Participation of Women in Promoting International Peace and Cooperation
The Declaration on the Participation of Women in Promoting International Peace and Cooperation was adopted by the General Assembly in 1982. It states that women and men have an equal and vital interest in contributing to international peace and cooperation and that, to this end, women must be enabled to exercise their right to participate in the economic, social, cultural, civil, and political affairs of society on an equal footing with men.

OTHER DECLARATIONS IN THE HUMAN RIGHTS FIELD

The Declaration of the Rights of the Child

In 1959, the General Assembly adopted the Declaration of the Rights of the Child, which proclaims that every child, without distinction or discrimination on account of race, color, sex, language, religion, political or other opinion, national or social origin, property, birth, or other status, whether of the child or of the child's family, shall enjoy special protection and be given opportunities and facilities to develop physically, mentally, morally, spiritually, and socially in a healthy and normal manner and in conditions of freedom and dignity. Every child shall be entitled from birth to a name and nationality and shall enjoy the benefits of social security. The child who is physically, mentally, or socially handicapped shall be given the special treatment, education, and care required by his or her particular condition. Every child is entitled to receive education that shall be free and compulsory, at least in the elementary stages. Every child shall be protected against all forms of neglect, cruelty, and exploitation and from practices that may foster racial, religious, or any other form of discrimination.

In November 1989 the General Assembly adopted the Convention on the Rights of the Child.

The Declaration on the Granting of Independence to Colonial Countries and Peoples

The Declaration on the Granting of Independence to Colonial Countries and Peoples, adopted by the General Assembly in 1960, declares that the subjection of peoples to alien subjugation, domination, and exploitation constitutes a denial of fundamental human rights, is contrary to the Charter, and is an impediment to the promotion of world peace and cooperation. The declaration proclaims that all peoples have the right to self-determination.

In 1961, the General Assembly established a Special Committee on the Situation with Regard to the Implementation of the Declaration. (See also the chapter on Independence of Colonial Peoples.)

The Declaration on Territorial Asylum

The Declaration on Territorial Asylum, adopted by the General Assembly in 1967, supplements Article 14 of the Universal Declaration of Human Rights and provides that asylum granted by a state, in the exercise of its sovereignty, to persons entitled to invoke Article 14 of the Universal Declaration, including persons struggling against colonization, shall be respected by all other states. It rests with the state granting asylum to evaluate the grounds for asylum. Where a state finds difficulty in granting or continuing to grant asylum, states individually or jointly or through the UN shall consider, in the spirit of international solidarity, appropriate measures to lighten the burden on that state. No person entitled to invoke Article 14 of the Universal Declaration shall be subjected to measures such as retention at the frontier or, if he has already entered the territory in which he seeks asylum, expulsion or compulsory return to any state where he may be subjected to persecution.

The Declaration on Social Progress and Development

In 1969, the General Assembly solemnly proclaimed the Declaration on Social Progress and Development, which sets forth the principles, objectives, means, and methods to eliminate obstacles to social progress, particularly inequality, exploitation, war, colonialism, and racism. The declaration shows the close connections between social development policies and endeavors to promote respect for human rights. Article 1 provides that all peoples and all human beings, without distinction as to race, color, sex, language, religion, nationality, ethnic origin, family or social status, or political or other conviction, shall have the right to live in dignity and freedom and to enjoy the fruits of social progress and should, on their part, contribute to it.

The Declaration on Principles of International Law Concerning Friendly Relations and Cooperation Among States

On 24 October 1970, the 25th anniversary of the entry into force of the Charter, the General Assembly adopted the Declaration on Principles of International Law Concerning Friendly Relations and Cooperation Among States in Accordance with the Charter of the United Nations. One of the principles thus proclaimed is that states "shall cooperate in the promotion of universal respect for, and observance of, human rights, and fundamental freedoms for all, and in the elimination of all forms of racial discrimination and all forms of religious intolerance."

The Declaration on the Rights of Mentally Retarded Persons

The Declaration on the Rights of Mentally Retarded Persons, adopted in 1971, proclaims that the mentally retarded person has, to the maximum degree of feasibility, the same rights as other human beings: the right to proper medical care and physical therapy, education, training, rehabilitation, and guidance; the right to economic security and to perform productive work; and the right, when necessary, to a qualified guardian and to protection from exploitation, abuse, and degrading treatment. Whenever mentally retarded persons are unable to exercise all their rights in a meaningful way or if it should become necessary to restrict or deny them, the procedure used must contain proper safeguards against abuse.

The Declaration on the Protection of Women and Children in Emergency and Armed Conflicts

In 1974, the General Assembly proclaimed the Declaration on the Protection of Women and Children in Emergency and Armed Conflicts. The declaration states that attacks on civilians, "especially on women and children, who are the most vulnerable members of the population," shall be prohibited and condemned and that states involved in armed conflicts shall make all efforts "to spare women and children from the ravages of war."

The Declaration on the Rights of Disabled Persons

The Declaration on the Rights of Mentally Retarded Persons was confirmed and expanded by the Declaration on the Rights of Disabled Persons, adopted in 1975. The term "disabled person" means any person unable to ensure by himself or herself wholly or partly the necessities of a normal individual and/or social life, as a result of a deficiency in his or her physical or mental capacities. While the formulation of some of the rights set forth in the Declaration on the Rights of Disabled Persons occasionally differs from that contained in the earlier instrument, there are no differences as regards the principles and purposes, except that the later declaration applies also to persons who are physically, not mentally, handicapped.

The Declaration on the Use of Scientific and Technological Progress in the Interests of Peace

In 1975, the General Assembly adopted the Declaration on the Use of Scientific and Technological Progress in the Interests of Peace and for the Benefit of Mankind. The declaration provides that all states shall promote international cooperation to ensure that the results of scientific and technological developments are used in the interests of strengthening international peace and security, freedom, and independence and that they are also used for economic and social development and the realization of human rights and freedoms. The declaration calls on all states to help prevent the use of scientific and technological developments to limit or interfere with the enjoyment of the human rights of the individual.

The Declaration on the Elimination of All Forms of Religious Intolerance

The Declaration on the Elimination of All Forms of Intolerance and of Discrimination Based on Religion and Belief, prepared by the Commission on Human Rights and adopted by the General Assembly in 1981, states that everyone shall have the right of freedom of thought, conscience, and religion and that no one shall be subject to discrimination on the grounds of religion or other beliefs.

The Declaration on the Human Rights of Individuals Who Are Not Nationals of the Country in Which They Live

In 1985, the General Assembly adopted the Declaration on the Human Rights of Individuals Who Are Not Nationals of the Country in Which They Live. The declaration defines the term "alien" as any individual who is not a national of the state in which he or she is present. It declares that all aliens shall enjoy a wide range of civil rights, as well as the right to safe and healthy working conditions, fair wages, and equal remuneration for work of equal value; the right to join trade unions and other associations; and the right to health protection, medical care, social security, education, rest, and leisure. No alien shall be deprived of his or her lawfully acquired assets, and aliens shall be free at any time to communicate with the consulate or diplomatic mission of the state of which they are nationals.

The Declaration on the Right to Development

The Declaration on the Right to Development was adopted by the General Assembly in 1986. In the declaration, the right to development is proclaimed as an inalienable human right by virtue of which every person and all peoples are entitled to participate in, contribute to, and enjoy economic, social, cultural, and political development, in which all human rights and fundamental freedoms can be fully realized. The right to development also implies the full realization of the right of peoples to self-determination, including their inalienable right to exercise full sovereignty over all their natural wealth and resources.

Declaration on the Rights of Persons belonging to National or Ethnic, Religious and Linguistic Minorities

In December 1992, the General Assembly reaffirmed that one of the basic aims of the United Nations was to promote and encourage respect for human rights and fundamental freedoms for all, without distinction as to race, sex, language, or religion. The Declaration on the Rights of Persons belonging to National or Ethnic, Religious and Linguistic Minorities invites states to protect the identity of minorities within their respective territories, in particular through appropriate legislation.

Declaration on the Protection of All Persons from Enforced Disappearance

In December 1992, the General Assembly also adopted the Declaration on the Protection of All Persons from Enforced Disappearance, which urges states to contribute by all means to the prevention and eradication of this gross offense to human dignity and flagrant violation of human rights. Acts of enforced disappearance should be considered offenses under criminal law punishable by appropriate penalties that take into account their extreme seriousness. The victims of acts of enforced disappearance, and their families, have the right to obtain redress and adequate compensation, including complete rehabilitation.

RECENT EVENTS

The World Conference on Human Rights

The World Conference on Human Rights was held in Vienna between 15–25 June 1993. It was attended by some 7,000 partic-ipants who represented governments, the human rights community, over 800 non-governmental organizations, and academic specialists. It was in 1989 when the General Assembly called for the convening of a world meeting that would review and assess progress made in the field of human rights since the adoption of the Universal Declaration of Human Rights, and identify obstacles and the ways in which they may be overcome.

The conference agenda, as set by the General Assembly in 1992, included the examination of the link between development, democracy, and economic, social, cultural, civil, and political rights, and the evaluation of the effectiveness of United Nations methods and mechanisms. During the first of four Preparatory Committee meetings, it was clear that the agenda raised many difficult issues regarding national sovereignty, universality, the role of non-governmental organizations, and questions as to the feasibility and impartiality of new or strengthened human rights instruments. But a search for common ground on these and many other issues was successful, after intense dialogue among all the parties.

The conference agreed to a final document that has become known as The Vienna Declaration and Programme of Action. This reaffirmed the principles that had evolved over the previous 45 years. In particular, the declaration recognizes the interdependence between democracy, development, and human rights as well as the serious need to promote and protect the rights of women, children, and indigenous people. It supported the creation of a Special Rapporteur on Violence against Women, called for universal ratification of the Convention on the Rights of the Child, and recommended that the General Assembly proclaim an international decade on behalf of the world's indigenous people.

The Vienna Declaration also made concrete recommendations for strengthening and harmonizing the monitoring capacities of the United Nations system. It emphasized the need for speedy ratification of human rights instruments and it recommended that the General Assembly consider establishing a post of United Nations High Commissioner for Human Rights.

International Year for the World's Indigenous People

The United Nations designated 1993 as the International Year for the World's Indigenous People in order to provide an opportunity to focus attention on one of the most neglected and vulnerable groups of people on earth. The year was a landmark in the history of indigenous peoples' struggle for survival and recognition of their rights. As its contribution—under the theme "Indigenous people: a new partnership"—the United Nations undertook a series of activities to strengthen global cooperation for solving the problems faced by indigenous communities in such areas as human rights, environment, development, education, and health. Representatives of some 300 million indigenous people from over 70 countries were given a platform to convey their messages and to promote an understanding of their cultures and way of life.

The Establishment of United Nations High Commissioner for Human Rights

Because of efforts undertaken at the World Conference on Human Rights, held in Vienna between 14–25 June 1993, the question of establishing a post of United Nations High Commissioner for Refugees gained momentum. Later that year, the General Assembly decided to create just such a post, and on 14 February 1994, it approved the appointment of José Ayala Lasso of Ecuador to the position of High Commissioner for Human Rights. The appointment is for four years and the High Commissioner will be based in the United Nations Office at Geneva. In its resolution A/RES/48/141, adopted in December 1993, the General Assembly charged the High Commissioner with coordinating the United Nation's human rights activities and supervision of the Centre for Human Rights in Geneva.

INDEPENDENCE OF COLONIAL PEOPLES

Since the creation of the UN, more than 80 territories that were formerly under foreign rule have become sovereign states and members of the UN. In this radical transformation of the world's political map, the UN has played a significant role that stems from the basic precepts of its charter as laid down in Article 1, which states that one of the purposes of the UN is to "develop friendly relations among nations based on respect for the principle of equal rights and self-determination of peoples, . . ." Chapters XI, XII, and XIII of the charter are devoted specifically to measures that are designed to promote the welfare of dependent peoples.

In its efforts to implement these measures, the UN has dealt with two types of territories: (1) former colonial territories administered by designated member states as UN trust territories pending independence, and (2) non-self-governing dependencies or colonies of UN member states. Since the UN powers and responsibilities differ considerably in regard to the two categories of territories, this chapter has been divided into two sections.

TRUST TERRITORIES
The main features of the trusteeship system are outlined in the chapter on the Trusteeship Council. What follows here is a brief description of the territories originally placed under UN trusteeship in 1946.

Trust Territories that have Achieved Independence
Three types of countries became part of the UN's trusteeship system: (1) territories still administered by a nation under a League of Nations mandate, (2) territories detached from enemy states as a result of the Second World War, and (3) territories voluntarily placed under the system by states responsible for their administration. All 11 territories that were placed under the trusteeship system in 1946 have since achieved the goals of the charter, either as independent states or as parts of independent states.

Following is a list of the territories that have achieved independence. The territories are listed under their administering powers.

Australia
Nauru (coadministered with New Zealand and the United Kingdom). The territory became independent on 31 January 1968, in accordance with a 1965 General Assembly resolution setting this date as the target for accession to independence.
New Guinea. The trust territory of New Guinea was administered by Australia together with the non-self-governing territory of Papua until the two were united and became the independent state of Papua New Guinea in 1975.

Belgium
Ruanda-Urundi under Belgian administration. In a special session convened in June 1962, the General Assembly approved separate independence for the two territories, which were established on 1 July 1962 as the Republic of Rwanda and the Kingdom of Burundi.

France
Togoland. In 1958, with the agreement of France, the UN supervised elections, and the territory became the independent state of Togo on 27 April 1960.
Cameroons. Following a notification in 1958 by its legislative assembly of the desire of the territory to become independent and

acting upon the recommendation of the Trusteeship Council, the General Assembly, in agreement with France, resolved that on 1 January 1960 trusteeship status would end and the territory would become independent as Cameroon.
Italy
Somaliland. In union with the dependency of British Somaliland, the territory became the sovereign state of Somalia on 1 July 1960.
New Zealand
Western Samoa. In agreement with the administering authority, the UN conducted a plebiscite in May 1961, following which the territory attained independence on 1 January 1962.
United Kingdom
Togoland. To ascertain the freely expressed wishes of the people as to their political future, the UN, in agreement with the United Kingdom, conducted a plebiscite in 1956. As a result of the plebiscite, the territory united in March 1957 with the former Gold Coast to form the independent state of Ghana.
Cameroons. Both the northern and southern sectors of the territory were administered as part of the federation of Nigeria, a British dependency. Following a plebiscite held under UN supervision in March 1961, the northern sector became part of newly independent Nigeria on 1 June 1961. Following a similar plebiscite, the peoples of the southern sector joined the newly independent state of Cameroon on 1 October 1961.
Tanganyika. Following negotiations between the United Kingdom and African leaders, the territory attained independence on 9 December 1961. It united with Zanzibar in 1964 to become the United Republic of Tanzania.
United States
Trust Territory of the Pacific Islands. By the end of 1975, only the Trust Territory of the Pacific Islands remained under the UN trusteeship system. It was administered by the United States under an agreement approved by the Security Council. Because it is a "strategic" trust territory, it was under the ultimate authority of the Security Council rather than the General Assembly. (See the chapter on the Trusteeship Council.)

The Pacific Islands, collectively known as Micronesia, include the former Japanese-mandated islands of the Marshalls, the Carolines, and the Northern Marianas (except Guam, which was ceded to the United States by Spain in 1898). In 1975, a covenant for political union with the United States was approved by the people of the Northern Marianas. In February 1976, the United States Congress gave final approval for granting commonwealth status to the Northern Marianas. The Commonwealth Covenant with the Northern Marianas came into force on 3 November 1986.

In a referendum held on 12 July 1978, Kosrae, Ponape, Truk, and Yap—in the Caroline archipelago—approved and ratified a draft constitution for a proposed Federated States of Micronesia. The four districts subsequently held elections, and the Congress of the Federated States of Micronesia was inaugurated on 10 May 1979. The Compact of Free Association with the Federated States of Micronesia also came into force on 3 November 1986.

On 21 December 1978, the Marshall Islands Constitutional Convention approved a draft constitution, and in a referendum held on 1 March 1979, the voters of those islands adopted it by a substantial majority. Legislative power in the Marshall Islands was vested in the Nitijela (legislature); the first general election under the new constitution took place on 10 April 1979. The Compact of Free Association with the Marshall Islands came into force on 21 October 1986.

On 2 April 1979, the Constitutional Convention of Palau adopted a draft constitution, which was approved by a referendum on 9 July. Elections were held on 4 November 1980, and the new constitution came into force on 1 January 1981. However, since its constitution required a 75 percent majority for the approval of the Compact of Free Association with the United States, Palau was unable to obtain approval for the compact in seven different referendums over the next 10 years.

In November 1992, Palau held a constitutional amendment referendum and changed the requirement for approval to simple majority (50 plus 1 percent). Thereafter, the eighth plebiscite was held in November 1993 and the compact was approved by 68 per cent of Palauans voting in favor. In January 1994, the United States informed the Trusteeship Council that its government and the government of Palau intended to implement the compact as soon as practicable. Planning for the smooth transition to Palau's new status was under way. The Trusteeship Council recommended that the two countries set 1 October 1994, as a target date for the full implementation of the Compact of Free Association and the official end of Palau's status as a trusteeship territory.

Non-self-governing Territories

The delegates attending the 1945 San Francisco Conference, at which the UN was founded, included many spokesmen for anti-colonialist sentiment. As a result of their efforts and generous proposals by Australia and the United Kingdom (which possessed the world's largest colonial empire at the time), the charter incorporates a pledge on the part of the colonial powers to assume certain obligations toward the peoples of their dependencies.

Charter Declaration on Non-self-governing Territories

The pledge takes the form of a declaration regarding non-self-governing territories that is embodied in Article 73, Chapter XI, of the charter. Under Article 73, all UN members "which have or assume responsibilities for the administration of territories whose peoples have not yet attained a full measure of self-government recognize the principle that the interests of the inhabitants of these territories are paramount, and accept as a sacred trust the obligation to promote to the utmost, within the system of international peace and security established by the present Charter, the well-being of the inhabitants of these territories, . . ." This general obligation is then divided into five specific obligations: (a) to "ensure, with due respect for the culture of the peoples concerned, their political, economic, social, and educational advancement, their just treatment, and their protection against abuses"; (b) to "develop self-government, to take due account of the political aspirations of the peoples, and to assist them in the progressive development of their free political institutions, according to the particular circumstances of each territory and its peoples . . . "; (c) to "further international peace and security"; (d) to "promote constructive measures of development . . . "; and (e) to "transmit regularly to the Secretary-General for information purposes, subject to such limitations as security and constitutional considerations may require, statistical and other information of a technical nature relating to economic, social, and educational conditions in the territories for which they are respectively responsible. . . ."

Today, when so many of these people have claimed and won their independence, the obligations contained in the declaration may not seem very far-reaching. For example, nothing is said about preparing non-self-governing territories for actual independence—indeed, the word "independence" appears nowhere in the declaration. Although due account is to be taken of the "political

aspirations of the peoples," all that is explicitly acknowledged is the obligation to develop "self-government," which does not necessarily imply independence.

However, the validity of the declaration must be considered in the context of its era. Few people at the San Francisco Conference foresaw how intense or universal the desire of colonial peoples for full political sovereignty would be. All told, the obligations included in the declaration probably represented the maximum that reasonably could be expected from colonial countries at that time. Moreover, in the circumstances then prevailing, the agreement by the colonial nations, under paragraph (e) of Article 73, to submit information to an international body concerning their own territories—in effect, to yield up a degree of their sovereignty—was a considerable concession.

TERRITORIES COVERED BY THE DECLARATION

The somewhat unwieldy term "non-self-governing territory" was chosen primarily because it was broad enough to include the various constitutional designations given by administering powers to their dependencies—colony, protectorate, and so on—as well as all stages of political development short of actual self-government or independence. The declaration includes all those territories "whose peoples have not yet attained a full measure of self-government." However, the precise meaning of the phrase "a full measure of self-government" was not specified in the charter, an omission that left the door open for subsequent dispute and controversy.

At the outset, it was considered the responsibility of the eight colonial powers that were UN members to identify the dependencies they regarded as non-self-governing within the meaning of Article 73 of the charter. At its first working session, in 1946, the General Assembly adopted a resolution enumerating 74 non-self-governing territories that the administering countries had identified as falling within the provisions of the declaration. The eight colonial countries were Australia, Belgium, Denmark, France, the Netherlands, New Zealand, the United Kingdom, and the United States. The combined population of their dependencies—which ranged from tiny Pitcairn Island, with a population of 100 persons, to the Netherlands Indies, with 73 million—was estimated at 215 million. The dependencies of Spain and Portugal could not be included in the 1946 list, since these two colonial powers were not UN members at the time. (For the non-self-governing territories listed by the General Assembly in 1946 and subsequently, see Table 1 on page 162.)

THE ROLE OF THE UN

The charter does not assign any particular task to the UN with respect to non-self-governing territories. It does not even specify what should be done with the information transmitted to the Secretary-General. Hence, the General Assembly has considered itself free to define its own functions.

Since, even in the very beginning, the majority of UN members were vehemently anticolonial, the immediate task that the General Assembly set for itself was to induce the colonial countries by every means in its power to fulfill their obligations under the charter declaration. Judging from the disputes and controversies that arose even as early as 1946, it seems safe to assume that this development was totally unforeseen by the colonial countries at the time of the San Francisco Conference.

Although the General Assembly lacks the power to enforce its recommendations, the colonial powers had no wish to see themselves recorded as being in constant opposition in majority decisions. Consequently, they fought from the start to maintain the right to take the initiative in affairs concerning their own territories and to prevent the UN from expanding its role in colonial matters. However, they were fighting a losing battle against an irreversible trend of world opinion; in effect, the story of the UN's role has essentially been one of increasing involvement in the process of decolonization.

Disputes over the Transmission of Information
The first dispute that arose between the colonial powers and the other UN members concerned the General Assembly's desire to discuss the reports that had been submitted on the various territories. Some of the colonial governments, particularly Belgium, contended that the mere submission of reports fulfilled the charter's requirements under paragraph (e) of Article 73. Disregarding these protests, the 1947 General Assembly set up a special committee to report on the information received. In 1949, this committee was established as the Committee on Information from Non-Self-Governing Territories, composed of an equal number of administering and nonadministering countries. In the same year, the General Assembly adopted a standard questionnaire, which the administering powers were expected to answer in annual reports. The questionnaire covered virtually every aspect of the social, economic, and educational conditions in the territories. However, because of the controversies discussed below, the committee received reports on only 56 of the 74 territories.

Cessation of Information
By 1949, some of the administering powers had unilaterally interpreted paragraph (e) of Article 73 to mean that when they themselves considered a territory to have attained self-government, they no longer needed to submit reports on it to the UN. On this basis, the United Kingdom ceased sending information on Malta after its first report in 1946. Likewise, France, after 1946, stopped sending reports on certain of its territories, including Guadeloupe, Martinique, and New Caledonia, that it regarded as overseas departments with rights equal to those of the metropolitan departments of France or as having reached a requisite stage of "internal autonomy." Nor did the United States send reports on the Panama Canal Zone after 1946 (though this decision may have been made because Panama itself contested classification of the Canal Zone as a non-self-governing territory). Concerned about these developments, the 1949 General Assembly, over the opposition of the colonial powers (the United States abstaining), decided that it was "within the responsibility of the General Assembly to express its opinion on the principles which have guided or which may in future guide the Members concerned in enumerating the territories for which the obligation exists to transmit information under Article 73 (e) of the Charter."

The General Assembly, in 1952, established a special committee to draw up a list of criteria of self-government and, at its next session, voted itself competent to decide on the basis of this list whether reports were due on a given territory. Since that time, the General Assembly has formally approved the cessation of reports on a number of territories, finding that they had "attained a full measure of self-government." However, in each case the administering power in question had already announced, prior to that approval, that it would no longer transmit information on these territories. The territories and the dates of General Assembly approval were as follows: from 1953 to 1955, Puerto Rico (United States), Greenland (Denmark), Suriname and Curaçao (Netherlands); in 1959, Alaska and Hawaii (United States); in 1965, the Cook Islands (New Zealand); and in 1974, Niue (New Zealand).

It should be noted, however, that so long as a territory is not actually independent, the General Assembly considers that it has the right to reopen the question of the territory's status at any time. Thus, although France ceased transmitting information on New Caledonia in 1947, the General Assembly decided on 2 December 1986 that New Caledonia was a non-self-governing territory within the meaning of Chapter XI of the charter and it was again included in the list of such territories.

In 1967, the United Kingdom announced that since a number of its small Caribbean dependencies—namely, Antigua, Dominica, Grenada, St. Kitts-Nevis-Anguilla, and St. Lucia—had achieved the status of associated states with a "full measure of self-government," it would no longer submit reports on those territories. The General Assembly did not, however, accept the territories' new status as constituting full self-government and continued to consider them as non-self-governing. (All the associated states except Anguilla subsequently attained independence, and the United Kingdom resumed transmission of information regarding Anguilla in 1984.) A similar situation arose with respect to Brunei, in 1972, when the United Kingdom informed the Secretary-General that the territory had attained full internal self-government and that, consequently, the United Kingdom considered the transmission of information about it to be no longer appropriate. (Brunei became independent in 1984.)

Refusal to Transmit Information
Until the General Assembly began to assert a competence in the matter, the inclusion of a territory in the list of non-self-governing territories to which Article 73 applies was at the discretion of the administering power concerned. For instance, in 1946, the United Kingdom did not include Southern Rhodesia in the list of dependent territories under its administration because the territory was self-govern,g but subsequently changed its position after the unilateral declaration of independence by the white-majority regime in 1965.

When Spain and Portugal became UN members in 1955, they also refused to transmit information on their overseas territories, maintaining that these were not colonial possessions but "overseas provinces." Spain retreated from this position in 1960, to the "satisfaction" of the General Assembly, and began to submit reports. However, Portugal maintained its stand until 1974, when an internal upheaval brought about a change of government.

These differences concerning the obligation to transmit information under Article 73 (e) led the Assembly in 1960 to adopt a resolution that defined a "full measure of self-government" to mean one of three specific conditions: (1) emergence of the territory as a sovereign independent state, (2) free association with an independent state, or (3) integration with an independent state, both (2) and (3) to be the result of a free and voluntary choice of the people concerned and the people to possess certain specified rights and safeguards in their new status. Unless one of these three conditions pertained, the General Assembly asserted, the administering power had an obligation to transmit information on any territory that is "geographically separate and is distinct ethnically and/or culturally from the country administering it."

THE 1960 ASSEMBLY DECLARATION ON THE ENDING OF COLONIALISM
Throughout the 1950s, the various disputes with colonial powers over the transmission of information on non-self-governing territories took place against a background of steady decolonization. Whether gracefully granted or bitterly fought for, sovereignty was achieved by a growing number of former colonial dependencies. In 1946, at the first working session of the General Assembly, only a handful of members had memories of recent foreign rule: India, the Philippines, and the four Arab countries that had been League of Nations mandate territories (Iraq, Jordan, Lebanon, and Syria). By 1959, eight Asian countries (Burma, Cambodia, Ceylon, Indonesia, Laos, Malaya, Nepal, and Pakistan) and two African countries (Ghana and Guinea) had become sovereign independent states. As these nations joined the UN, many of them after years of struggle against their former masters or with humiliating memories of the indignities of foreign rule, anticolonialist sentiment became increasingly bitter and significantly influenced the tone of the debates in the General Assembly. Wholeheartedly

supported by the Soviet-bloc nations, the newly independent nations began a drive to put a speedy end to colonialism altogether, thus going far beyond anything specifically spelled out in the charter.

The 1960 General Assembly proved to be decisive for the triumph of the anticolonialist forces in the UN. At the opening of that session, 16 new African states and Cyprus became members, thereby bringing the total number of African and Asian nations to 44 out of a total UN membership of 100. In addition, members of the Afro-Asian Group, as it was called, knew that they could count on the support of the Soviet bloc, many Latin American countries, and the Scandinavian countries. By the end of the session, they had drafted the text of a Declaration on the Granting of Independence to Colonial Countries and Peoples that was designed to serve as the UN's basic framework for its work in colonial matters, complementing the charter declaration.

Main Provisions of the Declaration

Whereas the charter declaration had been a gentlemanly agreement among masters to look after the welfare of their subjects, the General Assembly declaration, in effect, was an assertion of the right of these subject peoples to be subjects no longer. Written from the viewpoint of the colonial peoples themselves, the declaration in its preamble recognizes "the passionate yearning for freedom in all dependent peoples"; the existence of "increasing conflicts resulting from the denial . . . of the freedom of such peoples, which constitute a serious threat to world peace"; and "the important role of the United Nations in assisting the movement for independence in Trust and Non-Self-Governing Territories." The declaration then lists seven provisions: (1) the subjection of peoples to alien domination "is contrary to the Charter of the United Nations and is an impediment to the promotion of world peace and cooperation"; (2) "all peoples have the right to self-determination"; (3) inadequacy of preparedness "should never serve as a pretext for delaying independence"; (4) all armed action or repressive measures against dependent peoples "shall cease in order to enable them to exercise peacefully and freely their right to complete independence"; (5) "immediate steps shall be taken . . . to transfer all powers to the peoples of those territories, without any conditions or reservations"; (6) any attempt to disrupt the national unity and territorial integrity of a country "is incompatible with the purposes and principles of the Charter"; and (7) all states "shall observe faithfully and strictly" the provisions of the Charter, the Universal Declaration of Human Rights, and "the present Declaration" on the basis of equality, noninterference in the internal affairs of states, and respect for the sovereign rights of all peoples.

Although the phrase "colonial powers" does not appear, the declaration was clearly and firmly directed against those countries. Nevertheless, such was the force of anticolonial sentiment that no colonial power cared to record a negative vote. Accordingly, on 14 December 1960, the Declaration on the Granting of Independence to Colonial Countries and Peoples was adopted 89–0, with only nine abstentions (Australia, Belgium, the Dominican Republic, France, Portugal, South Africa, Spain, the United Kingdom, and the United States).

Establishment of the Special Committee

A year after the adoption of the declaration, the USSR took the initiative by asking the General Assembly to discuss the problem of implementing it. The ensuing debate led to the creation of a 17-member Special Committee on the Situation with Regard to the Implementation of the Declaration on the Granting of Independence to Colonial Countries and Peoples. Because of the importance attached to its work, seven additional members were added in the following year. Since that time, the composition of the Special Committee (in its early days called "the Special Committee of 24") has changed slightly when certain countries have withdrawn for various reasons, to be replaced by countries representing the same geopolitical grouping as the outgoing members. Originally, the committee included three colonial or administering powers—Australia, the United Kingdom, and the United States—but France, Spain, and the two most recalcitrant administering countries, Portugal and South Africa, were never members. In later developments, both the United Kingdom and the United States suspended their cooperation. Thus, the committee's deliberations have always been anticolonialist in tone.

In 1963, the committee's functions were expanded to include the work of the 1947 Committee on Information from Non-Self-Governing Territories, which was dissolved. At the same time, the General Assembly gave the committee the right to apprise the Security Council of any developments in any territory that it had examined that might threaten international peace and security. (Normally, subsidiary bodies do not have this right but must act through the General Assembly.) In addition, the General Assembly empowered the committee to examine information on the trust territories, as well as on non-self-governing territories—although the Trusteeship Council continued to exercise its normal functions until the graduation of the last trusteeship territory in 1994. The committee was also empowered to send visiting missions to dependent territories. Hence, since 1963, the committee has been the General Assembly's chief executive arm in colonial matters.

Besides considering problems connected with individual colonial territories, the committee debates topics of a more general nature assigned to it by the General Assembly—for example, the role played by foreign economic and military interests that are impeding the attainment of independence or exploiting the natural resources of the territories that rightfully belong to the indigenous inhabitants. The committee has been particularly active in the dissemination of information on colonial problems and in mobilizing international support and assistance for the colonial peoples and their efforts to achieve self-determination and independence.

In 1988, the General Assembly declared the decade 1990–2000 the Decade for the Eradication of Colonialism. In 1991, it approved a plan of action for the Special Committee which it hoped would achieve the total elimination of colonialism by the year 2000. The plan of action called for the Special Committee to, among other things: formulate specific proposals for the elimination of the remaining manifestations of colonialism, and to report its findings each year to the General Assembly; to make concrete suggestions to the Security Council about developments in colonial territories that threaten international peace and security; to pay special attention to small territories, and dispatch visiting missions to those territories to gather information firsthand; and to continue to collect, prepare, and disseminate studies and articles on the problems of decolonization, including continuation of the periodical *Objective: Justice* and the special series called *Decolonization*.

In January, 1986, the United Kingdom informed the Special committee's chairman that it would no longer take part in the Committee's work, since, in its own opinion, all the remaining territories under its administration had chosen to remain in close association with the United Kingdom. However, the United Kingdom agreed to continue to fulfill its obligations under the charter and to transmit information to the committee under Article 73e. The U.K. also reiterated to the Fourth Committee in 1990 that it would respect the wishes of the people of any of its 10 remaining territories, no matter what the size of their population.

In February 1992, the United States suspended its cooperation with the Special Committee, claiming that it had focused on an outmoded agenda instead of new approaches aimed at addressing the needs of the few remaining non-self-governing territories.

In January 1993, the following 25 countries were represented on the Special Committee: Afghanistan, Bulgaria, Chile, China, Congo, Côte d'Ivoire, Cuba, Czech Republic, Ethiopia, Fiji, Grenada, India, Indonesia, Iran (Islamic Republic of), Iraq, Mali, Papua New Guinea, Russian Federation, Sierra Leone, Syrian Arab Republic, Trinidad and Tobago, Tunisia, United Republic of Tanzania, Venezuela, and Yugoslavia.

PROGRESS OF DECOLONIZATION

In the 10 years following the adoption of the declaration on the ending of colonialism (1960 to 1970), 27 territories (with a total population of over 53 million) attained independence. Some 44 territories (with a population of approximately 28 million) remained under foreign rule or control, however, and the General Assembly's work in hastening the process of decolonization was far from completed. In Africa, an ever-widening confrontation had emerged between the colonial and white-minority regimes and the roughly 18 million Africans in Portuguese Guinea (now Guinea-Bissau), Angola, Mozambique, Cape Verde, and São Tomé and Príncipe; in Southern Rhodesia, which was legally still a British possession; and in the old League of Nations mandate territory of South West Africa, officially designated as Namibia by the UN. Resisting all efforts by the UN to bring an end to white-minority rule by peaceful means, these regimes refused to change despite pressures brought upon them both by the international community and by the demands of the African peoples of the territories.

This refusal had led to the emergence of African national liberation movements within the territories and to a series of armed conflicts that were seen by independent African states as a menace to peace and stability and as the potential cause of a bloody racial war engulfing the whole of Africa. Armed conflict, beginning in 1960 in Angola, had, in fact, spread to all the Portuguese-controlled territories on the African mainland and, as the African liberation movements gained strength and support, had developed into full-scale warfare in Angola, Portuguese Guinea, and Mozambique, engaging large Portuguese armies and putting a serious strain on Portugal's economy.

In Southern Rhodesia and Namibia, armed struggle for liberation was slower to develop, but despite the essential differences in the problems presented by these territories, the General Assembly—partly in response to a growing collaboration between South Africa, Portugal, and the white-minority regime in Southern Rhodesia—had come to view them as aspects of a single consuming issue of white-minority rule versus black-majority rights.

The strategy advocated by the Afro-Asian Group, supported by the Soviet-bloc countries and many others, for rectifying the situation in these territories was essentially to obtain recognition and support for their African national liberation movements and to seek the application, through a Security Council decision made under Chapter VII of the charter, of mandatory enforcement measures, including full economic sanctions and military force as circumstances warranted. However, in each case, except partially in that of Southern Rhodesia, the use of mandatory enforcement measures was decisively resisted by two permanent members of the Security Council, the United Kingdom and the United States, which, together with several other Western nations, felt that they could not afford to embark upon a policy of confrontation with the economically wealthy white-minority regimes of southern Africa.

Despite this resistance, the African and Asian nations continued to maintain the spotlight of attention on issues of decolonization. Year after year, one or another of the cases mentioned above was brought before the Security Council. Each session of the General Assembly, and of the Special Committee on decolonization, was the scene of lengthy and often acrimonious debates. This constant pressure led to greater recognition and status for the national liberation movements of the territories in Africa and brought about widespread condemnation and isolation of the white regimes. In 1971, for the first time, a mission of the Special Committee visited the liberated areas of Guinea-Bissau at the invitation of the African liberation movement concerned and found that the liberation movement had established an effective administration.

In 1972, the General Assembly affirmed for the first time that "the national liberation movements of Angola, Guinea-Bissau and Cape Verde, and Mozambique are the authentic representatives of the true aspirations of the peoples of those territories" and recommended that, pending the independence of those territories, all governments and UN bodies should, when dealing with matters pertaining to the territories, ensure the representation of those territories by the liberation movements concerned. In the following year, the General Assembly extended similar recognition to the national liberation movements of Southern Rhodesia and Namibia.

On 25 April 1974, largely as a result of internal and external pressures resulting from its colonial wars, a change of regime occurred in Portugal that had major repercussions on the situation in its African territories. The new regime pledged itself to ending the colonial wars and began negotiations with the national liberation movements. By the end of 1974, Portuguese troops had been withdrawn from Guinea-Bissau and the latter had become a UN member. This was followed by the independence and admission to UN membership of Cape Verde, Mozambique, and São Tomé and Príncipe in 1975 and Angola in 1976.

Southern Rhodesia (now Zimbabwe)

The problem of Southern Rhodesia, which in 1977 had a population of almost 7 million, of whom 6.5 million were Africans, was not resolved until the end of the decade.

Southern Rhodesia had been given full internal self-government by the United Kingdom in 1923, although under a constitution that vested political power exclusively in the hands of the white settlers. Hence, the United Kingdom did not include this dependency in its original 1946 list of non-self-governing territories and did not transmit information on it to the UN. Although, by the terms of the 1923 constitution, the United Kingdom retained the residual power to veto any legislation contrary to African interests, this power was never used, and no attempt was made to interfere with the white settlers' domination of the territorial government.

UN involvement in the question of Southern Rhodesia began in 1961, when African and Asian members tried, without success, to bring pressure to bear upon the United Kingdom not to permit a new territorial constitution to come into effect. While giving Africans their first representation in the Southern Rhodesian parliament, the 1961 constitution restricted their franchise through a two-tier electoral system heavily weighted in favor of the European community.

In June 1962, acting on the recommendation of the Special Committee, the General Assembly adopted a resolution declaring Southern Rhodesia to be a non-self-governing territory within the meaning of Chapter XI of the charter, on the grounds that the vast majority of the people of Southern Rhodesia were denied equal political rights and liberties. The General Assembly requested the United Kingdom to convene a conference of all political parties in Rhodesia for the purpose of drawing up a new constitution that would ensure the rights of the majority on the basis of "one-man, one-vote." However, the United Kingdom continued to maintain that it could not interfere in Rhodesia's domestic affairs. The 1961 constitution duly came into effect in November 1962.

On 11 November 1965, the government of Ian Smith unilaterally declared Southern Rhodesia independent. The United Kingdom, after branding the declaration an "illegal act," brought the matter to the Security Council on the following day, and a resolution was adopted condemning the declaration and calling upon all states to refrain from recognizing and giving assistance to the "rebel" regime. On 20 November, the council adopted a resolution condemning the "usurpation of power," calling upon the United Kingdom to bring the regime to an immediate end, and requesting all states, among other things, to sever economic relations and institute an embargo on oil and petroleum products. In 1968, the Security Council imposed wider mandatory sanctions against Southern Rhodesia and established a committee to oversee the application of the sanctions. The General Assembly urged countries to render moral and material assistance to the national liberation movements of Zimbabwe, the African name for the territory.

On 2 March 1970, Southern Rhodesia proclaimed itself a republic, thus severing its ties with the United Kingdom. After Mozambique became independent in 1975, guerrilla activity along the border with Southern Rhodesia intensified; the border was then closed, further threatening the economy of Southern Rhodesia, already hurt by UN-imposed sanctions.

In 1977, Anglo-American proposals for the settlement of the Southern Rhodesian problem were communicated to the Security Council by the United Kingdom. The proposals called for the surrender of power by the illegal regime, free elections on the basis of universal suffrage, the establishment by the United Kingdom of a transitional administration, the presence of a UN force during the transitional period, and the drafting of an independence constitution. The proposals were to be discussed at a conference of all political parties in Southern Rhodesia, white and African. However, the regime rejected the idea of such a conference. Attempts by the regime in 1978 and early 1979 to draft a new constitution giving some political power to Africans but maintaining effective control by the white minority failed, and the struggle by forces of the liberation movement, called the Patriotic Front, intensified.

In August 1979, British prime minister Margaret Thatcher stated at the Conference of Commonwealth Heads of State and Government that her government intended to bring Southern Rhodesia to legal independence on a basis acceptable to the international community. To this end, a constitutional conference was convened in London on 10 September, to which representatives of the Patriotic Front and the Rhodesian administration in Salisbury were invited. On 21 December, an agreement was signed on a draft independence constitution and on transitional arrangements for its implementation, as well as on a cease-fire to take effect on 28 December. Lord Soames was appointed governor of the territory until elections, which took place in February 1980 in the presence of UN observers. On 11 March, Lord Soames formally appointed Robert G. Mugabe, whose party had received the majority of seats in the House of Assembly, as prime minister. The independence of Zimbabwe was proclaimed on 18 April 1980, and on 25 August, Zimbabwe became a member of the UN.

Remaining Colonial Issues

The 17 remaining dependent territories are almost all small islands scattered about the globe. Their tiny populations and minimal economic resources render it almost impossible for them to survive as viable, fully independent states. Table 2 on page 163 sets forth all the former non-self-governing territories that have become independent or joined neighboring independent states.

Although the administering powers joined with the rest of the UN membership in asserting that the peoples of these small territories have an inalienable right to the exercise of self-determination, the leaders of the drive to end colonialism have doubted the genuineness of the preparations for achieving this goal. As evidence to justify their skepticism, the African and Asian nations

pointed out that military bases were established in some of the small territories, which they declared "incompatible with the purposes and principles of the Charter." Moreover, in the case of territories that the administering powers have declared their intention of preparing for self-governing status rather than for full independence, the majority of UN members feel that the General Assembly should be granted an active role in ascertaining the wishes of the inhabitants and furnished with more comprehensive information on conditions prevailing in the territories. The General Assembly has approved numerous resolutions requesting the administering states to allow UN missions to visit the remaining non-self-governing territories to ascertain, firsthand, the wishes of the inhabitants, but has met with little cooperation.

Two of the territories that have been brought under the General Assembly's surveillance through the Special Committee are United Kingdom possessions in which the issue of decolonization is complicated by conflicting claims of sovereignty by other nations—the Falkland Islands (Malvinas), claimed by Argentina, and Gibraltar, claimed by Spain.

In regard to another territory, East Timor, the administering power, Portugal, informed the General Assembly in 1977 that developments in the territory had prevented it from carrying out its responsibilities or exercising its authority. With regard to Western Sahara, Spain informed the Secretary-General in 1976 that it had terminated its presence in the territory and considered itself henceforth exempt from any international responsibility in connection with its administration. Both territories, however, continued to be listed by the General Assembly as non-self-governing.

The Special Committee annually reviews the list of territories to which the declaration on decolonization is applicable. In 1986, France, the administering power of New Caledonia, refused to recognize the competence of the committee over the territory or to transmit to the UN the information called for under Article 73 (e) of the charter. France has, however, asserted that it will respect the wishes of the majority of the people of New Caledonia, in accordance with the provisions of the Matignon Agreement agreed to by all the parties in 1988. Under the terms of that agreement, a national referendum on self-determination will take place between 1 March and 31 December 1998.

The Problem of Namibia (South West Africa)

The status of South West Africa (officially designated as Namibia by the General Assembly in June 1968), a pre–World War I German colony that was administered by South Africa under a League of Nations mandate beginning in 1920, has preoccupied the General Assembly almost from the first moment of the UN's existence. In 1946, South Africa proposed that the Assembly approve its annexation of the territory. Fearing that the South African government would seek to extend its apartheid system to South West Africa, the General Assembly did not approve the proposal and recommended instead that the territory be placed under the UN trusteeship system. In the following year, South Africa informed the General Assembly that while it agreed not to annex the territory, it would not place it under trusteeship. Although South Africa had reported on conditions in the territory in 1946, it declined to submit further reports, despite repeated requests from the General Assembly.

In 1950, the International Court of Justice, in an advisory opinion requested by the General Assembly, held that South Africa continued to have international obligations to promote to the utmost the material and moral well-being and social progress of the inhabitants of the territory as a sacred trust of civilization, and that the UN should exercise the supervisory functions of the League of Nations in the administration of the territory. South Africa refused to accept the court's opinion and continued to oppose any form of UN supervision over the territory's affairs.

In October 1966, the General Assembly, declaring that South Africa had failed to fulfill its obligations under the League of Nations mandate to ensure the well-being of the people of the territory and that it had, in fact, disavowed the mandate, decided that the mandate was therefore terminated, that South Africa had no other right to administer the territory, and that thenceforth the territory came under the direct responsibility of the UN. In May 1967, the General Assembly established the UN Council for South West Africa (later renamed the UN Council for Namibia) to administer the territory until independence "with the maximum possible participation of the people of the territory." It also decided to establish the post of UN Commissioner for Namibia to assist the council in carrying out its mandate. Later in the same year, in the face of South Africa's refusal to accept its decision and to cooperate with the UN Council for Namibia, the General Assembly recommended that the Security Council take measures to enable the UN Council for Namibia to carry out its mandate.

In its first resolution on the question, in 1969, the Security Council recognized the termination of the mandate by the General Assembly, described the continued presence of South Africa in Namibia as illegal, and called on South Africa to withdraw its administration from the territory immediately. In the following year, the Security Council explicitly declared for the first time that "all acts taken by the government of South Africa on behalf of or concerning Namibia after the termination of the mandate are illegal and invalid." This view was upheld in 1971 by the International Court of Justice, which stated, in an advisory opinion requested by the Security Council, that "the continued presence of South Africa in Namibia being illegal, South Africa is under obligation to withdraw its administration from Namibia immediately and thus put an end to its occupation of the territory." South Africa, however, again refused to comply with UN resolutions on the question of Namibia, and it continued to administer the territory.

To secure for the Namibians "adequate protection of the natural wealth and resources of the territory which is rightfully theirs," the UN Council for Namibia enacted a Decree for the Protection of the Natural Resources of Namibia in September 1974. Under the decree, no person or entity may search for, take, or distribute any natural resource found in Namibia without the council's permission, and any person or entity contravening the decree "may be held liable in damages by the future government of an independent Namibia." The council also established, in the same year, the Institute for Namibia (located in Lusaka, Zambia, until South Africa's withdrawal from Namibia) to provide Namibians with education and training and equip them to administer a future independent Namibia.

In 1976, the Security Council demanded for the first time that South Africa accept elections for the territory as a whole under UN supervision and control so that the people of Namibia might freely determine their own future. It condemned South Africa's "illegal and arbitrary application . . . of racially discriminatory and repressive laws and practices in Namibia," its military buildup, and its use of the territory "as a base for attacks on neighboring countries."

In the same year, the General Assembly condemned South Africa "for organizing the so-called constitutional talks at Windhoek, which seek to perpetuate the apartheid and homelands policies as well as the colonial oppression and exploitation of the people and resources of Namibia." It decided that any independence talks regarding Namibia must be between the representatives of South Africa and the South West Africa People's Organization (SWAPO), which it recognized as "the sole and authentic representative of the Namibian people." In 1977, the General Assembly declared that South Africa's decision to annex Walvis Bay, Namibia's main port, was "illegal, null, and void" and "an act of colonial expansion," and it condemned the annexation as an attempt "to undermine the territorial integrity and unity of Namibia."

At a special session on Namibia in May 1978, the General Assembly adopted a declaration on Namibia and a program of action in support of self-determination and national independence for Namibia. Expressing "full support for the armed liberation struggle of the Namibian people under the leadership of the SWAPO," it stated that any negotiated settlement must be arrived at with the agreement of SWAPO and within the framework of UN resolutions.

The UN Plan for Namibian Independence. In July 1978, the Security Council met to consider a proposal by the five Western members of the council—Canada, France, the Federal Republic of Germany, the United Kingdom, and the United States—for a settlement of the Namibian question. The proposal comprised a plan for free elections to a constituent assembly under the supervision and control of a UN representative, assisted by a UN transition assistance group that would include both civilian and military components. The council took note of the Western proposal and requested the Secretary-General to appoint a special representative for Namibia. In September 1978, after approving a report by the Secretary-General based on his special representative's findings, the council, in Resolution 435 (1978), endorsed the UN plan for the independence of Namibia, and it decided to establish, under its authority, the UN Transition Assistance Group (UNTAG) to ensure the early independence of Namibia through free and fair elections under UN supervision and control.

The Secretary-General's report stated that the implementation of the UN plan would be carried out in three stages: (1) cessation of all hostile acts by all parties; (2) the repeal of discriminatory or restrictive laws, the release of political prisoners, and the voluntary return of exiles and refugees; and (3) the holding of elections after a seven-month pre-electoral period, to be followed by the entry into force of the newly adopted constitution and the consequent achievement of independence by Namibia.

Since 1978, the General Assembly has continually reaffirmed that Security Council Resolution 435 (1978), in which the council endorsed the UN plan for the independence of Namibia, is the only basis for a peaceful settlement. It has condemned South Africa for obstructing the implementation of that resolution and other UN resolutions, for "its manoeuvres aimed at perpetuating its illegal occupation of Namibia," and for its attempts to establish a "linkage" between the independence of Namibia and "irrelevant, extraneous" issues, such as the presence of Cuban troops in Angola. In furtherance of the objective of bringing to an end South Africa's occupation of Namibia, the General Assembly has called upon all states to sever all relations with South Africa, and it has urged the Security Council to impose mandatory comprehensive sanctions against South Africa. The General Assembly also has continued to authorize the UN Council for Namibia, as the legal administering authority for Namibia, to mobilize international support for the withdrawal of the illegal South African administration from Namibia, to counter South Africa's policies against the Namibian people and against the UN, to denounce and seek the rejection by all states of South Africa's attempts to perpetuate its presence in Namibia, and to ensure the nonrecognition of any administration or political entity installed in Namibia, such as the so-called interim government imposed in Namibia on 17 June 1985, that is not the result of free elections held under UN supervision and control.

In April 1987, the Secretary-General reported to the Security Council that agreement had been reached on the system of proportional representation for the elections to be held in Namibia as envisaged in Council Resolution 435 (1978). Thus, he noted, all outstanding issues had been resolved, and the only reason for the delay in the emplacement of UNTAG and an agreement on a cease-fire was South Africa's unacceptable precondition that the

Cuban troops be withdrawn from Angola before the implementation of the UN plan for Namibian independence.

In December 1988, after eight months of intense negotiations brokered by the United States, Angola, Cuba, and South Africa signed agreements on the withdrawal of Cuban troops from Angola and the achievement of peace in south-western Africa. On 16 January 1989 the Security Council officially declared that Namibia's transition to independence would begin on 1 April 1989 (Security Council Resolution 628/1989). The council also authorized sending the UNTAG to Namibia to supervise the transition (Security Council Resolution 629/1989).

In one short year, from 1 April 1989 to 21 March 1990, the 8,000-member UNTAG force established 200 outposts, including 42 regional or district centers and 48 police stations. During the transition the UN High Commissioner for Refugees (UNHCR) had supervised the repatriation of 433,000 Namibian exiles who had been scattered throughout 40 countries. UNTAG supervised the registration of more than 700,000 voters, more than 97 percent of whom cast ballots in the historic election from 7–11 November 1989 that marked the end of Namibia's colonial history. The Special Committee also dispatched a visiting mission to observe and monitor the election process. In that election Sam Nujoma, head of SWAPO, was elected the country's first president. The mission reported to the Special Committee that the people of Namibia had, in accordance with Security Council resolution 435 (1978), exercised their inalienable right to self-determination by choosing their representatives to a constituent assembly that was charged with drafting a constitution for an independent Namibia.

In March 1990, Secretary-General Perez de Cuéllar administered the oath of office to the new Namibian president at a historic celebration. In a moving show of good faith, President F.W. DeKlerk of South Africa took part in the inauguration ceremony. Nelson Mandela, then leader of South Africa's African National Congress party and only recently released from prison in South Africa, also attended, as did hundreds of dignitaries from 70 countries.

On 23 April 1990 Namibia became the 159th member of the United Nations.

Table 1
Non-Self-Governing Territories, Listed by the General Assembly in 1946 and Subsequent Years, That Have Become Independent States or Joined Neighboring Independent States

Australia
  Cocos (Keeling) Islands (integrated with Australia)
  Papua (now part of Papua New Guinea)
Belgium
  Belgian Congo (now Zaire)
France
  Comoros
  French Equatorial Africa (now Central African Republic, Chad, Congo, and Gabon)
  French Somaliland (now Djibouti)
  French West Africa (now Burkina Faso, Côte d'Ivoire, Dahomey, Guinea, Mali, Mauritania, Niger, and Senegal)
  Indochina (now Kampuchea, Laos, and Viet Nam)
  Madagascar
  Morocco
  New Hebrides (Anglo-French condominium; now Vanuatu)
  Tunisia
Netherlands
  Netherlands Indies (now Indonesia)
  Suriname
  West New Guinea (West Irian; now part of Indonesia)
New Zealand
  Cook Islands (self-governing in free association with New Zealand)
  Niue (self-governing in free association with New Zealand)
Portugal
  Angola
  Cape Verde
  Goa (united with India)
  Mozambique
  Portuguese Guinea (now Guinea-Bissau)
  São Tomé and Principe
Spain
  Fernando Poo and Rio Muni (now Equatorial Guinea)
  Ifni (returned to Morocco)
United Kingdom
  Aden (now part of Yemen)
  Antigua (now Antigua and Barbuda)
  Bahamas
  Barbados
  Basutoland (now Lesotho)
  Bechuanaland (now Botswana)
  British Guiana (now Guyana)
  British Honduras (now Belize)
  British Somaliland (now Somalia)
  Brunei (now Brunei Darussalam)
  Cyprus
  Dominica
  Ellice Islands (now Tuvalu)
  Fiji
  Gambia
  Gilbert Islands (now Kiribati)
  Gold Coast (now Ghana)
  Grenada
  Jamaica
  Kenya
  Malaya (now Malaysia)
  Malta
  Mauritius
  Nigeria
  New Hebrides (Anglo-French condominium; now Vanuatu)
  North Borneo (now part of Malaysia)
  Northern Rhodesia (now Zambia)
  Nyasaland (now Malawi)
  Oman
  St. Kitts and Nevis
  St. Lucia
  St. Vincent and the Grenadines
  Sarawak (now part of Malaysia)
  Seychelles
  Sierra Leone
  Singapore
  Solomon Islands
  Southern Rhodesia (now Zimbabwe)
  Swaziland
  Trinidad and Tobago
  Uganda
  Zanzibar (now part of Tanzania)
United Nations
  Namibia (formerly South West Africa)[1]
United States
  Trust Territory of the Pacific Islands (Federated States of Micronesia, Marshall Islands, Palau (in free association with the United States))

1. In 1966, the General Assembly terminated South Africa's mandate over South West Africa and placed the territory under the direct responsibility of the UN. In 1968, the General Assembly declared that the territory would be called Namibia, in accordance with its people's wishes. Until independence, the legal administering authority for Namibia was the UN Council for Namibia.

Table 2
Remaining Non-Self-Governing Territories Listed by the General
Assembly, as of 30 June 1994

France[2]
New Caledonia
New Zealand
Tokelau Islands
Portugal
East Timor[3]
Spain
Western Sahara[4]
United Kingdom
Anguilla
Bermuda
British Virgin Islands
Cayman Islands
Falkland Islands (Malvinas)
Gibraltar
Montserrat
Pitcairn Island
St. Helena
Turks and Caicos Islands
United States
American Samoa
Guam
United States Virgin Islands

2. On 2 December 1986, the General Assembly decided that New Caledonia was a non-self-governing territory within the meaning of Chapter XI of the UN Charter.

3. On 20 April 1977, Portugal informed the Secretary-General that effective exercise of its sovereignty of the territory had ceased in August 1975 and that the only information that could be transmitted would concern the first months of 1975. In subsequent years, Portugal further informed the Secretary-General that conditions prevailing in East Timor continued to prevent it from assuming its responsibilities for the administration of the territory.

4. Spain informed the Secretary-General on 26 February 1976 that as of that date, it had terminated its presence in the territory of the Sahara and deemed it necessary to place the following on record: "Spain considers itself henceforth exempt from any responsibility of an international nature in connection with the administration of the territory in view of the cessation of its participation in the temporary administration established for the territory." On 5 December 1984, and in many subsequent resolutions, the General Assembly reaffirmed that the question of Western Sahara was a question of decolonization, which remained to be resolved by the people of Western Sahara. In August 1988 the Kingdom of Morocco and the Frente Popular para la Liberación (Polisario Front) agreed in principle to the proposals put forward by Secretary-General Perez de Cuéllar and the Organization of African Unity. By its Resolutions 658 (1990) and 690 (1991) the Security Council adopted a settlement plan for Western Sahara that included a referendum for self-determination by the people of the country. In September 1991, the UN achieved a cease-fire in Western Sahara between the factions. In 1993, however, talks were still continuing between the parties on the final arrangements for the referendum.

INTERNATIONAL LAW

The idea of developing international law through the restatement of existing rules is not of recent origin. In the last quarter of the eighteenth century, Jeremy Bentham proposed a codification of the whole of international law. Since his time, numerous attempts at codification have been made by private individuals, by learned societies and by governments. Enthusiasm for the "codification movement"—the name sometimes given to such attempts—generally stems from the belief that written international law would remove the uncertainties of customary international law by filling existing gaps in the law, as well as by giving precision to abstract general principles whose practical application is not settled.

MODERN ANTECEDENTS OF THE INTERNATIONAL LAW COMMISSION

The intergovernmental effort to promote the codification and development of international law made an important advance with the resolution of the assembly of the League of Nations of 22 September 1924, envisaging the creation of a standing organ called the Committee of Experts for the Progressive Codification of International Law, which was to be composed so as to present the "main forms of civilization and the principal legal systems of the world." This committee, consisting of 17 experts, was to prepare a list of subjects "the regulation of which by international agreement" was most "desirable and realizable" and thereafter to examine the comments of governments on this list and report on the questions which "were sufficiently ripe," as well as on the procedure to be followed in preparing for conferences for their solutions. This was the first attempt on a worldwide basis to codify and develop whole fields of international law rather than simply regulating individual and specific legal problems.

After certain consultations with governments and the League Council, the League Assembly decided, in 1927, to convene a diplomatic conference to codify three topics out of the five that had been considered to be "sufficiently ripe," namely: (1) nationality; (2) territorial waters; and (3) the responsibility of states for damage done in their territory to the person and property of foreigners. Delegates from 47 governments participated in the Codification Conference which met at The Hague, from 13 March to 12 April 1930. Unfortunately, nationality was the only subject for which an international instrument was agreed on. No further experiment in codification was made by the League of Nations after 1930, but on 25 September 1931, the League Assembly adopted an important resolution on the procedure of codification, the main theme of which was the strengthening of the influence of governments at every stage of the codification process.

PROVISIONS OF THE UNITED NATIONS CHARTER

Article I of the UN Charter calls for the adjustment or settlement of international disputes by peaceful means in conformity with the principles of justice and international law. In Article 13, the charter also requires the General Assembly to "initiate studies and make recommendations for the purpose of . . . encouraging the progressive development of international law and its codifica-

tion." To help it fulfill this mandate, the General Assembly set up two law commissions.

The International Law Commission was established in 1947 as a permanent subsidiary organ with its own separate statute. It began meeting in 1949 and since that time has completed a significant body of work.

At its 1966 session, the General Assembly established another commission with the specific object of promoting the harmonization and unification of international law in the field of trade. The UN Commission on International Trade Law (UNCITRAL) held its first meeting in 1968.

INTERNATIONAL LAW COMMISSION

Like the judges of the International Court of Justice, the 34 (originally 15) members of the International Law Commission are not representatives of governments. Instead, they are chosen in their individual capacity "as persons of recognized competence in international law" and with due consideration to representation of "the main forms of civilization" and "the principal legal systems of the world." No two members of the commission may be nationals of the same country. They are elected for five-year terms by the General Assembly, from a list of candidates nominated by UN member states.

The members of the International Law Commission do not serve in a full-time capacity on the International Law Commission and need not give up their other professional activities. They meet each year, normally in Geneva, for a session of approximately 12 weeks. The various topics under consideration are usually assigned to individual members, who then serve as special rapporteurs on the item concerned, carry out the necessary studies between sessions, and submit reports to the commission at its annual sessions.

Functions

Although the UN Charter does not lay down any principles for determining a desirable "progressive development" of international law, Article 1 of the Statute of the International Law Commission provides that the "Commission shall have for its object the promotion of the progressive development of international law and its codification." From the outset the discussions in the International Law Commission and the General Assembly have made very clear the main considerations involved. The traditional legal norms prevailing at the time of the San Francisco Conference were inherited from an era when world politics was dominated by a handful of Western European nations. As a consequence, international law itself reflected the values and interests of those nations. In essence, therefore, what has been required is an adjustment of the entire international legal order so as to take account of the interests and traditions of a much broader community of nations.

Article 15 of the Statute of the International Law Commission defines "progressive development" as the preparation of draft conventions on subjects which have not yet been regulated by international law, or in regard to which the law has not yet been sufficiently developed in the practice of states. It defines "codification" as meaning the more precise formulation and systemization of rules of international law in fields where there already has been extensive state practice, precedent, and doctrines.

Progressive Development. Under the Statute of the International Law Commission, proposals for the progressive development of international law are not formulated by the commission, but are referred to it by the General Assembly, or by members of the United Nations and other authorized agencies. On the other hand, the commission itself may select topics for codification.

Progressive development of international law is a conscious effort towards the creation of new rules of international law, whether by means of the regulation of a new topic or by means of the comprehensive vision of existing rules. Accordingly, the drafters of the statute considered that when the commission is engaged in the progressive development of any branch of law, the consummation of the work could be achieved only by means of an international convention. Thus the statute contemplates that the commission prepares a draft convention, and the General Assembly then decides whether steps should be taken to bring about the conclusion of an international convention.

Codification. On the other hand, when the commission's task is one of codification (the mere precise formulation and systematization of existing customary law), the statute envisages two other possible conclusions to its work: (a) simple publication of its report; and (b) a resolution of the General Assembly, taking note of or adopting the report. The statute also lays down the specific steps to be taken by the commission in the course of its work on progressive development and on codification.

Methods of Work
The commission follows essentially the same method for both progressive development and codification. A "special rapporteur" is appointed for each topic; an appropriate plan of work is formulated; where desirable, governments are requested to furnish the texts of relevant laws, decrees, judicial decisions, treaties, and diplomatic correspondence; the special rapporteur submits reports; the commission approves a provisional draft based on those reports in the form of articles, with a commentary setting forth precedents, any divergence of views, and alternative solutions considered. The provisional draft is issued as a commission document and submitted to the General Assembly, and also to governments for their written observations. On the basis of comments received from governments, together with any comments made in the debates of the Sixth Committee of the General Assembly, the special rapporteur submits a further report, recommending the changes in the provisional draft that seem appropriate. The commission then, on the basis of that report and the comments, adopts a final draft. The final draft is submitted to the General Assembly with a recommendation regarding further action.

Special Assignments. The General Assembly has from time to time requested the International Law Commission to examine particular texts or to report on particular legal problems. For example, at the specific request of the General Assembly, the commission dealt with the following topics: draft declaration on the rights and duties of states (1949); formulation of the Nürnberg principles (1950); questions of international criminal jurisdiction (1950); the question of defining aggression (1951); reservations to multilateral conventions (1951); draft code of offenses against the peace and security of mankind (1951 and 1954); extended participation in general multilateral treaties concluded under the auspices of the League of Nations (1962); question of the protection and inviolability of diplomatic agents and other persons entitled to special protection under international law (1972); and review of the multilateral treaty-making process (1979). The commission's reports on some of these topics were presented in the form of draft articles with commentaries. Conclusions reached on some other topics did not lend themselves to draft articles.

Scope of the Commission's Work
The General Assembly does not assign all legal issues with which it is concerned to the International Law Commission. Thus, the legal aspect of an agenda item that relates to another sphere of the General Assembly's work is often handled by a special committee set up to study that particular subject. This is the case, for example, with the legal aspects of the peaceful uses of outer space and with many matters of human rights and economic and social development. On occasion, too, the General Assembly has established a special committee to consider certain legal topics that directly affect the conduct of nations in the area of international peace and security and are therefore highly political. Thus, the agenda item entitled "Consideration of principles of international law concerning friendly relations and cooperation among states in accordance with the Charter of the United Nations" was assigned to a special 31-member committee. After eight years of discussion, the committee completed a draft declaration, as requested, in time for the commemorative session to celebrate the UN's 25th anniversary in 1970. The declaration embodies seven principles: the nonuse of force, peaceful settlement of disputes, nonintervention, sovereign equality, the duty to cooperate, equal rights and self-determination, and fulfillment of obligations under the charter.

Another example of a legal topic having a strongly political character is the definition of aggression. The International Law Commission originally was asked to draw up a definition of aggression. The task was taken over by the General Assembly only after the commission had failed to reach agreement. A special committee of the General Assembly drafted the text of the Definition of Aggression, which was adopted by the General Assembly in 1974.

Another special committee of the General Assembly drafted the International Convention on the Taking of Hostages, which was adopted in 1979, and still another prepared the draft of what became, after being approved by the General Assembly in 1982, the Manila Declaration on the Peaceful Settlement of International Disputes. A special committee, originally established by the General Assembly in 1977, completed a draft Declaration on the Enhancement of the Effectiveness of the Principle of Refraining from the Threat or Use of Force in International Relations, which the General Assembly approved in 1987. The General Assembly also has established an ad hoc committee to recommend practical measures for elimination of the problem of international terrorism. The committee, in 1979, submitted its final report and recommendations to the General Assembly, which welcomed the results achieved. In 1980, the General Assembly established an ad hoc committee on the drafting of an international convention against the recruitment, use, financing, and training of mercenaries. The committee completed its work in 1989. In the same year, the General Assembly adopted a convention on the subject. In 1993, the General Assembly entrusted an ad hoc committee with the task of elaborating an international convention dealing with the safety and security of United Nations and associated personnel, with particular reference to responsibility for attacks on such personnel. The ad hoc committee held its first session in March–April 1994.

Topics Selected for Codification
At its first session, in 1949, the commission considered 25 topics for possible study. It selected 14 of these for codification. The list was only provisional, and it was understood that changes might be made after further study by the commission or in compliance with the wishes of the General Assembly. The list, however, still constitutes the commission's basic long-term program of work.

Topics on which the commission has completed its work and submitted final drafts or reports to the General Assembly include the following: rights and duties of states; ways and means for making the evidence of customary international law more readily available; formulation of Nürnberg principles; the question of international criminal jurisdiction; reservations to multilateral conventions; the question of defining aggression; nationality, including statelessness; law of the sea; arbitral procedure; diplomatic intercourse and immunities; extended participation in general multilateral treaties concluded under the auspices of the League of Nations; law of treaties; special missions; relations between states and international organizations; succession of states in respect of treaties; question of protection and inviolability of diplomatic agents and other persons entitled to special protection under international law; the most-favored-nation clause; succession of states in respect of matters other than treaties; question of treaties concluded between states and international organizations or between two or more international organizations; status of the diplomatic courier and the diplomatic bag not accompanied by diplomatic courier; and jurisdictional immunities of states and their property.

The Sixth Committee itself sometimes functions as a codification body. On two occasions, with regard to the topics "Special Missions" and "Draft Convention on the Prevention and Punishments of Crimes against Diplomatic Agents and other Internationally Protected Persons," the Sixth Committee was assigned the finalization of the relevant conventions. The General Assembly subsequently adopted both conventions.

In 1994, the General Assembly, on the recommendation of the Sixth Committee, established an ad hoc committee to elaborate an international convention dealing with the safety and security of UN personnel. The committee's task was to consolidate, in a single document, the set of principles and obligations contained in existing treaties as well as to codify customary international law. The Sixth Committee also decided to convene in New York, in 1995, a United Nations Congress on Public International Law as part of the activities of the UN Decade for International Law (1990–1999).

Extended Participation in Multilateral Treaties Concluded Under the Auspices of the League of Nations

The commission's conclusions on the question of extended participation in multilateral treaties concluded under the auspices of the League of Nations were submitted to the General Assembly in 1963. On the basis of those conclusions, the General Assembly decided that it was the appropriate organ of the UN to exercise the functions of the League Council with respect to 21 general multilateral treaties of a technical and nonpolitical character concluded under the auspices of the former world body.

Law of Treaties

The most far-reaching task undertaken by the International Law Commission has been its work on the law of treaties—the laws governing the way in which treaties are to be negotiated, adopted, altered, and abrogated. The commission, which began work on this project in 1949, finally completed it in 1966, after 18 sessions. Throughout this period, the commission regularly submitted provisional draft articles to the General Assembly's Sixth Committee and to individual governments for comment. Accordingly, the final draft of 75 articles adopted by the commission and submitted to the General Assembly's 1966 session included many revisions. At a conference that met in two sessions in Vienna in 1968 and 1969, the Vienna Convention on the Law of Treaties was adopted. It came into force in 1980.

During the preparation of the draft articles on the law of treaties, the commission considered whether the articles should apply not only to treaties between states but also to treaties concluded by other entities, particularly by international organizations. The commission decided to confine its work to treaties between states, but following adoption of the Vienna Convention on the Law of Treaties, it took up, in consultation with the principal international organizations, the question of treaties concluded between states and international organizations or between two or more international organizations.

At a conference that met in Vienna in 1986, the Vienna Convention on the Law of Treaties Between States and International Organizations or Between International Organizations was adopted. It has not yet come into force.

Law of the Sea

In accordance with its 1949 program, the commission worked for a number of years on the codification of the law of the sea. Following a request of the 1954 General Assembly, the commission grouped together the articles that it had previously adopted and submitted a final draft on the law of the sea in 1956. The General Assembly called a special conference on the law of the sea at Geneva in 1958. At that conference, four conventions were adopted: (1) the Convention on the High Seas, which came into force on 30 September 1962; (2) the Convention on the Continental Shelf, on 24 April 1964; (3) the Convention on the Territorial Sea and the Contiguous Zone, on 10 September 1964; and (4) the Convention on Fishing and Conservation of the Living Resources of the High Seas, on 20 March 1966. (See also the chapter on the Law of the Sea.)

Reduction of Statelessness

In 1954, the commission prepared two drafts, one for a convention on the elimination of statelessness and another, which would impose fewer obligations on states, on the reduction of statelessness. General Assembly discussions showed that the first and more sweeping draft had no chance of acceptance. Even the measures on which countries would have to agree in order to reduce the number of stateless persons raised so many problems that two special conferences were eventually required, one in 1959 and one in 1961, to arrive at a Convention on the Reduction of Statelessness. It came into force in 1975.

Diplomatic and Consular Relations

In 1959, the commission adopted final draft articles on diplomatic intercourse and immunities. The General Assembly endorsed the drafts and convened an international conference, which met in Vienna in 1961 and adopted the Vienna Convention on Diplomatic Relations and two optional protocols, one concerning acquisition of nationality and the other compulsory settlement of disputes. The convention adapts to twentieth century requirements the rules for diplomatic intercourse formulated by the 1815 Congress of Vienna, which since that time have essentially governed diplomatic relations. It came into force on 24 April 1964.

Final draft articles on consular relations were submitted by the commission to the General Assembly in 1961. On the basis of these drafts, an international conference, held in Vienna in 1963, adopted the Vienna Convention on Consular Relations and two protocols. It came into force in 1967.

Special Missions

In 1968 and 1969, the General Assembly considered the question of a draft convention on special missions on the basis of draft articles prepared by the commission. On 8 December 1969, the General Assembly adopted the Convention on Special Missions and an optional protocol concerning the compulsory settlement of disputes. The convention, which came into force on 21 June 1985, provides rules applying to forms of ad hoc diplomacy—itinerant envoys, diplomatic conferences, and special missions sent to a state for limited purposes—that are not covered by the Vienna conventions of 1961 and 1963 relating to diplomatic and consular relations among states.

Protection of Diplomats

In 1973, the General Assembly adopted the Convention on the Prevention and Punishment of Crimes Against Internationally Protected Persons, Including Diplomatic Agents, on the basis of draft articles prepared by the commission. The convention's preamble states that crimes against diplomatic agents and other internationally protected persons, jeopardizing their safety, create a serious threat to the maintenance of normal international relations necessary for cooperation among states. It came into force on 20 February 1977.

Relations Between States and International Organizations

On the basis of draft articles prepared by the commission, the Vienna Convention on the Representation of States in Their Relations with International Organizations of a Universal Character was adopted in 1975 by an international conference. This convention is not yet in force.

Succession of States

Work on the subject of the succession of states was begun by the commission in 1962. Succession of states deals with cases in which dependent territories gain independence, as well as those involving the transfer of territory and the union, dissolution, and separation of states. In 1967, the commission divided the subject into three subtopics: succession in regard to treaties; in regard to matters other than treaties; and in regard to membership of international organizations.

Subsequently, two conferences were convened by the General Assembly to consider the subject on the basis of drafts prepared by the commission. The first conference, held in April 1977 and resumed in August 1978, adopted the Vienna Convention on Succession of States in Respect of Treaties. The second, which met in March–April 1983, adopted the Vienna Convention on Succession of States in Respect of State Property, Archives and Debts. Neither of these conventions is in force.

TOPICS PENDING BEFORE THE GENERAL ASSEMBLY

Status of the diplomatic courier and the diplomatic bag not accompanied by the diplomatic courier

The commission completed its work on this topic in 1989 and recommended that the General Assembly convene an international conference of plenipotentiaries to examine the draft articles and conclude a convention on the subject. The Sixth Committee of the General Assembly considered the issue in 1990, 1991, and 1992 and decided to return to it at its 49th session in 1995.

Jurisdictional immunities of states and their property

The commission completed its work on this topic in 1991 and recommended that the General Assembly convene an international conference to examine the draft articles and conclude a convention. The Sixth Committee examined the draft articles in a working group in 1992 and 1993 in order to resolve differences of views on some of the substantive issues raised. The Sixth Committee will again consider the subject at its 48th session in 1994 and will decide whether to convene an international conference to conclude a convention.

Current Topics

Topics on which the commission is currently working include: the elaboration of a Draft Code of Crimes Against the Peace and Security of Mankind; a Draft Statute for an International Criminal Court; the Law of the Non-Navigational Uses of International Watercourses; State Responsibility; and International Liability for Injurious Consequences Arising out of Acts Not Prohibited by International Law.

UN COMMISSION ON INTERNATIONAL TRADE LAW (UNCITRAL)

Like the International Law Commission, UNCITRAL is a permanent subsidiary organ of the General Assembly, which elects its members, observing the principle of balance among the geographical regions and the main economic and legal systems of the world.

In contrast to the International Law Commission, whose members serve in their individual capacities, the UN Commission on International Trade Law (UNCITRAL) is composed of the representatives of 36 (originally 29) states. Members serve six-year terms and are eligible for reelection. States not members of UNCITRAL, representatives of United Nations organs (the IMF and the World Bank), and some other international organizations (for example, the Inter-American Development Bank and the Organization of African Unity) may attend its sessions as observers.

The commission holds one regular session a year. At its 26th session, in July 1993, the following states were members: Argentina, Austria, Bulgaria, Cameroon, Canada, Chile, China, Costa Rica, Denmark, Ecuador, Egypt, France, Germany, Hungary, India, Iran, Italy, Japan, Russian Federation, Saudi Arabia, Singapore, Slovak Republic, Spain, Sudan, Thailand, Togo, Uganda, United Kingdom, United Republic of Tanzania, United States, and Uruguay. The following countries sent observers: Albania, Armenia, Australia, Bangladesh, Belarus, Belgium, Bolivia, Brazil, Colombia, Côte d'Ivoire, Croatia, Cuba, Czech Republic, Democratic People's Republic of Korea, Ethiopia, Finland, Gabon, Guatemala, Holy See, Indonesia, Jordan, Kuwait, Libyan Arab Jamahiriya, Malaysia, Nicaragua, Paraguay, Peru, Republic of Korea, Romania, Slovenia, South Africa, Swaziland, Sweden, Switzerland, Syrian Arab Republic, Turkey, Ukraine, and Venezuela.

Between sessions, working groups designated by the commission meet on specific topics. At its 26th session, the members of UNCITRAL heard reports from the Working Group on the New International Economic Order (15th session); the Working Group on International Contract Practices (18th session); the Working Group on Electronic Data Interchange (EDI) (25th session); and the Working Group on International Contract Practice (19th session).

Functions

A clear understanding of the respective rights and obligations of buyers, sellers, and other commercial parties facilitates the flow of trade from one country to another. When the laws of countries in this field are at variance, impediments may arise. In establishing UNCITRAL, the UN recognized that there was a need for it to play a more active role in removing or reducing legal obstacles to international trade.

UNCITRAL is charged with the task of seeking to resolve differences in national laws by providing texts that may become the basis of international conventions or other agreements. The 1966 General Assembly resolution establishing UNCITRAL invests it with seven specific functions in the furtherance of "progressive harmonization and unification of the law of international trade": coordinating the work of international organizations active in this field; promoting wider participation in existing international conventions, preparing new international conventions; promoting the means of ensuring the uniform interpretation and application of international conventions, collecting and disseminating information on national legislation and legal development in the field of international law; maintaining a close collaboration with UNCTAD; and maintaining liaison with other concerned UN organs and specialized agencies.

The Work of UNCITRAL

The commission draws up its own program of work, subject to the approval of the General Assembly. It selects topics that are both intrinsically capable of unification and ripe for final settlement by virtue of a sufficiently close convergence in their treatment among bodies of national law. Three topics have been given priority: the international sale of goods, international payments, and commercial arbitration.

The first treaty elaborated under the auspices of UNCITRAL was the Convention on the Limitation Period on the International Sale of Goods, adopted in 1974 and called the "Limitation Convention." The convention fixes at four years the period of time in which parties to a contract for the international sale of goods may sue under the contract, and it regulates various matters in regard to the commencement, prolongation, and termination of that period.

Other treaties elaborated by UNCITRAL include the UN Convention on the Carriage of Goods by Sea, adopted at Hamburg, Germany, in 1978 (the "Hamburg Rules"), which entered into force in 1992; the UN Convention on Contracts for the International Sale of Goods, adopted in 1980 (the "United Nations Sales Convention"); the 1988 Convention on International Bills of Exchange and International Promissory Notes (the "UNCITRAL Bills and Notes Convention"); and the 1991 United Nations Convention on the Liability of Operators of Transport Terminals in International Trade (the "United Nations Terminal Operators Convention").

Projects currently under way include: a draft Convention on Independent Guarantees and Stand-by Letters of Credit; model statutory provisions on procurement of services; uniform rules on legal aspects of the use of electronic data interchange (EDI) in international trade; draft Guidelines for Preparatory Conferences in Arbitration; and legal aspects of cross-border insolvencies.

At its 26th session in 1993, the commission noted that there was some uncertainty as to whether newly formed states considered themselves bound by the conventions to which their predecessor states were parties. It called upon those newly formed states to clarify their position and notify the Secretary-General.

In the field of commercial arbitration, UNCITRAL has adopted arbitration and conciliation rules and a Model Law on International Commercial Arbitration. In 1993, at its 26th session, UNCITRAL adopted the Model Law on the Procurement of Goods and Construction and recommended that it be transmitted to governments and other interested bodies.

In May 1992, the commission held the UNCITRAL Congress on International Trade Law in New York. The congress had as its theme "Uniform commercial law in the twenty-first century." One of the aims of the congress was to provide practicing lawyers, government officials, judges, arbitrators, and academics a forum to voice their practical needs as a basis for future work by the commission. Some of the topics emanating from the congress included: procurement of services; guidelines for pre-hearing conferences in arbitral proceedings; assignment of claims; cross-border insolvency; and legal issues in privatization. At its 26th session, in 1993, UNCITRAL decided to postpone study of privatization, but it instructed its secretariat to study and report on the other topics suggested by the congress.

UNCITRAL also conducts a substantial training and technical assistance program, designed to disseminate information concerning UNCITRAL legal texts to government officials, legislators, practicing lawyers, judges, traders, and academics.

UNIVERSAL DECLARATION OF HUMAN RIGHTS

On December 10, 1948 the General Assembly of the United Nations adopted and proclaimed the Universal Declaration of Human Rights. Following this act, the Assembly called upon all member countries to publicize the text of the Declaration and "to cause it to be disseminated, displayed, read and expounded principally in schools and other educational institutions, without distinction based on the political status of countries or territories." The full text of the final authorized version follows:

PREAMBLE

Whereas recognition of the inherent dignity and of the equal and inalienable rights of all members of the human family is the foundation of freedom, justice and peace in the world,

Whereas disregard and contempt for human rights have resulted in barbarous acts which have outraged the conscience of mankind, and the advent of a world in which human beings shall enjoy freedom of speech and belief and freedom from fear and want has beep proclaimed as the highest aspiration of the common people,

Whereas it is essential, if man is not to be compelled to have recourse, as a last resort, to rebellion against tyranny and oppression, that human rights should be protected by the rule of law,

Whereas it is essential to promote the development of friendly relations between nations,

Whereas the peoples of the United Nations have in the Charter reaffirmed their faith in fundamental human rights, in the dignity and worth of the human person and in the equal rights of men and women and have determined to promote social progress and better standards of life in larger freedom,

Whereas Member States have pledged themselves to achieve, in co-operation with the United Nations, the promotion of universal respect for and observance of human rights and fundamental freedoms,

Whereas a common understanding of these rights and freedoms is of the greatest importance for the full realization of this pledge,

Now, Therefore,

THE GENERAL ASSEMBLY
proclaims

THIS UNIVERSAL DECLARATION OF HUMAN RIGHTS

as a common standard of achievement for all peoples and all nations, to the end that every individual and every organ of society, keeping this Declaration constantly in mind, shall strive by teaching and education to promote respect for these rights and freedoms and by progressive measures, national and international, to secure their universal and effective recognition and observance, both among the peoples of Member States themselves and among the peoples of territories under their jurisdiction.

Article 1
All human beings are born free and equal in dignity and rights They are endowed with reason and conscience and should act towards one another in a spirit of brotherhood.

Article 2
Everyone is entitled to all the rights and freedoms set forth in this Declaration, without distinction of any kind, such as race, colour, sex, language, religion, political or other opinion, national or social origin, property, birth or other status. Furthermore, no distinction shall be made on the basis of the political, jurisdictional or international status of the country or territory to which a person belongs, whether it be independent, trust, non-self-governing or under any other limitation of sovereignty.

Article 3
Everyone has the right to life, liberty and security of person.

Article 4
No one shall be held in slavery or servitude; slavery and the slave trade shall be prohibited in all their forms.

Article 5
No one shall be subjected to torture or to cruel, inhuman or degrading treatment or punishment.

Article 6
Everyone has the right to recognition everywhere as a person before the law.

Article 7
All are equal before the law and are entitled without any discrimination to equal protection of the law All are entitled to equal protection against any discrimination in violation of this Declaration and against any incitement to such discrimination.

Article 8
Everyone has the right to an effective remedy by the competent national tribunals for acts violating the fundamental rights granted him by the constitution or by law.

Article 9
No one shall be subjected to arbitrary arrest, detention or exile.

Article 10
Everyone is entitled in full equality to a fair and public hearing by an independent and impartial tribunal, in the determination of his rights and obligations and of any criminal charge against him.

Article 11
(1) Everyone charged with a penal offense has the right to be presumed innocent until proved guilty according to law in a public trial at which he has had all the guarantees necessary for his defense.

(2) No one shall be held guilty of any penal offense on account of any act or omission which did not constitute a penal offense,

under national or international law, at the time when it was committed Nor shall a heavier penalty be imposed than the one that was applicable at the time the penal offense was committed.

Article 12
No one shall be subjected to arbitrary interference with his privacy, family, home or correspondence, nor to attacks upon his honor and reputation Everyone has the right to the protection of the law against such interference or attacks.

Article 13
(1) Everyone has the right to freedom of movement and residence within the borders of each state.

(2) Everyone has the right to leave any country, including his own, and to return to his country.

Article 14
(1) Everyone has the right to seek and to enjoy in other countries asylum from persecution.

(2) This right may not be invoked in the case of prosecutions genuinely arising from non-political crimes or from acts contrary to the purposes and principles of the United Nations.

Article 15
(1) Everyone has the right to a nationality.

(2) No one shall be arbitrarily deprived of his nationality nor denied the right to change his nationality.

Article 16
(1) Men and women of full age, without any limitation due to race, nationality or religion, have the right to marry and to found a family They are entitled to equal rights as to marriage, during marriage and at its dissolution.

(2) Marriage shall be entered into only with the free and full consent of the intending spouses.

(3) The family is the natural and fundamental group unit of society and is entitled to protection by society and the State.

Article 17
(1) Everyone has the right to own property alone as well as in association with others.

(2) No one shall be arbitrarily deprived of his property.

Article 18.
Everyone has the right to freedom of thought, conscience and religion; this right includes freedom to change his religion or belief, and freedom, either alone or in community with others and in public or private, to manifest his religion or belief in teaching, practice, worship and observance.

Article 19
Everyone has the right to freedom of opinion and expression; this right includes freedom to hold opinions without interference and to seek, receive and impart information and ideas through any media and regardless of frontiers.

Article 20
(1) Everyone has the right to freedom of peaceful assembly and association.

(2) No one may be compelled to belong to an association.

Article 21
(1) Everyone has the right to take part in the government of his country, directly or through freely chosen representatives.

(2) Everyone has the right of equal access to public service in his country.

(3) The will of the people shall be the basis of the authority of government; this will shall be expressed in periodic and genuine elections which shall be by universal and equal suffrage and shall be held by secret vote or by equivalent free voting procedures.

Article 22
Everyone, as a member of society, has the right to social security and is entitled to realization, through national effort and international co-operation and in accordance with the organization and resources of each State, of the economic, social and cultural rights indispensable for his dignity and the free development of his personality.

Article 23
(1) Everyone has the right to work, to free choice of employment, to just and favorable conditions of work and to protection against unemployment.

(2) Everyone, without any discrimination, has the right to equal pay for equal work.

(3) Everyone who works has the right to just and favorable remuneration ensuring for himself and his family an existence worthy of human dignity, and supplemented, if necessary, by other means of social protection.

(4) Everyone has the right to form and to join trade unions for the protection of his interests.

Article 24
Everyone has the right to rest and leisure, including reasonable limitation of working hours and periodic holidays with pay.

Article 25
(1) Everyone has the right to a standard of living adequate for the health and well-being of himself and of his family, including food, clothing, housing and medical care and necessary social services, and the right to security in the event of unemployment, sickness, disability, widowhood, old age or other lack of livelihood in circumstances beyond his control.

(2) Motherhood and childhood are entitled to special care and assistance All children, whether born in or out of wedlock, shall enjoy the same social protection.

Article 26
(1) Everyone has the right to education. Education shall be free, at least in the elementary and fundamental stages Elementary education shall be compulsory Technical and professional education shall be made generally available and higher education shall be equally accessible to all on the basis of merit.

(2) Education shall be directed to the full development of the human personality and to the strengthening of respect for human rights and fundamental freedoms It shall promote understanding, tolerance and friendship among all nations, racial or religious groups, and shall further the activities of the United Nations for the maintenance of peace.

(3) Parents have a prior right to choose the kind of education that shall be given to their children.

Article 27

(1) Everyone has the right freely to participate in the cultural life of the community, to enjoy the arts and to share in scientific advancement and its benefits.

(2) Everyone has the right to the protection of the moral and material interests resulting from any scientific, literary or artistic production of which he is the author.

Article 28

Everyone is entitled to a social and international order in which the rights and freedoms set forth in this Declaration can be fully realized.

Article 29

(1) Everyone has duties to the community in which alone the free and full development of his personality is possible.

(2) In the exercise of his rights and freedoms, everyone shall be subject only to such limitations as are determined by law solely for the purpose of securing due recognition and respect for the rights and freedoms of others and of meeting the just requirements of morality, public order and the general welfare in a democratic society.

(3) These rights and freedoms may in no case be exercised contrary to the purposes and principles of the United Nations.

Article 30

Nothing in this Declaration may be interpreted as implying for any State, group or person any right to engage in any activity or to perform any act aimed at the destruction of any of the rights and freedoms set forth herein.

ADDRESSES OF THE PRINCIPAL UNITED NATIONS ORGANIZATIONS

United Nations Headquarters
One United Nations Plaza
New York, NY 10017
212/963 1234
Centre for Human Rights
UN Office at Geneva
Palais des Nations
CH-1211 Geneva 10
Switzerland

Economic and Social Commission for Asia and the Pacific (ESCAP)
United Nations Building
Hajadamnern Avenue
Bangkok 10200
Thailand
66/2/282 9161-200

Economic and Social Commission for Europe (ECE)
Palais des Nations
CH-1211 Geneva 20
Switzerland
41/22/917 1234

Economic and Social Commission for Western Asia (ESCWA)
PO Box 927115
AMMAN
Jordan
962/6/694 351

Economic Commission for Africa (ECA)
PO Box 3001
Addis Ababa
Ethiopia
251/1/51 72 00

Economic Commission for Latin America and the Caribbean (ECLAC)
Casila 179 D
Santiago
Chile
56/2/210 2000

The Food and Agriculture Organization of the United Nations (FAO)
Via delle Terme di Caracalla
00100 Rome
Italy
39/6/57971

FAO
Suite 300
1001 22nd Street NW
Washington, D.C. 20437
202/653-2400

General Agreement on Tariffs and Trade (GATT)
World Trade Organization (WTO)
Centre William Rappard
154 Rue de Lausanne
1211 Geneva 21
Switzerland
41/22/739 51 11

International Atomic Energy Agency (IAEA)
Vienna International Centre
P.O. Box 100
A-1400 Vienna
Austria
43/1/23600

International Civil Aviation Organization (ICAO)
1000 Sherbrooke Street West
Suite 327
Montreal, PQ H3A 2R2
Canada
514/285 8219

International Court of Justice
Peace Palace
2517 KJ
The Hague
The Netherlands
31/70 392 44 41

International Labour Organization (ILO)
4, route des Morillons
CH-1211 Geneva 22
Switzerland
41/22/799 61 11

International Labour Organization (ILO)
1828 L Street NW
Suite 801
Washington, D.C. 20036
202/653-7652

International Labour Organization (ILO)
220 East 42nd Street
Suite 3101
New York, NY 10017
212/697-0150

ILO Publications Center
49 Sheridan Ave.
Albany, NY 12210
518/436-9686 x 123

International Maritime Organization (IMO)
4 Albert Embankment
London SE1 7SR
United Kingdom
44/71/735 7611

International Monetary Fund (IMF)
700 19th Street NW
Washington, D.C. 20431
202/623 7000

International Narcotics Control Board (INCB)
Vienna International Center
PO Box 500
A-1400 Vienna
Austria
43/1/211 310

International Telecommunications Union (ITU)
Place des Nations
CH-1211 Geneva 20
Switzerland
41/22/730 51 11

International Criminal Tribunal
for the Former Yugoslavia
PO Box 13888
2501 EW - The Hague
Netherlands
31/70/344 53 47

International Fund for Agricultural Development (IFAD)
Via del Serafico 107
I-00142 Rome
Italy
39/6/54591

International Fund for Agricultural Development (IFAD)
1889 F Street NW
Washington, D.C. 20006
202/289-3812

Office for Outer Space Affairs
Vienna International Centre
PO Box 500
A-1400 Vienna
Austria
43/1/211 31 - 4951

UN 50th Anniversary Secretariat
Room S-3161A
New York, NY 10017
212/963 1960

UN Commission on International Trade Law (UNCITRAL)
International Centre
PO Box 5500
A-1400 Vienna
Austria
43/1/211 31 4060

UN Conference on Trade and Development (UNCTAD)
Palais des Nations
CH-1211 Geneva 10
Switzerland
41/22/734 60 11

UN Conference on Trade and Development (UNCTAD)
United Nations Headquarters
Room S-927
New York, NY 10017
212/963-6896

UN Crime Prevention & Criminal Justice Branch
UN International Center
A-1400 Vienna
Austria
43/1/211 310

UN Department of Public Information (UNDPI)
United Nations
Room 1027A
New York, NY 10017
212/963 6830

UN Development Fund for Women (UNIFEM)
304 East 45th Street
Room FF-616
New York, NY 10017
212/906-6925

UN High Commissioner for Refugees (UNHCR)
Centre William Rappard
154 rue de Lausanne
CH-1202 Geneva
Switzerland
41/22/739 81 11

UN High Commissioner for Refugees (UNHCR)
Room S-931
United Nations
New York, NY 10017
212/963-6200

UN Industrial Development Organization (UNIDO)
PO Box 300
Vienna International Centre
A-1400 Vienna
Austria
43/1/21131

UN Institute for Training and Research (UNITAR)
Place des Nations
CH-1211 - Geneva 10
Switzerland
41/22/798 5850

UN International Research Training Institute for the Advancement of Women (INSTRAW)
PO Box 21747
Santo Domingo
Dominican Republic
809/685 2111

UN Interregional Crime and Justice Research Institute (UNICRI)
Via Giulia 52
I-00186 Rome
Italy
39/6/687 7437

UN Relief and Works Agency for Palestine Refugees (UNRWA)
Vienna International Centre
PO Box 700
A-1400 Vienna
Austria
43/1/211 310

UN Educational, Scientific and Cultural Organisation (UNESCO)
7 Place de Fontenoy
B.P. 3.07 Paris
F-75700 Paris
France
33/1/45 68 10 00

UNESCO
Room DC2-0934
Two United Nations Plaza
New York, NY 10017
212/963-5978

UN Childrens' Fund (UNICEF)
Three United Nations Plaza
New York, NY 10017
212/326 7000

United Nations Centre for Human Settlements (UNHCHS - Habitat)
PO Box 30030
Nairobi
Kenya
254/2/621234

United Nations Development Program (UNDP)
One United Nations Plaza
New York, NY 10017
212/906 5000

United Nations Environment Programme (UNEP)
P.O. Box 30552
Nairobi
Kenya
254/2/333 930

United Nations Environment Programme (UNEP)
United Nations
Room DC2-0816
New York, NY 10017
212/963-8138

United Nations Fund for Population Activities (UNFPA)
220 East 42nd St
New York, NY 10017
212/297-5000

United Nations International Drug Control Programme (UNDCP)
Vienna International Centre
PO Box 500
A-1400 Vienna
Austria
43/1/211 31 4115
United Nations Office at Vienna (UNOV)
Vienna International Center
P.O. Box 500 (Wagrammer Strasse 5)
A-1400 Vienna
Austria
43/1/211 310
United Nations Research Institute for Social Development (UNRISD)
Palais des Nations
CH-1211 Geneva 10
Switzerland
41/22/798 84 00
United Nations University (UNU)
Toho Seimei Building
15-1 Shibuya 2-chome, Shibuya-ku
TOKYO 150
Japan
81/3/3499 2811
United Nations University (UNU)
United Nations
Room DC2-1462-1470
New York, NY 10017
212/963 6387
Universal Postal Union (UPU)
Union postale universelle
Case postale
3000 Berne 15
Switzerland
41/31/350 31 11
World Bank
1818 H Street NW
Washington, D.C. 20433
202/477 1234
World Food Program (WFP)
Via Cristoforo Colombo, 426
I-00145 Rome
Italy
39/6/57971
World Food Program (WFP)
United Nations
Room DC1-1027
New York, NY 10017
212/963 8364
World Health Organization (WHO)
20 avenue Appia
1211 Geneva 27
Switzerland
41/22/791 21 11
World Health Organization (WHO)
Room DC2-0956
United Nations
New York, NY 10017
212/963 6004
World Health Organization
Regional Office for Africa (AFRO)
P.O. Box No.6
Brazzaville/Congo
Tel: +242 83 38 60 or 64
World Health Organization
Regional Office for the Americas (AMRO)

525, 23rd Street, NW
Washington, D.C. 20037
USA
Tel: +1 202 861 3200
World Health Organization
Regional Office for the Eastern Mediterranean (EMRO)
P.O. Box 1517
Alexandria - 21511
Egypt
Tel: +203 48 202 23 or 48 202 24 or 48 300 90
World Health Organization
Regional Office for Europe (EURO)
8, Scherfigsvej
DK -2100 Copenhagen 0
Tel: +45 39 17 17 17
World Health Organization
Regional Office for South-East Asia (SEARO)
World Health House
Indraprastha Estate
Mahatma Gandhi Road
New Delhi 110002
India
Tel: +91 11 331 7804 or 11 331 7823
World Health Organization
Regional Office for the Western Pacific (WPRO)
P.O. Box 2932
1099 Manila
Philippines
632 521 84 21
World Intellectual Property Organization (WIPO)
34 Chemin des Columbettes
CH-1211 Geneva 20
Switzerland
41/22/730 91 11
World Meteorlogical Organization (WMO)
41 Avenue Giuseppe-Motta
CH-1211 Geneva 20
Switzerland
41/22/730 81 11

ADDRESSES OF UNITED NATIONS INFORMATION CENTERS AND SERVICES

Centers and Services in Africa
Center: United Nations Information Center
              Gamel Abdul Nassar/Liberia Roads
              Post Office Box 2339
              Accra, Ghana
Services to: Ghana
              Sierra Leone

Center: United Nations Information Service
              Economic Commission for Africa
              Africa Hall
              Post Office Box 3001
              Addis Ababa, Ethiopia
Services to: Ethiopia

Center: United Nations Information Centre
              19, avenue Chahid El Ouali
              Mustapha Sayed
              Boîte Postale 823
              Algiers, Algeria
Services to: Algeria

Center: United Nations Information Centre
              22, rue Rainitovo, Antsahavola

Boîte Postale 1348
Antananarivo, Madagascar
Services to: Madagascar

Center: United Nations Information Centre
Avenue Foch
Case Ortf 15
Boîte Postale 13210
Brazzaville, Congo
Services to: Congo

Center: United Nations Information Centre
117, avenue de la Poste
Boîte Postale 2160
Bujumbura, Burundi
Services to: Burundi

Center: United Nations Information Centre
1 Osiris Street
Tagher Building (Garden City)
Boîte Postale 262
Cairo, Egypt
Services to: Egypt
Saudi Arabia
Yemen

Center: United Nations Information Centre
72, boulevard de la République
Boîte Postale 154
Dakar, Senegal
Services to: Cape Verde
Côte d'Ivoire
Gambia
Guinea
Guinea-Bissau
Mauritania
Senegal

Center: United Nations Information Centre
Matasalamat Building, 1st Floor
Samora Machel Avenue
Post Office Box 9224
Dar es Salaam, Tanzania
Services to: Tanzania

Center: United Nations Information Centre
Dolphin House, Ground Floor
123 L. Takawira Street
Post Office Box 4408
Harare, Zimbabwe
Services to: Zimbabwe

Center: United Nations Information Centre
United Nations Compound
University Avenue
Post Office Box 1992
Khartoum, Sudan
Services to: Somalia
Sudan

Center: United Nations Information Centre
Bâtiment Deuxième République
Boulevard du 30 Juin
Boîte Postale 7248
Kinshasa, Zaire
Services to: Zaire

Center: United Nations Information Centre
17 Kingsway Road, Ikoyi
Post Office Box 1068
Lagos, Nigeria
Services to: Nigeria

Center: United Nations Information Centre
107, Boulevard due 13 Janvier
Boîte Postale 911
Lomé, Togo
Services to: Benin
Togo

Center: United Nations Information Centre
Post Office Box 32905
Lusaka, Zambia
Services to: Botswana
Malawi
Swaziland
Zambia

Center: United Nations Information Centre
Corner Kingsway and Hilton Hill Road
Post Office Box 301
Maseru 100, Lesotho
Services to: Lesotho

Center: United Nations Information Centre
LBDI Building
Tubman Boulevard
Post Office Box 274
Monrovia, Liberia
Services to: Liberia

Center: United Nations Information Centre
United Nations Office
Post Office Box 34135
Nairobi, Kenya
Services to: Kenya
Seychelles
Uganda

Center: United Nations Information Centre
218 Rue de la Gare, Secteur No. 3
Boîte Postale 135
Ouagadougou 01, Burkina Faso
Services to: Burkina Faso
Chad
Mali
Niger

Center: United Nations Information Centre
Angle Charia Ibnouzaid et Zankat
Boîte Postale 601
Rabat, Morocco
Services to: Morocco

Center: United Nations Information Centre
Muzzafar Al Aftas Street
Hay El-Andolous 2
Post Office Box 286
Tripoli, Libyan Arab Jamahiriya
Services to: Libyan Arab Jamahiriya

Center: United Nations Information Centre
61, Boulevard Bab-Benat
Boîte Postale 863

Tunis, Tunisia
Services to: Tunisia

Center: United Nations Information Centre
             Immeuble Kamden, Rue Josef Clère
             Boîte Postale 836
             Yaoundé, Cameroon
Services to: Cameroon
             Central African Republic
             Gabon

Center: Centres and Services in the Americas
             United Nations Information Centre
             Casilla de Correo 1107
             Asunción, Paraguay
Services to: Paraguay

Center: United Nations Information Centre
             Junín 9140, 1er piso
             1113 **Buenos Aires**, Argentina
Services to: Argentina
             Uruguay

Center: United Nations Information Centre
             Edificio Naciones Unidas
             Plaza Isabel la Católica
             Apartado Postal 686
             La Paz, Bolivia
Services to: Bolivia

Center: United Nations Information Centre
             Mariscal Blas Cerdeña 450, San Isidro
             Apartado Postal 14-0199
             Lima, Peru
Services to: Peru

Center: United Nations Information Centre
             Bolonia, de Plaza España
             Apartado Postal 3260
             Managua, Nicaragua
Services to: Nicaragua

Center: United Nations Information Centre
             Presidente Mazaryk 29, 7° Piso
             México 11570, D.F.
             México
Services to: Dominican Republic
             Mexico

Center: United Nations Information Centre
             Urbanización Obarrio
             Apartado Postal 6-9083 El Dorado
             Panama City, Panama
Services to: Panama

Center: United Nations Information Centre
             16 Victoria Ave.
             Post Office Box 130
             Port of Spain, Trinidad
Services to: Antigua and Barbuda
             Bahamas
             Barbados
             Belize
             Dominica
             Grenada
             Guyana
             Jamaica

Netherlands Antilles
Saint Kitts and Nevi
Saint Lucia
Saint Vincent and the Grenadines
Suriname
Trinidad and Tobago

Center: United Nations Information Centre
             Palacio Itamaraty
             Avenida Marechal Floriano 196
             20060 **Rio de Janeiro**, RJ, Brasil
Services to: Brazil

Center: United Nations Information Centre
             Edificio Escalón, 2° Piso
             Apartado Postal 2157
             San Salvador, El Salvador
Services to: El Salvador

Center: United Nations Information Centre
             Calle 72, No. 12-65, Piso 2
             Apartado Aéreo 058964
             Santa Fé de Bogotá 2, Colombia
Services to: Colombia
             Ecuador
             Venezuela

Center: United Nations Information Service
             Edificio Naciones Unidas
             Avenida Dag Hammarskjöld
             Casilla 179-D
             Santiago, Chile
Services to: Chile

Center: United Nations Information Centre
             1889 F Street, NW
             Washington, D.C. 20006
             United States
Services to: United States

Centres and Services in Asia and Oceania
Center: United Nations Information Centre
             197 Ataturk Bulvari
             P.K. 407
             Ankara, Turkey
Services to: Turkey

Center: United Nations Information Service
             Amiriya, Airport Street
             Post Office Box 27
             Baghdad, Iraq
Services to: Iraq

Center: United Nations Information Service
             United Nations Building
             Rajadamnern Avenue
             Bangkok 10200, Thailand
Services to: Cambodia
             Hong Kong
             Lao People's Dem. Republic
             Malaysia
             Singapore
             Thailand
             Viet Nam

Center: United Nations Information Centre
             Apartment No. 1, Fakhoury Building

Monté Bain Militaire
Post Office Box 4656
Beirut, Lebanon
Services to: Jordan
Kuwait
Lebanon
Syrian Arab Republic

Center: United Nations Information Centre
202-204 Bauddhaloka Mawatha
Post Office Box 1505
Colombo 7, Sri Lanka
Services to: Sri Lanka

Center: United Nations Information Centre
House 25, Road 11
General Post Office Box 3658
Dhaka 100, Bangladesh
Services to: Bangladesh

Center: United Nations Information Centre
House No. 26, 88th Street, Ramna 6/3
Post Office Box 1107
Islamabad, Pakistan
Services to: Pakistan

Center: United Nations Information Centre
Gedung Dewan Pers, 5th Floor
32-34 Jalan Kebon Sirih
Jakarta 1001, Indonesia
Services to: Indonesia

Center: United Nations Information Centre
Shah Mahmoud Ghazi Watt
Post Office Box 5
Kabul, Afghanistan
Services to: Afghanistan

Center: United Nations Information Centre
Pulchowk, Patan
Post Office Box 107
Pulchowk, **Kathmandu**, Nepal
Services to: Nepal

Center: United Nations Information Centre
House No. 131, Road 2803
Segaya 328
Post Office Box 26004
Manama, Bahrain
Services to: Bahrain
Qatar
United Arab Emirates

Center: United Nations Information Centre
Post Office Box 7285 (ADC)
MIA Road, Pasay City
Metro Manila, Philippines
Services to: Papua new Guinea
Philippines
Solomon Islands

Center: United Nations Information Centre
55 Lodi Estate
New Delhi 110003, India
Services to: Bhutan
India

Center: United Nations Information Centre
2nd Floor, Suite 1, 125 York Street
Post Office Box 4045
Sydney, N.S.W. 2001
Australia
Services to: Australia
Fiji
Kiribati
Nauru
New Zealand
Samoa
Tonga
Tuvalu
Vanuatu

Center: United Nations Information Centre
Avenue Boharest Maydan
Argantine No. 74
Post Office Box 15875-4557
Teheran, Iran
Services to: Iran

Center: United Nations Information Centre
Shin Aoyama Building Nishika
22nd Floor
1-1 Minami Aoyama 1-chome
Minato-ku, **Tokyo** 107
Japan
Services to: Japan

Center: United Nations Information Centre
6 Natmauk Road
Post Office Box 230
Yangon, Myanmar
Services to: Myanmar

Centres and Services in Europe
Center: United Nations Information Centre
36 Amalia Avenue
GR-105
58 **Athens**, Greece
Services to: Cyprus
Greece
Israel

Center: United Nations Information Centre
Svetozara Markovica 58
Post Office Box 157
Belgrade, Yugoslavia YU-11001
Services to: Albania
Yugoslavia

Center: United Nations Information Centre
and Liaison Office with the
European Economic Community
Avenue de Broqueville 40
1200 **Brussells**, Belgium
Services to: Belgium
Luxembourg
Netherlands

Center: United Nations Information Centre
16 Aurel Vlaic Street
Post Office Box 1-701
Bucharest, Romania
Services to: Romania

Center: United Nations Information Centre
37 H.C. Andersens Boulevard
DK-1553 **Copenhagen** V, Denmark
Services to: Denmark
Finland
Iceland
Norway
Sweden

Center: United Nations Information Service
United Nations Office at Geneva
Palais des Nations
1211 **Geneva** 10, Switzerland
Services to: Bulgaria
Poland
Switzerland

Center: United Nations Information Centre
Rua Latino Coelho No. 1
Edificio Aviz, Bloco A-1, 10°
1000 **Lisbon**, Portugal
Services to: Portugal

Center: United Nations Information Centre
20 Buckingham Gate
London SW1E 6LB
United Kingdom
Services to: Ireland
United Kingdom

Center: United Nations Information Centre
Avenida General Perón, 32-1
Post Office Box 3400
28080 **Madrid**, Spain
Services to: Spain

Center: United Nations Information Centre
4/16 Ulitsa Lunacharskogo
Moscow 121002, Russian Federation
Services to: Belarus
Russian Federation
Ukraine

Center: United Nations Information Centre
1, rue Miollis
75732, **Paris** Cedex 15, France
Services to: France

Center: United Nations Information Centre
Panska 5
11000 **Prague** 1, Czech Republic
Services to: Czech Republic
Slovak Republic

Center: United Nations Information Centre
Palazzetto Venezia
Piazza San Marco 50
00186 **Rome,** Italy
Services to: Holy See
Italy
Malta

Center: United Nations Information Service
United Nations Office at Vienna
Services to: Austria and Germany

Center: Vienna International Centre
Wagramerstrasse 5
Post office Box 500
A-1400 **Vienna**, Austria
Services to: Hungary

UNITED NATIONS ONLINE DATABASES

Readers with access to a computer and modem may be able to access online sources of information about the United Nations via the internet. Current United Nations press releases, resolutions, and documents and breaking information on the UN's international conferences are maintained on the internet. Many public library systems and university library systems in the United States offer free, local dial-up access to these. A call to the closest public or university library would be the best way to determine if local dial-up access is available. Access will also be available to readers belonging to commercial online services that provide internet access and gopher software.

Although the following databases were developed for use by United Nations personnel and are not available free on the internet, a qualified researcher may be able to obtain online access to the following resources by making arrangements with the contact listed.

Database of United Nations Databases and Information Services (DUNDIS)
Subject: Databases; information services; information systems; UN system.
   Contact: ACCIS Secretariat
             Palais des Nations
             1211 GENEVA 10
             41/22/798 85 91

United Nations Press Release Retrieval System (UNPRESS)
Subject: Press releases on economic development; emergency relief; environment; international trade; law; natural resources; politics; population; science and technology; social conditions.
   Contact: Senior Information Officer
             Department of Public Information
             United Nations
             United Nations Plaza
             NEW YORK, NY 10017
             212/963 4176

Agenda Item File
Subject: ECOSOC; international relations; political problems; Trusteeship Council; UN; UN General Assembly; UN Secretariat; UN Security Council; UN system.
   Contact: Chief, Technical Operations and Publications Service
             Dag Hammarskjöld Library
             United Nations Plaza
             NEW YORK, NY 10017
             212/963 7436 879

External Materials File (CATFILE)
Subject: Economic development; human rights; international law; international relations; political problems; population; public administration; social development; UN; UN system.
   Contact: Chief, Technical Operations and Publications Service
             Dag Hammarskjöld Library
             United Nations Plaza
             NEW YORK, NY 10017
             212/963 7436 879

Resolutions File (RESFILE)
Subject: Economic development; ECOSOC; international relations; political problems; resolutions; Trusteeship Council; UN; UN General Assembly; UN Secretariat; UN Security Council; UN system
   Contact: Chief, Technical Operations and Publications Service
             Dag Hammarskjöld Library
             United Nations Plaza
             NEW YORK, NY 10017
             212/963 7436 879

United Nations Documents File (DOCFILE)
Subjects: Economic development; ECOSOC; international relations; political problems; Trusteeship Council; UN; UN General Assembly; UN Secretariat; UN Security Council; UN system.
   Contact: Chief, Technical Operations and Publications Service
             Dag Hammarskjöld Library
             United Nations Plaza
             NEW YORK, NY 10017
             212/963 7436 879

WORLD HEALTH ORGANIZATION COMPUTERIZED DATABASES

The following scientific databases are available either online or on diskette to qualified individuals, as indicated. For each database, specific information is presented, including: the type of data stored in the database; the principal areas of interest or specific subject content of the data; the user groups for whom the database, or parts of it, are used; the form in which the database, or parts of it, is made available; and the name of online services which provide online access to the data from the database. If the online file name in which the data is found is different from the database name given at the beginning of the entry, the file name is given. Finally, contact information is provided. This list was accurate as of September 1994.

AFRO/CDC - Morbidity/Mortality AFRO
Database type: Factual; numeric.
Subject scope: Morbidity; mortality.
Availability: UN system organizations; external users with restrictions.
Distribution media: Diskette; magnetic tape; printout.
   Contact: Dr. Nguyen-Khanh
             WHO/AFRO
             PO Box 6
             BRAZZAVILLE
             Republic of Congo
Telephone: 242/83 38 60
Telefax: 242/83 18 79

AFRO/CEIS - Immunization AFRO
Database type: Numeric.
Subject scope: Immunization.
Availability: UN system organizations; external users with restrictions.
Printed products: Information system: summary for WHO/AFRO.

Distribution media: Diskette; printout.
Contact: Dr. Arevshatian
　　　　WHO/AFRO
　　　　PO Box 6
　　　　BRAZZAVILLE
　　　　Republic of Congo
Telephone: 242/83 38 60
Telefax: 242/83 18 79

AFRO/PHS - Health Indicators in AFRO

Database type: Factual; numeric.
Subject scope: Health indicators.
Availability: UN system organizations; external users with restrictions
Distribution media: Diskette; printout.
Contact: Dr. Nguyen-Khanh
　　　　WHO/AFRO
　　　　PO Box 6
　　　　BRAZZAVILLE
　　　　Republic of Congo
Telephone: 242/83 38 60
Telefax: 242/83 18 79

Antimalaria Activities Status

Database type: Factual; numeric.
Subject scope: Malaria.
Availability: UN system organizations; external users.
Printed products: Weekly epidemiological record; WHO health statistics quarterly.
Contact: Director, Control of Tropical Diseases
　　　　WHO
　　　　20, avenue Appia
　　　　1211 GENEVA 27
　　　　Switzerland
Telephone: 41 22/791 21 11
Telefax: 41 22/791 07 46

Breast Feeding

Database type: Bibliographic; numeric.
Subject scope: Breast feeding.
Contact: Maternal and Child Health
　　　　Division of Family Health
　　　　WHO
　　　　20, avenue Appia
　　　　1211 GENEVA 27
　　　　Switzerland
Telephone: 41 22/791 21 11
Telefax: 41 22/791 07 46

Catalogue of WHO/WPRO Library (WPROLIB)

Database type: Bibliographic.
Subject scope: Chronic diseases; economic development; environment; food; health; infectious diseases; medicine; nutrition; primary health care; public health; social development.
Availability: UN system organizations; external users with restrictions.
Printed products: Recent acquisitions list; various bibliographies.
Contact: Librarian
　　　　WPRO Library
　　　　PO Box 2932
　　　　United Nations cor Taft Avenues
　　　　MANILA
　　　　Philippines
Telephone: 63 2/521 8421
Telefax: 63 2/521 1036

Communicable Disease Data Base

Database type: Numeric.
Subject scope: Disease transmission; epidemiology; infectious diseases.
Availability: UN system organizations; external users: data is made available on demand to health workers, especially for research and planning.
Printed products: Annual review of communicable diseases; CAREC surveillance report.
Distribution media: Printout.
Contact: Statistician
　　　　PAHO/CAREC
　　　　PO Box 164
　　　　16-18 Jamaica Boulevard
　　　　Federation Park
　　　　PORT-OF-SPAIN
　　　　Trinidad & Tobago
Telephone: 500 809/24261; 23404; 23745

Decade Monitoring

Database type: Numeric.
Subject scope: Sanitation; water supply.
Availability: UN system organizations; external users.
Printed products: International drinking water supply and sanitation decade status reports: 1980, 1983, 1985.
Distribution media: Diskette; printout.
Contact: Manager, CWS
　　　　Division of Environmental Health
　　　　WHO
　　　　20, avenue Appia
　　　　1211 GENEVA 27
　　　　Switzerland
Telephone: 41 22/791 21 11
Telefax: 41 22/791 07 46

Directory of Current Medical and Health-related Periodicals Published in the Western Pacific Region of WHO

Database type: Bibliographic; numeric.
Subject scope: Health; medicine; serials.
Availability: UN system organizations; external users.
Printed products: Directory of current medical and health-related periodicals published in the Western Pacific region of WHO.
Contact: Librarian
　　　　WPRO Library
　　　　PO Box 2932
　　　　United Nations cor Taft Avenues
　　　　MANILA
　　　　Philippines
Telephone: 63 2/521 8421
Telefax: 63 2/521 1036

Directory of On-going Research in Cancer Epidemiology Data Base

Database type: Full text.
Subject scope: Cancer; epidemiology; research.
Availability: UN system organizations; external users: directory distributed free to contributors; for sale through Oxford University Press.
Printed products: Directory of on-going research in cancer epidemiology.
Distribution media: Diskette (indexes); printout.
Contact: Unit of Descriptive Epidemiology
　　　　IARC
　　　　150, cours Albert Thomas
　　　　69372 LYON
　　　　France

Telephone: 33 7/7273 8485
Telefax: 33 7/7273 8575

Directory of Selected Medical and Health-related Libraries in the Western Pacific Region of WHO
Database type: Referral.
Subject scope: Health; information services; libraries.
Availability: UN system organizations; external users.
Printed products: Directory of selected medical and health-related libraries in the Western Pacific region of WHO.
Contact: Librarian
WPRO Library
PO Box 2932
United Nations cor Taft Avenues
MANILA
Philippines
Telephone: 63 2/521 8421
Telefax: 63 2/521 1036

ECO-Line
Subject scope: Environmental legislation; pesticides; pollution; toxic substances; toxicology.
Availability: UN system organizations; external users with restrictions.
Printed products: ECO-bibliograflas/ECO-bibliographies; ECO-boletin de adquisiciones bibliograficas/ECO-bibliographic acquisitions bulletin; ECO-library catalog; ECO-publications catalog.
Distribution media: Diskette; printout.
Contact: Head Librarian
ECO
Apartado Postal 37-473
06696 MEXICO CITY D.F.
Mexico

EURODOC
Database type: Bibliographic; referral.
Subject scope: Health; health services.
Availability: UN system organizations; WHO Member States.
Distribution media: Online; printout.
Online hosts: Health Documentation Service.
Contact: Librarian, WHO/EURO
8 Scherfigsvej
2100 COPENHAGEN 0
Denmark
Telephone: 45 31/29 01 11
Telefax: 45 31/18 11 20

Global Oral Epidemiology Data Bank
Database type: Bibliographic; full text; numeric; referral.
Subject scope: Dentistry; periodontal diseases.
Availability: UN system organizations; external users with restrictions: data is provided by printout on receipt of requests indicating countries' entities and age groups for which data is needed.
Distribution media: Diskette; printout.
Contact: Chief, ORH
WHO
20, avenue Appia
1211 GENEVA 27
Switzerland
Telephone: 41 22/791 34 90
Telefax: 41 22/791 07 46

Health for All Global Indicators
Database type: Numeric.
Subject scope: Health indicators.

Availability: UN system organizations; external users.
Printed products: Health situation report.
Distribution media: Diskette; printout.
Contact: Chief, HST/GSP
WHO
20, avenue Appia
1211 GENEVA 27
Switzerland
Telephone: 41 22/791 21 11
Telefax: 41 22/791 07 46

Health Legislation
Database type: Bibliographic; full text; referral.
Subject scope: AIDS; environmental legislation; health; human nutrition; legislation; occupational hygiene; pharmaceuticals; tobacco.
Availability: UN system organizations; external users.
Printed products: International digest of health legislation (English and French editions).
Contact: Chief, HLE
WHO
20, avenue Appia
1211 GENEVA 27
Switzerland
Telephone: 41 22/791 21 11
Telefax: 41 22/791 07 46

Health Legislation Notification System Data Base (EURO-HLE)
Database type: Full text; referral.
Subject scope: Health; legislation.
Availability: UN system organizations; external users (online); yearly report: free of charge to WHO Headquarters, the other WHO Regional Offices and Member States.
Printed products: Report.
Distribution media: Online; printout.
Online hosts: WHO-NET.
Contact: Regional Officer for Health Legislation, Health Legislation Unit
WHO/EURO
8 Scherfigsvej
2100 COPENHAGEN 0
Denmark
Telephone: 45 31/29 01 11
Telefax: 45 31/18 11 20

Health Statistics—Mortality
Database type: Numeric.
Subject scope: Health statistics; mortality.
Availability: UN system organizations; external users.
Printed products: World health statistics annual.
Distribution media: Magnetic tape.
Contact: Chief, HST/GSP
WHO
20, avenue Appia
1211 GENEVA 27
Switzerland
Telephone: 41 22/791 21 11
Telefax: 41 22/791 07 46

Health Statistics—Population & Live Births
Database type: Numeric.
Subject scope: Birth rate; demographic statistics; health statistics.
Availability: UN system organizations; external users.
Printed products: World health statistics annual.
Contact: Chief, HST/GSP
WHO

20, avenue Appia
1211 GENEVA 27
Switzerland
Telephone: 41 22/791 21 11
Telefax: 41 22/791 07 46

HQ/FHE—Health of Women
Database type: Bibliographic; numeric.
Subject scope: Health; women.
Availability: UN system organizations; external users: selected users in developing countries.
Printed products: Coverage of maternity care; Maternal mortality rates.
Distribution media: Printout.
Contact: Division of Family Health
          WHO
          20, avenue Appia
          1211 GENEVA 27
          Switzerland
Telephone: 41 22/791 21 11
Telefax: 41 22/791 07 46

HQ/NUT—Nutritional Status
Database type: Factual; numeric.
Subject scope: Nutrition.
Contact: Chief, Division of Family Health
          WHO
          20, avenue Appia
          1211 GENEVA 27
          Switzerland
Telephone: 41 22/791 21 11
Telefax: 41 22/791 07 46

HQ/NUT—Physical Growth of Children
Database type: Bibliographic; numeric.
Subject scope: Children; nutrition.
Contact: Nutrition
          Division of Family Health
          WHO
          20, avenue Appia
          1211 GENEVA 27
          Switzerland
Telephone: 41 22/791 21 11
Telefax: 41 22/791 07 46

Immunization Articles
Database type: Bibliographic.
Subject scope: Immunization.
Availability: UN system organizations; external users.
Printed products: Listing of EPI articles by subject/author.
Distribution media: Diskette; printout.
Contact: Expanded Programme on Immunization
          WHO
          20, avenue Appia
          1211 GENEVA 27
          Switzerland
Telephone: 41 22/791 41 67
Telefax: 41 22/791 07 46

Immunization Cold Chain Products
Database type: Full text; numeric.
Subject scope: Immunization; refrigeration; vaccination.
Availability: UN system organizations; external users.
Printed products: Product information sheets.
Contact: Technical Officer, EPI
          WHO
          20, avenue Appia

1211 GENEVA 27
Switzerland
Telephone: 41 22/791 21 11
Telefax: 41 22/791 07 46

Immunization Coverage Surveys
Database type: Numeric.
Subject scope: Immunization.
Availability: UN system organizations; external users.
Printed products: EPI information system.
Distribution media: Diskette; printout.
Contact: Expanded Programme on Immunization
          WHO
          20, avenue Appia
          1211 GENEVA 27
          Switzerland
Telephone: 41 22/791 41 67
Telefax: 41 22/791 07 46

Immunization Demographic Data
Database type: Numeric.
Subject scope: Immunization.
Availability: UN system organizations; external users.
Printed products: EPI information system.
Distribution media: Diskette; printout.
Contact: Expanded Programme on Immunization
          WHO
          20, avenue Appia
          1211 GENEVA 27
          Switzerland
Telephone: 41 22/791 41 67
Telefax: 41 22/791 07 46

Immunization Morbidity
Database type: Numeric.
Subject scope: Immunization.
Availability: UN system organizations; external users.
Printed products: EPI information system.
Distribution media: Diskette; printout.
Contact: Expanded Programme on Immunization
          WHO
          20, avenue Appia
          1211 GENEVA 27
          Switzerland
Telephone: 41 22/791 41 67
Telefax: 41 22/791 07 46

Immunization Programme Reviews
Database type: Factual.
Subject scope: Immunization.
Availability: UN system organizations; external users.
Printed products: EPI information system.
Distribution media: Diskette; printout.
Contact: Expanded Programme on Immunization
          WHO
          20, avenue Appia
          1211 GENEVA 27
          Switzerland
Telephone: 41 22/791 41 67
Telefax: 41 22/791 07 46

International Nonproprietary Names for Pharmaceutical Substances Data Base
Database type: Full text; referral.
Subject scope: Pharmaceuticals; terminology.
Availability: UN system organizations; external users: data provided free of charge on tape provided by request.

Printed products: International nonproprietary names (INN) for pharmaceutical substances (Cumulative List No. 7).
Distribution media: Magnetic tape; printout.
Contact: Chief, PHA
      DMP
      WHO
      20, avenue Appia
      1211 GENEVA 27
      Switzerland
Telephone: 41 22/791 21 11
Telefax: 41 22/791 07 46

Latin American Literature in the Health Sciences (LILACS)
Database type: Bibliographic.
Subject scope: Health; medical research; medical sciences.
Printed products: Index medicus latinoamericano (IMLA).
Distribution media: CD-ROM; magnetic tape; printout.
Contact: A.L. Packer
      Latin American Health Sciences Information Center
      R. Botucatu 862
      04023 SAO PAULO
      Brazil
Telephone: 55 11/549 2611

Leprosy Cases on Multidrug Treatment
Database type: Factual; numeric.
Subject scope: Leprosy.
Availability: UN system organizations.
Contact: LEP Unit
      WHO
      20, avenue Appia
      1211 GENEVA 27
      Switzerland
Telephone: 41 22/791 26 46
Telefax: 41 22/791 07 46

Low Birthweight/Perinatal Mortality
Database type: Bibliographic; numeric.
Subject scope: Maternal and child health.
Availability: UN system organizations; external users.
Distribution media: Diskette; printout.
Contact: Maternal and Child Health
      Division of Family Health
      WHO
      20, avenue Appia
      1211 GENEVA 27
      Switzerland
Telephone: 41 22/791 21 11
Telefax: 41 22/791 07 46

Malaria Cases
Database type: Factual; numeric.
Subject scope: Malaria.
Availability: UN system organizations; external users.
Printed products: Weekly epidemiological record; WHO health statistics quarterly.
Contact: Director, Control of Tropical Diseases
      WHO
      20, avenue Appia
      1211 GENEVA 27
      Switzerland
Telephone: 41 22/791 21 11
Telefax: 41 22/791 07 46

Management Information System for the Special Programme for Research and Training in Tropical Diseases (MISTR)
Database type: Bibliographic; factual; referral.

Subject scope: Development projects; research projects; tropical diseases.
Availability: UN system organizations; external users with restrictions.
Printed products: Management summary report; List of TDR funded projects.
Distribution media: Diskette; magnetic tape; online; printout.
Online hosts: ICC.
Contact: Management Officer (Information), TDR
      WHO
      20, avenue Appia
      1211 GENEVA 27
      Switzerland
Telephone: 41 22/791 21 11; 791 37 74
Telefax: 41 22/791 07 46

PAHO Document Retrieval System On-line (PAHOINFO)
Database type: Bibliographic; full text.
Subject scope: Health; health planning; health services; medical education.
Availability: UN system organizations; external users.
Printed products: PAHO disaster update; PAHO nutrition; PAHO-MEET; PAHODOC; PAHOSTC; TABCONT.
Distribution media: COM; magnetic tape; online.
Online hosts: DIALOG; MDC; PAHO, file: BIRS FILE; U.S. National Library of Medicine.
Contact: Chief, HBL
      Regional Office for the Americas (AMRO)
      525, 23rd Street, N.W.
      WASHINGTON, D.C. 20037
      USA
Tel: 1 202 861 3200
Fax: 1 202 223 5971

Pharmaceuticals Section/(UN Consolidated List of Products Whose Consumption and/or Sale Have Been Banned, Withdrawn, Severely Restricted or Not Approved by Governments)
Database type: Factual; full text.
Subject scope: Pharmaceuticals; regulations.
Availability: UN system organizations; external users with restrictions.
Printed products: Pharmaceuticals section/(UN consolidated list of products whose consumption and/or sale have been banned, withdrawn, severely restricted, or not approved by governments).
Distribution media: Magnetic tape; printout.
Contact: Chief, PHA
      DMP
      WHO
      20, avenue Appia
      1211 GENEVA 27
      Switzerland
Telephone: 41 22/791 21 11
Telefax: 41 22/791 07 46

REPIDISCA Data Base
Database type: Bibliographic.
Subject scope: Environmental engineering; sanitation; waste management; water pollution; water supply.
Availability: UN system organizations; external users.
Printed products: REPINDEX.
Distribution media: CD-ROM; magnetic tape.
Contact: Manager, REPIDISCA
      WHO
      Casilla 4337-Lima 100
      Los Pinos 259
      Urbanizacion Camacho

LIMA 3
Peru
Telephone: 51 14/35 41 35

Reported AIDS Cases
Database type: Numeric.
Subject scope: AIDS.
Contact: Global Programme on AIDS
WHO
20, avenue Appia
1211 GENEVA 27
Switzerland
Telephone: 41 22/791 21 11
Telefax: 41 22/791 07 46

WHO Library Information System (WHOLIS)
Database type: Bibliographic.
Subject scope: Health; health economics; public health; WHO.
Availability: UN system organizations; external users with restrictions.
Distribution media: Diskette; printout.
Contact: Head, Technical Services
HLT
WHO
20, avenue Appia
1211 GENEVA 27
Switzerland
Telephone: 41 22/791 20 73
Telefax: 41 22/791 07 46

WHO Terminology Information System (WHOTERM)
Database type: Factual.
Subject scope: Health; medicine; terminology.
Availability: UN system organizations.
Printed products: Glossaries; list of terms.
Distribution media: Diskette.
Contact: Chief, Technical Terminology Service
WHO
20, avenue Appia
1211 GENEVA 27
Switzerland
Telephone: 41 22/791 24 58; 791 24 55
Telefax: 41 22/791 07 46

World Health Statistics Data Base
Database type: Numeric.

Subject scope: Causes of death; demographic statistics; diseases; health personnel; health statistics; hospitals; infectious diseases; mortality.
Availability: UN system organizations; external users with restrictions: for national health authorities and government research institutes data is readily available.
Printed products: World health statistics annual; World health statistics quarterly.
Distribution media: Diskette; magnetic tape; printout.
Contact: Chief, HST/GSP
WHO
20, avenue Appia
1211 GENEVA 27
Switzerland
Telephone: 41 22/791 21 11
Telefax: 41 22/791 07 46

WPRO/CRP-Collaborating Centers in WPRO
Database type: Referral.
Subject scope: Health centres.
Availability: Agency staff.
Distribution media: Diskette.
Contact: WPRO
PO Box 2932
United Nations Cor Taft Avenues
MANILA
Philippines
Telephone: 63 2/521 8421
Telefax: 63 2/521 1036

WPRO/HSO-Indicators WPRO
Database type: Numeric.
Subject scope: Health indicators.
Availability: UN system organizations; external users with restrictions.
Printed products: Country health information profile; Western Pacific region data bank on socioeconomic and health indicators.
Distribution media: Printout.
Contact: WPRO
PO Box 2932
United Nations Cor Taft Avenues
MANILA
Philippines
Telephone: 63 2/521 8421
Telefax: 63 2/521 1036

UNITED NATIONS DEPOSITORY LIBRARIES

Listed below are the libraries where United Nations publications and other documents are available. Specific information on holdings in available by contacting the library directly.

LIBRARIES IN THE UNITED STATES

California
Los Angeles Public Library, Los Angeles
Stanford University Libraries, Stanford
University of California, General Library, Berkeley
University of California, University Research Library, Los Angeles

Colorado
University of Colorado at Boulder

Connecticut
Yale University Library, New Haven

District of Columbia
Library of Congress, Washington, D.C.

Florida
Florida State University, Robert M. Strozier Library, Tallahassee

Hawaii
University of Hawaii Library, Honolulu

Illinois
Library of International Relations, Chicago
Northwestern University Library, Evanston
University of Chicago, The Joseph Regenstein Library, Chicago
University of Illinois Library, Education and Social Sciences Library, Urbana

Indiana
Indiana University Library, Documents Department, Bloomington
Indiana University, School of Law Library, Indianapolis

Iowa
University of Iowa Library, Iowa City

Kansas
University of Kansas Libraries, Lawrence

Kentucky
University of Kentucky, Margaret I. King Library, Lexington

Louisiana
Louisiana State University Library, Baton Rouge

Maryland
Johns Hopkins University The Milton S. Eisenhower Library, Baltimore

Massachusetts
Harvard College Library, Cambridge
Boston Public Library

Michigan
University of Michigan, Harlan Hatcher Graduate Library, Ann Arbor

Minnesota
University of Minnesota, Wilson Library, Minneapolis

Nevada
University of Nevada Library, Reno

New Jersey
Princeton University, Pliny Fisk Library, Princeton

New York
Columbia University Law Library, New York
Cornell University, Olin Library, Ithaca
Council of Foreign Relations, New York
New York Public Library, Economics Division, New York
New York University, Elmer Holmes Bobst Library, New York

North Carolina
University of North Caroline, Davis Library, Chapel Hill

Ohio
Cleveland Public Library, Cleveland

Pennsylvania
University of Pennsylvania, C. Patterson Van Pelt Library, Philadelphia

Rhode Island
Brown University, The John D. Rockefeller, Jr. Library, Providence

Tennessee
Vanderbilt University Library, Nashville

Texas
University of Texas Library, Perry-Castañeda Library, Austin

Utah
University of Utah, Marriott Library, Salt Lake City

Virginia
University of Virginia, Alderman Library, Charlottesville

Washington
University of Washington Libraries, Seattle

LIBRARIES IN PUERTO RICO

Puerto Rico
Universidad de Puerto Rico, Biblioteca General, Rio Piedras
Universidad Católica de Puerto Rico, Escuela de Derecho, Ponce

LIBRARIES IN THE U.S. VIRGIN ISLANDS

St. Thomas
Enid M. Baa Library and Archives, Charlotte Amalie

LIBRARIES IN CANADA

Alberta
University of Alberta, The Library, Edmonton

British Columbia
University of British Columbia Library, Vancouver

Manitoba
Legislative Library, Winnipeg

New Brunswick
University of New Brunswick, Harriet Irving Library, Fredericton

Nova Scotia
Dalhousie University Library, Halifax

Ontario
Queens University, Documents Library, Mackintosh-Corry
  Hall, Kingston
University of Ottawa, Bibliothèque Morrisset, Ottawa
University of Toronto Library, Toronto

Québec
McGill University, McLennan Library, Montreal
Université de Montréal, Bibliothèque des Sciences Humaines
  et Sociales, Montréal
Université Laval, Bibliothèque, Québec

Saskatchewan
University of Saskatchewan, Murray Memorial Library,
  Saskatoon

Staff of the United Nations System

ORGANIZATION	FINANCED FROM REGULAR BUDGETS			EXTRA-BUDGETARY (VOLUNTARY FUNDS)			TOTAL	
	Prof.	G.S.	Total	Prof.	G.S.	Total	Prof.	G.S.
United Nations[1]	3,265	5,829	9,094	1,604	3,198	4,802	4,869	9,027
UNHCR	106	179	285	643	1,198	1,841	749	1,377
UNITAR	—	1	—	10	8	18	10	9
UNRWA	51	2	53	67	7	74	118	9
ITC	1		1	181	192	373	182	192
ICSC	18	22	40	—	—	—	18	22
ICJ	19	28	47	—	—	—	19	28
UNU	—	—	—	36	65	101	36	65
UNDP	—	—	—	1,571	5,033	6,604	1,571	5,033
UNICEF	—	—	—	1,179	2,623	3,802	1,179	2,623
ILO	678	1,012	1,690	695	692	1,387	1,373	1,704
FAO	1,051	2,062	3,113	1,608	1,649	3,257	2,659	3,711
UNESCO	808	1,406	2,214	248	341	589	1,056	1,747
WHO	1,269	2,350	3,619	564	1,208	1,772	1,833	3,558
ICAO	248	350	598	231	223	454	479	573
UPU	62	84	146	25	1	26	87	85
ITU	240	395	635	135	99	234	375	494
WMO	104	124	228	78	72	150	182	196
IMO	88	146	234	34	47	81	122	193
WIPO	114	237	351	4	18	22	118	255
UNIDO	355	665	1,020	305	458	763	660	1,123
IAEA	684	958	1,642	15	108	123	699	1,066
TOTALS	9,161	15,850	25,011	9,233	17,240	26,473	18,394	33,090

Grand Total UN System: 51,484

[1]These figures include staff for the central UN Secretariat in New York, Geneva, Vienna, the five Regional Commissions and many other units around the world, as of the end of 1990.

Note: "Prof." denotes professional grade positions; "G.S." denotes general service positions. "Regular Budget" positions are considered long-term worldwide civil service positions and are funded by legally binding assessments made upon all members of an organization; "Extra-budgetary" denotes positions for special development and humanitarian programs, which are funded by voluntary contributions from member governments. (Source: *Renewing the United Nations System* by Erskine Childers with Brian Urquhart, Dag Hammarskjöld Foundation, Sweden, 1994. Reprinted with permission.)

BIBLIOGRAPHY

The following is a selected list of titles for further reading about the United Nations. If no publisher is attributed, the book is published by the United Nations and available through the annual *United Nations Publications Catalog*. UN publicatios may be ordered from: the Sales Section, 2 United Nations Plaza, Room DC2-853, Dept. 421, New York, NY 10017, (800) 253-9646; or from UNIPUB, 4611-F Assembly Drive, Lanham, MD 20706, (800) 274-4888. In Europe, UN publications may be obtained from United Nations Publications, Sales Office and Bookshop, CH-1211 Geneva 10, Switzerland, 41(22) 734-1473.

GENERAL INFORMATION
A Global Agenda: Issues before the 46th General Assembly of the United Nations, John Tessitore, Susan Woolfson, editors, UN Association of the USA, University Press of America, 1992.

A Global Agenda: Issues before the 47th General Assembly of the United Nations, John Tessitore, Susan Woolfson, editors, UN Association of the USA, University Press of America, 1993.

About the United Nations, a series of VHS videos and texts providing insight into the issues facing the world organization today. Includes: *Human Rights, Environment and Development, Palestine, Literacy, Africa Recovery, Peace-Keeping,* and *Decolonization,* 1991–1992.

Acronyms and Abbreviations Covering the United Nations System and Other International Organizations, 1981. Contains the acronyms and abbreviations of approximately 825 titles within the UN system, in English, French, Russian, Spanish, Chinese, and Arabic.

Anarchy or Order: Annual Reports 1982–1991, by Javier Pérez de Cuéllar. A chronological assessment of the work of the organization during his tenure. 1991.

Basic Facts About the United Nations, annual.

International Institutions at Work, Paul G. Taylor, St. Martin's Press, 1988.

Peace by Pieces—United Nations Agencies and Their Roles: a Reader and Selective Bibliography, Robert N. Wells, Jr., Scarecrow Press, Metuchen, NJ, 1991, .

Programme budget for the biennium 1994–95, General Assembly, UN, 22 February 1994, A/RES/48/231.

Report of the Secretary General on the Work of the Organization, United Nations, annual.

Resolutions and Decisions Adopted by the General Assembly, United Nations, annual.

UN Chronicle, bi-monthly.

United Nations, Divided World, 2nd edition, Adam Roberts and Benedict Kingsbury, editors, Clarendon Press, 1993.

United Nations Yearbook, irregular.

Who's Who in the United Nations and Related Agencies, Detroit: Omnigraphics, 1992.

HISTORY OF THE UNITED NATIONS
A Dangerous Place, Daniel P. Moynihan, New York: Little Brown, 1978.

A Life in Peace and War, Brian Urquhart, New York: Harper & Row, 1987.

Hammarskjöld, Brian Urquhart, New York: Knopf, 1972.

Ralph Bunche: An American Life, Brian Urquhart, New York:

W.W. Norton, 1993.

The Structure of the United Nations General Assembly: An Organizational Approach to Its Work, 1974–1980s, Blanche Finley, Kraus International Publications, 1988.

The US, the UN, and the Management of Global Change, New York: New York University Press, 1983.

The United Nations at Forty: A Foundation to Build On, 1985.

THE FUTURE OF THE UNITED NATIONS
A World in Need of Leadership: Tomorrow's United Nations (Development Dialogue 1990: 1–2), Erskine Childers with Brian Urquhart, Dag Hammarskjöld Foundation, Uppsala, 1990.

Future Role of the United Nations in an Interdependent World, 1989.

Global Outlook 2000, 1990.

Renewing the United Nations System, Erskine Childers with Brian Urquhart, Dag Hammarskjöld Foundation, Uppsala, 1994.

Third Generation World Organization, 1989.

Towards a More Effective United Nations, (Development Dialogue, 1991: 1–2), Erskine Childers with Brian Urquhart, Dag Hammarskjold Foundation, Uppsala, 1991.

DISARMAMENT
Concepts of Security Disarmament, 1986.

Disarmament, Environment and Development and their Relevance to the Least Developed Countries, 1991.

International Law of Disarmament and Arms Control, 1991.

Study on Conventional Disarmament, 1945–1985, 1985.

The United Nations and Disarmament, 1945–1985, 1985.

United Nations Disarmament Yearbook, annual.

PEACEFUL USES OF OUTER SPACE
Maintaining Outer Space for Peaceful Uses, 1985.

Prevention of an Arms Race in Outer Space: A Guide to the Discussions in the Conference on Disarmament, 1991.

Report of the Committee on the Peaceful Uses of Outer Space, 1991.

Space Activities of the United Nations and International Organizations, 1992.

INTERNATIONAL PEACE AND SECURITY
An Agenda for Peace, Boutros Boutros-Ghali, United Nations, June 1992, DPI/1247.

The Blue Helmets: A Review of UN Peace-Keeping, 2nd edition, United Nations, 1990.

Reference Paper: The United Nations and the Situation in the Former Yugoslavia, UNDPI document, March 1994, DPI/1312/Rev.2.

The Evolution of UN Peacekeeping: Case Studies and Comparative Analysis, William Durch, editor, New York: St. Martins Press, 1993.

The United Nations and Collective Management of International Conflict, 1986.

United Nations Peace-keeping Update: May 1994, UNDPI document, DPI/1306/Rev.3, June 1994.

ENVIRONMENT AND SUSTAINABLE DEVELOPMENT

Climate Change and Transnational Corporations: Analysis and Trends, 1992.

Global Partnership for Environment and Development: A Guide to Agenda 21, 1992.

UNEP 1992 Annual Report: Twenty Years Since Stockholm, 1993.

State of the World Environment, 1991.

Sustainable Development and the Environment, UNDP.

ECONOMIC DEVELOPMENT

Conclusions on Accounting and Reporting by Transnational Corporations, 1988.

Development Update, UN Department of Public Information (UNDPI), United Nations, (bi-monthly).

Handbook of International Trade and Development Statistics 1991, 1992.

Industry and Development: A Global Report 1991/1992, 1991.

International Development Strategy and Establishment of a New International Economic Order: Third Regional Appraisal, 1981.

International Trade Statistics, annual.

International Development Strategy for the Fourth United Nations Development Decade (1991-2000), UN Dept. of Public Information, DPI/1107, 1991.

INSTRAW Report, annual.

The Least Developed Countries Report, UNCTAD, annual.

Paris Declaration and Programme of Action for the Least Developed Countries for the 1990s, 1992.

Report of the Commission on Science and Technology for Development, annual.

Source, (Magazine of the UNDP/World Bank Water and Sanitation Program), UNDP.

Trade and Development Report, UNCTAD, annual.

Transnational Corporations and the Transfer of New and Emerging Technologies to Developing Countries, 1990.

UNCTAD Review, biennial.

United Nations Development Programme: Compendium of Ongoing Projects, 1991.

United Nations University Annual Report.

UNU Press Publications to 1993.

World Economic Survey, annual.

World Statistics in Brief, annual.

SOCIAL DEVELOPMENT

Accelerating the Development Process: Challenges for National and International Policies in the 1990s, 1991.

Aging and Urbanization, 1991. Presents the reports and recommendations of the UN International Conference on Aging Populations in the Context of Urbanization.

An Agenda for Development, by Secretary General Boutros Boutros-Ghali, 1994.

Child Mortality in Developing Countries, 1991.

Crisis or Reform: Breaking the Barriers to Development, 1984.

Development for People: Goals and Strategies for the Year 2000, 1989.

Human Development Report 1993, UNDP, Oxford University Press.

The Least Developed Countries, 1990 Report, 1991.

The State of World Population, UNFPA, annual.

The World's Women, 1970–1990: Trends and Statistics, 1991.

UNFPA Annual Report.

UNFPA Publications & Audio Visual Guide, annual.

United Nations Demographic Yearbook, 42nd Issue, 1990, 1991.

Vienna International Plan of Action on Aging, UNDPI document, 1983, DPI/932.

Women: Challenges to the Year 2000, 1992.

World Survey on the Role of Women in Development, 1989.

World Food Programme 1993 Food Aid Review.

World Food Programme Journal, periodical.

HUMANITARIAN AFFAIRS AND DISASTER RELIEF

Images of Exile: 1951–1991, UNHCR, 1991. A visual record of the work of the UN High Commissioner for Refugees between 1951 and 1991.

Mitigating Natural Disasters: Phenomena, Effects and Options, 1991.

INTERNATIONAL CRIME AND ILLICIT TRAFFIC IN NARCOTIC DRUGS

Combating Drug Abuse and Related Crime, 1984.

Commission on Narcotic Drugs—Cumulative Index, 1987–1990, 1991. Covers all national laws and regulations on narcotic drugs and psychotropic substances which governments have communicated to the UN Secretariat during 1987–1990.

Eighth United Nations Congress on the Prevention of Crime and the Treatment of Offenders, 1991.

Report of the Commission on Crime Prevention and Criminal Justice, annual ECOSOC document.

Report of the Commission on Narcotic Drugs, annual ECOSOC document.

Report of the International Conference on Drug Abuse and Illicit Trafficking, June 1987, 1987.

The United Nations and Crime Prevention and Criminal Justice, UNDPI document, June 1990, DPI/1045.

The United Nations and Drug Abuse Control, UN International Drug Control Programme, United Nations (UNDPI), 1992.

United Nations Convention Against Illicit Traffic in Narcotic Drugs and Psychotropic Substances, 1991.

APARTHEID

Assembly accepts credentials of South African representatives after 24 years; deletes item on elimination of apartheid from its Agenda, UNDPI document, GA/8682.

Elimination of Apartheid and Establishment of a United Democratic and Non-racial South Africa, General Assembly document, 21 June 1994, A/48/L.58.

Progress Made in the Implementation of the Declaration on Apartheid and its Destructive Consequences in Southern Africa, Secretary General, General Assembly document, September 1991, A/45/1052.

Recent Developments on the Issue of Apartheid in South Africa (III); Upcoming Milestone: Democratic Parliamentary Elections, UNDPI document, March 1994, DPI/1469.

South Africa's Democratic Elections: The UN's Observer Role, UNDPI document, March 1994, DPI/1469.

INDEPENDENCE OF COLONIAL PEOPLES

Decolonization and World Peace, Brian Urquhart, University of Texas Press, Austin, 1989.

Decolonization: The Task Ahead; Profiles of 18 Trust and Non-Self-Governing Territories, United Nations, April 1991, DPI/1109.

HUMAN RIGHTS

Human Rights Committee: Its Role in the Development of the International Covenant on Civil and Political Rights, Dominic McGoldrick, Clarendon, Oxford University Press, 1991.

United Nations Actions in the Field of Human Rights, 40th Anniversary, 1989.

Universal Declaration of Human Rights.

Yearbook on Human Rights.

INTERNATIONAL LAW

International Court of Justice Bibliography, 1991.

International Court of Justice Reports and Judgments, Advisory Opinions and Orders, 1992.

Multilateral Treaties Deposited with the Secretary-General, annual.

The Law of the Sea: A Select Bibliography 1991, 1992.

The Law of the Sea: Multilateral Treaties Relevant to the United Nations Convention on the Law of the Sea, 1985.

United Nations Commission on International Trade Law Yearbook, annual.

United Nations Treaty Series. Treaties and international agreements entered into by UN member states.

Yearbook of the International Law Commission.

REGIONAL DEVELOPMENT

Economic and Social Survey for Asia and the Pacific, annual.

Economic Bulletin for Asia and the Pacific, semi-annual.

Economic Bulletin for Europe, issued periodically.

Economic Commission for Europe (ECE) Annual Report .

Economic and Social Commission for Asia and the Pacific (ESCAP), annual report.

Economic Survey of Europe, annual.

Economic Survey of Latin America and the Caribbean, annual.

Report of the Executive Secretary of ESCWA, annual.

Report of the Economic Commission for Africa (ECA), annual.

Report of the Economic Comission for Latin America and the Caribbean (ECLAC), annual.

Regional Cooperation: Report of the Secretary General, annual ECOSOC document.

Statistical Yearbook for Asia and the Pacific.

Statistical Yearbook for Latin America and the Caribbean.

Survey of Economic and Social Conditions in Africa, annual.

THE UNITED NATIONS

RELATED AGENCIES

AGENCIES OF THE UNITED NATIONS SYSTEM

The following organizations are often called part of the United Nations "family." The previous chapters have been concerned with the organs, programs, or funds of the United Nations that are directly governed by the General Assembly and/or the Security Council, and which have the Secretary General as their executive head. The following organizations all have their own separate member states, governing bodies, executive heads, and secretariats. While these organizations are bound to the UN by legal agreements, they are not governed directly by UN organs.

Most organizations in the system are related to the United Nations through legal agreements executed pursuant to Articles 57 and 63 of the Charter. A key purpose of these special agreements, as stated in Article 58, was coordination of activities in the pursuit of economic, social, and cultural objectives. However, some provisions have never been fully implemented.

The Specialized Agencies
The ILO, FAO, UNESCO and WHO all had predecessor organizations in the League of Nations but were re-established as part of the UN system between 1946–1994. UNIDO became a full specialized agency in 1985. Voting in the main governing bodies of these agencies is on the same one-nation-one-vote principle as in the United Nations.

Technical Agencies
Among this group are the very first truly international organizations, such as the International Telecommunications Union (ITU) and the Universal Postal Union (UPU), which were both established over a century ago. This group of agencies has a very specific focus, and countries are often represented by the head of the national ministry in charge of the relevant area, such as weather, telecommunications, postal service, intellectual property.

However, the International Atomic Energy Association (IAEA) was established in 1956 by the United Nations General Assembly, and is legally bound directly to the General Assembly. The other specialized and technical agencies report to the United Nations through the Economic and Social Council (ECOSOC).

GATT/WTO
The General Agreement on Tariffs and Trade, and its successor institution, the World Trade Organization, are not officially part of the UN system. However, GATT has been described as having a de facto specialized-agency relationship. In 1994, the WTO was still in an embryonic stage, and its exact relationship to the United Nations had not yet been spelled out.

The Bretton Woods Institutions
The IMF and the World Bank Group are structured very differently from the specialized agencies. These agencies were established under the charter of the United Nations at a special conference held at Bretton Woods, New Hampshire in 1944. The World Bank Group comprises five separate organizations: the IBRD, the IDA, the IFC, MIGA, and the ICSD. Members of the IBRD can choose which of the four remaining organizations they wish to join.

One of the most fundamental differences between the UN and the Bretton Woods institutions is that voting in these organizations is governed according to the number of shares held by each member state. Therefore, the wealthier countries have more voting power.

IFAD, while not a Bretton Woods institution, is a more recent addition to the specialized agency family that deals with capital funding operations. It raises money through replenishments. Its governing council is made up of three groups of countries—industrialized, oil-producing, and other developing countries. Each group has equal voting rights.

THE AGENCIES IN CHRONOLOGICAL ORDER—WITH EFFECTIVE DATES OF ESTABLISHMENT

Universal Postal Union	1 July 1875
International Labor Organization	11 April 1919
International Telecommunication Union	1 January 1934
Food and Agriculture Organization of the United Nations	16 October 1945
International Bank for Reconstruction and Development	27 December 1945
International Monetary Fund	27 December 1945
United Nations Educational, Scientific and Cultural Organization	4 November 1946
International Civil Aviation Organization	4 April 1947
General Agreement on Tariffs and Trade	1 January 1948
World Health Organization	7 April 1948
World Meteorological Organization	23 March 1950
International Finance Corporation	24 July 1956
International Atomic Energy Agency	29 July 1957
International Maritime Organization	17 March 1958
International Development Association	24 September 1960
World Intellectual Property Organization	26 April 1970
International Fund for Agricultural Development	30 November 1977
United Nations Industrial Development Organization	1 January 1986

The arrangement of articles on the United Nations related agencies follows the order of the chart on the Structure of the United Nations System shown in the first chapter. Each article is structured in the following sections: Background, Creation, Purposes, Membership, Structure, Budget, Activities, Bibliography.

THE INTERNATIONAL ATOMIC ENERGY AGENCY (IAEA)

BACKGROUND: The UN came into existence at the beginning of the atomic age. Man's success in harnessing atomic energy has made the UN's objectives not only important but even indispensable. The primary purpose of the UN is to prevent war. A major war involving the use of atomic weapons would be not simply catastrophic but very probably suicidal. The second objective of the UN is to promote the economic and social welfare of peoples throughout the world. Atomic energy promises to contribute greatly to worldwide prosperity. Although "atoms for peace" has been a continuing concern of the UN itself, and although a number of organizations of the UN family, such as FAO and WHO, have been concerned with specific aspects of peaceful uses of atomic energy, it was not until 1957 that a special organization, the International Atomic Energy Agency, came into being for the express purpose of accelerating and enlarging the contribution of atomic energy to peace, health, and prosperity throughout the world.

CREATION

Addressing the UN General Assembly in December 1953, US president Dwight D. Eisenhower called for the establishment of an international atomic energy organization to "serve the peaceful pursuits of mankind." The president said that he hoped the atomic powers, through such an organization, would dedicate "some of their strength to serve the needs rather than the fears of mankind."

President Eisenhower stated that the USSR "must, of course, be one" of the countries principally involved in the proposed organization. Accordingly, as a first step, the US State Department in the spring and summer of 1954 submitted a series of memoranda to the USSR suggesting the principles that should be incorporated in the statute of such an agency. It was, however, impossible for the two powers to reach agreement at that time. The USSR maintained that the issues of disarmament and peaceful uses of atomic energy were inseparable and that agreement on a general prohibition of nuclear weapons would have to precede the creation of the agency. The US countered with the argument that effective international control of nuclear weapons would have to precede their prohibition, and it announced that it was prepared to go ahead with international negotiations even without the participation of the USSR.

In the summer of 1954, the US issued invitations to seven other countries, including both "atomic powers" and important uranium-producing states—Australia, Belgium, Canada, France, Portugal, South Africa, and the UK—to meet with it in Washington, D.C., to prepare a draft statute for the proposed agency. In September, the USSR reversed its previous position. It announced its willingness to separate the issues of disarmament and peaceful uses of atomic energy and to accept the eight-power draft statute as a basis for further negotiations and guidance.

In December 1954, the General Assembly unanimously adopted an "Atoms for Peace" resolution expressing the hope that the International Atomic Energy Agency would be established "without delay" in order to assist "in lifting the burdens of hunger, poverty and disease." An international conference on the statute was convened at UN headquarters in New York on 20 September 1956, with the participation of 81 nations, including some, such as the Federal Republic of Germany, that were not yet members of the UN itself. After adopting a number of amendments, proposed for the most part by the atomic "have-not" powers, the conference unanimously adopted the statute as a whole on 26 October 1956.

On 29 July 1957, the statute came into force after 26 states had deposited instruments of ratification, and the International Atomic Energy Agency officially came into existence. The first General Conference of the IAEA was held in Vienna in October 1957, at which time it was decided to make Vienna the permanent headquarters site of the agency. The address of the IAEA is Wagramerstrasse 5, P.O. Box 100, A-1011 Vienna.

PURPOSES

According to the statute of the IAEA, the agency "shall seek to accelerate and enlarge the contribution of atomic energy to peace, health and prosperity throughout the world. It shall ensure, so far as it is able, that assistance provided by it or at its request or under its supervision and control is not used in such a way as to further any military purpose."

The IAEA acts as a clearinghouse for the pooling and coordination of experience and research in the peaceful uses of nuclear power. It helps its member countries acquire the necessary skills and materials to share in the benefits of the atomic age. In practice, the IAEA has been particularly concerned with bringing the advantages of atomic energy to underdeveloped regions.

The IAEA is obliged under its statute to "ensure, so far as it is able," that all the activities in which it takes part are directed exclusively to civilian uses. A second important task of the IAEA, then, is to establish a system of supervision and control to make certain that none of the assistance programs that it fosters and none of the materials whose distribution it supervises are used for military purposes. This aspect of the work assumed significance far beyond its primary objective when the Treaty on the Non-Proliferation of Nuclear Weapons came into force in March 1970, since the IAEA is the body responsible for the necessary control system under that treaty.

MEMBERSHIP

Any member of the UN or of any of the specialized agencies that signed the statute within 90 days after 26 October 1956 thereby became a charter member of the IAEA upon ratification of the statute. Other countries, even if not members of the UN or any of the specialized agencies, may be admitted by the General Conference of the IAEA upon recommendation of the Board of Governors.

As of 1 July 1994 the IAEA had 121 members. Latvia and Yemen have applied for membership and been approved by the General Council, but have not yet deposited an instrument of acceptance of the statute.

STRUCTURE
The three organs of the IAEA are the General Conference, the Board of Governors, and the secretariat, headed by a director-general.

General Conference
The General Conference consists of all members, each having one vote. It meets once a year at IAEA headquarters in Vienna. Special sessions may be convened by the director-general at the request of the Board of Governors or a majority of the IAEA members. The General Conference elects 22 of the 35 members of the Board of Governors for a period of two years. It considers the board's annual report and approves reports for submission to the UN and agreements with the UN and other organizations. It approves the budget recommended by the board and the appointment of the director-general. The General Conference may discuss any matter concerning the IAEA and may make recommendations to the Board of Governors or to any of the member states.

Board of Governors
The 35-member Board of Governors is the body actually vested with "the authority to carry out the functions of the Agency in accordance with (the) Statute." It is composed as follows: the outgoing Board of Governors designates for membership on the board the 13 members most advanced in the technology of atomic energy and the production of source materials and the member most advanced in the technology of atomic energy and the production of source materials in two of the following areas in which none of the aforesaid 13 is located—North America, Latin America, Western Europe, Eastern Europe, Africa, the Middle East and South Asia, Southeast Asia and the Pacific, and the Far East.

The General Conference also elects to membership of the Board of Governors the following: (1) 20 members, with due regard to geographical representation, so that the board at all times will include in this category 5 representatives of Latin America, 4 representatives of Western Europe, 3 representatives of Eastern Europe, 4 representatives of Africa, 2 representatives of the Middle East and South Asia, 1 representative of Southeast Asia and the Pacific, and 1 representative of the Far East; (2) in addition, 1 further member from among the members of the following areas: the Middle East and South Asia, Southeast Asia and the Pacific, and the Far East; (3) and 1 further member from among the members in the following areas: Africa, the Middle East and South Asia, and Southeast Asia and the Pacific.

The Board of Governors for 1993–94 was composed of representatives of Argentina, Australia, Brazil, Canada, Chile, China, Colombia, Cuba, Egypt, Ethiopia, Finland, France, Germany, Hungary, India, Indonesia, Ireland, Italy, Japan, Lebanon, Libyan Arab Jamahiriya, Malaysia, Nigeria, Paraguay, Philippines, Poland, Russian Federation, Saudi Arabia, Sweden, Switzerland, Syrian Arab Republic, Tunisia, Ukraine, United Kingdom, and United States.

Director-General and Secretariat
The staff of the IAEA is headed by a director-general, appointed by the Board of Governors with the approval of the General Conference for a term of four years. The statute describes the director-general as "the chief administrative officer of the Agency," but it closely limits his independent powers by providing that he "shall be under the authority and subject to the control of the Board of Governors." The director-general is responsible for "the appointment, organization, and functioning of the staff."

The first director-general, who held the post from 1957 to 1961, was Sterling Cole of the US, a former congressman. Dr. Sigvard Eklund, a Swedish physicist and administrator, served as director-general from 1961 to 1981. He was succeeded by Dr. Hans Blix of Sweden, a former foreign minister, who last was reappointed in 1993 for a fourth four-year term. He heads a staff of about 2,200 from some 85 countries.

Position in the UN System
The IAEA is an autonomous international organization occupying its own position in the UN family of organizations. Under the relationship agreement between the UN and the IAEA, the IAEA is recognized as being "responsible for international activities concerned with the peaceful uses of atomic energy." One of the statutory objectives of the IAEA is to ensure that none of the assistance it gives to member states is "used in such a way as to further any military purpose," and the IAEA has a staff of inspectors to report violations of this rule. In case of noncompliance, the agency's Board of Governors reports to the Security Council and the General Assembly of the UN.

The agency has relationship agreements with eight specialized agencies of the UN (UNESCO, ILO, WHO, WMO, ICAO, FAO, IMO, and UNIDO), as well as working contracts with UNEP, UNDP, UNDRO, the World Bank, and the UN Scientific Committee on the Effects of Atomic Radiation. Cooperation agreements have also been concluded with organizations not a part of the UN system that are concerned with the peaceful uses of atomic energy, such as the Inter-American Nuclear Energy Commission, the Agency for the Prohibition of Nuclear Weapons in Latin America, the League of Arab States, the OAU, the Nuclear Energy Agency of the OECD, and the European Atomic Energy Community. Finally, the IAEA maintains contact with 19 nongovernmental organizations having consultative status with it.

BUDGET
The IAEA is financed by regular and voluntary contributions from member states. The regular budget for 1994 amounted to US$200 million. The target for voluntary contributions to finance the IAEA program of technical cooperation was US$58.5 million for 1994.

ACTIVITIES

A. Assistance to Member States
The initial program of the IAEA, unanimously adopted by the 1957 General Conference, emphasized activities that could be undertaken while the IAEA's experience and resources were still relatively limited. High priority was given "to those activities which will give the maximum possible benefit from the peaceful applications of atomic energy in improving the conditions and raising the standard of living of the peoples in the underdeveloped areas."

In the light of these considerations, two of the IAEA's major objectives are to help member states prepare for the eventual use of nuclear power and to encourage them in the wider use of radioisotopes. Although it cannot undertake actual programs of development for its members, it can assist them in initiating and carrying out such programs. By 1992 IAEA was active in assisting its developing members in an impressive number of fields:

Basic human needs.

- water resources development
- agriculture (mutation breeding, fertilizer and soil nutrition, pest control, use of agrochemicals)
- livestock (reproduction, health, nutrition)
- health care (radiation therapy, nuclear medicine and diagnostics)

Industrial applications

- nondestructive testing
- hydrology (silt movements, geothermal studies)
- radiation processing (surface coating, radiation sterilization, food preservation, sterilization of medical products)
- isotopic tracers for industry
- nuclear gauging for industry (paper, steel, food processing, mining industries)
- radioisotope and radiopharmaceutical production
- research reactor design and use

Electricity generation

- geology, mining and processing of nuclear raw materials
- fuel element fabrication
- metallurgy and materials testing
- power reactor design
- reactor electronics instrumentation and control
- reactor engineering and quality assurance
- electricity system planning

Support activities

nuclear centers and laboratories
- nuclear safety (regulation, safety standards, radiation protection, waste management, safety assessment)
- physics (atomic, nuclear, high-energy and solid-state physics)
- chemistry (nuclear, radio, radiation, and nuclear analytical chemistry)

Technical Assistance

The IAEA has been providing technical assistance to developing member countries since 1959, in the form of expert services, equipment, and training, with the objective of facilitating technology transfer in various fields related to nuclear energy. The major fields in which assistance is provided are nuclear safety, the application of isotopes and radiation in agriculture, and nuclear engineering and technology. Other important areas for assistance are general atomic energy development, nuclear physics and chemistry, prospecting for and mining and processing of nuclear materials, and the application of isotopes and radiation in industry and hydrology, in medicine, and in biology.

Financial support for the IAEA's technical cooperation programs comes mainly from its own voluntary technical assistance and cooperation fund; other sources are extrabudgetary donations and contributions in kind from member states and UNDP. In 1992 a total of 1,094 technical cooperation projects were operational. In that year, IAEA's technical assistance cooperation was divided between the world's regions as follows: Asia and the Pacific, 26.3 percent; Africa, 22.5 percent; Middle East, 2.8 percent; Latin America, 25.1 percent; Europe, 15.2 percent; Interregional, 8.1 percent.

Provision of Materials

Under the IAEA statute, any member desiring to set up an atomic energy project for peaceful purposes "may request the assistance of the Agency in securing special fissionable and other materials."

The IAEA acts, on request, as an intermediary in arranging the supply of reactor fuel and specialized equipment from one member state to another. Argentina, Finland, Japan, Mexico, Norway, Pakistan, Uruguay, and Zaire, among other countries, have been beneficiaries of such arrangements. Small quantities of special fissionable materials have also been supplied to a number of countries for research purposes.

Training of Technical Personnel

The IAEA's training program has retained its importance, not only because the need for trained staff is pressing but also because less elaborate preparations are required for assistance of this kind than for technical assistance operations involving the provision of expert services and demonstration equipment.

To meet the shortage of scientific and technical workers, the IAEA has initiated a fivefold program:

1. *Fellowships.* Fellowships are awarded in all subjects involving the peaceful uses of atomic energy, such as nuclear physics; the production, handling, and application of isotopes in agriculture, industry, medicine, biology, and hydrology; nuclear chemistry; the planning, construction, and operation of research and power reactors; health physics; and radiological protection.
2. *Assignment of experts and consultants.* The program provides for scientists and engineers to give advice and in-service training to developing countries on various subjects.
3. *Survey of available facilities in member states.* The IAEA collects detailed information from its member states about their training and research programs, training facilities, and the experts that they are prepared to make available to the IAEA. It is thus in a position to act as an international clearinghouse for training in atomic energy and to promote technical cooperation among developing countries.
4. *Training courses.* The organization of these courses for participants from various countries requires elaborate preparations and cooperation with other organizations, national governments, universities, and scientific institutions. Such courses, which are given in different parts of the world, vary in duration from a few weeks to several months. Regional and interregional courses have been organized on such subjects as the application of isotopes and radiation in medicine, nuclear instrumentation for laboratory technicians, the use and maintenance of nuclear and related electronic equipment, radiological and safety protection, physics, the utilization of research reactors, nuclear-power projects and other high-technology subjects, the preparation and control of radiopharmaceuticals, and uranium prospecting and ore analysis.
5. *Expanded training programs.* A number of developing countries, faced with the need to introduce nuclear power, require special assistance in the training of their key staff; the agency has therefore initiated an expanded training program on nuclear-power project planning, implementation, and operation. Special training courses contribute to the development of efficient legal and organizational infrastructures for nuclear-power programs, including instruction in quality assurance and safety aspects. In addition, on-the-job training is arranged on subjects for which no formal courses are available.

B. Exchange of Information

While its assistance programs are directed primarily to the needs of economically developing areas, the IAEA's program of conferences and exchange of information is designed to benefit all of its members—even the most technically advanced.

The International Nuclear Information System (INIS), set up by the agency in 1970, provides worldwide coverage of the literature dealing with all aspects of peaceful uses of atomic energy and is the first fully decentralized computer-based information system. Countries and organizations participating in the INIS collect and process all the relevant literature within their geographic areas and send it to the IAEA. In Vienna, the information is checked, merged, and further processed, and the resulting output is distributed to individuals and organizations around the world. The major products of the system are the magnetic tape service, the *INIS Atomindex,* and the direct availability of the INIS data base on-line from the IAEA computer in Vienna. The magnetic tapes and the on-line service, available to member states and participating organizations only, contain bibliographic descriptions, subject indexing, and abstracts and are utilized for current selective dissemination of information and retrospective searching. The *INIS Atomindex,* an international nuclear abstract journal, is published twice a month and is available to the public on a subscription basis. An additional service is the provision on microfiche of texts of all nonconventional literature submitted to the system. In 1994, INIS membership included 86 countries and 17 international organizations; it reported on over 1,700,000 documents. In 1992 the INIS data base was made available to INIS member states on five CD-ROM disks.

The IAEA also cooperates with FAO in the provision of a similar information system for agriculture, known as *AGRIS.*

A second important information service of the IAEA concerns nuclear data—numerical and associated information on neutron cross-sections, related fission, capture, and scattering parameters of neutron-induced reactions, as well as other nuclear physical constants. The IAEA maintains an efficient system for collection of these data and, together with three other regional centers, in France, the Russian Federation, and the US, issues *CINDA,* an index to the literature on microscopic neutron data. It also compiles *WRENDA,* the world request list for nuclear-data measurements needed both for the development of fission and fusion reactors and for nuclear-material safeguards.

The IAEA plays a leading role in promoting the dissemination of scientific and technical information by organizing each year 15 to 20 conferences, symposia, and seminars and a large number of smaller technical meetings. The IAEA has organized major international meetings dealing with specific aspects of the peaceful uses of nuclear energy. For example, some important 1994 meetings included: the IAEA Symposium on International Safeguards (Vienna); Conference on Nuclear Power Option (Vienna); 15th International Conference on Plasma Physics and Controlled Nuclear Fusion Research (Vienna); FAO/IAEA International Symposium on Nuclear and Related Techniques in Soil/Plant Studies on Sustainable Agriculture and Environmental Preservation (Vienna); International Conference on Radiation, Health and Society: Comprehending Radiation Risks (Paris); Seminar on Developments in Radioactive Waste Transport (Vienna); Interregional Seminar on Isotope Techniques in Arid and Semi-Arid Land Hydrology (Vienna); Interregional Seminar on Radiotherapy Dosimetry: Radiation Dose in Radiotherapy from Prescription to Delivery (Rio de Janeiro); Second IAEA/FAO Seminar for Africa on Animal Trypanosomiasis: Vector and Disease Control using nuclear Techniques (Uganda); Seminar on Radioactive Waste Management Practices and Issues in Developing Countries (Beijing). A major conference reviewing the progress of the NPT has been scheduled for 1995.

C. Research

The International Center for Theoretical Physics, in Trieste, set up by the IAEA in 1964, brings together specialists from developing and developed countries to carry out research and to enable scientists from developing countries to keep abreast of progress without having to leave their own countries permanently or for long periods. Fellowships are awarded to candidates from developing countries for training and research, and an international forum is provided for personal contacts. Associate memberships are awarded by election to enable distinguished physicists to spend one to three months every year at the center. Senior and junior positions are offered by invitation, and a federation

scheme is designed to forge a partnership with institutions in developing countries. Assistance has been given by Italy and by the university and city of Trieste. Further aid has come from the Ford Foundation and from UNESCO, which in 1970 undertook joint management of the center.

The IAEA has three laboratories: a small one at its headquarters in Vienna, the main laboratory at Seibersdorf (20 miles from Vienna), and one at Monaco for research on the effects of radioactivity in the sea. The laboratories undertake work in agriculture, hydrology, medicine, physics, chemistry, low-level radioactivity, and environment.

A research contract program has been established with various institutions in member states. The subjects include nuclear power and reactors; physics and chemistry; radioisotope and radiation applications in agriculture, food technology, industry, and medicine; water resources development; protection of humans against ionizing radiation; radiation biology; medical and biological radiation dosimetry; health physics and radiation protection; environmental contamination; and waste treatment and disposal.

To keep abreast of scientific developments, members of the IAEA's scientific staff visit institutions in member states and conduct various studies. The IAEA has made a survey of research trends in the sterilization of food and drugs by ionizing radiation, a problem of considerable interest to both developed and developing countries.

D. Nuclear Power

Nuclear power is already an important source of electrical generation, particularly in industrialized countries, and technically and economically ripe for an even larger application worldwide. By the end of 1992 there were 496 nuclear-power plants operating or under construction around the world.

In response to the interest of developing countries in nuclear power, the IAEA has played an increasing role in objective nuclear-power planning studies for individual member states. Energy planning methodologies have been developed and made available. The IAEA has cooperated with interested member states in applying these methodologies to specific country cases and in assessing the economic role of nuclear power in meeting increasing requirements for electricity. IAEA efforts to help strengthen infrastructures for the planning, implementation, and operation of nuclear-power projects take the form of interregional and national training courses; technical assistance projects, often in cooperation with the World Bank; advisory missions to interested countries; and the publication of guidebooks.

The IAEA started to collect operating experience data from nuclear-power plants in the late 1960s and has now established a Power Reactor Information System (PRIS), which monitors the performance of the nuclear-power plants in operation in the world. In addition to performance indices and data on energy production, the system contains information about full and partial plant outages affecting plant operation and about power-reactor operating experience in the world. Periodic publications by the IAEA make this information available to planners and operators in member states. In 1992, information services were provided to 64 on-line users of PRIS in 26 countries and several international organizations. A subset of PRIS was distributed to 147 users in 50 states.

As an increasing number of countries are interested in the use of nuclear plants for heat-only production and cogeneration (for example, desalination combined with electricity generation), the IAEA periodically reviews progress in this area. In addition, scientific meetings on nuclear power are organized to discuss such matters as economic competitiveness of nuclear power, integration of nuclear-power plants in electric grids, operating experience, introduction of small and medium power reactors, development of fast-breeder and high-temperature reactors, and fusion technology.

E. Nuclear Safety

Although each state is responsible for nuclear safety with regard to nuclear activities within its own territory, nuclear safety is a field in which international cooperation can be very helpful, particularly in developing safety standards and providing assistance. The IAEA's activities in the field of nuclear safety include plant siting and design, the transport of radioactive waste, emergency planning and preparedness, and decommissioning. The IAEA also began work on an historic International Nuclear Safety Convention in 1991, the text of which was finalized at a major international conference held in Vienna in June 1994. (See Nuclear Law below.)

The IAEA maintains a 24-hour Emergency Response System (ERS) staffed by 30 emergency duty officers. In 1992 the system underwent its second comprehensive exercise to test procedures developed in support of the conventions on early nuclear accidents signed as a result of the 1986 Chernobyl incident (see below).

Regulations for the safe transport of nuclear material were developed by the IAEA in 1961. These were followed by Basic Safety Standards for Radiation Protection, which have been extensively revised in accordance with the new system of dose limitation recommended by the International Commission on Radiological Protection. The revised safety standards, carried out jointly with the ILO, WHO, and the Nuclear Energy Agency of the OECD, mark an important milestone in establishing international standards for radiation protection. In 1992 IAEA published the first biennial issue of waste management research abstracts. The publication contains 700 research abstracts from 35 countries and international organizations.

The IAEA's Nuclear Safety Standards program provides member states with internationally acceptable safety codes and guides on the many aspects of safety associated with nuclear-power plants. The program, which deals with protection against the harmful effects of ionizing radiations, is based on experience in safety practices gained by countries advanced in nuclear technology. Two types of safety documents—codes of practice and safety guides—are being developed in the areas of government organization, siting, design, operation, and quality assurance of nuclear-power plants. For each area there is a code of practice and a number of related safety guides. The codes outline basic objectives and minimum requirements that must be fulfilled to provide an adequate safety level. The safety guides recommend procedures and acceptable technical solutions to implement the requirements and achieve the objectives of the codes.

In recognition of the increasing emphasis on operational safety, the IAEA initiated the Operational Safety Review Team program in 1983 to assist regulatory authorities in the review of operating nuclear-power plants. The program provides an opportunity for member states to benefit from outside expertise and experience. An Operational Safety Review Team is composed of about 10 experts, including IAEA staff, to cover subject areas common to all reactor types, and consultants to cover those areas that are reactor-specific. Experts from developing countries have frequently been included. The reviews, which take up to three weeks, help provide an international frame of reference for regulatory and operating personnel and also provide the IAEA with valuable insights in regard to updating its regular and technical assistance programs.

Additional highlights of IAEA safety activities are: work on the management of severe accidents and on emergency response; the man-machine interface; probabilistic safety assessment; and advanced safety technology. There is also a nuclear incident reporting system and an International Nuclear Event Scale System

(INES). ASSET Missions assess, upon invitation, safety significant events involving nuclear power plants. In recent years, there has been a greater emphasis on evaluation and assistance to improve the safe operation of Eastern European nuclear reactors.

As the number of reactor years of operation increases, the feedback of experience is becoming a valuable means of enhancing safety and reliability. Systematic reporting and evaluation of safety-related events can make it possible to identify necessary plant modifications and develop improved plant procedures. To facilitate the exchange of experience, both the Nuclear Energy Agency of the OECD and the IAEA have established incident reporting systems to collect and examine details of events submitted by national organizations. National coordinators screen accounts of all events, passing on to the OECD and the IAEA the most important data.

Response of the IAEA to the Chernobyl Accident

In response to the accident that occurred in the fourth unit of the Chernobyl nuclear-power station in the USSR on 26 April 1986, resulting in loss of life, injuries, and considerable radioactive releases, the IAEA's Board of Governors met to elaborate proposals for expanded international cooperation in nuclear safety and radiological protection. Through a group of experts who convened in July–August 1986, it prepared drafts of two international conventions on nuclear accidents; at a post-accident review meeting convened by the IAEA in late August, about 600 experts from 62 countries and 21 international organizations discussed a comprehensive report presented by the USSR delegation. In September 1986, a special session of the IAEA's General Conference, attended by delegates from 94 countries and 27 national and international organizations, adopted the two draft conventions: the Convention on Early Notification of a Nuclear Accident and the Convention on Assistance in the Case of a Nuclear Accident or Radiological Emergency. The two conventions were immediately signed by more than 50 countries. By July 1994, the Early Notification Convention had 73 parties. The Accident Assistance Convention had 70 parties.

In March 1994, an international expert safety assessment team examined the safety situation at Chernobyl, at the invitation of the Ukrainian government. It concluded that there were numerous safety deficiencies in the two units of the plant that remain operational. The team determined that the shelter enclosing the destroyed reactor was experiencing accelerated deterioration. The IAEA recommended to the government of Ukraine that an urgent meeting on the situation at the Chernobyl reactor be held, to which the government agreed. At that meeting, the Ukrainian government pleaded severe economic hardship and an impending shortage of energy as a reason to delay closing the damaged plant. It asserted that, with international financial assistance, safety conditions at the plant could be improved. The government also asserted that the output of the Chernobyl station was a least-cost alternative for energy supply in the immediate future. Five new nuclear plants in planning and under construction would not be operational until 1999 at the earliest, and would cost more than US$2 billion to complete. Although a majority of the experts at that meeting wished to see the operation at Chernobyl discontinued, the meeting concluded that no simple, one-step solution to this dangerous problem existed.

F. Radioactive Waste Management

Safe management of radioactive wastes produced in all the stages of the nuclear fuel cycle is essential for the growth of nuclear power. The IAEA has been active since its establishment in all aspects of this field, including the publication of *Safety Series* and *Technical Reports*, which give guidelines and recommendations; the holding of seminars, symposia, and conferences; and the arranging of study tours for the benefit of member states. Major areas currently being studied by the IAEA are underground dis-

Members of the IAEA
as of 25 February 1994

Afghanistan	Ethiopia	Liechtenstein	Senegal
Albania	Finland	Lithuania	Sierra Leone
Algeria	France	Luxembourg	Singapore
Argentina	Gabon	Madagascar	Slovakia
Armenia	Germany	Malaysia	Slovenia
Australia	Ghana	Mali	South Africa
Austria	Greece	Marshall Islands	Spain
Bangladesh	Guatemala	Mauritius	Sri Lanka
Belarus	Haiti	Mexico	Sudan
Belgium	Holy See (Vatican)	Monaco	Sweden
Bolivia	Hungary	Mongolia	Switzerland
Brazil	Iceland	Morocco	Syrian Arab Republic
Bulgaria	India	Myanmar	Thailand
Cambodia	Indonesia	Namibia	The Former Yugoslav Republic of
Cameroon	Iran	Netherlands	Macedonia
Canada	Iraq	New Zealand	Tunisia
Chile	Ireland	Nicaragua	Turkey
China	Israel	Niger	Uganda
Colombia	Italy	Nigeria	Ukraine
Costa Rica	Jamaica	Norway	United Arab Emirates
Côte d'Ivoire	Japan	Pakistan	United Kingdom
Croatia	Jordan	Panama	United Republic of Tanzania
Cuba	Kazakhstan	Paraguay	United States
Cyprus	Kenya	Peru	Uruguay
Czech Republic	Korea, Democratic People's	Philippines	Uzbekistan
Denmark	Republic of	Poland	Venezuela
Dominican Republic	Korea, Republic of	Portugal	Viet Nam
Ecuador	Kuwait	Qatar	Yugoslavia
Egypt	Lebanon	Romania	Zaire
El Salvador	Liberia	Russian Federation	Zambia
Estonia	Libyan Arab Jamahiriya	Saudi Arabia	Zimbabwe

posal, waste handling and treatment, and environmental aspects of waste disposal.

Safety standards and codes of practice have been prepared on the management of wastes produced by users of radioactive materials; the management of wastes from the mining and milling of uranium and thorium ores; the disposal of wastes in shallow ground, rock cavities, and deep geological formations; and criteria for underground disposal of wastes.

G. Nuclear Law

From its inception, the IAEA has been faced with the need for international coordination and harmonization of the principles governing third-party liability in the event of nuclear damage. The absence of special legislation might leave injured victims without redress. Great difficulties might arise if different nations were to incorporate different principles and procedures in their legislation concerning third-party liability.

Some steps toward worldwide harmonization of compensation for damage arising from nuclear operations were taken through the adoption of two international conventions: the Brussels Convention on the Liability of Operators of Nuclear Ships (1962) and the Vienna Convention on Civil Liability for Nuclear Damage (1963). These two conventions set the minimum standards concerning the liability of the operator of a nuclear installation or a nuclear ship in the event of accidents occuring during the international transport of nuclear materials.

Another convention was adopted in 1971 by an international conference held in Brussels under the joint auspices of the IMO, the Nuclear Energy Agency of the OECD, and the IAEA: the Convention on Civil Liability in the Field of Maritime Carriage of Nuclear Matter, which came into force on 15 July 1975. This convention exonerates shipowners from liability under international maritime law in the case of nuclear damage falling within the purview of the Paris Convention on Third Party Liability in the Field of Nuclear Energy (1960), which came into force in

1968, or the Vienna Convention on Civil Liability for Nuclear Damage (1963), which came into force in 1977, whenever the carriage of nuclear material is involved; it thus eliminates what was previously a serious impediment to sea transport of such material. A joint protocol relating to the application of the Vienna Convention and the Paris Conventions entered into force on 27 April 1992.

The Convention on the Physical Protection of Nuclear Material was adopted on 26 October 1979 at a meeting of governmental representatives held at IAEA headquarters. The convention, which came into force on 9 February 1987, is designed to ensure that the prescribed levels of physical protection are applied to potentially hazardous nuclear materials during international transport.

As already noted, two conventions on nuclear accidents were adopted at a special session of the IAEA's General Conference in September 1986, in the aftermath of the Chernobyl accident in April of that year: the Convention on Early Notification of a Nuclear Accident, which came into force on 27 October 1986; and the Convention on Assistance in the Case of a Nuclear Accident or Radiological Emergency, which came into force on 27 February 1987.

In 1991, in recognition of the interdependence of nations in the nuclear fuel cycle, the General Conference supported the idea of an international nuclear safety convention. A draft convention elaborated by legal and technical experts from more than 50 countries was submitted to the General Conference at that time. In June 1994, delegations from 83 member states and four international organizations met in Vienna to consider and adopt the final text of the International Nuclear Safety Convention. The main features of the convention are the establishment of a reporting system on the implementation by contracting states of the obligations of the convention; the assurance of a proper legislative and regulatory framework to govern the safety of nuclear installations; general safety considerations to reinforce the priority of safety; sufficient financial and human resources; quality assurance; radiation protection, and emergency preparedness. The Nuclear Safety Convention was opened for signature by states and international organizations at the September 1994 session of the General Conference.

In conjunction with the increasing number of states embarking on nuclear programs, there has also been a growing awareness of the necessity for establishing both a proper legislative framework and specialized regulations for the licensing and control of nuclear installations. The IAEA has provided advisory services to several developing countries in the framing of statutory and regulatory provisions in such areas as the establishment of competent bodies on atomic energy; radiation and environmental protection; transport of radioactive materials; licensing of nuclear installations; nuclear liability; and nuclear merchant ships. In-service training at IAEA headquarters on various legal aspects of atomic energy has been provided to a number of officials nominated by member states under the IAEA fellowships program or through other arrangements.

H. Safeguards

The basic science and technology of nuclear energy are the same for both peaceful and military purposes. Therefore, the IAEA statute requires the agency "to establish and administer safeguards" to ensure that materials, services, equipment, facilities, and information that the IAEA makes available are not used "in such a way as to further any military purpose." Such safeguards may also be applied, "at the request of the parties, to any bilateral or multilateral arrangement, or, at the request of a state, to any of that state's activities in the field of atomic energy."

Under the IAEA safeguards system, which was first developed by the Board of Governors on the basis of these statutory provisions in 1961 and has been continuously revised to cover all major aspects of the fuel cycle, the IAEA exercises its control either over assistance provided directly by it or under its auspices, or over items placed voluntarily under IAEA safeguards by any state or group of states—for instance, over reactors, their fuel, and fuel-reprocessing plants.

A major development greatly affecting the significance of the IAEA's work was the coming into force in 1970 of the Treaty on the Non-Proliferation of Nuclear Weapons (NPT), under which states without nuclear weapons and party thereto agreed to accept IAEA safeguards on all their peaceful nuclear activities.

The objective of safeguards applied under agreements concluded in connection with the NPT is the timely detection of diversion of significant quantities of nuclear material from peaceful nuclear activities for the manufacture of nuclear weapons or other nuclear explosive devices or for purposes unknown, and the deterrence of such diversion by the risk of early detection. This objective is achieved by the independent verification of the findings of the national system of accountancy and control of nuclear materials, which a state without nuclear weapons must establish and maintain under the agreement. IAEA verification is accomplished by material accountancy, containment, and surveillance, including inspections, whose number, intensity, and duration must be kept to the minimum consistent with the effective implementation of safeguards.

Another important development in the furtherance of the IAEA's safeguards system was the adoption in 1967 of the Treaty for the Prohibition of Nuclear Weapons in Latin America (Treaty of Tlatelolco). The IAEA has the obligation of administering safeguards in connection with the treaty. The same applies to the parties to the South Pacific Nuclear Free Zone (Rarotonga Treaty).

As of 31 December 1993, safeguards agreements pursuant to NPT were in force with 100 states. For 57 non-nuclear-weapon states party to NPT there was still no safeguards agreement in force in accordance with Article III.4 of the treaty. As far as IAEA was aware, five of these states have significant nuclear activities (Armenia, Belarus, Azerbaijan, Niger, and Namibia. Safeguards were being applied in Colombia pursuant to other safeguards agreements, and technical arrangements are under discussion with the other four states pending the entry into force of a safeguards agreement pursuant to NPT.

NPT safeguards agreements are in force with all 11 signatories of the South Pacific Nuclear Free Zone Treaty (Rarotonga Treaty), and safeguards were applied in one of these states pursuant to such an agreement.

Twenty of the 24 Latin American states party to the Treaty of Tlatlolclco have concluded safeguards agreements with the IAEA pursuant to that Treaty. Seventeen of these agreements are in force.

By Resolution 687, adopted by the United Nations Security Council in April 1991, the IAEA was requested to carry out, with the assistance and cooperation of the Special Commission of the United Nations, immediate on-site inspection of Iraq's nuclear capabilities; to develop and carry out a plan for the destruction, removal, or rendering harmless, as appropriate, of all nuclear weapons and nuclear-weapons-usable material and any subsystems or components or any research, development, support, or manufacturing facilities related thereto; and to develop for the approval of the Security Council a plan for the future ongoing monitoring and verification of Iraq's compliance with its obligations under Resolution 687. By 1994 all nuclear material was moved out of Iraq and all related facilities were rendered harmless or destroyed in the course of 24 inspection missions.

In both 1993 and 1994, the IAEA Board of Governors reported to the UN Security Council that the Democratic People's Republic of Korea (DPRK) was not in compliance with its obligations under the NPT safeguards agreement with the IAEA which entered into force on 10 April 1992. Beginning in February 1993, the DPRK refused to permit IAEA inspectors to verify if reactor fuel had been diverted from a nuclear reactor to possible development of a nuclear weapon. In June 1994 the government of DPRK, in defiance of its commitments as a member of IAEA, removed the spent six-foot-long fuel rods from a small reactor at a complex at Yongbyon, about 60 miles north of the capital, Pyongyang. On 13 June 1994, the DPRK notified the IAEA of its decision to withdraw from the membership in the agency, touching off an international crisis that continued to simmer as this encyclopedia goes to press. The agency maintained that the country's withdrawal from membership did not affect the validity of the safeguards agreement contained in the Treaty on the Non-Proliferation of Nuclear Weapons.

The IAEA also applies safeguards to some of the peaceful nuclear activities in five nuclear-weapon states—France, the Russian Federation, the United Kingdom, and the United States—under voluntary offer agreements.

BIBLIOGRAPHY

INIS Atomindex. Bimonthly.
International Atomic Energy Agency Bulletin. Quarterly.
IAEA Newsbriefs. Bimonthly.
Meetings on Atomic Energy. Quarterly.
Nuclear Fusion. Monthly.
Nuclear Safety Review. Issued annually.
Safety Series. Manuals on the safe handling and transport of radioactive materials, monitoring of personnel, and disposal of radioactive wastes.

(The IAEA also publishes proceedings of scientific meetings covering an extensive range of nuclear-related subjects, including life sciences, nuclear safety and environmental protection, physics, chemistry, geology and raw materials, reactors and nuclear power, industrial applications, and nuclear law and safeguards.)

THE INTERNATIONAL LABOR ORGANIZATION (ILO)

BACKGROUND: The ILO is the only major organization originally part of the League of Nations system that has existed from the founding of the League in 1919 down to the present day. Its name is actually too narrow, for it is an organization neither of nor for labor alone. As the late James T. Shotwell, president emeritus of the Carnegie Endowment for International Peace, pointed out long ago, the ILO might more accurately have been termed an International Organization for Social Justice. Furthermore, as the organization's responsibilities have widened, it has given increasing attention to measures designed to help raise general standards of living. Its work now even includes activities such as productivity training courses for management personnel and high government. Michel Hansenne, Director General of the ILO since 1989, said, "Employment—the best possible employment for all—has always been, and will remain, the principal objective of our Organization, whose mission is to link economic growth, social justice and the creation and distribution of wealth."

CREATION

The International Labor Organization (ILO) was created by the 1919 Peace Conference that followed World War I. Its original constitution, which formed part of the Treaty of Versailles, established it on 11 April 1919 as an autonomous organization associated with the League of Nations.

A statement made in the constitution's preamble—"Conditions of labor exist involving such injustice, hardship, and privation to large numbers of people as to produce unrest so great that the peace and harmony of the world are imperilled"—was not mere rhetoric. World War I had shaken many countries to their foundations. The revolution in Russia had succeeded. All over the world there was labor unrest, and the conviction of the need to improve the lot of working people was by no means limited to labor itself. Organized labor, however, had been especially active during the war in demanding that the peace treaty include recognition of the rights of labor and that labor be given a voice in international matters. The American Federation of Labor (AFL) and other powerful trade-union bodies demanded in particular an international organization of labor that would wield "tremendous authority."

At the 1919 Paris Peace Conference, the president of the AFL, Samuel Gompers, was chairman of the conference's Commission on Labor Legislation. The Peace Conference, instead of establishing an international organization of labor, created an organization in which labor, employers, and governments were to be represented on an equal footing. As so constituted, the ILO was, and still is, unique among international governmental organizations—the only one in which private citizens, namely representatives of labor and of employers, have the same voting and other rights as are possessed by governments.

The ILO's principal function was to establish international labor and social standards through the drafting and adoption of international labor conventions. Prior to the existence of the ILO, only two international labor conventions had been adopted: one, designed to protect the health of workers in match factories, prohibited the use of white phosphorus, a poison, in the manufacture of matches; the other prescribed modest restrictions on night work by women. Neither of these had been widely ratified. By contrast, more than 174 international labor

conventions and 181 recommendations have been adopted by the ILO since 1919. At the end of 1993 ILO reported nearly 6,000 ratifications of these far-ranging standards from its 169 member countries.

PURPOSES

The aims and objectives of the ILO were set forth in the preamble to its constitution, drawn up in 1919. The preamble declares that "universal and lasting peace can be established only if it is based upon social justice." Hence, the basic objective of the organization is to help improve social conditions throughout the world. The following examples of concrete measures "urgently required" are specifically mentioned in the preamble: regulation of the hours of work, including the establishment of a maximum working day and week; regulation of the labor supply; prevention of unemployment; provision of an adequate living wage; protection of the worker against sickness, disease, and injury arising out of his employment; protection of children, young persons, and women; provision for old age and injury; protection of the interests of workers when employed in countries other than their own; recognition of the principle of equal remuneration for work of equal value; and recognition of the principle of freedom of association.

International action in these matters is required, the preamble makes clear, because "the failure of any nation to adopt humane conditions of labor is an obstacle in the way of other nations which desire to improve the conditions in their own countries." Finally, in agreeing to the ILO constitution, the member governments declare in the preamble that they are "moved by sentiments of justice and humanity as well as by the desire to secure the permanent peace of the world."

Meeting in Philadelphia in 1944, the International Labor Conference adopted a declaration that rephrased and broadened the "aims and purposes" of the ILO and "the principles which should inspire the policy of its members." President Roosevelt stated that the Declaration of Philadelphia, as it was called, summed up the aspirations of an epoch that had known two world wars and that it might well acquire a historical significance comparable to that of the US Declaration of Independence. The declaration, which was incorporated into the amended constitution of the ILO, affirms that labor is not a commodity; that freedom of expression and association are essential to sustained progress; that poverty anywhere constitutes a danger to prosperity everywhere; and that the war against want must be carried on not only with unrelenting vigor within each nation but also by "continuous and concerted international effort in which the representatives of workers and employers, enjoying equal status with those of Governments, join with them in free discussion and democratic decision with a view to the promotion of the common welfare."

The Declaration of Philadelphia recognizes the "solemn obligation" of the ILO to further among nations of the world programs that will achieve the following:

- full employment and the raising of standards of living;
- employment of workers in the occupations for which they are best suited and where they can make their greatest contribution to the common well-being;
- facilities for training and the transfer of labor, including migration for employment and settlement;
- policies in regard to wages and earnings, hours, and other conditions of work calculated to ensure a just share of the fruits of progress to all and a minimum living wage to all employed and in need of such protection;
- effective recognition of the right of collective bargaining, the cooperation of management and labor in the continuous improvement of productive efficiency, and the collaboration of workers and employers in the preparation and application of social and economic measures;
- extension of social security measures to provide a basic income to all in need of such protection and comprehensive medical care;
- adequate protection for the life and health of workers in all occupations;
- child welfare and maternity protection;
- adequate nutrition, housing, and facilities for recreation and culture; and
- assurance of equality of educational and vocational opportunity.

MEMBERSHIP

Originally, ILO membership was identical with League of Nations membership, since adherence to the League carried with it participation in the ILO. However, several countries that were not members of the League were admitted to the ILO, notably the US, which joined in 1934. In 1946, the ILO became the first specialized agency associated with the UN. The constitution of the ILO now provides that any nation that is a member of the UN can become a member of the ILO by unilaterally notifying the Director General that it accepts the obligations of the ILO constitution. Other nations may be admitted to ILO membership by a two-thirds vote of the International Labor Conference.

The ILO constitution originally made no provision for the expulsion of a member. However, two amendments adopted by the International Labor Conference in 1964 would have empowered the ILO membership, by a two-thirds vote, to expel or suspend any member that had been expelled or suspended by the UN or that had been found by the UN to be flagrantly and persistently pursuing by its legislation a policy of racial discrimination. The amendments were adopted in response to South Africa's policy of apartheid. These amendments never came into force for lack of ratifications. However, in 1972, the conference adopted another Instrument of Amendment about expulsions, which came into force on 1 November 1974.

A state may withdraw from the ILO by formal notification of its intent to do so, such withdrawal to be effective two years after

ILO receives the notification. Germany, one of the original members, withdrew in 1935. South Africa notified the organization of its intent to withdraw before the amendments that could have led to its expulsion were adopted. Its withdrawal became effective on 11 March 1966. South Africa rejoined the ILO on 26 May 1994. Albania withdrew in 1967. Viet Nam withdrew in 1985, but rejoined in 1992. Fourteen other countries withdrew their membership at various times (11 of them during the World War II period), but all sooner or later rejoined the organization. The rules that govern original admission to membership also apply to readmission.

In November 1975, the US filed a two-year notice of intent to withdraw, stating at the same time that it did not desire or expect to leave the ILO but hoped to help the ILO "return to basic principles." US Secretary of State Henry Kissinger said that the ILO had been "falling back" in four fundamental areas: workers' and employers' groups in the ILO falling under the domination of governments; an "appallingly selective" concern for human rights; "disregard of due process" in condemning member states "which happen to be the political target of the moment"; and "increasing politicization of the organization." The notice of intent to withdraw was allowed to run its course, thereby ending US membership in the ILO in November 1977. On the return of the US to membership in February 1980, President Jimmy Carter said: "As a member of the ILO and with the support of other countries, the United States will seek to ensure that the ILO continues to serve the interests of the world's working men and women by promoting more and better jobs while protecting human rights and dignity."

At 1 July 1994, the ILO had 169 members.

STRUCTURE

The principal organs of the ILO are the International Labor Conference, the Governing Body, and the International Labor Office, headed by a Director General.

International Labor Conference

The International Labor Conference is the organization's policy-making and legislative body, in which every member state is represented. It holds one session a year at ILO headquarters in Geneva.

Each member country sends to the International Labor Conference a national delegation consisting of four delegates. Two represent the government, one represents the country's employers, and one represents the country's workers. Alternates and advisers may be sent as well. Each delegate has one independent vote. Discussing this system of tripartite representation in 1959, the Director General noted that the ILO is "the only intergovernmental agency in whose work nongovernment delegates take part on an equal footing with government representatives as a matter of constitutional right. Representatives of employers' and workers' organizations are included in its policy-making, standard-setting, and executive machinery and participate, with full voting rights, in all these aspects of its work."

The government, employers', and workers' representatives to the conference act in many respects as three separate groups, functioning somewhat as political parties function in a national legislature: the three groups meet separately for informal discussions of strategy; they hold caucuses; and, voting separately, they elect the government, the employers', and the workers' delegates to the Governing Body and to tripartite committees. If the tripartite system is to function as intended, it is essential that employers' and workers' delegates be true representatives of their respective groups. The ILO constitution provides that governments must appoint these delegates in agreement with the "most representative" organizations of employers or workers "if such organizations exist."

Members of the ILO
(as of 1 July 1994)

Afghanistan	Djibouti	Latvia	Saudi Arabia
Albania	Dominica	Lebanon	Senegal
Algeria	Dominican Republic	Lesotho	Seychelles
Angola	Ecuador	Liberia	Sierra Leone
Antigua and Barbuda	Egypt	Libyan Arab Jamahiriya	Singapore
Argentina	El Salvador	Lithuania	Slovakia
Armenia	Equatorial Guinea	Luxembourg	Slovenia
Australia	Eritrea	Madagascar	Solomon Islands
Austria	Estonia	Malawi	Somalia
Azerbaijan	Ethiopia	Malaysia	Spain
Bahamas	Fiji	Mali	Sri Lanka
Bahrain	Finland	Malta	Sudan
Bangladesh	France	Mauritania	Suriname
Barbados	Gabon	Mauritius	Swaziland
Belarus	Georgia	Mexico	Sweden
Belgium	Germany	Moldova, Republic of	Switzerland
Belize	Ghana	Mongolia	Syrian Arab Republic
Benin	Greece	Morocco	Tajikistan
Bolivia	Grenada	Mozambique	Tanzania, United Republic of
Bosnia-Herzegovina	Guatemala	Myanmar	Thailand
Botswana	Guinea	Namibia	The Former Yugoslav
Brazil	Guinea-Bissau	Nepal	Republic of Macedonia
Bulgaria	Guyana	Netherlands	Togo
Burkina Faso	Haiti	New Zealand	Trinidad and Tobago
Burundi	Honduras	Nicaragua	Tunisia
Cambodia	Hungary	Niger	Turkey
Cameroon	Iceland	Nigeria	Turkmenistan
Canada	India	Norway	Uganda
Cape Verde	Indonesia	Pakistan	Ukraine
Central African Republic	Iran, Islamic Republic of	Panama	United Arab Emirates
Chad	Iraq	Papua New Guinea	United Kingdom
Chile	Ireland	Paraguay	United States of America
China	Israel	Peru	Uruguay
Colombia	Italy	Philippines	Uzbekistan
Comoros	Jamaica	Poland	Venezuela
Congo	Japan	Portugal	Viet Nam
Costa Rica	Jordan	Qatar	Yemen
Côte d'Ivoire	Kazakhstan	Romania	Yugoslavia
Croatia	Kenya	Russian Federation	Zaire
Cuba	Korea, Republic of	Rwanda	Zambia
Cyprus	Kuwait	St. Lucia	Zimbabwe
Czech Republic	Kyrgystan	San Marino	
Denmark	Lao People's Democratic Republic	São Tomé and Principe	

Governing Body

The Governing Body is the executive council of the ILO. It is composed of 56 members, 14 representing employers, 14 representing workers, and 28 representing governments.

Members of the Governing Body are elected by the corresponding groups in the International Labor Conference, except that 10 of the government representatives are appointed by countries that do not participate in the election of the other government representatives since these 10 countries are entitled to permanent seats as "states of chief industrial importance." The 10 governments permanently represented on the Governing Body are Brazil, China, France, Germany, India, Italy, Japan, the Russian Federation, the United Kingdom, and the United States of America. The remaining government members, elected in 1993 for three years, were from Argentina, Australia, Chile, Congo, Czech Republic, Ghana, the Islamic Republic of Iran, Kenya, Mexico, Nicaragua, Niger, Norway, Philippines, Qatar, Romania, Tunisia, Venezuela, and Zimbabwe.

Employers' representatives on the Governing Body, elected for three years by the 1993 conference, included leading industrialists or ranking employers' association officers from Argentina, Australia, Brazil, Côte d'Ivoire, Egypt, Finland, France, Germany, Japan, Kenya, Lebanon, Pakistan, United Kingdom, and the United States.

The 14 members of the workers' group, elected in 1993 for three years, were ranking trade union officials from Australia, Canada, the Czech Republic, Finland, Germany, India, Japan, Kenya, Mali, Mexico, Morocco, United Kingdom, the United States, and Venezuela.

Under amendments to the ILO constitution adopted by the International Labor Conference in 1986—to become effective when ratified or accepted by two-thirds of the members, including 5 of the 10 permanent members of the Governing Body—the members of the Governing Body will be increased to 112 (56 representing governments, 28 representing employers, and 28 representing workers) and the 10 permanent seats will be eliminated. As of June 1994, this amendment had not yet received sufficient ratifications to enter into force.

Meeting several times a year, the Governing Body coordinates and in many ways shapes the work of the organization. It draws up the agenda for each session of the International Labor Conference; while the conference is empowered to change this agenda, it rarely does. The Governing Body appoints the Director General of the International Labor Office. It examines the proposed budget submitted to it each year by the Director General and approves it for adoption by the conference. The Governing Body also is responsible for convening the scores of other conference and committee meetings held under ILO auspices every year in various parts of the world and decides what action ought to be taken on their resolutions and reports.

International Labor Office and Director General

The International Labor Office in Geneva, headed by the Director General, is the ILO's headquarters and its permanent secretariat. In December 1993, its staff consisted of about 1,800 persons from more than 110 countries.

During World War II, when for a time Switzerland was entirely surrounded by Axis forces, the International Labor Office and a skeleton staff were temporarily moved to Montreal, where, thanks to the hospitality of the Canadian government and McGill University, the office was able to continue its more urgent work.

The International Labor Office services the sessions of the conference, the Governing Body, and the various subsidiary organs and committees. It prepares the documents for these meetings; publishes periodicals, studies, and reports; and collects and distributes information on all subjects within the ILO's competence. As directed by the conference and the Governing Body, it carries out ILO operational programs that have been decided on in various fields.

The ILO has had eight Directors General—Albert Thomas, France, 1919–32; Harold Butler, UK, 1932–38; John G. Winant, US, 1939–41; Edward J. Phelan, Ireland, 1941–48; David A. Morse, US, 1948–70; Wilfred Jenks, UK, 1970–73; Francis Blanchard, France, 1973–89; and Michel Hansenne, Belgium, 1989 to present.

The ILO has regional, area, and branch offices in more than 40 countries. The eight branch offices are located in Washington, Ottawa, Tokyo, Paris, Bonn, Rome, London, and Brazil. The three regional offices are located in Abidjan (Africa), Peru (the Americas), and Bangkok (Asia). Thirty other ILO offices are located in the capitals of Algeria, Argentina, Bangladesh, Belgium, Cameroon, Chile, China, Costa Rica, Egypt, Ethiopia, Fiji, India, Indonesia, Kenya, Kuwait, Madagascar, Mexico, Nigeria, Pakistan, Philippines, Russian Federation, Senegal, Sri Lanka, Tanzania, Trinidad and Tobago, Turkey, Uruguay, Zaire, Zambia, and Zimbabwe. Since late 1992, a multidisciplinary team of ILO experts has been based in Budapest, Hungary. Its focus is to assist new ILO members from the former Soviet bloc in their transition to market economies.

THE ISSUE OF INDEPENDENT WORKER AND EMPLOYER REPRESENTATION

Since its early days, the ILO has been troubled by a basic constitutional issue: can the organization, without violating its own principles, countenance the seating of workers' and employers' delegates from countries where workers' and employers' organizations are not free from domination or control by the government?

Challenges to the Credentials of Workers

When, in the early 1920s, a member of the Italian Fascist labor corporations appeared at Geneva to take his seat as the workers' member of the Italian delegation to the ILO, his credentials were challenged, though unsuccessfully, by the workers' group, which maintained that he was not a true spokesman for Italian labor. Every session of the conference from 1923 to 1938 saw the credentials of one or more workers' delegates challenged on the grounds that these delegates did not represent an independent labor point of view. Among them were workers' delegates from Austria, Bulgaria, Germany, Greece, Italy, Latvia, Lithuania, and Poland. In all cases, however, the delegates were seated.

Since World War II, the conference has on several occasions actually refused to seat a workers' delegate whose credentials had been challenged. In 1945, it refused to seat the workers' delegate chosen by the Perón regime in Argentina on the ground

that workers' organizations in Argentina did not at that time enjoy freedom of association, action, or speech. In 1950, it refused to seat the workers' delegate appointed by the government of Venezuela on the ground that the delegate could not have been nominated in agreement with the country's most representative workers' associations since the government had at that time dissolved all trade unions. Challenges to the credentials of Argentinian and Venezuelan workers' delegates on other occasions were overruled by the credentials committee, however, as was a 1955 challenge to the credentials of the Chilean workers' delegate.

The Question of Employers' Delegates from Communist Countries

Much greater difficulties arose in the past over the seating of employers' delegates from former communist countries. When the first employers' delegate from the USSR, Mr. Kaoulin of the People's Commissariat of Water Transport, appeared at the 1936 maritime conference, the employers' group acquiesced in his seating but requested an examination of the constitutional questions involved. A study duly carried out by the International Labor Office concluded that the ILO constitution did not require an employer to be a private person and that in countries where the state was the chief employer, it was for the state to choose the employers' delegate. The employers' group at the conference voted unanimously to reject this interpretation.

At the 1945 International Labor Conference, held in Paris shortly after the end of World War II, two constitutional amendments were proposed that aimed at increasing the size of the national delegations so as to give representation to both the public and private sectors of the economy. Both proposed amendments were, for a variety of reasons, rejected by the conference. The employers' group, however, issued a declaration stating that if the USSR, which had withdrawn from the ILO in 1940, were to resume membership, "it would naturally appoint as employers' delegates a representative of the socialized management of the USSR."

At the 1953 conference, the employers' group challenged the credentials of the Czechoslovakian employers' delegate and, when the USSR did rejoin the organization in 1954, challenged those of the Soviet employers' delegate as well. On both occasions, the group was overruled by the credentials committee, which held that the delegates in question performed executive and managerial functions corresponding to those normally exercised by employers under other economic systems.

When the Governing Board met in November 1954, it was sharply divided on the question of employers' delegates from countries with nationalized economies. In hopes of facilitating a compromise, it appointed a special fact-finding committee, headed by Sir Arnold McNair, former president of the International Court of Justice, to report on the "extent of the freedom of employers' and workers' organizations" in ILO member countries "from government domination or control." The lengthy report, which the committee submitted in February 1956, was based on a study of the situation in 59 countries, including five in the Soviet bloc.

The report recognized at the outset that the unique feature of the ILO—cooperation among representatives of government, employers, and workers—could only be meaningful if the latter represented their constituents in the true sense of the word and had the right "to speak and vote freely without government control." On the other hand, the report noted, major changes had occurred in the economic structure of many countries since 1919, with governments participating in their countries' economic and social life in a wide variety of new ways. The ILO had long maintained that the principle of freedom of association is violated if the right to organize is subject to government authorization. However, the report found, the constitutions of no less than 21 ILO countries subjected the right of association to statutory regulation.

The Hungarian uprising of 1956 had sharp repercussions in the ILO, which were reflected in the credentials dispute. The Governing Body expressed solidarity with the Hungarian workers "who were struggling to secure their fundamental rights," and the 1957 International Labor Conference rejected the credentials of the employers' and workers' delegates appointed by the Kádár government, which had, in effect, restored the Hungarian status quo ante. In 1958 and 1959, the conference took the unprecedented step of not only rejecting the credentials of the Hungarian workers' and employers' delegates, but also refusing admission to the government delegates.

In the meantime, various attempts were made to find a general solution to the problem that would satisfy all concerned, including the Western employers' delegates. Involved in the problem was the fact that, under the International Labor Conference rules, each group—government, employers, and workers—could refuse to seat delegates whose credentials it did not accept. In 1959, acting on a plan proposed by a tripartite committee headed by Roberto Ago of Italy, the ILO established a five-member Appeals Board composed of persons of "internationally recognized independence and impartiality" to rule on such matters.

The demise of the Soviet bloc in the late 1980s heralded the arrival of a new era of consensus. Now that so many formerly communist governments no longer adhere to a managed economy, challenges to credentials are much less significant.

BUDGET

The ILO's activities are financed by a biennial budget fixed by the International Labor Conference and raised from the governments of member states according to a scale of contributions approved by the conference. The scale ranges from 0.01 percent for 75 least developed countries (LDCs) to 6.69 percent for the Russian Federation, 8.9 percent for Germany, 12.41 percent for Japan, and 25 percent for the US. In addition, the ILO receives for its technical assistance programs a share of the funds raised from voluntary government contributions to UNDP.

A net expenditure budget of US$446,211,000 was adopted by the 1993 conference.

ACTIVITIES

A. International Labor Code

One of the principal achievements of the ILO has been the formulation of an extensive international labor code through the drafting and adoption of various standard-setting conventions and recommendations. The first international convention adopted was the 1919 Hours of Work Convention, establishing the eight-hour day and the six-day week in industry.

A convention is similar to an international treaty and is subject to ratification. Recommendations do not require ratification. They serve as guidelines for national policy.

By 1994, the various sessions of the International Labor Conference had built up the edifice of the international labor code through the adoption of 174 conventions and 181 recommendations, covering such questions as the following:

- employment and unemployment: employment services, national development programs, and provisions for unemployment;
- various aspects of conditions of work: wages, hours, weekly rest periods, annual holidays with pay, and allied topics;
- employment of children and young persons: minimum age of admission to employment, medical examination for fitness for employment, vocational training and apprenticeship, and night work;

- employment of women: maternity protection, night work, and employment in unhealthy work;
- industrial health, safety, and welfare;
- social security;
- industrial (i.e., management-labor) relations;
- labor inspection;
- social policy in nonmetropolitan areas and concerning indigenous and tribal populations;
- protection of migrants; and
- trade unionism and collective bargaining.

At first, the effort to build up minimum labor and social standards that would be internationally valid was considered by many as utopian. In these fields, international action used to be virtually unknown. But the freely accepted conventions and recommendations and the ILO machinery of mutual supervision have helped to improve working conditions and management-labor relations, protect the fundamental rights of labor, promote social security, and lessen the frequency and intensity of labor conflicts.

The international labor code is continually being revised and extended, not only to broaden its scope but also to keep pace with advancing concepts of social and economic welfare. The following conventions represent the heart and soul of the organization's commitment to its mandate to social justice:

Important ILO Conventions

NUMBER	NAME	(RATIFICATIONS AS OF 1992)
No. 29	Forced Labor Convention (1930)	130
No. 87	Freedom of Association and Protection of the Right to Organize (1948)	102
No. 98	Right to Organize and Collective Bargaining Convention (1949)	107
No. 100	Equal Remuneration Convention (1951)	114
No. 105	Abolition of Forced Labor Convention (1957)	111
No. 111	Discrimination (Employment and Occupation) Convention (1958)	112
No. 122	Employment Policy Convention (1964)	77
No. 135	Workers' Representatives Convention (1971)	46
No. 141	Rural Workers' Organizations Convention (1978)	31
No. 144	Tripartite Consultation (International Labor Standards) Convention (1976)	144
No. 151	Labor Relations (Public Service) (1978)	24

Other important conventions are, for example, the 1960 convention and a recommendation on the protection of workers against ionizing radiations. These instruments, in essence, provide for the establishment of maximum permissible doses and amounts of radioactive substances that may be taken into the body. Appropriate radiation levels are fixed for workers over 16. Under these international instruments, workers under 16 are prohibited from working in direct contact with ionizing radiations.

In pursuit of ILO efforts to help extend the scope of social security coverage throughout the world and eliminate discrimination based upon nationality, the 1962 International Labor Conference adopted a convention on the equal treatment of nationals and non-nationals in social security. Under this convention, a ratifying country shall give to nationals of other ratifying countries, within its territory, equal treatment with its own nationals under its social security legislation. Countries may accept the obligations of the convention in any or all of the following types of social security: medical care, sickness benefits, maternity benefits, unemployment benefits, and family allowances.

The adoption of protective standard measures against occupationally caused cancer was taken up at the 1974 session of the International Labor Conference. Two international agreements were drawn up, aimed at limiting the use and the adverse effects of carcinogenic (cancer-causing) substances and strengthening protective measures to be used against them.

In 1983, a convention was adopted on the rights of handicapped people, aimed at increasing employment opportunities for the disabled. In 1986, a convention to protect workers against serious risks from the use of asbestos was adopted.

The following recommendations have been adopted since the seventh revision of this encyclopedia:

No. 175   Safety and Health in Construction Recommendation (1988)
No. 176   Employment Promotion and Protection against Unemployment Recommendation (1988)
No. 177   Chemicals Recommendation (1990)
No. 178   Night Work Recommendation (1990)
No. 179   Working Conditions in Hotels, Restaurants and Similar Establishments (1991)
No. 180   Protection of Workers' Claims in the Event of the Insolvency of Their Employer (1992)
No. 181   Prevention of Major Industrial Accidents (1993)

The following conventions have been adopted since the seventh revision of this encyclopedia:

No. 167   Safety and Health in Construction Convention (1988)
No. 168   Employment Promotion and Protection against Unemployment Convention (1988)
No. 169   Indigenous and Tribal Peoples Convention (1989)
No. 170   Chemicals Convention (1990)
No. 171   Night Work Convention (1990)
No. 172   Working Conditions in Hotels, Restaurants and Similar Establishments Convention (1991)
No. 173   Protection of Workers' Claims in the Event of the Insolvency of Their Employer Convention (1992)
No. 174   Prevention of Major Industrial Accidents (1993)

B. Obligation of Members after Adoption of International Labor Standards

The ILO, it should be borne in mind, is not a world lawgiver. The International Labor Conference cannot pass legislation that by itself is binding on any country. However, ingenious arrangements have been written into the ILO constitution to make sure that conventions and recommendations adopted by the International Labor Conference are not regarded as mere pious pronouncements. Member governments must report back to the ILO on the measures they have taken to bring the ILO convention or recommendation before their competent legislative authorities, and they must also keep the ILO informed of decisions made by those authorities.

Supervision of Application of Ratified Conventions

Once a convention has been ratified and has come into force, every country that ratified it is obligated to take all necessary measures to make its provisions effective.

By ratifying a convention, a country automatically agrees to report every year to the International Labor Office on how the convention is being applied in its territory. These reports are much more than a formality. For each convention, the Governing Body formulates a number of questions that include requests for information on the results of labor inspection, relevant court decisions, and statistics on the number of persons covered. Copies of each annual report prepared by a government are to be sent to the country's most representative employers' and workers' organizations, and the report, as finally submitted to the ILO, has to state whether the government has received any comments from them on the practical implementation of the convention in question.

These annual reports on the application of ratified conventions

are first considered by a committee of independent experts and then by an employer-worker-government committee, which in turn reports to the full International Labor Conference. The object of this whole system of supervision is to enable the conference to determine what progress has been made in implementing the standards set forth in the conventions. On the basis of the intelligence it receives, the conference may, if it feels this to be necessary, make "observations" to governments, that is, suggest to them ways in which they may overcome discrepancies between the provisions of the conventions that they have ratified and existing national laws or practices.

The effectiveness of this supervisory machinery depends, naturally, on the cooperation of member governments in submitting their annual reports. On the whole, an increasing number of governments have been living up to their obligations in this respect. If required reports are not forthcoming or if the reports submitted by certain countries are not really informative, the ILO supervisory committees express their dissatisfaction in polite but quite unmistakable terms. These criticisms are included in the printed reports of the committees and may occasion debates in the conference itself, thus giving the matter further publicity.

The ILO constitution provides two other procedures that may be followed to induce governments to carry out the provisions of conventions that they have ratified. First, workers' or employers' organizations may make representations to the International Labor Office if they believe that any government, even their own, has failed to live up to a convention that it has ratified. If the government concerned fails to provide a satisfactory answer to the allegation, the Governing Body may decide to publish the allegation and, if one has been submitted, the government reply. Second, any ILO member government may file a complaint against any other member for alleged noncompliance with a ratified convention. The ILO constitution provides that, in this event, a commission of inquiry shall examine the matter, report on its findings, and recommend such remedial steps as it thinks proper. The fact that the ILO constitution provides for specific machinery to take up such complaints itself has contributed to the observance of ratified international labor conventions on the part of member governments.

In his report to the 81st ILC in 1994, Director General Michel Hansenne reported that in the preceding 30 years, close to 2,000 cases of progress were recorded by supervisory bodies. "That means 2,000 situations in which national legislation and policy have been brought into line with the requirements of ratified Conventions," said the Director General.

Reports on Recommendations and Unratified Conventions

Recommendations adopted by the International Labor Conference, unlike the conventions that it adopts, are not international treaties and are not subject to ratification. Hence, these recommendations can never be binding on a member government in the sense that the provisions of a ratified convention are binding. Nevertheless, the recommendations constitute an important part of the international labor code, and, since 1948, the Governing Body of the ILO has had the right to ask member governments periodically to what extent they have given or intend to give effect to conventions not ratified and to recommendations. In such case, the governments also have to state the reasons that have so far prevented or delayed the ratification of conventions and the modification of national law and practices according to recommendations.

Ratifications

By 1994 there were more than 6,000 ratifications, as compared with 1960, when only about 1,900 conventions had been ratified.

The number of ratifications that a given convention has received is not, in itself, an accurate measure of its acceptance or impact. The fact that a convention has not been ratified by a particular country does not necessarily mean that that country has not met the standards prescribed in the convention. The UK, for example, advised the ILO that it did not intend to propose parliamentary ratification of the convention requiring a minimum 24-hour weekly rest period for commercial and office workers. It explained that such workers in the UK were already assured a rest period of at least that length through established custom and that it was not the policy of the government to intervene in matters that had already been satisfactorily settled by the parties concerned.

New Zealand, which in many ways has pioneered in labor legislation, waited until 1938 to ratify the eight-hour-day, six-day-week convention of 1919. At the same time, New Zealand also ratified the more restrictive 40-hour-week convention of 1935 and, in fact, remained for 18 years the only country ratifying it. Ratifications may be withheld for various reasons by a country for a number of years, after which a number of ratifications may be approved at once. Thus, in 1962 alone, Peru ratified 31 different international labor conventions.

Very often, countries do not ratify conventions on subjects that they feel do not concern them. The various maritime conventions, for example, are primarily of interest to nations with sizable merchant marine fleets. Occasionally, however, countries as a matter of principle ratify conventions on conditions quite alien to them. Thus, Switzerland ratified the 1957 Convention on the Abolition of Forced Labor on the recommendation of the Swiss Federal Council, which called for ratification because of the convention's humanitarian significance, although "forced labor in any of the forms mentioned in the Convention has never existed in Switzerland."

For a growing number of workers in an increasing number of countries, wages, working conditions, vacations, and so-called fringe benefits are being determined not through government legislation but through collective bargaining. The international standards embodied in the ILO's conventions, even though they may not show on the statute books, frequently serve as guides for labor-management agreements. The widening impact of ILO standards owes much to the various arrangements that have been worked out to make the provisions of the international labor code more widely known to employers' and workers' organizations.

The significance of the sharply increased rate at which governments have been ratifying ILO conventions since 1960 is very great. Ratification, particularly in a developing country, regularly signifies a step forward.

C. The ILO as a Promoter of Human Rights
Freedom of Association

World War II stimulated the growth of trade unions and increased their responsibilities. In many countries, labor was recognized as an equal partner in the effort that won the war. Nevertheless, in various parts of the world, the position of unions was far from secure, and in many countries, such a basic freedom as the worker's right to join a union of his choice was respected neither in law nor in practice.

In 1948, the International Labor Conference adopted the Convention on Freedom of Association and the Right to Organize, and in 1949, it adopted the Convention on the Right to Organize and Collective Bargaining. These conventions stipulate that all workers and employers shall possess the right to establish and join organizations of their own choosing without having to obtain government authorization. Such organizations shall have the right to function freely and without interference from public authorities; they may be dissolved or suspended only by normal judicial procedure and never by administrative authority. Workers must be protected against discrimination on the grounds of union membership or activities; thus, a worker may not be discharged because he joins or is active in a union. Employers and

workers must not interfere in the establishment or operation of one another's organizations; this provision outlaws such devices as employer-dominated unions. By June 1994, the first of the two conventions had been ratified by 108 countries and the second by 121.

The ILO Committee on Freedom of Association has recorded a dramatic rise in the numbers of complaints lodged under this convention: before 1990 a total of 61 complaints were received; 49 complaints were received in 1990 alone; 52 complaints were received in 1991; 73 complaints were received in 1992; and more than 113 complaints were received in 1993.

The ILO has been particularly concerned with safeguarding the rights enumerated in these two conventions. It has made full use of its regular procedure to ascertain whether all member states have presented the conventions to the appropriate domestic authorities for ratification and to supervise the implementation of the conventions by states that have ratified them. In addition, the International Labor Conference has conducted reviews concerning the extent to which member states, whether bound by the conventions or not, have put their provisions into effect.

In 1969, a special review was made, in connection with the 50th anniversary of the ILO, of the problems and prospects of ratification of 17 key conventions. Special bodies were set up to deal with complaints against governments for violation of trade-union rights: a committee of the Governing Body, known as the Committee on Freedom of Association, composed of government, employer, and worker representatives; and the quasi-judicial Fact-Finding and Conciliation Commission, composed of nine independent persons serving as individuals. The Fact-Finding and Conciliation Commission is authorized to make on-the-scene investigations, but it cannot consider a case unless the government concerned gives its consent. Japan, in 1964, was the first to do so; Greece was the second, in 1965. The government-employer-worker Committee on Freedom of Association, however, not being a semi-judicial body, may consider complaints whether or not the government concerned gives its consent.

Feeling that fuller factual information was needed about conditions in various countries affecting freedom of association, the ILO Governing Body decided in 1958 to inaugurate a worldwide survey to be carried out through on-the-spot studies. The first country to invite such a survey was the US; the second was the USSR. An ILO survey mission visited both countries in 1959. At the invitation of the governments of Sweden, the United Kingdom, Burma, and Malaya, surveys on freedom of association in those countries were made in 1960 and 1961.

The Committee on Freedom of Association considered complaints of infringements of trade union rights in Poland following the proclamation of martial law in that country in December 1981 and in response to measures taken against the Solidarity trade union. In November 1982, the Governing Body urged the Polish government to lift martial law; it noted with deep concern that the government had dissolved all existing trade unions, including Solidarity, and deplored the fact that fundamental provisions of the new Polish labor law did not conform with ILO principles of freedom of association and collective bargaining. A commission of inquiry set up by the ILO in 1983 reported in the following year that Poland had infringed trade union rights laid down in two ILO conventions to which it was a party, and it rejected Poland's objection to its inquiry.

Forced Labor

Before World War II, ILO's efforts in regard to forced labor, including the adoption of the 1930 Convention on Forced Labor and the 1936 Convention on Recruiting of Indigenous Workers, were directed primarily toward stamping out abuses in non-self-governing territories. A convention adopted in 1939 prescribed that contracts for the employment of indigenous labor must always be made in writing, and an accompanying recommendation called for regulation of the maximum period of time for which an indigenous worker could bind himself under contract. Another convention adopted in 1939 required all penal sanctions exacted against indigenous labor for breach of contract to be progressively abolished "as soon as possible"; when applicable to juvenile workers, the sanctions against breach of contract were to be abolished without delay.

After World War II, emphasis shifted from protection against exploitation in colonial areas to the abolition of systems of forced labor wherever they occur, as part of the promotion of human rights. The first step in this broader attack was an impartial inquiry into the nature and extent of forced labor, including prison labor, gang labor, labor service, and the like. A joint UN-ILO committee studied the existence in the world of systems of forced or "corrective" labor as a means of political coercion or as punishment for political views. In 1953, the committee reported that it had found two principal forms of forced labor existing in fully self-governing countries: one used mainly as a means of political coercion or political punishment, and the other used mainly for economic reasons.

In 1957, the International Labor Conference, by a vote of 240 to 0, with 1 abstention, adopted the Convention on the Abolition of Forced Labor. The convention outlaws any form of forced or compulsory labor (a) as a means of political coercion or education or as punishment for political or ideological views, (b) as a means of obtaining labor for economic development, (c) as a means of labor discipline, (d) as punishment for participation in strikes, or (e) as a means of racial, social, national, or religious discrimination. The convention, one of the farthest-reaching adopted by the ILO, has been in force since 17 January 1959. By 1991 the convention had received 110 ratifications.

Discrimination in Employment and Occupation

The Convention on Discrimination in Employment and Occupation, adopted by the International Labor Conference in 1958, constitutes another effort to promote the principle of equal rights. The convention defines such discrimination as any distinction, exclusion, or preference based on race, color, sex, religion, political opinion, national extraction, or social origin that impairs equal access to vocational training, equal access to employment and to certain occupations, or equal terms and conditions of employment. Measures affecting a person justifiably suspected of being engaged in activities prejudicial to the security of the state are not to be deemed discrimination, provided such a person is guaranteed the right of appeal. Furthermore, special measures of protection or assistance required because of sex, age, disablement, family responsibility, or social or cultural status are not to be considered discriminatory, but workers' and employers' organizations must in certain cases be consulted on such measures.

Every state ratifying the convention thereby undertakes to declare and pursue a national policy designed to promote, by methods appropriate to national conditions and practice, equality of opportunity and treatment in respect of employment and occupation, with a view to eliminating discrimination. This goal is to be accomplished through cooperation with employers' and workers' organizations, through legislation, and through educational programs. Ratifying states also agree to pursue nondiscriminatory public employment policies and to ensure the observance of such policies by public vocational guidance, training, and placement services. By 1991 this convention had received 109 ratifications.

D. Maritime Questions

The problems of merchant sailors differ in many respects from those of other workers. When plans for an international labor organization were being worked out in 1919, world seafarers' organizations urged the creation of a separate "permanent general conference for the international regulation of maritime labor" and of a separate "supervisory office for maritime labor."

Although it was eventually decided to include maritime questions as falling within the purview of the ILO, special ILO machinery was established to deal with them, including special maritime sessions of the International Labor Conference and a Joint Maritime Commission.

Maritime sessions of the International Labor Conference are periodic full-scale sessions of the conference devoted exclusively to maritime questions. The first such conference was held in 1920. Since then, some 50 conventions and recommendations concerning seafarers have been adopted, pertaining to conditions of employment, health and safety, welfare, and social security. Together, these conventions and recommendations form the International Seafarers' Code, which is binding on all subscribing countries.

The Joint Maritime Commission keeps questions regarding the merchant marine under review on a year-to-year basis. Since it began its work in 1920, the commission has been enlarged several times, mainly to provide wider geographical representation.

Conditions of Employment

The first of the ILO's maritime conventions, adopted in 1920, forbids the employment of children under 14 at sea, except on family-operated vessels. A convention adopted in 1936 raises the minimum age to 15. A convention adopted in 1926 prescribes the standard form and content of seafarers' articles of agreement or employment contracts, signing procedures, and the conditions under which such contracts may be terminated.

At the 1987 maritime session of the International Labor Conference, a number of conventions and recommendations were adopted, some of which revised and updated earlier instruments. A 1926 convention guaranteeing repatriation of seafarers was broadened to take into account developments in the shipping industry. The new instrument lists the circumstances under which repatriation rights shall apply, including cessation of employment, illness, shipwreck, and bankruptcy of the shipowner. Another revision of previous instruments was adopted on seafarers' welfare at sea and in port. States ratifying it will undertake to ensure that cultural and recreational facilities and information services are provided in appropriate ports and on board ship. A convention on health protection and medical care aims at providing seafarers with care comparable to that which is generally available to workers ashore.

Social Security for Seafarers

The first step toward social insurance for seafarers was taken by a 1920 convention which required a shipowner to pay two months' wages to crew members of a lost or foundered vessel.

Three conventions affecting seafarers were adopted at the 1976 maritime session: continuity of employment, annual leave with pay, and merchant shipping (minimum standards). The third convention provides that a state which has ratified the convention and in whose port a ship calls may take account of a complaint or evidence that the ship does not conform to the standards of the convention.

A new convention adopted in 1987 revised a number of existing instruments dealing with social security and insurance against illness; it requires ratifying states to provide seafarers with social security protection not less favorable than that enjoyed by shore workers for which the state has legislation in force. Member states would be bound to apply either minimum standards, as specified in the Social Security (Minimum Standards) Convention, or superior standards, as laid down in other ILO instruments.

The standards set by these conventions, even when not ratified by many countries, have an influence on collective agreements, national statutes, and regulations.

E. Technical Cooperation

Member states have always been able to count on the direct cooperation of the ILO. The expression "technical assistance" is to be found in an ILO report as early as 1930. ILO officials who were then sent on consultative missions to governments were the precursors of today's experts.

Depending on priority programs established by governments, the activities of consultants have become an increasingly integral feature of national development plans. Among these priorities are the development of human resources, the raising of living standards, and the promotion of full employment. The ILO works actively with the authorities to set up and put into effect concrete cooperative projects. These tasks range from brief preliminary missions to major projects, such as the setting up of networks of vocational training or management development centers, to the establishment of full-scale rural development programs.

A cooperative project is deemed a success when it can be fully taken over by the national counterparts of the country concerned after the ILO experts have left. To encourage this trend, the ILO has made it possible for national officials to complete their training overseas. Many cooperative projects also provide for study grants and the organization of training courses and seminars. The supply of specialized equipment for certain services is another form of ILO aid—for example, equipment to set up vocational training centers.

The international technical cooperation effort is financed in part by UNDP. Some of the industrialized countries also make funds available to the ILO for cooperative projects.

In the budget for the 1994–95 biennium, a total of US$124,602,892 was allocated for technical cooperation programs. Another US$105,483,121 was allocated for field programs. The ILO concentrates its efforts on activities that produce maximum long-term results, such as the creation of institutions of various kinds or of training centers for trainers. It also seeks to enlist the aid of employers and workers in the technical cooperation effort.

Technical cooperation is linked to action promoting adherence to international labor standards, such as aid in the area of labor legislation and administration. This policy improves workers' conditions while taking into account the realities of the situation in the country concerned.

Unemployment and Underemployment

The ILO considers help to member states in the struggle against unemployment to be one of its major responsibilities. Much work has been carried out in this area. Guided by international labor standards, and often with the practical aid of the ILO, many countries have taken steps to ease the lot of the unemployed, to organize employment bureaus, and to develop vocational training facilities. However, these measures are far from enough to solve the immense unemployment problem facing the world today.

A coherent set of measures is needed to solve the unemployment and underemployment problem: development of rural areas, as well as urban industrialization; training of citizens in modern employment techniques; and taking a census of the active population and concentrating the development effort on the sectors and techniques calculated to absorb the maximum number of workers. In short, employment does not automatically flow from economic expansion unless it is geared to a policy designed to promote employment systematically. The International Labor Conference recognized this point when, in 1964, it adopted a convention and a recommendation on unemployment policy; the promotion and planning of employment are now an integral part of the development effort.

Faced with the unemployment crisis, the ILO launched the World Employment Program in 1969. This program was the starting point in the ILO's efforts to help combat unemployment and underemployment.

It was in keeping with the recognition that growing world poverty required new initiatives that the World Employment Conference was held in 1976. The resulting declaration of principles and program of action called the world's attention to the need for full employment and an adequate income for every inhabitant in the shortest possible time.

The ILO-developed concept of basic needs is paramount to the effort to get to the root of poverty. Basic needs include two elements: certain minimum requirements of a family for private consumption—adequate food, shelter, and clothing are obviously included, as would be certain household equipment and furniture; and essential services provided for the community at large, such as safe drinking water, sanitation, public transportation, and health and education facilities.

The program of the 1976 conference emphasized that strategies and national development plans and policies should include explicitly, as a priority objective, the promotion of employment and the satisfaction of the basic needs of each country's population. The people should participate in making the decisions that affect them through organizations of their own choice. The concept of freely chosen employment is an integral part of a basic needs strategy. Among measures to be taken by governments to meet the target of creating sufficient jobs for all in developing countries by the year 2000 are ratification of selected ILO conventions; selection of development projects with a view to their employment and income distribution potential; and implementation of active labor market policies, with consideration given to social policies designed to increase the welfare of working people, especially women, the young, and the aged.

ILO operational activities and advisory missions remain important elements of the program. Regional employment teams in Asia, Africa, and Latin America provide technical advisory services and training courses in response to requests from a large number of countries.

Technical cooperation projects in the fields of employment planning, personnel planning, and labor-market information range from multiexpert, long-term projects to short-term consultancies and special advisory missions.

ILO technical advisory missions for special public works programs not only help governments define and, where appropriate, expand the scope of special public works programs and determine the technical feasibility of projects and organizational and staffing needs, but also assist in the preparation of technical cooperation components and in management reviews of ongoing programs.

At the 78th Session of the ILC in 1991, Director General Michel Hansenne raised the issue of the "working poor," the approximately 300 million people around the world who work in jobs that fall into what is called the "informal sector." Almost one-third of the world's gross domestic product is believed to be contributed by these millions working on the fringes of the recognized labor market. Such activities range from small manufacturing enterprises to a single person selling rolled cigarettes on a street corner. Generally, products of the informal sector require a low level of capital investment, technology, and skills.

The ILO initiatives focussed on the informal sector are the Regional Employment Program for Latin America and the Caribbean (PREALC) and the Jobs and Skills Program for Africa (JASPA). These initiatives include gathering data, providing training and technical cooperation, promoting income-generating projects for specific vulnerable groups, studying ways to open traditional apprenticeship and training for production schemes to women, and examining case studies of regulatory barriers.

Development of Human Resources

In an age when production techniques and structures are rapidly changing, simultaneously with a rapid increase in the world's active population, the entire concept of labor and vocational training must be viewed in a new light.

Many trades for which young people are being prepared will undergo radical transformation, and the qualifications that workers hold today will be obsolete without frequent refresher courses. Moreover, there will be a steady increase in the number of workers switching from one sector to another—for example, from agriculture to industry or from industry to commerce.

Any modern conception of developing human resources must take these factors into account by extending and diversifying vocational training facilities: apprenticeships, technical training and education, advanced training, and refresher courses. Vocational guidance must be developed not only to aid young people to make a wise choice of a career but also to retrain adult workers for different jobs. A coherent policy aimed at utilizing human resources must, therefore, include measures that make it possible for the worker to continue education and training, depending on the person's aptitudes and the opportunities in the labor market.

Vocational training is one of the key elements of ILO's technical cooperation program. Hundreds of projects have been mounted on all continents, some designed to create or strengthen national vocational training systems and others aimed at specific sectors of the economy: specialized industries, agriculture, handicrafts, commerce, the hotel trade, and tourism, among others. The ILO also cooperates in projects for management development and is active in the field of vocational rehabilitation. Its long-standing interest in handicapped people was expressed anew in 1983 with the adoption of a recommendation and a convention recognizing the importance that it attaches to the formulation and implementation of coherent national policies. The convention emphasizes collective participation—notably that of the representatives of employers' and workers' organizations and of the disabled themselves—in determining needs and developing vocational rehabilitation services at national as well as community levels.

The ILO's International Training Centre at Turin has trained 50,000 people from 170 countries since 1965, particularly in development management and national capacity building. In 1992 alone, the Turin Centre organized 118 group training courses and seminars, supported 600 fellowships, and welcomed 1,960 participants.

Social Institutions

The ILO's efforts to foster social justice in order to improve working and living conditions and to encourage balanced economic and social development would be wasted if there were no social structures promoting large-scale participation.

To assist governments, employers' associations, and trade unions in building or consolidating the necessary institutions and mechanisms, the ILO is active in such fields as labor law and administration, labor relations, workers' education, promotion of cooperatives, and rural institutions.

The ILO's work in standard-setting has had a formative effect on social legislation and labor law throughout the world. The ILO also has supplied expert advice to countries requesting it on the measures needed to bring their legislation up to the level of international labor standards or to solve certain social problems. Many developing countries have sought ILO help in establishing or codifying their labor and social legislation. To ensure that the legislation is effectively applied, a country must have a labor administration that includes the necessary services. To meet this need and to help labor ministries play an active role in designing a development policy, the ILO has mounted an increasing number of projects in this field.

The ILO has always been keenly concerned with labor-management relations and with the relations among trade unions, employers' organizations, and governments. When such relations are cordial, they foster a climate conducive to economic and social progress. When they are unsatisfactory, they can impede united national development. The ILO considers labor relations to be good when they are based on the full recognition of freedom of association, in law and in practice, and when they permit

labor, management, and government representatives to handle common problems.

Here again, technical cooperation is an extension of the action designed to set up standards and guidelines. ILO help is increasingly being sought in the field of industrial relations. Bipartite ILO missions comprising trade-union and management experts from industrialized countries have been sent to developing nations to encourage the establishment of a healthy working relationship between workers and employers. Study courses and seminars have been organized in various parts of the world.

Adequate training of workers' representatives is a prerequisite if they are to play an effective role in economic and social life. The trade unions themselves are aware of this fact and are increasing their own training programs accordingly. To assist them in this task, the ILO has established a workers' education program to enable trade unions and workers' education bodies to develop their services and to provide workers and their representatives with the social and economic training they need. ILO efforts have been directed to such objectives as the training of unionists to help them take part in the planning and execution of development policies, the encouragement of cooperative action, and the organization of union research and information services.

As part of this program, the ILO has organized seminars, study courses, and technical discussions, often on a regional basis. An average of 50 courses of this type, including discussions on such matters as population and family planning, are held each year in different parts of the world. There is also a publications program, consisting of handbooks, booklets, bulletins, and educational material, in addition to a film and filmstrip lending library.

Since its earliest days, the ILO has played an important role in developing the cooperative movement. Its range of activities in this field has grown with the introduction of the cooperative system in many developing countries. The governments of these countries recognize that cooperatives provide an instrument that can facilitate social and economic advancement. With their built-in system of controls and internal management, their freely elected councils, and public discussion of their programs, cooperatives can be compared to grass-roots civics classes, giving their members a true sense of responsibility and involvement in national development. They are a unifying agent in bringing men and women together for constructive tasks, and they contribute to training for leadership. Above all, cooperatives are a key factor in rural development, for both production and marketing.

The creation of processing cooperatives in rural areas for handling produce, as well as the organization of cooperatives for small enterprises and handicraft workshops, can aid progress toward industrialization. Whatever form they take, cooperatives raise living standards and increase employment opportunities. At the request of the governments, and with the financial support of UNDP, ILO experts are helping countries set up or develop cooperative movements.

The interregional project for the production of materials and techniques for cooperative management training ended in 1990 after 13 years of operation. The terminal evaluation considered the project to have achieved results of high quality and relevance, with almost 200,000 people having been trained in more than 60 countries.

Enterprise and Cooperative Development.

A major program to promote the establishment and effective operation of enterprises in the formal and informal sectors, in both rural and urban areas, was implemented in 1991. The Entrepreneurship and Management Development Program seeks to develop managerial resources at various levels and in various sectors of the economy in an environment characterized by rapid change.

In 1991, 153 projects were in operation focussing on four

major areas: strengthening national institutional mechanisms to monitor and manage productivity improvement; developing small and microenterprises; assisting structural adjustment processes; and strengthening management development institutions.

F. Problems of Certain Key Industries

During World War II, and even earlier, it was felt that a gap existed in the structure of the ILO: special machinery was needed for the detailed and continuing study of specific industries by people with a thorough practical knowledge of their particular problems. Acting on a plan prepared by British Minister of Labor and National Services Ernest Bevin, submitted in 1943 by the UK government, the Governing Body established seven ILO industrial committees in 1945 "to provide machinery through which the special circumstances of the principal international industries [could] receive special and detailed consideration." By 1946, industrial committees had been created to deal with the problems of the following key industries: inland transport; coal mines; iron and steel; textiles; petroleum; building, civil engineering, and public works; and chemicals. In 1994 a total of 12 industrial committees were active: the Inland Transport; Coal Mines; Iron and Steel; Metal Trades; Textiles; Building, Civil Engineering, and Public Works; Chemical Industries; Committee on Work on Plantations; Advisory Committee on Salaried Employees and Professional Workers; Hotel, Catering and Tourism; Forestry and Wood Industries; Food and Drink Industries.

Other ILO committees that deal with special problems of international significance include the Advisory Committee on Salaried Employees and Professional Workers, the Permanent Agricultural Committee, and the Committee on Work on Plantations. The ILO has also established Asian, African, and inter-American advisory committees, which provide information on special regional problems. The ILO industrial committees are, in effect, small-scale specialized international labor conferences.

Resolutions adopted by these committees may call for further action on the part of the ILO. They may also be designed for the guidance of employers' associations and trade unions in their collective bargaining, and they may contain suggestions addressed to the UN, to other specialized agencies, or to governments. The following are a few examples of subjects concerning which important resolutions or recommendations have been adopted:

Inland transport: prevention of accidents involving dock labor; inland transport working conditions in Asia and Africa; automatic coupling of railway cars; transport and handling of dangerous goods; limitation of loads carried by one person; marking of weights on loads; and interport competition;

Coal mines: principles for incorporation in a coal miners' charter; coal miners' housing; productivity in coal mines; safety in coal mines; and the social consequences of fuel and power consumption trends;

Iron and steel: regularization of production and employment at a high level; dismissal pay and payment for public holidays; and cooperation at the industry level;

Metal trades: regularization of production and employment at a high level; and long-term estimates of raw material requirements;

Textiles: disparities in wages in the textile industries of different countries;

Building, civil engineering, and public works: reduction of seasonal unemployment in the construction industry; social aspects of the world timber situation and outlook; and national housing programs;

Work on plantations: the place of the plantation in the general economy of the countries concerned; living and working conditions as related to plantation productivity; and the need for international action on commodity regulation; and

Salaried employees and professional workers: rights of the inventor who is an employee; migration of salaried and professional workers; hygiene in shops and offices; employment problems of musicians, actors, and other public performers; employment conditions of teachers; professional problems of journalists; problems involved in collective bargaining for white-collar and professional workers; wages and working conditions of hospital and health-service staff; and wages and working conditions of civil servants.

G. Other Activities

The Occupational Safety and Health Information Center (CIS)

In 1976, the ILO launched the International Program for the Improvement of Working Conditions and Environment (PIACT), aimed at giving governments and employers' and workers' organizations help in drawing up and implementing programs for the improvement of working conditions and environment. The various means of action included standard-setting; technical cooperation, including the sending of multidisciplinary teams to member states at their request; tripartite meetings, particularly meetings of industrial committees, regional meetings, and meetings of experts; action-oriented research and studies; and gathering and dissemination of information, particularly through the International Occupational Safety and Health Information Center.

The International Occupational Safety and Health Information Center (CIS) has as its objective to collect and disseminate world information that can contribute to the prevention of occupational accidents and diseases. The center is assisted by 70 national centers representing all continents. The CIS also offers on-line compact disc and microcomputer databases.

The conditions in which men and women work are at the very heart of the ILO's mandate. Despite the progress achieved, the working conditions of a great many workers remain arduous or give rise to new problems as a result of technological developments. In this arena the ILO is concerned with the safety and healthfulness of the working environment, working time, organization and content of work, working conditions and choice of technology, and working and living environment.

In 1991, with the assistance of a grant from the German government, the International Program on the Elimination of Child Labor (IPEC) was launched. More than 80 projects with government institutions, trade unions, employers' organizations, and non-governmental organizations (NGOs) were implemented in at least 12 countries.

International Health Hazard Alert System

A new approach to dealing with newly discovered or suspected occupational hazards, which spread very quickly around the world, is the ILO's International Health Hazard Alert System, established in 1977. When a new hazard is discovered, an alert is sent out by the ILO to the participating countries for their assessment and reply. For example, the communication concerning possible health hazards in the use of carbonless copy papers was widely disseminated in several countries. In 1993 the Health Hazard Alert System circulated requests to member states for up-to-date information on major occupational health hazards and their prevention.

Tripartite Declaration Concerning Multinational Enterprises and Social Policy

The 1977 Tripartite Declaration Concerning Multinational Enterprises and Social Policy applies to the fields of employment, training, conditions of work and life, and industrial relations. While already operational in the ILO, where it will continue to affect its purposes, it is foreseen as the employment and labor chapter of the proposed UN Code of Conduct on Transnational Corporations that has been the subject of prolonged debate (as of 1994, formal negotiations concerning this code of conduct had been suspended). The declaration stresses the positive contributions that multinational enterprises can make to economic and social progress and aims at minimizing and resolving the difficulties that their various operations may create. The principles are commended to governments and employers' and workers' organizations of home and host countries and to the multinational enterprises themselves for their voluntary observance.

The subject areas covered by the declaration conform to the areas of substantive competence of the ILO within the overall program of the UN. There are 22 ILO conventions and 27 recommendations referenced in the declaration. The declaration is universal in scope; it is addressed to all of the parties in the ILO's tripartite structure; it ascribes a leading role to multinational enterprises when they operate in developing countries; and, finally, it is voluntary.

BIBLIOGRAPHY

Conditions of Work Digest. Legal, policy, and program information on significant issues and emerging trends in the field of conditions of work and quality of working life. Annotated bibliographies, guides to information sources. Worldwide coverage.

International Labour Review. Notes and comments on the social and labor situation in the world and articles based on recent ILO and other research into economic and social topics of international interest affecting labor. Notes on new books published or received by the ILO. Six issues per year.

LABORDOC. (database) Machine-readable version of International Labour Documentation, available for interactive and retrospective on-line searching through several information hosts. Offers worldwide coverage of labor questions, especially industrial relations, labor law, employment, working conditions, vocational training, labor related aspects of economics, social development, rural development, and technological change.

Labour Law Documents. Formerly Legislative Series (founded in 1919), includes the most important texts of international conventions, laws, and regulations enacted throughout the world on labor and social security. Three issues per year.

Official Bulletin, Series A. Information on activities of the ILO, texts adopted by the ILC, and other official documents. Three issues per year. *Series B*. Reports of the Committee on Freedom of Association of the Governing Body and related material. Three issues per year.

World Labour Report. Reviews significant recent events and policy experiences in: human rights at work; employment; labor relations; social protection and working conditions. Yearly.

World of Work. A newsletter covering ILO activities throughout the world. Quarterly.

Year Book of Labor Statistics. A comprehensive survey of annual data from all parts of the world relating to total and economically active population, employment, unemployment, hours of work, wages, labor cost, strikes, and lockouts.

All publications may be ordered from the Secretariat in Geneva, or, in North America, from the ILO Publications Center, 49 Sheridan Avenue, Albany, NY 12210.

THE FOOD AND AGRICULTURE ORGANIZATION OF THE UNITED NATIONS (FAO)

"To the millions who have to go without two meals a day the only acceptable form in which God dare appear is food."
Mahatma Gandhi

BACKGROUND: Hunger is still the most urgent problem confronting the greater part of humanity. Hundreds of millions of the world's inhabitants are seriously and chronically undernourished. Not only is their diet quantitatively insufficient, but it is qualitatively insufficient as well, lacking the protein essential to health and vigor. Only about one person in four in the world is really well fed and adequately nourished.

CREATION

From the mid-19th century, reflecting a growing recognition of the interdependence of nations in agriculture and associated sciences, international conferences were held at which there were exchanges of knowledge relating to biology, biochemistry, crop diversification, and animal health. However, it was not until 1905 that these individually valuable but unrelated efforts were coordinated with the founding of the International Institute of Agriculture (IIA).

One of the institute's aims, which were necessarily modest because of public and governmental apathy, was "to get the farmer a square deal." The words were those of David Lubin, a prosperous California dry-goods dealer, born in a Polish ghetto, who almost single-handedly founded the institute. Depressed by the plight of his farmer customers during the agricultural crisis of the 1890s, he bought and managed his own fruit farm in order to study their problems. Rebuffed in his adopted country, he toured the chancelleries of Europe, preaching the importance of a healthy agriculture as a requisite of a healthy international society. Finally, Lubin found a sympathetic listener in King Victor Emmanuel III of Italy. Under his patronage, the institute started functioning in Rome in 1908 as a center for the dissemination of farming news, trends, prices, statistics, and techniques. Though lacking the capacity to initiate or directly assist projects in the field, the IIA's experience as a "head office" for the collection, collation, analysis, and dissemination of data formed a useful platform for the later launching of FAO's similar but wider reaching activities in agriculture.

The League of Nations did not directly concern itself with agriculture, but work done under its auspices in the relatively new field of nutrition proved of great practical significance. Ironically, Nazi Germany, although a sardonic critic of the League, was the first country to base its wartime rationing system on the scientific standards of diet drawn up by the League for heavy workers, expectant mothers, children, and others. Soon, other countries did the same, often with striking results. In the UK, for example, the meager and often uninteresting but balanced diet dictated by the ration card actually led to an improvement in the nation's nutritional health.

FAO was the end product of a series of conferences held during World War II. In 1941, the US Nutrition Conference for Defense, attended by 900 delegates, resolved that it should be a goal of the democracies to conquer hunger, "not only the obvious hunger that man has always known, but the hidden hunger revealed by modern knowledge of nutrition." In line with President Franklin D. Roosevelt's call in 1942 for the Four Freedoms, the Australian economist Frank McDougal proposed the creation of a "United Nations program for freedom from want of food" and urged the president that food be the first economic problem tackled by the UN system being proposed for establishment when the war ended.

President Roosevelt convened the UN Conference on Food and Agriculture at Hot Springs, Virginia, in May and June 1943. The first UN conference, antedating the San Francisco Conference by two years, it established an Interim Commission on Food and Agriculture, headed by Lester B. Pearson of Canada. The commission drew up a draft constitution for FAO, thus paving the way for the first FAO Conference, held in Quebec in October 1945 and attended by 44 nations and a number of observers. On 16 October 1945, 34 nations signed the constitution that brought FAO into existence. By the end of the conference, the new organization, headed by British nutritionist Sir John Boyd Orr, had 42 member nations.

PURPOSES

As expressed in the preamble to the FAO constitution, member states are pledged to promote the common welfare through separate and collective action to raise levels of nutrition and standards of living, improve the efficiency of the production and distribution of all food and agricultural products, better the conditions of rural populations, and thus contribute toward an expanding world economy and ensure humanity's freedom from hunger. Specifically, FAO is charged with collecting, evaluating, and disseminating information relating to nutrition, food, and agriculture and associated areas, including fisheries, marine products, forestry, and primary forestry products.

FAO is committed to promoting and, where appropriate, recommending national and international action with respect to the following: (a) scientific, technological, social, and economic research relating to nutrition, food, and agriculture; (b) improvement of education and administration relating to nutrition, food, and agriculture and the spread of public knowledge of nutritional and agricultural science and practice; (c) conservation of natural resources and the adoption of improved methods of agricultural

213

production; (d) improvement of the processing, marketing, and distribution of food and agricultural products; (e) adoption of policies for the provision of adequate agricultural credit, national and international; and (f) adoption of international policies on agricultural commodity arrangements. The FAO also plays a major role in dealing with food and agricultural emergencies such as drought, famine, plant diseases, and insect plagues.

Other functions of FAO are to furnish such technical assistance as governments may request; to organize, in cooperation with the governments concerned, such missions as may be needed to assist them in fulfilling obligations arising from their acceptance of the recommendations of the UN Conference on Food and Agriculture and of its constitution; and, generally, to take all necessary and appropriate action to implement the purposes of the organization as set forth in the preamble.

MEMBERSHIP

The 45 countries represented on the interim commission were entitled to original membership. The Russian Federation retains the entitlement to original membership previously held by the USSR, to be made effective at any time through the ratification of FAO's constitution. The other former members of the USSR must undergo the normal application process for new members; to date, Armenia, Estonia, Latvia, Lithuania, and the Kyrgyz Republic have done so.

Any nation may withdraw after four years. Among the countries that have withdrawn and later rejoined are Czechoslovakia (withdrew 1950, rejoined 1969), Poland (withdrew 1951, rejoined 1957), Hungary (withdrew 1952, rejoined 1967), and South Africa (withdrew 1964, rejoined 1993). Taiwan withdrew in 1952.

As of November 1993, FAO had 169 member nations. In addition, Puerto Rico was an associate member. The European Economic Community was a member organization.

STRUCTURE

The principal organs of FAO are the FAO Conference, the FAO Council, and the secretariat, headed by a Director General.

FAO Conference

The supreme body of FAO is the all-member FAO Conference, which holds its regular biennial sessions in Rome in odd-numbered years. The conference determines the policy of FAO and adopts its budget. It makes recommendations relating to food, agriculture, fisheries, forestry, and related matters to member nations and to other international organizations. It approves conventions and agreements for submission to member governments. It may establish commissions, working parties, and consultative groups and may convene special conferences. It periodically elects the Director General, as well as the member nations to be represented on the FAO Council. Each FAO member has one vote in the conference.

FAO Council

The FAO Council, consisting of 49 member nations elected by the FAO Conference for three-year terms on a rotating basis, meets at least once a year, under an independent chairman, as an interim governing body between meetings of the conference. The committees of the Council include the program and finance committees and committees on commodity problems, fisheries, agriculture, forestry, food aid, and legal matters.

Director General and Secretariat

Under the supervision of the conference and the Council, the Director General has full power and authority to direct the work of FAO. Edouard Saouma of Lebanon was Director General from 1975 to 1993. Dr. Jacques Diouf of Senegal was elected Director

General by the conference in 1993. He heads a staff of more than 6,000, including close to 3,000 persons working in various development projects in the field.

Headquarters and Regional Offices. FAO headquarters were in Washington, DC, until 1951. Since then, they have been located in Rome on extraterritorial grounds near the Colosseum and the Baths of Caracalla. The headquarters building was planned originally by the government of Mussolini, but construction was halted by World War II. Completed after the war, it was leased by the Italian government for the "permanent use and occupancy" of FAO at an annual rental of us$1.

Growth in staff and activities over the years created a need for more work space. Aside from additions to the main complex, office space was for some time rented away from the headquarters building. In 1993, the Italian government completed a major expansion of headquarters facilities, bringing all FAO staff together at the Terme di Caracalla address for the first time in 32 years.

Aside from headquarters in Rome, which also serves as the European regional office, FAO has regional offices for Africa in Accra, Ghana; Asia and the Pacific in Bangkok, Thailand; Latin America and the Caribbean in Santiago, Chile; and the Near East in Cairo, Egypt. There is also a North American liaison office in Washington, DC, as well as UN liaison offices in New York and in Geneva, Switzerland.

The Organization

The FAO comprises eight departments: Economic and Social Policy, Agriculture, Fisheries, Forestry, Sustainable Development, Technical Cooperation, Administration and Finance, and General Affairs and Information. The Technical Cooperation and Sustainable Development Departments were recently created through a process of restructuring to respond more effectively to evolving needs among the organization's member nations.

BUDGET

FAO's biennial internal budget, or Regular Programme, covers internal operations, including the maintenance of the highly qualified staff who conduct field work, advise governments on policy and planning, and service a wide range of development needs. The Regular Programme is financed by contributions from member nations. It covers the costs of the organization's secretariat, its Technical Cooperation Programme, and part of several special action programs. The 27th session of the FAO Conference unanimously approved, in November 1993, a budget of us$676.9 million for 1994–95.

The Technical Cooperation Program (TCP) was initiated in 1976. It enables the organization to provide speedy assistance to, for instance, a country when disasters affect its food and agricultural situation; practical and vocational training to complement training financed from trust funds and other sources; and short-term, small-scale supplementary technical assistance and policy advice that can be immediately useful to a country's food and agricultural situation. The amount of funds allocated to TCPs has been increased in each FAO budget; funds rose to us$77.4 million in 1992–93 from us$47.4 million in 1982–83.

The Field Programme implements FAO's development strategies and provides assistance to governments and rural communities. Projects are usually undertaken in cooperation with national governments and other agencies. Nearly half of Field Programme finances come from national trust funds and just over 40 percent is provided by the United Nations Development Program. FAO contributes about 10 percent from the Regular Programme budget through its Technical Cooperation Programme. In 1993, FAO disbursed close to us$110.3 million in UNDP funds in some 130 countries. An increasing amount of money comes from donor countries that ask FAO to carry out part of their aid activities for them. Many of these countries also assign and finance young technicians to work in FAO projects. During 1993, FAO trust fund activities accounted for total expenditures of approximately US$163.8 million.

ACTIVITIES

FAO collects, analyzes and disseminates information, provides policy and planning advice to governments, offers direct development assistance, and acts as an international forum for debate on food and agriculture issues.

Despite considerable progress in recent decades, the world still falls short of the goal of adequate food and nutrition for all. FAO estimates that more than 780 million people in the developing world are chronically undernourished, consuming too little food to meet even minimal energy and protein needs. Millions suffer from lack of essential micronutrients; their symptoms include blindness, vulnerability to infectious diseases, anemia, and mental retardation. Those most at risk include the poor, the elderly, refugees and displaced persons, drought-prone populations, and children. Nearly 13 million children under age five die every year as a direct or indirect result of hunger and malnutrition. FAO advocates equitable, participatory rural development as the key to eradication of poverty, the first and foremost cause of undernutrition and food insecurity.

Widespread hunger and malnutrition is not simply a problem of inadequate food production; it is the most critical and cruel element of poverty. Farmers in the developing world are discouraged from increasing food production by the lack of purchasing power among rural and urban populations as much as by a lack of technical assistance or inputs such as improved seeds and fertilizers. People go hungry because they do not have the money to buy food, rather than because local farmers cannot produce more. The fight against world hunger is a major part of the battle against world poverty. Building up a country's agriculture provides both food for the hungry and jobs for the rural populace; it contributes to the overall prosperity of the nation.

Food Security

The goal of eradicating hunger and malnutrition and ensuring food security for all is central to FAO's mandate. Following the serious depletion of world grain reserves caused by poor harvests in 1972, FAO saw the need to develop an international system to maintain minimum world food security and offset the effects of crop failures. The organization made a proposal under which all countries, be they developed or developing, would cooperate in building up national food reserves under a structure of international cooperation. Special efforts were called for to increase the self-reliance of developing countries. The proposal was endorsed by the World Food Conference held in Rome in November 1974, and FAO was requested to prepare an International Undertaking on World Food Security. In 1976, the organization established the Food Security Assistance Scheme to carry out the work of the International Undertaking.

In 1983, FAO's Committee on World Food Security adopted a broader concept of world food security, with the ultimate objective of ensuring that all people at all times have both physical and economic access to the food they need, and in 1986, the FAO Council endorsed a World Food Security Compact, which provides a clearly defined moral basis for action by governments, organizations, and individuals directed toward securing food supplies for all. The compact urged developing countries to promote domestic food production as the first line of defense and to reexamine, and if necessary revise, national policies to ensure adequate incentives to farmers, particularly small-scale producers. It recommended that governments of developing countries prepare to maintain food security in times of shortage by such measures as early-warning systems and emergency food reserves and to

promote rural development that helps increase the purchasing power of the poor. Developed countries, both importers and exporters, were asked to consider world as well as national interests when setting policies concerning food production, stocks, imports, and prices. They were encouraged to continue providing emergency food aid to less fortunate countries, as well as to assist in increasing agricultural production in those countries, and to help low-income countries to secure imports of food, fertilizers, and other agricultural inputs in times of difficulty. They were also requested to take into account, in negotiations on trade questions, the fact that the food security of many developing countries depends on their ability to export agricultural and other products in order to meet the cost of food imports.

The World Food Security Compact called on nongovernmental organizations to help stimulate public interest in food-security issues, thereby facilitating additional action by governments, and it called for a commitment to food security on the part of individuals throughout the world. The individual was called upon not only to work for his own food security and that of his family but also to recognize that he has "a sacred obligation" to concern himself with the food security of those less fortunate than himself. "Failure to provide succor when it is needed," the compact stated, "is a betrayal of man's duty to his fellow men."

In 1992, the International Conference on Nutrition (ICN) was convened at FAO headquarters in Rome. Organized jointly by FAO and WHO, the conference brought together almost 1,400 delegates from 159 countries and the EEC to address ways of channeling greater resources to the eradication of hunger and malnutrition worldwide. The ICN addressed eight important nutritional issues: preventing micronutrient deficiencies; preventing and managing infectious diseases; improving household food security; promoting healthy diets and lifestyles; enhancing the capacity for care; improving food quality and safety; assessing, analyzing, and monitoring nutrition situations; and incorporating nutrition objectives in development policies. Attention was drawn to the fact that, though enough food is produced yearly to provide an adequate diet for all, the distribution of these resources is very uneven.

FAO's activities are increasingly focused on food security as a question of household access to food as much as of overall food availability. In this context, proper identification of vulnerable groups is fundamental. FAO is developing, at national and subregional levels, an Aggregate Household Food Security Index. The conceptual basis for the index was approved by the FAO Council in 1993. Once fully developed, it will serve as a tool to help monitor food security trends worldwide.

Information for Agriculture

Among its information functions, FAO provides technical information for specialists through an active publishing program in the form of statistical yearbooks, periodicals, technical reports, scientific monographs, training materials, and other studies of agriculture worldwide (see Bibliography). Most of these publications are translated from their original language into at least one of the organization's other official languages: Arabic, Chinese, English, French, and Spanish.

FAO's David Lubin Memorial Library serves as a coordinating center for the Worldwide Network of Agricultural Libraries (AGLINET). It houses over 1 million items covering agriculture, statistics, economics, food and nutrition, forestry, fisheries, and rural development. The library's computerized facilities supply on-demand bibliographies to field projects, individuals, and institutions in FAO's member nations.

FAO's filmstrips and its radio, television, and video programs cover a wide range of topics from improved farming techniques to animal husbandry, aquaculture, and soil conservation. Translation of these materials into local languages is encouraged in order to reach small farmers and extension workers unable to use one of the five official languages. In addition, the organization provides users with access to over 40 databases on agriculture, fisheries, and forestry, as well as satellite-based information on climate that is crucial to monitoring and responding in a timely fashion to signs of drought, crop failure, and insect plagues.

Every decade, FAO sponsors a worldwide agricultural census, continuing and expanding the first world census carried out by the International Institute of Agriculture in 1930.

FAO has made considerable efforts to identify future demands on agriculture and how these demands might be met, based on the results of data collection and analysis, policy reviews, and practical knowledge of agricultural development. In 1969, FAO published a provisional World Plan for Agricultural Development, an attempt to analyze the major issues that would confront world agriculture in the 1970s and early 1980s. Building on this base, FAO submitted to the FAO Conference in 1979 a study entitled *Agriculture: Toward 2000*. The study's main purpose was to provide a framework for the analysis of options and consideration of policy issues relevant to the development of world agriculture until the end of the century. The study was global in scope, but the major emphasis was on developing countries. Approximately 90 developing countries, which, excluding China, together account for over 98 percent of the population of the developing countries, were studied individually.

In 1993, the FAO Conference launched *Agriculture: Towards 2010*, the revised and updated version of a study originally published by FAO in 1987. Designed to address how the future may unfold, rather than how it ought to develop, the document analyzes trends in food security, nutrition, and agricultural development to determine the most likely outcomes by the year 2010. Among the success stories, it foresees that world agricultural growth, although lower than in the past, will continue to outpace population increases. Also, the majority of people in the developing countries are expected to experience improvement in their per capita food availability and nutritional situation. At the policy level, the study notes a growing awareness of—and greater capabilities to respond to—the need to increase agricultural sustainability. Trade agreements are also seen as becoming more liberal and less trade-distorting, even though the progress may not be smooth.

Yet despite these favorable predictions, many problems are foreseen as remaining, especially for the less developed nations. Significant chronic undernutrition will continue to prevail in many countries and will likely affect significant proportions of the population in entire regions such as sub-Saharan Africa. According to the study, if present trends continue, sub-Saharan Africa will replace South Asia as the global area with the highest number of chronically undernourished people—close to 300 million by the year 2010. Though improvements will be made in South Asia, that region will still have 200 million undernourished.

The pressures on agriculture, on forest and fisheries resources, and on the environment will continue to build. Coupled with this, there will be few prospects for expansion of the main agricultural exports of the developing countries. The study presents detailed assessments of land resources potential for future crop production in the developing countries. These assessments are accompanied and sustained by maps illustrating the dominant land classes for each major geographical area. Aside from providing projections, the study proposes to assist planning at the national and international level, making recommendations designed to aid people and governments in taking early action to reverse negative trends. While doing so, it calls for continued vigilance and preparedness to deal with newly emerging problems.

To help in assessing potential food availability, FAO and UNESCO published in 1978 the Soil Map of the World. By combining the data in the Soil Map with inputs on climate and population, institutes undertaking global studies on climate change, agricultural production, and soil degradation can make efficient projections. In 1992, FAO completed a digitized version of the Soil Map in a form that allows it to be used as an input into climate change models. The data was also updated and the symbols were modified to make it accessible to nonspecialists. The Soil Map is part of FAO's Geographic Information System (GIS), which also provides data on vegetation cover and other aspects of land use.

The locust and grasshopper menace that threatened Africa in 1986 and 1987 gave new urgency to FAO's efforts to improve its Rome-based Global Information and Early Warning System for Food and Agriculture. The system, established in 1975 to monitor the world's food supply, sounds the alarm when food security is threatened. FAO prepares monthly, quarterly, and annual reports that provide comprehensive, up-to-date analyses of the world food situation and identify countries threatened by shortages. The reports also serve as a guide to potential donors and help avoid food crises.

FAO's Remote Sensing Center collects and interprets data and helps establish data-receiving stations, particularly in Africa; these stations can interpret information on precipitation, soil moisture, and biomass in order to forecast harvests and can transmit the information to national early-warning systems. ARTEMIS, FAO's Africa Real Time Environmental Monitoring Information System, uses high frequency environmental satellite data to produce, at regular intervals, images indicating the rainfall situation and the development of vegetation at continental scales. In combination with data from other sources, ARTEMIS enables specialists to make assessments of crop growing conditions, detect droughts at an early stage, and locate potential breeding grounds for desert locusts. ARTEMIS is an important tool for the GIEWS.

Research and Technical Information. FAO has stressed the importance of agricultural research in developing countries, where the shortage of trained personnel for research remains a major problem. Its Research and Technology Development Division, established in 1984, helps developing countries make the best use of their research resources and assists in the transfer of the fruits of research and technology to developing countries.

The Information System for the Agricultural Sciences and Technology (AGRIS) and the Current Agricultural Research Information System (CARIS) are two worldwide networks coordinated by FAO in support of research and development programs in food and agriculture. As of February 1994, 153 national and 24 regional multinational centers were reporting information to AGRIS. CARIS links 120 developing countries and 11 regional international centers, enabling them to exchange information on their current research activities.

FAO operates the world's most comprehensive bank of agricultural information and statistics. Called AGROSTAT, it brings together FAO's major data files, including data compiled since 1961 on annual supplies and utilization of crops, livestock, and fishery and forest products, as well as on producer prices, population, and other topics. AGROSTAT PC provides an electronic version of FAO's AGROSTAT yearbooks. Other important statistical information maintained by FAO's technical divisions include the Fisheries Statistical Database (FISHDAB), the Globefish Databank and Electronic Library, the Forest Resources Information System (FORIS), and the Geographic Information System (GIS).

To meet increasing demand for agricultural data, FAO is preparing the World Agricultural Information Centre (WAICENT). WAICENT will give governments, institutions, universities, and individuals easy, economical access to information from over 40 FAO databases. Users will be able to access the composite database employing a variety of methods including diskette, CD-ROM, computer networks, and telephone lines.

Advice to Governments

One of FAO's important mandates is to provide member nations with advice on agricultural and food topics. This involves a very broad range of technical, policy, and planning support, principally aimed at building awareness towards key issues, generating appropriate action, and helping countries to develop their own capacities. The recent restructuring of FAO's Policy Formulation, Investment Centre, and Field Operations divisions into a Technical Cooperation Department is intended to provide a consolidated base at headquarters for the provision of direct assistance to member nations in policy, investment, and implementation of field operations.

FAO's Food Security Assistance Scheme (FSAS) helps member countries formulate comprehensive food security program. A fundamental aspect of the FSAS methodology is the use of national multidisciplinary teams of experts in program planning and implementation. This approach contributes to accurate diagnosis of problems, realistic formulation of solutions, capacity building at the national level and anchoring of programs within the national institutional framework.

FAO's Investment Centre helps developing countries construct sound development programs and projects for funding by multilateral organizations, linking the interests of governments and donors to forge viable partnerships. During project identification, the center carefully assesses the development priority of investment proposals, working closely with local staff to promote self-sufficiency and to complement national expertise. This is followed by detailed project preparation for consideration by financing institutions.

The prime source of funding for FAO-assisted investment projects is the World Bank, particularly the IDA, but the Investment Centre also cooperates with most of the principal multilateral financing institutions, including the International Fund for Agricultural Development (IFAD) and regional development banks. Rural poverty alleviation is especially important in projects formulated in conjunction with IFAD.

FAO assists governments in using pesticides safely and rationally through the International Code of Conduct on the Distribution and Use of Pesticides. The code includes a clause for Prior Informed Consent (PIC), which establishes a mechanism for information exchange, enabling importing countries to decide whether they want to receive pesticides that have been banned or severely restricted because of threats to human health or the environment.

The organization's Codex Alimentarius is an international code of food standards. It is designed to guide the world's food industry and to protect the health of consumers by establishing definitions and requirements for foods, assisting in their harmonization, and, in doing so, facilitating international trade.

Aside from these activities, FAO is involved in a continuous process of consultation with its member governments, providing information, advice, and technical assistance that can help them make the best choices in promoting sustainable rural development.

Development Assistance

To promote sustainable agriculture and contribute to development that will provide long-term solutions to the fundamental problems of poverty and hunger, FAO gives practical help to developing countries through a wide range of technical assistance projects. The organization encourages an integrated approach, with environmental, social, and economic considerations included in the formulation of development projects. By encouraging people's participation, FAO aims to draw on local expertise and ensure a cooperative approach to development.

Emergency Assistance and Rehabilitation

FAO's Office for Special Relief Operations (OSRO) began operations in 1973 in response to the disastrous drought in 1972–73 in the semiarid countries on the southern edge of the Sahara Desert. In 1975, following an improvement in the Sahel situation, FAO's work was extended to cover emergencies elsewhere. The emphasis in these operations is on speedy approval and delivery of assistance. When disaster strikes a country, the FAO representative assesses needs in close collaboration with local authorities and with other UN agencies. At the request of the government, emergency missions are organized by FAO to assess in detail the damages and losses and to prepare assistance projects for consideration by multilateral and bilateral agencies. Most emergency projects are funded by governments, nongovernmental organizations, and UN agencies. In many cases, FAO, through its Technical Cooperation Program, offers an immediate source of funding for special relief operations. Supplies and equipment provided include seeds, fertilizers, pesticides, and livestock supplies and equipment, as well as logistical support. Disaster-prone countries may also receive preventive assistance to cope with calamities.

Through its Agricultural Rehabilitation Program for Africa, conceived in 1984 at the height of the Ethiopian famine, FAO helped channel some US$194 million into 25 countries to supply farmers with seeds and fertilizers, repair irrigation systems, and rebuild cattle herds.

Since the early 1950s, FAO has coordinated the campaign against the destructive desert locust, which intermittently swarms in the Middle East, Africa, and other regions. Campaigns were almost continuous until 1963, when the pest was brought under control. There have, however, been serious outbreaks of swarms since then, particularly between 1967 and 1970, and in 1978 in desert areas in India.

In 1986, FAO led the battle against the grasshopper and locust plagues that threatened to devastate crops in all parts of Africa. The Emergency Center for Locust Operations, established at FAO headquarters, directed what was to become a US$50 million continent-wide campaign that helped save more than 90 percent of crops in the Sahel alone. FAO monitored breeding areas with satellite imagery, implemented projects carrying out spraying missions, sent pest-control experts to advise African authorities, and helped set up coordinating committees of government and donor representatives in the most directly threatened countries. More than 40 donors, including both developed and developing countries, UN agencies, and nongovernmental organizations, contributed to the fight in 13 countries. The center was deactivated in the spring of 1989 when locusts were brought under control in some 40 countries in Africa, the Near East, and Southwest Asia. In late 1992, with the reappearance of the desert locust on the coastal plains around the Red Sea, the ECLO was immediately brought back into full operation.

FAO continues to strengthen its ability to prevent and respond to emergencies caused by pests and diseases, placing special emphasis on locusts and rinderpest.

INCREASING FOOD AND AGRICULTURAL PRODUCTION

FAO devotes a large share of the resources of its field and regular programs each year to increasing the output of crops, livestock, food fish, and forest products.

Crop Production and Protection

FAO's work in crop production includes collecting, conserving, and evaluating genetic resources; improving seed quality, production, and distribution; increasing crop output; and preventing losses before harvest. Particularly important in developing countries is the supply of high-quality food-crop seed to small farmers, who are responsible in some countries for more than 90 percent of domestic food production. National seed services and centers often are crucial for the supply of seeds to farmers, and much of

FAO's seed development work is concerned with building up these national institutions.

Many countries give high priority to cash crop production, and urban populations often have easier access to imported cereals, including wheat, than to traditional staples, such as cassavas, breadfruit, sweet potatoes, yams, and plantains. The danger of these trends is twofold: increased dependency on food imports and lagging production of traditional crops often used in rural communities as insurance against food scarcity and famine. FAO activities to combat these trends range from training sessions for extension staff to pilot projects, such as helping women's groups to start home vegetable gardens and working on ways to improve processing and storage of perishable vegetables. FAO also has helped develop varieties of wheat and barley suited to arid conditions, as well as more nutritive varieties.

Requests for technical assistance in horticulture are a constant on the FAO agenda. FAO projects cover, for example, citrus production in the Mediterranean, date palm production in the Near East and the Mediterranean, protected cultivation of vegetables in the Near East and North Africa, promotion of tropical fruit-tree production in humid and subhumid areas, and improved vegetable production in tropical semiarid and humid regions.

FAO has played a pivotal role in international crop protection activities for over four decades. The International Plant Protection Convention (IPPC) was vested in FAO in 1951. In order to strengthen FAO's role as coordinator, an IPPC secretariat was created in 1992-93. FAO's general objective in this field is to reduce or if possible prevent crop losses caused by pests. Specific objectives include reducing the spread of pests across national borders and promoting Integrated Pest Management (IPM), which consists of a "best mix" of natural control methods with a need-only-based use of selective pesticides (see Pest Control). In cooperation with the World Health Organization, FAO is conducting studies on the effects of pesticide residues on humans.

Plant diseases remain one of the major checks on crop production. The easiest and most economical way of coping with plant parasites is to breed varieties that are resistant to them. FAO-supported research has been aimed at breeding varieties with durable or long-term resistance. FAO recently established a Plant Genetic Resources Information and Seed Exchange Unit, which disseminates technical information and exchanges seeds and planting material samples for experimental purposes. The main beneficiaries are national and international research centers, plant breeders, and FAO field projects. On a national level, FAO advises governments on seed production and legislation.

Examples of FAO activities aimed at increasing crop output include:

- Over the 1986–92 period, there were 579 field projects in the area of crop protection with a total budget of US$265.6 million. Integrated Pest Management (IPM) accounted for the majority of the projects—57 percent of the total amount. Fifty percent of all crop protection projects by budget and number were in Africa.
- Since the early 1950s, FAO has coordinated the campaign against the destructive desert locust, which intermittently swarms in the Middle East, Africa, and other regions (see Emergency Assistance and Rehabilitation). FAO's Emergency Center for Locust Operations is fundamental in conducting these campaigns.
- The Geographic Information and Early Warning System (see Information for Agriculture) also contributes to crop protection, warning against potential difficulties and disasters.
- The Global System on Plant Genetic Resources supports international and regional networks for *in situ* and *ex situ* conservation under the auspices of FAO. The system also promotes evaluation, management, and enhanced use of plant genetic

resources (PGR), and prepares periodic reports on the state of the world's PGR. The Commission on Plant Genetic Resources coordinates the Code of Conduct for Biotechnology applied in the conservation and use of PGR, as well as work on farmers' rights and support for an international fund for PGR.

- FAO's agricultural research program strengthens countries' capabilities to generate and develop appropriate technology for crop protection and production. Special attention is given to traditional technologies and their use by farmers, as well as the role of rural women and the constraints they face.
- The Joint FAO/IAEA Division of Nuclear Techniques in Food and Agriculture operates a laboratory at Seibersdorf, near Vienna. The division's program is based on two fundamental approaches. Under the first, the movements and transformations of isotopically labeled chemical compounds of importance in relation to soils, water, air, plants, and livestock are studied. This information is used to improve management of soils and water, nutrition of plants and animals, and the safety of agrochemical use. The second approach uses ionizing radiation to induce mutations for selection of useful traits in plants, to sterilize insects for control purposes, and to improve the safety and preservation of food. In the field of food irradiation, for example, researchers have found that doses as low as 150 Gy (equivalent to heat energy of 0.0036 degrees C.) were sufficient to rid fruit and vegetables of fruit fly. The discovery may provide one answer to developing countries' quest to meet strict import standards set by the West.
- FAO provides information on crops through a global database of crop environmental requirements, with initial data for 360 species.

Animal Production and Health

Livestock often forms a key component of the "production systems approach" promoted by FAO in agricultural development schemes. The approach is based on the principle that the production of different commodities is often linked and that increased production of one may result in increased output of another. In India, for example, the production of food grain has increased markedly in villages where dairy cooperatives are functioning well. Milk sales provide the small farmer with the cash income to purchase inputs such as fertilizers, improved seeds, and irrigation water essential for increased grain yields. Thus, increased milk production has led to significant improvements in farm output and living standards. This approach also is being applied to sheep, goat, poultry, and rabbit production.

FAO's International Dairy Development Program is designed to help low-income countries modernize the complex chain linking milk producers and consumers. It helps coordinate efforts aimed at improving all aspects of the dairy industry, from farmers' organizations and veterinary services to processing plants and marketing channels. The program is aimed at assisting in the planning, coordination, and implementation of model projects for integrated dairy development, with the full participation of small-scale milk producers, the firm commitment of cooperating governments, and the active involvement of donors, and at making dairying a more effective force in rural development through its socioeconomic impact in rural areas and its contribution to nutrition.

FAO also works to improve livestock feeding and management by reducing to a minimum the amount of grain consumed by animals and making maximum use of pasture and fodder, crop residues, and agro-industrial by-products. An FAO database entitled *Tropical Feeds* offers concise and updatable information on over 500 tropical feed materials in published form and on diskette. This information is updated regularly.

Rapidly expanding human populations are increasing the demand for agricultural products—among them livestock—and in response, production is being intensified. To help foresee and forestall possible negative side effects of intensified production and enhance positive ones, FAO is conducting studies on the influence of livestock development practices on the natural resource base. These studies involve livestock feed quality, use of biomass for animal fodder, avoidance of overgrazing, manure management, animal waste disposal, domestic animal genetic diversity, plant and animal wildlife diversity, and integration of cropping and livestock systems.

FAO has joined hands with animal welfare organizations to initiate joint activities that will promote humane treatment of slaughter animals while heightening the quality of meat products and by-products. The organization also has helped boost the efficiency of village-level meat processing by developing modular designs for slaughtering and processing facilities. The designs employ affordable, easily available materials and modules that can be selected and adapted by users according to their needs. Use of the facilities helps reduce losses and limit contamination while increasing employment—particularly for rural women—as well as income for small producers.

Disease continues to check animal production in most developing countries. FAO focuses concerted attention on animal health involving the control of important diseases such as foot-and-mouth, rinderpest, swine fever, Rift-valley fever, trypanosomiasis, and Newcastle disease. Veterinary policy development and education also are stressed.

The control of African animal trypanosomiasis, a disease spread by the tsetse fly, is a priority. In sub-Saharan Africa, FAO has applied a community-based approach to disseminate a technology that uses colored cloth traps to capture tsetse flies. An FAO regional project to improve the quality of veterinary vaccines has helped to reduce rinderpest disease dramatically among cattle in Africa. In 1989–91, FAO was involved in an emergency campaign in Turkey that vaccinated 12 million cattle and buffalo threatened by rinderpest. One of FAO's greatest recent livestock success stories involves the defeat of the New World screwworm fly, which surfaced in Libya in 1989. The screwworm, which feeds on living flesh, can kill full grown cattle within 10 days. By 1991, FAO's Screwworm Emergency Center for North Africa, working with Libya, intergovernmental agencies, and donors, eradicated the pest using a technique for sterilizing the insects, thus inhibiting breeding.

FAO and the International Atomic Energy Agency (IAEA) have established a laboratory to promote nuclear-based ELISA methodology and related molecular techniques for diagnosis of livestock diseases. Accurate diagnosis is fundamental to disease control and eradication. The laboratory cooperates closely with national and international organizations to promote standardization and transfer of techniques designed specifically for the difficult conditions often experienced in less advanced countries. Priority is being given to the diseases of greatest importance such as rinderpest, trypanosomiasis, and foot-and-mouth disease.

In 1993, FAO and UNEP published the *World Watch List for Domestic Animal Diversity*, the first attempt to document the state of global livestock genetic diversity. Monitoring, description, and characterization of existing breeds constitute a vital part of conservation, allowing people to understand each species' status, as well as its members' unique qualities and potential. The *World Watch List* is based on the FAO Global Databank, part of the Global Information System for Domestic Animal Diversity. Developed as an early warning system to help prevent erosion of genetic diversity in animal species, the first edition of the list covers ass, buffalo, cattle, goat, horse, pig, and sheep. Future editions will add other species and wild relatives as the databank is updated and expanded; it currently comprises 3,000 entries and is expected to reach 4,000.

Fisheries

In the 1970s, the concepts of national sovereignty over marine resources off the shores of coastal countries began to emerge. FAO assumed a key role in helping member nations to develop priorities and build up capacities to assess, allocate, exploit, and manage fisheries resources through a comprehensive Programme of Assistance in the Development and Management of Fisheries in Exclusive Economic Zones.

To respond to the demands arising from this situation, FAO convened a World Conference on Fisheries and Development in 1984. The conference was the largest of its sort ever assembled, bringing together representatives of nearly 150 countries and over 60 international organizations to confront the fundamental problems and potential of world fisheries as a vital source of food, employment, and income. Principles and guidelines for fisheries management were endorsed by the conference to cover the contribution of fisheries to national economic, social, and nutritional goals; improved national self-reliance in fisheries management and development; national management and optimum use of fish resources; the special role and needs of small-scale fisheries; international trade in fish and fishery products; investment in fisheries; and international cooperation in fisheries management and development.

FAO's fisheries policy is based on the five programs of action endorsed by the conference: fisheries planning, management, and development; small-scale fisheries; aquaculture; international trade in fish and fishery products; and the use of fish in alleviating undernutrition.

To aid in fisheries management, FAO collects statistics, monitors fishing trends in the world fishing fleet, collects biological information on resources, and assists member countries in the areas of fishery analysis, research, and management.

A network of regional fishery bodies established under the auspices of FAO provides an important framework for coordinating fisheries development and management. The first of these regional fishery bodies, the Indo-Pacific Fisheries Commission (IPFC), was established in 1948. There now are nine bodies in all, covering almost 50 percent of the total area of the world's oceans and the inland waters of Asia, Africa, Latin America, and Europe. The FAO Review of the State of World Fishery Resources provides the only worldwide watch on fishery resources. Priority is given to helping developing countries map their Exclusive Economic Zones (EEZs) in order to better manage resources and coastlines and resolve disputes.

National fish inspection and quality assurance programs have been upgraded in several countries. This is an area of some urgency because of more stringent health and sanitary requirements imposed in recent years by major importing countries, such as the United States and Japan.

Because of over-fishing, global landings of all living marine resources have declined to about 82.5 million tons from the peak of 86.5 million tons reached in 1989. Many species, especially long-lived fish with high commercial value such as cod, haddock, snappers, and groupers, have registered downward trends. A progressively higher proportion of the global catch now comes from short-lived species, among them anchovies, sardines, and squids.

Only relatively recently has it been officially recognized that the world's oceans must be regulated and protected as natural resources, though FAO has for many years promoted activities to achieve this goal. Among its current endeavors to conserve and enhance marine resources, the organization is formulating an international Code of Conduct for Responsible Fishing. The code is intended to address unregulated fishing and associated activities, countering negative effects on marine ecosystems.

In November 1993, the 27th session of the FAO Conference took a first step toward the development of the code of conduct, adopting the "Agreement to Promote Compliance with International Measures by Fishing Vessels on the High Seas." The agreement demonstrates international consensus regarding the need to establish regulatory frameworks for fishing fleets that operate in areas beyond national jurisdiction. The Agreement for the Establishment of the Indian Ocean Tuna Fish Commission was also adopted by the FAO Council in November 1993. The commission will foster international cooperation among FAO members located in the region as well as those whose vessels fish in the area for tuna.

Small-scale fisherfolk supply much of the fish for consumption, though they remain the least privileged members of the world fishing community. An example of FAO assistance to small-scale fisheries is its Bay of Bengal Programme. Active since 1979 in Bangladesh, India, Indonesia, Malaysia, the Maldives, Sri Lanka, and Thailand, the Bay of Bengal Programme develops numerous educational, technical assistance, and training projects to improve the living standards of small-scale fishing communities. Particular emphasis is directed to bringing women into the development process as a vital means of improving community health, nutrition, and general well-being.

As capture fisheries reach their peak, aquaculture is helping to fill gaps in supply. FAO promotes aquaculture development in rural communities as a valuable source of animal protein as well as of income and export earnings. The organization is supporting the development of a system to report aquaculture data separately from catch statistics, while concentrating on fish nutrition and breeding strain selection.

Reliable market information is a key ingredient of successful trade development for fish and fish products. The Fish Marketing Information System set up by FAO establishes contacts between buyers and sellers, provides price and market information, and offers technical assistance and advice on post-harvest aspects of fisheries including handling, processing, equipment selection, and quality.

Forestry
The importance of forests has become increasingly recognized, especially for people in developing countries. One problem is that more than 250 million rural people throughout the world practice some form of shifting cultivation. They slash and burn trees against a backdrop of rapidly disappearing forests. FAO has a number of community forestry projects aimed at settling shifting cultivators or integrating their activities into rural development plans.

Another problem is that wood, which is the major source of energy in developing countries, is in chronically short supply and women and children often have to walk many miles a day to gather it. With inadequate, and expensive, fuel supplies, many people are unable to cook their food properly, and lack of fuelwood can lead directly to malnutrition and disease. As the people harvest whatever woodland is available, the trees disappear, to be replaced by rangelands or deserts. In Nepal, for example, the loss of soil-protecting trees used mainly for fuelwood and animal fodder has led to landslides in the foothills and the loss of lives, homes, and crops. The situation is being improved, however, through projects to restore and manage the watersheds and to bring the population together in community forestry development, including the establishment of plantations of quickly maturing trees to provide fodder and fuelwood.

FAO's Tropical Forests Action Programme is fundamental in contributing to the objectives set forth in UNCED's Agenda 21. The program is a major international undertaking uniting 90 partners in the battle to combat deforestation and to promote the conservation and sustainable development of tropical forests. Together, the partners are following an international strategy to integrate forestry into farming systems, develop waste forest

industries, increase supplies of fuelwood, and conserve tropical forest ecosystems while helping countries solve social and economic problems.

FAO's recently completed Forest Resources Assessment 1990 Project analyzed satellite images and existing survey data of 90 tropical countries to assess deforestation between 1981 and 1990. It found, among other things, that about 154 million hectares of forest, an area more than three times the size of France, were cut down during the decade. It also found that about 400 tree species are endangered in whole or part of their gene pools. FAO stresses the importance of people's participation in forestry management. The organization has carried out a wide variety of studies to develop participatory approaches and mechanisms for the management, production, and utilization of renewable natural resources—and of forests in particular—by rural people. FAO's Forests Trees and People Programme promotes self-reliance of rural groups in the sustainable management of forest resources.

Other forestry priorities include planning and policy formulation, national resources assessment, fire prevention and control, tree planting, conservation of genetic resources, plantation development, seed improvement, and development of harvesting and wood industries. Wildlife conservation and utilization also receive attention.

IMPROVING HANDLING AND DISTRIBUTION
Inadequate distribution of agricultural products causes waste of precious outputs and hinders agricultural development by reducing farmers' economic returns. FAO is involved at every stage in the distribution chain, from prevention of food losses in storage to attempts to bring about more equitable international trade. Programs deal with reduction of post-harvest losses, development of marketing skills, and promotion of trade terms that will help producers and exporters get a fair return.

Prevention of Post-Harvest Losses
In 1978, FAO began operations of its Action Program for the Prevention of Food Losses (PFL), designed primarily to reduce post-harvest losses of staple foods. The program focuses particular attention on women, major actors in the post-harvest system, through specific training activities and promotion of suitable technologies. Activities range from the development of adequate facilities for handling, drying, and storage to research on post-harvest practices that will protect harvests while reducing or avoiding the use of pesticides. For instance, FAO has successfully helped the Pacific Island nations develop control measures that will allow them to discontinue the use of ethylene dibromide, a pesticide banned by the major importers of fresh fruits and vegetables produced by the island countries.

Marketing
Poor marketing of local agricultural products often seriously impedes distribution and trade. Assistance is given to people involved in marketing from the grass-roots level to the senior management of marketing boards, as well as to officials responsible for marketing policy, legislation, and infrastructure. Direct assistance to marketing boards is aimed primarily at strengthening their management capacity and systems. FAO's field projects also support development of rural marketing centers and strengthening of the role of cooperatives.

FAO has recently developed the computerized version of *FAO Agri-Market*. This computer software program will help governments develop and perfect their price information systems, particularly during the transition from centrally planned to market-based economies. The organization also produces Marketing Extension Training Series videos focusing on techniques to be used by extension officers in providing marketing support to farmers.

Commodities and Trade

FAO's work on commodities and trade covers three main areas: commodity and trade policy, early warning, and food security.

In commodity policies and trade, FAO plays a lead role in the development of agricultural commodity projections. FAO's Intergovernmental Commodity Groups debate on developments in national policies, particularly those relating to protectionism, to analyze problems in commodity development and develop programs of work and projects.

FAO's Global Information and Early Warning System is housed in the Commodities and Trade Division (see Information for Agriculture). The preparation of information for the GIEWS entails continuous fielding of crop and food supply assessment missions to individual countries. GIEWS collects and analyzes a great variety of information from member nations, the private sector, and organizations active in the food, agriculture, and rural sectors, primarily in developing countries. When there are indications of unsatisfactory conditions, GIEWS intensifies its monitoring, most often involving on-the-spot missions to affected countries.

In the area of food security, FAO relies on national teams and workshops to derive and internalize realistic policy conclusions. The growing realization that food security is as much a question of household access to food as overall food availability has led to the development of composite indices of household food security in countries worldwide. These will serve as a tool to governments in addressing the needs of vulnerable groups. The Food Security Assistance Scheme (see Advice to Governments) supports member nations in the formulation of comprehensive national food security programs.

SUSTAINABLE AGRICULTURAL RESOURCES DEVELOPMENT

In November 1991, the FAO Conference launched the International Cooperative Framework for Sustainable Agriculture and Rural Development. The SARD framework, as it has come to be known, supports the integration of sustainability criteria in the programs and activities of the organization. Guidelines for achieving SARD were set down in the Den Bosch Declaration at a major international conference organized by FAO and the Netherlands in 1991. Preparations for the Den Bosch Conference also contributed to FAO's input to the UN Conference on Environment and Development in 1992.

FAO helps member countries plan and implement environmentally positive projects through sustainability assessment and review of policies and plans in the agriculture and related natural resources sectors. Assessment and preparation of investment projects by FAO's Investment Centre focus on sustainability criteria. At the same time, FAO is the "task master" for the "land cluster" of Agenda 21: water resources, forests, fragile mountain ecosystems, and sustainable agriculture and rural development. The organization also chairs two UN sub-committees to coordinate the implementation of Agenda 21 chapters on oceans and water resources.

To meet growing needs for food, FAO advocates equitable, participatory rural development as the key to eradication of poverty, the first and foremost cause of undernutrition. At the same time, FAO's approach includes fine-tuning programs and projects to the continuing challenges of balancing increased production with environmental and sustainability concerns.

Land and Water Management

Among the most basic of resources for agriculture, water and soil are quickly reaching their limits. As burgeoning populations demand more food, the realization of the finiteness of resources, and of the need to manage them carefully, becomes increasingly acute. The effects of soil and water degradation are especially severe in the developing countries, and in particular among the rural poor who have the most limited access to these vital resources. FAO has initiated many research projects to help farmers in developing nations make the most of the resources available to them.

FAO helps national and nongovernmental institutions and organizations study the effects of erosion on soil productivity, develop methods for soil reclamation, improve management of arid and semi-arid soils, disseminate appropriate tillage techniques, and monitor soil micro-organisms and bacteria as well as waterlogging and salinity. The organization also helps rural communities combat deforestation and concomitant soil degradation, developing knowledge and self-reliance that makes them more efficient managers of the resources under their custody.

On the information side, in addition to providing data on soil use for scientists, FAO's new digitized version of the Soil Map of the World (see Information for Agriculture) has been modified to make it accessible to nonspecialists. FAO contributes to technical seminars and general policy conferences on various aspects of soil and water management. For instance, the organization played a key role in the International Conference on Water and the Environment held in Dublin in 1992. The Dublin Statement emphasized water's economic value, and warned that this resource cannot be taken for granted.

In 1993, FAO completed two computer programs designed as tools for increasing the efficiency of water use in agriculture. AQUASTAT, as the first of these is called, is a global database on water use in rural development. Though irrigation is the major issue, AQUASTAT will provide information on such diverse aspects as drainage, environmental impact of water resources development, and water balance to users worldwide. The other computer-based system, SIMIS (Scheme Irrigation Management Information System), was developed to help reduce losses in irrigation systems. Many complex and shifting factors must be considered in irrigation schemes. Designed to be adaptable to diverse local situations in the developing world, the SIMIS system's 17 independent modules cover a range of irrigation management topics, from human resources administration, to information on climate, crops, soils, and machinery, to accounting codes. SIMIS can process information on one or several projects, making rapid and precise calculations to assess needs and possibilities while streamlining routine activities such as billing and registration.

Through the International Action Plan on Water and Sustainable Agricultural Development, FAO has launched programs in numerous member nations to help them manage water resources efficiently and meet the water needs of rural people.

A joint FAO/IAEA/SIDA research program uses neutron moisture meters to measure how water is used by crops and crop varieties. The study has shown that some varieties of cereals, for example, are up to three times more efficient in water use than others. The possibility of choosing water-efficient varieties will provide farmers in water-scarce areas with welcome relief.

Nutrient Management

After land and water, fertilizers are the most important input for increasing agricultural yield. Increased efficiency in fertilizer use can cut farmers' costs while helping to protect the environment, increase yields, and heighten consumer satisfaction. One of the Agenda 21 missions spearheaded by FAO is the achievement of increased food production through improvements in plant nutrition systems. In 1993, the organization renamed its Fertilizer Programme to reflect essential changes in approach. The new Plant Nutrition Programme focuses on the application of Integrated Plant Nutrition Systems (IPNS).

Under the new program, FAO promotes IPNS activities at the farm level for sustainable nutrient management based on a comprehensive vision of the cropping cycle. The objective is to help farmers establish the best association of biological (manure, crop residues), mineral, and naturally occurring (soil) nutrients to achieve a balanced supply while controlling losses and enhancing labor productivity.

Breeding research for improved plant nutrition concentrates on selecting and incorporating traits that will enhance a variety's nutrient uptake and utilization. In addition, the Plant Nutrition Programme helps governments develop sound policies and strategies at the national level, encouraging them to adapt or create institutions and organizations for the regulation of nutrient production, supply, and use.

Pest Control

FAO has numerous programs and projects aimed at reducing and rationalizing use of potentially harmful pesticides. The International Code of Conduct on the Distribution and Use of Pesticides (see Advice to Governments) identifies potential hazards and sets standards for those engaged in the regulation, distribution, and use of pesticides—governments, industry, traders, and users—to increase safety, efficacy, and economy.

FAO focuses its field work in plant protection on the application of the IPM strategy (see Crop Production and Protection) at the farm level, encouraging governments to support farmers who seek to improve production using these integrated methods. In Asia, over half a million rice growers have been able to minimize pesticide use and raise profits using techniques learned in IPM field schools. FAO has organized study tours to help plant protection specialists from countries in Africa, Latin America, and the Near East learn from the Asian experience.

PROMOTING RURAL DEVELOPMENT

Agrarian Reform and Rural Development

The World Conference on Agrarian Reform and Rural Development (WCARRD), sponsored by FAO in cooperation with other agencies of the UN system, was held at FAO headquarters in Rome in 1979. It was attended by more than 100 ministers and deputy ministers and some 1,400 other delegates from 145 countries. The conference approved a Declaration of Principles and a Program of Action to provide a framework for the reorientation of development policy and strategy toward greater participation and equity for rural people in the development process. FAO is the UN's lead agency for the implementation of the WCARRD program of action. Much of the work involves field projects to promote agrarian reform, land tenure improvement, and land settlement.

FAO helped to establish three regional centers to assist countries in the implementation of the program of action, and more generally, to coordinate activities in the area of integrated rural development at national level. The Centre on Integrated Rural Development for Asia and the Pacific (CIRDAP) is located in Dakha, Bangladesh; the Centre on Integrated Rural Development for Africa (CIRDAFRICA) is located in Arusha, Tanzania; and the Centre for Agrarian Reform and Rural Development for the Near East (CARDNE) is located in Amman, Jordan.

Activities related to rural development form an integral and permanent part of FAO's mainstream program. Every four years, the secretariat assists governments in the preparation of progress reports on implementation of the WCARRD program of action. FAO has organized intergovernmental consultations on WCARRD follow-up in Africa, Asia and the Pacific, and Latin America and the Caribbean. Interagency and Expert Consultations have been convened by FAO regional offices. Finally, at the request of member countries, FAO has fielded high-level WCARRD follow-up missions to assist governments in reviewing national rural development and agrarian reform strategies.

This support is especially crucial in the context of the transi-

tion from central planning and control to market orientation being undergone by numerous countries.

Aid to Small Farmers

Close to half of the world's population lives in the rural areas of the developing countries. The majority of these people can be considered poor, they have very small agricultural holdings from which to derive their existence. It is often difficult for small farmers to make their voices heard in the social, economic, and political power structures.

FAO has numerous programs devoted to helping small farmers, taking into consideration the smallholders' needs, motivations, capabilities, risks, and resources, and how these factors affect the production and marketing of produce or its use by the farm family. Governments are encouraged to consider the rural poor in their policies and planning, providing the necessary inputs at the right time, in reasonable quantities, and at acceptable prices. Emphasis is also placed on building collective strength among farmers for identifying and finding solutions to their problems and preparing production plans on the basis of their particular needs and priorities. Farmer self-help organizations are assisted in planning and managing their credit requirements, and improved access to credit is stressed.

The Role of Women

Women play a crucial role in agricultural development, yet they are perhaps the least integrated of the players in the development process. FAO recognizes the vital importance of the full integration of women, and has developed a Plan of Action for the Integration of Rural Women into the Development Process. The plan outlines four principal areas of activity, focusing on the civil status, economic, social, and decision-making spheres of rural women. The plan of action outlines activities in each of these spheres to remove existing barriers to women and foster their potential. FAO's approach involves implementation of projects directed exclusively at women, as well as support for the concerns of women in all FAO's projects and activities.

Nutrition

FAO plays a key role in helping countries improve nutrition, promote healthy diets, and ensure access to safe food. Prime areas of interest include food quality control; handling, processing, and storage; household food security; forestry, fisheries, crop production, and local foods; and nutrition monitoring, assessment, planning, education, and information.

In 1992, the organization cosponsored with WHO the International Conference on Nutrition (see Food Security). The conference adopted a Declaration and Plan of Action for Nutrition. The countries at the conference composed a World Declaration on Nutrition and pledged their adherence to a plan of action for the coming decades. The World Declaration reaffirmed that "poverty and lack of education, which are often the effects of underdevelopment, are the primary causes of hunger and undernutrition." It emphasized the need to identify the groups most in need, targeting nutritional resources first and foremost to alleviating their lot. It also stressed that food should not be used as a tool for political pressure. The importance of building knowledge among vulnerable groups through nutrition education was highlighted, as was the need for better preparedness for food emergencies resulting from civil strife and natural disasters.

The plan of action provides guidelines for governments, acting in partnership with NGOs, the private sector, local communities, families and households, and the international community. It contains recommendations on policies, programs, and activities identified through the intensive ICN consultative process and brings together a wide range of expert opinion from around the world. The 159 nations that participated in the ICN

Members of FAO
(as of November 1993)

Afghanistan	Fiji	Netherlands
Albania	Finland	New Zealand
Algeria	France	Nicaragua
Angola	Gabon	Niger
Antigua and Barbuda	Gambia	Nigeria
Argentina	Germany	Norway
Armenia	Ghana	Oman
Australia	Greece	Pakistan
Austria	Grenada	Panama
Bahamas	Guatemala	Papua New Guinea
Bahrain	Guinea	Paraguay
Bangladesh	Guinea-Bissau	Peru
Barbados	Guyana	Philippines
Belgium	Haiti	Poland
Belize	Honduras	Portugal
Benin	Hungary	Puerto Rico (Associate Member)
Bhutan	Iceland	Qatar
Bolivia	India	Romania
Bosnia and Herzegovina	Indonesia	Rwanda
Botswana	Iran, Islamic Republic of	St. Kitts and Nevis
Brazil	Iraq	St. Lucia
Bulgaria	Ireland	St. Vincent and the Grenadines
Burkina Faso	Israel	Samoa
Burundi	Italy	Sâo Tomé and Principe
Cambodia	Jamaica	Saudi Arabia
Cameroon	Japan	Senegal
Canada	Jordan	Seychelles
Cape Verde	Kenya	Sierra Leone
Central African Republic	Korea, Democratic People's Republic of	Slovakia
Chad	Korea, Republic of	Slovenia
Chile	Kuwait	Solomon Islands
China	Kyrgyz Republic	Somalia
Colombia	Laos	South Africa
Comoros	Latvia	Spain
Congo	Lebanon	Sri Lanka
Cook Islands	Lesotho	Sudan
Costa Rica	Liberia	Suriname
Côte d'Ivoire	Libyan Arab Jamahiriya	Swaziland
Croatia	Lithuania	Sweden
Cuba	Luxembourg	Switzerland
Cyprus	Madagascar	Syria
Czech Republic	Malawi	Tanzania
Denmark	Malaysia	Thailand
Djibouti	Maldives	The Former Yugoslav Republic of Macedonia
Dominica	Mali	Togo
Dominican Republic	Malta	Tonga
Ecuador	Mauritania	Trinidad and Tobago
Egypt	Mauritius	Tunisia
El Salvador	Mexico	Turkey
Equatorial Guinea	Mongolia	Uganda
Eritrea	Morocco	United Arab Emirates
Estonia	Mozambique	United Kingdom
Ethiopia	Myanmar	United States of America
European Economic Community (Member Organization)	Namibia	Uruguay
	Nepal	Vanuatu

committed themselves to developing national nutrition plans with attainable goals and measurable targets. In the continuing follow-up to the ICN, FAO is assisting many governments in preparing national plans of action for nutrition. To support the process, the document "Guidelines for Developing National Plans of Action for Nutrition" was distributed to member governments.

Many FAO nutrition projects work towards improving knowledge of nutrition within households, and particularly among women. Awareness of the need to improve the frequency and quality of meals is built up through participatory, pilot-family programs concentrating on nutrition education and home gardening. Households are encouraged either to grow the foods they need to fill their dietary gaps or to use income from home gardens to purchase vitamin-and-mineral-rich fruits and vegetables they cannot easily cultivate.

FAO has produced country nutrition profiles for 100 developing countries to provide a concise view of their food and nutrition status, agricultural production, and economic and demographic situation. Country profiles are used by governments and institutions for planning and training. FAO advocates incorporating nutritional information in early warning networks to supplement agricultural production data.

The Codex Alimentarius (see Advice to Governments) contributes to raising nutritional status by developing international standards, codes of practice, and other recommendations for food quality to protect consumer health and encourage fair trading practices in the food trade. To date some 210 international regulations and guidelines have been issued. As of 1993, 144 countries were members of the Codex Alimentarius Commission.

FAO's World Food Survey, published about once a decade, provides as complete a picture as possible of the world food and nutrition situation. It includes food balance sheets for almost all countries and, increasingly, household food-consumption surveys for developing countries.

BIBLIOGRAPHY

Animal Health Yearbook.
Ceres - The FAO Review. Bimonthly.
Commodity Review and Outlook. Annual.
FAO Annual Review.
FAO Bulletin of Statistics. Quarterly.
FAO Fertilizer Yearbook.
FAO Plant Protection Bulletin. Quarterly.
FAO Production Yearbook.
FAO Trade Yearbook.
Food and Agriculture Legislation. Annual.
Food Outlook. Monthly.
Rural Development. Annual.
The State of Food and Agriculture. Annual.
Unasylva: An International Journal of Forestry and Forest Products. Quarterly.
World Annual Review. Quarterly.
Yearbook of Fisheries Statistics.
Yearbook of Forest Products.

THE UNITED NATIONS EDUCATIONAL, SCIENTIFIC AND CULTURAL ORGANIZATION (UNESCO)

BACKGROUND: "Since wars begin in the minds of men," the preamble to the UNESCO constitution states, "it is in the minds of men that the defenses of peace must be constructed." As also stated in the preamble, "the great and terrible war which has now ended was a war made possible by the denial of the democratic principles of the dignity, equality and mutual respect of men and by the propagation, in their place, through ignorance and prejudice, of the doctrine of the inequality of men and races." World War II was too recent an event when UNESCO was created for its founders to forget that fact. UNESCO's purpose as a member of the UN family of organizations is "to contribute to peace and security by promoting collaboration among the nations through education, science and culture in order to further universal respect for justice, for the rule of law and for the human rights and fundamental freedoms which are affirmed for the peoples of the world, without distinction of race, sex, language or religion, by the Charter of the United Nations."

CREATION

Occasional attempts at international cooperation in educational, scientific, and cultural matters were made before World War I, but no machinery existed to promote these efforts on a worldwide scale. Even the League of Nations Covenant, when it was drawn up after the war, failed to mention international cooperation in these matters. However, thanks in great part to the efforts of the Belgian delegate Henri La Fontaine, a League of Nations Committee on Intellectual Cooperation was formed. Composed of 12 eminent persons, the committee met for the first time in the summer of 1922 under the chairmanship of the French philosopher Henri Bergson. Among those who served on the committee were Marie Curie, Gilbert Murray, and Albert Einstein. The intellectual atmosphere that prevailed in the committee was a lofty one, but at the same time the committee established precedents in practical matters that have proved useful to UNESCO. Thus, the 40-odd national committees on intellectual cooperation whose creation this committee promoted were a precedent for the national commissions now operating in over 173 countries to further the work of UNESCO. The International Institute of Intellectual Cooperation, established with the aid of the French government and located in Paris, began work early in 1926 and provided a permanent secretariat for the committee.

The League was thus provided with a technical body to promote international activity and was active in many fields, especially those of interest to scholars, professionals, learned societies, librarians, and the like. Numerous conferences and symposia were held under the auspices of the International Institute in Paris. Among the topics taken up by these conferences as the world situation became more menacing were the psychological causes of war and methods of promoting peaceful change as a substitute for war.

More intensive international cooperation in the field of educational problems began during World War II itself. A Conference of Allied Ministers of Education was convened in London in November 1942 to consider how the devastated educational systems of the countries under Nazi occupation could be restored after the war. The first meeting of the conference was attended by representatives of eight governments in exile and the French National Committee of Liberation. The conference met at frequent intervals throughout the war, with the participation of a growing number of representatives of other allied governments. The United States delegation to the April 1944 meeting of the conference included J. William Fulbright, then congressman and later senator from Arkansas, and the poet Archibald MacLeish, at that time Librarian of Congress, who was later to participate in the drafting of UNESCO's constitution.

It was decided at San Francisco that one of the objectives of the UN should be to promote international cultural and educational cooperation. Addressing the closing plenary session, President Truman declared: "We must set up an effective agency for constant and thorough interchange of thoughts and ideas, for there lies the road to a better and more tolerant understanding among nations and among peoples."

The conference creating UNESCO was convened by the United Kingdom and France in London in November 1945. It was decided that the new organization should deal not only with the transmission of existing knowledge but also with the pursuit of new knowledge. Hence, the encouragement of natural and social sciences through international cooperation was one of the principal tasks assigned UNESCO. UNESCO's constitution was adopted by the London conference after only two weeks of discussion and went into effect on 4 November 1946, when 20 states had deposited instruments of acceptance with the United Kingdom government.

PURPOSES

UNESCO's functions, as prescribed in its 1945 constitution, are as follows:

(a) to collaborate in the work of advancing the mutual knowledge and understanding of peoples through all means of mass communication;

(b) to give fresh impulse to popular education and to the spread of culture by collaborating with members, at their request, in the development of educational activities; by instituting collaboration among the nations to advance the ideal of equality of educational opportunities without regard to race, sex, or any distinctions, economic or social; and by suggesting educational methods best suited to prepare the children of the world for the responsibilities of freedom; and

(c) to maintain, increase, and diffuse knowledge by ensuring the conservation and protection of the world's heritage of books, works of art, and monuments of history and science; by encouraging cooperation among the nations in all branches of intellectual activity, including the international exchange of persons active in the fields of education, science, and culture and the exchange of publications, objects of artistic and scientific interest, and other materials of information; and by initiating methods of international cooperation calculated to give the people of all countries access to the printed and published materials produced by any of them."

Since UNESCO's constitution specifically emphasizes the need to preserve "the independence, integrity and fruitful diversity of the cultures and educational systems" of the member states, the organization cannot impose any particular standard either on all its members or on any of them, and it is "prohibited from intervening in matters . . . within their domestic jurisdiction."

MEMBERSHIP

Any UN member may join UNESCO. Other states may be admitted to UNESCO membership upon the recommendation of the organization's Executive Board and the approval of its General Conference by a two-thirds majority. Austria, Hungary, and Japan joined UNESCO years before entering the UN.

Under a United Kingdom-proposed amendment to the constitution adopted in 1951, territories or groups of territories not responsible for their international relations can be admitted as associate members upon application of member states or other authorities responsible for their international relations. Associate members do not have the right to vote.

A state may withdraw from UNESCO by notifying the organization's director-general of its intention to do so; the withdrawal takes effect as of the end of the respective calendar year. South Africa withdrew as of 31 December 1956. Czechoslovakia, Hungary, and Poland suspended their participation in UNESCO activities in 1952 but returned as active participants in 1954. Portugal withdrew in 1972 but returned in 1974. In November 1974, a vote dominated by Arab and Communist delegations excluded Israel from UNESCO's European regional group and withheld aid from it on the ground that it persists "in altering the historic features" of Jerusalem during excavations—an allegation not sustained by UNESCO's archaeological expert.

At the end of 1984, the United States withdrew from UNESCO, stating that "trends in the policy, ideological emphasis, budget, and management of UNESCO were detracting from the organization's effectiveness." One year later, the United Kingdom and Singapore withdrew. In February 1994, the *New York Times* reported that the United States State Department had recommended that the US rejoin UNESCO, which had cut its staff by nearly 1,800 people and changed its stand on the controversial New World Information and Communications Order (NWICO). However, the report stated that the State Department also recommended delaying a return to membership until 1996 or 1997, due to budgetary constraints. Until its departure, the United States had been responsible for 25 percent of UNESCO's budget. Upon rejoining, the United States' annual assessment would be approximately us$65 million.

As of February 1994, UNESCO had 182 members and 3 associate members.

STRUCTURE

UNESCO is an autonomous organization affiliated with the UN through a relationship agreement signed in 1946. Its three principal organs are the General Conference, the Executive Board, and the secretariat, headed by a director-general.

General Conference

All UNESCO members have the right to be represented in the General Conference, which determines UNESCO's policies and decides on its major undertakings. Each member state has one vote in the conference but may be represented by five delegates. The constitution of UNESCO requires that member governments are to consult with national educational, scientific, and cultural bodies before selecting these delegates; in countries where UNESCO commissions have been established, these too are to be consulted.

From 1946 through 1952, the General Conference met every year. Since then it has met generally every two years. As a rule, the conference takes place in Paris, but it has also met in Mexico City, Beirut, Florence, Montevideo, New Delhi, Nairobi, Belgrade, and Sofia.

Decisions of the General Conference are made by a simple majority vote, except for certain constitutionally specified matters that require a two-thirds majority, such as amending the UNESCO constitution or adopting an international convention. Member nations are not automatically bound by conventions adopted by the General Conference, but the UNESCO constitution requires them to submit such conventions to their appropriate national authority for ratification within one year. The same applies to recommendations, which the General Conference is empowered to adopt by simple majority vote.

Executive Board

Since the 1993 General Conference, the Executive Board, elected by the General Conference, consists of 51 member states. It supervises the execution of UNESCO's program. It meets at least twice a year. Before the General Conference convenes, the Executive Board reviews the budget estimates and work program for the following two-year period, as prepared by the director-general. It submits these with its recommendations to the General Conference and prepares the agenda for the conference.

Originally, the UNESCO constitution provided that "although the members of the Executive Board are representatives of their respective governments, they shall exercise the powers delegated to them by the General Conference on behalf of the Conference as a whole." Until 1993, the members of the board were not member states, but personalities designated by name. UNESCO's constitution only designated that the General Conference should "endeavor to include persons competent in the arts, the humanities, the sciences, education and the diffusion of ideas." In 1993, the General Conference changed this criteria. Since that time, the member states of the Executive Board are requested to appoint a person qualified in one or more of the fields of competence of UNESCO and with the necessary experience and capacity to fulfill the administrative and executive duties of the board. The General Conference, in electing member states to the Executive Board, must also take into account the diversity of cultures and balanced geographical distribution.

Following a constitutional amendment adopted by the General Conference in 1972, board members are elected for four years and are not immediately eligible for a second term. At each session, the General Conference elects members to succeed those whose terms end with that session. A system of electoral groups of member states, governing only elections to the Executive Board, was established in 1968.

Director-General and Secretariat

The secretariat carries out UNESCO's programs. It is headed by a director-general, nominated by the Executive Board and elected by the General Conference. The staff members are appointed by the director-general. Julian Huxley of the United Kingdom was UNESCO's first director-general. Federico Mayor Zaragoza of Spain was elected director-general in November 1987, succeeding Amadou-Mahtar M'Bow of Senegal, who had held the post since 1974. At the 1993 General Conference, Mr. Mayor Zaragoza was elected for a second six-year term.

Headquarters. UNESCO's first headquarters were in the Hotel Majestic, in Paris, a building which, ironically, had served as the headquarters for the German army during its occupation of France. In 1958, the organization's headquarters were transferred to a 3-hectare (7.5-acre) site, located at 7 place de Fontenoy, donated to UNESCO by the government of France.

UNESCO headquarters originally consisted of a conference building, a secretariat building, and a building for the permanent delegations assigned to UNESCO. In 1965, a new building constructed around underground patios was added, and in 1970 and 1977, two supplementary buildings. The buildings were designed and approved by several leading architects. Works by contemporary artists are an integral part of the headquarters.

Field Offices

UNESCO has been criticized by the United States since the 1980s for the concentration of its staff at its headquarters office in Paris, rather than in the field. A 1992 report by the United States State Department said that 73 percent of UNESCO's total staff of 2,697 persons were located in Paris. The same report also conceded that, despite this fact, 44 percent of the organization's regular and extra-budgetary resources were spent in the field. This disparity, however, may simply reflect the vastly different nature of UNESCO's mandate, as opposed to the mandate of technically-oriented specialized agencies. In any case, the fact remains that UNESCO maintains 42 field offices.

In Africa, UNESCO offices are located in Dar es Salaam, Ouagadougou, Yaoundé, Addis Ababa, Windhoek, Lagos, Kinshasa and Lusaka. UNESCO's Regional Office for Education in Africa is located in Dakar. The Regional Office for Science and Technology for Africa is located in Nairobi. The Subregional Office for Education in Southern Africa is located in Harare.

In the Arab world, UNESCO offices are located in Amman, Rabat and Tunis. The UNESCO Regional Office for Education in the Arab States is located in Beirut. The Regional Office for Science and Technology for the Arab States is located in Cairo. A Coordination Unit of the Educational Innovation Programme for Development in the Arab States is located in Kuwait.

In Asia and the Pacific, UNESCO offices are located in Kuala Lumpur, Beijing and Phnom Penh. The UNESCO Principal Regional Office for Asia and the Pacific is located in Bangkok. The Regional Office for Science and Technology for South and Central Asia is located in New Delhi. The Regional Office for Science and Technology for South-East Asia is located in Jakarta. The Regional Office for Book Development in Asia and the Pacific is located in Islamabad. The UNESCO Office for the Pacific States is located in Apia.

In Europe and North America, UNESCO maintains offices in Moscow and Quebec. The Regional Office for Science and Technology for Europe is located in Venice, including a special Liaison Bureau for Safeguarding Venice. The UNESCO European Centre for Higher Education is located in Bucharest.

In Latin America and the Caribbean, UNESCO maintains offices in Quito, San José, Port-of-Spain, Kingston, Cartagena, Brasilia, and Mexico City. The UNESCO Regional Office for Education in Latin America and the Caribbean is located in Santiago. The Regional Office for Science and Technology for Latin America and the Caribbean is located in Montevideo. The Regional Office for Culture for Latin America and the Caribbean is located in Havana. The Regional Centre for Higher Education in Latin America and the Caribbean is located in Caracas. The Caribbean network of Educational Innovation for Development is located in Bridgetown.

National Commissions for UNESCO

The UNESCO constitution requests every member state to associate "its principal bodies interested in educational, scientific, and cultural matters with the work of the Organization, preferably by the formation of a National Commission. . . ." By June 1994, 173 member states had established such broadly representative national commissions to collaborate with UNESCO in attaining its objectives. These commissions are not official UNESCO organs, but they provide a vital link between UNESCO and the public at large. They advise their governments and the delegations that attend the UNESCO General Conference on pertinent matters and serve as liaison agencies and information outlets.

The various national commissions vary greatly in size and composition. Often the country's minister of education is the commission's president, and its members may include high government officials, leaders in the fields of education, science, and the arts, and representatives of professional organizations. Through meetings, publications, broadcasts, contests, and exhibitions, the commissions stimulate public interest in specific UNESCO projects. National UNESCO commissions of several countries often meet for regional conferences. National commissions are frequently given contracts to translate UNESCO publications and to handle printing and distribution of these translations.

Cooperation with Nongovernmental Organizations

The constitution of UNESCO states that "a peace based exclusively upon the political and economic arrangements of governments would not be a peace which could secure the unanimous, lasting and sincere support of the peoples of the world" and that "peace must therefore be founded, if it is not to fail, upon the intellectual and moral solidarity of mankind."

In order to attain that objective, the founders of UNESCO sought ways of associating the peoples of the world as closely as possible in the preparation and implementation of the organization's aims and programs. Thus, from its inception, UNESCO has sought the collaboration of international nongovernmental organizations (NGOs). The NGOs with which UNESCO cooperates, now numbering over 587, have activities and interests paralleling those of the organization, ranging from specialized or scholarly organizations (of teachers, scientific researchers, philosophers, sociologists, journalists, writers, and legal experts) to mass organizations (trade unions, cooperatives, women's associations, and youth movements) and denominational organizations.

UNESCO consults and cooperates with NGOs so as to receive the broadest possible assistance from them in the preparation and implementation of its programs, thus strengthening international cooperation in the fields of education, science, and culture.

BUDGET

For the biennium 1994–95, the 1993 session of the General Conference voted a regular budget of us$455.5 million, of which us$95.5 million was for program services and operations in education, us$55.8 million for the natural sciences, us$42.8 million for culture, us$28.2 million for communication, information and informatics, us$23.3 million for the social and human sciences, and us$25 million for intersectoral and transverse programs.

UNESCO's budget is financed through contributions assessed against member states on a sliding scale. For the biennium 1994–95, these assessments ranged from a minimum of 0.01 percent of the total amount to 12.32 percent.

UNESCO receives funds from other specialized agencies of the UN system-mainly UNDP, UNFPA, UNEP and the World Bank-and regional banks for operational assistance to member states. For the 1994–95 biennium, it was estimated that these funds, when added to funds from other sources, would make a grand total of US$274.9 million in extrabudgetary resources devoted to operational projects.

ACTIVITIES

UNESCO's work is carried out principally in the fields of education, the natural sciences, the social and human sciences, culture, and communication.

At the 27th session of the General Conference (1993), a broad consensus emerged on the need to concentrate efforts on two of the objectives common to the United Nations system as a whole - the consolidation of peace and the promotion of sustainable human development. The General Conference also underlined the importance of UNESCO's role in promoting international intellectual cooperation, that is, acting as an international "think tank."

The Organization's Constitution outlines UNESCO's fundamental mission of promoting access to, and the transfer and sharing of knowledge. UNESCO's continued role of offering guidance, advice, and assessment when needed calls for strengthening activities in the following areas: anticipating and preparing innovative strategies, gathering and circulating reliable information on the present situation and probable trends in the Organization's fields of competence; and encouraging political leaders at the highest level to make firm commitments.

UNESCO's recent actions have been largely determined by commitments made at the major intergovernmental conferences it has recently convened-solely or jointly with other UN agencies-or in which it has participated, in particular the World Conference on Education For All, held in Jomtien, Thailand, in March 1990 and the United Nations Conference on Environment and Development (UNCED), held in Rio de Janeiro, Brazil, in June 1992.

The increasingly global nature and growing complexity of the problems in today's world call for a multidisciplinary or transdisciplinary approach in many of UNESCO's activities. A good example is the interdisciplinary project "Environment and population education and information for human development," conceived following the Rio Conference and aimed at the adoption of an integrated approach in order to achieve a development that is people-centered, equitable, and sustainable.

UNESCO's transdisciplinary Action Programme to Promote a Culture of Peace was created in 1993 to initiate activities in favor of the consolidation of peace following conflict. This involves reconstituting social infrastructures, fostering national reconciliation, reintegrating displaced persons, constructing a basis for a democratic citizenship, helping to create endogenous capabilities and ensuring the broadest possible involvement of the population in development efforts.

Since the fall of the Berlin Wall in 1989, UNESCO has been at the forefront of UN and international action in Central and Eastern Europe. The 26th Session of the General Conference (1991) called for UNESCO "to establish intersectoral coordination to support the introduction of democratic reforms" and "to establish close cooperation for carrying out this activity with international intergovernmental and non-governmental organizations, funds and other bodies" in support of Central and eastern Europe and in the newly independent states of the former Soviet Union. It was decided that the many existing activities in the region could be better focused if they were brought together under a single

program, and the Programme for Central and Eastern European Development (PROCEED) was created.

Finally, the Organization's action in recent years has been focused on satisfying the needs of three priority target groups–the least developed countries, the UNESCO member states of Africa, and women.

A. Education

UNESCO's largest sectoral activity, education, is the field for constant but changing endeavor. From originally helping to reconstruct educational systems in war-torn Europe and carrying out isolated, modest projects elsewhere, UNESCO has progressed to large-scale undertakings, such as literacy campaigns, rural development, science teaching, educational planning and administration, and teacher training.

In recent years, UNESCO's major education activities have focused on basic education, the renewal of educational systems and educational advancement and policy.

In activities following up the 1990 World Conference on Education-for-All, UNESCO has assisted member states in diagnosing basic learning needs, setting national education-for-all (EFA) objectives, and devising effective strategies to move towards EFA.

In cooperation with UNFPA, UNESCO organized the International Congress on Population Education and Development (Istanbul, April 1993) which adopted the Istanbul Declaration and Action Framework for Population Education on the Eve of the Twenty-first Century.

Emergency assistance programs and reconstruction operations in the field of education were carried out in such countries as Afghanistan, Albania, Angola, Bosnia and Herzegovina, Cambodia, Croatia, Iraq, Lebanon, Mozambique, Slovenia, and Somalia. Following the international meeting on "Peace, the day after," held in Granada, Spain in December 1993, activities aimed at the rebuilding of Palestinian educational and cultural institutions were initiated.

The Scheme of Humanitarian Assistance for Refugee Education (SHARE) responds specifically to the needs of refugee children. The program goes beyond the urgent but short-term goal of providing shelter, food, and medicines, to develop a coherent policy of refugee education in cooperation with local and national authorities. After initial experiences in Cambodia, Somalia, and Afghanistan, SHARE activities were also carried out in Slovenia and Croatia.

UNESCO also promotes studies and teaching in the fields of drugs, population, and the environment. In cooperation with WHO, the Organization has elaborated a joint prototype curriculum for AIDS education in schools and disseminated documents and guidelines to support AIDS education programs in member states.

The UNITWIN/UNESCO Chairs Programme, launched in 1991 to strengthen cooperation between universities through twinning arrangements and promote the development of inter-university networks in order to facilitate the exchange of knowledge and improve teacher training, involved, as of June 1994, 136 UNESCO Chairs and 21 Inter-University Networks, covering a wide range of disciplines and institutions from all regions of the world. Two additional networks are in the process of being set up, and 33 more are presently under consideration.

The World Education Report, a biennial first published in 1991, presents a broad but concise analysis of major trends and policy issues in education, including many tables, graphs, and a unique set of statistics—"World Education Indicators"—which give a country-by-country summary of key aspects of education in over 160 countries.

In January 1993, UNESCO set up the International Commission on Education for the Twenty-First Century, under the Chairmanship of Jacques Delors, President of the Commission of the

European Community, to study and reflect on the challenges facing education in the coming years, and to make recommendations that can serve as an agenda for renewal, innovation, and action for policy-makers. The Commission will focus its reflection on one central question—what kind of education is needed for what kind of society of tomorrow?—and will present its report at the end of 1995.

The Associated Schools Project (ASP), an international network set up to experiment with ways and means for enhancing the role of education in preparing young people to live in a world community, celebrated its 40th anniversary in 1993. Some 3,200 pre-school, primary, and secondary schools and teacher-training institutions in 121 countries are involved in the project.

Closely linked with the Associated Schools Project, often carrying out joint projects in crucial fields such as literacy work and the environment, are the 4,700 UNESCO Associations, centers and clubs, the first of which was founded in 1947. Found in 110 countries, with members from all age groups, they are set up in schools, universities, as associations or as permanent centers and, since 1981, are grouped together as part of the World Federation of UNESCO clubs, centers and associations.

In specific educational areas, UNESCO's work is supported by three separate institutes which conduct research and training programs. The International Bureau of Education (IBE), located in Geneva, serves as an international center for studies and publications on comparative education. The Institute for Educational Planning (IIEP), in Paris, organizes an annual nine-month training program for education planners and administrators, and offers training courses in the planning, financing and management of education. The Institute for Education (UIE), located in Hamburg, focuses on adult and non-formal education, within the framework of lifelong learning.

B. The Natural Sciences

UNESCO is the only organization within the UN system to have a mandate for the basic sciences. This mandate implies UNESCO's commitment to the promotion of multilateral, international, and regional cooperation for the training of specialists from developing countries in university science education and basic research in the four core areas of basic science, namely mathematics, physics, chemistry, and biology. Projects to be implemented in these and allied, interdisciplinary areas are selected for the impact they will have on strengthening national capacities, enabling access to current scientific information, human resources development, and their real or potential impact on sustainable development.

One of the main accomplishments of the Rio Conference on Environment and Development was Agenda 21, an international program of action for global sustainable development into the 21st century. Because of its broad mandate and long experience, UNESCO is implicated in many aspects of UNCED follow-up, with particular emphasis on Agenda 21 and the conventions on biological diversity and climate change.

In UNESCO's Natural Sciences sector, priority is therefore being given to implementing the recommendations of Agenda 21 by promoting multidisciplinary scientific programs which combine training, information and research and which are at the interface between environment and development. Special attention is also being accorded to the promotion of teaching (especially at the university level) and research in the basic sciences and engineering.

Environment and development problems have been a major focus of the Organization's work for the past 40 years. Beginning with the Arid Zone Programme in 1951, numerous UNESCO programs have been launched to address research, education, training, and policy needs related to specific environment and development issues, such as water resources management and the

conservation of biological diversity and ecological systems such as islands, tropical forests, and arid lands.

The activities of the Intergovernmental Oceanographic Commission (IOC), with 124 countries participating, primarily center around narrowing down the uncertainties about the role of the ocean in climate and global systems. In response to Agenda 21, the IOC adopted new strategies and action plans, especially in the field of oceanography.

IOC has developed global and regional ocean science programs related to living and non-living resources, and marine pollution research and monitoring, and enhanced the efficiency of the International Tsunami Warning System in the Pacific. It also organizes training and assistance and provides information, together with WMO, to coastal and island member states on events in the oceans and adjacent seas through a quarterly "Products Bulletin of the Integrated Global Ocean Services System," a precursor of the Global Ocean Observing System (GOOS).

The International Hydrological Decade, another intergovernmental program, was launched by UNESCO in 1965. In 1975 it became a long-term endeavor, the International Hydrological Programme (IHP). Now in its fourth phase (1990–95), the IHP is actively involved with some 150 countries in the development of scientific bases for the rational management of water resources. The objectives of IHP-IV have been divided into three sub-programs: Hydrological research in a changing environment; Management of water resources for sustainable development; and Education, training, the transfer of knowledge and public information.

UNESCO's first *World Science Report* was produced in 1993. It aims to provide an understanding of the present state of science around the world, including the ways in which scientific research is organized and how it works.

Under the "Diversitas" program, in cooperation with the International Union of Biological Sciences (IUBS) and the Special Committee on Pollution and the Environment (SCOPE) of the International Council of Scientific Unions (ICSU), UNESCO is promoting worldwide coordinated research on, and inventories and the monitoring of, biological diversity.

A Biotechnological Information Exchange System (BITES) has also been developed.

The Man and the Biosphere (MAB) Programme was launched in 1971 as an international program of applied research on the interactions between man and his environment. The program aims to provide the scientific knowledge and trained personnel to manage natural resources in a rational and sustained manner, giving priority to work in the field at the local level, within general frameworks for scientific cooperation at the international level. Based on a network of 110 MAB national committees, the program monitors the international biosphere reserve network, composed of 324 sites located in 82 countries, and has developed a number of problem-oriented research programs involving specialists from developing countries.

The International Geological Correlation Programme is a joint environmental activity between UNESCO and the International Union of Geological Sciences (IUGS), whose objectives are increasing knowledge of geological processes through correlation studies of many locations around the world, developing more effective ways of finding and assessing energy and mineral resources, and improving research methods and techniques. The transfer of traditional and new technologies, such as computerized information handling (GIS, DAS and PANGIS) and remote sensing analysis (e.g. GARS) to developing countries is privileged.

C. The Social and Human Sciences

UNESCO encourages the development of the social and human sciences at the international and regional levels by promoting training and research activities, as well as international exchanges.

In the fields of peace, human rights, and democracy, UNESCO's activities are aimed at the promotion and protection of human rights, consolidation of peace and democracy, as well as at the prevention and elimination of all forms of discrimination by means of research and education, dissemination of information and publications, and organization of meetings in cooperation with governments, intergovernmental and non-governmental organizations. UNESCO's activities in this field have led to the elaboration of important international instruments.

The emergence of multicultural and multiethnic societies, urbanization, and globalization are the transformation processes at the heart of the Management of Social Transformations Programme (MOST), established by the 1993 General Conference to foster policy-relevant, interdisciplinary and comparative social science research in three fields—the management of multiethnic societies, cities as arenas of accelerated social transformations, and coping locally and regionally with transnational phenomena.

The International Bioethics Committee, composed of specialists in biology, genetics, medicine, law, philosophy, and the social and human sciences, was set up to meet the ethical concern arising from progress in life sciences.

Within the framework of a UNESCO/UNFPA project, research is being conducted on socio-cultural factors affecting demographic change. This research will also serve as relevant input to the International Conference on Population and Development (Cairo, September 1994).

UNESCO's has an extensive program on the improvement of women's condition, stressing the principle of equality between men and women and against all forms of discrimination. This program will provide inputs for the preparation of the Fourth UN World Conference on Women: Action for Equality, Development and Peace (Beijing, September 1995).

The Organization's youth program deals with the analysis of problems and dissemination of information concerning youth, enrollment of young people in the service of international cooperation, development and peace, and action on behalf of disadvantaged young people, and has set up the International Youth Clearing House and Information Service (INFOYOUTH), an interactive, decentralized network for exchanges and contacts with some 400 partners.

D. Culture

UNESCO's main cultural activities are devoted to safeguarding of the cultural heritage, preserving and fostering respect for cultural identities and diversity, and promoting creative and intellectual expression. Almost two thousand projects have been launched worldwide in the context of the World Decade for Cultural Development (1988–97), including projects on the "Maya World," "Espaces du Baroque," "Slave Route" and "Iron Road." "The Silk Roads: Routes of Dialogue" project continues to assess the findings of four expeditions carried out in previous years and a joint UNESCO/World Tourism Organization project for cultural tourism on the Silk Roads in Central Asia was launched in 1993.

Safeguarding of Cultural Heritage

Under the terms of its constitution, UNESCO was entrusted with the task of "ensuring the preservation and protection of the world heritage of works of art and monuments of historic or scientific interest."

Training activities aimed at strengthening the application of the 1954 Hague Convention for the Protection of Cultural Property in the Event of Armed Conflict and the 1970 Convention on the Means of Prohibiting and Preventing the Illicit Import, Export and Transfer of Ownership of Cultural Property continue to be an important part of UNESCO's activities in this field.

UNESCO's activities in safeguarding the world's cultural heritage are best known through its campaigns to mobilize international support. The first such campaign was devoted to safeguarding the monuments of Nubia, in Egypt, and led to the successful reconstruction of the Temple of Abu Simbel, a US$40 million undertaking. Another project, successfully brought to a conclusion in 1983, was the restoration of Borobudur in Indonesia. A second Egyptian campaign was devoted to the creation of museums in Aswan and Cairo. Today, 27 such international campaigns are underway.

The growing determination of member states to preserve their national cultural heritage has led to an increase in museum development and in activities to preserve historical monuments and sites, works of art, and other cultural property. UNESCO's contribution in this field has consisted mainly in the provision of consultant services, equipment, supplies, and financial assistance to individual projects throughout the world. Improving the training of specialists in the conservation, preservation, and presentation of cultural heritage has involved the provision of lecturers and fellowships for international, regional, and subregional training projects.

UNESCO's activities have also resulted in the adoption of a number of conventions and recommendations, such as the International Convention Concerning the Protection of the World Cultural and National Heritage—called the World Heritage Convention—adopted by the General Conference in 1972. The convention provides, for the first time, a permanent legal, administrative, and financial framework for international cooperation. It also relates sectors that had previously been considered very different—the protection of cultural heritage and that of natural heritage--and introduces the concept of "world heritage," transcending political and geographical boundaries. The convention aims to foster a greater awareness among all peoples of the irreplaceable value of world heritage and the perils to which it is exposed. It is intended to complement, assist, and stimulate national endeavors without either competing with or replacing them. By April 1994, the convention had been ratified or accepted by 138 member states. The World Heritage Committee has thus far included 411 properties on the World Heritage List and has regularly approved financial support for technical cooperation through the World Heritage Fund.

Under its research, study, and information exchange activities, UNESCO has contributed to the advancement and spread of specialized knowledge concerning heritage preservation. It has issued a series of technical manuals on such subjects as museums, underwater archaeology, preserving and restoring monuments and historic buildings, the man-made landscape, conservation standards for works of art in transit and on exhibition, and conservation of stone. In response to the need for more elementary and accessible practical guidance, particularly in developing countries, a new series of technical handbooks was launched in 1975. The quarterly, *Museum*, published since 1948, is an international forum of information and reflection on museums of all kinds.

Study and Promotion of Cultures

An important part of UNESCO's activities in the field of culture focus on cultural identity, including the preparation of general histories and works on various geocultural areas. The eight volumes of the *General History of Africa* have now been published in English. Three of the ten volumes of the *General History of Latin America* will be published, in Spanish only, in 1995, and the first volume of the *General History of the Caribbean* will appear in 1994, while the first two volumes of the *General History of Central Asia* were published in 1993/94. Volume I of the *History of the Scientific and Cultural Development of Humanity* was published in 1994.

Dissemination of Cultures

The catalog of the UNESCO *Collection of Representative Works* listed more than 900 titles by 1994. Most are translations into widely spoken languages—English and French—of classics in more than 100 different languages from Europe, Asia, Africa, and Oceania, and from over 80 countries.

Cultural Development

The Universal Declaration of Human Rights asserts that everyone has the right to participate freely in the cultural life of society. This principle implies the right of people in different societies to share in the cultural heritage of the world community, and it implies that culture cannot be the privilege of an elite few but must be regarded as a dimension of human life. In this spirit, since the end of the 1960s, UNESCO has attached increased importance to cultural policies and activities related to cultural development. The principles governing UNESCO's activities in the field of culture stress the strengthening of the cultural dimension of development, that is, viewing culture not only in itself but also in relation to certain key areas of development, such as educational systems (including the cultural content of education and the adaptation of teaching models to local culture), the environment, science, and communication.

In 1970 the Intergovernmental Conference on Institutional, Administrative, and Financial Aspects of Cultural Policies, held in Venice, examined the role of public authorities in defining and achieving the objectives of cultural development and acknowledged for the first time the responsibility of governments to provide and plan for the cultural needs of society by implementing appropriate cultural policies. The Venice conference was followed by a series of regional conferences on cultural policies. Discussions at these meetings reflected a need to locate humanity and culture at the heart of the development process, rather than considering development as only economic progress.

The World Conference on Cultural Policies, held in Mexico City in 1982, took stock of the experience acquired in policies and practices in the field of culture and gave new impetus to the worldwide action carried out under UNESCO's auspices. The conference unanimously adopted the Mexico City Declaration on Cultural Policies, which proclaimed the guiding principles for promoting culture and strengthening the cultural dimension of development.

The World Commission on Culture and Development, under the Chairmanship of former UN Secretary-General Javier Pérez de Cuéllar was set up in December 1992 to focus on interrelations between culture and development in general and cultural policies and development models in particular. The Commission, composed of 12 members and five honorary members, will present its final report at the end of 1995 to the UN General Assembly and UNESCO's General Conference. The Commission's work is centered around five fundamental questions: the impact of cultural and socio-cultural factors on development; the impact of social and economic development on culture; the relationship between culture and models of development; the influence of cultural development on individual and collective well-being; and the role of cultural activities and artistic creativity in development and international cooperation.

E. Communication, Information, and Informatics

UNESCO is enjoined by its constitution to "collaborate in the work of advancing the mutual knowledge and understanding of peoples, through all means of mass communication." It is also authorized to recommend international agreements to facilitate "the free flow of ideas by word and image" and to encourage the international exchange of persons active in intellectual affairs and the exchange of "publications, objects of scientific interest, and other materials of information."

New World Information and Communication Order (NWICO)

In the 1970s, developing countries began to express their concern that the world's news media were predominantly Western-controlled. Major syndicated newspapers, press agencies like UPI, Reuters and Agence France Presse, the US networks, the BBC,

and the ORTF of France, were seen to be innately biased in their reporting on third world countries. It was felt that those organizations were able to greatly influence public opinion both in their own nations and in the developing countries themselves. The new nations of the UN system called for a New World Information and Communication Order (NWICO) which would allow them greater access to the sources of global information. At that time, UNESCO considered it a constitutional responsibility, and one especially pertinent to communication, to contribute to the removal of imbalances and inequalities in the capacity to produce, disseminate, and receive messages, and to eliminate the obstacles to a wider and better balanced flow of information.

In 1976, following a decision of the General Conference inviting UNESCO to undertake a review of all the problems of communication in contemporary society in the context of technological progress and recent developments in international relations, an international commission was appointed to study communication problems. The commission's recommendations were published by UNESCO in 1980 under the title *Many Voices, One World*. The General Conference considered the commission's report in 1980 and proposed 11 considerations on which a New World Information and Communication Order could be based. It also urged UNESCO "to contribute to the clarification, elaboration and application of the concept of a New World Information and Communication Order."

In 1978 the General Conference adopted the Declaration on Fundamental Principles Concerning the Contribution of the Mass Media to Strengthening Peace and International Understanding, to the Promotion of Human Rights and to Countering Racialism, Apartheid and Incitement to War. This declaration raised alarm in Western media organizations and governments. The declaration was interpreted as implying controls on press freedom. In later debates some Soviet countries proposed the licensing of journalists. However these proposals were never adopted, and no program of action based on them was ever put into action.

In the belief that high tariffs were an obstacle to the free flow of information, a UNESCO Working Group on Telecommunication Tariffs, established in 1979, recommended special tariffs under a Development Press Bulletin Service and a Conventional Press Bulletin Service to be applied to developing and developed countries, respectively.

The 1980 General Conference urged UNESCO "to contribute to the clarification, elaboration and application of the concept of a New World Information and Communication Order." However, the acrimonious public debate about NWICO had already damaged UNESCO's image in the West, and prompted the United States Congress to insert provisos in its 1982–83 appropriation for UNESCO stating that the funds would be withheld: "if that organization implements any policy or procedure the effect of which is to license journalists or their publications, to censor or otherwise restrict the free flow of information within or among countries, or to impose mandatory codes of journalistic practice or ethics."

Although the General Conference's espousal of NWICO was not cited in the United States' 1984 decision to withdraw from UNESCO (see "Membership"), concern over the "politicization" it represented was emblematic of the suspicion with which the Western countries (in particular the United States and the United Kingdom) regarded Soviet influence in the developing world. Now that developing nations greatly outnumbered industrialized nations, it was perceived that programs of action could be passed in UNESCO that were contrary to the interests of the West.

In 1989 the General Conference decided, by general agreement, to adopt a "New Strategy" in communication. The objective of this new strategy is "to render more operational the concern of the Organization to ensure a free flow of information at international as well as national levels, and its wider and better balanced dissemination, without any obstacle to the freedom of expression, and to strengthen communication capacities in the developing countries, so that they can participate more actively in the communication process." This last goal is implemented through UNESCO's International Program for the Development of Communication.

In February 1990, UNESCO organized an informal meeting of East-West media representatives to learn more about the needs of an independent press in Eastern Europe and how it could help to meet them. Since then, a number of regional seminars have been held to secure international support for strengthening press freedom and diversity.

The Windhoek Declaration

In April 1991, UNESCO and the United Nations convened a round table for media professionals in Windhoek, Namibia. Participants assessed the situation of the press in Africa and, on 3 May 1989, adopted the Windhoek Declaration, which declared that "independence, pluralism and diversity" were essential for the media in democracy. The United Nations declared May 3rd, the anniversary of the signing of the Windhoek Declaration, as International Press Freedom Day. UNESCO Director General Federico Mayor declared in a speech to the World Press Freedom Committee in 1992: "UNESCO is fully committed to the advance of press and media freedom. This means leaving codes of journalistic ethics and similar issues in the new and emerging democratic systems strictly within the purview of the press and media professionals themselves."

Communication technologies for development

UNESCO has been particularly concerned with the problem of disparities in communication existing between the developed and developing countries, which the great strides in communication technologies have only served to emphasize. In this field, UNESCO relies on three programs for the implementation of its activities: the International Programme for the Development of Communication (IPDC), the General Information Programme (known by its French acronym, PGI), and the Intergovernmental Informatics Programme (IIP).

One of the most important ways of improving information flow is by building up the resources of developing countries. The International Programme for the Development of Communication (IPDC), set up in 1980, aims to strengthen the resources of developing countries in terms of both personnel and equipment, to facilitate production and dissemination of news and other programming, thereby diminishing the imbalances that exists in the flow of information. In the 1994–95 biennium, the IPDC concentrated its support mainly on Africa's budding independent press.

The General Information Programme (PGI) was launched in 1976 to assist member states, particularly in the developing world, to increase their capacity to gather, organize, diffuse and utilize information. It combines professional and technical training, standard-setting and institution-building. It provides access to knowledge and technical know-how in the treatment of information and research, by training specialists and coordinating information systems in developing countries. It will also undertake a new project in 1994–95, the "Memory of the World," aimed at safeguarding library collections and archives.

UNESCO's Intergovernmental Informatics Programme (IIP) carries out regional and national activities in its priority areas of training, computer networking, software production, informatics research and development, and national informatics strategies. Among the projects recently approved by the IIP Bureau are the "Computer network for the countries of the Maghreb—MaghrebNet" and the "Strengthening of the Regional Informatics Network for Eastern Europe—RINEE." The IIP had some 40 new projects planned for the 1994–95 biennium.

In recent years, the Organization has reinforced its program in favor of independent and pluralist media, notably through the International Freedom of Expression Exchange Network (IFEX). UNESCO encourages movements towards the liberalization of media in Africa, Asia (including Central Asia), and Central and Eastern Europe, by assisting member states in restructuring their broadcasting systems, preparing appropriate legislation, and training media specialists.

Infrastructural projects supported by the United Nations, UNHCR and professional organizations for peace-building have been carried out in Cambodia, South Africa, and the former Yugoslavia.

Other activities in communications

Many of UNESCO's activities in the field of communications involve extensive data collection, analysis, and dissemination. The *World Communication Report*, a reference tool which focuses on trends in information and communication technologies and their impact on the work of media professionals and on society at large, was published in 1989, with an updated version due out in 1996.

An agreement with the International Telecommunication Union (ITU) came into effect in 1993 and a joint study on telecommunication tariffs in the field of education, science, and culture was completed.

UNESCO also prepared the booklet *Island Agenda,* which analyzes the problems facing small island states and the way in which UNESCO's expertise in education, science, culture, and communication can be used to catalyze sustainable development.

In preparation for the Fourth World Conference on Women to be held in Beijing in September 1995, UNESCO organized regional workshops on the theme of women in the media.

F. Agreement on the Importation of Educational, Scientific, and Cultural Materials

The states that are parties to the Agreement on the Importation of Educational, Scientific, and Cultural Materials and its protocol, adopted by the General Conference of UNESCO at Florence in 1950 and at Nairobi in 1976, respectively, exempt all the following materials from customs duties and any other importation charges: books, newspapers, and periodicals; various other categories of printed or duplicated matter; manuscripts, including typescripts; music; geographical, hydrographic, and astronomical maps and charts, irrespective of language and destination; works of art (paintings, drawings, and sculpture) and antiques, defined as articles more than 100 years old; visual and auditory materials, such as films, filmstrips, microfilms, sound recordings, glass slides, models, wall charts, and posters of an educational, scientific, or cultural character; and scientific instruments and apparatus, under the conditions that they be intended exclusively for educational purposes or pure scientific research, that they be consigned to public or private institutions approved by the importing country as entitled to exemption from customs duty, and that instruments or apparatus of equivalent scientific value not be manufactured in the importing country. Books and other publications for the blind and other materials of an educational, scientific, or cultural character for the use of the blind are also exempt.

Any individual living in a country where the agreement is in force may import duty-free books, works of art, or antiques from any other country where the agreement is in force, in accordance with the provisions of the agreement and protocol.

G. The UNESCO Coupon Program

UNESCO coupons are a type of international money order permitting persons living in countries with foreign-exchange restrictions to purchase from abroad books and many other articles of a scientific or cultural nature.

A person living in a country that participates in the UNESCO coupon plan who wishes to obtain from another participating country an item covered by the plan buys the required UNESCO

Members of UNESCO
(as of 10 February 1994)

Afghanistan
Albania
Algeria
Andorra
Angola
Antigua and Barbuda
Argentina
Armenia
Australia
Austria
Azerbaijan
Bahamas
Bahrain
Bangladesh
Barbados
Belarus
Belgium
Belize
Benin
Bhutan
Bolivia
Bosnia and Herzegovina
Botswana
Brazil
Bulgaria
Burkina Faso
Burundi
Cambodia
Cameroon
Canada
Cape Verde
Central African Republic
Chad
Chile
China
Colombia
Comoros
Congo
Cook Islands
Costa Rica
Côte d'Ivoire
Croatia
Cuba
Cyprus
Czech Republic
Denmark
Djibouti
Dominica

Dominican Republic
Ecuador
Egypt
El Salvador
Equatorial Guinea
Eritrea
Estonia
Ethiopia
Fiji
Finland
France
Gabon
Gambia
Georgia
Germany
Ghana
Greece
Grenada
Guatemala
Guinea
Guinea-Bissau
Guyana
Haiti
Honduras
Hungary
Iceland
India
Indonesia
Iran
Iraq
Ireland
Israel
Italy
Jamaica
Japan
Jordan
Kazakhstan
Kenya
Kiribati
Korea, Democratic People's
   Republic of
Korea, Republic of
Kuwait
Kyrgyzstan
Lao People's Democratic Republic
Latvia
Lebanon
Lesotho

Liberia
Libyan Arab Jamahiriya
Lithuania
Luxembourg
Madagascar
Malawi
Malaysia
Maldives
Mali
Malta
Mauritania
Mauritius
Mexico
Monaco
Mongolia
Morocco
Mozambique
Myanmar
Namibia
Nepal
Netherlands
New Zealand
Nicaragua
Niger
Nigeria
Niue
Norway
Oman
Pakistan
Panama
Papua New Guinea
Paraguay
Peru
Philippines
Poland
Portugal
Qatar
Republic of Moldova
Romania
Russian Federation
Rwanda
St. Christopher and Nevis
St. Lucia
St. Vincent and the Grenadines
Samoa
San Marino
Sâo Tomé and Principe
Saudi Arabia

Senegal
Seychelles
Sierra Leone
Slovakia
Slovenia
Solomon Islands
Somalia
Spain
Sri Lanka
Sudan
Suriname
Swaziland
Sweden
Switzerland
Syria
Tajikistan
Thailand
The Former Yugoslav
   Republic of Macedonia
Togo
Tonga
Trinidad and Tobago
Tunisia
Turkey
Turkmenistan
Tuvalu
Uganda
Ukraine
United Arab Emirates
United Republic of Tanzania
Uruguay
Uzbekistan
Vanuatu
Venezuela
Viet Nam
Yemen
Yugoslavia
Zaire
Zambia
Zimbabwe

ASSOCIATE MEMBERS
Aruba
British Virgin Islands
Netherlands Antilles

coupons, pays for them in local currency at the official UN rate, and mails them abroad without having to go through any formalities. To redeem the coupons, the seller sends them to Bankers Trust Company in New York (for the Americas), the Japan Society for the Promotion of Science in Tokyo (for Asia and the Far East), or to UNESCO's headquarters in Paris (for Europe and Africa). They are redeemed in the seller's national currency at the official UN exchange rate, after the deduction of a handling charge. In 1994, some 96 countries were participating in the UNESCO coupon plan. In the 1992–93 biennium, more than us$22,400,000 in coupons were distributed.

H. Encouragement of International Exchanges
As a means of promoting education, research, and international understanding, UNESCO aids and encourages various forms of exchange between its member states. It acts as a clearinghouse for governments, as well as international organizations, on all questions of exchange; administers its own program of fellowships and exchange of experts; and promotes study, training, and teaching abroad with the cooperation of governments and organiza-

tions. The principal publication issued by the exchange service is *Study Abroad,* a trilingual publication issued every two years, listing opportunities for subsidized higher education and training abroad through a wide variety of fellowships, scholarships, and educational exchange programs of some 3,000 awarding agencies in 128 different countries and territories.

I. Cooperative Action Program
UNESCO's Cooperative Action Program (Co-Action) enables individuals and groups to make direct contributions to community development projects such as schools, libraries, and vocational institutions for the disabled in developing countries. An illustrated catalog of selected Co-Action projects describing some of the priority needs and estimated costs is issued by UNESCO.

As of December 1993, contributions through the Co-Action program have totaled more than us$17,500,00, but its significance is more than a matter of money. Direct "people-to-people" relationships are established between donors and recipients that often develop into lasting friendships. In addition, the program has a special appeal for school groups.

THE WORLD HEALTH ORGANIZATION (WHO)

BACKGROUND: In taking the pulse of global health in 1974, WHO member states concluded that despite vaccines, antibiotic drugs, and a host of extraordinary advances in medical technology, the world was far from healthy. There was a "signal failure," the 27th World Health Assembly concluded, to provide basic services to two-thirds of the world's population, particularly to rural inhabitants and the urban poor, who, despite being the most needy and in the majority, were the most neglected. That assessment—made 24 years after WHO's establishment—led to a reorientation of WHO's outlook and to the adoption of the goal of "health for all by the year 2000" through the approach of primary health care. Although WHO's great achievement remained the eradication of smallpox, the HIV/AIDS pandemic and a virulent resurgence of preventable diseases like malaria and tuberculosis posed grave challenges to the goal of "health for all" as the year 2000 approached. The main task of WHO through the end of this century is to work to ensure that people everywhere have access to health services that will enable them to lead socially and economically productive lives.

CREATION

During the 19th century, waves of communicable diseases swept Europe, accompanying the growth of railways and steam navigation. Yet the first international sanitary conference, attended by 12 governments, was not held until 1851. An international convention on quarantine was drawn up, but it was ratified by only three states. Progress was slow.

The limited objectives of the nations participating in these early conferences also militated against the success of international health efforts. International public health did not come of age until the 20th century. The first international health bureau with its own secretariat was established by the republics of the Americas in 1902—the International Sanitary Bureau. The name was changed in 1923 to the Pan American Sanitary Bureau.

The idea of a permanent international agency to deal with health questions was seriously discussed for the first time at the 1874 conference, but it was not until 1903 that the establishment of such an agency was recommended. By that time, scientific discoveries concerning cholera, plague, and yellow fever had been generally accepted. The agency, known as the Office International d'Hygiène Publique (OIHP), was created in December 1907 by an agreement signed by 12 states (Belgium, Brazil, Egypt, France, Italy, the Netherlands, Portugal, Russia, Spain, Switzerland, the UK, and the US). The OIHP was located in Paris, and its first staff consisted of nine persons. Originally a predominantly European institution, the OIHP grew to include nearly 60 countries and colonies by 1914.

World War I left in its wake disastrous pandemics. The influenza wave of 1918–19 was estimated to have killed 15 to 20 million people, and in 1919, almost 250,000 cases of typhus were reported in Poland and more than 1.6 million in the USSR. Other disasters also made heavy demands on the OIHP, which found itself overburdened with work.

Early in 1920, a plan for a permanent international health organization was approved by the League of Nations. United official action to combat the typhus epidemic then raging in Poland was urged by the League's Council. The OIHP, however, was unable to participate in an interim combined League-OIHP committee. This was partly because the US, which was not a member of the League, wished to remain in the OIHP but could not if the

OIHP were absorbed into a League-connected agency. The OIHP existed for another generation, maintaining a formal relationship with the League of Nations.

The OIHP's main concern continued to be supervision and improvement of international quarantine measures. Smallpox and typhus were added to the quarantinable diseases by the International Sanitary Convention in 1926. Also adopted were measures requiring governments to notify the OIHP immediately of any outbreak of plague, cholera, or yellow fever or of the appearance of smallpox or typhus in epidemic form.

The League of Nations established a permanent epidemiological intelligence service to collect and disseminate data worldwide on the status of epidemic diseases of international significance. The Malaria Commission was founded and adopted a new international approach: to study and advise on control of the disease in regions where it existed rather than to work out the conventional precautions needed to prevent its spread from country to country. The annual reports of the League's Cancer Commission on such matters as results of radiotherapy in cancer of the uterus became an important source of international information on that disease. Other technical commissions included those on typhus, leprosy, and biological standardization.

Most of the work of the OIHP and the League's health units was cut short by World War II, although the *Weekly Epidemiological Record* continued. Fear of new postwar epidemics prompted the Allies to draw up plans for action. At its first meeting in 1943, the newly created United Nations Relief and Rehabilitation Administration (UNRRA) put health work among its "primary and fundamental responsibilities."

At its first meeting, in 1946, the UN Economic and Social Council decided to call an international conference to consider the establishment of a single health organization of the UN. The conference met in New York and on 22 July adopted a constitution for the World Health Organization, which would carry on the functions previously performed by the League and the OIHP.

WHO did not come into existence until 7 April 1948, when its constitution was ratified by the required 26 UN member states. In the meantime, UNRRA was dissolved, and a WHO Interim Commission carried out the most indispensable of UNRRA's health functions. The first WHO assembly convened in June 1948.

Among the severe problems that beset the Interim Commission was a cholera epidemic in Egypt in 1947. Three cases were reported on 22 September; by October, 33,000 cases were reported in widely separated areas on both sides of the Red Sea and the Suez Canal. Urgent calls for vaccine were sent out by the Interim Commission within hours after the first three cases were reported, and by means of a history-making cholera airlift, 20 million doses of vaccine were flown to Cairo from the US, the USSR, India, and elsewhere, one-third of them outright gifts. The cholera epidemic claimed 20,472 lives in Egypt by February 1948. During the epidemic the number of countries ratifying WHO's constitution increased by almost 50 percent.

PURPOSES

WHO's main functions can be summed up as follows: to act as a directing and coordinating authority on international health work, to ensure valid and productive technical cooperation, and to promote research.

The objective of WHO is the attainment by all peoples of the highest possible level of health. Health, as defined in the WHO Constitution, is a state of complete physical, mental, and social well-being and not merely the absence of disease or infirmity. In support of its main objective, the Organization has a wide range of functions, including the following:

- To act as the directing and coordinating authority on international health work;
- To promote technical cooperation;
- To assist Governments, upon request, in strengthening health services;
- To furnish appropriate technical assistance and, in emergencies, necessary aid, upon the request or acceptance of Governments;
- To stimulate and advance work on the prevention and control of epidemic, endemic, and other diseases;
- To promote, in cooperation with other specialized agencies where necessary, the improvement of nutrition, housing, sanitation, recreation, economic or working conditions, and other aspects of environmental hygiene;
- To promote and coordinate biomedical and health services research;
- To promote improved standards of teaching and training in the health, medical and related professions;
- To establish and stimulate the establishment of international standards for biological, pharmaceutical, and similar products, and to standardize diagnostic procedures;
- To foster activities in the field of mental health, especially those activities affecting the harmony of human relations.

WHO also proposes conventions, agreements, and regulations and makes recommendations about international nomenclature of diseases, causes of death, and public health practices. It develops, establishes, and promotes international standards concerning foods and biological, pharmaceutical, and similar substances.

MEMBERSHIP

UN members can join WHO by unilateral, formal notification to the UN secretary-general that they accept the WHO constitution. A non-UN member may be admitted if its application is approved by a simple majority vote of the World Health Assembly. Territories or groups of territories "not responsible for the conduct of their international relations" may be admitted as associate members upon application by the authority responsible for their international relations.

As of May 1994, WHO had 189 member states and 2 associate members.

STRUCTURE

The principal organs of WHO are the World Health Assembly, the Executive Board, and the secretariat, headed by a director general.

World Health Assembly

All WHO members are represented in the World Health Assembly. Each member has one vote but may send three delegates. According to the WHO constitution, the delegates are to be chosen for their technical competence and preferably should represent national health administrations. Delegations may include alternates and advisers. The assembly meets annually, usually in May, for approximately three weeks. Most assemblies have been held at WHO headquarters in Geneva. A president is elected by each assembly.

The World Health Assembly determines the policies of the organization and deals with budgetary, administrative, and similar questions. By a two-thirds vote, the assembly may adopt conventions or agreements. While these are not binding on member governments until accepted by them, WHO members have to "take action" leading to their acceptance within 18 months. Thus, each member government, even if its delegation voted against a convention in the assembly, must act. For example, it must submit the convention to its legislature for ratification. It must then notify WHO of the action taken. If the action is unsuccessful, it must notify WHO of the reasons for nonacceptance.

In addition, the assembly has quasi-legislative powers to adopt regulations on important technical matters specified in the WHO constitution. Once such a regulation is adopted by the assembly, it applies to all WHO member countries (including those whose delegates voted against it) except those whose governments specifically notify WHO that they reject the regulation or accept it only with certain reservations.

WHO is empowered to introduce uniform technical regulations on the following matters:

1. sanitary and quarantine requirements and other procedures designed to prevent international epidemics;
2. nomenclature with respect to disease, causes of death, and public health practices;
3. standards with respect to diagnostic procedures for international use;
4. standards with respect to safety, purity, and potency of biological, pharmaceutical, and similar products in international commerce; and
5. advertising and labeling of biological, pharmaceutical, and similar products in international commerce.

The assembly, at its first session in 1948, adopted World Health Regulation No. 1, *Nomenclature with Respect to Diseases and Causes of Death*. This regulation guides member countries in compiling statistics on disease and death and, by providing for a standardized nomenclature, facilitates their comparison. World Health Regulation No. 2 deals with quarantinable diseases.

Each year, the assembly doubles as a scientific conference on a specific topic of worldwide health interest, selected in advance. These technical discussions are held in addition to other business. They enable the delegates, who as a rule are top-ranking public health experts, to discuss common problems more thoroughly than formal committee debates would permit. Governments are asked to contribute special working papers and studies to these discussions and, if practicable, to send experts on the matters to be discussed with their delegations.

Executive Board

The World Health Assembly may elect any 31 member countries (the only rule being equitable geographical distribution) for three-year terms, and each of the countries elected designates one person "technically qualified in the field of health" to the WHO Executive Board. The countries are elected by rotation, one-third of the membership being replaced every year, and may succeed themselves. Board members serve as individuals and not as representatives of their governments.

The Executive Board meets twice a year, for sessions of a few days to several weeks, but it may convene a special meeting at any time. One of its important functions is to prepare the agenda of the World Health Assembly. The WHO constitution authorizes the board "to take emergency measures within the functions and financial resources of the Organization to deal with events requiring immediate action. In particular, it may authorize the director-general to take the necessary steps to combat epidemics and to participate in the organization of health relief to victims of a calamity."

In 1994, the Executive Board consisted of representatives from Afghanistan, Bolivia, Bulgaria, Cameroon, Canada, Costa Rica, Denmark, Greece, Israel, Jamaica, Japan, Maldives, Mexico, Mongolia, Morocco, Nepal, Philippines, Portugal, Qatar, Sierra Leone, Swaziland, Syrian Arab Republic, Togo, Tunisia, Turkey, Uganda, United Kingdom, United Republic of Tanzania, Uruguay, Viet Nam, and Zaire.

Director General and Secretariat

The secretariat comprises the technical and administrative personnel of the organization. It is headed by a director-general, appointed by the World Health Assembly. The first director general of WHO was Dr. Brock Chisholm of Canada. He was succeeded in 1953 by Dr. Marcolino G. Candau of Brazil and in 1973 by Dr. Halfdan T. Mahler of Denmark. Dr. Mahler served WHO for 15 years and was declared Director General Emiritus upon his retirement in 1988. Dr. Hiroshi Nakajima of Japan was elected Director General in 1988 and re-elected to a second five-year term in 1993.

In 1993, WHO had a total staff of about 4,448, of whom 1,587 were in the professional category and 2,861 were in the general services (support staff) category. Those figures excluded the Pan American Health Organization, which functions as its regional office for the Americas. Although WHO had set a target of hiring women in 30 percent of its professional openings, it reported that by 1992 the organization had hired women candidates for only 25 percent of those positions.

WHO has six regional offices, each covering a major geographic region of the world. These are located in Alexandria for the Eastern Mediterranean area, in Manila for the Western Pacific area, in New Delhi for the Southeast Asia area, in Copenhagen for Europe, in Brazzaville for the African area, and in Washington, D.C., where the directing council of the Pan American Health Organization acts as the regional committee of WHO in the Americas.

While all work of direct assistance to individual member governments is decentralized to the regional offices, the Geneva headquarters is where the work of the regions is coordinated and worldwide technical services are organized, including collection and dissemination of information. The headquarters cooperates with the UN, the other specialized agencies, and voluntary organizations and is responsible for medical research.

WHO assistance is given in response to a request from a government. Member governments meet annually in regional committees to review and plan WHO activities for their areas. Requests are consolidated by the regional directors and forwarded to the director-general, who incorporates regional programs and their estimated costs into the overall WHO draft program and budget. The program and budget, after review by the Executive Board, are submitted to the World Health Assembly.

BUDGET

For 1949, the first year of WHO's existence, its regular budget amounted to US$5 million. A regular working budget of US$872,496,000 was approved by the World Health Assembly for the 1994–95 biennium. WHO estimated that extrabudgetary contributions would bring the total budget for the biennium to US$1.8 billion. WHO reported that among programs supported were the following: Tropical disease control and research programs received US$200 million; malaria prevention and control received US$188 million; US$180 million was earmarked for the Global AIDS Programme; programs for environmental health in the developing world (combating, for example, the pollution problems that encourage water-borne diseases like cholera) received US$79 million; programs in human reproduction research received US$61 million; eradication of poliomyelitis received close to US$40 million; immunization programs received US$33.4 million; control of a resurgence of tuberculosis received US$20 million; WHO's programs to fight hunger and malnutrition received US$20 million. WHO's emergency and humanitarian relief operations also received additional funds, reflecting the increased demands by the world community on all UN organizations to respond to natural and man-made disasters in places like Mozambique, Somalia, the former Yugoslavia, and other Eastern European nations.

ACTIVITIES

Under the global "health for all" strategy, WHO and its member states have resolved to place special emphasis on the developing countries. Nevertheless, the benefits of WHO's international health work are reaped by all countries, including the most developed. For example, all nations have benefited from their contributions to the WHO programs that led to the global eradication of smallpox and to better and cheaper ways of controlling tuberculosis.

Prevention is a key word in WHO. The organization believes that immunization, which prevents the six major communicable diseases of childhood—diphtheria, measles, poliomyelitis, tetanus, tuberculosis, and whooping cough—should be available to all children who need it. WHO is leading a worldwide campaign to provide effective immunization for all children by the year 2000, in cooperation with UNICEF.

Provision of safe drinking water and adequate excreta disposal for all are the objectives of the International Drinking Water Supply and Sanitation Decade proclaimed by the UN General Assembly in 1980 and supported by WHO.

WHO is also active in international efforts to combat the diarrheal diseases, killers of infants and young children. The widespread introduction of oral rehydration salts, together with improved drinking water supply and sanitation, will, it is hoped, greatly reduce childhood mortality from diarrhea.

WHO's program for primary health care comprises eight essential elements:

1. education concerning prevalent health problems and the methods of preventing and controlling them;
2. promotion of food supply and proper nutrition;
3. maintenance of an adequate supply of safe water and basic sanitation;
4. provision of maternal and child health care, including family planning;
5. immunization against the major infectious diseases;
6. prevention and control of locally endemic diseases;
7. appropriate treatment of common diseases and injuries; and
8. provision of essential drugs. These eight elements were defined in the Declaration of Alma-Ata, which emerged from the International Conference on Primary Health Care, held in Alma-Ata, USSR, in 1978.

A. Disease Research, Control and Prevention

The Global Programme on AIDS (GPA)

The Acquired Immune Deficiency Syndrome (AIDS) pandemic is an international health problem of extraordinary scope and urgency. The GPA's mission is to mobilize an effective, equitable, and ethical response to the pandemic. It strives to raise awareness, stimulate solidarity, and unify worldwide action. The GPA works with countries to develop programs to prevent HIV transmission and reduce the suffering of people already affected. It provides technical and policy guidance to governments, other United Nations agencies, and non-governmental organizations. It also promotes and supports research to develop new technologies, interventions, and approaches to AIDS prevention and care. Since its inception in 1988, GPA has been assisted by other UN system organizations, including UNDP, the World Bank, UNICEF, UNFPA, and UNESCO. In 1994, the executive boards of these organizations approved a new joint and co-sponsored UN Programme on HIV/AIDS, to better coordinate fund raising and prevention efforts.

WHO estimated in 1994 that 16 million adults and one million children had been infected with the human immunodeficiency virus (HIV), which causes AIDS, since the epidemic came to public attention in the 1980s. In July 1994, WHO reported that the estimated number of full-blown AIDS cases worldwide increased from 2.5 million to 4 million in the preceding 12 months, an increase of 60 percent. Asia, however, reported an eight-fold increase in that same time period, from 30,000 cases in 1992 to 250,000 reported cases in 1993. By the end of the century, WHO estimated that 30 million to 40 million people will have been infected with the HIV virus. More than 90 percent of those infected will be in developing countries.

The disease is caused by a virus which destroys the body's innate capacity to withstand disease (the immune system). As the immune system is weakened, infected persons can no longer resist diseases which cause diarrhea, fatigue, severe weight loss, and skin lesions. Eventually, the AIDS-related illnesses cause death. Persons become infected with the HIV virus by contact with body fluids like semen (during sexual intercourse) or blood (if they receive contaminated blood during a transfusion). Intravenous drug users who share hypodermic needles have been shown to be at great risk for contracting HIV. Studies have proven, however, that HIV cannot be transmitted by air or simple touch. The insidious nature of the disease contributed to its silent explosion into the world population, since infected persons do not show signs of infection for as many as six to ten years.

AIDS was already an international epidemic (a "pandemic") by the time it was first recognized in 1981. In late 1983, WHO held the first international meeting on AIDS in Geneva. In February 1987, WHO established its Special Programme on AIDS in order to develop a global strategy for AIDS control, obtain financial resources, and begin implementation of the program. In 1988, the Executive Board renamed it the Global Programme on AIDS (GPA). The main objectives of the global strategy are:

- to prevent HIV infections;
- to reduce the personal and social impact of HIV infection; and
- to mobilize and unify national and international efforts against AIDS.

The global strategy was updated in 1992 to place increased emphasis on:

- health care for AIDS patients;
- treatment for sexually transmitted diseases;
- improving the status of women in developing countries in order to reduce the risk of infection;
- providing more frank information about AIDS;

- planning for the socio-economic impact of the pandemic;
- overcoming stigmatization and discrimination directed at persons infected with HIV/AIDS.

A World Summit of Ministers of Health on Programmes for AIDS Prevention was held in London in January 1988. The summit proclaimed 1 December as Worlds AIDS Day. In 1989 the World Health Assembly resolved to make World AIDS Day the annual focus for worldwide efforts against AIDS. That same year, WHO established a Global Commission on AIDS to provide the Director General with broad policy and scientific guidance from eminent experts representing a wide variety of disciplines. By the end of 1991, AIDS programs had been established in every WHO member country.

Tuberculosis

In April 1993, WHO declared a tuberculosis (TB) global emergency. WHO said that 35 years of neglect by governments, and a linkage to the HIV/AIDS pandemic, had led to a resurgence of the bacillus that causes tuberculosis. In New York City, the incidence of TB rose 150 percent between 1980 and 1993. The link between HIV/AIDS and tuberculosis, which were fueling each other, was so pronounced that by 1994 WHO called the phenomenon a co-epidemic. Between 1990 and the year 2000, WHO estimated that there would be a 35 percent increase in annual cases of tuberculosis, and a 38 percent increase in annual mortality due to tuberculosis. By the year 2000, WHO predicted that 10,222,000 people a year would contract tuberculosis and 3,509,000 of them would die—95 percent of those deaths would be in the developing world. To add to the danger, the bacillus that causes TB was becoming resistant to the very antibiotics that had held it in check for more than 30 years.

Tuberculosis is an age-old killer, traces of which have been found in the lungs of 3,000-year-old Egyptian mummies. It is caused by a bacillus that infects the lungs, forming knobby lesions called "tubercles." Up until the present century it was commonly called "consumption." Today the bacillus responsible for TB is called *Mycobacterium tuberculosis*. The first diagnostic test was discovered in 1905 and the first vaccine was created in France in 1921. The first antibiotic effective against TB, streptomycin, was discovered in 1944 in the United States. By 1960, chemotherapy for TB was so effective, sanitoria in mountain areas which had been used for more than a century to care for TB patients were closed. TB was presumed dead, at least in the industrialized world: public health measures for TB control were dismantled, and funding for research fell to a trickle. However, multidrug-resistant (MDR) strains began to flourish as patients being treated with antibiotics neglected to completely finish a course of treatment. In New York City, MDR strains accounted for only 7 percent of all TB strains in the early 1980s. By 1992, more than one-third of the strains tested were resistant to one drug, and almost one-fifth were resistant to the two main drugs.

WHO contends that the rise of tuberculosis in the industrialized world is linked not only to HIV/AIDS, but also to inadequate funding of international programs to combat tuberculosis in the developing world. The organization has insisted that it will be impossible to control TB in the industrialized countries unless it is sharply reduced in Africa, Asia, and Latin America.

The WHO Tuberculosis Programme aims to cut the annual death toll from TB from 3 million deaths in 1992 to 1.6 million within ten years. WHO predicts that about US$100 million needs to be spent each year to provide medicines, microscopes, and a modest infrastructure enabling poor countries to undertake successful tuberculosis programs. WHO reports that in the developing world, a complete cure could cost as little as US$13 per patient. However, the treatment of a patient with a multidrug-resistant strain of TB in New York City could cost US$180,000 per patient.

The Tropical Disease Research Programme

The UNDP/World Bank/WHO Special Programme for Research and Training in Tropical Diseases (TDR) was set up in 1975 to target malaria, schistosomiasis (bilharzia or "snail fever"), leishmaniasis, African trypanosomiasis (sleeping sickness), American trypanosomiasis (Chagas disease), lymphatic filariasis (which leads to elephantiasis), onchocerciasis (river blindness), and leprosy. Almost 500 million people, nearly all of them in developing countries, suffer from these diseases, which can cause terrible anguish, deformity, and death. At the same time, they cause considerable economic losses and frequently interfere with development projects (particularly water projects such as dams and irrigation schemes, and planned and unplanned forestry).

The death toll from the diseases—particularly among children from malaria in Africa—is expected to double by 2010, possibly reaching four million lives a year, unless radical solutions are found. Population increase, the spread of parasite resistance, mass migrations, environmental disturbance, and disruption of control programs through economic devastation, civil unrest, and wars, all contribute to the tropical disease problem.

TDR has a mandate to:

1. Develop new methods of preventing, diagnosing, and treating tropical diseases, methods that would be applicable, acceptable, and affordable by developing countries, require minimal skills or supervision, and be readily integrated into the health services of these countries.
2. Strengthen—through training in biomedical and social sciences and through support to institutions—the capability of developing countries to undertake the research required to develop and apply these new methods.

In this work, TDR collaborates closely with WHO's Division of Control of Tropical Diseases (CTD), and with many other WHO programs and outside bodies concerned with tropical disease research and control.

TDR acts to some extent like a research council, supporting investigator-initiated projects selected by peer-review, and to some extent as a pro-active agency commissioning the research required to reach its objectives. Its budget for 1994–95 is US$66.7 million, some 70 percent of which will be spent directly on project support. A quarter of TDR's funds goes to research capability strengthening (RCS) in developing countries. This RCS work is being increasingly combined with the performance of needed research: "training by doing."

Over the eighteen years of TDR's existence, a large number of drugs, diagnostic techniques, vector control agents, and other products have been developed, and in conjunction with national and international control programs there has been considerable success in applying these to reduce (or potentially reduce) the burden of some of the tropical diseases—notably leprosy, onchocerciasis, and Chagas disease. The other diseases still pose major problems, either globally or regionally.

TDR's research targets, and the appropriate management and decision-making structure to reach those targets have been thoroughly reviewed during 1992–93. A new structure, which will give the program greater focus on priority targets and more flexibility to identify and respond to the practical health and control needs of populations, will operate from 1 January 1994.

In the new structure, TDR's research is to be divided into three basic functional areas: "strategic" research, "applied field research," and "product research and development."

Strategic research. TDR defines "strategic research" (SR) as basic research, usually on the diseases, the parasites that cause them, or the vectors that carry them, aimed at a specified long-term goal in tropical disease control—such as the genetic engineering of the mosquito to make it unable to carry malaria. The amount of strategic research supported by TDR is decreasing, but not vanishing; important opportunities must always be grasped, subject to the availability of funds.

Applied field research. The research, development, and even introduction of a new tool does not automatically lead to improved control. Experience has shown that the ultimate success of TDR's efforts to control tropical diseases depends on social and economic factors in the endemic communities and on control programs' awareness of people's needs, perceptions, and wishes. Thus there is an urgent need for applied field research to develop cost-effective and sustainable control strategies which are based on a thorough understanding of social and economic factors, on the needs of the people in the endemic communities as identified by them, and on the availability and use of health facilities. Thus TDR's applied field research (AFR) will be a crucial area in the new Programme structure. AFR will address a multitude of practical community-level and health-system control questions which will help apply effectively the products of earlier research and will provide new appropriate directions for research. Around a dozen AFR Task Forces are being established in areas including operations research in Chagas disease and onchocerciasis, women and tropical disease, the use of bed nets, an integrated approach to the sick child of tropical diseases, and health financing.

Product research and development. TDR's product research and development (PRD) covers the process of transforming scientific knowledge into usable disease control products, through Phase I-IV field trials, registration, and the negotiation of production at an affordable price. The Product Development Unit focuses most resources on a short list of a few such projects, such as artemisinin derivatives, tumor necrosis factor antagonists, transmission-blocking vaccines for malaria, and the codelivery of praziquantel and albendazole for helminth infections.

TDR's particular strength is that, as part of the United Nations system, it enjoys a world view of the tropical disease scene and the standing conferred by a lack of partisan or profit-making motivation. These assets explain in large measure TDR's rapid success in creating an international network of over 5000 scientists, which gives it access to a broad range of expertise and scientific disciplines.

Through its WHO connection, TDR has ready access to programs and units working in related fields and—most importantly, with its new focus on the field and on national control programs—to WHO's 185 Member States. TDR can call on government support in endemic regions in order to engage populations and facilities in multi-center field trials rapidly and at very low cost.

Leprosy

Leprosy is a serious public health problem in the developing countries, particularly because the populations exposed to the risk of contracting the disease are very large (about 1.4 billion), and more than one-third of leprosy patients face the threat of permanent and progressive physical and social disability. In 1994, WHO estimated that there were 2.4 million existing cases of leprosy in the world. Five countries accounted for 81 percent of those cases: Brazil, India, Indonesia, Myanmar, and Nigeria. Each year, 650,000 new cases were being detected.

In 1991, WHO's member states pledged their commitment to eliminating leprosy as a public health problem by the year 2000. This would involve reducing the proportion of leprosy patients in a given community to less than one case per 10,000 population. This had become possible because of the development of powerful antileprosy drugs—rifampicin and clofazimine. By using multidrug therapy (MDT), it became possible to eliminate the bacterium. The number of registered cases reached a high of 5.4 million in 1985, and fell to 1.76 million in 1993, largely as a result of MDT treatment. In the eight years between 1985 and 1993, 4.3 million patients were cured through multidrug therapy.

Malaria

In 1993, WHO estimated that there were 300 to 500 million cases of malaria in the world, causing 1.5 to 3 million deaths annually. The majority of deaths were occurring in tropical Africa, but serious malaria problems were reported in Afghanistan, Brazil, India, Sri Lanka, Thailand, and Viet Nam. The rise of drug-resistant parasites, especially in Africa, posed a major problem.

By 1993, multidrug resistance had led to a rise in the drug cost per case from about US$0.15 to US$2.00 in countries of South-East Asia and the Amazon region of Brazil. WHO predicts a similar development in Africa, which may put drugs beyond the means of populations at greatest risk. In 1993, WHO began testing insecticide-impregnated materials for bed nets and curtains in an attempt to control the parasites that carry the disease. Benin, Burundi, Cameroon, Côte d'Ivoire, and other countries had incorporated them into their national malaria control programs.

In 1992, WHO convened a Ministerial Conference on Malaria in Amsterdam which was attended by health leaders from 102 countries and representatives of United Nations bodies and nongovernmental organizations. The conference endorsed a global malaria control strategy. WHO plans to implement control programs in 90 percent of the countries affected by the disease no later than 1997. The target is to reduce mortality by at least 20 percent between 1995 and the year 2000.

WHO has published many books in support of its fight against malaria, including: *A Global Strategy for Malaria Control, Basic Malaria Microscopy, Parasitic Diseases in Water Resources Development,* and books in many languages on the diagnosis and treatment of malaria.

In 1992–93 , WHO provided technical support to 31 countries for the strengthening of their malaria control programs. In September 1993, WHO convened a meeting of donor countries, international agencies, and intergovernmental and nongovernmental organizations to analyze the resource needs for malaria control at the national and international level. US$3.5 million was pledged by donor countries to help finance WHO's efforts to combat malaria in 1993–94.

Smallpox

The eradication of smallpox is among the finest achievements of WHO, which coordinated the international effort to combat this disease. It is the first time in history that a human malady has ever been totally eliminated. This became feasible because the virus causing the disease was transmitted only by direct human contagion; there were no animal reservoirs or human "carriers." Victims of the disease were immune to further attacks, while successful vaccination at three-year intervals gave essentially complete protection.

Eradication was based on a twofold strategy of surveillance-containment and vaccination. Rapid detection of cases, their immediate isolation, and the vaccination of anyone with whom the patient could have come in contact during the infective period, lasting about three weeks after the onset of rash, prevented further transmission. Implementation of these procedures, coupled with the basic immunity level attributable to routine immunization, resulted in the eradication of smallpox everywhere in the world.

Although a global program of eradication was initiated in 1959, it was not until 1967, when a special WHO budget with increased bilateral and multilateral support was prepared, that a definitive target date of 10 years was set for global eradication. By the end of 1977, this goal was achieved.

In 1967, 131,776 cases of smallpox were reported from 43 countries, 31 of which were classified as smallpox-endemic; however, the actual number of cases was estimated to have been between 10 million and 15 million, among whom possibly 1.5 to 2 million died. Since that time, WHO has convened many international commissions which certified smallpox eradication in 79 recently endemic countries. The global eradication of the disease was declared by the World Health Assembly in 1980. By 1985, all WHO member states had discontinued routine smallpox vaccination, and no country required smallpox vaccination certificates from international travelers.

By 1993, the complete nucleotide sequence of the genomes of several strains of the virus had been determined, fulfilling the requirements set in 1990 for the final destruction of the remaining stock of variola virus. On 9 September 1994, an expert committee agreed that the destruction of the remaining clinical specimens of variola virus should take place on 30 June 1995, after confirmation by the May 1995 meeting of the World Health Assembly. The committee also recommended that 500,000 doses of smallpox vaccine be kept by WHO in case of an emergency and that the vaccine seed virus be maintained in the WHO Collaborating Centre on Smallpox Vaccine in Bilthoven, Netherlands.

Cholera

In 1961, cholera caused by *Vibrio cholerae 01 El Tor* began to spread from its endemic locations and gradually invaded practically all countries in the Western Pacific and Southeast Asia regions, most of which had been free from cholera for many years. Cholera continued to spread westward, reaching Pakistan, Afghanistan, Iran, and Uzbekistan (USSR) in 1965 and Iraq in 1966. In 1969 and 1970, it created great problems in the Middle East, North and West Africa, and Europe and has since spread to most countries of Africa, becoming endemic in many of them. Its spread has been facilitated by the fact that most of the persons who come in contact with *El Tor vibrio* become mild cases or carriers of the disease. Between 1984 and 1990, reported cases of cholera had increased from 28,893 to 70,084, a 142 percent increase. By 1991, cholera had completed its spread around the globe and appeared in Latin America for the first time in this century. Extensive epidemics also recurred in Africa. In 1991, reports received by WHO indicated that 594,694 people contracted cholera, and of that number, 19,295 people died, more than in the previous five years combined.

Numerous field and laboratory studies showed that the control measures were not sufficiently effective. The anticholera vaccines in use, when tested in controlled field trials, were shown to protect at most about half the persons vaccinated and for less than six months. Some vaccines provided no protection at all.

In view of these findings, WHO has intensified its research activities in improving treatment and vaccines; it is also trying to reinforce the ability of governments to face the problem of cholera within the framework of control programs directed against diarrheal diseases in general.

A simple and inexpensive oral-rehydration treatment, proven effective in the 1970s for all acute diarrhea, has made cholera treatment substantially easier. As most of the cases of *El Tor vibrio* cholera cannot be differentiated from other diarrheal diseases on clinical grounds, WHO has developed a comprehensive and expanded program for the control of all diarrheal diseases, including cholera.

In April 1991, WHO created a Global Task Force on Cholera to strengthen global control efforts and improve preparedness. A new strain *Vibrio cholerae O139* emerged in the period 1992–93, causing new epidemics and largely replacing *El Tor vibrio*.

Other communicable diseases

WHO continues to monitor and sponsor research on influenza, viral hepatitis, arthropod-borne viruses, yellow fever, Japanese encephalitis, bubonic plague, meningitis, Legionellosis, and streptococcal infections.

Diseases Transmissible Between Animals and Man (Zoonoses) and Related Problems

Since its inception, WHO has been developing veterinary public health programs in cooperation with its member states. In the

1970s, WHO's veterinary public health program was reoriented toward more direct collaboration with member states in the development of national and intercountry programs in which zoonoses and food-borne disease control receive the highest priority. This action was justified because these diseases have become increasingly prevalent in many countries mainly as a result of the following factors: the greatly expanded international and national trade in live animals, animal products, and animal feedstuffs, which facilitates the spread of infection; the growth of urbanization, coupled with the increased numbers of domestic and half-wild animals living in close association with city populations, which exposes more people to zoonoses; and changing patterns of land use, such as irrigation, together with new systems of animal farming, which may lead to changes in the ecology that disseminate and increase animal reservoirs of zoonoses.

The 1978 World Health Assembly adopted a resolution on "prevention and control of zoonoses and food-borne diseases due to animal products" in which member states were invited to formulate and implement appropriate country-wide programs for the control of zoonoses; to strengthen cooperation between national veterinary and public health services in improving the surveillance, prevention, and control of these diseases; and to collaborate further in ensuring the appropriate development of zoonoses centers. The resolution also requested the director-general of WHO to continue development of national, regional, and global strategies and of methods for the surveillance, prevention, and control of zoonoses, and to promote the extension of the network of zoonoses centers in all regions so that the necessary support could be provided to country health programs dealing with these diseases.

WHO cooperates with member states in planning, implementing, and evaluating their national zoonoses and food-borne disease control programs. WHO centers, such as those in Athens (Mediterranean Zoonoses Control Center) and Buenos Aires (Pan American Zoonoses Control Center), play an increasing role in direct collaboration with countries and in organizing intercountry technical cooperation.

Global Epidemiological Surveillance

In the *Weekly Epidemiological Record,* WHO publishes notes on communicable diseases of international importance and information concerning the application of international health regulations. In the past, the publication was chiefly a summary of the weekly or daily notifications of diseases under the regulations, with declarations of infected areas or of freedom from infection when attained. It then became the vehicle for timely reports, narrative summaries, and interpretative comments on a variety of communicable disease topics. Annual, semiannual, or quarterly summaries are published on major trends in diseases and on special programs, such as those on malaria and AIDS. Data from special surveillance programs, such as the global influenza program, the European program for salmonella, and dengue-hemorrhagic fever surveillance, are summarized and published at appropriate intervals. The *Weekly Epidemiological Record* also communicates important changes in international health regulations and policies of member states.

Global Programme for Vaccines and Immunization

Immunization, one of the most powerful and cost-effective weapons of disease prevention, remains tragically underutilized. Diseases such as neonatal tetanus and poliomyelitis, which have been virtually eliminated in most of the developed world, continue to take a heavy toll in developing countries. Measles, whooping cough, diphtheria, and tuberculosis are serious health threats to children in developing countries, causing blindness, deafness, and even death. In 1993, WHO reported that 8 million children die annually in developing countries from viral and bacterial illnesses, and 900 million become severely ill.

The Expanded Programme on Immunization (EPI). In 1974,

with the help of UNICEF, UNDP, national donor agencies, and voluntary agencies, WHO initiated the Expanded Programme on Immunization, with the goal of providing immunizations for all children of the world by 1990.

In 1974, it was estimated that immunization coverage in the developing world was less than 5 percent. By 1987, coverage of children in developing countries in their first year of life with one dose of BCG and measles vaccines and three doses of DPT and poliomyelitis vaccines was reported to be between 45 percent and 55 percent. That level of immunization coverage was preventing over 1 million deaths and almost 200,000 cases of paralytic poliomyelitis a year in the developing world. In its coordinating role, WHO gave priority to the managerial training of health workers and the development of cold-chain systems in order to provide for the establishment of vaccine delivery mechanisms capable of achieving high coverage of susceptible populations with vaccines known to be safe and effective. WHO estimated that in 1990 alone, immunization programs reached more than 100 million infants each year, and saved 3.2 million children annually from measles, neonatal tetanus and pertussis. However, approximately 2.1 million children were still dying each year from the preventable diseases included in the EPI. Little progress had been made in extending coverage to hard-to-reach populations, and coverage in Africa had even begun to decline.

In 1993, WHO, UNICEF, UNDP, the World Bank, and the Rockefeller Foundation founded the *Children's Vaccine Initiative (CVI).* The Initiative undertook the research and development of a heat-stable oral poliomyelitis vaccine, a single-dose tetanus toxoid vaccine, and an improved measles vaccine which could be given earlier in life. In 1994, the EPI and the Children's Vaccine Initiative were merged into the *Global Programme for Vaccines and Immunization (GPV)* , which also took over the activities of the WHO/UNDP Programme for Vaccine Development. The GPV was established to sustain the accomplishments of the EPI and the CVI, to achieve the goals for immunization and disease control set by the World Health Assembly and the World Summit for Children, and to add new and improved vaccines as they become available. The GPV's principal targets are:

- to eradicate polio by the year 2000;
- to reduce measles deaths by 95 percent by 1995;
- to reduce measles incidence by 90 percent by 1995;
- to reduce neonatal tetanus to one per 1,000 live births worldwide by 1995;
- to develop immunization services to reach 90 percent of women and children world-wide by the year 2000.

B. Prevention and Control of Noncommunicable Diseases
Cancer

Cancer, a noncommunicable disease, has recently been ranked as the second or third main cause of death globally among persons who survive the first five years of life. Contrary to the general belief that cancer occurs mainly in the industrialized world, it is estimated that more than half of all cancer patients today are in developing countries. WHO estimates that 9 million cases of cancer occur in the world every year. By the year 2015, the annual figure is expected to reach 15 million cases, two-thirds of them in developing countries.

In May 1982, the World Health Assembly endorsed the WHO cancer program, which urges countries to take, without delay, positive control measures that are already known, such as the cessation of tobacco smoking and chewing, vaccination against virus B hepatitis, and early detection of cancers of the mouth, skin, and cervix uteri. Such measures, if implemented, would have an important effect on cancer globally.

WHO assists member countries in setting up national cancer control programs. In 1993, it reported it had provided guidance to more than 40 countries, each of which was establishing a cancer control program. WHO has set a goal of getting half its member states to formulate strategies and programs for cancer control by the year 2000.

The International Agency for Research on Cancer, located in Lyons, France, is associated with WHO and conducts research on identification of carcinogenic factors in the environment, as well as lifestyle factors in cancer development.

Cardiovascular Disease

The MONICA Project. WHO coordinates the Monitoring of Trends and Determinants of Cardiovascular Diseases (MONICA) which was established in 1979 and became operational in 39 collaborating centers located in 26 countries in October 1984. The MONICA project is the largest collaborative epidemiological study of these diseases ever carried out. It followed 25 million people between 25 and 64 years of age over a 10-year period, collecting data on coronary deaths, non-fatal heart attacks, coronary risk factors, and coronary care. By 1993, the main results from the MONICA study were: cross-sectional comparisons of risk factor levels; relations between various risk factors; five-year trends in risk factors; acute coronary care; medical services; cross-sectional comparisons of incidence rates for stroke; and management of stroke around the world. Several optional studies are being carried out in connection with MONICA on nutrition, antioxidant vitamins, polyunsaturated fatty acids, physical activity and psychosocial studies, and drug monitoring.

The MONICA data center was established at the National Public Health Institute in Finland, and prepared the data collection instruments and methodology for the study. It receives and analyzes the data collected. In 1993 the MONICA study entered its final stage of data collection. It was expected that the final results of the study would be available in 1998.

Substance Abuse

Tobacco Use. Cigarette smoking is one of the principal preventable causes of premature mortality and ill health, particularly in industrialized countries but also in developing countries, where it is spreading. Cigarette smoking is estimated to be responsible for about 90 percent of lung cancer deaths, 75 percent of bronchitis deaths, and 25 percent of deaths from coronary disease. In 1994, WHO estimated that at least three million premature deaths annually are caused by cigarette smoking and one-third of those deaths are in developing countries. Smoking has been shown to be linked with circulatory complications in women using oral contraceptives, cause lower body weight in newborns of smoking mothers, decrease male and female fertility, and be associated with cancers of organs other than the lungs. Passive smoking causes a higher frequency of upper respiratory tract infections in children exposed to tobacco smoke. In adults, it is associated with a significantly higher risk of lung cancer among exposed nonsmokers. Tobacco chewing, which is again becoming fashionable in some countries, causes cancer of the mouth.

Tobacco use is considered as a dependence disorder in WHO's 9th International Classification of Diseases. WHO has taken the lead in international action to stem the spread of smoking and its harmful health consequences. It collaborates with numerous national smoking and health associations around the world, as well as with nongovernmental organizations and other UN agencies. WHO collaborating reference centers assist in analyses of toxic components of cigarettes. Seminars and conferences muster scientific knowledge and political support.

In 1988, the World Health Assembly declared 31 May as a "World No Tobacco Day" to focus public attention and recognize contributions to healthy life-style free from tobacco use. In 1989 the WHA approved a plan of action on a program called "Tobacco or Health." The program promoted national tobacco control programs; provided advocacy and information services; and acted as a clearinghouse for activities in the field.

Alcohol and Drug Abuse. WHO is the executing agency for the United Nations Fund for Drug Abuse Control. In collaboration with the International Narcotics Control Board and the United Nations Division of Narcotic Drugs, WHO has prepared guidelines on drug-abuse reporting systems that give special attention to data on health, to complement the law enforcement data that are traditionally gathered. In 1991, WHO held an Interregional Meeting on Alcohol-Related Problems in Tokyo, which recommended a number of actions to reduce alcohol dependence in member states. In the 1992/93 biennium, the Abuse Trends Linkage Alerting System (ATLAS) was set up to gather health-related data from a variety of sources in order to assist in mobilizing efforts to reduce demand for dependence-producing substances. In 1993, WHO supplied global data on substance abuse for the World Bank's publication of *World Development Report 1993: Investing in Health.*

C. Primary Healthcare and Health Building
Maternal and Child Health

"Health for all" requires that special attention be paid to specific population groups whose health and welfare have profound social, demographic, and economic implications for society. The health of mothers and children is particularly important because of the special biological and psychosocial needs inherent in the rapid process of human growth, needs which must be met in order to ensure the survival and healthy development of the fetus and the child, as well as to maintain the health and development of the mother. The health of young people is also important, since the energy and idealism of youth are important resources that can be channeled to the benefit of their societies.

WHO assists governments in the application of preventive, curative, and rehabilitative measures aimed at promoting and protecting the health of women and children and at strengthening the role of all family members in health care and child rearing. WHO's primary approaches are the following: (1) to identify the extent and nature of the major health needs of mothers, children, and young people; (2) to develop and adapt methods for the promotion of healthy behavior and the protection of women, children, and adolescents during vulnerable periods of rapid physiological and social changes, particularly relating to reproduction; (3) to provide technical guidance in the planning, management, and evaluation of preventive and curative programs of maternal and child health, including family planning; (4) to introduce and adapt training approaches for improving knowledge and skills in interpersonal and group communication and counseling, the health rationale for family planning, and innovative maternal and child health/family planning technologies; (5) to disseminate information on the health needs of women, children, and adolescents and on new ways of addressing those needs; (6) to identify and support research in basic clinical and applied aspects of pediatrics, adolescent medicine, gynecology and obstetrics, social psychology, and health systems; (7) to collaborate in the activities of national and international organizations concerned with maternal and child health/family planning and young people; and (8) to contribute to the development of intersectoral policies and programs.

In 1992, the World Health Assembly established the Global Commission on Women's Health, which met for the first time in April 1994. The commission is composed of 30 eminent persons from different professional fields and acts as an advisory body to the Directory General, providing independent scientific and technical advice on policies and strategies relating to women's health. The commission meets once a year.

Reproductive Health

In 1993, the WHO Global Policy Council approved the following definition of reproductive health to provide a basis for action in this field. "Within the framework of WHO's definition of health as a state of complete physical, mental and social well-being, and not merely the absence of disease or infirmity, reproductive health addresses the reproductive processes, functions, and system at all stages of life. Reproductive health implies that people are able to have a responsible, satisfying, and safe sex life and that they have the capability to reproduce and the freedom to decide if, when, and how often to do so. Implicit in this last condition are the right of men and women to be informed of and to have access to safe, effective, affordable, and acceptable methods of fertility regulation of their choice, and the right of access to appropriate health care services that will enable women to go safely through pregnancy and childbirth and provide couples with the best chance of having a healthy infant."

Nutrition

In addition to developing criteria and norms for assessing nutritional status, WHO strives to strengthen the capacities of countries to assess and evaluate their nutritional problems and associated factors and to develop and implement sectoral strategies to deal with the causes of those problems. Increasing the awareness of the world community of those problems for which solutions have been designed and tested has resulted in a significant increase in national programs to control iodine-deficiency disorders and vitamin A deficiency. At the same time, improvements in factors that have an influence on nutrition, such as disease prevention and management, food production, and education, have resulted in a decreased prevalence of undernutrition.

The International Conference on Nutrition, held in Rome in December 1992, was the culmination of more than two years' joint effort by WHO and FAO to promote awareness of the extent and seriousness of nutritional and diet-related problems. The conference was attended by more than 1,300 people representing 159 governments and some 160 international and non-governmental organizations. The conference adopted the *World Declaration and Plan of Action for Nutrition* which declared its determination to eliminate hunger and reduce all forms of malnutrition, and called on the United Nations to declare an International Decade of Food and Nutrition. It was estimated at the conference that 780 million people in developing countries do not have access to enough food to meet their basic daily needs. It reaffirmed the right of women and adolescent girls to adequate nutrition. The conference set ambitious goals of eliminating famine and famine-related deaths by the end of the decade and substantially reducing starvation and widespread chronic hunger, especially among children, women, and the aged. It also called for the total elimination of inadequate sanitation and poor hygiene, including unsafe drinking water. Governments were urged to promote national plans of action based on the strategies developed at the conference and to allocate the financial and human resources needed to implement the necessary programs. In its report, the conference referred to the nutritional goals set by the Fourth United Nations Development Decade and the World Summit for Children.

In January 1994, WHO reported that 30 percent of the world's children under the age of five (approximately 192 million children) were malnourished and underweight. The report urged member nations to implement the International Code of Marketing of Breast-milk Substitutes, adopted by the WHA in 1981, to protect women in developing world from being manipulated into feeding their infants breast-milk substitutes, a practice which had been shown to put infants at risk. A wide range of illnesses and nutrition-related disorders are prevented by breast-feeding children. WHO considers direct advertising of infant formula to mothers with infants in the first four to six months of life singularly inappropriate. The 1994 report stated that large sums were being spent misguidedly to provide breast-milk substitutes to the countries of Central and Eastern Europe within the context of

food aid programs. The report noted that an adequate diet is more crucial in infancy than at any other time of life because infants have a high nutritional requirement in relation to body weight. Faulty nutrition during the first months has been proved to influence future health and development.

Rehabilitation of the Disabled

Since the early 1950s, WHO has had a program for rehabilitation of the disabled. The program was initially set up to increase awareness of the problems faced by war veterans and to stimulate governments to provide increased services for this group.

During the 1970s, the program was reoriented to promote rehabilitation in developing countries. A new policy was accepted by the World Health Assembly in 1976, making rehabilitation part of primary health care services. WHO then developed a whole series of teaching-training materials to be used at the community level. All of this material has been published in a manual entitled *Training in the Community for People with Disabilities*.

The basic idea governing the program is that training for disabled people can be successfully given by family members, under the guidance and supervision of a local health worker. Referral services are needed for some 30 percent, mostly for short-term interventions. The program stresses the importance of involving the family and community in rehabilitation.

New plans will concentrate on development of the personnel needed for providing community-based rehabilitation services at the community and district levels. Efforts are concentrated on strengthening the management capability of supervisors at the district level, thus broadening the population coverage so that by the year 2000, most people with disabilities will have access to at least the essential services.

Occupational Health

WHO's Occupational Health Program has four main aims: (1) health protection of the underserved working populations who constitute the bulk of the economically productive persons in developing countries; (2) strengthening of general health services through the application of occupational health technologies and approaches; (3) workers' participation in their health care delivery systems; and (4) development of occupational health science, technology, and practice.

The program incorporates identification and control of "work-related diseases," recognition of neuro-behavioral changes from occupational exposure to health hazards, control of occupational impairment in reproductive functions and other delayed effects and of adverse occupational psychosocial hazards, and the application of ergonomics as a factor in health promotion. WHO cooperates with countries in the development of their institutional framework for the health care of working people. Special attention is given to occupational health concerns of employed women, children, the elderly, migrant workers, and other groups.

Environmental Health

Safe drinking water, proper community sanitation (sewage disposal systems), rural and urban development, and housing standards are the focus of WHO's environmental health program. Many of WHO's projects in this area are carried out in collaboration with other United Nations agencies, including UNICEF, the World Bank, UNDP, and FAO.

Since 1986, WHO has sponsored a series of international consultations on cost recovery in community water supply and sanitation. Its *Guidelines for Drinking-water Quality* have been applied in developing countries. WHO has studied the technical aspects of wastewater reuse in agriculture and collaborated with UNEP, the World Bank, and FAO in formulating guidelines and defining strategies for safe wastewater reuse in agriculture.

WHO is also concerned with prevention and control of environmental pollution, and has produced technical manuals on the disposal of hazardous waste. The WHO/ILO/UNEP International Programme on Chemical Safety (IPCS) was established in 1980.

It provides information on the risks to human health and the environment of potentially toxic chemicals, and guidance in the safe use of chemicals. The IPCS was designated by UNCED as the nucleus for international cooperation on environmentally sound management of toxic chemicals.

In 1991, WHO set up a Global Environmental Technology Network (GETNET) to link specialists in environmental management technology. In 1993 GETNET was expanded to include 340 members in 87 countries.

In 1992, the WHO Commission on Health and the Environment published *Our Planet, Our Health*, one of several documents that served as the basis of WHO's contribution to the United Nations Conference on Environment and Development (the Earth Summit) held in Rio de Janeiro in June 1992. The WHA endorsed a new global strategy for health and environment based on the Commission's recommendations.

Mental Health

WHO's Mental Health Programme has as its major task, the improvement of care for the mentally ill. In 1992, WHO estimated that at least 52 million people in the world suffer from severe mental diseases such as schizophrenia or severe depression. Over the years, the program has promoted the provision of mental health care through primary and general health care rather than through specialized services. The program reviews legislation concerning mental illness and issues guidelines about revising or drafting legislation. It has also launched programs on prevention of mental illness and developed treatment guidelines.

The objectives of WHO's program in mental heath are the reduction of psychiatric and neurological morbidity, the utilization of mental health skills in the improvement of general health services, and an increased awareness of mental health aspects of social action. Activities range from improvement in the delivery of mental health services, personnel development, and information exchange to research into the epidemiology and biology of mental disorders.

A number of international collaborative studies have been sponsored and coordinated by WHO. These have focused on the form and course of mental disorders in different cultures, the development of prevention and treatment methods, the operation of mental health services, and psychosocial aspects of health and health care. International exchange of information is fostered through publications, training courses, seminars, and networks of collaborating research and training centers in some 40 countries.

The mental health program also includes projects concerned with the development of standardized procedures, diagnostic classifications, and statistics necessary for an improved mental health information system and collaboration in mental health research, and a major program concerned with the prevention and treatment of alcohol and drug dependence.

In the late 1980s WHO launched an Initiative of Support to People Disabled by Mental Illness, intended to facilitate the dissemination of information about good practice in community services for people with chronic mental illnesses. The initiative seeks to reduce the disabling effects of chronic mental illness and highlight social and environmental barriers which hinder treatment and rehabilitation. The Initiative sought to involve the patient in decisions affecting his or her care. The prerequisites to that involvement were considered to be: the right to be empowered; the right to representation; the right to have access to one's own medical records; the right to be free of stigmatizing labels.

In 1989, WHO began a major study to investigate the types and frequency of psychological problems in 14 countries. By 1992, it had screened 25,000 patients aged 18 to 65. The patients were classified in different categories according to the symptoms, and their progress was followed for a one-year period.

In December 1991, the United Nations General Assembly, in its resolution 46/119, approved the Principles for the Protection of Persons with Mental Illness and the Improvement of Mental Health Care. This gave mental health advocacy groups a tool to publicize their views on empowerment. The Initiative has produced publications, including *Schizophrenia: Information for Families*, which has been translated into 15 languages.

WHO considers the promotion of mental health—that is, the improvement of the position that mental health occupies in the scale of values of individuals, communities, and societies—as one of its fundamental tasks and as being essential for human development and the quality of life.

D. Pharmaceuticals

Pharmaceutical Products in International Commerce

Since 1964, WHO has studied ways of ensuring that all drugs exported from a country comply with its domestic drug quality requirements. A Certification Scheme on the Quality of Pharmaceutical Products Moving in International Commerce was adopted by the World Health Assembly in 1969, and a revised version in 1975. According to the scheme, in which about 124 countries are participating, the health authorities of the exporting countries provide a certificate that the product is authorized for sale in the exporting country and that the plant in which the product is produced is subject to regular inspection to ensure that it conforms to good practices of manufacture and quality control as recommended by WHO. Also under the scheme, the importing country may request from the authorities of the exporting country additional information on the controls exercised on the product. In addition to the product certificate issued by the competent authority of the exporting country, batch certificates, stating that the quality of the batch complies with quality specifications and indicating the expiration date and storage conditions, may be issued either by the competent authority of the exporting country or by the manufacturer.

International Biological Standardization

Biological substances cannot be characterized entirely by physical or chemical means. Their activity can be controlled only by tests in which laboratory animals, microorganisms, cell cultures, or antigen-antibody reactions are used. Such assays use biological reference materials which have previously been determined, usually under the form of an international unitage system, by calibration against appropriate international reference materials.

Much work in this field was done under League of Nations auspices. By 1945, 34 international biological standards had been established for such substances as antibiotics, antibodies, antigens, blood products and related substances, and hormones. Since then, WHO has enlisted the collaboration of more than 100 laboratories to conduct international collaborative studies, and there are now more than 200 international standards available to national control authorities throughout the world.

The work on biological standardization has expanded considerably and comprises a number of additional activities, including the establishment of international reference reagents, mainly for the purpose of diagnosis and identification. Furthermore, in order for manufacturers and national control authorities to achieve the production of biological substances which are safe and potent, international requirements on production and control have been prepared and are published in the *Technical Report Series*. Such requirements are kept up to date in the light of developing technology. By the end of 1986, 40 sets of international requirements had been published. In addition, guidelines have been published on such subjects as the setting up of biological standards, the testing of kits used for the assay of biological substances, and the use of interferon therapy.

A complete list of international standards and international reference reagents is published by WHO in *Biological Substances*.

Pharmaceutical Quality Control

International Pharmacopoeia. Attempts to establish internationally agreed-upon specifications for therapeutic agents have been made since the 1850s. By 1910, limited agreements were reached concerning certain potent drugs. Since 1951, WHO has published the *International Pharmacopoeia*, which provides internationally acceptable standards for the purity and potency of pharmaceutical products moving in international commerce that are available for adoption by member states in accordance with the WHO constitution and resolutions of the World Health Assembly.

The first edition, consisting of two volumes and a supplement, was issued between 1951 and 1959. The second edition was published in 1967; a supplement was added in 1971 and additional monographs in 1972. Work on the third edition, started in 1975, aims to accommodate the needs of developing countries by offering sound standards for the essential drugs. The first two volumes were issued in 1979 and 1981, respectively.

International Nonproprietary Names for Drugs. Many pharmaceutical substances are known not only by their nonproprietary, generic, or scientific names but by various trade names as well. In order to identify each pharmaceutical substance by a unique, universally available nonproprietary name, WHO has set up a procedure to select international nonproprietary names for pharmaceutical substances. Such names are published regularly in the *WHO Chronicle*. By the end of 1987, over 5,400 names had been proposed and published in 48 lists. A seventh cumulative list was published in 1987.

WHO Collaborating Center for Chemical Reference Substances. As a further service in the area of drug quality control, the WHO Collaborating Center for Chemical Reference Substances was established in Sweden, at the Apotekens Centrallaboratorium, in 1955. Its function is to collect, assay, and store international chemical reference substances and to make them available free to national and nonprofit laboratories and institutes and, for a nominal fee, to commercial firms. About 140 chemical reference substances needed for tests and assays described in the *International Pharmacopoeia* are available.

Good Practices in the Manufacture and Quality Control of Drugs. To assist member states with technical advice on adequate control processes in drug manufacture, the World Health Assembly, in 1969, recommended the requirements in a publication entitled *Good Practices in the Manufacture and Quality Control of Drugs.* A revised text was adopted in 1975 by the assembly. The text contains requirements pertaining to personnel, premises, and equipment of manufacturing establishments and general hygienic and sanitation measures. Special requirements pertain to raw materials, manufacturing operations, and labeling and packaging of products. The organization and duties of a quality-control department and a quality-control laboratory are specified.

Essential Drugs. As early as 1975, the WHA had received reports of the experiences of a few countries who had adopted schemes of basic or essential drugs. The purpose was to help people in developing countries whose basic health needs could be met through the existing supply system by giving them access to the most necessary drugs. The WHA recommended that member states draw up national drug policies to ensure that the most essential drugs were available at a reasonable price, and to stimulate research and development to produce new drugs adapted to the real health requirements of developing countries. There was recognition that developing countries could not afford to waste scarce resources on drugs which either did not meet majority needs, or which were priced at a level which their societies could not afford.

In 1977, a WHO committee of experts met to determine how many drugs were really needed to ensure a reasonable level of healthcare for as many people as possible. It was determined that, in country after country, a surprisingly uniform picture of drug selection emerged. At the village health post or dispensary level, 10 to 15 drugs meet immediate needs. At the health center level,

where the diagnostic and local facilities are better and the staff more highly trained, about 30 to 40 drugs will suffice for 80 percent to 90 percent of all complaints. District and provincial hospitals may need around 100 to 120 drugs, and the large referral and teaching hospitals the full range of 200 to 400. The committee's first *Model List of Essential Drugs* appeared in 1977 and contained some 200 items. By 1994 the list numbered 270 drugs. All of the drugs and vaccines on the list were of proven safety and efficacy, and possessed well understood therapeutic qualities. Most were no longer protected by patent and could be produced in quantity at reasonable cost. The *Model List* is revised every two years in order to respond to evolving needs and pharmaceutical advances. The list is not meant to be definitive, but to serve as a guideline for each country to pick and choose from in order to adopt a list of essential drugs according to its own priorities.

In 1981, WHO launched its Action Programme on Essential Drugs to help narrow the list of drugs that would be essential for small medical units in developing countries. This program assists countries in developing their own legislation and methods of financing comprehensive drug programs. It also assists them in implementing the quality control monitoring regimes mentioned above. The Action Programme also provides support for training personnel in the areas of drug management and rational use. It supports national and regional seminars at which hundreds of health staff from countries throughout the world receive practical training. In the area of research, the program encourages research aimed at filling gaps in existing knowledge about the best means of selecting, procuring, and distributing drugs. This research seeks to discover how providers make decisions on which drugs to prescribe, or how and why patients use—or fail to use—medicines. This research has direct bearing on the ways in which vital medicines can be made available and accessible to the greatest number of people. Today more than 113 countries have adapted the Model List to match their own patterns of disease and financial resources.

E. Research Promotion and Development

Through its advisory committees on medical research—one for each of the six WHO regions and one at the global level—WHO provides guidelines for research planning, execution, and implementation in health programs directly linked to national priorities. The committees also offer an appropriate forum for the discussion of national and regional experiences and for the detailed formulation of scientific and technological policies in the field of health. Research programs and activities are developed in close coordination with medical research councils or analogous bodies, with particular emphasis on the strengthening of managerial capacities at all levels.

WHO's coordinating role in research calls for the development of a system for the exchange of scientific information and the enlistment of the collaboration of groups of scientists and research workers in various areas on solving key problems and developing methods for most effectively combining their efforts.

Over the years, more than 1200 institutions with the necessary expertise and facilities have been designated by WHO as "WHO Collaborating Centers." In the 1992/93 biennium, WHO also had designated 54 expert advisory panels composed of more than 2,000 experts. Financial assistance is sometimes provided by WHO through technical services agreements, partially offsetting the much larger expenses borne by the centers themselves.

In order to increase the research potential of member countries, WHO has developed a program to train research workers. The duration of grants varies, but as far as possible, they are made sufficiently long to permit the candidate to gain an adequate knowledge of methods and techniques and, very often, to carry out, under supervision, a specific piece of research.

Communication among scientists is also promoted. A scientist

Members of the World Health Organization
(as of 9 May 1994)

Afghanistan	Ecuador	Lithuania	Senegal
Albania	Egypt	Luxembourg	Seychelles
Algeria	El Salvador	Madagascar	Sierra Leone
Angola	Equatorial Guinea	Malawi	Singapore
Antigua and Barbuda	Eritrea	Malaysia	Slovak Republic
Argentina	Estonia	Maldives	Slovenia
Armenia	Ethiopia	Mali	Solomon Islands
Australia	Fiji	Malta	Somalia
Austria	Finland	Marshall Islands	South Africa
Azerbaijan	France	Mauritania	Spain
Bahamas	Gabon	Mauritius	Sri Lanka
Bahrain	Gambia	Mexico	Sudan
Bangladesh	Georgia	Micronesia (Federated States of)	Suriname
Barbados	Germany	Monaco	Swaziland
Belarus	Ghana	Mongolia	Sweden
Belgium	Greece	Morocco	Switzerland
Belize	Grenada	Mozambique	Syria
Benin	Guatemala	Myanmar	Tajikistan
Bhutan	Guinea	Namibia	Thailand
Bolivia	Guinea-Bissau	Nauru	The Former Yugoslav
Bosnia and Herzegovina	Guyana	Nepal	Republic of Macedonia
Botswana	Haiti	Netherlands	Togo
Brazil	Honduras	New Zealand	Tonga
Brunei Darussalam	Hungary	Nicaragua	Trinidad and Tobago
Bulgaria	Iceland	Niger	Tunisia
Burkina Faso	India	Nigeria	Turkey
Burundi	Indonesia	Niue	Turkmenistan
Cambodia	Iran	Norway	Tuvalu
Cameroon	Iraq	Oman	Uganda
Canada	Ireland	Pakistan	Ukraine
Cape Verde	Israel	Panama	United Arab Emirates
Central African Republic	Italy	Papua New Guinea	United Kingdom
Chad	Jamaica	Paraguay	United Republic of Tanzania
Chile	Japan	Peru	United States
China	Jordan	Philippines	Uruguay
Colombia	Kazakhstan	Poland	Uzbekistan
Comoros	Kenya	Portugal	Vanuatu
Congo	Kiribati	Qatar	Venezuela
Cook Islands	Korea, Democratic People's	Republic of Moldova	Viet Nam
Costa Rica	Republic of	Romania	Yemen
Côte d'Ivoire	Korea, Republic of	Russian Federation	Yugoslavia
Croatia	Kuwait	Rwanda	Zaire
Cuba	Kyrgyz Republic	St. Kitts and Nevis	Zambia
Cyprus	Lao People's Democratic Republic	St. Lucia	Zimbabwe
Czech Republic	Latvia	St. Vincent and the Grenadines	
Denmark	Lebanon	Samoa	ASSOCIATE MEMBERS
Djibouti	Lesotho	San Marino	Puerto Rico
Dominica	Liberia	São Tomé and Principe	Tokelau
Dominican Republic	Libyan Arab Jamahiriya	Saudi Arabia	

from one country is enabled to visit scientists in other countries for a period of up to three months, thus facilitating personal contact and the exchange of ideas.

WHO promotes meetings, symposia, seminars, and training courses in special techniques, bringing together scientists from various parts of the world. Reports of such meetings are circulated, when appropriate, to the scientific community, as are the reports of expert committees and scientific and consultant groups.

F. Health Personnel Development

WHO's role in health personnel development is to collaborate with member states in their efforts to plan, train, deploy, and manage teams of health personnel made up of the numbers and types that are required (and that they can afford) and to help ensure that such personnel are socially responsible and possess appropriate technical, scientific, and management competence.

WHO is attempting to raise the political, economic, and social status of women as health care providers in the formal and infor-

mal health care system and in the community and to ensure that they receive the education, training, and orientation to enable them to expand the scope and improve the quality of the health care that they provide to themselves, each other, their families, and other members of the community.

Promotion of community-oriented educational programs with team and problem-based methods of teaching/learning is another approach. The programs are designed to prepare personnel to perform tasks directly related to identified service requirements of specific concern to the country.

Appropriate teaching and learning materials, including those for self-teaching and audiovisual purposes, adapted to different cultures and languages, are promoted for all categories of health personnel contributing to health development, particularly primary health workers and their teachers and supervisors.

Fellowships occupy an important place in WHO's program as one of the ways to provide opportunities for training and study in health matters which are not available in the fellow's own country and for the international exchange of scientific knowledge and techniques relating to health. WHO encourages the nomination, selection, and evaluation of fellows based on and determined by a member state's personnel development policy, in line with its national policy for health development, so that fellowships can contribute to the training of the type and amount of personnel needed to achieve the global target of "health for all." WHO awards fellowships preferably to candidates who will be directly involved in primary health care programs and tries to ensure that the program of studies is relevant to the long-term goals of a country's health policy.

In many countries, however, the problem is no longer one of shortage of health professionals, but rather of establishing or maintaining the right balance between them to ensure that the necessary knowledge and skills are available. WHO is sponsoring studies to develop information systems and methods to help countries achieve this balance.

Nursing. The WHA, in 1992, recommended that each country develop a national action plan for nursing. A global advisory group on nursing and midwifery was established by the 45th WHA, and held its first meeting in 1992. It recommended that, as the largest group of health personnel in any country, nursing and midwifery be declared a priority area for WHO action. A WHO study group on nursing beyond the year 2000 convened in July 1993. It adopted the Nursing Declaration of Alma-Ata, which recognized that a multiprofessional, multidisciplinary approach would be needed to prepare healthcare providers to work in a rapidly changing environment. As a starting point, every health ministry was urged to establish a position of chief nurse, with appropriate staff and budget.

G. Public Information and Education for Health

To integrate health education and information for health, WHO established the Division of Public Information and Education for Health. Its major tasks, in close cooperation with all regions, are to work with governments in developing coordinated information/education programs aimed at promoting healthy behavior and increasing self-reliance among individuals and communities, and to work with technical units in planning, developing, and implementing an information/education component in their programs.

The need for promotion, advocacy, and greater public awareness of health issues is a recurring theme in virtually all WHO programs. WHO considers health education as the sum of activities that will encourage people who want to be healthy to know how to stay healthy, to do what they can individually and collectively to maintain health, and to seek help whenever it may be needed.

WHO has developed many computerized information resources over the years, including WHOLIS, the WHO library information system, which is available on diskette and on the Internet. WHODOC, a regular listing of new WHO publications and documents is also available on diskette and on the Internet. See the appendix on "United Nations Databases" for a descriptive listing of WHO's computerized databases.

H. Health Legislation

While WHO is aware of the importance of health and related legislation to the delivery of personal and environmental health services in countries, it has no mandate to propose model legislation. On the other hand, it recognizes member states' need for relevant and timely information. WHO is mandated to maintain an awareness of all significant new laws and regulations in the field of health, and to disseminate information thereon as rapidly as possible. The main vehicle for information transfer is its *International Digest of Health Legislation* which appears four times a year. A demand for information on HIV/AIDS legislation prompted WHO to develop a computerized data base that covers relevant legislation as well as literature on the legal, ethical, and judicial aspects of AIDS. Data on other subjects, such as legislation to combat smoking, have also been computerized.

In February 1994, the First International Conference of Medical Parliamentarians was held in Bangkok, organized by the Asian Forum of Parliamentarians on Population Development and the International Medical Parliamentarians Organization in close cooperation with WHO. More than 80 medical parliamentarians from 33 countries attended the conference to discuss five specific areas: environmental health, population and development; narcotics drug abuse; organ transplantation; public health and development; and maternal and child health and AIDS. The conference adopted the Bangkok Declaration and Call for Action which set forth goals and priorities for the establishment of national legislation in the five subject areas.

BIBLIOGRAPHY

Bulletin of the World Health Organization. The principal scientific periodical of WHO; bimonthly.

International Travel and Health Vaccination Requirements and Health Advice.

Pharmaceutical Newsletter. Monthly.

Weekly Epidemiological Record. Contains notifications and other information relating to diseases designated as "quarantinable" in the International Sanitary Regulations. For the guidance of national health administrations and quarantine services.

WHO Drug Information. A quarterly journal with reports on major drug regulatory action in different countries and information on medicinal products and selected essential drugs from WHO's Model List.

World Directory of Medical Schools.

World Health. Illustrated WHO periodical for the nontechnical reader; bimonthly.

World Health Forum. An international journal of health development which provides a platform for the international exchange of experience, ideas, and opinion on all aspects of public health. Quarterly.

World Health Statistics Report. Monthly. Contains statistics on notifiable infectious diseases, natality, mortality, causes of death, and other topics.

THE INTERNATIONAL CIVIL AVIATION ORGANIZATION (ICAO)

BACKGROUND: In December 1903, the first heavier-than-air craft, designed by the Wright brothers, managed to fly 37 m (120 ft) under its own power carrying one person. In 1992, scheduled airlines alone flew 1,953 billion passenger-km, carrying 1,167 million passengers. Total operating revenues (passenger, cargo, mail) of the world's airlines had reached US$3.7 billion a year by 1958 and US$212 billion by 1992. Although in a number of countries regulation of domestic flights was established fairly soon, little was accomplished until 1944 to solve the multifarious technical, economic, and legal problems posed by international civil aviation.

CREATION

The first international civil aviation conference, held in 1910 and attended by European governments only, since transoceanic flight was then regarded as no more than a wild dream, was a failure. Almost another decade elapsed before an international convention, signed in Paris in 1919, created the International Commission for Air Navigation. The commission was to meet at least once a year and concern itself with technical matters. An international committee of jurists was also established, to concern itself with the intricate legal questions created by cross-border aviation. In 1928, a Pan-American convention on commercial aviation was adopted at a conference held in Havana to deal with problems then emerging as international flights became more frequent in the Western Hemisphere. Although some progress in obtaining agreement on international flight regulations had been made by the end of the 1930s, most nations still granted very few concessions to each other's airlines, and no agreement existed permitting foreign planes to fly nonstop over the territory of one country en route to another country.

The Chicago Conference of 1944

The tremendous development of aviation during World War II demonstrated the need for an international organization to assist and regulate international flight for peaceful purposes, covering all aspects of flying, including technical, economic, and legal problems. For these reasons, in early 1944, the US conducted exploratory discussions with its World War II allies, on the basis of which invitations were sent to 55 allied and neutral states to meet in Chicago in November 1944.

In November and December 1944, delegates of 52 nations met at the International Civil Aviation Conference in Chicago to plan for international cooperation in the field of air navigation in the postwar era. It was this conference that framed the constitution of the International Civil Aviation Organization—the Convention on International Civil Aviation, also called the Chicago Convention. This convention stipulated that ICAO would come into being after the convention was ratified by 26 nations. To respond to the immediate needs of civil aviation, a provisional organization was created and functioned for 20 months until, on 4 April 1947, ICAO officially came into existence.

In essence, the conference was faced with two questions: (1) whether universally recognized navigational signals and other navigational and technical standards could be agreed upon, and (2) whether international rules concerning the economics of air transport could be established. One group of countries, led by the US, wanted an international organization empowered only to make recommendations regarding standard technical procedures and equipment. In its economic aspects, these countries believed, air transportation should be freely competitive. This policy would also best serve the interests of the "consumer nations" that had no international airlines of their own. Another group of countries, led by the UK, favored a stronger organization, which would have a great deal to say about the economics of civil aviation. It would be empowered to allocate the international routes that the airlines of different countries would be allowed to fly, regulate the frequency of flights, and fix rates. A radical proposal, advanced by New Zealand and supported by Australia, called for international ownership and operation of international air transport.

The Convention on International Civil Aviation finally adopted by the conference was something of a compromise between the American and British positions. The convention established for the first time an independent international body, the International Civil Aviation Organization, to supervise "order in the air," obtain maximum technical standardization for international aviation, recommend certain practices that member countries should follow, and carry out other functions. Countries ratifying or acceding to the convention thereby agreed in advance to conform to the greatest possible extent to ICAO-adopted civil aviation standards and to endeavor to conform to ICAO-adopted recommendations.

In the economic field, ICAO has no regulatory powers, but one of its constitutional objectives is to "prevent economic waste caused by unreasonable competition." In addition, under the convention, member states undertake to have their international airlines furnish ICAO with traffic reports, cost statistics, and financial statements showing, among other things, all receipts from operations and the sources of such revenues.

The Chicago Convention affirms every state's "complete and exclusive sovereignty over the airspace above its territory." It provides that nonscheduled flights may, subject to certain permissible conditions and limitations, be made by the civil aircraft of one country into or over the territory of another. Scheduled international air service, however, may be operated from one country into or over the territory of another country only with the latter's authorization, and member states are permitted to establish areas prohibited to foreign aircraft as long as these regulations are nondiscriminatory. Pilotless as well as conventional aircraft are covered by these provisions. The term *airspace* is not precisely defined, however, and with the development of rockets and long-range missiles, the problem of deciding where a country's airspace ends and where outer space begins has become a matter of practical concern. This problem has come under study by the UN Committee on the Peaceful Uses of Outer Space.

An important matter considered by the Chicago conference was the question of the exchange of commercial rights in international civil aviation. It was not possible to reach an agreement satisfactory to all states attending the conference. Hence, the question was covered not in the Convention on International Civil Aviation that serves as ICAO's constitution but in two supplementary agreements adopted by the conference: the International Air Services Transit Agreement and the International Air Transport Agreement. These two treaties do not form part of the ICAO constitution and are binding only on the ICAO member states that have ratified them.

The International Air Services Transit Agreement guarantees (1) the freedom of civil aircraft to fly over foreign countries and territories as long as they do not land, and (2) the freedom of civil aircraft to make nontraffic landings, for refueling or overhaul only, in foreign territory. The agreement thus established for the first time the principle of automatic right of transit and of emergency landing.

The International Air Transport Agreement, also known as the Five Freedoms Agreement, affirms, in addition to the two freedoms covered by the transit agreement, three other freedoms of the air: (3) freedom to transport passengers and cargo from an aircraft's homeland to other countries, (4) freedom to transport passengers and cargo from other countries to an aircraft's homeland, and (5) freedom to carry air traffic between countries other than the aircraft's homeland.

Because the Chicago Convention was adopted in December 1944, ICAO possesses a constitution older than the UN Charter. Countries were much slower in ratifying the Chicago Convention, however, than they were in ratifying the UN Charter. For this reason, ICAO did not come into being until 4 April 1947, 30 days after the convention had been ratified by the required 26 states.

PURPOSES
ICAO's aims and objectives, as stated in the Chicago Convention, are to foster the planning and development of international air transport so as to ensure the safe and orderly growth of international civil aviation throughout the world; encourage the arts of aircraft design and operation for peaceful purposes; encourage the development of airways, airports, and air navigation facilities for international civil aviation; meet the needs of the peoples of the world for safe, regular, efficient, and economical air transport; prevent economic waste caused by unreasonable competition; ensure that the rights of contracting states are fully respected and that every contracting state has a fair opportunity to operate international airlines; avoid discrimination between contracting states; promote safety of flight in international air navigation; and promote generally the development of all aspects of international civil aeronautics.

MEMBERSHIP
As of March 1994, ICAO had 183 member states.

STRUCTURE
The three main organs of ICAO are the assembly, the council, and the secretariat, headed by the Secretary-General.

Assembly
The all-member assembly meets every three years. Every member state has one vote in the assembly, and decisions are made by a simple majority vote unless otherwise specified by the Chicago Convention. Sessions have been held in many different cities.

The assembly makes policy recommendations, reviews the work of ICAO, offers guidance to other ICAO bodies, elects the council, and determines the budget. The assembly may amend the

ICAO constitution by a two-thirds majority vote, and it has done so on several occasions. But amendments come into force for the states that ratify them only after they have been ratified by at least two-thirds of the ICAO member states as specified by the assembly. In other words, the assembly may feel that it would not be fair to introduce a particular innovation in international civil aviation unless certain states would abide by it. On the other hand, the assembly possesses a rather unusual prerogative to induce wide ratification of an amendment it has adopted: if a member state does not ratify a particular amendment within a given period of time, the assembly has the right to revoke that country's membership in ICAO. However, this provision (Article 94[b]) has never been invoked.

Council
The council is a permanent body, composed of 33 member states elected by the assembly for three-year terms. In selecting the membership of the council, the assembly is required by the Chicago Convention to give adequate representation to nations of major importance in air transport, to nations that provide the largest share of facilities for international civil air navigation, and to nations whose inclusion on the council will ensure broad geographical representation.

Assad Kotaite of Lebanon, president of the council since 1976, was reelected in November 1992 for another three-year term.

The council's powers are unusually broad, as compared with those of the executive councils of most other specialized agencies. It adopts international standards and recommended practices regarding civil air navigation and transport. It may act as arbiter between member states on disputes relating to the interpretation or application of the Chicago Convention and its annexes. It may investigate any situation that presents avoidable obstacles to the development of international air navigation. In general, it may take whatever steps are necessary to maintain the safety and regularity of operation of international air transport.

Secretary-General and Secretariat
The ICAO secretariat is headed by a Secretary-General, who is appointed by the council. The Secretary-General appoints the staff of the ICAO secretariat and supervises and directs its activities. Philippe Rochat of Switzerland was appointed Secretary-General in 1991.

ICAO headquarters are at International Aviation Square, 1000 Sherbrooke Street West, in the center of Montreal, occupying 18 floors of a 27-story building, as well as a complete conference complex adjacent to it. ICAO maintains regional offices in Paris, Bangkok, Cairo, Mexico City, Nairobi, Lima, and Dakar to assist member states in providing aeronautical services.

BUDGET
The 1992 assembly voted the following net budgets: 1993, US$50.0 million; 1994, US$51.3 million; 1995, US$52.2 million. Contributions by member states are assessed on a sliding scale determined by the assembly.

ACTIVITIES

A. International Standards and Recommended Practices
By joining ICAO—that is, by accepting the Chicago Convention—states undertake to collaborate in securing the highest practicable degree of uniformity in regulations, standards, procedures, and organization in all matters in which such uniformity will facilitate and improve air navigation. Hence, one of ICAO's chief tasks is to adopt such international standards and recommendations and to keep them up-to-date through modifications and amendments.

A standard, as defined by the first ICAO Assembly, is "any

specification for physical characteristics, configuration, material, performance, personnel, or procedures, the uniform application of which is recognized as *necessary* for the safety or regularity of international air navigation and to which member states *will conform*." Standards may thus include specifications for such matters as the length of runways, the materials to be used in aircraft construction, and the qualifications to be required of a pilot flying an international route. A recommendation is any such specification, the uniform application of which is recognized as "*desirable* in the interest of safety, regularity, or efficiency of international air navigation and to which member states will *endeavor to conform*."

Preparing and revising these standards and recommendations is largely the responsibility of ICAO's Air Navigation Commission, which plans, coordinates, and examines all of ICAO's activities in the field of air navigation. The commission consists of 15 persons, appointed by the council from among persons nominated by member states. If the council approves the text, it is submitted to the member states. While recommendations are not binding, standards automatically become binding on all member states, except for those who find it impracticable to comply and file a difference under Article 38 of the Chicago Convention.

Annexes to the Chicago Convention

The various standards and recommendations that have been adopted by ICAO are grouped into 18 annexes to the Chicago Convention. The aim of most of the annexes is to promote progress in flight safety, particularly by guaranteeing satisfactory minimum standards of training and safety procedures and by ensuring uniform international practices. The 18 annexes are the following:

1. Personnel Licensing—licensing of flight crews, air traffic controllers, and aircraft maintenance personnel.
2. Rules of the Air—rules relating to the conduct of visual and instrument flights.
3. Meteorological Services—provision of meteorological services for international air navigation and reporting of meteorological observations from aircraft.
4. Aeronautical Charts—specifications for aeronautical charts for use in international aviation.
5. Units of Measurement—dimensional systems to be used in air-ground communications.
6. Operation of Aircraft. Part I: International Commercial Air Transport; Part II: International General Aviation; Part III: International Operations–Helicopters. These specifications will ensure in similar operations throughout the world a level of safety above a prescribed minimum.
7. Aircraft Nationality and Registration Marks—requirements for registration and identification of aircraft.
8. Airworthiness of Aircraft—certification and inspection of aircraft according to uniform procedures.
9. Facilitation—simplification of customs, immigration, and health inspection regulations at international airports.
10. Aeronautical Telecommunications—standardization of communications equipment and systems and of communications procedures.
11. Air Traffic Services—establishment and operation of air traffic control, flight information, and alerting services.
12. Search and Rescue—organization and operation of facilities and services necessary for search and rescue.
13. Aircraft Accident Investigation—uniformity in the notification, investigation, and reporting of aircraft accidents.
14. Aerodromes—specifications for the design and equipment of aerodromes.
15. Aeronautical Information Services—methods for the collection and dissemination of aeronautical information required for flight operations.
16. Environmental Protection. Vol. I: Aircraft Noise—specifications for aircraft noise certification, noise monitoring, and noise exposure units for land-use planning; Vol. II: Aircraft Engine Emissions—standards relating to vented fuel and emissions certification requirements.
17. Security—specifications for safeguarding international civil aviation against acts of unlawful interference.
18. Safe Transport of Dangerous Goods by Air—specifications for the labeling, packing, and shipping of dangerous cargo.

B. Air Navigation

It is evident that air navigation covers an extremely broad spectrum of activities, ranging from short take-off and landing airplanes to supersonic transports, from security questions to the impact of aviation on the environment, from training and operating practices for pilots to the facilities required at airports.

ICAO's program regarding the environment provides a case in point. Growing air traffic and increased use of jet engines have heightened public awareness of the environmental impact of civil aviation. In 1968, ICAO instituted activities aimed at reducing aircraft noise. The first measures involved development of internationally agreed standards for the noise certification of aircraft (contained in Vol. I of Annex 16 to the Chicago Convention), which resulted in a quieter generation of jet aircraft.

Comparable studies of aviation's share in air pollution have resulted in the development of standards (Vol. II of Annex 16) relating to the control of fuel venting and of smoke and gaseous emissions from newly manufactured turbojet and turbofan engines for subsonic airplanes.

Concern about the continuing threat of violence against international civil aviation and its facilities, including the unlawful seizure and the sabotage of aircraft, led to adoption by the council of Annex 17 to the Chicago Convention, containing standards and recommended practices aimed at safeguarding international civil aviation against acts of unlawful interference. In addition, comprehensive guidance material on the subject has been developed. As part of its continuing effort to improve air safety, ICAO has adopted standards for the safe transport of dangerous goods by air. These form Annex 18 to the Chicago Convention. ICAO studies many other important subjects, such as all-weather operations, supersonic operations, application of space techniques to aviation, automated-data interchange systems, and visual aids.

C. Facilitation of International Air Transport

From the beginning of ICAO's history, the need to facilitate international air transport—to remove obstacles that would impede the free passage of aircraft, passengers, crew, baggage, cargo, and mail across international boundaries—was evident. This need is inherent in the speed of air travel itself; if, for example, customs, immigration, public health, and other formalities require one hour at each end of a transoceanic flight of six hours, the total duration of the trip is increased by 33 percent.

ICAO has therefore developed, over the years, a comprehensive facilitation program that is reflected in the international standards and recommended practices of Annex 9 to the Chicago Convention, as well as in the recommendations and statements of the ICAO Council and the Facilitation Division. Broadly speaking, the program aims at eliminating all nonessential documentary requirements, simplifying and standardizing the remaining forms, providing certain minimum facilities at international airports, and simplifying handling and clearance procedures. The program is concerned with such measures as liberalization of visa requirements and entry procedures for temporary visitors; the development of machine-readable passports and visas; speedy handling and clearance procedures for cargo, mail, and baggage; and the elimination, as far as possible, of requirements for documentation or examination in regard to transit traffic.

In addition to reducing procedural formalities, ICAO's efforts are aimed at providing adequate airport terminal buildings for passengers and their baggage and for air cargo, with all related facilities and services. Special attention is given to improving the accessibility of air transport to elderly and disabled passengers. The continuous growth in air traffic makes it necessary for airport administrations to review the adequacy of their facilities at regular intervals. When modifications in existing terminals or the building of new ones are contemplated, close coordination and cooperation between planners and users must be established from the earliest moment, even before any design is made. Proper airport traffic flow arrangements, with a sufficient number of clearance channels, baggage delivery positions, and cargo handling facilities, are necessary for the speedy processing of traffic through clearance control.

D. Regional Planning for Air Navigation

While worldwide uniformity is desirable for certain matters pertaining to civil aviation, others are best approached on a regional basis, since operating conditions vary a great deal from region to region. In the North Atlantic region, for example, long-range ocean flying predominates, whereas in Europe many international flights are short overland jumps. To deal with these different conditions and to facilitate detailed planning, ICAO has mapped out nine geographical regions: Africa and the Indian Ocean, Asia, the Caribbean, Europe, the Middle East, North America, the North Atlantic, the Pacific, and South America. At meetings held for each of them, detailed plans are drawn up for the facilities, services, and procedures appropriate to that region. The regional plans specify the air navigation facilities and services that are required, and the locations where they are required, for communications, air traffic control, search and rescue, meteorology, and so on. ICAO's plans for the nine regions are regularly revised or amended to meet the needs of increasing traffic and to take into account technical developments in civil aviation.

ICAO's regional offices are its principal agents in advising and assisting states in regard to implementation. The offices direct as much of their resources as possible to giving practical help, among other ways through frequent visits to states by members of the technical staff. In addition, ICAO allots funds for long-duration advisory implementation missions to help member countries overcome local deficiencies.

Shortcomings are taken up by the regional offices and the ICAO secretariat with the governments concerned. More complex cases may require study by the Air Navigation Commission and, if necessary, by the ICAO Council. The problem of eliminating deficiencies in navigational services and facilities is one that ICAO considers critical.

The major difficulties are lack of funds for facilities and services, a shortage of trained personnel, and administrative and organizational difficulties. ICAO has encouraged governments to upgrade their facilities through loans for capital expenditures, technical assistance, and other means. It also produces manuals and other documentation to assist states in setting up aviation training programs for flight and ground personnel and offers advice on maintenance and improvement of technical standards.

E. Jointly Operated or Financed Services

Under the Chicago Convention, every ICAO member state is required to provide air navigation facilities and services on its own territory. Navigational facilities and services must also be provided for air routes traversing the high seas and regions of undetermined sovereignty. The ICAO Council is constitutionally authorized at the request of a member state to "provide, man, maintain, and administer any or all of the airports and other air navigation facilities, including radio and meteorological services, required in its territory for the safe, regular, efficient, and eco-

nomical operation of the international air services of the other contracting states." The council also may act on its own initiative to resolve a situation that might impair the "safe, regular, efficient, and economical operation" of international air services. Although ICAO has not yet undertaken the actual supervision of any nation's international air navigation facilities and services, two international agreements are in effect to furnish such services and facilities in parts of the North Atlantic region through so-called "joint-support" programs.

Under these joint-support agreements, the nations concerned provide services, facilities, or cash payments based on the use by their own aircraft of the routes involved. The two existing agreements are the Agreement on the Joint Financing of Certain Air Navigation Services in Greenland and the Faroe Islands and the Agreement on the Joint Financing of Certain Air Navigation Services in Iceland.

The vast majority of aircraft that utilize the special traffic-control, navigational, and meteorological services furnished from Iceland and Greenland for transatlantic crossings are neither Icelandic nor Danish. Hence, some 20 countries, including Iceland and Denmark, provide the funds necessary for the operation of these services.

ICAO administers these two agreements, the Secretary-General having certain responsibilities and the ICAO Council having others. A special standing body, the Committee on Joint Support of Air Navigation Services, advises the council in these matters. The operation and costs of the services are constantly reviewed, and international conferences are held. In the early 1970s, charges for the use of the aeronautical facilities and services were imposed on all civil aircraft crossing the North Atlantic. These "user charges" covered only 40 percent of the costs allocable to civil aviation but were increased to 50 percent for the years 1975 to 1978, 60 percent for 1979 and 1980, 80 percent for 1981, and 100 percent thereafter.

F. Technical Assistance

In recognition of the importance of the airplane for international and domestic transport in countries where road and railway services are lacking, and as a means of aiding these countries in their social and economic development, ICAO has, from its inception, operated technical assistance programs through UNDP and other UN organs.

Assistance programs executed by ICAO fall into three main categories. UNDP obtains its funds from donor countries and allocates these funds among recipient countries in the form of country, intercountry, and interregional projects. The Funds-in-Trust program provides financial assistance for specific projects in the country receiving the technical assistance. The Associate Experts program provides experts from certain countries to work under ICAO guidance.

Each civil aviation project may include one or more of the following forms of assistance: experts to provide specialist advice to the civil aviation administration or national airline; fellowships to allow nationals to be trained abroad in civil aviation disciplines, often at civil aviation training centers that have been established through ICAO technical assistance; and equipment, such as radio navigational aids or communication facilities, to ensure safe and regular air service.

Fellowships have been awarded in many fields, including training as pilots, aircraft maintenance technicians, air traffic controllers, radio and radar maintenance technicians, communication officers, airport engineers, electronics engineers, air transport economists, aeronautical information officers, aeronautical meteorologists, aviation medicine specialists, accident investigation experts, flight operations officers, airport fire officers, and instructors.

Major types of equipment provided include air traffic control, radar, and flight simulators; training aircraft; radio communication and radar systems; distance-measuring equipment; very high frequency omni radio ranges; instrument landing systems; nondirectional beacons; "navaid" flight-test units; airworthiness data-acquisition systems; language laboratories; audiovisual aids; visual approach slope indicator systems; and firefighting vehicles.

Major training institutions assisted by ICAO include civil aviation training centers in Egypt, Ethiopia, Gabon, Indonesia, Kenya, Mexico, Nigeria, Singapore, Thailand, Trinidad and Tobago, and Tunisia.

Expenditures for ICAO technical assistance programs in 1992 totalled nearly US$40 million, of which more than half came from UNDP. UNDP expenditures by region were as follows: US$5.4 million for the Americas; US$6.1 million for Europe, the Mediterranean, and the Middle East; and US$1.5 million for intercountry projects.

G. International Conventions Prepared Under ICAO

The increasing number of incidents of unlawful interference with civil aviation, beginning in the 1960s—aircraft hijacking, the placing of bombs on board aircraft, and attacks on aircraft, passengers, and crew members at airports—led to the adoption of three conventions.

- *The Tokyo Convention of 1963.* The Convention on Offenses and Certain Other Acts Committed on Board Aircraft does not define specific offenses, but it does have the virtue of ensuring that there will always be a jurisdiction (namely, that of the state of registry of the aircraft) in which a person who has committed an offense on board an aircraft can be tried. The convention also provides for the powers and duties of the aircraft commander and others respecting restraint and disembarkation of the suspected offender. It provides a detailed code of behavior for states in whose territory the suspected offender has disembarked and also stipulates the steps to be taken in the event of the hijacking of an aircraft.
- *The Hague Convention of 1970.* The Convention for the Suppression of the Unlawful Seizure of Aircraft defines the offense of unlawful seizure and provides for universal jurisdiction over, and arrest and custody of, the suspected offender. It also stipulates that prosecution or extradition of the suspected offender should take place without many restrictions.
- *The Montreal Convention of 1971.* The Convention for the Suppression of Unlawful Acts Against the Safety of Civil Aviation defines a number of acts of unlawful interference directed against international civil aviation. It provides for universal jurisdiction over the offender and, in general, contains rules for custody, extradition, and prosecution similar to those in the Hague Convention.

All three conventions are concerned with the preservation of the means of international communication and provide specifically that in the case of the unlawful seizure of an aircraft, any contracting state in which the aircraft or its passengers or crew are present shall facilitate the continuation of the journey of the passengers and crew as soon as practicable and shall return the aircraft and its cargo to the person lawfully entitled to possession.

The cooperative international action contemplated by the Tokyo, Hague, and Montreal conventions is intended to eliminate safe havens for hijackers and saboteurs.

Two additional international instruments in the field of aviation security have been developed under the auspices of ICAO.

- *The Protocol for the Suppression of Unlawful Acts of Violence at Airports Serving International Civil Aviation, Supplementary to the Convention for the Suppression of Unlawful Acts against the Safety of Civil Aviation.* The protocol was signed at Montreal on 24 February 1988 and came into force as of 6 August 1989. This protocol adds to the definition of "offence" given in the Montreal Convention of 1971, including actions that are likely to endanger airport safety. It establishes universal jurisdiction over the offender and applies the Montreal Convention's rules of custody, extradition, and prosecution.
- *The Convention on the Marking of Plastic Explosives for the Purposes of Detection*, opened for signature at Montreal in 1991 has not yet come into force. This convention requires that each state party prohibit and prevent the manufacture of unmarked plastic explosives. Four detection agents are defined in the convention's technical annex. The convention also requires each state party to prevent the movement of unmarked explosives out of its territory. It also provides for the destruction of certain kinds of existing stocks of plastic explosives.

Regime and Liability of Air Carriers

Much of ICAO's work has been devoted to keeping up-to-date the regime and limits of liability of air carriers in the case of death of, or injury to, passengers and in the carriage of cargo and postal items by air.

- *The Warsaw Convention of 1929.* The Convention on the Unification of Certain Rules Relating to International Carriage by Air, adopted during the early days of aviation, dominated the field of aviation passenger liability for almost half a century. It limits the liability, except in cases of gross negligence on the part of the carrier, to a maximum of 125,000 Poincaré gold francs (about US$10,000). The Hague Protocol of 1955 doubled the existing limits of liability. In 1971, by the Guatemala City Protocol, the rule of the Warsaw Convention based on presumption of fault yielded to *strict* liability, irrespective of fault. However, it will be some time before the 1971 protocol comes into force because at least 30 states, including five with major air traffic, must ratify it. An interesting feature of the Guatemala City Protocol is that although it provides for a limit of about US$100,000 per passenger, there is also provision for a domestic supplement if a state that is party to the protocol wishes to have a higher limit.

  In 1975, an International Conference on Air Law, convened under the auspices of ICAO, adopted new amendments to the Warsaw Convention, as amended by the Hague Protocol. Under the new provisions, the carrier is responsible for cargo damage, irrespective of fault. Another major change concerns the method of calculating the liability limits by turning from a solely gold monetary basis to a dual system, allowing countries that are members of the IMF to base passenger, baggage, and cargo liability on Special Drawing Rights, whereas countries not members of the IMF would declare liability limits in monetary units based on gold.
- *The Guadalajara Convention of 1961.* The Guadalajara Convention, supplementary to the Warsaw Convention, contains rules with regard to carriage performed by other than the contracting carrier, that is to say, by a carrier that had not issued the ticket to the passenger, or the air waybill to the consignor. In this case, both the contracting carrier and the actual carrier would be held jointly and severally liable under the Warsaw Convention or that convention as amended by the Hague Protocol.
- *The Rome Convention of 1952.* The Convention on Damage Caused by Foreign Aircraft to Third Parties on the Surface includes the principle of absolute liability of the aircraft operator for damage caused to third parties on the surface but places a limitation on the amount of compensation, expressed in Poincaré gold francs and calculated in relation to the aircraft concerned. However, a diplomatic conference convened in

1978 under ICAO auspices adopted a protocol for the amendment of the Rome Convention. The basic feature of the protocol is a substantial increase in the limits of liability and the expression of the limits in the Special Drawing Rights of the IMF.

The Geneva Convention of 1948. The Convention on the International Recognition of Rights in Aircraft was prepared in order to promote the use of loans in financing the sale of aircraft by providing protection of the lender's rights in an aircraft whenever the aircraft is in the territory of another state that is party to the Geneva Convention.

Other legal subjects on ICAO's work program include the establishment of a legal framework for global navigation of satellite systems; expediting the ratification of Montreal protocols Nos. 3 and 4 of the "Warsaw System"; study of the instruments of the "Warsaw System"; liability rules that might be applicable to air traffic services providers; and the implication of the UN Convention on the Law of the Sea for the application of ICAO's Chicago Convention.

BIBLIOGRAPHY

Air Navigation Plans. For all nine ICAO regions of the world.

ICAO Journal. Provides a concise account of the activities of ICAO and features additional information of interest to contracting states and to the international aeronautical world. Issued ten times a year.

ICAO publications and audio visual training aids. A catalog of reference materials from ICAO, including texts of conventions, procedures for air navigation services, technical publications, air transport studies, and videos on subjects such as air traffic control, airport emergency planning, aviation medicine, safety, and meteorology. Published annually.

ICAO Contracting States
(as of 20 February 1994)

Afghanistan	Dominican Republic	Lebanon	São Tomé and Principe
Albania	Ecuador	Lesotho	Saudi Arabia
Algeria	Egypt	Liberia	Senegal
Angola	El Salvador	Libyan Arab Jamahiriya	Seychelles
Antigua and Barbuda	Equatorial Guinea	Lithuania	Sierra Leone
Argentina	Eritrea	Luxembourg	Singapore
Armenia	Estonia	Madagascar	Slovakia
Australia	Ethiopia	Malawi	Slovenia
Austria	Federated States of Micronesia	Malaysia	Solomon Islands
Azerbaijan	Fiji	Maldives	Somalia
Bahamas	Finland	Mali	South Africa
Bahrain	France	Malta	Spain
Bangladesh	Gabon	Marshall Islands	Sri Lanka
Barbados	Gambia	Mauritania	Sudan
Belarus	Georgia	Mauritius	Suriname
Belgium	Germany	Mexico	Swaziland
Belize	Ghana	Moldova	Sweden
Benin	Greece	Monaco	Switzerland
Bhutan	Grenada	Mongolia	Syrian Arab Republic
Bolivia	Guatemala	Morocco	Tajikistan
Bosnia and Herzegovina	Guinea	Mozambique	Thailand
Botswana	Guinea-Bissau	Myanmar	The Former Yugoslav Republic of
Brazil	Guyana	Namibia	Macedonia
Brunei Darussalam	Haiti	Nauru	Togo
Bulgaria	Honduras	Nepal	Tonga
Burkina Faso	Hungary	Netherlands	Trinidad and Tobago
Burundi	Iceland	New Zealand	Tunisia
Cambodia	India	Nicaragua	Turkey
Cameroon	Indonesia	Niger	Turkmenistan
Canada	Iran, Islamic Republic of	Nigeria	Uganda
Cape Verde	Iraq	Norway	Ukraine
Central African Republic	Ireland	Oman	United Arab Emirates
Chad	Israel	Pakistan	United Kingdom
Chile	Italy	Panama	United Republic of Tanzania
China	Jamaica	Papua New Guinea	United States
Colombia	Japan	Paraguay	Uruguay
Comoros	Jordan	Peru	Uzbekistan
Congo	Kazakhstan	Philippines	Vanuatu
Cook Islands	Kenya	Poland	Venezuela
Costa Rica	Kiribati	Portugal	Viet Nam
Côte d'Ivoire	Korea, Democratic People's Republic of	Qatar	Yemen
Croatia		Romania	Yugoslavia
Cuba	Korea, Republic of	Russian Federation	Zaire
Cyprus	Kuwait	Rwanda	Zambia
Czech Republic	Kyrgyzstan	St. Lucia	Zimbabwe
Denmark	Lao People's Democratic Republic	St. Vincent and the Grenadines	
Djibouti	Latvia	San Marino	

THE UNIVERSAL POSTAL UNION (UPU)

BACKGROUND: Every year, over 435 billion pieces of mail are channelled into the inland stream of some 700,000 post offices around the globe, employing about 6 million persons. Of this mass, 9 billion pieces cross international boundaries with a minimum of formalities and are swiftly and safely delivered to their destinations. The orderly and economical movement of international mail is made possible by the Constitution and Convention of the Universal Postal Union, the basic Acts under which the UPU operates. Since 187 countries now come under these Acts, the provisions affect virtually the entire world population. Under the Constitution, UPU member countries form a single postal territory for the reciprocal exchange of letter-post items, and freedom of transit is guaranteed throughout the entire territory of the Union.

CREATION

Although generally taken for granted, present-day postal service is of relatively recent origin. The use of postage stamps for prepayment of postage was not introduced until 1840, when the UK established a unified postage charge, the famous penny rate, to be paid by the sender of a letter regardless of the distance it had to travel. Until that year, the postal fee based on distance was often very high and was not paid by the sender but by the addressee. If the addressee could not pay, the letter was returned. Gradually, other countries introduced adhesive stamps, and their use spread to international mail. In 1863, on the initiative of the US, representatives of 15 postal administrations met in Paris to consider the problem of standardizing international postal practices.

The decisive development came with the meeting of the first international Postal Congress at Bern in 1874, at the suggestion of the German government. The Bern Congress was attended by delegates from 22 countries: 20 European countries (including Russia), Egypt, and the US. The congress adopted a treaty concerning the establishment of a General Postal Union—commonly known as the Bern Treaty—signed on 9 October 1874. This was the forerunner of the series of multilateral Universal Postal Union conventions and came into force in the following year, when the union was formally established, on 1 July 1875, to administer its operative regulations.

The 1874 Convention provided for subsequent postal congresses to revise the convention in the light of economic and technical developments. The second congress, held in Paris in 1878, changed the name of the General Postal Union to the Universal Postal Union (UPU). Four more congresses were held prior to World War I: Lisbon, 1885; Vienna, 1891; Washington, 1897; and Rome, 1906. There were five congresses between the wars: Madrid, 1920; Stockholm, 1924; London, 1929; Cairo, 1934; and Buenos Aires, 1939. The first post–World War II congress met in Paris in 1947 and arranged for the UPU to be recognized as a specialized agency of the UN family in 1948. Other congresses met at Brussels, 1952; Ottawa, 1957; Vienna, 1964; Tokyo, 1969; Lausanne, 1974; Rio de Janeiro, 1979; Hamburg, 1984, and Washington, 1989. The 21st congress was scheduled to take place in Seoul in 1994.

PURPOSES

The basic objective of the union was stated in the 1874 Convention, reiterated in all successive revisions, and embodied in the constitution: "The countries adopting this Constitution comprise, under the title of the Universal Postal Union, a single postal territory for the reciprocal exchange of letter-post items." The 1924 congress added: "It is also the object of the Postal Union to secure the organization and improvement of the various international postal services." The 1947 congress added another clause: "and to promote the development of international collaboration in this sphere."

In recognition of the union's continued interest and newly assumed responsibilities in the field of development aid, the congress held in Vienna in 1964 enlarged the UPU's goals to include the provision of postal technical assistance to member states. Under the single-territory principle, all the union's member countries are bound by the constitution and convention to observe certain fundamental rules pertaining to ordinary mail. Ordinary mail under the Lausanne Convention includes letters, postcards, printed papers, small packets, and literature for the blind, such as books in Braille. Although the convention lays down basic postage rates for ordinary mail sent to addresses in UPU territory, variations are permitted within generous limits. Postal authorities of all member states are pledged to handle all mail with equal care, regardless of its origin and destination, and to expedite mail originating in other UPU countries on a level comparable to the best means of conveyance used for their own mail.

In the past, foreign mail was delivered to its destination without charge to the country where it was posted, and each country retained the postage collected on international mail. Since mid-1971, however, where there is an imbalance between mail sent and received, the postal administration of the country receiving the larger quantity is authorized to ask for repayment at a standard rate (fixed by the Postal Congress) to offset its excess costs. However, each country reimburses, at standard rates fixed by the Universal Postal Congress, all intermediary countries through which its mail passes in transit.

Freedom of transit—the basic principle of the union—is guaranteed throughout UPU territory. Specific regulations provide for the dispatch of mail and for the return of undeliverable mail to the sender. Certain articles, such as opium and other drugs and inflammable or explosive agents, are excluded from the international mails.

Four optional postal agreements supplement the convention. They cover parcel mail, money orders, giro (postal checks), and cash on delivery.

MEMBERSHIP

The original treaty allowed "overseas" countries to be admitted to the union subject to the agreement of administrations having postal relations with them. The 1878 congress decreed, however, that any country could accede directly to the union merely by unilateral declaration and communication of that declaration to the Swiss government. This system was revised by the Paris congress of 1947, which ruled that applications for membership in the union could be filed only by sovereign states and had to be channelled through the Swiss government. Approval is then required by at least two-thirds of the full membership. At the 1964 Vienna Congress, it was also decided that any member nation of the UN could accede directly to the UPU by a formal declaration addressed to the Swiss government. Since Washington Congress 1989, the government of the country concerned will address it directly to the Director General of the International Bureau, who will notify the member countries of the accession or consult with them on the application for admission, as the case may be.

Dependent territories were granted collective membership by a special postal conference held in Bern in 1876. Membership in the UPU as of 1 March 1994 had reached 187, including 185 independent states and two collective members of dependent territories.

RESTRICTED POSTAL UNIONS

Members of the UPU may establish restricted unions and make special agreements concerning the international postal service, provided always that they do not introduce provisions less favorable to the public than those provided for by the Acts of the UPU to which the member countries concerned are parties. Restricted unions are the Association of European Public Postal Operators (POSTEUROP), the Arab Permanent Postal Commission (APPC), the European Postal Financial Services Commission (CSFPE), the Regional Community for Posts and Telecommunications (RCPT), the Conference of Posts and Telecommunications Administrations of Central Africa (CAPTAC), the European Conference of Postal and Telecommunications Administrations (CEPT), the African Posts and Telecommunications Union (APTU), the Baltic Postal Union (BPU), the Postal Union of the Americas, Spain and Portugal (PUASP), the African Postal Union (APU), the Pan African Postal Union (PAPU), the Asian-Pacific Postal Union (APPU), the Nordic Postal Union (UPPN), and the South and West Asia Postal Union (SWAPU).

STRUCTURE

The permanent organs of the UPU are the Universal Postal Congress, the Executive Council, the Consultative Council for Postal Studies, and the International Bureau.

Universal Postal Congress

The Universal Postal Congress, which meets in principle every five years, is the supreme authority of the UPU. The congress consists of representatives of member countries who are plenipotentiaries furnished by their governments with the necessary powers. Its main function is to revise the acts of the union on the basis of proposals submitted to it.

It also appoints the members of the Executive Council and the Consultative Council for Postal Studies and considers the reports on the work of those two bodies, and it elects the Director General and Deputy Director General of the International Bureau. The congress approves the union's accounts for the years that have elapsed since the previous congress and fixes the ceiling of the union's annual expenditures pending the enforcement of the acts of the next congress. It issues instructions regarding the operation of the union's various bodies and lays down their respective duties, and it takes certain decisions of principle on the subject of technical assistance.

Members of the UPU
(as of 30 May 1994)

Afghanistan	Georgia	Oman
Albania	Germany	Pakistan
Algeria	Ghana	Panama
Angola	Greece	Papua New Guinea
Antigua and Barbuda	Grenada	Paraguay
Argentina	Guatemala	Peru
Armenia	Guinea	Philippines
Australia and Austra-	Guinea-Bissau	Poland
lian territories	Guyana	Portugal (and Macau)
Austria	Haiti	Qatar
Azerbaijan	Honduras	Romania
Bahamas	Hungary	Russian Federation
Bahrain	Iceland	Rwanda
Bangladesh	India	St. Kitts and Nevis
Barbados	Indonesia	St. Lucia
Belarus	Iran	St. Vincent and the
Belgium	Iraq	Grenadines
Belize	Ireland	San Marino
Benin	Israel	São Tomé and Principe
Bhutan	Italy	Saudi Arabia
Bolivia	Jamaica	Senegal
Bosnia and	Japan	Seychelles
Herzegovina	Jordan	Sierra Leone
Botswana	Kazakhstan	Singapore
Brazil	Kenya	Slovakia
Brunei Darussalam	Kiribati	Slovenia
Bulgaria	Korea, Democratic Peo-	Solomon Islands
Burkina Faso	ple's Republic of	Somalia
Burundi	Korea, Republic of	Spain
Cambodia	Kuwait	Sri Lanka
Cameroon	Kyrgyzstan	Sudan
Canada	Laos	Suriname
Cape Verde	Latvia	Swaziland
Central African	Lebanon	Sweden
Republic	Lesotho	Switzerland
Chad	Liberia	Syria
Chile	Libya	Tanzania
China	Liechtenstein	Thailand
Colombia	Lithuania	Togo
Comoros	Luxembourg	Tonga
Congo	Madagascar	Trinidad and Tobago
Costa Rica	Malawi	Tunisia
Côte d'Ivoire	Malaysia	Turkey
Croatia	Maldives	Turkmenistan
Cuba	Mali	Tuvalu
Cyprus	Malta	Uganda
Czech Rep	Mauritania	Ukraine
Denmark (including	Mauritius	United Arab Emirates
Faroe Islands and	Mexico	United Kingdom
Greenland)	Moldova	United Kingdom
Djibouti	Monaco	overseas territories
Dominica	Mongolia	United States
Dominican Republic	Morocco	United States
Ecuador	Mozambique	territories
Egypt	Myanmar	Uruguay
El Salvador	Namibia	Uzbekistan
Equatorial Guinea	Nauru	Vanuatu
Eritrea	Nepal	Vatican
Estonia	Netherlands	Venezuela
Ethiopia	Netherlands	Viet Nam
Fiji	Antilles and Aruba	Western Samoa
Finland	New Zealand and New	Yemen
France and French	Zealand territories	Yugoslavia
overseas departments	Nicaragua	Zaire
and territories	Niger	Zambia
Gabon	Nigeria	Zimbabwe
Gambia	Norway	

Independent countries whose situation with regard to the UPU has not yet been settled:
Andorra, Marshall Islands, Micronesia (Federated States of), Tajikistan
Territory in a special situation:
East Timor

Executive Council

The Executive Council was created under the title Executive and Liaison Committee by the 1947 congress to ensure the continuity of the work of the UPU between congresses. Its name was changed by the 1964 Vienna Congress. The Executive Council consists of a chairman and 39 members. The chairmanship (held by the United States from 1990 to 1994) devolves by right on the host country of each congress: the 39 members are elected by the congress on the basis of equitable geographical distribution. At least half the membership is renewed at each congress, and no member may be elected by three successive congresses.

Broadly speaking, the Executive Council maintains close working relations with the postal administrations of member countries with a view to improving international postal service. It has legislative power as regards the Detailed Regulations and takes the necessary provisional measures to settle urgent matters that may arise between congresses. It studies administrative, legislative, and legal problems of interest to the postal service, draws up proposals, and makes recommendations to the congress. It is also responsible, within the framework of international technical cooperation, for promoting, supervising, and coordinating all aspects of postal technical assistance, including vocational training.

To some extent, the Executive Council supervises the activities of the International Bureau, considering and approving the annual report of the bureau. It also examines the annual report of the Consultative Council for Postal Studies and makes contacts, for the purpose of studies, with the UN and the specialized agencies and other international bodies.

Ten standing committees of the Executive Council deal, respectively, with human resources management, finance, general matters and structure of the union, regulatory aspects of letter post, pricing and remuneration of letter post, air conveyance and quality control, parcel post, postal financial services, technical cooperation, and Washington General Action Plan.

Consultative Council for Postal Studies

Originally, the Consultative Committee for Postal Studies was composed of all the member countries of the UPU, and worked through a Management Council of 26 members meeting annually. The 1969 Tokyo Congress abolished the Consultative Committee and replaced its Management Council by a Consultative Council for Postal Studies (CCPS), with the same function and a membership of 30, increased to 35 by the 1974 Lausanne Congress. The members are elected by the congress, in principle on the basis of as wide a geographical distribution as possible. The CCPS meets annually at the UPU headquarters in Bern (Switzerland).

The present CCPS is composed of 35 member countries elected by the Washington Congress (1989) and the current chairmanship is held by the Federation of Russia (1989–94) until the 21st (Seoul 1994) Universal Postal Congress (a five-year interval between congresses). The chairman, the vice-chairman (Canada from 1989 to 1994), and the committee chairmen of the CCPS constitute the steering committee, which meets at the chairman's request and prepares and directs the work of each CCPS session.

The CCPS exercises its functions during the period between congresses, and is responsible for carrying out studies of major problems affecting postal administrations in all UPU member countries. The current CCPS work program reviewed the considerable progress made in the implementation of the Washington General Action Plan through the work of various symposia, working parties, action groups, and committees in the technical, operational, and economic fields. Technical cooperation and vocational training for new and developing countries constitute an important activity. Seven standing committees deal, respectively, with the post and its markets, development of rapid services, operations and quality of service, modernization,

management, human resources, and postal development. Symposia, in particular, continue to constitute the most dynamic work method, resulting in important recommendations. They focus on key CCPS activities, namely, the EMS service, marketing, security, development of new products, human resources, research and technology, and the environment.

The work of the Electronic Transmission Standards Group (ETSG) (a Joint EC/CCPS Group) resulted in the establishment of a UPU worldwide postal electronic data transmission network, POST*NET. Postal security issues continued to be endorsed by the CCPS and EC based on proposals put forth by the Postal Security Action Group of the UPU (PSAG) (also a Joint EC/CCPS Group).

The Postal Development Action Group (also a Joint EC/CCPS Group) focussed on lobbying international financial institutions with regard to financing postal projects and on the need to incorporate postal needs into the national economic planning process.

The new edition of the Multilingual Vocabulary of the International Postal Service was available at the end of 1992. Specialized modules or supplements were developed on "marketing of the postal service" and "automation and computerization."

The work of the Joint ISO–UPU Working Party resulted in the adoption of the international standard ISO 11180 on postal addressing and its publication in 1993.

An urgent study on the post and the environment was launched in 1992, which culminated into a congress resolution aimed at putting forth a strategy for the UPU and its member countries in favor of protecting the environment. The "Green Paper on the future of postal services," published by the Commission of the European Communities, was also closely monitored.

The 1993 CCPS approved a work program for the 1995–99 period proposing 15 major study areas. This program was incorporated into the UPU's new strategic planning and budget programming activities. The Seoul Congress (August–September 1994) will be asked to make major decisions regarding the restructuring of the UPU, including the replacement of the current CCPS by a more dynamic Postal Operations Council (POC).

International Bureau

Since the establishment of the union, a central office known as the International Bureau has functioned at Bern. The bureau has five primary duties. (1) It serves as the UPU's permanent secretariat; (2) it acts as a clearinghouse for information concerning postal matters, being responsible, among other things, for the coordination, publication, and dissemination of all manner of information regarding the union and the international postal service; (3) it functions as a clearinghouse for the settlement between postal administrations of debts relating to transit charges, terminal dues, and international reply coupons; (4) it acts as a conciliator and arbitrator in disputes over postal matters between administrations; and (5) it promotes technical cooperation of all types. The bureau is headed by a Director General, who serves also as the secretary-general of the union's bodies; since 1985, the office has been held by A.C. Botto de Barros of Brazil.

BUDGET

The Universal Postal Congress sets a ceiling for the ordinary annual expenditure of the UPU. However, the ceiling may be exceeded, if circumstances so require, on the authority of the Executive Council and subject to certain conditions. The 1989 Washington Congress set the following ceilings: SwFr26.1 million for 1991; SwFr26.6 million for 1992; SwFr 26.8 million for 1993; SwFr26.8 million for 1994; SwFr26.9 million for 1995 (SwFr1.43=US$1).

The UPU's expenses are shared by all member countries, which, for this purpose, are divided into 11 contribution classes. The 1979 congress introduced a system of self-financing of the

UPU; previously, the funds needed for running the union were advanced by the Swiss Confederation, and member countries settled their contribution afterward on the basis of actual expenditure. The congress has authorized the Executive Council to exceed the ceilings of expenditure in order to deal with situations created by unforeseen circumstances that entail unavoidable expenditure. The 20th congress (Washington, 1989) replaced the gold franc by the International Monetary Fund (IMF) Special Drawing Right (SDR) as the official currency of the UPU and as the monetary unit for settlement of international postal accounts.

ACTIVITIES

A. Clearing accounts for international services

The UPU acts as a central office for the international postal traffic carried on by its members. In principle, UPU member states retain the revenue they derive from the sale of postage stamps and from other fees and charges for foreign-bound mail. Administrations must, however, reimburse one another for the transportation of foreign mail in intermediate transit and for the imbalance between international mail sent and received (terminal dues). At the end of each year, the International Bureau draws up an annual general clearing account for transit and terminal charges, stating the balances due. For 1993, 95 postal administrations settled transit and terminal charges through the bureau's clearing account.

Every two years the International Bureau publishes a general clearing account for the international reply coupons that it supplies to facilitate payment of international correspondence. Some 165 countries now sell these coupons, and all countries must accept them as payment for postage.

B. Information services

The UPU acts as an international clearinghouse for postal information. At the request of postal administrations, the International Bureau circulates inquiries concerning the operation of the various postal systems and makes the replies available to all UPU members. Inquiries may concern domestic, as well as international, postal practices and cover subjects as diverse as the texts of propaganda permitted on letters and packages, mobile post offices on motorboats, the opening of new offices of exchange, introduction of summer time, and national regulations for the dispatch of radioactive substances.

The International Bureau publishes a number of international postal handbooks, including the following: *Postal Statistics* (internal and international); *List of Prohibited Articles* (prohibited from the mails); *International List of Post Offices*; and *Recueil de transit*. The CCPS has prepared the *Multilingual Vocabulary of the International Postal Service*, designed to ensure that terms used by different national postal services convey an identical meaning. The bureau also prepares an annotated edition of UPU legislation, which includes discussion of principles, opinions, decisions, and practices underlying current international postal procedures and the present organization of the union.

C. Arbitration and interpretation of international postal rules

If a difference of opinion on the interpretation of UPU legislation between two or more postal administrations cannot be resolved by direct negotiations, the matter is settled by in-house arbitration. The countries concerned may also designate a single arbitrator, such as the International Bureau of the UPU.

D. Revision of rules and adoption of guidelines for international services

The main function of the Universal Postal Congress, as noted above, is to study and revise the acts of the union on the basis of proposals put forward by member countries, the Executive Council, and the CCPS. At the 1989 congress, which was attended by representatives of 162 countries, 881 proposals were considered. The main results included the following: conversion of basic letter-post charges into guideline charges; adoption of a Framework Agreement for EMS (international expedited mail), strengthening the service while retaining the flexibility required to adapt the agreement to changing customers' needs; generalization of the use of bar codes and standardized methods of identification for such purposes as tracking and tracing of items; introduction of an optional international business reply service; introduction of an international recorded delivery service; approval of separate terminal dues rates for exchanges of letters and printed papers exceeding an annual threshold of 150 tons and of a single combined rate for exchanges of letters and printed papers below that threshold, as well as a 12.5 percent increase in rates; approval of new statistical and accounting systems for the new terminal dues structure based on actual weights; restructuring of the convention and its detailed regulations in order to incorporate provisions concerning airmail in the corresponding letter-post provisions; recasting of the Postal Financial Services Agreements and of their related detailed regulations. The 20th congress also adopted a permanent project to safeguard and enhance the quality of and to modernize the international postal service. The project includes these main components: monitoring the quality of postal exchanges, transport flow studies, development of EMS, monitoring the competition, and market research.

On the subject of technical assistance, the congress laid down general principles and guidelines. It decided that first priority should be given to the least developed countries, and it instructed the Executive Council and the Director General of the International Bureau to take the necessary measures to provide more substantial aid to those countries. The congress also instructed them to encourage the use of TCDC as a technical assistance modality.

E. Technical assistance

The principle of technical assistance is contained in Article 1 of the UPU constitution; it was couched in general terms in order to give the union flexibility in the use of all forms of technical cooperation, present and future.

Requests for UPU assistance in technical cooperation matters cover all sectors: planning, organization, management, operations, training, and financial services. The aid provided comes in three forms: recruiting and sending experts, consultants, or volunteers; granting vocational training or further training fellowships for individual or group courses; and supplying equipment and training or demonstration aids.

Within the framework of UNDP, which as of 1993 was the main source of financing, the UPU executes country and intercountry projects covering all aspects of the postal services and the three components of experts, fellowships, and equipment. Projects common to several countries, which form a very important part of this program, make it possible to solve, economically and rationally, the problems that arise in a given region, especially by setting up intercountry postal training schools. These regional and interregional projects are carried out in conjunction with the restricted postal unions and the UN regional commissions.

Funds from the UPU budget make it possible to provide additional assistance to that of UNDP—namely, in the form of short consultant missions of three months at most, at the request of the postal administration concerned. A noteworthy feature is that, for many missions, the consultants' countries of origin also share the cost of this form of technical cooperation by continuing to pay all or part of the salaries of their officials during the mission. At the same time, since 1991 the UPU also has funded integrated projects incorporating short-term consultants' missions, vocational training fellowships, and items of minor equipment. The UPU Special Fund, set up in 1966 and maintained by voluntary contributions from member countries, is mainly designed to finance training and to further training activities in the form of fellowships, equipment, and training courses or study cycles. Some developed countries provide the International Bureau with funds for the management of associate experts in order to supplement the staff of ongoing projects and to give young people with sufficient training the opportunity to improve their professional qualifications.

Lastly, under a resolution adopted by the Executive Council in 1967, governments may avail themselves of technical assistance instead of payment, which they finance themselves from funds in trust; the International Bureau then undertakes to manage the projects implemented in this way. Of course, the UPU, through the International Bureau, continues to act as an intermediary, wherever expedient, for supplying assistance in kind to developing countries on the basis of offers from developed countries. It also has made a special effort in the field of vocational training by assessing the needs to be met and listing the facilities available in the various member countries. This effort is reflected in the establishment or reinforcement of national or multinational schools and the organization of study cycles for the further training of senior staff and of instructor-training courses; with this aid, a large number of postal administrations now have qualified postal instructors.

F. Postal Studies

The 1989 Washington Congress adopted a more rational approach to the CCPS work programme by having major studies divided into specific sub-study areas. The major technical studies covered the following areas: the post and its markets (commercial strategies, delivery network and customer analysis, press and publishing, parcel-post products/services), development of rapid services (EMS and electronic mail), operations and quality of service (improvement of the postal system, monitoring, mail circulation standards), modernization (automation, coding, telematics, technology research), management (international accounting, productivity indices, security, decentralization), human resources (adapting to the demands of competition, training), and postal development.

CCPS reports have been published as a Collection of Postal Studies, which includes over 200 studies to date. In the future, a new presentation of certain CCPS documents and studies and the rationalized use of others will provide administrations with operational binders for better management and follow-up of UPU decisions in key areas.

BIBLIOGRAPHY

Annual Report of the Work of the Union. Résumé and general review of UPU activities.

Collection of Postal Studies. A series of publications concerning topics studied by the CCPS.

Union Postale. Quarterly. Parallel text in the seven languages of the union—Arabic, Chinese, English, French, German, Russian, and Spanish. Contains articles on postal services and information on UPU activities.

The Universal Postal Union. A brief outline of UPU features.

THE INTERNATIONAL TELECOMMUNICATION UNION (ITU)

BACKGROUND: The International Telecommunication Union is the oldest of the intergovernmental organizations that have become specialized agencies related to the UN. In 1865, a convention establishing an International Telegraph Union was signed in Paris by the plenipotentiaries of 20 continental European states, including two extending into Asia—Russia and Turkey. Three years later, a permanent international bureau for the union was established in Bern, Switzerland. This bureau, which operated until 1948, was the forerunner of the present General Secretariat of the ITU. In 1885, at Berlin, the first regulations concerning international telephone services were added to the telegraph regulations annexed to the Paris convention. By the end of the nineteenth century, radiotelegraphy, or "wireless," had been developed, and for the first time it was possible to communicate directly between shore stations and ships at sea. Rival wireless companies frequently refused to accept one another's messages, however. In 1903, an international conference was called to consider the problem, and in 1906, in Berlin, 29 maritime states signed the International Radiotelegraph Convention, establishing the principle of compulsory intercommunication between vessels at sea and the land. The International Radiotelegraph Conference, which met in Washington in 1927, drew up for the first time a table of frequency allocations.

CREATION

Two plenipotentiary conferences were held in 1932 at Madrid—one covering telephone and telegraph and the other radiotelegraph communication. The two existing conventions were amalgamated into a single International Telecommunication Convention (the word *telecommunication* signifying "any transmission, emission or reception of signs, signals, writing, images and sounds, or intelligence of any nature by wire, radio, optical, or other electromagnetic systems"). The countries accepting the new convention, which came into force on 1 January 1934, formed the International Telecommunication Union.

The International Telecommunication Convention of 1932 has been revised six times. The Plenipotentiary Conference of the ITU, meeting in Atlantic City in 1947, radically changed the organization to keep up with developments in telecommunication: for example, a new permanent organ, the International Frequency Registration Board, was created to cope with the overcrowding of certain transmission frequencies; and an agreement was drawn up under which the ITU was recognized by the UN as the specialized agency for telecommunication. The convention was further modified in certain respects by plenipotentiary conferences in 1952, 1959, 1965, 1973, and 1982.

In 1989, the Plenipotentiary Conference held in Nice created a High-Level Committee to propose wide-ranging recommendations about the role of ITU in a world totally transformed by the convergence of telecommunications and computer technology and the globalization and privatization of telecommunications providers. An historic Additional Plenipotentiary Conference was convened in Geneva in December 1992 to adopt far-reaching structural changes to the union and a thoroughly revised constitution and convention. The new constitution officially entered into force on 1 July 1994. However, the structural changes were considered so important to maintaining the organization's relevance in the rapidly changing technological world that the new structure was implemented as of 1 March 1993.

PURPOSES

The new Constitution of the International Telecommunication Union (Geneva, 1992) cites the following purposes for the union:

- to maintain and extend international cooperation between all members of the union for the improvement and rational use of telecommunications of all kinds;
- to promote and to offer technical assistance to developing countries in the field of telecommunications;
- to promote the development of technical facilities and their efficient operation;
- to promote the extension of the benefits of the new telecommunication technologies to all the world's inhabitants;
- to harmonize the actions of members in the attainment of these ends;
- to promote, at the international level, the adoption of a broader approach to telecommunications issues, an approach that includes other world and regional organizations and nongovernmental organizations concerned with telecommunications.

MEMBERSHIP

As of 28 April 1994 ITU had 184 member nations. Although membership in the union itself is open only to sovereign states, the union's three sectors and their various conferences are open to telecommunications companies, scientific organizations, industrial groups, financing and development institutions, international and regional telecommunication organizations, and the United Nations itself as well as its specialized agencies. Indeed, the 1992 constitution makes it clear that the participation of private sector organizations in the union's work is encouraged. In 1994 more than 235 private sector companies and nearly 40 international organizations took part in ITU's standardization work.

STRUCTURE

The new structure of ITU combines the activities of its previous bodies into three "pillars" supporting the work mandated by the Plenipotentiary Conference: the Radiocommunication Sector, the Telecommunication Standardization Sector, and the Development Sector. Each sector's work is directed by international and regional conferences, supported by a bureau under the administration of a director. The bureau directors are assisted by "Advisory Groups" that are open to representatives of national telecommunication administrations, authorized organizations, and study groups. The Plenipotentiary Conference also elects the ITU Council, which acts as an intersessional administrative body guiding the work of the organization in the four-year intervals between conferences. The organization's General Secretariat, headquartered in Geneva, is administered by a Secretary-general, assisted by a deputy secretary-general. The secretary-general is assisted by both the secretariat and a World Telecommunication Advisory Committee.

Plenipotentiary Conference

The supreme body of the ITU is the Plenipotentiary Conference, in which each member has one vote. Previously, it met at intervals of five or more years—in Atlantic City in 1947, Buenos Aires in 1952, Geneva in 1959, Montreux in 1965, Torremolinos in 1973, Nairobi in 1982, and Nice in 1989. In 1992 the extraordinary Additional Plenipotentiary Conference met in Geneva to fundamentally revamp the organization. The first session of the Plenipotentiary Conference since the restructuring was held in Kyoto, Japan, in September 1994.

The Plenipotentiary Conference sets general policies for fulfilling the purposes of the union; receives reports on the organization's activities since the previous conference and takes decisions on those reports; establishes the budget in light of decisions taken by the ITU Council; fixes salary scales; elects member nations to the ITU Council; elects the secretary-general; the deputy secretary-general; the directors of the bureaus of the three sectors, and the members of the Radio Regulations Board; considers and adopts amendments to the constitution and the convention; concludes agreements between ITU and other organizations that may be concluded by the ITU Council. In general the conferences focus on long-term policy issues.

The ITU Council

The ITU Council (formerly called the Administrative Council) traces its history back to the New Jersey Plenipotentiary Conference of 1947. It is composed of 43 member nations elected by the plenipotentiary along a regional formula: the Americas have eight seats, Western Europe has seven seats, Eastern Europe and Northern Asia have four seats, Africa has 12 seats, and Asia and Australasia has 12 seats. The council members hold office until the next plenipotentiary, at which time they may be reelected.

The ITU Council guides the work of the union between sessions of the plenipotentiary. It approves the budgets of the union and controls its finances. It is responsible for the coordination of ITU's work with other United Nations organizations.

The members of the ITU Council from 1989 to 1994 were: Region A (Americas): Argentina, Brazil, Canada, Colombia, Cuba, Jamaica, Mexico, United States. Region B (Western Europe): France, Germany, Italy, Greece, Spain, Sweden, Switzerland. Region C (Eastern Europe and Northern Asia): Bulgaria, Russia, Romania. Region D (Africa) Algeria, Benin, Burkina Faso, Cameroon, Cape Verde, Egypt, Kenya, Mali, Morocco, Nigeria, Senegal, Tanzania. Region E (Asia and Australasia): Australia, China, India, Indonesia, Korea (Republic of), Kuwait, Malaysia, Pakistan, Philippines, Saudi Arabia, Thailand.

The Radiocommunications Sector

World Conferences on International Telecommunications

The plenipotentiary empowers these conferences to revise telecommunications regulations and establish general principles for international telecommunications services. World conferences are open to all ITU member administratios, the United Nations and its specialized agencies, regional telecommunication organizations, and intergovernmental organizations operating satellite systems.

Radiocommunication Conferences and Assemblies

Every two years the Radiocommunication Conference and a Radiocommunication Assembly meet to review and revise the Radio Regulations on the basis of an agenda adopted by the ITU Council. Radiocommunication conferences are open to all ITU member administrations and to the United Nations and its specialized agencies, regional telecommunication organizations, and intergovernmental organizations operating satellite systems. In addition, telecommunication operators authorized by their country to participate in the work of the Radio Sector are admitted to the conferences.

The Radiocommunication Assemblies provide the technical basis for the work of the conferences. The assemblies create study groups of experts and decide on the priority, urgency, and timescale for study of specific issues. The study groups are made up of experts from both administrations and public/private sector entities. By March 1994, 120 companies and 50 international regional organizations participated in the work of the assembly's study groups.

Radiocommunication Bureau

Headed by a director elected by the plenipotentiary, the bureau is the part of the ITU secretariat that coordinates the preparatory work of the study groups and communicates this information to members. It makes preparations for the Radiocommunication Conferences and Assemblies. It provides assistance to developing countries in preparing their own radiocommunication conferences.

Radio Regulations Board

The Radio Regulations Board is a part-time, nine-member body of experts that approves the rules of procedure to register radio frequency assignments and equitable utilization of the geo-stationary satellite orbit. It also investigates complaints by ITU members about frequency interference, and formulates recommendations to resolve such problems. It holds up to four meetings a year. The board members serve as custodians of international public trust and not as representatives of their respective member states or region, hence they cannot be part of national delegations at conferences. The Radio Regulations Board replaces the former five-member International Frequency Registration Board (IFRB), which was a full time body.

The Telecommunication Standardization Sector

World Telecommunication Standardization Conferences

These conferences are held every four years to approve, modify, or reject draft standards (called "Recommendations" because of their voluntary character). The conferences set the work program for the study groups that elaborate these recommendations. The Telecommunication Standardization Study Groups are groups of experts in which administrations and public/private sector entities participate. They focus on the standardization of telecommunication services, operation and performance of equipment, systems, networks, services, tariffs, and accounting methods.

Telecommunication Standardization Bureau

The bureau is headed by a director elected by the plenipotentiary. It prepares for conferences and meetings and processes and publishes information received from administrations about the application of the International Telecommunication Regulations. This information includes international telephone routes, statistics, notifications, and operational bulletins. It also is responsible for updating the documents and data bases of the Telecommunication Standardization Sector.

The Development Sector

World Telecommunication Development Conferences

These conferences fix objectives and strategies for balancing worldwide and regional development in telecommunications.

They serve as a forum for studying policy, organization, operation, regulatory, technical, and financial questions related to the needs of developing countries. Usually there will be one world conference and five regional conferences (one in each of the five regions) between sessions of the Plenipotentiary Conference. The resolutions, decisions, recommendations, and reports of the conferences are submitted to the plenipotentiary. The development conferences direct the work of the Telecommunications Development Bureau. The conferences also set up study groups on issues specific to developing countries.

The Telecommunication Development Bureau

This body was first established in 1990, as a direct result of the recommendations of the Nairobi Plenipotentiary, which directed the union to transform its ad hoc development arrangements into a comprehensive program to aid developing countries in creating and upgrading their national telecommunications systems. The director is elected by the plenipotentiary and supervises the bureau in its work.

The bureau prepares for development conferences, processes information received from administration, exchanges information with members, and updates the data bases of the Telecommunications Sector.

General Secretariat

The General Secretariat is at ITU headquarters in Geneva, Switzerland. It handles arrangements for ITU conferences and meetings and maintains liaison with member states and with the UN, the specialized agencies, and other international organizations. It also carries out the ITU's extensive publication program. It is headed by the secretary-general. Pekka Tarjanne of Finland was elected secretary-general by the Nice Plenipotentiary in 1989. In December 1993 the secretariat employed 719 persons, representing 74 nationalities.

The Secretariat also organizes an international commercial telecommunications exhibition called TELECOM, held in Geneva every four years. It also cosponsors regional telecommunications exhibitions with member administrations (Asia TELECOM, Africa TELECOM, Americas TELECOM, and Europa TELECOM). These trade shows feature a comprehensive display of telecommunication equipment and services, including digital transmission, switching technologies, and digital networks. In conjunction with TELECOM, ITU sponsors a FORUM which deals with emerging trends in telecommunications technology, administration, management, financing, research, and equipment supply.

BUDGET

The ordinary budget includes expenditures pertaining to the ITU Council, the Geneva headquarters, and the various conferences and meetings. The technical cooperation special accounts budget includes administrative expenditure for technical assistance to developing nations and is financed by the UNDP. The publications budget includes production costs of all publications and is self-financed through sales.

At each Plenipotentiary Conference, member countries choose a class of contribution. The lowest classes are reserved for countries designated least developed countries by the United Nations. The ordinary budget is then divided by the number of units assigned to each member. However, regional radio conferences require additional contributions.

All other organizations (private enterprises, international organizations, etc.) that take part in the work of the union's three sectors must also choose a contribution class; however, their units are 1/5th the value of the member countries' contributory unit. Separate contributions must be made for participation in any of the various conferences of the union.

The total budgets for 1994 amounted to Swiss francs 154,768,000. On this basis, a single contributory unit for a member state was Swiss francs 319,200.

ACTIVITIES

Background

In the early 1980s ITU members recognized that advances in technology were fundamentally changing the nature of telecommunications and the very principles upon which the union was founded. These fundamental changes were behind the restructuring of the union, which was completed in 1994. An understanding of these changes is fundamental to understanding ITU's activities in the rapidly evolving world of telecommunications.

From 1900 to the 1980s telecommunication was generally understood to mean essentially the transmission of voice telephone signals. Governments and the telecommunications industry shared easily communicable goals: provide telephone service for every business and home and arrive at international technological standards that would allow telephone connections between all countries. Until the 1980s telecommunication equipment technology evolved comparatively slowly, allowing enough time for ITU's international bodies to set standards without inhibiting the progress of technology development. In the area of pricing (tariffs) there was widespread acceptance that densely populated areas would produce enough income for telephone companies to cover their expenses for providing coverage for remote, sparsely populated areas.

In the 1980s technological advances in the digitization of telephone signals, software control, component miniaturization, and sharply decreasing switching and transmission costs brought about an explosion in products and services that could now transmit not only voice, but also data, text, image, and video information. Telecommunications became less a stand-alone industry and more intimately connected with the computer industry. It could be said that the two technologies had "converged," fundamentally reshaping the way all kinds of information services could be delivered to people and businesses. Similarly, wired and "wireless" telecommunications also began to converge. Wireless systems (cellular telephones, for example) began to compete with existing networks at every level through terrestrial and satellite-based communications systems.

At the same time, the equipment supply industry was transformed by shorter innovation cycles and global marketing efforts. This drastically shortened the time available for consultation and adoption of international standards. Finally, the profitability ethic of the computer industry began to replace the universal coverage ethic of the telecommunications industry. Businesses began to demand cost-based pricing, which would reduce their costs in increasingly competitive global markets. However, the growth of cost-based pricing would effectively deny telecommunications to isolated or sparsely populated countries or regions, since they could never afford to pay enough to be as profitable as densely populated areas. In other words, the competitive environment produced "islands" of high telecommunication capability where profitable customers existed and "deserts" of low telecommunications capability where profitable returns could not be achieved.

This trend strengthened towards the end of the 1980s with the end of the cold war. An international consensus emerged that market-based economies were the most efficient way to deliver goods and services and promote economic growth. Previously, most of the world's countries had government-controlled telecommunications departments. In the new atmosphere of deregulation and privatization, many state-owned telecommunications departments would become state-owned corporations, and perhaps eventually private corporations. Telecommunications companies in industrialized countries found their main opportunity for growth was to change from offering only domestic services to offering services region-wide or even globally, competing with the domestic services of other nations.

ITU's secretary-general, Dr. Pekka Tarjanne, told an international gathering in Tokyo in 1994 that: "Today's ITU does not fully reflect the dramatic changes that have taken place in telecommunications. The Union remains largely the preserve of dominant carriers, with little active participation by new players in the telecommunications industry or by major users. This trend strongly suggests the need for greater private sector participation by the new players in the telecommunications industry. . . . How can non-governmental players be given a greater voice in ITU decision-making processes without infringing on the sovereign rights of nations?" The future evolution of the organization and its activities will revolve around this dilemma.

The activities of the organization were defined in the 1992 constitution as:

- allocating bands of the radio frequency spectrum, alloting radio frequencies, registering radio frequency assignments, and registering orbital positions in the geostationary-satellite orbit in order to avoid harmful interference between radio stations of different countries;
- coordinating efforts to eliminate harmful intereference between radio stations of different countries;
- facilitating worldwide standardization of telecommunications;
- delivering technical assistance to developing countries that want to create, develop, and improve their telecommunications systems;
- fostering collaboration among its members to establishing rates at levels as low as possible while ensuring efficient service;
- promoting measures that would save lives through the cooperation of telecommunications services; and
- promoting the establishment of preferential and favorable lines of credit from international financial and development organizations for extending telecommunications services to the most isolated areas in countries.

Activities of the Radiocommunication Sector

The work of ITU, although invisible to the public, affects every individual on the planet every time he or she turns on a radio. Regulating the use of radio frequencies is one of the union's most fundamental and important jobs. These radio frequencies are also commonly used in everyday life for: telephone calls or data transmission by satellite or microwave systems, television broadcasts, radio broadcasts, aircraft communications, taxi communication networks, ambulance communication networks, police communication networks, and car telephones. While the possible uses for radio frequencies are always increasing, the usable range is not. Because of the physical nature of radio waves, the frequency spectrum is a limited natural resource. Similarly, the space available for geostationary-satellites to circle the earth also is finite.

The role of the Radiocommunication Sector is to ensure the efficient and economical use of the radio-frequency spectrum by all radiocommunication services, including those using the geostationary orbit. It also carries out studies that form the basis of its recommendations for the use of the frequency spectrum. The Radiocommunication Sector covers the following subjects:

- spectrum utilization and monitoring;
- inter-service sharing and compatibility;
- science services;
- radio wave propagation;
- fixed-satellite service;
- fixed service;
- mobile services;
- sound broadcasting; and
- television broadcasting.

The first Radio Regulations were drawn up in 1906 and now apply to frequencies between 9 kHz and 400 GHz. The first Table of Frequency Allocations appeared in 1912. These documents have the status of international treaties and are legally binding on ITU member countries. Changes to the Radio Regulations and the Table of Frequency Allocations are made by negotiations between national delegations at world radio conferences. Any proposed modification to these documents must be carefully studied because it will affect the manufacture of satellites and communication equipment used by aircraft, emergency services, and users of mobile phones. For example, a technique called single sideband operation (SSB) would make it possible to virtually double spectrum capacity. However, because existing radio transmitters and receivers are configured for double sideband operation (DSB), a sudden switch to SSB would render the enormous existing equipment base useless. Instead, ITU recommended that, as of 1991, its members should begin producing equipment that could operate in both SSB and DSB environments, so that the transition to SSB could be as seamless as possible.

Activities of the Telecommunication Standardization Sector

The Telecommunication Standardization Sector studies technical, operating, and tariff questions and issues recommendations to standardize worldwide telecommunications. These recommendations cover: services; network operations; tariffs; accounting principles; maintenance; protection of the outside of telecommunication facilities; data communication; terminals for telematic services; television and sound transmission; switching; signalling and man-machine language; transmission performance for systems and equipment; general network aspects.

Between 1990 and 1994 ITU adopted 379 new telecommunication standards applicable to public networks. It substantially amended 484 existing standards. This represented a dramatic increase in productivity, due mainly to the restructuring begun in 1989. This increased activity was considered essential to keeping ITU at the center of the international standardization effort and preventing the fragmentation of the industry into regional markets created on a de facto basis by the adoption of one manufacturer's equipment. The threat of fragmentation is very serious, since the growth of the world's economy (for example in the financial sector) would be seriously curbed if systems are not compatible.

ITU's standard-setting activities ensure global compatibility and interconnectivity of equipment and systems. This allows consumers a choice of suppliers and ensures competition among manufacturers and service providers. In order to keep up with the pace of technological change, ITU instituted a mechanism through which standards are adopted as they are readied by study groups, instead of waiting for formal approval by an international standardization conference (which are held only every four years).

The following ITU standards allow services in any country to be access other services all over the world:

- the X.400 recommendations cover interconnection of electronic message handling systems;
- the X.500 recommendations cover the transmission of electronic directory information;
- the F.710 recommendations cover teleconferencing services;
- the V-series of recommendations cover data transmission by modems over telephone networks; and
- the X.25 recommendation covers data transmission over dedicated networks.

Activities of the Telecommunication Development Sector

In the early 1980s, the members of ITU commissioned an independent study of progress made in telecommunications in the developing world. The study, called the Maitland Commission's

Green Paper, was released in 1984 and indicated that there was a growing chasm between industrialized and developing countries in telecommunications technology. In 1989, the Nice Plenipotentiary established ITU's newest sector, the Telecommunications Development Bureau (TDB), to focus the union's previously ad hoc efforts in this area. The TDB began operations in 1990 and was incorporated into the structure of the Telecommunications Development Sector by the 1992 constitution.

The role of this sector is to coordinate and focus the union's efforts, as a specialized agency of the UN system, to help developing countries develop and improve their telecommunication services. It also coordinates telecommunications activities funded by the United Nations Development Program (UNDP). Between 1989 and 1994, ITU administered each year on average some 600 expert missions of two to three months' duration; granted 1,200 training fellowships; implemented 180 technical cooperation projects worth around US$30 million; procured equipment for its field projects worth about US$8 million; and offered more than 700 telecommunication training courses to telecommunication administrations.

The most important contribution of this sector in its short history was the production of the first World Telecommunication Development Conference (WTDC), held in Buenos Aires, Argentina, in March 1994. For this conference it produced the World Telecommunication Development Report, which analyzed the state of the world's telecommunications infrastructure. One of the most shocking statistics revealed in that report was that there are an average of 49 telephone lines per 100 inhabitants of the 24 developed countries that are members of the Organization of Economic Cooperation and Development (OECD). However, there are only 3.5 lines per 100 inhabitants for the countries of the rest of the world. This number drops to less than one line per 100 inhabitants in the least developed countries. These statistics demonstrate the extent of the gulf which must be bridged to allow developing countries access to the world's global economy.

The WTDC attracted worldwide attention and was addressed by the vice president of the United States, Al Gore. The conference adopted the Buenos Aires Declaration and an action plan (Buenos Aires Action Plan) which charted the union's activities in this sector into the twenty-first century.

The declaration included the following points:

- telecommunications is considered to be an essential component of development and ITU members have a duty to make communications available to all individuals, groups, and peoples;
- special attention must be paid to the least developed countries;
- the governments of developing countries must establish appropriate telecommunication policies and regulatory structures;
- developing countries should foster liberalization, private investment, and competition in their telecommunication sector in order to attract investment;
- ITU has an important role to play as a catalyst among all the entities whose cooperation is necessary to help developing countries;
- the fostering and development of skilled staff in developing countries is critical to the development of their telecommunications networks.

The action plan addressed seven areas: policies, strategies and financing; human resources management and development; the creation of development plans; integrated rural development; broadcasting; and information services. One of the plan's concrete goals is to double the telephone density in developing countries by the year 2000.

One of the themes emerging from the WTDC was that government-run telecommunication administrations in developing countries are ultimately responsible for developing their own vibrant national telecommunication networks. To this end, it recommended widespread adoption of the principles of corporatization, privatization, and competition of telecommunication services in their countries. However, the WTDC stopped short of recommending specific goals or ways of financing such development. The estimated cost of implementation of the Buenos Aires Action Plan was Swiss francs 14.8 millions, 41 percent of which was to be financed by ITU and 59 percent from other development "partners" like the World Bank.

The World Telecommunications Development Report criticized existing financial assistance methods. It said that developing countries had been inconsistent in their support for telecommunication projects when applying for financial assistance for public works. The report projected that US$58.3 billion will have to be spent between 1995 and 2000 for most nations to achieve a basic level of infrastructure. The World Bank, however, called for more private investment, and calculated that the cost could be as high as US$80 billion. It was generally agreed, however, that developing countries run the risk of being permanently exiled from the international, information-based economy of the twenty-first century, if they fail to acquire and apply substantial resources to their telecommunications systems.

PUBLICATIONS

One of the most important duties of ITU headquarters is to collect and collate essential telecommunication data and to edit and publish the numerous documents essential for the day-to-day operation of the various telephone, telegraph, and broadcasting systems of the world. Among the documents regularly issued by the ITU are the *International Frequency List;* the quarterly *High Frequency Broadcasting Schedules;* yearly radio statistics; lists of coast, ship, and fixed stations; codes and abbreviations in general use; lists of radiolocation stations; an alphabetical list of call signs; summaries of international monitoring information; the *ITU Newsletter* (formerly the *Telecommunication Journal*) and similar publications, all generally issued in English, French, and Spanish editions, or in a single trilingual edition. Many of ITU's technical documents are available in electronic forms: online as part of ITUDOC, on CD-ROM discs, or on other computer-readable media.

Telecom Information Exchange Services (TIES) and ITUDOC

This on-line computer communication service is based at ITU headquarters for telecommunications-related information exchange. The system offers electronic mail, bulletin boards, document interchange, computer conferencing, and distributed access to ITU data bases such as global telecom services and tariffs, as well as notification of telecommunication information. It also contains a terminology infobase of 30,000 telecommunications terms in English, French, and Spanish.

ITUDOC allows users of the Internet to retrieve ITU documents and publications from a central computer server at ITU headquarters. It also allows participants in ITU's work to submit their contributions electronically.

ITU MEMBER COUNTRIES
(as of 1 May 1994)

Afghanistan
Albania
Algeria
Andorra
Angola
Antigua and Barbuda
Argentina
Armenia
Australia
Austria
Azerbaijan
Bahamas
Bahrain
Bangladesh
Barbados
Belarus
Belgium
Belize
Benin
Bhutan
Bolivia
Botswana
Bosnia and Herzegovina
Brazil
Brunei Darussalam
Bulgaria
Burkina Faso
Burundi
Cambodia
Cameroon
Canada
Cape Verde
Central African Republic
Chad
Chile
China
Colombia
Comoros
Congo
Costa Rica
Côte d'Ivoire
Croatia
Cuba
Cyprus
Czech Republic
Denmark
Djibouti
Dominican Republic
Ecuador
Egypt
El Salvador
Equatorial Guinea
Eritrea
Estonia
Ethiopia
Fiji
Finland
France
Gabon
Gambia
Georgia
Germany

Ghana
Greece
Grenade
Guatemala
Guinea
Guinea-Bissau
Guyana
Haiti
Honduras
Hungary
Iceland
India
Indonesia
Iran (Islamic Republic of)
Iraq
Ireland
Israel
Italy
Jamaica
Japan
Jordan
Kazakhstan
Kenya
Kiribati
Korea, Democratic People's Republic of
Korea, Republic of
Kuwait
Kyrgyzstan
Lao People's Democratic Republic
Latvia
Lebanon
Lesotho
Liberia
Libya
Liechtenstein
Lithuania
Luxembourg
Madagascar
Malawi
Malaysia
Maldives
Mali
Malta
Mauritania
Mauritius
Mexico
Micronesia
Moldova
Monaco
Mongolia
Morocco
Mozambique
Myanmar
Namibia
Nauru
Nepal
Netherlands
New Zealand
Nicaragua
Niger
Nigeria
Norway

Oman
Pakistan
Panama
Papua New Guinea
Paraguay
Peru
Philippines
Poland
Portugal
Qatar
Romania
Russia
Rwanda
St. Vincent and the Grenadines
San Marino
São Tomé and Principe
Saudi Arabia
Senegal
Sierra Leone
Singapore
Slovakia
Slovenia
Solomon
Somalia
South Africa
Spain
Sri Lanka
Sudan
Suriname
Swaziland
Sweden
Switzerland
Syria
Tadjikistan
Tanzania
Thailand
The Former Yugoslav Republic of Macedonia
Togo
Tonga
Trinidad and Tobago
Tunisia
Turkmenistan
Turkey
Uganda
Ukraine
United Arab Emirates
United Kingdom
United States
Uruguay
Uzbekistan
Vanuatu
Vatican
Venezuela
Viet Nam
Western Samoa
Yemen
Yugoslavia
Zaire
Zambia
Zimbabwe

THE WORLD METEOROLOGICAL
ORGANIZATION (WMO)

BACKGROUND: The practical uses of meteorology are to instruct, advise, and warn mankind about the weather. Thus, it can help prevent devastation caused by flood, drought, and storm; it can also assist the peoples of the world in best adapting their agriculture and industry to the climatic conditions under which they live.

For meteorology, international cooperation is indispensable. The reasons are expressed in the following words of President John F. Kennedy: ". . . there is the atmosphere itself, the atmosphere in which we live and breathe and which makes life on this planet possible. Scientists have studied the atmosphere for many decades, but its problems continue to defy us. The reasons for our limited progress are obvious. Weather cannot be easily reproduced and observed in the laboratory. It must, therefore, be studied in all of its violence wherever it has its way. Here, new scientific tools have become available. With modern computers, rockets and satellites, the time is ripe to harness a variety of disciplines for a concerted attack. . . . The atmospheric sciences require worldwide observation and, hence, international cooperation."

CREATION

Beginning in 1853, many of the world's leading maritime countries tried to establish an international system for collecting meteorological observations made by ships at sea.

The first international meteorological congress was held in Vienna in 1873; it led to the founding of the International Meteorological Organization, composed of directors of meteorological services from various countries and territories throughout the world. This body carried out ambitious programs to perfect and standardize international meteorological practices.

As transportation, communications, agriculture, and industry developed in the 20th century, they increasingly relied on meteorology, while meteorology itself relied to an increasing extent on advances in science and technology to perfect its methods of observing and predicting weather phenomena. Hence, the closest possible collaboration was called for between the International Meteorological Organization and other international bodies.

A conference of directors of national meteorological services met in Washington in 1947 under the auspices of the International Meteorological Organization and adopted the World Meteorological Convention, establishing the World Meteorological Organization as a UN specialized agency. On 23 March 1950, after 30 signers had ratified or acceded to the convention, it came into force. The first WMO congress opened in Paris on 19 March 1951.

PURPOSES

As set forth in the World Meteorological Convention, the purposes of the WMO are sixfold:

1. to facilitate worldwide cooperation in the establishment of networks of stations for meteorological, hydrological, and other geophysical observations and to promote the establishment and maintenance centers charged with the provision of meteorological and related services;
2. to promote the estabishment and maintenance of systems for rapid exchange of weather information;
3. to promote standardization of meteorological and related observations and ensure uniform publication of observations and statistics;

4. to further the application of meteorology to aviation, shipping, water problems, agriculture, and other human activities;
5. to promote activities in operational hydrology and cooperation between meteorological and hydrological services; and
6. to encourage research and training in meteorology and, as appropriate, to assist in coordinating the international aspects of such research and training.

MEMBERSHIP

Membership in the WMO is not limited to sovereign states; it may include territories that maintain their own meteorological services. Membership is open to any of the 45 states and 30 territories attending the 1947 conference in Washington that signed the convention or to any member of the UN with a meteorological service. Any of these automatically becomes a member of the WMO upon ratifying or acceding to the convention. Any other state, territory, or group of territories maintaining its own meteorological services may become eligible for membership upon approval of two-thirds of the WMO membership. As of 30 April 1994, the WMO had 175 members, including 170 states and five territories.

STRUCTURE

The WMO is headed by a president and three vice-presidents, elected by the World Meteorological Congress. There is also an Executive Council and a secretariat.

World Meteorological Congress

The World Meteorological Congress is the supreme body of the organization and is composed of the delegates representing its member states and territories. (According to the World Meteorological Convention, the principal delegate of each member "should be the director of its meteorological service.") The congress, which meets every four years, determines changes in the constitution and functions of the various WMO bodies, adopts regulations covering meteorological practices and procedures, and determines general policies for carrying out the purposes of the organization and related matters. It also establishes the regional associations and technical commissions.

Each member of the congress has one vote. Election of individuals to serve in any capacity in the organization is by a simple majority of the votes cast; other questions are decided by two-thirds of the votes cast for and against. On certain subjects, only members that are states may vote.

Executive Council

The Executive Council has 36 members: the president and the three vice-presidents of the WMO; the presidents of the six regional associations; and 26 directors of meteorological services from the member countries, elected by the congress. Meeting at least once a year, the council carries out the activities of the organization and the decisions of the congress. Its own decisions are reached by a two-thirds majority.

Regional Associations

There are six regional associations: one each for Africa, Asia, South America, North and Central America, the Southwest Pacific, and Europe. The regional associations are composed of the WMO members whose meteorological networks lie in or extend into the respective regions. They meet when necessary and examine from a regional point of view all questions referred to them by the Executive Council. Each association has the responsibility for coordinating meteorological activity.

Technical Commissions

The technical commissions are composed of experts in meteorology. They study various meteorological problems and make recommendations to the executive committee and the congress. The WMO has established eight commissions for the following areas: basic systems; instruments and methods of observation; atmospheric sciences; aeronautical meteorology; agricultural meteorology; marine meteorology; hydrology; and climatology.

Secretary-General and Secretariat

The secretariat, in Geneva, completes the structure of the WMO. Its staff, under the direction of a Secretary-General, undertakes studies, prepares publications, acts as secretariat during meetings of the various WMO bodies, and provides liaison between the various meteorological services of the world. The president of the WMO, elected in 1987, is Zou Jingmeng of China. The Secretary-General is G. O. P. Obasi of Nigeria. He is assisted by a staff of about 250.

BUDGET

Contributions to the WMO's regular budget are assessed upon members by the congress. For 1992–95, the budget was SFr236.1 million (approximately US$177 million). Estimates for 1994, approved by the Executive Council, amounted to SFr61.2 million (approximately US$45.9 million). In addition, a budget of SFr15.6 million (approximately US$11.7 million) was approved for technical cooperation activities, the funds being obtained from extrabudgetary sources. Total extrabudgetary expenditures for 1992–93 amounted to SFr13.98 million (approximately US$10.49 million), funded through UNDP, the WMO Voluntary Cooperation Program, and funds-in-trust.

ACTIVITIES

A. World Weather Watch

The World Weather Watch (WWW) was established by the Fifth World Meteorological Congress, held in Geneva in 1967. Its purpose is to make available to each national meteorological service meteorological and related environmental information required in order to enjoy the most efficient and effective meteorological and related environmental services possible in both applications and research. No other scientific discipline has such

international interdependence. The WWW has three essential elements:

1. The Global Data-Processing System provides meteorological analyses and forecast products to all meteorological services. It is composed of three world meteorological centers, in Melbourne, Moscow, and Washington, DC; 26 regional meteorological centers; and more than 150 national meteorological centers.
2. The Global Observing System provides observational data from surface-based observing stations and platforms and from meteorological satellites of its space-based subsystem.
3. The Global Telecommunication System consists of telecommunication facilities and arrangements necessary for the rapid and reliable exchange of the observational data and processed products required by meteorological services. The system is organized into the main telecommunication network (the core of the system), six regional meteorological telecommunication networks, and national meteorological telecommunication networks that interconnect meteorological centers through approximately 240 data links.

The WWW also has three support functions:

1. WWW Data Management is concerned with the overall real-time management of data and product selection and presentation to recipients in appropriate standard formats and codes and with the monitoring of the data availability, quality, and operational status of the WWW system.
2. WWW Implementation Support Activity makes available to WMO members information on new WWW technology, operational experience, and proven methodology.
3. WWW Implementation Coordination ensures that WWW activities are carried out in a coordinated and cost-effective way. The present GOS component of WWW includes about 10,000 land observing stations, 7,000 mobile ship stations, 3,000 aircraft stations, 300 fixed and drifting buoys, and 200 special-purpose stations measuring such parameters as background air pollution, radiation, and atmospheric ozone. A vast amount of global data and information is provided by several near-polar-orbiting weather satellites, and an almost continual surveillance in tropical and temperature latitudes is carried out by the geostationary satellites. Meteorological data, weather analyses, forecasts for several days ahead, and warnings for severe weather are exchanged by the Global Telecommunication System in digital and pictorial forms. Series of internationally agreed-upon WMOL character/figure codes and binary codes are in use. Details of agreed-upon international WWW procedures are prescribed in the WMO manuals on the Global Data-Processing System, the Global Observing System, the Global Telecommunication System, and codes.

The WWW also incorporates four other components.

1. *The Instruments and Methods of Observation Programme,* which aims at improving the accuracy of observational data, the standardization of meteorological instruments and observing techniques, and the incorporation of new technological developments.
2. *WMO Satellite Activities,* aimed at providing high-quality global satellite data and products and strengthening members' capabilities to receive and effectively use satellite data.
3. *The Tropical Cyclone Programme,* which is designed to assist some 60 countries in minimizing loss of life and property damage caused by tropical cyclones and storm surges by improving forecasting and warning systems, and disaster pre-

vention and preparedness awareness. Established in 1971, the program is effected through five TCP regional bodies: the ESCAP/WMO Typhoon Committee; the WMO/ESCAP Panel on Tropical Cyclones; the RAI (Africa) Tropical Cyclone Committee for the South-West Indian Ocean; the RAIV (North and Central America) Hurricane Committee; the RAV (south-west Pacific) Tropical Cyclone Committee for the South Pacific and South East Indian Ocean; and through projects that are implemented by small groups of experts.

4. *WMO Antarctic Activities,* aimed at promoting and coordinating the implementation and operation of the basic elements of the WWW to meet the requirements of meteorological services and research activities in the Antarctic, as well as for environmental monitoring and climate change.

B. World Climate Programme

The World Climate Programme (WCP) established by the eighth WMO Congress in 1979 comprises four major component programs: the World Climate Applications and Services Programme (WCASP); the World Climate Data and Monitoring Programme (WCDMP); the World Climate Research Programme (WCRP); and the World Climate Impact Assessment and Response Strategies Programme (WCIRP).

The objectives of the WCP are:

1. facilitate the effective collection and management of climate data and the monitoring of the global climate system, including the detection and assessment of climate variability and changes;
2. foster the effective application of climate knowledge and information for the benefit of society and the provision of climate services, including the prediction of significant climate variations both natural and as a result of human activity;
3. assess the impacts of climate variability and changes that could markedly affect economic or social activities and advise governments thereon and contribute to the development of a range of socioeconomic response strategies that could be used by governments and community;
4. improve the understanding of climate processes for determining the predictability of climate, including its variability and change; identifying the extent of human influence on climate; and developing the capability for climate prediction.

WMO is directly responsible for WCASP and WCDMP and for the overall coordination of the WCP, but has joint responsibility with the International Council of Scientific Union (ICSU) and the Intergovernmental Oceanographic Commission (IOC) of UNESCO for the WCRP. UNEP is responsible for the WCIRP. Several other international organizations such as FAO, UNESCO, WHO, and UNDP are actively involved.

The close cooperation required for the WCP, which is complex and multidisciplinary, is achieved through interagency meetings and through the Climate Exchange Co-ordination Activities. Within the program, priority attention is given to the food, water, and energy sectors.

The World Climate Programme provides an interagency, interdisciplinary framework to address the full range of climate change issues, including research into the economic and social consequences of climate change. It is the major international program supporting the work of the Intergovernmental Panel on Climate Change, the process of implementation of the Framework Convention on Climate Change, and relevant to the implementation of Agenda 21, the seminal statement of the 1992 UN Conference on Environment and Development (the "Earth Summit").

The eleventh World Meteorological Congress decided that the WCP should be supported by the Global Climate Observing System (GCOS) as an essential activity associated with the World Climate Programme.

The basic objectives of the WCRP are to increase understanding of climate mechanisms and to determine to what extent climate can be predicted and the possible influence of man's activities on climate. Achieving these objectives requires input from many scientific disciplines. To assist in this, coordination and overall guidance is provided by the WMO/ICSU Joint Scientific Committee. The eleventh WMO Congress decided that UNESCO's Intergovernmental Oceanographic Commission (IOC) should be invited to join in WCRP. Continuing efforts are made at model development and global climate analysis, in particular the assessment of cloud prediction schemes and the representation of ocean-atmosphere interface fluxes in atmospheric general circulation models. Projects to assemble quality-controlled, consistent global climatological sets of sea-surface temperature and precipitation also have been established. Continual support is given to WCRP activities concerned with the study of climate forcing, including research on radiation codes used in climate models, aerosol sensitivity investigations and the global ozone research and monitoring projects.

C. Applications of Meteorology

The WMO's Aeronautical Meteorology Programme serves to further the application of meteorology to aviation. It is keyed to ensure, jointly with ICAO, the continuous development of regulatory and guidance material required for the provision of services to aviation in accordance with the operational requirements of aviation. It also contributes to the implementation and improvement of meteorological services necessary to ensure the safety, regularity, and efficiency of air transport.

The overall purpose of the WMO's Marine Meteorological Programme is the promotion of the required marine meteorological services over the high seas and coastal areas, including specialized ocean services and the application of marine climatological information for planning marine activities. The program also includes development of a comprehensive marine environmental monitoring service, a coordinated ocean data management system, and activities within the Integrated Global Ocean Services System, a joint venture of the WMO and the Intergovernmental Oceanographic Commission.

The purpose of the Agricultural Meteorology Programme is to help WMO members develop the capability to provide the agricultural community with practical information—based on knowledge of the climate, recent weather, and short-, medium-, and long-term forecasts—that can be used to improve production, reduce risks and crop losses, decrease pollution by agricultural chemicals, diminish costs, and increase the efficiency of the use of energy in agriculture. In turn, these immediate goals can help members achieve self-sufficiency in food production and increase export earnings from agriculture. At the international and regional levels, the program helps to identify requirements for information in agricultural meteorology, assess the impact of weather and climate fluctuations on food production, and apply agrometeorological methods to improve land use, crop selection, and management practices.

D. Atmospheric Research and Environment Programme

The purpose of the Atmospheric Research and Environment Programme (AREP) is to contribute to the advancement of atmospheric sciences and to assist members in providing better meteorological services by fostering research in meteorology and related environmental fields. It also is aimed at ensuring that members have relevant information and guidance to make the best use of the results of research applied for the benefit of their national economies and quality of life. The transfer of technology is ensured through support, within available resources, for the participation of scientists from developing countries in AREP.

AREP has five main components: the Global Atmosphere Watch (GAW); the Programme on Short- and Medium-Range Weather Prediction Research; the Programme on Long-range Forecasting Research; the Tropical Meteorology Research Programme; and the Programme on Physics and Chemistry of Clouds and Weather Modification Research.

Global Atmosphere Watch (GAW). This worldwide system integrates most monitoring and research activities involving the measurement of atmospheric composition. It is intended to serve as an early warning system to detect further changes in the ozone layer and in long-range transport of pollutants, including acidity and toxicity of rain, as well as the atmospheric burden of aerosols. The instruments of these globally standardized observations and related research are the WMO Global Ozone Observing System (GOOS), operating about 140 stations in more than 60 countries, and the WMO Background Air Pollution Monitoring Network (BAPMoN), which has nearly 200 stations in more than 90 countries. GAW is the main contributor of data on chemical composition and physical characteristics of the atmosphere to the Global Environment Monitoring Systems (GEMS) of UNEP. GAW will be a main component of the Global Climate Observing System (GCOS). Through GAW, WMO collaborates with the UN Economic Commission for Europe (ECE) and is responsible for the meteorological part of the Monitoring and Evaluation of the Long-Range Transmission of Air Pollutants in Europe. In this respect WMO has arranged for the establishment of two Meteorological Synthethizing Centres (in Oslo and Moscow) that provide daily analysis of the transport of pollution over Europe. GAW also gives attention to atmospheric chemistry studies, prepares assessments, and encourages integrated environmental monitoring.

Weather Prediction Research Programs. These programs assist members in improving their weather services by exchanging the results of research on weather prediction. It accomplishes this goal by means of international conferences, technical reports, and progress reports on numerical weather prediction. The Programme on Short- and Medium-Range Weather Prediction Research aims at strengthening members' research with emphasis on improving the accuracy of short- and medium-range weather forecasting, including forecasting of local weather phenomena (particularly severe phenomena). The main objective of the Programme on Long-Range Forecasting Research is to foster members' research efforts in the development, introduction, and improvement of operational long-range weather forecasting systems.

Tropical Meteorology Research Programme. This program aims at the promotion and coordination of members' efforts into such important problems as monsoons, tropical cyclones, droughts in the arid zones of the tropics, rain-producing tropical weather systems, and the interaction between tropical and mid-latitutde weather systems. The goal is to be of economic benefit to tropical countries by improving members' forecasting abilities.

Physics and Chemistry of Clouds and Weather Modification Research Programme. This program encourages scientific research in physics and chemistry of clouds and its application to all fields where clouds have a major role. Examples include weather enhancement (rain making) and hail suppression. The program provides information on worldwide weather modification projects and guidance in the design and evaluation of experiments. It also studies the role of clouds in the transport, transformation, and dispersion of pollution.

E. Hydrology and Water Resources

The purpose of the WMO's Hydrology and Water Resources Programme is to promote worldwide cooperation in the assessment of water resources and their development through the coordinated establishment of hydrological networks and services,

including data collection and processing, hydrological forecasting and warnings, and the supply of meteorological and hydrological data to be used for the design of projects. The five primary components of the program are: the Operational Hydrological Programme (OHP); Basic Systems, Including the Hydrological Operational Multipurpose Systems (HOMS); the Operational Hydrology Programme (OHP); Applications and Environment; and the Programme on Water-Related Issues.

The emphasis is on the operational hydrology program, and particularly its hydrological operational multipurpose subprogram, the main aim of which is to provide an efficient means and systematic institutional framework for transfer of operational hydrological technology to and between developing countries.

The program for applications and services in regard to water resources provides technical support for WMO activities dealing with environmental problems, such as the Tropical Cyclone Programme, the World Climate Programme, and WMO activities relating to droughts and desertification.

The program for cooperation with water-related programs of other international organizations includes a wide range of activities undertaken jointly with other organizations, notably support by the WMO to the International Hydrological Programme of UNESCO.

F. Education and Training

The Education and Training Programme is designed to support the scientific and technical programs of the WMO, as well as to assist in the development of the required personnel in the national meteorological and hydrological services of member countries. The program thus ensures that the full benefit of meteorological and hydrological skills and knowledge are obtained at national levels.

Activities under the program include surveys of personnel training requirements; the development of appropriate training programs; the establishment and improvement of regional training centers; the organization of training courses, seminars, and conferences; and the preparation of training materials in the form of compendia of lecture notes, problem workbooks, and visual and audiovisual aids. Emphasis is being placed on audiovisual aids and computer-assisted learning materials. The program also arranges individual training programs and provides fellowships. There are, on the average, 500 WMO trainees a year, and about 300 fellowships are awarded annually from the WMO's regular budget and from extrabudgetary resources, such as UNDP, funds-in-trust, and the Voluntary Cooperation Programme.

The program provides advice on education and training in meteorology and operational hydrology and on the availability of suitable training facilities. A training library is maintained. Films are provided on a loan basis to members on request.

The Panel of Experts on Education and Training serves as the focal point of the program.

G. Regional Program

The main objectives of the regional program are to give the required support to the organization and implementation of WMO programs on a regional and subregional basis. Within the regional program, as part of the WMO secretariat, three offices have been established: for Africa, in Bujumbura, Burundi; for Asia and the Pacific, in Geneva; and for the Americas, in Asuncion, Paraguay.

H. Technical Cooperation

The WMO's technical cooperation activities—in the form of fellowships, expert missions, equipment, and assistance for group training, such as workshops and seminars—are carried out through UNDP, the Voluntary Cooperation Programme, trust-fund arrangements, and the regular budget of the organization.

Assistance has been given in support of projects ranging from the establishment, organization, and operation of meteorological and hydrological services to the application of meteorology in increasing food production and assessing alternative energy sources.

UNDP funding is provided to individual countries and regional projects. The WMO provides assistance in formulating and overseeing the implementation of projects involving meteorology and operational hydrology. The financial value of the assistance provided to 130 countries under UNDP and trust-fund arrangements in 1992 is estimated at US$17.8 million. More than 50 large-scale projects were under execution during 1992. Several of these were directly related to the expansion and strengthening of national meteorological and hydrological services, while others were concerned with the evaluation of water resources, flood forecasting, meteorological services for agriculture, meteorological training and research, and improvement of facilities for the detection and warning of tropical cyclones. Special attention was made to the new project covering assistance to drought-stricken countries in eastern and southern Africa. There was also a continuing project for strengthening the agrometeorological and hydrological services of the Sahelian countries. A center for training in the application of agrometeorology and operational hydrology formed a part of this program.

WMO's Voluntary Cooperation Program (VCP) is maintained by contributions from members to the Voluntary Cooperation Fund and to the Equipment and Services Program. Although priority is given to the implementation of the World Weather Watch, the VCP also provides assistance and supports other WMO programs in such fields as agrometeorology, hydrology, and climate. It grants fellowships to nationals of developing countries. Assistance totalling almost US$7.7 million was provided through the program in 1993. A total of 16 VCP projects were completed in 1992. As of 31 December 1992, 101 VCP projects benefitting 67 countries were being implemented.

Under trust-fund arrangements, countries make funds available through the WMO for technical cooperation activities either in the country providing the funds or in another country.

Activities under the WMO's regular budget represent only a very small percentage of the total assistance and are confined mainly to the awarding of fellowships and participation in group training.

BIBLIOGRAPHY

International Glossary of Hydrology
Manual on the Global Data Processing System
Manual on the Global Observing System
Manual on Marine Meteorological Services
Operational Hydrology Reports
Special Environmental Reports
Technical Regulations—Manual on Codes
WMO Annual Report.
WMO Bulletin. Summarizes the work of the WMO and of developments in international meteorology. Quarterly.
WMO Training Series
World Weather Watch—The Plan and Implementation Programme.
(The WMO Library carries 35,000 monographs and 200 periodicals on the topics of meteorology, climatology, hydrology, marine and agricultural meteorology, and related topics of pollution and environment.)

Members of the World Meteorological Organization
(as of 1 June 1994)

Afghanistan	Comoros	Indonesia	Myanmar	Sri Lanka
Azerbaijan	Congo	Iran	Namibia	Sudan
Albania	Costa Rica	Iraq	Nepal	Suriname
Algeria	Côte d'Ivoire	Ireland	Netherlands	Swaziland
Angola	Croatia	Israel	New Zealand	Sweden
Antigua and	Cuba	Italy	Nicaragua	Switzerland
Barbuda	Cyprus	Jamaica	Niger	Syria
Argentina	Czech Republic	Japan	Nigeria	Tajikistan
Armenia	Denmark	Jordan	Norway	Tanzania
Australia	Djibouti	Kazakhstan	Oman	Thailand
Austria	Dominica	Kenya	Pakistan	The Former
Bahamas	Dominican Republic	Korea, Democratic	Panama	Yugoslav Republic
Bahrain	Ecuador	People's Republic of	Papua New Guinea	of Macedonia
Bangladesh	Egypt	Korea, Republic of	Paraguay	Togo
Barbados	El Salvador	Kuwait	Peru	Trinidad and
Belarus	Eritrea	Latvia	Philippines	Tobago
Belgium	Estonia	Lao Peoples	Poland	Tunisia
Belize	Ethiopia	Democratic Republic	Portugal	Turkey
Benin	Fiji	Lebanon	Qatar	Turkmenistan
Bolivia	Finland	Lesotho	Romania	Uganda
Botswana	France	Liberia	Russian Federation	Ukraine
Brazil	Gabon	Libya	Rwanda	United Arab
Brunei Darussalam	Gambia	Lithuania	St. Lucia	Emirates
Bulgaria	Georgia	Luxembourg	São Tomé and	United Kingdom
Burkina Faso	Germany	Madagascar	Principe	United States
Burundi	Ghana	Malawi	Saudi Arabia	of America
Cambodia	Greece	Malaysia	Senegal	Uruguay
Cameroon	Guatemala	Maldives	Seychelles	Uzbekistan
Canada	Guinea	Mali	Sierra Leone	Vanuatu
Cape Verde	Guinea-Bissau	Malta	Singapore	Venezuela
Central African	Guyana	Mauritania	Slovakia	Viet Nam
Republic	Haiti	Mauritius	Slovenia	Yemen
Chad	Honduras	Mexico	Solomon Islands	Yugoslavia
Chile	Hungary	Mongolia	Somalia	Zaire
China	Iceland	Morocco	South Africa	Zambia
Colombia	India	Mozambique	Spain	Zimbabwe

THE INTERNATIONAL MARITIME ORGANIZATION (IMO)

BACKGROUND: The seven seas, accounting for about two-thirds of the earth's surface, are the only truly international part of our globe. Except for a marginal belt a very few miles wide, touching on the shores of countries, the greater part of the world's oceans and maritime resources are the common property of all nations. Since ancient times, however, "freedom of the seas" has too often been a theoretical ideal rather than a reality. In each historic era, the great maritime powers tended to use their naval might to dominate the sea. Some of those powers, while serving their own interests, served the world as a whole, as in the great explorations of unknown continents. Many sought to use the waters for purely national interests, particularly in matters affecting straits and other narrow waterways. Private shipping interests, often supported by their national governments, have been even more competitive, and international cooperation in maritime matters has been very limited.

The need for an international organization to develop and coordinate international maritime cooperation was expressed by President Woodrow Wilson, who called for "universal association of the nations to maintain the inviolate security of the highway of the seas for the common and unhindered use of all the nations of the world." However, it was not until after the creation of the UN that such an organization came into being.

CREATION

The convention establishing the International Maritime Organization (originally called the Inter-Governmental Maritime Consultative Organization) was drawn up in 1948 by the UN Maritime Conference in Geneva, but it was 10 years before the convention went into effect. The conference decided that the IMO's success depended on participation by most of the nations with large merchant navies, and it specified that the organization would come into being only when 21 states, including seven having at least 1 million gross tons of shipping each, had become parties to the convention. On 17 March 1958, the convention went into effect. The first IMO Assembly met in London in January 1959. The relationship of the IMO to the UN as a specialized agency was approved by the UN General Assembly on 18 November 1958 and by the IMO Assembly on 13 January 1959.

PURPOSES

The purposes of the IMO, as set forth in the convention, are the following:

1. to facilitate cooperation among governments on technical matters of all kinds affecting shipping engaged in international trade;
2. to encourage the general adoption of the highest practicable standards in matters concerning maritime safety, efficiency of navigation, and the prevention and control of marine pollution;
3. to encourage the removal of discriminatory action and unnecessary restrictions by governments engaged in international trade, so as to promote the availability of shipping services to world commerce without discrimination;
4. to consider matters concerning unfair restrictive practices by shipping concerns; and
5. to consider any matters concerning shipping that may be referred to the IMO by any UN organ or specialized agency.

MEMBERSHIP

Any state invited to the 1948 Maritime Conference or any member of the UN may become a member of the IMO by accepting the 1948 convention. Any other state whose application is approved by two-thirds of the IMO membership becomes a member by accepting the convention. If an IMO member responsible for the international relations of a territory (or group of territories) declares the convention to be applicable to that territory, the territory may become an associate member of the IMO. As of 3 May 1994 there were 148 IMO members and two associate members.

STRUCTURE

The IMO's structure comprises the Assembly, the Council, the Maritime Safety Committee, the Marine Environment Protection Committee, the Legal Committee, the Technical Cooperation Committee, and the secretariat, headed by a Secretary-General.

Assembly

The policymaking body of the IMO is the Assembly, composed of all IMO members. The Assembly determines the work program and votes on the budget to which all members contribute. Meetings are held every two years.

Council

Between sessions of the Assembly, the Council performs all functions of the organization except that of recommending the adoption of maritime safety regulations, a prerogative of the Maritime Safety Committee. The Council also has an important policymaking role. Drafts of international instruments and formal recommendations must be approved by the Council before they can be submitted to the Assembly.

The Council is made up of 32 members elected by the Assembly: eight members represent states with the largest international shipping services; eight represent states with the largest international seaborne trade; and 16 represent states, not elected under the foregoing categories, that have special interests in maritime transport or navigation and whose presence in the Council will ensure representation of the world's major geographic areas. The Council normally meets twice a year.

Committees

The Maritime Safety Committee is made up of all IMO member states. Its work is carried out mainly through subcommittees dealing with safety of navigation; radiocommunications; lifesaving, search, and rescue; standards of training and watchkeeping; carriage of dangerous goods; ship design and equipment; fire protection; stability and load lines, and fishing vessel safety; containers and cargoes; flag state implementation; and bulk chemicals.

The Marine Environment Protection Committee is responsible for all matters relating to the prevention and control of marine pollution from ships.

The Legal Committee, established in the aftermath of the *Torrey Canyon* disaster of 1967 to deal with the legal problems arising from that incident, is responsible for any legal matter within the scope of the IMO.

The Technical Cooperation Committee coordinates the work of the IMO in providing technical assistance in the maritime field, especially to developing countries.

Secretary-General and Secretariat

The secretariat consists of a Secretary-General, appointed by the Council with the approval of the Assembly, and an international staff of about 300. IMO headquarters are at 4 Albert Embankment, London, SE1, 7SR.

The Secretary-General is William A. O'Neill, of Canada, who was appointed to a four-year term beginning on 1 January 1994.

BUDGET

The IMO Assembly approved a budget of US$34.33 million for the 1994–95 biennium.

ACTIVITIES

The IMO's general functions, as stipulated in its convention, are "consultative and advisory." It thus serves as a forum where members can consult and exchange information on maritime matters. It discusses and makes recommendations on any maritime question submitted by member states or by other bodies of the UN and advises other international bodies, including the UN itself, on maritime matters. Various other intergovernmental agencies deal with specialized maritime matters, such as atomic propulsion for ships (IAEA), health at sea (WHO), maritime labor standards (ILO), meteorology (WMO), oceanography (UNESCO), and ship-to-ship and ship-to-shore communications (ITU). One of the functions of the IMO is to help coordinate the work in these different fields.

The IMO is also authorized to convene international conferences when necessary and to draft international maritime conventions or agreements for adoption by governments. These conferences, and the conventions resulting from them, have been mainly concerned with two subjects of primary concern to the IMO: safety at sea and the prevention of marine pollution.

A. Safety at Sea

A conference convened by the IMO in 1960 adopted the International Convention on Safety of Life at Sea to replace an earlier (1948) instrument. The convention covers a wide range of measures designed to improve the safety of shipping, including subdivision and stability; machinery and electrical installations; fire protection, detection, and extinction; lifesaving appliances; radiotelegraphy and radiotelephony; safety of navigation; carriage of grain; carriage of dangerous goods; and nuclear ships. A new

convention, incorporating amendments to the 1960 agreement, was adopted in 1974.

In 1966, an IMO conference adopted the International Convention on Load Lines, which sets limitations on the draught to which a ship may be loaded, an important consideration in its safety. The 1969 International Convention on Tonnage Measurement of Ships is designed to establish a uniform system for tonnage measurement.

Two conventions were adopted in 1972, following IMO conferences: the Convention on the International Regulations for Preventing Collisions at Sea, which concerns traffic separation schemes; and the Convention for Safe Containers, which provides uniform international regulations for maintaining a high level of safety in the carriage of containers by providing generally acceptable test procedures and related strength requirements.

The International Convention on the International Maritime Satellite Organization, adopted in 1976, concerns the use of space satellites for improved communication, enabling distress messages to be conveyed much more effectively than by conventional radio.

Three additional conventions concern safety at sea: the 1977 Torremolinos Convention for the Safety of Fishing Vessels, which applies to new fishing vessels of 24 m (79 ft) in length or longer; the 1978 Convention on Standards of Training, Certification, and Watch-keeping for Seafarers, which aims to establish internationally acceptable minimum standards for crews; and the 1979 International Convention on Maritime Search and Rescue, which is designed to improve existing arrangements for carrying out search and rescue operations following accidents at sea.

B. Prevention of Marine Pollution

The 1954 Oil Pollution Convention, for which the IMO became depositary in 1959, was the first major attempt by the maritime nations to curb the impact of oil pollution. Following a conference convened by the IMO, the 1954 convention was amended in 1962, but it was the wreck of the oil tanker *Torrey Canyon* in March 1967 that fully alerted the world to the great dangers that the transport of oil posed to the marine environment. In 1969, two new conventions were adopted: the Convention on Intervention on the High Seas in Cases of Oil Pollution Casualties, which gives states the right to intervene in incidents on the high seas that are likely to result in oil pollution; and the Convention on Civil Liability for Oil Pollution Damage, which is intended to ensure that adequate compensation is available to victims and which places the liability for the damage on the shipowner.

Two years later, a conference convened by the IMO led to the adoption of the Convention for the Establishment of an International Fund for Compensation for Oil Pollution Damage. The fund, with headquarters in London, is made up of contributions from oil importers. If an accident at sea results in pollution damage which exceeds the compensation available under the Civil Liability Convention, the fund is made available to pay an additional amount.

These three conventions all deal with the legal aspects of oil pollution, but the continuing boom in the transportation of oil showed that more work needed to be done on the technical side as well. The problem of oil pollution—not only as a result of accidents but also through normal tanker operations, especially the cleaning of cargo tanks—was so great in some areas that there was serious concern for the marine environment.

In 1973, a major conference was convened by the IMO to discuss the whole problem of marine pollution from ships. The result of the conference was the International Convention for the Prevention of Pollution from Ships, which deals not only with oil but also with other sources of pollution, including garbage, sewage, and chemicals. The convention greatly reduces the amount of oil that can be discharged into the sea by ships and bans such dis-

Membership of IMO
(as of 3 May 1994)

Albania	El Salvador	Lebanon	Seychelles
Algeria	Equatorial Guinea	Liberia	Sierra Leone
Angola	Eritrea	Libyan Arab Jamahiriya	Singapore
Antigua and Barbuda	Estonia	Luxembourg	Slovakia
Argentina	Ethiopia	Madagascar	Slovenia
Australia	Fiji	Malawi	Solomon Islands
Austria	Finland	Malaysia	Somalia
Bahamas	France	Maldives	Spain
Bahrain	Gabon	Malta	Sri Lanka
Bangladesh	Gambia	Mauritania	Sudan
Barbados	Georgia	Mauritius	Suriname
Belgium	Germany	Mexico	Sweden
Belize	Ghana	Monaco	Switzerland
Benin	Greece	Morocco	Syrian Arab Republic
Bolivia	Guatemala	Mozambique	Thailand
Bosnia and Herzegovina	Guinea	Myanmar	The Former Yugoslav Republic
Brazil	Guinea-Bissau	Netherlands	of Macedonia
Brunei Darussalam	Guyana	New Zealand	Togo
Bulgaria	Haiti	Nicaragua	Trinidad and Tobago
Cambodia	Honduras	Nigeria	Tunisia
Cameroon	Hungary	Norway	Turkey
Canada	Iceland	Oman	Turkmenistan
Cape Verde	India	Pakistan	Ukraine
Chile	Indonesia	Panama	United Arab Emirates
China	Iran, Islamic Republic of	Papua New Guinea	United Kingdom
Colombia	Iraq	Paraguay	United Republic
Congo	Ireland	Peru	of Tanzania
Costa Rica	Israel	Philippines	United States
Côte D'Ivoire	Italy	Poland	Uruguay
Croatia	Jamaica	Portugal	Vanuatu
Cuba	Japan	Qatar	Venezuela
Cyprus	Jordan	Romania	Viet Nam
Czech Republic	Kazakhstan	Russian Federation	Yemen
Denmark	Kenya	St. Lucia	Yugoslavia
Djibouti	Korea, Democratic People's	St. Vincent and	Zaire
Dominica	Republic of	the Grenadines	
Dominican Republic	Korea, Republic of	São Tomé and Principe	ASSOCIATE MEMBERS
Ecuador	Kuwait	Saudi Arabia	Hong Kong
Egypt	Latvia	Senegal	Macau

charges completely in certain areas, such as the Black Sea and the Red Sea. It gives statutory support for such operational procedures as "load on top," which greatly reduces the amount of mixtures to be disposed of after tank cleaning, and for segregated ballast tanks.

A series of tanker accidents that occurred in the winter of 1976/77 led to demands for further action and to the convening of the Conference on Tanker Safety and Pollution Prevention in 1978. The most important measures adopted by the conference were incorporated in protocols to the 1974 Convention on Safety of Life at Sea and the 1973 Marine Pollution Convention.

The protocol to the 1973 convention greatly strengthened the provisions regarding oil pollution and at the same time was modified to incorporate the parent convention. It was amended in 1984, and further amendments were made in 1985 to Annex II, which deals with pollution by noxious liquid substances carried in bulk.

In 1989, a conference of leading industrial nations in Paris called upon IMO to develop further measures to prevent oil pollution from ships. In 1990 IMO adopted the International Convention on Oil Pollution Preparedness, Response and Cooperation. The convention provides a global framework for international cooperation in combating major incidents or threats of marine pollutions. Parties to the convention will be required to establish measures for dealing with pollution incidents and ships and operators of offshore oil units will be required to have oil pollution emergency plans. The convention also calls for the

establishment of stockpiles of oil spill-combating equipment, the holding of oil spill-combating exercises, and the development of detailed plans for dealing with pollution incidents. As of January 1994 the convention had, as yet, received no acceptances and had not entered into force.

In addition, through its Marine Environment Protection Committee, the IMO has been working on various other projects designed to reduce the threat of oil pollution—for example, the Regional Oil-Combating Center, established in Malta in 1976 in conjunction with UNEP. The Mediterranean is particularly vulnerable to pollution, and a massive oil pollution incident there could be catastrophic. The center's purpose is to coordinate antipollution activities in the region and to help develop contingency plans that could be put into effect should a disaster occur. The IMO has also taken part in projects in other regions, including the Caribbean and West Africa.

C. Other Maritime Questions

In 1965, the IMO adopted the Convention on Facilitation of Maritime Traffic, the primary objectives of which are to prevent unnecessary delays in maritime traffic, to aid in cooperation between states, and to secure the highest practicable degree of uniformity in formalities and procedures.

In association with the IAEA and the European Nuclear Energy Agency of the OECD, the IMO convened a conference in 1971, which adopted the Convention on Civil Liability in the Field of Maritime Carriage of Nuclear Matter.

The Convention on Carriage of Passengers and Their Luggage, adopted in 1974, establishes a regime of liability for damage suffered by passengers carried on seagoing vessels. It declares the carrier liable for damage or loss suffered by passengers if the incident is due to the fault or neglect of the carrier. The limit of liability is set at US$55,000 per carriage.

Another convention on liability, the 1976 Convention on Limitation of Liability for Maritime Claims, covers two types of claims: claims arising from loss of life or personal injury and claims arising from damage to ships, harbor works, or other property.

Liability, compensation, and various other matters, including consideration of a new convention on maritime salvage, are dealt with by the IMO's Legal Committee.

In addition to such conventions, whose requirements are mandatory for nations that ratify them, IMO has produced numerous codes, recommendations, and other instruments dealing with maritime questions. These do not have the legal power of conventions but can be used by governments as a basis for domestic legislation and for guidance. Some of the recommendations deal with bulk cargoes, safety of fishermen and fishing vessels, liquefied gases, dangerous goods, timber deck cargoes, mobile offshore drilling units, noise levels on board ships, and nuclear merchant ships.

Some codes, such as those dealing with the transport of bulk chemicals and liquefied gas, have been made mandatory through amendments to the International Convention on Safety of Life at Sea.

In 1988, IMO adopted the Convention for the Suppression of Unlawful Acts Against the Safety of Maritime Navigation, which entered into force in 1992. The main purpose of the convention is to ensure that appropriate action is taken against persons committing unlawful acts against ships. The convention obliges contracting governments either to extradite or prosecute alleged offenders. A concurrent protocol extended this convention to fixed platforms engaged in the exploitation of offshore oil and gas.

The International Convention on Salvage was adopted in 1989, and, as of January 1994, had been accepted by two states. The convention is intended to replace an instrument adopted in Brussels in 1910. That convention incorporated the "no cure, no pay" principle that has been in existence for many years and is the basis of most salvage operations today. However, it did not take compensation into account. The new convention seeks to remedy this by making provisions for "special compensation" to be paid to salvers when there is a threat to the environment.

D. Technical Assistance and Training

While the adoption of conventions, codes, and recommendations has been the IMO's most important function, in recent years the agency has devoted increasing attention to securing the effective implementation of these measures throughout the world. As a result, the IMO's technical assistance activities have become more important, and in 1975 it established the Technical Cooperation Committee. The purpose of the technical assistance program is to help states, many of them developing countries, to ratify IMO conventions and to reach the standards contained in the conventions and other instruments.

Advisors and consultants employed by the IMO, in the field and at headquarters, deal with such matters as maritime safety administration, maritime legislation, marine pollution, training for deck and engineering personnel, the technical aspects of ports, and the carriage of dangerous goods.

Through its technical assistance program, the IMO is able to offer advice in these and other areas and to assist in the acquisition of equipment and the provision of fellowships. In some cases, financial aid can be provided through such other UN agencies as UNDP and UNEP and by donor countries.

The World Maritime University, in Malmö, Sweden, which was established under the auspices of the IMO and opened in 1983, provides advanced training for up to 200 maritime personnel annually—senior maritime teachers, surveyors, inspectors, technical managers, and administrators from developing countries. Funded by UNDP and by Sweden and other countries, the university offers two-year courses in maritime education and training, maritime safety administration, general maritime administration, and technical management of shipping companies, as well as field and other training. It is designed to help meet the urgent need of developing countries for high-level maritime personnel and to contribute to maintaining international standards for maritime safety and preventing pollution of the seas by ships. The university serves as the apex of an international system of training in the maritime field, collaborating with regional, subregional, and national maritime training institutions throughout the world.

BIBLIOGRAPHY

IMO News. Quarterly.
IMO—What It Is, What It Does. Descriptive leaflet.

(The IMO also publishes the texts of all its conventions, codes, and recommendations, as well as a number of specialized manuals and guides, such as the *Manual on Oil Pollution; Regulations on Subdivision and Stability of Passenger Ships; Merchant Ship Search and Rescue Manual; International Maritime Dangerous Goods Code; Pocket Guide to Cold Water Survival; and Noise Levels on Board Ships.*)

THE WORLD INTELLECTUAL PROPERTY ORGANIZATION (WIPO)

BACKGROUND: Intellectual property includes industrial property, such as inventions, trademarks, and designs, on the one hand, and the objects of copyright and neighboring rights on the other. Until a century ago, there were no international instruments for the protection of intellectual property. Legislative provisions for the protection of inventors, writers, dramatists, and other creators of intellectual property varied from country to country and could be effective only within the borders of states adopting them. It came to be widely recognized that adequate protection of industrial property encourages industrialization, investment, and honest trade. That the arts would be advanced by legal safeguards in favor of their practitioners had long been argued, but such safeguards were difficult to devise and enact into law. The Paris Convention of 20 March 1883 and the Bern Convention of 9 September 1886 represented initial steps toward systematic provision of the two sorts of international protection that led eventually to the creation of the World Intellectual Property Organization (WIPO).

CREATION

The 1883 Paris Convention established the International Union for the Protection of Industrial Property, also called the Paris Union. The convention is open to all states. Its most important functions have to do with patents for inventions and marks for goods and services.

The term industrial property is applied in its widest sense in the convention. In addition to inventions, industrial designs, trademarks, service marks, indications of source, and appellations of origin, it covers small patents called utility models in a few countries, trade names or the designations under which an industrial or commercial activity is carried on, and the suppression of unfair competition.

The convention states that members must provide the same protection of rights in industrial property to nationals of the other members as they provide to their own nationals. It permits foreigners to file for a patent that will apply in all member states within a year after first filing in the country of origin. Additionally, it defines conditions under which a state may license the use of a patent in its own territory—for example, if the owner of the patent does not exploit it there.

The 1886 Bern Convention established the International Union for the Protection of Literary and Artistic Works, also called the Bern Union. It also is open to all states. Its function is the protection of copyright, the main beneficiaries of which include authors of books and articles; publishers of books, newspapers, and periodicals; composers of music; painters; photographers; sculptors; film producers; and creators of certain television programs. Under the convention, each member state must accord the same protection to the copyright of the nationals of the other member states as it accords to that of its own nationals. The convention also prescribes some minimum standards of protection—for example, that copyright protection generally continues throughout the author's life and for 50 years thereafter. It includes special provisions for the benefit of developing countries.

In 1893, the secretariats of the Paris Union and the Bern Union were joined in the United International Bureaus for the Protection of Intellectual Property (BIRPI).

The World Intellectual Property Organization (WIPO) was established by a convention signed at Stockholm 14 July 1967 by 51 states. When the convention entered into force on 26 April 1970, WIPO incorporated BIRPI and perpetuated its functions. BIRPI still has a function for members of the Paris or Bern unions that have not yet joined WIPO.

WIPO became the fourteenth specialized UN agency, the first new one since 1961, when the General Assembly approved that status on 17 December 1974.

PURPOSES

The purposes of WIPO are twofold: (1) to promote the protection of intellectual property throughout the world through cooperation among states and, where appropriate, in collaboration with any other international organization; and (2) to ensure administrative cooperation among the unions.

Intellectual property comprises two main branches: *industrial property,* chiefly in inventions, trademarks, and industrial designs; and *copyright,* chiefly in literary, musical, artistic, photographic, and cinematographic works.

The WIPO Convention lists rights in intellectual property relating to literary, artistic, and scientific works; performances of artists; phonograms; broadcasts; inventions in all fields of human endeavor; scientific discoveries; industrial designs; trademarks; service marks; and commercial names and designations. The convention also offers protection against unfair competition and covers all other rights resulting from intellectual activity in the industrial, scientific, literary, or artistic fields.

On 1 January 1994, WIPO administered the following unions or treaties, listed in the chronological order of their creation:

1. *Industrial property:* the Paris Union (1883), for the protection of industrial property; the Madrid Agreement (1891), for the repression of false or deceptive indications of source on goods; the Madrid Union (1891), for the international registration of marks; the Hague Union (1925), for the international deposit of industrial designs; the Nice Union (1957), for the international classification of goods and services for the purpose of registration of marks; the Lisbon Union (1958), for the protection of appellations of origin and their international registration; the Locarno Union

(1968), establishing an international classification for industrial designs; the International Patent Cooperation (IPC) Union (1970), for the establishment of worldwide uniformity of patent classification; the Patent Cooperation Treaty (PCT) Union (1971), for cooperation in the filing, searching, and examination of international applications for the protection of inventions where such protection is sought in several countries; the Trademark Registration Treaty (TRT) Union (1973), for the filing of international applications for the registration of trademarks where protection is sought in several countries; the Vienna Union (1973), establishing an international classification of the figurative elements of marks; the Budapest Union (1977), for the international recognition of the deposit of microorganisms for the purpose of patent procedure; and the Nairobi Treaty (1981), on the protection of the Olympic symbol.

2. *Copyright and neighboring rights:* the Bern Union (1886), for the protection of literary and artistic works; the Rome Convention (1961), for the protection of performers, producers of phonograms, and broadcasting organizations, jointly administered with the ILO and UNESCO; the Geneva Convention (1971), for the protection of producers of phonograms against unauthorized duplication of their phonograms; the Brussels Convention (1974), relating to the distribution of program-carrying signals transmitted by satellite; and the International Convention for the Protection of New Varieties of Plants (1961).

Three additional treaties are to be administered by WIPO when they come into effect: the Vienna Agreement, on the protection of typefaces and their international deposit; the Geneva Treaty, on the international recording of scientific discoveries; and the Madrid Multilateral Convention, on the question of double taxation of copyright royalties.

MEMBERSHIP

Membership in WIPO is open to any state that is a member of any of the unions, is a member of the UN or any of the specialized agencies or the IAEA, is party to the Statute of the International Court of Justice, or is invited by the General Assembly of WIPO to become a party to the WIPO Convention. The 147 members of WIPO (W), 120 members of the Paris Union (P), and 107 members of the Bern Union (B) as of 1 April 1994 are listed in the table on the next page.

STRUCTURE

The Paris and Bern unions each have an assembly consisting of the member states, meeting biennially. An executive committee elected by the General Assembly, consisting of one-fourth of the member states, meets annually. The other unions, in most cases, have an assembly but no executive committee.

WIPO itself has four organs: the General Assembly, the Conference, the Coordination Committee, and a secretariat called the International Bureau.

General Assembly

The General Assembly consists of all states party to the WIPO Convention that are also members of any of the unions. It meets biennially and has the highest authority of all the organs.

Conference

The Conference consists of all states party to the WIPO Convention, whether or not they are members of one or more of the unions. It meets biennially to discuss matters of general interest in the field of intellectual property, as well as to establish WIPO's program of technical legal assistance and the budget for that program.

Coordination Committee

The Coordination Committee meets annually. It consists of executive committee members of the Paris or the Bern union or both.

International Bureau

The International Bureau, located in Geneva, is the secretariat of the various governing bodies of WIPO and the unions. It consists of a staff of about 450 people from 57 different countries, headed by a Director General. Arpad Bogsch, of the US, has been elected to successive terms as Director General since the establishment of WIPO in 1974.

BUDGET

Until January 1994, the budget was entirely met from contributions of member states; from fees paid by applicants for international protection of inventions, international registration of trademarks and appellations of origin, and deposit of industrial designs; and from the sale of publications. In 1994 fees represented 73 percent of the total income, contributions represented 18 percent, and 9 percent came from the sale of WIPO publications and other sources. For the 1994–95 and 1996–97 bienniums the governing bodies decided to institute a trial of a unitary contribution system. The advantages of the unitary contribution system are that it makes the administration of contributions simpler, and will be an incentive for states to join more unions, since adherence will not increase the amount of their contribution. In addition, the governing bodies adopted a new formula for contributions that was intended to significantly lower overall cost of contributions for developing countries. For the 1994–95 biennium, the budget was approximately SwFr230 million (depending on exchange rates, approximately US$172.5 million).

ACTIVITIES

A. Assistance to Developing Countries

One of the main objectives of WIPO is to assist developing countries in the fields of both industrial property and copyright.

In the field of industrial property, WIPO's chief aims are the following: (1) to encourage and increase, in quantity and quality, the creation of patentable inventions in developing countries by their own nationals and in their own enterprises and thereby to increase their technological self-reliance; (2) to improve conditions for the acquisition of foreign patented technology; (3) to increase the competitiveness of developing countries in international trade through better protection of trademarks; and (4) to make it easier and cheaper for developing countries to locate the technological information contained in patent documents.

In the field of copyright, the main objectives are the following:

1. to encourage and increase the creation of literary and artistic works in developing countries by their own nationals and thereby to maintain their national culture in their own languages and corresponding to their own ethnic and social traditions and aspirations; and

2. to improve conditions for the acquisition of the right to use or enjoy the literary and artistic works in which copyright is owned by foreigners.

In order to attain these objectives, most developing countries need to create or modernize domestic legislation and governmental institutions, accede to international treaties, and have more specialists in the fields of industrial property and copyright.

WIPO's assistance consists mainly of advice, training, and the furnishing of documents and equipment. Advice is given by the staff of WIPO, by experts chosen by WIPO, or at international meetings convened by WIPO. Training may be individual (on-the-job) or collective (in courses, seminars, and workshops) and may

Members of WIPO and of the Paris and Bern Unions
(P=Paris, B=Bern)
(as of 1 January 1994)

Country		Country		Country		Country	
Albania	B	Egypt	P, B	Libya	P, B	Sierra Leone	
Algeria	P	El Salvador	P, B	Liechtenstein	P, B	Singapore	
Angola		Estonia		Lithuania		Slovakia	P, B
Argentina	P, B	Fiji	B	Luxembourg	P, B	Slovenia	P, B
Armenia		Finland	P, B	Madagascar	P, B	Somalia	
Australia	P, B	France	P, B	Malawi	P, B	South Africa	P, B
Austria	P, B	Gabon	P, B	Malaysia	P, B	Spain	P, B
Bahamas	P, B	Gambia	P, B	Mali	P, B	Sri Lanka	P, B
Bangladesh	P	Germany	P, B	Malta	P, B	Sudan	P
Barbados	P, B	Ghana	P, B	Mauritania	P, B	Suriname	P, B
Belarus	P	Greece	P, B	Mauritius	P, B	Swaziland	P
Belgium	P, B	Guatemala		Mexico	P, B	Sweden	P, B
Benin	P, B	Guinea	P, B	Monaco	P, B	Switzerland	P, B
Bhutan		Guinea-Bissau	P, B	Mongolia	P	Thailand	B
Bolivia		Haiti	P	Morocco	P, B	The Former Yugoslav	
Bosnia and Herzegovina	P, B	Holy See (Vatican)	P, B	Namibia	B	Republic of Macedonia	P, B
Brazil	P, B	Honduras	P, B	Netherlands	P, B	Togo	P, B
Bulgaria	P, B	Hungary	P, B	New Zealand	P, B	Trinidad and Tobago	P, B
Burkina Faso	P, B	Iceland	P, B	Nicaragua		Tunisia	P, B
Burundi	P	India	B	Niger	P, B	Turkey	P, B
Cameroon	P, B	Indonesia	P	Norway	P, B	Uganda	P
Canada	P, B	Iraq	P	Pakistan	B	Ukraine	P
Central Africa Republic	P, B	Ireland	P, B	Panama		United Arab Emirates	
Chad	P, B	Israel	P, B	Paragua	B	United Kingdom	P, B
Chile	P, B	Italy	P, B	Peru	B	United Republic of	
China	P, B	Jamaica	B	Philippines	P, B	Tanzania	P
Colombia	B	Japan	P, B	Poland	P, B	United States of	
Congo	P, B	Jordan	P	Portugal	P, B	America	P, B
Costa Rica	B	Kazakhstan	P	Qatar		Uruguay	P, B
Côte d'Ivoire	P, B	Kenya	P, B	Republic of Moldova	P	Uzbekistan	P
Croatia	P, B	Korea, Democratic People's		Romania	P	Venezuela	B
Cuba	P	Republic of	P	Russian Federation	P	Viet Nam	P
Cyprus	P, B	Korea, Republic of	P	Rwanda	P, B	Yemen	
Czech Republic	P, B	Latvia	P	St. Lucia	B	Yugoslavia	P, B
Denmark	P, B	Lebanon	P, B	San Marino	P	Zaire	P, B
Ecuador	B	Lesotho	P, B	Saudi Arabia		Zambia	P, B
Egypt	P, B	Liberia	B	Senegal	P, B	Zimbabwe	P, B

take place in the interested developing country, in an industrialized country, or in another developing country. The resources for such activities are provided in WIPO's budget or from donor countries or organizations, particularly UNDP.

In 1993, WIPO organized some 90 courses, workshops, and seminars on industrial property and copyright law in developing countries and sponsored 80 study visits for officials of developing countries to both industrialized and developing nations. About 6,000 men and women from 118 developing countries attended these events.

In addition, the International Bureau gave advice and assistance to officials from newly independent governments of the former Soviet Union in connection with the preparation and enactment of intellectual property laws, the establishment of industrial property offices, as well as adherence to WIPO-administered treaties. In particular, the International Bureau advised the Interstate Council on the Protection of Industrial Property (which groups nine states from the former Soviet Union: Armenia, Belarus, Kazakhstan, Kyrgyzstan, the Republic of Moldova, the Russian Federation, Tajikistan, Ukraine, and Uzabekistan) on a plan to set up a regional patent system under the proposed Eurasian Patent Convention.

B. Other Activities

In order to adapt the treaties administered by WIPO to changing circumstances and needs, a constant watch is kept to see whether they need to be revised. The Paris Convention, for example, has had six revisions, the last in Stockholm in 1967, and the Bern Convention has had five, the last in Paris in 1971. WIPO also keeps international classifications of patents, trademarks, and industrial designs under review in order to keep them up-to-date.

In addition, WIPO observes changes in international industrial, trade, and cultural relations that seem to call for adaptations not only in the treaties administered by WIPO but also in national laws, regional arrangements, contractual practices, and professional activities in the field of intellectual property.

Thus, for example, in the field of industrial property, WIPO is considering the possibilities of uniform provisions in national patent laws, particularly concerning the effects on the patentability of an invention or a public disclosure of the invention by the inventor prior to filing a patent application. It also advocates laws and treaty provisions that would give more efficient protection against the counterfeiting of goods and would protect the intellectual creators of microchips or integrted circuits and inventions in biotechnology, including genetic engineering.

In the field of copyright, WIPO has been engaged, in some cases jointly with UNESCO, in recommending laws for the protection of computer programs, for works created by employee-authors, for expressions of folklore, for more effective protection of authors and performers in connection with cable television, and for protection against piratical editions of books, phonograms, and videotapes and excessive unauthorized reproduction. WIPO is also studying the copyright law aspects of the rental of phonograms and videograms, of direct broadcast satellites, and of electronic libraries and the possibility of creating an international register of audiovisual works.

In 1993, WIPO established the WIPO Academy to conduct encounter sessions on current intellectual property issues at the policy level for government officials from developing countries. The academy sponsored three such sessions in 1993 for 35 officials from 33 developing countries. WIPO also awarded to three nationals from developing countries the first long-term scholarships to institutions in industrialized countries for intellectual property law studies.

The WIPO Arbitration Center was established in July 1994 to offer enterprises and individuals four dispute-settlement procedures: mediation, arbitration, expedited arbitration (for small-scale disputes), and a combined procedure of mediation and arbitration.

International Registrations

The International Patent Documentation Center, established in Vienna in 1972 under an agreement between WIPO and the government of Austria, puts on computer the principal bibliographic data of almost 1 million patent documents a year and permits the retrieval of the data required for various purposes by patent offices, industry, and research and development institutions. The financial and operational responsibility lies with the Austrian government, but WIPO assists the center in its contacts with the patent offices of the various countries.

The International Bureau of WIPO, in Geneva, maintains four registration services in the fields of patents, trademarks, industrial designs, and appellations of origin.

BIBLIOGRAPHY

Copyright. Monthly review of the Bern Union in English and French. Covers ratifications and contains texts of laws, court decisions, studies.

Industrial Property. Monthly review of the Paris Union in English and French. Covers ratifications and contains texts of laws, court decisions, studies.

International Designs Bulletin. Monthly review in English and French. Contains notifications and modifications concerning the international registration of industrial designs.

Model Laws for Developing Countries on Inventions, on Marks, Trade Names and Acts of Unfair Competition and on Designs. In English, French, and Spanish.

(WIPO also publishes the texts of conventions, treaties, and agreements on intellectual property; international classifications; and model laws.)

THE INTERNATIONAL FUND FOR AGRICULTURAL DEVELOPMENT (IFAD)

BACKGROUND: The International Fund for Agricultural Development (IFAD) is the first international institution established exclusively to provide additional resources for agricultural and rural development in developing countries and to channel those resources to the poorest rural populations in Africa, Near East and North Africa, Asia, and Latin America and the Caribbean that suffer from chronic hunger and malnutrition.

CREATION

IFAD was one of the major initiatives of the World Food Conference, held in Rome in 1974, following two years of negotiations. The agreement establishing the fund was adopted by 91 governments on 13 June 1976 and was opened for signature or ratification on 20 December 1976, following attainment of the target of US$ 1 billion in initial pledges. The agreement came into force on 30 November 1977.

PURPOSES

The objective of the fund is to mobilize additional resources to be made available on concessional terms to help developing countries improve their food production and nutrition. The fund is unique in that its projects are focused exclusively on agricultural development, concentrating on the poorest sections of the rural populations in developing countries. It deals with all aspects of agriculture, including crops, irrigation, agricultural credit, storage, livestock, and fisheries.

MEMBERSHIP

IFAD had a total of 157 member nations in June 1994, compared with 91 at the time of its establishment. Of these, 22 were in Category I (developed countries), 12 in Category II (oil-exporting developing countries), and 123 in Category II (other developing countries). (The members of IFAD are shown in the table.)

STRUCTURE

IFAD is a new kind of institution in the UN system. The governing bodies that supervise its operations reflect an innovative formula that brings together the interests of industrialized countries, each of the three categories having the same number of votes (600). As an action-oriented organization, the fund normally works by consensus rather than by voting.

The three main organs are the Governing Council, the Executive Board, and the secretariat, headed by a president.

Governing Council

The highest governing body of the fund is the Governing Council, which meets once a year and on which all members are represented. The council adopts the fund's budget, approves the applications of new members, and elects the president of the fund and members of the Executive Board.

Executive Board

The 18-member Executive Board, composed of six executive directors from each of the three categories, with 17 alternates,

oversees the operations of the fund, including its investments and work program. The board holds three sessions a year.

President and Secretariat

The president of the fund, elected for four years, is responsible for its management. He is chairman of the Executive Board and heads the secretariat, composed of about 259 staff members from some 50 countries. Fawzi Al-Sultan of Kuwait was elected president of the fund in January 1993. The fund's headquarters are located at 107, Via del Serafico 00142 Rome, Italy.

BUDGET

Total revenue under the Regular Programme for 1993 was US$176 million, mainly income from investments. Total operational and administrative expenses for the same year amounted to US$44 million.

ACTIVITIES

A. Loans and Resources

The first project loans were approved by IFAD's Executive Board in April 1978. At the end of the three-year period, 1978–80, the fund's cumulative commitments amounted to nearly US$900 million in loans and grants for some 70 of its developing member states.

For the period 1981–83, IFAD expanded its operational program. By 1983, IFAD's total financial commitments since April 1978 exceeded US$1.4 billion for projects and programs in some 80 member countries in Africa, Near East and North Africa, Asia, and Latin America and the Caribbean. By mid-1987, IFAD had extended loans totalling US$2.3 billion to 89 developing countries to finance 204 projects. By the end of 1993, the fund's cumulative commitments reached US$3.9 billion to 100 developing countries to finance 370 projects.

The first replenishment of IFAD resources was unanimously approved by the fund's Governing Council in January 1982. Member countries offered to provide contributions totalling US$1 billion for the period 1981–83, including US$620 million from Category I (developed) countries, US$450 million from Category II (oil-exporting developing) countries, and US$32 million from Category III (other developing) countries.

In 1986, the Governing Council agreed on a second replenishment of IFAD's resources totalling US$488 million, of which Category I countries pledged US$276 million; Category II countries, US$184 million; and Category III countries, US$28 million. In 1990, the Governing Council agreed on a third replenishment.

Member countries offered to provide contributions totalling US$567 million of which Category I countries pledged US$378 million; Category II countries, US$124 million, and Category III, US$65 million.

B. Lending Policies and Operations

IFAD loan operations fall into two groups: projects initiated by the fund and projects cofinanced with other financial and development institutions. IFAD-initiated projects are those for which the fund has taken the lead in project identification and preparation and in mobilizing additional resources from other financial agencies where necessary.

Most of IFAD's assistance has been provided on highly concessional terms —loans repayable over 50 years with a 10-year grace period and an annual service charge of 1 percent. About one-quarter of the loans are repayable over 20 years at 4 percent annual interest, while a few have been offered at 8 percent over 15–18 years. However, at its 17th session of January 1994, the Governing Council adopted a resolution which amended the lending terms and conditions for the first time since the fund's establishment.

In the future, those developing members countries having a Gross National Product (GNP) per capita of US$805 or less in 1992 prices, or which qualify for loans from the World Bank's "soft loan" agency, the International Development Association, will normally be eligible to receive loans from IFAD on highly concessional terms. Loans on highly concessional terms will be free of interest but will bear a service charge of 0.75 percent per annum and have a repayment period of 40 years, including a grace period of 10 years. The total amount of loans provided each year on highly concessional terms will be approximately two-thirds of the total lent annually by IFAD.

Member countries having a GNP per capita of between US$806 and US$1,305 inclusive in 1992 prices normally will be eligible to receive loans from IFAD on intermediate terms. Those having a GNP per capita of US$1,306 or more in 1992 prices normally will be eligible to receive loans on ordinary terms.

IFAD loans represent only a part of the total project costs; the governments concerned contribute a share. In most of the projects approved so far, IFAD also has cooperated with the World Bank (IBRD and IDA); the African, Asian, Inter-American, and Islamic development banks; the Arab Fund for Economic and Social Development; the Central American Bank for Economic Integration; the World Food Programme; the EEC; OPEC; and other multilateral and bilateral institutions.

IFAD, while seeking to preserve an appropriate balance in its regional allocations, also has attempted to respond to the special needs of the 74 low-income, food-deficit countries. Well over 80 percent of the fund's loans were channelled to these countries in the 1978–93 period. The regional shares of IFAD-supported projects approved between 1978–93 under both regular and special programs stand as follows: Africa (sub-Sahara), 35.2 percent; Asia and the Pacific, 33.7 percent; Latin America and the Caribbean, 14.8 percent; and Near East and North Africa, 16.4 percent.

In January 1986, IFAD, as the first international financial institution to respond to the socioeconomic crisis in sub-Saharan Africa, in the wake of the disastrous droughts and famines of 1983–85, launched the Special Programme for Sub-Saharan African Countries Affected by Drought and Desertification (SPA), with a target for resource mobilization of US$300 million. This target was outrun by contributions reaching US$322.8 million from five developing countries and the European Community.

The program aims to restore the productive capacity of small farmers, promote traditional food crops mainly grown by smallholders, and initiate small-scale water control schemes, in addition to recommending measures for environmental protection and providing assistance to governments in regard to policy.

Members of IFAD
(as of 28 January 1994)

CATEGORY I: DEVELOPED COUNTRIES

Australia	Greece	Portugal
Austria	Ireland	Spain
Belgium	Italy	Sweden
Canada	Japan	Switzerland
Denmark	Luxembourg	United Kingdom
Finland	Netherlands	United States
France	New Zealand	
Germany	Norway	

CATEGORY II: OIL-EXPORTING DEVELOPING COUNTRIES

Algeria	Iraq	Qatar
Gabon	Kuwait	Saudi Arabia
Indonesia	Libyan Arab	United Arab Emirates
Iran, Islamic	Jamahiriya	Venezuela
Republic of	Nigeria	

CATEGORY III: OTHER DEVELOPING COUNTRIES

Afghanistan	Fiji	Paraguay
Albania	Gambia	Peru
Angola	Ghana	Philippines
Antigua and Barbuda	Grenada	Romania
Argentina	Guatemala	Rwanda
Armenia	Guinea	Saint Kitts and
Azerbaijan	Guinea-Bissau	Nevis
Bangladesh	Guyana	Saint Lucia
Barbados	Haiti	Saint Vincent and
Belize	Honduras	the Grenadines
Benin	India	São Tomé and
Bhutan	Israel	Principe
Bolivia	Jamaica	Senegal
Bosnia and	Jordan	Seychelles
Herzegovina	Kenya	Sierra Leone
Botswana	Korea, Democratic	Solomon Islands
Brazil	People's Republic of	Somalia
Burkina Faso	Korea, Republic of	Sri Lanka
Burundi	Kyrgystan	Sudan
Cambodia	Lao Peoples Demo-	Suriname
Cameroon	cratic Republic	Swaziland
Cape Verde	Lebanon	Syrian Arab Republic
Central African	Lesotho	Tajikistan
Republic	Liberia	Tanzania, United
Chad	Madagascar	Republic of
Chile	Malawi	Thailand
China	Malaysia	The Former Yugoslav
Colombia	Maldives	Republic of
Comoros	Mali	Macedonia
Congo	Malta	Togo
Cook Islands	Mauritania	Tonga
Costa Rica	Mauritius	Trinidad and Tobago
Côte d'Ivoire	Mexico	Tunisia
Croatia	Mongolia	Turkey
Cuba	Morocco	Uganda
Cyprus	Mozambique	Uruguay
Djibouti	Myanmar	Viet Nam
Dominica	Namibia	Western Samoa
Dominican Republic	Nepal	Yemen
Ecuador	Nicaragua	Yugoslavia
Egypt	Niger	Zaire
El Salvador	Oman	Zambia
Equatorial Guinea	Pakistan	Zimbabwe
Eritrea	Panama	
Ethiopia	Papua New Guinea	

By January 1993, a second phase of the program became effective. While it preserves the focus of the first phase, it extends its conceptual frame and operational scope. Specifically it carries environmental and soil conservation objectives from on-farm to off-farm (particularly in the common property resource domain), and addresses overall coping strategies of households and communities through economic diversification. By the end of 1993 SPA had financed 40 loans, supporting 39 projects in 24 countries.

Projects by Region under the Regular Programme and Special Programme for Africa, 1978–93
(in millions of US$)

REGION	NUMBER OF PROJECTS	AMOUNT
Africa	152	$1,384.8
Asia	95	1,327.2
Latin America and the Caribbean	65	581.5
Near East and North Africa	58	644.9
TOTAL	370	$3,938.4

IFAD Projects by Type under the Regular Programme and the Special Programme for Africa, 1978–93
(SDR million)

REGION	NUMBER OF PROJECTS	AMOUNT
Agricultural Development	123	934.8
Rural Development	92	836.1
Livestock	20	167.2
Irrigation	31	356.6
Settlement	3	36.4
Research/extension/training	16	117.7
Credit	54	524.0
Fisheries	19	75.2
Marketing/storage/processing	2	9.8
PROGRAMME LOAN	9	112.7 million

In selecting an area of a country for assistance, IFAD determines whether the area is geographically or functionally isolated from the rest of the national economy; the extent to which its population has a lower average per capita income than the national average; the degree to which the area is food-deficient; whether it has relatively inadequate delivery systems and infrastructure in comparison with the rest of the country; and the proportion of poverty—for example, the proportion of landless—in comparison with other rural areas. In terms of impact, IFAD's projects, at full development, will help some 30 million poor rural households out of hunger and poverty.

C. Technical Assistance

IFAD provides grant financing for technical assistance in project preparation, institutional development, agricultural research, training, and other activities which support the fund's activities. Between 1978 and 1993, 481 research and technical assistance grants amounting to US$191.73 million were extended under both regular and special programs.

BIBLIOGRAPHY

Africa: Sowing the Seeds of Self-Sufficiency.
A Fund for the Rural Poor.
IFAD Annual Report. Annual.
Latin America and the Caribbean: Bringing the Harvest Home.
Meeting the Challenge of Hunger and Poverty.
The Poor Are Bankable; Rural Credit the IFAD Way.
The Role of Rural Credit Projects in Reaching the Rural Poor: IFAD's Experience.
Rural Women in Agricultural Investment Projects.
The State of World Rural Poverty.

(IFAD also publishes basic texts and guidelines, including the agreement establishing IFAD; guidelines on lending policies and criteria, on relending rates, and on procurement; and guiding principles for the design and use of monitoring and evaluation in rural development projects and programs.)

THE UNITED NATIONS INDUSTRIAL DEVELOPMENT ORGANIZATION (UNIDO)

BACKGROUND: Industrialization is one of the primary goals of the developing countries, to increase their share of world manufacturing output and decrease their dependence on imported goods and services and on their traditional raw-materials export economies. The United Nations Industrial Development Organization (UNIDO), the newest specialized agency of the UN, seeks to further that goal through its programs of technical cooperation with developing countries, designed to aid in the planning and implementation of industrial projects, the training of personnel in manufacturing and managerial skills, the transfer of technology and the provision of information, and the promotion of investment in industry in developing countries.

CREATION

UNIDO was established by the General Assembly in November 1966 as an autonomous organization within the UN to promote and accelerate the industrialization of developing countries and to coordinate the industrial development activities of the UN system.

The first General Conference of UNIDO was held in Vienna in 1971. The second General Conference, held in Lima in 1975, proposed the conversion of UNIDO into a specialized agency "in order to increase its ability to render assistance to developing countries in the most efficient ways." The conference also adopted the Lima Declaration and Plan of Action, which called for developing countries to reach the target of 25 percent of world industrial output by the year 2000.

In 1979, a conference of plenipotentiaries, meeting in Vienna, adopted a constitution for UNIDO, to become effective when at least 80 states had ratified it. This was achieved on 21 June 1985, and UNIDO's conversion into a specialized agency became effective on 1 January 1986.

PURPOSES

UNIDO's mandate from the General Assembly is to act as the central coordinating body for industrial activities within the United Nations system and to promote industrial development and cooperation at global, regional, national, and sectoral levels.

In the wake of the reorganization of the activities of the United Nations and its specialized agencies in the early 1990s, UNIDO identified five development objectives that provide a new conceptual framework for the organization's future programs:

- industrial and technological growth and competitiveness;
- human resource development;
- equitable development through industrialization;
- environmentally sustainable industrial development; and
- international cooperation in industrial investment and technology.

By applying its expertise at three levels—policy, institution, and enterprise—UNIDO acts as:

- the central coordinating agency for matters related to industrial development;

- a focal point for industrial technology;
- an honest broker for industrial cooperation;
- a center of excellence on industrial development issues; and
- a global source of industrial information.

MEMBERSHIP

As of December 1993, UNIDO had a membership of 166, an increase of 18 countries since 1987. The 11 percent growth in membership was mainly caused by the emergence of the newly independent nations of Central and Eastern Europe in the wake of the collapse of the former Soviet Union. This increase in membership further strained UNIDO's already tightly-stretched resources to cover the need for its services by countries whose industries were disrupted by the transition to market economies. However, these same countries were not in a position to enhance its resource base.

STRUCTURE

The four organs of UNIDO are the General Conference, the Industrial Development Board, the program and budget committee, and the secretariat, headed by a Director General.

General Conference

UNIDO's strategies and policies in regard to industrial development are outlined at its General Conference, which meets every two years and is composed of representatives of all members. Since the organization's inception, the General Conference has met nine times: 1971 (Vienna), 1975 (Lima), 1980 (New Delhi), 1984 (Vienna), 1985 (Vienna—UNIDO's transition to a specialized agency), 1987 (Bangkok), 1989 (Vienna), 1991 (Vienna), 1993 (Yaoundé).

Industrial Development Board

The Industrial Development Board consists of 53 members elected by the General Conference for four-year terms. In 1993, the following states were members of the board:

Austria, Belarus, Belgium, Bolivia, Brazil, Cameroon, Chile, China, Costa Rica, Cuba, Egypt, Ethiopia, Finland, France, Germany, Ghana, Greece, Guinea, Hungary, India, Indonesia, Iran, Iraq, Italy, Japan, Kuwait, Mexico, Morocco, Netherlands, Nigeria, Norway, Pakistan, Peru, Republic of Korea, Romania, Russian Federation, Saudi Arabia, Senegal, Slovakia, Spain, Sudan, Switzerland, Syrian Arab Republic, Thailand, Trinidad and

Tobago, Tunisia, Turkey, Uganda, United Kingdom, United States, Venezuela, Zaire, and Zimbabwe.

Program and Budget Committee

The program and budget committee is composed of 27 members elected for two-year terms. In 1993, its members were:

Algeria, Austria, Brazil, Bulgaria, China, Colombia, Cuba, Egypt, France, Germany, India, Italy, Japan, Kenya, Malawi, Mexico, Netherlands, Nigeria, Philippines, Poland, Qatar, Russian Federation, Rwanda, Sweden, United Kingdom, United States, and Yugoslavia.

Director General and Secretariat

The Director General of UNIDO, elected by the General Conference on 1 April 1993 for a four-year term, is Mauricio de Maria y Campos of Mexico.

Prior to its conversion into a specialized agency, UNIDO was headed by an executive director appointed by the Secretary-General of the UN. The first two executive directors were Ibrahim Helmi Abdel-Rahman (1967–74) and Abd-El Rahman Khane (1975–85). Domingo L. Siazo, Jr., of the Philippines was the first Director General of UNIDO when it became a specialized agency in 1985. He served as Director General from 1985 to 1993.

The secretariat, with a staff of about 1,238, comprises the office of the Director General and eight divisions: human resources and enterprise development; operational support; funds mobilization; country strategy and program development; information and research; industrial sectors and environment; investment and technology promotion; and administration.

There are, in addition, some 100 UNIDO country directors and junior professional officers who work in developing countries with UNDP resident representatives. They are financed by UNDP, by voluntary contributions, and from the regular budget of UNIDO.

Offices

UNIDO is headquartered in Vienna, Austria. It maintains liaison offices at UN headquarters in New York and at the UN office in Geneva. It also operates two "centers of excellence": the International Centre for Genetic Engineering and Biotechnology (ICGEB), with components in New Delhi, India, and Trieste, Italy; and the International Centre for Science and High Technology (ICS), with headquarters in Trieste. In collaboration with the UNDP, UNIDO maintains 38 country directors in field offices that cover more than 100 countries.

BUDGET

At its fourth session in 1991, the General Conference appropriated approximately us$181,013,400 for the regular budget in the biennium 1992–93, to be financed from assessed contributions of member states. For the Regular Programme of Technical Cooperation, the General Conference appropriated us$10,755,700, to be used as seed money to mobilize additional financial resources for technical assistance and to meet needs in the context of the Second IDDA. Most costs of expert advice, equipment, and other forms of technical assistance, in partnership with and at the request of developing countries, are met by the UNDP, for which UNIDO is an executing agency. Special UNIDO projects use the Industrial Development Fund, established in 1976 with a "desirable funding level of us$50 million annually."

ACTIVITIES

A. Technical Cooperation

In 1993, UNIDO had 1,713 technical cooperation projects under implementation worldwide at a cost of $118.8 million, distributed as follows:

DISTRIBUTION BY GEOGRAPHICAL AREA	SHARE OF TOTAL (PERCENT)
Asia and the Pacific	26.2
Africa	34.2
Arab States (including the African Arab States)	13.0
Latin America and the Caribbean	9.2
Europe	3.3
Interregional and global	24.2

DISTRIBUTION BY PRODUCT COMPONENT	SHARE OF TOTAL (PERCENT)
Project personnel (experts)	66
Equipment	20
Fellowships and training	14
Subcontracts	14
Miscellaneous	5

DISTRIBUTION BY FIELD OF ACTIVITY	NUMBER OF PROJECTS
Agro-based activities	165
Chemical industries	280
Metallurgical industries	81
Engineering industries	162
Industrial strategies and policies	79
Institutional infrastructure	211
Industrial management and rehabilitation	63
Industrial human resource development	104

UNIDO's objectives in technical cooperation are the following:

1. To elaborate programs and projects for the industrial development of developing countries, including special measures for the least developed countries;
2. To formulate policies and strategies for the development of UNIDO's operational activities, from different sources of finance and with particular focus on the country, subregion, and region concerned;
3. To prepare technical cooperation programs and formulate specific projects, in collaboration with other UN bodies and with governments, as well as through participation in round-table meetings or consultative groups;
4. To help improve the effectiveness of technical cooperation programs by assessing the progress made and the results achieved by projects at intermediate and final stages and by feeding back into the programming process the results of their impact; and
5. To maintain a program of UNIDO country directors that enhances the services rendered to the developing countries.

In seeking to industrialize their economies, developing countries face a wide spectrum of problems, ranging from preparation of national plans, development of sectoral programs, and elaboration of appropriate policies and strategies of industrial development, to concerns relating to the technical processes to be employed in manufacturing any specific product, preparation of preinvestment studies, organization of production facilities, training of personnel in new skills, management of factory operations, and establishment of an industrial infrastructure to support industrial enterprises and to mobilize financial resources for investment in industrial production.

UNIDO assists in addressing these problems by in-depth studies on specific priority problems of industrialization in particular countries, with consideration given to important concerns, such as the rehabilitation of troubled industries, international cooperation for small- and medium-sized industry development, institutional development for technology transfer and adaptation, and technical cooperation among developing countries.

UNIDO also works to increase the resources available for technical cooperation purposes, working with traditional as well as new funding sources, such as trust funds under which the developing countries themselves finance UNIDO technical assistance projects, and mobilizing the support of nongovernmental organizations.

Industrial Operations Technology

A common problem of developing countries is how best to exploit their natural resources and other comparative advantages in order to ensure a worthwhile share for themselves in world production and trade in manufactured products, including replacement of imported industrial products with locally manufactured ones. In order to increase industrial production in developing countries, UNIDO assists them, through the implementation of technical cooperation projects, in acquiring the technological base and know-how that will enable them to establish, expand, rehabilitate, and improve the efficiency and productivity of industrial facilities in the main branches of industry. It provides this help through direct assistance to manufacturing enterprises or through the establishment or strengthening of specialized technology centers servicing individual industrial sectors.

UNIDO also extends assistance in the efficient utilization of energy resources by industry, in the industrial-scale production of fuel and feedstock from renewable resources, and in promoting environmentally sustainable industrial development. Continued attention is given to the establishment of pilot and demonstration plants to accelerate the utilization of locally available raw materials, including industrial and agricultural wastes. Particular attention is given to technical assistance in chemical industries and in the production of capital goods, including equipment for telecommunications and transportation, especially in support of rural development and in the manufacture of pesticides, fertilizers, and agricultural equipment.

Industrial Institutions and Services

In order to increase industrial production, developing countries have to make extensive use of planning techniques and preinvestment studies and also need to establish and strengthen institutional infrastructures and support services and the skills required to set up and operate manufacturing enterprises. Institutional infrastructures are particularly critical in order to compensate, at least in part, for the absence of a long tradition of industrial development in most developing countries. There is a continuous demand for the establishment or strengthening of institutions dealing with standardization and quality control, industrial research, small-scale industries, and rural development. The lack of production, managerial, and entrepreneurial skills is frequently the greatest obstacle to industrial development.

Through its technical cooperation programs, UNIDO seeks to assist developing countries, particularly in the development of human resources, by identifying priority areas for industrial training and for the establishment of national institutes for research and development and for training and consultancy that may become centers for training of personnel, including training in management and in the preparation of preinvestment studies, project implementation, and operation of industrial enterprises. UNIDO extends assistance through fellowships, study tours, and group training programs.

B. Investment Promotion

Another major focus of UNIDO activities is the acceleration of investment in the private and public sectors of developing countries, in a manner consistent with their national plans and policies, and through the implementation of technical cooperation projects in the field of industrial investment.

Although there is a need for a massive flow of financial and technical resources from outside sources to implement projects necessary to achieve the targets of industrial growth laid down in the plans of developing countries, the lack of sound and well-prepared investment projects backed by suitable entrepreneurs has been a more serious obstacle to the flow of these needed resources than the lack of investment funds. Information is scarce regarding the sources of financing and the identification of enterprises that are suitable and willing to participate in manufacturing projects in developing countries or to redeploy their industrial plants to developing countries. At the same time, there is often a lack of awareness among development finance institutions and entrepreneurs in industrialized and selected developing countries of the possibilities for cooperation with project sponsors in developing countries.

UNIDO seeks to stimulate industrial development in developing countries by promoting cooperation between industrialists in both developed and developing countries in the generation, formulation, and promotion of investment projects through investment promotion services, access to information stored in computer data banks, and links with international, regional, subregional, and national development finance institutions.

UNIDO's Investment Promotion Resources Information System contains thousands of records on industrial investment project proposals, potential partners, development finance institutions, investment-related institutions, and project sponsors. UNIDO also maintains investment service offices in Athens, Vienna, Paris, Cologne, Seoul, Tokyo, Zurich, Warsaw, Washington, and Milan, which serve as a direct link to businesses and governments in developing countries and can be the "eyes and ears" of firms in industrialized countries interested in investment opportunities in developing countries.

C. Information and Consultations

Through its Industrial and Technological Information Bank, UNIDO seeks to accelerate the flow of information to developing countries, many of which lack access to such information and to technological trends and advances. It also assists in advancing the capacities of developing countries for acquisition of technology through workshops and advisory services and through its System of Consultations. At both the regional and interregional levels, UNIDO's System of Consultations is an instrument in promoting industrial cooperation among developing countries.

BIBLIOGRAPHY

Annual Report of UNIDO.

Handbook of Industrial Statistics (annual).

Industry and Development: Global Report (annual).

UNIDO Update (quarterly).

Industrial Development Abstracts (IDA). The main source of information on UNIDO activities in developing countries. Also available as an electronic database.

Referral Database on Energy and the Environment (REED). A database system relevant to industry and environment, containing bibliographic information, information on institutions, experts, computerized sources, technology descriptions, and vendors.

Micro-Metadex Plus. A database for microcomputer containing selected information from the world's leading metallurgical database.

THE GENERAL AGREEMENT ON TARIFFS AND TRADE (GATT)

BACKGROUND: Efforts to foster international trade go back to antiquity; so do national efforts to expand exports to the detriment of competitors and to restrict or even prohibit imports. Wars have been fought over such issues, and, for long periods of time in many countries, controversy between protectionists and free traders has dominated the political scene. In the 1930s, when the world was suffering from an intense economic depression, many governments attempted to find shelter behind protective trade barriers: high tariff walls, quota restrictions on imports, exchange controls, and the like. If anything, these uncoordinated and mutually antagonistic policies prolonged the international economic crisis. During World War II, serious thought was given to ways and means of preventing such restrictive trade practices from becoming permanently fastened upon the world. Postwar attempts to create a full-fledged international agency to foster and liberalize world trade failed. The General Agreement on Tariffs and Trade is the major result of the efforts that were made in this direction. In the absence of a true international trade organization, it serves as the only intergovernmental instrument that lays down rules for trade and harmonizes trading relations among the nations of the international community.

CREATION

The origin of the General Agreement on Tariffs and Trade can be traced to the Atlantic Charter and to the lend-lease agreements in which the wartime allies bound themselves to seek a world trading system based on nondiscrimination and aimed at higher standards of living to be achieved through fair, full, and free exchange of goods and services.

Three agencies to operate in the specialized field of economic affairs were contemplated: an International Monetary Fund (IMF), an International Bank for Reconstruction and Development (IBRD), and an International Trade Organization (ITO). The IMF and the IBRD were duly established at the Bretton Woods Conference of 1944, but for various reasons, including the complexity of the problems involved, the drafting of the ITO charter was delayed. The UN Economic and Social Council took up the matter at its first session, in February 1946, and appointed a 17-nation preparatory committee to draft such a charter. The committee's draft was submitted to a 56-nation conference that met in Havana from 21 November 1947 to 24 March 1948 and, after considering some 800 separate amendments, hammered out a document known as the Havana Charter to serve as the constitution of the ITO.

The Havana Charter dealt not only with the reduction of trade barriers but also with a number of other complex (and sometimes controversial) matters, including employment and investment policies, mutual cooperation for economic development, commodity control agreements, and the control of international cartels. In view of the preponderant economic position of the US at that time, US participation in the proposed agency was indispensable. The US government favored ratification, but opinion in the country and in Congress was sharply divided. Some opponents argued that the Havana Charter contained too many escape clauses to be effective; others argued that it was too strong and would stifle private enterprise. In December 1950, US president Harry Truman decided not to submit the Havana Charter to the US Senate for ratification, since it was evident that the requisite two-thirds majority could not be obtained. After it became clear

that the US would not join the ITO, the plan to create the agency was abandoned.

While the draft charter of the ITO was being worked out prior to the Havana Conference, the governments of the 17-nation preparatory committee agreed to sponsor negotiations for an interim agreement aimed at lowering customs tariffs and reducing the other trade restrictions among themselves. The first tariff negotiating conference was held in Geneva in 1947. The tariff concessions resulting from these special negotiating sessions were embodied in a multilateral agreement called the General Agreement on Tariffs and Trade (GATT), which included a set of rules designed to prevent the tariff concessions from being frustrated by other protective devices. The agreement was signed on 30 October 1947 and came into force on 1 January 1948. GATT was intended as no more than a stopgap arrangement pending the creation of the ITO, but, as events worked out, it has functioned since 1948 as an agency fulfilling some of the proposed ITO's most important functions.

PURPOSES

GATT is a multilateral trade treaty embodying reciprocal rights and duties. It contains the world's first common code of commercial conduct and fair trading, the objective of which is to expand the production and exchange of goods and so to promote economic development, full employment, and higher standards of living. Under the agreement, all parties are to accord to one another the same "most-favored-nation" treatment in the application of import and export duties and charges and in their administration. Protection is to be afforded to domestic industries exclusively through customs tariffs, import quotas being specifically outlawed as a protectionist device (though they may be used for certain other purposes, such as redressing a country's balance of payments). Countries adhering to GATT agree to avoid, through consultations, damage to the trading interests of any of the contracting parties. GATT itself provides a framework within which negotiations can be held for the reduction of tariffs and other barriers to trade and within which the results of such negotiations can be embodied in a legal instrument. The importance of this "fair trading" code can be measured by the fact that it is accepted and applied by countries accounting for well over 80 percent of world exports.

MEMBERSHIP

Since GATT is a treaty rather than an organization, adhering governments are designated as "contracting parties." When the agreement was brought into operation on 1 January 1948, it was applied by eight governments only. As of 1 July 1994 there were 123 contracting parties to the General Agreement. In addition, there were 14 other countries to whose territories GATT had been applied before their independence and which, as independent states, maintained a de facto application of GATT pending final decisions as to their future commercial policy. At 1 July 1994, 21 countries and territories were negotiating their access to the GATT: Albania, Algeria, Armenia, Belarus, Bulgaria, China, Croatia, Ecuador, Estonia, Jordan, Latvia, Lithuania, Moldova, Mongolia, Nepal, Panama, Russian Federation, Saudi Arabia, Slovenia, Chinese Taipei, and Ukraine.

New adherents to the General Agreement are welcomed. Countries that are former dependencies of existing contracting parties may, on achieving independence, adhere to GATT by stating that they accept the obligations of membership. Other applicants must negotiate the terms of their adherence with the existing members, offering trade concessions to balance those that they will enjoy as a result of accession. The proposed terms of accession are submitted to a vote and must be approved by two-thirds of all GATT members. Developing countries are not expected to make concessions inconsistent with their developmental, financial, and trade needs. A number of Eastern European countries have negotiated their accession, even though many lack meaningful tariff systems and therefore cannot offer tariff concessions, on the basis of assurances regarding their expected trade with GATT members.

Under a special provision (Article XXXV) of the General Agreement, a GATT country that has not yet entered into tariff negotiations with another GATT country is permitted to declare that the GATT obligations will not apply between the two of them.

STRUCTURE

Sessions of the Contracting Parties

The central forum in which the GATT countries act collectively is the Session of the Contracting Parties to the General Agreement on Tariffs and Trade. The sessions, which are usually held annually, in Geneva, provide an opportunity to review developments and trends in international trade and in the operations of the General Agreement itself.

Council of Representatives

Between sessions, the work of GATT is largely carried on by the 93-nation Council of Representatives, established in 1960. Capable of being called together at a few days' notice, it can deal with both routine and urgent matters. Although it cannot make decisions where these require a vote by the contracting parties as a whole, it can and frequently does submit such decisions to a postal ballot. The council can as necessary set up committees, working groups, or panels of experts to assist it in its work. The questions that come before it are extremely varied; they may range from routine reports of standing committees to urgent complaints by governments alleging violation of GATT obligations by other countries.

Committees

The Committee on Trade and Development has the duty to fol-

low all activities of GATT, ensuring that problems of concern to developing countries are given priority attention. A number of standing committees deal with, respectively, the situation of countries using trade restrictions to protect their balance of payments; textiles; tariff concessions; antidumping practices; customs valuation; government procurement; subsidies and countervailing measures; import licensing; technical barriers to trade; agriculture; trade in meat; trade in dairy products; trade in civil aircraft; quantitative restrictions and other nontariff measures; and budget, financial, and administrative questions.

Director-General and Secretariat

In 1994 GATT was administered by a secretariat of about 400 people under Director-General Peter Sutherland of Ireland. The headquarters address is Centre William Rappard, CH 1211 Geneva 21, Switzerland.

BUDGET

Governments that are parties to GATT are assessed for its administrative expenses according to their share in the total trade of the contracting governments. Contributions for 1994 were assessed at SF94.14 million (approximately US$127.1 million).

ACTIVITIES

The General Agreement on Tariffs and Trade consists of 38 articles.

Articles I and II deal directly with tariffs. The first article is the mutual guarantee of most-favored-nation treatment among all contracting parties. It states that any "advantage, favor, privilege or immunity" in regard to duties, payments, and formalities in connection with imports and exports granted by a GATT country to another must automatically be extended to all other GATT countries. Article II provides detailed schedules for tariff reductions agreed to as a result of GATT negotiations.

Article III prohibits the use of internal taxes to protect domestic products against imports.

Articles IV to X—known as the technical articles—provide general rules and principles relating to such matters as transit trade, antidumping duties, customs valuation, customs formalities, and marks of origin. For example, all countries adhering to GATT are required to grant freedom of transit to goods en route to or from other GATT countries; and if a country can prove that another country is injuring its industry by dumping a product on its markets at less than normal value, it may levy a special duty on the product in question.

Articles XI to XIV include a general prohibition of quantitive import restrictions except to safeguard balance of payments, while Article XV deals with relations between contracting parties and the IMF.

Subsequent articles deal with the progressive elimination of export subsidies (XVI), and with state trading enterprises (XVII), emergency measures (XIX), and general and security exceptions to the General Agreement (XX and XXI). Article XVIII recognizes that the less developed countries need to maintain a special degree of tariff flexibility to protect vulnerable new industries and may need to apply some import quotas in order to have sufficient foreign exchange for imports that are vital.

The important provisions for action by contracting parties to settle differences arising out of the application of the General Agreement are contained in Articles XXII and XXIII. Article XXIV, which has assumed great importance, lays down conditions under which a customs union or free-trade area is accepted as a basis for an exception to the most-favored-nation principle.

One of the most important provisions is that in Article XXV, which provides for joint action by the contracting parties. This article is the legal basis that has allowed GATT, as a collective enterprise rather than just a treaty, to work toward the expansion of international trade and serve as a forum for the discussion of international trade problems.

Articles XXVI to XXXV are rules about the operation of GATT itself.

In 1965, a chapter on trade and development, consisting of Articles XXXVI to XXXVIII, was added to the General Agreement. These articles provide a legal basis for collective action on the part of the contracting parties aimed at enlarging the export earnings of developing countries.

A. Trade Negotiations

"The substantial reduction of tariffs and other barriers to trade" is laid down in the General Agreement as one of the principal means of obtaining its broad objectives. Before this agreement, tariffs were generally established by simple unilateral action, each government acting independently or through bilateral negotiations, in which one government would trade reciprocal concessions with another. The General Agreement provided the first machinery for multilateral tariff negotiations, aimed at reducing tariffs simultaneously among all the contracting parties, in accordance with the most-favored-nation principle.

During GATT's first 35 years there have been eight major trade negotiations: 1947 (Geneva), 1949 (Annecy, France), 1951 (Torquay, England), 1956 (Geneva), 1960–61 (Geneva, the "Dillon Round"), 1964–67 (Geneva, the "Kennedy Round"), and 1973–79 (Tokyo and Geneva, the "Tokyo Round"). The eighth round (the "Uruguay Round") was launched in Punta del Este, Uruguay, in September 1986 and concluded in April 1994 in Marrakech, Morocco. As a result of these negotiations, the tariff rates for thousands of items entering into world commerce were reduced or frozen ("bound," in GATT parlance) to prevent their being increased.

The tariff and nontariff concessions agreed upon in the negotiations have affected a high proportion of the trade of GATT countries and, indirectly, the trade of many nonmembers as well. GATT has thus contributed greatly to the spectacular growth in world trade since 1948.

B. The Tokyo Round

Ninety-nine countries participated in the Tokyo Round of negotiations, which began in Tokyo in 1973 and were concluded in Geneva in November 1979 with agreements that covered an improved legal framework for the conduct of world trade (including recognition of tariff and nontariff treatment in favor of and among developing countries as a permanent legal feature of the world trading system), nontariff measures (subsidies and countervailing measures), technical barriers to trade, government procurement, customs valuation, import licensing procedures, a revision of the 1967 GATT Antidumping Code, bovine meat, dairy products, tropical products, and civil aircraft. The agreements contained provisions for special and more favorable treatment for developing countries. Participating countries reduced tariffs on thousands of industrial and agricultural products, the cuts being gradually implemented over a period of seven years ending on 1 January 1987.

Tariffs

The tariff reductions agreed to in the Tokyo Round were completed by 1 January 1987. The total value of trade affected by the Tokyo Round most-favored-nation tariff reductions, and by bindings of prevailing tariff rates, amounts to more than $300 billion, measured on most-favored-nation imports. As a result of these cuts, the weighted average tariff (that is, the average tariff measured against actual trade flows) on manufactured products in the world's nine major industrial markets declined from 7 to 4.7 percent, representing a one-third reduction of customs collection, a cut comparable to that achieved in the Kennedy Round (1964–67). Since the tariff-cutting formula adopted by most industrialized

countries has the result that the largest reductions are generally made in the highest duties, the customs duties of different countries were brought closer together, or "harmonized." Developing countries made tariff-cutting commitments, in the form of tariff bindings or reductions, on $3.9 billion of their imports in 1977.

Nontariff Measures

As the general level of tariff protection declined in the post–World War II period, the distorting effects of nontariff measures on world trade became more pervasive. The complex and often very difficult negotiations to counter the negative effects of these measures distinguished the Tokyo Round from earlier GATT trade negotiations. The core of the Tokyo Round results consisted of the binding agreements, or codes, aimed at reducing, and bringing under more effective international discipline, these nontariff measures. All the agreements provided for consultation and dispute settlement; they also provided for special and more favorable treatment for developing countries. The following agreements were made on nontariff measures.

The agreement on *subsidies and countervailing measures* commits signatory governments to ensuring that any use of subsidies by them does not harm the trading interests of other signatories and that countervailing measures do not unjustifiably impede international trade; these measures may be applied only if it can be shown that the subsidized imports in question are in fact responsible for causing material injury, or threatening such injury, to the domestic industry that has lodged the complaint.

The agreement on *technical barriers to trade* (also known as the Standards Code) commits signatories to making sure that when governments or other bodies adopt technical regulations or standards, for reasons of safety, health, or consumer or environmental protection, among others, these regulations or standards, and the testing and certification schemes related to them, do not create unnecessary obstacles to trade.

The agreement on *import licensing procedures* recognizes not only that these procedures can have acceptable uses but also that their inappropriate use may hamper international trade; it aims at ensuring that they do not in themselves act as restrictions on imports. By becoming parties to the agreement, governments commit themselves to simple import licensing procedures and to administering them in a neutral and fair way.

The agreement on *government procurement* aims to secure greater international competition in the bidding for government procurement contracts. It contains detailed rules on the way in which tenders for government purchasing contracts should be invited and awarded. It is designed to make laws, regulations, procedures, and practices regarding government procurement more transparent and to ensure that they do not protect domestic products or suppliers or discriminate among foreign products or suppliers. The provisions of the agreement apply to individual government contracts worth more than SDR 130,000 (about $150,000). Listed in an annex to the agreement are all the government agencies in each signatory country whose purchases are covered by the agreement.

The agreement on *customs valuation* sets a fair, uniform, and neutral system for the valuation of goods for customs purposes, a system that conforms to commercial realities and that outlaws the use of arbitrary or fictitious customs values. The code provides a revised set of valuation rules, expanding and giving greater precision to the provisions on customs valuation already found in GATT. Developing countries may delay applying the code for five years and are given greater powers to counter potentially unfair valuation practices.

Under the *revised GATT Antidumping Code,* "dumped" goods are broadly defined as imports that are sold at prices below those charged by the producer in his domestic market. Participants in the Tokyo Round agreed on a revision of the earlier GATT Antidumping Code negotiated by a group of major industrialized countries during the Kennedy Round (1964–67). The new code interprets the provisions of Article VI of GATT, which lays down the conditions under which antidumping duties may be imposed as a defense against dumped imports, and brings certain of its provisions into line with the relevant provisions of the Code on Subsidies and Countervailing Measures.

Agreement on Trade in Civil Aircraft

Several industrialized countries agreed in the Tokyo Round to eliminate, by 1 January 1980, all customs duties and similar charges of any kind on civil aircraft, aircraft parts, and repairs on civil aircraft. These zero duties are legally "bound" under GATT and, according to the most-favored-nation rule, apply to all GATT member countries. The agreement contains an annex listing all the products covered, ranging from passenger airliners, helicopters, and ground flight simulators to food warmers and oxygen masks. In 1983 and 1984, further civil aircraft products were added to the duty-free items listed in the annex; these provisions came into force on 1 January 1985.

The Multilateral Safeguard System and Adjustment Assistance

The Tokyo Round decided that "with a view to furthering trade liberalization and preserving its results," the negotiations would include an examination of the adequacy of the multilateral safeguard system and in particular of the way in which Article XIX of the General Agreement is applied. This issue was not resolved during the Tokyo Round, and a committee was established within GATT to continue the safeguards negotiations.

Article XIX is the main GATT "escape clause." It allows member countries to take emergency action of a nondiscriminatory character to restrict imports of particular products when they "cause or threaten serious injury to domestic producers." The question of internal adjustment policies is closely linked with that of safeguards.

Agricultural Products

The agreements on tariff and nontariff concessions, and all the multilateral agreements reached in the Tokyo Round, apply to world trade in farm products, as well as to industrial products. Participating countries also drew up multilateral agreements on bovine meat and on dairy products, which came into force on 1 January 1980.

The *Arrangement Regarding Bovine Meat* aims to promote expansion, liberalization, and stabilization of international trade in meat and livestock, as well as to improve international cooperation in this sector. The arrangement covers beef and veal, as well as live cattle. The International Meat Council within GATT reviews the functioning of the arrangement, evaluates the world supply and demand situation for meat, and provides a forum for regular consultation on all matters affecting international trade in bovine meat.

The *International Dairy Arrangement* aims to expand and liberalize world trade in dairy products; to achieve greater stability in this trade and, therefore, in the interests of exporters and importers, to avoid surpluses, shortages, and undue fluctuations in prices; to further the economic and social development of developing countries; and to improve international cooperation in the dairy products sector. The arrangement covers all dairy products. Annexed to the arrangement are three protocols setting specific provisions, including minimum prices, for international trade in certain milk powders, milk fats (including butter), and certain cheeses. The International Dairy Products Council within GATT reviews the functioning of the arrangement and evaluates the situation in, and future outlook for, the world dairy market, including bilateral and multilateral commitments on trade in this sector.

Tropical Products

The reduction by industrialized countries of import duties and other trade barriers facing exports of tropical products from developing countries was the first concrete result of the Tokyo Round; most reductions were implemented in 1976 and 1977.

Further concessions offered during the later stages of the negotiations took effect from 1980 onward. The concessions cover such products as coffee, cocoa, tea, spices, and a variety of other goods in raw, processed, and semiprocessed forms. A new set of negotiations in this area is being undertaken in the Uruguay Round.

C. The Uruguay Round

In December 1988, trade ministers met in Montreal for the mid-term review meeting of the Uruguay Round. Agreements on the future conduct of the round were reached in 11 of the 15 negotiating areas. At the same time, ministers were able to agree to a package of concessions on tropical products; a series of measures to streamline the disputes settlement system; and a new trade policy review mechanism under which the trade policies of individual GATT contracting parties are subject to regular assessment. Each of these was implemented provisionally in 1989. In April 1989, a meeting of the Trade Negotiations Committee (TNC)—the most senior body of the round—in Geneva, succeeded in securing mid-term agreements on the remaining four negotiating areas: agriculture, safeguards, textiles and clothing, and intellectual property.

It was intended that the round would be concluded at a ministerial TNC meeting in December 1990 in Brussels. Significant progress was made in most negotiating areas before and during the meeting. However, among other problems, it was found impossible to reach an understanding on possible commitments to reduce government financial support and market access restrictions in agriculture. This failure led to a decision by the ministers to prolong the Uruguay Round.

In February 1991, the TNC adopted a work program for the resumption of the negotiations. In December 1991, GATT's Director-General tabled a draft Final Act of the Uruguay Round. In November 1992, negotiators for the European Community and the United States concluded an agriculture agreement in Washington, D.C., which sparked hopes for an imminent conclusion of the round. However, negotiations in Geneva did not gain the expected momentum.

The negotiations resumed in July 1993. After intensive negotiations in November and December, GATT's director-general gaveled the seven-year Uruguay Round negotiations to a close at a meeting of the TNC in Geneva on 15 December 1993. He described the Uruguay Round package as a truly remarkable achievement, pointing out that the results would mean more trade, investment, jobs and income growth for all countries. The major achievements of the round included:

- The General Agreement on Trade in Services provided for a new set of multilateral rules for the conduct of services trade. It simultaneously created a framework for a continuing process of liberalization. This greatly improved the outlook for job creation in this fast-growing sector, which accounts for over 60 percent of world production.
- Trade in intellectual property became the subject of a comprehensive set of new rules (the Agreement on Trade-Related Aspects of Intellectual Property Rights, Including Trade in Counterfeit Goods; also known as TRIPS). This agreement was intended to promote creative activities and innovation and to safeguard investments in intellectual property.
- Agriculture became subject to new disciplines designed to establish a fair and market-oriented agricultural trading system. It was intended that reductions in subsidies would lead to more sustainable markets for farmers worldwide and create opportunities for governments to relieve excess burdens borne by taxpayers and consumers.
- Textiles and clothing also were to be brought back under GATT disciplines, although the process will take 10 years, considerably longer than for other sectors.

The following trade agreements, while forming a part of the Uruguay Round, will be optional for countries that become members of the World Trade Organization: the Agreement on Trade in Civil Aircraft; the Agreement on Government Procurement; the International Dairy Arrangement; and the Arrangement Regarding Bovine Meat.

The results on market access for goods represented a major milestone in the history of the GATT. Tariffs were expected to be reduced by around 40 percent. It was estimated that the United States alone would lose US$18 billion over five years as a result of this reduction. On the other hand, it was estimated that the United States would gain US$26 billion in international trade by the year 2002. The European Economic Community estimated its member countries would gain nearly US$800 billion annually (in 1991 prices) by the year 2002.

On 15 April 1994, more than a hundred ministers, in the ancient trading crossroad of Marrakesh, signed the Final Act of the Uruguay Round. The ministers also made decisions ensuring that the proposed successor to GATT, the World Trade Organization (WTO), would begin operations on 1 January 1995. Under the terms of the "Agreement Establishing the Multilateral Trade Organization," the secretariat and director-general of GATT will become the secretariat and director-general of WTO.

The Final Act contained 28 agreements and 26,000 appended pages of national tariff and services schedules. Referred to as GATT 94, GATT economists estimate the new agreement will add some US$755 billion to world exports and raise incomes by some US$235 billion annually.

The establishment of a Preparatory Committee for the World Trade Organization was one of the four "Decisions" taken by the ministers on 14 April 1994. The other three were: the Decision on Acceptance of and Accession to the Agreement Establishing the World Trade Organization; the Decision on Trade and Environment; and the Decision on Organizational and Financial Consequences flowing from Implementation of the Agreement Establishing the WTO. The Preparatory Committee, headed by the current director-general of GATT, Peter Sutherland, in his personal capacity, was charged with ensuring an orderly transition from the GATT to the WTO.

The Uruguay Round Agreement establishing the WTO envisages a single institutional framework encompassing the GATT, as modified by the Uruguay Round, all agreements and arrangements concluded under its auspices, and the complete results of the Uruguay Round. Its structure will be headed by a Ministerial Conference meeting at least once every two years. A General Council will be established to oversee the operation of the agreement and ministerial decisions on a regular basis. This General Council will itself act as a Dispute Settlement Body and a Trade Policy Review Mechanism, which will concern itself with the full range of trade issues covered by the WTO, and will also establish subsidiary bodies such as a Goods Council, a Services Council, and a Council on Trade-Related Aspects of Intellectual Property Rights (TRIPS). The WTO framework will ensure a "single undertaking approach" to the results of the Uruguay Round. Thus, membership in the WTO will entail accepting all the results of the round without exception.

The Uruguay Round went further than any previous negotiations to extend and strengthen the rule of law in international trade, both by bringing GATT principles to apply in areas where they have been lacking, and by strengthening the existing rules, especially by ensuring their application through a more effective dispute settlement system.

Central to the functioning of the WTO will be the dispute settlement mechanism embodied by the "Understanding on Rules and Procedures Governing the Settlement of Disputes." This agreement sets forth a detailed mechanism for the bringing of trade disputes. Its principal features include:

1. Any member of the WTO may request a "consultation" on practices of another member that it deems contrary to the rules of GATT 94 (and therefore of the WTO).
2. The member receiving the request must respond within 10 days and must enter into good faith consultations within 30 days of receipt of the request.
3. If, after 60 days, no agreement has been reached, the complaining party may request that a three-member dispute settlement panel (DSP) be formed to consider its complaint. If the subject of the complaint is particularly urgent (concerning perishable goods, for example), the waiting period is reduced to 20 days.
4. The secretariat of the WTO will maintain a comprehensive list of qualified individuals who may be called upon to serve on a DSP. The expenses of such individuals incurred in the discharge of their duties will be met by the WTO.
5. Members of WTO, in acceding to the WTO, will have agreed not to dispute the membership of a DSP, except for compelling reasons. However, if both parties do not agree to the membership of the panel the director-general of WTO shall choose a panel.
6. The duties of a DSP will be to assist the Dispute Settlement Board by providing an objective assessment of the facts of the case and the applicability of and conformity with the relevant covered agreements. They are intended to consult with both parties to a dispute and help them arrive at a mutually acceptable agreement. A very specific timetable for this process is defined.

Obstacles to the entry into force of GATT 94 and the creation of the WTO remained at the time of publication. For example, protectionist forces inside the United States were rising to attempt to block its passage in the U.S. Congress. In addition, environmentalists in the United States were concerned that the new GATT agreement would weaken hard-won environmental protection laws already passed in developed countries. This, despite the fact that the agreement's preamble cites the express goal of creating a multilateral trading system that would "allow optimal use of the world's resources in accordance with the objective of sustainable development, seeking both to protect and preserve the environment. . . ."

However, it was expected that the inestimable advantages for the world economy of increased security in international trade from replacement of the piecemeal agreements embodied in GATT 47 with the more comprehensive provisions of GATT 94 (including international consensus on reduction of trade barriers and quick resolution of trade disputes) would lead to widespread adherence to its provisions.

D. GATT and Developing Countries

About two-thirds of the member countries of GATT are developing countries, and it is GATT's responsibility, as the organization under whose rules the greater part of world trade moves, to assist their economic growth.

The developing countries take full part in GATT's work. Their presence underlines not only their determination to promote their own trading interests but also their recognition that the success of their own efforts to promote their economic development is closely linked with the continued expansion of world trade. This expansion of trade, in turn, is largely dependent on GATT's success in its efforts to maintain an open world trading system. Promotion of the trade interests of the developing countries was a priority aim of the Tokyo Round, while a number of provisions of the General Agreement have for many years permitted flexibility to these countries in their application of some GATT rules.

Part IV of the General Agreement

In 1965, a new chapter—Part IV—on trade and development was

added to the General Agreement, committing developed countries to assist the developing countries "as a matter of conscious and purposeful effort." Part IV laid down the important principle, subsequently elaborated in the Tokyo Round "framework" agreements, that developed countries would not expect developing countries, in the course of trade negotiations, to make contributions inconsistent with their individual development, financial, and trade needs. Developed countries also agreed that except when compelling reasons made it impossible, they would refrain from increasing barriers to exports of primary and other products of special interest to developing countries and would give high priority to reducing existing barriers, including fiscal taxes. Consultation procedures were also established, and the Committee on Trade and Development was set up. The committee's role was strengthened following the Tokyo Round by the creation of two new subcommittees, one to examine any new protective measures taken by developed countries against imports from developing countries and the other to consider the trade problems of the least developed countries.

One of the most important issues agreed upon for developing countries during the Tokyo Round was the differential and more favorable treatment, reciprocity, and fuller participation of developing countries, which marked a turning point in international trade relations by recognizing tariff and nontariff preferential treatment in favor of and among developing countries as a permanent legal feature of the world trading system. This "enabling clause" includes provision of a permanent legal basis for the extension of the generalized system of preferences by developed countries to developing countries (previously authorized by a temporary waiver from the provisions of Article I). It also permits special trade treatment for the least developed countries.

Developed countries state that they do not expect reciprocity for commitments made by them in trade negotiations to reduce or remove tariffs and other barriers to the trade of developing countries, while developing countries recognize that as their economies grow stronger, they would expect to participate more fully in the GATT framework of rights and obligations.

Three other important agreements emerged from negotiations on the framework for the conduct of world trade.

The agreement on *trade measures taken for balance-of-payments purposes* states principles and codifies practices and procedures regarding the use of trade measures by governments to safeguard their external financial position and their balance of payments.

The agreement on *safeguard action for development purposes* concerns facilities accorded to developing countries under Article XVIII of the General Agreement, giving them greater flexibility in applying trade measures to meet their development needs.

The *understanding on notification, consultation, dispute settlement, and surveillance* in GATT provides for improvements in the existing mechanisms concerning notification of trade measures, consultations, dispute settlement, and surveillance of developments in the international trading system.

Preferential Agreement Among Developing Countries

An agreement embodying the exchange of preferential tariff concessions among developing countries (17 in 1987), the first multilateral effort by these countries to expand their mutual trade, was successfully concluded in November 1971, when the agreement was approved by the GATT contracting parties, and came into force in February 1973. The participants, who account for about half of all developing-country exports of manufactured goods, exchanged concessions on some 500 tariff headings or subheadings, 30 percent of which concern agricultural products and raw materials. The concessions granted are generally in the form of a preferential duty rate or the binding of a margin of preference expressed either as a percentage of the most-favored-nation rate or, in some cases, as a reduction of that rate. In 1985, according to data from 10 participating countries, aggregate trade with other participating countries in products included in the schedules of concessions amounted to approximately $350 million. The agreement is open to all developing countries, whether or not they are members of GATT.

Technical Assistance and Training

Since 1955, GATT has provided training in commercial policy for officials from developing countries at its headquarters in Geneva. Assistance to developing countries is also provided through a Technical Cooperation Division within the GATT secretariat in all fields of GATT's work, including in particular follow-up action in regard to the Tokyo Round of multilateral trade negotiations.

International Trade Center

In 1964, GATT established the International Trade Center to provide trade information and trade promotion advisory services for developing countries. Since January 1968, the center has been jointly operated by GATT and UNCTAD.

The center responds to requests from developing countries for assistance in formulating and implementing export promotion programs. It provides information and advice on export markets and marketing techniques and assists in establishing export promotion and marketing services and in training personnel for these services.

E. Other GATT Activities

Settlement of Differences

Among the matters that are referred to the GATT Council are trade disputes over the application of Articles XXII and XXIII of the agreement, concerning the settlement of differences. If a GATT country believes that a benefit that should accrue to it is being nullified or impaired (or that the attainment of any objective of the agreement is being impeded), it is first expected to seek redress through diplomatic channels. If no satisfactory adjustment can be reached through bilateral consultations, the country may lodge a complaint with GATT. The contracting parties are then required to carry out prompt investigations and to make recommendations or rulings. Such trade differences as are not settled through bilateral consultations are submitted to a group of experts from countries that have no direct interest in the matter. These panels, as they are called, have frequently succeeded in bringing about an agreement.

Improvements in the procedures for dispute settlement, especially to take into account problems of developing countries, were adopted during the Tokyo Round.

Textiles

Trade in textiles has long been a major concern of GATT. From 1962 until 1973, world trade in cotton textiles was largely regulated by the so-called Long-Term Arrangement, which was drawn up to ensure the orderly development of this trade. Since 1974, world trade in textiles and clothing has largely been regulated by the Arrangement Regarding International Trade in Textiles, otherwise known as the Multi-Fiber Arrangement. Negotiated under GATT auspices, the arrangement took effect on 1 January 1974. It is intended to reconcile the interests of importing and exporting countries in the sensitive and difficult field of textiles by permitting the expansion of trade while avoiding disruption of markets. The safeguard provisions of the arrangement may be invoked by participants if their domestic market is disrupted, or threatened with disruption, as a result of imports; any restrictions imposed must permit exports from an affected supplying country to expand in an orderly and equitable manner. Most safeguard measures under the arrangement have taken the form of bilateral agreements. Supervision of the arrangement is entrusted to the Textiles Surveillance Body, consisting of an independent chairman and eight members so chosen as to provide balanced representation of the countries participating in the Multi-Fiber Arrangement.

GATT Membership
(as of June 1994)

Angola	Denmark	Kenya	Philippines	United Kingdom
Antigua and Barbuda	Dominica	Korea, Republic of	Poland	United States
Argentina	Dominican Republic	Kuwait	Portugal	Uruguay
Australia	Egypt	Lesotho	Qatar	Venezuela
Austria	El Salvador	Liechtenstein	Romania	Yugoslavia
Bahrain	Fiji	Luxembourg	Rwanda	Zaire
Bangladesh	Finland	Macau	St. Kitts and Nevis	Zambia
Barbados	France	Madagascar	St. Lucia	Zimbabwe
Belgium	Gabon	Malawi	St. Vincent and the	
Belize	Gambia	Malaysia	Grenadines	DE FACTO ADHERENTS TO
Benin	Germany	Maldives	Senegal	GATT
Bolivia	Ghana	Mali	Sierra Leone	Algeria
Botswana	Greece	Malta	Singapore	Bahamas
Brazil	Grenada	Mauritania	Slovak Republic	Cambodia
Brunei Darussalam	Guatemala	Mauritius	South Africa	Cape Verde
Burkina Faso	Guinea-Bissau	Mexico	Spain	Djibouti
Burundi	Guyana	Morocco	Sri Lanka	Equatorial Guinea
Cameroon	Haiti	Mozambique	Suriname	Kribati
Canada	Honduras	Myanmar	Swaziland	Papua New Guinea
Central African Republic	Hong Kong	Namibia	Sweden	Sâo Tomé and Principe
Chad	Hungary	Netherlands	Switzerland	Seychelles
Chile	Iceland	New Zealand	Tanzania	Solomon Islands
Colombia	India	Nicaragua	Thailand	Tonga
Congo	Indonesia	Niger	Togo	Tuvalu
Costa Rica	Ireland	Nigeria	Trinidad and Tobago	Yemen
Côte d'Ivoire	Israel	Norway	Tunisia	
Cuba	Italy	Pakistan	Turkey	
Cyprus	Jamaica	Paraguay	Uganda	
Czech Republic	Japan	Peru	United Arab Emirates	

There is no precedent in international trade relations for a multilateral surveillance group of this kind. The Textiles Surveillance Body reports to the Textiles Committee, which reviews the operation of the arrangement once a year.

One major result of the Uruguay Round has been agreement to integrate trade in textiles and clothing back into GATT over a 10-year period.

Regional Arrangements

If two or more countries form a customs union or free-trade area, goods moving between them are liberated from import and export duties and other trade barriers. Under a free-trade-area arrangement, the participating countries maintain their right to determine separate customs tariffs toward the outside. Under a customs union, the participating countries go further; they set up a common customs tariff for trade with the outside. Clearly, both arrangements affect the commercial interests of third countries.

The European Economic Community (EEC) and the European Free Trade Association (EFTA) are the two regional arrangements that have posed the greatest problems in respect to the most-favored-nation principles of the General Agreement, since the countries belonging to the EEC and EFTA are all parties to the agreement and since their combined foreign commerce accounts for a very high proportion of total world trade.

The position of the EEC as the world's largest trading entity was further reinforced by the accession of Denmark, Ireland, and the UK to membership in 1973, the accession of Greece in 1981, and the accession of Spain and Portugal in 1986. All the member countries of the community are contracting parties to GATT. Careful scrutiny of the trade effects of the community's enlargement was therefore necessary.

The rules in the General Agreement relating to customs unions and free-trade areas are contained in Article XXIV, which states that integration of national economies is conceived of as a means of contributing to the objectives of GATT. It lays down the conditions under which a customs union or free-trade area is accepted as a basis for an exception to the most-favored-nation clause, and sets out a series of rules designed to ensure that a customs union

or a free-trade area shall in effect lead to the reduction and elimination of barriers within the area without raising new barriers to trade with the outside.

Since its enlargement, the EEC has signed trade agreements with all the remaining countries of the EFTA (Austria, Finland, Iceland, Norway, Sweden, and Switzerland). This means that a high proportion of trade between Western European countries takes place on a tariff-free basis.

The compatibility of these agreements with Article XXIV of the General Agreement was examined by special working groups, but no unanimous conclusions were reached. The parties to the agreements, supported by some other countries, maintain that these agreements are fully compatible with the rules of GATT, which specifically allow the formation of free-trade areas since these encourage the growth and liberalization of world trade. Against this position, other countries argue that the agreements are preferential trade arrangements for industrial products rather than instruments of free trade, since the agricultural sector as a whole is excluded. The many agreements which have been negotiated between the EEC and a number of Mediterranean and developing countries have given rise to similar controversy.

Other regional trading arrangements are examined regularly by the contracting parties within the framework of Article XXIV of the General Agreement.

BIBLIOGRAPHY

Guide to GATT Law and Practice, 6th edition, 1994 An article-by-article handbook on the provisions of GATT. Available in English, French, and Spanish.

GATT: What It Is, What It Does. Information brochure.

GATT Activities. Annual report on the work of GATT and account of developments of the year under review.

GATT Focus. Newsletter published six times a year.

International Trade. Annual. Report on developments in world trade.

(GATT also publishes the texts of agreements, as well as studies on specific sectors of international trade.)

THE INTERNATIONAL MONETARY FUND (IMF)

BACKGROUND: The 1930s was a period not only of great political upheaval but also of grave financial and economic difficulty. The gold standard was largely abandoned, and currency exchange rates fluctuated wildly. Economic chaos was aggravated by a lack of coordination between governments that imposed controls on international financial transactions and engaged in ruthless economic warfare.

During World War II, most countries realized that they would emerge from the conflict with depleted economic resources just when they would have to confront a reconstruction effort of staggering dimensions. It was also known that the United Kingdom would emerge from the war as the world's principal debtor nation and the United States, whose productive capacity had greatly increased during the war, as the world's principal creditor nation.

CREATION

The United Kingdom, the United States, and their allies were convinced that international economic and financial cooperation through intergovernmental institutions was required to prevent a more serious recurrence of the economic and monetary chaos of the 1930s. Two plans were proposed almost simultaneously in 1943: a United States plan for an International Stabilization Fund, referred to as the White plan, after H. D. White, then assistant to the United States secretary of the treasury; and a British plan for an International Clearing Union, referred to as the Keynes plan, after the British economist John Maynard Keynes. Both plans called for international machinery to stabilize currencies and—a radical innovation—a prohibition against altering exchange rates beyond narrow limits without international approval. Both would have introduced a new international currency unit defined in terms of gold. The American plan called for participating nations to contribute to a relatively limited stabilization fund of about $5 billion, on which they would be permitted to draw in order to bridge balance-of-payments deficits. The British plan would have established a system of international clearing accounts, under which each member country could borrow up to its own quota limit, while its creditors would be credited with corresponding amounts, expressed in international currency units. Both plans were discussed with financial experts of other powers, including the Republic of China, the French Committee for Liberation, and the USSR. The International Monetary Fund as finally constituted resembled the United States-suggested stabilization fund. The proposal to establish a new international monetary unit was deferred for the time being.

The Bretton Woods Conference

A conference called by President Franklin D. Roosevelt and attended by delegates from all 44 United and Associated Nations was held from 1 to 22 July 1944 at Bretton Woods, New Hampshire. The Bretton Woods Conference produced the constitutions, or Articles of Agreement, of two agencies conceived as sister institutions: the International Monetary Fund (IMF) and the International Bank for Reconstruction and Development (IBRD).

The IMF came into existence on 27 December 1945, when 29 governments, responsible for 80 percent of the quotas to be contributed to the Fund, signed the IMF Articles of Agreement. An agreement with the UN, under which the IMF became a specialized agency, entered into force on 15 November 1947.

PURPOSES

The purposes of the IMF are the following:

1. to promote international monetary cooperation;
2. to facilitate the expansion and balanced growth of international trade and contribute thereby to the promotion and maintenance of high levels of employment and real income;
3. to promote exchange stability, maintain orderly exchange arrangements among member states, and avoid competitive currency depreciations;
4. to assist in establishing a multilateral system of payments of current transactions among members and in eliminating foreign-exchange restrictions that hamper world trade; and
5. to alleviate serious disequilibrium in the international balance of payments of members by making the resources of the Fund available under adequate safeguards, so as to prevent the members from resorting to measures that endanger national or international prosperity.

MEMBERSHIP

The original members of the IMF were the 29 nations whose governments had ratified the Articles of Agreement by 27 December 1945. Any other state, whether or not a member of the UN, may become a member of the IMF in accordance with terms prescribed by the Board of Governors. The IMF had 178 members as of 31 December 1993. (See membership list at the end of this section.) Membership in the IMF is a prerequisite to membership in the IBRD. A member may withdraw from the IMF at any time, and its withdrawal becomes effective on the day that a written notice to that effect is received by the Fund.

If a member state fails to fulfill its obligations under the IMF Articles of Agreement, the Fund may declare that country ineligible to use its resources. If, after a reasonable period has elapsed, the member state persists in its failure to live up to its obligations, the Board of Governors may require it to withdraw from membership.

The Third Amendment of the IMF's Articles of Agreement came into force on 11 November 1992. It allows for the suspension of voting and related rights of a member that persists in its failure to fulfill its obligations under the Articles.

STRUCTURE

The Fund has a Board of Governors, composed of as many governors as there are member states; 24 executive directors; and a managing director and staff.

Board of Governors

All powers of the IMF are vested in its Board of Governors, on which all member states are represented. Each member state appoints one governor and one alternate governor, who may vote when the principal governor is absent. A government customarily appoints its minister of finance, the president of its central bank, or another high-ranking official as its governor. For example, in September 1993, the United States governor was Secretary of the Treasury Lloyd M. Bentsen, and the alternate, Federal Reserve Board Chairman Alan Greenspan.

The principle that applies in most international bodies—one nation, one vote—does not apply in the IMF Board of Governors. Multiple votes are assigned to IMF member states, more votes being assigned to those subscribing larger quotas to the Fund's resources. Each member has 250 votes plus 1 additional vote for each SDR 100,000 of its quota. (The SDR is an international reserve asset created by the Fund. See section F.) The total number of votes of all IMF members was 1,490,550 on 31 December 1993, of which the United States held about 17.8 percent and the United Kingdom about 5.6 percent.

Each governor is entitled to cast all the votes allotted to his country as a unit. On certain matters, however, voting power varies according to the use made of the Fund's resources by the respective member. IMF decisions are made by a simple majority of the votes cast, unless otherwise stipulated in the constitution. The Board of Governors regularly meets once a year. It may also be convened for other than annual meetings.

Except for such basic matters as admission of new members, quota changes, and the like, the Board of Governors delegates most of its powers to the Executive Directors of the Fund.

The Articles of Agreement, as amended effective 1 April 1978, provide that the Board of Governors may decide to establish a new council at the ministerial level which would "supervise the management and adaptation of the international monetary system." Pending establishment of the council, a 22-member Interim Committee on the International Monetary System, established in 1974, advises the Board of Governors.

Executive Directors

The 24 executive directors of the IMF are responsible for the Fund's general operations, and for this purpose they exercise all the powers delegated to them by the Board of Governors. They "function in continuous session" at the Fund's headquarters and meet as often as business may require, usually several times a week.

Of the 24 executive directors, five have been appointed by individual countries (United States, Germany, Japan, France and the United Kingdom) and the other 19 have been elected by groups of the remaining members.

Managing Director and Staff

The managing director, who is chosen by the executive directors, is responsible for the conduct of the ordinary business of the Fund. He is appointed for a five-year term and may not serve concurrently as a governor or executive director of the IMF. The managing director chairs meetings of the executive directors but may vote only in case of a tie.

The permanent headquarters of the IMF are at 700 19th Street, N.W., Washington, DC 20431. As of December 1993, the staff consisted of about 2,300 persons from 122 countries.

BUDGET

The budget for the fiscal year ending April 1994 was SDR 476,815,000. The Fund's income considerably exceeds its administrative expenditures. This income is derived principally from charges on the Fund's transactions.

ACTIVITIES

A. Resources of the IMF

The Fund obtains its necessary financial resources from the accumulated subscriptions made by its members. How much a member government subscribes to the Fund's resources is determined by the quota assigned to that country. As mentioned above, the quota also determines the country's voting strength in the IMF. Furthermore, the quota, which is expressed in SDRs, determines the amounts that the country may draw from the Fund's currency pool, as well as the country's allocations of SDRs.

In determining a member's quota, the IMF considers relevant economic data, including the country's national income, its international reserves, and the volume of its imports and exports.

The method of payment for initial quota subscriptions or increases in quotas was modified when the Second Amendment to the Articles of Agreement went into effect in 1978. Under the original Articles, members were required to pay 25 percent of their quota in gold and the remainder in their own currencies. Following the Second Amendment, an amount not exceeding 25 percent of new members' initial quotas, or existing members' increases in quotas, is paid in reserve assets, while the remainder is paid in the members' own currencies.

The Fund is required by its constitution to review its members' quotas every five years and to propose called-for adjustments in quotas. All quota changes must be approved by an 85 percent majority of the total voting power.

Several reviews of the adequacy of members' quotas have led to general and selective increases of Fund quotas. A special review in 1958/59 resulted in a 50 percent increase in quotas, which was followed by a 25 percent general increase in 1965 and a further 25 percent general increase in 1970. The 1976 review of quotas was affected by developments in the international monetary system, including the quadrupling of oil prices. As a result of that review, total quotas were increased by 32.5 percent, to SDR 39 billion, reflecting a doubling of the collective share in total quotas of the major oil-exporting countries. The share of all other developing countries was maintained at its then existing level. The 1978 review provided for a 50 percent general quota increase for most members and additional special increases for 11 members. Consents to increases under this review raised total quotas to SDR 59.6 billion. The 1983 review increased quotas by 47.5 percent, to SDR 90 billion.

The most recent review of IMF resources resulted in an increase in total quotas to SDR 144.7 billion, as of 16 August 1993.

The Fund is authorized under its Articles to supplement its resources by borrowing. In January 1962, a four-year agreement was concluded with 10 industrial members (the Group of 10)—subsequently joined by Switzerland as an associate and by Saudi Arabia under a special arrangement in 1983—by which they undertook to lend to the Fund to finance drawings by participants of the General Arrangements to Borrow (GAB) "if this should be needed to forestall or cope with an impairment of the international monetary system." These General Arrangements to Borrow have been extended several times and are effective until 26 December 1998.

On 19 January 1983, the ministers of the Group of 10 agreed in principle to enlarge the GAB to SDR 17 billion, from approximately SDR 6.4 billion, and to permit the Fund to borrow under the enlarged credit arrangements to finance exchange transactions with members that are not GAB participants. In addition, the ministers agreed to authorize Swiss participation in the agreement. The amounts of credit arrangements (in millions of SDRs) are as follows: the United States, 4,250; Germany, 2,380; Japan, 2,125; France, 1,700; the United Kingdom, 1,700; Saudi Arabia, 1,500; Italy, 1,105; Switzerland, 1,020; Canada, 892.5; the Netherlands, 850; Belgium, 595; and Sweden, 382.5.

The Fund has also, in the past, supplemented its resources by borrowing, for example, for the oil facility for 1974 and 1975 and for the supplementary financing facility, whose resources of SDR 7,784 billion were borrowed from 14 members or institutions.

B. General Obligations of IMF Members

The economic philosophy of the Bretton Woods Agreement holds that monetary stability and cooperation and the unhampered movement of money, especially in payment of current international transactions, will promote national and international prosperity. This principle is reflected in certain general obligations that countries undertake by accepting the IMF's Articles of Agreement. The Articles favor stabilization measures to help overcome short-term balance-of-payments difficulties, and they discourage exchange controls under normal conditions. The Agreement also enables the Fund to help governments in short-term payments difficulties.

C. Consultations

Consultations with members are an essential component of the Fund's work and provide a major instrument for Fund surveillance of members' policies in several key areas.

Article IV of the Articles of Agreement, entitled "Obligations Regarding Exchange Arrangements," allows individual members considerable freedom in the selection of their exchange arrangements, but it also stipulates general obligations and specific undertakings.

In order to help the Fund ensure observance of these obligations through the exercise of "firm surveillance" over exchange-rate policies, members are required to consult with the Fund regularly under Article IV, in principle on an annual basis. These consultations provide an opportunity for detailed review of the economic and financial situation and the policies of members from both the national and international viewpoints. They also help the Fund deal expeditiously with members' requests for the use of Fund resources and for proposed changes in policies or practices that are subject to Fund approval. For the individual member, regular consultations provide the occasion for an external appraisal of policies and for discussion of any special difficulties that may arise from the actions of other members.

Members availing themselves of the transitional arrangements permitted under Article XIV of the Articles of Agreement to maintain multiple exchange rates or other restrictions on current international payments are required to consult annually with the Fund. Article VIII countries have accepted the obligation to avoid such practices. Consultations under Article IV include the regular consultations under Article VIII and Article XIV and are required for all members.

Between annual consultations, there is a supplemental surveillance procedure under which the managing director initiates an informal and confidential discussion with a member whenever he thinks that a modification in the member's exchange arrangements or exchange-rate policies or the behavior of the exchange rate of its currency may be important or may have important effects on other members.

Special consultations with selected countries also supplement regular consultations in connection with the periodic reviews of the world economic outlook undertaken by the Executive Board. The purpose of these consultations is to provide up-to-date knowledge of the economic situation in countries whose external policies are regarded as being of major importance to the world economy.

D. Transactions Between the Fund and Its Members

Use of Resources

Members of the Fund may draw on its financial resources to meet their balance-of-payments needs. They may use the reserve tranche and, under tranche policies, the four credit tranches (see below). In addition, there are four permanent facilities for specific purposes—the Compensatory and Contingency Financing Facility (CCFF); the buffer stock financing facility (established in 1969); the extended Fund facility (established in 1974); and the structural adjustment facility (SAF) (established in 1986).

In addition, members may make use of temporary facilities established by the Fund with borrowed resources. For 1974 and 1975, for example, following the sharp rise in oil prices, the Fund provided assistance under a temporary oil facility designed to help members meet the increased cost of imports of petroleum and petroleum products. During the period 1978–84, a supplementary financing facility, funded with borrowed resources amounting to SDR 7,784 billion from 13 member countries or their institutions and the Swiss National Bank, assisted members whose payments imbalances were large in proportion to their quotas. In March 1981, a policy of enlarged access to the Fund's resources was adopted, allowing the Fund to continue to provide assistance on a scale similar to that under the supplementary financing facility. This enlarged access policy was terminated in November 1992, when the Ninth General Review of Quotas became effective.

In December 1987, the IMF established the enhanced structural adjustment facility (ESAF). It is similar to the SAF in objective, eligibility and program features, but differs in scope, terms of access, and funding sources. The ESAF has been renewed and extended since its creation and will be in operation for commitments through 1996, with disbursements extending through 1999.

In April 1993, the IMF created the systematic transformation facility (STF) to address the special needs of its members experiencing severe disruptions in their trade and payments arrangements owing to the shift to market-oriented systems. The STF will remain in effect through 1994.

For any drawing, a member is required to indicate to the Fund that the desired purchase is needed to stabilize its balance-of-payments or reserve position or to deal with adverse developments in its reserves.

When a member draws on the Fund, it uses its own currency to purchase the currencies of other member countries or SDRs held by the General Resources Account. Thus, a drawing results in an increase in the Fund's holdings of the purchasing member's currency and a corresponding decrease in the Fund's holdings of other currencies or SDRs that are sold. Within a prescribed time, a member must reverse the transaction (unless it is a reserve tranche purchase) by buying back its own currency with SDRs or currencies specified by the Fund. Usually, repurchases are to be made within three to five years after the date of purchase. However, under the extended Fund facility, the period for repurchases is within four and a half to ten years, and under the supplementary financing facility, within three and a half to seven years. In addition, a member is expected normally to repurchase as its balance-of-payments or reserve position improves.

Reserve Tranche. The difference between a member's quota and the Fund's holdings of that member's currency is referred to as the member's reserve tranche. Purchases in the reserve tranche—a reserve asset that can be mobilized by the member with minimum delay—are subject to balance-of-payments need but not to prior challenge, economic policy conditions, or repurchase requirements. A member using Fund resources in the credit tranches has the option either to use or to retain a reserve tranche position.

Credit Tranches. Further purchases are made in four credit tranches, each of 25 percent of the member's quota. In the past, the total of purchases under credit tranche policies was normally limited to 100 percent of the member's quota, an amount that would raise the Fund's holdings of the member's currency to 200 percent of its quota. However, in response to the structural and deep-rooted nature of the payments imbalance currently confronting many members, the Fund is placing greater emphasis on programs involving adjustment periods of longer duration, and provision has been made for a larger access above these limits. As of November 1992, access was limited to 68 percent of quota annually and 300 percent cumulatively.

All requests for the use of the Fund's resources other than use of the reserve tranche are examined by the Fund to determine whether the proposed use would be consistent with the provisions of the Articles of Agreement and with Fund policies.

The criteria used by the Fund in determining whether its assistance should be made available are more liberal when the request is in the first credit tranche (that is, when the Fund holdings of a member's currency are above 100 percent but not above 125 percent of the member's quota) than when it is in the higher credit tranches (that is, when the Fund's holdings following the drawing exceed 125 percent of quota).

A member requesting a direct purchase expects to draw the full amount immediately after approval of the request; under a standby arrangement, a member may make the agreed drawing at any time during the period of the standby arrangement.

Requests for purchases in the higher credit tranches require substantial justification. Such purchases are almost always made under standby or similar arrangements. The amount available under a standby arrangement in the upper credit tranches is phased to be available in portions at specified intervals during the standby period, and the member's right to draw is always subject to the observance of certain key policy objectives described in the program or to a further review of the situation.

In November 1987, the Executive Board began to examine the need to address external contingencies in Fund arrangements and the design of appropriate contingency financing mechanisms. These deliberations resulted in the establishment of the Compensatory and Contingency Financing Facility (CCFF) in August 1988. The CCFF incorporated existing facilities—the compensatory financing facility (established in 1963), which provided financial assistance to members experiencing temporary export shortfalls, and the facility providing compensatory financing for excesses in cereal import costs that were largely attributable to circumstances beyond the members' control. The CCFF also introduced a new element—the "external contingency mechanism." This mechanism gave members with fund arrangements the opportunity to protect themselves from unexpected, adverse external developments. In December 1990, an additional, temporary element was introduced to compensate members for sharp rises in oil import costs.

As of November 1992, the amounts of financing available to a member under the CCFF are 30 percent of quota each on account of the export shortfall and the external contingency elements, and 15 percent of quota for the cereal import cost element. Members may also choose to apply an "optional tranche" of 20 percent of quota to supplement any of the three elements. Members may draw up to 65 percent of quota to finance either export shortfalls or cereal import costs (or both) when their balance of payments difficulties are due only to the effects of these circumstances. They may draw up to 80 percent of quota on the use of all three elements.

In accordance with the criteria set forth in the decision establishing the BSFF, the IMF has so far authorized the use of its resources in connection with buffer stocks of tin, sugar, and natural rubber.

Extended Facility. Under the extended facility, the Fund may provide assistance to members to meet their balance-of-payments deficits for longer periods and in amounts larger in relation to quotas than under the credit tranche policies. For example, a member might apply for assistance under the facility if it has serious payments imbalances relating to structural maladjustments in production, trade, and prices and if it intends to implement a comprehensive set of corrective policies for two or three years. Use of the facility might also be indicated by an inherently weak balance-of-payments position that prevents the pursuit of an active development policy.

Drawings under extended arrangements generally take place over periods of up to three years, although this may be extended to four years.

Structural Adjustment Facility. In response to the particularly difficult situation confronting the low-income members of the Fund, the Executive Board established in March 1986 a structural adjustment facility within the Fund's Special Disbursement Account. This facility provides concessional balance-of-payments assistance—in conjunction with the World Bank and other lenders—to low-income countries eligible for IDA loans that are facing protracted balance-of-payments problems and are undertaking comprehensive efforts to strengthen their balance-of-payments position. In 1993, 61 members of the Fund were eligible for assistance under this facility, the use of which requires the adoption of a comprehensive three-year framework that incorporates the structural policy elements of a member's reform program. The World Bank participates jointly with the Fund in assisting the member in the formulation of the policy framework, which is also reviewed by the Bank's Executive Board. The initial resources for this facility were derived from repayments of Trust Fund loans (about SDR 2.7 billion).

Conditionality

A country making use of the Fund's resources is generally required to implement economic policies aimed at achieving a viable balance-of-payments position over an appropriate period of time. This requirement is known as "conditionality," and it reflects the principle that balance-of-payments financing and adjustment must go hand in hand.

A comprehensive review of the guidelines for conditionality was undertaken in 1979. These guidelines include the use of consultation clauses in Fund-supported programs, the phasing of purchases, and the injunction that objective indicators for monitoring performance be limited only to those variables necessary to ensure achievement of the objectives of the programs. In addition, the guidelines emphasize the need to encourage members to adopt corrective measures at an early stage of their balance-of-payments difficulties; to recognize that in many cases adjustment will take longer than the period associated with standby arrangements; to provide for the adoption of a flexible approach for the treatment of external borrowing in adjustment programs; and to stress the necessity to pay due regard to the domestic social and political objectives, the economic priorities, and the circumstances of members, including the causes of their payments problems.

Within the context of the guidelines, Fund-supported programs emphasize a number of major economic variables, including certain financial aggregates, such as domestic credit, public sector financial needs, and external debt, as well as some key elements of the price system, including the exchange rate, interest rates, and, in exceptional cases, the prices of commodities that bear significantly upon public finances and foreign trade.

The Fund-supported corrective strategy provides for a reorientation of the economy toward sustained growth and avoids purely deflationary policies that may have a deleterious effect on investment and fail to encourage the required shift of resources to the external sector.

Charges for Use of Resources and Remuneration on Creditor Positions

The Fund applies charges for the use of its resources, except for reserve tranche purchases. A service charge of 0.5 percent is payable on purchases other than reserve tranche purchases. In addition, the Fund levies charges on balances of members' currencies resulting from purchases. The rate of charge on purchases in the four credit tranches and under the extended Fund facility, the compensatory financing facility, and the buffer-stock financing facility is determined at the beginning of each financial year on the basis of the estimated income and expense of the Fund during the year and a target amount of net income. The average rate of charge on the use of the Fund's ordinary resources for financial year 1993 was 6.6 percent. Members that use the Fund's borrowed resources pay charges that reflect the Fund's borrowing costs plus a margin. In 1992/93, the average rate of charge for the supplementary financing facility was 6.53 percent; for the enlarged access policy, it was 6.60 percent.

When the Fund's holdings of a member's currency are reduced below a specified level, the member acquires a creditor position in the Fund on which it earns remuneration (that is, interest). The Fund pays remuneration on creditor positions at a rate determined by a formula based on short-term market interest rates in the United States, the United Kingdom, Germany, France, and Japan. For financial year 1993, the average rate of remuneration paid to members in creditor positions was 4.57 percent.

E. Technical Assistance

Technical assistance is a major activity of the Fund. Staff officials are sent to member countries, sometimes for extended periods, to give advice on stabilization programs, the simplification of exchange systems, the modification of central banking machinery, the reform of fiscal systems and budgetary controls, or the preparation of financial statistics. The Fund collects and publishes a considerable number of statistics supplied by members. As part of its technical cooperation, the Fund established the IMF Institute in May 1964 to coordinate and expand its training program for staff members of finance ministries and central banks. The IMF established the Joint Vienna Institute in the Fall of 1992. During 1992/93, the IMF Institute offered 13 courses and three seminars at IMF headquarters and eight courses and one seminar at the Joint Vienna Institute, training 816 persons in a wide range of subjects.

F. Special Drawing Rights (SDRs)

The SDR is an international reserve asset created by the Fund and allocated to its members as a supplement to existing reserve assets. The Fund has allocated a total of SDR 21.4 billion in six allocations.

The last allocation of SDRs in the third basic period was made on 1 January 1981, when a total of SDR 4,052 million was allocated to the 141 countries that were members of the Fund at that time. Similar amounts were allocated in each of the two previous years. The Fund allocates SDRs to its members in proportion to their quotas at the time of allocation. In deciding on the timing and amount of SDR allocations, the Fund considers whether there exists a global need to supplement existing reserve assets, and it takes into account the objectives of the Fund's Articles of Agreement, which call upon Fund members to collaborate with each other and with the Fund with a view to making the SDR the principal reserve asset of the international monetary system.

All 178 member countries of the Fund are participants in the SDR Department and are eligible to receive allocations. They may use SDRs in transactions and operations among themselves, with prescribed "other holders," of which there are now 15, and with the Fund itself. The SDR is the Fund's unit of account, and, increasingly, commercial transactions and private financial obligations are being denominated in SDRs.

Members with a balance-of-payments need may use SDRs to acquire foreign exchange in a transaction with designation—that is, one in which another member, designated by the Fund, provides currency in exchange for SDRs. The Fund designates members to provide currency on the basis of the strength of their balance-of-payments and reserve positions. However, a member's obligation to provide currency does not extend beyond the point at which its holdings are three times the net cumulative allocation that it has received. Fund members and "other holders" may also use SDRs in a variety of voluntary transactions and operations by agreement. They may buy and sell SDRs, both spot and forward, use SDRs in swaps and in settlement of financial obligations, or make donations (grants) with SDRs.

The valuation of the SDR is determined on the basis of a basket of five currencies—the United States dollar, the German deutsche mark, the Japanese yen, the French franc, and the British pound sterling. The value of the SDR is calculated daily by the Fund as the sum of the values in United States dollars, based on market exchange rates, of specified amounts of the five currencies in the basket. These amounts, or "currency units," are derived from agreed percentage weights for the currencies in the basket. As of 31 December 1991, the agreed weights are: 40 percent for the United States dollar, 21 percent for the deutsche mark, 17 percent for the Japanese yen, and 11 percent each for the French franc and the pound sterling. The weights broadly reflect the relative importance of the currencies in international trade and payments, based on the value of the exports of goods and services of the member countries issuing these currencies and the balances of these currencies held as reserves by members of the Fund over the five-year period 1985–89. The SDR interest rate is based on the short-term obligations in the money markets of the same five countries whose currencies are used in the valuation.

G. Gold Sales by the Fund

The Fund's original Articles of Agreement required members to pay one-fourth of their quota subscription in gold. The establishment of the SDR in 1969 and the Second Amendment to the Articles of Agreement in 1978 virtually eliminated the monetary role of gold from the Articles, although gold still remains an important component in the reserve holdings of member countries. As a result of these developments, the Executive Board decided to sell off a portion of the Fund's gold holdings, beginning in 1976. In May 1980, the Fund completed a four-year gold sales program, through which 50 million oz, or one-third of the Fund's gold holdings at the beginning of the period, were sold. One-sixth of the gold (25 million oz) was sold to members at the former official price of SDR 35 an ounce. Another one-sixth was sold at auction for the benefit of developing countries. Some of the profits from these auctions were used to finance a trust fund, providing concessional balance-of-payments assistance to eligible developing countries. Repayments of these concessional loans (amounting to about SDR 2.7 billion) form the basic funding for the structural adjustment facility.

BIBLIOGRAPHY

Annual Report of the Executive Board. Reviews the Fund's activities and surveys the world economy.

Annual Report on Exchange Restrictions.

Balance of Payments Yearbook.

Direction of Trade. Monthly. Contains trade-by-country statistics of some 100 countries and summaries by geographic and monetary areas. Compiled by the IMF and the IBRD and published jointly by the Fund, the Bank, and the UN.

Government Finance Statistics Yearbook.

IMF Survey. Twice a month.

International Financial Statistics. Monthly. Contains statistics on all aspects of domestic and international finance (exchange rates, gold and foreign exchange holdings, money supply, bank assets, international trade, prices, production, interest rates, etc.).

Quotas of IMF Members
(as of 16 August 1993)

MEMBER	QUOTA	MEMBER	QUOTA	MEMBER	QUOTA
Afghanistan	120.4	Grenada	8.5	Paraguay	72.1
Albania	35.3	Guatemala	153.8	Peru	466.1
Algeria	914.4	Guinea	78.7	Philippines	633.4
Angola	207.3	Guinea-Bissau	10.5	Poland	988.5
Antigua and Barbuda	8.5	Guyana	67.2	Portugal	557.6
Argentina	1,537.1	Haiti	44.1	Qatar	190.5
Armenia	67.5	Honduras	95.0	Republic of Moldova	90.0
Australia	2,333.2	Hungary	754.8	Romania	754.1
Austria	1,188.3	Iceland	85.3	Russian Federation	4,313.1
Azerbaijan	117.0	India	3,055.5	Rwanda	59.5
Bahamas	94.9	Indonesia	1,497.6	St. Kitts and Nevis	6.5
Bahrain	82.8	Iran	1,078.5	Saint Lucia	11.0
Bangladesh	392.5	Iraq	504.0	Saint Vincent and the Grenadines	6.0
Barbados	48.9	Ireland	525.0	Samoa	8.5
Belarus	280.4	Israel	662.2	San Marino	10.0
Belgium	3,102.3	Italy	4,590.7	São Tomé and Principe	5.5
Belize	13.5	Jamaica	200.9	Saudi Arabia	5,130.6
Benin	45.3	Japan	8,241.5	Senegal	118.9
Bhutan	4.5	Jordan	121.7	Seychelles	6.0
Bolivia	126.2	Kazakhstan	247.5	Sierra Leone	57.9
Botswana	36.6	Kenya	199.4	Singapore	357.6
Brazil	2,170.8	Kiribati	4.0	Slovakia	257.4
Bulgaria	464.9	Korea, Republic of	799.6	Slovenia	150.5
Burkina Faso	44.2	Kuwait	995.2	Solomon Islands	7.5
Burundi	57.2	Kyrgyz Republic	64.5	Somalia	44.2
Cambodia	25.0	Lao People's Democratic Republic	39.1	South Africa	1,365.4
Cameroon	135.1	Latvia	91.5	Spain	1,935.4
Canada	4,320.3	Lebanon	78.7	Sri Lanka	303.6
Cape Verde	7.0	Lesotho	23.9	Sudan	169.7
Central African Republic	41.2	Liberia	71.3	Suriname	49.3
Chad	41.3	Libya	817.6	Swaziland	36.5
Chile	621.7	Lithuania	103.5	Sweden	1,614.0
China	3,385.2	Luxembourg	135.5	Switzerland	2,470.4
Colombia	561.3	Madagascar	90.4	Syria	209.9
Comoros	6.5	Malawi	50.9	Tajikistan	40.0
Congo	57.9	Malaysia	832.7	Thailand	573.9
Costa Rica	119.0	Maldives	5.5	The Former Yugoslav Republic of Macedonia	49.6
Côte d'Ivoire	238.2	Mali	68.9	Togo	54.3
Croatia	261.6	Malta	67.5	Tonga	5.0
Cyprus	100.00	Marshall Islands	2.5	Trinidad and Tobago	246.8
Czech Republic	589.6	Mauritania	47.5	Tunisia	206.0
Denmark	1,069.9	Mauritius	73.3	Turkey	642.0
Djibouti	11.5	Mexico	1,753.3	Turkmenistan	48.0
Dominica	6.0	Micronesia (Federated States of)	3.5	Uganda	133.9
Dominican Republic	158.8	Mongolia	37.1	Ukraine	997.3
Ecuador	219.2	Morocco	427.7	United Arab Emirates	392.1
Egypt	678.4	Mozambique	84.0	United Kingdom	7,414.6
El Salvador	125.6	Myanmar	184.9	United Republic of Tanzania	146.9
Equatorial Guinea	24.3	Namibia	99.6	United States	26,526.8
Estonia	46.5	Nepal	52.0	Uruguay	225.3
Ethiopia	98.3	Netherlands	3,444.2	Uzbekistan	199.5
Fiji	51.1	New Zealand	650.1	Vanuatu	12.5
Finland	861.8	Nicaragua	96.1	Venezuela	1,951.3
France	7,414.6	Niger	48.3	Viet Nam	176.8
Gabon	110.3	Nigeria	1,281.6	Yemen	176.5
Gambia	22.9	Norway	1,104.6	Zaire	291.0
Georgia	111.0	Oman	119.4	Zambia	270.3
Germany	8,241.5	Pakistan	758.2	Zimbabwe	261.3
Ghana	274.0	Panama	149.6		
Greece	587.6	Papua New Guinea	95.3		

Executive Directors of the IMF and Voting Power
(as of 30 April 1993)

DIRECTOR	CASTING VOTES OF	VOTES BY COUNTRY	TOTAL VOTES	% OF FUND TOTAL
APPOINTED				
Thomas C. Dawson II	United States	265,518	265,518	17.82
Stefan Schoenberg	Germany	82,665	82,665	5.55
Hiroo Fukui	Japan	82,665	82,665	5.55
Jean-Pierre Landau	France	74,396	74,396	4.99
David Peretz	United Kingdom	74,396	74,396	4.99
ELECTED				
Jacques de Groote (Belgium)	Austria	12,133		
	Belarus	3,054		
	Belgium	31,273		
	Czech Republic	6,146		
	Hungary	7,798		
	Kazakhstan	2,725		
	Luxembourg	1,605		
	Slovak Republic	2,824		
	Turkey	6,670	74,228	4.98
Godert A. Posthumus (Netherlands)	Armenia	925		
	Bulgaria	4,899		
	Cyprus	1,250		
	Georgia	1,360		
	Israel	6,912		
	Moldova	1,150		
	Netherlands	34,692		
	Romania	7,791		
	Ukraine	10,223	69,202	4.64
Roberto Marino (Mexico)	Costa Rica	1,440		
	El Salvador	1,506		
	Guatemala	1,788		
	Honduras	1,200		
	Mexico	17,783		
	Nicaragua	1,211		
	Spain	19,604		
	Venezuela	19,763	64,295	4.31
Giulio Lanciotti (Italy)	Albania	603		
	Greece	6,126		
	Italy	46,157		
	Malta	925		
	Portugal	5,826		
	San Marino	350	59,987	4.03
Douglas E. Smee (Canada)	Antigua and Barbuda	335		
	Bahamas	1,199		
	Barbados	739		
	Belize	385		
	Canada	43,453		
	Dominica	310		
	Grenada	335		
	Ireland	5,500		
	Jamaica	2,259		
	St. Kitts and Nevis	315		
	St. Lucia	360		
	St. Vincent and the Grenadines	310	55,500	3.72
Ingimundur Fridriksson (Iceland)	Denmark	10,949		
	Estonia	715		
	Finland	8,868		
	Iceland	1,103		
	Latvia	1,165		
	Lithuania	1,285		
	Norway	11,296		
	Sweden	16,390	51,771	3.47
Muhammad Al-Jasser (Saudi Arabia)	Saudi Arabia	51,556	51,556	3.46
Ewen L. Waterman (Australia)	Australia	23,582		
	Kiribati	290		
	Korea	8,246		
	Marshall Islands	275		
	Mongolia	621		
	New Zealand	6,751		
	Papua New Guinea	1,203		
	Philippines	6,584		
	Seychelles	310		
	Solomon Islands	325		
	Vanuatu	375		
	Western Samoa	335	48,897	3.28
A. Shakour Shaalan (Egypt)	Bahrain	1,078		
	Egypt	7,034		
	Iraq	5,290		
	Jordan	1,467		
	Kuwait	10,202		
	Lebanon	1,037		
	Libya	8,426		
	Maldives	305		
	Oman	1,444		
	Qatar	2,155		
	Syrian Arab Republic	1,641		
	United Arab Emirates	4,171		
	Yemen	2,015	46,265	3.10
Konstantin G. Kagalovsky (Russia)	Russia	43,381	43,381	2.91
Daniel Kaeser (Switzerland)	Azerbaijan	1,420		
	Kyrgyzstan	895		
	Poland	10,135		
	Switzerland	24,954		
	Turkmenistan	730		
	Uzbekistan	2,245	40,379	2.71
J.E. Ismael (Indonesia)	Fiji	761		
	Indonesia	15,226		
	Lao People's Dem. Rep.	641		
	Malaysia	8,577		
	Myanmar	2,099		
	Nepal	770		
	Singapore	3,826		
	Thailand	5,989		
	Tonga	300		
	Viet Nam	2,018	40,207	2.70
Abbas Mirakhor (Iran)	Afghanistan	1,454		
	Algeria	9,394		
	Ghana	2,990		
	Iran	11,035		
	Morocco	4,527		
	Pakistan	7,832		
	Tunisia	2,310	39,542	2.65

Executive Directors of the IMF and Voting Power—*cont.*
(as of 30 April 1993)

DIRECTOR	CASTING VOTES OF	VOTES BY COUNTRY	TOTAL VOTES	% OF FUND TOTAL	DIRECTOR	CASTING VOTES OF	VOTES BY COUNTRY	TOTAL VOTES	% OF FUND TOTAL
Alexandre Kafka					A. Guillermo Zoccali				
(Brazil)	Brazil	21,958			(Argentina)	Argentina	15,621		
	Colombia	5,863				Bolivia	1,512		
	Dominican Republic	1,838				Chile	6,467		
	Ecuador	2,442				Paraguay	971		
	Guyana	922				Peru	4,911		
	Haiti	691				Uruguay	2,503	31,985	2.15
	Panama	1,746							
	Suriname	743			Corentino V. Santos				
	Trinidad and Tobago	2,718	38,921	2.61	(Cape Verde)	Benin	703		
						Burkina Faso	692		
K.P. Geethakrishnan						Cameroon	1,601		
(India)	Bangladesh	4,175				Cape Verde	320		
	Bhutan	295				Central African Republic	662		
	India	30,805				Chad	663		
	Sri Lanka	3,286	38,561	2.59		Comoros	315		
						Congo	829		
L.J. Mwananshiku						Côte d'Ivoire	2,632		
(Zambia)	Angola	2,323				Djibouti	365		
	Botswana	616				Equatorial Guinea	493		
	Burundi	822				Gabon	1,353		
	Ethiopia	1,233				Guinea	1,037		
	Gambia	479				Guinea-Bissau	355		
	Kenya	2,244				Madagascar	1,154		
	Lesotho	489				Mali	939		
	Liberia	963				Mauritania	725		
	Malawi	759				Mauritius	983		
	Mozambique	1,090				Niger	733		
	Namibia	1,246				Rwanda	845		
	Nigeria	13,066				Sâo Tomé and Principe	305		
	Sierra Leone	829				Senegal	1,439		
	Sudan	1,947				Togo	793		
	Swaziland	615				Zaire	3,160	23,096	1.55
	Tanzania	1,719							
	Uganda	1,589							
	Zambia	2,953							
	Zimbabwe	2,863	37,845	2.54					
Zhang Ming									
(China)	China	34,102	34,102	2.29					

Note: Voting power varies on certain matters pertaining to the General Department with use of the Fund's resources in that Department. Percentage refers to total votes in the General Department and the SDR Department. The votes of Cambodia, Croatia, the former Yugoslav Republic of Macedonia, Slovenia, Somalia, South Africa and Tajikistan are not included, because they did not participate in the 1992 Regular Election of Executive Directors. The combined votes of those members total 20,952-1.51% of those in the General Department and SDR Department. Percentages subject to rounding.

THE WORLD BANK GROUP

The World Bank Group comprises five organizations: the International Bank for Reconstruction and Development (IBRD), the International Development Association (IDA), the International Finance Corporation (IFC), the Multilateral Investment Guarantee Agency (MIGA), and the International Centre for the Settlement of Investment Disputes (ICSID).

INTERNATIONAL BANK FOR RECONSTRUCTION AND DEVELOPMENT (IBRD)

Background

As early as February 1943, United States Undersecretary of State Sumner B. Welles urged preparatory consultation aimed at the establishment of agencies to finance reconstruction and development of the world economy after WWII. The US and the UK took leading roles in the negotiations that were to result in the formation of the IBRD and the IMF. The IBRD is the main lending organization of the World Bank Group and, like its sister institution, the International Monetary Fund (IMF), was born of the Allies' realization during World War II that tremendous difficulties in reconstruction and development would face them in the postwar transition period, necessitating international economic and financial cooperation on a vast scale. The IBRD, frequently called the "World Bank," was conceived in July 1944 at the United Nations Monetary and Financial Conference in Bretton Woods, New Hampshire, US.

Purposes

Although one of the Bank's early functions was to assist in bringing about a smooth transition from wartime to peaceful economies, economic development soon became the Bank's main object. Today, the goal of the World Bank is to promote economic development that benefits poor people in developing countries. Loans are provided to developing countries to help reduce poverty and to finance investments that contribute to economic growth. Investments include roads, power plants, schools, and irrigation networks, as well as activities like agricultural extension services, training for teachers, and nutrition-improvement programs for children and pregnant women. Some World Bank loans finance changes in the structure of countries' economies to make them more stable, efficient, and market oriented. The World Bank also provides technical assistance to help governments make specific sectors of their economies more efficient and more relevant to national development goals.

Membership

The Bank's founders envisioned a global institution, the membership of which would eventually comprise all nations. Membership in the IBRD rose gradually from 41 governments in 1946 to 177 as of June 30, 1994.

A government may withdraw from membership at any time by giving notice of withdrawal. Membership also ceases for a member suspended by a majority of the governors for failure to fulfill an obligation, if that member has not been restored to good standing by a similar majority within a year after the suspension.

Although the Soviet Union took part in the 1944 Bretton Woods Conference, and signed the final act establishing the IMF and the IBRD, it never ratified the Articles of Agreement or paid in the 20 percent of its subscribed capital that was due within 60 days after the Bank began operations. Had it joined, the Soviet Union would have been the Bank's third largest shareholder, after the United States and the United Kingdom. Over the next four decades, as the Bank grew in size and scope, it couldn't fulfill its founders' intentions of being a truly global institution due to the absence of the Soviet Union. Then, at the beginning of the 1990s, as political and economic change swept through the 15 republics of the USSR, the Soviet government indicated its interest in participating in the international financial system and sought membership in the IMF and World Bank. On 15 July 1991, Soviet President Mikhail Gorbachev formally applied for membership for the USSR in the IBRD and its three affiliates (IFC, IDA and MIGA). However, by December 1991, the USSR had ceased to exist. During 1992, the Russian Federation and 15 former Soviet republics (including the Baltic states) applied for membership and were accepted. Eleven of them also applied to IDA, 14 to IFC and 15 to MIGA. To accommodate these countries, the total authorized capital of the bank was increased.

Structure

Board of Governors

All powers of the Bank are vested in its Board of Governors, composed of one governor and one alternate from each member state. Ministers of Finance, central bank presidents, or persons of comparable status usually represent member states on the Bank's Board of Governors. The board meets annually.

The Bank is organized somewhat like a corporation. According to an agreed-upon formula, member countries subscribe to shares of the Bank's capital stock. Each governor is entitled to cast 250 votes plus 1 vote for each share of capital stock subscribed by his country. As of 30 June 1993, the United States, with 243,109 shares, was the largest shareholder.

Executive Directors

The Bank's Board of Governors has delegated most of its authority to 24 executive directors. According to the Articles of Agreement, each of the five largest shareholders—the United States, Japan, Germany, France and the United Kingdom—appoints one executive director. The other countries are grouped in 19 constituencies, each represented by an executive director who is elected by a group of countries. The number of countries each of these 19 directors represents varies widely. For example, the executive directors for China, the Russian Federation, and Saudi Arabia represent one country each, while one director speaks for 24

Francophone African countries and another director represents 21 mainly English-speaking African countries.

President and Staff

The president of the Bank, elected by the executive directors, is also their chairman, although he is not entitled to a vote, except in case of an equal division. Subject to their general direction, the president is responsible for the conduct of the ordinary business of the Bank. Action on Bank loans is initiated by the president and the staff of the Bank. The amount, terms, and conditions of a loan are recommended by the president to the executive directors, and the loan is made if his recommendation is approved by them.

Past presidents of the Bank include Robert S. McNamara (1968–1981), A. W. Clausen (1981–1986), and Barber B. Conable (1986–1991). Lewis T. Preston is the current president of the Bank, serving a five-year term which began in September 1991. He heads a staff of more than 7,100 persons from over 130 countries.

The IBRD's headquarters are at 1818 H Street, N.W., Washington, D.C. 20433.

Budget

The IBRD's administrative budget for the fiscal year ending 30 June 1993 was us$679 million. Administrative expenses are paid from the IBRD's income.

Activities

A. FINANCIAL RESOURCES

Authorized capital. At its establishment, the IBRD had an authorized capital of us$10 billion. Countries subscribing shares were required to pay in only one-fifth of their subscription on joining, the remainder being available on call but only to meet the IBRD's liabilities if it got into difficulties. Moreover, not even the one-fifth had to be paid in hard cash at that time. The sole cash requirement was the payment in gold or US dollars of 2 percent of each country's subscription. A further 18 percent of the subscription was payable in the currency of the member country concerned, and although this sum was technically paid in, in the form of notes bearing no interest, it could not be used without the member's permission. In 1959, each member was given an opportunity to double its subscription without any payment. Thus, for countries joining the IBRD after the 1959 capital increase and for those subscribing to additional capital stock, the statutory provisions affecting the 2 percent and 18 percent portions have been applied to only one-half of their total subscriptions, so that 1 percent of each subscription that is freely usable in the IBRD's operations has been payable in gold or US dollars, and 9 percent that is usable only with the consent of the member is in the member's currency. The remaining 90 percent is not paid in but is subject to call by the IBRD.

Financial Resources for Lending Purposes. The subscriptions of the IBRD's members constitute the basic element in the financial resources of the IBRD. Altogether, the paid portion of the subscriptions was about us$10.5 billion on 30 June 1993. However, the Bank draws much more money from borrowings in the market and from earnings. The Bank's outstanding borrowings as of 30 June 1993 were us$96.3 billion, raised in the capital markets of the world. These obligations were denominated in some 24 different currencies and were placed with investors, including central banks and government institutions, in more than 100 countries. The IBRD has raised this large sum, at interest rates little or no higher than are paid by governments, because of confidence in the Bank engendered by its record of reliability since 1947 and the investors' knowledge that if the IBRD should ever be in difficulty, it can call in unpaid portions of member countries' subscription. In connection with its borrowing operations, the Bank also undertakes a substantial volume of currency and interest rate swap transactions. These swaps have enabled the

IBRD to lower its fund-raising costs and to expand its direct borrowing transactions to markets and currencies in which it otherwise would not have borrowed.

B. LENDING OPERATIONS

The IBRD lends to member governments, or, with government guarantee, to political subdivisions, or to public or private enterprises.

The IBRD's first loan, us$250 million for postwar reconstruction, was made in the latter part of 1947. Altogether, it lent us$497 million for postwar reconstruction, all to European countries. The IBRD's first development loans were made in the first half of 1948. As of 30 June 1993, the cumulative total of loans made by the Bank was over us$312 billion.

Loan Terms and Interest Rates. The IBRD normally makes long-term loans, with repayment commencing after a certain period. The length of the loan is generally related to the estimated useful life of the equipment or plant being financed. Since July 1982, IBRD loans have been made at variable rates. The lending rate on all loans made under the variable-rate system is adjusted semiannually, on 1 January and 1 July, by adding a spread of 0.5 percent to the IBRD's weighted average cost during the prior six months of a "pool" of borrowings drawn down after 30 June 1982. Since July 1989, only borrowings allocated to lending have been included in the cost of borrowings with respect to new loans and existing variable rate loans that are amended to apply the new cost basis. For interest periods beginning from 1 January through 30 June 1994, the applicable rates are 7.27 percent for such new or amended loans and 7.25 percent for all other outstanding variable rate loans. Before July 1982, loans were made at fixed rates, and, accordingly, the semiannual interest-rate adjustments do not apply to payments made on these older loans.

C. PURPOSES OF THE LOANS

The main purpose of the Bank's operations is to lend to developing member countries for productive projects in such sectors as agriculture, energy, industry, and transportation and to help improve basic services considered essential for development. The main criterion for assistance is that it should be provided where it can be most effective in the context of the country's specific lending programs developed by the Bank in consultation with its borrowers. In the late 1980s, the World Bank came under criticism that its policies, intended to encourage developing countries to restructure their economies in order to render them more efficient, were actually imposing too heavy a burden on the world's poorest peoples. This, and charges by environmentalists that World Bank lending had underwritten projects that were severely detrimental to the environment of developing countries, led to a re-thinking of the Bank's policies in the 1990s.

Implementing the Bank's Poverty Reduction Strategy. The fundamental objective of the World Bank is sustainable poverty reduction. Underpinning this objective is a two-part strategy for reducing poverty that was proposed in the World Development Report 1990. The first element is to promote broad-based economic growth that makes efficient use of the poor's most abundant asset, labor. The second element involves ensuring widespread access to basic social services to improve the well being of the poor and to enable them to participate fully in the growth of the economy. Progress in implementing the poverty-reduction strategy is clearly visible in Bank-wide statistics on new lending. While shares of lending for agriculture and rural development and for water supply and sanitation—two sectors that are among the key targets of poverty reduction efforts—have remained roughly constant recently, lending for human resource development has increased fivefold (by dollar amount) since the early 1980s (from 5 percent of total Bank lending in fiscal 1981–83 to 15 percent in fiscal 1991–93).

Sector and Structural Adjustment Lending. Bank lending for sector adjustment and structural adjustment increasingly supports the establishment of social safety nets and the protection of public spending for basic social services. The share of adjustment lending that addresses social issues climbed from 5 percent in fiscal 1984–86 to 50 percent in fiscal 1990–92. In fiscal year 1993, 6 of 17 adjustment operations included specific poverty-reduction measures.

In its assistance to countries that are preparing adjustment programs, the Bank works with them to (a) design the phasing of programs to accommodate the needs of the poor, (b) give priority to relative price changes in favor of the poor early in the reform process, (c) secure adequate resources for the provision of basic social services aimed at the poor, and (d) design social safety nets into economic-reform programs. These efforts better position of the poor to be major beneficiaries of the economic growth and associated employment opportunities that are facilitated by the implementation of adjustment programs.

Human Resource Development. Over the past two decades, Bank lending for human resource development has largely been committed for education, and its focus has been towards development of basic education. Lending for education has increased from an average US$700 million during the 1980s to an average US$1,907 million during the first four years of the 1990s. In fiscal 1993, 32 projects with total commitments of US$2,006 million were approved.

Bank lending for population, health, and nutrition has expanded even more rapidly. Average yearly lending to this sector during the 1980s was US$207 million, while lending during fiscal 1991–93 has averaged US$1,447 million. In fiscal 1993, Bank lending amounted to US$1,812 million for 25 projects.

The Environment. The Bank has continued to support environmental protection efforts with 23 loans totaling nearly US$2 billion in fiscal 1993, compared to US$404 million in fiscal 1990. But the full story cannot be told by stand-alone environmental projects. Half of all World Bank projects now have an environmental component of some kind.

The Bank will continue to ensure that individual projects it finances are environmentally benign. More than a project-by-project approach is needed, however. The Bank is now working at two levels: rigorous assessment of individual projects, and efforts to help developing country governments build environmental concerns into policy-making at all levels.

In fiscal 1993 the World Bank undertook structural changes to respond to growing borrower demand for Bank assistance in environmental issues, and to the need for internal strengthening of monitoring and implementation. A Vice Presidency for Environmentally Sustainable Development was established. Three departments were placed under this vice presidency—the Environment Department, the Agriculture and Natural Resources Department, and the Transport and Urban Development Department.

The Global Environment Facility is a cooperative venture between the World Bank, the United Nations Development Programme, the United Nations Environment Programme, and national governments. The Facility provides grants to help developing countries deal with environmental problems that transcend boundaries, such as airborne pollution produced by smokestacks or hazardous waste dumped into rivers. The GEF gives priority to four objectives: limiting emissions of greenhouse gases; preserving biodiversity; protecting international waters; and protecting the ozone layer.

Private Sector Development. The promotion of private sector growth in developing member countries has always been central to the Bank's overall mission of fostering sustainable growth and reducing poverty. Two Bank Group affiliates, The International Bank for Reconstruction and Development and the International Development Association, committed total loans of US$23.7 billion to developing countries for private sector development in the

fiscal year 1993. In addition, another member of the Bank Group, the International Finance Corporation, (which invests directly in the private sector), invested US$2.1 billion in developing countries in fiscal 1993.

The Bank's private sector development strategy has three themes: improving the business environment by supporting procedural, regulatory, and legal reforms; public sector restructuring by reorienting public spending—through privatization of state-owned enterprises, upgrading of public administrative capacities in areas important to private sector development (such as trade and investment promotion), and encouraging, where appropriate, private provision of services traditionally provided by the state-to achieve more efficient use of private and public resources; and financial sector development by supporting the development of efficient financial systems that mobilize savings and channel them to the most productive end uses.

D. OTHER ACTIVITIES

Technical Assistance. The Bank provides its members with a wide variety of technical assistance, much of it financed under its lending program. The volume of technical assistance in which the Bank is involved as lender, provider, or administrator has more than doubled (in current dollars) in the past decade. It amounted to US$2.7 billion in 1992. Much of the growth has occurred in the area of institutional development.

Interagency Cooperation. The Bank's overarching purpose is helping to reduce global poverty. To this end, the institution encourages the involvement of other development agencies in preparing poverty assessments and works closely with other UN agencies in preparing proposals to improve the quality of poverty-related data. At the country level, the Bank is broadening its efforts to coordinate work with UNDP, UNICEF, and the International Fund for Agricultural Development in specific countries on preparing or following up poverty assessments and planned human development assessments.

Coordination between the Bank and the UN system on poverty at the project level is extensive, particularly in the design of social funds and social action programs. Together with other UN agencies, the World Bank has taken the lead in mobilizing groups of donors, both multilateral and bilateral, to tackle specific areas of concern—for example, the Consultative Group on International Agricultural Research (CGIAR), which is cosponsored by the FAO, UNDP, and the World Bank. The Bank is an active partner in interagency activities which include the follow-up to the World Conference on Education for All and the World Summit for Children; the Safe Motherhood Inter-Agency Group; the Onchocerciasis (riverblindness) Control Programme; the Global Programme for AIDS; and the Task Force for Child Survival. The Bank also has links with the United Nations at the political and policy making level in the work of the General Assembly and its related committees, and the Economic and Social Council.

The Economic Development Institute is the Bank's department responsible for such dissemination. Through seminars, workshops and courses, EDI enables policy makers to assess and use the lessons of development to benefit their own policies. In 1993, EDI organized 152 activities for nearly 5,000 officials and other development practitioners. The two largest users of EDI's services were the transitional economies of Europe and Central Asia and the developing economies of Sub-Saharan Africa.

Economic Research and Studies. The Bank's economic and social research program, inaugurated in 1972, is undertaken by the Bank's own research staff and is funded out of its administrative budget. The research program is shaped by the Bank's own needs, as a lending institution and as a source of policy advice to member governments, and by the needs of member countries. Its main purposes are to gain new insights into the development process and the policies affecting it; to introduce new techniques or methodologies into country, sectoral, and project analyses; to provide the analytical bases for major Bank documents, such as the World Development Report; and to help strengthen indigenous research capacity in developing countries.

Total IBRD Loans by Region in Millions of US Dollars
(as of 30 June 1993)

REGION	AMOUNT
Africa	2,817.3
East Asia and Pacific	5,569.8
South Asia	3,416.2
Europe and Central Asia	3,843.9
Latin America and the Caribbean	6,168.5
Middle East and North Africa	1,880.2
TOTAL	23,695.9

Total IBRD Loans by Major Purpose in Millions of US Dollars
(as of 30 June 1993)

PURPOSE	AMOUNT
Agriculture and rural development	42,469.5
Development finance companies	22,005.4
Education	10,437.8
Energy	50,245.0
Industry	16,652.4
Nonproject	22,024.4
Population, health, and nutrition	3,363.0
Public-sector management	2,717.0
Small-scale industry	4,586.8
Technical assistance	865.1
Telecommunications	4,097.5
Transportation	33,604.7
Urban development	11,609.0
Water supply and sewerage	0,476.2
TOTAL	235,154.4

INTERNATIONAL CENTRE FOR SETTLEMENT OF INVESTMENT DISPUTES (ICSID)

Developing countries depend heavily on foreign private capital to finance development. Such capital flows are sensitive to legal and political conditions in developing countries. The International Centre for Settlement of Investment Disputes is an autonomous institution founded in 1966 to promote increased flows of international investment by providing facilities for the conciliation and arbitration of disputes between governments and foreign investors. ICSID also provides advice, carries out research, and produces publications in the area of foreign investment law. Its publications include a semiannual law journal, *ICSD Review-Foreign Investment Law Journal,* and multivolume collections of *Investment Laws of the World* and *Investment Treaties.* As of 30 June 1993, ICSID had 109 member countries.

MULTILATERAL GUARANTEE INVESTMENT AGENCY (MIGA)

MIGA was established in 1988. Its main purpose is to promote the flow of foreign direct investment among member countries by insuring investments against non-commercial (political) risk, and by providing promotional and advisory services to help member countries create an attractive investment climate. MIGA offers four basic types of coverage:

Currency Inconvertibility. Protects against losses arising from an inability to convert local currency investment returns into foreign exchange for transfer outside the host country;

Expropriation. Protects against loss from acts by the host government that may reduce or eliminate ownership of, or control over, rights to the insured investment;

War and Civil Disturbance. Protects against losses arising

from military action or civil disturbance that destroys or damages tangible assets of the project enterprise or interferes with its operations; and

Breach of Contract. Protects against losses from the investor's inability to obtain and/or enforce a decision or award against a host country that has repudiated or breached an investment contract.

The demand for MIGA's services has been strong. By the end of 1993, it had subscribed capital of US$948 million. As of 31 December 1993, MIGA had issued a total of 86 guarantee contracts. MIGA's total maximum contingent liability as of that date was about US$1 billion. As of 10 February 1994, 118 countries have completed membership requirements with an additional 26 countries in the process of becoming members.

THE INTERNATIONAL DEVELOPMENT ASSOCIATION (IDA)

Background

The world's poorer countries have gone heavily into debt to finance their development. The total outstanding debt of 90 such countries rose from US$51 billion in 1970 to an estimated US$485 billion in 1985. Annual interest and amortization charges on this debt had, by 1985, reached over US$100 billion. Many countries have long since arrived at the point where they can no longer afford to raise all the development capital that they are in a position to use at ordinary rates of interest and in the time span of conventional loans, IBRD loans included.

The International Development Association (IDA), an affiliate of the World Bank, was established in 1960 to promote economic development in the world's poorest countries—those that cannot afford to borrow from the IBRD. It is the largest single multilateral source of concessional lending to low-income countries. IDA loans, known as "credits," are provided mainly to countries with annual per capita incomes of about US$800 or less. IDA financing helps these countries build the human capital, institutions, and physical infrastructure required to bring about equitable and sustainable economic development.

The IDA's loans are interest-free and repayable over very long terms, with extended grace periods. As a result, the IDA's resources, unlike the resources of a regular lending institution, must be regularly replenished through contributions if the agency is to continue in business.

Creation

The creation of an international agency such as the IDA was discussed in the UN at various times during the 1950s. A report drawn up in 1951 by a group of experts on financing and economic development referred to the need for an "international development authority." Although such proposals were at first opposed by the US, the IDA as it was finally launched was largely the result of US initiative. In 1958, the US Senate passed a resolution introduced by Senator A. S. ("Mike") Monroney calling for cooperative international action along these lines. On 1 October 1959, the IBRD's Board of Governors approved, without objections, a motion of US Secretary of the Treasury Robert Anderson that a new agency, under the name International Development Association, be established as an affiliate of the Bank.

The debate that preceded the Board's action revealed potential disagreements among members of the Bank on a number of points, such as the terms that the IDA should set for its loans, the permissible restrictions that countries subscribing to the IDA's capital could place on the use of funds supplied in their national currencies, and related matters. Rather than decide these matters itself, the Board of Governors asked the Executive Directors of the IBRD to draw up Articles of Agreement for the IDA, which would then be submitted to the Bank's member governments.

The IDA's Articles of Agreement were accordingly drafted by the Executive Directors of the IBRD and early in 1960 transmitted to the member governments of the Bank. The next step was for those governments desiring to join the IDA to take whatever legislative or other action might be required to accept membership and to subscribe funds.

The new lending association came into existence on 24 September 1960, when governments whose subscriptions to its capital aggregated US$650 million, or 65 percent of the projected one-billion-dollar goal, had accepted membership. The IDA started operations in November of that year.

As of 30 March 1994, IDA has 155 member countries, about 77 of which are eligible to borrow. Since it was established, the Association has extended more than US$80 billion in credits to more than 90 countries, and 21 countries which were once borrowers have "graduated" from IDA. Today, 2 of them, Korea and Turkey, are donor members.

Purposes

In the preamble to the Articles of Agreement, the signatory governments declare their conviction that mutual cooperation for constructive economic purposes, healthy development of the world economy, and balanced growth of international trade foster peace and world prosperity; that higher standards of living and economic and social progress in the less developed countries are desirable not only in the interest of the latter but also for the international community as a whole; and that achievement of these objectives would be facilitated by an increase in the international flow of capital, public and private, to assist in the development of the resources of less developed countries.

As stated in its Articles of Agreement, the purposes of the IDA are "to promote economic development, increase productivity, and thus raise standards of living in the less-developed areas of the world included within the Association's membership, in particular by providing financing to meet their important developmental requirements on terms which are more flexible and bear less heavily on the balance of payments than those of conventional loans, thereby furthering the developmental objectives of the [IBRD] and supplementing its activities."

Membership

For the purposes of the IDA, members are divided into two categories. Part I members of which there were 24 as of 30 June 1993, are economically advanced countries. These countries pay their subscriptions in convertible currencies and have made further agreed contributions to replenish the Association's resources. Part II members, 128 in mid-1993, are the less-developed countries, which pay 10 percent of their subscriptions in convertible currencies and the remaining 90 percent, and any additional subscriptions, in their own currency.

Structure

The IDA is administered by the same officers and staff who administer the affairs of the IBRD. The president of the Bank also serves as the president of the IDA, and the governors and the executive directors of the Bank serve in the same capacity in the IDA.

As in the IBRD, a member's voting power in the IDA is roughly proportionate to its capital subscription. As of 30 June 1993, the 24 Part I countries had 61.4 percent of the total votes, and the 128 Part II countries had 38.6 percent of the total votes.

Budget

Since the IDA relies entirely on the IBRD's staff and facilities for all its activities, it reimburses the Bank through a management fee for administrative expenses incurred on its behalf. The management fee was US$467 million for the fiscal year ending 30 June 1993.

Activities

A. Financial Resources

The IDA's funds are obtained from three main sources: members' subscriptions; periodic "replenishments" provided by richer members and certain special contributions; and transfer of income from the IBRD and repayments on IDA credits. As of June 30, 1993, members' subscriptions and supplementary resources totaled nearly US$73 billion.

Initial subscriptions alone were never envisaged as the sole source of the IDA's lending funds, but by the early 1960s, it became clear that more funding would be needed much earlier than expected. Thus, IDA members began the practice of replenishments, of which there have been 10 since 1964, the first totaling US$750 million and the latest (the tenth replenishment), for the three-year period from 1 July 1993 to 30 June 1996, totaling US$18 billion.

Aside from their contributions under replenishment agreements, a number of countries have agreed over the years to make voluntary increases and special contributions in excess of their normal shares. Since 1964, the IDA has received regular support from the IBRD through the transfer of some of its net income not needed for the Bank's own purposes. When combined with repayments by IDA borrowers and contributions from the World Bank's net income, the 10th replenishment will finance a total of about US$22 billion in development credits.

The IDA's income in fiscal 1993, ending 30 June 1993, including income from development credits and from investments, was US$1.1 billion.

B. Terms of IDA Lending

IDA provides credits to its borrowers, interest-free with a 35- to 40-year final maturity and a 10-year grace period. Although IDA does not charge interest, it does charge a small administrative fee of 0.75 percent against the outstanding balance of credits to meet administrative expenses. There is also a commitment fee of 0.5 percent of 50 basis points, but this has been waived since fiscal year 1989. IDA's credits are thus highly concessional with a grant element of about 85 percent.

C. IDA Operations

While the IDA's financial terms are liberal, its economic and technical criteria for development credits are exactly the same as those applied by the IBRD in lending on conventional terms. Each credit must be justified by the borrowing country's economic position, prospects, and policies. Credits are extended only for high-priority purposes that, in the words of the IDA's Articles of Agreement, will "promote economic development, increase productivity, and thus raise standards of living in the less-developed areas of the world."

Since the IDA's resources have been considerably less than the need of developing countries for additional external finance on easy terms, they must be carefully rationed on the basis of need and prospects for their most effective use. Borrowing countries typically have per capita incomes of less than US$805. In general, countries which move above an annual per capita income level of US$805 or are deemed creditworthy for World Bank or commercial bank loans are not eligible for IDA credits.

D. IDA's Evolving Role

IDA has taken an active role in helping governments undertaking structural adjustment to protect and expand social and environmental programs. It supports rural development programs and projects which aim to increase agricultural productivity and ensure adequate food supplies. IDA also finances projects that give special attention to improving women's incomes and status in their communities. The Association has markedly increased its support for population, health, and nutrition projects.

Environmental concerns have been integrated into all aspects of IDA's operations. The Association is helping borrowers develop their own Environmental Action Plans to identify the policy changes and investments that are required for environmentally sustainable development.

Two vital contributions that IDA makes to economic development in low- income countries are the funds it mobilizes in support of countries' development programs and the role it plays in coordinating the use of resources by borrowers.

IDA is the largest single source of multilateral concessional funds. Its annual net disbursements of around US$4 billion are about 30 percent of net concessional multilateral disbursements, and 12 percent of Official Development Assistance. The Association also helps mobilize and coordinate aid from other multilateral organizations and donor countries. IDA's involvement is often a catalyst for other bilateral aid donors and regional development banks to participate in providing assistance. On average, for every dollar IDA commits, 50 cents of cofinancing is mobilized.

Total IDA Credits By Region in Millions of US Dollars
(as of 30 June 1993)

REGION	AMOUNT
Africa	US$2,770.3
East Asia and Pacific	1,165.0
South Asia	2,271.2
Europe and Central Asia	104.4
Latin America and the Caribbean	316.7
Middle East and North Africa	123.8
TOTAL	6,751.4

Total IDA Credits by Major Purpose in Millions of US Dollars
(as of 30 June 1993)

PURPOSE	AMOUNT
Agricultural and rural development	US$1,347.9
Education	1,038.2
Energy	565.1
Industry	401.6
Nonproject	600.8
Population, health, and nutrition	1,104.8
Public-sector management	32.6
Technical assistance	300.6
Telecommunications	89.1
Transportation	584.1
Urban development	291.2
Water supply and sewerage	395.4
TOTAL	6,751.4

THE INTERNATIONAL FINANCE CORPORATION (IFC)

Background
The International Finance Corporation is the member of the World Bank Group that promotes the growth of the private sector in less developed member countries. The IFC's principal activity is helping finance individual private enterprise projects that contribute to the economic development of the country or region where the project is located. The IFC is the World Bank Group's investment bank for developing countries. It lends directly to private companies and makes equity investments in them, without guarantees from governments, and attracts other sources of funds for private-sector projects. IFC also provides advisory services and technical assistance to governments and businesses.

Creation
Within a few years of the founding of the International Bank for Reconstruction and Development (IBRD), it became evident that sufficient provision had not been made for financing the develop-

ment of the private sector in countries looking to the UN system for aid. The Bank's charter restrained it from making equity (capital stock) investments or from lending money, directly or indirectly, to a private company without a governmental guarantee. Yet "venture capital" was the very thing needed in many developing countries to get a variety of productive enterprises underway, and the amount of venture capital available through private banking and investment channels was inadequate.

The first public suggestion for an international institution to close this gap appeared in a report, "Partners and Progress," which Nelson Rockefeller (then chairman of the advisory board of the Point 4 Program) had submitted to President Harry S. Truman in 1951. The matter was taken up by the staff of the IBRD, and in 1952, the Bank submitted proposals for such an institution to the UN Economic and Social Council. Some members of the Council, including the UK and the US, voiced the fear that the proposed institution might deter the flow of private capital to the developing countries. They also objected in principle to an intergovernmental organization's having the right to purchase shares in private companies.

The majority of members of the Economic and Social Council, however, strongly endorsed the idea of an international financial institution to aid private sector development, and by late 1954, a compromise was worked out. The International Finance Corporation, as originally established, could lend money to private enterprises without government guarantees, but it was not empowered to make equity investments, though loans with certain equity features, such as stock options, were allowed. The 31 countries necessary to launch the IFC pledged their consent over the next 18 months, and the IFC formally came into existence on 14 July 1956 as a separate legal entity affiliated with the IBRD.

The IFC's early investments often included such features as stock options and other profit-sharing devices in lieu of direct equity financing, but the terms were complex and difficult to negotiate, and it soon became apparent to all concerned that IFC's effectiveness was severely circumscribed by the restriction on equity investment. Proposals to amend the charter so as to permit the IFC to hold shares were put to the Board of Directors and the Board of Governors and approved in 1961—with the support, this time, of both the UK and the US. The revision of IFC's charter in 1961 to permit investment in equities made it possible to broaden and diversify operations, as well as to simplify the terms of investment. With the demand for IFC's services steadily expanding, the Board of Directors amended the charter again in 1965 to permit the IFC to borrow from the IBRD up to four times its unimpaired subscribed capital and surplus.

Purposes
IFC's purpose is to foster economic growth by promoting private sector investment in its developing member countries. It accomplishes this by providing venture capital for productive private enterprises in association with local investors and management, by encouraging the development of local capital markets, and by stimulating the flow of private capital. The Corporation is designed to supplement, rather than replace, private capital. It plays an important catalytic role in mobilizing additional project funding from other investors and lenders, either in the form of cofinancing or through loan syndications, the underwriting of debt and equity securities issues, and guarantees. In addition to project finance and resource mobilization, IFC offers a full array of advisory services and technical assistance in such areas as capital market development, corporate restructuring, risk management, and project preparation and evaluation, and advises governments on creating an environment that encourages the growth of private enterprise and foreign investment.

Membership
Membership in the IFC is open to all members of IBRD. On 30 June 1993, IFC had 155 member states.

Structure
The structure of IFC is similar to that of the IBRD. IFC's Board of Governors consists of those governors of the Bank (IBRD) whose countries are also members of IFC. Its Board of Directors is composed of all the Executive Directors of the Bank. The annual meeting of the IFC Board of Governors is held in conjunction with the annual meeting of the Board of Governors of the IBRD. IFC headquarters, like those of the IBRD, are at 1818 H Street, N.W., Washington, D.C.

The first president of the IFC was Robert L. Garner, formerly vice-president of the IBRD. Since 1961, the president of the Bank also has been the president of the Corporation. The immediate direction of the Corporation is the responsibility of the executive vice-president, Jannik Lindbaek, who has served in that post since 1 January 1994. IFC has more than 800 staff from 99 countries.

ACTIVITIES

A. Financial Resources Capital Subscriptions
The authorized capital of IFC is US$2.45 billion. Each member country subscribes to it, and the amount of the subscription determines its voting power. As of 30 June 1993, US$1.4 billion has been subscribed by 155 members.

Earnings and Borrowings
IFC's operating income in fiscal 1993 was US$648.1 million. Net income, after deducting operating and administrative expenses, was US$141.7 million. As of 30 June 1993, the Corporation's net worth, the total of paid-in capital and retained earnings, came to US$2.7 billion.

IFC may borrow from the IBRD for use in its lending operations as long as the Corporation's total borrowings do not exceed four times its unimpaired subscribed capital and surplus. During fiscal 1993, IFC borrowed the equivalent of US$948 million from IBRD.

Disbursements
New commitments signed during fiscal 1993 reached US$1.5 billion. Disbursements reached US$1.1 billion in fiscal 1993. IFC's disbursed portfolio was US$5.4 billion as of 30 June 1993.

B. Investment Policies
Unlike the IBRD, IFC lends to private companies and does not accept guarantees from host-country governments. It also makes equity investments in developing-country businesses, and mobilizes additional loan and equity financing in the international financial markets. Because of the success of IFC's operations, its bond issues in the international markets have earned triple-A ratings from Moody's and Standard and Poor's.

IFC is the single largest source of direct financing for private sector projects in developing countries. Although IFC invests and lends on market terms, it does not compete with private capital. It finances projects unable to obtain sufficient funding on reasonable terms from other sources. Normally, IFC does not finance more than 25 percent of total project costs, so as to ensure that most of the project financing comes from private investors and lenders. And while IFC may buy up to 35 percent of the stock of a company, it is never the largest shareholder and does not take part in a firm's management. But since IFC does not accept government guarantees, it shares all project risks with its partners.

IFC finances the creation of new companies as well as the expansion or modernization of established companies in sectors ranging from agribusiness to manufacturing to energy to mining. A number of IFC projects involve building up the financial sectors of developing countries, for example by financing the creation of institutions such as investment banks and insurance companies.

IFC can provide loans, equity investments, and arrange quasi-equity instruments—in whatever combination is necessary to ensure that a project is soundly funded from the outset. The Corporation can provide additional financial support through contingent financing or full or partial guarantees of other sources of financing. In the past few years, IFC has made derivative products, such as currency and interest rate swaps, available to companies in developing countries. It has intermediated several such swaps for companies in Bolivia, Egypt, Ghana, and Mexico, helping them gain access to risk-management techniques commonly used by companies in industrialized countries but not normally available to companies in the developing world.

C. IFC Investments
The IFC's history has been marked by growth in the number and size of investments and by a continued search for new ways to assist its member countries. An improved policy environment in many of IFC's developing member countries has helped the Corporation to make a larger contribution to economic development. During fiscal year 1993, IFC approved US$2.1 billion in financing for 185 projects. Helping companies in developing countries achieve a proper balance between debt and equity financing is a key IFC objective. Equity and quasi-equity investment approved during fiscal 1993 came to US$519 million, 24 percent of total approvals.

In addition to approving debt and equity financing for its own account, the Corporation approved the mobilization of US$1.8 billion in financing from other investors and lenders through loan syndications and the underwriting of securities issues. It also mobilized considerable cofinancing. The total costs of the projects approved during the year were estimated to be US$17 billion. Thus, for every US$1 of financing approved by IFC for its own account, other investors and lenders will provide US$7.

The efficient provision of services in such sectors as power, water, transportation, and communications is critical to successful private sector development. A growing number of IFC's member countries are opening these sectors, once the preserve of the state, to private investment and management. During fiscal 1993 financing approved by IFC for infrastructure projects came to US$379 million. The Corporation approved an additional US$357 million to be mobilized through its loan syndications program.

The countries of Eastern and Central Europe and the former Soviet republics are a new focus of IFC's work. IFC's role includes financing private-sector projects and advising governments on creating a modern financial sector, selling off state-owned enterprises, and attracting foreign investment.

IFC advised governments officials in Russia and Ukraine on different techniques for privatizing state enterprises, and developed privatization programs that can be used as models by local authorities in both republics. It helped design and implement the auction of small enterprises in three regions in Russia—Nizhny Novgorod, Volgograd, and Tomsk—and in the city of L'viv, Ukraine, and produced a manual on the privatization of small enterprises.

In many developing countries small-scale entrepreneurs with promising ideas are often unable to get the financing or advice they need to start or expand businesses. IFC has set up project development facilities in Sub-Saharan Africa, Central America and the Caribbean, the South Pacific Islands, and Poland to help entrepreneurs prepare project proposals. Although these facilities do not themselves fund projects, they help entrepreneurs find loans and equity financing on reasonable terms. The Africa Enterprise Fund, established in 1989, is a special program devoted to financing small and medium-sized businesses in Sub-Saharan Africa.

Advisory Services and Technical Assistance

In the course of conducting project appraisals, IFC may provide considerable technical assistance to companies—for example, by helping them select a technical partner or a technology, identify markets for their products, and put together the most appropriate financial package. The Corporation also advises companies on financial restructuring, helping them reduce their debt.

IFC advises member governments on an array of issues, such as capital markets development. It helps governments create and put in place the regulatory, legal, and fiscal frameworks necessary for financial institutions to operate efficiently. IFC also provides advice on privatization and on restructuring state enterprises slated for privatization. The Foreign Investment Advisory Service, established by IFC and operated jointly with the Multilateral Investment Guarantee Agency and IBRD, advises governments on attracting direct foreign investment.

MIGA Shares and Voting Power

(as of 30 June 1993)

MEMBER	SHARES	VOTING POWER NUMBER OF VOTES	% OF TOTAL	MEMBER	SHARES	VOTING POWER NUMBER OF VOTES	% OF TOTAL
Albania	58	235	0.22	Luxembourg	106	283	0.27
Angola	187	364	0.34	Madagascar	116	293	0.28
Argentina	1,254	1,431	1.34	Malawi	100	277	0.26
Azerbaijan	115	292	0.27	Malaysia	77	254	0.24
Bahrain	77	254	0.24	Maldives	579	756	0.71
Bangladesh	340	517	0.49	Mali	81	258	0.24
Barbados	68	245	0.23	Malta	75	252	0.24
Belarus	233	410	0.38	Mauritania	63	240	0.23
Belgium	2,030	2,207	2.07	Mauritius	87	264	0.25
Belize	50	227	0.21	Moldova	96	273	0.26
Bolivia	125	302	0.28	Morocco	348	525	0.49
Botswana	50	227	0.21	Namibia	107	284	0.27
Brazil	1,479	1,656	1.55	Netherlands	2,169	2,346	2.20
Bulgaria	365	542	0.51	Nicaragua	102	279	0.26
Burkina Faso	61	238	0.22	Nigeria	844	1,021	0.96
Cameroon	107	284	0.27	Norway	699	876	0.82
Canada	2,965	3,142	2.95	Oman	94	271	0.25
Cape Verde	60	227	0.21	Pakistan	660	837	0.79
Chile	485	662	0.62	Papua New Guinea	96	273	0.26
China	3,138	3,315	3.11	Paraguay	80	257	0.24
Congo	65	242	0.23	Peru	373	550	0.52
Côte d'Ivoire	176	353	0.33	Poland	764	941	0.88
Croatia	187	364	0.34	Portugal	382	559	0.52
Cyprus	104	281	0.26	Romania	555	732	0.63
Czech Republic	445	622	0.58	Russian Federation	3,137	3,314	3.11
Denmark	718	895	0.84	St. Lucia	50	227	0.21
Dominica	50	227	0.21	St. Vincent and the Grenadines	50	227	0.21
Ecuador	182	359	0.34	Samoa	50	227	0.21
Egypt	459	636	0.60	Saudi Arabia	3,137	3,314	3.11
El Salvador	122	299	0.28	Senegal	145	322	0.30
Estonia	65	242	0.23	Seychelles	50	227	0.21
Ethiopia	70	247	0.23	Slovakia	222	399	0.37
Fiji	71	248	0.23	Slovenia	102	279	0.26
Finland	600	777	0.73	Spain	1,285	1,462	1.37
France	4,860	5,037	4.73	Sri Lanka	271	448	0.42
Gambia	50	227	0.21	Sudan	206	383	0.36
Georgia	111	288	0.27	Swaziland	58	235	0.22
Germany	5,071	5248	4.93	Sweden	1,049	1,226	1.15
Ghana	245	422	0.40	Switzerland	1,500	1,677	1.57
Grenada	50	227	0.21	Togo	77	254	0.24
Guyana	84	261	0.25	Trinidad and Tobago	203	380	0.36
Honduras	101	278	0.26	Tunisia	156	333	0.31
Hungary	564	741	0.70	Turkey	462	639	0.60
Indonesia	1,049	1,226	1.15	Uganda	132	309	0.29
Ireland	369	546	0.51	United Kingdom	4,860	5,037	4.73
Israel	474	651	0.61	United Republic of Tanzania	141	318	0.30
Italy	2,820	2,997	2.81	United States	20,509	20,696	19.43
Jamaica	181	358	0.34	Uruguay	202	379	0.36
Japan	5,095	5,272	4.95	Vanuatu	50	227	0.21
Jordan	97	274	0.26	Zaire	338	515	0.48
Kenya	172	349	0.33	Zambia	—	495	0.46
Korea, Republic of	449	626	0.59	Zimbabwe	—	413	0.39
Lesotho	930	1,107	1.04				
Libya	50	227	0.21	TOTAL	87,581	106,520	100%
Lithuania	549	726	0.68				

Member countries of IBRD, IDA, MIGA and ICSD
(as of listed date)

	IBRD (12/31/93)	IDA (12/31/93)	IFC (6/30/93)	MIGA (6/30/93)	ICSD (8/18/94)
Afghanistan	X	X	X		X
Albania	X	X	X	X	X
Algeria	X	X	X		
Angola	X	X	X	X	
Antigua and Barbuda	X		X		
Argentina	X	X	X	X	X
Armenia	X				X
Australia	X	X	X		X
Austria	X	X	X		X
Azerbaijan	X			X	X
Bahamas	X		X		
Bahrain	X		X	X	
Bangladesh	X	X	X	X	X
Barbados	X		X	X	X
Belarus	X		X	X	X
Belgium	X	X	X	X	X
Belize	X	X	X	X	X
Benin	X	X	X		X
Bhutan	X	X			
Bolivia	X	X	X	X	X
Botswana	X	X	X	X	X
Brazil	X	X	X	X	
Bulgaria	X		X	X	
Burkina Faso	X	X	X	X	X
Burundi	X	X	X		X
Cambodia	X	X			X
Cameroon	X	X	X	X	X
Canada	X	X	X	X	
Cape Verde	X	X	X	X	
Central African Republic	X	X	X		X
Chad	X	X			X
Chile	X	X	X	X	X
China	X	X	X	X	X
Colombia	X	X	X		X
Comoros	X	X	X		X
Congo	X	X	X	X	X
Costa Rica	X	X	X		X
Côte d'Ivoire	X	X	X	X	X
Croatia	X	X	X	X	
Cyprus	X	X	X	X	
Czech Republic	X	X	X	X	X
Denmark	X	X	X	X	X
Djibouti	X	X	X		
Dominica	X	X	X	X	
Dominican Republic	X	X	X		
Ecuador	X	X	X		X
Egypt	X	X	X	X	X
El Salvador	X	X	X	X	X
Equatorial Guinea	X	X	X		
Estonia	X		X	X	X
Ethiopia	X	X	X	X	X
Fiji	X	X	X	X	X
Finland	X	X	X	X	X
France	X	X	X	X	X
Gabon	X	X	X		X
Gambia	X	X	X	X	X
Georgia	X	X		X	X
Germany	X	X	X	X	X
Ghana	X	X	X	X	X
Greece	X	X	X		X
Grenada	X	X	X	X	X
Guatemala	X	X	X		
Guinea	X	X	X		X
Guinea-Bissau	X	X	X		X
Guyana	X	X	X	X	X
Haiti	X	X	X		X
Honduras	X	X	X		X
Hungary	X	X	X	X	X
Iceland	X	X	X		X
India	X	X	X		
Indonesia	X	X	X	X	X
Iran	X	X	X		
Iraq	X	X	X		
Ireland	X		X	X	X
Israel	X	X	X	X	X
Italy	X	X	X	X	X
Jamaica	X		X	X	X
Japan	X	X	X	X	X
Jordan	X	X	X	X	X
Kazakhstan	X	X			X
Kenya	X	X	X	X	X
Kiribati	X	X	X		
Korea, Republic of	X	X	X	X	X
Kuwait	X	X	X	X	X
Kyrgyzstan	X	X	X		
Lao People's Dem. Rep.	X	X	X		
Latvia	X	X	X		
Lebanon	X	X	X		
Lesotho	X	X	X	X	X
Liberia	X	X	X		X
Libya	X	X	X	X	
Lithuania	X		X	X	X
Luxembourg	X	X	X	X	X
Madagascar	X	X	X	X	X
Malawi	X	X	X		
Malaysia	X	X	X	X	X
Maldives	X	X	X		
Mali	X	X	X	X	X
Malta	X	X		X	
Marshall Islands	X	X	X		
Mauritania	X	X	X	X	X
Mauritius	X	X	X	X	X
Mexico	X	X	X		
Micronesia	X	X	X		X
Moldova	X			X	X
Mongolia	X	X	X		X
Morocco	X	X	X	X	X
Mozambique	X	X	X		
Myanmar	X	X	X		
Namibia	X		X	X	
Nepal	X	X	X		X
Netherlands	X	X	X	X	X
New Zealand	X	X	X		X
Nicaragua	X	X	X	X	
Niger	X	X	X		
Nigeria	X	X	X	X	X
Norway	X	X	X	X	X
Oman	X	X	X	X	
Pakistan	X	X	X	X	X
Panama	X	X	X		
Papua New Guinea	X	X	X	X	X
Paraguay	X	X	X	X	X
Peru	X	X	X	X	X
Philippines	X	X	X		X
Poland	X	X	X	X	
Portugal	X	X	X	X	X
Qatar	X				
Romania	X		X	X	X
Russian Federation	X	X	X	X	X
Rwanda	X	X	X		
St. Kitts and Nevis	X	X			
St. Lucia	X	X	X	X	X
St. Vincent and the Grenadines	X	X		X	
Samoa	X	X	X		X
São Tomé and Principe	X	X			
Saudi Arabia	X	X	X	X	X
Senegal	X	X	X	X	X

Member countries of IBRD, IDA, MIGA and ICSD—*cont.*

(as of listed date)

	IBRD (12/31/93)	IDA (12/31/93)	IFC (6/30/93)	MIGA (6/30/93)	ICSD (8/18/94)
Seychelles	X		X	X	X
Sierra Leone	X	X	X		X
Singapore	X		X		X
Slovakia	X	X	X	X	X
Slovenia	X	X	X	X	X
Solomon Islands	X	X	X		
Somalia	X	X	X		X
South Africa	X	X	X		
Spain	X	X	X	X	X
Sri Lanka	X	X	X	X	X
Sudan	X	X	X	X	X
Suriname	X				
Swaziland	X		X	X	X
Sweden	X	X	X	X	X
Switzerland	X	X	X	X	X
Syria	X	X	X		
Tajikistan	X	X			
Thailand	X	X	X		X
Togo	X	X	X	X	X
Tonga	X	X	X		X
Trinidad and Tobago	X	X	X	X	X
Tunisia	X	X	X	X	X
Turkey	X	X	X	X	X
Turkmenistan	X				X
Uganda	X	X	X	X	X
Ukraine	X				
United Arab Emirates	X		X		X
United Kingdom	X	X	X	X	X
United Republic of Tanzania	X	X	X	X	X
United States	X	X	X	X	X
Uruguay	X		X	X	X
Uzbekistan	X	X			X
Vanuatu	X	X	X	X	
Venezuela	X		X		X
Viet Nam	X	X	X		
Yemen	X	X	X		
Zaire	X	X	X	X	X
Zambia	X	X	X	X	X
Zimbabwe	X	X	X	X	X

Executive Directors of the IFC and Voting Power

(on 30 June 1993)

DIRECTOR	CASTING VOTES OF	TOTAL VOTES	% OF TOTAL
APPOINTED			
E. Patrick Coady	United States	347,305	24.08
Yasuyuki Kawahara	Japan	100,504	6.97
Fritz Fischer	Germany	84,321	5.85
Jean-Pierre Landau	France	79,173	5.49
David Peretz	United Kingdom	79,173	5.49
ELECTED			
Bernard Snoy (Belgium)	Austria, Belarus, Belgium, Czech Republic, Hungary, Luxembourg, Slovak Republic, Turkey	69,861	4.84
Bimal Jalan (India)	Bangladesh, India, Sri Lanka	61,941	4.29
Frank Potter (Canada)	Antigua and Barbuda, Bahamas, Barbados, Belize, Canada, Dominica, Grenada, Guyana, Ireland, Jamaica, St. Lucia	60,664	4.21
Enzo Grilli (Italy)	Albania, Greece, Italy, Portugal	57,022	3.95
Angel Torres (Spain)	Costa Rica, El Salvador, Guatemala, Honduras, Mexico, Nicaragua, Panama, Spain, Venezuela	56,234	3.90
Jorunn Maehlum (Norway)	Denmark, Finland, Iceland, Lithuania, Norway, Sweden	53,887	3.74
Pedro Malan (Brazil)	Brazil, Colombia, Dominican Republic, Ecuador, Haiti, Philippines, Trinidad and Tobago	46,699	3.24
John H. Cosgrove (Australia)	Australia, Kiribati, Korea (Rep. of), Marshall Islands, Mongolia, New Zealand, Papua New Guinea, Solomon Islands, Vanuatu, Western Samoa	42,728	2.96

World Bank Group

Executive Directors of the IFC and Voting Power—*cont.*

(on 30 June 1993)

DIRECTOR	CASTING VOTES OF	TOTAL VOTES	% OF TOTAL	DIRECTOR	CASTING VOTES OF	TOTAL VOTES	% OF TOTAL
Aris Othman (Malaysia)	Fiji				Mozambique		
	Indonesia				Namibia		
	Lao Peoples' Dem. Rep.				Nigeria		
	Malaysia				Seychelles		
	Myanmar				Sierra Leone		
	Nepal				Sudan		
	Singapore				Swaziland		
	Thailand				Tanzania		
	Tonga				Uganda		
					Zambia		
	Viet Nam	40,486	2.81		Zimbabwe	27,815	1.93
Eveline Herfkens (Netherlands)				Faisal A. Al-Khaled (Kuwait)			
	Bulgaria				Egypt		
	Cyprus				Jordan		
	Israel				Kuwait		
	Netherlands				Lebanon		
	Romania	39,102	2.71		Libya		
Boris G. Federov (Russian Federation)	Russian Federation	35,863	2.49		Maldives		
					Oman		
Nicolás Flaño (Chile)	Argentina				Syrian Arab Republic		
	Bolivia				United Arab Emirates		
	Chile				Yemen	19,968	1.38
	Paraguay			Jean-Pierre Le Bouder (Central African Republic)			
	Peru				Benin		
	Uruguay	35,106	2.43		Burkina Faso		
Jean-Daniel Gerber (Switzerland)					Cameroon		
	Kyrgzstan				Cape Verde		
	Poland				Central African Republic		
	Switzerland	34,121	2.37		Comoros		
Mohamed Benhocine (Algeria)					Congo		
	Afghanistan				Côte d'Ivoire		
	Algeria				Djibouti		
	Ghana				Equatorial Guinea		
	Iran				Gabon		
	Morocco				Guinea-Bissau		
	Pakistan				Madagascar		
	Tunisia	28,163	1.95		Mali		
O.K. Matambo (Botswana)					Mauritania		
	Angola				Mauritius		
	Botswana				Niger		
	Burundi				Rwanda		
	Ethiopia				Senegal		
	Gambia				Togo		
	Guinea				Zaire	16,638	1.15
	Kenya			Ibrahim A. Al-Assaf (Saudi Arabia)	Saudi Arabia	14,697	1.02
	Lesotho			Wang Liansheng (China)			
	Liberia				China	10,769	.75
	Malawi						

SUPPLEMENTS

POLAR REGIONS

ANTARCTICA

Antarctica, the coldest and second-smallest continent (after Australia), is centered on the South Pole and is situated almost entirely within the Antarctic Circle at 66 1/2°s. Some 97% of the total area of about 13,924,000 sq km (5,376,000 sq mi) is covered by ice, and the continent contains about 90% of the world's ice and 70% of the fresh water. Antarctica is bounded by the South Atlantic, Indian, and South Pacific oceans. The nearest points of land are the southern tip of South America, South Georgia, the South Sandwich Islands, the South Orkney Islands, and the South Shetland Islands. All of these islands are located within the Antarctic Convergence, which encircles Antarctica at approximately 1,600 km (1,000 mi) from the coast and divides the cold Antarctic waters from the warmer waters of the three oceans, in a zone of perpetual turbulence.

Some 200 million years ago, Antarctica was joined to South America, Africa, India, and Australia in a large single continent, Gondwanaland; subsequent geological changes caused the breakup into separate continental masses. Recent geological studies and fossil finds indicate that Antarctica once had a tropical environment, but that its present ice sheet is at least 20 million years old.

The Transantarctic Mountains divide the continent into two parts: the larger East Antarctic ice sheet, with land mostly above sea level; and the smaller West Antarctic ice sheet, with land mostly below sea level. The highest point is the Vinson Massif (4,897 m/16,066 ft), in the Ellsworth Mountains of West Antarctica. The South Pole lies at an altitude of about 3,000 m (9,800 ft). The Antarctic ice sheet averages 2,160 m (7,090 ft) in depth and is 4,776 m (15,670 ft) deep at its thickest point. Glaciers form ice shelves along nearly half the coastline. The larger ice shelves—the Amery in the east, Ross in the south, and Ronne in the northwest—move seaward at speeds of from 900 to 1,300 m (2,950–4,250 ft) per year. Sea ice up to 3 m (10 ft) thick forms a belt about 500 km (300 mi) wide that encircles the continent in winter. Ice-free areas are located generally along the coast and include the dry valleys in southern Victoria Land and the Bunger Oasis in Wilkes Land. Largely ice-free areas where much scientific activity takes place are on the coast of the Antarctic Peninsula, and on Ross Island in McMurdo Sound.

The severity of the Antarctic cold varies with location and altitude. East Antarctica has the coldest climate; the Antarctic Peninsula in the west has the mildest, with summer temperatures generally remaining above freezing. The mean annual temperature of the interior regions is −57°C (−71°F); mean temperatures at the coastal McMurdo station range from −28°C (−18°F) in August to −3°C (27°F) in January. The world's record low temperature of −89.2°C (−128.6°F) was registered at what was the Soviet's Vostok station on 24 August 1960; highs of 15°C (59°F) have been measured on the northernmost Antarctic Peninsula. The interior is a vast desert, with annual precipitation averaging below 3 cm (1 in). The coastland is considerably more humid, with annual precipitation of about 25 cm (10 in) along the coasts of East Antarctica and the Antarctic Peninsula. Adélie Coast, in the southeast near the South Magnetic Pole, has recorded average wind speeds of 64 km/hr (40 mph), with gusts of nearly 320 km/hr (200 mph).

Because of its polar location, Antarctica has six months of continuous daylight from mid-September to mid-March, with the maximum 24 hours of light received at the summer solstice on 22 December; and six months of continuous darkness from mid-March to mid-September, with the winter solstice occurring on 22 June. In summer, the continent receives more solar radiation than even the Equator over a 24-hour period.

Although Antarctica has no native humans or large terrestrial mammals, it does have a varied marine life ranging from microscopic plankton to the largest whales and including about 100 species of fish. Land life includes bacteria, lichens, mosses, two kinds of flowering plants (in the ice-free areas), penguins, and some flying birds. Six types of seal—the crabeater, Weddell, elephant, leopard, fur, and Ross—thrive in Antarctica and together number about 32.7 million, with the crabeaters accounting for nearly 94% of the total. The once-numerous fur seals were reduced by uncontrolled slaughter (about 1 million were killed on South Georgia alone in 1820–22) to near extinction by 1870. This ended the Antarctic fur-sealing industry; since then, the number of fur seals has gradually increased, to more than 1 million, mostly on South Georgia. In 1972, the 12 nations active in the Antarctic signed the Convention for the Conservation of Antarctic Seals, which prohibits the killing of fur, elephant, and Ross seals, and sets annual quotas for the harvest of crabeater, leopard, and Weddell seals. The treaty entered into force in 1978, and as of 1987 had been ratified by 12 nations. In 1982, the Convention on the Conservation of Antarctic Marine Living Resources entered into force, assuring the protection of ecosystems found in the Antarctic waters; as of 1994, over 20 countries and the EC were parties to the treaty.

Exploitation by humans threatens the survival of the Antarctic whales—the sperm, blue, humpback, fin, minke, and sei—which decreased in number from more than 1,500,000 at the beginning of the 20th century to fewer than 700,000 by the mid-1980s. Since 1972, the International Whaling Commission (IWC) has set quotas by species on the taking of whales, and the survival of all species of Antarctic whales seemed assured by the early 1980s. In 1982, the IWC approved a moratorium on the commercial killing of all whales that began in 1985. However, Japanese fishermen caught 3,087 whales in 1985 and 2,769 in 1986. Japan promised to end commercial whaling in 1988 but announced plans to harvest 300 minke (nonendangered) whales in Antarctic waters for "research" purposes during the winter of 1987–88; these plans were criticized by the IWC. As recently s May 14, 1993 the IWC voted to uphold the ban on commerical whaling. Immediately after the IWC's decision Norway said it would withdraw its membership. Canada is a former member of the IWC but is generally adheres to IWC regulations and decisions.

Exploration

The ancient Greeks reasoned that there must be an "Antarctic" (opposite the Arctic) to balance the large land mass in the Northern Hemisphere, but it was not until the 19th century that definite proof was found that the continent existed. British Capt. James Cook had crossed the Antarctic Circle and circumnavigated the continent without sighting land (1772–75). In 1820, however, two other British mariners, William Smith and James

Bransfield, discovered and mapped the Antarctic Peninsula, which was also explored by the American sea captain Nathaniel Palmer and the Englishman James Weddell, who discovered the sea that bears his name. Russian Adm. Fabian von Bellingshausen sailed around Antarctica during his 1819–21 voyage and found Queen Maud Land and Peter I Island.

On 7 February 1821, US Capt. John Davis made the first known landing on the continent at Hughes Bay, in the northwest. Many other British and US sealers explored the area, including 11 shipwrecked Englishmen who spent the winter of 1821 on King George Island, in the South Shetlands. Palmer and Benjamin Pendleton led a pioneering expedition in 1828–30 that included James Eights, the first American scientist to visit Antarctica. In 1837, a French expedition under J .S .C. Dumont d'Urville discovered the Adélie Coast (named for his wife) in eastern Antarctica. A year later, Lt. Charles Wilkes of the US Navy sailed along the coast of eastern Antarctica for about 2,400 km (1,500 mi), thereby definitely establishing that Antarctica was a continent, not a cluster of islands. During his 1839–43 Antarctic voyage, British Capt. James C. Ross discovered Victoria Land and the sea and the ice shelf that were later named in his honor.

With the decline of the fur seal industry, Antarctic exploration was neglected for about 50 years, until Norwegian and Scottish whalers began operating in the area. A Norwegian whaling captain, Carl Anton Larsen, explored the east coast of the Antarctic Peninsula in 1892 and found the first fossils. Thus began a period of intensive exploration during which 9 countries sent 16 expeditions to Antarctica. Another Norwegian captain, Leonard Kristensen, landed at Cape Adare, on McMurdo Sound, in 1895. It was there that a British expedition, led by a Norwegian, Carsten Egeberg Borchgrevink, established a base in 1899; Borchgrevink became the first explorer to probe inland by sledge. Swedish, Scottish, Belgian, and French expeditions also arrived, and four British expeditions set up bases on Ross Island. From there, Sir Ernest Henry Shackleton sledged to within 156 km (97 mi) of the South Pole on 9 January 1909.

This feat encouraged five national expeditions to compete for the goal in 1911, and the competition narrowed to a "race to the pole" between Capt. Robert F. Scott and Roald Amundsen of Norway. Amundsen and four companions, with sledges and 52 dogs, left their base on the Ross Ice Shelf on 20 October, scaled 3,000-m (10,000-ft) glaciers in the Queen Maud Mountains, ascended to the icy plateau, and located the South Pole by celestial observation on 14 December. They returned to their base by late January 1912. Meanwhile, Scott's party of five explorers, who had left McMurdo Sound on 1 November, reached the pole on 18 January 1912, only to find that Amundsen had beaten them there by more than a month. Disheartened, they met with mishaps on the return journey and, weakened by food shortages and exhausted from man-hauling their sledges, they all perished on the ice in late March. Another expedition that ended badly was led in 1914–15 by Shackleton, who lost his ship *Endurance* in heavy pack ice in the Weddell Sea and, with five companions, made a perilous 1,300-km (800-mi) journey in an open whale boat to South Georgia Island, where he got help to rescue his stranded men. Shackleton died at South Georgia in 1922, while preparing another expedition.

Technological advances were applied to Antarctic exploration after World War I. An Australian, Sir Hubert Wilkins, in 1928 became the first man to fly an airplane along the Antarctic Peninsula. The following year, US Navy Adm. Richard Evelyn Byrd flew over the South Pole, with his Norwegian-American pilot Bernt Balchen; Byrd established the Little America base on the Ross Ice Shelf, and was the first explorer to coordinate airplanes, radios, aerial cameras, and other technological aids for the purpose of exploration. Another American, Lincoln Ellsworth, was the first to complete a transantarctic flight, from the Antarctic Peninsula to the Ross Ice Shelf, in 1935. American, British, German, and Norwegian scientific expeditions did considerable aerial mapping of the continent throughout the 1930s; research in oceanography and marine biology by a British expedition resulted in the discovery of the Antarctic Convergence. The US expedition of 1939–41, headed by Byrd, established two continuing bases in the Antarctic, but the program ended with the outbreak of World War II.

Scientific Research

After the war, the US took the lead in conducting scientific research in Antarctica. The Navy's Operation Highjump (1946–47), the largest expedition ever made to the continent, involved 4,700 men, 13 ships, and 25 airplanes to map extensive coastal areas by aerial photography. The Antarctic Research Expedition (1947–48), headed by Finn Ronne, was a privately sponsored US expedition to the continent. A major joint international expedition (1949–52), mounted by the UK, Norway, and Sweden, initiated the use of geophysical methods on a large scale to determine the thickness of ice caps. The former USSR also mounted expeditions, in 1946–47 and 1951–52.

The greatest scientific undertaking involving the Antarctic was the International Geophysical Year (IGY) of 1957/58, in which 67 nations participated. The purpose of the IGY's Antarctic program was to study the effects of the continent's huge ice mass on global weather, the oceans, the aurora australis, and the ionosphere. More than 50 Antarctic stations were established by 12 countries: Argentina, Australia, Belgium, Chile, France, Japan, New Zealand, Norway, South Africa, the UK, the US, and the former USSR. The US built a supply base and airfield on Ross Island, a station at the South Pole that was provisioned by air, and four other stations. The former USSR had 4 bases, the UK 14, Argentina 8, and Chile 6. The South Pole was the terminus of three pole-to-pole observation chains along three meridians, and the US station at Little America analyzed meteorological reports from all over the world. Valuable information was gleaned from meteorological and seismic observations, studies of the upper atmosphere, magnetic measurements, and ice-sheet core drillings. The first surface transantarctic crossing, between the Weddell and Ross seas, was accomplished by the Commonwealth Transantarctic Expedition. After the IGY, very little of the continent remained to be explored.

An important result of the IGY's success was the continuation of significant research programs in Antarctica after 1958. Old stations were either closed or replaced with new buildings, and new stations were opened. The US constructed a year-round scientific village at McMurdo Sound, heated and lighted by a small atomic power plant that also used waste heat to distill seawater (the atomic reactor was replaced by diesel-powered units in 1972). Besides McMurdo Station, the US maintains two other year-round stations, at the South Pole and on Anvers Island, off the Antarctic Peninsula. Other countries maintaining year-round stations are the former USSR 7, Argentina 6, the UK 4, Chile 3, Australia 3, Japan 2, and 1 each by Brazil, China, the Federal Republic of Germany (FRG), France, India, Italy, New Zealand, Poland, and South Africa.

Transportation services are essential to Antarctic operations; for example, transportation expenses accounts for about half of the US's yearly expenditure in Antarctica The US, along with Argentina and New Zealand, routinely uses aircraft to carry both passengers and priority supplies to Antarctic stations. However, only four airfields can handle wheeled aircraft, those of Argentina, Chile, the former USSR, and the US. France reportedly built a fully equipped airport on the Adélie Coast. Air transport to other bases is by ski-equipped aircraft. The US has a fleet of transport airplanes which can carry large loads virtually anywhere in Antarctica. Transport between stations in the interior is

ANTARCTIC REGION

500   1000 km
500   1000 mi

■ Research Stations

South

Atlantic

Ocean

AFRICA

South
Sandwich
Is.
(UK)

South
Georgia
(UK)

Antarctic   Circle

SANAE III
(SOUTH AFRICA)

Dashkin Gangotri
(INDIA)

Falkland Is. (UK)
(Islas Malvinas)

South Orkney Is.
(UK)

Georg von
Neumayer (FRG)

Syowa (JAPAN)

SOUTH AMERICA

Elephant I.

Queen Maud Land

Molodezhnaya
(USSR)

Drake
Passage

Capitán Arturo Prat (CHILE)

Mizuho
(JAPAN)

South
Shetland
Is.
(UK)

Graham

New Halley (UK)
Halley (UK)

Antarctic
Pen.

Weddell Sea

Mawson
(AUSTRALIA)

Palmer (US)

Land

General Belgrano II
(ARGENTINA)

Filchner
Ice Shelf

Amery Ice Shelf

Rothera (UK)

Ronne
Ice Shelf

Berkner I.

Progress (USSR)

Alexander I.

DUFEK
MASSIF

Davis
(AUSTRALIA)

Bellingshausen

Sea

ELLSWORTH
MTS.

SOUTH POLE

Mirnyy
(USSR)

Peter I I.

Siple (US)

Ellsworth

Amundsen-Scott (US)

Shackleton
Ice Shelf

Land

Vostok
(USSR)

Amundsen

Sea

Ross

Casey
(AUSTRALIA)

Ice Shelf

Russkaya
(USSR)

McMurdo (US)

Scott
(NEW ZEALAND)

Ross Sea

McMurdo
Sound

Terra Nova
(ITALY)

Adélie   Coast

Leningradskaya
(USSR)

Dumont d'Urville
(FRANCE)

Scott I.

Balleny Is.

South

Pacific

Ocean

TASMANIA

WORLDMARK
ENCYCLOPEDIA
OF THE NATIONS

NEW

ZEALAND

AUSTRALIA

© WORLDMARK PRESS Ltd.

Tropic of Capricorn

provided mainly by tractor-trains and ski-equipped light aircraft. The longest surface supply route is from the former Soviet's Mirnyy station on the east coast to Vostok station in the interior, a distance of nearly 1,400 km (860 mi). Most nations operating in Antarctica rely on shipping for long-distance transportation and employ icebreakers to clear channels of pack ice. When conditions are favorable, ships offload cargo directly onto land or the ice shelf; when harbors are blocked by ice, tractors and helicopters carry passengers and cargo to shore.

Territorial Claims and International Cooperation
Seven nations have made separate territorial claims in Antarctica. Five of the claims begin at 60°s latitude and continue in the shape of a pie wedge to the South Pole. The exceptions are the claims of the UK, which start at 50°s in order to include the South Sandwich and South Georgia Islands of the Falkland chain; and of Norway, the northern and southern boundaries of which are undefined. The UK, the first nation to claim a "slice" of the continent (in 1908), was followed by New Zealand (1923), France (1924), Australia (1933), Norway (1939), Chile (1940), and Argentina (1943). The claims of Argentina and Chile overlap with each other and with that of the UK. Neither the US nor the former USSR has claimed any Antarctic territory, and neither recognizes the claims of other nations. Since international law requires "effective occupation" as the basis for ownership, and since no nation has met the criteria by sustaining such permanent occupation in Antarctica, these territorial claims have not been recognized by other countries, by the UN, or by any other international body.

In order to clarify the issue of territorial claims and to form a legal framework for the activities of nations in Antarctica, the 12 countries that had participated in the IGY signed the Antarctic Treaty on 1 December 1959: Argentina, Australia, Belgium, Chile, France, Japan, New Zealand, Norway, South Africa, the former USSR, the UK, and the US. All 12 had ratified the treaty by 23 June 1961, when it duly entered into force. Other nations that conduct Antarctic research are entitled to consultative membership; as of May 1989, seven countries—Poland (1977), Germany (1981), Brazil (1983), India (1983), China (1985), Uruguay (1985), and Italy (1987) —had attained consultative status. By that year, 23 countries in addition to the signatory nations had acceded to the terms of the treaty: Poland (1961), The Czech Republic (1962), Denmark (1965), the Netherlands (1967), Romania (1971), Brazil (1975), Bulgaria (1978), Germany (1979), Uruguay (1980), Papua New Guinea (1981), Italy (1981), Peru (1981), Spain (1982), China (1983), India (1983), Hungary (1984), Sweden (1984), Finland (1984), Cuba (1984), the Republic of Korea (1986), Austria (1987), the Democratic People's Republic of Korea (1987), and Ecuador (1987).

The Antarctic Treaty provides that "Antarctica shall be used for peaceful purposes only," and prohibits military bases, weapons testing (including nuclear explosions), and disposal of radioactive wastes. It seeks to foster freedom of scientific investigation and cooperation between nations, with the free exchange of scientific programs, observations, results, and personnel guaranteed. The treaty neither recognizes nor nullifies any preexisting territorial claims, but it does forbid any new claim or enlargement of any existing claim. The document specifies that contracting parties have the right to designate observers, and that such observers shall at all times have the right to inspect any station or installation. The treaty provides for the peaceful settlement of all disputes by the parties concerned or by the International Court of Justice. It also specifies periodic meetings between member states to exchange information and to enact measures in furtherance of treaty objectives; from 1961 to 1987, 14 consultative meetings were held. In 1991 the treaty was reviewed and renewed by 39 nations. The nations agreed to maintain the unique status of Ant-

arctica for another 50 years. The nations also agreed to establish regulations and guidelines with respect to Antarctica's mineral and natural resources.

Scientific research has continued under the provisions of the treaty, but the emphasis has shifted from short-term reconnaissance to long-term, large-scale investigations of Antarctic phenomena. Detailed study of the ice sheet has brought about increased understanding of global weather and climatic changes. The largest cooperative program completed to date has been the International Antarctic Glaciological Project (1971–81), conducted by Australia, France, the former USSR, the UK, and the US. The principal objectives are to measure precisely the East Antarctic ice sheet by means of core drillings through the ice to bedrock at several coastal and interior locations, and to make extensive aerial surveys of the area. Another collaborative project, Polar Experiment (POLEX)–South (1975–85), mounted by Argentina, the former USSR, and the US, expanded on existing national research programs on the atmosphere, ocean currents, and the ice sheet. The Dry Valley Drilling Project (1971–76), a joint project conducted by Japan, New Zealand, and the US, included geophysical exploration and bedrock drilling in the McMurdo Sound area. The Ross Ice Shelf Project, an ongoing US endeavor begun in 1973, has incorporated contributions from at least 12 other nations to measure the surface and under-ice topography, ice thickness, gravity, and seismic activity of the Ross Ice Shelf. Another US project, inaugurated in November 1983, involved the most intensive study yet of the relationship between the West Antarctica ice sheet and the global climate. A Soviet exploration project (1975–80) in the Filchner Ice Shelf of West Antarctica used aerial photography and geological surveys to evaluate the area's mineral resources. During the austral summers of 1983–86, international research resulted in significant discoveries of plant and animal fossils in Antarctica that provided new data on the geologic, climatic, and oceanic history of the Southern Hemisphere; enabled glaciologists to learn more about cycles of ice ages; and facilitated studies of Antarctic sea-ice algae and bacteria thought to be vital to the advancement of genetic engineering. In addition, a satellite link was established between the US and the McMurdo and South Pole stations. In the late 1980s, some of the most compelling research in Antarctica was focused on study of the springtime depletion of stratospheric ozone—a phenomenon popularly termed "the ozone hole"—allowing high levels of potentially harmful ultraviolet radiation to reach the earth's surface.

Resources
Estimates of Antarctica's mineral deposits are imprecise. A US Geological Survey study has concluded that the continent may contain some 900 major mineral deposits, but that only about 20 of these are likely to be found in ice-free areas. Two minerals, iron ore and coal, have been discovered in quantities that, were they accessible, would be commercially attractive. Small amounts of copper, chromium, platinum, nickel, gold, and hydrocarbons have also been found. Mineral exploration has been limited to comparatively small ice-free areas, but the Dufek Massif in the Pensacola Mountains of the Transantarctic Range shows the most potential for discovery of valuable metals. Offshore deposits of oil and natural gas show the greatest economic promise: traces of natural gas were discovered in a core taken from the Weddell Sea in 1972. However, the difficulty of operating in the harsh Antarctic climate, the inaccessibility of the deposits, and the high cost involved in mining and transportation make mineral exploitation of Antarctica unlikely for some time, if ever.

THE ARCTIC
The northernmost area of the earth's surface, the Arctic may be defined as all land and water within the Arctic Circle at 66°31′N.

However, the regional boundary may also be considered the 10°C (50°F) atmospheric isotherm for the warmest month (July), which extends well below the Arctic Circle in some places and coincides roughly with the tree line. The region, centered around the North Pole, includes the ice-covered Arctic Ocean basin, which is surrounded by the northern mainland and islands of North America and Eurasia, with outlets to the Bering Sea and the North Atlantic Ocean. The Arctic Ocean, with an area of about 14 million sq km (5.4 million sq mi), comprises nearly two-thirds of the total area. Principal land masses are the northern reaches of the former USSR, Scandinavia, Greenland, Canada, and Alaska.

Unlike Antarctica, the Arctic region has a year-round habitable climate at its fringes, a permanent population, and established territorial sovereignty over all land areas. The Arctic also is of great strategic importance because of its central location between North America and Eurasia; the northern tip of Canada lies only about 4,000 km (2,500 mi) from what was the Soviet city of Murmansk on the great circle route. As a consequence of such proximity, the Arctic region is the site of many radar stations maintained by Canada, the former USSR, and the US to monitor air traffic and to provide early warning of an air attack.

The continental shelf around the Arctic basin occupies more than half the ocean area, a much larger proportion than in any other ocean; the edge of the continental shelf near Franz Josef Land lies about 1,500 km (930 mi) from the Eurasian mainland. The landmasses that extend above the Arctic Circle exhibit three major types of landforms: rugged uplands and deep fjords formed by glaciation; swampy coastal plains and high ice plateaus covered by glacial deposits; and folded mountains, including the high peaks of the Canadian Rocky Mountains, Alaska's Brooks Range, and the rounded slopes of the Ural Mountains of the former USSR. Principal rivers flowing into the Arctic Ocean are the Mackenzie, in Canada, and the Ob', Yenisey, Lena, and Kolyma, in the former USSR. Major seas in the Arctic include the Chukchi, East Siberian, Laptev, Kara, Barents, Norwegian, Greenland, and Beaufort.

The Arctic Ocean remains frozen throughout the year (except for its fringes during summer) and is virtually icelocked from October to June. The vast Arctic ice pack expands from an average area of 7.8 million sq km (3 million sq mi) in summer to an average of 14.8 million sq km (5.7 million sq mi) during winter. The average thickness of the ice pack is estimated at 3–3.5 m (9.8–11.5 ft). Ice "islands" up to 60 m (200 ft) thick and 30 km (19 mi) wide break away from the moving ice pack off North America and float slowly in erratic circles before disintegrating or exiting to the North Atlantic. Smaller fragments called icebergs break off glaciers in Greenland and northeastern Canada and move southward via the East Greenland and Labrador currents into Atlantic shipping lanes. An estimated 1,000 icebergs each year cross 55°N, and nearly 400 reach the Grand Banks off Newfoundland. A few icebergs have traveled as far as 4,000 km (2,500 mi) over a three-year period and have been sighted as far south as Bermuda.

The most recent Ice Age climaxed about 15,000 years ago, when continental ice sheets covered most of the Northern Hemisphere. The retreat of the glaciers was stabilized some 8,500 years ago in Europe and 7,000 years ago in North America. The warming period that followed reached its maximum in historic times during AD 800–1000, making possible the Viking colonization of Arctic lands, and from the 1880s to the 1940s, when extensive Arctic exploration occurred. However, a minor cooling trend that began in the 1940s (and is expected to last well into the 1990s) has had severe effects in the Arctic, increasing the ice-covered area substantially and reducing the annual mean air temperatures by several degrees, thereby shortening the summer season along the Arctic coast of Eurasia by nearly a month.

The Arctic experiences alternating six-month periods of winter darkness and summer daylight, including 24 hours of daylight within the Arctic Circle during the summer equinox (hence the designation "land of the midnight sun"). The region is subject to long, cold winters and short, cool summers. The snow cover is relatively light, averaging 20–50 cm (8–20 in) and lasting for about 10 months over the frozen ocean. Air temperatures above the pack ice average –30°C (–22°F) in January and near 0°C (32°F) in July. Annual mean temperatures on land vary from –12°C (10°F) at Barrow, Alaska, and –16°C (3°F) on Resolute Island, in northern Canada, to 0°C (32°F) at Murmansk, in what was the western USSR. Annual mean temperatures in Greenland are low because of the island's high elevation and vast interior ice sheet; they range from –40°C (–40°F) in January to –10°C (14°F) in July, temperatures significantly colder than those of the North Pole. Total annual precipitation varies from 10 to 25 cm (4–10 in) on the Arctic ice pack to 45 cm (18 in) or more in Greenland.

A climate-dependent phenomenon is the presence of perennially frozen ground, or permafrost, which has impeded human use of land in the Arctic region. Permafrost, occurring wherever ground temperatures remain below freezing for two or more years, underlies most of the Arctic landmass of Alaska and Greenland, half of that in Canada and the former USSR, and parts of Scandinavia. It also has been found under coastal seabeds of the Arctic Ocean. The maximum thickness of permafrost has been measured at 500 m (1,640 ft) in Canada, 900 m (2,950 ft) in Alaska, and 1,500 m (4,920 ft) in the former USSR. Alternate freezing and thawing of the outer permafrost layer shortens the growing season during the summer and causes serious engineering problems for construction and mining operations in the Arctic region.

Vegetation on the Arctic tundra, or treeless plain, is limited to mosses, lichens, sedges, and a few flowering plants which blossom during the brief spring and summer seasons. The outer edges of the Arctic ice pack support a small number of animal species by providing an overhead platform for algae and plankton, which are eaten by fish that, in turn, serve as food for seals, walruses, and birds; the food chain is continued by foxes and polar bears which feed upon young seals. Altogether, the Arctic has about 20 species of land mammals, including the moose, caribou, reindeer, wolf, and squirrel. The arrival of migratory birds each spring increases the bird population enormously.

Principal fish are cod, herring, and capelin, a true Arctic fish; all of these have great commercial value, as do shrimp and crab. Since 15 October 1975, when Iceland extended its fishing zone to 200 nautical mi, all nations bordering the Arctic have done the same, and fish catch quotas are now under national management.

The ecological cycle of Arctic life has been damaged by human encroachment, but in recent years the natural environment has been increasingly protected by the five circumpolar countries (Canada, Denmark, Norway, the former USSR, and the US). In 1956, the former USSR prohibited hunting of the polar bear, and in 1973 the five nations agreed to protect the bear's habitat. During construction in the 1970s of the trans-Alaska oil pipeline from Prudhoe Bay on the Arctic coast to the port of Valdez on the Gulf of Alaska, the US government required contractors to clean up the work site and to restore displaced vegetation; drillers were directed to trap and remove spilled oil. The pipeline carrying hot oil was suspended above ground level to prevent the permafrost from thawing, and crossings under the pipeline were provided at intervals for caribou and moose migrations. The Alaska Native Claims Settlement Act (1971) set aside about one-fourth of the state's area for wilderness preserves, wildlife refuges, and national parks. To prevent or control oil spills in the Arctic Ocean, Canada in 1970 authorized a 161-km (100-mi) offshore pollution control zone north of the 60° line. The former USSR has established nature preserves on several islands off the Kola Peninsula, east of the Barents Sea, and on Wrangel Island. In 1973, Norway established nature reserves and national parks in its Svalbard territory in the Barents Sea, and the next year, Denmark designated the northeastern third of Greenland as a national park.

Settlement and Exploration

The Arctic region was settled some 10,000 to 12,000 years ago, after the last Ice Age, by peoples of Central Asia, probably of Mongoloid stock, who pursued animal herds northward in the wake of retreating glaciers. The ancestors of the Lapps migrated to northern Scandinavia and the Kola Peninsula, while further east diverse peoples settled along the Arctic coast. At about the same time, the forebears of the American Indians came from Asia via a land bridge across the Bering Strait or traveled along the Aleutian Islands to North America. It is believed that the Eskimos arrived in Alaska much later.

These migratory peoples adapted to the harsh Arctic environment by inventing snowshoes, the kayak, the igloo, and primitive tools. They fashioned clothing and tents of caribou or reindeer skins, perfected efficient hunting techniques, and evolved distinctive forms of social organization. Gradually, over the course of centuries, these hunter-gatherers made the transition to herding and trading; especially for the Indians and Eskimos of Canada and the US, however, intense contact with modern culture in the 20th century has meant abrupt change. In addition to Indians and Eskimos, principal indigenous Arctic population groups include the mixed Eskimo-Caucasian peoples of Greenland; the Lapps in Scandinavia; and the Samoyedic, Yakuts, Tungus-Manchurian, and Chukchi peoples of the former USSR. These aboriginal peoples constituted about half of the Arctic's total population.

The first explorers in Arctic waters were the Vikings (Northmen) from Scandinavia, who ventured into the North Atlantic as far as Greenland and the North American continent in the 10th and 11th centuries. It is generally accepted that the Norse chieftain Leif Ericson explored part of the northeastern North American mainland, which he called Vinland, although its actual location is disputed. During the 16th and 17th centuries, European explorers such as Martin Frobisher, William Baffin, and William Barents probed the Arctic Ocean for the fabled Northwest Passage around North America to the Orient. Arctic geographical landmarks have been named after them and for Vitus Bering, the Danish explorer who sailed in the service of Russia in 1728 through the strait that bears his name. In the late 18th century, while developing trade routes for English fur companies, Alexander Mackenzie and Samuel Hearne followed Canadian rivers to reach the Arctic coast. In 1819, William Parry sailed west through the northern Canadian islands as far as M'Clure Strait before being stopped by heavy pack ice. That year, Swedish explorer Nils Nordenskjöld became the first to complete the Northeast Passage along the Russian Arctic coast. The disappearance in 1845 of Sir John Franklin's expedition spurred further exploration and the mapping of many Canadian islands in the Arctic Ocean. Norwegian explorer Roald Amundsen successfully transited the Northwest Passage for the first time, from 1903 to 1906.

Amundsen's accomplishment shifted the emphasis of Arctic exploration to reaching the North Pole. American explorer Robert E. Peary came within 280 km (174 mi) of the goal in his 1905–06 expedition, and on 6 April 1909, he and his party, including four Eskimos, were the first men to reach the North Pole. In 1926, Adm. Richard E. Byrd, of Antarctic exploration fame, and his copilot Floyd Bennett were the first to fly over the pole, and Amundsen and Lincoln Ellsworth flew from Spitsbergen (now Svalbard) across the pole to Alaska. Much later, in 1958, the US atomic-powered submarine *Nautilus* was the first underwater vessel to navigate the North Pole, and in 1960, another US submarine, the *Skate,* became the first to surface at

the pole. The Soviet icebreaker *Arktika* was the first surface vessel to reach it, in 1977.

Unresolved Arctic territorial disputes concern Norway's exclusive claim to the resources of the Svalbard continental shelf and conflicting Norwegian-Soviet claims in the Barents Sea. After the Antarctic Treaty was signed in 1959, hopes were raised for a similar agreement in regard to the Arctic, but the strategic importance of the Arctic region, its increasing economic value, and complex legal problems involving national sensitivities have thus far prevented the attainment of such an accord.

Arctic Development

The five nations with territories within the Arctic Circle have all developed the area's natural resources to some degree, but the former USSR has taken the lead both in populating the region and in exploiting its rich mineral deposits and other resources. The largest Arctic city is Murmansk, with a population of about 400,000, and there are some 30 other ex-Soviet cities and towns in the Arctic with more than 10,000 inhabitants. In contrast, the largest town on the North American mainland located north of the Arctic Circle is Inuvik, in Canada's Northwest Territories, with a population of about 3,000; Godthaab, the capital of Greenland, has less than 12,000 residents. The former USSR estimated the population of what it terms its "far north" (including areas in eastern Siberia as far south as 55°N) at about 4 million in the late 1970s. Of the total, about 65% lived in mining districts or coastal settlements based on fishing and military activities, 20% were concentrated in northern river valleys, and 15% were scattered in the hinterlands. Canada's Yukon Territory and Northwest Territories have over 40% of the country's land area but less than 1% of the total population. Alaska is the largest but second least populous of all the states of the US.

Beginning in the 1930s, with the establishment of the northern sea route to link coastal and river settlements, the Soviet government undertook the exceptionally costly task of fostering industrial development of the Arctic region. Because the harsh climate, the shortage of housing and amenities, and the low level of social services discouraged voluntary migration to the area, the Soviet government offered special resettlement inducements to workers, such as high wages and extensive fringe benefits. As a result, Soviet migration to the far north was nearly equal to the region's natural population increase between 1940 and 1970. However, labor turnover was rapid, with most new workers staying only one to three years. The most important economic activity was the mining of large nickel, copper, tin, platinum, cobalt, iron, and coal deposits. Eastern Siberia produced more than half the country's total output of nickel and much of the nation's copper, while the Kola Peninsula's apatite deposits provided at least two-thirds of the raw materials used to produce phosphate fertilizer. Eastern Siberia also produced about 90% of the former USSR's annual output of diamonds and tin. In addition, valuable oil fields and about two-thirds of proved Soviet natural gas reserves was located in western Siberia. Expansion of Soviet mining operations in the Arctic region continued into the 1980s and up until its collapse in the early 1990s.

The most significant economic development in the Arctic during the 1970s was the $4.5-billion trans-Alaska oil pipeline project and the exploitation of vast petroleum reserves (estimated at more than 10 billion barrels) at Alaska's Prudhoe Bay. Construction began on the 1,270-km (789-mi) pipeline to Valdez in 1974, and oil began to flow through the pipeline in 1977. Tens of thousands of American workers migrated to Alaska to take part in the project (earning the highest average wage rates in the US), and many stayed there after its completion, thereby contributing to Alaska's population increase of 32.4% during the decade. Coal reserves estimated at 5 trillion tons are located on Alaska's North Slope; coal is mined at Healy, between Anchorage and Fairbanks.

ARCTIC REGION

500   1000 km
500   1000 mi

North Pacific Ocean

Aleutian Is.

Bering   Sea

Anadyr'

Evensk

Bethel

Bering
Strait

Provid'eniya

Arctic Circle

R.

Anchorage

Nome

Cherskiy

Kolyma

Aldan

Valdez

UNITED STATES
(Alaska)

*Chukchi
Sea*

Yakutsk

Healy

Verkhoyansk

Fairbanks

BROOKS   North
Slope
Barrow

Wrangel I.

R.

Viluy

Skagway

Whitehorse

RANGE

*East
Siberian
Sea*

Dawson

Yukon

Prudhoe
Bay

Lensk

ROCKY   MTS.

Liard R.

R.

Inuvik

*Beaufort
Sea*

New
Siberian
Is.

Tiksi

Lena

UNION OF SOVIET

Hay River

Mackenzie

*Great
Bear
Lake*

Arctic   Ocean

*Laptev
Sea*

*Great
Slave
Lake*

Echo Bay

Banks I.

*Ozero
Taymyr*

Tura

SOCIALIST

Yellowknife

Victoria I.

M'Clure Strait

Severnaya
Zemlya

Noril'sk

Cambridge Bay

Yenisey R.

Churchill

C A N A D A

Queen

NORTH POLE

Urengoy

R E P U B L I C S

*Hudson
Bay*

Repulse Bay

Elizabeth
Is.

Resolute

*Kara
Sea*

Dikson

Surgut

Arctic Bay

Ellesmere I.

Franz
Josef
Land

Vorkuta

Ob' R.

Irtysh R.

Inuvik

Baffin
I.

Alert

*Baffin
Bay*

Nord

Novaya
Zemlya

U R A L   M T S.

Thule

Frobisher
Bay

*Davis
Strait*

Godhavn

GREENLAND
(DENMARK)

Longyearbyen

Svalbard
(NORWAY)

Pechora R.

Pechora

Danmark
Havn

Arkhangel'sk

Kotlas

*Severnaya
Dvina R.*

Godthaab

*Greenland
Sea*

Bjørnøya
(NORWAY)

*Barents
Sea*

Murmansk
Kola Pen.

Angmagssalik

Scoresbysund

Hammerfest

*Lake
Onega*

Pefrozavodsk

Julianehåb

*Denmark
Strait*

Jan Mayen
(NORWAY)

Narvik

Arctic   Circle

Kiruna

Oulu

*Lake
Ladoga*

Reykjavík   **ICELAND**

NORWAY

Umeå

FINLAND

Leningrad

Faroe Is.
Tórshavn   (DENMARK)

Trondheim

SWEDEN

Tampere

Helsinki

North

Shetland
Is.
(UK)

Bergen

Gävle

Atlantic

Ocean

WORLDMARK
ENCYCLOPEDIA
OF THE NATIONS

© WORLDMARK PRESS Ltd.

Gold, copper, lead, zinc, tin, platinum, tungsten, and uranium have been mined in the past, and there are known reserves of silver, lead, nickel, cobalt, mercury, molybdenum, and asbestos. However, the remoteness of mining sites and the high production costs continued to hinder mineral development (except for oil) in the 1980s and early 1990s.

Valuable minerals produced in the Canadian Arctic include gold, silver, lead, zinc, copper, nickel, platinum, cadmium, and uranium. Canada also has proved oil reserves totaling 1.5 billion barrels in the Mackenzie River delta and offshore areas of the Beaufort Sea. Although Greenland also has considerable mineral resources, only lead, zinc, and coal were being mined in the early 1990s. The two largest iron mines in Scandinavia are situated in the vicinity of Kiruna, in Swedish Lapland, and in Norway, near the Soviet border. Both Norway and the former USSR operate coal mines in Svalbard, and both have explored for offshore oil beneath the Barents Sea.

Lack of adequate transportation facilities long hampered Arctic development. Since World War II, however, a network of air, water, and land routes has been developed, and modern technology has made most polar areas accessible. Scheduled flights from many airfields scattered throughout the region link cities and remote towns in Alaska, Canada, and the former USSR. In Greenland, where the rugged terrain makes the building of airstrips both difficult and costly, there is scheduled jet helicopter service. Air transport serves both military and civilian needs in Norway's polar region and links Svalbard with the mainland. Although water transport is seasonal because of ice-blocked channels in winter, large quantities of cargo generally move by ship. Several hundred Russian vessels, including icebreakers, ply the 2,800-km (1,740-mi) northern sea route between Novaya Zemlya and the Bering Strait, moving an estimated 4 million tons of cargo annually during 2–4 months of navigability.

The former USSR and Norway use waterborne shuttles to supply Svalbard and to convey coal to their respective home ports. Canada's shipping service for Hudson Bay, the Arctic islands, and the Mackenzie River delta is provided by the coast guard and by private companies. The Alaskan ports of Prudhoe Bay and Barrow are served by ships for a two-month period during late summer. Inland waterways provide important supply links in the Soviet Arctic and northwestern Canada.

Land routes in the Arctic are relatively undeveloped in the colder regions. However, there are four railroad lines in North America that penetrate the Arctic Circle. In addition to Alaska's heavily used Anchorage–Fairbanks line, there are three Canadian railroads, providing links to Churchill, on Hudson Bay; to Hay River, on the Great Slave Lake; and to Skagway, on the Alaskan border. Six Russian railroads serve the Arctic region, including the ports of Murmansk and Arkhangel'sk. Canada's two Arctic highways connect Inuvik with Dawson and with the Great Slave Lake towns of Hay River and Yellowknife. The most heavily traveled highway is Alaska's Arctic haul road between the Yukon River and Prudhoe Bay; this road was instrumental in hauling supplies and equipment to build the trans-Alaska oil pipeline. The Soviet Arctic has few roads, but the Murmansk area in the west connects with a well-developed Scandinavian road network.

Scientific Research

Scientific research in the Arctic region is directed mainly toward economic development and military applications. Research studies have dealt primarily with the Arctic's role in global air and water circulation and with such natural phenomena as pack ice, permafrost, geomagnetism, the aurora borealis, and other upper atmospheric conditions.

International cooperation has long played a vital role in Arctic research, dating back to the 1882/83 and 1932/33 International

Polar Years. The most intensive multinational scientific study of the Arctic was accomplished during the International Geophysical Year (1957/58), in which some 300 Arctic stations were set up to monitor polar phenomena. The US and the former USSR each launched two drifting stations on the pack ice to gather data on Arctic currents and the topography of the Arctic seabed. It was found that little marine life existed on the Arctic Ocean floor and that rocks were scattered in profusion on the ocean bottom. The land stations obtained detailed information on the aurora borealis, ionosphere, and polar magnetic field. During 1969–75, Canada and the US jointly conducted an Arctic ice experimental program involving manned and unmanned drifting stations to determine the dynamics of sea-ice movement within the polar environment.

Scientific efforts by the former USSR in the Arctic have exceeded the combined activities of all the other circumpolar nations. By the late 1970s, the former USSR operated at least 100 polar stations and more than a dozen specially equipped sea and air vehicles to collect data on weather, ocean currents, and sea ice, with the aim of maintaining shipping services over the northern sea route. Drifting ice stations maintained year-round make a variety of meteorological observations and conduct oceanographic and geophysical experiments. Each year, Russia mounts air expeditions to hundreds of sites along the ice pack, emplacing nearly two dozen automatic buoys to radio data on environmental conditions to the mainland.

US Arctic research centers mainly on Alaska but extends also to northern Canada, Greenland, and the Arctic Ocean. Civilian research is coordinated by the National Science Foundation (NSF), which awards funds for research to universities; the principal research centers are at Fairbanks and Barrow. Small outposts to gather weather information have been established at US military facilities in Alaska and at radar stations on the 4,800-km (3,000-mi) Distant Early Warning (DEW) line extending from Alaska to Greenland. In 1986/87, the NSF allocated approximately $19 million for Arctic research studies. In the same year, total US government outlay for Arctic research was approximately $93 million.

The US operates an average of one drifting ice station per year in the Arctic Ocean, supplemented by automatic data buoys. Ice reconnaissance flights are conducted, as well as ocean surveys by icebreakers and submarines in the Bering and Greenland seas. In the early 1980s, the NSF conducted a six-year project, called Processes and Resources of the Bering Sea Shelf (PROBES), to study the marine ecosystem of the Bering Sea in order to predict the environmental impact of both natural events and human activities. In 1987, the NSF initiated a follow-up program, Inner Shelf Transfer and Recycling (ISHTAR), conducted in the Bering and Chukchi seas to study the ways in which seasonal and annual variations in the northward transport of water influence life processes. In 1985, scientists from the National Oceanic and Atmospheric Administration (NOAA) embarked on a study of a 5,200-sq km (2,000-sq mi) polynya (open water in pack ice that is a source of heat in an extremely cold area) in the Bering Sea, hoping to assess its effects on weather patterns, wind behavior, and ocean currents. In the summer of 1981, the US cooperated with Denmark and Switzerland to obtain ice cores from the bottom of the Greenland ice sheet, which represents a record of the climate over the past 130,000 years. Other recent US programs include studies of the geology and geophysics of the Arctic basin and research in Alaska on so-called surging glaciers, which move forward at the unusually rapid rate of several miles a year.

Other circumpolar nations have concentrated their Arctic research on the land and continental shelf. Canada's ongoing Polar Continental Shelf Project, begun in 1959, makes intensive studies of the North American continental shelf, Arctic islands, and Arctic Ocean. From March to October of each year, Canada also conducts aerial surveys of sea ice in the Arctic Ocean, Baffin Bay, and Beaufort Sea. Norway's Polar Institute, in Oslo, supervises mapping and scientific surveys of Svalbard, Jan Mayen, and the Arctic Ocean. In Greenland, the US participates in geophysical and weather studies at Thule Air Base. Scientists from Russia, the UK, France, and other countries also conduct geological and biological research on the Danish dependency.

BIBLIOGRAPHY

Armstrong, Terrence, *et al. The Circumpolar North: A Political and Economic Geography of the Arctic and Sub-Arctic*. New York: Methuen, 1978.

Auburn, F. M. *Antarctic Law and Politics*. Bloomington: Indiana University Press, 1982.

Bonner, W. N., and R. J. Berry (eds.). *Ecology in the Antarctic*. New York: Academic Press, 1981.

Bush, W. M. *Basic Documents on Antarctica*. 2 vols. Dobbs Ferry, N.Y.: Oceana, 1982.

Federal Arctic Research. Springfield, Va.: Interagency Arctic Research Policy Committee, National Technical Information Service, 1985.

McWhinnie, Mary A. (ed.). *Polar Research: To the Present and the Future*. Boulder, Colo.: Westview Press, 1978.

Mirsky, Jeanette. *To the Arctic: The Story of Northern Exploration from Earliest Times to the Present*. Chicago: University of Chicago Press, 1970.

Parker, Bruce C. (ed.). *Environmental Impact in Antarctica*. Charlottesville: University Press of Virginia, 1978.

Polar Regions Atlas. Washington, D.C.: Central Intelligence Agency, 1978.

Porter, Eliot. *Antarctica*. New York: Dutton, 1978.

Pyne, Stephen J. *The Ice: A Journey to Antarctica*. Ames: University of Iowa Press, 1987.

Quigg, P. W. *A Pole Apart: The Emerging Issues of Antarctica*. New York: McGraw-Hill, 1982.

Ray, G. Carleton, and M. G. McCormick-Ray. *Wildlife of the Polar Regions*. New York: Abrams, 1981.

Sugden, David. *Arctic and Antarctic: A Modern Geographical Synthesis*. Totowa, N.J.: Barnes & Noble, 1982.

UN Economic Commission for Europe. *Human Settlements in the Arctic: An Account of the ECE Symposium on Human Settlements Planning and Development in the Arctic, Godthöab, Greenland, Aug. 18–25, 1978*. Elmsford, N.Y.: Pergamon, 1980.

WORLD TABLES

Table 1. World Demographic Indicators

321

COUNTRY	POPULATION 1992 IN THOUSANDS	POPULATION GROWTH RATE % 1985-92	TOTAL FERTILITY RATE-BIRTHS PER WOMEN 1992	CRUDE BIRTH RATE (EST) 1992	CRUDE DEATH RATE (EST) 1992	LIFE EXPECTANCY (YEARS EST) 1992
AFRICA						
Algeria	26,375	2.7	4.9	31	7	66
Angola	9,732	2.9	6.6	46	19	46
Benin	5,042	3.2	6.2	49	15	51
Botswana	1,360	3.4	4.7	35	8	68
Burkina Faso	9,537	2.8	6.5	49	16	48
Burundi	5,818	2.9	6.8	46	14	48
Cameroon	12,245	3.0	5.8	44	11	56
Cape Verde	389	2.7	4.3	48	10	68
Central African Republic	3,166	2.7	5.8	43	18	47
Chad	5,977	2.5	5.9	42	21	47
Comoros	510	3.7	6.7	47	12	56
Congo	2,428	3.3	6.6	42	13	51
Côte d'Ivoire	12,841	4.0	6.6	47	12	52
Djibouti	465	2.9	6.6	43	16	49
Egypt	54,805	2.4	4.1	33	9	62
Equatorial Guinea	437	2.3	5.5	42	15	48
Eritrea	—	—	—	—	—	—
Ethiopia	54,790	3.4	6.9	45	14	49
Gabon	1,201	2.7	5.9	29	14	54
Gambia	929	3.2	6.5	47	17	45
Ghana	15,824	3.3	6.1	45	13	55
Guinea	6,048	2.8	6.5	46	21	44
Guinea-Bissau	1,022	2.1	6.0	42	18	39
Kenya	25,838	3.5	6.4	44	8	59
Lesotho	1,860	2.7	5.1	35	10	57
Liberia	2,179	3.1	6.2	44	13	55
Libya	4,873	3.6	6.4	36	6	63
Madagascar	12,384	3.1	6.2	46	14	51
Malawi	9,085	3.4	7.6	52	17	44
Mali	8,962	2.8	7.1	52	17	48
Mauritania	2,082	2.7	6.8	48	17	48
Mauritius	1,099	1.1	2.0	19	7	70
Morocco	26,262	2.5	4.2	29	8	63
Mozambique	16,565	2.7	6.5	46	17	47
Namibia	1,529	3.1	6.0	45	9	58
Niger	8,171	3.2	7.4	58	23	46
Nigeria	101,884	2.9	5.9	46	16	52
Rwanda	7,310	3.0	6.2	52	14	46
São Tomé and Principe	121	2.3	5.0	38	8	68
Senegal	7,845	3.0	6.1	44	13	48
Seychelles	69	0.8	2.7	23	7	71
Sierra Leone	4,354	2.5	6.5	46	20	43
Somalia	8,302	2.9	5.4	46	13	65
South Africa	39,763	2.4	4.1	34	8	63
Sudan	26,587	2.8	6.2	44	13	52
Swaziland	860	3.9	6.6	44	12	57
Tanzania	25,965	3.0	6.3	49	15	51
Togo	3,899	3.7	6.5	48	12	54
Tunisia	8,405	2.0	3.4	25	5	68
Uganda	17,475	3.1	7.3	51	14	46
Zaire	39,794	3.3	6.2	45	13	52
Zambia	8,589	3.5	6.5	48	11	48
Zimbabwe	10,352	3.0	4.6	40	8	60
AMERICAS						
Antigua and Barbuda	81	1.0	1.9	18	6	74
Argentina	33,099	1.3	2.8	20	9	71
Bahamas	263	1.9	2.1	19	5	70
Barbados	259	0.3	1.8	16	9	75
Belize	200	2.6	4.5	31	5	69
Bolivia	7,527	2.5	4.7	33	9	60
Brazil	153,850	1.8	2.8	25	7	66
Canada	27,844	1.4	1.9	14	7	78
Chile	13,599	1.7	2.7	21	6	72
Colombia	33,405	1.8	2.7	24	5	69
Costa Rica	3,135	2.5	3.1	27	4	76
Cuba	10,841	1.0	1.9	17	6	76
Dominica	72	1.6	2.5	24	5	72
Dominican Republic	7,321	1.9	3.0	26	7	68
Ecuador	11,028	2.5	3.6	28	6	67

Table 1. World Demographic Indicators—*cont.*

COUNTRY	POPULATION 1992 IN THOUSANDS	POPULATION GROWTH RATE % 1985-92	TOTAL FERTILITY RATE-BIRTHS PER WOMEN 1992	CRUDE BIRTH RATE (EST) 1992	CRUDE DEATH RATE (EST) 1992	LIFE EXPECTANCY (YEARS EST) 1992
El Salvador	5,387	1.8	4.0	33	5	66
Grenada	91	-0.3	2.9	34	7	70
Guatemala	9,746	2.9	5.3	34	8	65
Guyana	806	0.3	2.6	21	7	65
Haiti	6,715	2.0	4.7	42	15	55
Honduras	5,418	3.1	4.9	42	15	66
Jamaica	2,394	0.8	2.6	23	6	74
Mexico	84,967	1.8	3.2	29	5	70
Nicaragua	3,916	2.8	5.0	37	7	67
Panama	2,514	2.1	2.9	25	5	73
Paraguay	4,519	2.9	4.3	33	5	67
Peru	22,370	2.1	3.3	27	7	65
St. Kitts and Nevis	—	—	—	—	—	—
St. Lucia	—	—	—	—	—	—
St. Vincent and the Grenadines	—	—	—	—	—	—
Suriname	467	2.3	3.2	26	6	69
Trinidad and Tobago	1,268	1.3	2.7	21	6	71
United States	255,414	0.9	2.1	14	9	76
Uruguay	3,131	0.6	2.3	17	10	74
Venezuela	20,310	2.5	3.1	27	4	70
ASIA AND OCEANIA						
Afghanistan	21,558	2.5	6.9	44	20	43
Armenia	3,499	1.2	3.0	22	7	72
Australia	17,540	1.6	1.9	15	7	77
Azerbaijan	7,145	1.0	3.2	26	7	71
Bahrain	532	3.2	4.6	27	4	70
Bangladesh	112,832	2.2	4.3	36	12	53
Bhutan	1,497	2.2	5.9	40	17	48
Brunei Darussalam	273	3.2	3.7	27	5	74
Burma (Myanmar)	43,718	2.2	4.2	29	10	60
China	1,166,144	1.5	2.4	22	7	71
Cyprus	715	1.0	2.4	18	8	77
Federated States of Micronesia	108	2.4	4.5	29	7	71
Fiji	750	0.9	3.0	25	7	72
India	883,473	2.1	3.9	30	11	60
Indonesia	184,274	1.8	2.9	25	8	60
Iran	59,791	3.7	6.1	44	8	65
Iraq	19,184	3.3	5.7	44	8	64
Israel	5,113	2.7	2.7	21	6	77
Japan	124,318	0.4	1.6	10	7	79
Jordan	3,949	5.8	5.2	45	3	70
Kampuchea	9,010	2.7	4.5	37	15	51
Kazakhstan	16,954	1.0	2.7	23	8	69
Kiribati	75	2.1	4.1	33	12	56
Korea, (DPRK)	22,614	1.9	2.4	24	6	71
Korea, Republic of (ROK)	43,663	1.0	1.8	16	6	71
Kuwait	1,400	—	3.7	32	2	75
Kyrgyzstan	4,472	1.7	3.9	31	8	66
Laos	4,384	2.9	6.7	44	16	51
Lebanon	3,781	2.3	3.1	28	7	66
Malaysia	18,610	2.5	3.6	29	6	71
Maldives	228	3.3	5.9	45	8	62
Marshall Islands	50	3.9	7.0	47	8	62.5
Mongolia	2,311	2.8	4.6	34	7	64
Nauru	9,460	1.3	2.1	18	5	67
Nepal	19,892	2.6	5.5	38	14	54
New Zealand	3,415	0.7	2.1	16	8	76
Oman	1,647	3.8	6.7	41	6	70
Pakistan	119,347	3.1	5.6	43	13	59
Palau	—	—	—	—	—	—
Papua New Guinea	4,055	2.3	4.9	34	11	56
Philippines	64,187	2.3	3.5	28	7	65
Qatar	524	6.0	4.4	21	4	71
Saudi Arabia	15,909	3.5	6.4	39	6	69
Singapore	2,814	1.8	1.8	18	5	75
Solomon Islands	335	2.9	5.4	40	5	65
Sri Lanka	17,396	1.3	2.5	20	6	72
Syria	12,951	3.3	6.2	44	7	67
Taiwan	20,878	1.0	1.8	16	5	75
Tajikistan	5,634	3.0	5.3	40	8	69

Table 1. World Demographic Indicators—*cont.*   323

COUNTRY	POPULATION 1992 IN THOUSANDS	POPULATION GROWTH RATE % 1985-92	TOTAL FERTILITY RATE-BIRTHS PER WOMEN 1992	CRUDE BIRTH RATE (EST) 1992	CRUDE DEATH RATE (EST) 1992	LIFE EXPECTANCY (YEARS EST) 1992
Thailand	57,992	1.7	2.2	20	6	69
Tonga	101	0.9	3.8	26	7	68
Turkey	58,467	2.2	3.3	27	6	67
Turkmenistan	3,852	2.5	4.5	36	9	66
Turks and Caicos Islands	—	—	—	—	—	—
Tuvalu	—	—	—	—	—	—
United Arab Emirates	1,668	3.1	4.5	29	3	72
Uzbekistan	21,285	2.4	4.3	34	7	69
Vanuatu	155	2.4	5.5	35	5	65
Viet-Nam	69,225	2.3	3.7	29	8	6.7
Western Samoa	162	0.5	4.5	34	6	66
Yemen	13,128	4.4	7.4	51	16	53
EUROPE						
Albania	3,338	1.7	3.0	23	5	73
Andorra	60	2.2	1.3	11	4	77
Austria	7,906	0.6	1.6	12	11	77
Belarus	10,346	0.5	1.9	15	11	71
Belgium	10,039	0.3	1.8	12	10	76
Bosnia and Herzegovina	4,383	0.2	1.6	14.5	6.5	72
Bulgaria	8,952	0.0	1.7	12	12	71
Croatia	4,773	0.4	1.7	12.2	11.3	73
Czech Republic	10,383	0.1	1.7	13	11	73
Denmark	5,166	0.1	1.7	13	12	76
Estonia	1,544	0.2	1.8	16	12	70
Finland	5,062	0.4	1.9	12	10	76
France	57,338	0.6	1.8	13	9	77
Georgia	5,493	0.5	2.1	17	9	73
Germany	80,553	0.6	1.5	11	11	76
Greece	10,454	0.7	1.5	11	9	78
Hungary	10,202	-0.1	1.8	12	13	70
Iceland	261	1.2	2.2	18	7	78
Ireland	3,536	0.2	2.0	15	9	75
Italy	57,844	0.2	1.3	10	10	78
Latvia	2,617	0.6	2.0	15	12	69
Liechtenstein	28,642	0.6	1.5	13	7	77
Lithuania	3,754	0.7	2.0	15	11	70
Luxembourg	389	0.8	1.8	12	10	76
Malta	360	0.7	2.2	14	8	76
Moldova	4,359	0.6	2.5	19	10	68
Monaco	30	0.9	1.1	7	7	75
Netherlands	15,167	0.7	1.7	13	8	77
Norway	4,281	0.4	1.9	14	10	77
Poland	38,365	0.4	2.1	14	10	71
Portugal	9,843	0.4	1.4	12	10	74
Romania	22,865	0.1	1.9	14	10	70
Russian Federation	148,920	0.5	1.8	15	11	69
San Marino	23,404	0.6	1.3	8	7	76.5
Slovakia	5,346	0.4	2.0	—	—	72
Slovenia	2,017	0.7	1.7	—	—	73
Spain	39,077	0.2	1.3	11	9	77
Sweden	8,707	0.6	2.1	13	11	78
Switzerland	6,864	0.9	1.8	12	9	78
Ukraine	52,118	0.3	1.8	14	12	70
United Kingdom	57,701	0.3	1.9	14	11	76
Vatican	—	—	—	—	—	—
Yugoslavia (the former)	10,597	0.8	2.1	—	—	72

—Nil, not available, or does not apply.

Table 2. World Agriculture

COUNTRY	1994 LAND AREA (SQ MI)	1994 CROP LAND (IN ACRES)	%LABOR FORCE IN AGRICULTURE 1990	TOTAL LIVESTOCK (MILLIONS)	GRAINS OUTPUT (1,000 METRIC TONS) 1992	ROOTS AND TUBERS OUTPUT (1,000 METRIC TONS) 1992
AFRICA						
Algeria	919,591	29,355	15.9	18.8	3,219	900
Angola	481,352	13,127	71.4	4.9	465	2,095
Benin	43,483	7,181	61.1	3.6	541	2,139
Botswana	224,606	5,328	3.3	5.2	15	8
Burkina Faso	105,869	13,757	85.8 (1985)	12.3	2,332	90
Burundi	10,745	5,166	92.3 (1985)	1.8	309	1,487
Cameroon	183,568	27,058	70.4	13.1	905	1,952
Cape Verde	1,556	151	33.2	0.2	6	10
Central African Republic	240,533	7,745	80.4	4.4	74	866
Chad	495,753	12,375	77.4	9.8	915	643
Comoros	—	386	80.8 (1985)	0.2	14	59
Congo	132,046	649	61.1 (1985)	0.5	27	857
Côte d'Ivoire	124,502	14,247	58.8 (1985)	3.4	191	4,096
Djibouti	8,958	—	76.8	1.1	—	—
Egypt	386,660	10,066	39.5	15.5	14,702	2,019
Equatorial Guinea	10,831	—	57.9	—	—	82
Eritrea	48,000	—		—	—	
Ethiopia	471,776	53,784	75.7	73.9	7,000	2,074
Gabon	103,348	1,764	60.0	0.4	25	447
Gambia	4,363	687	82.6 (1985)	0.8	123	6
Ghana	92,100	10,502	54.5 (1985)	5.9	970	6,200
Guinea	94,927	2,811	78.1 (1985)	2.8	1,022	885
Guinea-Bissau	13,946	1,293	83.1 (1985)	1.2	171	61
Kenya	224,081	9,382	19.1	29.2	3,019	1,620
Lesotho	11,718	1,236	66.2	3.2	88	8
Liberia	37,741	1,440	72.5 (1985)	0.6	110	351
Libya	679,359	8,320	19.2	6.6	298	150
Madagascar	226,656	11,977	77.9	13.7	2,617	3,136
Malawi	45,745	9,340	81.1	2.6	685	459
Mali	478,838	8,081	82.4	17.1	2,156	145
Mauritania	395,954	792	66.0	9.8	74	6
Mauritius	718	409	15.7	0.1	2	16
Morocco	172,413	36,012	39.7 (1985)	22.9	2,954	912
Mozambique	309,494	12,085	83.4 (1985)	2.1	239	3,371
Namibia	317,873	2,556	19.5	7.4	32	220
Niger	489,189	13,938	78.0	10.7	2,258	253
Nigeria	356,668	124,710	43.1 (1986)	74.2	12,583	41,602
Rwanda	10,170	4,459	90.1	2.3	301	1,530
São Tomé and Principe	372	—	40.4	—	1	20
Senegal	75,954	9,073	79.5	8.8	857	62
Seychelles	175	—	9.1	—	—	—
Sierra Leone	27,699	2,510	10.4	—	478	105
Somalia	246,201	4,012	71.8	47.0	202	93
South Africa	471,444	50,865	9.8	53.7	4,646	1,250
Sudan	967,495	49,807	70.3 (1985)	58.4	5,691	159
Swaziland	6,703	788	18.8 (1986)	1.1	58	10
Tanzania	364,900	13,000	82.0	25.4	3,538	7,577
Togo	21,925	—	70.1	—	459	884
Tunisia	63,170	17,668	23.0	8.2	2,199	218
Uganda	91,073	25,907	82.6	10.9	1,636	5,789
Zaire	905,564	30,347	67.4	6.3	1,377	19,126
Zambia	290,583	20,340	68.9	3.7	600	299
Zimbabwe	150,803	10,857	20.2	9.2	505	136
AMERICAS						
Antigua and Barbuda	171	—	9.0 (1982)	—	—	—
Argentina	1,068,298	105,019	11.7 (1985)	90.3	24,750	3,200
Bahamas	5,382	—	3.9	—	1	2
Barbados	166	127	4.7	0.2	2	7
Belize	8,865	216	17.6	0.1	27	4
Bolivia	424,162	8,911	42.3	22.7	761	1,298
Brazil	3,286,477	231,660	22.0	221.5	44,165	26,005
Canada	3,851,794	177,413	3.1	23.8	49,147	3,529
Chile	292,259	17,475	17.1	12.4	2,901	1,030
Colombia	439,734	20,927	31.8 (1985)	32.8	3,674	4,021
Costa Rica	19,730	2,042	24.8	2.1	249	125
Cuba	42,803	12,857	20.4	7.9	404	813
Dominica	18,680		25.8		—	26
Dominican Republic	18,815	5,583	22.0	3.7	576	347
Ecuador	109,483	10,521	30.8	8.8	1,557	474

Table 2. World Agriculture—*cont.*   325

COUNTRY	1994 LAND AREA (SQ MI)	1994 CROP LAND (IN ACRES)	%LABOR FORCE IN AGRICULTURE 1990	TOTAL LIVESTOCK (MILLIONS)	GRAINS OUTPUT (1,000 METRIC TONS) 1992	ROOTS AND TUBERS OUTPUT (1,000 METRIC TONS) 1992
El Salvador	8,124	2,830	10.4	1.7	992	53
Grenada	133	—	14.3	—	—	4
Guatemala	42,042	7,278	58.1	3.9	1,404	21
Guyana	83,000	1,911	24.4 (1985)	0.5	276	32
Haiti	10,714	3,494	67.6 (1985)	4.2	240	673
Honduras	43,278	7,027	46.1	3.4	692	35
Jamaica	4,243	1,039	23.0	1.0	4	287
Mexico	756,062	95,405	26.2	69.7	24,742	1,342
Netherlands Amer Dependencies	13,103	—	—	—	—	—
Nicaragua	50,193	4,915	30.0	2.6	463	96
Panama	29,761	2,525	27.4 (1985)	1.8	281	1,282
Paraguay	157,046	8,556	46.5 (1985)	11.6	803	3,388
Peru	496,224	14,402	34.0	21.1	1,497	1,819
St. Kitts and Nevis	101	—	29.6 (1984)	—	—	1
St. Lucia	238	—	22.9 (1985)	—	—	11
St. Vincent and the Grenadines	150	—	25.7 (1980)	—	1	18
Suriname	63,039	263	2.9	0.1	190	4
Trinidad and Tobago	1,981	463	42.9	0.2	17	11
United States	3,618,770	733,263	2.8	170.6	353,353	19,207
Uruguay	68,037	5,035	14.5 (1985)	34.6	1,337	215
Venezuela	352,143	15,039	11.5	18.7	2,027	722
ASIA AND OCEANIA						
Afghanistan	251,772	31,097	57.7	18.0	2,400	224
Armenia	11,500	—	—	—	275	343
Australia	2,978,133	188,876	4.8	197.2	24,939	1,139
Azerbaijan	33,400	—	32.3	—	1,305	170
Bahrain	263	8	2.3	0.0	—	—
Bangladesh	55,598	35,236	64.2	45.9	28,538	1,850
Bhutan	18,147	510	87.2	0.6	106	55
Brunei Darussalam	10,747	—	3.5	—	1	1
Burma (Myanmar)	261,216	38,876	67.6	15.0	14,340	230
China	3,705,392	372,830	60.0	684.1	400,409	147,898
Cyprus	3,571	602	12.2	0.9	182	172
Federated States of Micronesia	271	—	41.6	—	24,742	1,342
Fiji	7,054	927	44.1 (1986)	0.3	35	66
India	1,269,340	652,819	81.4 (1986)	449.7	199,585	21,920
Indonesia	735,356	84,942	54.0	39.5	55,757	19,224
Iran	636,294	58,108	25.0 (1986)	75.9	16,602	2,800
Iraq	169,236	21,042	11.6	13.2	1,255	195
Israel	8,019	1,687	3.1	1.0	274	220
Japan	145,869	17,745	6.2	16.7	14,428	5,612
Jordan	34,444	1,544	7.3	2.0	148	59
Kampuchea	69,900	11,799	70.4	4.5	2,304	117
Kazakhstan	1,048,900	—	17.9	—	29,427	2,200
Kiribati	332	—	71.0	—	—	14
Korea, (DPRK)	46,540	7,722	44.1 1982	5.2	9,872	2,475
Korea, Republic of (ROK)	38,232	8,143	16.3	7.0	7,873	793
Kuwait	6,880	15	1.3	0.3	5	—
Kyrgyzstan	76,600	—	18.8	—	1,417	325
Laos	91,429	3,517	72.2	3.5	1,561	207
Lebanon	4,015	1,162	19.1 (1986)	0.7	75	252
Malaysia	127,317	18,842	25.3	4.0	1,896	524
Maldives	115	—	25.0	—	—	9
Marshall Islands	70	—	18.7	—	—	—
Mongolia	604,827	5,351	27.6	24.9	492	76
Nauru	8.2	—	—	—	—	—
Nepal	54,363	10,243	80.5	16.1	4,710	873
New Zealand	104,629	1,591	9.4	67.5	819	314
Oman	82,031	236	27.2	1.2	2	5
Pakistan	307,375	80,116	44.6	98.4	22,078	866
Palau	—	—	—	—	—	76
Papua New Guinea	178,703	1,525	77.0	—	3	1,282
Philippines	115,830	30,772	41.2	14.9	13,755	2,221
Qatar	4,416	—	1.6	—	4	—
Saudi Arabia	829,997	9,131	9.9	10.4	4,746	50
Singapore	239	4	0.3	0.4	—	—
Solomon Islands	11,158	220	23.7	0.1	—	111
Sri Lanka	25,332	7,336	40.9	3.4	2,285	411
Syria	71,498	21,722	26.3	16.4	4,363	420
Taiwan	13,900	—	12.2	—	3,303	5,430

COUNTRY	1994 LAND AREA (SQ MI)	1994 CROP LAND (IN ACRES)	%LABOR FORCE IN AGRICULTURE 1990	TOTAL LIVESTOCK (MILLIONS)	GRAINS OUTPUT (1,000 METRIC TONS) 1992	ROOTS AND TUBERS OUTPUT (1,000 METRIC TONS) 1992
Tajikistan	55,200	—	42.9	—	318	165
Thailand	198,116	85,483	45.4	15.6	22,266	21,348
Tonga	289	—	42.1 (1986)	—	—	90
Turkey	300,946	107,761	54.9	68.7	30,201	4,501
Turkmenistan	188,400	—	42.9	—	780	32
Turks and Caicos Islands	—	—	—	—	—	—
Tuvalu	10	—	68.0	—	—	—
United Arab Emirates	32,270	151	6.3	1.0	8	4
Uzbekistan	172,700	—	29.1	—	2,185	335
Vanuatu	4,707	—	61.1	—	1	51
Viet-Nam	128,066	25,483	72.7	18.8	22,165	5,400
Western Samoa	1,093	—	63.6 (1986)	—	—	41
Yemen	203,850	6,212	56.3 (1986)	8.4	811	165
EUROPE						
Albania	11,100	2,730	47.0	3.7	588	60
Andorra	—	—	1.2	—	—	2
Austria	32,375	5,811	7.2	6.7	4,310	780
Belarus	80,100	—	20.1	—	6,340	8,000
Belgium	12,780	3,162	2.4	9.7	2,244	1,800
Bosnia and Herzegovina	19,736	—	3.8	—	1,348	296
Bulgaria	42,822	16,046	13.1	14.6	5,845	550
Croatia	21,824	—	4.0	—	2,355	480
Czech Republic	78,864	—	11.6	—	10,319	2,686
Denmark	16,637	9,927	5.4	11.7	7,106	1,500
Estonia	17,400	—	12.8	—	594	648
Finland	130,552	9,405	8.1	2.8	2,803	673
France	212,934	74,317	7.5	47.1	60,420	6,495
Georgia	26,900	—	27.1	—	459	200
Germany	137,819	47,931	3.0	59.2	34,749	10,975
Greece	50,961	15,189	22.2	18.0	5,458	967
Hungary	35,919	20,417	12.7	11.4	10,435	1,203
Iceland	39,768	31	4.8	0.9	—	11
Ireland	27,135	3,641	11.5	12.7	2,080	620
Italy	116,321	46,672	7.5	31.2	19,608	2,512
Latvia	24,900	—	5.7	—	1,103	1,000
Liechtenstein	61.8	—	2.4	—	—	127
Lithuania	25,200	—	18.6	—	2,198	12
Luxembourg	999	—	3.4	—	—	1,079
Malta	122	—	2.1	—	9	24
Moldova	13,000	—	35.7	—	2,106	300
Monaco	1.21	—	—	—	—	—
Netherlands	14,413	3,591	4.2	20.2	1,292	7,595
Norway	125,058	3,336	5.5	4.0	901	450
Poland	120,726	56,884	30.1	34.6	19,969	23,388
Portugal	35,672	12,251	11.3	10.3	1,275	1,317
Romania	91,699	38,764	29.1	35.3	12,285	2,600
Russian Federation	6,591,100	—	13.5	—	102,117	37,800
San Marino	23.4	—	2.1	—	—	—
Slovakia	30,457	—	13.9	—	—	—
Slovenia	7,817	—	12.7	—	434	368
Spain	194,896	78,475	9.5	49.1	14,358	5,314
Sweden	173,730	10,911	3.2	4.4	3,757	1,144
Switzerland	15,942	1,591	5.4	4.2	1,213	737
Ukraine	233,000	—	27.3	—	35,530	20,427
United Kingdom	94,548	25,703	2.1	49.0	22,190	7,882
Vatican	—	—	—	—	—	—
Yugoslavia (the former)	39,424	—	5.0	—	—	711

—Nil, not available, or does not apply.

Table 3. World Energy Production and Consumption 327

COUNTRY	ELECTRIC POWER TOTAL (1,000,000 KWH) 1991	HYDRO-POWER % 1991	NUCLEAR FUEL % 1991	COAL AND LIGNITE PRODUCTION (1,000 METRIC TONS) 1991	NATURAL GAS OUTPUT (1,000,000 CU M) 1991	CRUDE PETROLEUM PROVED RESERVES (1,000,000 BARRELS) 1993	CRUDE PETROLEUM PRODUCTION (1,000,000 BARRELS) 1992	(1,000,000 BARRELS) 1991
AFRICA								
Algeria	17,345	1.7	—	15	52,089	10,387	423	176
Angola	1,840	73.9	—	—	566	1,334	172	111
Benin	5	—	—	—	—	20	1.4	—
Botswana	522	—	—	400	—	—	—	—
Burkina Faso	157	—	—	—	—	—	—	—
Burundi	136	98.5	—	—	—	—	—	—
Cameroon	2,712	42.9	—	1	—	326	50	5
Cape Verde	36	—	—	—	—	—	—	—
Central African Republic	96	81.3	—	—	—	—	—	—
Chad	85	—	—	—	—	—	—	—
Comoros	16	12.5	—	—	—	—	—	—
Congo	482	99.4	—	1	2	725	63	5
Côte d'Ivoire	2,376	67.1	—	—	—	100	0.5	15
Djibouti	178	—	—	—	—	—	—	—
Egypt	40,460	24.5	—	1,200	8,917	3,593	346	177
Equatorial Guinea	18	11.1	—	—	—	4	0.4	—
Eritrea	—	—	—	—	—	—	—	—
Ethiopia	973	80.7	6.9	—	—	—	—	5
Gabon	914	77.4	—	—	102	768	107	8
Gambia	68	—	—	—	—	—	—	—
Ghana	6,152	99.3	—	—	—	0.5	—	7
Guinea	521	33.8	—	—	—	—	—	—
Guinea-Bissau	41	—	—	—	—	—	—	—
Kenya	3,227	85.8	9.3	—	—	—	—	15
Lesotho	—	—	—	—	—	—	—	—
Liberia	450	35.6	—	—	—	—	—	—
Libya	19,500	—	—	—	6,773	38,190	538	133
Madagascar	569	56.2	—	—	—	—	—	—
Malawi	750	98.1	—	—	—	—	—	—
Mali	276	67.0	—	—	—	—	—	—
Mauritania	143	17.5	—	—	—	—	—	6
Mauritius	813	9.2	—	—	—	—	—	—
Morocco	9,834	12.5	—	555	31	2	0.1	41
Mozambique	490	10.2	—	42	—	—	—	—
Namibia	—	—	—	—	—	—	—	—
Niger	168	—	—	157	—	—	—	—
Nigeria	9,955	22.3	—	90	4,703	18,213	704	88
Rwanda	179	98.9	—	—	—	—	—	—
São Tomé and Principe	15	53.3	—	—	—	—	—	6
Senegal	756	—	—	—	—	—	—	—
Seychelles	102	—	—	—	—	—	—	—
Sierra Leone	230	—	—	—	—	—	—	2
Somalia	110	—	—	—	—	—	—	0.8
South Africa	169,645	0.5	2.5	176,174	—	—	—	116
Sudan	1,329	70.6	—	—	—	300	—	8
Swaziland	—	—	—	—	—	—	—	—
Tanzania	901	69.0	—	4	—	—	—	—
Togo	60	8.3	—	—	—	—	—	—
Tunisia	5,555	0.8	—	—	238	468	38	13
Uganda	783	99.1	—	—	—	—	—	—
Zaire	6,168	97.4	—	128	—	87	10	3
Zambia	7,775	99.5	—	380	—	—	—	4
Zimbabwe	9,565	36.9	—	5,600	—	—	—	—
AMERICAS								
Afghanistan	1,015	68.0	—	135	297	—	—	—
Antigua and Barbuda	95	—	—	—	—	—	—	—
Argentina	54,048	30.4	14.4	292	17,166	1,630	202	174
Armenia	9,500	15.0	—	50	170	—	—	—
Bahamas	965	—	—	—	—	—	—	—
Barbados	527	—	—	—	22	6	0.5	2
Belize	105	—	—	—	—	—	—	—
Bolivia	2,150	58.8	—	—	3,078	118	8	8
Brazil	234,366	92.9	0.6	5,124	3,757	3,667	238	410
Canada	507,913	60.7	—	50,622	122,279	5,668	501	486
Chile	19,961	51.3	—	3,097	1,150	132	5	46
Colombia	36,661	75.6	—	6,553	4,078	1,643	160	92
Costa Rica	3,872	94.2	—	—	—	—	—	—
Cuba	16,255	0.5	—	200	3	128	18	7

COUNTRY	ELECTRIC POWER TOTAL (1,000,000 KWH) 1991	ELECTRIC POWER HYDRO-POWER % 1991	NUCLEAR FUEL % 1991	COAL AND LIGNITE PRODUCTION (1,000 METRIC TONS) 1991	NATURAL GAS OUTPUT (1,000,000 CU M) 1991	CRUDE PETROLEUM PROVED RESERVES (1,000,000 BARRELS) 1993	CRUDE PETROLEUM PRODUCTION (1,000,000 BARRELS) 1992	CRUDE PETROLEUM (1,000,000 BARRELS) 1991
Dominica	31	51.6	—	—	—	—	—	—
Dominican Republic	5,330	15.9	—	—	—	—	—	—
Ecuador	6,952	72.8	—	—	102	2,040	119	45
El Salvador	2,300	72.8	18.3	—	—	—	—	5
Grenada	52	—	—	—	—	—	—	—
Guatemala	2,330	89.7	—	—	8	207	2	5
Guyana	225	2.2	—	—	—	—	—	—
Haiti	475	68.4	—	—	—	—	—	—
Honduras	1,105	80.1	—	—	—	—	—	—
Jamaica	2,735	4.8	—	—	—	—	—	7
Mexico	126,375	19.2	6.6	10,700	25,499	51,225	1,009	471
Nicaragua	1,043	25.2	28.3	—	—	—	—	3
Panama	2,907	70.0	—	—	—	—	—	—
Paraguay	29,780	99.9	—	—	—	—	—	3
Peru	14,828	76.4	—	140	1,314	782	42	51
St. Kitts and Nevis	40	—	—	—	—	—	—	—
St. Lucia	105	—	—	—	—	—	—	—
St. Vincent and the Grenadines	51	76.5	—	—	—	—	—	—
Suriname	1,400	79.6	—	—	—	49	1.5	1.2
Trinidad and Tobago	3,640	—	—	—	4,635	541	51	41
United States	3,079,085	9.4	19.9	901,877	537,542	22,845	2,617	4,921
Uruguay	7,017	87.1	—	—	—	—	—	10
Venezuela	57,150	60	—	2,696	22,877	63,300	865	357
ASIA AND OCEANIA								
Australia	156,883	10.3	—	214,030	24,231	3,155	195	195
Azerbaijan	23,300	—	—	—	11,655	3,300	86	—
Bahrain	3,495	—	—	—	4,783	56	15	82
Bangladesh	8,930	9.4	—	—	5,335	1.5	1.8	9
Bhutan	513	99.9	—	2	—	—	—	—
Brunei Darussalam	1,242	—	—	—	8,396	1,130	66	0.01
Burma (Myanmar)	2,400	47.9	—	83	841	100	6	7
China	677,550	18.5	—	1,058,208	15,392	29,600	1,061	905
Cyprus	2,077	—	—	15	—	—	—	6
Federated States of Micronesia	—	—	—	—	—	—	—	—
Fiji	472	81.6	—	—	—	—	—	—
India	309,370	21.8	1.8	224,500	13,796	5,935	211	405
Indonesia	44,660	19.1	0.5	13,715	47,927	8,350	546	299
Iran	56,900	11.6	—	1,400	26,595	61,300	1,220	310
Iraq	20,810	1.5	—	—	1,620	99,840	161	100
Israel	21,320	—	—	—	23	3	0.1	60
Japan	888,086	11.9	24.0	8,069	2,326	60	6	1,432
Jordan	3,723	0.2	—	—	161	4	0.1	17
Kampuchea	70	42.9	—	—	—	—	—	—
Kazakhstan	86,128	—	—	130,315	7,885	—	194	—
Kiribati	7	—	—	—	—	—	—	—
Korea, (DPRK)	53,500	59.3	—	89,000	—	—	—	21
Korea, Republic of (ROK)	132,228	3.8	42.6	15,058	—	—	—	411
Kuwait	9,100	—	—	—	2,648	92,428	312	40
Kyrgyzstan	14,903	—	—	2,250	68	—	0.9	—
Laos	972	95.2	—	1	—	—	—	—
Lebanon	4,750	11.8	—	—	—	—	—	4
Malaysia	28,362	15.7	—	180	20,802	4,260	230	72
Maldives	28	—	—	—	—	—	—	—
Marshall Islands	—	—	—	—	—	—	—	4
Mongolia	3,500	—	—	7,775	—	—	—	—
Nauru	29	—	—	—	—	—	—	—
Nepal	890	97.0	—	—	—	—	—	—
New Zealand	29,556	73.9	5.1	2,714	6,308	160	13	32
Oman	5,548	—	—	—	3,457	4,740	270	25
Pakistan	47,334	38.7	0.8	3,054	13,470	147	22	52
Palau	—	—	—	—	—	—	—	—
Papua New Guinea	1,790	25.7	—	—	—	146	19	—
Philippines	22,484	22.9	25.6	1,265	—	180	6	80
Qatar	4,716	—	—	—	9,093	4,339	167	20
Saudi Arabia	47,710	—	—	—	32,808	250,600	2,975	534
Singapore	16,597	—	—	—	—	—	—	326
Solomon Islands	30	—	—	—	—	—	—	—
Sri Lanka	3,377	92.3	—	—	—	—	—	12
Syria	12,179	51.3	—	—	3,469	3,000	188	80

Table 3. World Energy Production and Consumption—*cont.* 329

COUNTRY	ELECTRIC POWER TOTAL (1,000,000 KWH) 1991	ELECTRIC POWER HYDRO-POWER % 1991	ELECTRIC POWER NUCLEAR FUEL % 1991	COAL AND LIGNITE PRODUCTION (1,000 METRIC TONS) 1991	NATURAL GAS OUTPUT (1,000,000 CU M) 1991	CRUDE PETROLEUM PROVED RESERVES (1,000,000 BARRELS) 1993	CRUDE PETROLEUM PRODUCTION (1,000,000 BARRELS) 1992	CRUDE PETROLEUM (1,000,000 BARRELS) 1991
Taiwan	89,639	6.1	37.8	403	767	4	0.4	—
Tajikistan	17,500	—	—	313	93	—	0.7	—
Thailand	52,486	8.7	—	14,689	8,376	242	18	87
Tonga	22	—	—	—	—	—	—	—
Turkey	60,338	37.7	0.2	46,178	201	281	30	161
Turkmenistan	17,171	—	—	—	84,300	740	43	—
Turks and Caicos Islands	—	—	—	—	—	—	—	—
Tuvalu	—	—	—	—	—	—	—	—
United Arab Emirates	13,790	—	—	—	25,516	67,747	837	65
Uzbekistan	57,400	—	—	6,200	41,600	—	21	62
Vanuatu	26	—	—	—	—	—	—	—
Viet Nam	8,550	61.7	—	5,000	711	350	38	0.3
Western Samoa	47	42.6	—	—	—	—	—	—
Yemen	1,750	—	—	—	—	2,010	69	34
EUROPE								
Albania	2,800	91.1	—	1,850	136	185	6	8
Andorra	—	—	—	—	—	—	—	—
Austria	51,484	63.6	—	2,081	1,433	76	8	59
Belarus	38,700	—	—	—	210	—	—	210
Belgium	71,945	1.3	59.6	634	14	—	—	—
Bosnia and Herzegovina	14,632	20.9	—	—	—	—	—	—
Bulgaria	38,917	6.2	33.9	28,451	11	13	0.3	32
Croatia	8,833	65.5	—	—	2,061	151	10	—
Czech Republic	83,274	3.8	28.6	101,395	702	9	0.6	77
Denmark	36,303	0.1	2.1	13,513	3,769	715	57	64
Estonia	14,627	—	—	—	—	—	—	—
Finland	58,137	22.5	33.6	—	—	—	—	—
France	454,702	13.6	72.9	12,092	3,356	166	23	555
Georgia	14,200	—	—	700	45	—	—	667
Germany	573,752	3.7	28.4	458,102	21,127	225	24	667
Greece	35,813	8.9	—	52,695	102	41	5	92
Hungary	30,039	0.6	45.9	16,957	4,774	122	14	49
Iceland	4,494	93.5	6.3	—	—	—	—	—
Ireland	15,147	6.4	—	1	2,352	—	—	—
Italy	222,041	20.5	1.5	961	16,469	822	31	533
Latvia	5,600	—	—	—	—	—	—	—
Liechtenstein	—	—	—	—	—	—	—	—
Lithuania	29,363	1.5	—	—	—	—	—	—
Luxembourg	1,415	56.4	—	—	—	—	—	—
Malta	1,100	—	—	—	—	—	—	—
Moldova	15,690	—	—	4,576	—	—	—	52
Monaco	—	—	—	—	—	—	—	—
Netherlands	74,252	0.2	4.5	—	58,656	329	24	355
Norway	110,950	99.6	—	339	26,114	16,788	800	94
Poland	134,696	2.5	—	209,782	3,617	36	1.4	87
Portugal	29,871	30.7	—	270	—	—	—	37
Romania	56,912	25.0	—	3,118	25,100	1,245	50	114
Russian Federation	1,068,000	15.4	10.9	353,000	643,000	156,700	2,911	3,700
San Marino	—	—	—	—	—	—	—	—
Slovakia	22,731	—	—	4,149	313	7	0.5,	—
Slovenia	12,399	24.0	37.3	—	24	—	0.02	—
Spain	155,704	18.2	35.7	33,562	1,308	23	8	396
Sweden	147,730	43.1	52.2	28	—	—	—	125
Switzerland	57,802	57.8	39.7	—	—	—	—	34
Ukraine	279,000	—	—	135,600	28,100	—	36	—
United Kingdom	322,133	1.9	21.9	96,144	53,669	4,554	684	591
Vatican	—	—	—	—	—	—	—	—
Yugoslavia (the former)	38,488	24.2	5.6	40,105	846	130	7	90

—Nil, not available, or does not apply.

COUNTRY	GROWTH RATE OF GDP 1992	CEMENT 1991 (1,000 METRIC TONS)	STEEL 1992 (NATIONS PRODUCING 2 MILLION METRIC TONS +)	MOTOR VEHICLES 1991	% SHARE OF EXPORTS IN GDP	% OF GDP IN INDUSTRY	SUGAR (1,000 METRIC TONS) 1990
AFRICA							
Algeria	2.6	—	—	—	27	30	16
Angola	1.7	—	—	—	43	60	29
Benin	-2.3	500	—	—	23	15	—
Botswana	6.5	—	—	—	—	53	—
Burkina Faso	0.5	—	—	—	12	23	22
Burundi	1.3	—	—	—	9	5	—
Cameroon	-5.7	—	—	—	20	30	—
Cape Verde	2.7	—	—	—	21	4	—
Central African Republic	-1.9	—	—	—	12	14	—
Chad	0.3	—	—	—	19	15	28
Comoros	1.6	—	—	—	16	10	—
Congo	-6.3	58	—	—	37	33	35
Côte d'Ivoire	-0.3	700	—	—	34	11	145
Djibouti	-1.0	—	—	—	60	11	—
Egypt	0.3	9,832	2.5	—	29	18	977
Equatorial Guinea	13.0	—	—	—	129	—	—
Eritrea	—	—	—	—	—	—	—
Ethiopia	-7.5	345	—	—	7	12	171.4
Gabon	2.2	—	—	—	42	45	—
Gambia	3	—	—	—	63	5.8	—
Ghana	3.6	678.6	—	—	16	15	—
Guinea	3.2	—	—	—	21	27	15
Guinea-Bissau	3.1	—	—	—	14	10	—
Kenya	0.4	1,512	—	—	27	13	414
Lesotho	1.3	50	—	—	19	11	—
Liberia	—	2,700	—	—	—	22	—
Libya	—	—	—	—	—	7.6	—
Madagascar	1.0	2000	—	—	17	—	111,000
Malawi	-8.0	101	—	—	24	18	178
Mali	4.0	20	—	—	14	10	23
Mauritania	1.8	—	—	—	39	33	—
Mauritius	5.8	—	—	—	64	25	634,224
Morocco	-3.0	5,381	—	—	22	27	—
Mozambique	-4.5	73.2	—	—	29	—	—
Namibia	3.9	—	—	—	58	35	—
Niger	-6.2	27	—	—	14	13	—
Nigeria	4.1	3,500	—	—	3539	8.5	—
Rwanda	2.5	57	—	—	6	17	—
São Tomé and Principe	1.5	—	—	—	24	—	—
Senegal	2.9	380	—	—	23	15	78
Seychelles	2.0	—	—	—	67	10	—
Sierra Leone	-4.0	—	—	—	26	—	—
Somalia	—	—	—	—	10	—	41.2
South Africa	-2.1	6,147	9.1	—	25	40	1,359
Sudan	11.3	—	—	—	5	11	—
Swaziland	-2.0	2,475	—	—	77	26	486,800
Tanzania	3.7	300	—	—	17	7	106
Togo	-9.7	370	—	—	32	20	—
Tunisia	8.0	3,215.1	—	—	38	25	—
Uganda	2.1	27	—	—	6	5	29
Zaire	-10.6	—	—	—	11	—	70
Zambia	—	432,000	—	—	28	50	147,000
Zimbabwe	-7.9	996	—	—	22	38	493
AMERICAS							
Antigua and Barbuda	3.0	—	—	—	—	—	—
Argentina	8.6	4,439	2.7	138,958	7	26	—
Bahamas	1.0	—	—	—	—	15	—
Barbados	-3.7	—	—	—	63	10	54,500
Belize	5.0	—	—	—	71	12	100,297
Bolivia	3.8	588,468	—	—	15	32	—
Brazil	-0.9	25,920	23.9	960,044	10	39	8,070
Canada	-1.1	—	13.9	1,872,708	25	34	—
Chile	10.3	2,251	—	—	31	34	281
Colombia	3.7	6,389.3	—	—	19	20	1,633.2
Costa Rica	7.3	315	—	—	39	19	210
Cuba	-20	3,758.8	—	—	—	—	7,328.8
Dominica	7.0	—	—	—	54	18	—
Dominican Republic	7.4	—	—	—	29	20	—

Table 4. World Industrial Production—*cont.* 331

COUNTRY	GROWTH RATE OF GDP 1992	CEMENT 1991 (1,000 METRIC TONS)	STEEL 1992 (NATIONS PRODUCING 2 MILLION METRIC TONS +)	MOTOR VEHICLES 1991	% SHARE OF EXPORTS IN GDP	% OF GDP IN INDUSTRY	SUGAR (1,000 METRIC TONS) 1990
Ecuador	3.5	—	—	—	31	40	—
El Salvador	4.2	641	—	—	14	22	213
Grenada	5.2	—	—	—	53	9	—
Guatemala	4.8	873	—	—	17	18	998
Guyana	8.3	211	—	—	—	24	163
Haiti	-5.0	—	—	—	12	15	—
Honduras	4.9	15,265	—	—	29	15	4,130
Jamaica	2.0	360	—	—	64	25	201
Mexico	2.6	24,683	8.4	989,373	14	28	3,406
Nicaragua	1.2	—	—	—	16	25	212
Panama	8.5	—	—	—	31	9	150.6
Paraguay	1.8	—	—	—	23	17	97,491
Peru	-2.8	2,103	—	—	10	24	6,711
St. Kitts and Nevis	2.1	—	—	—	47	11	20,159
St. Lucia	7.2	—	—	—	73	12	—
St. Vincent and the Grenadines	3.0	—	—	—	—	14	—
Suriname	-2.5	24,128	—	—	27	27	42
Trinidad and Tobago	0.1	438	—	—	44	40	118
United States	2.1	—	84.3	8,810,521	11	—	—
Uruguay	7.4	—	—	—	22	25	—
Venezuela	7.3	5,996	3.4	—	26	25	499
ASIA AND OCEANIA							
Afghanistan	0.0	70	—	—	—	25	—
Armenia	-52.2	1,466	—	—	—	—	—
Australia	-0.6	7,075	6.9	293,012	18	32	—
Azerbaijan	-35.5	—	—	—	—	—	—
Bahrain	—	—	—	—	119	44	—
Bangladesh	4.2	—	—	—	10	10	242
Bhutan	3.0	169,624	—	—	34	18	—
Brunei Darussalam	1.0	—	—	—	—	52.4	—
Burma (Myanmar)	11.2	262.4	—	—	2	10	24.5
China	12.0	209,710.8	80.0	708,820	20	—	5,819.5
Cyprus	6.0	—	—	—	46	16.5	—
Federated States of Micronesia	—	—	—	—	—	—	—
Fiji	3.1	78.9	—	—	55	13	389
India	4.3	51,660	18.1	353,564	10	25	12,852
Indonesia	6.3	15,600	3.1	—	29	40	—
Iran	6.4	11,926	2.9	—	17	30	418
Iraq	—	13,000	—	—	—	10	—
Israel	5.0	2,868	—	—	—	20	—
Japan	4.5	89,564	98.1	13,245,432	10	30	—
Jordan	11.3	1,780	—	—	43	20	—
Kampuchea	—	78	—	—	—	—	—
Kazakhstan	-14.0	—	4.0	—	—	30	—
Kiribati	1.0	—	—	—	—	4	—
Korea, (DPRK)	-2.0	16,300	7.0	—	—	—	—
Korea, Republic of (ROK)	4.8	43,270	28.1	1,497,818	29	45	1,077
Kuwait	80	800	—	—	36	—	—
Kyrgyzstan	—	1049.3	—	—	—	—	—
Laos	7.0	720	—	—	10	18	—
Lebanon	—	900	—	—	24	—	—
Malaysia	8.0	5,881	—	99,300	78	—	—
Maldives	10.1	—	—	—	—	6	—
Marshall Islands	—	—	—	—	—	—	—
Mongolia	-7.6	132.5	—	—	30	—	—
Nauru	—	—	—	—	—	—	—
Nepal	2.1	214,838	—	—	20	7	52,000
New Zealand	-0.4	581	—	—	29	20	—
Oman	7.7	—	—	—	—	—	—
Pakistan	7.8	4,153	—	—	17	20	2,298
Palau	—	—	—	—	—	21	—
Papua New Guinea	9.4	—	—	—	487	21	45
Philippines	0.0	6,360	—	—	29	34	1,740
Qatar	3	—	—	—	—	64	—
Saudi Arabia	2.9	10,000	—	—	46	37	—
Singapore	6.5	—	—	—	147	28	—
Solomon Islands	8.2	—	—	—	54	5	—
Sri Lanka	4.1	566	—	—	32	20	24
Syria	—	3,049	—	—	29	18	—

Table 4. World Industrial Production—*cont.*

COUNTRY	GROWTH RATE OF GDP 1992	CEMENT 1991 (1,000 METRIC TONS)	STEEL 1992 (NATIONS PRODUCING 2 MILLION METRIC TONS +)	MOTOR VEHICLES 1991	% SHARE OF EXPORTS IN GDP	% OF GDP IN INDUSTRY	SUGAR (1,000 METRIC TONS) 1990
Taiwan	5.2	19,398.6	10.7	—	—	40	398.9
Tajikistan	-25.0	999.9	—	—	—	—	—
Thailand	7.5	18,040	—	—	36	26	1,869
Tonga	2.5	—	—	—	—	11	—
Turkey	5.5	28,607	10.3	—	22	28	1,593
Turkmenistan	—	—	—	—	—	—	—
Turks and Caicos Islands	—	—	—	—	—	—	—
Tuvalu	—	—	—	—	—	—	—
United Arab Emirates	—	—	—	—	69	56	—
Uzbekistan	-9.6	—	—	—	—	—	—
Vanuatu	1.0	—	—	—	—	10	—
Viet-Nam	7.4	3,127.1	—	—	—	30	376.1
Western Samoa	-3.3	—	—	—	31	14	—
Yemen	—	700	—	—	16	18	—
EUROPE							
Albania	-35	646	—	—	12	—	—
Andorra	—	1,000	—	—	—	—	—
Austria	3.0	5,017	4.0	19,198	41	—	438
Belarus	-10.0	—	—	—	47	50	—
Belgium	1.4	7,184	10.3	337,661	73	—	1,121
Bosnia and Herzegovina	-37	797	—	—	—	—	—
Bulgaria	-6.1	4,710	—	—	45	37	185
Croatia	-25	1,705	—	—	—	—	100
Czech Republic	4	—	—	—	58	60	N.A
Denmark	2.0	2,019	—	—	37	—	—
Estonia	-25.8	—	—	—	33	—	—
Finland	-6.2	1,343	3.1	—	22	—	263
France	1.4	25,884	18.0	3,610,773	23	—	4,130
Georgia	-45.6	31,920	—	—	40	—	—
Germany	0.7	—	39.7	5,032,812	24	—	—
Greece	1.4	10,940	—	—	23	20	349
Hungary	-5.1	2,529	—	5,001	33	—	605.5
Iceland	0.3	106.2	—	—	33	—	—
Ireland	1.3	—	—	—	62	37	—
Italy	1.0	—	24.9	1,878,289	20	35	—
Latvia	-44.8	—	—	—	35	—	—
Liechtenstein	—	—	—	—	—	—	—
Lithuania	-39.3	—	—	—	—	—	150.5
Luxembourg	2.5	—	3.1	—	94	25	—
Malta	5.5	—	—	—	85	27	—
Moldova	-21.3	172	—	—	38	—	242.4
Monaco	—	—	—	—	—	—	—
Netherlands	2.2	3,546	5.4	110,812	54	25	1,047
Norway	4.1	1,137.3	—	—	45	—	—
Poland	1.8	12,012	9.8	193,172	19	—	1,639
Portugal	1.1	6,000	—	—	35	40	—
Romania	-14.9	7,405	5.4	—	28	48	344
Russian Federation	-19.0	—	67.0	2,012,600	—	—	3,758
San Marino	—	—	—	—	—	—	—
Slovakia	-7.0	2,680	—	—	28	—	189
Slovenia	10.0	974	—	—	64	—	50
Spain	2.5	28,092	12.3	2,081,711	17	—	—
Sweden	1.1	—	4.4	344,690	28	—	—
Switzerland	0.2	5,206	—	—	35	—	—
Ukraine	-14.0	22,729	41.8	—	—	—	5,388
United Kingdom	-1.9	12,297	16.1	1,454,041	24	—	1,220
Vatican	—	—	—	—	—	—	—
Yugoslavia (the former)	—	2,411	—	239,591	—	—	470

—Nil, not available, or does not apply.

Table 5. Economic Development Assistance: Millions of Dollars

333

COUNTRY	OECD (1881-90)	OPEC (1981-90)	OFFICIAL DEVELOPMENT RECEIVED (1946-90)
AFRICA			
Algeria	—	527	3,745.2
Angola	—	—	—
Benin	—	—	1,286.2
Botswana	—	—	1,024.8
Burkina Faso	—	—	1,805.4
Burundi	—	—	1,340.2
Cameroon	—	—	2,991.2
Cape Verde	—	—	—
Central African Republic	—	—	1,095.4
Chad	—	—	1,329.1
Comoros	—	—	—
Congo	—	—	971.0
Côte d'Ivoire	—	—	4,091.1
Djibouti	—	—	—
Egypt	—	—	15,121.8
Equatorial Guinea	—	—	—
Eritrea	—	—	—
Ethiopia	—	—	4,791.8
Gabon	—	—	702.2
Gambia	—	—	—
Ghana	—	—	3,050.6
Guinea	—	—	1,720.3
Guinea-Bissau	—	—	552.2
Kenya	—	—	5,834.9
Lesotho	—	—	727.6
Liberia	—	—	—
Libya	—	969	—
Madagascar	—	—	2,361.7
Malawi	—	—	2,568.7
Mali	—	—	2,516.0
Mauritania	—	—	1,286.0
Mauritius	—	—	587.6
Morocco	—	—	6,463.1
Mozambique	—	—	3,480.4
Namibia	—	—	—
Niger	—	—	1,895.6
Nigeria	—	459	4,193.1
Rwanda	—	—	1,554.4
São Tomé and Principe	—	—	—
Senegal	—	—	3,676.7
Seychelles	—	—	—
Sierra Leone	—	—	556.8
Somalia	—	—	2,457.2
South Africa	—	—	—
Sudan	—	—	4,843.1
Swaziland	—	—	—
Tanzania	—	—	5,373.2
Togo	—	—	1,234.1
Tunisia	—	—	—
Uganda	—	—	2,393.0
Zaire	—	—	—
Zambia	—	—	3,095.5
Zimbabwe	—	—	1,912.6
AMERICAS			
Antigua and Barbuda	—	—	—
Argentina	—	—	6,965.7
Bahamas	—	—	—
Barbados	—	—	—
Belize	—	—	—
Bolivia	—	—	3,145.2
Brazil	—	—	20,561.0
Canada	15,688	—	—
Chile	—	—	4,196.1
Colombia	—	—	7,541.9
Costa Rica	—	—	1,686.5
Cuba	—	—	—
Dominica	—	—	—
Dominican Republic	—	—	1,217.4
Ecuador	—	—	3,433.2
El Salvador	—	—	2,544.9
Grenada	—	—	—
Guatemala	—	—	2,391.5

COUNTRY	OECD (1881-90)	OPEC (1981-90)	OFFICIAL DEVELOPMENT RECEIVED (1946-90)
Guyana	—	—	—
Haiti	—	—	—
Honduras	—	—	2,661.8
Jamaica	—	—	1,953.4
Mexico	—	—	12,281.5
Nicaragua	—	—	1,735.6
Panama	—	—	1,441.3
Paraguay	—	—	—
Peru	—	—	4,591.9
St. Kitts and Nevis	—	—	—
St. Lucia	—	—	—
St. Vincent and the Grenadines	—	—	—
Suriname	—	—	—
Trinidad and Tobago	—	—	542.7
United States	79,174	—	—
Uruguay	—	—	995.9
Venezuela	—	697	1,414.9
ASIA AND OCEANIA			
Afghanistan	—	—	—
Armenia	—	—	—
Australia	7,674	—	—
Azerbaijan	—	—	—
Bahrain	—	—	—
Bangladesh	—	—	13,024.9
Bhutan	—	—	226.9
Brunei Darussalam	—	—	—
Burma (Myanmar)	—	—	11,927.7
China	—	—	11,925.7
Cyprus	—	—	—
Federated States of Micronesia	—	—	—
Fiji	—	—	—
India	—	—	33.194.7
Indonesia	—	—	20,432.5
Iran	—	-504	1,623.2
Iraq	—	-2	—
Israel	—	—	5,417.3
Japan	50,827	—	—
Jordan	—	—	—
Kampuchea	—	—	—
Kazakhstan	—	—	—
Kiribati	—	—	—
Korea, (DPRK)	—	—	—
Korea, Republic of (ROK)	—	—	9,033.9
Kuwait	—	8,062	—
Kyrgyzstan	—	—	—
Laos	—	—	610.1
Lebanon	—	—	—
Malaysia	—	—	4,371.5
Maldives	—	—	—
Marshall Islands	—	—	—
Mongolia	—	—	25.0
Nauru	—	—	—
Nepal	—	—	2,970.1
New Zealand	—	655	—
Oman	—	—	239.3
Pakistan	—	—	12,307.3
Palau	—	—	—
Papua New Guinea	—	—	2,552.0
Philippines	—	—	10,920.5
Qatar	—	434	—
Saudi Arabia	—	31,846	151.4
Singapore	—	—	137.0
Solomon Islands	—	—	—
Sri Lanka	—	—	3,976.8
Syria	—	—	2,508.7
Taiwan	—	—	—
Tajikistan	—	—	—
Thailand	—	—	8,828.5
Tonga	—	—	—
Turkey	—	—	10,306.6
Turkmenistan	—	—	—
Turks and Caicos Islands	—	—	—
Tuvalu	—	—	—

COUNTRY	OECD (1881-90)	OPEC (1981-90)	OFFICIAL DEVELOPMENT RECEIVED (1946-90)
United Arab Emirates	—	975	102.0
Uzbekistan	—	—	—
Vanuatu	—	—	—
Viet-Nam	—	—	—
Western Samoa	—	—	—
Yemen	—	—	2,273.0
EUROPE			
Albania	—	—	—
Andorra	—	—	—
Austria	2,218	—	—
Belarus	—	—	—
Belgium	2,251	—	—
Bosnia and Herzegovina	—	—	—
Bulgaria	—	—	—
Croatia	—	—	—
Czech Republic	—	—	—
Denmark	5,827	—	—
Estonia	—	—	—
Finland	3,294	—	—
France	23,945	—	—
Georgia	—	—	—
Germany	35,112	—	—
Greece	—	—	—
Hungary	—	—	—
Iceland	—	—	—
Ireland	163	—	—
Italy	17,166	—	—
Latvia	—	—	—
Liechtenstein	—	—	—
Lithuania	—	—	—
Luxembourg	—	—	—
Malta	—	—	—
Moldova	—	—	—
Monaco	—	—	—
Netherlands	15,056	—	—
Norway	—	—	—
Poland	—	—	—
Portugal	—	—	—
Romania	—	—	—
Russian Federation	—	—	—
San Marino	—	—	—
Slovakia	—	—	—
Slovenia	—	—	—
Spain	—	—	—
Sweden	10,714	—	—
Switzerland	3,752	—	—
Ukraine	—	—	—
United Kingdom	18,228	—	—
Vatican	—	—	—
Yugoslavia (the former)	—	—	—

—Nil, not available, or does not apply.

Table 6. World Social and Military Indicators

COUNTRY	ANNUAL % POP. INCREASE 1985-92	ANNUAL % INCREASE IN GNP PER CAPITA (1985-92)	MILITARY SPENDING % OF GDP 1993	DOCTORS PER 1,000 POP. 1988-92	NURSE-TO-DOCTOR-RATIO 1988-90	% OF SCHOOL AGED CHILDREN (6-23) ATTENDING SCHOOL 1990	% OF ILLITERATE ADULTS 1990
AFRICA							
Algeria	2.7	-2.0	2.5	0.26	4.7	60	42.6
Angola	2.9	—	—	0.07	16.4	32	58.3
Benin	3.2	-1.5	1.7	0.07	5.8	30	76.6
Botswana	3.4	8.1	4.9	—	—	64	—
Burkina Faso	2.8	0.9	—	0.03	8.2	17	81.1
Burundi	2.9	—	3.7	0.06	4.3	—	50.0
Cameroon	3.0	-6.7	2	0.08	6.4	52	45.9
Cape Verde	2.7	1.8	—	—	—	49	33.5
Central African Republic	2.7	-2.4	1.8	0.04	4.5	35	62.3
Chad	2.5	1.3	5.6	0.03	0.9	29	70.2
Comoros	3.7	-2.3	—	—	34	—	—
Congo	3.3	-3.0	—	—	—	—	43.4
Côte d'Ivoire	4.0	-5.7	2.3	0.06	4.8	37	46.2
Djibouti	2.9	—	—	—	—	—	—
Egypt	2.4	0.8	5	0.77	1.2	66	51.6
Equatorial Guinea	2.3	-0.3	—	—	—	64	49.8
Eritrea	—	—	—	—	—	—	—
Ethiopia	3.4	-2.0	—	0.03	2.4	17	—
Gabon	2.7	-2.1	3.2	—	—	29	39.3
Gambia	3.2	1.8	—	—	—	—	72.8
Ghana	3.3	1.2	1	0.04	9.1	46	39.7
Guinea	2.8	0.8	1.2	0.02	4.2	19	76.0
Guinea-Bissau	2.1	0.4	5-6	—	—	25	63.5
Kenya	3.5	0.6	2.9	0.14	3.2	58	31.0
Lesotho	2.7	0.8	13	—	—	58	—
Liberia	3.1	—	—	—	—	—	60.5
Libya	3.6	—	15	1.04	2.9	—	36.2
Madagascar	1.1	-1.7	2.2	0.12	3.5	38	19.8
Malawi	3.4	-0.3	1.6	0.02	2.8	11	—
Mali	2.8	-1.9	2	0.05	2.5	25	68.0
Mauritania	2.7	—	4.2	—	—	25	64.3
Mauritius	1.1	-0.1	0.2	—	—	57	20.1
Morocco	2.5	1.3	3.8	0.21	4.5	37	50.5
Mozambique	2.7	-1.3	8	0.02	13.1	24	67.1
Namibia	3.1	1.1	3.4	—	—	65	—
Niger	3.2	-1.5	1.3	0.03	11.3	14	71.6
Nigeria	2.9	3.5	1	0.15	6.0	37	49.8
Rwanda	3.0	-2.8	1.6	0.02	1.7	39	49.8
São Tomé and Principe	2.3	-1.8	—	—	—	—	—
Senegal	3.0	0.3	2	0.05	2.6	30	61.7
Seychelles	0.8	4.1	4	—	—	—	—
Sierra Leone	2.5	0.0	0.7	0.07	5.0	29	79.3
Somalia	3.1	—	—	0.07	7.1	—	75.9
South Africa	2.4	-1.3	2.5	0.61	4.5	—	—
Sudan	2.8	—	2.2	0.09	2.7	27	72.9
Swaziland	3.9	6.4	—	—	—	64	—
Tanzania	3.0	1.4	—	0.03	7.3	32	—
Togo	3.7	-1.5	3	0.08	6.2	54	56.7
Tunisia	2.0	2.1	3.7	.053	2.7	62	34.7
Uganda	3.1	1.8	15	0.04	8.4	41	51.7
Zaire	3.3	—	0.8	0.07	2.1	38	28.1
Zambia	3.5	-2.1	1	—	—	47	27.2
Zimbabwe	3.0	-0.6	6	0.16	6.1	66	33.1
AMERICAS							
Antigua and Barbuda	1.0	1.1	1	—	—	—	—
Argentina	1.3	0.5	—	2.99	0.2	82	4.7
Bahamas	1.9	-1.2	2.7	—	—	74	—
Barbados	0.3	0.6	0.7	—	—	67	—
Belize	2.6	6.3	2	—	—	—	—
Bolivia	2.5	1.0	1.6	0.48	0.7	55	22.5
Brazil	1.8	-0.7	3	1.46	0.1	60	18.9
Canada	1.4	0.3	2	2.22	4.7	89	—
Chile	1.7	6.1	3.4	0.46	0.8	66	6.6
Colombia	1.8	2.4	1.3	0.87	0.6	55	13.3
Costa Rica	2.5	2.6	0.5	—	—	56	7.2
Cuba	1.0	—	10	3.75	1.7	63	6.0
Dominica	-0.3	5.1	—	1.08	0.7	—	—
Dominican Republic	1.9	0.3	0.7	—	—	66	16.7

Table 6. World Social and Military Indicators—*cont.*   337

COUNTRY	ANNUAL % POP. INCREASE 1985-92	ANNUAL % INCREASE IN GNP PER CAPITA (1985-92)	MILITARY SPENDING % OF GDP 1993	DOCTORS PER 1,000 POP. 1988-92	NURSE-TO-DOCTOR-RATIO 1988-90	% OF SCHOOL AGED CHILDREN (6-23) ATTENDING SCHOOL 1990	% OF ILLITERATE ADULTS 1990
Ecuador	2.5	0.6	—	1.04	0.3	68	12.7
El Salvador	1.8	0.9	3-4	0.64	1.5	51	27.0
Grenada	-0.2	4.4	—	—	—	—	44.9
Guatemala	2.9	0.6	1	0.44	2.5	41	44.9
Guyana	0.3	-5.4	—	—	—	65	3.6
Haiti	2.0	-2.9	1.5	0.14	0.8	29	47.0
Honduras	3.1	0.5	1	0.32	1.0	50	26.9
Jamaica	0.8	2.9	1	—	—	61	1.6
Mexico	1.8	1.1	—	0.54	0.8	62	12.4
Nicaragua	2.8	-7.8	2.7	0.60	0.5	53	—
Panama	2.1	-1.2	1.7	—	—	62	11.2
Paraguay	2.9	1.0	1.4	0.62	1.7	52	9.9
Peru	2.1	-4.3	2	1.03	0.9	74	14.9
St. Kitts and Nevis	-0.4	5.3	—	—	—	—	—
St. Lucia	1.9	5.2	—	—	—	—	—
St. Vincent and the Grenadines	0.9	4.7	—	—	—	—	—
Suriname	2.3	-3.2	—	—	—	69	5.1
Trinidad and Tobago	1.3	-3.0	1-2	—	—	66	—
United States	0.9	1.1	5.3	2.28	2.8	86	—
Uruguay	0.6	2.9	2.3	2.90	0.2	73	3.8
Venezuela	2.5	1.1	4	1.55	0.5	63	11.9
ASIA AND OCEANIA							
Afghanistan	2.5	—	—	0.11	0.8	13	70.6
Armenia	1.2	-8.2	—	4.28	2.5	—	1.2
Australia	1.6	0.7	2.4	2.29	3.8	71	—
Azerbaijan	1.0	—	—	3.93	2.4	—	2.7
Bahrain	3.2	-1.7	6	—	—	75	22.6
Bangladesh	2.2	1.7	1.5	0.15	0.8	32	64.7
Bhutan	2.2	5.2	—	—	—	11	61.6
Brunei Darussalam	3.2	—	9	—	—	67	—
Burma (Myanmar)	2.2	1.0	—	0.08	4.0	39	19.4
China	1.5	6.0	3.5	1.37	0.5	43	22.2
Cyprus	1.0	5.1	5	—	—	—	—
Federated States of Micronesia	2.4	—	—	—	—	—	—
Fiji	0.9	2.6	2	—	—	70	—
India	2.1	3.3	2.4	0.41	1.1	50	51.8
Indonesia	1.8	4.7	1.5	.014	2.8	58	18.4
Iran	3.7	-1.4	8-13	0.32	1.1	61	46.0
Iraq	3.3	—	—	0.58	1.2	62	40.3
Israel	2.7	2.3	18	2.90	2.3	—	—
Japan	0.4	4.0	0.94	1.64	1.8	73	—
Jordan	5.8	-7.0	7.9	1.54	0.3	73	19.9
Kampuchea	2.7	—	—	0.04	8.0	—	64.8
Kazakhstan	1.0	—	—	4.12	3.0	—	2.5
Kiribati	2.1	-1.1	—	—	—	—	—
Korea, (DPRK)	1.9	—	20-25	2.72	—	—	—
Korea, Republic of (ROK)	1.0	8.5	3.6	0.73	1.0	74	3.7
Kuwait	-2.3	—	7.3	—	—	—	27.0
Kyrgyzstan	1.7	2.3	—	3.67	2.8	—	3.0
Laos	2.9	1.8	—	0.23	5.9	42	—
Lebanon	2.3	—	8.2	—	—	65	19.9
Malaysia	2.5	5.7	5	0.37	3.9	65	21.6
Maldives	3.3	8.5	—	—	—	58	—
Marshall Islands	—	—	—	—	—	—	—
Mongolia	2.8	—	1	—	—	56	—
Nauru	—	2.1	—	—	—	—	—
Nepal	2.6	2.1	2	0.06	2.7	41	74.4
New Zealand	0.7	-0.4	2	1.74	0.1	78	—
Oman	3.8	1.0	16	—	—	61	—
Pakistan	3.1	1.7	3.2	0.34	0.8	24	65.2
Palau	—	—	—	—	—	—	—
Papua New Guinea	2.3	-0.1	1.8	0.08	8.1	30	—
Philippines	2.3	1.9	1.9	0.12	3.1	64	10.3
Qatar	6.0	-6.9	—	—	—	78	—
Saudi Arabia	3.5	1.3	13	—	—	50	37.6
Singapore	1.8	5.9	4	1.09	3.8	68	—
Solomon Islands	2.9	2.7	—	—	—	—	—
Sri Lanka	1.3	2.2	4.7	0.14	5.1	68	11.6
Syria	3.3	0.0	6	0.85	1.2	66	35.5

COUNTRY	ANNUAL % POP. INCREASE 1985-92	ANNUAL % INCREASE IN GNP PER CAPITA (1985-92)	MILITARY SPENDING % OF GDP 1993	DOCTORS PER 1,000 POP. 1988-92	NURSE-TO-DOCTOR-RATIO 1988-90	% OF SCHOOL AGED CHILDREN (6-23) ATTENDING SCHOOL 1990	% OF ILLITERATE ADULTS 1990
Taiwan	—	—	5.4	—	—	—	—
Tajikistan	3.0	—	—	2.71	2.8	—	2.3
Thailand	1.7	8.3	2	0.20	5.5	45	7.0
Tonga	0.9	-0.1	—	—	—	—	—
Turkey	2.2	2.7	3.9	0.74	1.5	52	19.3
Turkmenistan	2.5	—	—	3.57	2.8	—	2.3
Turks and Caicos Islands	—	—	—	—	—	—	—
Tuvalu	—	—	—	—	—	—	—
United Arab Emirates	3.1	0.0	5.3	—	—	73	—
Uzbekistan	2.4	—	—	3.58	2.9	—	2.8
Vanuatu	2.4	0.5	—	—	—	—	—
Viet-Nam	2.3	—	—	0.35	4.9	52	12.4
Western Samoa	0.5	-0.1	—	—	—	—	—
Yemen	4.4	—	10	0.18	2.9	45	60.75
EUROPE							
Albania	1.7	—	—	1.39	2.5	—	—
Andorra	—	—	—	—	—	—	—
Austria	0.6	2.4	0.9	4.34	2.4	—	—
Belarus	0.5	—	—	4.05	—	—	2.1
Belgium	0.3	2.8	2	3.21	0.1	76	—
Bosnia and Herzegovina	0.2	—	—	—	—	—	26.4
Bulgaria	0.0	-3.6	—	3.19	2.1	67	—
Croatia	0.4	—	—	—	—	—	—
Czech Republic	0.1	-5.3	—	3.23	2.4	—	—
Denmark	0.1	1.2	2	2.56	5.6	77	—
Estonia	0.2	3.0	—	—	—	—	0.3
Finland	0.4	.0.7	2	2.47	4.3	84	—
France	0.6	2.2	3.1	2.89	1.6	78	—
Georgia	0.5	—	—	5.92	2.2	—	1.0
Germany	0.6	2.2	2.2	2.73	1.7	77	—
Greece	0.7	1.1	5.1	1.73	1.6	72	6.8
Hungary	0.9	-1.5	—	2.98	1.1	64	—
Iceland	1.2	0.5	—	—	—	81	—
Ireland	-0.1	5.0	1-2	1.58	4.7	73	—
Italy	0.2	2.3	2	4.69	0.6	64	2.9
Latvia	0.0	-3.6	3-5	—	—	—	0.5
Liechtenstein	—	—	—	—	—	—	—
Lithuania	0.7	-2.7	5.5	—	—	—	1.6
Luxembourg	0.8	3.1	1.2	—	—	58	—
Malta	0.7	5.4	1.3	—	—	76	—
Moldova	0.6	-2.9	—	4.00	3.0	—	3.6
Monaco	—	—	—	—	—	—	—
Netherlands	0.7	2.1	3	2.43	3.4	71	—
Norway	0.4	0.2	3.4	2.43	4.4	77	—
Poland	0.4	-1.9	1.8	2.06	—	71	—
Portugal	-0.7	5.5	2.9	2.57	0.8	66	15.0
Romania	0.1	-5.5	3	1.79	—	—	3.1
Russian Federation	0.5	—	6	4.69	—	—	1.3
San Marino	—	—	—	—	—	—	—
Slovakia	0.4	-7.0	—	—	—	—	—
Slovenia	0.7	—	4.5	—	—	—	—
Spain	0.2	3.8	1.6	3.60	1.1	83	—
Sweden	0.6	0.4	3.8	2.73	3.4	70	—
Switzerland	0.9	1.1	1.7	1.59	2.6	74	—
Ukraine	0.3	—	8.6	4.40	2.7	—	1.6
United Kingdom	0.3	1.5	3.6	1.40	2.0	72	—
Vatican	—	—	—	—	—	—	—
Yugoslavia (the former)	0.8	—	4-6	2.63	1.9	61	—

—Nil, not available, or does not apply.

Table 7. World Cultural Indicators   339

COUNTRY	POST-SECONDARY STUDENTS PER 100,000 POP. 1991	NUMBER OF MUSEUMS	TV SETS PER 1,000 POP. 1991	DAILY NEWSPAPER CIRCUALTION PER 1,000 POP. 1990	RADIOS PER 1,000 POP. 1991\
AFRICA					
Algeria	—	—	74	51	234
Angola	—	—	6.2	13	28
Benin	—	6	5.0	3	90
Botswana	306	—	16	15	122
Burkina Faso	—	1	5.3	0.3	26
Burundi	68	—	0.8	4	60
Cameroon	—	—	24	7	145
Cape Verde	—	—	—	—	164
Central African Republic	146	6	4.4	0.7	68
Chad	—	—	1.2	0.4	243
Comoros	—	—	0.4	—	128
Congo	524	—	5.9	8	113
Côte d'Ivoire	—	—	59	8	142
Djibouti	—	—	53	—	86
Egypt	—	—	116	57	326
Equatorial Guinea	—	—	9.4	6	425
Eritrea	—	—	—	—	—
Ethiopia	66	—	2.5	0.8	189
Gabon	368	—	37	17	143
Gambia	—	—	—	2	170
Ghana	—	—	15	13	268
Guinea	—	—	7	—	42
Guinea-Bissau	—	1	—	6	40
Kenya	—	—	9.6	15	86
Lesotho	232	—	5.9	11	32
Liberia	—	—	18	14	225
Libya	1,548	—	99	15	225
Madagascar	—	5	20	4	200
Malawi	—	3	—	3	220
Mali	—	—	1.1	1	44
Mauritania	281	—	23	0.5	144
Mauritius	—	5	217	74	359
Morocco	—	14	74	13	210
Mozambique	—	—	2.9	6	47
Namibia	280	—	21	153	127
Niger	—	3	4.6	0.6	60
Nigeria	—	12	33	16	173
Rwanda	—	—	—	0.1	64
São Tomé and Principe	—	—	—	—	269
Senegal	—	—	36	7	114
Seychelles	—	2	85	45	458
Sierra Leone	—	—	10	2	223
Somalia	—	—	12	1	37
South Africa	—	—	98	35	303
Sudan	—	—	77	24	250
Swaziland	418	—	19	13	165
Tanzania	—	—	1.6	8	25
Togo	—	7	6.2	3	211
Tunisia	925	—	79	37	199
Uganda	—	—	10	2	109
Zaire	—	—	1.0	—	97
Zambia	—	11	26	12	81
Zimbabwe	—	—	26	21	84
AMERICAS					
Antigua and Barbuda	—	—	355	92	415
Argentina	3,293	—	220	124	682
Bahamas	—	—	225	137	538
Barbados	—	3	265	117	876
Belize	—	—	165	—	577
Bolivia	2,028	—	103	56	625
Brazil	1,075	—	207	54	386
Canada	7,197	1,352	639	228	1,029
Chile	2,144	24	209	455	344
Colombia	—	—	116	62	177
Costa Rica	2,584	15	140	101	257
Cuba	—	216	163	172	345
Dominica	—	—	72	—	588
Dominican Republic	—	—	84	32	171
Ecuador	—	—	84	87	317

COUNTRY	POST-SECONDARY STUDENTS PER 100,000 POP. 1991	NUMBER OF MUSEUMS	TV SETS PER 1,000 POP. 1991	DAILY NEWSPAPER CIRCUALTION PER 1,000 POP. 1990	RADIOS PER 1,000 POP. 1991\
El Salvador	—	—	92	88	412
Grenada	—	—	330	—	597
Guatemala	—	—	52	21	66
Guyana	—	2	39	101	489
Haiti	—	4	5	7	47
Honduras	—	—	73	39	386
Jamaica	—	—	131	64	420
Mexico	—	93	148	133	255
Netherlands Amer Dependencies	—	625	—	—	
Nicaragua	—	—	65	68	262
Panama	2,377	11	166	70	224
Paraguay	—	—	50	39	171
Peru	—	—	98	79	253
St. Kitts and Nevis	—	—	205	—	645
St. Lucia	—	—	189	—	763
St. Vincent and the Grenadines	—	—	144	—	698
Suriname	—	—	130	95	637
Trinidad and Tobago	—	—	315	77	492
United States	5,687	—	814	249	2,118
Uruguay	2,367	11	231	233	604
Venezuela	—	—	162	145	477
ASIA AND OCEANIA					
Afghanistan	—	—	8.3	11	107
Armenia	—	—	—	—	—
Australia	3,082	1,893	480	246	1,268
Azerbaijan	—	—	—	—	—
Bahrain	—	—	415	57	537
Bangladesh	—	13	4.6	6	43
Bhutan	—	—	—	—	16
Brunei Darussalam	—	8	235	39	269
Burma (Myanmar)	—	—	1.9	5	82
China	181	—	31	—	182
Cyprus	—	18	144	110	292
Federated States of Micronesia	—	—	—	—	—
Fiji	1,080	—	15	37	612
India	—	462	35	—	79
Indonesia	—	131	59	28	146
Iran	1,061	52	63	26	231
Iraq	—	25	72	36	215
Israel	—	—	269	258	470
Japan	2,328	638	613	587	907
Jordan	—	11	80	56	256
Kampuchea	—	—	8.2	—	112
Kazakhstan	—	—	—	—	—
Kiribati	—	—	—	—	207
Korea, (DPRK)	—	—	15	230	119
Korea, Republic of (ROK)	4,023	—	208	277	1,001
Kuwait	1,135	7	283	210	343
Kyrgyzstan	—	—	—	—	—
Laos	—	—	5.8	3	125
Lebanon	3,071	—	325	117	833
Malaysia	—	43	149	140	430
Maldives	—	1	25	8	118
Marshall Islands	—	—	—	—	—
Mongolia	1,254	—	40	74	132
Nauru	—	—	—	—	575
Nepal	549	—	2.0	8	33
New Zealand	3,742	98	443	324	560
Oman	463	3	728	40	637
Pakistan	—	—	18	15	90
Palau	—	—	—	—	—
Papua New Guinea	—	—	2.3	13	475
Philippines	2,596	76	44	54	138
Qatar	—	6	450	187	443
Saudi Arabia	—	—	266	40	304
Singapore	—	—	378	282	646
Solomon Islands	—	1	—	—	575
Sri Lanka	—	—	981	32	198
Syria	1,718	33	60	23	—
Taiwan	—	—	—	—	—

Table 7. World Cultural Indicators—*cont.* 341

COUNTRY	POST-SECONDARY STUDENTS PER 100,000 POP. 1991	NUMBER OF MUSEUMS	TV SETS PER 1,000 POP. 1991	DAILY NEWSPAPER CIRCUALTION PER 1,000 POP. 1990	RADIOS PER 1,000 POP. 1991
Tajikistan	—	—	—	—	—
Thailand	—	180	114	73	255
Tonga	—	—	—	73	554
Turkey	1,418	154	175	71	191
Turkmenistan	—	—	—	—	—
Turks and Caicos Islands	—	—	—	—	512
Tuvalu	—	—	—	—	229
United Arab Emirates	638	—	107	157	325
Uzbekistan	—	1	8.6	—	300
Vanuatu	—	—	—	—	—
Viet-Nam	—	—	41	9	104
Western Samoa	—	—	21	—	—
Yemen	—	—	27	19	27
EUROPE					
Albania	—	—	87	42	176
Andorra	—	—	154	—	222
Austria	2,796	719	478	351	617
Belarus	—	86	—	286	—
Belgium	—	—	451	301	769
Bosnia and Herzegovina	—	—	—	—	—
Bulgaria	2,071	223	252	452	442
Croatia	—	—	221	—	244
Czech Republic	—	—	—	—	—
Denmark	—	285	536	352	1,031
Estonia	—	—	347	—	—
Finland	3,478	206	501	558	997
France	3,245	1,300	407	208	888
Georgia	—	—	—	—	—
Germany	—	4,034	556	—	876
Greece	1,017	478	197	139	421
Hungary	—	571	412	233	596
Iceland	2,397	—	319	—	786
Ireland	—	—	76	169	630
Italy	2,656	130	421	106	791
Latvia	—	—	372	—	—
Liechtenstein	—	5	345	307	719
Lithuania	—	—	374	—	379
Luxembourg	—	1	267	383	632
Malta	—	—	—	153	526
Moldova	—	—	—	—	—
Monaco	—	6	819	296	1,126
Netherlands	—	—	485	311	907
Norway	3,613	401	347	610	794
Poland	1,398	551	295	128	433
Portugal	—	314	187	39	228
Romania	—	471	196	—	199
Russian Federation	—	—	—	—	—
San Marino	—	9	351	87	589
Slovakia	—	—	—	—	—
Slovenia	—	—	284	—	360
Spain	—	9	400	82	310
Sweden	2,407	195	468	525	877
Switzerland	2,115	699	406	456	842
Ukraine	—	224	487	—	1,177
United Kingdom	—	—	434	374	1,143
Vatican	—	—	—	—	—
Yugoslavia (the former)	—	565	—	96	—

—Nil, not available, or does not apply.

Conversion Tables*

LENGTH

1 centimeter ....0.3937 inch
1 centimeter ....0.03280833 foot
1 meter (100 centimeters)..........................3.280833 feet
1 meter...1.093611 US yards
1 kilometer (1,000 meters) ....0.62137 statute mile
1 kilometer.............................0.539957 nautical mile
1 inch.......................................2.540005 centimeters
1 foot (12 inches) ....30.4801 centimeters
1 US yard (3 feet) ....0.914402 meter
1 statute mile (5,280 feet; 1,760 yards) ....1.609347 kilometers
1 British mile ....1.609344 kilometers
1 nautical mile (1.1508 statute miles
or 6,076.10333 feet) .... 1.852 kilometers
1 British nautical mile (6,080 feet) ....1.85319 kilometers

AREA

1 sq centimeter .... 0.154999 sq inch
1 sq meter (10,000 sq centimeters) ....10.76387 sq feet
1 sq meter.......................................1.1959585 sq yards
1 hectare (10,000 sq meters) ....2.47104 acres
1 sq kilometer (100 hectares) ....0.386101 sq mile
1 sq inch...6.451626 sq centimeters
1 sq foot (144 sq inches) .... 0.092903 sq meter
1 sq yard (9 sq feet) ....0.836131 sq meter
1 acre (4,840 sq yards) .... 0.404687 hectare
1 sq mile (640 acres) ....2.589998 sq kilometers

VOLUME

1 cubic centimeter ....0.061023 cubic inch
1 cubic meter
(1,000,000 cubic centimeters) ....35.31445 cubic feet
1 cubic meter..............................1.307943 cubic yards
1 cubic inch................................16.387162 cubic centimeters
1 cubic foot (1,728 cubic inches)............................0.028317 cubic meter
1 cubic yard (27 cubic feet) ....0.764559 cubic meter

LIQUID MEASURE

1 liter ....0.8799 imperial quart
1 liter .... 1.05671 US quarts
1 hectoliter ....21.9975 imperial gallons
1 hectoliter .... 26.4178 US gallons
1 imperial quart .... 1.136491 liters
1 US quart .... 0.946333 liter
1 imperial gallon ....0.04546 hectoliter
1 US gallon ....0.037853 hectoliter

WEIGHT

1 Kilogram (1,000 grams) ....35.27396 avoirdupois ounces
1 kilogram................................32.15074 troy ounces
1 kilogram................................2.204622 avoirdupois pounds
1 quintal (100 kg) ....220.4622 avoirdupois pounds
1 quintal...................................1.9684125 hundredweights
1 metric ton (1,000 kg) ....1.102311 short tons

1 metric ton .... 0.984206 long ton
1 avoirdupois ounce .... 0.0283495 kilogram
1 troy ounce .... 0.0311035 kilogram
1 avoirdupois pound .... 0.453592 kilogram
1 avoirdupois pound .... 0.00453592 quintal
1 hundred weight (cwt., 112 lb) .... 0.50802 quintal
1 short ton (2,000 lb) .... 0.907185 metric ton
1 long ton (2,240 lb) ....1.016047 metric tons

ELECTRIC ENERGY

1 horsepower (hp) .... 0.7457 kilowatt
1 kilowatt (kw)........................ 1.34102 horsepower

TEMPERATURE

Celsius (C)....................................Fahrenheit-32 X 5/9
Fahrenheit (F) .... 9/5 Celsius + 32

BUSHELS

	LB	METRIC TON	BUSHELS PER METRIC TON
Barley(US)	48	0.021772	45.931
(UK)	50	0.022680	44.092
Corn (UK, US)	56	0.025401	39.368
Linseed (UK)	52	0.023587	42.396
(Australia, US)	56	0.025401	39.368
Oats (US)	32	0.014515	68.894
(Canada)	34	0.015422	64.842
Potatoes (UK, U&S)	60	0.027216	36.743
Rice (Australia)	42	0.019051	52.491
(US)	45	0.020412	48.991
Rye (UK, US)	56	0.025401	39.368
(Australia)	60	0.027216	36.743
Soybeans (US)	60	0.027216	36.743
Wheat (UK, US)	60	0.027216	36.743

BAGS OF COFFEE

	LB	KG	BAGS PER METRIC TON
Brazil, Columbia Mexico, Venezuela	132.28	60	16.667
El Salvador	152.12	69	14.493
Haiti	185.63	84.2	11.876

BALES OF COTTON

	LB	METRIC TON	BALES PER METRIC TON
India	392	0.177808	5.624
Brazil	397	0.180000	5.555
US (net)	480	0.217724	4.593
US (gross)	500	0.226796	4.409

PETROLEUM

One barrel = 42 US gallons = 34.97 imperial gallons = 158.99 liters = 0.15899 cubic meter (or 1 cubic meter = 6.2898 barrels).

*Includes units of measure cited in the text, as well as certain other units employed in parts of the English-speaking world and in specified countries.

Abbreviations and Acronyms

AD—Anno Domini
ADB—African Development Bank
AsDB—Asian Development Bank
AFL-CIO—American Federation of Labor–Congress of Industrial Organizations
AID—Agency for International Development [of the US]
AIDS—Acquired Immune Deficiency Syndrome
AM—before noon
AM—Amplitude modulation
ANZUS—Security Treaty of Australia, New Zealand, and the United States
Arch.—Archipelago
ASEAN—Association of Southeast Asian Nations
ASSR—Autonomous Soviet Socialist Republic
b.—born
BC—Before Christ
BCEAO—Central Bank of the West African States (Banque Centrale des États de l'Afrique de l'Ouest)
BEAC—Bank of the Central African States (Banque des États de l'Afrique Centrale)
BENELUX—Benelux Economic Union (Belgium-Netherlands-Luxembourg Economic Union)
Bibliog.—bibliography
BIS—Bank for International Settlements
BLEU—Belgium-Luxembourg Economic Union
Br.—British
Brig.—brigadier
c.—circa (about)
C—Celsius
CACM—Central American Common Market
Capt.—Captain
CARE—Cooperative for American Remittances to Everywhere, Inc.
CARICOM—Caribbean Community and Common Market
CCC—Customs Cooperation Council
CDB—Caribbean Development Bank
CEAO—West African Economic Community (Communauté Économique de l'Afrique de l'Ouest; replaced UDEAO)
CEMA—see CMEA
CENTO—Central Treaty Organization
CERN—European Organization for Nuclear Research
CFA—Communauté Financière Africaine
CFP—Communauté Française du Pacifique
CGT—Confédération Générale du Travail
CIA—Central Intelligence Agency [of the US]
c.i.f.—cost, insurance, and freight
cm—centimeter(s)
CMEA—Council for Mutual Economic Assistance
Co.—company
Col.—colonel
COMECON—see CMEA
comp.—compiled, compiler
Cons.—Conservative
Corp.—corporation
cu—cubic
cu m—cubic meters
cwt—hundredweight
d.—daily

d.—died
DDT—dichlorodiphenyltrichloroethane
Dem.—Democratic
DPT—diphtheria, pertussis, and tetanus
Dr.—doctor
DPRK—Democratic People's Republic of Korea (North Korea)
DRV—Democratic Republic of Viet-Nam (North Viet-Nam)
dwt—deadweight tons
e—evening
E—east
EAC—East African Community
EAEC—see EURATOM
EC—European Communities
ECA—Economic Commission for Africa [of the UN]
ECAFE—see ESCAP
ECE—Economic Commission for Europe [of the UN]
ECLAC—Economic Commission for Latin America and the Caribbean [of the UN]
ECOWAS—Economic Community of West African States
ECSC—European Coal and Steel Community
ed.—editor, edited, edition
EEC—European Economic Community (Common Market)
EFTA—European Free Trade Association
e.g.—exempli gratia (for example)
ESCAP—Economic and Social Commission for Asia and the Pacific [of the UN]
ESCWA—Economic and Social Commission for Western Asia [of the UN]
ESRO—European Space Research Organization
est.—estimate(d)
et al.—et alii (and others)
EURATOM—European Atomic Energy Community
f.—founded
F—Fahrenheit
FAO—Food and Agriculture Organization [of the UN]
ff.—following
fl.—flourished
FM—frequency modulation
f.o.b.—free on board
Fr.—France, French
FRG—Federal Republic of Germany (West Germany)
FSM—Federated States of Micronesia
ft—foot, feet
ft^3—cubic foot, feet
Ft.—Fort
G-77—Group of 77
GATT—General Agreement on Tariffs and Trade
GCC—Gulf Cooperation Council
GDP—gross domestic product
GDR—German Democratic Republic (East Germany)
Gen.—General
GHz—gigahertz
gm—gram(s)
GMT—Greenwich Mean Time
GNP—gross national product
GRT—gross registered tons (tonnage)
GSP—gross social product
HIV—human immunodeficiency virus

343

HMSO—Her Majesty's Stationery Office [of the UK]
ha—hectare(s)
I.—Island
IADB—see IDB
IAEA—International Atomic Energy Agency
IATA—International Air Transport Association
IBRD—International Bank for Reconstruction and Development (World Bank)
ICAO—International Civil Aviation Organization
ICC—International Control Commission
ICFTU—International Confederation of Free Trade Unions
ICSU—International Council of Scientific Unions
IDA—International Development Association
IDB/IADB—Inter-American Development Bank
i.e.—id est (that is)
IFAD—International Fund for Agricultural Development
IFC—International Finance Corporation
IGO—intergovernmental organization
IGY—International Geophysical Year
ILO—International Labor Organization
IMCO—see IMO
IMF—International Monetary Fund
IMO—International Maritime Organization (formerly IMCO)
in—inch(es)
Inc.—incorporated
Indep.—Independent
INSTRAW—International Research and Training Institute for the Advancement of Women [of the UN]
INTELSAT—International Telecommunications Satellite Consortium
INTERPOL—International Criminal Police Organization
IRU—International Relief Union
Is.—islands
ITU—International Telecommunication Union
IUCN—International Union for the Conservation of Nature and Natural Resources
IWC—International Whaling Commission; International Wheat Council
kg—kilogram(s)
kHz—kilohertz
km—kilometer(s)
km/hr—kilometer(s) per hour
kw—kilowatt(s)
kwh—kilowatt-hour(s)
L.—Lake
LAFTA—Latin American Free Trade Association
LAIA—Latin American Integration Association
lb—pound(s)
Lieut.—lieutenant
Ltd.—limited
m—meter(s); morning
m^3—cubic meter(s)
mg—milligram(s)
MHz—megahertz
mi—mile(s)
mm—millimeter(s)
mph—mile(s) per hour
MPR—Mongolian People's Republic
Mt.—Mount
Mtn.—mountain(s)
Mw—Megawatt(s)
N—north
NA—not available
NATO—North Atlantic Treaty Organization
n.d.—no date
n.e.s.—not elsewhere specified
Neth.—Netherlands

NGO—nongovernmental organization
n.i.e.—not included elsewhere
NMP—net material product
NZ—New Zealand
OAPEC—Organization of Arab Petroleum Exporting Countries (subgroup of OPEC)
OAS—Organization of American States
OAU—Organization of African Unity
OCAM—African and Malagasy Common Organization
OECD—Organization for Economic Cooperation and Development
OIHP—International Office of Public Health (Office International d'Hygiène Publique)
O.M.—Order of Merit
OPEC—Organization of Petroleum Exporting Countries
orig.—original [edition]
oz—ounce(s)
p.—page
PAHO—Pan American Health Organization
PC of A—Permanent Court of Arbitration
PDRY—People's Democratic Republic of Yemen (South Yemen)
PL—Public Law
PLO—Palestine Liberation Organization
PM—after noon
pop.—population
Port.—Portugal, Portuguese
pp.—pages
PRC—People's Republic of China
r.—reigned
R.—river
Ra.—Range
Rep.—Republic
rev.—revised
ROC—Republic of China (Taiwan)
ROK—Republic of Korea (South Korea)
RVN—Republic of Viet-Nam (South Viet-Nam)
s—South
S.A.—Société Anonyme
SAARC—South Asian Association for Regional Cooperation
SDI—Strategic Defense Initiative
SDRs—Special Drawing Rights
SEATO—Southeast Asia Treaty Organization
SELA—Latin American Economic System (Sistema Económica Latinoamericano)
Sgt.—sergeant
SHAPE—Supreme Headquarters Allied Powers Europe
SPC—South Pacific Commission
sq—square
SRV—Socialist Republic of Viet-Nam
SSR—Soviet Socialist Republic
St.—Saint
tr.—translated
TB—tuberculosis
TV—television
UAE—United Arab Emirates
UAR—United Arab Republic
UCC—Universal Copyright Convention
UDEAC—Central African Customs and Economic Union (Union Douanière et Économique de l'Afrique Centrale)
UDEAO—see CEAO
UEAC—Central African Economic Union (Union des États de l'Afrique Centrale)
UHF—ultra high frequency
UK—United Kingdom of Great Britain and Northern Ireland
UMOA—West African Monetary Union (Union Monétaire Ouest Africaine)
UN—United Nations

UNCHS—UN Center for Human Settlements (Habitat)
UNCTAD—UN Conference on Trade and Development
UNDOF—UN Disengagement Observer Force
UNDP—UN Development Program
UNDRO—UN Disaster Relief Coordinator, Office of
UNEF—UN Emergency Force
UNEP—UN Environment Program
UNESCO—UN Educational, Scientific and Cultural Organization
UNFICYP—UN Peacekeeping Force in Cyprus
UNFPA—UN Population Fund
UNHCR—UN High Commissioner for Refugees
UNICEF—UN Children's Fund
UNIDO—UN Industrial Development Organization
UNIFIL—UN Interim Force in Lebanon
UNITAR—UN Institute for Training and Research
UNMOGIP—UN Military Observer Group in India and Pakistan
UNRWA—UN Relief and Works Agency for Palestine Refugees
UNSO—UN Sahelian Office
UNTSO—UN Truce Supervision Organization

UNU—UN University
UNV—UN Volunteers
UPU—Universal Postal Union
US—United States of America
USIA—US Information Agency
USSR—Union of Soviet Socialist Republics
VHF—very high frequency
vol., vols., Vol., Vols.—volume(s)
w—west
WEU—Western European Union
WFC—World Food Council
WFP—World Food Program
WFTU—World Federation of Trade Unions
WHO—World Health Organization
WIPO—World Intellectual Property Organization
WMO—World Meteorological Organization
WTO—Warsaw Treaty Organization; World Tourism Organization
YAR—Yemen Arab Republic (North Yemen)

Glossary of Religious Holidays

BUDDHIST HOLIDAYS

Buddhist religious practice stems from the Hindu belief that every new moon or full moon day should be set apart for observance. In Buddhism, the half-moon days also have special status. In Sri Lanka, each Poya day—the day of the rise of the full moon of each month of the Buddhist calendar—is a public holiday. The following observances are common in Southeast Asia.

Songran. The Buddhist New Year is a three-day springtime water festival, in which images of the Buddha are bathed.

Vesak. This last full moon day of Visakha highlights a three-day celebration of the birth, enlightenment, and death of the Buddha. It falls in April or May.

Waso (Varsa; Vassa). This holiday begins the Buddhist equivalent of Lent, a period between July and October (the rainy season in Southeast Asia), during which Buddhist monks may not leave their cloisters. The season starts with the full moon of the month of Asalha and ends with a festival during the full moon of the month of Thadingyut.

CHRISTIAN HOLIDAYS

The chief Christian holiday is **Easter,** the annual celebration of the resurrection of Jesus Christ. Like Passover, the Jewish feast from which it is derived, the date of observation is linked to the phases of the moon. Since the Christian calendar is a solar one rather than a lunar one, the date of Easter changes from year to year. Easter is celebrated on the first Sunday after the first full moon following the spring equinox; in the Gregorian calendar, it can occur as early as 22 March or as late as 25 April. The Easter date determines the date of many other Roman Catholic holidays, such as Ash Wednesday, Ascension, and Pentecost.

Important Christian celebrations and feasts that invariably occur on Sunday are not listed as holidays in the country articles because Sunday itself is a holiday ("holy day") in predominantly Christian countries. In these lands, it is the day of rest and worship, occurring on the day after the Jewish Sabbath, from which it is derived, in commemoration of Christ's resurrection on Easter Sunday.

The names and dates of the Christian holidays listed below are almost all based on Roman Catholic observances. Some of these holidays are also observed by Protestant denominations. By contrast, all countries where Eastern Orthodox rites predominate are Communist-ruled except Greece and the Greek-held portion of Cyprus; in the Communist countries, Christian holidays are not national holidays. For religious celebrations, some Eastern Orthodox churches retain the Julian calendar, which is 13 days behind the Gregorian calendar. Eastern Orthodox holidays do not fully correspond to the list of church holidays given below.

Solemnity of Mary, Mother of God. Observed on 1 January, this celebration was, before a 1969 Vatican reform, the Feast of the Circumcision of Our Lord Jesus Christ.

Epiphany of Our Lord. Traditionally observed on 6 January but now observable on the Sunday falling between 2 January and 7 January, this feast commemorates the adoration of the Magi, who journeyed to the place of Jesus' birth. In the Orthodox churches, however, it is the feast celebrating Jesus' baptism.

St. Dévôte Day. Observed on 27 January in Monaco in honor of the principality's patron saint, this day celebrates her safe landing after a perilous voyage, thanks to a dove who directed her ship to the Monaco shore.

Candlemas. A national holiday on 2 February in Liechtenstein, this observation is now called the Presentation of the Lord, commemorating the presentation of the infant Jesus in the Temple at Jerusalem. Before a 1969 Vatican reform, it commemorated the Purification of Mary 40 days after giving birth to a male child in accordance with a Jewish practice of the time.

St. Agatha's Day. On 5 February is celebrated the feast day of the patron saint of San Marino. St. Agatha is also the patron saint of nurses, firefighters, and jewelers.

Shrove Monday and Shrove Tuesday. These two days occur just prior to the beginning of Lent (a term which derives from the Middle English *lente,* "spring"), the Christian season of penitence that ends with Easter Sunday. These are days of **Carnival,** public holidays of feasting and merriment in many lands. Shrove Tuesday is also known as **Mardi Gras.**

Ash Wednesday. The first day of Lent, observed 46 days before Easter, is so called from the practice of placing ashes on the forehead of the worshiper as a sign of penitence. In the Roman Catholic Church, these ashes are obtained from burning palm branches used in the previous year's **Palm Sunday** observation. (Palm Sunday commemorates the entry of Jesus into Jerusalem a week before Easter Sunday, and it begins **Holy Week.** On Ash Wednesday, the ashes are placed on the forehead of the communicant during Mass. The recipient is told, "Remember that you are dust, and unto dust you shall return" or "Turn away from sin and be faithful to the Gospel."

St. Patrick's Day. This holiday, observed on 17 March, is celebrated in Ireland to honor its patron saint.

St. Joseph's Day. The feast day in honor of Mary's husband is observed on 19 March as a public holiday in several countries.

Holy (Maundy) Thursday. The Thursday preceding Easter commemorates the Last Supper, the betrayal of Jesus by Judas Iscariot, and the arrest and arraignment of Jesus. In Rome, the pope customarily performs a ceremony in remembrance of Jesus' washing of his apostles' feet (John 13:5–20).

Good Friday. The day after Holy Thursday is devoted to remembrance of the crucifixion of Jesus and is given to penance and prayer.

Holy Saturday. This day commemorates the time during which Jesus was buried and, like Good Friday, is given to solemn prayer.

Easter Monday. The day after Easter is a public holiday in many countries.

Prayer Day. This Danish public holiday is observed on the fourth Friday after Easter.

Ascension. One of the most important Christian feasts, Ascension is observed 40 days after Easter in commemoration of Jesus' ascension to heaven.

Pentecost Monday (Whitmonday). This public holiday in many countries occurs the day after Pentecost (derived from the ancient Green *pentekostos,* "fiftieth"), or **Whitsunday,** which commemorates the descent of the Holy Spirit upon Jesus' apostles on the seventh Sunday after Easter and is derived from the Jewish feast of Shavuot. It was an important occasion for baptism in the early church, and the name "Whitsunday" originated from the white robes worn by the newly baptized.

Corpus Christi. This holiday in honor of the Eucharist is observed on the Thursday or Sunday after **Trinity Sunday**, which is the Sunday after Pentecost. In the Roman Catholic and Eastern Orthodox Churches, the Eucharist is a sacrament in which the consecrated bread and wine literally become the body and blood of Jesus Christ, a belief stemming from New Testament accounts of the Last Supper.

Sacred Heart. The Friday of the week after Corpus Christi is a holiday in Colombia. The object of devotion is the divine person of Jesus, whose heart is the symbol of his love for mankind.

Day of St. Peter and St. Paul. This observance, on 29 June, commemorates the martyrdom of the two apostles traditionally believed to have been executed in Rome on the same day (c. AD 67) during the persecution of Christians ordered by Emperor Nero.

St. James' Day. Observed on 25 July, this day commemorates St. James the Greater, one of Jesus' 12 apostles. St. James is the patron saint of Spain.

Feast of Our Lady of Angels. This feast, on 2 August, is celebrated as a national holiday in Costa Rica in honor of the Virgin Mary. Pilgrimage is made to the basilica in Cartago, which houses a black stone statue of the Virgin.

Assumption. This holiday, observed on 15 August in many countries, celebrates the Roman Catholic and Eastern Orthodox dogma that, following Mary's death, her body was taken into heaven and reunited with her soul.

Crowning of Our Lady of Altagracia. Another holiday in honor of Mary, this day is celebrated in the Dominican Republic on 15 August with a pilgrimage to her shrine. (**Altagracia Day**, 21 January, is also a holiday in the Dominican Republic.)

Day of Santa Rosa of Lima. The feast day in honor of the first native-born saint of the New World, declared patron saint of South America by Pope Clement X in 1671, is 23 August, but in Peru, she is commemorated by a national holiday on 30 August.

Day of Our Lady of Mercy (Las Mercedes). Another holiday in honor of Mary, this observance on 24 September is a holiday in the Dominican Republic.

All Saints' Day. On 1 November, a public holiday in many countries, saints and martyrs who have no special festival are commemorated. In the Middle Ages, it was known as **All Hallows' Day**; the evening of the previous day, October 31, was called **All Hallow Even**, from which the secular holiday **Halloween** is derived.

All Souls' Day. This day, 2 November, is dedicated to prayer for the repose of the souls of the dead.

Immaculate Conception. This day, 8 December, celebrates the Roman Catholic dogma asserting that Mary's conception, as the future mother of God, was uniquely free from original sin. In Paraguay, it is observed as the Day of Our Lady of Caacupé.

Our Lady of Guadalupe. This Mexican festival, on 12 December, celebrates a miracle that the Virgin Mary is believed to have performed on this day in 1531, when she appeared before an Amerindian peasant and told him to build a shrine in her honor. The shrine is now the site of a basilica in the Mexico City area.

Christmas. The annual commemoration of the nativity of Jesus is held on 25 December. A midnight Mass ushers in this joyous celebration in many Roman Catholic churches. The custom of distributing gifts to children on **Christmas Eve** derives from a Dutch custom originally observed on the evening before **St. Nicholas' Day (6 December)**. The day after Christmas—often called **Boxing Day**, for the boxed gifts customarily given—is a public holiday in many countries.

St. Stephen's Day. The feast day in honor of the first martyred Christian saint is 26 December, the day after Christmas. St. Stephen is the patron saint of Hungary.

HINDU HOLIDAYS

Hindu holidays are based on various lunar calendars, with an extra month inserted at intervals that vary from year to year, in order to keep festivals from shifting in relation to the seasons. The bright half of the month is that in which the new moon advances to the full moon; the dark half lasts from full moon to new moon. It is said that no nation has more festivals than India. Most are of only local or regional importance, but the following are national holidays in India and other countries with large Hindu populations.

Raksha Bandhan. During this festival, which usually falls in August, bracelets of colored thread and tinsel are tied by women to the wrists of their menfolk, thus binding the men to guard and protect them during the year. It is celebrated on the full moon of Sravana.

Ganesh Chaturthi. The festival, honoring Ganesh (Ganesha), god of prosperity, is held on the fourth day of the bright fortnight of the month of Bhadrapada, corresponding to August or September.

Durga Puja. This holiday honors the Divine Mother, wife of Shiva and the principle of creation, in her victory over the demon Mashishasura. It is held during the first 10 days of the bright fortnight of Asvina (Navaratri), a period corresponding to September or October. The last day is Dussehra, an autumn festival that celebrates the victory of the god Rama over Ravana, king of demons.

Dewali (Deepavali; Divali). Dewali is the Hindu Festival of Lights, when Lakshmi, goddess of good fortune, is said to visit the homes of humans. The four- or five-day festival comes at the end of Asvina and the beginning of Karttika, a time corresponding to October or November.

Shivarati (Mahashivarati). Dedicated to the god Shiva, this holiday is observed on the 13th day of the dark half of Magha, corresponding to January or February.

Thaipusam. A holiday in Malaysia, Thaipusam honors Subrimaya, son of Shiva and an important deity in southern India. The three-day festival is held in the month of Magha according to when Pusam, a section of the lunar zodiac, is on the ascendant.

Holi. A festival lasting 3 to 10 days, Holi closes the old year with processions and merriment. It terminates on the full moon of Phalguna, the last month, corresponding to February or March.

JEWISH HOLIDAYS

The basic Jewish holy day is the **Sabbath**, the seventh day of each week, starting at sundown on Friday and ending at nightfall on Saturday. This is a day of rest and is devoted to worship, religious study, and the family.

Other Jewish holidays (all starting at sundown and ending at nightfall) occur on specific days of specific months of the Jewish calendar, which consists of 12 alternating months of 29 or 30 days (two months are variable), conforming to the lunar cycle of roughly 29½ days. In order to reconcile the lunar year of 353, 354, or 355 days with the solar year of 365¼ days, a 30-day month (Adar Sheni) is added 7 times within a 19-year cycle. In this way, Jewish festivals retain their seasonal origins. The following list, arranged in the order of the Jewish calendar, shows Jewish religious holidays observed in the State of Israel.

Rosh Hashanah. The Jewish New Year is celebrated on 1 Tishri, the first month. In synagogues, the sounding of the shofar (ram's horn) heralds the new year. Rosh Hashanah begins the observance of the Ten Penitential Days, which culminate in Yom Kippur. Orthodox and Conservative Jews outside Israel celebrate 2 Tishri, the next day, as well.

Yom Kippur. The Day of Atonement, spent in fasting, penitence, and prayer, is the most solemn day in Judaism. It takes place on 10 Tishri.

Sukkot. This ancient Jewish harvest festival, which begins on 15 Tishri, recalls the period in which harvesters left their homes to dwell in the fields in sukkot, or booths—small outdoor shelters of boards, leaves, and branches—in order to facilitate gathering the crops before the seasonal rains began. In religious terms, it commemorates the 40 years of wandering in the desert by the ancient Hebrews after their exodus from Egypt. The 8th day of Sukkot and the 22d day of Tishri is **Shmini Azeret/Simhat Torah**, a joyous holiday in which the annual cycle of reading the Torah (the Five Books of Moses) is completed and begun anew. Outside of Israel, Simhat Torah and the beginning of a new reading cycle are celebrated on the next day, 23 Tishri.

Hanukkah. The Festival of Lights, corresponding roughly to the winter solstice, is celebrated over an eight-day period beginning on 25 Kislev, the third month. Also known as the Feast of Dedication and Feast of the Maccabees, Hanukkah commemorates the rededication of the Temple at Jerusalem in 164 BC. According to tradition, the one ritually pure container of olive oil, sufficient to illuminate the Temple for one day, miraculously burned for eight days, until new oil could be prepared. A feature of the Hanukkah celebration is the lighting in each Jewish home of an eight-branched candelabrum, the menorah (hanukkiah). This festival, though not a public holiday in Israel, is widely observed with the lighting of giant hanukkiot in public places.

Purim. This holiday, celebrated on 14 Adar (Adar Sheni in a leap year), joyously commemorates the delivery of the Jews from potential annihilation at the hands of Haman, viceroy of Persia, as described in the Book of Esther, which is read from a scroll (megillah). The day, though not a public holiday in Israel, is widely marked by charity, exchange of edible gifts, and feasting.

Pesach (Passover). Pesach, lasting seven days in Israel and eight outside it, begins on 15 Nisan, at roughly the spring equinox, and recalls the exodus of the Hebrews from Egypt and their delivery from bondage. The chief festival of Judaism, Pesach begins with a ceremonial family meal, or seder, at which special foods (including unleavened bread, or matzoh) are eaten and the Passover story (Haggadah) is read.

Shavuot. This festival, on 6 Sivan, celebrates the presentation of the Ten Commandments to Moses on Mt. Sinai and the offering of the first harvest fruits at the temple in Jerusalem. The precursor of the Christian Pentecost, Shavuot takes place on the 50th day after the first day of Pesach.

Tishah b'Av. This holiday, which takes place on 9 Av, commemorates the destruction of the First Temple by the Babylonians (Chaldeans) in 586 BC and of the Second Temple by the Romans in AD 70. It is observed by fasting.

The Jewish calendar begins with the traditional date of Creation, equivalent to 3761 BC on the Christian calendar.

MUSLIM HOLIDAYS

Like the Jewish calendar, the Islamic calendar consists of 12 months alternating between 29 and 30 days. A normal year is 354 days; a leap day is added to the last month (Dhu'l-Hijja) 11 times during a 30-year cycle in order to keep the calendar in conformity with the phases of the moon. Like the Jewish day, the Islamic day runs from sundown to sundown. Unlike the Jewish calendar, however, the Islamic calendar makes no attempt to align itself with the solar year by the periodic addition of an extra month; therefore, over the course of time, Islamic festivals may occur at any season. Like the Christian and Jewish calendars, the Islamic calendar has a seven-day week. Friday is the principal day of worship; although work is not forbidden on that day, it is suspended during the midday prayer session. The following list gives Muslim holy days that are observed as public holidays in one or more of the predominantly Muslim countries. Except where noted, a transliteration style reflecting pronunciation practice in the Arab countries is given. Not given here are certain special Muslim holidays in Iran, the only Muslim country in which the Shi'i form of Islam predominates.

Muslim New Year. Although in some countries 1 Muharram, which is the first month of the Islamic year, is observed as a holiday, the new year is in other places observed on Sha'ban, the eighth month of the year. This practice apparently stems from pagan Arab times. Shab-i-Bharat, a national holiday in Bangladesh on this day, is held by many to be the occasion when God ordains all actions in the coming year.

'Ashura. This fast day was instituted by Muhammad as the equivalent of the Jewish Yom Kippur but later became voluntary when Ramadan replaced it as a penitential event. It also commemorates Noah's leaving the ark on Mt. Ararat after the waters of the Great Flood had subsided. In Iran, the martyrdom of Husayn, grandson of Muhammad, is commemorated with passion plays on this day.

Milad an-Nabi. The traditional birthday of Muhammad is celebrated on 12 Rabi al-Awwal, the third month of the Islamic year.

Laylat al-Miraj. This holiday, celebrated on 27 Rajab, the seventh month, commemorates the night of Muhammad's miraculous ascension to heaven, during which he received instructions from Allah on the requirements for daily prayer.

Ramadan. The first day of Ramadan (the ninth month) is a public holiday in many countries, although the religious festival does not officially begin until the new moon is sighted from the Naval Observatory in Cairo, Egypt. The entire month commemorates the period in which the Prophet received divine revelation and is observed by a strict fast from sunrise to sundown. This observance is one of Islam's five main duties for believers.

Laylat al-Qadr (Night of Power). This commemoration of the first revelation of the Koran (Qur'an) to Muhammad usually falls on 27 Ramadan.

'Id al-Fitr. The Little Festival, or Breaking-Fast-Festival, which begins just after Ramadan, on 1 Shawwal, the 10th month, is the occasion for three or four days of feasting. In Malaysia and Singapore, this festival is called Hari Raya Puasa; in Turkey, Şeker Bayrami.

'Id al-'Adha'. The Great Festival, or Sacrificial Feast, celebrates the end of the special pilgrimage season, or Hajj, to Mecca and Medina, an obligation for Muslims once in their lifetime if physically and economically feasible. The slaughter of animals pays tribute to Abraham's obedience to God in offering his son to the Lord for sacrifice; a portion of the meat is supposed to be donated to the poor. The feast begins on 10 Dhu'l-Hijja and continues to 13 Dhu'l-Hijja (14 Dhu'l-Hijja in a leap year). In Malaysia and Singapore, this festival is celebrated as Hari Raya Haji; in Indonesia, Lebaran Haji; in Turkey, Kurban Bayrami.

The Islamic calendar begins with the entry of Muhammad into Medina, equivalent to AD 622 on the Christian calendar.

Glossary of Special Terms

The following is a selected list, with brief definitions and explanations, of terms that appear frequently in these volumes. Not included below are UN organs and related agencies, which are discussed under their own headings elsewhere.

adult literacy: the capacity of adults to read and write, as defined by divergent national criteria of age and ability.

ad valorem tax: a levy based on a fixed percentage of an item's value; ad valorem taxes include sales taxes, property taxes, and the majority of import duties.

African Development Bank: IGO founded in 1963 and with its headquarters at Abidjan, Côte d'Ivoire; coordinates its members' development finances and provides loans.

animism: the belief that natural objects and phenomena have souls or innate spiritual powers.

Asian Development Bank: IGO founded in 1966 and with its headquarters at Manila, Philippines; seeks to encourage economic growth in Asia and the Far East and provides long-term, large-scale loans, with emphasis on the developing countries.

Association of South-East Asian Nations (ASEAN): IGO founded in 1967 and with its headquarters at Jakarta, Indonesia; promotes economic cooperation among its members.

balance of payments: a systematic record of all financial transactions between one country and the rest of the world.

bank of issue: a bank empowered to issue currency.

capital account: all additions to or subtractions from a stock of investment.

Caribbean Community and Common Market (CARICOM): IGO founded in 1973 and with its headquarters in Georgetown, Guyana; seeks the establishment of a common external tariff and common trade policy among its members and promotes increased cooperation in agricultural and industrial development in the Caribbean region.

cash economy: see **money economy**.

central bank: a financial institution that handles the transactions of the central government, coordinates and controls the nation's commercial banks, and regulates the nation's money supply and credit conditions.

Colombo Plan: formally known as the Colombo Plan for Cooperative Economic Development in Asia and the Pacific, a multinational mutual assistance program that took effect in 1951 and has its headquarters in Colombo, Sri Lanka.

commercial bank: a bank that offers to businesses and individuals a variety of banking services, including demand deposit and withdrawal by check.

Commonwealth of Nations: voluntary association of the UK and its present dependencies and associated states, as well as certain former dependencies and their dependent territories. The term was first used officially in 1926 and is embodied in the Statute of Westminster (1931). Within the Commonwealth, whose secretariat (established in 1965) is located in London, England, are numerous subgroups devoted to economic and technical cooperation.

constant prices: money values calculated so as to eliminate the effect of inflation on prices and income.

Council for Mutual Economic Assistance (CMEA): also known as COMECON, an IGO established to foster economic and technical cooperation within the Communist bloc, including the USSR, most Eastern European countries, and several other nations. Founded in 1949, CMEA has its headquarters in Moscow.

Council of Europe: IGO founded in 1949 and with its headquarters in Strasbourg, France; promotes consultation and cooperation among European countries.

crude birthrate: the number of births in a year per 1,000 estimated midyear population.

crude death rate: the number of deaths in a year per 1,000 estimated midyear population.

current account: the flow of goods and services, as measured by payments for and receipts from imports and exports, including interest and dividends.

currency in circulation: the tangible portion of a nation's money supply, composed of bank notes, government notes, and coins.

current prices: money values that reflect prevailing prices, without excluding the effects of inflation.

customs duty: a tax imposed on the importation or exportation of goods.

customs union: an arrangement between governments to establish a common tariff policy and remove customs barriers between them.

demand deposit: a bank deposit that can be withdrawn by the depositor without previous notice to the bank.

direct tax: a tax that cannot be shifted from the original payer to the ultimate consumer of a good or service; direct taxes include the income tax and the poll tax.

Economic Community of West African States (ECOWAS): IGO founded in 1975 and with its headquarters at Lagos, Nigeria; seeks to establish a common tariff policy and promote economic cooperation among its members.

economically active population: see **labor force**.

endangered species: a type of plant or animal threatened with extinction in all or part of its natural range. For the Seventh Edition, listings of endangered animal species are as compiled for each country by the International Union for Conservation of Nature and Natural Resources.

European Communities (EC): collective name for a supranational organization encompassing, among other entities, the European Coal and Steel Community, established in 1952; the European Economic Community (EEC, or European Common Market), founded in 1958; and the European Atomic Energy Community (EURATOM), also established in 1958. All EC members also participate in the European Parliament, which meets in Strasbourg and Luxembourg, and the Court of Justice, which sits in Luxembourg.

European Free Trade Association (EFTA): customs union established in 1960 and with its headquarters in Geneva, Switzerland.

factor cost: a concept used in determining the value of the national product in relation to the economic resources employed.

fertility rate: the average number of children that would be born to each woman in a population if she were to live through her childbearing lifetime bearing children at the same rate as women in that age range actually did in a given year.

fly: the part of a flag opposite and parallel to the one nearest the flagpole.

foreign exchange: all monetary assets that give residents of one country a financial claim on another.

gross domestic product (GDP): the total gross expenditure, in purchasers' values, on the domestic supply of goods and services (final use).

gross national product (GNP): the total monetary value of all final goods and services that a nation produces.

Group of 77 (G-77): IGO founded in 1967 to represent the interests of the developing countries and taking its name from the 77 developing nations that signed the Joint Declaration of the first UN Conference on Trade and Development (UNCTAD).

Gulf Cooperation Council (GCC): IGO founded in 1981 and with its headquarters in Riyadh, Sa'udi Arabia; aims at increasing cooperation among nations of the Persian (Arabian) Gulf region in matters of security and economic development.

hoist: the part of a flag nearest the flagpole.

indirect tax: a tax levied against goods and services; sales taxes, excise taxes, and import duties are generally regarded as indirect taxes.

infant mortality rate: the number of deaths of children less than one year old per 1,000 live births in a given year.

installed capacity: the maximum possible output of electric power at any given time.

Inter-American Development Bank (IDB): IGO established in 1959 and with its headquarters in Washington, D.C.; provides technical assistance and development financing to member nations in Latin America and the Caribbean.

intergovernmental organization (IGO): a body, such as the UN, to which only governments belong.

international reserves: cash and other international assets readily convertible into cash for the settlement of international accounts by a government.

invisibles: exports and imports of services (e.g., shipping charges, banking services, royalties, rents, and interest).

labor force: the number of people in a population available for work, whether actually employed or not.

Latin American Integration Association (LAIA): IGO founded in 1980 as the successor to the Latin American Free Trade Association and with its headquarters in Montevideo, Uruguay; seeks to foster economic cooperation among Latin American nations.

League of Arab States (Arab League): IGO founded in 1945 and with its headquarters in Tunis, Tunisia (formerly in Cairo, Egypt); attempts to coordinate national and international political activities of its members, to revive and diffuse the cultural legacy of Arabs, and to develop Arab social consciousness.

life expectancy: the expected life span of a newborn baby at any given date.

lingua franca: a language widely used as a means of communication among speakers of other languages.

Marshall Plan: formally known as the European Recovery Program, a joint project between the US and most Western European nations under which $12.5 billion in US loans and grants was expended to aid European recovery after World War II. Expenditures under the program, named for US Secretary of State George C. Marshall, were made from fiscal years 1949 through 1952.

money economy: a system or stage of economic development in which money replaces barter in the exchange of goods and services.

most-favored-nation clause: a provision in commercial treaties between two or more countries that guarantees that all partners to the agreement will automatically extend to each other any tariff reductions that they offer to nonmember countries.

Net material product: the total net value of goods and "productive" services, including turnover taxes, produced by the economy in the course of a given time period.

net natural increase: the difference between the crude birthrate and the crude death rate.

nongovernmental organization (NGO): a body, such as the International Chamber of Commerce or Amnesty International, in which organizations and individuals participate, often without government control or sponsorship.

Nordic Council: IGO founded in 1952 and with its headquarters in Stockholm, Sweden; a consultative body on matters of common interest to the Nordic (Scandinavian) countries.

North Atlantic Treaty Organization (NATO): IGO established in 1949 and with its headquarters in Brussels, Belgium; fosters cooperation in defense and other matters.

Organization of African Unity (OAU): IGO established in 1963 and with its headquarters in Addis Ababa, Ethiopia; attempts to promote African unity and development, eradicate colonialism, and coordinate members' economic, political, diplomatic, educational, cultural, health, scientific, and defense policies.

Organization of American States (OAS): IGO founded in 1948 and with its headquarters in Washington, D.C.; seeks to achieve peaceful settlement of members' disputes, promote solidarity in defense matters, and foster cooperation in the health, economic social and cultural fields.

Organization for Economic Cooperation and Development (OECD): IGO established in 1961 as the successor to the Organization for European Economic Cooperation and with its headquarters in Paris; attempts to promote economic growth, social welfare, higher living standards, and financial stability in member countries.

Organization of Petroleum Exporting Countries (OPEC): IGO founded in 1960 and with its headquarters in Vienna, Austria; seeks to coordinate its members' production and pricing of crude petroleum.

Pan American Health Organization (PAHO): IGO founded in 1902 as the International Sanitary Bureau and with its headquarters now in Washington, D.C. An OAS affiliate, PAHO seeks to improve health and environmental conditions in the Americas.

per capita: per person.

proved reserves: the quantity of a recoverable mineral resource (such as oil or natural gas) that is still in the ground.

public debt: the amount owed by a government.

retail trade: the sale of goods directly to the consumer.

smallholder: the owner or tenant of a small farm.

subsistence economy: the part of a national economy in which money plays little or no role, trade is by barter, and living standards are minimal.

supranational: transcending the limitations of the nation-state.

time deposit: money held in a bank account for which the bank may require advance notice of withdrawal.

turnkey project: a factory or other installation wholly built by a company of one country at a site in another country, which then assumes complete operational control over it, paying the builder in cash, credits, or a share of the proceeds.

turnover tax: a tax on transactions of goods and services at all levels of production and distribution.

value added by manufacture: the difference, measured in national currency units, between the value of finished goods and the cost of materials needed to produce them.

value-added tax (VAT): see **ad valorem tax**.

visibles: international transactions involving movement of tangible goods.

Warsaw Treaty Organization (WTO): IGO commonly known as the Warsaw Pact; attempts to promote the collective security of its members. Founded in 1955, the alliance has its headquarters in Moscow.

wholesale trade: the sale of goods, usually in bulk quantities, to intermediaries for ultimate resale to consumers.

work force: see **labor force**.

GENERAL BIBLIOGRAPHY

A

ABECOR. *Country Reports*. London: Barclays Bank PLC, 1994.

Ackerman, Robert H. "Economic and Medical Directions in the Czech Republic and Hungary." *The American Journal of Surgery*. Vol. 167 (February, 1994).

Agrentina, Republic of. Secretariat of Science and Technology, National Bureau of International Affairs. *National System of Science and Technology*. Washington, D.C.: Embassy of Argentina, 1994.

American Automobile Manufacturers Association. *World Motor Vehicle Data 1993 Edition*. Washington, D.C.: American Automobile Manufacturers Association, 1993.

Argakas, Kullo, et. al. *The Baltic States, A Reference Book*. Tallinn, Estonia: Estonian Encyclopedia Publishers, 1991.

Arthur Andersen & Co. *A Tax Guide to Europe*. New York: Arthur Andersen & Co., 1992.

———. *Asia and the Pacific, a Tax Tour*. New York: Arthur Andersen & Co., 1993.

———. *Tax Guide to the Americas*. New York: Arthur Andersen & Co., 1991.

Asian Development Bank. *Asian Development Outlook 1990*. Manila, Philippines: Asian Development Bank, 1990.

Asian Survey. *Survey of Asia 1993*. Berkeley: University of California Press, 1994.

Australian Bureau of Statistics. *Year Book Australia*. Canberra, Australia: Australian Bureau of Statistics, 1994.

B

Bowen, Thomas F. and Kelly S. Bowen. *Countries of the World and Their Leaders Yearbook 1994*. Detroit: Gale Research, 1994.

Briggs, Asa, ed. *A Dictionary of 20th-Century World Biography*. New York: Oxford University Press, 1993.

British Petroleum Company. *BP Statistical Review of World Energy*. London: BP Education Service, 1994.

Brown, W. Norman. *The United States and India, Pakistan,*

Bangladesh. Cambridge: Harvard University Press 1972.

Bungs, Dzintra. "Latvia: Transition to Independence Complicated." *RFE/RL Research Report* (7 January 1994): 96–98.

———."Russia Agrees to Withdraw Troops from Latvia." *RFE/RL Research Report* (3 June 1994): 1–9.

Business International Limited. *Country Profiles*. London: Business International Limited, 1991–1994.

C

Caribbean Latin American Action. *Caribbean Basin Profile*. Washington: Caribbean Latin American Action, 1994.

Centers for Disease Control and Prevention. *Health Information for International Travel 1993*. Washington, D.C.: U.S. Government Printing Office, August 1993.

Central Office of Information. *Britain 1993: An Official Handbook*. London: HMSO Publications Centre, 1993.

Chew, Allen. *An Atlas of Russian History*. rev. ed. New Haven: Yale University Press, 1970.

CIA Directorate of Intelligence. *Chiefs of State and Cabinet Members of Foreign Governments: A Directory*. Washington, D.C.: U.S. Government Printing Office, June 1994

Continuous Reporting System on Migration (SOPEMI). *Trends in International Migration*. Paris: Organization for Economic Co-operation and Development (OECD), 1992.

Coopers and Lybrand. *International Tax Summaries*. New York: John Wiley and Sons, 1992.

Current History. Philadelphia: Current History, Inc.

D

Department of Economic and Social Information and Policy Analysis. *World Urbanization Prospects. The 1992 Revision*. New York: United Nations, 1993.

Department for Economic and Social Information and Policy Analysis, Statistical Division. *Housing in the World: Graphical Presentation of Statistical Data.* New York: United Nations, 1993.

———. *Population and Vital Statistics Report.* Series A vol. XLVI, no. 1. New York: United Nations, 1994.

E

Economist Intelligence Unit. *Country Reports.* London: Economist Intelligence Unit, 1994.

———. *The Economist Book of Vital World Statistics.* New York: Random House, 1990.

Euromonitor. *International Marketing Data and Statistics.* London: Euromonitor, 1994.

———. The *World Healthcare Marketing Director.* London: Euromonitor, 1993.

Europa Publications Limited. *Africa South of the Sahara.* 23rd ed. London: Europa Publications Limited, 1994.

———. *The World of Learning.* 43rd edition. London: Europa Publications Limited, 1993.

F

Fairbank, John K., Edwin O. Reischauer, and Albert M. Craig. *East Asia: Tradition and Transformation.* Boston: Houghton Mifflin Company, 1989.

Far Eastern Economic Review. *All-Asia Travel Guide.* 16th ed. Hong Kong: Review Publishing Co. Ltd., 1993.

Food and Agriculture Organization of the United Nations. *FAO Yearbook: Trade.* vol. 46. New York: United Nations, 1992.

———. *FAO Yearbook: Production.* vol. 46. New York: United Nations, 1993.

———. *FAO Yearbook: Fishery Statistics, Catches and Landings.* vol. 72. New York: United Nations, 1993.

———. *FAO Yearbook: Fishery Statistics, Commodities.* vol. 73. New York: United Nations, 1993.

———. *FAO Yearbook: Forest Products.* New York: United Nations, 1993.

Foreign and Commonwealth Office. *Commonwealth Yearbook.* London: HMSO Publications Centre, 1992.

Foye, Stephen. "Russia Will Not Meet Deadline for Baltic Withdrawal." *RFE/RL Daily Report* (11 July 1994).

Fuller, Elizabeth. "Armenia's Constitutional Debate." *RFE/RL Research Report* (27 May 1994): 6–9.

———. "The Challenges to Armenia's Non-Communist Government." *RFE/RL Report on the USSR* (3 May 1991): 19–24.

———. "The Transcaucasus." *RFE/RL Research Report.* (22 April 1994): 38–41.

———. "Transcaucasia: Ethnic Strife Threatens Democra-

tization." *RFE/RL Research Report* (1 January 1993): 17–24.

———. "The Transcaucasus: War, Turmoil, Economic Collapse." *RFE/RL Research Report* (7 January 1994): 51–58.

G

Girnius, Saulius. "The Baltic States." *RFE/RL Research Report* (22 April 1994): 5–8.

———. "Lithuania: Former Communists Fail to Solve Problems." *RFE/RL Research Report* (7 January 1994): 99–102.

———. "Lithuania: Former Communists Return to Power." *RFE/RL Research Report* (1 January 1993): 99–101.

Goldstein, Melvyn C. and Cynthia M. Beall. *The Changing World of Mongolia's Nomads.* Berkeley: University of California Press, 1994.

Grant, James P. United Nations Children's Fund. *The State of the World's Children.* New York: Oxford University Press, 1994.

H

Hane, Mikiso. *Modern Japan, A Historical Survey* Boulder: Westview Press, 1986.

Hiatt, Fred. "Voters in Ukraine, Belarus Oust Their Leaders." *The Washington Post* (12 July 1994).

Hongkong and Shanghai Banking Corporation. *Business Profile Series.* Hong Kong: Hongkong and Shanghai Banking Corporation Limited.

Hubbard, Monica M. and Beverly Baer, eds. *Cities of the World.* 4th ed. Detroit: Gale Research, 1993.

I

Institute of the History of Natural Sciences, Chinese Academy of Sciences. *Ancient China's Technology and Science.* Beijing: Foreign Languages Press, 1983.

International Civil Aviation Organization. *ICAO Statistical Yearbook, Civil Aviation Statistics of the World.* 18th ed. Montreal: International Civil Aviation Organization, 1993.

International Committee of the Red Cross. *Annual Report.* Geneva: ICRC Publications, 1993.

International Finance Corporation. *Emerging Stock Markets Factbook 1993.* Washington, D.C.: International Finance Corporation, 1993.

International Institute for Environment and Development and World Resources Institute. *World Resources 1993.*

New York: Basic Books, 1993.

International Iron and Steel Institute. *World Steel in Figures*. Brussels: International Iron and Steel Institute, 1993.

International Labour Office. *1993 Year Book of Labour Statistics*. 52nd. issue. Geneva: International Labour Office, 1993.

International Monetary Fund. *Direction of Trade Statistics*. Washington, D.C.: International Monetary Fund, June 1994

———. *International Financial Statistics*. Washington, D.C.: International Monetary Fund, June 1994

J

Jamison, Ellen. *World Population Profile: 1991*. Washington, D.C.: U.S. Government Printing Office, 1991.

K

Kand, Villu "Estonia: A Year of Challenges." *RFE/RL Research Report*, 7 January 1994, 92–95.

Khader, Bichara and Bashir el-Wifati, eds. *The Economic Development of Libya*. London: Croom Helm, 1987.

L

Leppingwell, John W. R. "Ukrainian Parliament Removes START-1 Conditions." *RFE/RL Research Report* (25 February 1994): 37–42.

Lukashuk, Alexander, "Belarusian Draft Constitution: A Controversial Step Forward." *RFE/RL Research Report* (30 October 1992): 43–48.

M

MacFarquhar, Roderick, ed., *The Politics of China, 1949–1989*, Cambridge: Cambridge University Press, 1993.

Markus, Ustina. "Belarus: Slowly Awakening to New Realities." *RFE/RL Research Report* (7 January 1994): 42–46.

———. "Lukashenka Wins Election." *RFE/RL Daily Report* (11 July 1994).

Meisner, Maurice. *Mao's China and After, A History of the People's Republic*. New York: The Free Press, 1989.

Morgan, Barry, ed. *OPEC Annual Report 1991*. Vienna: Organization of the Petroleum Exporting Countries, 1992.

Morrison, Christian. *Adjustment and Equity in Morocco*. Paris: Development Centre Studies, 1991.

N

Nahaylo, Bohdan and Victor Swoboda. *Soviet Disunion: A History of the Nationalities Problem in the USSR*. New York: The Free Press, 1990.

Nahaylo, Bohdan. "More on Ukrainian Election Results." *RFE/RL Daily Report* (12 April 1994).

National Science Board. *Science and Engineering Indicators*. Washington, D.C.: U.S. Government Printing Office, 1993.

Nordic Statistical Secretariat, ed. *Yearbook of Nordic Statistics*. Stockholm: Nordic Council of Ministers, 1993.

O

OECD Tourism Committee. *Tourism Policy and International Tourism in OECD Member Countries*. Paris: Organization for Economic Co-operation and Development (OECD), 1992.

OECD. *Revenue Statistics of OECD Member Countries: 1965–1992*. Paris: Organization for Economic Co-operation and Development (OECD), 1993.

Office of Conference Services; Translation Division; Documentation, Reference and Terminology Section. *Terminology Bulletin No. 345: Country Names*. New York: United Nations, 1993.

Organization of American States. *OAS Annual Report of the Inter American Commission on Human Rights*. Washington, D.C.: Organization of American States, 1992–93.

P

Philippines: Asian Development Bank. *Key Indicators of Developing Asian and Pacific Countries*. Manila, Philippines: Asian Development Bank, vol. XXI, July 1990.

Population Council. *Family Planning and Population: A Compendium of International Statistics*. New York: The Population Council, 1993.

Price Waterhouse. *Information Guide Series: Doing Business in . . .* New York: Price Waterhouse, 1994.

Programme Evaluation and Communications Research Unit (PECRU). *World Media Handbook 1992–94*. New York: United Nations Department of Public Information (DPI), 1992

R

Rahr, Alexander. "The First Year of Russian Independence." *RFE/RL Research Report* (1 January 1993): 50–57.

S

Salt, John. *Migration and Population Change in Europe.* Research Paper No. 19. New York: United Nations, 1993.

Sayeed, Khalid B. *The Political System of Pakistan.* Boston: Houghton Mifflin Co. 1967.

Schirokauer, Conrad. *A Brief History of Chinese Civilization.* San Diego: Harcourt, Brace, Jovanovich, 1991.

Seton-Watson, Hugh. *The Russian Empire, 1801–1917.* Oxford: Oxford University Press, 1967.

Sivard, Ruth Leger. *World Military and Social Expenditures 1993.* Washington. D.C.: World Priorities, 1993.

Shafir, Shlomo. *American Jews and Germany after 1945, Points of Connection and Points of Departure.* Cincinnati: American Jewish Archives, 1993.

Slater, Wendy. "Russia: The Return of Authoritarian Government?" *RFE/RL Research Report* (7 January 1994): 22–31.

———. "Russian Duma Sidelines Extremist Politicians," *RFE/RL Research Report* (18 February 1994): 5–9.

Socor, Vladimir. "Moldova's Dniester Ulcer." *RFE/RL Research Report* (1 January 1993): 12–16.

———. "Moldova's Political Landscape: Profiles of the Parties." *RFE/RL Research Report* (11 March 1994): 6–14.

———. "Moldova: Democracy Advances, Independence at Risk." *RFE/RL Research Report* (7 January 1994): 47–50.

———. "Moldovan Election Results." *RFE/RL Daily Report* (15 March 1994).

———. "Ukraine: A Year of Crisis." *RFE/RL Research Report* (7 January 1994): 38–41.

———. "Political Parties in Ukraine's Elections." *RFE/RL Daily Report* (14 April 1994).

Solomon Brothers. *Economic and Market Analysis: International Bond Market Analysis.* New York: Solomon Brothers, Inc., September 1993.

Statistical Directorate. *National Accounts 1979–1991.* Paris: Organization for Economic Co-operation and Development (OECD), 1993.

Statistics Canada. *Canada Year Book 1994.* Ottawa: Statistics Canada, 1994.

Statistics Sweden. *Sweden in Figures.* Stockholm: Statistics Sweden, 1992.

Stetler, Susan L., ed. *Almanac of Famous People.* 4th ed. Detroit: Gale Research, 1989.

Stokcholm International Peace Research Institute. *SIPRI Yearbook 1993: World Armaments and Disarmament.* New York: Oxford University Press, 1993.

Svetova, Svetlana and Roman Solchanyk. "Chronology of Events in Crimea." *RFE/RL Research Report* (13 May 1994): 27–33.

T

Taylor, Richard and Kiki Thomas. "Mortality Patterns in the Modernized Pacific Island Nation of Nauru," *The American Journal of Public Health* (February, 1985) 75:2.

Teague, Elizabeth. "Russia's Local Elections Begin," *RFE/RL Research Report* (18 February 1994): 1–4.

Thorson, Carla. "Russia's Draft Constitution." *RFE/RL Research Report* (3 December 1993): 9–15.

Tolz, Vera. "Russia's New Parliament and Yeltsin: Cooperation Prospects," *RFE/RL Research Report* (4 February 1994): 1–6.

———. "Russia's Parliamentary Elections: What Happened and Why," *RFE/RL Research Report* (14 January 1994): 1–8.

Treadgold, Donald W. *Twentieth Century Russia.* 7th ed. Boulder: Westview Press, 1990.

U

U.S. Bureau of the Census. *Statistical Abstract of the United States.* Washington, D.C.: U.S. Government Printing Office, 1993.

U.S. Central Intelligence Agency. *World Factbook.* Washington, D.C.: U.S. Government Printing Office, 1994.

U.S. Department of Agriculture, Foreign Agricultural Service. *Wood Products Trade and Foreign Markets: EC Market Profile Issue.* Washington, D.C.: U.S. Government Printing Office, 1993.

———. *Wood Products Trade and Foreign Markets: Annual Production, Consumption, and Trade Issue.* Washington, D.C.: U.S. Government Printing Office, 1993.

U.S. Department of Commerce. *International Business Practices.* Washington, D.C.: U.S. Government Printing Office, 1993.

U.S. Department of Commerce, Economics and Statistics Administration, Office of Business Analysis. *NTDB: The Export Connection CD-ROM.* Washington, D.C.: U.S. Government Printing Office, March–August 1994. This CD-ROM includes a wide variety of U.S. Government publications including the following which were used in the compilation of this encyclopedia:

Commercial Activities Reports;

Country Marketing Plans;

Foreign Economic Trends;

Country Commercial Guides;

Country Reports on Economic Policy and Trade Practices;

Handbook of Economic Statistics;

International Labor Statistics;

U.S. Foreign Trade Highlights;
Market Research Reports;
International Business Practices;
Foreign Labor Trends;
Background Notes;
BINIS Bulletin (Newly Independent States)

U.S. Department of Energy, Energy Information Administration. *Country Profiles: 1993; An Energy Overview of Important Countries in the World Oil Market.* Washington, D.C.: U.S. Government Printing Office, 1993.

———. *Energy Use and Carbon Emission: Some International Comparisons.* Washington, D.C.: U.S. Government Printing Office, March 1994.

———. *International Energy Outlook 1993.* Washington, D.C.: U.S. Government Printing Office, April 1993.

———. *International Energy Annual, 1992.* Washington, D.C.: U.S. Government Printing Office, January 1994.

———. *International Petroleum Statistics Report.* Washington, D.C.: U.S. Government Printing Office, September 1993.

U.S. Department of Health, Education, and Welfare. *Social Security Programs Throughout the World.* Washington, D.C.: U.S. Government Printing Office, 1991.

U.S. Department of State. *Country Reports on Human Rights Practices 1993.* Washington, D.C.: U.S. Government Printing Office, 1994.

U.S. Department of State, Bureau of Intelligence and Research. *Geographic and Global Issues Quarterly* (U.S. Government Printing Office) vol. 3, no. 1–4 (1994).

U.S. Department of the Interior. *Endangered and Threatened Wildlife and Plants.* Washington, D.C.: U.S. Government Printing Office, 1992.

U.S. Department of the Interior, Bureau of Mines. *Mineral Perspectives: The Mineral Economy of Mexico.* Washington, D.C.: U.S. Government Printing Office, 1992.

———. *Minerals Today* (U.S. Government Printing Office) June 1993.

———. *Minerals Yearbook: Minerals in the World Economy.* Washington, D.C.: U.S. Government Printing Office, 1991.

U.S. Department of Transportation, Maritime Administration. *Merchant Fleets of the World.* Washington, D.C.: U.S. Government Printing Office, 1992.

U.S. Library of Congress. Congressional Research Service. *International Science and Technology: Issues for U.S. Policymakers* (a report for the Committee on Science, Space, and Technology of the U.S. House of Representatives). Coordinated by Glenn J. McLoughlin. June 1994.

U.S. Public Health Service. Health Information for the International Traveller. Washington, D.C.: US Government Printing Office, 1994.

UNESCO. *Statistical Yearbook.* New York: United Nations, 1993.

UNICEF. *The State of the World's Children.* Wallingford, United Kingdom.: UNICEF, 1994.

United Nations. *United Nations System of Organizations and Directory.* New York: United Nations, 1994.

United Nations. *National Accounts Statistics: Main Aggregates and Detailed Tables, 1991.* 2 vols. New York: United Nations, 1993.

United Nations Conference on Environment and Development. *Nations of the Earth Report.* New York: United Nations, 1993.

United Nations Conference on Trade and Development. *Handbook of International Trade and Development Statistics: 1992.* New York: United Nations, 1993

United Nations Department of Economic and Social Information and Policy Analysis. Statistical Yearbook, 1990/1991. 38th issue. New York: United Nations, 1992.

United Nations Development Program. *Human Development Report.* New York: Oxford University Press, 1993.

United Nations High Commissioner for Refugees. *The State of the World's Refugees: The Challenge of Protection.* New York: Penguin Books, 1993.

V

Velez, Orlando, ed. *Editor and Publisher Market Guide.* New York: The Editor and Publisher Company, 1994.

W

Wasylyk, Myron. "Ukraine on the Eve of Elections." *RFE/RL Research Report* (25 March 1994): 44–50.

Wenner, Manfred W. *The Yemen Arab Republic.* Boulder: Westview Press, 1991.

Wishnevsky, Julia. "Problems of Russian Regional Leadership." *RFE/RL Research Report* (13 May 1994): 6–13.

World Bank. *Emerging Stock Markets Factbook.* Washington, D.C.: The World Bank, 1993.

———. *Russian Economic Reform: Crossing the Threshold of Structural Change* (A World Bank Country Study). Washington, D.C.: World Bank, 1992.

———. *Trends in Developing Economies 1993.* Washington, D.C.: World Bank, 1993.

———. *World Bank Annual Report 1994.* Washington, D.C.: World Bank, 1994.

———. *World Bank Atlas 1994.* Washington, D.C.: World Bank, 1994.

———. *World Development Report 1993: Investing in*

Health. New York: Oxford University Press, 1993.

———. *World Tables 1994*. Baltimore: Johns Hopkins University Press, 1994.

World Health Organization. *1993 World Health Statistics Annual*. Geneva: World Health Organization, 1994.

World Tourism Organization. *Compendium of Tourism Statistics*. 13th ed. Madrid: World Tourism Organization, 1993.

———. *Yearbook of Tourism Statistics*. vol. 1–2, 45th ed. Madrid: World Tourism Organization, 1993.

INDEX TO COUNTRIES AND TERRITORIES

This alphabetical list includes countries and dependencies (colonies, protectorates, and other territories) described in the encyclopedia. Countries and territories described in their own articles are followed by the continental volume (printed in *italics*) in which each appears, along with the volume number and first page of the article. For example, Argentina, which begins on page 7 of *Americas* (Volume 3), is listed this way: Argentina—*Americas* 3:7. Dependencies are listed here with the title of the volume in which they are treated, followed by the name of the article in which they are dealt with. In a few cases, an alternative name for the same place is given in parentheses at the end of the entry. The name of the volume *Asia and Oceania* is abbreviated in this list to *Asia*.

INDEX TO THE UNITED NATIONS AND RELATED AGENCIES

UNITED NATIONS ORGANS, SPECIALIZED AGENCIES AND OTHER AUTONOMOUS ORGANIZATIONS WITHIN THE SYSTEM

UNITED NATIONS DEVELOPMENT PROGRAM FIELD OFFICES

UNITED NATIONS INFORMATION CENTERS/SERVICES

PEACEKEEPING OPERATIONS/ OBSERVER MISSIONS

PRINCIPAL ORGANS OF THE UNITED NATIONS

New York:
General Assembly
Security Council
Economic and Social Council
Trusteeship Council
Secretariat

The Hague:
The International Court
of Justice

OTHER UNITED NATIONS ORGANS
(representative list only)

Geneva:
UNCTAD -United Nations Conference on Trade
and Development
UNDRO -Office of the United Nations Disaster Relief
Co-ordinator
UNHCR -Office of the United Nations High Commissioner
for refugees
Nairobi:
UNCHS -United Nations Centre for Human Settlements
(Habitat)
UNEP -United Nations Environment Programme
New York:
UNDP -United Nations Development Programme
UNFPA -United Nations Population Fund
UNICEF -United Nations Children's Fund
UNITAR -United Nations Institute for Training
and Research

Rome:
-World Food Council
WCF -Joint UN/Fao World Food Programme
WFP

Santo Domingo:
INSTRAW -International Research and Training Institute
for the Advancement of Women
Tokyo:
UNU -United Nations University

PEACE-KEEPING OPERATIONS/OBSERVER MISSIONS

UNDOF -United Nations Disengagement Observer Force
UNFICYP -United Nations Peace-Keeping Force in Cyprus
UNIFIL -United Nations Interim Force in Lebanon
UNMOGIP -United Nations Military Observer Group in India
and Pakistan
UNTSO -United Nations Truce Supervision Organization